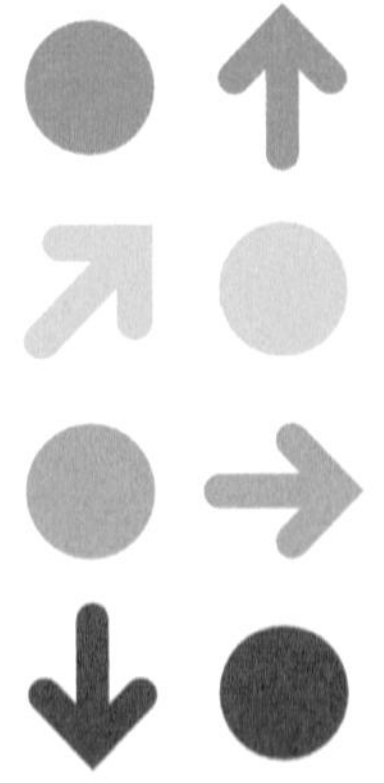

SUSTAINABLE DEVELOPMENT REPORT 2022

From Crisis to Sustainable Development: the SDGs as Roadmap to 2030 and Beyond

Includes the SDG Index and Dashboards

By Jeffrey D. Sachs, Guillaume Lafortune, Christian Kroll, Grayson Fuller, and Finn Woelm

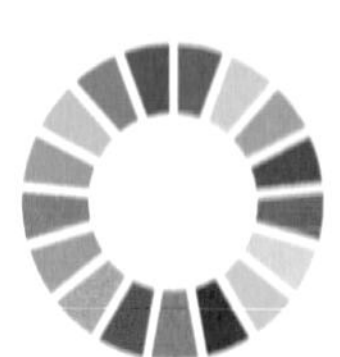

CAMBRIDGE
UNIVERSITY PRESS

University Printing House, Cambridge CB2 8BS, United Kingdom

One Liberty Plaza, 20th Floor, New York, NY 10006, USA

477 Williamstown Road, Port Melbourne, VIC 3207, Australia

314–321, 3rd Floor, Plot 3, Splendor Forum, Jasola District Centre, New Delhi – 110025, India

103 Penang Road, #05-06/07, Visioncrest Commercial, Singapore 238467

Cambridge University Press is part of the University of Cambridge.

It furthers the University's mission by disseminating knowledge in the pursuit of education, learning, and research at the highest international levels of excellence.

www.cambridge.org
Information on this title: www.cambridge.org/9781009210089
doi.org/10.1017/9781009210058

When citing this work, please include a reference to the DOI 10.1017/9781009210058

First published 2022

Printed in the United Kingdom by TJ Books Limited, Padstow Cornwall

A catalogue record for this publication is available from the British Library.

Library of Congress Cataloging-in-Publication Data

ISBN 978-1-009-21008-9 Hardback
ISBN 978-1-009-21003-4 Paperback

Contents

Figures

Tables

List of Boxes

Acknowledgments

The *Sustainable Development Report* (SDR) reviews progress made each year on the Sustainable Development Goals since their adoption by the 193 UN Member States in 2015. Fifty years after the release of *Limits to Growth* and the first UN Conference on the Environment, held in Stockholm in 1972, this 7th edition of the SDR is published amid multiple health, security and climate crises. The fundamental SDG principles of social inclusion, international cooperation, responsible production and consumption, and universal access to clean energy are needed more than ever to fight these major challenges of our times. Ahead of the SDG Summit in September 2023, which will convene at the level of heads of state under the auspices of the UN General Assembly, the SDR 2022 identifies major priorities to restore and accelerate SDG progress towards 2030 and beyond.

The report was coordinated by Guillaume Lafortune, in cooperation with Christian Kroll and under the overall supervision of Jeffrey D. Sachs. Lead writers are Jeffrey D. Sachs, Guillaume Lafortune, Christian Kroll, Grayson Fuller, and Finn Woelm. The statistical work was led by Grayson Fuller, Finn Woelm, and Guillaume Lafortune. The interactive website and data visualization that accompanies this report was developed by Max Gruber and Finn Woelm. Other major contributors to the data and analyses in this year's report include Leslie Bermont Diaz, Salma Dahir, Alainna Lynch, Isabella Massa, Samory Toure, and Rosalie Valentiny. We also thank Alyson Marks, Castelline Tilus, and Grant Cameron from the Thematic Research Network on Data and Statistics (SDSN TReNDS) for preparing Part 4. SDG Data Systems and Statistics.

The SDR 2022 combines data and analyses produced by international organizations, civil society organizations, and research centers. We thank all of these for their contributions and collaboration in producing the report, including during the annual public consultation process that took place in March and April 2022.

We also thank the regional and national SDSN networks, the SDSN secretariat, and experts and government officials for responding to the 2022 survey on "national implementation and coordination mechanisms for the SDGs at the central/federal level" and providing comments and feedback at various stages.

María Cortés Puch, Maëlle Voil, Cheyenne Maddox, and Ryan Swaney provided communication support for the launch of the report. We thank Philip Good and Roisin Munnelly from Cambridge University Press & Assessment and Roberto Rossi of Pica Publishing for preparing the manuscript for publication. We welcome feedback on the publication and data that may help to strengthen future iterations of this work.

Please notify us of any publications that use the SDG Index and Dashboards data or the *Sustainable Development Report* and share your publication with us at info@sdgindex.org.

An interactive online dashboard and all data used in this report can be accessed at: www.sdgindex.org

June 2022

Please cite this report as:

Sachs, J., Lafortune, G., Kroll, C., Fuller, G., Woelm, F. (2022). *From Crisis to Sustainable Development: the SDGs as Roadmap to 2030 and Beyond. Sustainable Development Report 2022*. Cambridge: Cambridge University Press.

This report has been prepared with the extensive advice and consultation of the SDSN Leadership Council members. Members of the Leadership Council serve in their personal capacities; the opinions expressed in this report may not reflect the positions or policies of their host institutions. Members are not necessarily in agreement on every detail of this report.

The views expressed in this report do not reflect the views of any organization, agency or programme of the United Nations.

Design and layout by Pica Publishing Ltd – www.pica-publishing.com

Executive Summary

Peace, diplomacy, and international cooperation are fundamental conditions for the world to progress on the SDGs towards 2030 and beyond. The war in Ukraine and other military conflicts are humanitarian tragedies. They also impact prosperity and social outcomes through the rest of the world, including exacerbating poverty, food insecurity, and access to affordable energy. The climate and biodiversity crises amplify the impact of these crises. At the time of this writing in early May 2022, the outcome of the war in Ukraine and other military conflicts, but also of the health crisis, remain highly uncertain. Yet, it is clear that these multiple and simultaneous crises have diverted policy attention and priorities away from medium and long-term goals such as the SDGs and the Paris Climate Agreement: a shift of focus towards short-term issues that threatens to slow down or even stall the adoption of ambitious and credible national and international plans but also squeezes available international funding for sustainable development. Global cooperation and commitment to the bedrock SDG principles of social inclusion, clean energy, responsible consumption, and universal access to public services are needed more than ever to respond to the major challenges of our times, including security crises, pandemics, and climate change. Despite these difficult times, the SDGs should remain the roadmap for achieving sustainable development by 2030 and beyond.

For the second year in a row, the world is no longer making progress on the SDGs. The average SDG Index score slightly declined in 2021, partly due to slow or nonexistent recovery in poor and vulnerable countries. Multiple and overlapping health and security crises have led to a reversal in SDG progress. Performance on SDG 1 (No Poverty) and SDG 8 (Decent Work and Economic Growth) remains below pre-pandemic levels in many low-income countries (LICs) and lower-middle-income countries (LMICs). This is a major setback, especially considering that before the pandemic, over the period 2015–2019, the world was progressing on the SDGs at a rate of 0.5 points per year (which was also too slow to reach the 2030 deadline), with poorer countries making greater gains than rich countries. Progress on climate and biodiversity goals is also too slow, especially in rich countries. Ahead of the heads of state SDG Summit in 2023, restoring and accelerating SDG progress in all countries, including the poorest and most vulnerable, should be a major priority of recovery plans and reforms to the international development finance system.

SDG Index Score over time, world average (2010–2021)

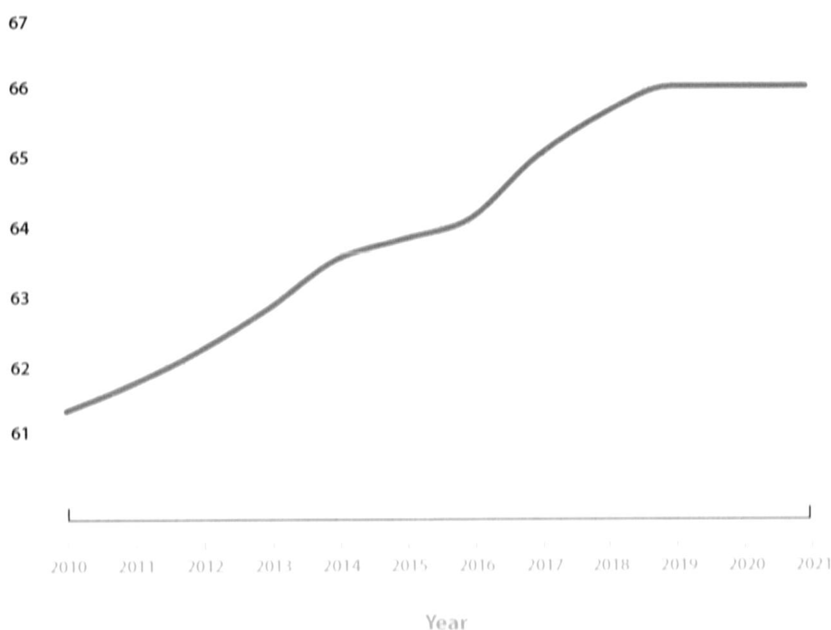

Source: Authors' analysis. *Note:* Population-weighted average

A global plan to finance the SDGs is needed. Achieving the SDGs is fundamentally an investment agenda in physical infrastructure (including renewable energy) and human capital. Yet the poorest half of the world – roughly speaking, the low-income countries (LICs) and lower-middle-income countries (LMICs) – lacks market access to capital on acceptable terms. We highlight five priorities towards a global plan to finance the SDGs. **First**, the G20 should declare clearly and unequivocally its commitment to channel far larger flows of financing to developing countries so that they can achieve economic development and meet the SDG targets. **Second**, the G20 should greatly increase the lending capacity and annual flows of the Multilateral Development Banks (MDBs), mainly through greater paid-in capital to these institutions, but also through greater leverage of their balance sheets. **Third**, the G20 should support other measures as well – notably increased ODA, large-scale philanthropy, and refinancing of debts falling due – to bolster SDG finance for the LICs and LMICs. **Fourth**, the IMF and the credit-rating agencies need to redesign the assessments of debt sustainability, taking into account the growth potential of developing countries and their need for far larger capital accumulation. **Fifth**, working together with the IMF and the MDBs, developing countries need to strengthen their debt management and creditworthiness by integrating their borrowing policies with tax policies, export policies, and liquidity management, all to prevent future liquidity crises.

At mid-point on the way to 2030, policy efforts and commitments supporting the SDGs vary significantly across countries, including among G20 countries. Ambitious and sound national targets, strategies, and plans are crucial to turning the SDGs into an action agenda. Every year, SDSN conducts a survey of government efforts for

Governments' Commitment and Efforts for the SDGs Score (pilot version) versus SDG Index Score

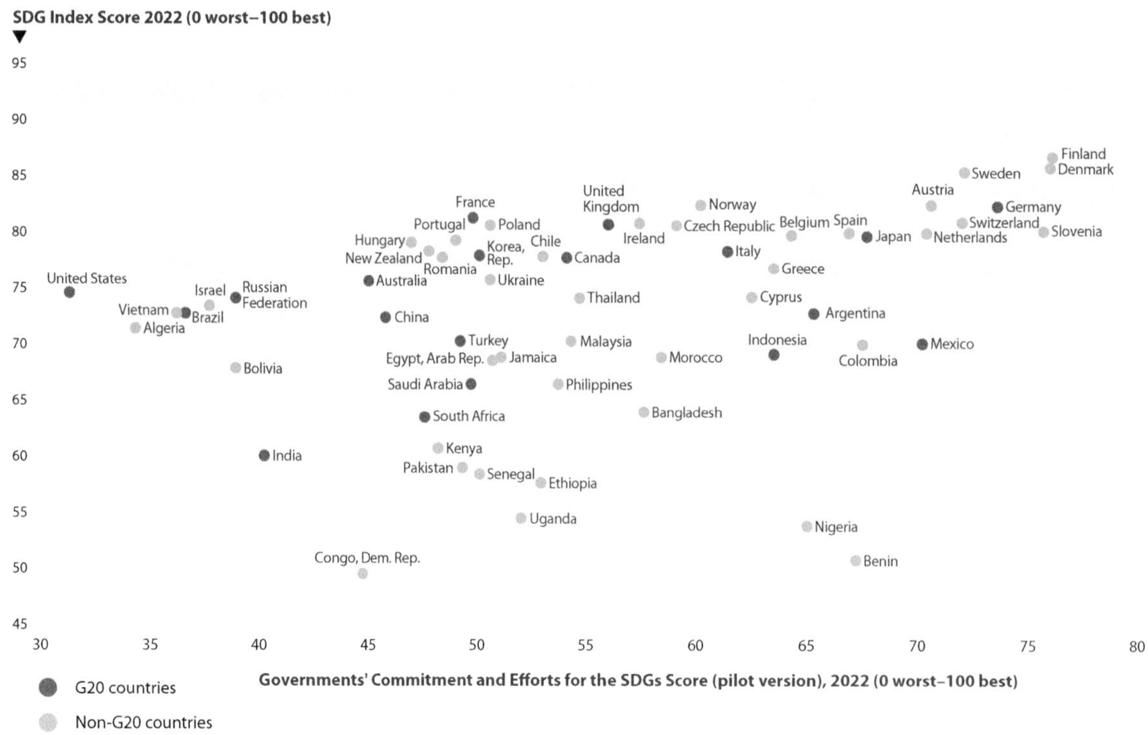

Note: G20 countries in red. The score for Ukraine reflects the situation as of January 2022.
Source: Authors' analysis. Details on the methodology and the indicators used are available on www.sdgindex.org

the SDGs, to monitor how the goals are integrated into official speeches, national plans, budgets and monitoring systems. SDSN also compiles metrics to gauge the alignment of national objectives and investments with the Six SDG Transformations. This year's pilot score of *Governments' Commitment and Efforts for the SDGs,* compiled for more than 60 countries, reveals that among G20 member states, the United States, Brazil, and the Russian Federation exhibit the least support for the 2030 Agenda and the SDGs. The United States is among the few UN Member States to have never submitted a Voluntary National Review (VNR). By contrast, Nordic countries demonstrate relatively high support for the SDGs, as do Argentina, Germany, Japan and Mexico (all G20 countries). Some countries, such as Benin and Nigeria, for example, have large gaps in their SDG Index yet also earn relatively high scores for their policy efforts. This may help them achieve better results in coming years. Interestingly, Benin and Mexico have both issued SDG Sovereign Bonds in recent years to scale up their sustainable development investments.

Rich countries generate negative international spillovers notably through unsustainable consumption; Europe is taking actions. The 2022 SDG Index is topped by three Nordic countries – Finland, Denmark and Sweden – and all top 10 countries are European countries. Yet even these countries face major challenges in achieving several SDGs. The 2022 International Spillover Index included in this report underlines how rich countries, including many European countries, generate negative socioeconomic and environmental spillovers, including through unsustainable trade and supply chains. The European Union has called for 'zero tolerance' of child labor and has proposed using trade to export European values throughout the world. Several instruments and legislations

SDG Index Score versus International Spillover Index Score

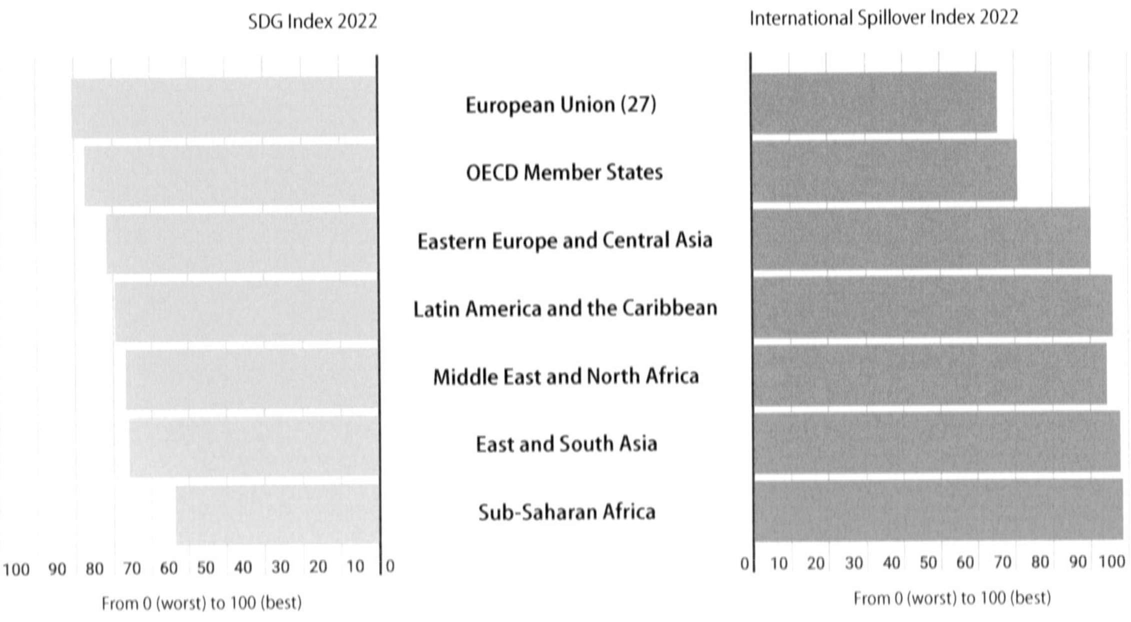

Source: Authors' analysis

are under discussion in the European Union to address international spillover effects in the context of the European Green Deal. At the member states' level, in 2022, Sweden became the first country to announce its intention to set a national target to curb imported CO_2 emissions. Ahead of the 2023 SDG Summit, we underline four major priorities to curb negative international spillovers generated by rich countries: (1) Scale up international development and climate finance; (2) Leverage technical cooperation and SDG diplomacy; (3) Adopt national targets and instruments to address consumption-based impacts on other countries (do no harm); (4) Strengthen monitoring and data systems at international, national, industrial, and corporate levels covering the full supply chains, and make them an integral part of SDG reporting.

The COVID-19 pandemic forced data providers to innovate and build new forms of partnerships; these should be leveraged and scaled up to promote SDG impacts by 2030 and beyond. The pandemic led to a massive and sudden shift in demand for timely and quality data to monitor the health impacts of COVID-19 and inform policy intervention at international and national levels. The health situation and lockdowns impacted traditional mechanisms for data collection, including traditional face-to-face surveys. Data providers were pushed to innovate and modernize their data collection methods and processes, notably leveraging mobile and wireless technologies. This was accompanied by a sharp acceleration in the use of non-traditional data sources, including citizen science, social media, and earth observation data. New dynamic dashboards, GIS instruments, and improved data visualizations and infographics have facilitated a greater understanding of data and statistics. Looking ahead, consolidating and scaling-up data innovations and new forms of partnerships – including between the public and private sectors (including technology providers) – while also maintaining high standards for data quality and privacy, could help to promote evidence-based SDG policies and interventions. More generally, science, technological innovations, and data systems can help identify solutions in times of crises and can provide decisive contributions to address the major challenges of our times. These require increased and prolonged investments in statistical capacities, R&D, and education and skills.

Acronyms and Abbreviations

AI	Artificial Intelligence
CAPI	Computer Assisted Personal Interviewing
CEPEI	Centro de Pensamiento Estratégico Internacional
CSA	Central Statistics Agency
DAC	Development Assistance Committee
DANE	National Administrative Department of Statistics
EO	Earth observation
EU	European Union
FAO	Food and Agriculture Organization
G20	Group of Twenty (intergovernmental forum comprising 19 countries and the European Union)
G7	Group of Seven (intergovernmental forum comprising of Canada, France, Germany, Italy, Japan, the United Kingdom, and the United States)
GDP	Gross Domestic Product
GeoGIAM	Group on Earth Observations Global Agricultural Monitoring Initiative
GIS	Geographic Information System
GSS	Ghana Statistical Service
HIC	High Income Country
ICLEI	Local Governments for Sustainability
ICS	International Continence Society
ILO	International Labour Organisation
IMF	International Monetary Fund
LAC	Latin American Countries
LIC	Low Income Country
LMIC	Lower Middle Income Country
LSMS	Living Standards Measurement Study
MENA	Middle East/ North Africa
MRIO	Multi-regional input-output
NBS	National Bureau of Statistics
NGO	Non Governmental Organisation
NSO	National Statistic Office
ODA	Official Development Assistance
OECD	Organisation for Economic Co-operation and Development
SDG	Sustainable Development Goal
SDR	Sustainable Development Report
SDSN	Sustainable Development Solutions Network
SIDS	Small Island Developing States
STATIN	Statistical Institute of Jamaica
TReNDS	Thematic Research Network on Data and Statistics
UCLG	United Cities and Local Governments
UHC	Universal Health Coverage
UMIC	Upper Middle Income Country
UN	United Nations
UNICEF	United Nations International Children's Emergency Fund
VNR	Voluntary National Review
WHO	World Health Organisation

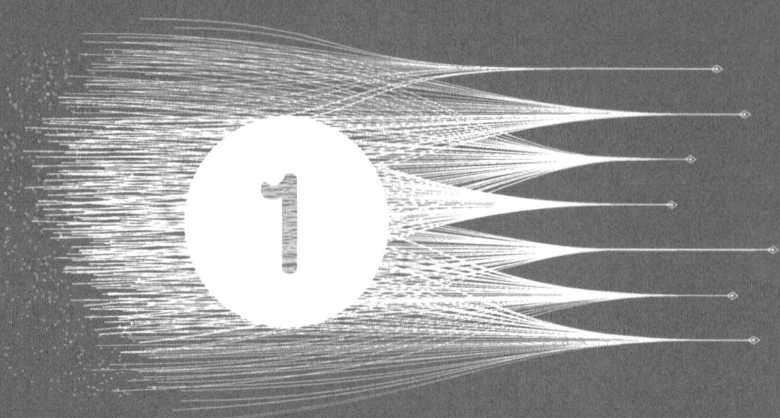

A Global Plan to Finance the Sustainable Development Goals

Part 1
A Global Plan to Finance the Sustainable Development Goals

The SDGs are not being achieved. Success is held back by severe financing constraints facing the developing countries: constraints that have been gravely aggravated by the COVID-19 pandemic and the war in Ukraine. The key to achieving the SDGs, besides preserving peace and lowering geopolitical tensions, is having a plan to finance them. This was emphasized by United Nations Secretary-General António Guterres in his briefing to the General Assembly on major priorities for 2022: "we must go into emergency mode to reform global finance" (UN, 2022a).

At last year's G20 Summit in Rome (October 30–31, 2021), the leaders of the world's largest economies recommitted to the SDGs:

> "We reaffirm our commitment to a global response to accelerate progress on the implementation of the SDGs and to support a sustainable, inclusive and resilient recovery across the world."

Financial constraints faced by developing countries have recently been highlighted by US Treasury Secretary Janet Yellen in a speech to the Atlantic Council in April 2022. Yellen's important words are worth quoting at length:

> "We've made great efforts to provide funding to support human development, the creation of needed infrastructure, and more recently the attainment of climate objectives. Multilateral development banks, bilateral official donors and creditors, and growing private-sector involvement deserve credit for important achievements. That said, the response to date is just not to the scale that's needed. *Experts put the funding needs in the trillions, and we've so far been working in billions*. The irony of the situation is that while the world has been awash in savings – so much so that real interest rates have been falling for several decades –we have not been able to find the capital needed for investments in education, health care, and infrastructure. There's little doubt that there are huge potential returns, both human and eventually financial, in equipping billions of people in developing countries with what they will need to succeed. Going forward, we need to evolve the development finance system, including the World Bank and the regional development banks, to our changing world, in particular to better mobilize private capital and fund global public goods. However, the multilateral development banks alone will never meet the scale of financing needed, so we also need to revisit our strategies for making capital markets work for people in developing countries." (Atlantic Council, 2022)

For these reasons, the G20 urgently needs to adopt a Global Plan to Finance the SDGs. The basis of the plan would be to significantly increase fiscal space in developing countries. The IMF, in particular, should work with developing countries to design SDG-based public investment strategies and the means to finance them.

Chronic underfinancing of sustainable development

According to the IMF's World Economic Outlook, low-income countries (LICs) constitute 8.4% of the world's population, but currently account for less than 1% of the world's investment spending (2019). Lower-middle-income countries (LMICs) constitute 42.9% of the world's population but account for only 15% of investment spending. High-income countries (HICs), by contrast, account for 15.8% of the world's population yet account for about half of the world's investment spending.

The LICs and LMICs make up the poorer half of the world (combined they equal 51% of the world's population), but they account for only around 15% of the world's investments. The UMICs and HICs comprise the richer 49% of the world's population, with more than 80% of the world's investments. The same discrepancy is found regarding fiscal outlays. The LICs and LMICs together account for around 10% of the world's fiscal outlays, while the UMICs and HICs account for about 90%. Annual average fiscal spending per person in the LICs amounted to US$133 in 2019 (USD, nominal), not enough to provide universal schooling, much less to meet all of the SDGs. The dire shortfall in public outlays is why the SDG agenda and the clean-energy transformation are both far off track. There is overall a positive and statistically significant correlation between total government outlays per capita per year (in USD PPP) and the SDG Index Score (Figure 1.1). Based on this simple correlation analysis, the association between government outlays and SDG outcomes is particularly strong among countries that spend relatively little. Beyond a certain threshold (approximately US$10,000 PPP per capita), the quality of spending and other factors seem to make a bigger difference (Table 1.2).

The need for greatly expanded SDG financing

The SDSN has identified six investment priorities: areas in which major societal "transformations" are needed to achieve the SDGs (Sachs et al., 2019):

1. **Education and social protection** to achieve universal secondary education (SDG 4) and poverty reduction (SDG 1)
2. **Health systems** to end the pandemic and to achieve Universal Health Coverage (SDG 3)
3. **Zero-carbon energy and circular economy to decarbonize** and slash pollution (SDG 7, SDG 12, SDG 13)
4. **Sustainable food**, land use, and protection of biodiversity and ecosystems (SDG 2, SDG 13, SDG 15)
5. **Sustainable urban infrastructure**, including housing, public transport, water, and sewerage (SDG 11)
6. **Universal digital services** (SDG 9) to support all other SDG investments, including online education, telemedicine, e-payments, e-financing, and e-government services.

Figure 1.1
Correlation between general government expenditure per capita (USD, PPP) and SDG Index Score

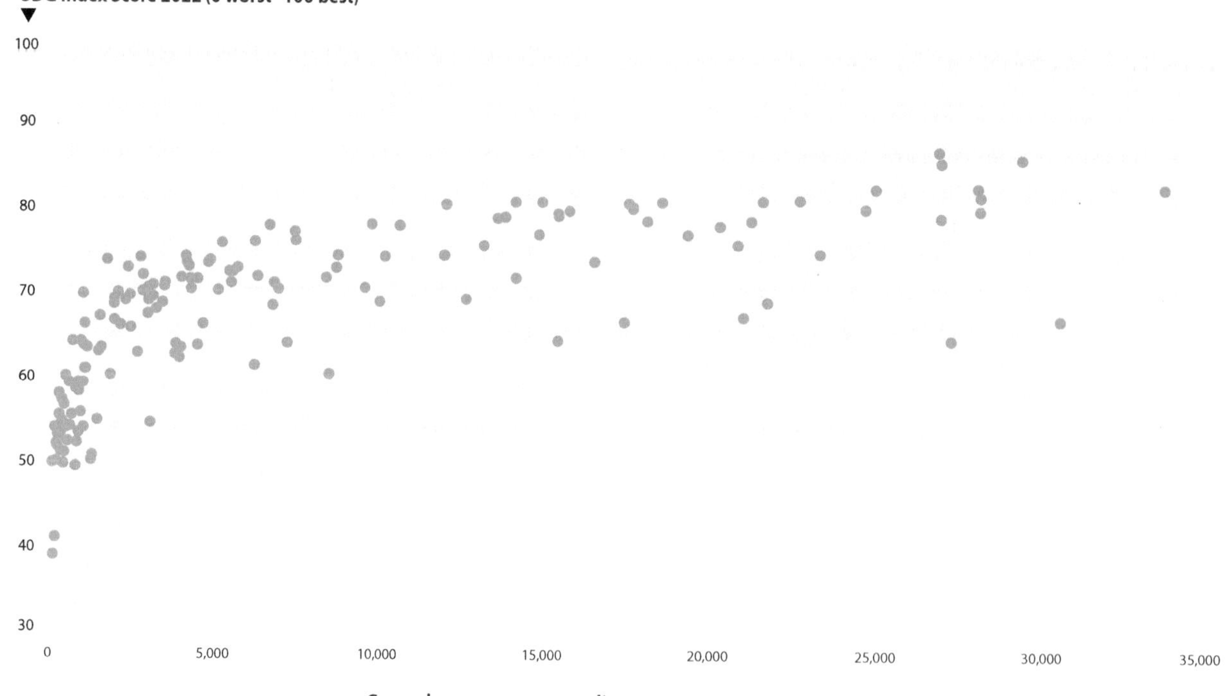

Note: See table at the end of this chapter for detailed regression results. Luxembourg is excluded from the chart (outlier).
Sources: Authors' analysis. Based on "World Economic Outlook Database, October 2021" (IMF, 2021).

At the core of each transformation is a large-scale, long-term public investment program. The major practical challenge facing developing countries is to mobilize the incremental financing needed for these six priority areas.

The need for increased SDG financing to achieve these six transformations is by now well established. Several excellent studies, especially by the IMF, have identified the scale of financing that developing countries need to achieve the SDGs (Senhadji et al., 2021).[1] The bottom line is clear: there is a sizable SDG financing gap for low-income countries (LICs) and lower-middle-income countries (LMICs) amounting to several hundred billion dollars per year, perhaps around US$500 billion per year. Adding in the needs of upper-middle-income countries (UMICs), the incremental financing needs come to more than US$1 trillion per year.

While the incremental SDG financing needs are large relative to the economies of the developing countries, perhaps 10–20% of gross domestic product (GDP) for many LICs and LMICs, the gap is actually quite modest relative to size of the world economy. With gross world product (GWP) now at around US$100 trillion, the global SDG financing gap is perhaps 1–2% of GWP. Global saving is currently around 27% of GWP, or roughly US$27 trillion per year: incremental financing to the order of only 4–8% of global saving is needed to cover the incremental SDG financing needs for approximately 80% of the world's population.

To facilitate a significant increase of funding for the SDGs, developing countries should enter into a new "SDG Investment Compact" with the Bretton Woods institutions, akin to the poverty reduction strategy frameworks under the previous MDG agenda. This would offer a framework for significant increases of SDG financing in line with long-term debt sustainability. The new SDG Investment Compact could be launched in conjunction with the IMF's new Resilience and Sustainability Trust (RST).

1. Studies to date have estimated SDG costs for social protection (SDG 1); sustainable agriculture and the end of hunger (SDG 2); universal health coverage (SDG 3); universal education from pre-K to upper secondary (SDG 4); universal access to safe water and sanitation (SDG 6); universal access to sustainable energy for all (SDG 7); universal access to digital technologies (SDG 9); sustainable housing and urban infrastructure (SDG 11); comprehensive decarbonization and climate adaptation/resilience (SDG 13); sustainable marine and coastal ecozones (SDG 14); sustainable land use and reforestation (SDG 15); and access of the poor to justice (SDG 16).

Six practical pathways for increased SDG financing

The incremental public financing required can be mobilized in six major ways: (1) increased domestic tax revenues; (2) increased sovereign (government) borrowing from international development finance institutions (DFIs); (3) increased sovereign borrowing from international private capital markets; (4) increased official development assistance (ODA); (5) increased funding by private foundations and philanthropies; and (6) debt restructuring for heavily indebted borrowers, mainly to lengthen maturities and reduce interest rates.

Increased domestic tax revenues. The SDGs require large-scale public investments: in education, health care, infrastructure (green energy, digital access, water and sanitation, transport), and environmental conservation. On top of that, government has ongoing obligations for social protection, public administration, and other public services. The levels of investment needed per year are far greater than current revenues collected by developing countries. A typical LIC collects 15–20% of its GDP in revenues, but SDG public investment needs can reach 40% of GDP or higher, and public administration adds another 5–10% of GDP to budget needs. In short, most countries should increase their public revenues to support needed levels of public spending. As a rule of thumb, LICs should aim for at least 25% of GDP in government revenues; LMICs for at least 30%; UMICs for at least 35%; and HICs for at least 40%.

Increased borrowing from multilateral development banks. Beyond the increase in domestic revenues, the LICs and LMICs need to borrow to finance SDG-related investments. The best source of increased finance will be the multilateral development banks (MDBs), which were created precisely to supply long-term low-interest financing to developing countries. The MDBs have the potential to borrow large sums from the international capital markets on favorable terms and then to use that borrowing to expand lending to developing countries on favorable terms (long maturities at low interest rates). The MDBs can leverage their paid-in capital base severalfold, so that an incremental US$50 billion of paid-in capital each year can support US$250 billion or more in increased annual lending. The G20 should work urgently with the MDBs on a strategy to multiply their SDG financing.

Sovereign borrowing on international capital markets. The LICs and LIMCs should also increase their direct sovereign borrowing from international capital markets, especially by floating sustainability-themed bonds (including sovereign SDG bonds). Yet the amounts and terms of international bond-market borrowing are inadequate. The basic reason is this: Not a single LIC, and only three LMICs – India, Indonesia and the Philippines – currently have an investment-grade rating from the international rating agencies, as shown in Table 1.1. The consequence is that the terms of sovereign bond-market borrowing facing most developing countries are very onerous: short maturities at very high interest rates (often 500–1000 basis points above the highest-rated borrowers). The G20 and IMF should undertake a series of reforms to unlock private capital flows at much larger amounts and on far more favorable terms. This would include a more accurate credit-rating system that recognizes the high long-term growth potential of the developing countries, and measures to increase the liquidity of the global sovereign bond market. We discuss this issue further in the next section.

Increased ODA. The donor countries in the OECD Development Assistance Committee (DAC) are supposed to give 0.7 percent of GNI in ODA, but in 2021 they gave only 0.33 percent (US$179 billion ODA/US$54.2 trillion GNI) (OECD, 2021). By reaching the 0.7 target, ODA would rise by US$200 billion per year. To increase ODA towards 0.7 percent of GNI, it is important to identify additional sources of funding for ODA. Two potential new sources are apparent. The first would be a levy on HICs and UMICs (upper-middle-income countries) on annual carbon dioxide (CO_2) emissions. A levy of US$5/t$CO_2$ on HICs and US$2.5/t$CO_2$ on UMICs would yield annual revenues of around US$100 billion. The second would be a globally coordinated wealth tax on ultra-high-net worth individuals. The world's 3,000 or so billionaires have a combined net worth of around US$15 trillion. Hence, a 2% wealth tax, assuming no leakage, would generate around US$300 billion per year.

Increased philanthropic giving. In 2021, Jeff Bezos donated US$10 billion into a new Bezos Earth Fund to help finance investments in climate change and biodiversity conservation. Mr. Bezos's net worth is around 1% of total billionaire net worth (roughly US$140 billion out of US$14 trillion). Following this model, the potential for a massive increase in philanthropic giving for the SDGs is vast, and could be mobilized in part by a giving campaign initiated by the G20 governments and the United Nations.

Debt restructuring for heavily indebted countries. Many developing countries are in a precarious situation regarding debt servicing, because they owe not only the interest on the debt, but large amortizations of principal as well, with little prospect of routinely refinancing the principal. In other words, many countries are facing a severe liquidity squeeze. In a few cases, there is also a solvency crisis, because the interest service is too high to pay even in the long term. The global official development system, especially the IMF, should take steps to help developing countries to refinance their debts falling due, so that we avoid a new wave of sovereign defaults. It takes years or even decades to re-establish a country's creditworthiness after such a default.

Re-thinking debt sustainability: a conceptual digression

One of the barriers to SDGs financing is conceptual: the widespread belief that sovereign borrowers should avoid building up public debt beyond an upper limit of 50–70% of GDP. This view is shared by the IMF and the credit rating agencies. The belief is that debt levels beyond such ratios are likely to result in default. This is a hasty over-generalization.

To understand why, consider briefly a quantitative illustration. Let us describe a country's GDP as a function of its capital stock per person, K, according to a standard aggregate production function familiar in macroeconomic theory. A typical assumption is that the GDP function has the Cobb-Douglas form:

$$\mathbf{GDP = tfp*K^b}$$

Here, tfp (total factor productivity) is a measure of overall productivity and the coefficient b is the share of capital in national income. Considering capital broadly to include both physical capital and human capital (mainly education), the coefficient b is around 0.7.

Net domestic product (NDP) equals GDP minus depreciation of capital, which we will take to be 5% per annum. Therefore:

NDP = GDP – 0.05*K

If the country has net international debt, it pays interest to foreign creditors, so that net national product (NNP) equals NDP minus the interest payments. NNP is the baseline measure of real income of the economy, net of depreciation and debt service. We will also assume that the international interest rate is 5%. The cost of capital equals 10%, the sum of the interest rate and the rate of depreciation:

NNP = GDP – 0.05*K – 0.05*Debt

For purposes of illustration, we will choose parameter values tfp = 6.8 and K = US$400,000 in order to mimic a HIC. With this level of capital per person, the GDP equals US$57,100 and NNP = US$37,100, with depreciation equal to US$20,000. The marginal product of capital (MPK) equals 10%, which is also the cost of capital.

Now consider a developing country with K = US$40,000, just one-tenth of the HIC capital per person. Assume also that the developing country starts with zero international debt. Because of the lower stock of capital per person, we can calculate that NNP = US$9,400. A middle-income country such as Egypt is roughly in this position. Now, we can determine that its MPK equals 20%, rather than 10% as in the HIC. That is, the marginal return on investment in the developing country is *higher* than that of the HIC because of the capital scarcity in the developing country.

Assume that the developing country can borrow internationally at a 5% interest rate to increase its capital stock, with all borrowing used to augment K. Let D be the debt per person, so that capital stock per person with borrowing equals K^{NEW} = US$40,000 + D. The new NNP equals:

NNP^{NEW} = tfp*(US$40,000+D)$^{0.7}$ – 5%x(US$40,000+D) – 5%xD

It's now easy to calculate the optimum amount of debt per person in order to maximize NNP^{NEW}. The answer is that the developing country should borrow enough to raise K^{NEW} *to the level of K in the HIC*. Debt per capita, in other words, should equal US$360,000, to increase the capital stock per person to US$400,000. The government should therefore borrow an astounding 32 times its initial GDP and channel it into increased capital per person!

By borrowing US$360,000, the country's GDP rises from US$11,400 to US$57,100, and its NNP rises from US$9,400 to US$19,100. The borrowing country takes on a massive amount of debt, but also enjoys a 5X increase in GDP and a 2X increase in NNP after interest payments. In the model, this rise in output happens all at once. In the real world, it takes one to two generations. Yet the principle is the same: large-scale borrowing can finance a dramatic rise in living standards and thereby justify a high level of borrowing relative to GDP.

Initially, in the model, the D/GDP ratio reaches 31.5, but after the five-fold growth, D/GDP settles at 6.3 (630%). This too seems to suggest insolvency by conventional standards, but with the interest rate at 5%, the interest servicing is 32% of GDP. That is huge, but in the modeling exercise it is a price worth paying to generate a 5X increase in GDP. Of course, this is merely a heuristic exercise, as it completely ignores the fact that raising 32% of GDP in tax revenues for interest payments would by itself create massive economic distortions. A realistic account of debt-servicing capacity must take into account not only the marginal productivity of investment, but also the ability to service sovereign debt through sufficient tax revenues, and the ability to convert GDP into net exports.

Still, the essential message remains. LICs and LMICs are capital scarce. They have high prospective growth rates and high marginal productivities of capital. They should borrow, and borrow heavily, in order to finance a broad-based increase in investments on human capital (education and health), public infrastructure (power, digital, water and sanitation, transport), and environmental protection.

Removing the barriers to increased capital market flows

Why don't the international capital markets direct such large lending to developing countries, so that they can massively increase their capital stocks and achieve rapid development? There are several important explanations.

First, to service heavy debts, the borrowing country has to run a large trade surplus to pay its interest abroad. In the illustration, the borrowing country would have to run a trade surplus equal to 32% of GDP. Many countries borrow abroad but then fail to take appropriate steps (such as maintaining a competitive exchange rate) to promote the increase in net exports needed to service the increased debts.

Second, the borrowing country needs to collect increased taxes to be able to service the increased interest payments. It's not enough for the national economy to borrow and grow. The sovereign borrower must take care to raise taxes sufficiently to service the higher level of interest payments.

Third, an irresponsible sovereign borrower might take on a huge stock of debt, but then use the debt for consumption or wasteful investment rather than for the kinds of investment really needed to raise national income. Therefore, sovereign borrowers must establish reliable and trusted systems of public administration, so as to prove that incremental borrowing gets translated into incremental, high-quality capital.

Fourth, there are inherent limits to a government's ability to rapidly boost capital stock. Most importantly, human capital investments require a timescale of a full generation: they must educate today's young children so that they can become skilled members of the workforce in twenty years time. Such investments therefore need time to come to full fruition, and sovereign borrowing should be paced according to the timeline of economic growth.

Fifth, governments often fall into unwanted liquidity crises that prevent them from servicing debts even with a growing economy. Typically, governments pay not only interest on the debt (as in the illustration) but on the principal as well. As the principal is paid down (amortized) it should in theory be refinanced with new loans, to keep the debt stock constant (or growing with GDP). In practice, governments are often unable to refinance debts coming due. Lenders often panic and refuse to supply new loans to refinance old debts coming due. If the government loses access to new borrowing, it is often pushed into default. At that point, the country's credit rating collapses, and a short-term liquidity problem quickly becomes a long-term financial crisis!

This analysis points to three main policy conclusions:

First, developing countries can and should take on much larger debts than is now considered normal, but to do so, they need to be able to borrow long-term at reasonable interest rates.

Second, the IMF and credit-rating agencies need to rethink the current rating systems and debt-sustainability indicators to take the future economic growth prospects of the developing countries into account, thereby revealing a much larger debt servicing capacity than is shown in static analyses.

Third, developing countries need to manage their budgets, trade policies, and liquid assets so that they can routinely service their external debts without fear of a liquidity crisis. Improved credibility and liquidity management will be essential to enable LICs and LMICs to tap the international capital markets on a much larger scale.

Next steps towards a global plan to finance the SDGs

First, the G20 should declare, clearly and unequivocally, its commitment to channel far larger flows of financing to developing countries: so that they can achieve economic development and meet the SDG targets. Second, the G20 should greatly increase the lending capacity and annual flows of the MDBs, mainly through greater paid-in capital to these institutions, but also through greater leverage of their balance sheets. Third, the G20 should support other measures as well – notably increased ODA, large-scale philanthropy, and refinancing of debts falling due – to bolster SDG finance for the LICs and LMICs. Fourth, the IMF and the credit-rating agencies need to redesign assessments of debt sustainability, taking into account the growth potential of developing countries and their need for far larger capital accumulation. Fifth, working together with the IMF and the MDBs, the developing countries need to strengthen their debt management and creditworthiness by integrating their borrowing policies with tax policies, export policies, and liquidity management, all to prevent future liquidity crises.

Table 1.1

Creditworthiness of Countries According to World Bank Income Category

	Number of UN Member States	Number with Moody's Ratings	Number with an Investment Grade Rating	% Countries with an Investment Grade Rating	% of population in WB Income Category with an Investment Grade Rating
LICs	27	9	0	0	0
LMICs	53	35	3	8.6	52.9
UMICs	54	40	10	25	72.5
HICs	59	52	44	84.6	97.3
WORLD	193	136	57	41.9	61.4

Source: Moody's (2021) and World Bank (2022b)

Table 1.2

Regression table: SDG Index vs General Government expenditure

SDG index vs. Government Outlays			
	Dependent variable		
	SDG index, 2022		
	All	**Expenditure below USD$10K per capita**	**Expenditure above US$10K per capita**
Log of government outlays per capita (USD PPP, 2019)	6.055***	6.704***	3.491
	-0.296	-0.407	-2.333
Constant	17.940***	13.320***	42.555*
	-2.405	-3.071	-22.748
Income group fixed effects	No	No	No
Observations	157	111	46
R^2	0.746	0.703	0.048
Adjusted R^2	0.744	0.7	0.027
Note	*p**p***p<0.01		

Source: Authors' analysis. Government outlays data are from the "World Economic Outlook Database, October 2021" (IMF, 2021)

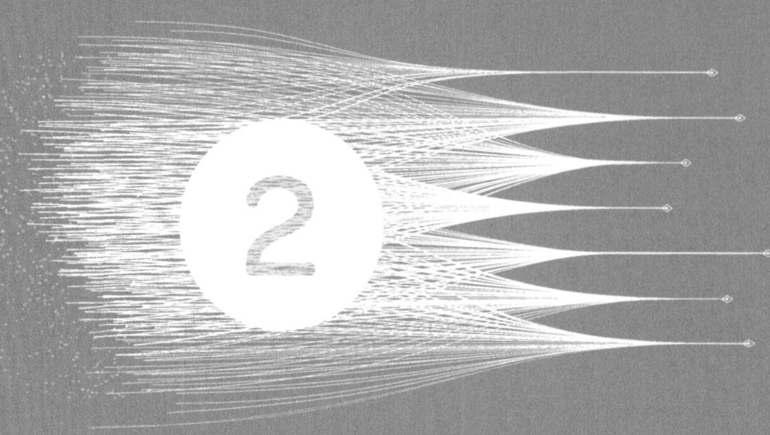

The SDG Index and Dashboards

Part 2
The SDG Index and Dashboards

The adoption in 2015 of three major international agreements – the 2030 Agenda and the SDGs, the Paris Climate Agreement, and the Addis Ababa Action Agenda on financing for development – represented major global breakthroughs for the international community. For the first time in history, all UN Member States agreed on a common set of goals for sustainable development (to be achieved by 2030, with mid-century goals for the Paris Climate Agreement) and established major principles and priorities for their financing. These commitments were made possible only through decades of work and advocacy by scientists, experts, governments, and civil society. In fact, 2022 marks the 50th anniversary of the first world conference on the global environment – the 1972 Stockholm Conference – and of the release of the landmark report, The Limits to Growth (Meadows et al., 1972). Multiple health and security crises, amplified by the climate and biodiversity crises, are now, however, putting the sustainable development agenda at risk. As the SDG Index highlights, since 2019 these crises have halted progress on sustainable development worldwide.

Although too slow, and unequal across countries and goals, progress was made globally on the SDGs between 2015 and 2019. But on top of their disastrous humanitarian cost, recent health and security crises have shifted attention away from long-term goals such as climate action, and exposed major fragmentation in multilateralism. These successive crises have also hit low-income and vulnerable countries particularly hard, and they may take longer to recover due to more limited access to financing. Members of the Leadership Council of the SDSN have released a statement calling for peace and diplomacy in the context of the war in Ukraine (SDSN, 2022).

Despite these difficult times, the SDGs should remain our roadmap for achieving sustainable development by 2030. They remain the only common language and vision across all UN member states on the triple bottom line of sustainable development: economic, social and environmental. As emphasized under SDG 16 (Peace, Justice and Strong Institutions) and SDG 17 (Partnerships for the Goals), peace and diplomacy are absolute prerequisites for progress on the goals. It is also crucial we learn from the COVID-19 pandemic if we are to prevent and respond in a more coordinated way to future outbreaks and pandemics and other major risks, as underscored by SDG 3 (Good Health and Well-Being). Achieving the SDGs is fundamentally an investment agenda, into building physical infrastructure and key services, while the bedrock principles of the SDGs of social inclusion, global cooperation, and universal access to public services are needed more than ever to fight the major challenges of our times, including security crises, pandemics, and climate change. Recovery plans, notably in high-income countries (HICs), and increased additional financing should be mobilized for restoring and accelerating SDG progress.

In September 2023, the world's heads of state will meet at the United Nations in New York for the second SDG Summit since the adoption of the 2030 Agenda. The Summit can and must be the opportunity to double down on efforts to transform societies by 2030 and beyond.

Box 1. The SDG Index and Dashboards

The SDG Index is an assessment of each country's overall performance on the 17 SDGs, giving equal weight to each Goal. The score signifies a country's position between the worst possible outcome (score of 0) and the target (score of 100). The dashboard and trend arrows help identify priorities for further actions and indicate whether countries are on-track or off-track based on latest trend data to achieve the goals and targets by 2030. Two-thirds of the data come from official statistics (typically UN custodian agencies) and one third from non-traditional statistics, including research centers, universities, and non-governmental organizations. Published since 2015, the SDG Index and Dashboards has been peer-reviewed (Schmidt-Traub et al., 2017) and statistically audited by the European Commission (Papadimitriou et al., 2019). More detailed information is available in the Annex (Method's Summary and Data Tables) and on our website (www.sdgindex.org).

2.1 Global trends and rankings

For the second year in a row, the world was no longer making progress on the SDGs in 2021. At 66.0 points, the average SDG Index score declined slightly from 2020: the pandemic and other crises have clearly been major setbacks for sustainable development.

From 2015 to 2019 the world progressed on the SDG Index at an average rate of 0.5 points a year. This was already too slow to achieve the SDGs by 2030. Progress also varied significantly across countries and goals, with trends for some countries and on some goals heading in the wrong direction. Poorer countries with lower SDG Index scores were progressing faster than richer countries. Since 2019, however, SDG Index scores have declined slightly: by 0.01 points per year on average. Overall, progress on the SDG Index has stagnated across all income groups.

The decline in the SDG Index score since 2019 has been driven primarily by a reversal in progress on socioeconomic goals. SDG 1 (No Poverty) and SDG 8 (Decent Work and Economic Growth) have been especially impacted by multiple crises in this period. The share of people facing extreme poverty has increased significantly since 2019, including in low-income countries (LICs). Small Island Developing States (SIDS) are also particularly vulnerable to international crises, partly due to their dependence on the international trade system, remittances, and tourism.

As recent editions of the *Sustainable Development Report* (SDR) have highlighted, progress on other SDGs has also been impacted, including SDG 2 (No Hunger), SDG 3 (Health and Well-Being) and SDG 4 (Quality Education), while temporary gains observed during lockdowns on environmental goals in 2020 were rapidly offset once restrictions were lifted (IPCC, 2022). The 2020 and 2021 editions of the SDR discussed and analyzed in detail the impact of COVID-19 on key SDG metrics (Sachs et al., 2020, 2021).

Due to time lags in data reporting, the full impact of the multiple crises including the COVID-19 pandemic is not fully reflected in this year's SDG Index. The ramifications that school closures have had on learning outcomes, as well as the pandemic's direct and indirect effects on health (such as long COVID, mental health impacts, or repercussions of delayed interventions and screening), may have long-term development impacts that could take years to be fully reflected in international statistics. This year's SDG Index also does not yet capture the war in Ukraine and its impact on

Figure 2.1
SDG Index Score over time, world average (2010-2021)

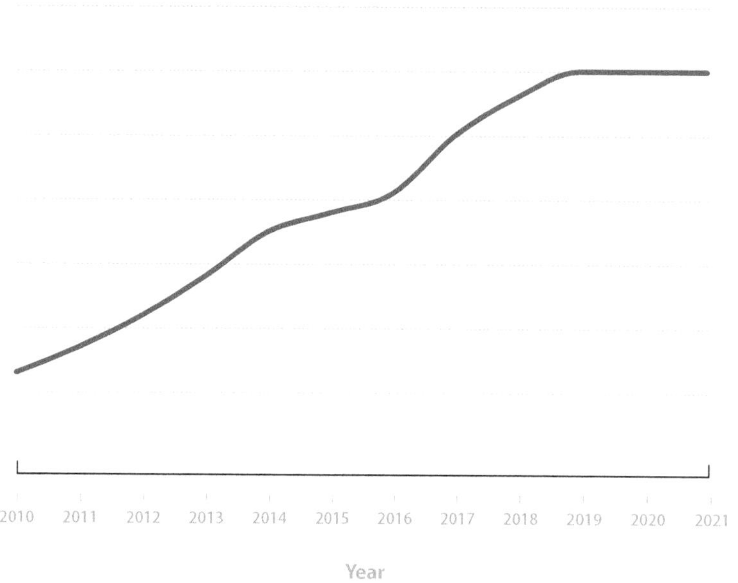

Note: Population-weighted averages. *Source:* Authors' analysis

Figure 2.2

Annualized growth rate of the SDG Index Score (2015-2019 vs 2019-2021)

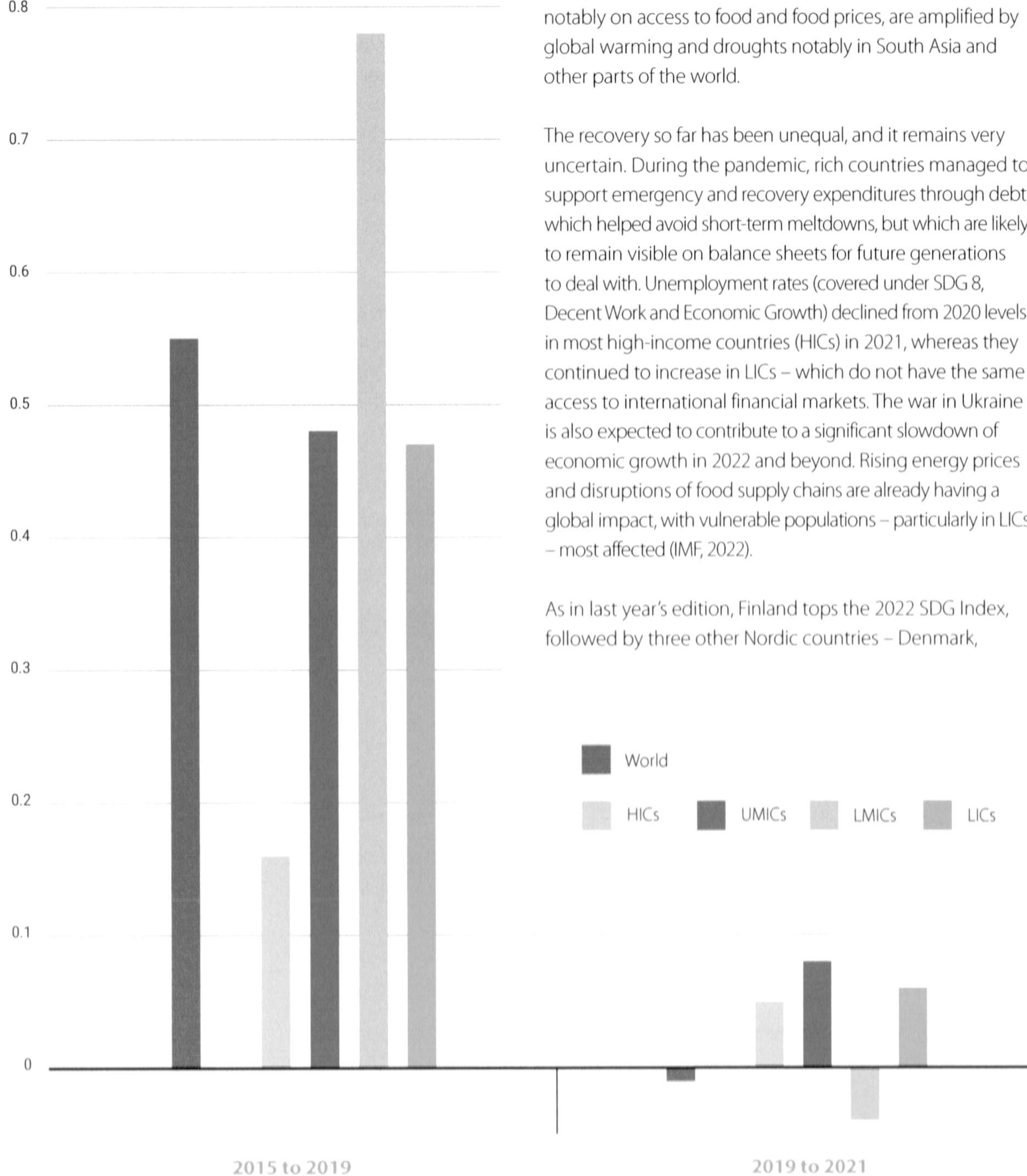

Note: Population weighted averages. *Source:* Authors' analysis

many countries. Other studies have already documented the impacts and likely impacts of the war in Ukraine on poverty, food security, and other SDGs (FAO, 2022; Wheatley, 2022; World Bank, 2022c). The impacts of the war in Ukraine, notably on access to food and food prices, are amplified by global warming and droughts notably in South Asia and other parts of the world.

The recovery so far has been unequal, and it remains very uncertain. During the pandemic, rich countries managed to support emergency and recovery expenditures through debt, which helped avoid short-term meltdowns, but which are likely to remain visible on balance sheets for future generations to deal with. Unemployment rates (covered under SDG 8, Decent Work and Economic Growth) declined from 2020 levels in most high-income countries (HICs) in 2021, whereas they continued to increase in LICs – which do not have the same access to international financial markets. The war in Ukraine is also expected to contribute to a significant slowdown of economic growth in 2022 and beyond. Rising energy prices and disruptions of food supply chains are already having a global impact, with vulnerable populations – particularly in LICs – most affected (IMF, 2022).

As in last year's edition, Finland tops the 2022 SDG Index, followed by three other Nordic countries – Denmark,

Sweden and Norway. Finland and the Nordic countries are also the happiest countries in the world according to the latest World Happiness Report (Helliwell et al., 2022). The top ten countries in the SDG Index are all in Europe, eight of them members of the European Union. While the detailed dashboards show that major SDG challenges remain even in these countries, especially on SDGs 12–15 (related to climate and biodiversity) and in relation to international spillovers, the European model of social democracies seems conducive to strong performance in the three major dimensions of sustainable development: economic, social and environmental.

Low-income countries tend to have lower SDG Index scores. This is partly due to the nature of the SDGs, which focus to a large extent on ending extreme poverty and providing access for all to basic services and infrastructure (SDGs 1–9). Moreover, poorer countries tend to lack adequate infrastructure and mechanisms to manage the key environmental challenges addressed by SDGs 12–15. Yet before the pandemic hit, most low-income countries, with the exception of those experiencing ongoing armed conflict or civil war, were making progress towards ending extreme poverty and providing access to basic services and infrastructure, particularly in relation to SDG 3 (Good Health and Well-Being) and SDG 8 (Decent Work and Economic Growth). As emphasized in Part 1 of this report, we interpret the performance of low-income countries (LICs) as a call to action for the world community to scale up SDG finance, especially for those countries at the bottom of the ladder.

Overall, East and South Asia has progressed on the SDGs more than any other region since their adoption in 2015, with Bangladesh and Cambodia showing the most progress of all countries. By contrast, Venezuela has declined the most on the SDG Index since 2015.

Figure 2.3

SDG 1 (No Poverty), Goal score by income group, 2010-2021

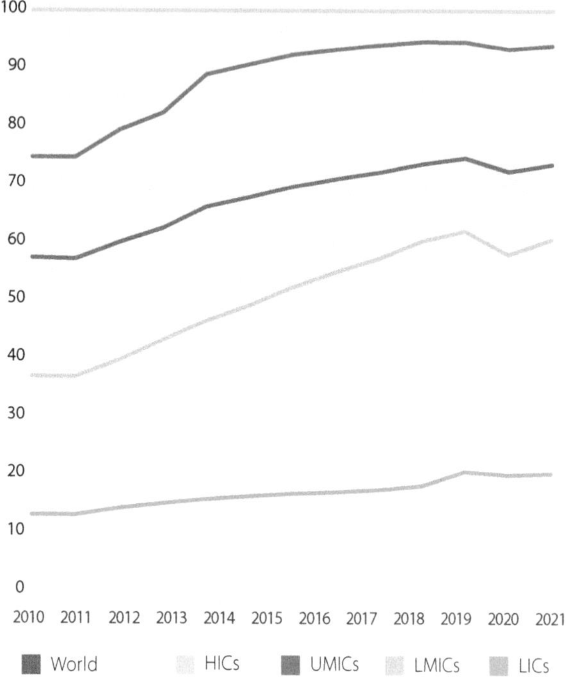

Note: Population-weighted averages. *Source:* Authors' analysis

Figure 2.4

SDG 8 (Decent Work and Economic Growth), Goal score by income group, 2010–2021

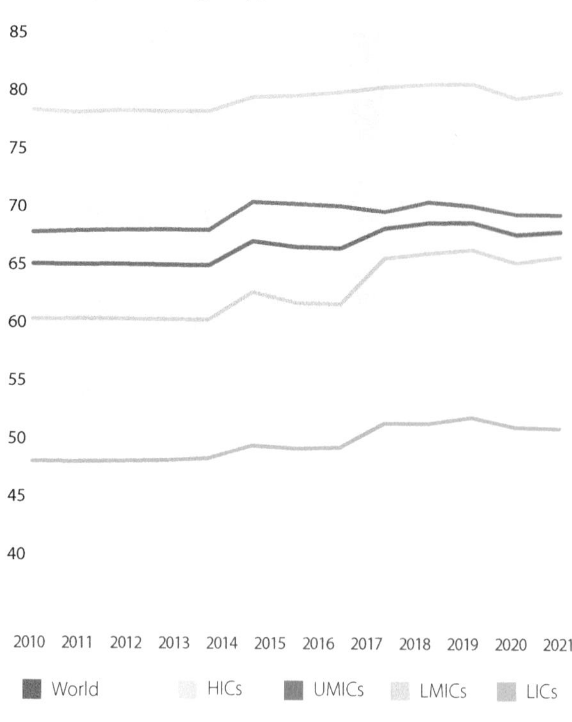

Note: Population-weighted averages. *Source:* Authors' analysis

Figure 2.5
Unemployment rates (SDG 8, Decent Work and Economic Growth) by income group, 2019, 2020, and 2021 (% of labor force)

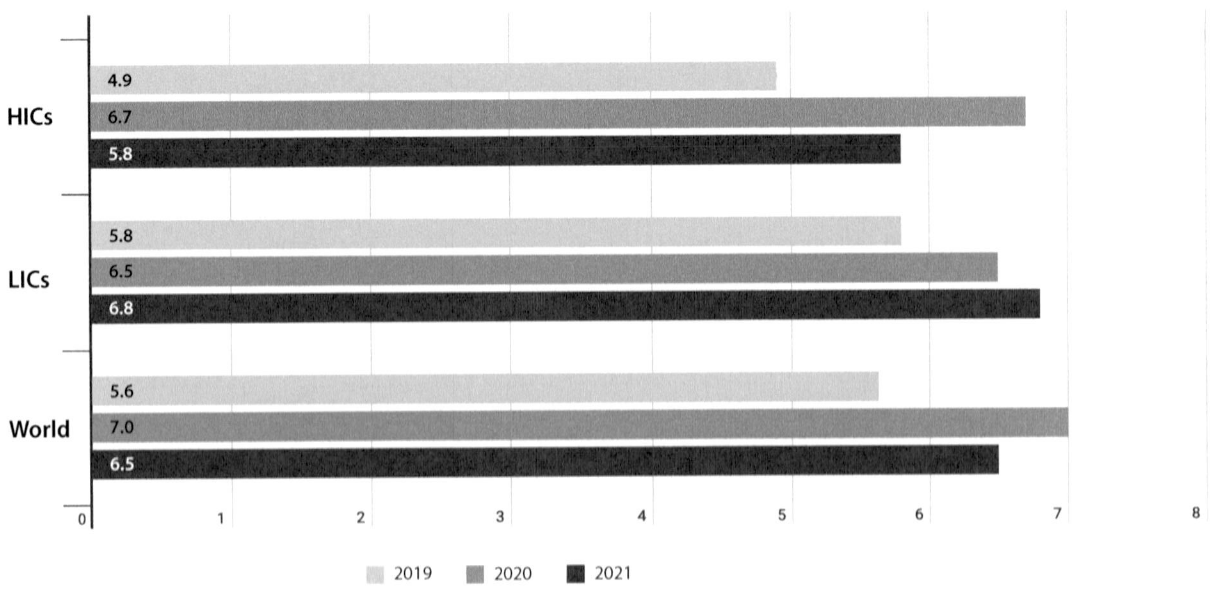

Note: Population-weighted averages. *Source:* Authors' calculations based on International Labour Organization (ILO)

Figure 2.6
Countries with the greatest change in SDG Index score between 2015 and 2021 (annualized point changes)

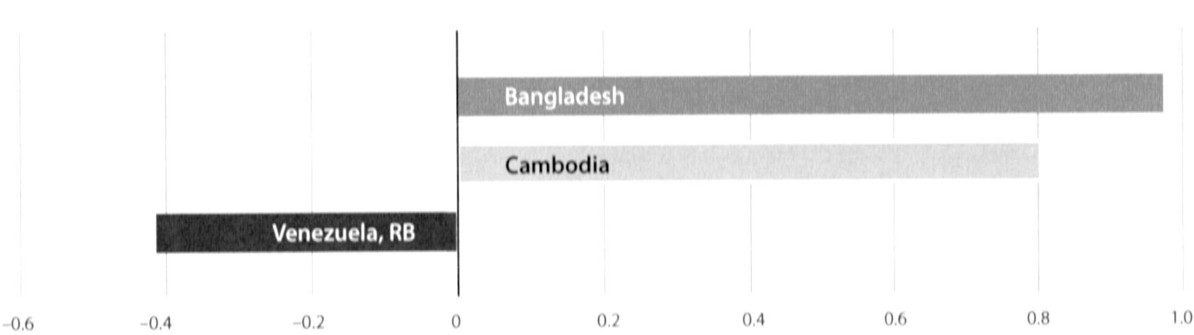

Source: Authors' analysis

Table 2.1
2022 SDG Index ranking and score

Rank	Country	Score	Rank	Country	Score
1	Finland	86.5	42	Bulgaria	74.3
2	Denmark	85.6	43	Cyprus	74.2
3	Sweden	85.2	44	Thailand	74.1
4	Norway	82.3	45	Russian Federation	74.1
5	Austria	82.3	46	Moldova	73.9
6	Germany	82.2	47	Costa Rica	73.8
7	France	81.2	48	Kyrgyz Republic	73.7
8	Switzerland	80.8	49	Israel	73.5
9	Ireland	80.7	50	Azerbaijan	73.5
10	Estonia	80.6	51	Georgia	73.4
11	United Kingdom	80.6	52	Fiji	72.9
12	Poland	80.5	53	Brazil	72.8
13	Czech Republic	80.5	54	Argentina	72.8
14	Latvia	80.3	55	Vietnam	72.8
15	Slovenia	80.0	56	China	72.4
16	Spain	79.9	57	North Macedonia	72.3
17	Netherlands	79.9	58	Peru	71.9
18	Belgium	79.7	59	Bosnia and Herzegovina	71.7
19	Japan	79.6	60	Singapore	71.7
20	Portugal	79.2	61	Albania	71.6
21	Hungary	79.0	62	Suriname	71.6
22	Iceland	78.9	63	Ecuador	71.5
23	Croatia	78.8	64	Algeria	71.5
24	Slovak Republic	78.7	65	Kazakhstan	71.1
25	Italy	78.3	66	Armenia	71.1
26	New Zealand	78.3	67	Maldives	71.0
27	Korea, Rep.	77.9	68	Dominican Republic	70.8
28	Chile	77.8	69	Tunisia	70.7
29	Canada	77.7	70	Bhutan	70.5
30	Romania	77.7	71	Turkey	70.4
31	Uruguay	77.0	72	Malaysia	70.4
32	Greece	76.8	73	Barbados	70.3
33	Malta	76.8	74	Mexico	70.2
34	Belarus	76.0	75	Colombia	70.1
35	Serbia	75.9	76	Sri Lanka	70.0
36	Luxembourg	75.7	77	Uzbekistan	69.9
37	Ukraine	75.7	78	Tajikistan	69.7
38	Australia	75.6	79	El Salvador	69.6
39	Lithuania	75.4	80	Jordan	69.4
40	Cuba	74.7	81	Oman	69.2
41	United States	74.6	82	Indonesia	69.2

Rank	Country	Score
83	Jamaica	69.0
84	Morocco	69.0
85	United Arab Emirates	68.8
86	Montenegro	68.8
87	Egypt, Arab Rep.	68.7
88	Iran, Islamic Rep.	68.6
89	Mauritius	68.4
90	Bolivia	68.0
91	Paraguay	67.4
92	Nicaragua	67.1
93	Brunei Darussalam	67.1
94	Qatar	66.8
95	Philippines	66.6
96	Saudi Arabia	66.6
97	Lebanon	66.3
98	Nepal	66.2
99	Turkmenistan	66.1
100	Belize	65.7
101	Kuwait	64.5
102	Bahrain	64.3
103	Myanmar	64.3
104	Bangladesh	64.2
105	Panama	64.0
106	Guyana	63.9
107	Cambodia	63.8
108	South Africa	63.7
109	Mongolia	63.5
110	Ghana	63.4
111	Lao PDR	63.4
112	Honduras	63.1
113	Gabon	62.8
114	Namibia	62.7
115	Iraq	62.3
116	Botswana	61.4
117	Guatemala	61.0
118	Kenya	61.0
119	Trinidad and Tobago	60.4
120	Venezuela, RB	60.3
121	India	60.3
122	Gambia, The	60.2
123	Sao Tome and Principe	59.4

Rank	Country	Score
124	Rwanda	59.4
125	Pakistan	59.3
126	Senegal	58.7
127	Cote d'Ivoire	58.4
128	Ethiopia	58.0
129	Syrian Arab Republic	57.4
130	Tanzania	57.4
131	Zimbabwe	56.8
132	Mauritania	55.8
133	Togo	55.6
134	Cameroon	55.5
135	Lesotho	55.1
136	Uganda	54.9
137	Eswatini	54.6
138	Burkina Faso	54.5
139	Nigeria	54.2
140	Zambia	54.2
141	Burundi	54.1
142	Mali	54.1
143	Mozambique	53.6
144	Papua New Guinea	53.6
145	Malawi	53.3
146	Sierra Leone	53.0
147	Afghanistan	52.5
148	Congo, Rep.	52.3
149	Niger	52.2
150	Yemen, Rep.	52.1
151	Haiti	51.9
152	Guinea	51.3
153	Benin	51.2
154	Angola	50.9
155	Djibouti	50.3
156	Madagascar	50.1
157	Congo, Dem. Rep.	50.0
158	Liberia	49.9
159	Sudan	49.6
160	Somalia	45.6
161	Chad	41.3
162	Central African Republic	39.3
163	South Sudan	39.0

Box 2. SDG Indices for regions and cities

This report – the SDR 2022 – focuses on global SDG priorities and trends. For more detailed regional and subnational analyses of SDG data and policies, see SDSN's special editions of the SDR for Africa (2019, 2020), the Arab Region (2019, 2022), Europe (2019, 2020, 2021), Latin America and the Caribbean (2019) and also for national and subnational entities in Benin, Bolivia, Brazil, Italy, Paraguay, Spain, the United States and Uruguay (among others) on our website (www.sdgindex.org). These are developed and prepared in close collaboration with SDSN's global, regional and national networks of experts and research institutions and other local partners.

Figure 2.7

SDG Index and Dashboards: Global, Regional and Subnational editions (2015-2022)

Global editions

Regional editions

Subnational editions

Source: Authors' analysis. Download the reports and databases at: www.sdgindex.org.

2.2 SDG dashboards and trends by income groups and major world regions

The SDG dashboards highlight each country's strengths and weaknesses in relation to the 17 goals, presenting performance in terms of levels and trends. As described in the methodology section, dashboard ratings for each goal are based on data for the two indicators on which the country performs worst. Good performance on five of seven indicators, for example, does not compensate for poor performance on the other two. In other words, our methodology assumes low substitutability or compensation across indicators in the construction of our composite index. The arrow system focuses on structural trajectories since the adoption of the SDGs (and less on year-on-year changes).

As in previous years, the dashboards include population-weighted averages for each region and income group, using the same set of indicators as the SDG Index (Figure 2.8). The OECD dashboards (Figure 2.9) incorporate more indicators than others owing to the greater availability of data for these countries. SDSN is also promoting regional editions of the SDG Index and Dashboards, including editions on Africa, the Arab Region, Europe, and Latin America as well as subnational editions – for instance looking at SDG gaps in cities in Bolivia, Brazil, Italy, Spain and the United States. These regional and subnational editions further contextualize the indicator selection and discuss more specific policy and implementation challenges. For instance, in this global assessment, performance on SDG 1 (No Poverty) only focuses on extreme poverty. In regional editions, we leverage other datasets to track material deprivation and poverty below poverty lines. Besides goal-level analyses, dashboards showing progress on each indicator are included in the country profiles and online database. Table 2.2 shows the ten SDG targets where high-income and low-income countries are facing the greatest challenges and assigns these targets to SDSN's Six SDG Transformations (Sachs et al, 2019).

Overall, high-income countries (HICs) and OECD countries are closer to achieving the targets than other country groups, yet none are on track to achieve all 17 SDGs. These countries perform better on goals related to socio-economic outcomes and basic access to infrastructure and services, including SDG 1 (No Poverty), SDG 3 (Good Health and Well-Being), SDG 6 (Clean Water and Sanitation), and SDG 7 (Affordable and Clean Energy). For SDG 3, the indicator set does not capture well a country's preparedness for global health security issues (such as pandemics), due to the absence of a robust international measure. The additional indicators included for OECD countries reveal that, while extreme poverty and basic access to services is mostly guaranteed in these countries, gaps persist in health and education outcomes across population groups, with income inequalities rising in some OECD countries. Further effort is also needed to reduce gender pay gaps to achieve SDG 5 (Gender Equality) in many OECD countries. Only moderate performance on SDG 16 (Peace, Justice and Strong Institutions), is partly driven by high homicide rates in large economies (including the United States), but also by persisting issues around access to affordable legal services and justice.

Major efforts are needed in HICs and OECD countries to accelerate progress towards climate mitigation and biodiversity protection (SDGs 12–15) and move towards more sustainable food systems and diets (covered under SDG 2, No Hunger). All HICs and OECD countries generate significant negative socioeconomic and environmental impacts outside their borders (spillovers) through trade and consumption, hampering other countries' efforts to achieve the SDGs. Historically these countries are also responsible for the bulk of greenhouse gas emissions and climate change and hence bear a special responsibility to take actions at the national and international level. Yet their progress on SDG 13 (Climate Action) and SDG 14 (Life Below Water) is mostly stagnant or insufficient to achieve internationally agreed targets.

HICs and OECD countries have very low levels of undernourishment and among the most productive agricultural systems, yet they perform poorly on SDG 2 (No Hunger) due to high and rising obesity rates and unsustainable agricultural systems and diets. Tax havens and profit-shifting in some OECD countries continue to undermine the ability of other countries to leverage resources to achieve the SDGs.

Overall, poorer countries – low-income countries (LICs) and lower-middle-income countries (LMICs), including many countries in sub-Saharan Africa – as well as Small Island

Table 2.2
Major SDG gaps for HICs and LICs by target

Major challenges for high-income countries

Percentage of countries in red	Official Target	Indicators included	Corresponding Transformations
66	17.2 Developed countries to implement fully their official development assistance commitments, including the commitment by many developed countries to achieve the target of 0.7 per cent of gross national income for official development assistance (ODA/GNI) to developing countries and 0.15 to 0.20 per cent of ODA/GNI to least developed countries; ODA providers are encouraged to consider setting a target to provide at least 0.20 per cent of ODA/GNI to least developed countries	For high-income and all OECD DAC countries: International concessional public finance, including official development assistance (% of GNI)	Other
58	13.2.2 Total greenhouse gas emissions per year (13.2 Integrate climate change measures into national policies, strategies and planning)	CO_2 emissions from fossil fuel combustion and cement production (tCO_2/capita), CO_2 emissions embodied in imports (tCO_2/capita), CO_2 emissions embodied in fossil fuel exports (kg/capita), Carbon Pricing Score at EUR60/tCO_2 (%, worst 0-100 best)	Transformation 3 - Energy Decarbonisation and Sustainable Industry
57.1	14.5 By 2020, conserve at least 10 per cent of coastal and marine areas, consistent with national and international law and based on the best available scientific information	Mean area that is protected in marine sites important to biodiversity (%)	Transformation 4 - Sustainable Food, Land, Water, and Oceans
56.7	12.5 By 2030, substantially reduce waste generation through prevention, reduction, recycling and reuse	Municipal solid waste (kg/capita/day), Electronic waste (kg/capita), Non-recycled municipal solid waste (kg/capita/day), Exports of plastic waste (kg/capita)	Transformation 5 - Sustainable Cities and Communities, Transformation 3 - Energy Decarbonisation and Sustainable Industry
44.1	15.1 By 2020, ensure the conservation, restoration and sustainable use of terrestrial and inland freshwater ecosystems and their services, in particular forests, wetlands, mountains and drylands, in line with obligations under international agreements	Mean area that is protected in terrestrial sites important to biodiversity (%), Mean area that is protected in freshwater sites important to biodiversity (%), Terrestrial and freshwater biodiversity threats embodied in imports (per million population)	Transformation 4 - Sustainable Food, Land, Water, and Oceans
41.6	14.1 By 2025, prevent and significantly reduce marine pollution of all kinds, in particular from land-based activities, including marine debris and nutrient pollution	Ocean Health Index: Clean Waters score (worst 0-100 best), Marine biodiversity threats embodied in imports (per million population)	Transformation 4 - Sustainable Food, Land, Water, and Oceans
33.0	6.4.2 Level of water stress: freshwater withdrawal as a proportion of available freshwater resources (6.4 By 2030, substantially increase water-use efficiency across all sectors and ensure sustainable withdrawals and supply of freshwater to address water scarcity and substantially reduce the number of people suffering from water scarcity)	Freshwater withdrawal (% of available freshwater resources), Scarce water consumption embodied in imports (m3 H_2O eq/capita)	Transformation 4 - Sustainable Food, Land, Water, and Oceans
32.0	17.1 Strengthen domestic resource mobilization, including through international support to developing countries, to improve domestic capacity for tax and other revenue collection	Other countries: Government revenue excluding grants (% of GDP), Corporate Tax Haven Score (best 0-100 worst), Financial Secrecy Score (best 0-100 worst), Shifted profits of multinationals (US$ billion)	Other
29.5	7.2 By 2030, increase substantially the share of renewable energy in the global energy mix	CO_2 emissions from fuel combustion per total electricity output ($MtCO_2$/TWh), Share of renewable energy in total primary energy supply (%)	Transformation 3 - Energy Decarbonisation and Sustainable Industry
23.8	2.2 By 2030, end all forms of malnutrition, including achieving, by 2025, the internationally agreed targets on stunting and wasting in children under 5 years of age, and address the nutritional needs of adolescent girls, pregnant and lactating women and older persons (2.2.2 wasting and overweight)	Prevalence of stunting in children under 5 years of age (%), Prevalence of wasting in children under 5 years of age (%), Prevalence of obesity, BMI ≥ 30 (% of adult population), Human Trophic Level (best 2-3 worst)	Transformation 4 - Sustainable Food, Land, Water, and Oceans

Table 2.2
(continued)

Major challenges for low-income countries

Percentage of countries in red	Official Target	Indicators included	Corresponding Transformations
100	1.2 By 2030, reduce at least by half the proportion of men, women and children of all ages living in poverty in all its dimensions according to national definitions	Poverty headcount ratio at $3.20/day (%)	Transformation 1 - Education, Gender, and Inequality
100	16.2 End abuse, exploitation, trafficking and all forms of violence against and torture of children	Children involved in child labor (% of population aged 5 to 14)	Transformation 1 - Education, Gender, and Inequality
95.8	6.2 By 2030, achieve access to adequate and equitable sanitation and hygiene for all and end open defecation, paying special attention to the needs of women and girls and those in vulnerable situations	Population using at least basic sanitation services (%), Population using safely managed sanitation services (%)	Transformation 5 - Sustainable Cities and Communities
95.8	6.3 By 2030, improve water quality by reducing pollution, eliminating dumping and minimizing release of hazardous chemicals and materials, halving the proportion of untreated wastewater and substantially increasing recycling and safe reuse globally	Anthropogenic wastewater that receives treatment (%), Population using safely managed water services (%)	Transformation 5 - Sustainable Cities and Communities
93.8	3.1 By 2030, reduce the global maternal mortality ratio to less than 70 per 100,000 live births	Maternal mortality rate (per 100,000 live births), Births attended by skilled health personnel (%)	Transformation 2 - Health, Well-being and Demography
93.8	9.c Significantly increase access to information and communications technology and strive to provide universal and affordable access to the Internet in least developed countries by 2020	Population using the internet (%), Mobile broadband subscriptions (per 100 population), Gap in internet access by income (percentage points)	Transformation 6 - Digital Revolution for Sustainable Development
91.7	16.5 Substantially reduce corruption and bribery in all their forms	Corruption Perceptions Index (worst 0-100 best)	Other
91.7	3.6 By 2020, halve the number of global deaths and injuries from road traffic accidents	Traffic deaths (per 100,000 population)	Transformation 2 - Health, Well-being and Demography
91.7	3.7 By 2030, ensure universal access to sexual and reproductive health-care services, including for family planning, information and education, and the integration of reproductive health into national strategies and programmes	Adolescent fertility rate (births per 1,000 females aged 15 to 19)	Transformation 2 - Health, Well-being and Demography
91.3	8.10 Strengthen the capacity of domestic financial institutions to encourage and expand access to banking, insurance and financial services for all	Adults with an account at a bank or other financial institution or with a mobile-money-service provider (% f population aged 15 or over)	Transformation 6 - Digital Revolution for Sustainable Development

Developing States (SIDS) tend to face the largest SDG gaps. This is largely driven by a lack of the physical, digital, and human infrastructure (schools, hospitals) needed to achieve the socioeconomic goals (SDGs 1–9) and manage key environmental challenges. Ongoing conflicts in some countries have led to poor and worsening performance on most SDGs for several years, and the pandemic halted years of progress towards eradicating extreme poverty. The war in Ukraine threatens access to food globally, including in countries already facing major challenges on SDG 2 (No Hunger). By contrast, these countries perform better than the rest of the world on SDG 12 (Responsible Consumption and Production) and SDG 13 (Climate Action). Many of them emit less than 2 tonnes of CO_2 per person each year. Yet they are often the countries that are most vulnerable to the impacts of climate change. Strengthening public-sector capacities as well as statistical capacities remain major priorities in all of these countries, as emphasized under SDG 16 (Peace, Justice and Strong Institutions).

Figure 2.8

2022 SDG dashboards by region and income group (levels and trends)

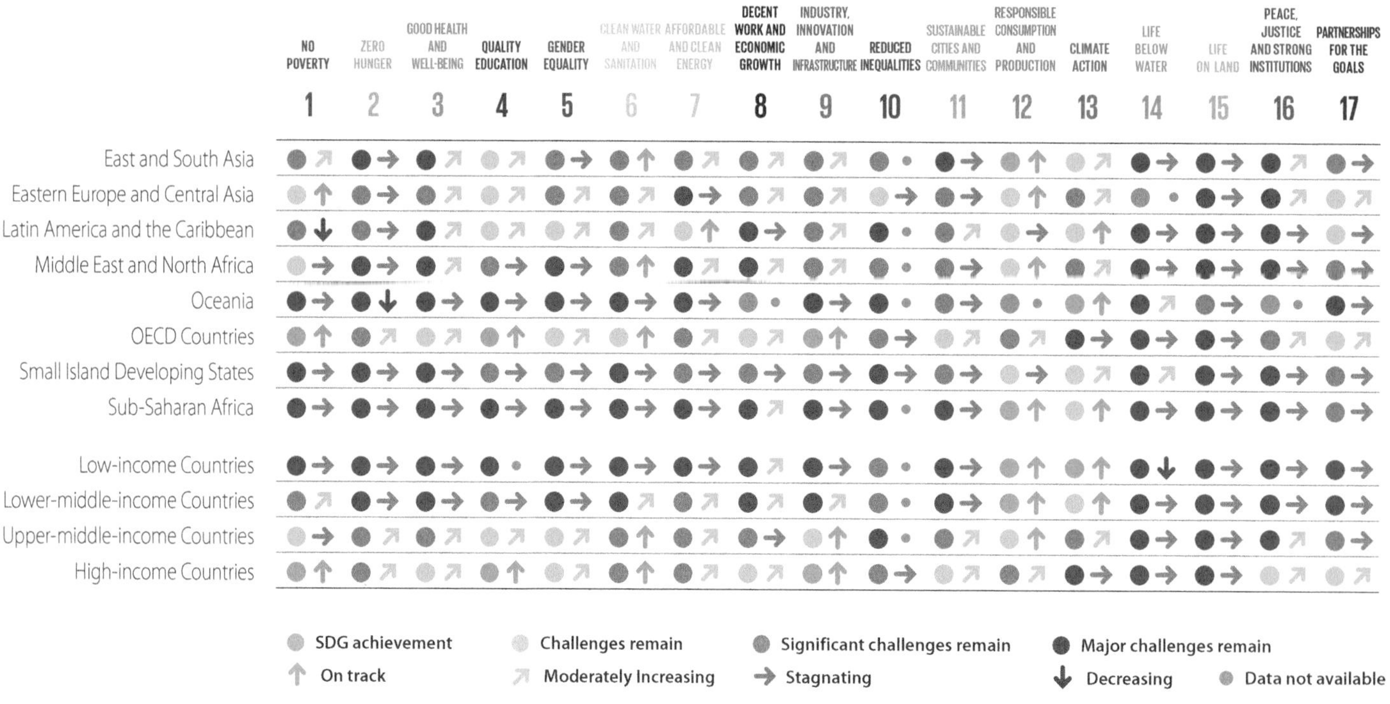

Note: Excluding OECD specific indicators. Population-weighted averages. *Source:* Authors' analysis

Figure 2.9
2022 SDG dashboards for OECD countries (levels and trends)

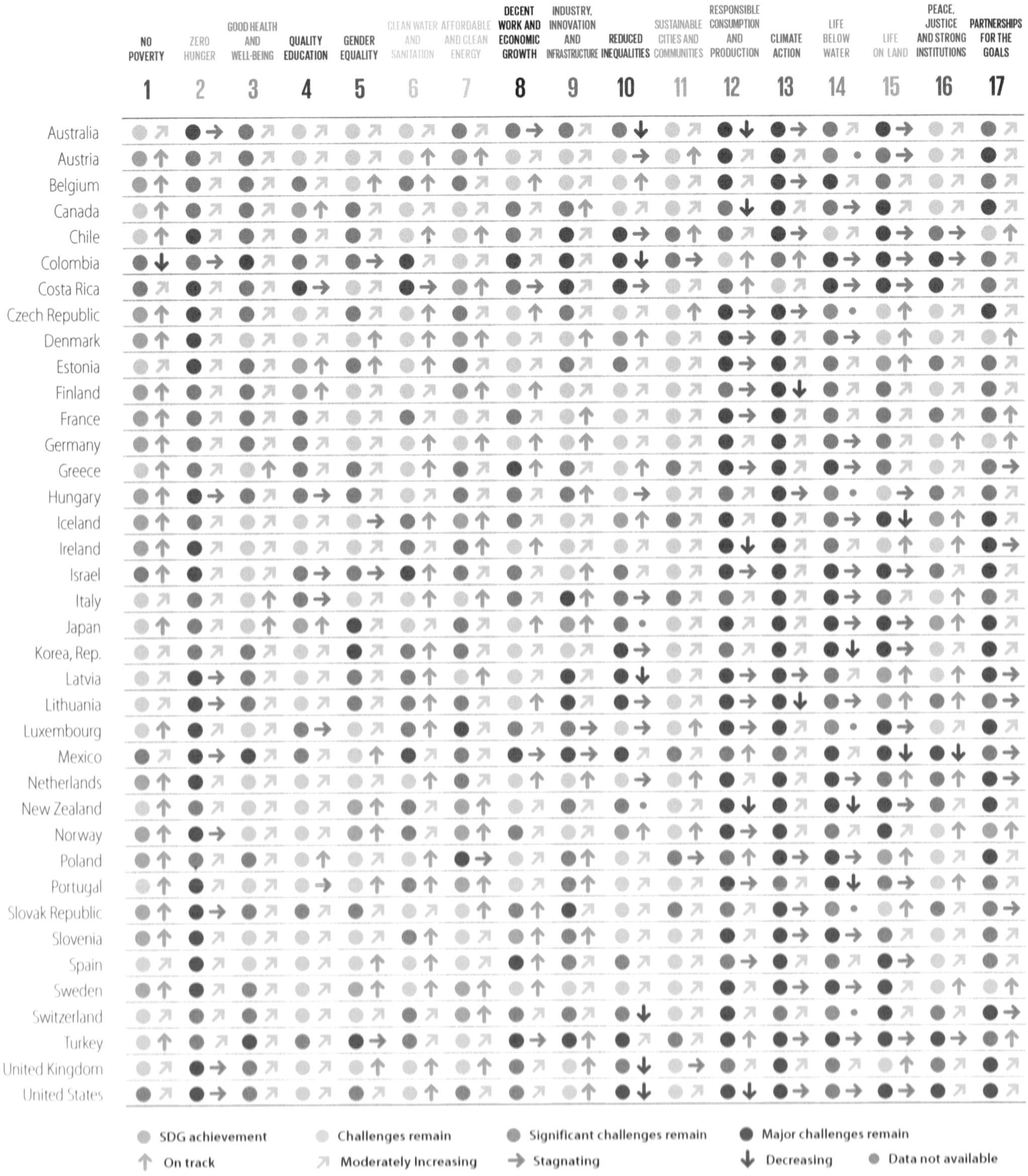

	NO POVERTY 1	ZERO HUNGER 2	GOOD HEALTH AND WELL-BEING 3	QUALITY EDUCATION 4	GENDER EQUALITY 5	CLEAN WATER AND SANITATION 6	AFFORDABLE AND CLEAN ENERGY 7	DECENT WORK AND ECONOMIC GROWTH 8	INDUSTRY, INNOVATION AND INFRASTRUCTURE 9	REDUCED INEQUALITIES 10	SUSTAINABLE CITIES AND COMMUNITIES 11	RESPONSIBLE CONSUMPTION AND PRODUCTION 12	CLIMATE ACTION 13	LIFE BELOW WATER 14	LIFE ON LAND 15	PEACE, JUSTICE AND STRONG INSTITUTIONS 16	PARTNERSHIPS FOR THE GOALS 17
Australia	↗	→	↗	↗	↗	↗	↗	→	↗	↓	↗	↓	→	↗	→	↗	↗
Austria	↑	↗	↗	↗	↗	↑	↑	↗	↗	→	↑	↗	↗	•	→	↗	↗
Belgium	↑	↗	↗	↗	↑	↑	↗	↑	↗	↑	↗	↗	→	↗	↗	↗	↗
Canada	↑	↗	↗	↑	↗	↗	↗	↗	↑	↗	↗	↓	↗	→	↗	↗	↗
Chile	↑	↗	↗	↗	↗	↑	↑	↗	↗	→	↑	↗	→	↗	→	→	↑
Colombia	↓	→	↗	↗	→	↗	↗	↗	↗	↓	→	↑	↑	→	→	→	↗
Costa Rica	↗	↗	↗	→	↗	→	↑	→	↗	→	↗	↑	↗	→	→	↗	↗
Czech Republic	↑	↗	↗	↗	↗	↑	↗	↑	↗	↗	↑	→	→	•	↑	↗	↗
Denmark	↑	↗	↗	↗	↑	↑	↑	↗	↑	↑	↗	→	↗	→	↑	↗	↑
Estonia	↗	↗	↗	↑	↑	↑	↗	↗	↗	↗	↗	→	↗	↗	↑	↗	↗
Finland	↑	↗	↗	↑	↗	↗	↑	↑	↗	↗	↗	→	↓	↗	↗	↗	↗
France	↑	↗	↗	↗	↗	↗	↗	↗	↑	↗	↗	→	↗	↗	↗	↗	↑
Germany	↑	↗	↗	↗	↗	↑	↑	↑	↑	↗	↗	↗	↗	→	↗	↑	↑
Greece	↑	↗	↑	↗	↗	↑	↗	↑	↗	↑	↗	→	↗	→	↗	↗	→
Hungary	↑	→	↗	→	↗	↗	↗	↗	↑	→	↗	↗	→	•	→	↗	↗
Iceland	↑	↗	↗	↗	→	↑	↑	↗	↗	↑	↗	↗	↗	→	↓	↑	↗
Ireland	↑	↗	↗	↗	↗	↗	↑	↑	↗	↗	↗	↓	↗	↗	↑	↑	→
Israel	↑	↗	↗	→	→	↑	↗	↗	↑	↗	↗	→	↗	→	→	↗	↗
Italy	↗	↗	↑	→	↗	↑	↑	↗	↑	→	↗	↗	↗	→	↗	↑	↗
Japan	↑	↗	↑	↑	↗	↗	↗	↑	↑	•	↗	↗	↗	→	→	↑	↗
Korea, Rep.	↗	↗	↗	↗	↗	↑	↗	↗	↗	→	↗	↗	↗	↓	→	↗	↗
Latvia	↗	→	↗	↗	↗	↑	↑	↗	↗	↓	↗	→	→	↗	↑	↑	→
Lithuania	↗	→	↗	↗	↗	↑	↗	↑	↗	→	↗	→	↓	→	↑	↑	→
Luxembourg	↑	↗	↗	→	↗	↑	↗	↗	→	→	↑	→	↗	•	→	↗	↗
Mexico	↗	→	↗	↗	↑	↗	↗	→	→	↗	↗	↑	↗	↗	↓	↓	→
Netherlands	↑	↗	↗	↗	↗	↑	↗	↑	↑	→	↑	↗	↗	→	↑	↑	→
New Zealand	↑	↗	↗	↗	↑	↗	↑	↗	↗	•	↗	↓	↗	↓	→	↗	↗
Norway	↑	→	↗	↗	↑	↗	↑	↗	↗	↑	↑	→	↗	↗	↗	↑	↑
Poland	↑	↗	↗	↑	↗	↑	→	↗	↑	↗	→	↑	→	→	↑	↗	↗
Portugal	↑	↗	↗	→	↑	↑	↑	↗	↑	↗	↗	→	↗	↓	→	↑	↗
Slovak Republic	↑	→	↗	↗	↗	↗	↑	↑	↗	↗	↗	↗	→	•	↑	↗	→
Slovenia	↑	↗	↗	↗	↗	↑	↗	↑	↑	↗	↗	↗	→	→	↗	↗	↗
Spain	↗	↗	↗	↗	↑	↑	↗	↑	↗	↗	↗	→	↗	↗	→	↗	↗
Sweden	↑	↗	↗	↗	↑	↑	↑	↑	↗	↗	↗	↗	→	→	↗	↑	↑
Switzerland	↗	↗	↗	↗	↗	↗	↑	↗	↗	↓	↗	↗	↗	•	↗	↗	→
Turkey	↑	↗	↗	↗	→	↗	↗	→	↑	↗	↗	↑	→	→	→	→	↑
United Kingdom	↗	→	↗	↗	↑	↑	↑	↗	↑	↓	→	↗	↗	↗	↑	↗	↗
United States	↗	→	↗	↗	↗	↑	↗	↗	↑	↓	↗	↓	→	→	→	↗	↗

● SDG achievement ● Challenges remain ● Significant challenges remain ● Major challenges remain
↑ On track ↗ Moderately increasing → Stagnating ↓ Decreasing • Data not available

Note: Including OECD specific indicators. *Source:* Authors' analysis.

Figure 2.10

2022 SDG dashboards for East and South Asia (levels and trends)

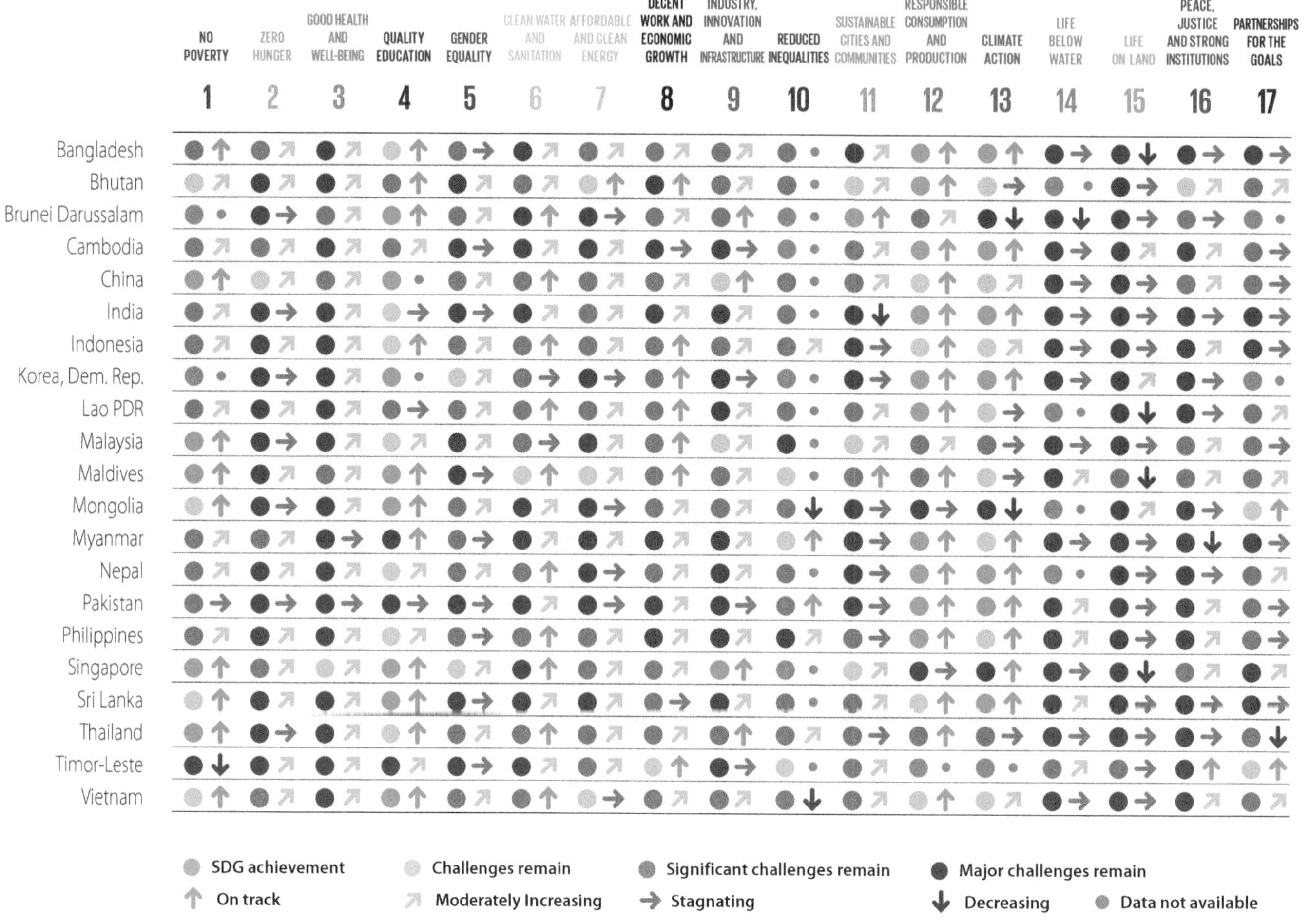

Source: Authors' analysis

Figure 2.11

2022 SDG dashboards for Eastern Europe and Central Asia (levels and trends)

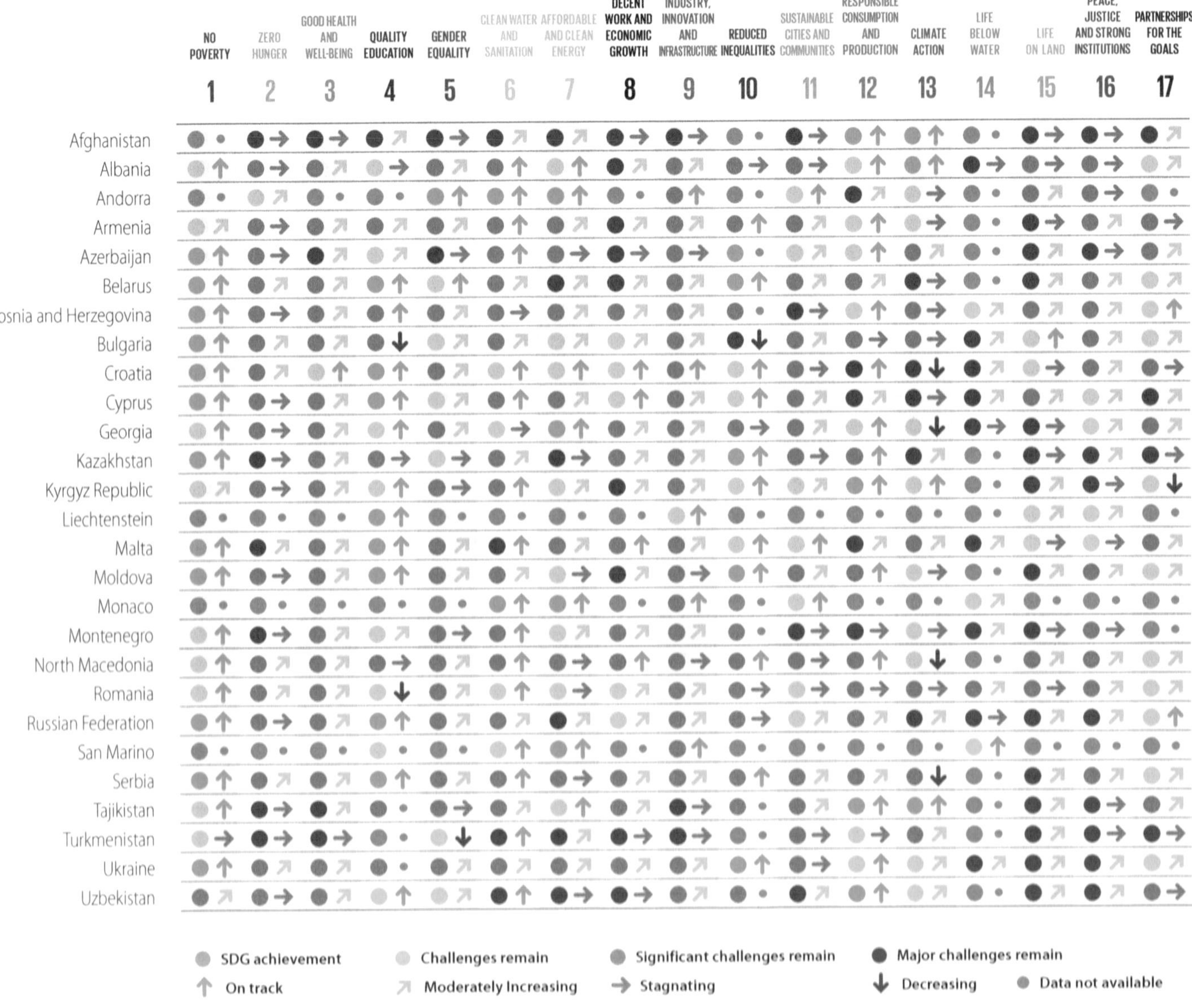

Source: Authors' analysis

Figure 2.12

2022 SDG dashboards for Latin America and the Caribbean (levels and trends)

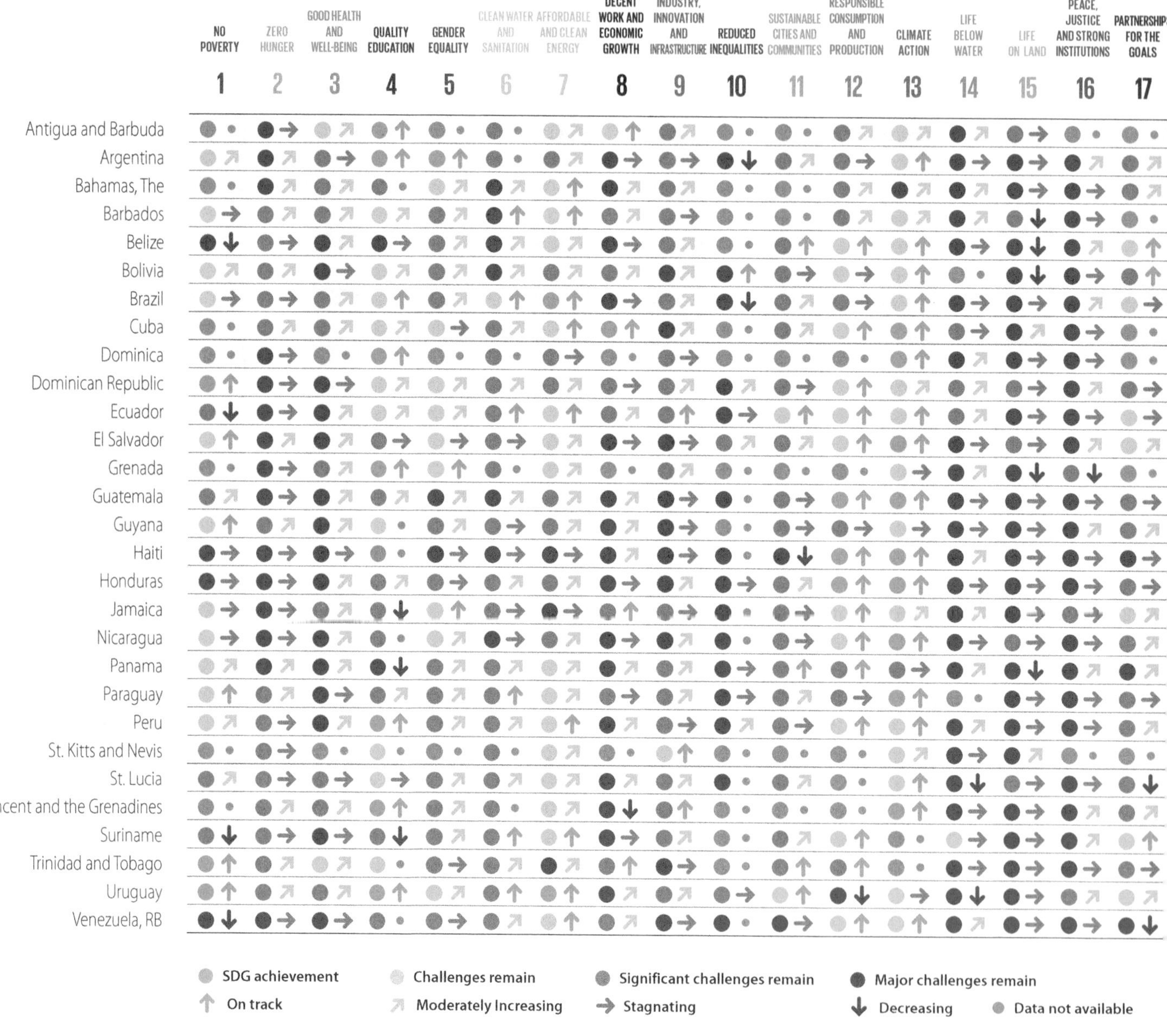

Source: Authors' analysis

Figure 2.13

2022 SDG dashboards for the Middle East and North Africa (levels and trends)

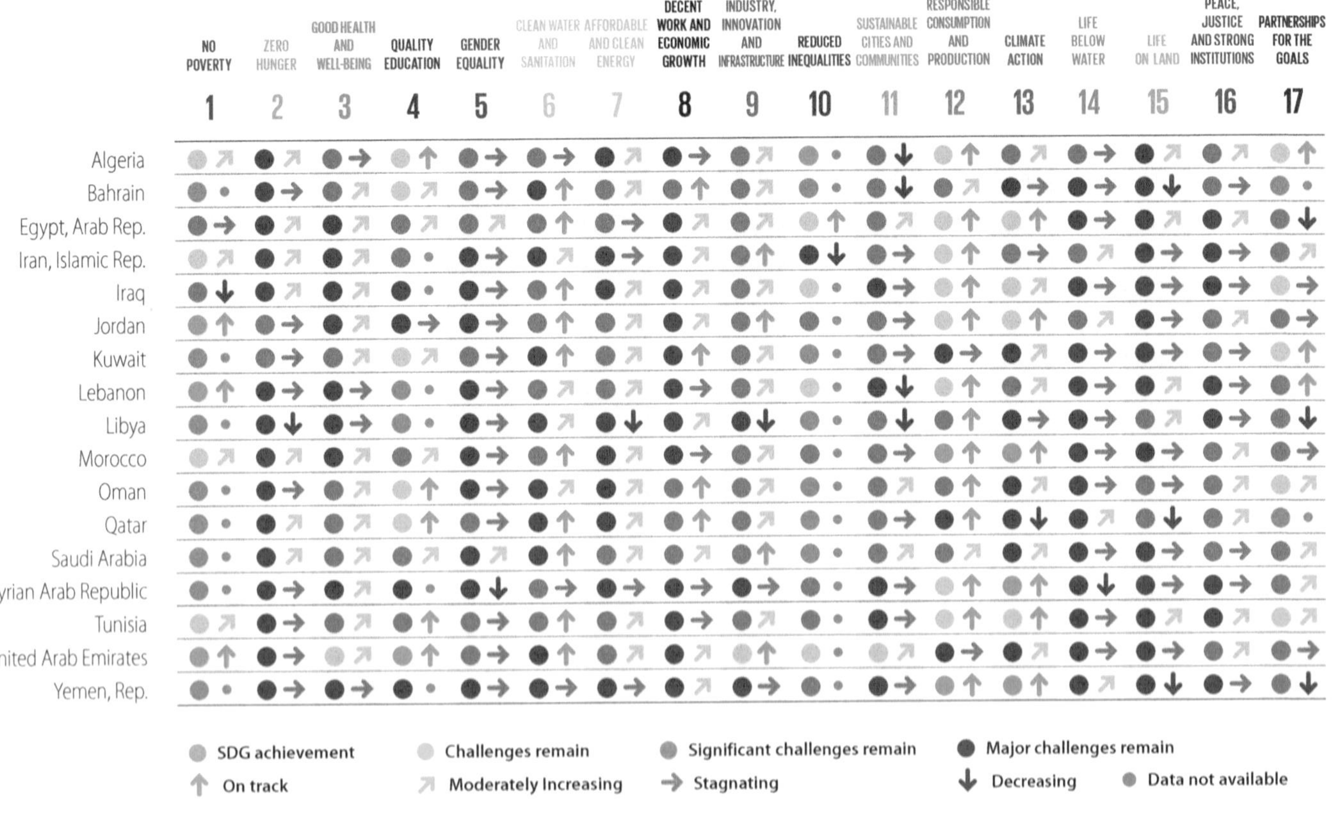

Source: Authors' analysis

Figure 2.14

2022 SDG dashboards for Oceania (levels and trends)

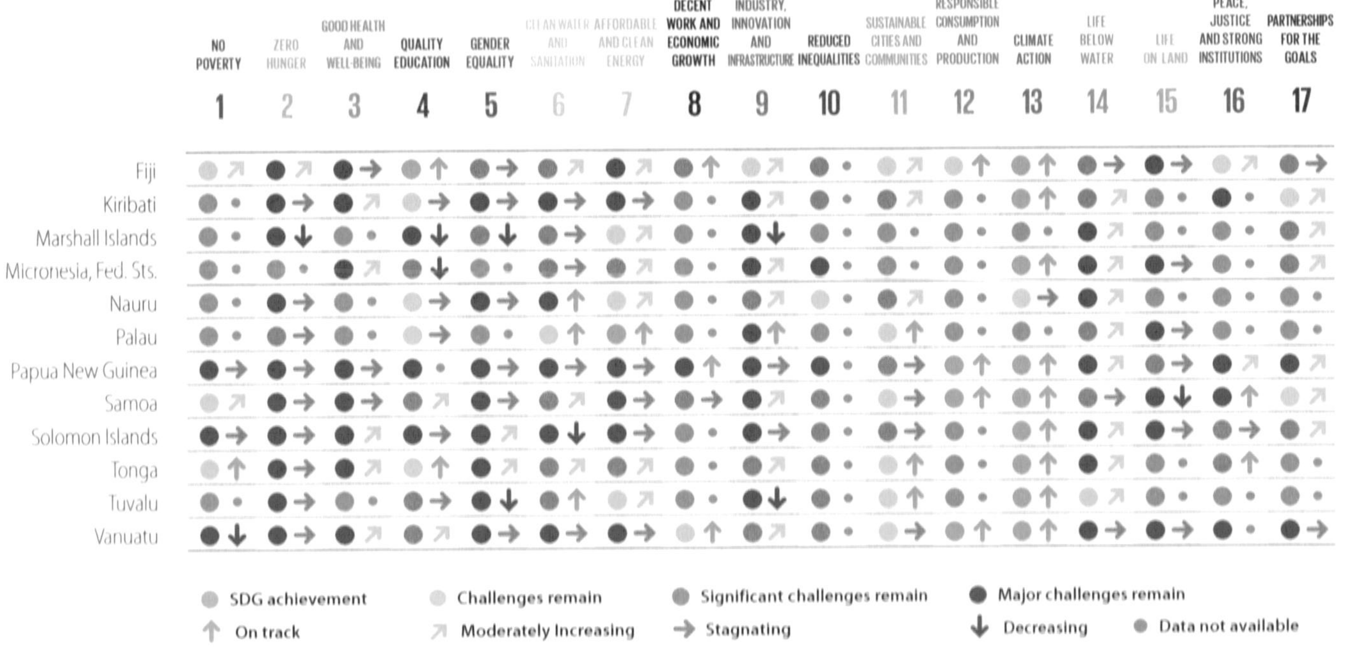

Source: Authors' analysis

Figure 2.15

2022 SDG dashboards for sub-Saharan Africa (levels and trends)

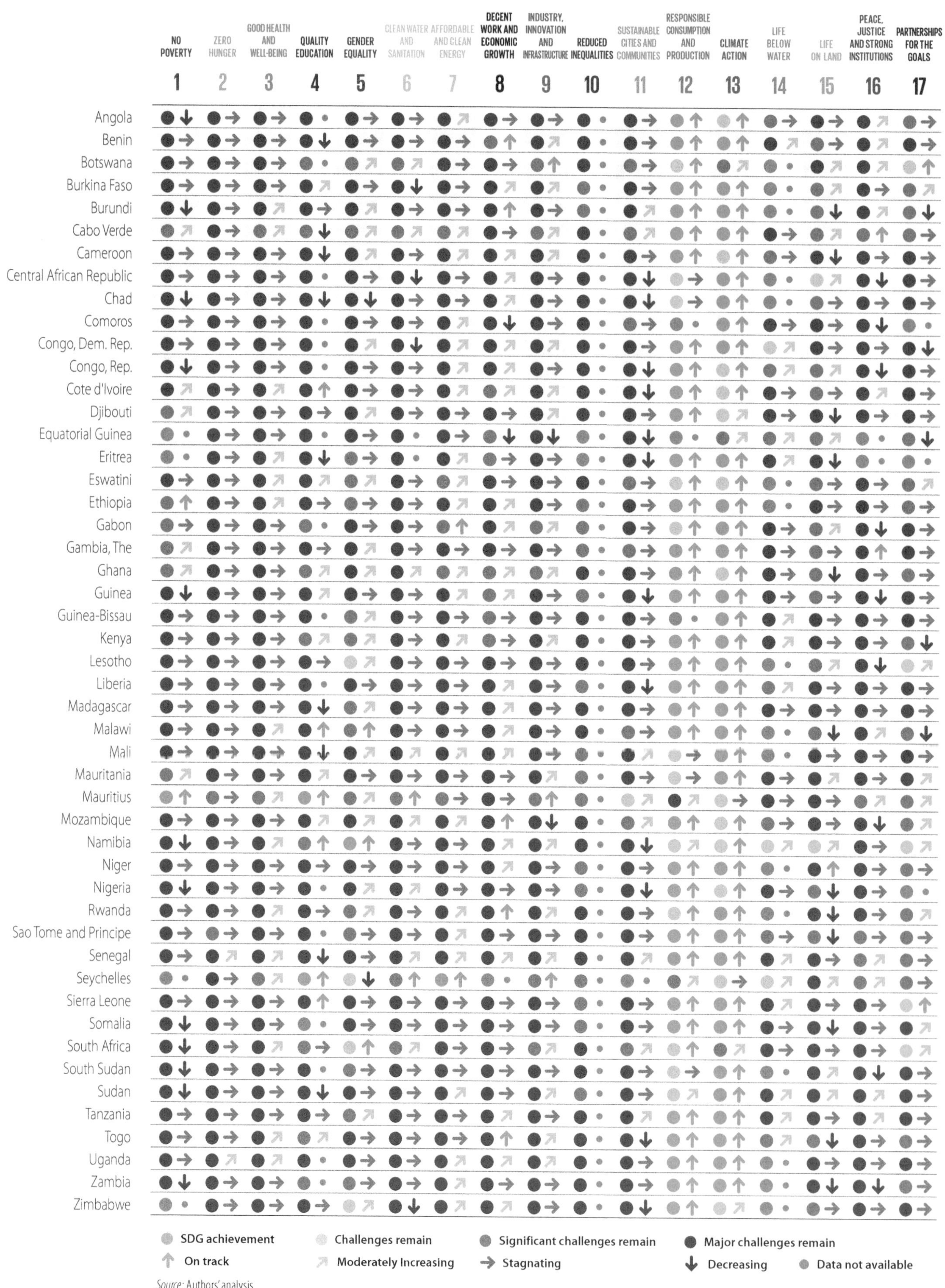

Figure 2.16

2022 SDG dashboards for Small Island Developing States (SIDS) (levels and trends)

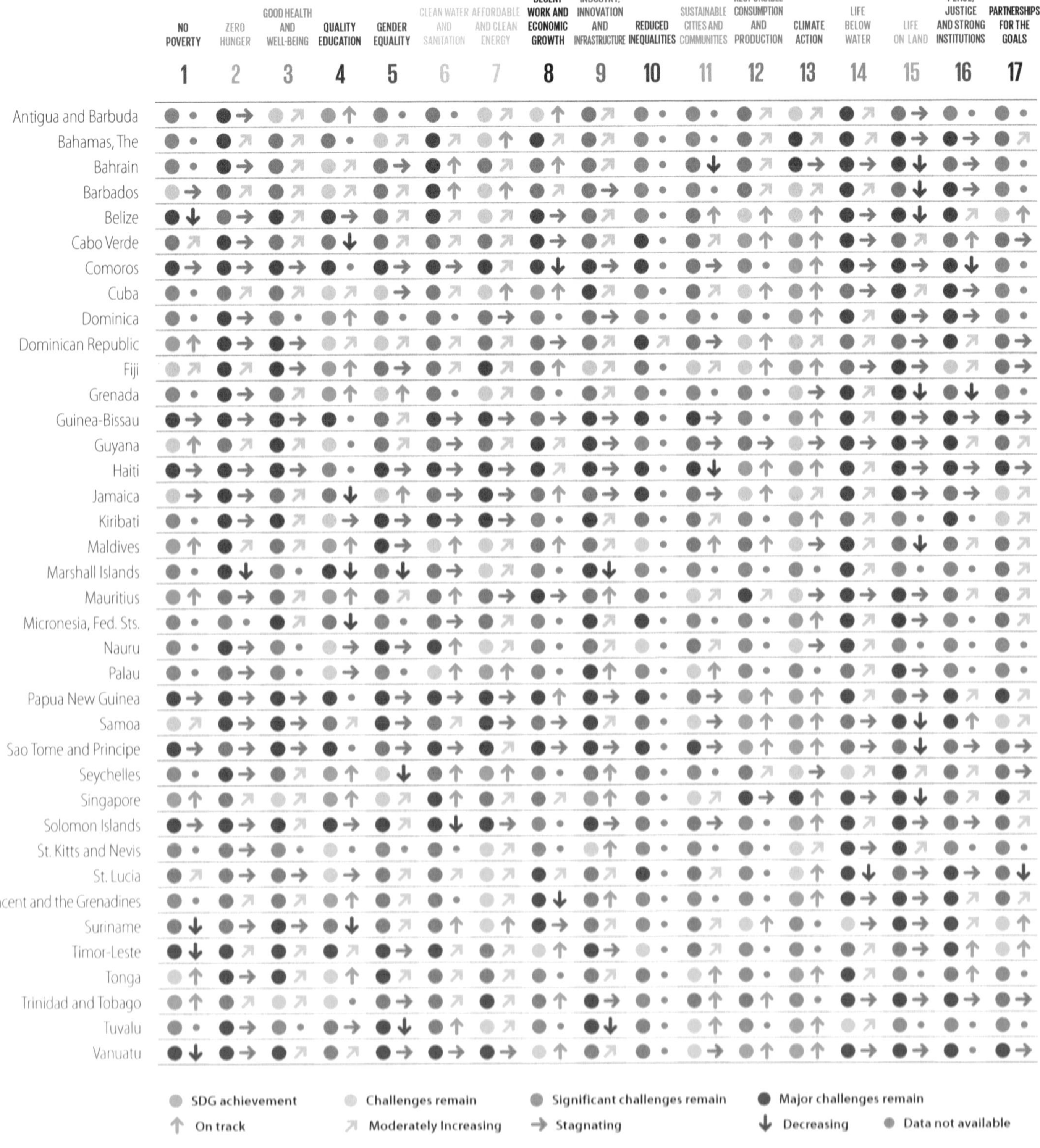

Source: Authors' analysis

2.3 International spillovers

Spillovers, both positive and negative, must be understood, measured, and carefully managed. These benefits or costs may be referred to as positive or negative externalities. Countries cannot achieve the SDGs if such negative externalities from other countries counteract their efforts (Schmidt-Traub et al., 2019). International spillover effects are said to occur when one country's actions generate benefits or impose costs on another country that are not reflected in market prices and therefore are not 'internalized' by the actions of consumers and producers (Sachs et al., 2017).

The 2030 Agenda and the SDGs recognize the importance of international spillovers in several crucial ways. SDG 17 (Partnerships for the Goals) calls for "policy coherence" for sustainable development, SDG 12 (Responsible Consumption and Production) stresses the need for more sustainable production and consumption, and SDG 8 (Decent Work and Economic Growth) demands the eradication of modern slavery and child labor.

Conceptually, international spillovers in the context of the SDGs can be grouped into four categories:

- **Environmental and social spillovers embodied into trade**. These cover international effects related to pollution, the use of natural resources, and social impacts generated by the consumption of goods and services. Multi-regional input-output (MRIO) models combined with satellite datasets provide powerful tools to track impacts generated worldwide by consuming countries. This category of spillovers also includes exports of toxic pesticides, trade in waste, and illegal wildlife trade. They are particularly connected to SDG 8 (Decent Work and Economic Growth), SDGs 12–15 (related to responsible consumption, climate and biodiversity) and SDG 17 (Partnerships for the Goals). They also indirectly affect all other SDGs.

- **Direct cross-border flows in air and water**. These cover effects generated through physical flows – for instance of air and water – from one country to another. Cross-border air and water pollution are difficult to attribute to a country of origin, and this remains an important data gap. Unfortunately, the International Spillover Index does not currently include any indicators to track these types of spillovers. They are particularly related to SDG 6 (Clean Water and Sanitation) and SDGs 12–15 on climate and biodiversity, but also concern many other goals, including SDG 3 (Good Health and Well-Being).

- **Spillovers related to economic and financial flows**. These include unfair tax competition, corruption, banking secrecy, profit shifting, tax havens, and stolen assets – which undermine the capacity of other countries to leverage resources to achieve the SDGs. They also include positive spillovers (or handprints) such as international development finance (for example, ODA). These types of spillovers are closely related to SDG 16 (Peace, Security and Strong Institutions) and SDG 17 (Partnerships for the Goals), and indirectly to all other SDGs, notably through ODA.

- **Peacekeeping and security spillovers**. These include negative externalities such as organized international crime or exports of major conventional weapons or small arms, which can have destabilizing impacts on poor countries. Among the positive spillovers in this category are investments in conflict prevention and peacekeeping. These spillovers are particularly related to SDG 16 (Peace, Security and Strong Institutions) and SDG 17 (Partnerships for the Goals), but also indirectly connected with most of the SDGs – including poverty, hunger, and health, as well as other socioeconomic goals.

The 2022 International Spillover Index includes 14 indicators. Each indicator is included in the total SDG Index score, and also used to generate a stand-alone International Spillover Index.

Rich countries tend to generate the largest negative spillover effects, undermining other countries' efforts to achieve the SDGs. While member states of the European Union and many OECD countries top the SDG Index and the World Happiness Report, they are among the worst performers when it comes to international spillover effects. Approximately 40 percent of the European Union's carbon footprint relating to its consumption of good and services takes place in other countries (SDSN et al., 2021).

Table 2.3
The SDGs and international spillover indicators

SDG	Spillover Indicator
SDG 2 (No Hunger)	Exports of hazardous pesticides (tonnes per million population)
SDG 6 (Clean Water and Sanitation)	Scarce water consumption embodied in imports (m3 H2O eq/capita)
SDG 8 (Decent Work and Economic Growth)	Fatal work-related accidents embodied in imports (per 100,000 population)
SDG 12 (Responsible Consumption and Production)	SO_2 emissions embodied in imports (kg/capita)
SDG 12 (Responsible Consumption and Production)	Nitrogen emissions embodied in imports (kg/capita)
SDG 12 (Responsible Consumption and Production)	Exports of plastic waste (kg/capita)
SDG 13 (Climate Action)	CO_2 emissions embodied in imports (tCO_2/capita)
SDG 14 (Life Below Water)	Marine biodiversity threats embodied in imports (per million population)
SDG 15 (Life on Land)	Terrestrial and freshwater biodiversity threats embodied in imports (per million population)
SDG 16 (Peace, Justice and Strong Institutions)	Exports of major conventional weapons (TIV constant million USD per 100,000 population)
SDG 17 (Partnerships for the Goals)	For high-income and all OECD DAC countries: International concessional public finance, including official development assistance (% of GNI)
SDG 17 (Partnerships for the Goals)	Corporate Tax Haven Score (best 0–100 worst)
SDG 17 (Partnerships for the Goals)	Financial Secrecy Score (best 0–100 worst)
SDG 17 (Partnerships for the Goals)	Shifted profits of multinationals (US$ billion)

Source: Authors' analysis

The European Union's consumption of good and services is responsible for 16 percent of the world's tropical deforestation (WWF, 2021), its imports of textile products are associated with 375 fatal and 21,000 non-fatal accidents at work, and its food demand contributes to 16 percent of the particulate matter emissions outside its borders (Malik, Lafortune, Carter, et al., 2021; Malik, Lafortune, Dahir, et al., 2021). Focusing on trajectories: while the European Union has managed to decouple economic growth from domestic CO_2 emissions in recent years, there are no signs of structural decline in its imported CO_2 emissions (CO_2 emissions generated abroad to satisfy EU consumption). Overall, HICs are responsible for more than 80% of cumulative imported CO_2 emissions over the period 2010-2018.

To ensure international legitimacy, the European Union and other rich countries must address negative international spillovers, including those embodied into unsustainable supply chains. The European Union and its member states are taking action. The current President of the European Commission has called for "zero tolerance" of child labor and has proposed using trade to export European values throughout the world (von der Leyen, 2019). The European Union is developing various regulations and tools to strengthen policy coherence and due diligence across supply chains. In 2022, Sweden became the first country in the world to announce its intention to define a target to reduce consumption-based CO_2 emissions (Naturskyddsföreningen, 2022).

Figure 2.17
SDG Index score vs International Spillover Index score

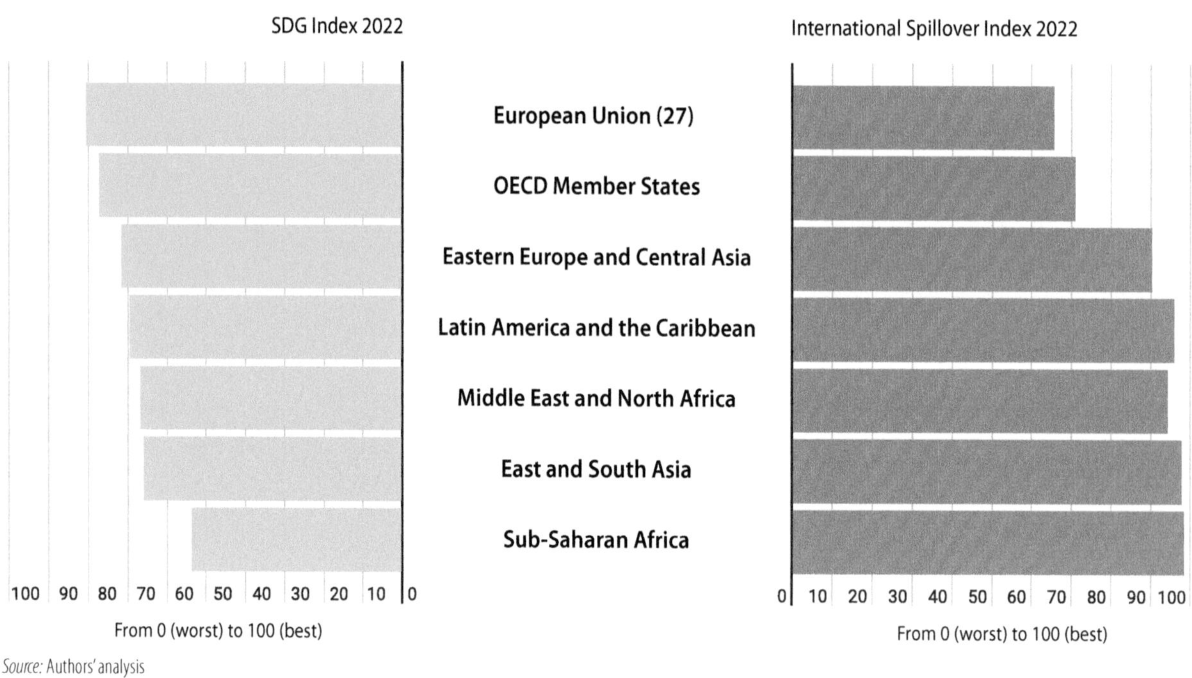

Source: Authors' analysis

Figure 2.18
Growth rate of GDP, production-based CO_2 emissions and imported CO_2 emissions, EU27, 2000–2019

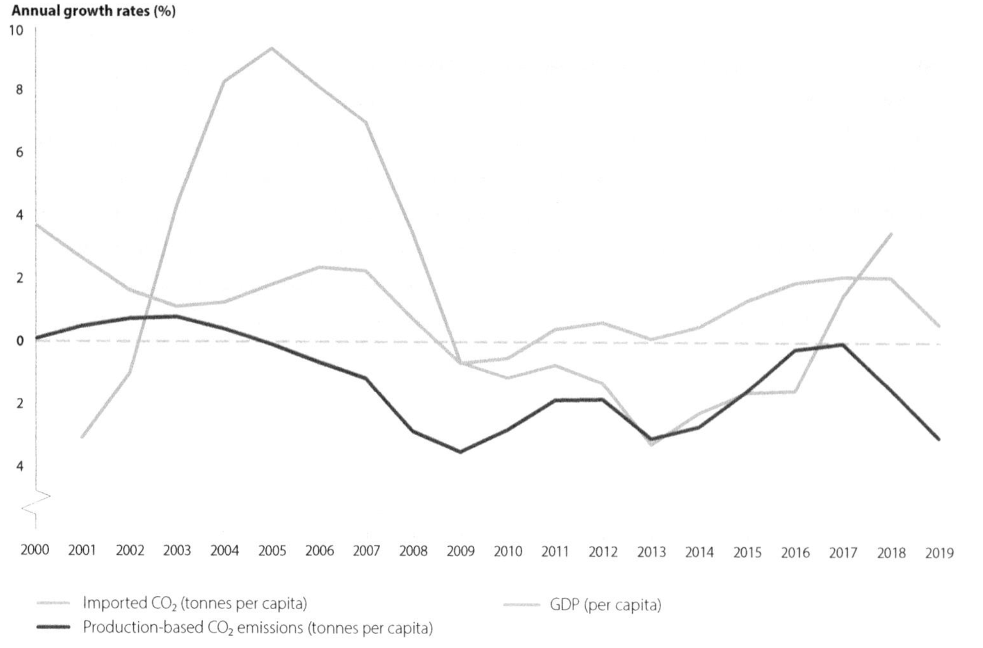

Note: Imported CO_2 emissions refer to CO_2 emissions emitted abroad (e.g., to produce cement or steel) to satisfy EU27 consumption of goods and services. Three-years moving averages. *Source:* Lafortune et al. (2021)

Finland's latest Voluntary National Review (VNR) includes a section on measuring and addressing international spillovers (Prime Minister's Office of Finland, 2020). Finally, EU technical agencies including the Joint Research Centre, Eurostat, and the European Environment Agency have developed tools and indicators to monitor international spillovers.

We have identified **four major priority areas** in addressing international spillovers:

1. **SDG Financing:** Rich countries bear a special responsibility when it comes to climate adaptation and mitigation and safeguarding the Global Commons. They should push for major reforms to the international development finance system to support key SDG Transformations (see Part 1). In 2021, only five OECD Development Assistance Committee member countries (Denmark, Germany, Luxembourg, Norway and Sweden) achieved the target of dedicating 0.7 percent of their gross national income to official development assistance. Multiple crises are putting further pressure on development finance. Rich countries fell short too in delivering on their commitment to mobilizing US$100 billion each year by 2020 to mitigate further rises in temperature and help poorer countries adapt to climate change. Several positive moves were made at COP26 in November 2021, including the US and European Union's pledge to slash methane emissions and the European Union's commitment of €1 billion to protect world forests. Rich countries must also lead the way in combating illicit financial flows, unfair tax competition, and profit shifting – all of which undermine other countries' capacity to leverage resources towards realizing the SDGs. The international agreement to implement a global minimum corporate tax rate by 2023 is a step in the right direction but will require effective implementation.

Figure 2.19

Imported CO_2 emissions by country income groups, cumulative average per person per year, 2010-2018

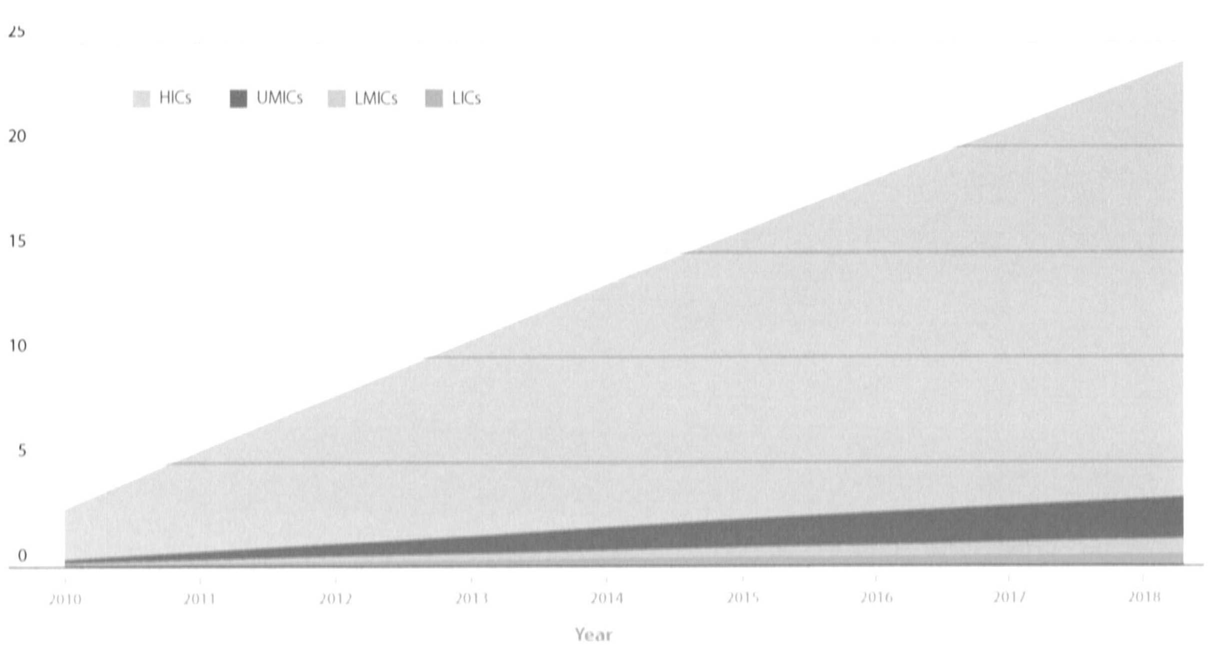

Source: Authors' analysis based on Lenzen et al. (2020)

2. **Technical Cooperation and SDG diplomacy:** Technical cooperation and knowledge transfer can support greater sustainability in producing countries. In the European Union, SDG/Green Deal diplomacy can help to achieve sustainable development worldwide while advancing the region's geopolitical interests. It is critical that major international infrastructure investment programs – including the United States' Build Back Better plan, the European Union's Global Gateway strategy, and China's Belt and Road Initiative – align with the SDGs and modernize production systems and connectivity in developing countries. Rich countries must leverage diplomacy to advance key multilateral processes towards achieving the SDGs: at the UN General Assembly, the High-Level Political Forum on Sustainable Development, the G7 (under German presidency in 2022), the G20 (under Indonesian presidency in 2022), and the Annual Meetings of the IMF and the World Bank.

3. **National targets and instruments:** In 2022, Sweden became the first country to commit to setting a national target to curb its imported consumption-based CO_2 emissions. National targets can help catalyze action. Due diligence regulations and other monitoring and regulatory instruments must be leveraged to hold businesses accountable for the impacts generated through their value chains. If well designed, measures such as the Carbon Border Adjustment Mechanism or mirror clauses currently under discussion in the European Union could boost policy coherence and encourage other countries to align with the European Green Deal goals and requirements. Yet these same measures might arguably be considered protectionist – since they will inevitably impact trade partners, including poorer countries that are not historically responsible for climate change. To counter this, they must be implemented alongside increased commitments to international financing and development cooperation. Rich countries should also curb trade in waste and toxic pesticides and reduce unsustainable consumption, including through improved diets and lower material consumption.

4. **Accountability, data, and statistics**: Robust data systems are paramount at the international, national, industrial, and corporation levels: to track negative impacts throughout the entire supply chain and to inform global action to address spillovers. Over time, consumption-based metrics should become part of official statistics. International spillovers must also be included more systematically in voluntary national reviews (VNRs) presented by rich countries, following the example of Finland.

Policy Efforts and Commitments for the SDGs

Part 3
Policy Efforts and Commitments for the SDGs

Restoring and accelerating SDG progress requires financing (see Part 1), data and statistics (see Parts 2 and 4) and sound and ambitious SDG policies and roadmaps. To operationalize the 17 SDGs and 169 targets, SDSN and partners promote six SDG Transformations that must be implemented in parallel and adapted to local contexts. These include quality education (SDG 4); access to good quality and affordable health care (SDG 3); renewable energy and a circular economy (SDGs 7, 12, and 13); sustainable land and marine management (SDGs 2, 14, and 15); sustainable urban infrastructure (SDGs 6, 9, and 11); and universal access to digital services (SDG 9). Scientific knowledge and networks are key to model structural changes over a time horizon of 10–30 years, which can inform policy discussions and consultations on the six SDG transformations.

This section discusses efforts made by governments (primarily the executive branch) to integrate the SDGs into public policies. The SDG Index and Dashboards focus on internationally standardized outcome statistics. Due to data gaps and time lags in international reporting, national policies and commitments must also be considered in gauging a country's efforts to achieve the SDGs. We present an assessment of governments' efforts to achieve the SDGs, including the 2022 SDSN Policy Coordination Survey for the SDGs and the Six Transformations Scorecards. For the first time, we also present prototype scores of government commitments and efforts in support of the SDGs.

3.1 Political leadership and policy environment: results from the 2022 SDSN Policy Coordination Survey for the SDGs

Every year, SDSN mobilizes its global network of experts to track public statements by governments and the strategic use of public practices in support of the SDGs. Since 2018, this information has been collected through the SDSN survey on national coordination and implementation mechanisms at the central/federal level of government. This year's survey covers 60 countries (13 more than the 48 covered in 2021) plus the European Union, including all countries in the G20 and most OECD members as well as many countries with a population greater than 100 million inhabitants. The results are presented in Table 3.1. Data are collected and analyzed in close partnership with SDSN's global network, and results are shared with UN Permanent Missions for comments prior to publication.

Six years after the adoption of the 2030 Agenda and the SDGs in 2015, a majority of governments had by 2021 developed strategies and action plans to implement the goals. For many governments, this takes the form of a national sustainability strategy that is explicitly linked to the 2030 Agenda goals and targets. Some governments though have preferred to take a mainstreaming approach, whereby the SDGs are implemented by each government ministry within the scope of its mandate (instead of via an overarching national action plan). Our survey is unable to evaluate, in practice, political and administrative support for the implementation of these strategies, although SDSN has published a detailed analysis of SDG integration in recovery and resilience plans within the European Union (Lafortune et al., 2021).

Regarding SDG coordination units and mechanisms: we find that most countries have appointed a lead unit or agency responsible for coordinating implementation of the SDGs (Figure 3.1). Yet less than a third of the countries surveyed have located this unit at the center of government (offices of the President or Prime Minister, or cabinet offices).

Many countries have also developed strategies for SDG monitoring. 46 out of the 61 governments covered in the survey have adapted the SDG framework to their context and identified a set of nationally relevant indicators. On average, such national sets comprise around 135 indicators. Several countries have also developed online platforms to report on progress towards the SDGs. These efforts to strengthen mechanisms to monitor sustainable development are critical to inform SDG interventions. Challenges related to the COVID-19 pandemic also sparked new innovations in monitoring and data collection, which are discussed in Part 4.

Figure 3.1
Designated lead unit for SDG coordination, at the central/federal level of government

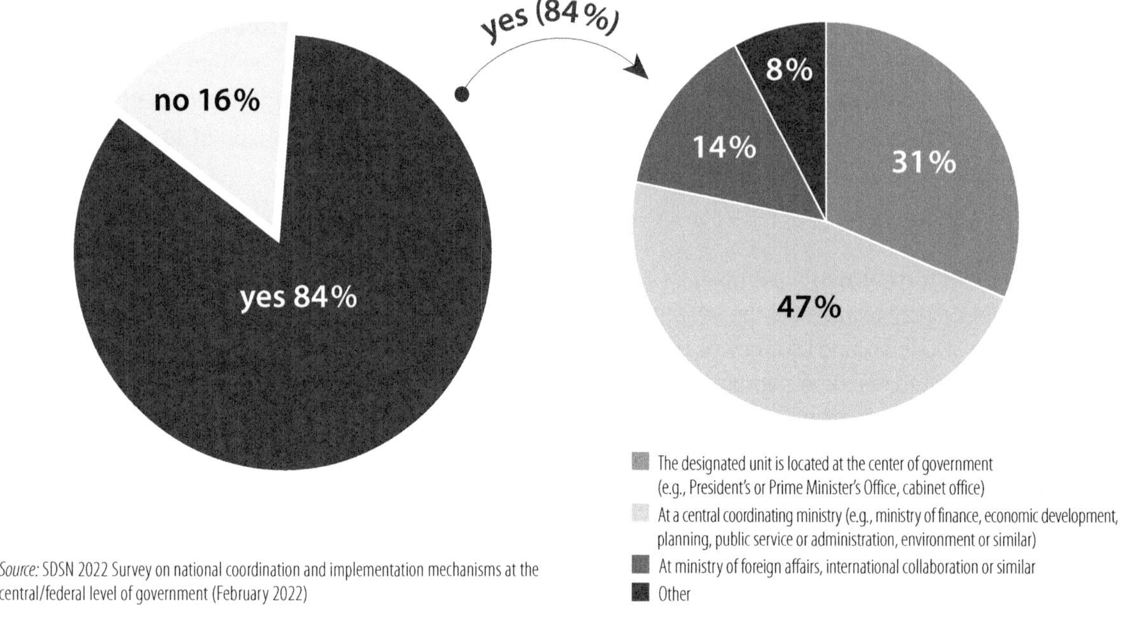

Source: SDSN 2022 Survey on national coordination and implementation mechanisms at the central/federal level of government (February 2022)

Official speeches and government efforts to prepare voluntary national reviews (VNRs) are also relevant proxy measures to gauge commitment to the SDGs. Over the past 12 months, just over half of the surveyed countries have reinforced their commitment to the SDGs in the context of an official speech or statement made by the head of state (president or prime minister). Since 2016, 187 UN Member States have prepared VNRs – the official government-led process to report on SDG progress, gaps, and policy efforts (see Figure 3.2). This year, 45 countries have committed to submitting a VNR, which is comparable to the pre-pandemic period. But while some countries are preparing their fourth VNR, six countries have still never submitted one – Haiti, Iran, Myanmar, South Sudan, the United States, and Yemen (UN, 2022b).

As in previous years, there is some discrepancy between expressed political support for the SDGs and integration of the goals into strategic public policy processes, most notably national budgets. About a third of the governments surveyed (21 out of 61) mention the SDGs or use related terms in their latest official budget document – no improvement over last year. And only half of these include the SDGs in a dedicated section of their national budgets or in a dedicated budget line. The other half refer to the SDGs only in the general narrative, providing less SDG-specific budget allocations. Several countries surveyed do specifically refer to the SDGs in their national budget to support both domestic SDG implementation (including national health, education, social protection, or economic development reforms) and SDG implementation abroad (for example, aid allocation or foreign policy).

This discrepancy is evident also in COVID-19 recovery plans. Among the 44 countries with national recovery plans in place, we found that most (26) do not refer to the SDGs at all. Only 9 have a COVID-19 recovery plan in which the SDGs form a central pillar to guide a sustainable, inclusive, and resilient recovery. This aligns with some of the findings from green recovery policy trackers (Green Economy Tracker, 2022; O'Callaghan et al., 2022; Vivid Economics, 2021; Wuppertal Institut and E3G, 2021). As countries work to recover from the pandemic, it is important to maintain – and increase – the focus on achieving the long-term goals agreed by the international community in 2015, including the SDGs, the 2030 Agenda, and the Paris Climate Agreement.

Figure 3.2
Submissions of voluntary national reviews (number of countries)

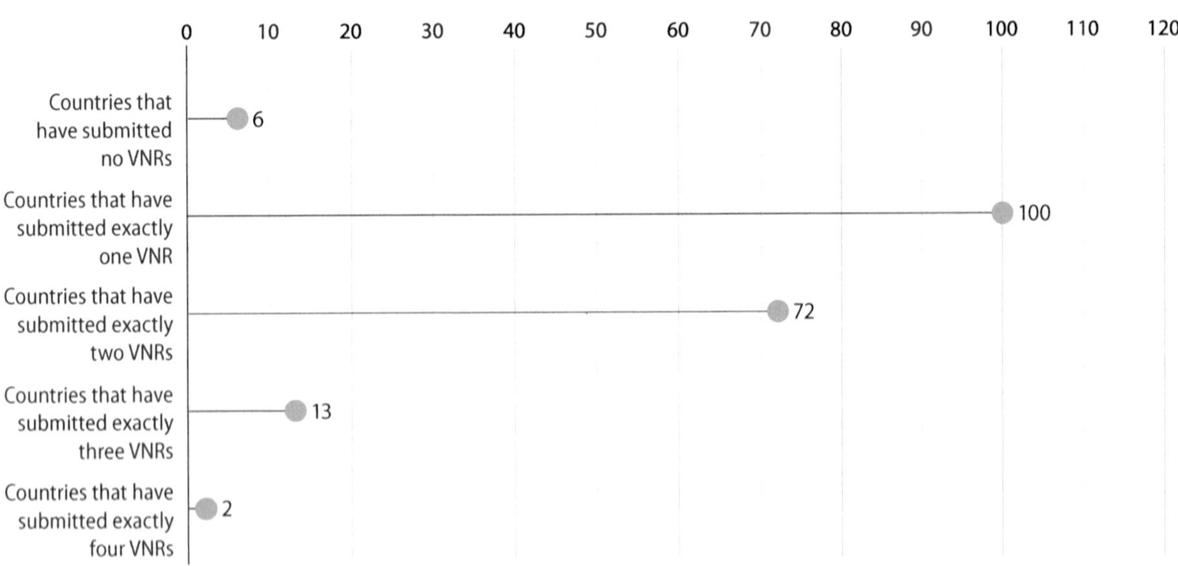

Note: Data includes VNRs that will be submitted by countries this year. *Source:* Authors' analysis. Based on data from the United Nations (2022).

Figure 3.3
Integration of the SDGs into key policy processes, G20 countries versus other countries

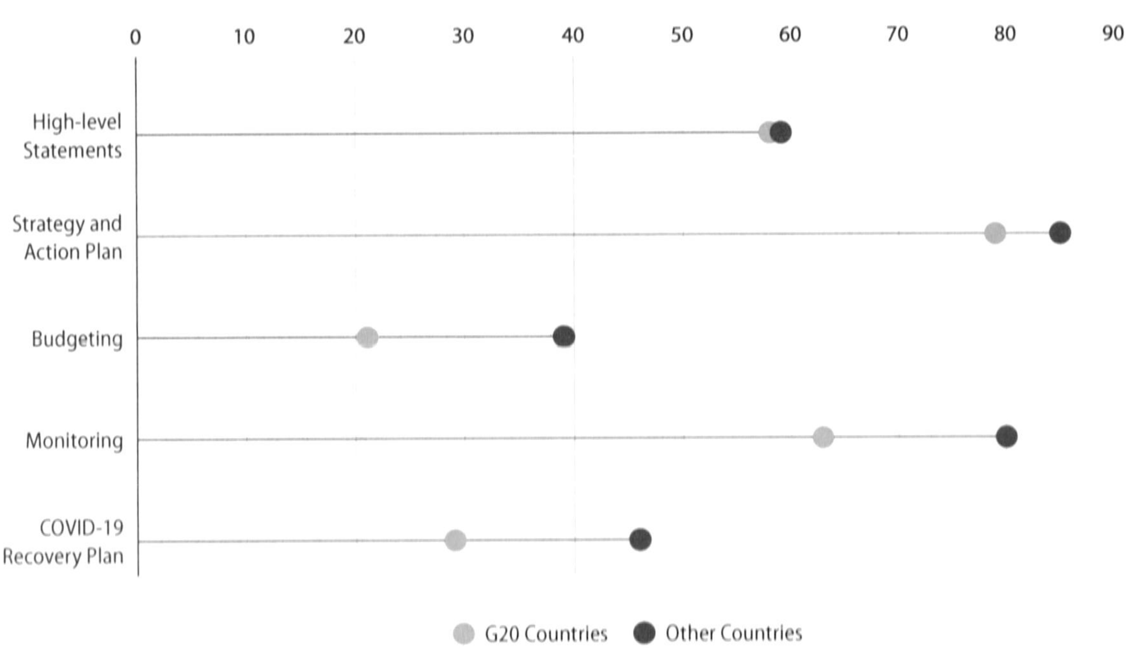

Note: Percentage of countries where Table 3.1 shows a "yes" for the respective question. For COVID-19 recovery plans: Percentage of countries where Table 3.1 shows a "yes" out of the number of countries that have adopted a recovery plan.
Source: Authors' analysis. Based on SDSN 2022 Survey on national coordination and implementation mechanisms at the central/federal level of government (February 2022).

Table 3.1. National government efforts to implement the SDGs

	VNR	High-level statements	SDG strategy/ SDGs into sectoral action plans	SDGs in national budget		National SDG monitoring		Designated lead unit	SDGs in national COVID-19 recovery plan
	Year submitted	yes/no	yes/no	yes/no	Overarching narrative/section or budget line	yes/no	no. of indicators	yes/no	- yes, as a central pillar (5 mentions or more) - yes, in the general narrative (1-4 mentions) - no
Algeria	2019	no	yes	no		yes	71	no	
Argentina	2017, 2020, & 2022	yes	yes	no		yes	242	yes	
Australia	2018	yes	no	no		no, but online reporting		no	no
Austria	2020	yes	yes	yes	section or budget line	yes	200	yes	no
Bangladesh	2017 & 2020	yes	yes	no		yes	40	yes	no
Belgium	2017	yes	yes	yes	overarching narrative	yes	86	yes	yes, as a central pillar
Benin	2017, 2018, & 2020	no	yes	yes	section or budget line	yes	164	yes	yes, in the general narrative
Bolivia	2021	yes	yes	no		yes	104	yes	no
Brazil	2017	no	yes	no		no, but online reporting		no	
Canada	2018	yes	yes	no		yes	76	yes	no
Chile	2017 & 2019	no	yes	no		yes	231	yes	no
China	2016 & 2021	yes	yes	no		no, but it is planned		yes	no
Colombia	2016, 2018, & 2021	yes	yes	yes	overarching narrative	yes	161	yes	no
Congo, Dem. Rep.	2020	no	yes	no		yes	59	yes	
Cyprus	2017 & 2021	yes	no	yes	overarching narrative	yes	140	yes	yes, as a central pillar
Czech Republic	2017 & 2021	no	yes	no		yes	192	yes	no
Denmark	2017 & 2021	yes	yes	yes	section or budget line	yes	197	yes	yes, as a central pillar
Egypt, Arab Rep.	2016, 2018, & 2021	no	yes	no		no, but online reporting		yes	
Ethiopia	2017 & 2022	no	yes	yes	section or budget line	yes	60	no	no
European Union	planned (TBC)	yes	yes	yes	overarching narrative	yes	102	yes	yes, in the general narrative
Finland	2016 & 2020	yes	yes	yes	overarching narrative	yes	48	yes	no
France	2016	no	yes	no		yes	98	yes	no
Germany	2016 & 2021	yes	yes	yes	overarching narrative	yes	75	yes	yes, in the general narrative
Greece	2018 & 2022	yes	yes	no		yes	158	yes	yes, as a central pillar
Hungary	2018	yes	no	no		yes	103	yes	no
India	2017 & 2020	no	no	no		no, but online reporting		no	
Indonesia	2017, 2019, & 2021	yes	yes	yes	overarching narrative	yes	319	yes	no
Ireland	2018	yes	yes	yes	overarching narrative	yes	143	yes	no
Israel	2019	no	yes	no		no, but online reporting		yes	
Italy	2017 & 2022	yes	yes	no		yes	130	yes	yes, in the general narrative
Jamaica	2018 & 2022	yes	yes	no		yes	119	yes	
Japan	2017 & 2021	yes	yes	yes	section or budget line	no, but online reporting		yes	
Kenya	2017 & 2020	no	no	no		no		no	
Korea, Rep.	2016	yes	yes	no		yes	214	yes	no
Malaysia	2017 & 2021	yes	yes	yes	section or budget line	yes	146	yes	no
Mexico	2016, 2018 & 2021	no	yes	yes	section or budget line	yes	54	yes	yes, as a central pillar
Morocco	2016 & 2020	no	yes	no		yes	102	yes	
Netherlands	2017 & 2022	yes	yes	no		yes	267	yes	
New Zealand	2019	yes	no	no		yes	166	no	no
Nigeria	2017 & 2020	yes	yes	yes	section or budget line	yes	141	yes	yes, as a central pillar
Norway	2016 & 2021	yes	yes	yes	section or budget line	no, but online reporting		yes	no
Pakistan	2019 & 2022	no	yes	yes	section or budget line	no, but online reporting		yes	no
Philippines	2016, 2019, & 2022	no	yes	no		no, but online reporting	155	yes	
Poland	2018	yes	yes	no		yes	65	yes	yes, as a central pillar
Portugal	2017	no	no	yes	overarching narrative	yes	46	yes	yes, in the general narrative
Romania	2018	yes	yes	no		yes	98	yes	no
Russian Federation	2020	no	no	no		yes	175	yes	no
Saudi Arabia	2018 & 2021	no	yes	no		yes	244	yes	
Senegal	2018 & 2022	no	yes	no		yes	142	yes	yes, in the general narrative
Slovenia	2017 & 2020	yes	yes	no		yes	54	yes	yes, in the general narrative
South Africa	2019	yes	yes	no		yes	258	yes	no
Spain	2018 & 2021	yes	yes	yes	section or budget line	no, but online reporting		yes	yes, as a central pillar
Sweden	2017 & 2021	yes	yes	yes	overarching narrative	yes	45	yes	yes, in the general narrative
Switzerland	2016, 2018, & 2022	yes	yes	no		yes	108	yes	
Thailand	2017 & 2021	yes	yes	no		no, but online reporting		yes	yes, as a central pillar
Turkey	2016 & 2019	no	yes	no		yes	131	yes	yes, in the general narrative
Uganda	2016 & 2020	no	yes	no		yes	64	yes	
Ukraine*	2020	no	no	no		yes	183	yes	yes, in the general narrative
United Kingdom	2019	yes	yes	no		no, but online reporting		no	no
United States		no	no	no		no, but online reporting		no	no
Vietnam	2018	no	yes	no		yes	158	yes	

Note: For the European Union, the answer to the question on the national COVID-19 recovery plan is based on the "Guidance to Member States Recovery and Resilience Plans". The answers for Ukraine reflect the situation as of January 2022. Due to the situation, we were not able to verify the answers for Ukraine with the Permanent Mission of Ukraine to the United Nations.
Source: SDSN 2022 Survey on national coordination and implementation mechanisms at the central/federal level of government (February 2022)

Figure 3.4. National government efforts to implement the SDGs

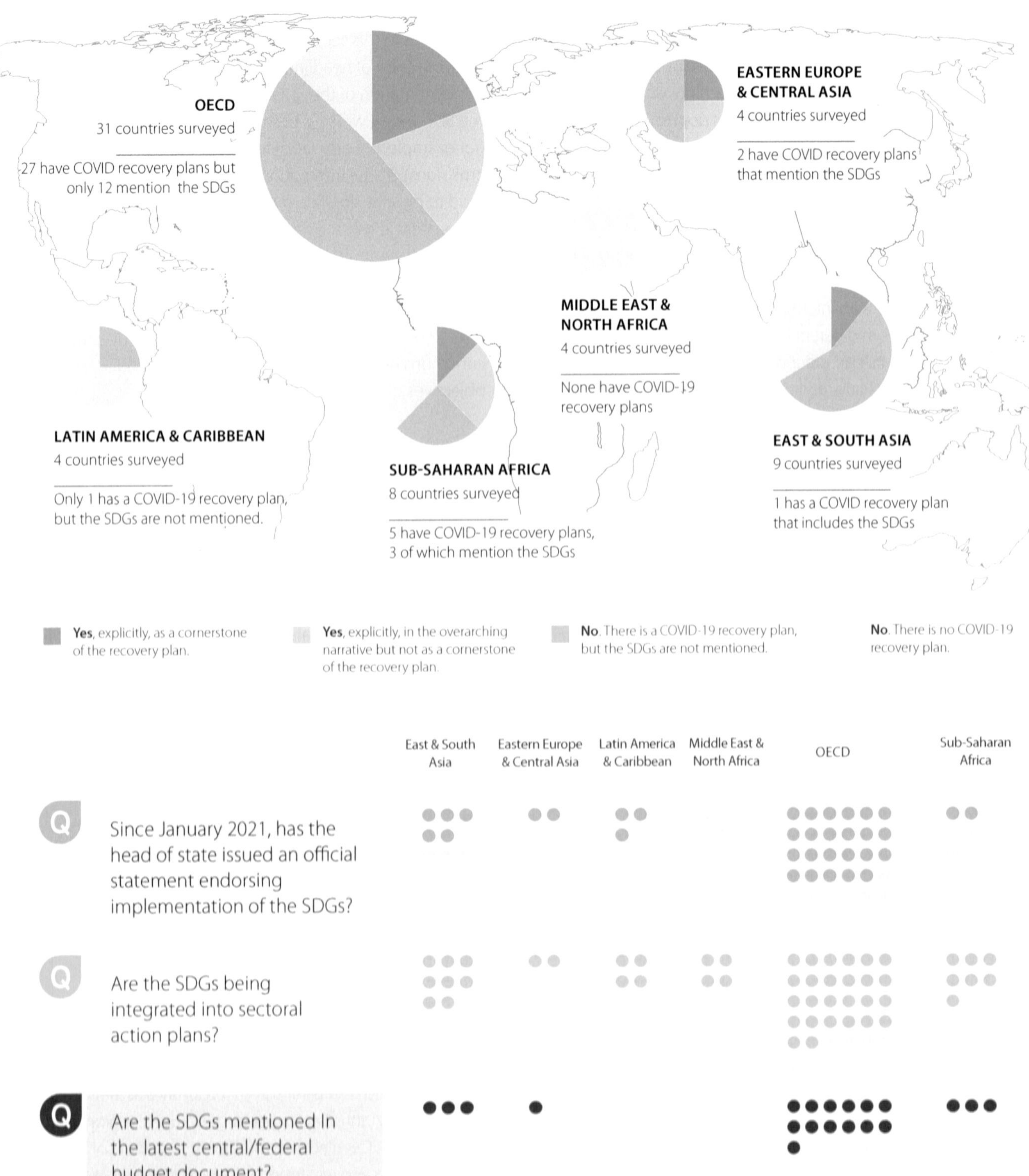

As shown in Figure 3.3, G20 countries are on average less ambitious than others when it comes to integrating the SDGs into key policy processes. Particularly with regards to linking budgets to the goals and developing national SDG indicator sets, G20 countries lag behind. As G20 countries represent two-thirds of the world's population and 85 percent of global GDP, integrating the SDGs into their governance systems is particularly important.

Besides the executive branch of government, parliamentary committees and groups promoting SDG action have also emerged over the years. For instance, the SDG Alliance is an informal group of European Parliament Members from different committees and political groups who are mobilized around the SDGs. In France in 2022, a Member of Parliament put together a comprehensive assessment of the country's SDG gaps and priorities (Provendier, 2022). Public participation processes at various levels (including regions and cities), whether organized through national legislature, citizen assemblies, or councils, can also help to identify better policy interventions, build legitimacy, and strengthen ownership of SDG actions.

3.2 The six SDG Transformations scorecards

The six SDG Transformations provide a detailed framework on which to construct integrated strategies for the SDGs (Sachs et al., 2019). They can be implemented in every country to help address trade-offs and synergies across the SDGs. They can also be used to recover from COVID-19 and to build back better (Sachs et al., 2020; Schmidt-Traub, 2020).

The core of the six Transformations is the recognition that all 17 SDGs can be achieved through six major societal transformations, focused on: (1) education and skills, (2) health and well-being, (3) clean energy and industry, (4) sustainable land use, (5) sustainable cities, and (6) digital technologies. All are guided by the twin principles to "leave no one behind" and "ensure circularity and decoupling" (see Sachs et al., 2019 for details, page 3). The six Transformations provide an action agenda for government ministries, businesses, and civil society.

Building on the work of last year, we present an updated and improved version of the SDG Transformation scorecards in this section. Each scorecard consists of a collection of headline policy measures to track implementation of the SDGs. The scorecards complement the SDG Index, which is based on outcome data (for example, poverty rate, life expectancy, and CO_2 emissions). At the international level, outcome data tend to present significant time lags: they may not adequately reflect the impact of transformative policies and investments introduced by governments since the adoption of the SDGs, as these often yield results only in the medium or longer term. The scorecards focus instead on the enabling legal, regulatory, and investment conditions needed to achieve the SDGs and the objectives of the Paris Climate Agreement.

This exercise has several caveats and limitations. First, internationally comparable policy trackers and measures (such as laws, regulations, investments, and subsidies) tend to be less available than international outcome data. They rely on more qualitative methods and require an advanced understanding of policy areas and country policies and contexts. Generally, more comparable policy trackers and measures are available for OECD countries than for others. Second, policy efforts need to be interpreted with an understanding of national challenges and contexts (for instance, the absence of an advanced cybersecurity policy matters less in a country with low internet access and poor digital infrastructure). Third, apart from a few exceptions, government pledges and policies do not capture their effective implementation. And fourth, fewer internationally agreed targets or thresholds for policy measures are defined at the international level.

The rest of this section provides a brief overview of countries' policy efforts and commitments relating to achieving the six SDG Transformations and highlights where more research and policy trackers are required to broaden our understanding of national SDG efforts. We present detailed results for the G20 countries as well as population-weighted averages by geographic region and income group. Detailed information on indicator sources and thresholds and results for all 193 UN Member States are accessible online at www.sdgindex.org.

Figure 3.5
Six SDG Transformations

Source: Sachs et al. (2019)

Transformation 1: Education, Gender and Inequality

Education builds human capital, which in turn promotes economic growth, innovation, decent work, and the elimination of extreme poverty and helps overcome gender and other inequalities. Countries must further expand and transform education systems. SDG target 4.1 calls for universal access to 12 years of free primary and secondary education, with at least 9 years compulsory. The scorecards show that many countries around the world currently fall short of this target. To reduce inequalities, governments also need to expand social safety nets. These should be complemented by anti-discrimination measures (including gender), improved labor standards, and measures to end all forms of modern slavery, trafficking, and child labor. Investments in research and development will also help to promote economic growth, which can contribute to reducing inequalities.

Table 3.2

Scorecard – Transformation 1: Education, Gender and Inequality

Note: Regional and income level averages are population weighted. Details on definitions, sources, and thresholds are available on www.sdgindex.org
Source: Authors' analysis

Transformation 1: Education, Gender and Inequality	Years of free education in the law (#, 2020, UNESCO)	Years of compulsory education in the law (#, 2020, UNESCO)	Commitment to Reducing Inequalities: Tax Progressivity & Protection of Labor Right (score, 2020, Oxfam & DFI)	Gender Equality in the Law (score, 2022, World Bank)	Expenditure on research and development (% of GDP, 2018, UNESCO)
G20 Countries					
Argentina	12	12	0.63	79.4	0.5
Australia	13	10	0.69	96.9	1.9
Brazil	12	12	0.57	85.0	1.2
Canada	12	10	0.74	100.0	1.5
China	9	9	0.54	75.6	2.1
France	12	10	0.72	100.0	2.2
Germany	13	13	0.75	97.5	3.1
India	8	8	0.45	74.4	0.7
Indonesia	12	9	0.54	64.4	0.2
Italy	8	12	0.67	97.5	1.4
Japan	9	9	0.69	78.8	3.3
Korea, Rep.	9	9	0.63	85.0	4.5
Mexico	12	12	0.56	88.8	0.3
Russian Federation	11	11	0.67	73.1	1.0
Saudi Arabia	12	9	NO DATA	80.0	0.8
South Africa	12	9	0.69	88.1	0.8
Turkey	12	12	0.56	82.5	1.0
United Kingdom	13	11	0.67	97.5	1.7
United States	12	12	0.66	91.3	2.8
By regions					
East and South Asia	8.9	8.7	0.51	72.1	1.1
Eastern Europe and Central Asia	11.3	10.4	0.62	73.6	0.6
Latin America and the Caribbean	11.6	11.2	0.57	84.1	0.7
Middle East and North Africa	10.9	9.6	0.54	50.2	0.6
Oceania	8.8	9.6	NO DATA	61.9	NO DATA
OECD members	11.4	11.1	0.66	91.3	2.1
Sub-Saharan Africa	8.8	8.1	0.44	71.8	0.3
By income level					
Low-income countries	9.0	7.9	0.45	65.8	0.3
Lower-middle-income countries	8.7	8.7	0.48	70.4	0.5
Upper-middle-income countries	10.3	9.6	0.56	74.8	1.4
High-income countries	11.4	10.8	0.68	91.3	2.3

More ambitious	≥ 12 years	≥ 12 years	≥ 0.7	≥ 90	≥ 2.3%
Moderately ambitious	≥ 9 years	≥ 9 years	≥ 0.5	≥ 70	≥ 1.0%
Less ambitious	less than 9 years	less than 9 years	below 0.5	below 70	below 1.0%

Transformation 2: Health, Well-Being and Demography

This Transformation promotes key investments in health and well-being. It aligns closely with SDG target 3.8, of achieving universal health coverage and ensuring that all people have access to the health services they need. In the SDGs, UHC is considered as a target in itself but for the purpose of the SDG Transformation scorecards we consider UHC as an enabler (input) for greater health outcomes. Even before the pandemic, the WHO and other international institutions had lamented the slow progress being made towards achieving universal health coverage (WHO, 2019). Compared with the rest of the world, a higher percentage of people in OECD countries tend to be covered by public or mandatory private health insurance, and incidence rates of catastrophic out-of-pocket health expenditures are lower – although there are exceptions, including Mexico, Costa Rica, Poland, and the United States. The SDGs also call on all countries to strengthen their capacity for early warning, risk reduction, and management of national and global health risks (SDG target 3.d). The Global Health Security Index, a measure of pandemic preparedness, turned out to be a rather poor predictor of effective early response to COVID-19, as measured in number of cases and deaths (Lafortune, 2020), indicating that there are important factors at play which are not yet adequately captured by existing policy trackers. Looking ahead, it will be important to define solid international measures and monitoring systems to better gauge countries' preparedness for global health security threats.

Transformation 3: Energy Decarbonization and Sustainable Industry

This Transformation aims to ensure universal access to modern energy sources, decarbonize the energy system by mid-century (in line with the Paris Agreement), and reduce industrial pollution of soil, water, and air. Many countries, especially OECD members and high-income countries, have made commitments to reaching net-zero emissions my mid-century. Over 130 countries are signatories to the UN Climate Ambition Alliance and more than 50 have anchored their net-zero commitment in a law or policy document (Net Zero Tracker, 2022; UNFCCC, 2022). However, there continues to be a major discrepancy between countries' self-declared ambitions and their tangible efforts and policies. The Climate Action Tracker, an independent scientific analysis of governments' climate actions, finds that not a single G20 country has adopted a sufficient mix of policies and actions compatible with achieving the objectives of the Paris Climate Agreement (2022). Many countries continue to provide significant subsidies for fossil fuels, undercutting efforts to decarbonize the energy system. Countries must also ensure that any economic stimulus provided by COVID-19 recovery packages aligns with Paris climate objectives and supports the transition to net-zero emissions by 2050.

Transformation 4. Sustainable Food, Land, Water, and Oceans

Today's land-use and food systems have led to persistent hunger, malnutrition, and obesity. They account for a quarter of greenhouse gas emissions, over 90 percent of scarcity-weighted water use, most biodiversity loss, the overexploitation of fisheries, eutrophication through nutrient overload, and the pollution of our water and air. At the same time, food systems are highly vulnerable to climate change and land degradation. Integrated strategies are needed to make food systems, land use, and oceans sustainable and healthy for people.

Efforts to track commitments and objectives on Transformation 4 are constrained by the complexity of policies relating to land use, oceans, and agriculture and the absence of internationally agreed targets for biodiversity and land degradation. The debate continues on the "30x30" target for biodiversity: a proposal to have at least 30 percent of the Earth's surface under conservation status by 2030. There is concern on whether the target is sufficient, whether the global community should instead focus on biodiversity "hot spots", and how to address potential negative impacts on communities living in surrounding areas.

We consider that for the moment there is no comprehensive tracker or headline policy indicators (apart from those related to protected areas) available to assess in a meaningful and comprehensive way countries' commitment and efforts on this Transformation. SDSN has launched the

Table 3.3
Scorecard – Transformation 2: Health, Well-being and Demography

Note: Regional and income level averages are population weighted. Details on definitions, sources, and thresholds are available on www.sdgindex.org
Source: Authors' analysis

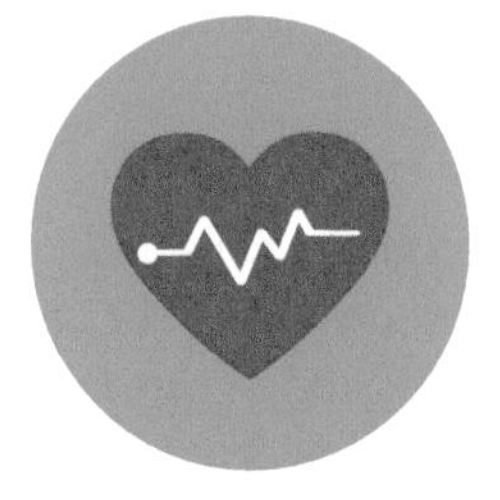

Transformation 2: Health, Well-being and Demography	UHC index of service coverage (score, 2019, WHO)	Catastrophic out-of-pocket health spending: Pop. spending 10%+ of household income on health (%, 2016, WHO)	Population coverage for health care (%, 2020, OECD)	Global Health Security Index: Pandemic Preparedness (score, 2021, NIS & Johns Hopkins)
G20 Countries				
Argentina	73.0	9.6	NO DATA	54.4
Australia	87.0	2.5	100.0	71.1
Brazil	75.0	11.8	NO DATA	51.2
Canada	89.0	3.5	100.0	69.8
China	82.0	24.0	NO DATA	47.5
France	84.0	NO DATA	99.9	61.9
Germany	86.0	1.5	100.0	65.5
India	61.0	17.3	NO DATA	42.8
Indonesia	59.0	4.5	NO DATA	50.4
Italy	83.0	9.3	100.0	51.9
Japan	85.0	10.5	100.0	60.5
Korea, Rep.	87.0	12.0	100.0	65.4
Mexico	74.0	1.6	72.4	57.0
Russian Federation	75.0	7.7	NO DATA	49.1
Saudi Arabia	73.0	1.3	NO DATA	44.9
South Africa	67.0	1.0	NO DATA	45.8
Turkey	79.0	3.2	98.8	50.0
United Kingdom	88.0	2.3	100.0	67.2
United States	83.0	4.3	90.3	75.9
By regions				
East and South Asia	67.7	17.3	NO DATA	44.3
Eastern Europe and Central Asia	69.1	10.3	NO DATA	43.2
Latin America and the Caribbean	72.6	10.4	NO DATA	45.4
Middle East and North Africa	68.5	16.4	NO DATA	30.7
Oceania	37.8	NO DATA	NO DATA	25.1
OECD members	82.5	5.9	94.4	63.5
Sub-Saharan Africa	44.5	8.4	NO DATA	32.9
By income level				
Low-income countries	42.4	7.9	NO DATA	28.6
Lower-middle-income countries	57.6	14.8	NO DATA	38.5
Upper-middle-income countries	76.4	15.5	NO DATA	48.0
High-income countries	83.1	6.4	96.7	64.0

	UHC index	Catastrophic out-of-pocket	Population coverage	Global Health Security Index
More ambitious	≥ 80	≤ 4%	≥ 99%	≥ 80
Moderately ambitious	≥ 60	≤ 10%	≥ 95%	≥ 50
Less ambitious	below 60	above 10%	below 95%	below 50

Table 3.4
Scorecard – Transformation 3: Energy Decarbonization and Sustainable Industry

Note: Regional and income level averages are population weighted. Details on definitions, sources, and thresholds are available on www.sdgindex.org
Source: Authors' analysis

Transformation 3: Energy Decarbonization and Sustainable Industry

	UN Climate Ambition Alliance Signatory (March 2022, UN)	Policy- or NDC-based commitment to reach net-zero emissions by 2050 (March 2022, Net Zero Tracker)	1.5°C Paris-agreement-compatible climate action (March 2022, Climate Action Tracker)	Unconditional fossil fuel subsidies (USD per capita, March 2022, Energy Policy Tracker)	Green COVID-19 Recovery (1 worst – 5 best, April 2022, Green Economy Tracker)
G20 Countries					
Argentina	✓	X	Highly Insufficient	29.82	2.00
Australia	X	✓	Highly Insufficient	65.53	2.00
Brazil	X	X	Highly Insufficient	2.71	2.00
Canada	✓	✓	Highly Insufficient	537.99	4.00
China	X	2060	Highly Insufficient	17.55	2.00
France	✓	✓	Insufficient	116.01	5.00
Germany	✓	✓	Insufficient	195.23	3.00
India	X	X	Highly Insufficient	27.19	2.00
Indonesia	X	X	Highly Insufficient	23.66	2.00
Italy	✓	✓	Insufficient	65.76	3.00
Japan	✓	✓	Insufficient	12.93	2.00
Korea, Rep.	✓	✓	Highly Insufficient	97.46	3.00
Mexico	✓	X	Highly Insufficient	61.88	2.00
Russian Federation	X	X	Critically Insufficient	35.50	NO DATA
Saudi Arabia	X	X	Highly Insufficient	158.17	1.00
South Africa	X	X	Insufficient	10.66	2.00
Turkey	X	2053	Critically Insufficient	165.68	2.00
United Kingdom	✓	✓	Almost Sufficient	589.53	4.00
United States	X	✓	Insufficient	217.32	3.00
By regions					
East and South Asia	10 of 21	6 of 21	NO DATA	NO DATA	NO DATA
Eastern Europe and Central Asia	14 of 27	7 of 27	NO DATA	NO DATA	NO DATA
Latin America and the Caribbean	22 of 30	7 of 30	NO DATA	NO DATA	NO DATA
Middle East and North Africa	4 of 17	0 of 17	NO DATA	NO DATA	NO DATA
Oceania	12 of 12	2 of 12	NO DATA	NO DATA	NO DATA
OECD members	32 of 37	32 of 37	NO DATA	171.45	NO DATA
Sub-Saharan Africa	40 of 49	4 of 49	NO DATA	NO DATA	NO DATA
By income level					
Low-income countries	26 of 29	3 of 29	NO DATA	NO DATA	NO DATA
Lower-middle-income countries	31 of 49	6 of 49	NO DATA	NO DATA	NO DATA
Upper-middle-income countries	31 of 54	10 of 54	NO DATA	NO DATA	NO DATA
High-income countries	46 of 61	39 of 61	NO DATA	NO DATA	NO DATA

More ambitious	signatory	net-zero by 2050	1.5°C compatible	0 USD/capita	≥ 4
Moderately ambitious	N/A	net-zero by 2060	Almost sufficient	≤ 50 USD/capita	≥ 3
Less ambitious	not a signatory	no commitment	Insufficient	50+ USD/capita	below 3

Food, Environment, Land and Development (FELD) Action Tracker to examine national commitments to achieving sustainable land use, resource management, and food systems – including policies, regulations, and investments. A first assessment of the integration of food and land issues in the Nationally Determined Contributions of G20 countries showed that current commitments and actions are largely insufficient (FOLU and FELD, 2021).

Transformation 5. Sustainable Cities and Communities

Cities and other urban areas are home to around 55 percent of humanity and account for 70 percent of global economic output. By 2050, these shares will increase to 70 and 85 percent, respectively (Jiang and O'Neill, 2017). The OECD estimates that 105 of the 169 SDG targets will not be reached without sufficiently engaging sub-national governments (OECD, 2020). The COVID-19 pandemic too will likely have lasting impacts on urban mobility, land use, and transport systems in developed and developing countries alike. Many urban organizations and associations have mainstreamed the SDGs into their work programs, including UN Habitat, the United Cities and Local Governments (UCLG), C40, the OECD, Local Governments for Sustainability (ICLEI), and others.

By design, Transformation 5 calls for regional and local policy trackers. These would notably track efforts at the regional and city level to curb urban pollution, increase the affordability of housing, and strengthen access to public transport and mobility. Other policy measures could be considered as proxies of local government commitment to achieving the triple objective of being economically productive, socially inclusive, and environmentally sustainable. SDSN is working with local partners to strengthen policy frameworks in regions and cities, and to reinforce the science–policy interface at the subnational level.

Transformation 6. Digital Revolution for Sustainable Development

Artificial Intelligence and other digital technologies are disrupting almost every sector of the economy, including agriculture (precision agriculture), mining (autonomous vehicles), manufacturing (robotics), retail (e-commerce), finance (e-payments, trading strategies), media (social networks), health (diagnostics, telemedicine), education (online learning), public administration (e-governance, e-voting), and science and technology. Digital technologies can raise productivity, lower production costs, reduce emissions, expand access, dematerialize production, improve matching in markets, enable the use of big data, and make public services more readily available. They can also improve resource-use efficiencies, support the circular economy, enable zero-carbon energy systems, help monitor and protect ecosystems, and assume other critical roles in support of the SDGs.

Tracking commitments and efforts towards Transformation 6 remains difficult, as countries face very different challenges depending on their current level of digitalization. For example, highly connected and digitized countries may need to prioritize issues surrounding cybersecurity, artificial intelligence, and e-government. Less-connected countries, however, may first need to focus on ensuring widespread and affordable internet access and computer literacy education. So far, we have been unable to come up with a reliable framework to gauge countries' commitments and efforts on Transformation 6 that would allow for such distinctions across country contexts. This remains an important item on our research agenda at SDSN.

3.3 Governments' SDG commitments versus SDG Index gaps

Building on the SDSN survey of government efforts for the SDGs as well as the Six Transformations scorecards, this year we present pilot scores rating the commitments and efforts that governments have made towards achieving the SDGs (Figure 3.6). These scores range from 0 (very low SDG commitment) to 100 (very high SDG commitment) and cover all 60 countries in the 2022 SDG Policy Coordination Survey presented in section 3.1, including all G20 countries and most OECD countries. It includes a total of 18 indicators on policy efforts and commitments.

As discussed earlier in this report, the policy data currently available is subject to several caveats and limitations, especially with regards to Transformations 4, 5, and 6. Therefore, this year's scores of government efforts and commitments should be considered as a pilot and interpreted with caution. The methodology and rationale for these scores are explained in a separate note that is available on www.sdgindex.org. We welcome critical comments and feedback that may help to strengthen future iterations of this work.

This pilot assessment reveals that policy efforts and commitments for the SDGs vary significantly across countries, including among G20 countries. The United States, Brazil, and the Russian Federation show the least support for the 2030 Agenda and the SDGs, with the United States being among the few UN Member States to have never submitted a VNR. But even in these countries, despite low federal or national support for the 2030 Agenda and the SDGs, notable commitments and efforts can be found at subnational levels: in regions, states, metropolitan areas, and cities. SDSN has worked, for instance, with associations of metropolitan and municipal areas in the United States and Brazil (ICS and SDSN, 2021; Lynch et al., 2019). By contrast, Nordic countries and, among G20 countries, Germany and Mexico, show more support for the SDGs.

Figure 3.7 shows pilot *Governments' Commitment and Efforts for the SDGs* scores in relation to national scores on this year's SDG Index. Benin and Nigeria, for example, have large gaps in their SDG Index yet also earn relatively high scores for their policy efforts. This may help them achieve better results in coming years. Interestingly, Benin and Mexico have both issued SDG Sovereign Bonds in recent years to scale up their sustainable development investments. Establishing the right policy frameworks for sustainable development, building on scientific knowledge and networks, and connecting these frameworks with discussions on access to financing should be major priorities of the international community towards restoring and accelerating SDG progress by 2030 and beyond.

None of the 60 countries included in this assessment attained a score of 80 or more for their commitments and efforts, indicating that none of them has an appropriate set of policies in place to achieve the objectives of the 2030 Agenda. Even among the top performers in Europe, the assessment made by the Climate Action Tracker considers that the strategies and actions of these governments are insufficient to achieve the objectives set out in the Paris Climate Agreement. Many of these countries could also further connect key instruments, such as the national budget and COVID-19 recovery plans, with the SDGs. Ambitious and sound national targets, strategies, and plans are crucial to turn the SDGs into an action agenda.

Figure 3.6

Governments' Commitments and Efforts for the SDGs scores (pilot version)

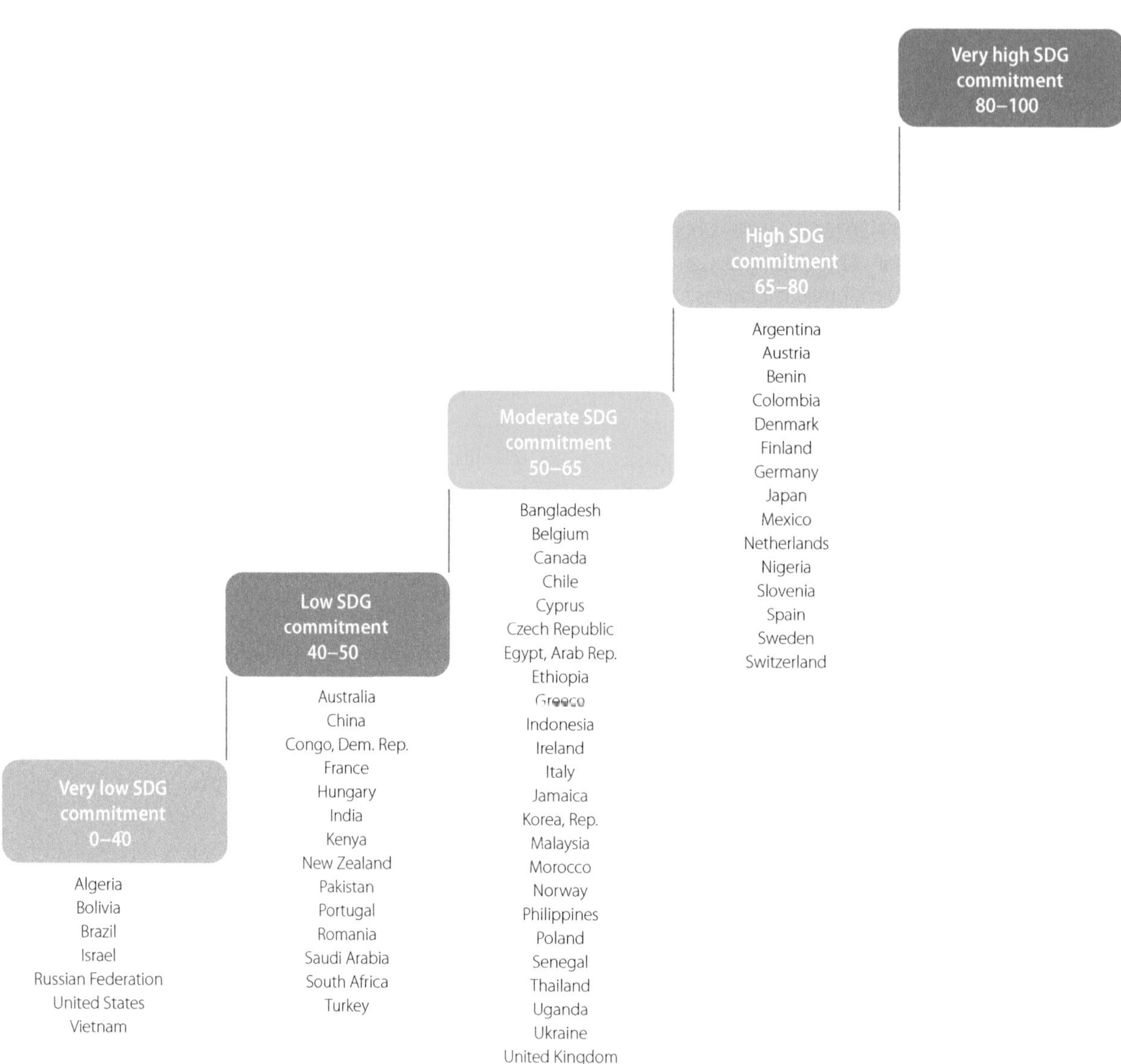

Note: G20 countries in orange. The score for Ukraine reflects the situation as of January 2022.
Source: Authors' analysis. Details on the methodology and the indicators used are available on www.sdgindex.org

Figure 3.7

Governments' Commitment and Efforts for the SDGs Score (pilot version) versus SDG Index Score

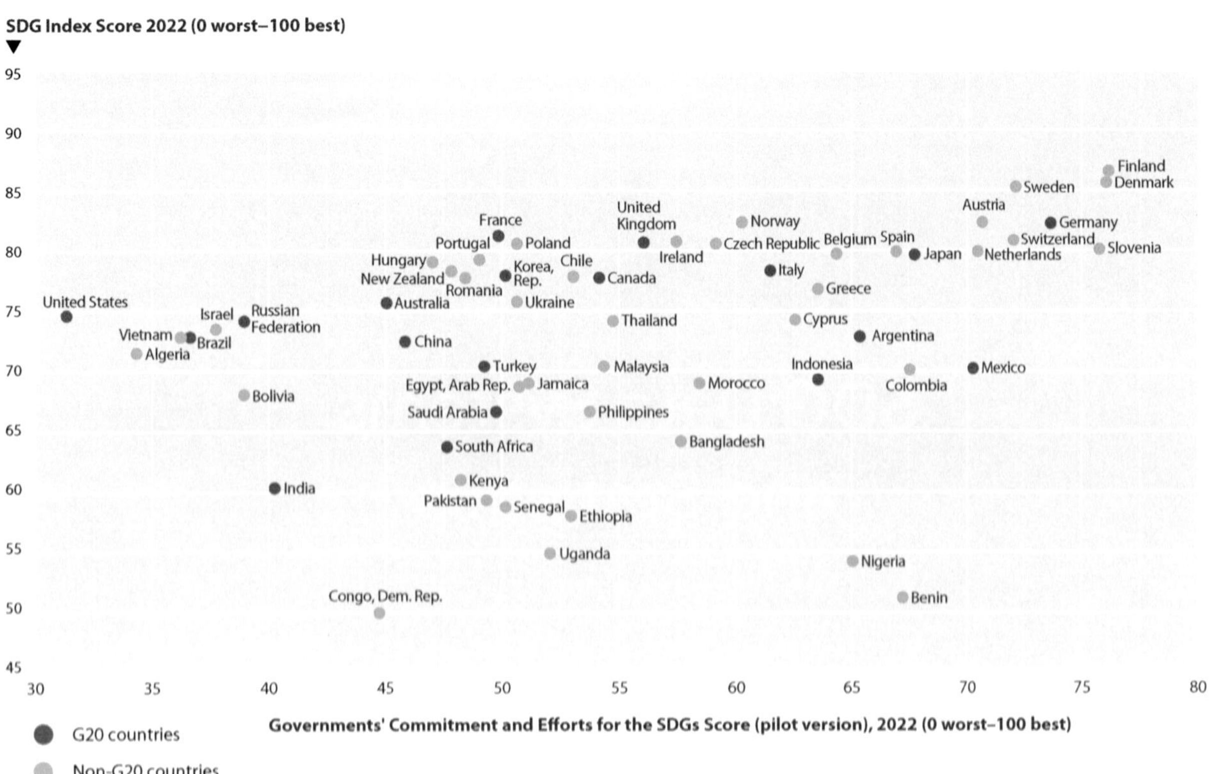

Note: G20 countries in red. The score for Ukraine reflects the situation as of January 2022.
Source: Authors' analysis. Details on the methodology and the indicators used are available on www.sdgindex.org

SDG Data Systems and Statistics

Part 4
SDG Data Systems and Statistics

The COVID-19 pandemic has prompted a massive shift in the demand for data, especially for timelier and higher-quality data (UNDESA, 2021). At the same time, socioeconomic impacts of the pandemic have rendered much of the pre-pandemic data less useful or outdated (Mahler et al., 2021). Governments have needed more rapid, geolocated, and granular data not only to track the trajectory of COVID-19 cases across their countries, but to ensure that basic resources for their citizens are targeted effectively and efficiently (UNStats, 2021b). With the elevated focus on and interest in data, COVID-19 has also set the stage for new user expectations, with many users – especially the general public – now expecting to obtain data in real time. As such, governments have had to find new ways to satisfy user demands with reduced budgets and staff resources, while also balancing data timeliness, precision, and quality needs. An SDSN initiative, the Thematic Research Network on Data and Statistics (TReNDS), mobilizes technical and policy-oriented solutions to advance the data revolution for sustainable devedevelopment.

Partnerships across sectors have proven critical in helping to meet this challenge (UNStats, 2022c). And in many countries, national statistics offices (NSOs) have become innovators during the pandemic. They have engaged in partnerships that were previously few and far between – working with stakeholders across sectors, including civil society, the private sector, academia, and NGOs to accelerate data innovations for policymaking and SDG attainment.

In this section, we highlight data innovations across sectors that have arisen as a result of the pandemic; discuss how these innovations have led to a greater focus on using data to enhance policymaking and SDG attainment; and share some of the key lessons learned to sustain and advance these developments to support SDG transformations.

4.1 Data innovations during the COVID-19 pandemic

Having timely, high-quality data has become the foundation of resilient and effective governments throughout the pandemic. However, COVID-19 has presented numerous obstacles to achieving this, including office closures; stretched government resources and budgets; significant disruptions to statistical operations; and delays in planned censuses, surveys, and other data programs (UN and World Bank, 2020; UNDESA, 2020).

Across countries, pragmatic decisions have been made to reprioritize staff and resources to modernize data capture methods and processes. Non-traditional sources, including citizen science, social media data, mobile phone data, and satellite imagery have been introduced to fill data gaps, while improved dissemination schemes have made it easier for policymakers and the public to consume the data. To realize these feats, countries have embarked on a range of multi-disciplinary and cross-sector partnerships.

Modernizing data-collection methods and processes

Health risks as well as government measures introduced in response to the COVID-19 pandemic severely limited traditional mechanisms of primary data collection, particularly face-to-face surveys and other in-person data-capture methods. At the onset of the pandemic, NSOs around the world suspended face-to-face interviews and asked staff to work from home, although many lacked adequate technology and infrastructure for remote work (Hammer et al., 2021). According to a UN Statistics Division survey, two-thirds of national statistics offices reported that these disruptions limited their ability to produce essential data and meet international reporting requirements (World Bank, 2020). But the pandemic also presented an opportunity for countries to modernize their methods and processes – with the support of key global stakeholders, such as the World Bank – notably leveraging mobile and other remote technologies to improve enumeration strategies and data collection processes.

In response to social distancing measures, for example, the World Bank helped countries quickly pivot to telephone surveys to conduct its flagship household survey, the Living Standards Measurement Study (LSMS), which collects socioeconomic and livelihood data in low-income and lower-middle-income countries. The LSMS also provided technical and financial assistance to several African countries, including Ethiopia, Malawi, Nigeria, Tanzania, and Uganda, to implement high-frequency telephone surveys of the pandemic's socioeconomic impacts (World Bank, 2022a).

To administer its 2020 census, Ethiopia's Central Statistics Agency piloted its use of a public-domain Computer Assisted Personal Interviewing (CAPI) software package. Compared to the traditional paper-based approach used for previous censuses, the CAPI system provided more timely and accurate monitoring of field activities, allowing field teams to monitor the progress of enumeration activities and to analyze, in near real-time, the quality of data collected (Bruno et al., 2020). The CAPI system also enabled Ethiopia to introduce geographic information system (GIS) technologies to its census methodology, allowing enumerators to capture geotagged data at the household level and create associated map products for real-time monitoring and reporting. Several other countries within the region (including South Africa and Sierra Leone) have similarly adopted CAPI systems since the start of the pandemic (Concord Times, 2021; Statistics South Africa, n.d.).

The Maldives National Bureau of Statistics was also able to continue key statistical activities during COVID-19 by adopting innovative methods (PARIS21, 2021b). The bureau moved from face-to-face interviews to telephone surveys to produce its monthly consumer price index, and reweighted variables in its 2019/2020 Household Income and Expenditure Survey to account for incomplete data collection during the pandemic (National Bureau of Statistics Maldives, n.d.). Individual weights were adjusted to account for non-interviewed enumeration blocks, enabling estimates to be produced that were representative of the entire population.

During the pandemic, governments also began to use artificial intelligence (AI) and other novel data-collection methods to improve service delivery and policymaking. The Swedish region of Halland, for example, developed a comprehensive data warehouse to collect timely financial and clinical healthcare data from hospitals, primary care facilities, and ambulatory care facilities, integrating these disparate data sources into a single repository for real-time delivery of healthcare services (Emilsson, 2021). As a result, providers and researchers were able to analyze patient pathways, identify trends, and predict impacts on the capacity of intensive care units throughout the pandemic. In Greece too, the government launched a system based on machine-learning algorithms to determine which travelers entering the country should be tested for COVID-19, which helped authorities to better assess mitigation measures ("Greece Used AI to Curb COVID," 2021).

Non-traditional data sources

The pandemic has demonstrated the value of innovation to fill data gaps for greater accuracy, timeliness, and granularity. Although governments have in the past relied primarily on traditional data sources, COVID-19 helped accelerate the use of non-traditional sources – including citizen science, social media, and earth observation data – to support evidence-based decision making and further SDG attainment at the local and national levels (Khanna and Ramachandran, 2022).

Marine litter inflicts significant damage on Africa's coastlines every year, particularly in Ghana. Yet continuous data to monitor marine litter in Ghana was lacking. To help fill the data gaps, Ghana turned to an innovative approach. In 2020, the country's statistical service partnered with a coalition of key stakeholders to introduce citizen science methods to monitor progress on SDG 14.1.1b (plastic debris density), aligning methodologies and existing initiatives within the country, building partnerships, and fostering more efficient data collection (SDSN TReNDS, 2021). And in 2021, Ghana became the first country to report on indicator 14.1.1b using citizen science data.

Another example can be found in Colombia, where DANE, Colombia's National Administrative Department of Statistics, has begun using social media data to complement measurement of SDG 16 (promotion of peaceful and inclusive societies) (UNStats, 2022c). By analyzing data culled from Facebook, exchanges among diverse segments of the population are used to determine the prevalence of discrimination within the country, and to establish a baseline for SDG indicators 16.b.1 (proportion of the population who have felt harassed or discriminated against in the past 12 months) and 16.7.2 (proportion of the population who believe decision-making is inclusive and responsive). Similarly, in Serbia, NSOs have supplemented their official statistics by analyzing Facebook advertising data to better measure emigration trends (IISD, 2021). Using social network data as a proxy for the number of Serbian emigrants and the rate of migration, they were able to determine how the pandemic had affected Serbian emigration rates.

Earth Observation (EO) data is also being increasingly used to support evidence-based decision-making. For instance, during the pandemic, Thailand and the Philippines both used EO imagery alongside household survey and census data to assess poverty levels more accurately (Ernst and Soerakoesoemah, 2021). Similarly, GEOGLAM (Group on Earth Observations Global Agricultural Monitoring Initiative) uses EO data to improve food security and market transparency by producing timely and actionable remote-sensing information on agricultural conditions at the national, regional, and global scale (GEOGLAM, 2020). GEOGLAM produces monthly global "Crop Monitors," providing near real-time information on crop conditions. Their EO datasets have been used by many low- and middle-income countries to make pre-harvest production forecasts, to identify anomalies associated with droughts and other weather-related events, and to assess the pandemic's impact on the global food supply (GEOGLAM, 2022).

New dissemination schemes

COVID-19 has also significantly increased the demand for timely data among users who may lack technical data skills – prompting stakeholders to reevaluate their user-engagement and dissemination strategies. New dynamic dashboards and GIS products have been developed, as well as stronger data visualizations and infographics to facilitate a better understanding of data and statistics.

For instance, in South America, the Colombian-based think-tank, Cepei *(Centro de Pensamiento Estratégico Internacional)* has partnered with Tableau and the UN Multi-Partner Trust Fund to launch the COVID-19 Data and Innovation Centre: a platform for sharing experiences, knowledge, and recommendations to enhance response and recovery efforts in the Global South (Cepei, 2020). The platform features data stories targeted toward the public and key decision-makers, as well as dashboards and open datasets relating to the pandemic.

Eurostat, the European Union's statistical office, has also launched a regional dashboard where users can find monthly and quarterly updates on a selection of COVID-19 indicators, as well as brief descriptions of the economic and social situation in the latest available period (Eurostat, 2022). The dashboard has proven very successful among users, with several additional features and functionalities added recently to help policymakers readily access the data they

Figure 4.1

Use of non-traditional data sources by national statistics offices to monitor the COVID-19 pandemic

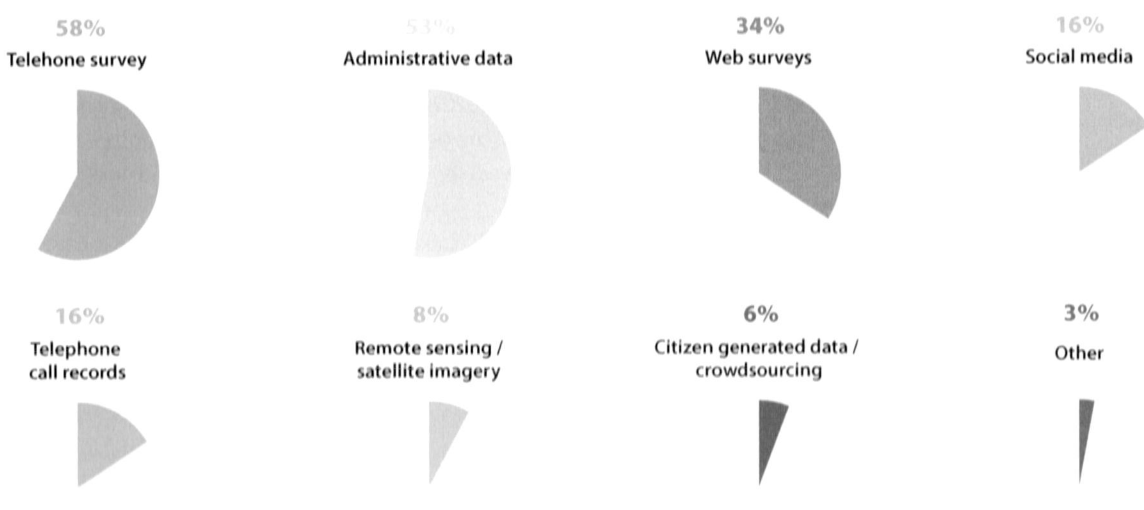

Note: Based on responses from 122 national statistical offices to the question: "Is your institution using alternative/non-traditional data sources/approaches to analyze or monitor aspects of the COVID-19 pandemic?"

need to make timely decisions in response to the COVID-19 crisis. In addition to the dashboard, Eurostat has enhanced its monthly commentary with graphical analyses and other features to keep pace with user demands (UNStats, 2021a).

At the national level, Canada leveraged investments in new analytics tools and dashboards during COVID-19 that enabled policymakers to make more informed decisions, providing them with richer context and much greater data disaggregation (Statistics Canada, 2022; UNStats, 2021c). For example, Canada's NSO has developed a statistical geospatial explorer that gives users the ability to generate data visualizations at a more granular level and produce custom tabs on a range of socioeconomic topics (Apolitical, 2021; Statistics Canada, 2020).

In addition to data visualization tools, several institutions – such as Paraguay's National Institute of Statistics – have launched open data portals on their websites to make COVID-19 data readily available to the public and to respond to growing demands for public health information from policy-makers and civil society organizations alike (PARIS21, 2020).

Innovative and cross-disciplinary partnerships

The range of innovative partnerships built across the data sector in response to COVID-19 has also been a clear upside of the pandemic. This has proven that in times of crisis, new ways of working are needed to be able to pivot quickly and strategically, and that cross-sector partnerships are essential for building resiliency and innovation across government.

This was especially true in Jamaica (UNStats, 2022b). Faced with a rapidly evolving pandemic situation and growing demand from users, the Statistical Institute of Jamaica (STATIN) acknowledged that a non-traditional approach to gathering data was required, and that they needed to improve research coordination and the production of data on COVID-19 impacts in the country. To achieve this, the institute established a national research agenda for COVID-19, linking research to policymaking and involving stakeholders from across sectors, including the Ministry of Health and Wellness, local academia, and the private sector. Additionally, they worked to improve research processes using a whole-of-society approach to data production, which led to the first nationally-representative telephone survey in Jamaica, conducted in collaboration with private-sector mobile phone networks. Moreover, partnerships with external actors prompted STATIN to reassess their administrative data sources and use them more efficiently, and to enhance their data-dissemination tools by including more user-friendly infographics.

To generate timely and accurate population and infrastructure data in response to COVID-19, the government of Sierra Leone, alongside the statistical office and some ministries, partnered with a range of leading data-science and geospatial organizations from the private sector (including Esri and Maxar), as well as regional commissions (including the UN Economic Commission for Africa) and NGOs (including GRID3 – Geo-Referenced Infrastructure and Demographic Data for Development). These partnerships enabled the country to produce critical geospatial datasets, analyses, and tools to support the government's COVID-19 response, publishing them under an open, non-commercial license (Government of Sierra Leone, 2020).

In Chile too, the government worked across sectors to develop a data platform to provide the public with timely updates on COVID-19 (UNStats, 2020). The country's National System of Coordination of Territorial Information (SNIT) worked alongside various ministries, the NSO, and private sector partners, such as Esri, to develop a COVID-19 Territorial Viewer so that all citizens could access territorial information on COVID-19 at the national, regional, and municipal levels (IDE Chile, 2022). A team of journalists and designers contributed to the development of the Viewer to ensure that the data was easy for the public to visualize and understand.

New multi-stakeholder partnerships for the SDGs have also taken shape during the pandemic. For instance, in Senegal, multi-stakeholder and cross-sectoral partnerships helped enhance capacity-building and knowledge-sharing around priority land-use indicators and small-area estimation methodologies (Global Partnership for Sustainable Development Data, 2022). As part of the multi-stakeholder Data For Now initiative, Senegal's National Agency of Statistics and Demography (ANSD, *Agence Nationale de Statistique et de la Démographie*) also partnered with UN Habitat, the UN Food and Agriculture Organization (FAO), and the UN Statistics Division to build capacity for measuring SDG indicators 2.3.1 and 2.3.2.

4.2 Emerging lessons for data systems

The country examples we have cited underscore recent shifts (in a large part due to COVID-19) towards better use of data to inform policymaking and SDG attainment. While the pandemic continues to evolve, lessons and trends that are likely to continue include the following:

- **The value of developing data that is fit-for-purpose.** The pandemic demonstrated that data is not valuable if it is not designed with users' needs in mind. Data must be timely, disaggregated, high-quality, and presented in a format and through a means that decision-makers can understand and act quickly on.

- **Post-pandemic, traditional approaches to survey taking, data production, and analysis will no longer satisfy user needs – non-traditional approaches are required.** As highlighted by the numerous country cases above, governments have successfully adopted new data approaches to keep pace with demands that have permanently raised user expectations. Partnerships are essential to continue to harness these innovations.

- **The importance and value of cross-sector partnerships**. Before the pandemic, multi-disciplinary and cross-sector partnerships within the data sector were still novel. Fortunately, COVID-19 has changed this for the better and enabled countries to take a whole-of-government approach to their data strategies.

- **Dissemination efforts should be prioritized alongside production efforts**. The pandemic prompted the development of hundreds of innovative platforms and dashboards to enable the public to understand the impact of COVID in near real time. It also encouraged governments to rethink their strategies to ensure that data production is accompanied by effective dissemination strategies that make data easier to use and understand for individuals who may lack technical aptitude and data literacy skills.

- **Data innovations are working.** As demonstrated, many countries are seeing positive, tangible results from the innovations they have adopted. For instance, since developing their new products, use of Statistics Canada's website has tripled (UNStats, 2021c).

- **Data innovations are emerging beyond the national level.** The pandemic has spurred innovations in data across other sectors, including within civil society (where we are seeing greater civic engagement in data to hold governments accountable) and the private sector (where there have been new efforts to improve ESG reporting) (Cameron, 2021; Chinn et al., 2021).

The COVID-19 pandemic is a major setback for sustainable development everywhere. Yet as with other major crises in the past, new ideas emerged during the pandemic that may help advance SDG policies and roadmaps to 2030 and beyond. Data systems and statistics were mobilized in new ways to inform countries' responses to the pandemic. In particular, the pandemic underscored the value of non-traditional data sources and approaches, including citizen science, social media, and earth observation data. It also catalyzed data partnerships and innovations across sectors and fostered the development of more fit-for-purpose, timely, and disaggregated data to support targeted policy interventions. Global efforts, including by the UN Statistical Commission, aim to solidify these improvements and innovations across nations and further greater cross-sector knowledge exchange (UNStats, 2022a).

Looking ahead, financing data systems continues to be a critical challenge, especially in LICs and LMICs. Despite heightened demand for data, its financing remains stagnant (PARIS21, 2021a). Cross-sectoral partnerships and initiatives to spur innovation – such as the Joint SDG Fund of the United Nations and the recently launched Clearinghouse for Financing Development Data – are positive developments, but to fully prepare countries for future epidemics and ensure the achievement of the 2030 agenda, significant investments in financing for national statistical and health information systems are paramount (Joint SDG Fund, 2022; PARIS21, 2021c).

Annex
Methods Summary and Data Tables

A.1 Interpreting the SDG Index and Dashboards results

The Sustainable Development Report describes countries' progress towards achieving the SDGs and highlights areas where progress is insufficient. A country's overall SDG Index score and the scores it receives on individual goals represent percentages of optimal performance. The difference between any score and the maximum value of 100 is therefore the distance in percentage points that a country must overcome to reach optimum SDG performance. The same indicators are used for all countries to generate the SDG Index score and rankings.

Substantial differences in rankings may be due to small differences in aggregate SDG Index scores. Differences of two or three places between countries' rankings should not be interpreted as "significant", whereas differences of 10 places or more may show a meaningful distinction. For details, see the statistical audit by Papadimitriou et al. (2019), conducted on behalf of the Joint Research Centre of the European Commission (EU JRC).

The SDG Dashboards provide a visual representation of each country's performance on the 17 SDGs. The "traffic light" color scheme (green, yellow, orange, and red) illustrates how far a country is from achieving a particular goal. As in previous years, the Dashboards and country profiles for OECD members include additional metrics for which data is not available for all countries.

The SDG Trend Dashboards indicate whether a country is on track to achieve a particular goal by 2030, based on recent performance of individual indicators. Indicator trends are then aggregated at the goal level to give an appraisal of how well the country is progressing towards that SDG.

This section provides a brief summary of the methods used to compute the SDG Index and Dashboards. A detailed methodology paper is accessible online (Lafortune et al., 2018). The European Commission Joint Research Centre (JRC) conducted an independent statistical audit of the methodology and results in 2019, reviewing the conceptual and statistical coherence of the index structure. Their audit and additional data tables are available on our website, www.sdgindex.org

This year's edition does not reflect the impact of the war in Ukraine.

A.2 Changes to the 2022 edition and main limitations

Changes to the 2022 SDG Index and Dashboards

The 2022 SDG Index covers 163 countries – two fewer than last year due to missing data (Cabo Verde and Vanuatu). This edition introduces an additional indicator (for SDG 12, see Table A1) to cover a previous data gap. We have also dropped two indicators due to insufficient periodicity of updates to the data and another one due to redundancy. Table A1 also identifies indicators that have been modified or replaced due to changes in methodologies or estimates of data providers. Data for this year's edition were extracted between February and March 2022.

Limitations and data gaps

Due to changes in the indicators and some refinements in the methodology, SDG Index rankings and scores cannot be compared with the results from previous years. However, Part 2 provides time series for the SDG Index, calculated retroactively using this year's indicators and methods. The full time series for the SDG Index are available for download online.

In spite of our best efforts to identify data for the SDGs, several indicator and data gaps persist at the international level (Table A2). Governments and the international community must increase investments in SDG data and

Table A.1

New indicators and modifications

SDG	Indicator	Modification	Source
4	Participation rate in pre-primary organized learning (% of children aged 4 to 6)	Modification, now global indicator	UNESCO
4	Resilient students in science (% of 15-year-olds)	Removed due to redundancy	OECD
5	Gender gap in time spent doing unpaid work (minutes/day)	Removed due to lack of timely data	OECD
6	Scarce water consumption embodied in imports (m^3 H_2O eq/capita)	Modification, now sourced from different Multi-regional input-output database, Gloria.	UNEP
7	Share of renewable energy in total primary energy supply (%)	Modification, now global indicator	OECD
9	Articles published in academic journals (per 1,000 population)	Changed source to Scimago Journal Rank	Scimago Jounal Rank
10	Gini coefficient	Replaces Adjusted Gini Coefficient	World Bank
10	Gini coefficient adjusted for top income	Removed due to insufficient update frequency	Chandy and Seidel (2017)
12	Municipal solid waste (kg/capita/day)	Changed calculation method. Now divided by entire country population since waste collection data covers urban & rural areas	World Bank
12	Production-based SO_2 emissions (kg/capita)	Modification, now sourced from different Multi-regional input-output database, Gloria.	Lenzen et al. (2020)
12	SO_2 emissions embodied in imports (kg/capita)	Modification, now sourced from different Multi-regional input-output database, Gloria.	Lenzen et al. (2020)
12	Exports of plastic waste (kg/capita)	New indicator	UN Comtrade
13	CO_2 emissions embodied in imports (tCO_2/capita)	Modification, now sourced from different Multi-regional input-output database, Gloria.	Lenzen et al. (2020)

Source: Authors' analysis

monitoring systems and build strong data partnerships to support informed SDG decisions and strategies.

To ensure maximum data comparability, we only use data from internationally comparable sources. These sources may adjust national data to ensure international comparability. As a result, some data points presented in this report may differ from data available from national statistical offices or other national sources. Moreover, the length of international organizations' validation processes can lead to significant delays in publishing some data. National statistical offices may therefore have more recent data for some indicators than what is presented in this report.

A.3 Methodology (overview)

The SDR2022 provides a comprehensive assessment of distance to targets based on the most up-to-date data available covering all 193 UN Member States. This year's report includes 94 global indicators as well as 26 additional indicators specifically for OECD countries (due to better data coverage).

The following sections provide an overview of the methodology for indicator selection, normalization, and aggregation and for generating indications on trends. Additional information including raw data, additional data tables, and sensitivity tests are available online.

A. Data selection

Where possible, the SDR2022 uses official SDG indicators endorsed by the UN Statistical Commission. Where there are data gaps or insufficient data available for an official indicator, we include other metrics from official and unofficial providers. Five criteria for indicator selection were used to determine suitable metrics for inclusion in the report:

1. Global relevance and applicability to a broad range of country settings.
2. Statistical adequacy: the indicators selected represent valid and reliable measures.
3. Timeliness: the indicators selected are up to date and published on a reasonably prompt schedule.

Table A.2
Major indicator and data gaps for the SDGs

SDG	Issue	Desired metrics
2	Agriculture and nutrition	Food loss and food waste Greenhouse gas emissions from land use Global yield gap statistics
3	Health	Health care system resilience and preparedness to face global health risks Internationally comparable survey data on unmet care needs
4	Education	Internationally comparable primary and secondary education outcomes Early childhood development (access and quality)
5	Women empowerment	Gender pay gap and other empowerment measures Violence against women
6	Water	Quality of drinking water and surface waters
8	Decent work	Decent work Child labor and modern slavery embodied into trade
10	Inequality	Wealth inequality Vertical mobility
12	Sustainable consumption and production	Environmental impact of transboundary physical flows (e.g. air pollution through wind, water pollution through rivers) Recycling and re-use (circular economy) Chemicals
13	Climate Action	Robust indicators of climate adaptation
14	Marine ecosystems	Maximum sustainable yields for fisheries Impact of high-sea and cross-border fishing Protected areas by level of protection
15	Terrestrial ecosystems	Leading indicators for ecosystem health Trade in endangered species Protected areas by level of protection
16	Peace and justice	Violence against children
17	Means of implementation	Climate finance Development impact of trade practices

Source: Authors' analysis

4. Coverage: data must be available for at least 80 percent of the UN Member States with a population greater than one million people.[1]
5. Capacity to measure distance to targets: optimal performance can be determined.

Data sources

The data included in the SDR2022 come from a mix of official and non-official data sources. Most of the data (around two-thirds) come from international organizations (including FAO, ILO, OECD, UNICEF, WHO, and the World Bank,) which have extensive and rigorous data validation processes. Other data sources (around a third) come from less traditional statistics: including household surveys (Gallup World Poll); civil society organizations and networks (such as Oxfam, Reporters sans Frontières, the Tax Justice Network, and the World Justice Project); and peer-reviewed journals (for example, to track international spillovers). The full list of indicators and data sources is available online.

B. Missing data and imputations

The Sustainable Development Report's purpose is to provide robust data that can guide countries in determining their SDG priorities. To minimize biases due to missing data, the SDG Index only includes countries for which data is available for at least 80% of the variables included in the global SDG. The list of countries not included in the SDG Index due to insufficient data availability is presented in Table A3. All UN Member States are included in both the SDG Dashboards and the country profiles – which also indicate any data gaps for each country.

Considering that many SDG priorities lack accepted statistical models that could be used to impute country-level data, missing data was only imputed or modelled in a few particular instances. The list of indicators for which imputations were performed is available online.

1. There are two exceptions to this rule: (i) Exports of hazardous pesticides; (ii) Children involved in child labor

C. Method for constructing the SDG Index and Dashboards

The procedure for calculating the SDG Index comprises three steps: (i) establish performance thresholds and remove extreme values from the distribution of each indicator; (ii) rescale the data to ensure comparability across indicators (normalization); (iii) aggregate the indicators within and across SDGs.

Establishing performance thresholds

To make the data comparable across indicators, each variable was rescaled from 0 to 100 with 0 denoting worst possible performance and 100 describing optimum performance. Rescaling is usually very sensitive to the choice of limits and to extreme values (outliers) at both ends of the distribution. These outliers can become unintended thresholds and introduce spurious variability to the data. Consequently, the choice of upper and lower bounds can affect the relative ranking of countries in the index.

The upper bound for each indicator was determined using a five-step decision tree:

1. Use absolute quantitative thresholds in SDGs and targets: for example, zero poverty, universal school completion, universal access to water and sanitation, full gender equality.
2. Where no explicit SDG target is available, apply the principle of "leave no one behind" in setting the upper bound to universal access or zero deprivation.
3. Where science based targets exist that must be achieved by 2030 or later, use these to set the upper bound (for example, zero greenhouse gas emissions from CO_2 by 2050 required for global warming to stay within 1.5°C, 100% sustainable management of fisheries).
4. Where several countries already exceed an SDG target, use the average of the top five performers (for example, child mortality).
5. For all other indicators, use the average of the top performers.

Table A.3
Countries excluded from the 2022 SDG Index due to insufficient data

Country	Missing Values	Percentage of Missing Values
Andorra	48	54%
Antigua and Barbuda	33	35%
Bahamas, The	22	23%
Cabo Verde	20	21%
Comoros	22	23%
Dominica	47	50%
Equatorial Guinea	29	31%
Eritrea	25	27%
Grenada	39	41%
Guinea-Bissau	22	23%
Kiribati	37	39%
Korea, Dem. Rep.	29	31%
Libya	23	24%
Liechtenstein	59	66%
Marshall Islands	52	55%
Micronesia, Fed. Sts.	44	47%
Monaco	59	63%
Nauru	51	54%
Palau	51	54%
Samoa	26	28%
San Marino	57	61%
Seychelles	30	32%
Solomon Islands	28	30%
St. Kitts and Nevis	47	50%
St. Lucia	25	27%
St. Vincent and the Grenadines	33	35%
Timor-Leste	25	27%
Tonga	33	35%
Tuvalu	51	54%
Vanuatu	23	24%

Source: Authors' analysis

These principles interpret the SDGs as "stretch targets" and focus attention on the indicators on which a country is lagging. The lower bound was defined at the 2.5th percentile of the distribution. Each indicator distribution was censored, so that all values exceeding the upper bound scored 100, and values below the lower bound scored 0.

Normalization

After establishing the upper and lower bounds, variables were transformed linearly to a scale between 0 and 100 using the following rescaling formula for the range [0; 100]:

$$x' = \frac{x - min.(x)}{max.(x) - min.(x)} \times 100$$

where x is the raw data value; max/min denote the upper and lower bounds, respectively; and x' is the normalized value after rescaling.

The rescaling equation ensured that all rescaled variables were expressed as ascending variables (higher values denoted better performance). In this way, the rescaled data became easy to interpret and compare across all indicators: a country that scores 50 on a variable is half-way towards achieving the optimum value, while one with a score of 75 has covered three-quarters of the distance from worst to best.

Weighting and aggregation

Several rounds of expert consultations on earlier drafts of the SDG Index made it clear that there was no consensus across different epistemic communities on assigning higher weights to some SDGs over others. As a normative assumption, we therefore opted to give fixed, equal weight to every SDG, reflecting the commitment of policymakers to treat all SDGs equally as part of an integrated and indivisible set of goals. To improve their SDG Index score, countries need to place attention on all goals, albeit with a particular focus on those they are furthest from achieving and where incremental progress might be expected to be fastest.

To compute the SDG Index, we first estimate a country's scores on each goal using the arithmetic mean of its scores on the goal indicators. These scores are then averaged across all 17 SDGs to obtain the country's 2022 SDG Index score. Various sensitivity tests are made available online, including Monte Carlo simulations and comparisons of arithmetic mean versus geometric mean at both the Index and goal levels. Monte Carlo simulations call for prudence in interpreting small differences in the Index scores and rankings between countries, as they may be sensitive to the weighting scheme used.

Dashboards

We also introduced quantitative thresholds for each indicator, to group countries into a "traffic light" table. Thresholds have been established via statistical techniques supported by various rounds of consultations with experts since 2016.

Averaging across all indicators for an SDG might hide areas of policy concern if a country performs well on most indicators but faces serious shortfalls on one or two metrics within the same SDG (often called the "substitutability" or "compensation" issue). This applies particularly to high-income and upper-middle-income countries that have made significant progress on many SDG dimensions but may face serious shortfalls on individual variables.

As a result, the SDG Dashboards focus exclusively on the two variables on which a country performs worst. We applied the added rule that a red rating is given only if the country scores red on *both* of its worst-performing indicators for that goal. Similarly, to score green, both of these indicators had to be green. More details on the construction of the Dashboards are accessible online.

SDG Trends

Using historic data, we estimate how fast a country has been progressing towards an SDG and determine whether – if extrapolated into the future – this pace will be sufficient to achieve the SDG by 2030. For each indicator, SDG achievement is defined by the green threshold set for the SDG Dashboards. The difference in percentage points between the green threshold and the normalized country score denotes the gap that must be closed to meet that goal. To estimate trends at the indicator level, we calculated the linear annual growth rates (annual percentage improvements) needed to achieve the target by 2030 (from 2015–2030), which we compared to the average annual growth rate over the most recent period since the adoption of the SDGs in 2015 (for example, 2015–2020). Progress towards achievement on a particular indicator is described using a four-arrow system (Figure A1). Figure A2 illustrates the methodology graphically.

Since the projections are based on average growth rate over recent years, a country might have observed a decline in performance over the past year (for instance due to the impact of COVID-19) but still be considered as being on track. This methodology emphasizes long-term structural changes over time since the adoption of the SDGs in 2015, with less emphasis given to annual changes that may be cyclical or temporary.

Figure A.1
The Four-arrow system for denoting SDG trends

Decreasing	Stagnating	Moderately improving	On track or Maintaining SDG achievement
Decreasing score, i.e. country moves in the wrong direction	Score remains stagnant or increases at a rate below 50% of the growth rate needed to achieve the SDG by 2030	Score increases at a rate above 50% of the required growth rate but below the rate needed to achieve the SDG by 2030	Score increases at the rate needed to achieve the SDG by 2030 or performance has already exceeded SDG achievement threshold

Figure A.2
Graphic representation of the methodology for SDG trends

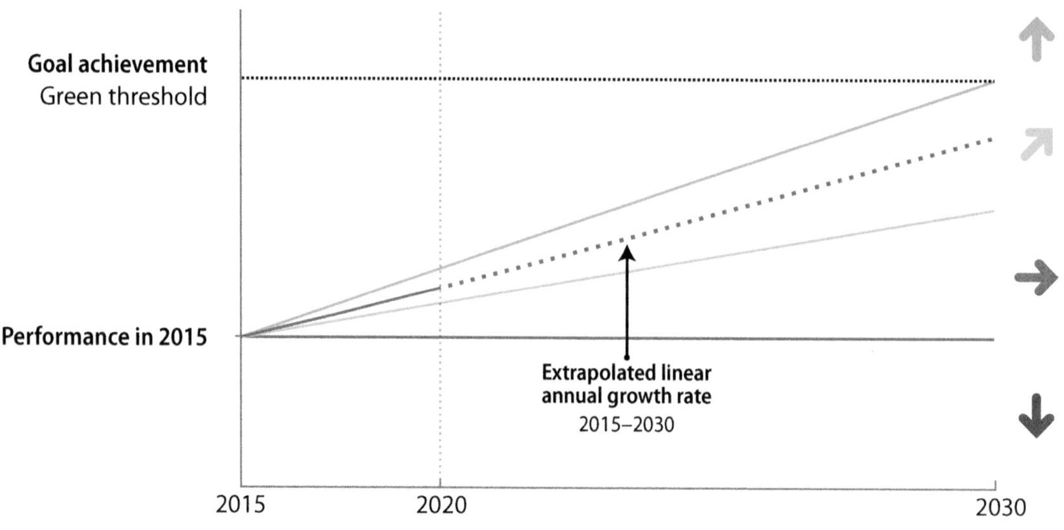

Source: Authors' analysis

Table A.4

Indicators included in the *Sustainable Development Report 2022*

Legend

[a] denotes OECD-only indicators
[b] denotes indicators not used in OECD dashboard but that are used in the calculation of OECD countries' index scores.

SDG	Notes	Indicator	Reference Year	Source	Description
1		Poverty headcount ratio at \$1.90/day (%)	2022	World Data Lab	Estimated percentage of the population that is living under the poverty threshold of US\$1.90 a day. Estimated using historical estimates of the income distribution, projections of population changes by age and educational attainment, and GDP projections.
1		Poverty headcount ratio at \$3.20/day (%)	2022	World Data Lab	Estimated percentage of the population that is living under the poverty threshold of US\$3.20 a day. Estimated using historical estimates of the income distribution, projections of population changes by age and educational attainment, and GDP projections.
1	[a]	Poverty rate after taxes and transfers (%)	2019	OECD	Relative poverty is measured as the share of the population whose incomes fall below half the median disposable income for the entire population. The income threshold for relative poverty changes over time with changes in median disposable income.
2		Prevalence of undernourishment (%)	2019	FAO	The percentage of the population whose food intake is insufficient to meet dietary energy requirements for a minimum of one year. Dietary energy requirements are defined as the amount of dietary energy required by an individual to maintain body functions, health and normal activity. FAO et al. (2015) report 14.7 million undernourished people in developed regions, which corresponds to an average prevalence of 1.17% in the developed regions. We assumed a 1.2% prevalence rate for each high-income country with missing data.
2		Prevalence of stunting in children under 5 years of age (%)	2019	UNICEF et al.	The percentage of children up to the age of 5 years that are stunted, measured as the percentage that fall below minus two standard deviations from the median height for their age, according to the WHO Child Growth Standards. UNICEF et al. (2016) report an average prevalence of wasting in high-income countries of 2.58%. We assumed this value for high-income countries with missing data.
2		Prevalence of wasting in children under 5 years of age (%)	2019	UNICEF et al.	The percentage of children up to the age of 5 years whose weight falls below minus two standard deviations from the median weight for their age, according to the WHO Child Growth Standards. UNICEF et al. (2016) report an average prevalence of wasting in high-income countries of 0.75%. We assumed this value for high-income countries with missing data.
2		Prevalence of obesity, BMI ≥ 30 (% of adult population)	2016	WHO	The percentage of the adult population that has a body mass index (BMI) of $30kg/m^2$ or higher, based on measured height and weight.
2		Human Trophic Level (best 2–3 worst)	2017	Bonhommeau et al. (2013)	Trophic levels are a measure of the energy intensity of diet composition and reflect the relative amounts of plants as opposed to animals eaten in a given country. A higher trophic level represents a greater level of consumption of energy-intensive animals.
2		Cereal yield (tonnes per hectare of harvested land)	2018	FAO	Cereal yield, measured as tonnes per hectare of harvested land. Production data on cereals relate to crops harvested for dry grain only and exclude crops harvested for hay or green for food, feed, or silage and those used for grazing.
2		Sustainable Nitrogen Management Index (best 0–1.41 worst)	2015	Zhang and Davidson (2019)	The Sustainable Nitrogen Management Index (SNMI) is a one-dimensional ranking score that combines two efficiency measures in crop production: Nitrogen use efficiency (NUE) and land use efficiency (crop yield).
2	[a]	Yield gap closure (% of potential yield)	2015	Global Yield Gap Atlas	A country's yield expressed as a percentage of its potential yield in the three annual crops using the most land area, weighted for the relative importance of each crop in terms of surface area.

Table A.4
(continued)

SDG	Notes	Indicator	Reference Year	Source	Description
2		Exports of hazardous pesticides (tonnes per million population)	2019	FAO	Exports of pesticides deemed hazardous to human health, standardized by population. Due to volatility, the calculation uses the average value over the last 5 years.
3		Maternal mortality rate (per 100,000 live births)	2017	WHO et al.	The estimated number of girls and women, between the ages of 15 and 49, who die from pregnancy-related causes while pregnant or within 42 days of termination of pregnancy, per 100,000 live births.
3		Neonatal mortality rate (per 1,000 live births)	2020	UNICEF et al.	The number of newborn infants (neonates) who die before reaching 28 days of age, per 1,000 live births.
3		Mortality rate, under-5 (per 1,000 live births)	2020	UNICEF et al.	The probability that a newborn baby will die before reaching age five, if subject to age-specific mortality rates of the specified year, per 1,000 live births.
3		Incidence of tuberculosis (per 100,000 population)	2020	WHO	The estimated rate of new and relapse cases of tuberculosis in a given year, expressed per 100,000 people. All forms of tuberculosis are included, including cases of people living with HIV.
3		New HIV infections (per 1,000 uninfected population)	2020	UNAIDS	Number of people newly infected with HIV per 1,000 uninfected population.
3		Age-standardized death rate due to cardiovascular disease, cancer, diabetes, or chronic respiratory disease in adults aged 30–70 years (%)	2019	WHO	The probability of dying between the ages of 30 and 70 years from cardiovascular diseases, cancer, diabetes or chronic respiratory diseases, defined as the percent of 30-year-old-people who would die before their 70th birthday from these diseases, assuming current mortality rates at every age and that individuals would not die from any other cause of death (for example injuries or HIV/AIDS).
3		Age-standardized death rate attributable to household air pollution and ambient air pollution (per 100,000 population)	2016	WHO	Mortality rate that is attributable to the joint effects of fuels used for cooking indoors and ambient outdoor air pollution.
3		Traffic deaths (per 100,000 population)	2019	WHO	Estimated number of fatal road traffic injuries per 100,000 people.
3		Life expectancy at birth (years)	2019	WHO	The average number of years that a newborn could expect to live, if he or she were to pass through life exposed to the sex- and age-specific death rates prevailing at the time of his or her birth, for a specific year, in a given country, territory, or geographic area.
3		Adolescent fertility rate (births per 1,000 females aged 15 to 19)	2019	WHO	The number of births per 1,000 females between the age of 15 to 19.
3		Births attended by skilled health personnel (%)	2018	UNICEF	The percentage of births attended by personnel trained to give the necessary supervision, care, and advice to women during pregnancy, labor, and the postpartum period, to conduct deliveries on their own, and to care for newborns.
3		Surviving infants who received 2 WHO-recommended vaccines (%)	2020	WHO and UNICEF	Estimated national routine immunization coverage of infants, expressed as the percentage of surviving infants, children under the age of 12 months, who received two WHO-recommended vaccines (3rd dose of DTP and 1st dose of measles). Calculated as the minimum value between the percentage of infants who have received the 3rd dose of DTP and the percentage who have received the 1st dose of measles.
3		Universal health coverage (UHC) index of service coverage (worst 0–100 best)	2019	WHO	Coverage of essential health services (defined as the average coverage of essential services based on tracer interventions that include reproductive, maternal, newborn and child health, infectious diseases, non-communicable diseases and service capacity and access, among the general and the most disadvantaged population). The indicator is an index reported on a unitless scale of 0 to 100, which is computed as the geometric mean of 14 tracer indicators of health service coverage.

Table A.4
(continued)

SDG	Notes	Indicator	Reference Year	Source	Description
3		Subjective well-being (average ladder score, worst 0–10 best)	2021	Gallup	Subjective self-evaluation of life, where respondents are asked to evaluate where they feel they stand on a ladder where 0 represents the worst possible life and 10 the best possible life.
3	[a]	Gap in life expectancy at birth among regions (years)	2019	OECD	Difference between maximum and minimum regional life expectancy at birth among regions.
3	[a]	Gap in self-reported health status by income (percentage points)	2020	OECD	Gap in percentage of people who perceive their health status as good or very good between the poorest 20% and the richest 20% of the population.
3	[a]	Daily smokers (% of population aged 15 and over)	2020	OECD	The percentage of the population aged 15 years and older who are reported to smoke daily.
4	[a]	Participation rate in pre-primary organized learning (% of children aged 4 to 6)	2020	UNESCO	Participation rate in organized learning one year before the official primary entry age.
4		Net primary enrollment rate (%)	2020	UNESCO	The percentage of children of the official school age population who are enrolled in primary education.
4		Lower secondary completion rate (%)	2020	UNESCO	Lower secondary education completion rate measured as the gross intake ratio to the last grade of lower secondary education (general and pre-vocational). It is calculated as the number of new entrants in the last grade of lower secondary education, regardless of age, divided by the population at the entrance age for the last grade of lower secondary education.
4		Literacy rate (% of population aged 15 to 24)	2020	UNESCO	The percentage of youth, aged 15 to 24, who can both read and write a short simple statement on everyday life with understanding.
4	[a]	Tertiary educational attainment (% of population aged 25 to 34)	2020	OECD	The percentage of the population, aged 25 to 34, who have completed tertiary education.
4	[a]	PISA score (worst 0–600 best)	2018	OECD	National scores in the Programme for International Student Assessment (PISA), an internationally standardized assessment that is administered to 15-year-olds in schools. It assesses how far students near the end of compulsory education have acquired some of the knowledge and skills that are essential for full participation in society. Country PISA scores for reading, mathematics, and science were averaged to obtain an overall PISA score.
4	[a]	Variation in science performance explained by socio-economic status (%)	2018	OECD	Percentage of variation in science performance explained by students' socio-economic status.
4	[a]	Underachievers in science (% of 15-year-olds)	2018	OECD	Percentage of students with a performance in science below level 2 (less than 409.54 score points).
5		Demand for family planning satisfied by modern methods (% of females aged 15 to 49)	2022	UNDESA	The percentage of women of reproductive age whose demand for family planning has been met using modern methods of contraception.
5		Ratio of female-to-male mean years of education received (%)	2019	UNESCO	The mean years of education received by women aged 25 and older divided by the mean years of education received by men aged 25 and older.
5		Ratio of female-to-male labor force participation rate (%)	2020	ILO	Modeled estimate of the proportion of the female population aged 15 years and older that is economically active, divided by the same proportion for men.
5		Seats held by women in national parliament (%)	2020	IPU	The number of seats held by women in single or lower chambers of national parliaments, expressed as a percentage of all occupied seats. Seats refer to the number of parliamentary mandates, or the number of members of parliament.
5	[a]	Gender wage gap (% of male median wage)	2020	OECD	The difference between male and female median wages of full-time employees and those self-employed, divided by the male median wage.

Table A.4
(continued)

SDG	Notes	Indicator	Reference Year	Source	Description
6		Population using at least basic drinking water services (%)	2020	JMP	The percentage of the population using at least a basic drinking water service, such as drinking water from an improved source, provided that the collection time is not more than 30 minutes for a round trip, including queuing.
6		Population using at least basic sanitation services (%)	2020	JMP	The percentage of the population using at least a basic sanitation service, such as an improved sanitation facility that is not shared with other households.
6		Freshwater withdrawal (% of available freshwater resources)	2018	FAO	The level of water stress: freshwater withdrawal as a proportion of available freshwater resources is the ratio between total freshwater withdrawn by all major sectors and total renewable freshwater resources, after taking into account environmental water requirements. Main sectors, as defined by ISIC standards, include agriculture, forestry and fishing, manufacturing, electricity industry, and services. This indicator is also known as water withdrawal intensity.
6		Anthropogenic wastewater that receives treatment (%)	2018	EPI	The percentage of collected, generated, or produced wastewater that is treated, normalized by the population connected to centralized wastewater treatment facilities. Scores were calculated by multiplying the wastewater treatment summary values, based on decadal averages, with the sewerage connection values to arrive at an overall total percentage of wastewater treated.
6		Scarce water consumption embodied in imports (m^3 H2O equivalent/capita)	2018	UNEP	Water scarcity is measured as water consumption weighted by scarcity indices. In order to incorporate water scarcity into the virtual water flow calculus, water use entries are weighted so that they reflect the scarcity of the water being used. The weight used is a measure of water withdrawals as a percentage of the existing local renewable freshwater resources.
6	[a]	Population using safely managed water services (%)	2020	JMP	The percentage of the population using a safely managed drinking water service. A safely managed drinking water service is one where people use an "improved" source meeting three criteria: it is accessible on premises, water is available when needed, and the water supplied is free from contamination. Improved sources are those that have the potential to deliver safe water by nature of their design and construction.
6	[a]	Population using safely managed sanitation services (%)	2020	JMP	The percentage of the population using safely managed sanitation services. Safely managed sanitation services are "improved" sanitation facilities that are not shared with other households, and where the excreta produced should either be treated and disposed of in situ, stored temporarily and then emptied, transported and treated off-site, or transported through a sewer with wastewater and then treated off-site. Improved sanitation facilities are those designed to hygienically separate excreta from human contact.
7		Population with access to electricity (%)	2019	SE4All	The percentage of the population who has access to electricity.
7		Population with access to clean fuels and technology for cooking (%)	2019	SE4All	The percentage of the population primarily using clean cooking fuels and technologies for cooking. Under WHO guidelines, kerosene is excluded from clean cooking fuels.
7		CO_2 emissions from fuel combustion per total electricity output ($MtCO_2$/TWh)	2019	IEA	A measure of the carbon intensity of energy production, calculated by dividing CO_2 emissions from the combustion of fuel by electricity output. The data are reported in Megatonnes per billion kilowatt hours.
7	[a]	Share of renewable energy in total primary energy supply (%)	2019	OECD	The share of renewable energy in the total primary energy supply. Renewables include the primary energy equivalent of hydro (excluding pumped storage), geothermal, solar, wind, tide and wave sources. Energy derived from solid biofuels, biogasoline, biodiesels, other liquid biofuels, biogases and the renewable fraction of municipal waste are also included.
8		Adjusted GDP growth (%)	2020	World Bank	The growth rate of GDP adjusted to income levels (where rich countries are expected to grow less) and expressed relative to the US growth performance. World Bank data on GDP per capita, PPP (current international $) annual data were used as the starting point. The growth rate over the last 3-year period (t-3 to t) was calculated where GRa=(At/At-3)^(1/3)-1 and where GRa is the growth rate for country A and At is the GDP per capita data for the year t in country A. Then our adjustment is as follows : ADJa= [GRa-(GRusa - 0,015*log(At-3/USAt-3))] * 100, where GRusa is the United States growth rate and USAt-3 is the United States GDP per capita 3 years ago.

Table A.4

(continued)

SDG	Notes	Indicator	Reference Year	Source	Description
8		Victims of modern slavery (per 1,000 population)	2018	Walk Free Foundation (2018)	Estimation of the number of people in modern slavery. Modern slavery is defined as people in forced labor or forced marriage. It is calculated based on standardized surveys and Multiple Systems Estimation (MSE).
8		Adults with an account at a bank or other financial institution or with a mobile-money-service provider (% of population aged 15 or over)	2017	Demirguc-Kunt et al. (2018)	The percentage of adults, 15 years and older, who report having an account (by themselves or with someone else) at a bank or another type of financial institution, or who have personally used a mobile money service within the past 12 months.
8	[b]	Unemployment rate (% of total labor force, ages 15+)	2022	ILO	Modeled estimate of the share of the labor force that is without work but is available and actively seeking employment. The indicator reflects the inability of an economy to generate employment for people who want to work but are not doing so.
8		Fundamental labor rights are effectively guaranteed (worst 0–1 best)	2020	World Justice Project	Measures the effective enforcement of fundamental labor rights, including freedom of association and the right to collective bargaining, the absence of discrimination with respect to employment, and freedom from forced labor and child labor.
8		Fatal work-related accidents embodied in imports (per 100,000 population)	2015	Alsamawi et al. (2017)	The number of fatal work-related accidents associated with imported goods. Calculated using extensions to a multiregional input-output table.
8	[a]	Employment-to-population ratio (%)	2021	OECD	The ratio of the employed to the working age population. Employed people are those aged 15 or older who were in paid employment or self-employed during a specified period. The working age population refers to people aged 15 to 64.
8	[a]	Youth not in employment, education or training (NEET) (% of population aged 15 to 29)	2020	OECD	The percentage of young people who are not in employment, education or training (NEET). Education includes part-time or full-time education, but exclude those in non-formal education and in educational activities of very short duration. Employment is defined according to the ILO Guidelines and covers all those who have been in paid work for at least one hour in the reference week or were temporarily absent from such work.
9		Population using the internet (%)	2020	ITU	The percentage of the population who used the Internet from any location in the last three months. Access could be via a fixed or mobile network.
9		Mobile broadband subscriptions (per 100 population)	2019	ITU	The number of mobile broadband subscriptions per 100 population. Mobile broadband subscriptions refer to subscriptions to mobile cellular networks with access to data communications (for example the Internet) at broadband speeds, irrespective of the device used to access the internet.
9		Logistics Performance Index: Quality of trade and transport-related infrastructure (worst 1–5 best)	2018	World Bank	Survey-based average assessment of the quality of trade and transport related infrastructure, for example ports, roads, railroads and information technology, on a scale from 1 (worst) to 5 (best).
9		The Times Higher Education Universities Ranking: Average score of top 3 universities (worst 0–100 best)	2022	Times Higher Education	The average score of the top three universities in each country that are listed in the global top 1,000 universities in the world. For countries with at least one university on the list, only the score of the ranked university was taken into account. When a university score was missing in the Times Higher Education World University Ranking, an indicator from the Global Innovation Index on the top 3 universities in Quacquarelli Symonds (QS) University Ranking was used as a source when available.
9		Articles published in academic journals (per 1,000 population)	2020	Scimago Jounal Rank	Number of citable documents published by a journal in the three previous years (selected year documents are excluded). Exclusively articles, reviews and conference papers are considered.
9		Expenditure on research and development (% of GDP)	2018	UNESCO	Gross domestic expenditure on scientific research and experimental development (R&D) expressed as a percentage of Gross Domestic Product (GDP). We assumed zero R&D expenditure for low-income countries that do not report any data.

Table A.4
(continued)

SDG	Notes	Indicator	Reference Year	Source	Description
9	[a]	Researchers (per 1,000 employed population)	2019	OECD	The number of researchers per thousand employed people. Researchers are professionals engaged in the conception or creation of new knowledge, products, processes, methods and systems, as well as in the management of the projects concerned.
9	[a]	Triadic patent families filed (per million population)	2019	OECD	A triadic patent family is defined as a set of patents registered in various countries (i.e. patent offices) to protect the same invention. Triadic patent families are a set of patents filed at three of these major patent offices: the European Patent Office (EPO), the Japan Patent Office (JPO) and the United States Patent and Trademark Office (USPTO). The number of triadic patent families is "nowcast" for timeliness.
9	[a]	Gap in internet access by income (percentage points)	2020	OECD	The difference in the percentage of household Internet access between the top and bottom income quartiles.
9		Female share of graduates from STEM fields at the tertiary level (%)	2018	World Bank	Female share of graduates from Science, Technology, Engineering and Mathematics (STEM) programmes, tertiary (%)
10		Gini coefficient	2019	World Bank	The Gini coefficient measures the extent to which the distribution of income among individuals or households within an economy deviates from a perfectly equal distribution.
10	[a]	Palma ratio	2019	OECD & UNDP	The share of all income received by the 10% people with highest disposable income divided by the share of all income received by the 40% people with the lowest disposable income.
10	[a]	Elderly poverty rate (% of population aged 66 or over)	2019	OECD	The percentage of people of 66 years of age or more whose income falls below half the median household income of the total population.
11		Proportion of urban population living in slums (%)	2018	UN Habitat	Population living in slums is the proportion of the urban population living in slum households. A slum household is defined as a group of individuals living under the same roof lacking one or more of the following conditions: access to improved water, access to improved sanitation, sufficient living area, housing durability, and security of tenure.
11		Annual mean concentration of particulate matter of less than 2.5 microns in diameter (PM2.5) ($\mu g/m^3$)	2019	IHME	Air pollution measured as the population-weighted mean annual concentration of PM2.5 for the urban population in a country. PM2.5 is suspended particles measuring less than 2.5 microns in aerodynamic diameter, which are capable of penetrating deep into the respiratory tract and can cause severe health damage.
11		Access to improved water source, piped (% of urban population)	2020	WHO and UNICEF	The percentage of the urban population with access to improved drinking water piped on premises. An "improved" drinking-water source is one that, by the nature of its construction and when properly used, adequately protects the source from outside contamination, particularly fecal matter.
11		Satisfaction with public transport (%)	2021	Gallup	The percentage of the surveyed population that responded "satisfied" to the question "In the city or area where you live, are you satisfied or dissatisfied with the public transportation systems?".
11	[a]	Population with rent overburden (%)	2019	OECD	Percentage of the population living in households where the total housing costs represent more than 40 % of disposable income.
12	[b]	Municipal solid waste (kg/capita/day)	2016	World Bank	The amount of waste collected by or on behalf of municipal authorities and disposed of through the waste management system. Waste from agriculture and from industries are not included.
12		Electronic waste (kg/capita)	2019	UNU-IAS	Waste from electrical and electronic equipment, estimated based on figures for domestic production, imports and exports of electronic products, as well as product lifespan data.
12		Production-based SO_2 emissions (kg/capita)	2018	Lenzen et al. (2020)	SO_2 emissions associated with the production of goods and services, which are then either exported or consumed domestically.

Table A.4

(continued)

SDG	Notes	Indicator	Reference Year	Source	Description
12		SO_2 emissions embodied in imports (kg/capita)	2018	Lenzen et al. (2020)	Emissions of SO_2 embodied in imported goods and services. SO_2 emissions have severe health impacts and are a significant cause of premature mortality worldwide.
12		Production-based nitrogen emissions (kg/capita)	2015	Oita et al. (2016)	Reactive nitrogen emitted during the production of commodities, which are then either exported or consumed domestically. Reactive nitrogen corresponds to emissions of ammonia, nitrogen oxides and nitrous oxide to the atmosphere, and of reactive nitrogen potentially exportable to water bodies, all of which can be harmful to human health and the environment.
12		Nitrogen emissions embodied in imports (kg/capita)	2015	Oita et al. (2016)	Emissions of reactive nitrogen embodied in imported goods and services. Reactive nitrogen corresponds here to emissions of ammonia, nitrogen oxides and nitrous oxide to the atmosphere, and of reactive nitrogen potentially exportable to water bodies, all of which can be harmful to human health and the environment.
12		Exports of plastic waste (kg/capita)	2021	UN Comtrade	The average annual amount of plastic waste exported over the last 5 years expressed per capita.
12	[a]	Non-recycled municipal solid waste (kg/capita/day)	2019	OECD	The amount of municipal solid waste (MSW), including household waste, that is neither recycled nor composted.
13		CO_2 emissions from fossil fuel combustion and cement production (tCO_2/capita)	2020	Global Carbon Project	Emissions from the combustion and oxidation of fossil fuels and from cement production. The indicator excludes emissions from fuels used for international aviation and maritime transport.
13		CO_2 emissions embodied in imports (tCO_2/capita)	2018	Lenzen et al. (2020)	CO_2 emissions embodied in imported goods and services.
13		CO_2 emissions embodied in fossil fuel exports (kg/capita)	2021	UN Comtrade	CO_2 emissions embodied in the exports of coal, gas, and oil. Calculated using a 5-year average of fossil fuel exports and converting exports into their equivalent CO_2 emissions. Exports for each fossil fuel are capped at the country's level of production.
13	[a]	Carbon Pricing Score at EUR60/tCO_2 (%, worst 0–100 best)	2018	OECD	The Carbon Pricing Score (CPS) measures the extent to which countries have attained the goal of pricing all energy related carbon emissions at certain benchmark values for carbon costs. The more progress that a country has made towards a specified benchmark value, the higher the CPS. For example, a CPS of 100% against a EUR 60 per tonne of CO_2 benchmark means that the country (or the group of countries) prices all carbon emissions in its (their) territory from energy use at EUR 60 or more.
14		Mean area that is protected in marine sites important to biodiversity (%)	2020	Birdlife International et al.	The mean percentage area of marine Key Biodiversity Areas (sites that are important for the global persistence of marine biodiversity) that are protected.
14		Ocean Health Index: Clean Waters score (worst 0–100 best)	2020	Ocean Health Index	The clean waters subgoal of the Ocean Health Index measures to what degree marine waters under national jurisdictions have been contaminated by chemicals, excessive nutrients (eutrophication), human pathogens, and trash.
14		Fish caught from overexploited or collapsed stocks (% of total catch)	2018	Sea around Us	The percentage of a country's total catch, within its exclusive economic zone (EEZ), that is comprised of species that are overexploited or collapsed, weighted by the quality of fish catch data.
14		Fish caught by trawling or dredging (%)	2018	Sea Around Us	The percentage of fish caught by trawling, a method of fishing in which industrial fishing vessels drag large nets (trawls) along the seabed.
14		Fish caught that are then discarded (%)	2018	Sea around Us	The percentage of fish that are caught only to be later discarded.
14		Marine biodiversity threats embodied in imports (per million population)	2018	Lenzen et al. (2012)	Threats to marine species embodied in imports of goods and services.

Table A.4
(continued)

SDG	Notes	Indicator	Reference Year	Source	Description
15		Mean area that is protected in terrestrial sites important to biodiversity (%)	2020	Birdlife International et al.	The mean percentage area of terrestrial Key Biodiversity Areas (sites that are important for the global persistence of biodiversity) that are protected.
15		Mean area that is protected in freshwater sites important to biodiversity (%)	2020	Birdlife International et al.	The mean percentage area of freshwater Key Biodiversity Areas (sites that are important for the global persistence of biodiversity) that are protected.
15		Red List Index of species survival (worst 0–1 best)	2021	IUCN and Birdlife International	The change in aggregate extinction risk across groups of species. The index is based on genuine changes in the number of species in each category of extinction risk on The IUCN Red List of Threatened Species.
15		Permanent deforestation (% of forest area, 3-year average)	2020	Curtis et al. (2018)	The mean annual percentage of permanent deforestation over the last 3-year period. Permanent deforestation refers to tree cover removal for urbanization, commodity production and certain types of small-scale agriculture whereby the previous tree cover does not return. It does not include temporary forest loss due to cuttings within the forestry sector or wildfires. Since data on tree cover gains are not available, the annual net loss cannot be calculated, thus the indicator is an estimate for gross permanent deforestation.
15		Terrestrial and freshwater biodiversity threats embodied in imports (per million population)	2018	Lenzen et al. (2012)	Threats to terrestrial and freshwater species embodied in imports of goods and services.
16		Homicides (per 100,000 population)	2020	UNODC	The number of intentional homicides per 100,000 people. Intentional homicides are estimates of unlawful homicides purposely inflicted as a result of domestic disputes, interpersonal violence, violent conflicts over land resources, intergang violence over turf or control, and predatory violence and killing by armed groups. Intentional homicide does not include all intentional killing, such as killing in armed conflict.
16		Unsentenced detainees (% of prison population)	2019	UNODC	Unsentenced prisoners as a percentage of overall prison population. Persons held unsentenced or pre-trial refers to persons held in prisons, penal institutions or correctional institutions who are untried, pre-trial or awaiting a first instance decision on their case from a competent authority regarding their conviction or acquittal.
16		Population who feel safe walking alone at night in the city or area where they live (%)	2020	Gallup	The percentage of the surveyed population that responded "Yes" to the question "Do you feel safe walking alone at night in the city or area where you live?"
16		Property Rights (worst 1–7 best)	2020	World Economic Forum	Survey-based assessment of protection of property rights, on a scale from 1 (worst) to 7 (best). The indicator reports respondents' qualitative assessment based on answers to several questions on the protection of property rights and intellectual property rights protection.
16		Birth registrations with civil authority (% of children under age 5)	2020	UNICEF	The percentage of children under the age of five whose births are reported as being registered with the relevant national civil authorities.
16		Corruption Perceptions Index (worst 0–100 best)	2021	Transparency International	The perceived levels of public sector corruption, on a scale from 0 (highest level of perceived corruption) to 100 (lowest level of perceived corruption). The CPI aggregates data from a number of different sources that provide perceptions of business people and country experts.
16		Children involved in child labor (% of population aged 5 to 14)	2019	UNICEF	The percentage of children, between the ages of 5–14 years, involved in child labor at the time of the survey. A child is considered to be involved in child labor under the following conditions: (a) children 5–11 years old who, during the reference week, did at least one hour of economic activity or at least 28 hours of household chores, or (b) children 12–14 years old who, during the reference week, did at least 14 hours of economic activity or at least 28 hours of household chores. We assumed 0% child labor for high-income countries for which no data was reported.

Table A.4

(continued)

SDG	Notes	Indicator	Reference Year	Source	Description
16		Exports of major conventional weapons (TIV constant million USD per 100,000 population)	2020	Stockholm Peace Research Institute	Volume of major conventional weapons exported, expressed in constant 1990 US$ millions (TIV) per 100,000 population. The trend-indicator value is based on the known unit production cost of a core set of weapons, and does not reflect the financial value of the exports. Small arms, light weapons, ammunition and other support material are not included. Values were calculated based on a 5-year rolling average.
16		Press Freedom Index (best 0–100 worst)	2021	Reporters sans frontières	Degree of freedom available to journalists in 180 countries and regions, determined by pooling the responses of experts to a questionnaire devised by RSF.
16		Access to and affordability of justice (worst 0–1 best)	2020	World Justice Project	Measures the accessibility and affordability of civil courts, including whether people are aware of available remedies; can access and afford legal advice and representation; and can access the court system without incurring unreasonable fees, encountering unreasonable procedural hurdles, or experiencing physical or linguistic barriers.
16	[a]	Persons held in prison (per 100,000 population)	2019	UNODC	The prison population is composed of persons held in prisons, penal institutions, or correctional institutions.
17		Government spending on health and education (% of GDP)	2020	UNESCO	The sum of public expenditure on health from domestic sources and general government expenditure on education (current, capital, and transfers) expressed as a percentage of GDP. This indicator is based on the World Bank health and education spending datasets, sourced from WHO & UNESCO respectively. Values are carried forward for both health and education, but a value in a given year is only reported if at least one data point is a real observation (not carried forward).
17		For high-income and all OECD DAC countries: International concessional public finance, including official development assistance (% of GNI)	2021	OECD	The amount of official development assistance (ODA) as a share of gross national income (GNI). It includes grants, "soft" loans (where the grant element is at least 25% of the total) and the provision of technical assistance, and excludes grants and loans for military purposes. There is a break in the series because from 2018, the ODA grant-equivalent methodology is used whereby only the "grant portion" of the loan, i.e. the amount "given" by lending below market rates, counts as ODA.
17		Other countries: Government revenue excluding grants (% of GDP)	2019	IMF	Government revenue measured as cash receipts from taxes, social contributions, and other revenues such as fines, fees, rent, and income from property or sales. Grants are also considered as revenue but are excluded here.
17		Corporate Tax Haven Score (best 0–100 worst)	2019	Tax Justice Network	The Corporate Tax Haven Score measures a jurisdiction's potential to poach the tax base of others, as enshrined in its laws, regulations and documented administrative practices. For countries with multiple jurisdictions, the value of the worst-performing jurisdiction was retained.
17	[a]	Financial Secrecy Score (best 0–100 worst)	2020	Tax Justice Network	The Index measures the contribution of each jurisdiction to financial secrecy, on a scale from 0 (best) to 100 (worst). It is calculated using qualitative data to prepare a secrecy score for each jurisdiction and quantitative data to create a global scale weighting for each jurisdiction according to its share of offshore financial services activity in the global total. For countries with multiple jurisdictions, the average score of the jurisdictions was used.
17	[a]	Shifted profits of multinationals (US$ billion)	2017	Zucman et al. (2019)	Estimation of how much profit is shifted into tax havens and how much non-haven countries lose in profits from such shifting. Based on macroeconomic data known as foreign affiliates statistics. Negative values indicate profit shifting.
17		Statistical Performance Index (worst 0–100 best)	2019	World Bank	The Statistical Performance Index is a weighted average of the statistical performance indicators that evaluate the performance of national statistical systems. It aggregates five pillars of statistical performance: data use, data services, data products, data sources, and data infrastructure.

Source: Authors' analysis

Table A.5

Indicator thresholds and justifications for optimal values

SDG	Indicator	Optimum (value = 100)	Green	Yellow	Orange	Red	Lower bound	Justification for optimum
1	Poverty headcount ratio at $1.90/day (%)	0	≤ 2	2 < x ≤ 7.5	7.5 < x ≤ 13	> 13	72.6	SDG Target
1	Poverty headcount ratio at $3.20/day (%)	0	≤ 2	2 < x ≤ 7.5	7.5 < x ≤ 13	> 13	51.5	SDG Target
1	Poverty rate after taxes and transfers (%)	6.1	≤ 10	10 < x ≤ 12.5	12.5 < x ≤ 15	> 15	17.7	Average of 3 best OECD performers
2	Prevalence of undernourishment (%)	0	≤ 7.5	7.5 < x ≤ 11.25	11.25 < x ≤ 15	> 15	42.3	SDG Target
2	Prevalence of stunting in children under 5 years of age (%)	0	≤ 7.5	7.5 < x ≤ 11.25	11.25 < x ≤ 15	> 15	50.2	SDG Target
2	Prevalence of wasting in children under 5 years of age (%)	0	≤ 5	5 < x ≤ 7.5	7.5 < x ≤ 10	> 10	16.3	SDG Target
2	Prevalence of obesity, BMI ≥ 30 (% of adult population)	2.8	≤ 10	10 < x ≤ 17.5	17.5 < x ≤ 25	> 25	35.1	Average of 5 best performers
2	Human Trophic Level (best 2–3 worst)	2.04	≤ 2.2	2.2 < x ≤ 2.3	2.3 < x ≤ 2.4	> 2.4	2.47	Average of 5 best performers
2	Cereal yield (tonnes per hectare of harvested land)	7	≥ 2.5	2.5 > x ≥ 2	2 > x ≥ 1.5	< 1.5	0.2	Average of 5 best performers minus outliers (1 & 1/2SD)
2	Sustainable Nitrogen Management Index (best 0–1.41 worst)	0	≤ 0.3	0.3 < x ≤ 0.5	0.5 < x ≤ 0.7	> 0.7	1.2	Technical Optimum
2	Yield gap closure (% of potential yield)	77	≥ 75	75 > x ≥ 62.5	62.5 > x ≥ 50	< 50	28	Average of 5 best performers
2	Exports of hazardous pesticides (tonnes per million population)	0	≤ 1	1 < x ≤ 25.5	25.5 < x ≤ 50	> 50	250	Technical Optimum
3	Maternal mortality rate (per 100,000 live births)	3.4	≤ 70	70 < x ≤ 105	105 < x ≤ 140	> 140	814	Average of 5 best performers
3	Neonatal mortality rate (per 1,000 live births)	1.1	≤ 12	12 < x ≤ 15	15 < x ≤ 18	> 18	39.7	Average of 5 best performers
3	Mortality rate, under-5 (per 1,000 live births)	2.6	≤ 25	25 < x ≤ 37.5	37.5 < x ≤ 50	> 50	130.1	Average of 5 best performers
3	Incidence of tuberculosis (per 100,000 population)	0	≤ 10	10 < x ≤ 42.5	42.5 < x ≤ 75	> 75	561	SDG Target
3	New HIV infections (per 1,000 uninfected population)	0	≤ 0.2	0.2 < x ≤ 0.6	0.6 < x ≤ 1	> 1	5.5	SDG Target
3	Age-standardized death rate due to cardiovascular disease, cancer, diabetes, or chronic respiratory disease in adults aged 30–70 years (%)	9.3	≤ 15	15 < x ≤ 20	20 < x ≤ 25	> 25	31	Average of 5 best performers
3	Age-standardized death rate attributable to household air pollution and ambient air pollution (per 100,000 population)	0	≤ 18	18 < x ≤ 84	84 < x ≤ 150	> 150	368.8	SDG Target
3	Traffic deaths (per 100,000 population)	3.2	≤ 8.4	8.4 < x ≤ 12.6	12.6 < x ≤ 16.8	> 16.8	33.7	Average of 5 best performers
3	Life expectancy at birth (years)	83	≥ 80	80 > x ≥ 75	75 > x ≥ 70	< 70	54	Average of 5 best performers
3	Adolescent fertility rate (births per 1,000 females aged 15 to 19)	2.5	≤ 25	25 < x ≤ 37.5	37.5 < x ≤ 50	> 50	139.6	Average of 5 best performers
3	Births attended by skilled health personnel (%)	100	≥ 98	98 > x ≥ 94	94 > x ≥ 90	< 90	23.1	Leave no one behind
3	Surviving infants who received 2 WHO-recommended vaccines (%)	100	≥ 90	90 > x ≥ 85	85 > x ≥ 80	< 80	41	Leave no one behind

Table A.5
(continued)

SDG	Indicator	Optimum (value = 100)	Green	Yellow	Orange	Red	Lower bound	Justification for optimum
3	Universal health coverage (UHC) index of service coverage (worst 0–100 best)	100	≥ 80	80 > x ≥ 70	70 > x ≥ 60	< 60	38.2	Leave no one behind
3	Subjective well-being (average ladder score, worst 0–10 best)	7.6	≥ 6	6 > x ≥ 5.5	5.5 > x ≥ 5	< 5	3.3	Average of 5 best performers
3	Gap in life expectancy at birth among regions (years)	0	≤ 3	3 < x ≤ 5	5 < x ≤ 7	> 7	11	Leave no one behind
3	Gap in self-reported health status by income (percentage points)	0	≤ 20	20 < x ≤ 30	30 < x ≤ 40	> 40	45	Leave no one behind
3	Daily smokers (% of population aged 15 and over)	10.1	≤ 18	18 < x ≤ 25	25 < x ≤ 32	> 32	35	Average of 3 best OECD performers
4	Participation rate in pre-primary organized learning (% of children aged 4 to 6)	100	≥ 90	90 > x ≥ 80	80 > x ≥ 70	< 70	35	SDG Target
4	Net primary enrollment rate (%)	100	≥ 97	97 > x ≥ 88.5	88.5 > x ≥ 80	< 80	53.8	SDG Target
4	Lower secondary completion rate (%)	100	≥ 90	90 > x ≥ 82.5	82.5 > x ≥ 75	< 75	18	SDG Target
4	Literacy rate (% of population aged 15 to 24)	100	≥ 95	95 > x ≥ 90	90 > x ≥ 85	< 85	45.2	Leave no one behind
4	Tertiary educational attainment (% of population aged 25 to 34)	52.2	≥ 40	40 > x ≥ 25	25 > x ≥ 10	< 10	0	Average of 3 best OECD performers
4	PISA score (worst 0–600 best)	525.6	≥ 493	493 > x ≥ 446.5	446.5 > x ≥ 400	< 400	350	Average of 3 best OECD performers
4	Variation in science performance explained by socio-economic status (%)	8.3	≤ 10.5	10.5 < x ≤ 15.25	15.25 < x ≤ 20	> 20	21.4	Average of 3 best OECD performers
4	Underachievers in science (% of 15-year-olds)	10	≤ 15	15 < x ≤ 22.5	22.5 < x ≤ 30	> 30	48	Average of 3 best OECD performers
5	Demand for family planning satisfied by modern methods (% of girls and women aged 15 to 49)	100	≥ 80	80 > x ≥ 70	70 > x ≥ 60	< 60	17.5	Leave no one behind
5	Ratio of female-to-male mean years of education received (%)	100	≥ 98	98 > x ≥ 86.5	86.5 > x ≥ 75	< 75	41.8	SDG Target
5	Ratio of female-to-male labor force participation rate (%)	100	≥ 70	70 > x ≥ 60	60 > x ≥ 50	< 50	21.5	SDG Target
5	Seats held by women in national parliament (%)	50	≥ 40	40 > x ≥ 30	30 > x ≥ 20	< 20	1.2	SDG Target
5	Gender wage gap (% of male median wage)	0	≤ 8	8 < x ≤ 14	14 < x ≤ 20	> 20	36.7	Technical Optimum
6	Population using at least basic drinking water services (%)	100	≥ 98	98 > x ≥ 89	89 > x ≥ 80	< 80	40	Leave no one behind
6	Population using at least basic sanitation services (%)	100	≥ 95	95 > x ≥ 85	85 > x ≥ 75	< 75	9.7	Leave no one behind
6	Freshwater withdrawal (% of available freshwater resources)	12.5	≤ 25	25 < x ≤ 50	50 < x ≤ 75	> 75	100	Technical Optimum
6	Anthropogenic wastewater that receives treatment (%)	100	≥ 50	50 > x ≥ 32.5	32.5 > x ≥ 15	< 15	0	Technical Optimum
6	Scarce water consumption embodied in imports (m^3 H2O equivalent/capita)	100	≤ 1000	1000 < x ≤ 2500	2500 < x ≤ 4000	> 4000	11000	Average of 5 best performers
6	Population using safely managed water services (%)	100	≥ 95	95 > x ≥ 87.5	87.5 > x ≥ 80	< 80	10.5	Leave no one behind
6	Population using safely managed sanitation services (%)	100	≥ 90	90 > x ≥ 77.5	77.5 > x ≥ 65	< 65	14.1	Leave no one behind
7	Population with access to electricity (%)	100	≥ 98	98 > x ≥ 89	89 > x ≥ 80	< 80	9.1	Leave no one behind
7	Population with access to clean fuels and technology for cooking (%)	100	≥ 85	85 > x ≥ 67.5	67.5 > x ≥ 50	< 50	2	Average of 3 best OECD performers

Table A.5
(continued)

SDG	Indicator	Optimum (value = 100)	Green	Yellow	Orange	Red	Lower bound	Justification for optimum
7	CO_2 emissions from fuel combustion per total electricity output ($MtCO_2$/TWh)	0	≤ 1	1 < x ≤ 1.25	1.25 < x ≤ 1.5	> 1.5	5.9	Technical Optimum
7	Share of renewable energy in total primary energy supply (%)	51	≥ 20	20 > x ≥ 15	15 > x ≥ 10	< 10	3	Average of 3 best OECD performers
8	Adjusted GDP growth (%)	5	≥ 0	0 > x ≥ -1.5	-1.5 > x ≥ -3	< -3	-14.7	Average of 5 best performers
8	Victims of modern slavery (per 1,000 population)	0	≤ 4	4 < x ≤ 7	7 < x ≤ 10	> 10	22	Leave no one behind
8	Adults with an account at a bank or other financial institution or with a mobile-money-service provider (% of population aged 15 or over)	100	≥ 80	80 > x ≥ 65	65 > x ≥ 50	< 50	8	Technical Optimum
8	Unemployment rate (% of total labor force, ages 15+)	0.5	≤ 5	5 < x ≤ 7.5	7.5 < x ≤ 10	> 10	25.9	Average of 5 best performers
8	Fundamental labor rights are effectively guaranteed (worst 0–1 best)	0.85	≥ 0.7	0.7 > x ≥ 0.6	0.6 > x ≥ 0.5	< 0.5	0.3	Average of 5 best performers
8	Fatal work-related accidents embodied in imports (per 100,000 population)	0	≤ 1	1 < x ≤ 1.75	1.75 < x ≤ 2.5	> 2.5	6	Technical Optimum
8	Employment-to-population ratio (%)	77.8	≥ 60	60 > x ≥ 55	55 > x ≥ 50	< 50	50	Average of 3 best OECD performers
8	Youth not in employment, education or training (NEET) (% of population aged 15 to 29)	8.1	≤ 10	10 < x ≤ 12.5	12.5 < x ≤ 15	> 15	28.2	Average of 3 best OECD performers
9	Population using the internet (%)	100	≥ 80	80 > x ≥ 65	65 > x ≥ 50	< 50	2.2	Leave no one behind
9	Mobile broadband subscriptions (per 100 population)	100	≥ 75	75 > x ≥ 57.5	57.5 > x ≥ 40	< 40	1.4	Leave no one behind
9	Logistics Performance Index: Quality of trade and transport-related infrastructure (worst 1–5 best)	3.8	≥ 3	3 > x ≥ 2.5	2.5 > x ≥ 2	< 2	1.6	Average of 5 best performers
9	The Times Higher Education Universities Ranking: Average score of top 3 universities (worst 0–100 best)	50	≥ 30	30 > x ≥ 15	15 > x ≥ 0	< 0	0	Average of 5 best performers
9	Articles published in academic journals (per 1,000 population)	1.2	≥ 0.7	0.7 > x ≥ 0.38	0.38 > x ≥ 0.05	< 0.05	0	Average of 5 best performers
9	Expenditure on research and development (% of GDP)	3.7	≥ 1.5	1.5 > x ≥ 1.25	1.25 > x ≥ 1	< 1	0	Average of 5 best performers
9	Researchers (per 1,000 employed population)	15.6	≥ 8	8 > x ≥ 7.5	7.5 > x ≥ 7	< 7	0.8	Average of 3 best OECD performers
9	Triadic patent families filed (per million population)	115.7	≥ 20	20 > x ≥ 15	15 > x ≥ 10	< 10	0.1	Average of 3 best OECD performers
9	Gap in internet access by income (percentage points)	0	≤ 7	7 < x ≤ 26	26 < x ≤ 45	> 45	63.6	Leave no one behind
9	Female share of graduates from STEM fields at the tertiary level (%)	50	≥ 30	30 > x ≥ 25	25 > x ≥ 20	< 20	15	Leave no one behind
10	Gini coefficient	27.5	≤ 30	30 < x ≤ 35	35 < x ≤ 40	> 40	63	Average of 5 best performers
10	Palma ratio	0.9	≤ 1	1 < x ≤ 1.15	1.15 < x ≤ 1.3	> 1.3	2.5	Average of 3 best OECD performers
10	Elderly poverty rate (% of population aged 66 or over)	3.2	≤ 5	5 < x ≤ 15	15 < x ≤ 25	> 25	45.7	Average of 3 best OECD performers
11	Proportion of urban population living in slums (%)	0	≤ 5	5 < x ≤ 15	15 < x ≤ 25	> 25	90	Leave no one behind

Table A.5
(continued)

SDG	Indicator	Optimum (value = 100)	Green	Yellow	Orange	Red	Lower bound	Justification for optimum
11	Annual mean concentration of particulate matter of less than 2.5 microns in diameter (PM2.5) ($\mu g/m^3$)	6.3	≤ 10	$10 < x \leq 17.5$	$17.5 < x \leq 25$	> 25	87	Average of 5 best performers
11	Access to improved water source, piped (% of urban population)	100	≥ 98	$98 > x \geq 86.5$	$86.5 > x \geq 75$	< 75	6.1	Leave no one behind
11	Satisfaction with public transport (%)	82.6	≥ 72	$72 > x \geq 57.5$	$57.5 > x \geq 43$	< 43	21	Average of 5 best performers
11	Population with rent overburden (%)	4.6	≤ 7	$7 < x \leq 12$	$12 < x \leq 17$	> 17	25.6	Average of 3 best OECD performers
12	Municipal solid waste (kg/capita/day)	0.1	≤ 1	$1 < x \leq 1.5$	$1.5 < x \leq 2$	> 2	3.7	Average of 5 best performers
12	Electronic waste (kg/capita)	0.2	≤ 5	$5 < x \leq 7.5$	$7.5 < x \leq 10$	> 10	23.5	Average of 5 best performers
12	Production-based SO_2 emissions (kg/capita)	0	≤ 30	$30 < x \leq 65$	$65 < x \leq 100$	> 100	525	Average of 5 best performers
12	SO_2 emissions embodied in imports (kg/capita)	0	≤ 5	$5 < x \leq 7.5$	$7.5 < x \leq 10$	> 10	30	Technical Optimum
12	Production-based nitrogen emissions (kg/capita)	2	≤ 20	$20 < x \leq 35$	$35 < x \leq 50$	> 50	100	Average of 5 best performers
12	Nitrogen emissions embodied in imports (kg/capita)	0	≤ 5	$5 < x \leq 10$	$10 < x \leq 15$	> 15	45	Technical Optimum
12	Exports of plastic waste (kg/capita)	0	≤ 1	$1 < x \leq 3$	$3 < x \leq 5$	> 5	12	Average of 5 best performers
12	Non-recycled municipal solid waste (kg/capita/day)	0.6	≤ 0.8	$0.8 < x \leq 0.9$	$0.9 < x \leq 1$	> 1	1.5	Average of 3 best OECD performers
13	CO_2 emissions from fossil fuel combustion and cement production (tCO_2 /capita)	0	≤ 2	$2 < x \leq 3$	$3 < x \leq 4$	> 4	20	Technical Optimum
13	CO_2 emissions embodied in imports (tCO_2/capita)	0	≤ 0.5	$0.5 < x \leq 0.75$	$0.75 < x \leq 1$	> 1	3.2	Technical Optimum
13	CO_2 emissions embodied in fossil fuel exports (kg/capita)	0	≤ 100	$100 < x \leq 4050$	$4050 < x \leq 8000$	> 8000	44000	Technical Optimum
13	Carbon Pricing Score at EUR60/tCO_2 (%, worst 0–100 best)	100	≥ 70	$70 > x \geq 50$	$50 > x \geq 30$	< 30	0	Technical Optimum
14	Mean area that is protected in marine sites important to biodiversity (%)	100	≥ 85	$85 > x \geq 75$	$75 > x \geq 65$	< 65	0	Technical Optimum
14	Ocean Health Index: Clean Waters score (worst 0–100 best)	100	≥ 80	$80 > x \geq 75$	$75 > x \geq 70$	< 70	28.6	Technical Optimum
14	Fish caught from overexploited or collapsed stocks (% of total catch)	0	≤ 25	$25 < x \leq 37.5$	$37.5 < x \leq 50$	> 50	90.7	Technical Optimum
14	Fish caught by trawling or dredging (%)	1	≤ 7	$7 < x \leq 33.5$	$33.5 < x \leq 60$	> 60	90	Average of 5 best performers
14	Fish caught that are then discarded (%)	0	≤ 5	$5 < x \leq 10$	$10 < x \leq 15$	> 15	20	Technical Optimum
14	Marine biodiversity threats embodied in imports (per million population)	0	≤ 0.2	$0.2 < x \leq 0.6$	$0.6 < x \leq 1$	> 1	2	Technical Optimum
15	Mean area that is protected in terrestrial sites important to biodiversity (%)	100	≥ 85	$85 > x \geq 75$	$75 > x \geq 65$	< 65	0	Technical Optimum
15	Mean area that is protected in freshwater sites important to biodiversity (%)	100	≥ 85	$85 > x \geq 75$	$75 > x \geq 65$	< 65	0	Technical Optimum
15	Red List Index of species survival (worst 0–1 best)	1	≥ 0.9	$0.9 > x \geq 0.85$	$0.85 > x \geq 0.8$	< 0.8	0.6	Technical Optimum

Table A.5

(continued)

SDG	Indicator	Optimum (value = 100)	Green	Yellow	Orange	Red	Lower bound	Justification for optimum
15	Permanent deforestation (% of forest area, 3-year average)	0	≤ 0.05	0.05 < x ≤ 0.28	0.28 < x ≤ 0.5	> 0.5	1.5	SDG Target
15	Terrestrial and freshwater biodiversity threats embodied in imports (per million population)	0	≤ 1	1 < x ≤ 2	2 < x ≤ 3	> 3	10	Technical Optimum
16	Homicides (per 100,000 population)	0.3	≤ 1.5	1.5 < x ≤ 2.75	2.75 < x ≤ 4	> 4	38	Average of 5 best performers
16	Unsentenced detainees (% of prison population)	7	≤ 30	30 < x ≤ 40	40 < x ≤ 50	> 50	75	Average of 5 best performers
16	Population who feel safe walking alone at night in the city or area where they live (%)	90	≥ 70	70 > x ≥ 60	60 > x ≥ 50	< 50	33	Average of 5 best performers
16	Property Rights (worst 1–7 best)	6.3	≥ 4.5	4.5 > x ≥ 3.75	3.75 > x ≥ 3	< 3	2.5	Average of 5 best performers
16	Birth registrations with civil authority (% of children under age 5)	100	≥ 98	98 > x ≥ 86.5	86.5 > x ≥ 75	< 75	11	Leave no one behind
16	Corruption Perceptions Index (worst 0–100 best)	88.6	≥ 60	60 > x ≥ 50	50 > x ≥ 40	< 40	13	Average of 5 best performers
16	Children involved in child labor (% of population aged 5 to 14)	0	≤ 2	2 < x ≤ 6	6 < x ≤ 10	> 10	39.3	Leave no one behind
16	Exports of major conventional weapons (TIV constant million USD per 100,000 population)	0	≤ 1	1 < x ≤ 1.75	1.75 < x ≤ 2.5	> 2.5	3.4	Technical Optimum
16	Press Freedom Index (best 0–100 worst)	10	≤ 30	30 < x ≤ 40	40 < x ≤ 50	> 50	80	Average of 5 best performers
16	Access to and affordability of justice (worst 0–1 best)	0.75	≥ 0.65	0.65 > x ≥ 0.58	0.58 > x ≥ 0.5	< 0.5	0.1	Average of 5 best performers
16	Persons held in prison (per 100,000 population)	25	≤ 100	100 < x ≤ 175	175 < x ≤ 250	> 250	475	Average of 5 best performers
17	Government spending on health and education (% of GDP)	15	≥ 10	10 > x ≥ 7.5	7.5 > x ≥ 5	< 5	0	Average of 5 best performers
17	For high-income and all OECD DAC countries: International concessional public finance, including official development assistance (% of GNI)	1	≥ 0.7	0.7 > x ≥ 0.52	0.52 > x ≥ 0.35	< 0.35	0.1	Average of 5 best performers
17	Other countries: Government revenue excluding grants (% of GDP)	40	≥ 30	30 > x ≥ 23	23 > x ≥ 16	< 16	10	Average of 5 best performers
17	Corporate Tax Haven Score (best 0–100 worst)	40	≤ 60	60 < x ≤ 65	65 < x ≤ 70	> 70	100	Average of best performers (EU Report)
17	Financial Secrecy Score (best 0–100 worst)	42.7	≤ 45	45 < x ≤ 50	50 < x ≤ 55	> 55	76.5	Average of 5 best performers
17	Shifted profits of multinationals (US$ billion)	0	≥ 0	0 > x ≥ -15	-15 > x ≥ -30	< -30	-70	Technical Optimum
17	Statistical Performance Index (worst 0–100 best)	100	≥ 80	80 > x ≥ 65	65 > x ≥ 50	< 50	25	Technical Optimum

Source: Authors' analysis

References

References cited in the text

Apolitical. (2021, March 25). *How to use data to "build back better" post-Covid-19*. https://vimeo.com/528752730

Atlantic Council. (2022, April 13). *Special address by US Treasury Secretary Janet L. Yellen*. https://www.atlanticcouncil.org/event/special-address-by-us-treasury-secretary-janet-l-yellen/

Bruno, M., Grassia, F., Handley, J., Abate, A. A., Mamo, D. D., and Girma, A. (2020). Census metadata-driven data collection monitoring: The Ethiopian experience. *Statistical Journal of the IAOS*, *36*(1), 67–76. https://doi.org/10.3233/SJI-190582

Cameron, G. (2021, December 22). 2022 Predictions For The Evolution of Data Use. *TReNDS*. https://www.sdsntrends.org/blog/2021/predictionsfor2022?locale=en

Cepei. (2020, December 3). *COVID-19 Data and Innovation Centre: Visualize the effects of the pandemic and the potential solutions*. Cepei. https://cepei.org/en/novedad/covid-19-data-innovation-centre-visualize-the-effects-of-the-pandemic-and-the-potential-solutions

Chinn, L., Carpenter, A., and Dunn, A. D. (2021, October 20). ESG trends: Improving and standardizing disclosure. *Reuters*. https://www.reuters.com/legal/legalindustry/esg-trends-improving-standardizing-disclosure-2021-10-20/

Concord Times. (2021, August 17). Sierra Leone: Stats SL commences computer assisted personal interview experts training. *Concord Times*. https://allafrica.com/stories/202108170175.html

Cuaresma, J. C., Fengler, W., Kharas, H., Bekhtiar, K., Brottrager, M., and Hofer, M. (2019). Will the Sustainable Development Goals be fulfilled? Assessing present and future global poverty. Palgrave Communications, 4(1), 29.

Emilsson, C. (2021, April 9). How Sweden uses data and AI to improve the health of citizens. *Towards Digital States*. https://medium.com/digital-states/how-sweden-uses-data-and-ai-to-improve-the-health-of-citizens-416c4c80705b

Ernst, J., and Soerakoesoemah, R. (2021, August 4). Enhancing poverty measurement through big data. ESCAP. https://www.unescap.org/blog/enhancing-poverty-measurement-through-big-data

Eurostat. (2022). *European Statistical Recovery Dashboard*. https://ec.europa.eu/eurostat/cache/recovery-dashboard/

FAO. (2022). Impact of the Ukraine-Russia conflict on global food security and related matters under the mandate of the Food and Agriculture Organization of the United Nations (FAO). Food and Agriculture Organization. https://www.fao.org/3/ni734en/ni734en.pdf

FOLU and FELD. (2021). From Global Commitments to National Action: A Closer Look at Nationally Determined Contributions from a Food and Land Perspective. https://www.foodandlandusecoalition.org/wp-content/uploads/2021/11/From-COP-to-national-action-Assessing-the-NDCs-from-a-food-land-perspective.pdf

GEOGLAM. (2020, May 7). *GEOGLAM and COVID-19: Responding to an emerging food security emergency*. GEO Observations Blog. http://www.earthobservations.org/geo_blog_obs.php?id=428

GEOGLAM. (2022). *GEOGLAM Crop Monitor*. https://cropmonitor.org

Global Partnership for Sustainable Development Data. (2022, February 23). *Insights From the Data for Now Initiative | UNSC 2022 side event*. https://www.youtube.com/watch?v=yeKD9NU7elk

Government of Sierra Leone. (2020, August 10). Press Release: Sierra Leone fights COVID-19 using innovative geospatial data and technology. https://www.data4sdgs.org/news/press-release-sierra-leone-fights-covid-19-using-innovative-geospatial-data-and-technology

Greece used AI to curb COVID: What other nations can learn. (2021). *Nature*, *597*(7877), 447–448. https://doi.org/10.1038/d41586-021-02554-y

Green Economy Tracker. (2022). *Green COVID-19 Recovery*. Green Economy Tracker. https://greeneconomytracker.org/policies/green-covid-19-recovery

Hammer, C., Morales, L. G., Contreras-González, I. M., and Wollburg, P. R. (2021, August 11). National statistical offices still face disruptions and challenges as they adapt to a "new normal." https://blogs.worldbank.org/opendata/national-statistical-offices-still-face-disruptions-and-challenges-they-adapt-new-normal

Helliwell, J. F., Layard, R., Sachs, J. D., De Neve, J.-E., Aknin, L. B., and Wang, S. (2022). *World Happiness Report 2022*. Sustainable Development Solutions Network (SDSN).

ICS and SDSN. (2021). *O Índice de Desenvolvimento Sustentável das Cidades—Brasil (IDSC-BR)*. Instituto Cidades Sustentáveis and Sustainable Development Solutions Network. https://www.sustainabledevelopment.report/reports/indice-de-desenvolvimento-sustentavel-das-cidades-brasil/

IDE Chile. (2022). *Visor territorial COVID-19*. https://covid.visorterritorial.cl/

IISD. (2021, November 18). *How Social Networks Can Track Migration*. http://sdg.iisd.org/news/how-social-networks-can-track-migration/

IMF. (2019). *World Economic Outlook*. https://www.imf.org/en/Publications/WEO/weo-database/2019/October

IMF. (2021). *World Economic Outlook*. https://www.imf.org/en/Publications/WEO/weo-database/2021/October

IMF. (2022). *World Economic Outlook: War Sets Back the Global Recovery*. International Monetary Fund. https://www.imf.org/en/Publications/WEO/Issues/2022/04/19/world-economic-outlook-april-2022

IPCC. (2022). Summary for Policymakers. In P. R. Sukhla, J. Skea, R. Slade, A. Al Khourdajie, R. van Diemen, D. McCollum, M. Pathak, S. Some, P. Vyas, R. Fradera, M. Belkacemi, A. Hasija, G. Lisboa, S. Luz, J. Malley (Eds.), *Climate Change 2022: Mitigation of Climate Change. Contribution of Working Group III to the Sixth Assessment Report of the Intergovernmental Panel on Climate Change*. Cambridge University Press. https://report.ipcc.ch/ar6wg3/pdf/IPCC_AR6_WGIII_FinalDraft_FullReport.pdf

Jiang, L., and O'Neill, B. C. (2017). Global urbanization projections for the Shared Socioeconomic Pathways. *Global Environmental Change*, *42*, 193–199. https://doi.org/10.1016/j.gloenvcha.2015.03.008

4. SDG Data Systems and Statistics

Joint SDG Fund. (2022). *Homepage*. Homepage | Joint SDG Fund. https://www.jointsdgfund.org/homepage

Khanna, D., and Ramachandran, S. (2022, February 1). Leveraging Non-Traditional Data For The Covid-19 Socioeconomic Recovery Strategy. *Forbes*. https://www.forbes.com/sites/deepalikhanna/2022/02/01/leveraging-non-traditional-data-for-the-covid-19-socioeconomic-recovery-strategy/

Lafortune, G. (2020, April 20). *How much do we know about countries preparedness to respond to pandemics? Insights from two country-level indices*. http://www.unsdsn.org/how-much-do-we-know-about-countries-preparedness-to-respond-to-pandemics-insights-from-two-country-level-indices

Lafortune, G., Cortés Puch, M., Mosnier, A., Fuller, G., Diaz, M., Riccaboni, A., Kloke-Lesch, A., Zachariadis, T., Carli, E., and Oger, A. (2021). *Europe Sustainable Development Report 2021: Transforming the European Union to achieve the Sustainable Development Goals*. SDSN, SDSN Europe and IEEP.

Lafortune, G., Fuller, G., Moreno, J., Schmidt-Traub, G., and Kroll, C. (2018). *SDG Index and Dashboards Detailed Methodological paper*. Sustainable Development Solutions Network. https://raw.githubusercontent.com/sdsna/2018GlobalIndex/master/2018GlobalIndexMethodology.pdf

Lenzen, M., Malik, A., Li, M., Fry, J., Weisz, H., Pichler, P-P., Chaves, L.S.M., Capon, A. Pencheon, D. 2020 (under review), The global environmental footprint of healthcare, The Lancet Planetary Health.

Lynch, A., LoPresti, A., and Fox, C. (2019). *The 2019 US Cities Sustainable Development Report*. Sustainable Development Solutions Network (SDSN). https://www.sustainabledevelopment.report/reports/2019-us-cities-sustainable-development-report/

Mahler, D. G., Yonzan, N., Lakner, C., Castaneda Aguilar, R. A., and Wu, H. (2021, June 24). Updated estimates of the impact of COVID-19 on global poverty: Turning the corner on the pandemic in 2021? https://blogs.worldbank.org/opendata/updated-estimates-impact-covid-19-global-poverty-turning-corner-pandemic-2021

Malik, A., Lafortune, G., Carter, S., Li, M., Lenzen, M., and Kroll, C. (2021). International spillover effects in the EU's textile supply chains: A global SDG assessment. *Journal of Environmental Management*, *295*, 113037. https://doi.org/10.1016/j.jenvman.2021.113037

Malik, A., Lafortune, G., Dahir, S., Wendling, Z. A., Carter, S., Li, M., and Lenzen, M. (2021). Making globalisation and trade work for people and planet: International spillovers embodied in EU's food supply chains.

Moody's. (2021, December). *Creditworthiness of Countries*. https://www.moodys.com

Meadows, D. H., Meadows, D. L., Randers, J., and Behrens, W. (1972). *The Limits to Growth: A Report for the Club of Rome's Project on the Predicament of Mankind*. Universe Books.

National Bureau of Statistics Maldives. (n.d.). *Maldives household income and expenditure survey (HIES): Sample design and estimation procedures for 2019*. Ministry of National Planning, Housing and Infrastructure. Retrieved April 24, 2022, from http://statisticsmaldives.gov.mv/nbs/wp-content/uploads/2021/02/HIES2019-Sampling-DesignEstimationProcedures.pdf

Naturskyddsföreningen. (2022, April 7). *Sweden Sets Historical Climate Target; Aims to Reduce Consumption-Based Emissions Created Abroad*. https://via.tt.se/pressmeddelande/sweden-sets-historical-climate-target-aims-to-reduce-consumption-based-emissions-created-abroad?publisherId=3236031&releaseId=3319935

Net Zero Tracker. (2022). *Net Zero Tracker*. https://zerotracker.net/

O'Callaghan, B., Yau, N., Murdock, E., Tritsch, D., Janz, A., Blackwood, A., Purroy, S., Sadler, A., Wen, E., Kope, H., Flodell, H., Tillman-Morris, L., Ostrovsky, N., Kitsberg, A., Lee, T., Hristov, D., Didarali, Z., Chowdhry, K., Karlubik, M., ... Heeney, L. (2022). *Global Recovery Observatory*. Oxford University Economic Recovery Project. https://recovery.smithschool.ox.ac.uk/tracking/

OECD. (2020). *A Territorial Approach to the Sustainable Development Goals: Synthesis report*. Organisation for Economic Co-operation and Development. https://doi.org/10.1787/e86fa715-en

OECD. (2021). *ODA levels in 2021—Preliminary data*. https://www.oecd.org/dac/financing-sustainable-development/development-finance-standards/ODA-2021-summary.pdf

Papadimitriou, E., Fragoso Neves, A., and Becker, W. E. (2019). *JRC Statistical Audit of the Sustainable Development Goals Index and Dashboards*. European Commission. https://ec.europa.eu/jrc/en/publication/jrc-statistical-audit-sustainable-development-goals-index-and-dashboards

PARIS21. (2020, November 19). *New video series tells story of how NSOs are innovating in the face of COVID-19*. Paris 21. https://paris21.org/news-center/news/new-video-series-tells-story-how-nsos-are-innovating-face-covid-19

PARIS21. (2021a). *The Partner Report on Support to Statistics 2021*. https://paris21.org/sites/default/files/2022-02/Press%202021_WEB.pdf

PARIS21. (2021b, February 14). The production of statistics in times of a pandemic—Maldives 1/3 (Full video). https://www.youtube.com/watch?v=rwybHgvJDHw

PARIS21. (2021c, October 4). World's first platform to track SDG data financing launched. *Paris 21*. https://paris21.org/news-center/news/worlds-first-platform-track-sdg-data-financing-launched

Prime Minister's Office of Finland. (2020). Voluntary National Review 2020 Finland: Report on the Implementation of the 2030 Agenda for Sustainable Development.

Provendier, F. (2022). ODD tout est lié! : Rapport autour des objectifs de développement durable, remis au Premier ministre, Jean Castex et à la ministre de la Transition écologique, Barbara Pompili. https://www.ecologie.gouv.fr/sites/default/files/23.02.2022_Rapport_mission_temporaire_autour_des_ODD.pdf

Sachs, J. D., Kroll, C., Lafortune, G., Fuller, G., and Woelm, F. (2021). *Sustainable Development Report 2021: The Decade of Action for the Sustainable Development Goals*. Cambridge University Press. https://www.cambridge.org/core/books/sustainable-development-report-2021/2843BDD9D08CDD80E6875016110EFDAE

Sachs, J. D., Schmidt-Traub, G., Kroll, C., Durand-Delacre, D., and Teksoz, K. (2017). *SDG Index and Dashboards Report 2017*. Bertelsmann Stiftung and Sustainable Development Solutions Network (SDSN).

Sachs, J. D., Schmidt-Traub, G., Kroll, C., Lafortune, G., Fuller, G., and Woelm, F. (2020). *Sustainable Development Report 2020: The Sustainable Development Goals and COVID-19*. Cambridge University Press. https://www.sdgindex.org/

Sachs, J. D., Schmidt-Traub, G., Mazzucato, M., Messner, D., Nakicenovic, N., and Rockström, J. (2019). Six Transformations to achieve the Sustainable Development Goals. *Nature Sustainability*, *2*(9), 805–814. https://doi.org/10.1038/s41893-019-0352-9

Schmidt-Traub, G. (2020, October 22). The SDGs can guide our recovery. https://www.sustainablegoals.org.uk/the-sdgs-can-guide-our-recovery/

Schmidt-Traub, G., Hoff, H., and Bernlöhr, M. (2019). International spillovers and the Sustainable Development Goals (SDGs): Measuring how a country's progress towards the SDGs is affected by actions in other countries [SDSN Working Papers]. Sustainable Development Solutions Network.

Schmidt-Traub, G., Kroll, C., Teksoz, K., Durand-Delacre, D., and Sachs, J. D. (2017). National baselines for the Sustainable Development Goals assessed in the SDG Index and Dashboards. *Nature Geoscience*, *10*(8), 547–555. https://doi.org/10.1038/ngeo2985

SDSN TReNDS. (2021, April 9). *Strengthening Measurement of Marine Litter in Ghana*. ArcGIS StoryMaps. https://storymaps.arcgis.com/stories/2622af0a0c7d4c709c3d09f4cc249f7d

SDSN, Yale Center for Environmental Law and Policy, and Center for Global Commons at the University of Tokyo. (2021). *Global Commons Stewardship Index 2021: Safeguarding the Shared Resources of the Planet*.

SDSN. (2022, April 15). *A Message to all UN Member States and Leaders of the United Nations*. https://www.unsdsn.org/a-message-to-all-un-member-states-and-leaders-of-the-united-nations

Senhadji, A., Tieman, A., Gemayel, E., & Benedek, D. (2021). A Post-Pandemic Assessment of the Sustainable Development Goals. *Staff Discussion Notes, 2021*(003), 1. https://doi.org/10.5089/9781498314909.006

Statistics Canada. (2020, April 23). *Canadian Statistical Geospatial Explorer Hub*. https://www150.statcan.gc.ca/n1/pub/71-607-x/71-607-x2020010-eng.htm?HPA=1

Statistics Canada. (2022). *Interact with data*. https://www.statcangc.ca/en/interact

Statistics South Africa. (n.d.). *Census 2021 New Methodologies Test*. Retrieved April 24, 2022, from https://www.statssa.gov.za/?page_id=11389 / *Statistics South Africa*.

UN. (2022a, January 21). *Secretary General outlines priorities for 2022*. https://www.un.org/press/en/2022/sgsm21113.doc.htm

UN. (2022b). Voluntary National Reviews, Sustainable Development Knowledge Platform. https://sustainabledevelopment.un.org/vnrs/

UN and World Bank. (2020). Monitoring the State of Statistical Operations under the COVID-19 Pandemic: Highlights from the Second Round of a Global COVID-19 Survey of National Statistical Offices. World Bank Group. http://documents.worldbank.org/curated/en/297221597442670485/Monitoring-the-State-of-Statistical-Operations-under-the-COVID-19-Pandemic-Highlights-from-the-Second-Round-of-a-Global-COVID-19-Survey-of-National-Statistical-Offices

UNDESA. (2020). Sustainable Development Goals Report 2020. United Nations.

UNDESA. (2021). Sustainable Development Goals Report 2021. United Nations.

UNFCCC. (2022). *GCAP UNFCCC – Initiative*. https://climateaction.unfccc.int/Initiatives?id=95

UNStats. (2020, September 1). UNWDF Webinar: COVID-19 data hubs for timely decision-making amidst the pandemic. https://www.youtube.com/watch?v=8LiFvhsRT4Y

UNStats. (2021a, September 17). *European Statistical Recovery Dashboard*. https://covid-19-response.unstatshub.org/ https:/covid-19-response.unstatshub.org/posts/european-statistical-recovery-dashboard/

UNStats. (2021b, October 5). TA2.01 (High-level plenary) How to innovate timely data for Covid-19 and the SDGs. https://www.youtube.com/watch?v=5twe1uJ2Va8

UNStats. (2021c, October 12). (TA5.14) Governing data for development: From normative frameworks to implementation (all virtual pa. https://www.youtube.com/watch?v=rDuUSjblhNc

UNStats. (2022a). *UNSD — United Nations Statistical Commission: 53rd session*. https://unstats.un.org/unsd/statcom/53rd-session/

UNStats. (2022b, February 17). Moving From Data Production to Impact: Discussion on the Role of NSO Facilitating Greater Data Use. https://www.youtube.com/watch?v=mR6Xu4jnn6U

UNStats. (2022c, February 17). UNSC53 side event: Mobilizing Innovation Through Partnerships and Collaboration. https://www.youtube.com/watch?v=dklhLocvjJQ

UNStats and World Bank. (2020). Monitoring the state of statistical operations under the COVID-19 Pandemic: Highlights from a global COVID-19 survey of National Statistical Offices. https://documents1.worldbank.org/curated/en/338481591648922978/pdf/Monitoring-the-State-of-Statistical-Operations-under-the-COVID-19-Pandemic.pdf

Vivid Economics. (2021). *Greenness of Stimulus Index*. https://www.vivideconomics.com/casestudy/greenness-for-stimulus-index/

von der Leyen, U. (2019). A Union that strives for more: My agenda for Europe : political guidelines for the next European Commission 2019 2024. Publications Office of the European Union. https://data.europa.eu/doi/10.2775/018127

Wheatley, J. (2022, March 29). Ukraine war will increase poverty in developing economies, warns World Bank. *Financial Times*.

World Bank. (2020, July 6). *Survey of National Statistical Offices (NSOs) during COVID-19* [Text/HTML]. World Bank. https://www.worldbank.org/en/research/brief/survey-of-national-statistical-offices-nsos-during-covid-19

World Bank. (2022a). *LSMS-Supported High-Frequency Phone Surveys on COVID-19* [Text/HTML]. World Bank. https://www.worldbank.org/en/programs/lsms/brief/lsms-launches-high-frequency-phone-surveys-on-covid-19

World Bank. (2022b). *The World by Income and Region*. https://datatopics.worldbank.org/world-development-indicators/the-world-by-income-and-region.html

World Bank. (2022c). *World Bank Group Response to Global Impacts of the War in Ukraine: A Proposed Roadmap*. World Bank Group. https://thedocs.worldbank.org/en/doc/bf544fb23105352f4aef132bd6f40cb8-0290032022/original/WBG-Response-to-Global-Impacts-of-the-War-in-Ukraine-A-Proposed-Roadmap.pdf

Wuppertal Institut and E3G. (2021). *Green Recovery Tracker*. https://www.greenrecoverytracker.org/

WWF. (2021, April 14). L'Union européenne, deuxième importateur mondial de déforestation tropicale derrière la Chine et devant les Etats-Unis, selon la dernière étude du WWF. https://www.wwf.fr/vous-informer/actualites/union-europeenne-deuxieme-importateur-mondial-de-deforestation-tropicale

Databases

BirdLife International, IUCN, UNEP-WCMC (2022). *Resources and Data*. BirdLife International, International Union for Conservation of Nature and United Nations Environment Programme – World Conservation Monitoring Center. https://unstats.un.org/sdgs/indicators/database/

Climate Action Tracker. (2022). *Climate Action Tracker*. https://climateactiontracker.org/countries/

Curtis et al. (2018). Classifying drivers of global forest loss. *Science*, Vol. 361 – 6407, pp. 1108– – 11. Data updated in 2020.

Demirguc-Kunt et al. (2018). *Global Financial Inclusion Database*. World Bank, Washington, D.C. https://data.worldbank.org/indicator/FX.OWN.TOTL.ZS

FAO (2022). AQUASTAT. Level of water stress: freshwater withdrawal as a proportion of available freshwater resources (%). Food and Agriculture Organization, Rome. http://www.fao.org/nr/water/aquastat/data/query/index.html?lang=en

FAO (2022). Cereal Yield (kg per hectare). Food and Agriculture Organization, Rome. http://data.worldbank.org/indicator/AG.YLD.CREL.KG

FAO (2022). Prevalence of undernourishment (% of population). Food and Agriculture Organization, Rome. http://data.worldbank.org/indicator/SN.ITK.DEFC.ZS

FAO (2022). Trade in hazardous peseticides. Food and Agriculture Organization, Rome. http://www.fao.org/faostat/en/#data/RT/metadata

Forti V., Baldé C.P., Kuehr R., Bel G. *The Global E-Waste Monitor 2020: Quantities, Flows and the Circular Economy Potential*. United Nations University (UNU)/United Nations Institute for Training and Research (UNITAR) – co-hosted SCYCLE Programme, International Telecommunication Union (ITU) and International Solid Waste Association (ISWA), Bonn/Geneva/Rotterdam.

Gallup (2022). *Gallup World Poll*. www.gallup.com.

Global Yield Gap Atlas (2015). A joint initiative of Wageningen University and Research and University of Nebraska-Lincoln. http://www.yieldgap.org

IEA (2019). *CO_2 Emissions from Fuel Combustion 2019*. International Energy Agency, Paris. https://www.iea.org/reports/co2-emissions-from-fuel-combustion-2019

IHME (2020). The Global Burden of Disease Study 2019. *The Lancet*, 17 October 2020, Volume 396, Issue 10258, Pages 1129–1306

ILO (2022). Ratio of female to male labor force participation rate (%) (modeled ILO estimate). International Labour Organization, Geneva. https://data.worldbank.org/indicator/SL.TLF.CACT.FM.ZS

ILO (2022). Unemployment, total (% of total labor force) (modeled ILO estimate). International Labour Organization, Geneva. http://data.worldbank.org/indicator/SL.UEM.TOTL.ZS

IMF (2022). *Government Finance Statistics Yearbook*. International Monetary Fund. https://data.worldbank.org/indicator/GC.REV.XGRT.GD.ZS?view=chart

IMF (2022). *World Economic Outlook Database, October 2021*. International Monetary Fund. Accessed May 13, 2022. https://www.imf.org/en/Publications/WEO/weo-database/2021/October.

IPU (2022). Proportion of seats held by women in national parliaments (%). Inter-Parliamentary Union, Geneva. http://data.worldbank.org/indicator/SG.GEN.PARL.ZS

ITU (2022). *World Telecommunication/ICT Indicators Database*. International Telecommunication Union, Geneva. http://www.itu.int/en/ITU-D/Statistics/Pages/publications/wtid.aspx

IUCN and BirdLife International (2022). *IUCN Red List*. International Union for Conservation of Nature and Birdlife International. http://unstats.un.org/sdgs/indicators/database/?indicator=15.5.1

Kaza, S., Yao, L., Bhada-Tata, P., and Van Woerden, F. 2018. *What a Waste 2.0: A Global Snapshot of Solid Waste Management to 2050*. Urban Development Series. Washington, DC: World Bank. doi:10.1596/978-1-4648-1329-0

Lenzen, M., Malik, A., Li, M., Fry, J., Weisz, H., Pichler, P-P., Chaves, L.S.M., Capon, A. Pencheon, D. 2020 (under review), The global environmental footprint of healthcare. *The Lancet Planetary Health*.

Lenzen, M., Moran, D., Kanemoto, K., Foran, B., Lobefaro, L., and Geschke, A. (2012). International trade drives biodiversity threats in developing nations, *Nature*, 486, 109-112. (Dataset updated to 2015 by Isaac Russell Peterson, Matthew Selinkske and colleagues). doi: 10.1038/nature11145

Ocean Health Index (2019). *Ocean Health Index 2019 Global Assessment*. National Center for Ecological Analysis and Synthesis, University of California, Santa Barbara. http://data.oceanhealthindex.org/data-and-downloads

OECD (2021). Environmental policy: effective carbon rates. *OECD Environment Statistics* (database), Organisation for Economic Cooperation and Development, Paris. https://doi.org/10.1787/108c55c1-en

OECD (2022). *OECD Statistics*. Organisation for Economic Cooperation and Development, Paris. http://stats.oecd.org/

OECD (2022). *PISA Database*. Organisation for Economic Cooperation and Development, Paris. http://pisadataexplorer.oecd.org/ide/idepisa/dataset.aspx.

OECD. *Affordable Housing Database*. Organisation for Economic Cooperation and Development, Paris. http://www.oecd.org/housing/data/affordable-housing-database/), indicator HC1.2.

Oita, A., et al. (2016). Substantial nitrogen pollution embedded in international trade. *Nature Geoscience*, 9, pp. 111–115. doi: 10.1038/ngeo2635

Pauly D, Zeller D, and Palomares M.L.D. (Editors) (2020) *Sea Around Us Concepts, Design and Data*. www.seaaroundus.org

Pauly D., Zeller D. (2018). *Sea Around Us Concepts, Design and Data*. www.seaaroundus.org.

Reporters Without Borders (2020). *World Press Freedom Index 2020*. https://rsf.org/en/ranking

Schwab, K. (2020). *The Global Competitiveness Report 2020*. World Economic Forum, Geneva. https://www.weforum.org/reports/the-global-competitiveness-report-2020

SCImago (2022). *SCImago Journal & Country Rank*. SCImago. http://www.scimagojr.com

SE4All (2022). Access to clean fuels and technologies for cooking (% of population). Sustainable Energy for All. https://data.worldbank.org/indicator/EG.CFT.ACCS.ZS

SE4All (2022). Access to electricity (% of population). Sustainable Energy for All. http://data.worldbank.org/indicator/EG.ELC.ACCS.ZS

SIPRI (2022). *SIPRI Arms Transfers Database*. Stockholm International Peace Research Institute, Stockholm. https://www.sipri.org/ databases/armstransfers.

Tax Justice Network (2020). *Financial Secrecy Index 2020*. Tax Justice Network, London. https://www.financialsecrecyindex.com/introduction/fsi-2018-results

Times Higher Education (2022). *World University Rankings 2022*. Times Higher Education. London. https://www.timeshighereducation.com/world-university-rankings/2022/world-ranking#!/page/0/length/25/sort_by/rank/sort_order/asc/cols/stats

Transparency International (2021). *Corruption Perceptions Index 2020*. Transparency International, Berlin. https://www.transparency.org/en/cpi/

UN Comtrade Database (2022). https://comtrade.un.org/data/ WHO (2022). World Health Expenditure Database. World Health Organization, Geneva. http://apps.who.int/nha/database

UN Habitat (2022). Proportion of urban population living in slums. United Nations Human Settlements Programme, Nairoibi, Kenya. https://data.unhabitat.org/datasets/52c52084f31a403397e2c3bbee37f378_0/data

UNAIDS (2022). HIV incidence per 1000 population (15–49). In AIDSinfo. Joint United Nations Programme on HIV and AIDS, Geneva. https://aidsinfo.unaids.org

UNDESA (2022). Proportion of women of reproductive age (aged 15–49 years) who have their need for family planning satisfied with modern methods (% of women aged 15–49 years). *World Contraceptive Use 2021*. (POP/DB/CP/Rev2022). Population Division, United Nations Department of Economic and Social Affairs, New York. https://www.un.org/en/development/desa/population/publications/dataset/contraception/wcu2022.asp

UNDESA (2022). *Family Planning – Model*. United Nations Department of Economic and Social Affairs, New York. http://www.un.org/en/development/desa/population/theme/family-planning/cp_model.shtml

UNEP (2022). *Hotspot Analysis Tool for Sustainable Consumption and Production (SCP-HAT)*. SCP-HAT database v2.0. United Nations Environment Programme, Life Cycle Initiative, One Planet Network, International Resource Panel. Paris. http://scp-hat.lifecycleinitiative.org/methods/

UNESCO (2022). Government expenditure on education. United Nations Educational, Scientific and Cultural Organization, Paris. http://data.worldbank.org/indicator/SE.XPD.TOTL.GD.ZS. WHO (2022).

UNESCO (2022). UIS.Stat. Lower secondary completion rate, total (% of relevant age group). United Nations Educational, Scientific and Cultural Organization, Paris. http://data.uis.unesco.org/

UNESCO (2022). UIS.Stat. Net enrolment rate, primary, both sexes (%). United Nations Educational, Scientific and Cultural Organization, Paris. http://data.uis.unesco.org/

UNESCO (2022). UIS.Stat. United Nations Educational, Scientific and Cultural Organization, Paris. http://data.uis.unesco.org/

UNESCO (2022). UIS.Stat. Youth literacy rate, population 15–24 years, both sexes (%). United Nations Educational, Scientific and Cultural Organization, Paris. http://data.uis.unesco.org/

UNICEF (2022). Birth registration. United Nations Children's Fund, New York. http://data.unicef.org/topic/child-protection/birth-registration/

UNICEF (2022). Births attended by skilled health staff (% of total). United Nations Children's Fund, New York. http://data.worldbank.org/indicator/SH.STA.BRTC.ZS

UNICEF (2022). *Child Labour*. United Nations Children's Fund, New York. http://data.unicef.org/topic/child-protection/child-labour/

UNICEF, et al. (2022). Mortality rate, neonatal (per 1,000 live births). United Nations Children's Fund, New York. http://data.worldbank.org/indicator/SH.DYN.NMRT

UNICEF, et al. (2022). Mortality rate, under-5 (per 1,000 live births). United Nations Children's Fund, New York. http://data.worldbank.org/indicator/SH.DYN.MORT

UNICEF, et al. (2022). Prevalence of stunting, height for age (% of children under 5). United Nations Children's Fund, New York. https://data.worldbank.org/indicator/SH.STA.STNT.ZS

UNICEF, et al. (2022). Prevalence of wasting, weight for height (% of children under 5). United Nations Children's Fund, New York. http://data.worldbank.org/indicator/SH.STA.WAST.ZS

UNODC (2022). *Global Study on Homicides*. United Nations Office on Drugs and Crime, Vienna. https://dataunodc.un.org/GSH_app

UNODC (2022). Total persons held unsentenced. United Nations Office on Drugs and Crime, Vienna. https://dataunodc.un.org/data/prison/total%20persons%20held%20unsentenced

UNODC (2022). Total prison population. United Nations Office on Drugs and Crime, Vienna. https://dataunodc.un.org/crime/total-prison-population

Walk Free Foundation (2018*). Global Slavery Index 2018*. Walk Free Foundation, Broadway Nedlands, Australia. https://www.globalslaveryindex.org/

Wendling, Z., Emerson, J., Esty, D., Levy, M, de Sherbinin, A., et al. (2018). *2018 Environmental Performance Index*. New Haven, CT: Yale Center for Environmental Law and Policy. http://epi.yale.edu.

WHO (2022). Age-standardized death rate attributable to household air pollution and ambient air pollution, per 100 000 population. World Health Organization, Geneva. https://apps.who.int/gho/data/view.main.GSWCAH37v

WHO (2022). Age-standardized death rate due to cardiovascular disease, cancer, diabetes, and chronic respiratory disease in populations age 30–70 years, per 100 000 population. World Health Organization, Geneva. https://apps.who.int/gho/data/view.main.GSWCAH21v

WHO (2022). GHO Adolescent birth rate. World Health Organization, Geneva. https://www.who.int/data/gho/data/indicators/indicator-details/GHO/adolescent-birth-rate-(per-1000-women-aged-15-19-years)

WHO (2022). GHO Life expectancy and healthy life expectancy. World Health Organization, Geneva. http://apps.who.int/gho/data/node.main.688

WHO (2022). GHO Obesity (ag-standardized estimate). World Health Organization, Geneva. http://apps.who.int/gho/data/view.main.CTRY2450A?lang=en

WHO (2022). GHO Road traffic deaths. World Health Organization, Geneva. http://apps.who.int/gho/data/node.main.A997

WHO (2022). Incidence of tuberculosis (per 100,000 people). World Health Organization, Geneva. http://data.worldbank.org/indicator/SH.TBS.INCD

WHO (2022). Tracking universal health coverage: 2022 Global Monitoring Report. World Health Organization, Geneva. http://www.who.int/healthinfo/universal_health_coverage/report/2022/en/

WHO, et al. (2022). Maternal mortality ratio (modeled estimate, per 100,000 live births). World Health Organization, Geneva. http://data.worldbank.org/indicator/SH.STA.MMRT

WHO, UNICEF (2022). *Immunization Coverage*. World Health Organization and United Nations Children's Fund, Geneva and New York. http://data.unicef.org/topic/child-health/immunization/

WHO, UNICEF (2022). People using at least basic drinking water services (% of population). *WHO / UNICEF Joint Monitoring Programme: Data and Estimates*. World Health Organization and United Nations Children's Fund, Geneva and New York. https://washdata.org/data

WHO, UNICEF (2022). People using at least basic sanitation services (% of population). *WHO / UNICEF Joint Monitoring Programme: Data and Estimates*. World Health Organization and United Nations Children's Fund, Geneva and New York. https://washdata.org/data

WHO, UNICEF (2022). *WHO / UNICEF Joint Monitoring Programme: Data and Estimates*. World Health Organization and United Nations Children's Fund, Geneva and New York. https://washdata.org/data

World Bank (2018). *2018 Logistics Performance Index*. World Bank, Washington, D.C. http://lpi.worldbank.org/international/global

World Bank (2022). Female share of graduates from science, technology, engineering and mathematics (STEM) programmes, tertiary (%). World Bank, Washington, D.C. https://databank.worldbank.org/reports.aspx?source=283&series=SE.TER.GRAD.FE.SI.ZS

World Bank (2022). GDP per capita, PPP (current international $). World Bank, Washington, D.C. https://data.worldbank.org/indicator/NY.GDP.PCAP.PP.CD

World Bank (2022). Gini Index (World Bank estimate). World Bank, Washington, D.C. https://data.worldbank.org/indicator/SI.POV.GINI

World Bank (2022). Statistical Performance Indicators, SPI Overall Score. World Bank, Washington D.C., https://databank.worldbank.org/Statistical-Performance-Indicators-(SPI)/id/c6cc9909

World Data Lab. *World Poverty Clock*. World Data Lab, Vienna, Austria. http://worldpoverty.io/

World Health Expenditure Database. World Health Organization, Geneva. http://apps.who.int/nha/database

World Justice Project (2020). *The World Justice Project: Rule of Law Index 2020*. The World Justice Project, Washington, D.C. https://worldjusticeproject.org/our-work/research-and-data/wjp-rule-law-index-2020

Zhang, X., and Davidson, E. (2019). Sustainable Nitrogen Management Index. Earth and Space Science Open Archive. https://doi.org/10.1002/essoar.10501111.1

Zucman, G. et al. (2019). The Missing Profits of Nations: 2016 Figures. https://missingprofits.world

Part 5
Country Profiles

AFGHANISTAN

Eastern Europe and Central Asia

AVERAGE PERFORMANCE BY SDG

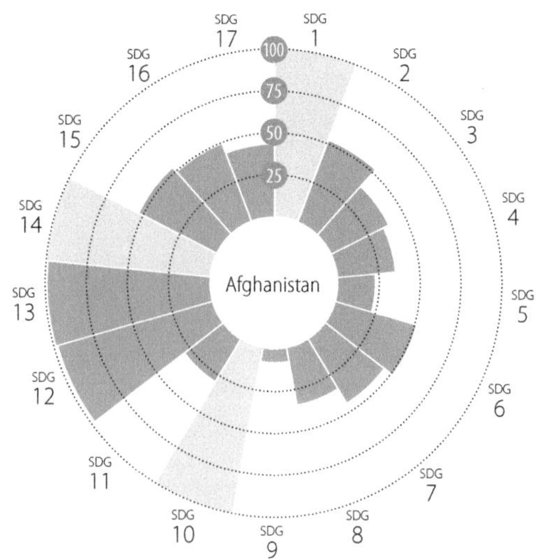

OVERALL PERFORMANCE

COUNTRY RANKING

AFGHANISTAN

147/163

COUNTRY SCORE

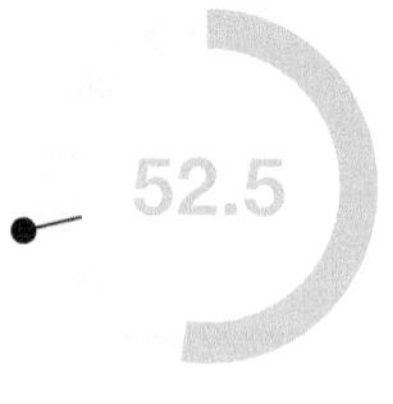

REGIONAL AVERAGE: 71.6

SDG DASHBOARDS AND TRENDS

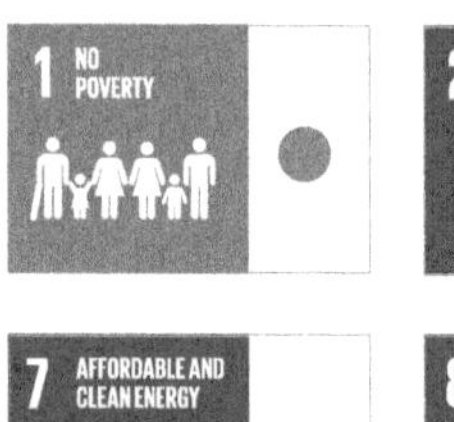

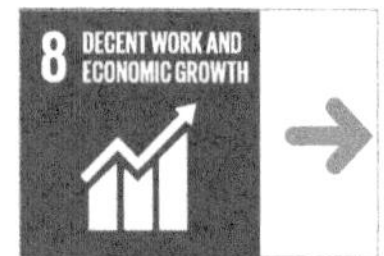

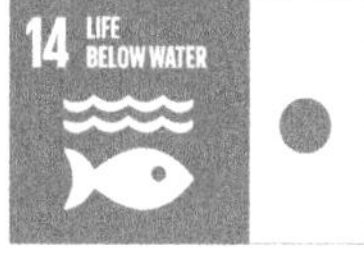

Major challenges · Significant challenges · Challenges remain · SDG achieved · Information unavailable

Decreasing · Stagnating · Moderately improving · On track or maintaining SDG achievement · Information unavailable

Note: The full title of each SDG is available here: https://sustainabledevelopment.un.org/topics/sustainabledevelopmentgoals

INTERNATIONAL SPILLOVER INDEX

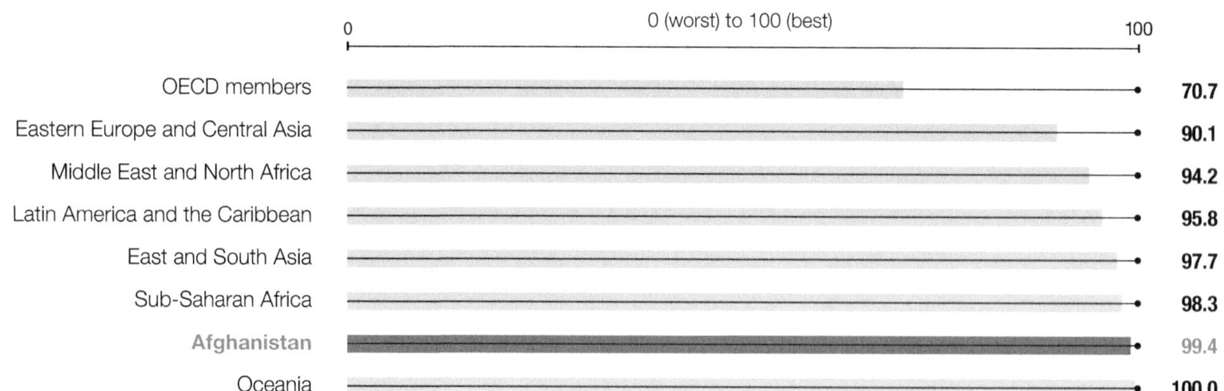

Region	Score
OECD members	70.7
Eastern Europe and Central Asia	90.1
Middle East and North Africa	94.2
Latin America and the Caribbean	95.8
East and South Asia	97.7
Sub-Saharan Africa	98.3
Afghanistan	99.4
Oceania	100.0

STATISTICAL PERFORMANCE INDEX

0 (worst) to 100 (best)

MISSING DATA IN SDG INDEX

10%

AFGHANISTAN

Performance by Indicator

	Value	Year	Rating	Trend
SDG1 – No Poverty				
Poverty headcount ratio at \$1.90/day (%)	* NA	NA	●	●
Poverty headcount ratio at \$3.20/day (%)	* NA	NA	●	●
SDG2 – Zero Hunger				
Prevalence of undernourishment (%)	25.6	2019	●	↓
Prevalence of stunting in children under 5 years of age (%)	38.2	2018	●	→
Prevalence of wasting in children under 5 years of age (%)	5.1	2018	●	→
Prevalence of obesity, BMI ≥ 30 (% of adult population)	5.5	2016	●	↑
Human Trophic Level (best 2–3 worst)	2.2	2017	●	↑
Cereal yield (tonnes per hectare of harvested land)	2.2	2018	●	→
Sustainable Nitrogen Management Index (best 0–1.41 worst)	0.7	2015	●	↓
Exports of hazardous pesticides (tonnes per million population)	NA	NA	●	●
SDG3 – Good Health and Well-Being				
Maternal mortality rate (per 100,000 live births)	638	2017	●	↑
Neonatal mortality rate (per 1,000 live births)	35.2	2020	●	↗
Mortality rate, under-5 (per 1,000 live births)	58.0	2020	●	↗
Incidence of tuberculosis (per 100,000 population)	193.0	2020	●	↓
New HIV infections (per 1,000 uninfected population)	0.0	2020	●	↑
Age-standardized death rate due to cardiovascular disease, cancer, diabetes, or chronic respiratory disease in adults aged 30–70 years (%)	35.3	2019	●	→
Age-standardized death rate attributable to household air pollution and ambient air pollution (per 100,000 population)	211	2016	●	●
Traffic deaths (per 100,000 population)	15.9	2019	●	↓
Life expectancy at birth (years)	63.2	2019	●	→
Adolescent fertility rate (births per 1,000 females aged 15 to 19)	62.0	2017	●	●
Births attended by skilled health personnel (%)	58.8	2018	●	↗
Surviving infants who received 2 WHO-recommended vaccines (%)	66	2020	●	→
Universal health coverage (UHC) index of service coverage (worst 0–100 best)	37	2019	●	→
Subjective well-being (average ladder score, worst 0–10 best)	2.4	2021	●	↓
SDG4 – Quality Education				
Participation rate in pre-primary organized learning (% of children aged 4 to 6)	NA	NA	●	●
Net primary enrollment rate (%)	NA	NA	●	●
Lower secondary completion rate (%)	58.3	2019	●	↗
Literacy rate (% of population aged 15 to 24)	55.9	2021	●	●
SDG5 – Gender Equality				
Demand for family planning satisfied by modern methods (% of females aged 15 to 49)	42.2	2016	●	●
Ratio of female-to-male mean years of education received (%)	31.7	2019	●	→
Ratio of female-to-male labor force participation rate (%)	24.7	2020	●	↓
Seats held by women in national parliament (%)	27.0	2020	●	↓
SDG6 – Clean Water and Sanitation				
Population using at least basic drinking water services (%)	75.1	2020	●	↑
Population using at least basic sanitation services (%)	50.5	2020	●	→
Freshwater withdrawal (% of available freshwater resources)	54.8	2018	●	●
Anthropogenic wastewater that receives treatment (%)	0.0	2018	●	●
Scarce water consumption embodied in imports (m^3 H_2O eq/capita)	453.6	2018	●	●
SDG7 – Affordable and Clean Energy				
Population with access to electricity (%)	97.7	2019	●	↑
Population with access to clean fuels and technology for cooking (%)	36.0	2019	●	→
CO_2 emissions from fuel combustion per total electricity output ($MtCO_2$/TWh)	8.9	2019	●	↓
Share of renewable energy in total primary energy supply (%)	NA	NA	●	●
SDG8 – Decent Work and Economic Growth				
Adjusted GDP growth (%)	-6.6	2020	●	●
Victims of modern slavery (per 1,000 population)	22.2	2018	●	●
Adults with an account at a bank or other financial institution or with a mobile-money-service provider (% of population aged 15 or over)	14.9	2017	●	→
Unemployment rate (% of total labor force)	18.5	2022	●	↓
Fundamental labor rights are effectively guaranteed (worst 0–1 best)	0.4	2020	●	↗
Fatal work-related accidents embodied in imports (per 100,000 population)	0.0	2015	●	↑

	Value	Year	Rating	Trend
SDG9 – Industry, Innovation and Infrastructure				
Population using the internet (%)	18.4	2020	●	→
Mobile broadband subscriptions (per 100 population)	19.2	2019	●	↗
Logistics Performance Index: Quality of trade and transport-related infrastructure (worst 1–5 best)	1.8	2018	●	↓
The Times Higher Education Universities Ranking: Average score of top 3 universities (worst 0–100 best)	* 0.0	2022	●	●
Articles published in academic journals (per 1,000 population)	0.0	2020	●	→
Expenditure on research and development (% of GDP)	* 0.0	2018	●	●
SDG10 – Reduced Inequalities				
Gini coefficient	NA	NA	●	●
Palma ratio	NA	NA	●	●
SDG11 – Sustainable Cities and Communities				
Proportion of urban population living in slums (%)	73.5	2018	●	↓
Annual mean concentration of particulate matter of less than 2.5 microns in diameter (PM2.5) (μg/m^3)	55.0	2019	●	↗
Access to improved water source, piped (% of urban population)	41.9	2020	●	→
Satisfaction with public transport (%)	34.0	2021	●	↓
SDG12 – Responsible Consumption and Production				
Municipal solid waste (kg/capita/day)	0.4	2016	●	●
Electronic waste (kg/capita)	0.6	2019	●	●
Production-based SO_2 emissions (kg/capita)	1.7	2018	●	●
SO_2 emissions embodied in imports (kg/capita)	0.1	2018	●	●
Production-based nitrogen emissions (kg/capita)	5.9	2015	●	↑
Nitrogen emissions embodied in imports (kg/capita)	0.2	2015	●	↑
Exports of plastic waste (kg/capita)	0.0	2019	●	●
SDG13 – Climate Action				
CO_2 emissions from fossil fuel combustion and cement production (tCO_2/capita)	0.3	2020	●	↑
CO_2 emissions embodied in imports (tCO_2/capita)	0.1	2018	●	↑
CO_2 emissions embodied in fossil fuel exports (kg/capita)	36.9	2019	●	●
SDG14 – Life Below Water				
Mean area that is protected in marine sites important to biodiversity (%)	NA	NA	●	●
Ocean Health Index: Clean Waters score (worst 0–100 best)	NA	NA	●	●
Fish caught from overexploited or collapsed stocks (% of total catch)	NA	NA	●	●
Fish caught by trawling or dredging (%)	NA	NA	●	●
Fish caught that are then discarded (%)	NA	NA	●	●
Marine biodiversity threats embodied in imports (per million population)	0.0	2018	●	●
SDG15 – Life on Land				
Mean area that is protected in terrestrial sites important to biodiversity (%)	5.7	2020	●	→
Mean area that is protected in freshwater sites important to biodiversity (%)	0.0	2020	●	→
Red List Index of species survival (worst 0–1 best)	0.8	2021	●	→
Permanent deforestation (% of forest area, 5-year average)	0.0	2020	●	↑
Terrestrial and freshwater biodiversity threats embodied in imports (per million population)	0.0	2018	●	●
SDG16 – Peace, Justice and Strong Institutions				
Homicides (per 100,000 population)	6.7	2018	●	↑
Unsentenced detainees (% of prison population)	31.3	2014	●	●
Population who feel safe walking alone at night in the city or area where they live (%)	22	2021	●	↓
Property Rights (worst 1–7 best)	NA	NA	●	●
Birth registrations with civil authority (% of children under age 5)	42.3	2020	●	●
Corruption Perception Index (worst 0–100 best)	16	2021	●	→
Children involved in child labor (% of population aged 5 to 14)	21.4	2019	●	●
Exports of major conventional weapons (TIV constant million USD per 100,000 population)	* 0.0	2020	●	●
Press Freedom Index (best 0–100 worst)	40.2	2021	●	↓
Access to and affordability of justice (worst 0–1 best)	0.5	2020	●	↗
SDG17 – Partnerships for the Goals				
Government spending on health and education (% of GDP)	4.3	2019	●	→
For high-income and all OECD DAC countries: International concessional public finance, including official development assistance (% of GNI)	NA	NA	●	●
Other countries: Government revenue excluding grants (% of GDP)	13.0	2017	●	●
Corporate Tax Haven Score (best 0–100 worst)	* 0.0	2019	●	●
Statistical Performance Index (worst 0–100 best)	49.8	2019	●	↑

* Imputed data point

ALBANIA

Eastern Europe and Central Asia

OVERALL PERFORMANCE

COUNTRY RANKING

ALBANIA

61 **/163**

COUNTRY SCORE

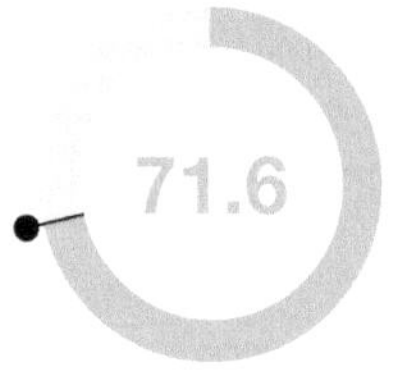

REGIONAL AVERAGE: 71.6

AVERAGE PERFORMANCE BY SDG

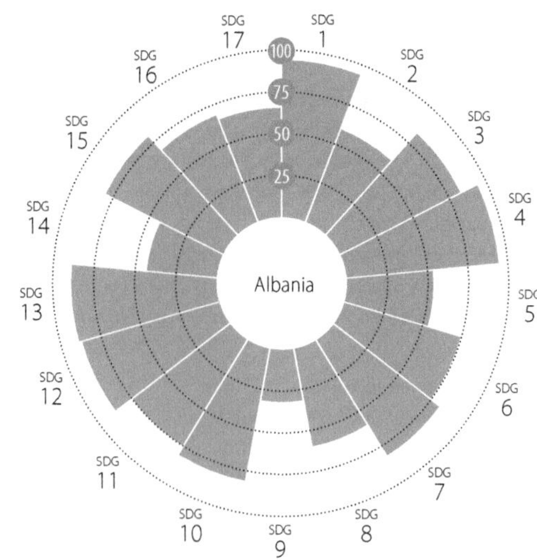

SDG DASHBOARDS AND TRENDS

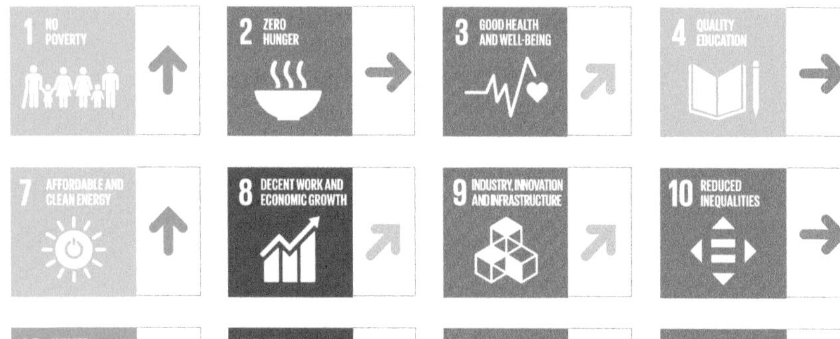

Major challenges · Significant challenges · Challenges remain · SDG achieved · Information unavailable

Decreasing · Stagnating · Moderately improving · On track or maintaining SDG achievement · Information unavailable

Note: The full title of each SDG is available here: https://sustainabledevelopment.un.org/topics/sustainabledevelopmentgoals

INTERNATIONAL SPILLOVER INDEX

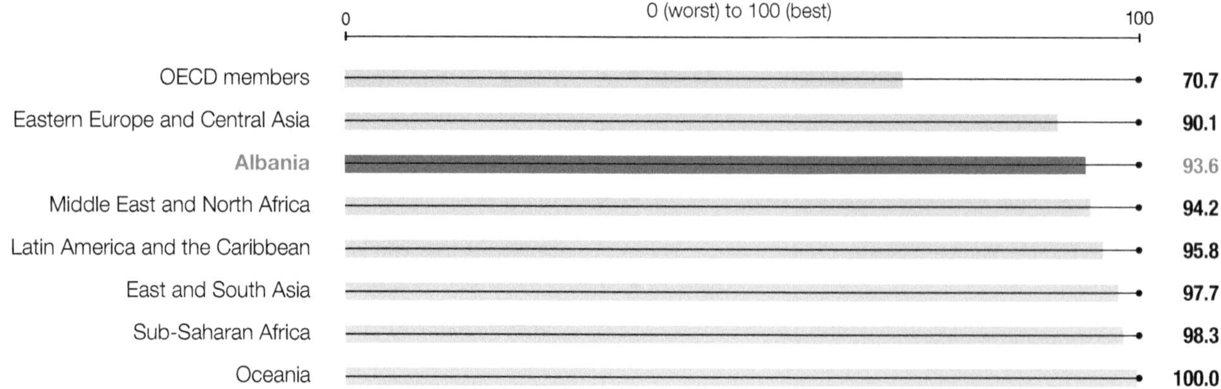

STATISTICAL PERFORMANCE INDEX

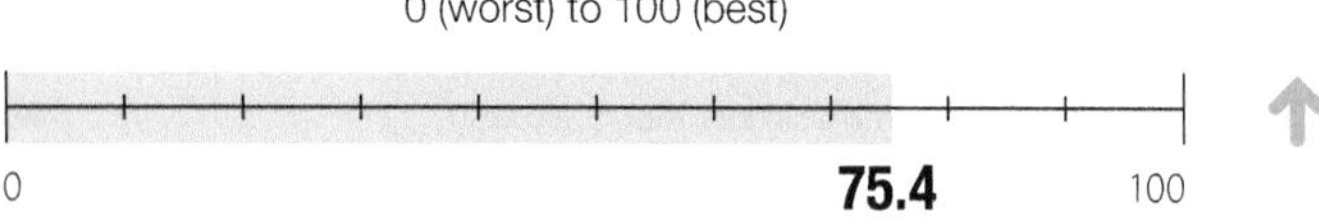

MISSING DATA IN SDG INDEX

4%

ALBANIA

SDG1 – No Poverty	Value	Year	Rating	Trend
Poverty headcount ratio at $1.90/day (%)	0.1	2022	●	↑
Poverty headcount ratio at $3.20/day (%)	5.8	2022	●	↑
SDG2 – Zero Hunger				
Prevalence of undernourishment (%)	3.9	2019	●	↑
Prevalence of stunting in children under 5 years of age (%)	11.3	2017	●	→
Prevalence of wasting in children under 5 years of age (%)	1.6	2017	●	↑
Prevalence of obesity, BMI ≥ 30 (% of adult population)	21.7	2016	●	↓
Human Trophic Level (best 2–3 worst)	2.4	2017	●	↓
Cereal yield (tonnes per hectare of harvested land)	4.8	2018	●	↑
Sustainable Nitrogen Management Index (best 0–1.41 worst)	0.8	2015	●	→
Exports of hazardous pesticides (tonnes per million population)	NA	NA	●	●
SDG3 – Good Health and Well-Being				
Maternal mortality rate (per 100,000 live births)	15	2017	●	↑
Neonatal mortality rate (per 1,000 live births)	7.8	2020	●	↑
Mortality rate, under-5 (per 1,000 live births)	9.8	2020	●	↑
Incidence of tuberculosis (per 100,000 population)	15.0	2020	●	↗
New HIV infections (per 1,000 uninfected population)	0.0	2020	●	↑
Age-standardized death rate due to cardiovascular disease, cancer, diabetes, or chronic respiratory disease in adults aged 30–70 years (%)	11.4	2019	●	↑
Age-standardized death rate attributable to household air pollution and ambient air pollution (per 100,000 population)	68	2016	●	●
Traffic deaths (per 100,000 population)	11.7	2019	●	↑
Life expectancy at birth (years)	78.0	2019	●	→
Adolescent fertility rate (births per 1,000 females aged 15 to 19)	14.2	2019	●	↑
Births attended by skilled health personnel (%)	99.8	2018	●	●
Surviving infants who received 2 WHO-recommended vaccines (%)	91	2020	●	↑
Universal health coverage (UHC) index of service coverage (worst 0–100 best)	62	2019	●	→
Subjective well-being (average ladder score, worst 0–10 best)	5.3	2021	●	↑
SDG4 – Quality Education				
Participation rate in pre-primary organized learning (% of children aged 4 to 6)	97.1	2018	●	●
Net primary enrollment rate (%)	96.2	2020	●	↓
Lower secondary completion rate (%)	92.7	2020	●	↑
Literacy rate (% of population aged 15 to 24)	99.3	2018	●	●
SDG5 – Gender Equality				
Demand for family planning satisfied by modern methods (% of females aged 15 to 49)	6.3	2018	●	●
Ratio of female-to-male mean years of education received (%)	91.5	2019	●	↓
Ratio of female-to-male labor force participation rate (%)	75.9	2020	●	↑
Seats held by women in national parliament (%)	29.5	2020	●	↑
SDG6 – Clean Water and Sanitation				
Population using at least basic drinking water services (%)	95.1	2020	●	↑
Population using at least basic sanitation services (%)	99.3	2020	●	↑
Freshwater withdrawal (% of available freshwater resources)	5.8	2018	●	●
Anthropogenic wastewater that receives treatment (%)	2.7	2018	●	●
Scarce water consumption embodied in imports (m^3 H_2O eq/capita)	2528.0	2018	●	●
SDG7 – Affordable and Clean Energy				
Population with access to electricity (%)	100.0	2019	●	↑
Population with access to clean fuels and technology for cooking (%)	80.7	2019	●	↑
CO_2 emissions from fuel combustion per total electricity output ($MtCO_2$/TWh)	0.9	2019	●	↑
Share of renewable energy in total primary energy supply (%)	31.8	2019	●	↑
SDG8 – Decent Work and Economic Growth				
Adjusted GDP growth (%)	-2.5	2020	●	●
Victims of modern slavery (per 1,000 population)	6.9	2018	●	●
Adults with an account at a bank or other financial institution or with a mobile-money-service provider (% of population aged 15 or over)	40.0	2017	●	→
Unemployment rate (% of total labor force)	10.9	2022	●	↑
Fundamental labor rights are effectively guaranteed (worst 0–1 best)	0.5	2020	●	→
Fatal work-related accidents embodied in imports (per 100,000 population)	0.2	2015	●	↑

* Imputed data point

SDG9 – Industry, Innovation and Infrastructure	Value	Year	Rating	Trend
Population using the internet (%)	72.2	2020	●	↑
Mobile broadband subscriptions (per 100 population)	62.1	2019	●	↑
Logistics Performance Index: Quality of trade and transport-related infrastructure (worst 1–5 best)	2.3	2018	●	●
The Times Higher Education Universities Ranking: Average score of top 3 universities (worst 0–100 best)	* 0.0	2022	●	●
Articles published in academic journals (per 1,000 population)	0.2	2020	●	→
Expenditure on research and development (% of GDP)	0.2	2008	●	●
SDG10 – Reduced Inequalities				
Gini coefficient	33.2	2017	●	→
Palma ratio	1.3	2018	●	●
SDG11 – Sustainable Cities and Communities				
Proportion of urban population living in slums (%)	13.2	2018	●	●
Annual mean concentration of particulate matter of less than 2.5 microns in diameter (PM2.5) (μg/m^3)	17.5	2019	●	↗
Access to improved water source, piped (% of urban population)	83.7	2020	●	↓
Satisfaction with public transport (%)	48.0	2021	●	↓
SDG12 – Responsible Consumption and Production				
Municipal solid waste (kg/capita/day)	1.0	2019	●	●
Electronic waste (kg/capita)	7.4	2019	●	●
Production-based SO_2 emissions (kg/capita)	3.9	2018	●	●
SO_2 emissions embodied in imports (kg/capita)	1.4	2018	●	●
Production-based nitrogen emissions (kg/capita)	14.4	2015	●	↑
Nitrogen emissions embodied in imports (kg/capita)	1.9	2015	●	↑
Exports of plastic waste (kg/capita)	NA	NA	●	●
SDG13 – Climate Action				
CO_2 emissions from fossil fuel combustion and cement production (tCO_2/capita)	1.6	2020	●	↑
CO_2 emissions embodied in imports (tCO_2/capita)	0.5	2018	●	↑
CO_2 emissions embodied in fossil fuel exports (kg/capita)	NA	NA	●	●
SDG14 – Life Below Water				
Mean area that is protected in marine sites important to biodiversity (%)	70.7	2020	●	→
Ocean Health Index: Clean Waters score (worst 0–100 best)	56.8	2020	●	→
Fish caught from overexploited or collapsed stocks (% of total catch)	NA	NA	●	●
Fish caught by trawling or dredging (%)	84.3	2018	●	↓
Fish caught that are then discarded (%)	24.7	2018	●	↓
Marine biodiversity threats embodied in imports (per million population)	0.0	2018	●	●
SDG15 – Life on Land				
Mean area that is protected in terrestrial sites important to biodiversity (%)	50.5	2020	●	→
Mean area that is protected in freshwater sites important to biodiversity (%)	96.6	2020	●	↑
Red List Index of species survival (worst 0–1 best)	0.8	2021	●	↓
Permanent deforestation (% of forest area, 5-year average)	0.0	2020	●	↑
Terrestrial and freshwater biodiversity threats embodied in imports (per million population)	0.6	2018	●	●
SDG16 – Peace, Justice and Strong Institutions				
Homicides (per 100,000 population)	2.1	2020	●	→
Unsentenced detainees (% of prison population)	44.9	2019	●	↗
Population who feel safe walking alone at night in the city or area where they live (%)	71	2021	●	↑
Property Rights (worst 1–7 best)	3.3	2020	●	↓
Birth registrations with civil authority (% of children under age 5)	98.4	2020	●	●
Corruption Perception Index (worst 0–100 best)	35	2021	●	↓
Children involved in child labor (% of population aged 5 to 14)	3.3	2019	●	●
Exports of major conventional weapons (TIV constant million USD per 100,000 population)	0.0	2020	●	●
Press Freedom Index (best 0–100 worst)	30.6	2021	●	↓
Access to and affordability of justice (worst 0–1 best)	0.6	2020	●	↗
SDG17 – Partnerships for the Goals				
Government spending on health and education (% of GDP)	6.8	2019	●	↗
For high-income and all OECD DAC countries: International concessional public finance, including official development assistance (% of GNI)	NA	NA	●	●
Other countries: Government revenue excluding grants (% of GDP)	25.1	2019	●	→
Corporate Tax Haven Score (best 0–100 worst)	* 0.0	2019	●	●
Statistical Performance Index (worst 0–100 best)	75.4	2019	●	↑

ALGERIA

Middle East and North Africa

OVERALL PERFORMANCE

COUNTRY RANKING

ALGERIA

64/163

COUNTRY SCORE

REGIONAL AVERAGE: 66.7

AVERAGE PERFORMANCE BY SDG

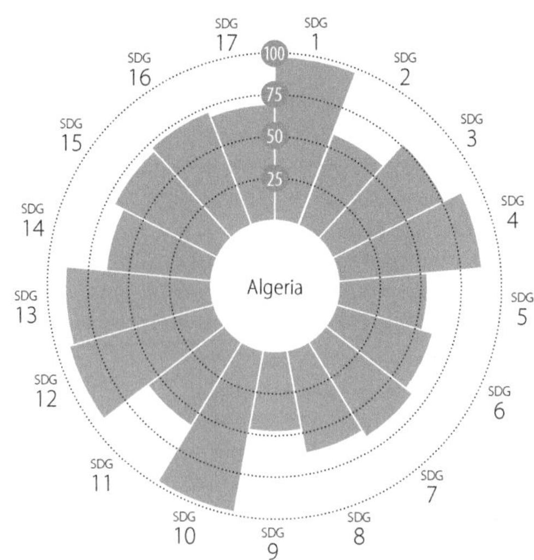

SDG DASHBOARDS AND TRENDS

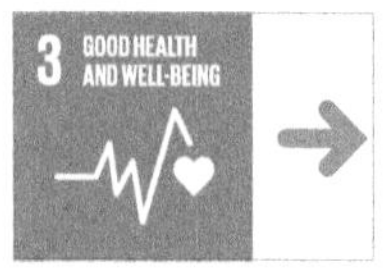

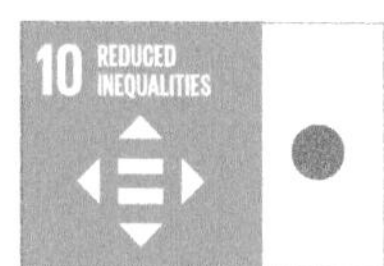

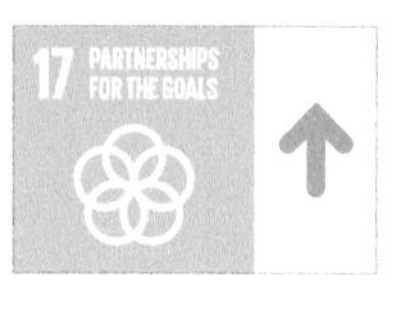

Major challenges | Significant challenges | Challenges remain | SDG achieved | Information unavailable

Decreasing | Stagnating | Moderately improving | On track or maintaining SDG achievement | Information unavailable

Note: The full title of each SDG is available here: https://sustainabledevelopment.un.org/topics/sustainabledevelopmentgoals

INTERNATIONAL SPILLOVER INDEX

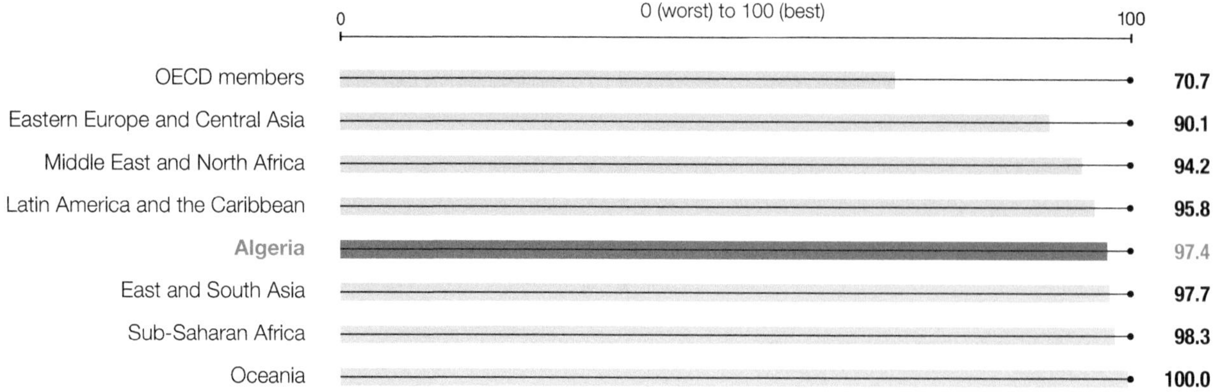

STATISTICAL PERFORMANCE INDEX

0 (worst) to 100 (best)

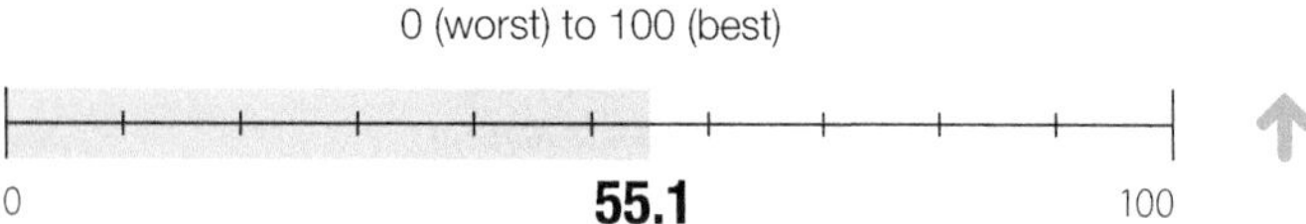

MISSING DATA IN SDG INDEX

3%

ALGERIA

Performance by Indicator

SDG1 – No Poverty	Value	Year	Rating	Trend
Poverty headcount ratio at $1.90/day (%)	0.3	2022	●	↑
Poverty headcount ratio at $3.20/day (%)	2.4	2022	●	↗

SDG2 – Zero Hunger	Value	Year	Rating	Trend
Prevalence of undernourishment (%)	2.5	2019	●	↑
Prevalence of stunting in children under 5 years of age (%)	9.8	2019	●	↗
Prevalence of wasting in children under 5 years of age (%)	2.7	2019	●	↑
Prevalence of obesity, BMI ≥ 30 (% of adult population)	27.4	2016	●	↓
Human Trophic Level (best 2–3 worst)	2.2	2017	●	↑
Cereal yield (tonnes per hectare of harvested land)	1.8	2018	●	↑
Sustainable Nitrogen Management Index (best 0–1.41 worst)	0.7	2015	●	→
Exports of hazardous pesticides (tonnes per million population)	NA	NA	●	●

SDG3 – Good Health and Well-Being	Value	Year	Rating	Trend
Maternal mortality rate (per 100,000 live births)	112	2017	●	→
Neonatal mortality rate (per 1,000 live births)	16.3	2020	●	→
Mortality rate, under-5 (per 1,000 live births)	22.7	2020	●	↑
Incidence of tuberculosis (per 100,000 population)	59.0	2020	●	↗
New HIV infections (per 1,000 uninfected population)	0.0	2020	●	↑
Age-standardized death rate due to cardiovascular disease, cancer, diabetes, or chronic respiratory disease in adults aged 30–70 years (%)	13.9	2019	●	↑
Age-standardized death rate attributable to household air pollution and ambient air pollution (per 100,000 population)	50	2016	●	●
Traffic deaths (per 100,000 population)	20.9	2019	●	→
Life expectancy at birth (years)	77.1	2019	●	↗
Adolescent fertility rate (births per 1,000 females aged 15 to 19)	12.0	2017	●	●
Births attended by skilled health personnel (%)	96.6	2013	●	●
Surviving infants who received 2 WHO-recommended vaccines (%)	80	2019	●	↓
Universal health coverage (UHC) index of service coverage (worst 0–100 best)	75	2019	●	→
Subjective well-being (average ladder score, worst 0–10 best)	5.2	2021	●	↓

SDG4 – Quality Education	Value	Year	Rating	Trend
Participation rate in pre-primary organized learning (% of children aged 4 to 6)	84.7	2011	●	●
Net primary enrollment rate (%)	99.8	2020	●	↑
Lower secondary completion rate (%)	82.9	2019	●	↑
Literacy rate (% of population aged 15 to 24)	97.4	2018	●	●

SDG5 – Gender Equality	Value	Year	Rating	Trend
Demand for family planning satisfied by modern methods (% of females aged 15 to 49)	77.2	2013	●	●
Ratio of female-to-male mean years of education received (%)	92.8	2019	●	↑
Ratio of female-to-male labor force participation rate (%)	24.1	2020	●	↓
Seats held by women in national parliament (%)	25.8	2020	●	↓

SDG6 – Clean Water and Sanitation	Value	Year	Rating	Trend
Population using at least basic drinking water services (%)	94.4	2020	●	↗
Population using at least basic sanitation services (%)	86.0	2020	●	→
Freshwater withdrawal (% of available freshwater resources)	137.9	2018	●	●
Anthropogenic wastewater that receives treatment (%)	33.1	2018	●	●
Scarce water consumption embodied in imports (m^3 H_2O eq/capita)	801.9	2018	●	●

SDG7 – Affordable and Clean Energy	Value	Year	Rating	Trend
Population with access to electricity (%)	99.5	2019	●	↑
Population with access to clean fuels and technology for cooking (%)	99.3	2019	●	↑
CO_2 emissions from fuel combustion per total electricity output ($MtCO_2$/TWh)	2.2	2019	●	→
Share of renewable energy in total primary energy supply (%)	0.1	2019	●	→

SDG8 – Decent Work and Economic Growth	Value	Year	Rating	Trend
Adjusted GDP growth (%)	-5.5	2020	●	●
Victims of modern slavery (per 1,000 population)	2.7	2018	●	●
Adults with an account at a bank or other financial institution or with a mobile-money-service provider (% of population aged 15 or over)	42.8	2017	●	↓
Unemployment rate (% of total labor force)	12.2	2022	●	↓
Fundamental labor rights are effectively guaranteed (worst 0–1 best)	0.5	2020	●	●
Fatal work-related accidents embodied in imports (per 100,000 population)	0.1	2015	●	↑

* Imputed data point

SDG9 – Industry, Innovation and Infrastructure	Value	Year	Rating	Trend
Population using the internet (%)	62.9	2020	●	↑
Mobile broadband subscriptions (per 100 population)	89.8	2019	●	↑
Logistics Performance Index: Quality of trade and transport-related infrastructure (worst 1–5 best)	2.4	2018	●	↓
The Times Higher Education Universities Ranking: Average score of top 3 universities (worst 0–100 best)	30.3	2022	●	●
Articles published in academic journals (per 1,000 population)	0.2	2020	●	→
Expenditure on research and development (% of GDP)	0.5	2017	●	●

SDG10 – Reduced Inequalities	Value	Year	Rating	Trend
Gini coefficient	27.6	2011	●	●
Palma ratio	1.0	2018	●	●

SDG11 – Sustainable Cities and Communities	Value	Year	Rating	Trend
Proportion of urban population living in slums (%)	NA	NA	●	●
Annual mean concentration of particulate matter of less than 2.5 microns in diameter (PM2.5) (μg/m^3)	41.3	2019	●	↓
Access to improved water source, piped (% of urban population)	76.1	2020	●	↓
Satisfaction with public transport (%)	47.0	2021	●	↓

SDG12 – Responsible Consumption and Production	Value	Year	Rating	Trend
Municipal solid waste (kg/capita/day)	0.8	2016	●	●
Electronic waste (kg/capita)	7.1	2019	●	●
Production-based SO_2 emissions (kg/capita)	2.1	2018	●	●
SO_2 emissions embodied in imports (kg/capita)	1.0	2018	●	●
Production-based nitrogen emissions (kg/capita)	6.5	2015	●	↑
Nitrogen emissions embodied in imports (kg/capita)	0.9	2015	●	↑
Exports of plastic waste (kg/capita)	0.0	2017	●	●

SDG13 – Climate Action	Value	Year	Rating	Trend
CO_2 emissions from fossil fuel combustion and cement production (tCO_2/capita)	3.5	2020	●	→
CO_2 emissions embodied in imports (tCO_2/capita)	0.3	2018	●	↑
CO_2 emissions embodied in fossil fuel exports (kg/capita)	3110.9	2017	●	●

SDG14 – Life Below Water	Value	Year	Rating	Trend
Mean area that is protected in marine sites important to biodiversity (%)	76.6	2020	●	→
Ocean Health Index: Clean Waters score (worst 0–100 best)	41.6	2020	●	→
Fish caught from overexploited or collapsed stocks (% of total catch)	19.6	2018	●	↑
Fish caught by trawling or dredging (%)	21.4	2018	●	↓
Fish caught that are then discarded (%)	13.5	2018	●	↓
Marine biodiversity threats embodied in imports (per million population)	0.0	2018	●	●

SDG15 – Life on Land	Value	Year	Rating	Trend
Mean area that is protected in terrestrial sites important to biodiversity (%)	36.5	2020	●	→
Mean area that is protected in freshwater sites important to biodiversity (%)	76.3	2020	●	→
Red List Index of species survival (worst 0–1 best)	0.9	2021	●	↑
Permanent deforestation (% of forest area, 5-year average)	0.6	2020	●	↑
Terrestrial and freshwater biodiversity threats embodied in imports (per million population)	0.3	2018	●	●

SDG16 – Peace, Justice and Strong Institutions	Value	Year	Rating	Trend
Homicides (per 100,000 population)	1.3	2020	●	↑
Unsentenced detainees (% of prison population)	12.0	2019	●	↑
Population who feel safe walking alone at night in the city or area where they live (%)	65	2021	●	●
Property Rights (worst 1–7 best)	4.1	2020	●	↑
Birth registrations with civil authority (% of children under age 5)	99.6	2020	●	●
Corruption Perception Index (worst 0–100 best)	33	2021	●	↓
Children involved in child labor (% of population aged 5 to 14)	4.3	2019	●	●
Exports of major conventional weapons (TIV constant million USD per 100,000 population)	0.0	2020	●	●
Press Freedom Index (best 0–100 worst)	47.3	2021	●	↓
Access to and affordability of justice (worst 0–1 best)	0.6	2020	●	●

SDG17 – Partnerships for the Goals	Value	Year	Rating	Trend
Government spending on health and education (% of GDP)	10.2	2019	●	↑
For high-income and all OECD DAC countries: International concessional public finance, including official development assistance (% of GNI)	NA	NA	●	●
Other countries: Government revenue excluding grants (% of GDP)	NA	NA	●	●
Corporate Tax Haven Score (best 0–100 worst)	* 0.0	2019	●	●
Statistical Performance Index (worst 0–100 best)	55.1	2019	●	↑

ANDORRA

Western Europe

OVERALL PERFORMANCE

COUNTRY RANKING

ANDORRA

NA /163

COUNTRY SCORE

na

REGIONAL AVERAGE: 71.6

AVERAGE PERFORMANCE BY SDG

SDG 17, SDG 1, SDG 2, SDG 3, SDG 4, SDG 5, SDG 6, SDG 7, SDG 8, SDG 9, SDG 10, SDG 11, SDG 12, SDG 13, SDG 14, SDG 15, SDG 16

100, 75, 50, 25

Andorra

SDG DASHBOARDS AND TRENDS

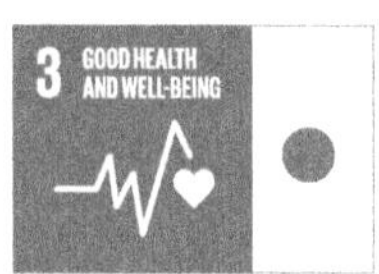

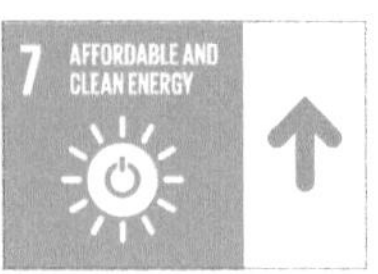

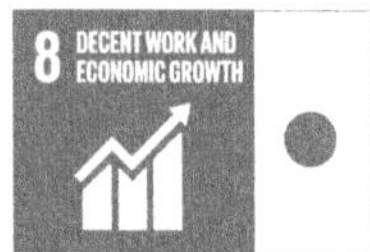

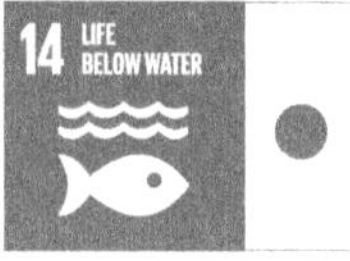

Major challenges · Significant challenges · Challenges remain · SDG achieved · Information unavailable

Decreasing · Stagnating · Moderately improving · On track or maintaining SDG achievement · Information unavailable

Note: The full title of each SDG is available here: https://sustainabledevelopment.un.org/topics/sustainabledevelopmentgoals

INTERNATIONAL SPILLOVER INDEX

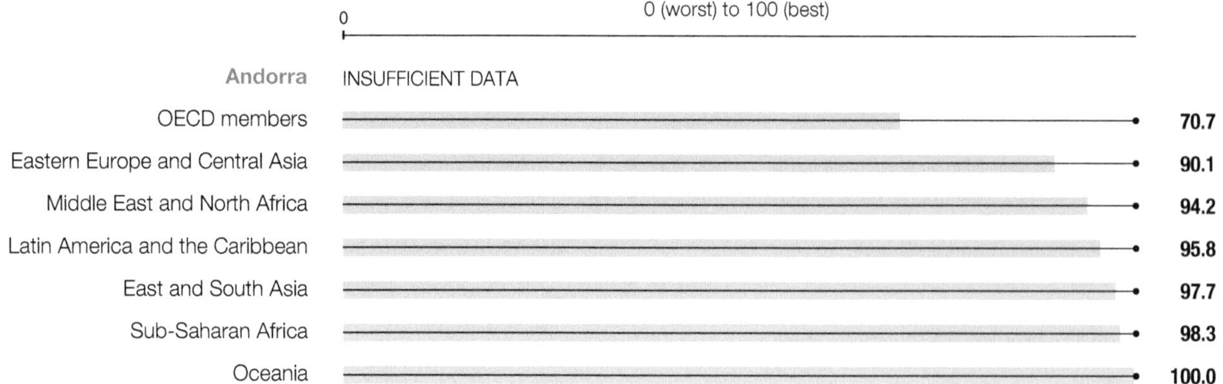

STATISTICAL PERFORMANCE INDEX

0 (worst) to 100 (best)

0 — 100

na

MISSING DATA IN SDG INDEX

54%

ANDORRA

Performance by Indicator

SDG1 – No Poverty	Value	Year	Rating	Trend
Poverty headcount ratio at $1.90/day (%)	NA	NA	•	•
Poverty headcount ratio at $3.20/day (%)	NA	NA	•	•
SDG2 – Zero Hunger				
Prevalence of undernourishment (%)	* 1.2	2019	•	•
Prevalence of stunting in children under 5 years of age (%)	* 2.6	2019	•	↑
Prevalence of wasting in children under 5 years of age (%)	* 0.7	2019	•	↑
Prevalence of obesity, BMI ≥ 30 (% of adult population)	25.6	2016	•	↓
Human Trophic Level (best 2–3 worst)	NA	NA	•	•
Cereal yield (tonnes per hectare of harvested land)	NA	NA	•	•
Sustainable Nitrogen Management Index (best 0–1.41 worst)	NA	NA	•	•
Exports of hazardous pesticides (tonnes per million population)	NA	NA	•	•
SDG3 – Good Health and Well-Being				
Maternal mortality rate (per 100,000 live births)	NA	NA	•	•
Neonatal mortality rate (per 1,000 live births)	1.3	2020	•	↑
Mortality rate, under-5 (per 1,000 live births)	2.5	2020	•	↑
Incidence of tuberculosis (per 100,000 population)	3.0	2020	•	↑
New HIV infections (per 1,000 uninfected population)	NA	NA	•	•
Age-standardized death rate due to cardiovascular disease, cancer, diabetes, or chronic respiratory disease in adults aged 30–70 years (%)	NA	NA	•	•
Age-standardized death rate attributable to household air pollution and ambient air pollution (per 100,000 population)	NA	NA	•	•
Traffic deaths (per 100,000 population)	NA	NA	•	•
Life expectancy at birth (years)	NA	NA	•	•
Adolescent fertility rate (births per 1,000 females aged 15 to 19)	2.7	2018	•	↑
Births attended by skilled health personnel (%)	100.0	2017	•	↑
Surviving infants who received 2 WHO-recommended vaccines (%)	98	2020	•	↑
Universal health coverage (UHC) index of service coverage (worst 0–100 best)	NA	NA	•	•
Subjective well-being (average ladder score, worst 0–10 best)	NA	NA	•	•
SDG4 – Quality Education				
Participation rate in pre-primary organized learning (% of children aged 4 to 6)	NA	NA	•	•
Net primary enrollment rate (%)	NA	NA	•	•
Lower secondary completion rate (%)	NA	NA	•	•
Literacy rate (% of population aged 15 to 24)	NA	NA	•	•
SDG5 – Gender Equality				
Demand for family planning satisfied by modern methods (% of females aged 15 to 49)	NA	NA	•	•
Ratio of female-to-male mean years of education received (%)	98.1	2019	•	↑
Ratio of female-to-male labor force participation rate (%)	NA	NA	•	•
Seats held by women in national parliament (%)	46.4	2020	•	↑
SDG6 – Clean Water and Sanitation				
Population using at least basic drinking water services (%)	100.0	2020	•	↑
Population using at least basic sanitation services (%)	100.0	2020	•	↑
Freshwater withdrawal (% of available freshwater resources)	NA	NA	•	•
Anthropogenic wastewater that receives treatment (%)	100.0	2018	•	•
Scarce water consumption embodied in imports (m^3 H_2O eq/capita)	NA	NA	•	•
SDG7 – Affordable and Clean Energy				
Population with access to electricity (%)	100.0	2019	•	↑
Population with access to clean fuels and technology for cooking (%)	100.0	2019	•	↑
CO_2 emissions from fuel combustion per total electricity output ($MtCO_2$/TWh)	NA	NA	•	•
Share of renewable energy in total primary energy supply (%)	NA	NA	•	•
SDG8 – Decent Work and Economic Growth				
Adjusted GDP growth (%)	NA	NA	•	•
Victims of modern slavery (per 1,000 population)	NA	NA	•	•
Adults with an account at a bank or other financial institution or with a mobile-money-service provider (% of population aged 15 or over)	NA	NA	•	•
Unemployment rate (% of total labor force)	NA	NA	•	•
Fundamental labor rights are effectively guaranteed (worst 0–1 best)	NA	NA	•	•
Fatal work-related accidents embodied in imports (per 100,000 population)	1.2	2015	•	↑

* Imputed data point

SDG9 – Industry, Innovation and Infrastructure	Value	Year	Rating	Trend
Population using the internet (%)	91.6	2017	•	•
Mobile broadband subscriptions (per 100 population)	66.1	2019	•	↑
Logistics Performance Index: Quality of trade and transport-related infrastructure (worst 1–5 best)	NA	NA	•	•
The Times Higher Education Universities Ranking: Average score of top 3 universities (worst 0–100 best)	* 0.0	2022	•	•
Articles published in academic journals (per 1,000 population)	0.5	2020	•	↑
Expenditure on research and development (% of GDP)	NA	NA	•	•
SDG10 – Reduced Inequalities				
Gini coefficient	NA	NA	•	•
Palma ratio	NA	NA	•	•
SDG11 – Sustainable Cities and Communities				
Proportion of urban population living in slums (%)	NA	NA	•	•
Annual mean concentration of particulate matter of less than 2.5 microns in diameter (PM2.5) (μg/m^3)	11.2	2019	•	↑
Access to improved water source, piped (% of urban population)	100.0	2020	•	↑
Satisfaction with public transport (%)	NA	NA	•	•
SDG12 – Responsible Consumption and Production				
Municipal solid waste (kg/capita/day)	1.4	2012	•	•
Electronic waste (kg/capita)	NA	NA	•	•
Production-based SO_2 emissions (kg/capita)	NA	NA	•	•
SO_2 emissions embodied in imports (kg/capita)	NA	NA	•	•
Production-based nitrogen emissions (kg/capita)	0.0	2015	•	↑
Nitrogen emissions embodied in imports (kg/capita)	18.1	2015	•	→
Exports of plastic waste (kg/capita)	13.0	2018	•	•
SDG13 – Climate Action				
CO_2 emissions from fossil fuel combustion and cement production (tCO_2/capita)	6.0	2020	•	→
CO_2 emissions embodied in imports (tCO_2/capita)	NA	NA	•	•
CO_2 emissions embodied in fossil fuel exports (kg/capita)	0.0	2017	•	•
SDG14 – Life Below Water				
Mean area that is protected in marine sites important to biodiversity (%)	NA	NA	•	•
Ocean Health Index: Clean Waters score (worst 0–100 best)	NA	NA	•	•
Fish caught from overexploited or collapsed stocks (% of total catch)	NA	NA	•	•
Fish caught by trawling or dredging (%)	NA	NA	•	•
Fish caught that are then discarded (%)	NA	NA	•	•
Marine biodiversity threats embodied in imports (per million population)	NA	NA	•	•
SDG15 – Life on Land				
Mean area that is protected in terrestrial sites important to biodiversity (%)	26.1	2020	•	→
Mean area that is protected in freshwater sites important to biodiversity (%)	NA	NA	•	•
Red List Index of species survival (worst 0–1 best)	0.9	2021	•	↑
Permanent deforestation (% of forest area, 5-year average)	0.0	2020	•	↑
Terrestrial and freshwater biodiversity threats embodied in imports (per million population)	0.6	2018	•	•
SDG16 – Peace, Justice and Strong Institutions				
Homicides (per 100,000 population)	2.6	2020	•	↓
Unsentenced detainees (% of prison population)	42.9	2019	•	→
Population who feel safe walking alone at night in the city or area where they live (%)	NA	NA	•	•
Property Rights (worst 1–7 best)	NA	NA	•	•
Birth registrations with civil authority (% of children under age 5)	100.0	2020	•	•
Corruption Perception Index (worst 0–100 best)	NA	NA	•	•
Children involved in child labor (% of population aged 5 to 14)	NA	NA	•	•
Exports of major conventional weapons (TIV constant million USD per 100,000 population)	* 0.0	2020	•	•
Press Freedom Index (best 0–100 worst)	23.3	2021	•	↑
Access to and affordability of justice (worst 0–1 best)	NA	NA	•	•
SDG17 – Partnerships for the Goals				
Government spending on health and education (% of GDP)	7.8	2019	•	→
For high-income and all OECD DAC countries: International concessional public finance, including official development assistance (% of GNI)	NA	NA	•	•
Other countries: Government revenue excluding grants (% of GDP)	NA	NA	•	•
Corporate Tax Haven Score (best 0–100 worst)	69.0	2019	•	•
Statistical Performance Index (worst 0–100 best)	NA	NA	•	•

5. Country Profiles

ANGOLA

Sub-Saharan Africa

OVERALL PERFORMANCE

COUNTRY RANKING

ANGOLA

154 /163

COUNTRY SCORE

AVERAGE PERFORMANCE BY SDG

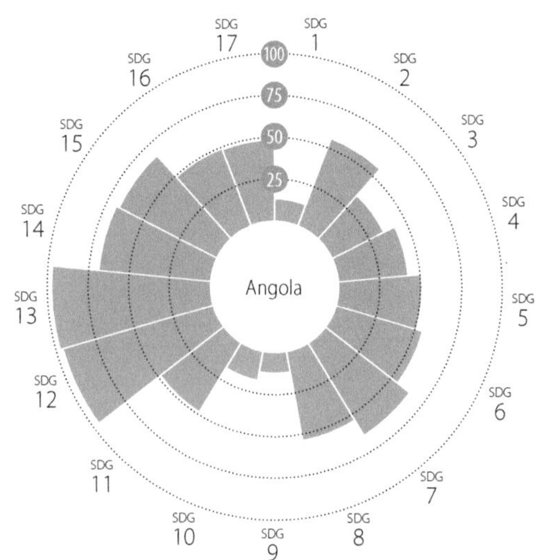

SDG DASHBOARDS AND TRENDS

Note: The full title of each SDG is available here: https://sustainabledevelopment.un.org/topics/sustainabledevelopmentgoals

INTERNATIONAL SPILLOVER INDEX

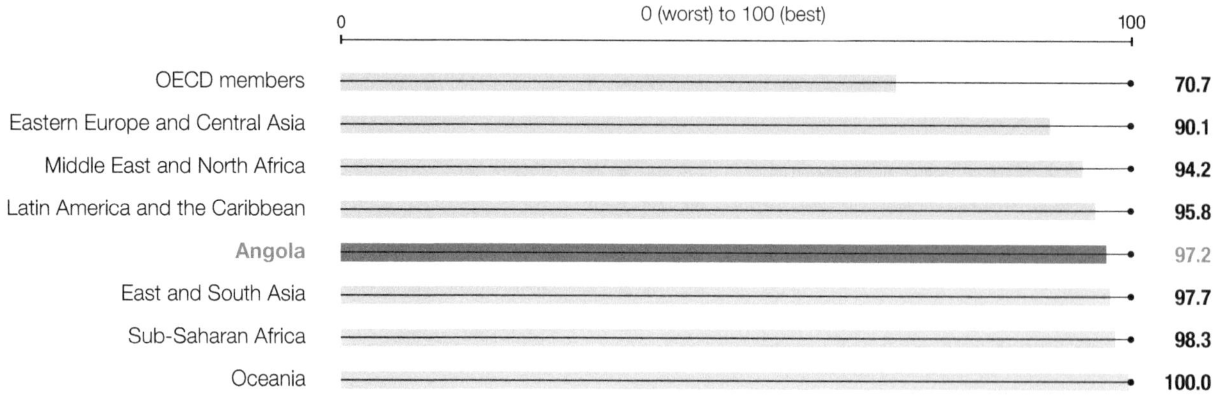

STATISTICAL PERFORMANCE INDEX

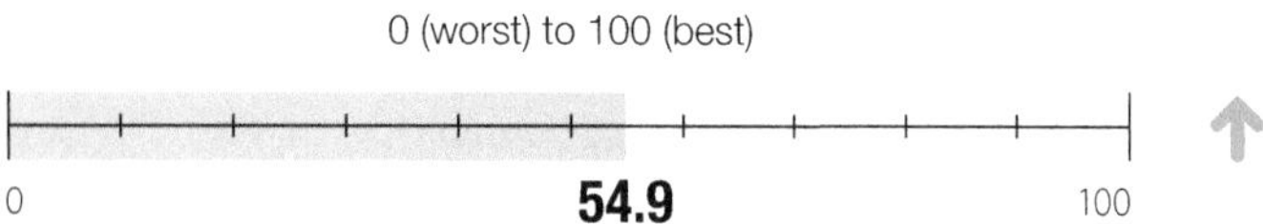

MISSING DATA IN SDG INDEX

Performance by Indicator

SDG1 – No Poverty	Value	Year	Rating	Trend
Poverty headcount ratio at $1.90/day (%)	53.8	2022	•	↓
Poverty headcount ratio at $3.20/day (%)	75.7	2022	•	↓
SDG2 – Zero Hunger				
Prevalence of undernourishment (%)	17.3	2019	•	↓
Prevalence of stunting in children under 5 years of age (%)	37.6	2015	•	→
Prevalence of wasting in children under 5 years of age (%)	4.9	2015	•	↑
Prevalence of obesity, BMI ≥ 30 (% of adult population)	8.2	2016	•	↑
Human Trophic Level (best 2–3 worst)	2.1	2017	•	↑
Cereal yield (tonnes per hectare of harvested land)	0.8	2018	•	↓
Sustainable Nitrogen Management Index (best 0–1.41 worst)	0.9	2015	•	↓
Exports of hazardous pesticides (tonnes per million population)	0.0	2019	•	•
SDG3 – Good Health and Well-Being				
Maternal mortality rate (per 100,000 live births)	241	2017	•	→
Neonatal mortality rate (per 1,000 live births)	27.3	2020	•	↗
Mortality rate, under-5 (per 1,000 live births)	71.5	2020	•	↗
Incidence of tuberculosis (per 100,000 population)	350.0	2020	•	→
New HIV infections (per 1,000 uninfected population)	0.7	2020	•	↑
Age-standardized death rate due to cardiovascular disease, cancer, diabetes, or chronic respiratory disease in adults aged 30–70 years (%)	22.3	2019	•	→
Age-standardized death rate attributable to household air pollution and ambient air pollution (per 100,000 population)	119	2016	•	•
Traffic deaths (per 100,000 population)	26.1	2019	•	↓
Life expectancy at birth (years)	63.1	2019	•	→
Adolescent fertility rate (births per 1,000 females aged 15 to 19)	163.0	2014	•	•
Births attended by skilled health personnel (%)	46.6	2016	•	•
Surviving infants who received 2 WHO-recommended vaccines (%)	44	2020	•	↓
Universal health coverage (UHC) index of service coverage (worst 0–100 best)	39	2019	•	→
Subjective well-being (average ladder score, worst 0–10 best)	3.8	2014	•	•
SDG4 – Quality Education				
Participation rate in pre-primary organized learning (% of children aged 4 to 6)	65.2	2016	•	•
Net primary enrollment rate (%)	81.6	2011	•	•
Lower secondary completion rate (%)	20.7	2011	•	•
Literacy rate (% of population aged 15 to 24)	77.4	2014	•	•
SDG5 – Gender Equality				
Demand for family planning satisfied by modern methods (% of females aged 15 to 49)	29.8	2016	•	•
Ratio of female-to-male mean years of education received (%)	62.5	2019	•	↓
Ratio of female-to-male labor force participation rate (%)	93.4	2020	•	↑
Seats held by women in national parliament (%)	30.0	2020	•	↓
SDG6 – Clean Water and Sanitation				
Population using at least basic drinking water services (%)	57.2	2020	•	→
Population using at least basic sanitation services (%)	51.7	2020	•	→
Freshwater withdrawal (% of available freshwater resources)	1.9	2018	•	•
Anthropogenic wastewater that receives treatment (%)	0.0	2018	•	•
Scarce water consumption embodied in imports (m^3 H_2O eq/capita)	493.2	2018	•	•
SDG7 – Affordable and Clean Energy				
Population with access to electricity (%)	45.7	2019	•	→
Population with access to clean fuels and technology for cooking (%)	49.6	2019	•	→
CO_2 emissions from fuel combustion per total electricity output ($MtCO_2$/TWh)	1.8	2019	•	↑
Share of renewable energy in total primary energy supply (%)	49.5	2019	•	↑
SDG8 – Decent Work and Economic Growth				
Adjusted GDP growth (%)	-9.2	2020	•	•
Victims of modern slavery (per 1,000 population)	7.2	2018	•	•
Adults with an account at a bank or other financial institution or with a mobile-money-service provider (% of population aged 15 or over)	29.3	2014	•	•
Unemployment rate (% of total labor force)	8.3	2022	•	↓
Fundamental labor rights are effectively guaranteed (worst 0–1 best)	0.5	2020	•	•
Fatal work-related accidents embodied in imports (per 100,000 population)	0.1	2015	•	↑

SDG9 – Industry, Innovation and Infrastructure	Value	Year	Rating	Trend
Population using the internet (%)	36.0	2020	•	↗
Mobile broadband subscriptions (per 100 population)	21.2	2019	•	→
Logistics Performance Index: Quality of trade and transport-related infrastructure (worst 1–5 best)	1.9	2018	•	↓
The Times Higher Education Universities Ranking: Average score of top 3 universities (worst 0–100 best)	* 0.0	2022	•	•
Articles published in academic journals (per 1,000 population)	0.0	2020	•	→
Expenditure on research and development (% of GDP)	0.0	2016	•	•
SDG10 – Reduced Inequalities				
Gini coefficient	51.3	2018	•	•
Palma ratio	3.4	2018	•	•
SDG11 – Sustainable Cities and Communities				
Proportion of urban population living in slums (%)	47.0	2018	•	↗
Annual mean concentration of particulate matter of less than 2.5 microns in diameter (PM2.5) (μg/m³)	32.3	2019	•	→
Access to improved water source, piped (% of urban population)	59.5	2020	•	→
Satisfaction with public transport (%)	32.0	2014	•	•
SDG12 – Responsible Consumption and Production				
Municipal solid waste (kg/capita/day)	0.5	2012	•	•
Electronic waste (kg/capita)	4.2	2019	•	•
Production-based SO_2 emissions (kg/capita)	1.8	2018	•	•
SO_2 emissions embodied in imports (kg/capita)	0.6	2018	•	•
Production-based nitrogen emissions (kg/capita)	5.1	2015	•	↑
Nitrogen emissions embodied in imports (kg/capita)	0.9	2015	•	↑
Exports of plastic waste (kg/capita)	0.0	2019	•	•
SDG13 – Climate Action				
CO_2 emissions from fossil fuel combustion and cement production (tCO_2/capita)	0.7	2020	•	↑
CO_2 emissions embodied in imports (tCO_2/capita)	0.2	2018	•	↑
CO_2 emissions embodied in fossil fuel exports (kg/capita)	116.0	2019	•	•
SDG14 – Life Below Water				
Mean area that is protected in marine sites important to biodiversity (%)	66.6	2020	•	→
Ocean Health Index: Clean Waters score (worst 0–100 best)	55.3	2020	•	↓
Fish caught from overexploited or collapsed stocks (% of total catch)	11.5	2018	•	↑
Fish caught by trawling or dredging (%)	26.8	2018	•	↓
Fish caught that are then discarded (%)	8.5	2018	•	→
Marine biodiversity threats embodied in imports (per million population)	0.2	2018	•	•
SDG15 – Life on Land				
Mean area that is protected in terrestrial sites important to biodiversity (%)	28.1	2020	•	→
Mean area that is protected in freshwater sites important to biodiversity (%)	42.8	2020	•	→
Red List Index of species survival (worst 0–1 best)	0.9	2021	•	↑
Permanent deforestation (% of forest area, 5-year average)	0.2	2020	•	→
Terrestrial and freshwater biodiversity threats embodied in imports (per million population)	0.6	2018	•	•
SDG16 – Peace, Justice and Strong Institutions				
Homicides (per 100,000 population)	4.9	2012	•	•
Unsentenced detainees (% of prison population)	48.0	2016	•	•
Population who feel safe walking alone at night in the city or area where they live (%)	46	2014	•	•
Property Rights (worst 1–7 best)	3.4	2020	•	↑
Birth registrations with civil authority (% of children under age 5)	25.0	2020	•	•
Corruption Perception Index (worst 0–100 best)	29	2021	•	↗
Children involved in child labor (% of population aged 5 to 14)	18.7	2019	•	•
Exports of major conventional weapons (TIV constant million USD per 100,000 population)	0.0	2020	•	•
Press Freedom Index (best 0–100 worst)	34.1	2021	•	↑
Access to and affordability of justice (worst 0–1 best)	0.5	2020	•	•
SDG17 – Partnerships for the Goals				
Government spending on health and education (% of GDP)	2.9	2019	•	↓
For high-income and all OECD DAC countries: International concessional public finance, including official development assistance (% of GNI)	NA	NA	•	•
Other countries: Government revenue excluding grants (% of GDP)	20.3	2019	•	→
Corporate Tax Haven Score (best 0–100 worst)	* 0.0	2019	•	•
Statistical Performance Index (worst 0–100 best)	54.9	2019	•	↑

* Imputed data point

ANTIGUA AND BARBUDA

Latin America and the Caribbean

OVERALL PERFORMANCE

COUNTRY RANKING

ANTIGUA AND BARBUDA

NA /163

COUNTRY SCORE

REGIONAL AVERAGE: 69.5

AVERAGE PERFORMANCE BY SDG

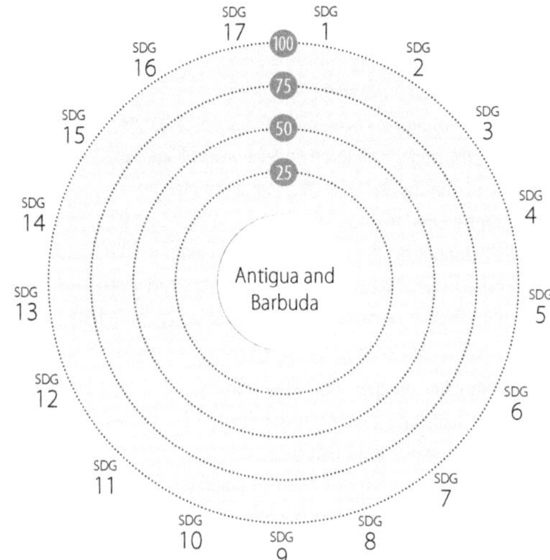

SDG DASHBOARDS AND TRENDS

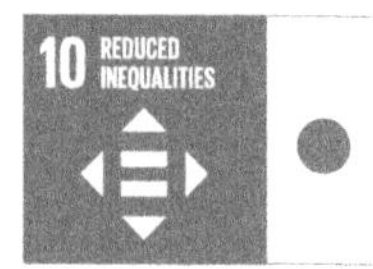

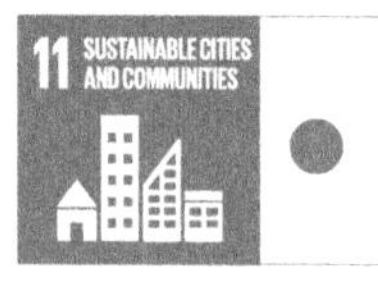

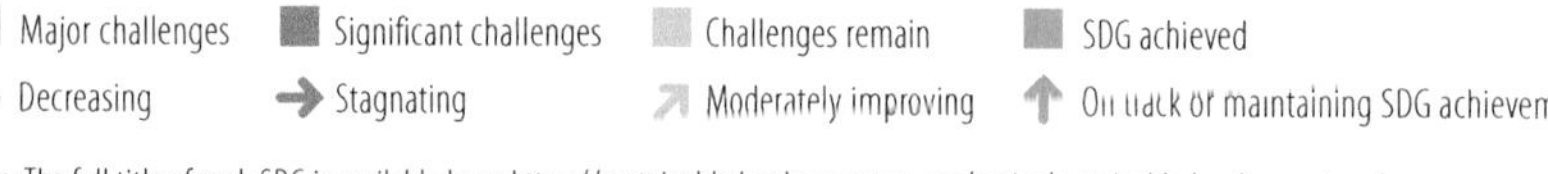

Note: The full title of each SDG is available here: https://sustainabledevelopment.un.org/topics/sustainabledevelopmentgoals

INTERNATIONAL SPILLOVER INDEX

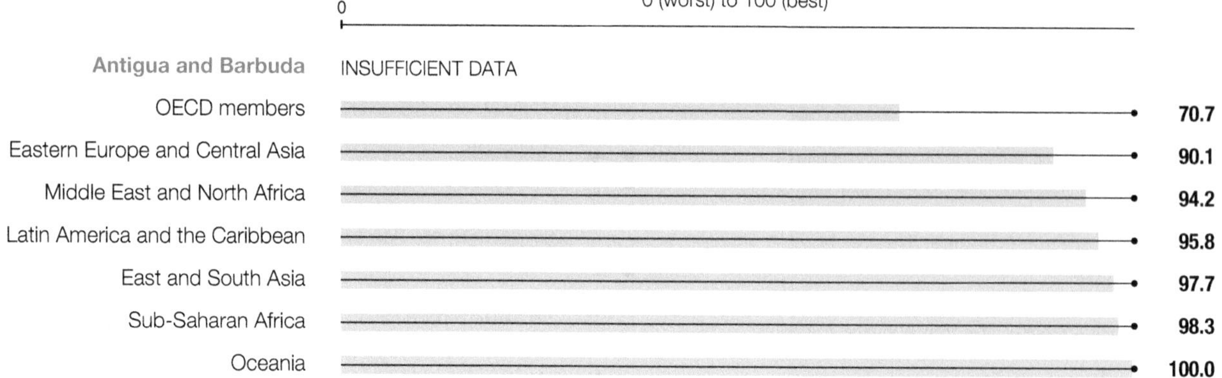

STATISTICAL PERFORMANCE INDEX

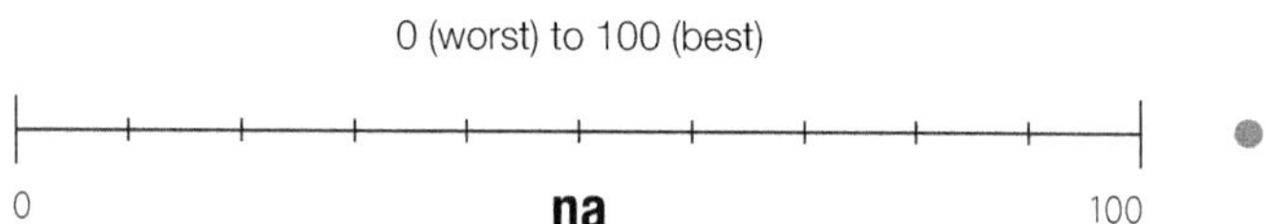

MISSING DATA IN SDG INDEX

35%

ANTIGUA AND BARBUDA

Performance by Indicator

SDG1 – No Poverty

Indicator		Value	Year	Rating	Trend
Poverty headcount ratio at \$1.90/day (%)		NA	NA	●	●
Poverty headcount ratio at \$3.20/day (%)		NA	NA	●	●

SDG2 – Zero Hunger

Indicator		Value	Year	Rating	Trend
Prevalence of undernourishment (%)	*	1.2	2019	●	●
Prevalence of stunting in children under 5 years of age (%)	*	2.6	2019	●	↑
Prevalence of wasting in children under 5 years of age (%)	*	0.7	2019	●	↑
Prevalence of obesity, BMI ≥ 30 (% of adult population)		18.9	2016	●	↓
Human Trophic Level (best 2–3 worst)		2.4	2017	●	→
Cereal yield (tonnes per hectare of harvested land)		1.6	2018	●	→
Sustainable Nitrogen Management Index (best 0–1.41 worst)		1.3	2015	●	→
Exports of hazardous pesticides (tonnes per million population)		NA	NA	●	●

SDG3 – Good Health and Well-Being

Indicator		Value	Year	Rating	Trend
Maternal mortality rate (per 100,000 live births)		42	2017	●	↑
Neonatal mortality rate (per 1,000 live births)		3.5	2020	●	↑
Mortality rate, under-5 (per 1,000 live births)		6.4	2020	●	↑
Incidence of tuberculosis (per 100,000 population)		2.3	2020	●	↑
New HIV infections (per 1,000 uninfected population)		NA	NA	●	●
Age-standardized death rate due to cardiovascular disease, cancer, diabetes, or chronic respiratory disease in adults aged 30–70 years (%)		17.6	2019	●	↗
Age-standardized death rate attributable to household air pollution and ambient air pollution (per 100,000 population)		30	2016	●	●
Traffic deaths (per 100,000 population)		0.0	2019	●	↑
Life expectancy at birth (years)		76.5	2019	●	→
Adolescent fertility rate (births per 1,000 females aged 15 to 19)		27.7	2018	●	↑
Births attended by skilled health personnel (%)		100.0	2017	●	↑
Surviving infants who received 2 WHO-recommended vaccines (%)		89	2020	●	↓
Universal health coverage (UHC) index of service coverage (worst 0–100 best)		72	2019	●	→
Subjective well-being (average ladder score, worst 0–10 best)		NA	NA	●	●

SDG4 – Quality Education

Indicator		Value	Year	Rating	Trend
Participation rate in pre-primary organized learning (% of children aged 4 to 6)		91.1	2018	●	●
Net primary enrollment rate (%)		99.3	2018	●	●
Lower secondary completion rate (%)		98.6	2018	●	↑
Literacy rate (% of population aged 15 to 24)		NA	NA	●	●

SDG5 – Gender Equality

Indicator		Value	Year	Rating	Trend
Demand for family planning satisfied by modern methods (% of females aged 15 to 49)		NA	NA	●	●
Ratio of female-to-male mean years of education received (%)		NA	NA	●	●
Ratio of female-to-male labor force participation rate (%)		NA	NA	●	●
Seats held by women in national parliament (%)		11.1	2020	●	→

SDG6 – Clean Water and Sanitation

Indicator		Value	Year	Rating	Trend
Population using at least basic drinking water services (%)		96.7	2017	●	●
Population using at least basic sanitation services (%)		87.5	2017	●	●
Freshwater withdrawal (% of available freshwater resources)		8.5	2018	●	●
Anthropogenic wastewater that receives treatment (%)		1.3	2018	●	●
Scarce water consumption embodied in imports (m^3 H_2O eq/capita)		NA	NA	●	●

SDG7 – Affordable and Clean Energy

Indicator		Value	Year	Rating	Trend
Population with access to electricity (%)		100.0	2019	●	↑
Population with access to clean fuels and technology for cooking (%)		100.0	2019	●	↑
CO_2 emissions from fuel combustion per total electricity output ($MtCO_2$/TWh)		1.6	2019	●	→
Share of renewable energy in total primary energy supply (%)		NA	NA	●	●

SDG8 – Decent Work and Economic Growth

Indicator		Value	Year	Rating	Trend
Adjusted GDP growth (%)		-6.3	2020	●	●
Victims of modern slavery (per 1,000 population)		NA	NA	●	●
Adults with an account at a bank or other financial institution or with a mobile-money-service provider (% of population aged 15 or over)		NA	NA	●	●
Unemployment rate (% of total labor force)		NA	NA	●	●
Fundamental labor rights are effectively guaranteed (worst 0–1 best)		0.8	2020	●	↑
Fatal work-related accidents embodied in imports (per 100,000 population)		0.6	2015	●	↑

SDG9 – Industry, Innovation and Infrastructure

Indicator		Value	Year	Rating	Trend
Population using the internet (%)		73.0	2016	●	●
Mobile broadband subscriptions (per 100 population)		49.4	2019	●	↑
Logistics Performance Index: Quality of trade and transport-related infrastructure (worst 1–5 best)		NA	NA	●	●
The Times Higher Education Universities Ranking: Average score of top 3 universities (worst 0–100 best)	*	0.0	2022	●	●
Articles published in academic journals (per 1,000 population)		0.2	2020	●	↗
Expenditure on research and development (% of GDP)		NA	NA	●	●

SDG10 – Reduced Inequalities

Indicator		Value	Year	Rating	Trend
Gini coefficient		NA	NA	●	●
Palma ratio		NA	NA	●	●

SDG11 – Sustainable Cities and Communities

Indicator		Value	Year	Rating	Trend
Proportion of urban population living in slums (%)		NA	NA	●	●
Annual mean concentration of particulate matter of less than 2.5 microns in diameter (PM2.5) (μg/m^3)		17.6	2019	●	↗
Access to improved water source, piped (% of urban population)		NA	NA	●	●
Satisfaction with public transport (%)		NA	NA	●	●

SDG12 – Responsible Consumption and Production

Indicator		Value	Year	Rating	Trend
Municipal solid waste (kg/capita/day)		0.9	2012	●	●
Electronic waste (kg/capita)		12.7	2019	●	●
Production-based SO_2 emissions (kg/capita)		NA	NA	●	●
SO_2 emissions embodied in imports (kg/capita)		NA	NA	●	●
Production-based nitrogen emissions (kg/capita)		5.7	2015	●	↑
Nitrogen emissions embodied in imports (kg/capita)		12.2	2015	●	→
Exports of plastic waste (kg/capita)		0.3	2018	●	●

SDG13 – Climate Action

Indicator		Value	Year	Rating	Trend
CO_2 emissions from fossil fuel combustion and cement production (tCO_2/capita)		4.4	2020	●	↗
CO_2 emissions embodied in imports (tCO_2/capita)		NA	NA	●	●
CO_2 emissions embodied in fossil fuel exports (kg/capita)		0.0	2020	●	●

SDG14 – Life Below Water

Indicator		Value	Year	Rating	Trend
Mean area that is protected in marine sites important to biodiversity (%)		29.1	2020	●	→
Ocean Health Index: Clean Waters score (worst 0–100 best)		61.7	2020	●	↓
Fish caught from overexploited or collapsed stocks (% of total catch)		20.7	2018	●	↑
Fish caught by trawling or dredging (%)		0.0	2018	●	↑
Fish caught that are then discarded (%)		0.0	2018	●	↑
Marine biodiversity threats embodied in imports (per million population)		0.9	2018	●	●

SDG15 – Life on Land

Indicator		Value	Year	Rating	Trend
Mean area that is protected in terrestrial sites important to biodiversity (%)		26.9	2020	●	→
Mean area that is protected in freshwater sites important to biodiversity (%)		NA	NA	●	●
Red List Index of species survival (worst 0–1 best)		0.9	2021	●	→
Permanent deforestation (% of forest area, 5-year average)		0.2	2020	●	↓
Terrestrial and freshwater biodiversity threats embodied in imports (per million population)		0.3	2018	●	●

SDG16 – Peace, Justice and Strong Institutions

Indicator		Value	Year	Rating	Trend
Homicides (per 100,000 population)		3.1	2019	●	●
Unsentenced detainees (% of prison population)		38.5	2016	●	●
Population who feel safe walking alone at night in the city or area where they live (%)		NA	NA	●	●
Property Rights (worst 1–7 best)		NA	NA	●	●
Birth registrations with civil authority (% of children under age 5)		NA	NA	●	●
Corruption Perception Index (worst 0–100 best)		NA	NA	●	●
Children involved in child labor (% of population aged 5 to 14)		NA	NA	●	●
Exports of major conventional weapons (TIV constant million USD per 100,000 population)	*	0.0	2020	●	●
Press Freedom Index (best 0–100 worst)		NA	NA	●	●
Access to and affordability of justice (worst 0–1 best)		0.7	2020	●	↑

SDG17 – Partnerships for the Goals

Indicator		Value	Year	Rating	Trend
Government spending on health and education (% of GDP)		5.9	2020	●	→
For high-income and all OECD DAC countries: International concessional public finance, including official development assistance (% of GNI)		NA	NA	●	●
Other countries: Government revenue excluding grants (% of GDP)		NA	NA	●	●
Corporate Tax Haven Score (best 0–100 worst)	*	0.0	2019	●	●
Statistical Performance Index (worst 0–100 best)		NA	NA	●	●

* Imputed data point

5. Country Profiles

ARGENTINA

Latin America and the Caribbean

OVERALL PERFORMANCE

COUNTRY RANKING

ARGENTINA

54/163

COUNTRY SCORE

REGIONAL AVERAGE: 69.5

AVERAGE PERFORMANCE BY SDG

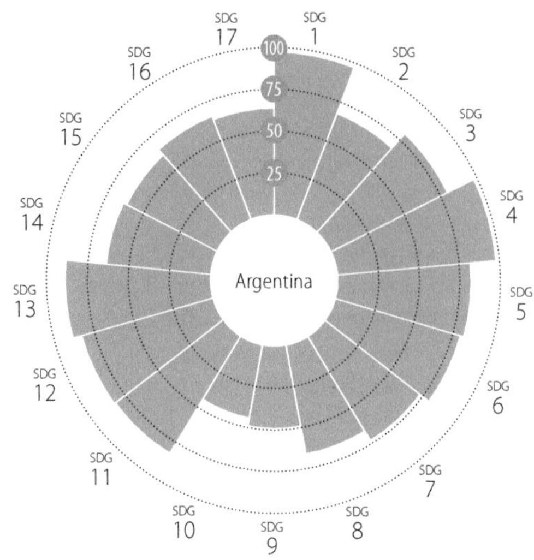

SDG DASHBOARDS AND TRENDS

Major challenges | Significant challenges | Challenges remain | SDG achieved | Information unavailable

Decreasing | Stagnating | Moderately improving | On track or maintaining SDG achievement | Information unavailable

Note: The full title of each SDG is available here: https://sustainabledevelopment.un.org/topics/sustainabledevelopmentgoals

INTERNATIONAL SPILLOVER INDEX

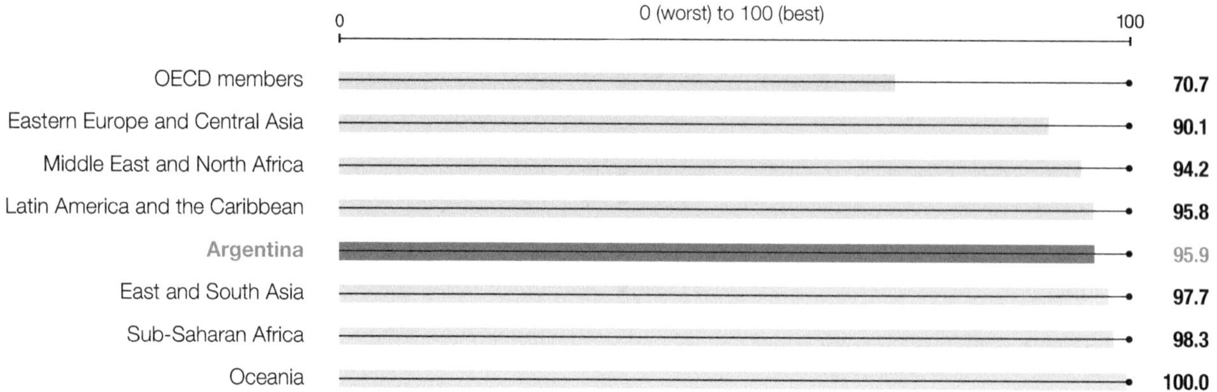

STATISTICAL PERFORMANCE INDEX

0 (worst) to 100 (best)

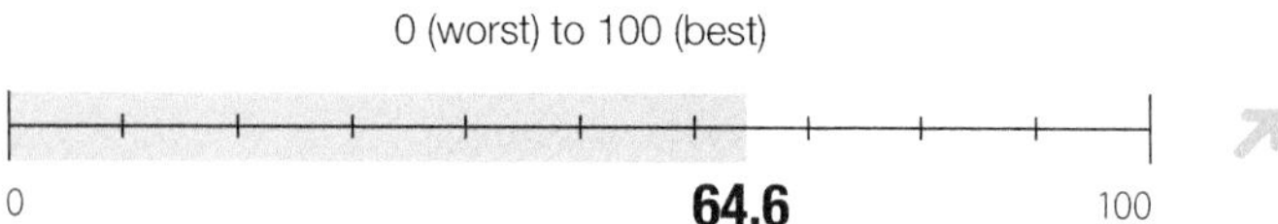

MISSING DATA IN SDG INDEX

2%

SDG1 – No Poverty	Value	Year	Rating	Trend
Poverty headcount ratio at $1.90/day (%)	0.7	2022	●	↑
Poverty headcount ratio at $3.20/day (%)	3.0	2022	●	→

SDG2 – Zero Hunger	Value	Year	Rating	Trend
Prevalence of undernourishment (%)	3.9	2019	●	↑
Prevalence of stunting in children under 5 years of age (%)	7.9	2019	●	↑
Prevalence of wasting in children under 5 years of age (%)	1.6	2019	●	↑
Prevalence of obesity, BMI ≥ 30 (% of adult population)	28.3	2016	●	↓
Human Trophic Level (best 2–3 worst)	2.4	2017	●	→
Cereal yield (tonnes per hectare of harvested land)	4.7	2018	●	↑
Sustainable Nitrogen Management Index (best 0–1.41 worst)	0.3	2015	●	↑
Exports of hazardous pesticides (tonnes per million population)	1.1	2019	●	●

SDG3 – Good Health and Well-Being	Value	Year	Rating	Trend
Maternal mortality rate (per 100,000 live births)	39	2017	●	↑
Neonatal mortality rate (per 1,000 live births)	4.6	2020	●	↑
Mortality rate, under-5 (per 1,000 live births)	8.6	2020	●	↑
Incidence of tuberculosis (per 100,000 population)	31.0	2020	●	→
New HIV infections (per 1,000 uninfected population)	0.1	2020	●	↑
Age-standardized death rate due to cardiovascular disease, cancer, diabetes, or chronic respiratory disease in adults aged 30–70 years (%)	15.7	2019	●	↑
Age-standardized death rate attributable to household air pollution and ambient air pollution (per 100,000 population)	27	2016	●	●
Traffic deaths (per 100,000 population)	14.1	2019	●	↓
Life expectancy at birth (years)	76.6	2019	●	→
Adolescent fertility rate (births per 1,000 females aged 15 to 19)	49.9	2018	●	↑
Births attended by skilled health personnel (%)	93.9	2017	●	↓
Surviving infants who received 2 WHO-recommended vaccines (%)	74	2020	●	↓
Universal health coverage (UHC) index of service coverage (worst 0–100 best)	73	2019	●	↓
Subjective well-being (average ladder score, worst 0–10 best)	5.9	2021	●	↓

SDG4 – Quality Education	Value	Year	Rating	Trend
Participation rate in pre-primary organized learning (% of children aged 4 to 6)	99.3	2019	●	↑
Net primary enrollment rate (%)	99.6	2019	●	↑
Lower secondary completion rate (%)	93.5	2019	●	↑
Literacy rate (% of population aged 15 to 24)	99.5	2018	●	↑

SDG5 – Gender Equality	Value	Year	Rating	Trend
Demand for family planning satisfied by modern methods (% of females aged 15 to 49)	NA	NA	●	●
Ratio of female-to-male mean years of education received (%)	103.7	2019	●	↑
Ratio of female-to-male labor force participation rate (%)	70.5	2020	●	↑
Seats held by women in national parliament (%)	40.9	2020	●	↑

SDG6 – Clean Water and Sanitation	Value	Year	Rating	Trend
Population using at least basic drinking water services (%)	99.0	2016	●	●
Population using at least basic sanitation services (%)	95.4	2016	●	●
Freshwater withdrawal (% of available freshwater resources)	10.5	2018	●	●
Anthropogenic wastewater that receives treatment (%)	5.9	2018	●	●
Scarce water consumption embodied in imports (m^3 H_2O eq/capita)	491.6	2018	●	●

SDG7 – Affordable and Clean Energy	Value	Year	Rating	Trend
Population with access to electricity (%)	100.0	2019	●	↑
Population with access to clean fuels and technology for cooking (%)	99.8	2019	●	↑
CO_2 emissions from fuel combustion per total electricity output ($MtCO_2$/TWh)	1.3	2019	●	↗
Share of renewable energy in total primary energy supply (%)	8.6	2019	●	→

SDG8 – Decent Work and Economic Growth	Value	Year	Rating	Trend
Adjusted GDP growth (%)	-7.5	2020	●	●
Victims of modern slavery (per 1,000 population)	1.3	2018	●	●
Adults with an account at a bank or other financial institution or with a mobile-money-service provider (% of population aged 15 or over)	48.7	2017	●	↓
Unemployment rate (% of total labor force)	10.6	2022	●	↓
Fundamental labor rights are effectively guaranteed (worst 0–1 best)	0.6	2020	●	↓
Fatal work-related accidents embodied in imports (per 100,000 population)	0.3	2015	●	↑

SDG9 – Industry, Innovation and Infrastructure	Value	Year	Rating	Trend
Population using the internet (%)	85.5	2020	●	↑
Mobile broadband subscriptions (per 100 population)	72.0	2019	●	↓
Logistics Performance Index: Quality of trade and transport-related infrastructure (worst 1–5 best)	2.8	2018	●	↓
The Times Higher Education Universities Ranking: Average score of top 3 universities (worst 0–100 best)	19.2	2022	●	●
Articles published in academic journals (per 1,000 population)	0.3	2020	●	→
Expenditure on research and development (% of GDP)	0.5	2018	●	↓

SDG10 – Reduced Inequalities	Value	Year	Rating	Trend
Gini coefficient	42.9	2019	●	↓
Palma ratio	2.0	2018	●	●

SDG11 – Sustainable Cities and Communities	Value	Year	Rating	Trend
Proportion of urban population living in slums (%)	14.7	2018	●	↗
Annual mean concentration of particulate matter of less than 2.5 microns in diameter (PM2.5) (μg/m^3)	12.6	2019	●	↑
Access to improved water source, piped (% of urban population)	98.9	2020	●	↑
Satisfaction with public transport (%)	54.0	2021	●	↓

SDG12 – Responsible Consumption and Production	Value	Year	Rating	Trend
Municipal solid waste (kg/capita/day)	1.2	2014	●	●
Electronic waste (kg/capita)	10.3	2019	●	●
Production-based SO_2 emissions (kg/capita)	11.5	2018	●	●
SO_2 emissions embodied in imports (kg/capita)	1.9	2018	●	●
Production-based nitrogen emissions (kg/capita)	36.1	2015	●	↓
Nitrogen emissions embodied in imports (kg/capita)	2.1	2015	●	↑
Exports of plastic waste (kg/capita)	0.1	2017	●	●

SDG13 – Climate Action	Value	Year	Rating	Trend
CO_2 emissions from fossil fuel combustion and cement production (tCO_2/capita)	3.5	2020	●	↑
CO_2 emissions embodied in imports (tCO_2/capita)	0.6	2018	●	↑
CO_2 emissions embodied in fossil fuel exports (kg/capita)	204.5	2020	●	●

SDG14 – Life Below Water	Value	Year	Rating	Trend
Mean area that is protected in marine sites important to biodiversity (%)	42.3	2020	●	→
Ocean Health Index: Clean Waters score (worst 0–100 best)	82.2	2020	●	↑
Fish caught from overexploited or collapsed stocks (% of total catch)	61.0	2018	●	↓
Fish caught by trawling or dredging (%)	34.4	2018	●	↓
Fish caught that are then discarded (%)	6.2	2018	●	→
Marine biodiversity threats embodied in imports (per million population)	0.0	2018	●	●

SDG15 – Life on Land	Value	Year	Rating	Trend
Mean area that is protected in terrestrial sites important to biodiversity (%)	32.1	2020	●	→
Mean area that is protected in freshwater sites important to biodiversity (%)	42.5	2020	●	→
Red List Index of species survival (worst 0–1 best)	0.8	2021	●	↓
Permanent deforestation (% of forest area, 5-year average)	0.4	2020	●	↗
Terrestrial and freshwater biodiversity threats embodied in imports (per million population)	0.5	2018	●	●

SDG16 – Peace, Justice and Strong Institutions	Value	Year	Rating	Trend
Homicides (per 100,000 population)	5.1	2019	●	↑
Unsentenced detainees (% of prison population)	45.4	2018	●	↑
Population who feel safe walking alone at night in the city or area where they live (%)	51	2021	●	↗
Property Rights (worst 1–7 best)	3.4	2020	●	↓
Birth registrations with civil authority (% of children under age 5)	99.5	2020	●	●
Corruption Perception Index (worst 0–100 best)	38	2021	●	↗
Children involved in child labor (% of population aged 5 to 14)	NA	NA	●	●
Exports of major conventional weapons (TIV constant million USD per 100,000 population)	0.0	2020	●	●
Press Freedom Index (best 0–100 worst)	29.0	2021	●	↑
Access to and affordability of justice (worst 0–1 best)	0.7	2020	●	↑

SDG17 – Partnerships for the Goals	Value	Year	Rating	Trend
Government spending on health and education (% of GDP)	10.7	2019	●	↑
For high-income and all OECD DAC countries: International concessional public finance, including official development assistance (% of GNI)	NA	NA	●	●
Other countries: Government revenue excluding grants (% of GDP)	18.5	2019	●	↓
Corporate Tax Haven Score (best 0–100 worst)	* 0.0	2019	●	●
Statistical Performance Index (worst 0–100 best)	64.6	2019	●	↗

* Imputed data point

ARMENIA

Eastern Europe and Central Asia

OVERALL PERFORMANCE

COUNTRY RANKING

ARMENIA

66/163

COUNTRY SCORE

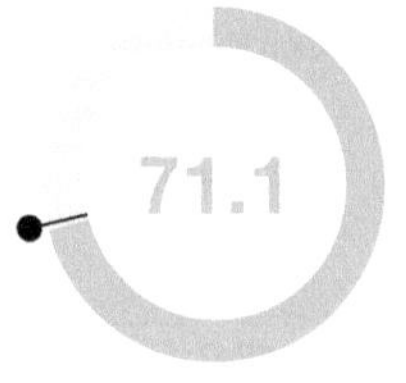

REGIONAL AVERAGE: 71.6

AVERAGE PERFORMANCE BY SDG

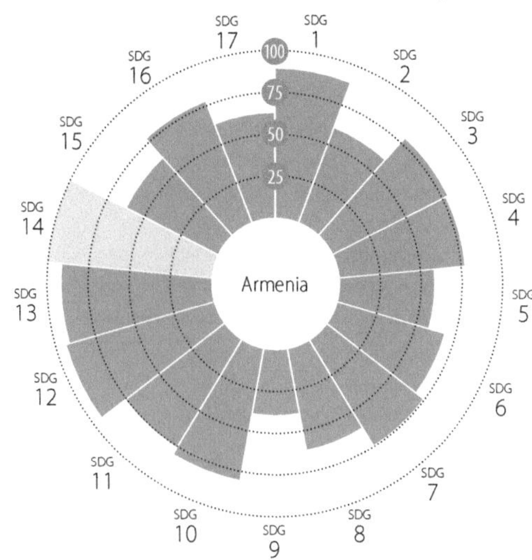

SDG DASHBOARDS AND TRENDS

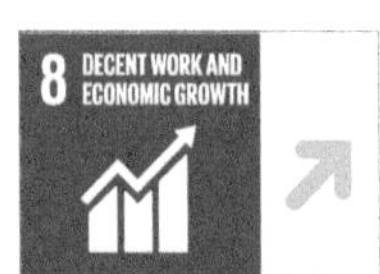

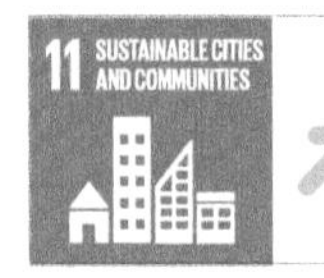

Note: The full title of each SDG is available here: https://sustainabledevelopment.un.org/topics/sustainabledevelopmentgoals

INTERNATIONAL SPILLOVER INDEX

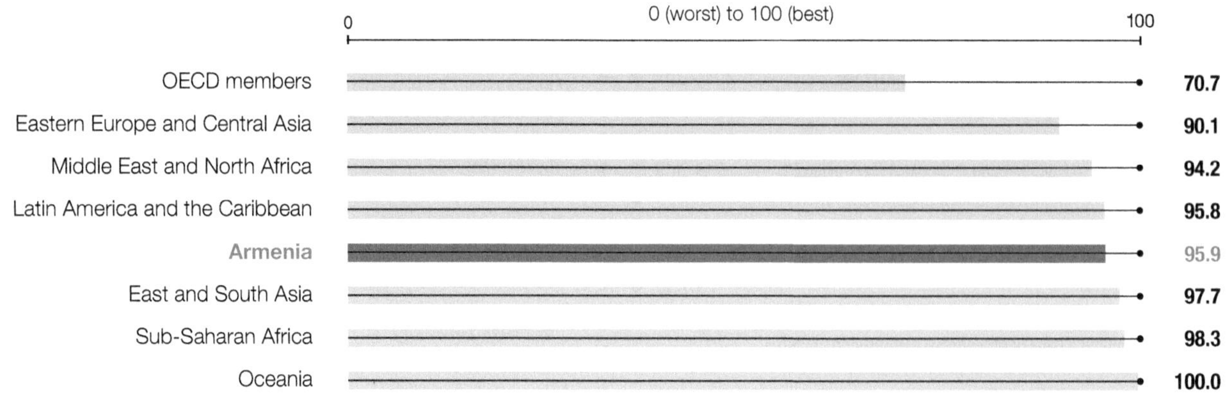

STATISTICAL PERFORMANCE INDEX

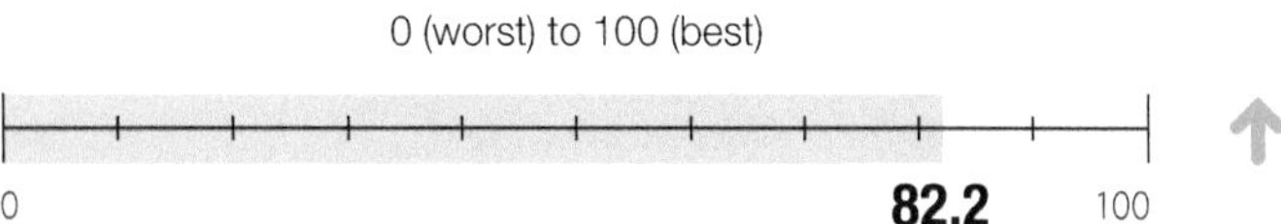

MISSING DATA IN SDG INDEX

3%

ARMENIA

SDG1 – No Poverty	Value	Year	Rating	Trend
Poverty headcount ratio at $1.90/day (%)	1.1	2022	●	↑
Poverty headcount ratio at $3.20/day (%)	10.7	2022	●	→
SDG2 – Zero Hunger				
Prevalence of undernourishment (%)	3.4	2019	●	↑
Prevalence of stunting in children under 5 years of age (%)	9.4	2016	●	↗
Prevalence of wasting in children under 5 years of age (%)	4.4	2016	●	↑
Prevalence of obesity, BMI ≥ 30 (% of adult population)	20.2	2016	●	↓
Human Trophic Level (best 2–3 worst)	2.3	2017	●	→
Cereal yield (tonnes per hectare of harvested land)	2.6	2018	●	↑
Sustainable Nitrogen Management Index (best 0–1.41 worst)	0.6	2015	●	↓
Exports of hazardous pesticides (tonnes per million population)	NA	NA	●	●
SDG3 – Good Health and Well-Being				
Maternal mortality rate (per 100,000 live births)	26	2017	●	↑
Neonatal mortality rate (per 1,000 live births)	5.7	2020	●	↑
Mortality rate, under-5 (per 1,000 live births)	10.9	2020	●	↑
Incidence of tuberculosis (per 100,000 population)	23.0	2020	●	↑
New HIV infections (per 1,000 uninfected population)	0.1	2020	●	↑
Age-standardized death rate due to cardiovascular disease, cancer, diabetes, or chronic respiratory disease in adults aged 30–70 years (%)	19.9	2019	●	↑
Age-standardized death rate attributable to household air pollution and ambient air pollution (per 100,000 population)	55	2016	●	●
Traffic deaths (per 100,000 population)	20.0	2019	●	↓
Life expectancy at birth (years)	76.0	2019	●	↑
Adolescent fertility rate (births per 1,000 females aged 15 to 19)	18.9	2018	●	↑
Births attended by skilled health personnel (%)	99.8	2016	●	●
Surviving infants who received 2 WHO-recommended vaccines (%)	91	2020	●	↑
Universal health coverage (UHC) index of service coverage (worst 0–100 best)	69	2019	●	↑
Subjective well-being (average ladder score, worst 0–10 best)	5.3	2021	●	↑
SDG4 – Quality Education				
Participation rate in pre-primary organized learning (% of children aged 4 to 6)	62.9	2020	●	↑
Net primary enrollment rate (%)	89.5	2020	●	↓
Lower secondary completion rate (%)	90.1	2020	●	↑
Literacy rate (% of population aged 15 to 24)	99.9	2020	●	●
SDG5 – Gender Equality				
Demand for family planning satisfied by modern methods (% of females aged 15 to 49)	40.2	2016	●	●
Ratio of female-to-male mean years of education received (%)	100.0	2019	●	↑
Ratio of female-to-male labor force participation rate (%)	67.2	2020	●	↓
Seats held by women in national parliament (%)	23.5	2020	●	↑
SDG6 – Clean Water and Sanitation				
Population using at least basic drinking water services (%)	100.0	2020	●	↑
Population using at least basic sanitation services (%)	93.9	2020	●	↑
Freshwater withdrawal (% of available freshwater resources)	54.8	2018	●	●
Anthropogenic wastewater that receives treatment (%)	8.8	2018	●	●
Scarce water consumption embodied in imports (m^3 H_2O eq/capita)	1556.1	2018	●	●
SDG7 – Affordable and Clean Energy				
Population with access to electricity (%)	100.0	2019	●	↑
Population with access to clean fuels and technology for cooking (%)	98.1	2019	●	↑
CO_2 emissions from fuel combustion per total electricity output ($MtCO_2/TWh$)	0.9	2019	●	↑
Share of renewable energy in total primary energy supply (%)	8.8	2019	●	→
SDG8 – Decent Work and Economic Growth				
Adjusted GDP growth (%)	-1.1	2020	●	●
Victims of modern slavery (per 1,000 population)	5.3	2018	●	●
Adults with an account at a bank or other financial institution or with a mobile-money-service provider (% of population aged 15 or over)	47.8	2017	●	↑
Unemployment rate (% of total labor force)	20.8	2022	●	↓
Fundamental labor rights are effectively guaranteed (worst 0–1 best)	NA	NA	●	●
Fatal work-related accidents embodied in imports (per 100,000 population)	0.1	2015	●	↑

SDG9 – Industry, Innovation and Infrastructure	Value	Year	Rating	Trend
Population using the internet (%)	76.5	2020	●	↑
Mobile broadband subscriptions (per 100 population)	78.8	2019	●	↑
Logistics Performance Index: Quality of trade and transport-related infrastructure (worst 1–5 best)	2.5	2018	●	↗
The Times Higher Education Universities Ranking: Average score of top 3 universities (worst 0–100 best)	* 0.0	2022	●	●
Articles published in academic journals (per 1,000 population)	0.4	2020	●	→
Expenditure on research and development (% of GDP)	0.2	2018	●	↓
SDG10 – Reduced Inequalities				
Gini coefficient	29.9	2019	●	↑
Palma ratio	1.4	2018	●	●
SDG11 – Sustainable Cities and Communities				
Proportion of urban population living in slums (%)	8.2	2018	●	↑
Annual mean concentration of particulate matter of less than 2.5 microns in diameter (PM2.5) (μg/m^3)	32.2	2019	●	→
Access to improved water source, piped (% of urban population)	100.0	2020	●	↑
Satisfaction with public transport (%)	47.0	2021	●	↓
SDG12 – Responsible Consumption and Production				
Municipal solid waste (kg/capita/day)	0.5	2014	●	●
Electronic waste (kg/capita)	5.8	2019	●	●
Production-based SO_2 emissions (kg/capita)	2.6	2018	●	●
SO_2 emissions embodied in imports (kg/capita)	1.5	2018	●	●
Production-based nitrogen emissions (kg/capita)	7.7	2015	●	↑
Nitrogen emissions embodied in imports (kg/capita)	1.0	2015	●	↑
Exports of plastic waste (kg/capita)	0.0	2021	●	●
SDG13 – Climate Action				
CO_2 emissions from fossil fuel combustion and cement production (tCO_2/capita)	2.0	2020	●	↑
CO_2 emissions embodied in imports (tCO_2/capita)	0.6	2018	●	↓
CO_2 emissions embodied in fossil fuel exports (kg/capita)	0.0	2020	●	●
SDG14 – Life Below Water				
Mean area that is protected in marine sites important to biodiversity (%)	NA	NA	●	●
Ocean Health Index: Clean Waters score (worst 0–100 best)	NA	NA	●	●
Fish caught from overexploited or collapsed stocks (% of total catch)	NA	NA	●	●
Fish caught by trawling or dredging (%)	NA	NA	●	●
Fish caught that are then discarded (%)	NA	NA	●	●
Marine biodiversity threats embodied in imports (per million population)	0.0	2018	●	●
SDG15 – Life on Land				
Mean area that is protected in terrestrial sites important to biodiversity (%)	22.6	2020	●	→
Mean area that is protected in freshwater sites important to biodiversity (%)	30.5	2020	●	→
Red List Index of species survival (worst 0–1 best)	0.8	2021	●	→
Permanent deforestation (% of forest area, 5-year average)	0.0	2020	●	↑
Terrestrial and freshwater biodiversity threats embodied in imports (per million population)	0.1	2018	●	●
SDG16 – Peace, Justice and Strong Institutions				
Homicides (per 100,000 population)	1.8	2020	●	↑
Unsentenced detainees (% of prison population)	45.8	2019	●	↓
Population who feel safe walking alone at night in the city or area where they live (%)	82	2021	●	↑
Property Rights (worst 1–7 best)	4.9	2020	●	↑
Birth registrations with civil authority (% of children under age 5)	98.7	2020	●	●
Corruption Perception Index (worst 0–100 best)	49	2021	●	↑
Children involved in child labor (% of population aged 5 to 14)	4.1	2019	●	●
Exports of major conventional weapons (TIV constant million USD per 100,000 population)	0.0	2020	●	●
Press Freedom Index (best 0–100 worst)	28.8	2021	●	↑
Access to and affordability of justice (worst 0–1 best)	NA	NA	●	●
SDG17 – Partnerships for the Goals				
Government spending on health and education (% of GDP)	4.1	2020	●	↓
For high-income and all OECD DAC countries: International concessional public finance, including official development assistance (% of GNI)	NA	NA	●	●
Other countries: Government revenue excluding grants (% of GDP)	23.9	2019	●	→
Corporate Tax Haven Score (best 0–100 worst)	* 0.0	2019	●	●
Statistical Performance Index (worst 0–100 best)	82.2	2019	●	↑

* Imputed data point

AUSTRALIA

OECD Countries

OVERALL PERFORMANCE

COUNTRY RANKING

AUSTRALIA

38/163

COUNTRY SCORE

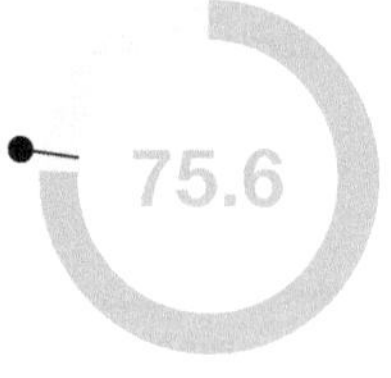

REGIONAL AVERAGE: 77.2

AVERAGE PERFORMANCE BY SDG

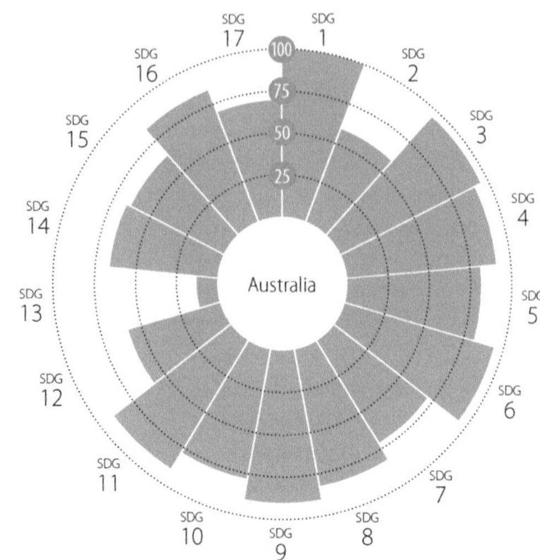

SDG DASHBOARDS AND TRENDS

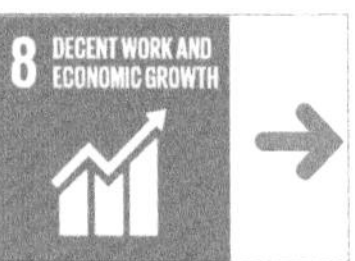

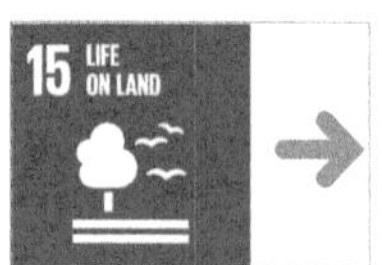

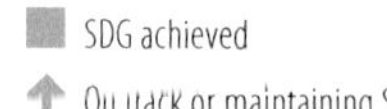

Major challenges | Significant challenges | Challenges remain | SDG achieved | Information unavailable

Decreasing | Stagnating | Moderately improving | On track or maintaining SDG achievement | Information unavailable

Note: The full title of each SDG is available here: https://sustainabledevelopment.un.org/topics/sustainabledevelopmentgoals

INTERNATIONAL SPILLOVER INDEX

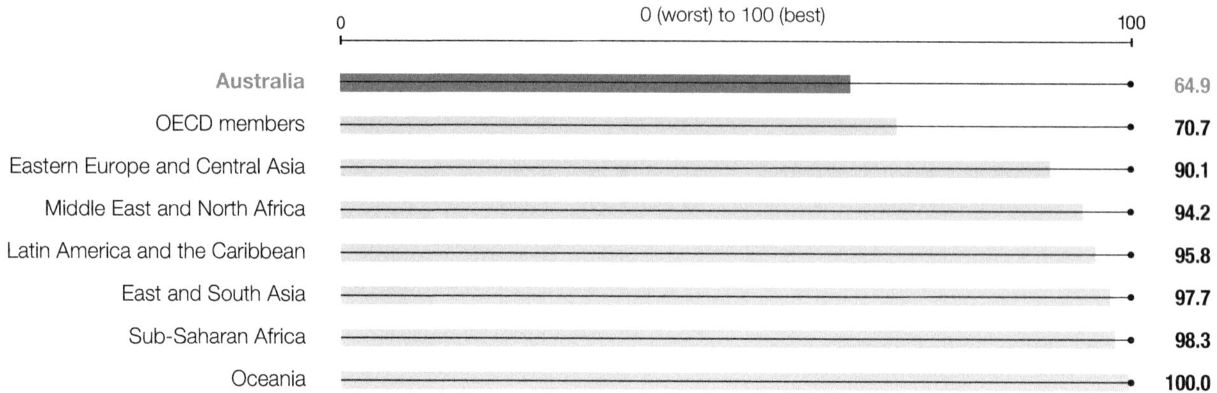

STATISTICAL PERFORMANCE INDEX

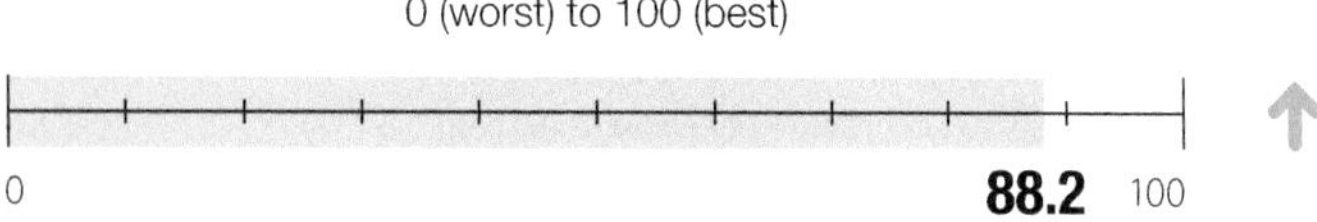

MISSING DATA IN SDG INDEX

1%

SDG1 – No Poverty	Value	Year	Rating	Trend
Poverty headcount ratio at $1.90/day (%)	0.2	2022	●	↑
Poverty headcount ratio at $3.20/day (%)	0.3	2022	●	↑
Poverty rate after taxes and transfers (%)	12.4	2018	●	↓

SDG2 – Zero Hunger	Value	Year	Rating	Trend
Prevalence of undernourishment (%)	2.5	2019	●	↑
Prevalence of stunting in children under 5 years of age (%)	2.0	2007	●	↑
Prevalence of wasting in children under 5 years of age (%)	0.0	2007	●	↑
Prevalence of obesity, BMI ≥ 30 (% of adult population)	29.0	2016	●	↓
Human Trophic Level (best 2–3 worst)	2.5	2017	●	→
Cereal yield (tonnes per hectare of harvested land)	2.0	2018	●	→
Sustainable Nitrogen Management Index (best 0–1.41 worst)	0.6	2015	●	→
Yield gap closure (% of potential yield)	47.7	2018	●	●
Exports of hazardous pesticides (tonnes per million population)	24.3	2019	●	●

SDG3 – Good Health and Well-Being	Value	Year	Rating	Trend
Maternal mortality rate (per 100,000 live births)	6	2017	●	↑
Neonatal mortality rate (per 1,000 live births)	2.4	2020	●	↑
Mortality rate, under-5 (per 1,000 live births)	3.7	2020	●	↑
Incidence of tuberculosis (per 100,000 population)	7.3	2020	●	↑
New HIV infections (per 1,000 uninfected population)	0.0	2020	●	↑
Age-standardized death rate due to cardiovascular disease, cancer, diabetes, or chronic respiratory disease in adults aged 30–70 years (%)	8.6	2019	●	↑
Age-standardized death rate attributable to household air pollution and ambient air pollution (per 100,000 population)	8	2016	●	●
Traffic deaths (per 100,000 population)	4.9	2019	●	↑
Life expectancy at birth (years)	83.0	2019	●	↑
Adolescent fertility rate (births per 1,000 females aged 15 to 19)	9.4	2018	●	↑
Births attended by skilled health personnel (%)	96.7	2017	●	↓
Surviving infants who received 2 WHO-recommended vaccines (%)	95	2020	●	↑
Universal health coverage (UHC) index of service coverage (worst 0–100 best)	87	2019	●	↑
Subjective well-being (average ladder score, worst 0–10 best)	7.1	2021	●	↑
Gap in life expectancy at birth among regions (years)	10.0	2019	●	↓
Gap in self-reported health status by income (percentage points)	8.9	2017	●	●
Daily smokers (% of population aged 15 and over)	11.2	2019	●	↑

SDG4 – Quality Education	Value	Year	Rating	Trend
Participation rate in pre-primary organized learning (% of children aged 4 to 6)	83.5	2019	●	↓
Net primary enrollment rate (%)	99.3	2019	●	↑
Lower secondary completion rate (%)	* 99.9	2019	●	↑
Literacy rate (% of population aged 15 to 24)	NA	NA	●	●
Tertiary educational attainment (% of population aged 25 to 34)	54.6	2020	●	↑
PISA score (worst 0–600 best)	499.0	2018	●	↑
Variation in science performance explained by socio-economic status (%)	10.0	2018	●	↑
Underachievers in science (% of 15-year-olds)	18.9	2018	●	↓

SDG5 – Gender Equality	Value	Year	Rating	Trend
Demand for family planning satisfied by modern methods (% of females aged 15 to 49)	85.6	2021	●	●
Ratio of female-to-male mean years of education received (%)	100.8	2019	●	↑
Ratio of female-to-male labor force participation rate (%)	86.0	2020	●	↑
Seats held by women in national parliament (%)	30.5	2020	●	↗
Gender wage gap (% of male median wage)	12.3	2020	●	↑

SDG6 – Clean Water and Sanitation	Value	Year	Rating	Trend
Population using at least basic drinking water services (%)	100.0	2020	●	↑
Population using at least basic sanitation services (%)	100.0	2020	●	↑
Freshwater withdrawal (% of available freshwater resources)	4.7	2018	●	●
Anthropogenic wastewater that receives treatment (%)	92.7	2018	●	●
Scarce water consumption embodied in imports (m^3 H_2O eq/capita)	2508.4	2018	●	●
Population using safely managed water services (%)	* 100.0	2020	●	●
Population using safely managed sanitation services (%)	82.2	2020	●	→

SDG7 – Affordable and Clean Energy	Value	Year	Rating	Trend
Population with access to electricity (%)	100.0	2019	●	↑
Population with access to clean fuels and technology for cooking (%)	100.0	2019	●	↑
CO_2 emissions from fuel combustion per total electricity output ($MtCO_2$/TWh)	1.5	2019	●	↗
Share of renewable energy in total primary energy supply (%)	7.3	2019	●	→

SDG8 – Decent Work and Economic Growth	Value	Year	Rating	Trend
Adjusted GDP growth (%)	1.1	2020	●	●
Victims of modern slavery (per 1,000 population)	0.6	2018	●	●
Adults with an account at a bank or other financial institution or with a mobile-money-service provider (% of population aged 15 or over)	99.5	2017	●	↑
Fundamental labor rights are effectively guaranteed (worst 0–1 best)	0.7	2020	●	↓
Fatal work-related accidents embodied in imports (per 100,000 population)	2.2	2015	●	↗
Employment-to-population ratio (%)	75.0	2021	●	↑
Youth not in employment, education or training (NEET) (% of population aged 15 to 29)	14.2	2020	●	↓

SDG9 – Industry, Innovation and Infrastructure	Value	Year	Rating	Trend
Population using the internet (%)	89.6	2020	●	↑
Mobile broadband subscriptions (per 100 population)	129.9	2019	●	↑
Logistics Performance Index: Quality of trade and transport-related infrastructure (worst 1–5 best)	4.0	2018	●	↑
The Times Higher Education Universities Ranking: Average score of top 3 universities (worst 0–100 best)	72.6	2022	●	●
Articles published in academic journals (per 1,000 population)	4.2	2020	●	↑
Expenditure on research and development (% of GDP)	1.9	2017	●	↑
Researchers (per 1,000 employed population)	9.0	2010	●	●
Triadic patent families filed (per million population)	14.5	2019	●	↓
Gap in internet access by income (percentage points)	57.0	2008	●	●
Female share of graduates from STEM fields at the tertiary level (%)	32.1	2017	●	↑

SDG10 – Reduced Inequalities	Value	Year	Rating	Trend
Gini coefficient	34.4	2014	●	●
Palma ratio	1.3	2018	●	↓
Elderly poverty rate (% of population aged 66 or over)	23.7	2018	●	↓

SDG11 – Sustainable Cities and Communities	Value	Year	Rating	Trend
Proportion of urban population living in slums (%)	* 0.0	2018	●	↑
Annual mean concentration of particulate matter of less than 2.5 microns in diameter (PM2.5) (μg/m^3)	8.1	2019	●	↑
Access to improved water source, piped (% of urban population)	92.4	2019	●	→
Satisfaction with public transport (%)	63.0	2021	●	↑
Population with rent overburden (%)	7.7	2019	●	↑

SDG12 – Responsible Consumption and Production	Value	Year	Rating	Trend
Electronic waste (kg/capita)	21.7	2019	●	●
Production-based SO_2 emissions (kg/capita)	36.6	2018	●	●
SO_2 emissions embodied in imports (kg/capita)	10.3	2018	●	●
Production-based nitrogen emissions (kg/capita)	71.8	2015	●	↓
Nitrogen emissions embodied in imports (kg/capita)	6.9	2015	●	→
Exports of plastic waste (kg/capita)	3.9	2021	●	●
Non-recycled municipal solid waste (kg/capita/day)	0.8	2017	●	●

SDG13 – Climate Action	Value	Year	Rating	Trend
CO_2 emissions from fossil fuel combustion and cement production (tCO_2/capita)	15.4	2020	●	→
CO_2 emissions embodied in imports (tCO_2/capita)	3.3	2018	●	↗
CO_2 emissions embodied in fossil fuel exports (kg/capita)	37396.5	2020	●	●
Carbon Pricing Score at EUR60/tCO_2 (%, worst 0–100 best)	20.4	2018	●	→

SDG14 – Life Below Water	Value	Year	Rating	Trend
Mean area that is protected in marine sites important to biodiversity (%)	64.6	2020	●	→
Ocean Health Index: Clean Waters score (worst 0–100 best)	80.5	2020	●	↑
Fish caught from overexploited or collapsed stocks (% of total catch)	38.8	2018	●	↑
Fish caught by trawling or dredging (%)	15.8	2018	●	→
Fish caught that are then discarded (%)	8.6	2018	●	→
Marine biodiversity threats embodied in imports (per million population)	0.8	2018	●	●

SDG15 – Life on Land	Value	Year	Rating	Trend
Mean area that is protected in terrestrial sites important to biodiversity (%)	56.6	2020	●	→
Mean area that is protected in freshwater sites important to biodiversity (%)	37.7	2020	●	→
Red List Index of species survival (worst 0–1 best)	0.8	2021	●	↓
Permanent deforestation (% of forest area, 5-year average)	0.1	2020	●	↓
Terrestrial and freshwater biodiversity threats embodied in imports (per million population)	2.7	2018	●	●

SDG16 – Peace, Justice and Strong Institutions	Value	Year	Rating	Trend
Homicides (per 100,000 population)	0.9	2020	●	↑
Unsentenced detainees (% of prison population)	31.5	2018	●	↓
Population who feel safe walking alone at night in the city or area where they live (%)	67	2021	●	↑
Property Rights (worst 1–7 best)	6.0	2020	●	↑
Birth registrations with civil authority (% of children under age 5)	100.0	2020	●	●
Corruption Perception Index (worst 0–100 best)	73	2021	●	↑
Children involved in child labor (% of population aged 5 to 14)	* 0.0	2019	●	●
Exports of major conventional weapons (TIV constant million USD per 100,000 population)	0.6	2020	●	●
Press Freedom Index (best 0–100 worst)	19.8	2021	●	↑
Access to and affordability of justice (worst 0–1 best)	0.6	2020	●	→
Persons held in prison (per 100,000 population)	176.5	2018	●	↓

SDG17 – Partnerships for the Goals	Value	Year	Rating	Trend
Government spending on health and education (% of GDP)	12.2	2019	●	↑
For high-income and all OECD DAC countries: International concessional public finance, including official development assistance (% of GNI)	0.2	2021	●	↓
Other countries: Government revenue excluding grants (% of GDP)	NA	NA	●	●
Corporate Tax Haven Score (best 0–100 worst)	* 0.0	2019	●	●
Financial Secrecy Score (best 0–100 worst)	50.1	2020	●	●
Shifted profits of multinationals (US$ billion)	25.2	2018	●	↑
Statistical Performance Index (worst 0–100 best)	88.2	2019	●	↑

* Imputed data point

5. Country Profiles

AUSTRIA

OVERALL PERFORMANCE

COUNTRY RANKING

AUSTRIA

5 **/163**

COUNTRY SCORE

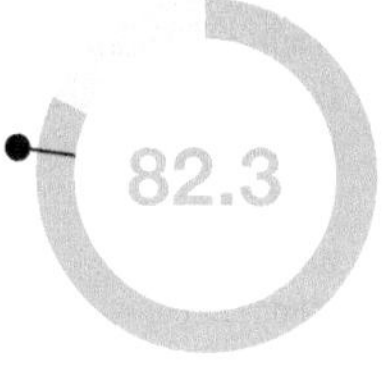

REGIONAL AVERAGE: 77.2

AVERAGE PERFORMANCE BY SDG

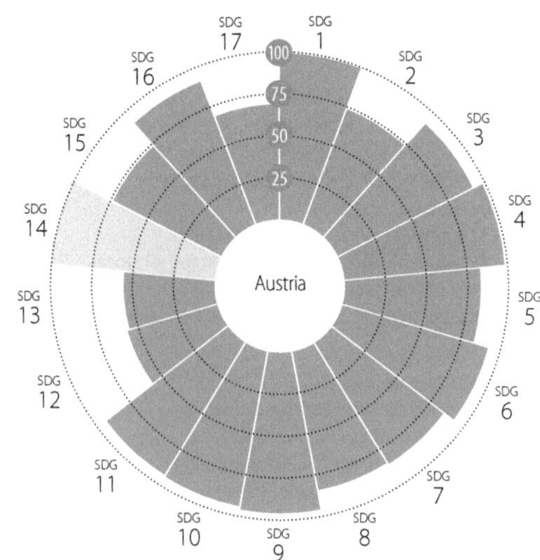

SDG DASHBOARDS AND TRENDS

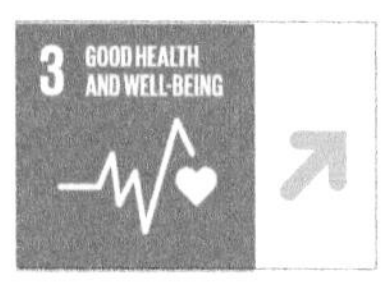

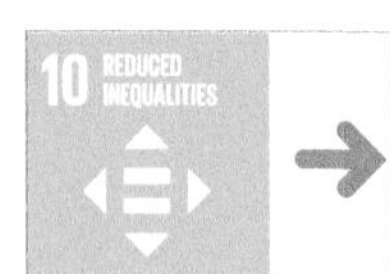

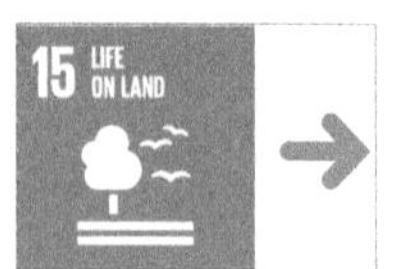

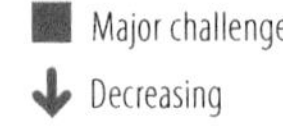

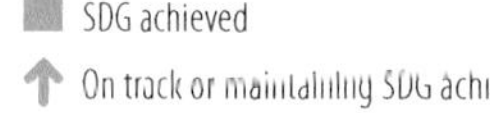

Major challenges | Significant challenges | Challenges remain | SDG achieved | Information unavailable

Decreasing | Stagnating | Moderately improving | On track or maintaining SDG achievement | Information unavailable

Note: The full title of each SDG is available here: https://sustainabledevelopment.un.org/topics/sustainabledevelopmentgoals

INTERNATIONAL SPILLOVER INDEX

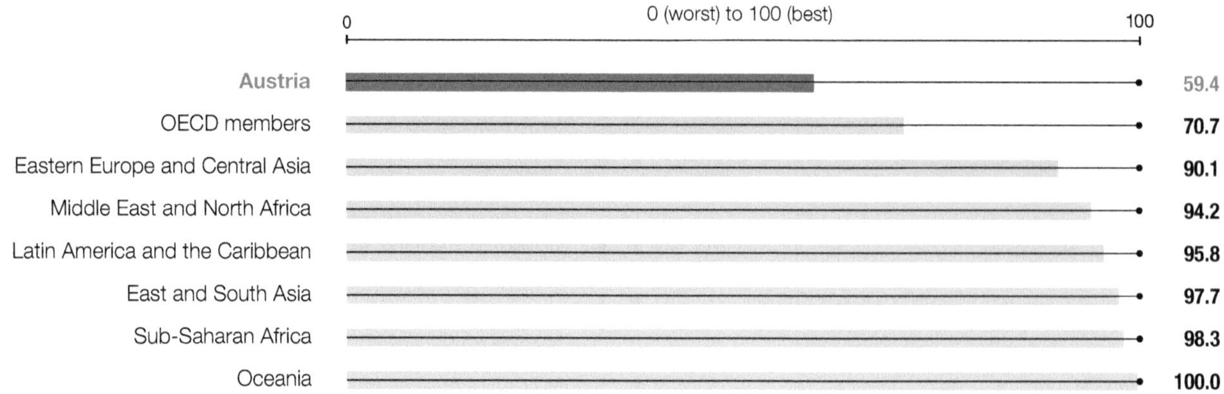

STATISTICAL PERFORMANCE INDEX

0 (worst) to 100 (best)

0 **89.1** 100

MISSING DATA IN SDG INDEX

3%

AUSTRIA

Performance by Indicator

SDG1 – No Poverty		Value	Year	Rating	Trend
Poverty headcount ratio at $1.90/day (%)		0.4	2022	●	↑
Poverty headcount ratio at $3.20/day (%)		0.4	2022	●	↑
Poverty rate after taxes and transfers (%)		10.0	2019	●	↑
SDG2 – Zero Hunger					
Prevalence of undernourishment (%)		2.5	2019	●	↑
Prevalence of stunting in children under 5 years of age (%)	*	2.6	2019	●	↑
Prevalence of wasting in children under 5 years of age (%)	*	0.7	2019	●	↑
Prevalence of obesity, BMI ≥ 30 (% of adult population)		20.1	2016	●	↓
Human Trophic Level (best 2–3 worst)		2.4	2017	●	↓
Cereal yield (tonnes per hectare of harvested land)		6.2	2018	●	↑
Sustainable Nitrogen Management Index (best 0–1.41 worst)		0.4	2015	●	↓
Yield gap closure (% of potential yield)		69.7	2018	●	●
Exports of hazardous pesticides (tonnes per million population)		25.7	2019	●	●
SDG3 – Good Health and Well-Being					
Maternal mortality rate (per 100,000 live births)		5	2017	●	↑
Neonatal mortality rate (per 1,000 live births)		2.3	2020	●	↑
Mortality rate, under-5 (per 1,000 live births)		3.6	2020	●	↑
Incidence of tuberculosis (per 100,000 population)		4.9	2020	●	↑
New HIV infections (per 1,000 uninfected population)		1.0	2020	●	→
Age-standardized death rate due to cardiovascular disease, cancer, diabetes, or chronic respiratory disease in adults aged 30–70 years (%)		10.4	2019	●	↑
Age-standardized death rate attributable to household air pollution and ambient air pollution (per 100,000 population)		15	2016	●	●
Traffic deaths (per 100,000 population)		4.9	2019	●	↑
Life expectancy at birth (years)		81.7	2019	●	↑
Adolescent fertility rate (births per 1,000 females aged 15 to 19)		5.5	2018	●	↑
Births attended by skilled health personnel (%)		98.4	2018	●	↑
Surviving infants who received 2 WHO-recommended vaccines (%)		85	2020	●	↓
Universal health coverage (UHC) index of service coverage (worst 0–100 best)		82	2019	●	↑
Subjective well-being (average ladder score, worst 0–10 best)		7.1	2021	●	↑
Gap in life expectancy at birth among regions (years)		2.2	2019	●	↑
Gap in self-reported health status by income (percentage points)		20.9	2020	●	↑
Daily smokers (% of population aged 15 and over)		20.6	2019	●	↑
SDG4 – Quality Education					
Participation rate in pre-primary organized learning (% of children aged 4 to 6)		98.5	2019	●	↑
Net primary enrollment rate (%)		99.9	2019	●	↑
Lower secondary completion rate (%)		97.6	2019	●	↑
Literacy rate (% of population aged 15 to 24)		NA	NA	●	●
Tertiary educational attainment (% of population aged 25 to 34)		41.4	2020	●	↑
PISA score (worst 0–600 best)		491.0	2018	●	→
Variation in science performance explained by socio-economic status (%)		14.8	2018	●	↗
Underachievers in science (% of 15-year-olds)		21.9	2018	●	↓
SDG5 – Gender Equality					
Demand for family planning satisfied by modern methods (% of females aged 15 to 49)		NA	NA	●	●
Ratio of female-to-male mean years of education received (%)		94.6	2019	●	→
Ratio of female-to-male labor force participation rate (%)		84.1	2020	●	↑
Seats held by women in national parliament (%)		39.3	2020	●	↑
Gender wage gap (% of male median wage)		13.3	2020	●	↑
SDG6 – Clean Water and Sanitation					
Population using at least basic drinking water services (%)		100.0	2020	●	↑
Population using at least basic sanitation services (%)		100.0	2020	●	↑
Freshwater withdrawal (% of available freshwater resources)		9.6	2018	●	●
Anthropogenic wastewater that receives treatment (%)		94.0	2018	●	●
Scarce water consumption embodied in imports (m^3 H_2O eq/capita)		3598.2	2018	●	●
Population using safely managed water services (%)		98.9	2020	●	↑
Population using safely managed sanitation services (%)		99.6	2020	●	↑
SDG7 – Affordable and Clean Energy					
Population with access to electricity (%)		100.0	2019	●	↑
Population with access to clean fuels and technology for cooking (%)		100.0	2019	●	↑
CO_2 emissions from fuel combustion per total electricity output ($MtCO_2$/TWh)		0.9	2019	●	↑
Share of renewable energy in total primary energy supply (%)		29.9	2019	●	↑
SDG8 – Decent Work and Economic Growth					
Adjusted GDP growth (%)		-1.1	2020	●	●
Victims of modern slavery (per 1,000 population)		1.7	2018	●	●
Adults with an account at a bank or other financial institution or with a mobile-money-service provider (% of population aged 15 or over)		98.2	2017	●	↑
Fundamental labor rights are effectively guaranteed (worst 0–1 best)		0.8	2020	●	↑
Fatal work-related accidents embodied in imports (per 100,000 population)		1.7	2015	●	↑
Employment-to-population ratio (%)		71.7	2020	●	↑
Youth not in employment, education or training (NEET) (% of population aged 15 to 29)		11.6	2020	●	↓

* Imputed data point

SDG9 – Industry, Innovation and Infrastructure		Value	Year	Rating	Trend
Population using the internet (%)		87.5	2020	●	↑
Mobile broadband subscriptions (per 100 population)		107.4	2019	●	↑
Logistics Performance Index: Quality of trade and transport-related infrastructure (worst 1–5 best)		4.2	2018	●	↑
The Times Higher Education Universities Ranking: Average score of top 3 universities (worst 0–100 best)		54.9	2022	●	●
Articles published in academic journals (per 1,000 population)		3.0	2020	●	↑
Expenditure on research and development (% of GDP)		3.2	2019	●	↑
Researchers (per 1,000 employed population)		11.6	2019	●	↑
Triadic patent families filed (per million population)		43.0	2019	●	↑
Gap in internet access by income (percentage points)		14.2	2020	●	↑
Female share of graduates from STEM fields at the tertiary level (%)		25.9	2016	●	↓
SDG10 – Reduced Inequalities					
Gini coefficient		30.8	2018	●	→
Palma ratio		1.0	2019	●	↑
Elderly poverty rate (% of population aged 66 or over)		10.1	2019	●	↓
SDG11 – Sustainable Cities and Communities					
Proportion of urban population living in slums (%)		0.0	2018	●	↑
Annual mean concentration of particulate matter of less than 2.5 microns in diameter (PM2.5) (μg/m³)		11.9	2019	●	↑
Access to improved water source, piped (% of urban population)		NA	NA	●	●
Satisfaction with public transport (%)		74.0	2021	●	↑
Population with rent overburden (%)		5.8	2019	●	↑
SDG12 – Responsible Consumption and Production					
Electronic waste (kg/capita)		18.8	2019	●	●
Production-based SO_2 emissions (kg/capita)		11.1	2018	●	●
SO_2 emissions embodied in imports (kg/capita)		9.3	2018	●	●
Production-based nitrogen emissions (kg/capita)		12.3	2015	●	↑
Nitrogen emissions embodied in imports (kg/capita)		16.9	2015	●	↓
Exports of plastic waste (kg/capita)		19.6	2020	●	●
Non-recycled municipal solid waste (kg/capita/day)		0.7	2019	●	↑
SDG13 – Climate Action					
CO_2 emissions from fossil fuel combustion and cement production (tCO_2/capita)		6.7	2020	●	→
CO_2 emissions embodied in imports (tCO_2/capita)		4.1	2018	●	→
CO_2 emissions embodied in fossil fuel exports (kg/capita)		191.9	2020	●	●
Carbon Pricing Score at EUR60/tCO_2 (%, worst 0–100 best)		47.6	2018	●	↑
SDG14 – Life Below Water					
Mean area that is protected in marine sites important to biodiversity (%)		NA	NA	●	●
Ocean Health Index: Clean Waters score (worst 0–100 best)		NA	NA	●	●
Fish caught from overexploited or collapsed stocks (% of total catch)		NA	NA	●	●
Fish caught by trawling or dredging (%)		NA	NA	●	●
Fish caught that are then discarded (%)		NA	NA	●	●
Marine biodiversity threats embodied in imports (per million population)		0.1	2018	●	●
SDG15 – Life on Land					
Mean area that is protected in terrestrial sites important to biodiversity (%)		67.4	2020	●	→
Mean area that is protected in freshwater sites important to biodiversity (%)		71.2	2020	●	→
Red List Index of species survival (worst 0–1 best)		0.9	2021	●	→
Permanent deforestation (% of forest area, 5-year average)		0.0	2020	●	↑
Terrestrial and freshwater biodiversity threats embodied in imports (per million population)		4.5	2018	●	●
SDG16 – Peace, Justice and Strong Institutions					
Homicides (per 100,000 population)		0.7	2020	●	↑
Unsentenced detainees (% of prison population)		20.0	2019	●	↑
Population who feel safe walking alone at night in the city or area where they live (%)		76	2021	●	↑
Property Rights (worst 1–7 best)		6.2	2020	●	↑
Birth registrations with civil authority (% of children under age 5)		100.0	2020	●	●
Corruption Perception Index (worst 0–100 best)		74	2021	●	↑
Children involved in child labor (% of population aged 5 to 14)	*	0.0	2019	●	●
Exports of major conventional weapons (TIV constant million USD per 100,000 population)		0.1	2020	●	●
Press Freedom Index (best 0–100 worst)		16.3	2021	●	↑
Access to and affordability of justice (worst 0–1 best)		0.7	2020	●	↑
Persons held in prison (per 100,000 population)		101.3	2019	●	↓
SDG17 – Partnerships for the Goals					
Government spending on health and education (% of GDP)		12.8	2019	●	↑
For high-income and all OECD DAC countries: International concessional public finance, including official development assistance (% of GNI)		0.3	2021	●	↓
Other countries: Government revenue excluding grants (% of GDP)		NA	NA	●	●
Corporate Tax Haven Score (best 0–100 worst)		51.6	2019	●	●
Financial Secrecy Score (best 0–100 worst)		56.5	2020	●	●
Shifted profits of multinationals (US$ billion)		5.3	2018	●	↑
Statistical Performance Index (worst 0–100 best)		89.1	2019	●	↑

AZERBAIJAN

Eastern Europe and Central Asia

OVERALL PERFORMANCE

COUNTRY RANKING

AZERBAIJAN

50/163

COUNTRY SCORE

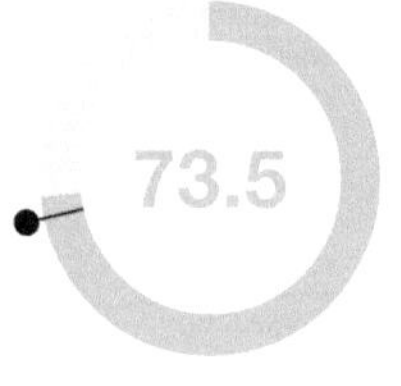

REGIONAL AVERAGE: 71.6

AVERAGE PERFORMANCE BY SDG

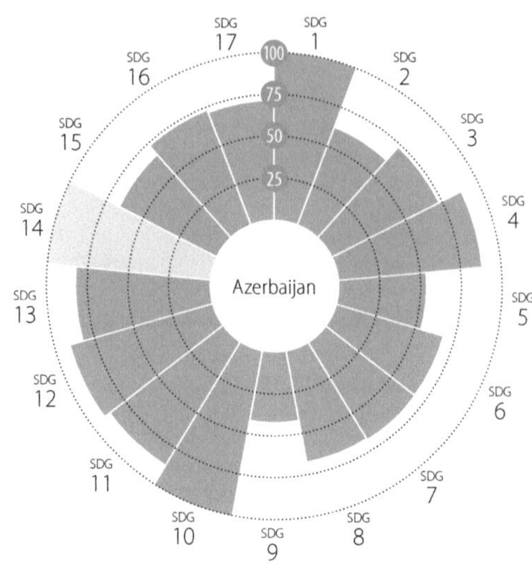

SDG DASHBOARDS AND TRENDS

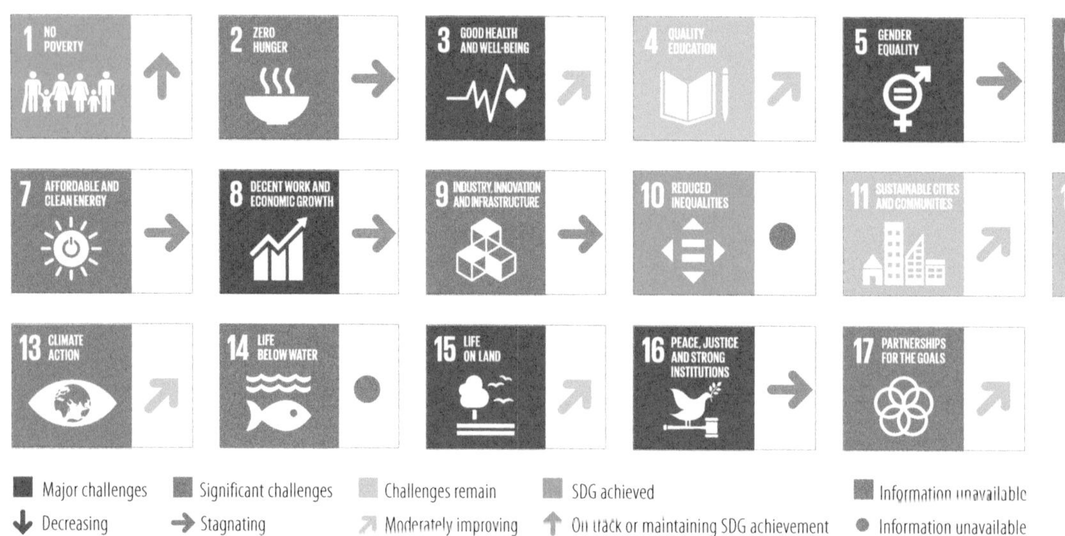

Major challenges | Significant challenges | Challenges remain | SDG achieved | Information unavailable

Decreasing | Stagnating | Moderately improving | On track or maintaining SDG achievement | Information unavailable

Note: The full title of each SDG is available here: https://sustainabledevelopment.un.org/topics/sustainabledevelopmentgoals

INTERNATIONAL SPILLOVER INDEX

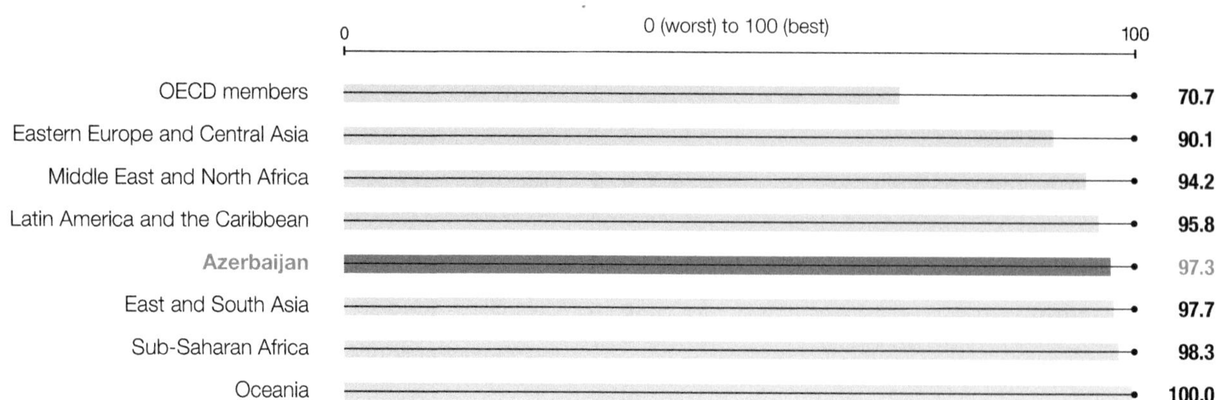

STATISTICAL PERFORMANCE INDEX

0 (worst) to 100 (best)

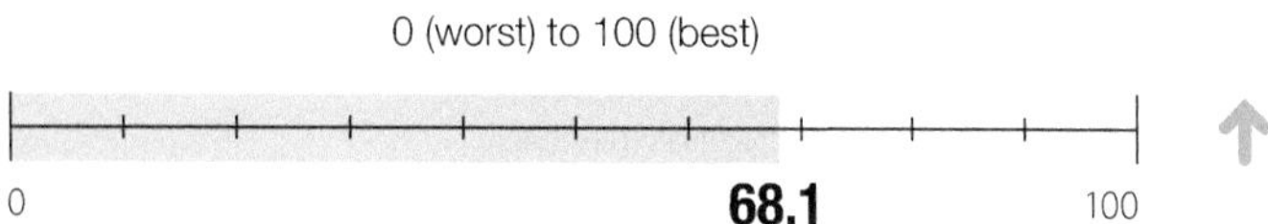

MISSING DATA IN SDG INDEX

AZERBAIJAN

	Value	Year	Rating	Trend
SDG1 – No Poverty				
Poverty headcount ratio at \$1.90/day (%)	0.0	2022	●	↑
Poverty headcount ratio at \$3.20/day (%)	0.0	2022	●	↑
SDG2 – Zero Hunger				
Prevalence of undernourishment (%)	2.5	2019	●	↑
Prevalence of stunting in children under 5 years of age (%)	17.8	2013	●	→
Prevalence of wasting in children under 5 years of age (%)	3.2	2013	●	↑
Prevalence of obesity, BMI ≥ 30 (% of adult population)	19.9	2016	●	↓
Human Trophic Level (best 2–3 worst)	2.2	2017	●	→
Cereal yield (tonnes per hectare of harvested land)	3.0	2018	●	↑
Sustainable Nitrogen Management Index (best 0–1.41 worst)	0.6	2015	●	→
Exports of hazardous pesticides (tonnes per million population)	NA	NA	●	●
SDG3 – Good Health and Well-Being				
Maternal mortality rate (per 100,000 live births)	26	2017	●	↑
Neonatal mortality rate (per 1,000 live births)	9.8	2020	●	↑
Mortality rate, under-5 (per 1,000 live births)	19.4	2020	●	↑
Incidence of tuberculosis (per 100,000 population)	58.0	2020	●	↗
New HIV infections (per 1,000 uninfected population)	0.0	2020	●	↑
Age-standardized death rate due to cardiovascular disease, cancer, diabetes, or chronic respiratory disease in adults aged 30–70 years (%)	27.2	2019	●	→
Age-standardized death rate attributable to household air pollution and ambient air pollution (per 100,000 population)	64	2016	●	●
Traffic deaths (per 100,000 population)	6.7	2019	●	↑
Life expectancy at birth (years)	71.4	2019	●	→
Adolescent fertility rate (births per 1,000 females aged 15 to 19)	48.1	2019	●	↗
Births attended by skilled health personnel (%)	99.4	2018	●	↑
Surviving infants who received 2 WHO-recommended vaccines (%)	79	2020	●	↓
Universal health coverage (UHC) index of service coverage (worst 0–100 best)	65	2019	●	↗
Subjective well-being (average ladder score, worst 0–10 best)	5.2	2019	●	●
SDG4 – Quality Education				
Participation rate in pre-primary organized learning (% of children aged 4 to 6)	83.2	2020	●	↑
Net primary enrollment rate (%)	89.5	2020	●	↓
Lower secondary completion rate (%)	101.3	2020	●	↑
Literacy rate (% of population aged 15 to 24)	99.9	2019	●	↑
SDG5 – Gender Equality				
Demand for family planning satisfied by modern methods (% of females aged 15 to 49)	21.5	2006	●	●
Ratio of female-to-male mean years of education received (%)	93.6	2019	●	→
Ratio of female-to-male labor force participation rate (%)	88.9	2020	●	↑
Seats held by women in national parliament (%)	17.4	2020	●	→
SDG6 – Clean Water and Sanitation				
Population using at least basic drinking water services (%)	96.0	2020	●	↑
Population using at least basic sanitation services (%)	96.1	2019	●	↑
Freshwater withdrawal (% of available freshwater resources)	53.7	2018	●	●
Anthropogenic wastewater that receives treatment (%)	3.8	2018	●	●
Scarce water consumption embodied in imports (m^3 H_2O eq/capita)	1028.4	2018	●	●
SDG7 – Affordable and Clean Energy				
Population with access to electricity (%)	100.0	2019	●	↑
Population with access to clean fuels and technology for cooking (%)	96.7	2019	●	↑
CO_2 emissions from fuel combustion per total electricity output ($MtCO_2$/TWh)	1.5	2019	●	→
Share of renewable energy in total primary energy supply (%)	1.4	2019	●	↓
SDG8 – Decent Work and Economic Growth				
Adjusted GDP growth (%)	-3.2	2020	●	●
Victims of modern slavery (per 1,000 population)	4.5	2018	●	●
Adults with an account at a bank or other financial institution or with a mobile-money-service provider (% of population aged 15 or over)	28.6	2017	●	↓
Unemployment rate (% of total labor force)	6.6	2022	●	↓
Fundamental labor rights are effectively guaranteed (worst 0–1 best)	NA	NA	●	●
Fatal work-related accidents embodied in imports (per 100,000 population)	0.1	2015	●	↑

* Imputed data point

	Value	Year	Rating	Trend
SDG9 – Industry, Innovation and Infrastructure				
Population using the internet (%)	84.6	2020	●	↑
Mobile broadband subscriptions (per 100 population)	62.1	2019	●	→
Logistics Performance Index: Quality of trade and transport-related infrastructure (worst 1–5 best)	2.7	2014	●	●
The Times Higher Education Universities Ranking: Average score of top 3 universities (worst 0–100 best)	16.5	2022	●	●
Articles published in academic journals (per 1,000 population)	0.2	2020	●	→
Expenditure on research and development (% of GDP)	0.2	2018	●	↓
SDG10 – Reduced Inequalities				
Gini coefficient	26.6	2005	●	●
Palma ratio	NA	NA	●	●
SDG11 – Sustainable Cities and Communities				
Proportion of urban population living in slums (%)	NA	NA	●	●
Annual mean concentration of particulate matter of less than 2.5 microns in diameter (PM2.5) (μg/m^3)	19.2	2019	●	↗
Access to improved water source, piped (% of urban population)	100.0	2020	●	↑
Satisfaction with public transport (%)	67.0	2019	●	●
SDG12 – Responsible Consumption and Production				
Municipal solid waste (kg/capita/day)	0.8	2015	●	●
Electronic waste (kg/capita)	8.0	2019	●	●
Production-based SO_2 emissions (kg/capita)	5.0	2018	●	●
SO_2 emissions embodied in imports (kg/capita)	0.9	2018	●	●
Production-based nitrogen emissions (kg/capita)	12.0	2015	●	↑
Nitrogen emissions embodied in imports (kg/capita)	0.7	2015	●	↑
Exports of plastic waste (kg/capita)	0.0	2021	●	●
SDG13 – Climate Action				
CO_2 emissions from fossil fuel combustion and cement production (tCO_2/capita)	3.7	2020	●	→
CO_2 emissions embodied in imports (tCO_2/capita)	0.4	2018	●	↑
CO_2 emissions embodied in fossil fuel exports (kg/capita)	11267.6	2021	●	●
SDG14 – Life Below Water				
Mean area that is protected in marine sites important to biodiversity (%)	NA	NA	●	●
Ocean Health Index: Clean Waters score (worst 0–100 best)	NA	NA	●	●
Fish caught from overexploited or collapsed stocks (% of total catch)	NA	NA	●	●
Fish caught by trawling or dredging (%)	NA	NA	●	●
Fish caught that are then discarded (%)	NA	NA	●	●
Marine biodiversity threats embodied in imports (per million population)	0.0	2018	●	●
SDG15 – Life on Land				
Mean area that is protected in terrestrial sites important to biodiversity (%)	36.6	2020	●	→
Mean area that is protected in freshwater sites important to biodiversity (%)	14.5	2020	●	→
Red List Index of species survival (worst 0–1 best)	0.9	2021	●	↑
Permanent deforestation (% of forest area, 5-year average)	0.0	2020	●	↑
Terrestrial and freshwater biodiversity threats embodied in imports (per million population)	0.1	2018	●	●
SDG16 – Peace, Justice and Strong Institutions				
Homicides (per 100,000 population)	2.3	2020	●	→
Unsentenced detainees (% of prison population)	15.9	2019	●	↑
Population who feel safe walking alone at night in the city or area where they live (%)	82	2019	●	●
Property Rights (worst 1–7 best)	5.1	2020	●	↑
Birth registrations with civil authority (% of children under age 5)	93.6	2020	●	●
Corruption Perception Index (worst 0–100 best)	30	2021	●	→
Children involved in child labor (% of population aged 5 to 14)	NA	NA	●	●
Exports of major conventional weapons (TIV constant million USD per 100,000 population)	* 0.0	2020	●	●
Press Freedom Index (best 0–100 worst)	58.8	2021	●	↓
Access to and affordability of justice (worst 0–1 best)	NA	NA	●	●
SDG17 – Partnerships for the Goals				
Government spending on health and education (% of GDP)	4.0	2019	●	↓
For high-income and all OECD DAC countries: International concessional public finance, including official development assistance (% of GNI)	NA	NA	●	●
Other countries: Government revenue excluding grants (% of GDP)	42.8	2019	●	↑
Corporate Tax Haven Score (best 0–100 worst)	* 0.0	2019	●	●
Statistical Performance Index (worst 0–100 best)	68.1	2019	●	↑

THE BAHAMAS

Latin America and the Caribbean

OVERALL PERFORMANCE

COUNTRY RANKING

THE BAHAMAS

NA /163

COUNTRY SCORE

REGIONAL AVERAGE: 69.5

AVERAGE PERFORMANCE BY SDG

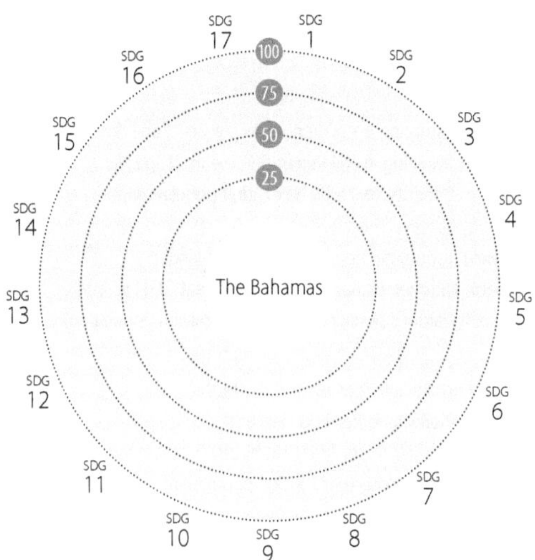

SDG DASHBOARDS AND TRENDS

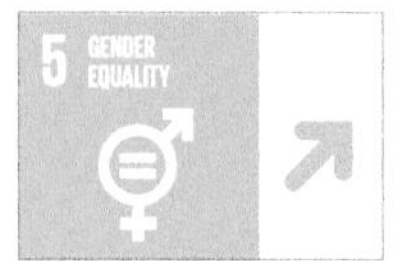

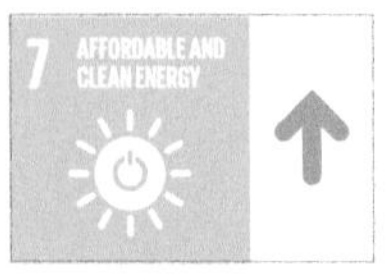

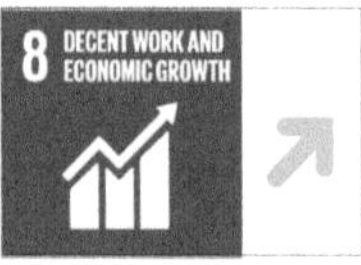

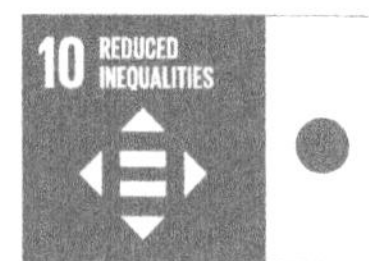

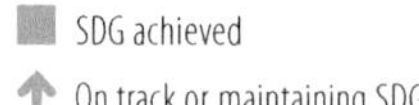

Major challenges | Significant challenges | Challenges remain | SDG achieved | Information unavailable

Decreasing | Stagnating | Moderately improving | On track or maintaining SDG achievement | Information unavailable

Note: The full title of each SDG is available here: https://sustainabledevelopment.un.org/topics/sustainabledevelopmentgoals

INTERNATIONAL SPILLOVER INDEX

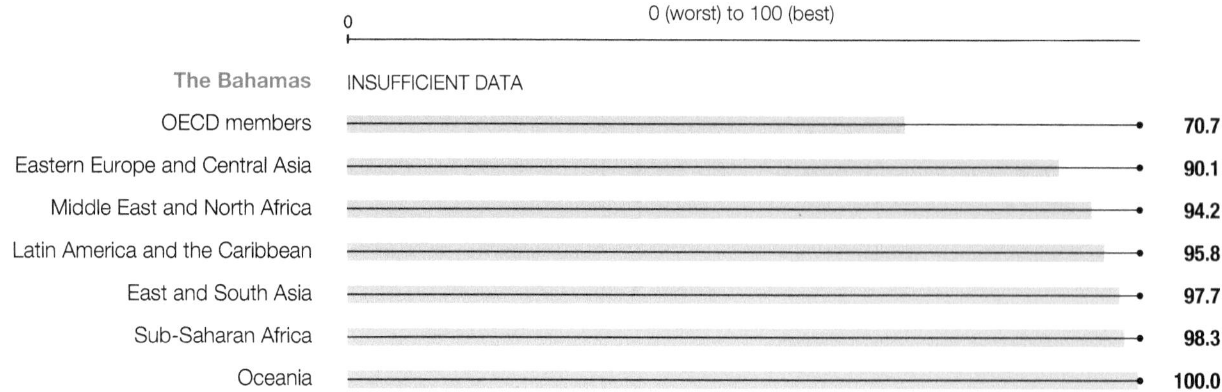

STATISTICAL PERFORMANCE INDEX

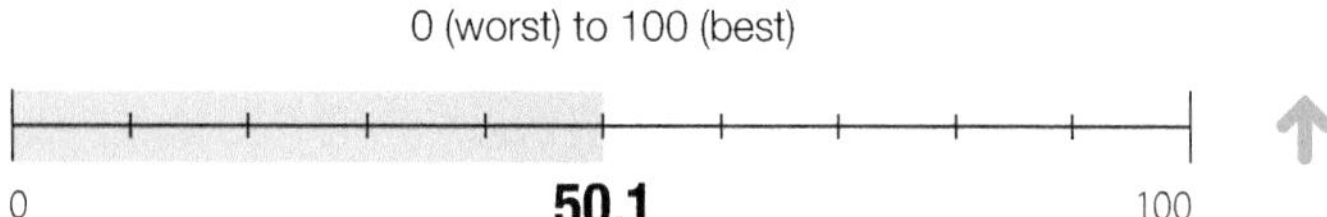

MISSING DATA IN SDG INDEX

23%

THE BAHAMAS

Performance by Indicator

Indicator		Value	Year	Rating	Trend
SDG1 – No Poverty					
Poverty headcount ratio at \$1.90/day (%)	*	NA	NA	●	●
Poverty headcount ratio at \$3.20/day (%)	*	NA	NA	●	●
SDG2 – Zero Hunger					
Prevalence of undernourishment (%)	*	1.2	2019	●	●
Prevalence of stunting in children under 5 years of age (%)	*	2.6	2019	●	↑
Prevalence of wasting in children under 5 years of age (%)	*	0.7	2019	●	↑
Prevalence of obesity, BMI ≥ 30 (% of adult population)		31.6	2016	●	↓
Human Trophic Level (best 2–3 worst)		2.3	2017	●	↗
Cereal yield (tonnes per hectare of harvested land)		8.7	2018	●	↑
Sustainable Nitrogen Management Index (best 0–1.41 worst)		1.1	2015	●	↓
Exports of hazardous pesticides (tonnes per million population)		NA	NA	●	●
SDG3 – Good Health and Well-Being					
Maternal mortality rate (per 100,000 live births)		70	2017	●	↑
Neonatal mortality rate (per 1,000 live births)		6.6	2020	●	↑
Mortality rate, under-5 (per 1,000 live births)		12.3	2020	●	↑
Incidence of tuberculosis (per 100,000 population)		9.1	2020	●	↑
New HIV infections (per 1,000 uninfected population)		0.3	2020	●	↑
Age-standardized death rate due to cardiovascular disease, cancer, diabetes, or chronic respiratory disease in adults aged 30–70 years (%)		19.9	2019	●	↓
Age-standardized death rate attributable to household air pollution and ambient air pollution (per 100,000 population)		20	2016	●	●
Traffic deaths (per 100,000 population)		7.8	2019	●	↑
Life expectancy at birth (years)		73.2	2019	●	→
Adolescent fertility rate (births per 1,000 females aged 15 to 19)		29.0	2013	●	●
Births attended by skilled health personnel (%)		99.0	2016	●	●
Surviving infants who received 2 WHO-recommended vaccines (%)		83	2020	●	↓
Universal health coverage (UHC) index of service coverage (worst 0–100 best)		70	2019	●	↗
Subjective well-being (average ladder score, worst 0–10 best)		NA	NA	●	●
SDG4 – Quality Education					
Participation rate in pre-primary organized learning (% of children aged 4 to 6)		37.6	2018	●	●
Net primary enrollment rate (%)		86.5	2006	●	●
Lower secondary completion rate (%)		92.2	2010	●	●
Literacy rate (% of population aged 15 to 24)		NA	NA	●	●
SDG5 – Gender Equality					
Demand for family planning satisfied by modern methods (% of females aged 15 to 49)		NA	NA	●	●
Ratio of female-to-male mean years of education received (%)		102.6	2019	●	↑
Ratio of female-to-male labor force participation rate (%)		90.5	2020	●	↑
Seats held by women in national parliament (%)		12.8	2020	●	↓
SDG6 – Clean Water and Sanitation					
Population using at least basic drinking water services (%)		98.9	2019	●	↑
Population using at least basic sanitation services (%)		94.9	2019	●	→
Freshwater withdrawal (% of available freshwater resources)		NA	NA	●	●
Anthropogenic wastewater that receives treatment (%)		1.4	2018	●	●
Scarce water consumption embodied in imports (m^3 H_2O eq/capita)		11758.3	2018	●	●
SDG7 – Affordable and Clean Energy					
Population with access to electricity (%)		100.0	2019	●	↑
Population with access to clean fuels and technology for cooking (%)		100.0	2019	●	↑
CO_2 emissions from fuel combustion per total electricity output ($MtCO_2$/TWh)		1.0	2019	●	↑
Share of renewable energy in total primary energy supply (%)		NA	NA	●	●
SDG8 – Decent Work and Economic Growth					
Adjusted GDP growth (%)		-5.9	2020	●	●
Victims of modern slavery (per 1,000 population)		NA	NA	●	●
Adults with an account at a bank or other financial institution or with a mobile-money-service provider (% of population aged 15 or over)		NA	NA	●	●
Unemployment rate (% of total labor force)		12.9	2022	●	↓
Fundamental labor rights are effectively guaranteed (worst 0–1 best)		0.6	2020	●	↑
Fatal work-related accidents embodied in imports (per 100,000 population)		0.4	2015	●	↑

* Imputed data point

Indicator		Value	Year	Rating	Trend
SDG9 – Industry, Innovation and Infrastructure					
Population using the internet (%)		87.0	2020	●	↑
Mobile broadband subscriptions (per 100 population)		93.0	2019	●	↑
Logistics Performance Index: Quality of trade and transport-related infrastructure (worst 1–5 best)		2.4	2018	●	↓
The Times Higher Education Universities Ranking: Average score of top 3 universities (worst 0–100 best)	*	0.0	2022	●	●
Articles published in academic journals (per 1,000 population)		0.2	2020	●	↗
Expenditure on research and development (% of GDP)		NA	NA	●	●
SDG10 – Reduced Inequalities					
Gini coefficient		NA	NA	●	●
Palma ratio		NA	NA	●	●
SDG11 – Sustainable Cities and Communities					
Proportion of urban population living in slums (%)		NA	NA	●	●
Annual mean concentration of particulate matter of less than 2.5 microns in diameter (PM2.5) (μg/m^3)		16.3	2019	●	↑
Access to improved water source, piped (% of urban population)		NA	NA	●	●
Satisfaction with public transport (%)		NA	NA	●	●
SDG12 – Responsible Consumption and Production					
Municipal solid waste (kg/capita/day)		1.9	2015	●	●
Electronic waste (kg/capita)		17.2	2019	●	●
Production-based SO_2 emissions (kg/capita)		78.1	2018	●	●
SO_2 emissions embodied in imports (kg/capita)		6.8	2018	●	●
Production-based nitrogen emissions (kg/capita)		3.6	2015	●	↑
Nitrogen emissions embodied in imports (kg/capita)		9.6	2015	●	→
Exports of plastic waste (kg/capita)		0.0	2018	●	●
SDG13 – Climate Action					
CO_2 emissions from fossil fuel combustion and cement production (tCO_2/capita)		5.9	2020	●	→
CO_2 emissions embodied in imports (tCO_2/capita)		2.9	2018	●	↑
CO_2 emissions embodied in fossil fuel exports (kg/capita)		0.0	2017	●	●
SDG14 – Life Below Water					
Mean area that is protected in marine sites important to biodiversity (%)		30.3	2020	●	→
Ocean Health Index: Clean Waters score (worst 0–100 best)		61.8	2020	●	→
Fish caught from overexploited or collapsed stocks (% of total catch)		30.9	2018	●	↑
Fish caught by trawling or dredging (%)		0.0	2018	●	↑
Fish caught that are then discarded (%)		0.0	2018	●	↑
Marine biodiversity threats embodied in imports (per million population)		1.7	2018	●	●
SDG15 – Life on Land					
Mean area that is protected in terrestrial sites important to biodiversity (%)		29.8	2020	●	→
Mean area that is protected in freshwater sites important to biodiversity (%)		0.0	2020	●	→
Red List Index of species survival (worst 0–1 best)		0.7	2021	●	↓
Permanent deforestation (% of forest area, 5-year average)		0.2	2020	●	↑
Terrestrial and freshwater biodiversity threats embodied in imports (per million population)		0.4	2018	●	●
SDG16 – Peace, Justice and Strong Institutions					
Homicides (per 100,000 population)		18.6	2020	●	↑
Unsentenced detainees (% of prison population)		58.7	2019	●	↓
Population who feel safe walking alone at night in the city or area where they live (%)		NA	NA	●	●
Property Rights (worst 1–7 best)		NA	NA	●	●
Birth registrations with civil authority (% of children under age 5)		NA	NA	●	●
Corruption Perception Index (worst 0–100 best)		64	2021	●	↑
Children involved in child labor (% of population aged 5 to 14)		NA	NA	●	●
Exports of major conventional weapons (TIV constant million USD per 100,000 population)		0.0	2020	●	●
Press Freedom Index (best 0–100 worst)		NA	NA	●	●
Access to and affordability of justice (worst 0–1 best)		0.6	2020	●	→
SDG17 – Partnerships for the Goals					
Government spending on health and education (% of GDP)		5.5	2020	●	→
For high-income and all OECD DAC countries: International concessional public finance, including official development assistance (% of GNI)		NA	NA	●	●
Other countries: Government revenue excluding grants (% of GDP)		NA	NA	●	●
Corporate Tax Haven Score (best 0–100 worst)		100.0	2019	●	●
Statistical Performance Index (worst 0–100 best)		50.1	2019	●	↑

BAHRAIN

Middle East and North Africa

OVERALL PERFORMANCE

COUNTRY RANKING

BAHRAIN

102/163

COUNTRY SCORE

REGIONAL AVERAGE: 66.7

AVERAGE PERFORMANCE BY SDG

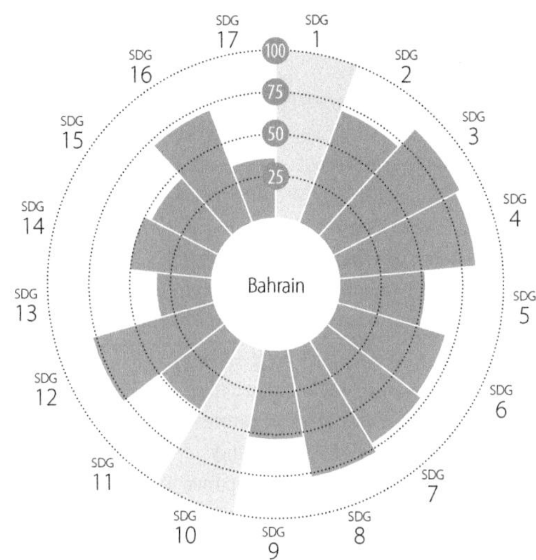

SDG DASHBOARDS AND TRENDS

Major challenges · Significant challenges · Challenges remain · SDG achieved · Information unavailable

Decreasing · Stagnating · Moderately improving · On track or maintaining SDG achievement · Information unavailable

Note: The full title of each SDG is available here: https://sustainabledevelopment.un.org/topics/sustainabledevelopmentgoals

INTERNATIONAL SPILLOVER INDEX

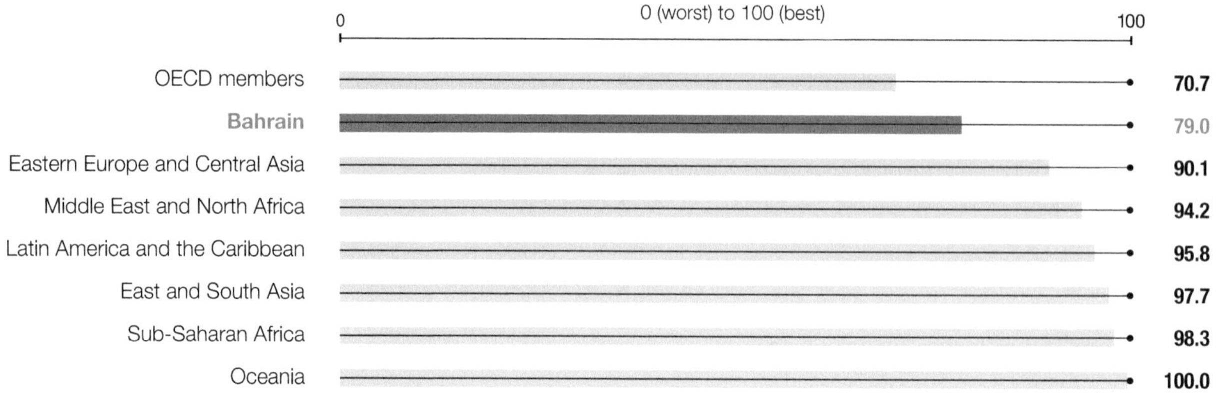

STATISTICAL PERFORMANCE INDEX

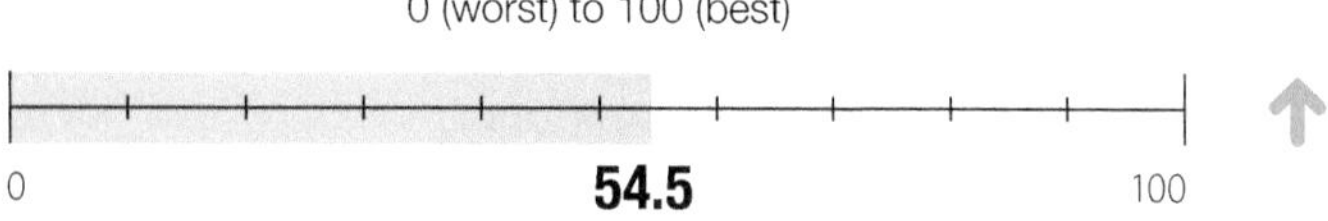

MISSING DATA IN SDG INDEX

20%

SDG1 – No Poverty		Value	Year	Rating	Trend
Poverty headcount ratio at \$1.90/day (%)	*	NA	NA	●	●
Poverty headcount ratio at \$3.20/day (%)	*	NA	NA	●	●
SDG2 – Zero Hunger					
Prevalence of undernourishment (%)	*	1.2	2019	●	●
Prevalence of stunting in children under 5 years of age (%)	*	2.6	2019	●	↑
Prevalence of wasting in children under 5 years of age (%)	*	0.7	2019	●	↑
Prevalence of obesity, BMI ≥ 30 (% of adult population)		29.8	2016	●	↓
Human Trophic Level (best 2–3 worst)		NA	NA	●	●
Cereal yield (tonnes per hectare of harvested land)		NA	NA	●	●
Sustainable Nitrogen Management Index (best 0–1.41 worst)		0.9	2015	●	↓
Exports of hazardous pesticides (tonnes per million population)		7.9	2019	●	●
SDG3 – Good Health and Well-Being					
Maternal mortality rate (per 100,000 live births)		14	2017	●	↑
Neonatal mortality rate (per 1,000 live births)		2.9	2020	●	↑
Mortality rate, under-5 (per 1,000 live births)		6.8	2020	●	↑
Incidence of tuberculosis (per 100,000 population)		13.0	2020	●	↑
New HIV infections (per 1,000 uninfected population)		1.0	2020	●	→
Age-standardized death rate due to cardiovascular disease, cancer, diabetes, or chronic respiratory disease in adults aged 30–70 years (%)		16.1	2019	●	↗
Age-standardized death rate attributable to household air pollution and ambient air pollution (per 100,000 population)		40	2016	●	●
Traffic deaths (per 100,000 population)		5.2	2019	●	↑
Life expectancy at birth (years)		75.8	2019	●	→
Adolescent fertility rate (births per 1,000 females aged 15 to 19)		12.5	2018	●	↑
Births attended by skilled health personnel (%)		99.9	2017	●	↑
Surviving infants who received 2 WHO-recommended vaccines (%)		98	2020	●	↑
Universal health coverage (UHC) index of service coverage (worst 0–100 best)		71	2019	●	↓
Subjective well-being (average ladder score, worst 0–10 best)		6.2	2020	●	↑
SDG4 – Quality Education					
Participation rate in pre-primary organized learning (% of children aged 4 to 6)		70.1	2019	●	↓
Net primary enrollment rate (%)		97.7	2019	●	↑
Lower secondary completion rate (%)		93.5	2019	●	↑
Literacy rate (% of population aged 15 to 24)		95.5	2010	●	●
SDG5 – Gender Equality					
Demand for family planning satisfied by modern methods (% of females aged 15 to 49)		NA	NA	●	●
Ratio of female-to-male mean years of education received (%)		93.8	2019	●	↓
Ratio of female-to-male labor force participation rate (%)		50.5	2020	●	→
Seats held by women in national parliament (%)		15.0	2020	●	↗
SDG6 – Clean Water and Sanitation					
Population using at least basic drinking water services (%)		100.0	2020	●	↑
Population using at least basic sanitation services (%)		100.0	2020	●	↑
Freshwater withdrawal (% of available freshwater resources)		133.7	2018	●	●
Anthropogenic wastewater that receives treatment (%)		86.9	2018	●	●
Scarce water consumption embodied in imports (m^3 H_2O eq/capita)		5166.9	2018	●	●
SDG7 – Affordable and Clean Energy					
Population with access to electricity (%)		100.0	2019	●	↑
Population with access to clean fuels and technology for cooking (%)		100.0	2019	●	↑
CO_2 emissions from fuel combustion per total electricity output ($MtCO_2$/TWh)		0.8	2019	●	↑
Share of renewable energy in total primary energy supply (%)		0.0	2019	●	→
SDG8 – Decent Work and Economic Growth					
Adjusted GDP growth (%)		-5.1	2020	●	●
Victims of modern slavery (per 1,000 population)	*	NA	NA	●	●
Adults with an account at a bank or other financial institution or with a mobile-money-service provider (% of population aged 15 or over)		82.6	2017	●	↑
Unemployment rate (% of total labor force)		1.8	2022	●	↑
Fundamental labor rights are effectively guaranteed (worst 0–1 best)		NA	NA	●	●
Fatal work-related accidents embodied in imports (per 100,000 population)		1.0	2015	●	↑

SDG9 – Industry, Innovation and Infrastructure		Value	Year	Rating	Trend
Population using the internet (%)		99.7	2020	●	↑
Mobile broadband subscriptions (per 100 population)		122.6	2019	●	↑
Logistics Performance Index: Quality of trade and transport-related infrastructure (worst 1–5 best)		2.7	2018	●	↓
The Times Higher Education Universities Ranking: Average score of top 3 universities (worst 0–100 best)	*	4.5	2019	●	●
Articles published in academic journals (per 1,000 population)		0.6	2020	●	↑
Expenditure on research and development (% of GDP)		0.1	2014	●	●
SDG10 – Reduced Inequalities					
Gini coefficient		NA	NA	●	●
Palma ratio		NA	NA	●	●
SDG11 – Sustainable Cities and Communities					
Proportion of urban population living in slums (%)		NA	NA	●	●
Annual mean concentration of particulate matter of less than 2.5 microns in diameter (PM2.5) (μg/m³)		72.8	2019	●	↓
Access to improved water source, piped (% of urban population)		NA	NA	●	●
Satisfaction with public transport (%)		70.0	2020	●	↓
SDG12 – Responsible Consumption and Production					
Municipal solid waste (kg/capita/day)		1.8	2016	●	●
Electronic waste (kg/capita)		15.9	2019	●	●
Production-based SO_2 emissions (kg/capita)		8.5	2018	●	●
SO_2 emissions embodied in imports (kg/capita)		7.6	2018	●	●
Production-based nitrogen emissions (kg/capita)		0.6	2015	●	↑
Nitrogen emissions embodied in imports (kg/capita)		6.0	2015	●	→
Exports of plastic waste (kg/capita)		0.6	2019	●	●
SDG13 – Climate Action					
CO_2 emissions from fossil fuel combustion and cement production (tCO_2/capita)		20.5	2020	●	→
CO_2 emissions embodied in imports (tCO_2/capita)		3.2	2018	●	→
CO_2 emissions embodied in fossil fuel exports (kg/capita)		0.0	2019	●	●
SDG14 – Life Below Water					
Mean area that is protected in marine sites important to biodiversity (%)		0.0	2020	●	→
Ocean Health Index: Clean Waters score (worst 0–100 best)		54.6	2020	●	→
Fish caught from overexploited or collapsed stocks (% of total catch)		NA	NA	●	●
Fish caught by trawling or dredging (%)		0.0	2018	●	↑
Fish caught that are then discarded (%)		16.8	2018	●	→
Marine biodiversity threats embodied in imports (per million population)		0.0	2018	●	●
SDG15 – Life on Land					
Mean area that is protected in terrestrial sites important to biodiversity (%)		0.0	2020	●	→
Mean area that is protected in freshwater sites important to biodiversity (%)		NA	NA	●	●
Red List Index of species survival (worst 0–1 best)		0.7	2021	●	↓
Permanent deforestation (% of forest area, 5-year average)		NA	NA	●	●
Terrestrial and freshwater biodiversity threats embodied in imports (per million population)		0.1	2018	●	●
SDG16 – Peace, Justice and Strong Institutions					
Homicides (per 100,000 population)		0.1	2019	●	↑
Unsentenced detainees (% of prison population)		NA	NA	●	●
Population who feel safe walking alone at night in the city or area where they live (%)		60	2011	●	●
Property Rights (worst 1–7 best)		5.8	2020	●	↑
Birth registrations with civil authority (% of children under age 5)		100.0	2020	●	●
Corruption Perception Index (worst 0–100 best)		42	2021	●	↓
Children involved in child labor (% of population aged 5 to 14)		NA	NA	●	●
Exports of major conventional weapons (TIV constant million USD per 100,000 population)		0.0	2020	●	●
Press Freedom Index (best 0–100 worst)		61.1	2021	●	↓
Access to and affordability of justice (worst 0–1 best)		NA	NA	●	●
SDG17 – Partnerships for the Goals					
Government spending on health and education (% of GDP)		4.7	2019	●	↓
For high-income and all OECD DAC countries: International concessional public finance, including official development assistance (% of GNI)		NA	NA	●	●
Other countries: Government revenue excluding grants (% of GDP)		NA	NA	●	●
Corporate Tax Haven Score (best 0–100 worst)	*	NA	NA	●	●
Statistical Performance Index (worst 0–100 best)		54.5	2019	●	↑

* Imputed data point

BANGLADESH

East and South Asia

OVERALL PERFORMANCE

COUNTRY RANKING

BANGLADESH

104/163

COUNTRY SCORE

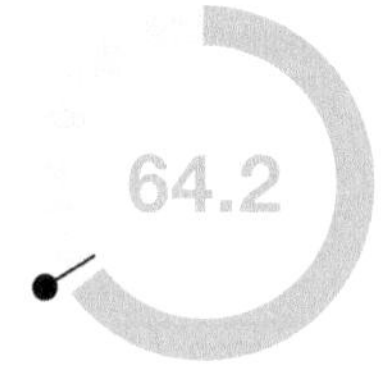

REGIONAL AVERAGE: 65.9

AVERAGE PERFORMANCE BY SDG

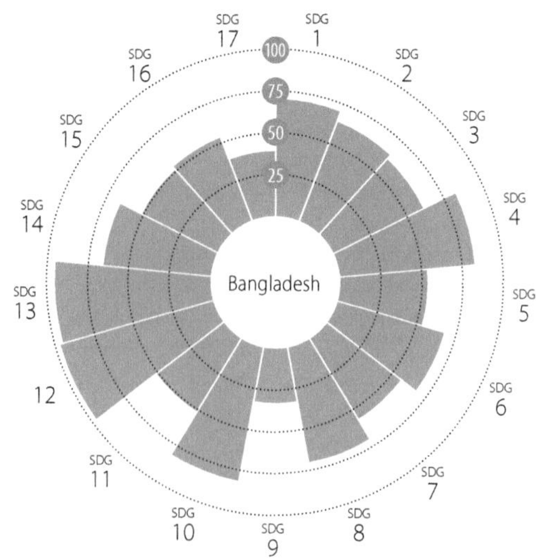

SDG DASHBOARDS AND TRENDS

Major challenges | Significant challenges | Challenges remain | SDG achieved | Information unavailable

Decreasing | Stagnating | Moderately improving | On track or maintaining SDG achievement | Information unavailable

Note: The full title of each SDG is available here: https://sustainabledevelopment.un.org/topics/sustainabledevelopmentgoals

INTERNATIONAL SPILLOVER INDEX

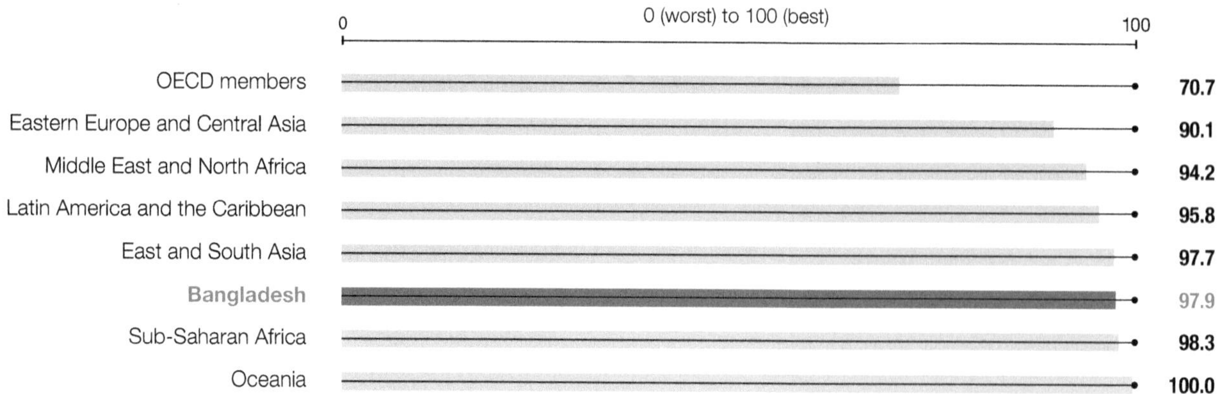

STATISTICAL PERFORMANCE INDEX

0 (worst) to 100 (best)

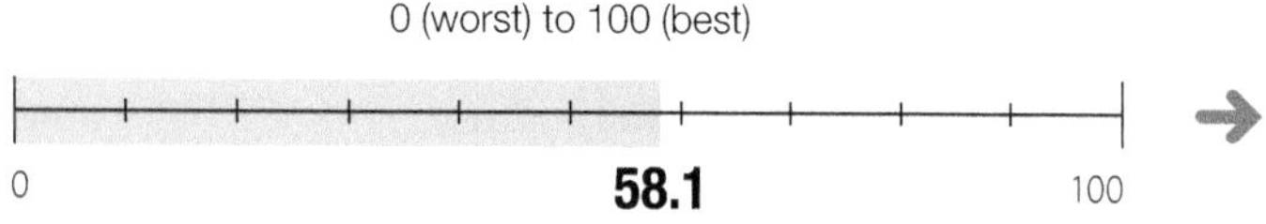

MISSING DATA IN SDG INDEX

4%

BANGLADESH

Performance by Indicator

SDG1 – No Poverty	Value	Year	Rating	Trend
Poverty headcount ratio at $1.90/day (%)	3.5	2022	●	↑
Poverty headcount ratio at $3.20/day (%)	28.2	2022	●	↑
SDG2 – Zero Hunger				
Prevalence of undernourishment (%)	9.7	2019	●	↑
Prevalence of stunting in children under 5 years of age (%)	28.0	2019	●	→
Prevalence of wasting in children under 5 years of age (%)	9.8	2019	●	→
Prevalence of obesity, BMI ≥ 30 (% of adult population)	3.6	2016	●	↑
Human Trophic Level (best 2–3 worst)	2.1	2017	●	↑
Cereal yield (tonnes per hectare of harvested land)	4.8	2018	●	↑
Sustainable Nitrogen Management Index (best 0–1.41 worst)	0.7	2015	●	→
Exports of hazardous pesticides (tonnes per million population)	NA	NA	●	●
SDG3 – Good Health and Well-Being				
Maternal mortality rate (per 100,000 live births)	173	2017	●	↑
Neonatal mortality rate (per 1,000 live births)	17.5	2020	●	↑
Mortality rate, under-5 (per 1,000 live births)	29.1	2020	●	↑
Incidence of tuberculosis (per 100,000 population)	218.0	2020	●	→
New HIV infections (per 1,000 uninfected population)	1.0	2020	●	→
Age-standardized death rate due to cardiovascular disease, cancer, diabetes, or chronic respiratory disease in adults aged 30–70 years (%)	18.9	2019	●	→
Age-standardized death rate attributable to household air pollution and ambient air pollution (per 100,000 population)	149	2016	●	●
Traffic deaths (per 100,000 population)	15.4	2019	●	→
Life expectancy at birth (years)	74.3	2019	●	→
Adolescent fertility rate (births per 1,000 females aged 15 to 19)	74.0	2019	●	↑
Births attended by skilled health personnel (%)	52.7	2018	●	→
Surviving infants who received 2 WHO-recommended vaccines (%)	97	2020	●	↑
Universal health coverage (UHC) index of service coverage (worst 0–100 best)	51	2019	●	↗
Subjective well-being (average ladder score, worst 0–10 best)	5.3	2020	●	↑
SDG4 – Quality Education				
Participation rate in pre-primary organized learning (% of children aged 4 to 6)	77.5	2019	●	●
Net primary enrollment rate (%)	95.0	2010	●	●
Lower secondary completion rate (%)	88.0	2018	●	↑
Literacy rate (% of population aged 15 to 24)	94.5	2020	●	↑
SDG5 – Gender Equality				
Demand for family planning satisfied by modern methods (% of females aged 15 to 49)	77.4	2019	●	●
Ratio of female-to-male mean years of education received (%)	82.6	2019	●	↗
Ratio of female-to-male labor force participation rate (%)	44.0	2020	●	→
Seats held by women in national parliament (%)	20.9	2020	●	→
SDG6 – Clean Water and Sanitation				
Population using at least basic drinking water services (%)	97.7	2020	●	↑
Population using at least basic sanitation services (%)	54.2	2020	●	→
Freshwater withdrawal (% of available freshwater resources)	5.7	2018	●	●
Anthropogenic wastewater that receives treatment (%)	0.0	2018	●	●
Scarce water consumption embodied in imports (m^3 H_2O eq/capita)	1053.7	2018	●	●
SDG7 – Affordable and Clean Energy				
Population with access to electricity (%)	92.2	2019	●	↑
Population with access to clean fuels and technology for cooking (%)	23.0	2019	●	→
CO_2 emissions from fuel combustion per total electricity output ($MtCO_2$/TWh)	1.2	2019	●	↑
Share of renewable energy in total primary energy supply (%)	18.3	2019	●	↓
SDG8 – Decent Work and Economic Growth				
Adjusted GDP growth (%)	1.4	2020	●	●
Victims of modern slavery (per 1,000 population)	3.7	2018	●	●
Adults with an account at a bank or other financial institution or with a mobile-money-service provider (% of population aged 15 or over)	50.0	2017	●	↑
Unemployment rate (% of total labor force)	5.0	2022	●	↓
Fundamental labor rights are effectively guaranteed (worst 0–1 best)	0.4	2020	●	↓
Fatal work-related accidents embodied in imports (per 100,000 population)	0.1	2015	●	↑

SDG9 – Industry, Innovation and Infrastructure	Value	Year	Rating	Trend
Population using the internet (%)	24.8	2020	●	↗
Mobile broadband subscriptions (per 100 population)	52.8	2019	●	↑
Logistics Performance Index: Quality of trade and transport-related infrastructure (worst 1–5 best)	2.4	2018	●	↑
The Times Higher Education Universities Ranking: Average score of top 3 universities (worst 0–100 best)	23.6	2022	●	●
Articles published in academic journals (per 1,000 population)	0.1	2020	●	→
Expenditure on research and development (% of GDP)	NA	NA	●	●
SDG10 – Reduced Inequalities				
Gini coefficient	32.4	2016	●	●
Palma ratio	1.3	2018	●	●
SDG11 – Sustainable Cities and Communities				
Proportion of urban population living in slums (%)	47.6	2018	●	↗
Annual mean concentration of particulate matter of less than 2.5 microns in diameter (PM2.5) (μg/m^3)	59.5	2019	●	↗
Access to improved water source, piped (% of urban population)	35.7	2020	●	→
Satisfaction with public transport (%)	78.0	2020	●	↑
SDG12 – Responsible Consumption and Production				
Municipal solid waste (kg/capita/day)	0.3	2012	●	●
Electronic waste (kg/capita)	1.2	2019	●	●
Production-based SO_2 emissions (kg/capita)	1.7	2018	●	●
SO_2 emissions embodied in imports (kg/capita)	0.6	2018	●	●
Production-based nitrogen emissions (kg/capita)	6.9	2015	●	↑
Nitrogen emissions embodied in imports (kg/capita)	0.2	2015	●	↑
Exports of plastic waste (kg/capita)	NA	NA	●	●
SDG13 – Climate Action				
CO_2 emissions from fossil fuel combustion and cement production (tCO_2/capita)	0.6	2020	●	↑
CO_2 emissions embodied in imports (tCO_2/capita)	0.2	2018	●	↑
CO_2 emissions embodied in fossil fuel exports (kg/capita)	NA	NA	●	●
SDG14 – Life Below Water				
Mean area that is protected in marine sites important to biodiversity (%)	34.5	2020	●	→
Ocean Health Index: Clean Waters score (worst 0–100 best)	33.6	2020	●	→
Fish caught from overexploited or collapsed stocks (% of total catch)	3.2	2018	●	↑
Fish caught by trawling or dredging (%)	15.4	2018	●	→
Fish caught that are then discarded (%)	5.1	2018	●	↓
Marine biodiversity threats embodied in imports (per million population)	0.0	2018	●	●
SDG15 – Life on Land				
Mean area that is protected in terrestrial sites important to biodiversity (%)	41.5	2020	●	→
Mean area that is protected in freshwater sites important to biodiversity (%)	0.0	2020	●	→
Red List Index of species survival (worst 0–1 best)	0.7	2021	●	↓
Permanent deforestation (% of forest area, 5-year average)	0.3	2020	●	↓
Terrestrial and freshwater biodiversity threats embodied in imports (per million population)	0.0	2018	●	●
SDG16 – Peace, Justice and Strong Institutions				
Homicides (per 100,000 population)	2.4	2018	●	↗
Unsentenced detainees (% of prison population)	81.3	2019	●	↓
Population who feel safe walking alone at night in the city or area where they live (%)	64	2020	●	↓
Property Rights (worst 1–7 best)	4.0	2020	●	↓
Birth registrations with civil authority (% of children under age 5)	56.0	2020	●	●
Corruption Perception Index (worst 0–100 best)	26	2021	●	→
Children involved in child labor (% of population aged 5 to 14)	6.8	2019	●	●
Exports of major conventional weapons (TIV constant million USD per 100,000 population)	* 0.0	2020	●	●
Press Freedom Index (best 0–100 worst)	49.7	2021	●	↓
Access to and affordability of justice (worst 0–1 best)	0.4	2020	●	↗
SDG17 – Partnerships for the Goals				
Government spending on health and education (% of GDP)	1.8	2019	●	↓
For high-income and all OECD DAC countries: International concessional public finance, including official development assistance (% of GNI)	NA	NA	●	●
Other countries: Government revenue excluding grants (% of GDP)	10.2	2016	●	●
Corporate Tax Haven Score (best 0–100 worst)	* 0.0	2019	●	●
Statistical Performance Index (worst 0–100 best)	58.1	2019	●	→

* Imputed data point

5. Country Profiles

BARBADOS

Latin America and the Caribbean

OVERALL PERFORMANCE

COUNTRY RANKING

BARBADOS

73/163

COUNTRY SCORE

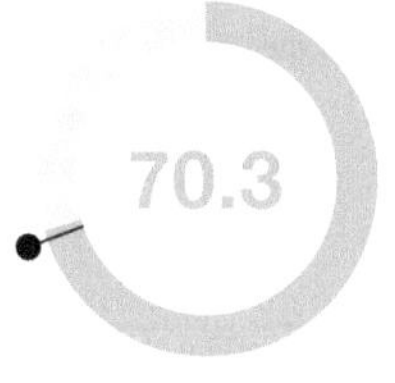

REGIONAL AVERAGE: 69.5

AVERAGE PERFORMANCE BY SDG

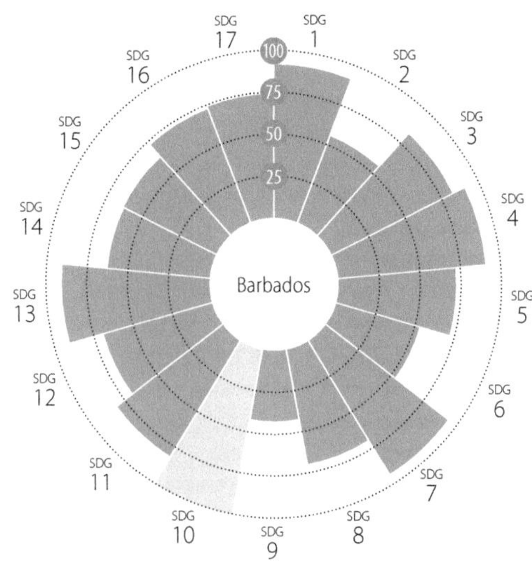

SDG DASHBOARDS AND TRENDS

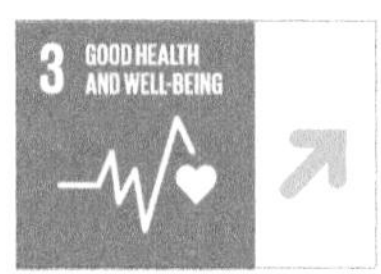

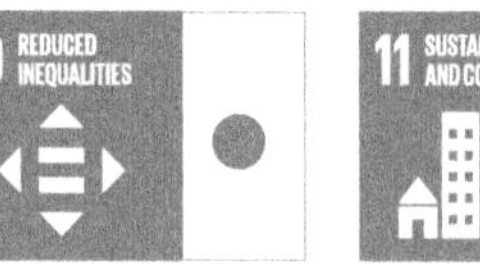

Major challenges | Significant challenges | Challenges remain | SDG achieved | Information unavailable

Decreasing | Stagnating | Moderately improving | On track or maintaining SDG achievement | Information unavailable

Note: The full title of each SDG is available here: https://sustainabledevelopment.un.org/topics/sustainabledevelopmentgoals

INTERNATIONAL SPILLOVER INDEX

STATISTICAL PERFORMANCE INDEX

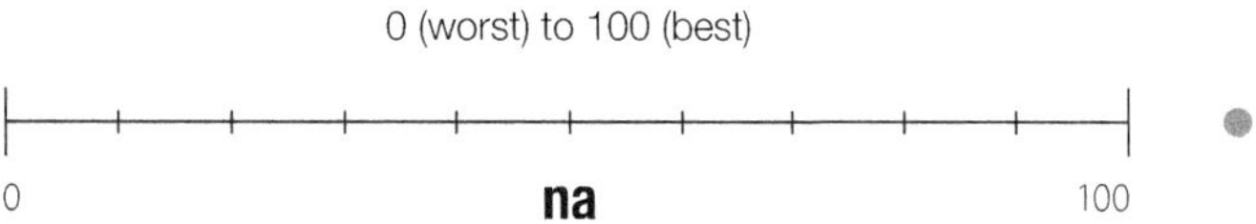

MISSING DATA IN SDG INDEX

20%

SDG1 – No Poverty	Value	Year	Rating	Trend
Poverty headcount ratio at $1.90/day (%)	2.7	2022	●	→
Poverty headcount ratio at $3.20/day (%)	7.1	2022	●	→
SDG2 – Zero Hunger				
Prevalence of undernourishment (%)	4.1	2019	●	↑
Prevalence of stunting in children under 5 years of age (%)	7.7	2012	●	↑
Prevalence of wasting in children under 5 years of age (%)	6.8	2012	●	↑
Prevalence of obesity, BMI ≥ 30 (% of adult population)	23.1	2016	●	↓
Human Trophic Level (best 2–3 worst)	2.3	2017	●	→
Cereal yield (tonnes per hectare of harvested land)	2.9	2018	●	↑
Sustainable Nitrogen Management Index (best 0–1.41 worst)	1.2	2015	●	→
Exports of hazardous pesticides (tonnes per million population)	0.0	2019	●	●
SDG3 – Good Health and Well-Being				
Maternal mortality rate (per 100,000 live births)	27	2017	●	↑
Neonatal mortality rate (per 1,000 live births)	8.1	2020	●	↑
Mortality rate, under-5 (per 1,000 live births)	12.2	2020	●	↑
Incidence of tuberculosis (per 100,000 population)	2.4	2020	●	↑
New HIV infections (per 1,000 uninfected population)	1.0	2020	●	→
Age-standardized death rate due to cardiovascular disease, cancer, diabetes, or chronic respiratory disease in adults aged 30–70 years (%)	16.0	2019	●	→
Age-standardized death rate attributable to household air pollution and ambient air pollution (per 100,000 population)	31	2016	●	●
Traffic deaths (per 100,000 population)	8.2	2019	●	↑
Life expectancy at birth (years)	76.0	2019	●	→
Adolescent fertility rate (births per 1,000 females aged 15 to 19)	49.7	2007	●	●
Births attended by skilled health personnel (%)	99.1	2016	●	●
Surviving infants who received 2 WHO-recommended vaccines (%)	85	2020	●	↓
Universal health coverage (UHC) index of service coverage (worst 0–100 best)	74	2019	●	↗
Subjective well-being (average ladder score, worst 0–10 best)	NA	NA	●	●
SDG4 – Quality Education				
Participation rate in pre-primary organized learning (% of children aged 4 to 6)	87.5	2020	●	↓
Net primary enrollment rate (%)	97.3	2020	●	↑
Lower secondary completion rate (%)	89.0	2020	●	●
Literacy rate (% of population aged 15 to 24)	99.9	2014	●	●
SDG5 – Gender Equality				
Demand for family planning satisfied by modern methods (% of females aged 15 to 49)	69.9	2012	●	●
Ratio of female-to-male mean years of education received (%)	106.8	2019	●	↑
Ratio of female-to-male labor force participation rate (%)	87.6	2020	●	↑
Seats held by women in national parliament (%)	20.0	2020	●	→
SDG6 – Clean Water and Sanitation				
Population using at least basic drinking water services (%)	98.5	2020	●	↑
Population using at least basic sanitation services (%)	98.1	2020	●	↑
Freshwater withdrawal (% of available freshwater resources)	87.5	2018	●	●
Anthropogenic wastewater that receives treatment (%)	1.2	2018	●	●
Scarce water consumption embodied in imports (m^3 H_2O eq/capita)	NA	NA	●	●
SDG7 – Affordable and Clean Energy				
Population with access to electricity (%)	100.0	2019	●	↑
Population with access to clean fuels and technology for cooking (%)	100.0	2019	●	↑
CO_2 emissions from fuel combustion per total electricity output ($MtCO_2$/TWh)	1.2	2019	●	↑
Share of renewable energy in total primary energy supply (%)	NA	NA	●	●
SDG8 – Decent Work and Economic Growth				
Adjusted GDP growth (%)	-9.3	2020	●	●
Victims of modern slavery (per 1,000 population)	2.7	2018	●	●
Adults with an account at a bank or other financial institution or with a mobile-money-service provider (% of population aged 15 or over)	NA	NA	●	●
Unemployment rate (% of total labor force)	9.8	2022	●	→
Fundamental labor rights are effectively guaranteed (worst 0–1 best)	0.7	2020	●	↑
Fatal work-related accidents embodied in imports (per 100,000 population)	0.6	2015	●	↑

SDG9 – Industry, Innovation and Infrastructure	Value	Year	Rating	Trend
Population using the internet (%)	81.8	2017	●	●
Mobile broadband subscriptions (per 100 population)	42.2	2019	●	↓
Logistics Performance Index: Quality of trade and transport-related infrastructure (worst 1–5 best)	NA	NA	●	●
The Times Higher Education Universities Ranking: Average score of top 3 universities (worst 0–100 best)	* 0.0	2022	●	●
Articles published in academic journals (per 1,000 population)	0.5	2020	●	↑
Expenditure on research and development (% of GDP)	NA	NA	●	●
SDG10 – Reduced Inequalities				
Gini coefficient	NA	NA	●	●
Palma ratio	NA	NA	●	●
SDG11 – Sustainable Cities and Communities				
Proportion of urban population living in slums (%)	NA	NA	●	●
Annual mean concentration of particulate matter of less than 2.5 microns in diameter (PM2.5) (μg/m³)	21.6	2019	●	↗
Access to improved water source, piped (% of urban population)	NA	NA	●	●
Satisfaction with public transport (%)	NA	NA	●	●
SDG12 – Responsible Consumption and Production				
Municipal solid waste (kg/capita/day)	1.7	2011	●	●
Electronic waste (kg/capita)	12.7	2019	●	●
Production-based SO_2 emissions (kg/capita)	NA	NA	●	●
SO_2 emissions embodied in imports (kg/capita)	NA	NA	●	●
Production-based nitrogen emissions (kg/capita)	5.6	2015	●	↑
Nitrogen emissions embodied in imports (kg/capita)	8.7	2015	●	→
Exports of plastic waste (kg/capita)	4.2	2021	●	●
SDG13 – Climate Action				
CO_2 emissions from fossil fuel combustion and cement production (tCO_2/capita)	3.8	2020	●	↗
CO_2 emissions embodied in imports (tCO_2/capita)	NA	NA	●	●
CO_2 emissions embodied in fossil fuel exports (kg/capita)	304.1	2021	●	●
SDG14 – Life Below Water				
Mean area that is protected in marine sites important to biodiversity (%)	2.9	2020	●	→
Ocean Health Index: Clean Waters score (worst 0–100 best)	64.1	2020	●	→
Fish caught from overexploited or collapsed stocks (% of total catch)	39.3	2018	●	↑
Fish caught by trawling or dredging (%)	0.0	2018	●	↑
Fish caught that are then discarded (%)	1.7	2018	●	↑
Marine biodiversity threats embodied in imports (per million population)	0.5	2018	●	●
SDG15 – Life on Land				
Mean area that is protected in terrestrial sites important to biodiversity (%)	1.8	2020	●	→
Mean area that is protected in freshwater sites important to biodiversity (%)	NA	NA	●	●
Red List Index of species survival (worst 0–1 best)	0.9	2021	●	↓
Permanent deforestation (% of forest area, 5-year average)	0.3	2020	●	↓
Terrestrial and freshwater biodiversity threats embodied in imports (per million population)	0.6	2018	●	●
SDG16 – Peace, Justice and Strong Institutions				
Homicides (per 100,000 population)	16.7	2019	●	↓
Unsentenced detainees (% of prison population)	84.1	2019	●	↓
Population who feel safe walking alone at night in the city or area where they live (%)	NA	NA	●	●
Property Rights (worst 1–7 best)	4.8	2020	●	●
Birth registrations with civil authority (% of children under age 5)	98.7	2020	●	●
Corruption Perception Index (worst 0–100 best)	65	2021	●	↑
Children involved in child labor (% of population aged 5 to 14)	1.4	2019	●	●
Exports of major conventional weapons (TIV constant million USD per 100,000 population)	* 0.0	2020	●	●
Press Freedom Index (best 0–100 worst)	NA	NA	●	●
Access to and affordability of justice (worst 0–1 best)	0.7	2020	●	↑
SDG17 – Partnerships for the Goals				
Government spending on health and education (% of GDP)	7.1	2020	●	↓
For high-income and all OECD DAC countries: International concessional public finance, including official development assistance (% of GNI)	NA	NA	●	●
Other countries: Government revenue excluding grants (% of GDP)	NA	NA	●	●
Corporate Tax Haven Score (best 0–100 worst)	* 0.0	2019	●	●
Statistical Performance Index (worst 0–100 best)	NA	NA	●	●

* Imputed data point

5. Country Profiles

BELARUS

Eastern Europe and Central Asia

OVERALL PERFORMANCE

COUNTRY RANKING

BELARUS

34/163

COUNTRY SCORE

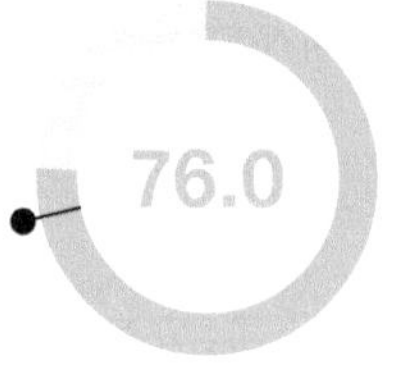

REGIONAL AVERAGE: 71.6

AVERAGE PERFORMANCE BY SDG

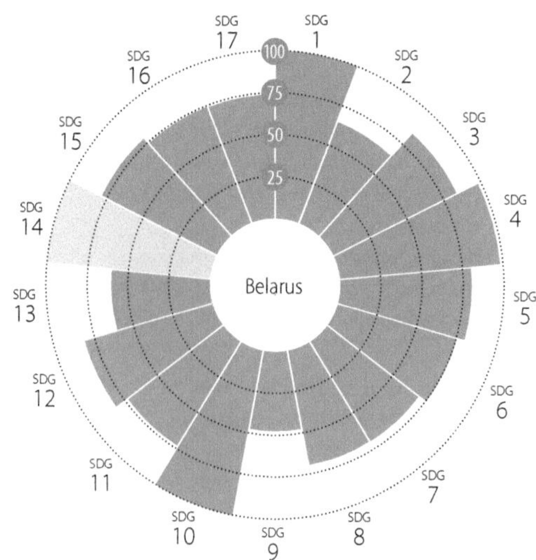

SDG DASHBOARDS AND TRENDS

Major challenges · Significant challenges · Challenges remain · SDG achieved · Information unavailable

Decreasing · Stagnating · Moderately improving · On track or maintaining SDG achievement · Information unavailable

Note: The full title of each SDG is available here: https://sustainabledevelopment.un.org/topics/sustainabledevelopmentgoals

INTERNATIONAL SPILLOVER INDEX

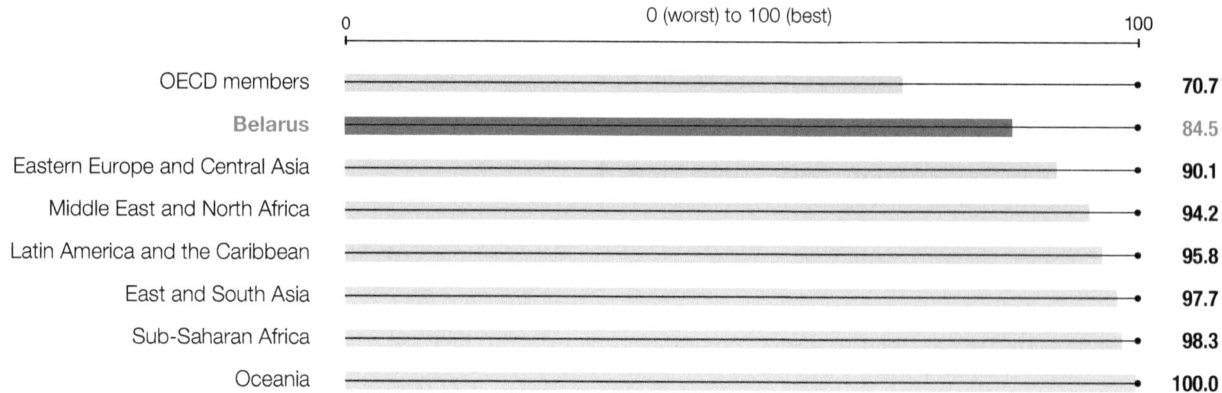

STATISTICAL PERFORMANCE INDEX

0 (worst) to 100 (best)

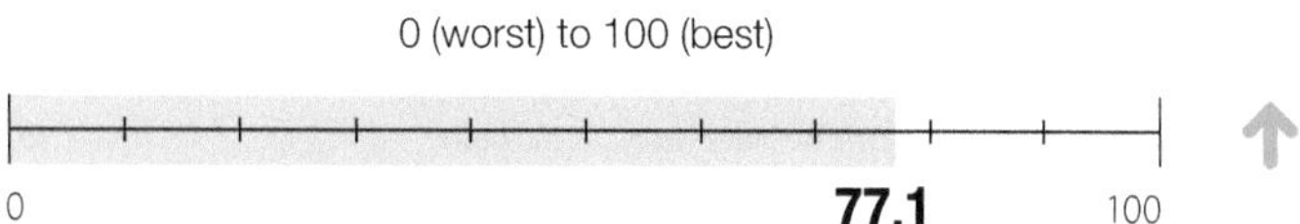

MISSING DATA IN SDG INDEX

1%

SDG1 – No Poverty	Value	Year	Rating	Trend
Poverty headcount ratio at $1.90/day (%)	0.0	2022	●	↑
Poverty headcount ratio at $3.20/day (%)	0.1	2022	●	↑
SDG2 – Zero Hunger				
Prevalence of undernourishment (%)	2.5	2019	●	↑
Prevalence of stunting in children under 5 years of age (%)	4.5	2005	●	↑
Prevalence of wasting in children under 5 years of age (%)	2.2	2005	●	↑
Prevalence of obesity, BMI ≥ 30 (% of adult population)	24.5	2016	●	↓
Human Trophic Level (best 2–3 worst)	2.3	2017	●	↗
Cereal yield (tonnes per hectare of harvested land)	2.7	2018	●	↑
Sustainable Nitrogen Management Index (best 0–1.41 worst)	0.8	2015	●	→
Exports of hazardous pesticides (tonnes per million population)	0.0	2019	●	●
SDG3 – Good Health and Well-Being				
Maternal mortality rate (per 100,000 live births)	2	2017	●	↑
Neonatal mortality rate (per 1,000 live births)	1.0	2020	●	↑
Mortality rate, under-5 (per 1,000 live births)	2.9	2020	●	↑
Incidence of tuberculosis (per 100,000 population)	26.0	2020	●	↑
New HIV infections (per 1,000 uninfected population)	0.1	2020	●	↑
Age-standardized death rate due to cardiovascular disease, cancer, diabetes, or chronic respiratory disease in adults aged 30–70 years (%)	23.8	2019	●	→
Age-standardized death rate attributable to household air pollution and ambient air pollution (per 100,000 population)	61	2016	●	●
Traffic deaths (per 100,000 population)	7.6	2019	●	↑
Life expectancy at birth (years)	74.8	2019	●	↗
Adolescent fertility rate (births per 1,000 females aged 15 to 19)	11.7	2018	●	↑
Births attended by skilled health personnel (%)	99.8	2014	●	●
Surviving infants who received 2 WHO-recommended vaccines (%)	97	2020	●	↑
Universal health coverage (UHC) index of service coverage (worst 0–100 best)	74	2019	●	↑
Subjective well-being (average ladder score, worst 0–10 best)	5.8	2019	●	●
SDG4 – Quality Education				
Participation rate in pre-primary organized learning (% of children aged 4 to 6)	98.1	2018	●	●
Net primary enrollment rate (%)	98.7	2018	●	●
Lower secondary completion rate (%)	97.8	2018	●	↑
Literacy rate (% of population aged 15 to 24)	99.9	2019	●	●
SDG5 – Gender Equality				
Demand for family planning satisfied by modern methods (% of females aged 15 to 49)	73.0	2012	●	●
Ratio of female-to-male mean years of education received (%)	98.4	2019	●	↑
Ratio of female-to-male labor force participation rate (%)	80.6	2020	●	↑
Seats held by women in national parliament (%)	40.0	2020	●	↑
SDG6 – Clean Water and Sanitation				
Population using at least basic drinking water services (%)	96.5	2020	●	→
Population using at least basic sanitation services (%)	97.9	2020	●	↑
Freshwater withdrawal (% of available freshwater resources)	4.6	2018	●	●
Anthropogenic wastewater that receives treatment (%)	7.2	2018	●	●
Scarce water consumption embodied in imports (m^3 H_2O eq/capita)	2642.6	2018	●	●
SDG7 – Affordable and Clean Energy				
Population with access to electricity (%)	100.0	2019	●	↑
Population with access to clean fuels and technology for cooking (%)	98.9	2019	●	↑
CO_2 emissions from fuel combustion per total electricity output ($MtCO_2$/TWh)	1.6	2019	●	↗
Share of renewable energy in total primary energy supply (%)	6.7	2019	●	→
SDG8 – Decent Work and Economic Growth				
Adjusted GDP growth (%)	-0.4	2020	●	●
Victims of modern slavery (per 1,000 population)	10.9	2018	●	●
Adults with an account at a bank or other financial institution or with a mobile-money-service provider (% of population aged 15 or over)	81.2	2017	●	↑
Unemployment rate (% of total labor force)	4.6	2022	●	↑
Fundamental labor rights are effectively guaranteed (worst 0–1 best)	0.5	2020	●	↓
Fatal work-related accidents embodied in imports (per 100,000 population)	0.0	2015	●	↑

* Imputed data point

SDG9 – Industry, Innovation and Infrastructure	Value	Year	Rating	Trend
Population using the internet (%)	85.1	2020	●	↑
Mobile broadband subscriptions (per 100 population)	89.5	2019	●	↑
Logistics Performance Index: Quality of trade and transport-related infrastructure (worst 1–5 best)	2.4	2018	●	↓
The Times Higher Education Universities Ranking: Average score of top 3 universities (worst 0–100 best)	16.5	2022	●	●
Articles published in academic journals (per 1,000 population)	0.3	2020	●	↗
Expenditure on research and development (% of GDP)	0.6	2018	●	↗
SDG10 – Reduced Inequalities				
Gini coefficient	25.3	2019	●	↑
Palma ratio	0.9	2018	●	●
SDG11 – Sustainable Cities and Communities				
Proportion of urban population living in slums (%)	45.2	2018	●	●
Annual mean concentration of particulate matter of less than 2.5 microns in diameter (PM2.5) (μg/m^3)	18.3	2019	●	↗
Access to improved water source, piped (% of urban population)	99.1	2020	●	↑
Satisfaction with public transport (%)	57.0	2019	●	●
SDG12 – Responsible Consumption and Production				
Municipal solid waste (kg/capita/day)	1.2	2015	●	●
Electronic waste (kg/capita)	9.3	2019	●	●
Production-based SO_2 emissions (kg/capita)	1.7	2018	●	●
SO_2 emissions embodied in imports (kg/capita)	5.6	2018	●	●
Production-based nitrogen emissions (kg/capita)	29.4	2015	●	→
Nitrogen emissions embodied in imports (kg/capita)	0.1	2015	●	↑
Exports of plastic waste (kg/capita)	1.4	2020	●	●
SDG13 – Climate Action				
CO_2 emissions from fossil fuel combustion and cement production (tCO_2/capita)	6.1	2020	●	→
CO_2 emissions embodied in imports (tCO_2/capita)	2.8	2018	●	→
CO_2 emissions embodied in fossil fuel exports (kg/capita)	496.6	2020	●	●
SDG14 – Life Below Water				
Mean area that is protected in marine sites important to biodiversity (%)	NA	NA	●	●
Ocean Health Index: Clean Waters score (worst 0–100 best)	NA	NA	●	●
Fish caught from overexploited or collapsed stocks (% of total catch)	NA	NA	●	●
Fish caught by trawling or dredging (%)	NA	NA	●	●
Fish caught that are then discarded (%)	NA	NA	●	●
Marine biodiversity threats embodied in imports (per million population)	0.0	2018	●	●
SDG15 – Life on Land				
Mean area that is protected in terrestrial sites important to biodiversity (%)	47.1	2020	●	→
Mean area that is protected in freshwater sites important to biodiversity (%)	53.3	2020	●	→
Red List Index of species survival (worst 0–1 best)	1.0	2021	●	↑
Permanent deforestation (% of forest area, 5-year average)	0.0	2020	●	↑
Terrestrial and freshwater biodiversity threats embodied in imports (per million population)	0.0	2018	●	●
SDG16 – Peace, Justice and Strong Institutions				
Homicides (per 100,000 population)	2.4	2019	●	↑
Unsentenced detainees (% of prison population)	9.2	2018	●	↑
Population who feel safe walking alone at night in the city or area where they live (%)	61	2019	●	●
Property Rights (worst 1–7 best)	NA	NA	●	●
Birth registrations with civil authority (% of children under age 5)	100.0	2020	●	●
Corruption Perception Index (worst 0–100 best)	41	2021	●	↗
Children involved in child labor (% of population aged 5 to 14)	1.0	2019	●	●
Exports of major conventional weapons (TIV constant million USD per 100,000 population)	1.0	2020	●	●
Press Freedom Index (best 0–100 worst)	50.8	2021	●	→
Access to and affordability of justice (worst 0–1 best)	0.6	2020	●	↑
SDG17 – Partnerships for the Goals				
Government spending on health and education (% of GDP)	9.1	2020	●	↑
For high-income and all OECD DAC countries: International concessional public finance, including official development assistance (% of GNI)	NA	NA	●	●
Other countries: Government revenue excluding grants (% of GDP)	29.6	2019	●	→
Corporate Tax Haven Score (best 0–100 worst)	* 0.0	2019	●	●
Statistical Performance Index (worst 0–100 best)	77.1	2019	●	↑

5. Country Profiles

BELGIUM

OVERALL PERFORMANCE

COUNTRY RANKING

BELGIUM

18 /163

COUNTRY SCORE

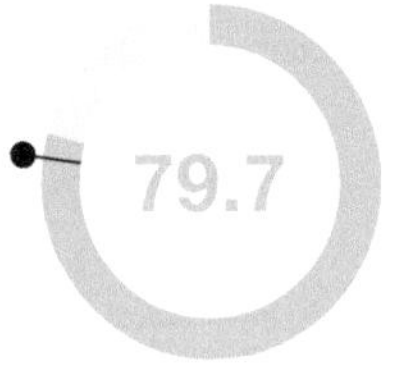

REGIONAL AVERAGE: 77.2

AVERAGE PERFORMANCE BY SDG

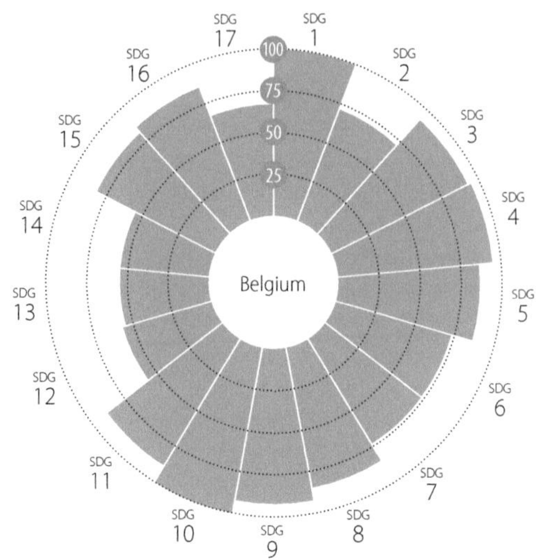

SDG DASHBOARDS AND TRENDS

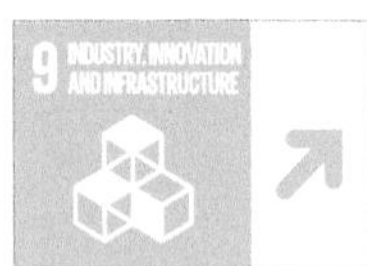

Information unavailable

Information unavailable

Note: The full title of each SDG is available here: https://sustainabledevelopment.un.org/topics/sustainabledevelopmentgoals

INTERNATIONAL SPILLOVER INDEX

STATISTICAL PERFORMANCE INDEX

0 (worst) to 100 (best)

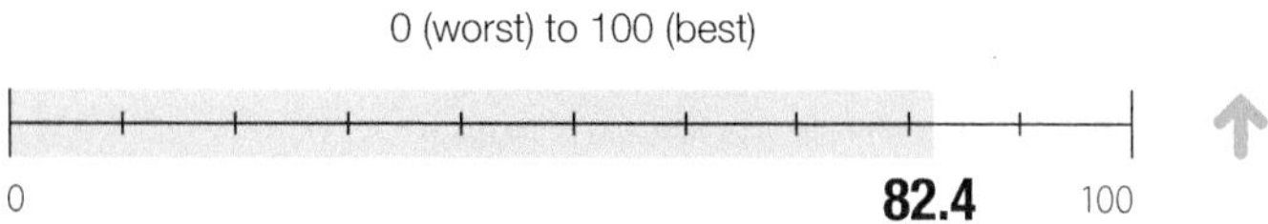

MISSING DATA IN SDG INDEX

4%

SDG1 – No Poverty	Value	Year	Rating	Trend
Poverty headcount ratio at \$1.90/day (%)	0.2	2022	●	↑
Poverty headcount ratio at \$3.20/day (%)	0.2	2022	●	↑
Poverty rate after taxes and transfers (%)	8.1	2019	●	●

SDG2 – Zero Hunger	Value	Year	Rating	Trend
Prevalence of undernourishment (%)	2.5	2019	●	↑
Prevalence of stunting in children under 5 years of age (%)	1.6	2014	●	↑
Prevalence of wasting in children under 5 years of age (%)	0.4	2014	●	↑
Prevalence of obesity, BMI ≥ 30 (% of adult population)	22.1	2016	●	↓
Human Trophic Level (best 2–3 worst)	2.4	2017	●	↗
Cereal yield (tonnes per hectare of harvested land)	8.2	2018	●	↑
Sustainable Nitrogen Management Index (best 0–1.41 worst)	0.7	2015	●	→
Yield gap closure (% of potential yield)	77.2	2018	●	●
Exports of hazardous pesticides (tonnes per million population)	42.3	2019	●	●

SDG3 – Good Health and Well-Being	Value	Year	Rating	Trend
Maternal mortality rate (per 100,000 live births)	5	2017	●	↑
Neonatal mortality rate (per 1,000 live births)	2.4	2020	●	↑
Mortality rate, under-5 (per 1,000 live births)	4.2	2020	●	↑
Incidence of tuberculosis (per 100,000 population)	7.7	2020	●	↑
New HIV infections (per 1,000 uninfected population)	1.0	2020	●	→
Age-standardized death rate due to cardiovascular disease, cancer, diabetes, or chronic respiratory disease in adults aged 30–70 years (%)	10.6	2019	●	↑
Age-standardized death rate attributable to household air pollution and ambient air pollution (per 100,000 population)	16	2016	●	●
Traffic deaths (per 100,000 population)	5.8	2019	●	↑
Life expectancy at birth (years)	81.4	2019	●	↑
Adolescent fertility rate (births per 1,000 females aged 15 to 19)	5.5	2018	●	↑
Births attended by skilled health personnel (%)	NA	NA	●	●
Surviving infants who received 2 WHO-recommended vaccines (%)	96	2020	●	↑
Universal health coverage (UHC) index of service coverage (worst 0–100 best)	85	2019	●	↑
Subjective well-being (average ladder score, worst 0–10 best)	6.9	2021	●	↑
Gap in life expectancy at birth among regions (years)	2.6	2019	●	↑
Gap in self-reported health status by income (percentage points)	29.7	2019	●	↓
Daily smokers (% of population aged 15 and over)	15.4	2018	●	●

SDG4 – Quality Education	Value	Year	Rating	Trend
Participation rate in pre-primary organized learning (% of children aged 4 to 6)	96.2	2019	●	↑
Net primary enrollment rate (%)	99.1	2019	●	↑
Lower secondary completion rate (%)	92.5	2019	●	↑
Literacy rate (% of population aged 15 to 24)	NA	NA	●	●
Tertiary educational attainment (% of population aged 25 to 34)	48.5	2020	●	↑
PISA score (worst 0–600 best)	500.0	2018	●	↑
Variation in science performance explained by socio-economic status (%)	20.0	2018	●	↓
Underachievers in science (% of 15-year-olds)	20.0	2018	●	↓

SDG5 – Gender Equality	Value	Year	Rating	Trend
Demand for family planning satisfied by modern methods (% of females aged 15 to 49)	NA	NA	●	●
Ratio of female-to-male mean years of education received (%)	97.5	2019	●	↑
Ratio of female-to-male labor force participation rate (%)	84.4	2020	●	↑
Seats held by women in national parliament (%)	41.3	2020	●	↑
Gender wage gap (% of male median wage)	3.8	2019	●	↑

SDG6 – Clean Water and Sanitation	Value	Year	Rating	Trend
Population using at least basic drinking water services (%)	100.0	2020	●	↑
Population using at least basic sanitation services (%)	99.5	2020	●	↑
Freshwater withdrawal (% of available freshwater resources)	49.1	2018	●	●
Anthropogenic wastewater that receives treatment (%)	67.9	2018	●	●
Scarce water consumption embodied in imports (m^3 H_2O eq/capita)	6802.1	2018	●	●
Population using safely managed water services (%)	99.9	2020	●	↑
Population using safely managed sanitation services (%)	88.8	2020	●	↑

SDG7 – Affordable and Clean Energy	Value	Year	Rating	Trend
Population with access to electricity (%)	100.0	2019	●	↑
Population with access to clean fuels and technology for cooking (%)	100.0	2019	●	↑
CO_2 emissions from fuel combustion per total electricity output ($MtCO_2$/TWh)	1.1	2019	●	↑
Share of renewable energy in total primary energy supply (%)	7.8	2019	●	→

SDG8 – Decent Work and Economic Growth	Value	Year	Rating	Trend
Adjusted GDP growth (%)	-0.5	2020	●	●
Victims of modern slavery (per 1,000 population)	2.0	2018	●	●
Adults with an account at a bank or other financial institution or with a mobile-money-service provider (% of population aged 15 or over)	98.6	2017	●	↑
Fundamental labor rights are effectively guaranteed (worst 0–1 best)	0.8	2020	●	↑
Fatal work-related accidents embodied in imports (per 100,000 population)	1.6	2015	●	↑
Employment-to-population ratio (%)	64.5	2020	●	↑
Youth not in employment, education or training (NEET) (% of population aged 15 to 29)	12.5	2020	●	↑

SDG9 – Industry, Innovation and Infrastructure	Value	Year	Rating	Trend
Population using the internet (%)	91.5	2020	●	↑
Mobile broadband subscriptions (per 100 population)	87.0	2019	●	↑
Logistics Performance Index: Quality of trade and transport-related infrastructure (worst 1–5 best)	4.0	2018	●	↑
The Times Higher Education Universities Ranking: Average score of top 3 universities (worst 0–100 best)	64.7	2022	●	●
Articles published in academic journals (per 1,000 population)	3.0	2020	●	↑
Expenditure on research and development (% of GDP)	2.8	2018	●	↑
Researchers (per 1,000 employed population)	12.4	2019	●	↑
Triadic patent families filed (per million population)	37.9	2019	●	↑
Gap in internet access by income (percentage points)	18.3	2020	●	↑
Female share of graduates from STEM fields at the tertiary level (%)	25.8	2017	●	↓

SDG10 – Reduced Inequalities	Value	Year	Rating	Trend
Gini coefficient	27.2	2018	●	↑
Palma ratio	0.9	2019	●	●
Elderly poverty rate (% of population aged 66 or over)	10.5	2019	●	●

SDG11 – Sustainable Cities and Communities	Value	Year	Rating	Trend
Proportion of urban population living in slums (%)	* 0.0	2018	●	↑
Annual mean concentration of particulate matter of less than 2.5 microns in diameter (PM2.5) (μg/m^3)	12.3	2019	●	↑
Access to improved water source, piped (% of urban population)	100.0	2020	●	↑
Satisfaction with public transport (%)	59.0	2021	●	↓
Population with rent overburden (%)	7.0	2019	●	↑

SDG12 – Responsible Consumption and Production	Value	Year	Rating	Trend
Electronic waste (kg/capita)	20.4	2019	●	●
Production-based SO_2 emissions (kg/capita)	15.4	2018	●	●
SO_2 emissions embodied in imports (kg/capita)	11.9	2018	●	●
Production-based nitrogen emissions (kg/capita)	12.5	2015	●	↑
Nitrogen emissions embodied in imports (kg/capita)	15.6	2015	●	↓
Exports of plastic waste (kg/capita)	29.2	2021	●	●
Non-recycled municipal solid waste (kg/capita/day)	0.5	2019	●	↑

SDG13 – Climate Action	Value	Year	Rating	Trend
CO_2 emissions from fossil fuel combustion and cement production (tCO_2/capita)	7.2	2020	●	↗
CO_2 emissions embodied in imports (tCO_2/capita)	5.2	2018	●	↓
CO_2 emissions embodied in fossil fuel exports (kg/capita)	0.0	2020	●	●
Carbon Pricing Score at EUR60/tCO_2 (%, worst 0–100 best)	33.6	2018	●	↗

SDG14 – Life Below Water	Value	Year	Rating	Trend
Mean area that is protected in marine sites important to biodiversity (%)	94.0	2020	●	↑
Ocean Health Index: Clean Waters score (worst 0–100 best)	32.0	2020	●	↓
Fish caught from overexploited or collapsed stocks (% of total catch)	NA	NA	●	●
Fish caught by trawling or dredging (%)	13.0	2018	●	↑
Fish caught that are then discarded (%)	34.6	2018	●	↓
Marine biodiversity threats embodied in imports (per million population)	0.2	2018	●	●

SDG15 – Life on Land	Value	Year	Rating	Trend
Mean area that is protected in terrestrial sites important to biodiversity (%)	75.6	2020	●	→
Mean area that is protected in freshwater sites important to biodiversity (%)	85.6	2020	●	↑
Red List Index of species survival (worst 0–1 best)	1.0	2021	●	↑
Permanent deforestation (% of forest area, 5-year average)	0.0	2020	●	↑
Terrestrial and freshwater biodiversity threats embodied in imports (per million population)	4.7	2018	●	●

SDG16 – Peace, Justice and Strong Institutions	Value	Year	Rating	Trend
Homicides (per 100,000 population)	3.1	2002	●	●
Unsentenced detainees (% of prison population)	35.6	2018	●	↓
Population who feel safe walking alone at night in the city or area where they live (%)	71	2021	●	↑
Property Rights (worst 1–7 best)	5.2	2020	●	↑
Birth registrations with civil authority (% of children under age 5)	100.0	2020	●	●
Corruption Perception Index (worst 0–100 best)	73	2021	●	↑
Children involved in child labor (% of population aged 5 to 14)	* 0.0	2019	●	●
Exports of major conventional weapons (TIV constant million USD per 100,000 population)	0.3	2020	●	●
Press Freedom Index (best 0–100 worst)	11.7	2021	●	↑
Access to and affordability of justice (worst 0–1 best)	0.7	2020	●	↑
Persons held in prison (per 100,000 population)	87.7	2018	●	↑

SDG17 – Partnerships for the Goals	Value	Year	Rating	Trend
Government spending on health and education (% of GDP)	14.6	2019	●	↑
For high-income and all OECD DAC countries: International concessional public finance, including official development assistance (% of GNI)	0.5	2021	●	→
Other countries: Government revenue excluding grants (% of GDP)	NA	NA	●	●
Corporate Tax Haven Score (best 0–100 worst)	67.8	2019	●	●
Financial Secrecy Score (best 0–100 worst)	45.1	2020	●	●
Shifted profits of multinationals (US\$ billion)	45.7	2018	●	↓
Statistical Performance Index (worst 0–100 best)	82.4	2019	●	↑

* Imputed data point

BELIZE

Latin America and the Caribbean

OVERALL PERFORMANCE

COUNTRY RANKING

BELIZE

100/163

COUNTRY SCORE

REGIONAL AVERAGE: 69.5

AVERAGE PERFORMANCE BY SDG

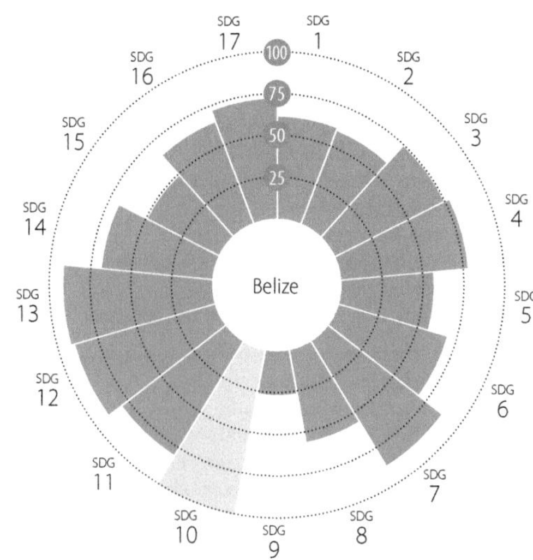

SDG DASHBOARDS AND TRENDS

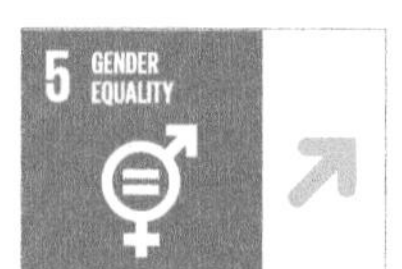

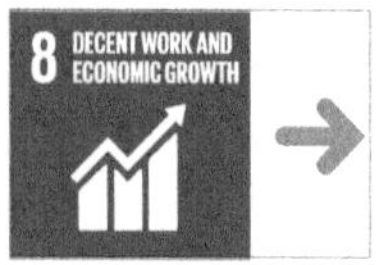

Major challenges · Significant challenges · Challenges remain · SDG achieved · Information unavailable

Decreasing · Stagnating · Moderately improving · On track or maintaining SDG achievement · Information unavailable

Note: The full title of each SDG is available here: https://sustainabledevelopment.un.org/topics/sustainabledevelopmentgoals

INTERNATIONAL SPILLOVER INDEX

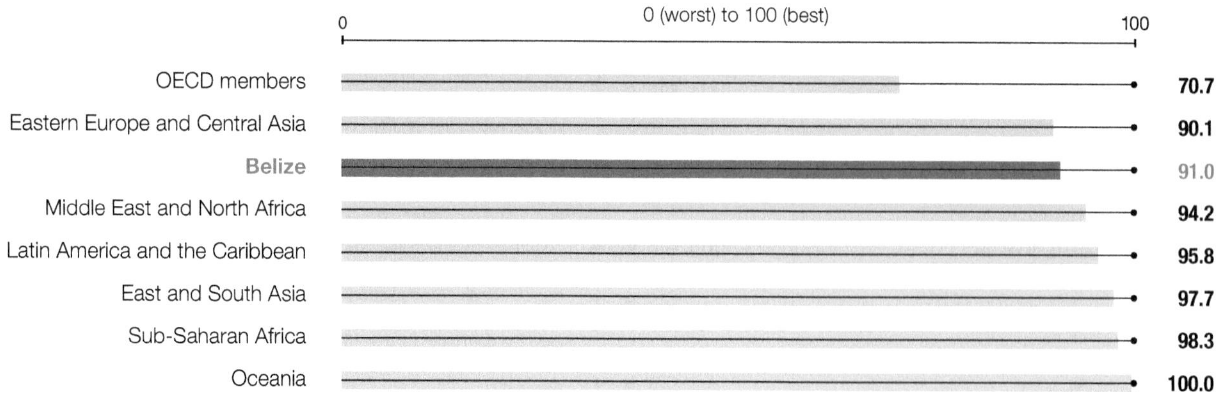

STATISTICAL PERFORMANCE INDEX

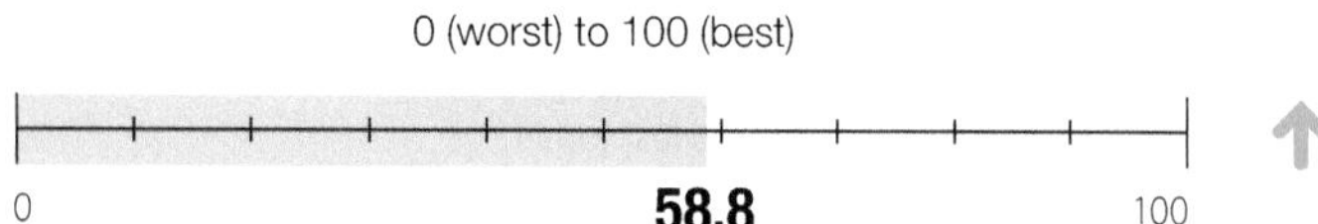

MISSING DATA IN SDG INDEX

11%

	Value	Year	Rating	Trend
SDG1 – No Poverty				
Poverty headcount ratio at \$1.90/day (%)	14.5	2022	●	↓
Poverty headcount ratio at \$3.20/day (%)	29.3	2022	●	↓
SDG2 – Zero Hunger				
Prevalence of undernourishment (%)	5.9	2019	●	↑
Prevalence of stunting in children under 5 years of age (%)	15.0	2015	●	→
Prevalence of wasting in children under 5 years of age (%)	1.8	2015	●	↑
Prevalence of obesity, BMI ≥ 30 (% of adult population)	24.1	2016	●	↓
Human Trophic Level (best 2–3 worst)	2.2	2017	●	↓
Cereal yield (tonnes per hectare of harvested land)	4.0	2018	●	↑
Sustainable Nitrogen Management Index (best 0–1.41 worst)	0.9	2015	●	↓
Exports of hazardous pesticides (tonnes per million population)	NA	NA	●	●
SDG3 – Good Health and Well-Being				
Maternal mortality rate (per 100,000 live births)	36	2017	●	↑
Neonatal mortality rate (per 1,000 live births)	7.7	2020	●	↑
Mortality rate, under-5 (per 1,000 live births)	11.7	2020	●	↑
Incidence of tuberculosis (per 100,000 population)	23.0	2020	●	→
New HIV infections (per 1,000 uninfected population)	0.5	2020	●	→
Age-standardized death rate due to cardiovascular disease, cancer, diabetes, or chronic respiratory disease in adults aged 30–70 years (%)	16.5	2019	●	→
Age-standardized death rate attributable to household air pollution and ambient air pollution (per 100,000 population)	69	2016	●	●
Traffic deaths (per 100,000 population)	22.6	2019	●	↗
Life expectancy at birth (years)	74.4	2019	●	→
Adolescent fertility rate (births per 1,000 females aged 15 to 19)	58.2	2019	●	↗
Births attended by skilled health personnel (%)	94.0	2017	●	↑
Surviving infants who received 2 WHO-recommended vaccines (%)	79	2020	●	↓
Universal health coverage (UHC) index of service coverage (worst 0–100 best)	67	2019	●	↗
Subjective well-being (average ladder score, worst 0–10 best)	6.0	2014	●	●
SDG4 – Quality Education				
Participation rate in pre-primary organized learning (% of children aged 4 to 6)	84.4	2020	●	→
Net primary enrollment rate (%)	99.8	2020	●	↑
Lower secondary completion rate (%)	69.5	2020	●	→
Literacy rate (% of population aged 15 to 24)	84.2	2000	●	●
SDG5 – Gender Equality				
Demand for family planning satisfied by modern methods (% of females aged 15 to 49)	64.9	2016	●	●
Ratio of female-to-male mean years of education received (%)	100.0	2019	●	↑
Ratio of female-to-male labor force participation rate (%)	60.4	2020	●	↓
Seats held by women in national parliament (%)	9.7	2020	●	↗
SDG6 – Clean Water and Sanitation				
Population using at least basic drinking water services (%)	98.4	2020	●	↑
Population using at least basic sanitation services (%)	88.2	2020	●	→
Freshwater withdrawal (% of available freshwater resources)	1.3	2018	●	●
Anthropogenic wastewater that receives treatment (%)	0.6	2018	●	●
Scarce water consumption embodied in imports (m^3 H_2O eq/capita)	4765.9	2018	●	●
SDG7 – Affordable and Clean Energy				
Population with access to electricity (%)	92.7	2019	●	↗
Population with access to clean fuels and technology for cooking (%)	82.4	2019	●	→
CO_2 emissions from fuel combustion per total electricity output ($MtCO_2$/TWh)	0.8	2019	●	↑
Share of renewable energy in total primary energy supply (%)	NA	NA	●	●
SDG8 – Decent Work and Economic Growth				
Adjusted GDP growth (%)	-8.6	2020	●	●
Victims of modern slavery (per 1,000 population)	NA	NA	●	●
Adults with an account at a bank or other financial institution or with a mobile-money-service provider (% of population aged 15 or over)	48.2	2014	●	●
Unemployment rate (% of total labor force)	7.8	2022	●	→
Fundamental labor rights are effectively guaranteed (worst 0–1 best)	0.5	2020	●	↓
Fatal work-related accidents embodied in imports (per 100,000 population)	0.3	2015	●	↑

	Value	Year	Rating	Trend
SDG9 – Industry, Innovation and Infrastructure				
Population using the internet (%)	50.8	2019	●	↗
Mobile broadband subscriptions (per 100 population)	43.9	2019	●	↑
Logistics Performance Index: Quality of trade and transport-related infrastructure (worst 1–5 best)	NA	NA	●	●
The Times Higher Education Universities Ranking: Average score of top 3 universities (worst 0–100 best)	* 0.0	2022	●	●
Articles published in academic journals (per 1,000 population)	0.1	2020	●	→
Expenditure on research and development (% of GDP)	NA	NA	●	●
SDG10 – Reduced Inequalities				
Gini coefficient	NA	NA	●	●
Palma ratio	NA	NA	●	●
SDG11 – Sustainable Cities and Communities				
Proportion of urban population living in slums (%)	3.5	2018	●	↑
Annual mean concentration of particulate matter of less than 2.5 microns in diameter (PM2.5) (μg/m^3)	21.3	2019	●	↗
Access to improved water source, piped (% of urban population)	96.4	2020	●	↑
Satisfaction with public transport (%)	49.0	2014	●	●
SDG12 – Responsible Consumption and Production				
Municipal solid waste (kg/capita/day)	0.8	2015	●	●
Electronic waste (kg/capita)	5.8	2019	●	●
Production-based SO_2 emissions (kg/capita)	13.8	2018	●	●
SO_2 emissions embodied in imports (kg/capita)	1.3	2018	●	●
Production-based nitrogen emissions (kg/capita)	10.3	2015	●	↑
Nitrogen emissions embodied in imports (kg/capita)	3.2	2015	●	↑
Exports of plastic waste (kg/capita)	1.0	2021	●	●
SDG13 – Climate Action				
CO_2 emissions from fossil fuel combustion and cement production (tCO_2/capita)	1.5	2020	●	↑
CO_2 emissions embodied in imports (tCO_2/capita)	0.6	2018	●	↑
CO_2 emissions embodied in fossil fuel exports (kg/capita)	289.5	2021	●	●
SDG14 – Life Below Water				
Mean area that is protected in marine sites important to biodiversity (%)	31.2	2020	●	→
Ocean Health Index: Clean Waters score (worst 0–100 best)	66.3	2020	●	→
Fish caught from overexploited or collapsed stocks (% of total catch)	NA	NA	●	●
Fish caught by trawling or dredging (%)	0.4	2018	●	↑
Fish caught that are then discarded (%)	7.4	2018	●	↓
Marine biodiversity threats embodied in imports (per million population)	0.1	2018	●	●
SDG15 – Life on Land				
Mean area that is protected in terrestrial sites important to biodiversity (%)	43.3	2020	●	→
Mean area that is protected in freshwater sites important to biodiversity (%)	15.3	2020	●	→
Red List Index of species survival (worst 0–1 best)	0.8	2021	●	↓
Permanent deforestation (% of forest area, 5-year average)	0.8	2020	●	↓
Terrestrial and freshwater biodiversity threats embodied in imports (per million population)	0.2	2018	●	●
SDG16 – Peace, Justice and Strong Institutions				
Homicides (per 100,000 population)	25.7	2020	●	↗
Unsentenced detainees (% of prison population)	50.8	2019	●	↑
Population who feel safe walking alone at night in the city or area where they live (%)	50	2014	●	●
Property Rights (worst 1–7 best)	NA	NA	●	●
Birth registrations with civil authority (% of children under age 5)	95.7	2020	●	●
Corruption Perception Index (worst 0–100 best)	NA	NA	●	●
Children involved in child labor (% of population aged 5 to 14)	3.3	2019	●	●
Exports of major conventional weapons (TIV constant million USD per 100,000 population)	* 0.0	2020	●	●
Press Freedom Index (best 0–100 worst)	27.6	2021	●	↑
Access to and affordability of justice (worst 0–1 best)	0.5	2020	●	→
SDG17 – Partnerships for the Goals				
Government spending on health and education (% of GDP)	12.1	2020	●	↑
For high-income and all OECD DAC countries: International concessional public finance, including official development assistance (% of GNI)	NA	NA	●	●
Other countries: Government revenue excluding grants (% of GDP)	29.0	2017	●	●
Corporate Tax Haven Score (best 0–100 worst)	* 0.0	2019	●	●
Statistical Performance Index (worst 0–100 best)	58.8	2019	●	↑

* Imputed data point

BENIN

Sub-Saharan Africa

OVERALL PERFORMANCE

COUNTRY RANKING

BENIN

153/163

COUNTRY SCORE

AVERAGE PERFORMANCE BY SDG

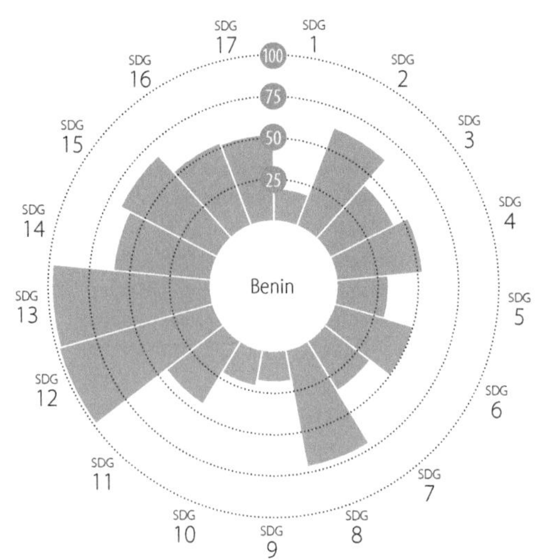

SDG DASHBOARDS AND TRENDS

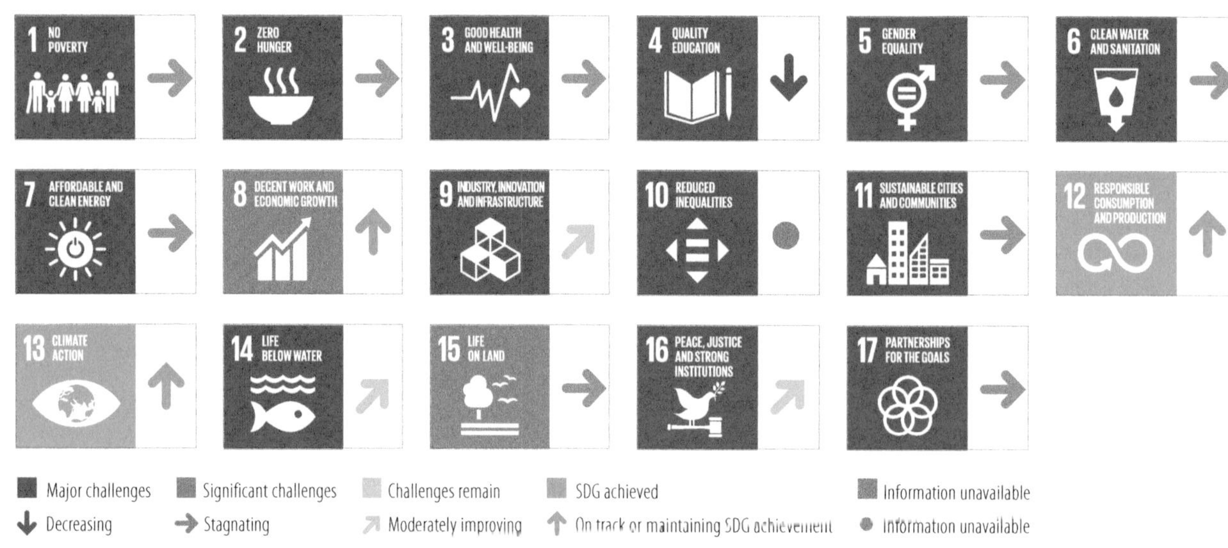

Major challenges | Significant challenges | Challenges remain | SDG achieved | Information unavailable

Decreasing | Stagnating | Moderately improving | On track or maintaining SDG achievement | Information unavailable

Note: The full title of each SDG is available here: https://sustainabledevelopment.un.org/topics/sustainabledevelopmentgoals

INTERNATIONAL SPILLOVER INDEX

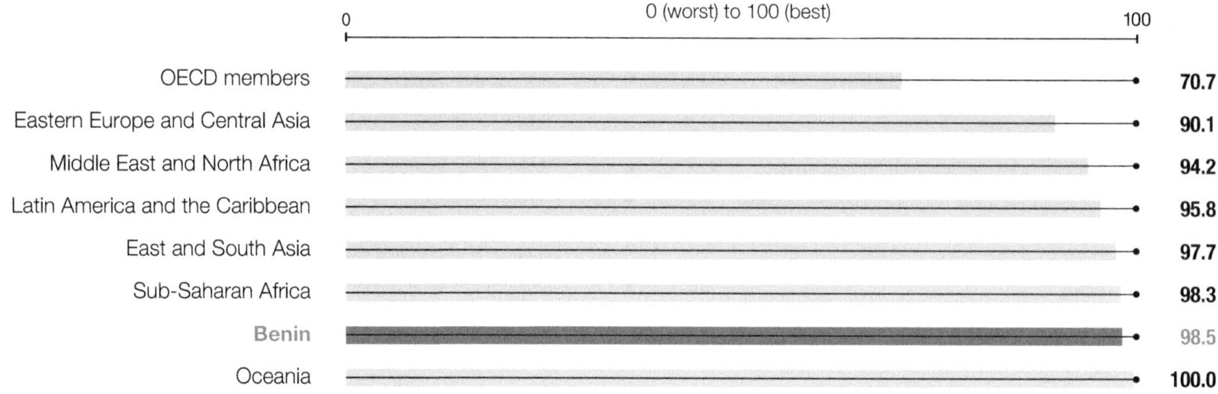

STATISTICAL PERFORMANCE INDEX

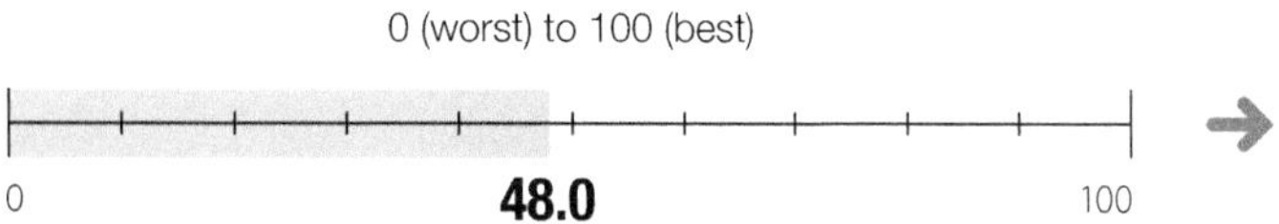

MISSING DATA IN SDG INDEX

5%

SDG1 – No Poverty	Value	Year	Rating	Trend
Poverty headcount ratio at $1.90/day (%)	45.5	2022	●	→
Poverty headcount ratio at $3.20/day (%)	69.5	2022	●	→
SDG2 – Zero Hunger				
Prevalence of undernourishment (%)	7.6	2019	●	↓
Prevalence of stunting in children under 5 years of age (%)	32.2	2018	●	→
Prevalence of wasting in children under 5 years of age (%)	5.0	2018	●	↑
Prevalence of obesity, BMI ≥ 30 (% of adult population)	9.6	2016	●	↑
Human Trophic Level (best 2–3 worst)	2.1	2017	●	↑
Cereal yield (tonnes per hectare of harvested land)	1.4	2018	●	→
Sustainable Nitrogen Management Index (best 0–1.41 worst)	0.8	2015	●	→
Exports of hazardous pesticides (tonnes per million population)	13.6	2019	●	●
SDG3 – Good Health and Well-Being				
Maternal mortality rate (per 100,000 live births)	397	2017	●	↗
Neonatal mortality rate (per 1,000 live births)	29.7	2020	●	→
Mortality rate, under-5 (per 1,000 live births)	85.9	2020	●	→
Incidence of tuberculosis (per 100,000 population)	55.0	2020	●	→
New HIV infections (per 1,000 uninfected population)	0.2	2020	●	↑
Age-standardized death rate due to cardiovascular disease, cancer, diabetes, or chronic respiratory disease in adults aged 30–70 years (%)	22.6	2019	●	→
Age-standardized death rate attributable to household air pollution and ambient air pollution (per 100,000 population)	205	2016	●	●
Traffic deaths (per 100,000 population)	26.8	2019	●	→
Life expectancy at birth (years)	63.4	2019	●	→
Adolescent fertility rate (births per 1,000 females aged 15 to 19)	108.0	2016	●	●
Births attended by skilled health personnel (%)	78.1	2018	●	→
Surviving infants who received 2 WHO-recommended vaccines (%)	65	2020	●	↓
Universal health coverage (UHC) index of service coverage (worst 0–100 best)	38	2019	●	→
Subjective well-being (average ladder score, worst 0–10 best)	4.5	2021	●	↗
SDG4 – Quality Education				
Participation rate in pre-primary organized learning (% of children aged 4 to 6)	84.8	2018	●	●
Net primary enrollment rate (%)	93.3	2020	●	↓
Lower secondary completion rate (%)	33.0	2020	●	↓
Literacy rate (% of population aged 15 to 24)	60.9	2018	●	●
SDG5 – Gender Equality				
Demand for family planning satisfied by modern methods (% of females aged 15 to 49)	28.0	2018	●	→
Ratio of female-to-male mean years of education received (%)	43.6	2019	●	↓
Ratio of female-to-male labor force participation rate (%)	95.7	2020	●	↑
Seats held by women in national parliament (%)	7.2	2020	●	→
SDG6 – Clean Water and Sanitation				
Population using at least basic drinking water services (%)	65.4	2020	●	→
Population using at least basic sanitation services (%)	17.0	2020	●	→
Freshwater withdrawal (% of available freshwater resources)	1.0	2018	●	●
Anthropogenic wastewater that receives treatment (%)	0.0	2018	●	●
Scarce water consumption embodied in imports (m^3 H_2O eq/capita)	462.6	2018	●	●
SDG7 – Affordable and Clean Energy				
Population with access to electricity (%)	40.3	2019	●	↗
Population with access to clean fuels and technology for cooking (%)	4.0	2019	●	↓
CO_2 emissions from fuel combustion per total electricity output ($MtCO_2$/TWh)	34.0	2019	●	↓
Share of renewable energy in total primary energy supply (%)	54.6	2019	●	↑
SDG8 – Decent Work and Economic Growth				
Adjusted GDP growth (%)	-1.6	2020	●	●
Victims of modern slavery (per 1,000 population)	5.5	2018	●	●
Adults with an account at a bank or other financial institution or with a mobile-money-service provider (% of population aged 15 or over)	38.5	2017	●	↑
Unemployment rate (% of total labor force)	1.5	2022	●	↑
Fundamental labor rights are effectively guaranteed (worst 0–1 best)	0.6	2020	●	●
Fatal work-related accidents embodied in imports (per 100,000 population)	0.0	2015	●	↑

* Imputed data point

SDG9 – Industry, Innovation and Infrastructure	Value	Year	Rating	Trend
Population using the internet (%)	25.8	2020	●	↗
Mobile broadband subscriptions (per 100 population)	21.5	2019	●	↗
Logistics Performance Index: Quality of trade and transport-related infrastructure (worst 1–5 best)	2.5	2018	●	↗
The Times Higher Education Universities Ranking: Average score of top 3 universities (worst 0–100 best)	* 0.0	2022	●	●
Articles published in academic journals (per 1,000 population)	0.1	2020	●	→
Expenditure on research and development (% of GDP)	NA	NA	●	●
SDG10 – Reduced Inequalities				
Gini coefficient	47.8	2015	●	●
Palma ratio	2.9	2018	●	●
SDG11 – Sustainable Cities and Communities				
Proportion of urban population living in slums (%)	59.2	2018	●	→
Annual mean concentration of particulate matter of less than 2.5 microns in diameter (PM2.5) (μg/m³)	41.9	2019	●	↓
Access to improved water source, piped (% of urban population)	48.6	2020	●	↓
Satisfaction with public transport (%)	46.0	2021	●	↗
SDG12 – Responsible Consumption and Production				
Municipal solid waste (kg/capita/day)	NA	NA	●	●
Electronic waste (kg/capita)	0.8	2019	●	●
Production-based SO_2 emissions (kg/capita)	0.7	2018	●	●
SO_2 emissions embodied in imports (kg/capita)	0.5	2018	●	●
Production-based nitrogen emissions (kg/capita)	6.5	2015	●	↑
Nitrogen emissions embodied in imports (kg/capita)	0.4	2015	●	↑
Exports of plastic waste (kg/capita)	0.0	2020	●	●
SDG13 – Climate Action				
CO_2 emissions from fossil fuel combustion and cement production (tCO_2/capita)	0.6	2020	●	↑
CO_2 emissions embodied in imports (tCO_2/capita)	0.2	2018	●	↑
CO_2 emissions embodied in fossil fuel exports (kg/capita)	0.0	2020	●	●
SDG14 – Life Below Water				
Mean area that is protected in marine sites important to biodiversity (%)	0.0	2020	●	→
Ocean Health Index: Clean Waters score (worst 0–100 best)	23.9	2020	●	→
Fish caught from overexploited or collapsed stocks (% of total catch)	NA	NA	●	●
Fish caught by trawling or dredging (%)	0.0	2018	●	↑
Fish caught that are then discarded (%)	0.0	2018	●	↑
Marine biodiversity threats embodied in imports (per million population)	0.0	2018	●	●
SDG15 – Life on Land				
Mean area that is protected in terrestrial sites important to biodiversity (%)	66.7	2020	●	→
Mean area that is protected in freshwater sites important to biodiversity (%)	0.0	2020	●	→
Red List Index of species survival (worst 0–1 best)	0.9	2021	●	↑
Permanent deforestation (% of forest area, 5-year average)	0.2	2020	●	↗
Terrestrial and freshwater biodiversity threats embodied in imports (per million population)	0.0	2018	●	●
SDG16 – Peace, Justice and Strong Institutions				
Homicides (per 100,000 population)	NA	NA	●	●
Unsentenced detainees (% of prison population)	62.3	2017	●	●
Population who feel safe walking alone at night in the city or area where they live (%)	54	2021	●	↗
Property Rights (worst 1–7 best)	4.3	2020	●	↑
Birth registrations with civil authority (% of children under age 5)	85.6	2020	●	●
Corruption Perception Index (worst 0–100 best)	42	2021	●	↗
Children involved in child labor (% of population aged 5 to 14)	24.8	2019	●	●
Exports of major conventional weapons (TIV constant million USD per 100,000 population)	* 0.0	2020	●	●
Press Freedom Index (best 0–100 worst)	38.2	2021	●	↓
Access to and affordability of justice (worst 0–1 best)	0.4	2020	●	●
SDG17 – Partnerships for the Goals				
Government spending on health and education (% of GDP)	3.5	2019	●	↓
For high-income and all OECD DAC countries: International concessional public finance, including official development assistance (% of GNI)	NA	NA	●	●
Other countries: Government revenue excluding grants (% of GDP)	NA	NA	●	●
Corporate Tax Haven Score (best 0–100 worst)	* 0.0	2019	●	●
Statistical Performance Index (worst 0–100 best)	48.0	2019	●	→

BHUTAN

East and South Asia

OVERALL PERFORMANCE

COUNTRY RANKING

BHUTAN

70 /163

COUNTRY SCORE

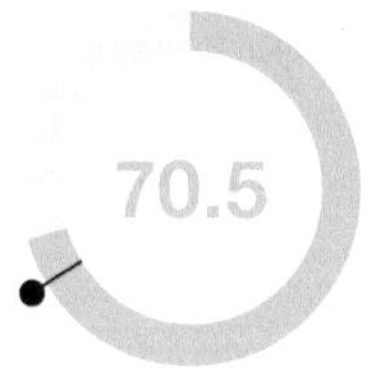

REGIONAL AVERAGE: 65.9

AVERAGE PERFORMANCE BY SDG

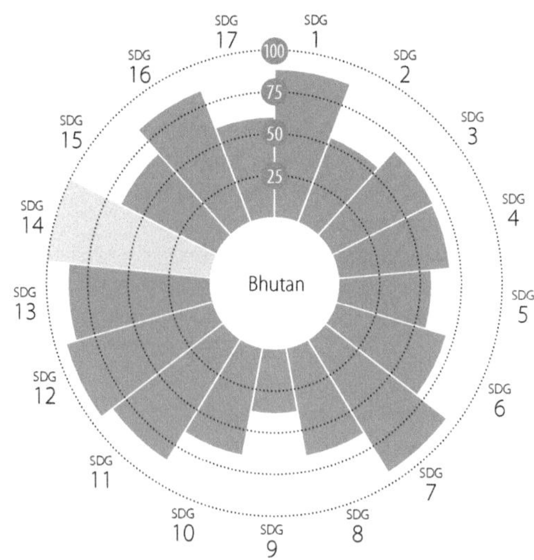

SDG DASHBOARDS AND TRENDS

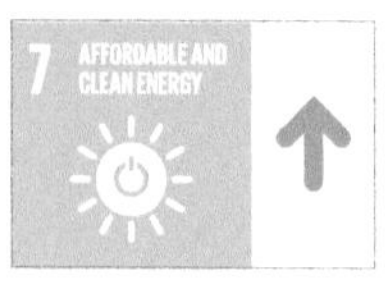

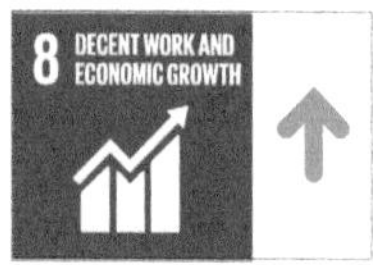

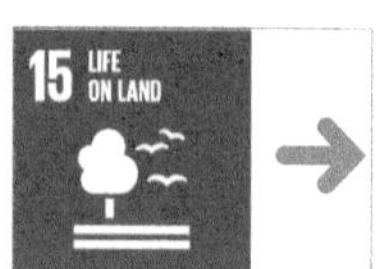

Major challenges | Significant challenges | Challenges remain | SDG achieved | Information unavailable

Decreasing | Stagnating | Moderately improving | On track or maintaining SDG achievement | Information unavailable

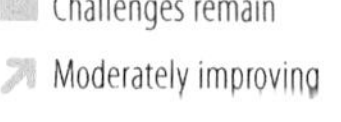

Note: The full title of each SDG is available here: https://sustainabledevelopment.un.org/topics/sustainabledevelopmentgoals

INTERNATIONAL SPILLOVER INDEX

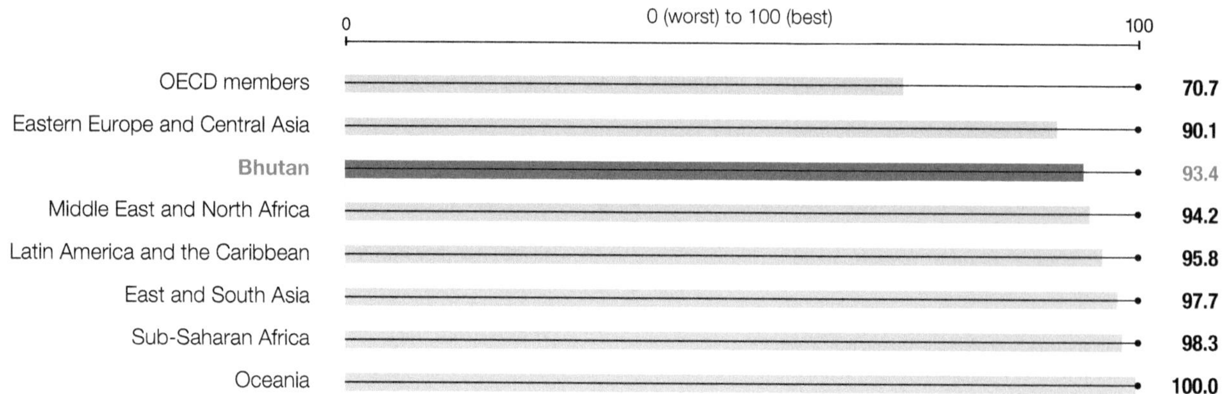

Region	Score
OECD members	70.7
Eastern Europe and Central Asia	90.1
Bhutan	93.4
Middle East and North Africa	94.2
Latin America and the Caribbean	95.8
East and South Asia	97.7
Sub-Saharan Africa	98.3
Oceania	100.0

STATISTICAL PERFORMANCE INDEX

0 (worst) to 100 (best)

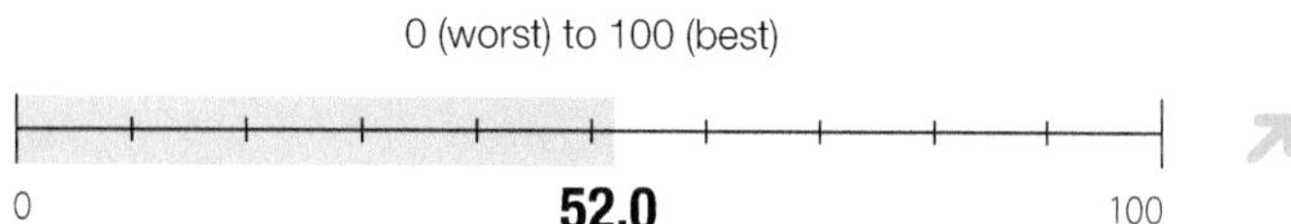

MISSING DATA IN SDG INDEX

13%

BHUTAN

Performance by Indicator

SDG1 – No Poverty	Value	Year	Rating	Trend
Poverty headcount ratio at $1.90/day (%)	0.0	2022	●	↑
Poverty headcount ratio at $3.20/day (%)	11.7	2022	●	↗

SDG2 – Zero Hunger	Value	Year	Rating	Trend
Prevalence of undernourishment (%)	NA	NA	●	●
Prevalence of stunting in children under 5 years of age (%)	33.5	2010	●	→
Prevalence of wasting in children under 5 years of age (%)	5.9	2010	●	↗
Prevalence of obesity, BMI ≥ 30 (% of adult population)	6.4	2016	●	↑
Human Trophic Level (best 2–3 worst)	NA	NA	●	●
Cereal yield (tonnes per hectare of harvested land)	3.5	2018	●	↑
Sustainable Nitrogen Management Index (best 0–1.41 worst)	0.7	2015	●	→
Exports of hazardous pesticides (tonnes per million population)	NA	NA	●	●

SDG3 – Good Health and Well-Being	Value	Year	Rating	Trend
Maternal mortality rate (per 100,000 live births)	183	2017	●	↑
Neonatal mortality rate (per 1,000 live births)	15.3	2020	●	↑
Mortality rate, under-5 (per 1,000 live births)	27.6	2020	●	↑
Incidence of tuberculosis (per 100,000 population)	165.0	2020	●	→
New HIV infections (per 1,000 uninfected population)	0.1	2020	●	↑
Age-standardized death rate due to cardiovascular disease, cancer, diabetes, or chronic respiratory disease in adults aged 30–70 years (%)	18.5	2019	●	→
Age-standardized death rate attributable to household air pollution and ambient air pollution (per 100,000 population)	124	2016	●	●
Traffic deaths (per 100,000 population)	16.2	2019	●	↓
Life expectancy at birth (years)	73.1	2019	●	→
Adolescent fertility rate (births per 1,000 females aged 15 to 19)	59.0	2009	●	●
Births attended by skilled health personnel (%)	96.2	2018	●	↑
Surviving infants who received 2 WHO-recommended vaccines (%)	93	2020	●	↑
Universal health coverage (UHC) index of service coverage (worst 0–100 best)	62	2019	●	↗
Subjective well-being (average ladder score, worst 0–10 best)	5.1	2015	●	●

SDG4 – Quality Education	Value	Year	Rating	Trend
Participation rate in pre-primary organized learning (% of children aged 4 to 6)	41.4	2020	●	●
Net primary enrollment rate (%)	96.3	2020	●	↑
Lower secondary completion rate (%)	85.1	2020	●	↑
Literacy rate (% of population aged 15 to 24)	93.1	2017	●	●

SDG5 – Gender Equality	Value	Year	Rating	Trend
Demand for family planning satisfied by modern methods (% of females aged 15 to 49)	84.6	2010	●	●
Ratio of female-to-male mean years of education received (%)	68.8	2019	●	↗
Ratio of female-to-male labor force participation rate (%)	76.2	2020	●	↑
Seats held by women in national parliament (%)	14.9	2020	●	↗

SDG6 – Clean Water and Sanitation	Value	Year	Rating	Trend
Population using at least basic drinking water services (%)	97.3	2020	●	↑
Population using at least basic sanitation services (%)	76.5	2020	●	↗
Freshwater withdrawal (% of available freshwater resources)	1.4	2018	●	●
Anthropogenic wastewater that receives treatment (%)	0.0	2018	●	●
Scarce water consumption embodied in imports (m^3 H_2O eq/capita)	2455.0	2018	●	●

SDG7 – Affordable and Clean Energy	Value	Year	Rating	Trend
Population with access to electricity (%)	100.0	2019	●	↑
Population with access to clean fuels and technology for cooking (%)	79.1	2019	●	↑
CO_2 emissions from fuel combustion per total electricity output ($MtCO_2$/TWh)	0.1	2019	●	↑
Share of renewable energy in total primary energy supply (%)	NA	NA	●	●

SDG8 – Decent Work and Economic Growth	Value	Year	Rating	Trend
Adjusted GDP growth (%)	-4.5	2020	●	●
Victims of modern slavery (per 1,000 population)	NA	NA	●	●
Adults with an account at a bank or other financial institution or with a mobile-money-service provider (% of population aged 15 or over)	33.7	2014	●	●
Unemployment rate (% of total labor force)	4.4	2022	●	↑
Fundamental labor rights are effectively guaranteed (worst 0–1 best)	NA	NA	●	●
Fatal work-related accidents embodied in imports (per 100,000 population)	0.4	2015	●	↑

* Imputed data point

SDG9 – Industry, Innovation and Infrastructure	Value	Year	Rating	Trend
Population using the internet (%)	53.5	2020	●	↑
Mobile broadband subscriptions (per 100 population)	99.9	2019	●	↑
Logistics Performance Index: Quality of trade and transport-related infrastructure (worst 1–5 best)	1.9	2018	●	↓
The Times Higher Education Universities Ranking: Average score of top 3 universities (worst 0–100 best)	* 0.0	2022	●	●
Articles published in academic journals (per 1,000 population)	0.3	2020	●	↗
Expenditure on research and development (% of GDP)	NA	NA	●	●

SDG10 – Reduced Inequalities	Value	Year	Rating	Trend
Gini coefficient	37.4	2017	●	●
Palma ratio	1.6	2018	●	●

SDG11 – Sustainable Cities and Communities	Value	Year	Rating	Trend
Proportion of urban population living in slums (%)	NA	NA	●	●
Annual mean concentration of particulate matter of less than 2.5 microns in diameter (PM2.5) (μg/m^3)	33.1	2019	●	→
Access to improved water source, piped (% of urban population)	99.3	2020	●	↑
Satisfaction with public transport (%)	75.0	2015	●	●

SDG12 – Responsible Consumption and Production	Value	Year	Rating	Trend
Municipal solid waste (kg/capita/day)	0.5	2007	●	●
Electronic waste (kg/capita)	4.0	2019	●	●
Production-based SO_2 emissions (kg/capita)	7.9	2018	●	●
SO_2 emissions embodied in imports (kg/capita)	1.3	2018	●	●
Production-based nitrogen emissions (kg/capita)	4.8	2015	●	↑
Nitrogen emissions embodied in imports (kg/capita)	3.5	2015	●	↑
Exports of plastic waste (kg/capita)	NA	NA	●	●

SDG13 – Climate Action	Value	Year	Rating	Trend
CO_2 emissions from fossil fuel combustion and cement production (tCO_2/capita)	2.5	2020	●	↓
CO_2 emissions embodied in imports (tCO_2/capita)	0.5	2018	●	↑
CO_2 emissions embodied in fossil fuel exports (kg/capita)	NA	NA	●	●

SDG14 – Life Below Water	Value	Year	Rating	Trend
Mean area that is protected in marine sites important to biodiversity (%)	NA	NA	●	●
Ocean Health Index: Clean Waters score (worst 0–100 best)	NA	NA	●	●
Fish caught from overexploited or collapsed stocks (% of total catch)	NA	NA	●	●
Fish caught by trawling or dredging (%)	NA	NA	●	●
Fish caught that are then discarded (%)	NA	NA	●	●
Marine biodiversity threats embodied in imports (per million population)	0.1	2018	●	●

SDG15 – Life on Land	Value	Year	Rating	Trend
Mean area that is protected in terrestrial sites important to biodiversity (%)	47.0	2020	●	→
Mean area that is protected in freshwater sites important to biodiversity (%)	34.8	2020	●	→
Red List Index of species survival (worst 0–1 best)	0.8	2021	●	↓
Permanent deforestation (% of forest area, 5-year average)	0.0	2020	●	↑
Terrestrial and freshwater biodiversity threats embodied in imports (per million population)	0.2	2018	●	●

SDG16 – Peace, Justice and Strong Institutions	Value	Year	Rating	Trend
Homicides (per 100,000 population)	2.5	2020	●	→
Unsentenced detainees (% of prison population)	14.2	2019	●	●
Population who feel safe walking alone at night in the city or area where they live (%)	63	2015	●	●
Property Rights (worst 1–7 best)	NA	NA	●	●
Birth registrations with civil authority (% of children under age 5)	99.9	2020	●	●
Corruption Perception Index (worst 0–100 best)	68	2021	●	↑
Children involved in child labor (% of population aged 5 to 14)	3.5	2019	●	●
Exports of major conventional weapons (TIV constant million USD per 100,000 population)	* 0.0	2020	●	●
Press Freedom Index (best 0–100 worst)	28.9	2021	●	↑
Access to and affordability of justice (worst 0–1 best)	NA	NA	●	●

SDG17 – Partnerships for the Goals	Value	Year	Rating	Trend
Government spending on health and education (% of GDP)	9.5	2019	●	↓
For high-income and all OECD DAC countries: International concessional public finance, including official development assistance (% of GNI)	NA	NA	●	●
Other countries: Government revenue excluding grants (% of GDP)	22.2	2018	●	↑
Corporate Tax Haven Score (best 0–100 worst)	* 0.0	2019	●	●
Statistical Performance Index (worst 0–100 best)	52.0	2019	●	↗

BOLIVIA

Latin America and the Caribbean

OVERALL PERFORMANCE

COUNTRY RANKING

BOLIVIA

90/163

COUNTRY SCORE

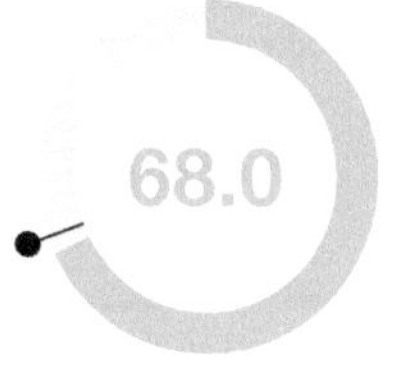

REGIONAL AVERAGE: 69.5

AVERAGE PERFORMANCE BY SDG

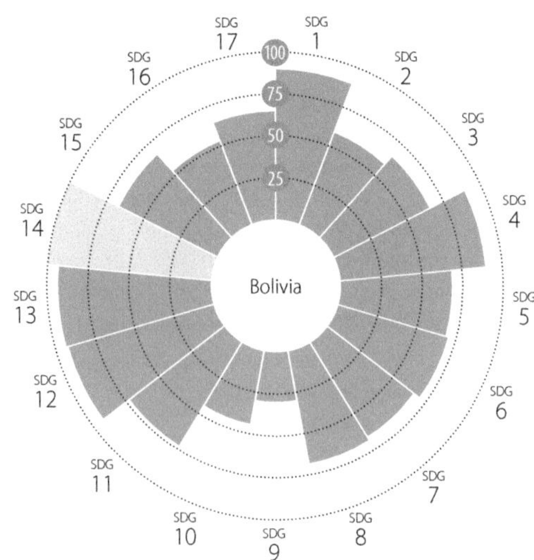

SDG DASHBOARDS AND TRENDS

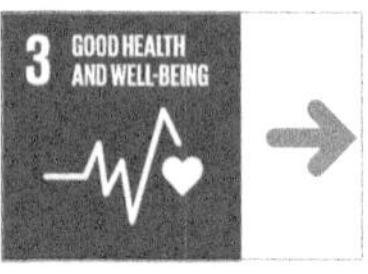

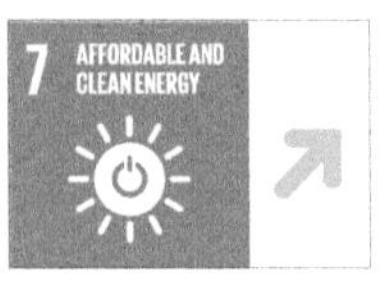

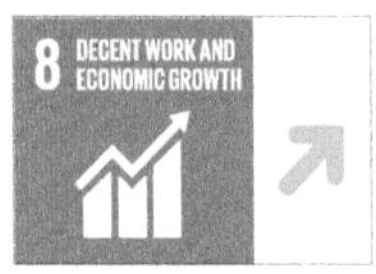

Major challenges | Significant challenges | Challenges remain | SDG achieved | Information unavailable

Decreasing | Stagnating | Moderately improving | On track or maintaining SDG achievement | Information unavailable

Note: The full title of each SDG is available here: https://sustainabledevelopment.un.org/topics/sustainabledevelopmentgoals

INTERNATIONAL SPILLOVER INDEX

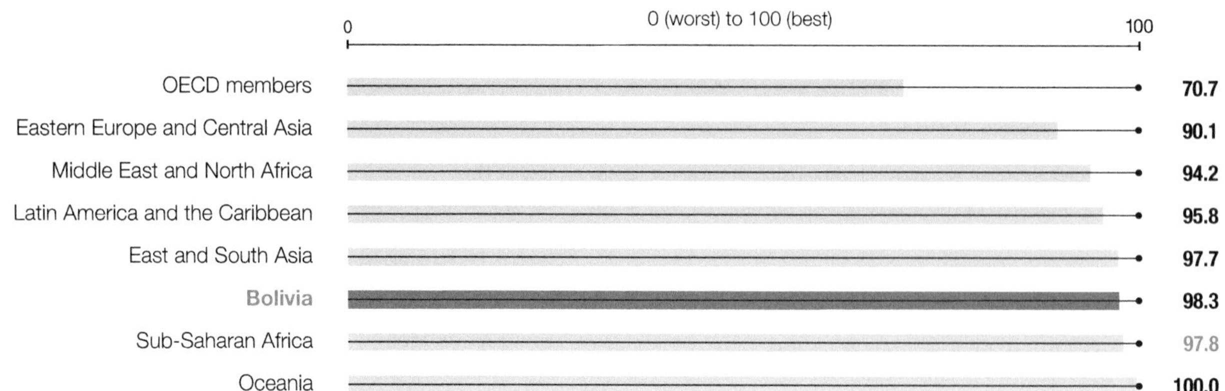

STATISTICAL PERFORMANCE INDEX

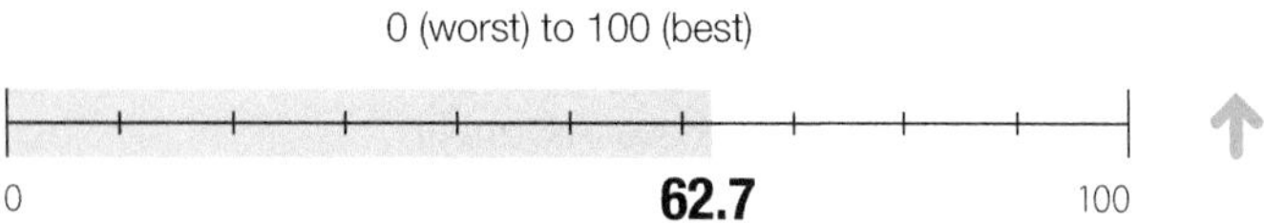

MISSING DATA IN SDG INDEX

2%

BOLIVIA

SDG1 – No Poverty	Value	Year	Rating	Trend
Poverty headcount ratio at $1.90/day (%)	2.6	2022	●	↑
Poverty headcount ratio at $3.20/day (%)	8.8	2022	●	↗

SDG2 – Zero Hunger	Value	Year	Rating	Trend
Prevalence of undernourishment (%)	12.6	2019	●	↗
Prevalence of stunting in children under 5 years of age (%)	16.1	2016	●	↗
Prevalence of wasting in children under 5 years of age (%)	2.0	2016	●	↑
Prevalence of obesity, BMI ≥ 30 (% of adult population)	20.2	2016	●	↓
Human Trophic Level (best 2–3 worst)	2.3	2017	●	→
Cereal yield (tonnes per hectare of harvested land)	2.3	2018	●	↑
Sustainable Nitrogen Management Index (best 0–1.41 worst)	0.5	2015	●	↗
Exports of hazardous pesticides (tonnes per million population)	NA	NA	●	●

SDG3 – Good Health and Well-Being	Value	Year	Rating	Trend
Maternal mortality rate (per 100,000 live births)	155	2017	●	↑
Neonatal mortality rate (per 1,000 live births)	13.5	2020	●	↑
Mortality rate, under-5 (per 1,000 live births)	25.4	2020	●	↑
Incidence of tuberculosis (per 100,000 population)	105.0	2020	●	→
New HIV infections (per 1,000 uninfected population)	0.1	2020	●	↑
Age-standardized death rate due to cardiovascular disease, cancer, diabetes, or chronic respiratory disease in adults aged 30–70 years (%)	17.9	2019	●	→
Age-standardized death rate attributable to household air pollution and ambient air pollution (per 100,000 population)	64	2016	●	●
Traffic deaths (per 100,000 population)	21.1	2019	●	↓
Life expectancy at birth (years)	72.1	2019	●	→
Adolescent fertility rate (births per 1,000 females aged 15 to 19)	71.0	2015	●	●
Births attended by skilled health personnel (%)	71.5	2018	●	↓
Surviving infants who received 2 WHO-recommended vaccines (%)	68	2020	●	↓
Universal health coverage (UHC) index of service coverage (worst 0–100 best)	67	2019	●	●
Subjective well-being (average ladder score, worst 0–10 best)	5.6	2021	●	↓

SDG4 – Quality Education	Value	Year	Rating	Trend
Participation rate in pre-primary organized learning (% of children aged 4 to 6)	91.7	2019	●	↑
Net primary enrollment rate (%)	94.7	2019	●	↑
Lower secondary completion rate (%)	85.8	2019	●	↓
Literacy rate (% of population aged 15 to 24)	99.4	2015	●	●

SDG5 – Gender Equality	Value	Year	Rating	Trend
Demand for family planning satisfied by modern methods (% of females aged 15 to 49)	50.3	2016	●	●
Ratio of female-to-male mean years of education received (%)	84.7	2019	●	↓
Ratio of female-to-male labor force participation rate (%)	73.7	2020	●	↑
Seats held by women in national parliament (%)	46.2	2020	●	↑

SDG6 – Clean Water and Sanitation	Value	Year	Rating	Trend
Population using at least basic drinking water services (%)	93.4	2020	●	↑
Population using at least basic sanitation services (%)	65.8	2020	●	↗
Freshwater withdrawal (% of available freshwater resources)	1.2	2018	●	●
Anthropogenic wastewater that receives treatment (%)	3.5	2018	●	●
Scarce water consumption embodied in imports (m^3 H_2O eq/capita)	720.4	2018	●	●

SDG7 – Affordable and Clean Energy	Value	Year	Rating	Trend
Population with access to electricity (%)	96.3	2019	●	↑
Population with access to clean fuels and technology for cooking (%)	85.5	2019	●	↑
CO_2 emissions from fuel combustion per total electricity output ($MtCO_2$/TWh)	2.0	2019	●	→
Share of renewable energy in total primary energy supply (%)	10.0	2019	●	↓

SDG8 – Decent Work and Economic Growth	Value	Year	Rating	Trend
Adjusted GDP growth (%)	-5.4	2020	●	●
Victims of modern slavery (per 1,000 population)	2.1	2018	●	●
Adults with an account at a bank or other financial institution or with a mobile-money-service provider (% of population aged 15 or over)	54.4	2017	●	↑
Unemployment rate (% of total labor force)	5.6	2022	●	↓
Fundamental labor rights are effectively guaranteed (worst 0–1 best)	0.5	2020	●	→
Fatal work-related accidents embodied in imports (per 100,000 population)	0.1	2015	●	↑

SDG9 – Industry, Innovation and Infrastructure	Value	Year	Rating	Trend
Population using the internet (%)	59.9	2020	●	↑
Mobile broadband subscriptions (per 100 population)	83.0	2019	●	↑
Logistics Performance Index: Quality of trade and transport-related infrastructure (worst 1–5 best)	2.2	2018	●	↓
The Times Higher Education Universities Ranking: Average score of top 3 universities (worst 0–100 best)	* 0.0	2022	●	●
Articles published in academic journals (per 1,000 population)	0.0	2020	●	→
Expenditure on research and development (% of GDP)	0.2	2009	●	●

SDG10 – Reduced Inequalities	Value	Year	Rating	Trend
Gini coefficient	41.6	2019	●	↑
Palma ratio	2.1	2018	●	●

SDG11 – Sustainable Cities and Communities	Value	Year	Rating	Trend
Proportion of urban population living in slums (%)	49.9	2018	●	↓
Annual mean concentration of particulate matter of less than 2.5 microns in diameter (PM2.5) (μg/m^3)	19.7	2019	●	↗
Access to improved water source, piped (% of urban population)	86.7	2020	●	↓
Satisfaction with public transport (%)	67.0	2021	●	↑

SDG12 – Responsible Consumption and Production	Value	Year	Rating	Trend
Municipal solid waste (kg/capita/day)	0.6	2015	●	●
Electronic waste (kg/capita)	3.6	2019	●	●
Production-based SO_2 emissions (kg/capita)	2.5	2018	●	●
SO_2 emissions embodied in imports (kg/capita)	0.7	2018	●	●
Production-based nitrogen emissions (kg/capita)	24.7	2015	●	↓
Nitrogen emissions embodied in imports (kg/capita)	1.2	2015	●	↑
Exports of plastic waste (kg/capita)	0.1	2020	●	●

SDG13 – Climate Action	Value	Year	Rating	Trend
CO_2 emissions from fossil fuel combustion and cement production (tCO_2/capita)	1.8	2020	●	↑
CO_2 emissions embodied in imports (tCO_2/capita)	0.2	2018	●	↑
CO_2 emissions embodied in fossil fuel exports (kg/capita)	2323.5	2020	●	●

SDG14 – Life Below Water	Value	Year	Rating	Trend
Mean area that is protected in marine sites important to biodiversity (%)	NA	NA	●	●
Ocean Health Index: Clean Waters score (worst 0–100 best)	NA	NA	●	●
Fish caught from overexploited or collapsed stocks (% of total catch)	NA	NA	●	●
Fish caught by trawling or dredging (%)	NA	NA	●	●
Fish caught that are then discarded (%)	NA	NA	●	●
Marine biodiversity threats embodied in imports (per million population)	0.0	2018	●	●

SDG15 – Life on Land	Value	Year	Rating	Trend
Mean area that is protected in terrestrial sites important to biodiversity (%)	48.2	2020	●	→
Mean area that is protected in freshwater sites important to biodiversity (%)	58.7	2020	●	→
Red List Index of species survival (worst 0–1 best)	0.9	2021	●	→
Permanent deforestation (% of forest area, 5-year average)	0.6	2020	●	↓
Terrestrial and freshwater biodiversity threats embodied in imports (per million population)	0.2	2018	●	●

SDG16 – Peace, Justice and Strong Institutions	Value	Year	Rating	Trend
Homicides (per 100,000 population)	7.0	2019	●	→
Unsentenced detainees (% of prison population)	64.3	2019	●	→
Population who feel safe walking alone at night in the city or area where they live (%)	47	2021	●	→
Property Rights (worst 1–7 best)	2.8	2020	●	↗
Birth registrations with civil authority (% of children under age 5)	91.9	2020	●	●
Corruption Perception Index (worst 0–100 best)	30	2021	●	↓
Children involved in child labor (% of population aged 5 to 14)	13.6	2019	●	●
Exports of major conventional weapons (TIV constant million USD per 100,000 population)	* 0.0	2020	●	●
Press Freedom Index (best 0–100 worst)	35.5	2021	●	↓
Access to and affordability of justice (worst 0–1 best)	0.5	2020	●	→

SDG17 – Partnerships for the Goals	Value	Year	Rating	Trend
Government spending on health and education (% of GDP)	NA	NA	●	●
For high-income and all OECD DAC countries: International concessional public finance, including official development assistance (% of GNI)	NA	NA	●	●
Other countries: Government revenue excluding grants (% of GDP)	23.3	2007	●	●
Corporate Tax Haven Score (best 0–100 worst)	* 0.0	2019	●	●
Statistical Performance Index (worst 0–100 best)	62.7	2019	●	↑

* Imputed data point

BOSNIA AND HERZEGOVINA

Eastern Europe and Central Asia

OVERALL PERFORMANCE

COUNTRY RANKING

BOSNIA AND HERZEGOVINA

59/163

COUNTRY SCORE

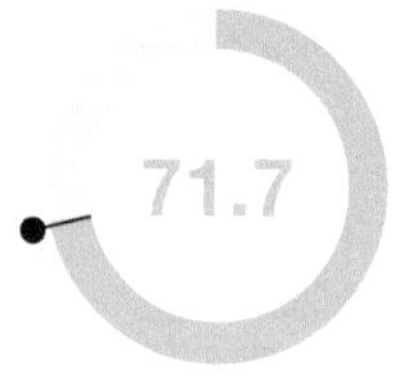

REGIONAL AVERAGE: 71.6

AVERAGE PERFORMANCE BY SDG

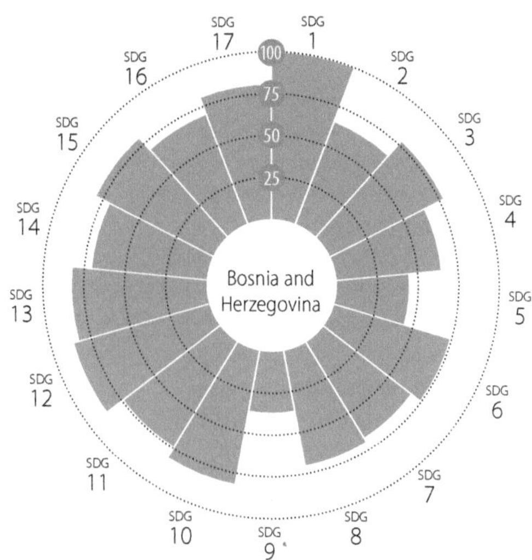

SDG DASHBOARDS AND TRENDS

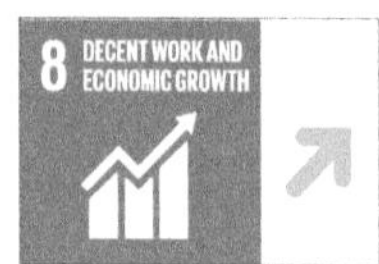

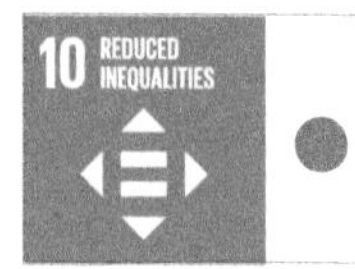

Major challenges · Significant challenges · Challenges remain · SDG achieved · Information unavailable

Decreasing · Stagnating · Moderately improving · On track or maintaining SDG achievement · Information unavailable

Note: The full title of each SDG is available here: https://sustainabledevelopment.un.org/topics/sustainabledevelopmentgoals

INTERNATIONAL SPILLOVER INDEX

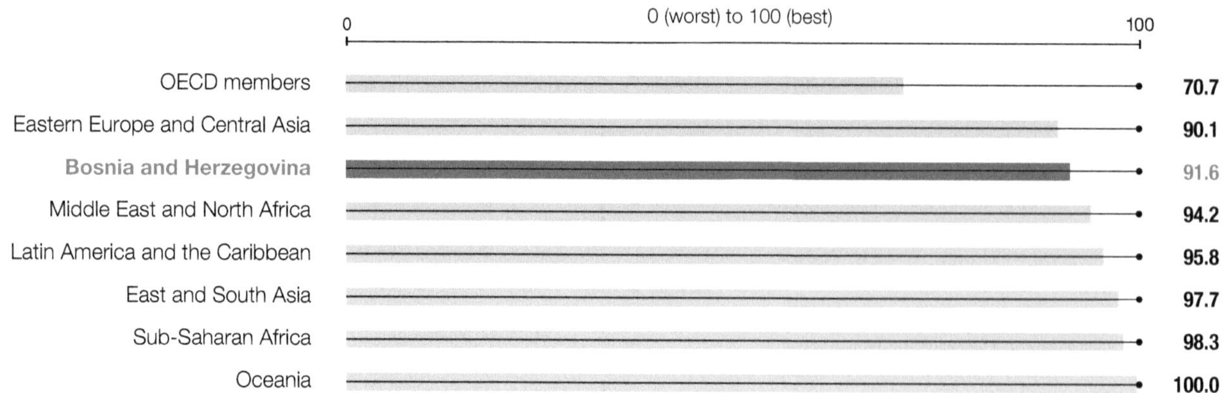

Region	Score
OECD members	70.7
Eastern Europe and Central Asia	90.1
Bosnia and Herzegovina	91.6
Middle East and North Africa	94.2
Latin America and the Caribbean	95.8
East and South Asia	97.7
Sub-Saharan Africa	98.3
Oceania	100.0

STATISTICAL PERFORMANCE INDEX

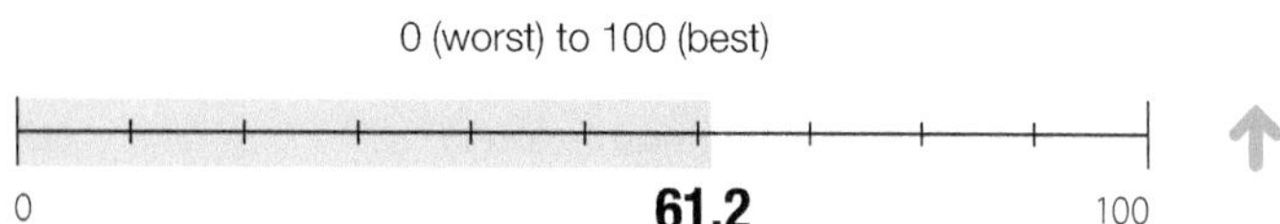

MISSING DATA IN SDG INDEX

7%

BOSNIA AND HERZEGOVINA

Performance by Indicator

SDG1 – No Poverty	Value	Year	Rating	Trend
Poverty headcount ratio at \$1.90/day (%)	0.1	2022	●	↑
Poverty headcount ratio at \$3.20/day (%)	0.2	2022	●	↑
SDG2 – Zero Hunger				
Prevalence of undernourishment (%)	2.5	2019	●	↑
Prevalence of stunting in children under 5 years of age (%)	8.9	2012	●	→
Prevalence of wasting in children under 5 years of age (%)	2.3	2012	●	↑
Prevalence of obesity, BMI ≥ 30 (% of adult population)	17.9	2016	●	↓
Human Trophic Level (best 2–3 worst)	2.3	2017	●	↗
Cereal yield (tonnes per hectare of harvested land)	5.5	2018	●	↑
Sustainable Nitrogen Management Index (best 0–1.41 worst)	1.0	2015	●	↓
Exports of hazardous pesticides (tonnes per million population)	NA	NA	●	●
SDG3 – Good Health and Well-Being				
Maternal mortality rate (per 100,000 live births)	10	2017	●	↑
Neonatal mortality rate (per 1,000 live births)	4.1	2020	●	↑
Mortality rate, under-5 (per 1,000 live births)	5.7	2020	●	↑
Incidence of tuberculosis (per 100,000 population)	26.0	2020	●	↑
New HIV infections (per 1,000 uninfected population)	1.0	2020	●	→
Age-standardized death rate due to cardiovascular disease, cancer, diabetes, or chronic respiratory disease in adults aged 30–70 years (%)	18.7	2019	●	→
Age-standardized death rate attributable to household air pollution and ambient air pollution (per 100,000 population)	80	2016	●	●
Traffic deaths (per 100,000 population)	13.5	2019	●	↑
Life expectancy at birth (years)	76.8	2019	●	→
Adolescent fertility rate (births per 1,000 females aged 15 to 19)	10.1	2019	●	↑
Births attended by skilled health personnel (%)	99.9	2018	●	↑
Surviving infants who received 2 WHO-recommended vaccines (%)	68	2019	●	↓
Universal health coverage (UHC) index of service coverage (worst 0–100 best)	65	2019	●	↗
Subjective well-being (average ladder score, worst 0–10 best)	5.7	2021	●	↑
SDG4 – Quality Education				
Participation rate in pre-primary organized learning (% of children aged 4 to 6)	29.3	2020	●	●
Net primary enrollment rate (%)	NA	NA	●	●
Lower secondary completion rate (%)	94.2	2018	●	↑
Literacy rate (% of population aged 15 to 24)	99.7	2013	●	●
SDG5 – Gender Equality				
Demand for family planning satisfied by modern methods (% of females aged 15 to 49)	21.9	2012	●	●
Ratio of female-to-male mean years of education received (%)	81.7	2019	●	↗
Ratio of female-to-male labor force participation rate (%)	61.6	2020	●	→
Seats held by women in national parliament (%)	26.2	2020	●	↗
SDG6 – Clean Water and Sanitation				
Population using at least basic drinking water services (%)	96.1	2020	●	→
Population using at least basic sanitation services (%)	95.4	2018	●	●
Freshwater withdrawal (% of available freshwater resources)	2.7	2018	●	●
Anthropogenic wastewater that receives treatment (%)	1.1	2018	●	●
Scarce water consumption embodied in imports (m^3 H_2O eq/capita)	2518.9	2018	●	●
SDG7 – Affordable and Clean Energy				
Population with access to electricity (%)	100.0	2019	●	↑
Population with access to clean fuels and technology for cooking (%)	46.3	2019	●	→
CO_2 emissions from fuel combustion per total electricity output ($MtCO_2$/TWh)	1.4	2019	●	→
Share of renewable energy in total primary energy supply (%)	24.9	2019	●	↑
SDG8 – Decent Work and Economic Growth				
Adjusted GDP growth (%)	0.2	2020	●	●
Victims of modern slavery (per 1,000 population)	3.4	2018	●	●
Adults with an account at a bank or other financial institution or with a mobile-money-service provider (% of population aged 15 or over)	58.8	2017	●	↑
Unemployment rate (% of total labor force)	15.0	2022	●	↑
Fundamental labor rights are effectively guaranteed (worst 0–1 best)	0.6	2020	●	↓
Fatal work-related accidents embodied in imports (per 100,000 population)	0.1	2015	●	↑

* Imputed data point

SDG9 – Industry, Innovation and Infrastructure	Value	Year	Rating	Trend
Population using the internet (%)	73.2	2020	●	↑
Mobile broadband subscriptions (per 100 population)	47.3	2019	●	↗
Logistics Performance Index: Quality of trade and transport-related infrastructure (worst 1–5 best)	2.4	2018	●	↓
The Times Higher Education Universities Ranking: Average score of top 3 universities (worst 0–100 best)	* 7.0	2019	●	●
Articles published in academic journals (per 1,000 population)	0.5	2020	●	↑
Expenditure on research and development (% of GDP)	0.2	2018	●	↓
SDG10 – Reduced Inequalities				
Gini coefficient	33.0	2011	●	●
Palma ratio	1.3	2018	●	●
SDG11 – Sustainable Cities and Communities				
Proportion of urban population living in slums (%)	8.3	2018	●	●
Annual mean concentration of particulate matter of less than 2.5 microns in diameter (PM2.5) (μg/m^3)	26.8	2019	●	↗
Access to improved water source, piped (% of urban population)	97.6	2018	●	●
Satisfaction with public transport (%)	40.0	2021	●	↓
SDG12 – Responsible Consumption and Production				
Municipal solid waste (kg/capita/day)	1.0	2015	●	●
Electronic waste (kg/capita)	7.8	2019	●	●
Production-based SO_2 emissions (kg/capita)	49.0	2018	●	●
SO_2 emissions embodied in imports (kg/capita)	1.7	2018	●	●
Production-based nitrogen emissions (kg/capita)	9.3	2015	●	↑
Nitrogen emissions embodied in imports (kg/capita)	1.6	2015	●	↑
Exports of plastic waste (kg/capita)	1.9	2020	●	●
SDG13 – Climate Action				
CO_2 emissions from fossil fuel combustion and cement production (tCO_2/capita)	6.5	2020	●	→
CO_2 emissions embodied in imports (tCO_2/capita)	0.7	2018	●	→
CO_2 emissions embodied in fossil fuel exports (kg/capita)	70.1	2020	●	●
SDG14 – Life Below Water				
Mean area that is protected in marine sites important to biodiversity (%)	NA	NA	●	●
Ocean Health Index: Clean Waters score (worst 0–100 best)	40.7	2020	●	→
Fish caught from overexploited or collapsed stocks (% of total catch)	NA	NA	●	●
Fish caught by trawling or dredging (%)	0.0	2018	●	↑
Fish caught that are then discarded (%)	1.2	2018	●	↑
Marine biodiversity threats embodied in imports (per million population)	NA	NA	●	●
SDG15 – Life on Land				
Mean area that is protected in terrestrial sites important to biodiversity (%)	29.0	2020	●	→
Mean area that is protected in freshwater sites important to biodiversity (%)	100.0	2020	●	↑
Red List Index of species survival (worst 0–1 best)	0.9	2021	●	↑
Permanent deforestation (% of forest area, 5-year average)	0.0	2020	●	↑
Terrestrial and freshwater biodiversity threats embodied in imports (per million population)	0.5	2018	●	●
SDG16 – Peace, Justice and Strong Institutions				
Homicides (per 100,000 population)	1.2	2019	●	↑
Unsentenced detainees (% of prison population)	31.8	2019	●	↓
Population who feel safe walking alone at night in the city or area where they live (%)	73	2021	●	↑
Property Rights (worst 1–7 best)	3.4	2020	●	↗
Birth registrations with civil authority (% of children under age 5)	99.5	2020	●	●
Corruption Perception Index (worst 0–100 best)	35	2021	●	↓
Children involved in child labor (% of population aged 5 to 14)	NA	NA	●	●
Exports of major conventional weapons (TIV constant million USD per 100,000 population)	0.0	2020	●	●
Press Freedom Index (best 0–100 worst)	28.3	2021	●	↑
Access to and affordability of justice (worst 0–1 best)	0.6	2020	●	↑
SDG17 – Partnerships for the Goals				
Government spending on health and education (% of GDP)	NA	NA	●	●
For high-income and all OECD DAC countries: International concessional public finance, including official development assistance (% of GNI)	NA	NA	●	●
Other countries: Government revenue excluding grants (% of GDP)	38.1	2019	●	↑
Corporate Tax Haven Score (best 0–100 worst)	* 0.0	2019	●	●
Statistical Performance Index (worst 0–100 best)	61.2	2019	●	↑

BOTSWANA

Sub-Saharan Africa

OVERALL PERFORMANCE

COUNTRY RANKING

BOTSWANA

116 /163

COUNTRY SCORE

REGIONAL AVERAGE: 53.6

AVERAGE PERFORMANCE BY SDG

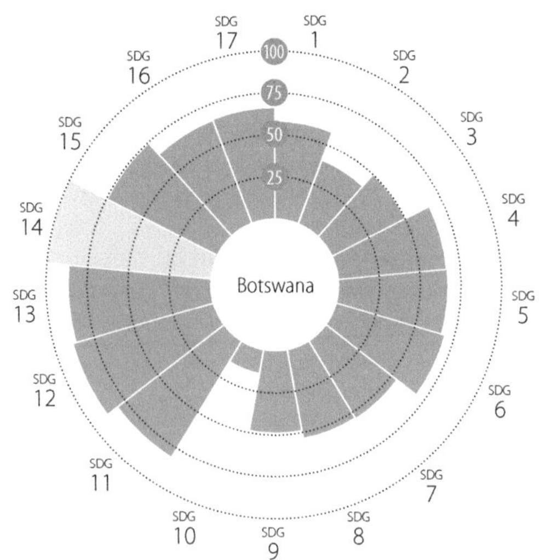

SDG DASHBOARDS AND TRENDS

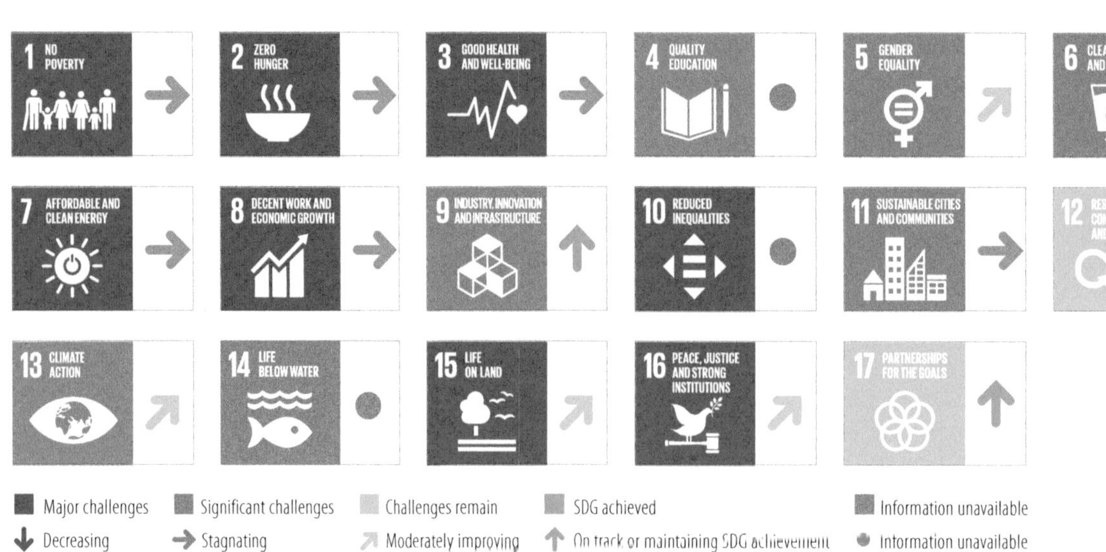

Major challenges | Significant challenges | Challenges remain | SDG achieved | Information unavailable

Decreasing | Stagnating | Moderately improving | On track or maintaining SDG achievement | Information unavailable

Note: The full title of each SDG is available here: https://sustainabledevelopment.un.org/topics/sustainabledevelopmentgoals

INTERNATIONAL SPILLOVER INDEX

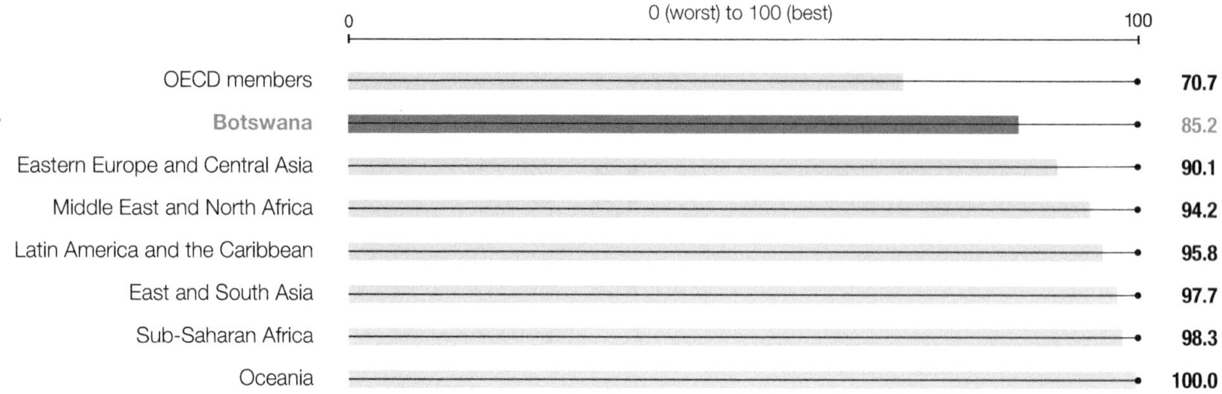

STATISTICAL PERFORMANCE INDEX

0 (worst) to 100 (best)

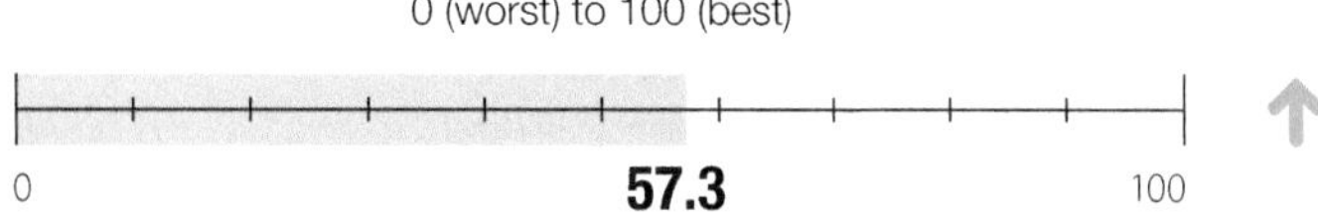

MISSING DATA IN SDG INDEX

3%

BOTSWANA

Performance by Indicator

SDG1 – No Poverty	Value	Year	Rating	Trend
Poverty headcount ratio at \$1.90/day (%)	16.5	2022	●	→
Poverty headcount ratio at \$3.20/day (%)	31.7	2022	●	→
SDG2 – Zero Hunger				
Prevalence of undernourishment (%)	29.3	2019	●	↓
Prevalence of stunting in children under 5 years of age (%)	28.9	2007	●	→
Prevalence of wasting in children under 5 years of age (%)	7.3	2007	●	→
Prevalence of obesity, BMI ≥ 30 (% of adult population)	18.9	2016	●	↓
Human Trophic Level (best 2–3 worst)	2.3	2017	●	↑
Cereal yield (tonnes per hectare of harvested land)	0.4	2018	●	↓
Sustainable Nitrogen Management Index (best 0–1.41 worst)	1.3	2015	●	↓
Exports of hazardous pesticides (tonnes per million population)	1.4	2019	●	●
SDG3 – Good Health and Well-Being				
Maternal mortality rate (per 100,000 live births)	144	2017	●	↗
Neonatal mortality rate (per 1,000 live births)	21.9	2020	●	→
Mortality rate, under-5 (per 1,000 live births)	44.8	2020	●	↗
Incidence of tuberculosis (per 100,000 population)	236.0	2020	●	↑
New HIV infections (per 1,000 uninfected population)	4.4	2020	●	↗
Age-standardized death rate due to cardiovascular disease, cancer, diabetes, or chronic respiratory disease in adults aged 30–70 years (%)	27.0	2019	●	↗
Age-standardized death rate attributable to household air pollution and ambient air pollution (per 100,000 population)	101	2016	●	●
Traffic deaths (per 100,000 population)	26.4	2019	●	↓
Life expectancy at birth (years)	62.3	2019	●	→
Adolescent fertility rate (births per 1,000 females aged 15 to 19)	51.9	2018	●	→
Births attended by skilled health personnel (%)	99.8	2017	●	↑
Surviving infants who received 2 WHO-recommended vaccines (%)	87	2020	●	↓
Universal health coverage (UHC) index of service coverage (worst 0–100 best)	54	2019	●	→
Subjective well-being (average ladder score, worst 0–10 best)	3.5	2019	●	●
SDG4 – Quality Education				
Participation rate in pre-primary organized learning (% of children aged 4 to 6)	21.3	2015	●	●
Net primary enrollment rate (%)	89.0	2014	●	●
Lower secondary completion rate (%)	92.8	2017	●	●
Literacy rate (% of population aged 15 to 24)	97.5	2013	●	●
SDG5 – Gender Equality				
Demand for family planning satisfied by modern methods (% of females aged 15 to 49)	NA	NA	●	●
Ratio of female-to-male mean years of education received (%)	97.9	2019	●	↑
Ratio of female-to-male labor force participation rate (%)	86.2	2020	●	↑
Seats held by women in national parliament (%)	10.8	2020	●	→
SDG6 – Clean Water and Sanitation				
Population using at least basic drinking water services (%)	92.2	2020	●	↑
Population using at least basic sanitation services (%)	80.0	2020	●	↗
Freshwater withdrawal (% of available freshwater resources)	2.0	2018	●	●
Anthropogenic wastewater that receives treatment (%)	1.0	2018	●	●
Scarce water consumption embodied in imports (m^3 H_2O eq/capita)	2735.8	2018	●	●
SDG7 – Affordable and Clean Energy				
Population with access to electricity (%)	70.2	2019	●	↗
Population with access to clean fuels and technology for cooking (%)	52.8	2019	●	↓
CO_2 emissions from fuel combustion per total electricity output ($MtCO_2$/TWh)	2.3	2019	●	→
Share of renewable energy in total primary energy supply (%)	18.9	2019	●	→
SDG8 – Decent Work and Economic Growth				
Adjusted GDP growth (%)	-4.9	2020	●	●
Victims of modern slavery (per 1,000 population)	3.4	2018	●	●
Adults with an account at a bank or other financial institution or with a mobile-money-service provider (% of population aged 15 or over)	51.0	2017	●	↓
Unemployment rate (% of total labor force)	23.7	2022	●	↓
Fundamental labor rights are effectively guaranteed (worst 0–1 best)	0.5	2020	●	↗
Fatal work-related accidents embodied in imports (per 100,000 population)	0.8	2015	●	↑

* Imputed data point

SDG9 – Industry, Innovation and Infrastructure	Value	Year	Rating	Trend
Population using the internet (%)	64.0	2020	●	↑
Mobile broadband subscriptions (per 100 population)	88.4	2019	●	↑
Logistics Performance Index: Quality of trade and transport-related infrastructure (worst 1–5 best)	3.0	2016	●	●
The Times Higher Education Universities Ranking: Average score of top 3 universities (worst 0–100 best)	16.5	2022	●	●
Articles published in academic journals (per 1,000 population)	0.3	2020	●	↗
Expenditure on research and development (% of GDP)	0.5	2013	●	●
SDG10 – Reduced Inequalities				
Gini coefficient	53.3	2015	●	●
Palma ratio	3.8	2018	●	●
SDG11 – Sustainable Cities and Communities				
Proportion of urban population living in slums (%)	NA	NA	●	●
Annual mean concentration of particulate matter of less than 2.5 microns in diameter (PM2.5) (μg/m³)	22.6	2019	●	→
Access to improved water source, piped (% of urban population)	96.4	2020	●	→
Satisfaction with public transport (%)	62.0	2019	●	●
SDG12 – Responsible Consumption and Production				
Municipal solid waste (kg/capita/day)	0.3	2010	●	●
Electronic waste (kg/capita)	7.9	2019	●	●
Production-based SO_2 emissions (kg/capita)	23.3	2018	●	●
SO_2 emissions embodied in imports (kg/capita)	3.3	2018	●	●
Production-based nitrogen emissions (kg/capita)	16.2	2015	●	↑
Nitrogen emissions embodied in imports (kg/capita)	4.9	2015	●	↑
Exports of plastic waste (kg/capita)	0.2	2020	●	●
SDG13 – Climate Action				
CO_2 emissions from fossil fuel combustion and cement production (tCO_2/capita)	2.8	2020	●	→
CO_2 emissions embodied in imports (tCO_2/capita)	0.9	2018	●	↑
CO_2 emissions embodied in fossil fuel exports (kg/capita)	106.3	2020	●	●
SDG14 – Life Below Water				
Mean area that is protected in marine sites important to biodiversity (%)	NA	NA	●	●
Ocean Health Index: Clean Waters score (worst 0–100 best)	NA	NA	●	●
Fish caught from overexploited or collapsed stocks (% of total catch)	NA	NA	●	●
Fish caught by trawling or dredging (%)	NA	NA	●	●
Fish caught that are then discarded (%)	NA	NA	●	●
Marine biodiversity threats embodied in imports (per million population)	0.5	2018	●	●
SDG15 – Life on Land				
Mean area that is protected in terrestrial sites important to biodiversity (%)	51.1	2020	●	→
Mean area that is protected in freshwater sites important to biodiversity (%)	52.1	2020	●	→
Red List Index of species survival (worst 0–1 best)	1.0	2021	●	↑
Permanent deforestation (% of forest area, 5-year average)	0.0	2020	●	↑
Terrestrial and freshwater biodiversity threats embodied in imports (per million population)	2.5	2018	●	●
SDG16 – Peace, Justice and Strong Institutions				
Homicides (per 100,000 population)	15.3	2010	●	●
Unsentenced detainees (% of prison population)	22.2	2016	●	●
Population who feel safe walking alone at night in the city or area where they live (%)	36	2019	●	●
Property Rights (worst 1–7 best)	4.7	2020	●	↑
Birth registrations with civil authority (% of children under age 5)	87.5	2020	●	●
Corruption Perception Index (worst 0–100 best)	55	2021	●	↓
Children involved in child labor (% of population aged 5 to 14)	NA	NA	●	●
Exports of major conventional weapons (TIV constant million USD per 100,000 population)	* 0.0	2020	●	●
Press Freedom Index (best 0–100 worst)	23.3	2021	●	↑
Access to and affordability of justice (worst 0–1 best)	0.5	2020	●	↗
SDG17 – Partnerships for the Goals				
Government spending on health and education (% of GDP)	11.7	2019	●	↑
For high-income and all OECD DAC countries: International concessional public finance, including official development assistance (% of GNI)	NA	NA	●	●
Other countries: Government revenue excluding grants (% of GDP)	30.4	2019	●	↑
Corporate Tax Haven Score (best 0–100 worst)	55.3	2019	●	●
Statistical Performance Index (worst 0–100 best)	57.3	2019	●	↑

BRAZIL

Latin America and the Caribbean

OVERALL PERFORMANCE

COUNTRY RANKING

BRAZIL

53/163

COUNTRY SCORE

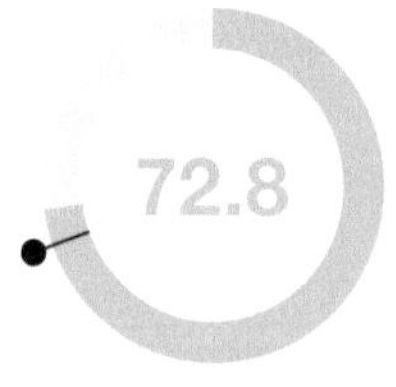

REGIONAL AVERAGE: 69.5

AVERAGE PERFORMANCE BY SDG

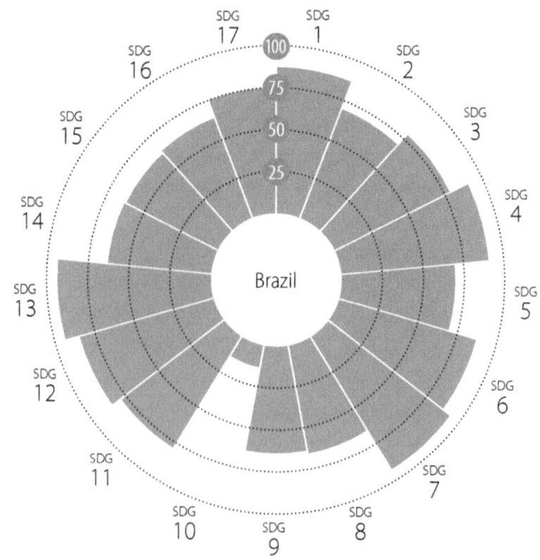

SDG DASHBOARDS AND TRENDS

Major challenges | Significant challenges | Challenges remain | SDG achieved | Information unavailable

Decreasing | Stagnating | Moderately improving | On track or maintaining SDG achievement | Information unavailable

Note: The full title of each SDG is available here: https://sustainabledevelopment.un.org/topics/sustainabledevelopmentgoals

INTERNATIONAL SPILLOVER INDEX

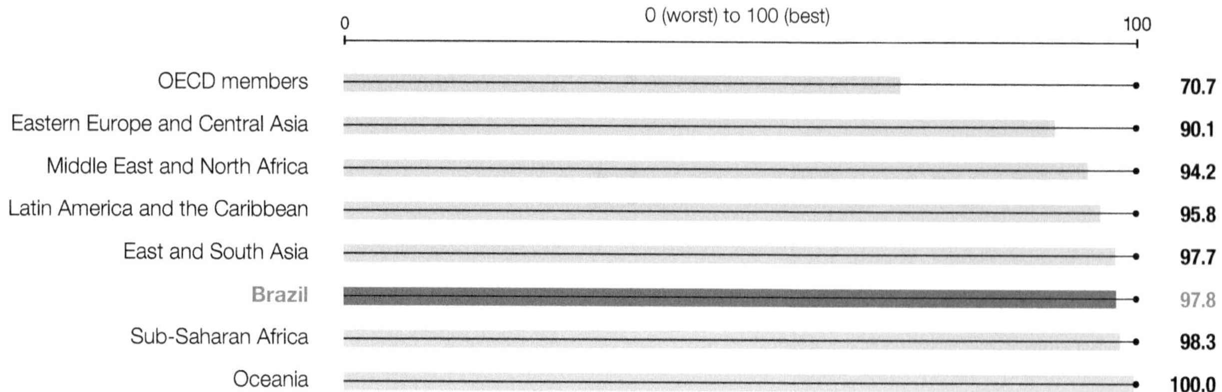

STATISTICAL PERFORMANCE INDEX

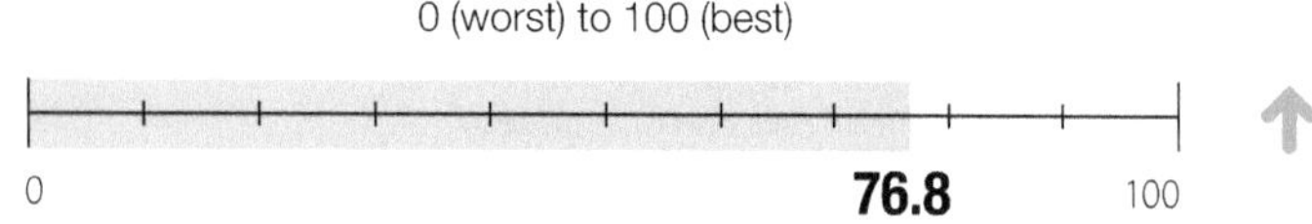

MISSING DATA IN SDG INDEX

0%

SDG1 – No Poverty

Indicator	Value	Year	Rating	Trend
Poverty headcount ratio at $1.90/day (%)	4.1	2022	●	→
Poverty headcount ratio at $3.20/day (%)	10.5	2022	●	→

SDG2 – Zero Hunger

Indicator	Value	Year	Rating	Trend
Prevalence of undernourishment (%)	2.5	2019	●	↑
Prevalence of stunting in children under 5 years of age (%)	7.0	2007	●	↑
Prevalence of wasting in children under 5 years of age (%)	1.8	2007	●	↑
Prevalence of obesity, BMI ≥ 30 (% of adult population)	22.1	2016	●	↓
Human Trophic Level (best 2–3 worst)	2.4	2017	●	→
Cereal yield (tonnes per hectare of harvested land)	4.8	2018	●	↑
Sustainable Nitrogen Management Index (best 0–1.41 worst)	0.5	2015	●	↓
Exports of hazardous pesticides (tonnes per million population)	0.2	2019	●	●

SDG3 – Good Health and Well-Being

Indicator	Value	Year	Rating	Trend
Maternal mortality rate (per 100,000 live births)	60	2017	●	↑
Neonatal mortality rate (per 1,000 live births)	8.7	2020	●	↑
Mortality rate, under-5 (per 1,000 live births)	14.7	2020	●	↑
Incidence of tuberculosis (per 100,000 population)	45.0	2020	●	→
New HIV infections (per 1,000 uninfected population)	0.2	2020	●	→
Age-standardized death rate due to cardiovascular disease, cancer, diabetes, or chronic respiratory disease in adults aged 30–70 years (%)	15.5	2019	●	↑
Age-standardized death rate attributable to household air pollution and ambient air pollution (per 100,000 population)	30	2016	●	●
Traffic deaths (per 100,000 population)	16.1	2019	●	↑
Life expectancy at birth (years)	75.9	2019	●	↗
Adolescent fertility rate (births per 1,000 females aged 15 to 19)	49.1	2019	●	↑
Births attended by skilled health personnel (%)	99.1	2017	●	↑
Surviving infants who received 2 WHO-recommended vaccines (%)	77	2020	●	↓
Universal health coverage (UHC) index of service coverage (worst 0–100 best)	75	2019	●	→
Subjective well-being (average ladder score, worst 0–10 best)	6.0	2021	●	↑

SDG4 – Quality Education

Indicator	Value	Year	Rating	Trend
Participation rate in pre-primary organized learning (% of children aged 4 to 6)	99.4	2019	●	↑
Net primary enrollment rate (%)	99.4	2019	●	↑
Lower secondary completion rate (%)	71.8	2011	●	●
Literacy rate (% of population aged 15 to 24)	99.2	2018	●	↑

SDG5 – Gender Equality

Indicator	Value	Year	Rating	Trend
Demand for family planning satisfied by modern methods (% of females aged 15 to 49)	89.0	2007	●	●
Ratio of female-to-male mean years of education received (%)	106.5	2019	●	↑
Ratio of female-to-male labor force participation rate (%)	70.8	2020	●	↑
Seats held by women in national parliament (%)	14.6	2020	●	→

SDG6 – Clean Water and Sanitation

Indicator	Value	Year	Rating	Trend
Population using at least basic drinking water services (%)	99.3	2020	●	↑
Population using at least basic sanitation services (%)	90.1	2020	●	↑
Freshwater withdrawal (% of available freshwater resources)	3.1	2018	●	●
Anthropogenic wastewater that receives treatment (%)	49.3	2018	●	●
Scarce water consumption embodied in imports (m^3 H_2O eq/capita)	267.3	2018	●	●

SDG7 – Affordable and Clean Energy

Indicator	Value	Year	Rating	Trend
Population with access to electricity (%)	99.8	2019	●	↑
Population with access to clean fuels and technology for cooking (%)	95.9	2019	●	↑
CO_2 emissions from fuel combustion per total electricity output ($MtCO_2$/TWh)	0.7	2019	●	↑
Share of renewable energy in total primary energy supply (%)	45.6	2019	●	↑

SDG8 – Decent Work and Economic Growth

Indicator	Value	Year	Rating	Trend
Adjusted GDP growth (%)	-3.3	2020	●	●
Victims of modern slavery (per 1,000 population)	1.8	2018	●	●
Adults with an account at a bank or other financial institution or with a mobile-money-service provider (% of population aged 15 or over)	70.0	2017	●	↗
Unemployment rate (% of total labor force)	13.6	2022	●	↓
Fundamental labor rights are effectively guaranteed (worst 0–1 best)	0.5	2020	●	↓
Fatal work-related accidents embodied in imports (per 100,000 population)	0.1	2015	●	↑

* Imputed data point

SDG9 – Industry, Innovation and Infrastructure

Indicator	Value	Year	Rating	Trend
Population using the internet (%)	81.3	2020	●	↑
Mobile broadband subscriptions (per 100 population)	87.1	2019	●	↑
Logistics Performance Index: Quality of trade and transport-related infrastructure (worst 1–5 best)	2.9	2018	●	→
The Times Higher Education Universities Ranking: Average score of top 3 universities (worst 0–100 best)	43.2	2022	●	●
Articles published in academic journals (per 1,000 population)	0.4	2020	●	↗
Expenditure on research and development (% of GDP)	1.2	2018	●	↓

SDG10 – Reduced Inequalities

Indicator	Value	Year	Rating	Trend
Gini coefficient	53.4	2019	●	↓
Palma ratio	2.9	2016	●	●

SDG11 – Sustainable Cities and Communities

Indicator	Value	Year	Rating	Trend
Proportion of urban population living in slums (%)	15.2	2018	●	↑
Annual mean concentration of particulate matter of less than 2.5 microns in diameter (PM2.5) ($\mu g/m^3$)	11.8	2019	●	↑
Access to improved water source, piped (% of urban population)	99.8	2020	●	↑
Satisfaction with public transport (%)	44.0	2021	●	↓

SDG12 – Responsible Consumption and Production

Indicator	Value	Year	Rating	Trend
Municipal solid waste (kg/capita/day)	1.0	2018	●	●
Electronic waste (kg/capita)	10.2	2019	●	●
Production-based SO_2 emissions (kg/capita)	7.6	2018	●	●
SO_2 emissions embodied in imports (kg/capita)	0.7	2018	●	●
Production-based nitrogen emissions (kg/capita)	31.9	2015	●	↓
Nitrogen emissions embodied in imports (kg/capita)	2.1	2015	●	↑
Exports of plastic waste (kg/capita)	0.0	2020	●	●

SDG13 – Climate Action

Indicator	Value	Year	Rating	Trend
CO_2 emissions from fossil fuel combustion and cement production (tCO_2/capita)	2.2	2020	●	↑
CO_2 emissions embodied in imports (tCO_2/capita)	0.2	2018	●	↑
CO_2 emissions embodied in fossil fuel exports (kg/capita)	655.5	2020	●	●

SDG14 – Life Below Water

Indicator	Value	Year	Rating	Trend
Mean area that is protected in marine sites important to biodiversity (%)	66.5	2020	●	→
Ocean Health Index: Clean Waters score (worst 0–100 best)	60.2	2020	●	↓
Fish caught from overexploited or collapsed stocks (% of total catch)	14.1	2018	●	↑
Fish caught by trawling or dredging (%)	14.4	2018	●	→
Fish caught that are then discarded (%)	33.5	2018	●	↓
Marine biodiversity threats embodied in imports (per million population)	0.0	2018	●	●

SDG15 – Life on Land

Indicator	Value	Year	Rating	Trend
Mean area that is protected in terrestrial sites important to biodiversity (%)	43.8	2020	●	→
Mean area that is protected in freshwater sites important to biodiversity (%)	28.3	2020	●	→
Red List Index of species survival (worst 0–1 best)	0.9	2021	●	↓
Permanent deforestation (% of forest area, 5-year average)	0.5	2020	●	↑
Terrestrial and freshwater biodiversity threats embodied in imports (per million population)	0.3	2018	●	●

SDG16 – Peace, Justice and Strong Institutions

Indicator	Value	Year	Rating	Trend
Homicides (per 100,000 population)	20.9	2019	●	↑
Unsentenced detainees (% of prison population)	30.4	2019	●	↑
Population who feel safe walking alone at night in the city or area where they live (%)	48	2021	●	↗
Property Rights (worst 1–7 best)	4.2	2020	●	↓
Birth registrations with civil authority (% of children under age 5)	96.4	2020	●	●
Corruption Perception Index (worst 0–100 best)	38	2021	●	→
Children involved in child labor (% of population aged 5 to 14)	5.4	2019	●	●
Exports of major conventional weapons (TIV constant million USD per 100,000 population)	0.0	2020	●	●
Press Freedom Index (best 0–100 worst)	36.3	2021	●	↓
Access to and affordability of justice (worst 0–1 best)	0.6	2020	●	↑

SDG17 – Partnerships for the Goals

Indicator	Value	Year	Rating	Trend
Government spending on health and education (% of GDP)	10.0	2019	●	↓
For high-income and all OECD DAC countries: International concessional public finance, including official development assistance (% of GNI)	NA	NA	●	●
Other countries: Government revenue excluding grants (% of GDP)	29.1	2019	●	→
Corporate Tax Haven Score (best 0–100 worst)	* 0.0	2019	●	●
Statistical Performance Index (worst 0–100 best)	76.8	2019	●	↑

5. Country Profiles

BRUNEI DARUSSALAM

East and South Asia

OVERALL PERFORMANCE

COUNTRY RANKING

BRUNEI DARUSSALAM

93/163

COUNTRY SCORE

REGIONAL AVERAGE: 65.9

AVERAGE PERFORMANCE BY SDG

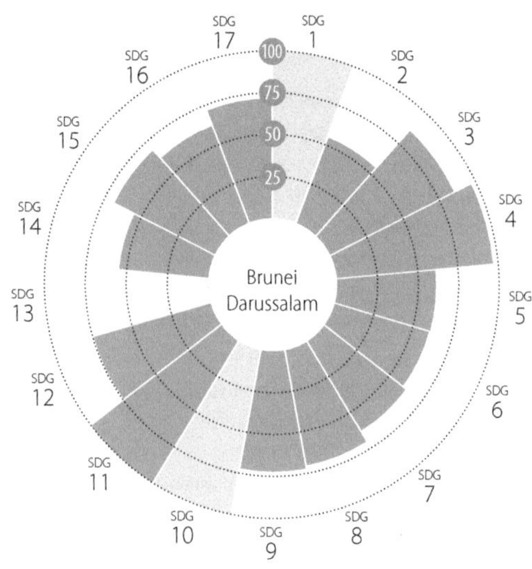

SDG DASHBOARDS AND TRENDS

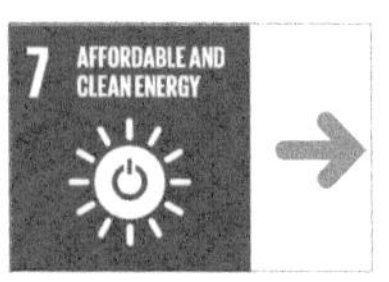

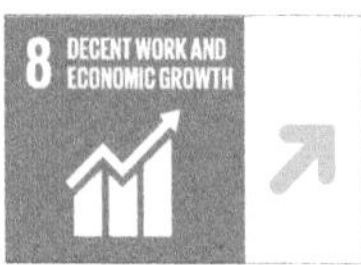

Major challenges · Significant challenges · Challenges remain · SDG achieved · Information unavailable

Decreasing · Stagnating · Moderately improving · On track or maintaining SDG achievement · Information unavailable

Note: The full title of each SDG is available here: https://sustainabledevelopment.un.org/topics/sustainabledevelopmentgoals

INTERNATIONAL SPILLOVER INDEX

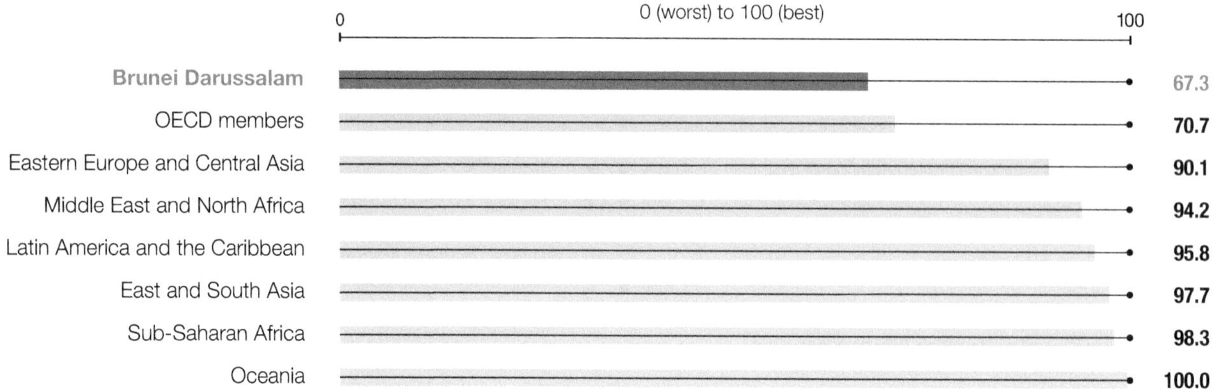

STATISTICAL PERFORMANCE INDEX

0 (worst) to 100 (best)

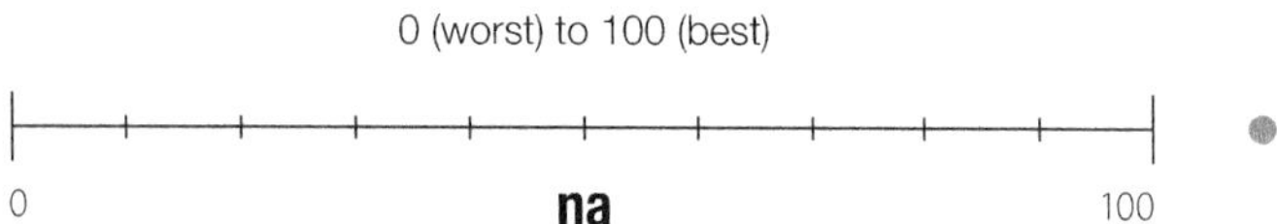

MISSING DATA IN SDG INDEX

18%

BRUNEI DARUSSALAM

Performance by Indicator

SDG1 – No Poverty	Value	Year	Rating	Trend
Poverty headcount ratio at $1.90/day (%)	* NA	NA	•	•
Poverty headcount ratio at $3.20/day (%)	* NA	NA	•	•

SDG2 – Zero Hunger	Value	Year	Rating	Trend
Prevalence of undernourishment (%)	2.5	2019	•	↑
Prevalence of stunting in children under 5 years of age (%)	19.7	2009	•	→
Prevalence of wasting in children under 5 years of age (%)	2.9	2009	•	↑
Prevalence of obesity, BMI ≥ 30 (% of adult population)	14.1	2016	•	↓
Human Trophic Level (best 2–3 worst)	2.4	2013	•	•
Cereal yield (tonnes per hectare of harvested land)	2.0	2018	•	↓
Sustainable Nitrogen Management Index (best 0–1.41 worst)	1.4	2015	•	→
Exports of hazardous pesticides (tonnes per million population)	0.0	2019	•	•

SDG3 – Good Health and Well-Being	Value	Year	Rating	Trend
Maternal mortality rate (per 100,000 live births)	31	2017	•	↑
Neonatal mortality rate (per 1,000 live births)	6.1	2020	•	↑
Mortality rate, under-5 (per 1,000 live births)	11.5	2020	•	↑
Incidence of tuberculosis (per 100,000 population)	83.0	2020	•	→
New HIV infections (per 1,000 uninfected population)	1.0	2020	•	→
Age-standardized death rate due to cardiovascular disease, cancer, diabetes, or chronic respiratory disease in adults aged 30–70 years (%)	18.5	2019	•	→
Age-standardized death rate attributable to household air pollution and ambient air pollution (per 100,000 population)	13	2016	•	•
Traffic deaths (per 100,000 population)	7.5	2019	•	↑
Life expectancy at birth (years)	74.3	2019	•	↓
Adolescent fertility rate (births per 1,000 females aged 15 to 19)	9.9	2018	•	↑
Births attended by skilled health personnel (%)	99.8	2017	•	↑
Surviving infants who received 2 WHO-recommended vaccines (%)	99	2020	•	↑
Universal health coverage (UHC) index of service coverage (worst 0–100 best)	77	2019	•	↑
Subjective well-being (average ladder score, worst 0–10 best)	NA	NA	•	•

SDG4 – Quality Education	Value	Year	Rating	Trend
Participation rate in pre-primary organized learning (% of children aged 4 to 6)	94.3	2020	•	↑
Net primary enrollment rate (%)	98.3	2020	•	↑
Lower secondary completion rate (%)	111.0	2020	•	↑
Literacy rate (% of population aged 15 to 24)	99.7	2018	•	•

SDG5 – Gender Equality	Value	Year	Rating	Trend
Demand for family planning satisfied by modern methods (% of females aged 15 to 49)	NA	NA	•	•
Ratio of female-to-male mean years of education received (%)	98.9	2019	•	↑
Ratio of female-to-male labor force participation rate (%)	75.0	2020	•	↑
Seats held by women in national parliament (%)	9.1	2020	•	→

SDG6 – Clean Water and Sanitation	Value	Year	Rating	Trend
Population using at least basic drinking water services (%)	99.9	2020	•	↑
Population using at least basic sanitation services (%)	96.3	2015	•	•
Freshwater withdrawal (% of available freshwater resources)	3.5	2018	•	•
Anthropogenic wastewater that receives treatment (%)	6.1	2018	•	•
Scarce water consumption embodied in imports (m^3 H_2O eq/capita)	13635.5	2018	•	•

SDG7 – Affordable and Clean Energy	Value	Year	Rating	Trend
Population with access to electricity (%)	100.0	2019	•	↑
Population with access to clean fuels and technology for cooking (%)	100.0	2019	•	↑
CO_2 emissions from fuel combustion per total electricity output ($MtCO_2$/TWh)	2.8	2019	•	→
Share of renewable energy in total primary energy supply (%)	0.0	2019	•	↓

SDG8 – Decent Work and Economic Growth	Value	Year	Rating	Trend
Adjusted GDP growth (%)	0.6	2020	•	•
Victims of modern slavery (per 1,000 population)	10.9	2018	•	•
Adults with an account at a bank or other financial institution or with a mobile-money-service provider (% of population aged 15 or over)	NA	NA	•	•
Unemployment rate (% of total labor force)	7.4	2022	•	→
Fundamental labor rights are effectively guaranteed (worst 0–1 best)	NA	NA	•	•
Fatal work-related accidents embodied in imports (per 100,000 population)	1.2	2015	•	↗

* Imputed data point

SDG9 – Industry, Innovation and Infrastructure	Value	Year	Rating	Trend
Population using the internet (%)	95.0	2020	•	↑
Mobile broadband subscriptions (per 100 population)	148.1	2019	•	↑
Logistics Performance Index: Quality of trade and transport-related infrastructure (worst 1–5 best)	2.5	2018	•	•
The Times Higher Education Universities Ranking: Average score of top 3 universities (worst 0–100 best)	45.1	2022	•	•
Articles published in academic journals (per 1,000 population)	1.6	2020	•	↑
Expenditure on research and development (% of GDP)	0.3	2018	•	•

SDG10 – Reduced Inequalities	Value	Year	Rating	Trend
Gini coefficient	NA	NA	•	•
Palma ratio	NA	NA	•	•

SDG11 – Sustainable Cities and Communities	Value	Year	Rating	Trend
Proportion of urban population living in slums (%)	NA	NA	•	•
Annual mean concentration of particulate matter of less than 2.5 microns in diameter (PM2.5) (μg/m^3)	5.1	2019	•	↑
Access to improved water source, piped (% of urban population)	99.6	2020	•	↑
Satisfaction with public transport (%)	NA	NA	•	•

SDG12 – Responsible Consumption and Production	Value	Year	Rating	Trend
Municipal solid waste (kg/capita/day)	1.4	2016	•	•
Electronic waste (kg/capita)	19.7	2019	•	•
Production-based SO_2 emissions (kg/capita)	17.5	2018	•	•
SO_2 emissions embodied in imports (kg/capita)	9.5	2018	•	•
Production-based nitrogen emissions (kg/capita)	5.9	2015	•	↑
Nitrogen emissions embodied in imports (kg/capita)	6.9	2015	•	→
Exports of plastic waste (kg/capita)	0.7	2020	•	•

SDG13 – Climate Action	Value	Year	Rating	Trend
CO_2 emissions from fossil fuel combustion and cement production (tCO_2/capita)	23.2	2020	•	↓
CO_2 emissions embodied in imports (tCO_2/capita)	4.3	2018	•	→
CO_2 emissions embodied in fossil fuel exports (kg/capita)	65919.4	2020	•	•

SDG14 – Life Below Water	Value	Year	Rating	Trend
Mean area that is protected in marine sites important to biodiversity (%)	5.4	2020	•	→
Ocean Health Index: Clean Waters score (worst 0–100 best)	57.5	2020	•	→
Fish caught from overexploited or collapsed stocks (% of total catch)	NA	NA	•	•
Fish caught by trawling or dredging (%)	31.9	2018	•	↓
Fish caught that are then discarded (%)	7.2	2017	•	↓
Marine biodiversity threats embodied in imports (per million population)	0.0	2018	•	•

SDG15 – Life on Land	Value	Year	Rating	Trend
Mean area that is protected in terrestrial sites important to biodiversity (%)	41.7	2020	•	→
Mean area that is protected in freshwater sites important to biodiversity (%)	50.0	2020	•	→
Red List Index of species survival (worst 0–1 best)	0.9	2021	•	→
Permanent deforestation (% of forest area, 5-year average)	0.1	2020	•	↑
Terrestrial and freshwater biodiversity threats embodied in imports (per million population)	0.4	2018	•	•

SDG16 – Peace, Justice and Strong Institutions	Value	Year	Rating	Trend
Homicides (per 100,000 population)	0.5	2013	•	•
Unsentenced detainees (% of prison population)	7.1	2016	•	•
Population who feel safe walking alone at night in the city or area where they live (%)	NA	NA	•	•
Property Rights (worst 1–7 best)	4.3	2020	•	↓
Birth registrations with civil authority (% of children under age 5)	NA	NA	•	•
Corruption Perception Index (worst 0–100 best)	60	2020	•	↑
Children involved in child labor (% of population aged 5 to 14)	NA	NA	•	•
Exports of major conventional weapons (TIV constant million USD per 100,000 population)	2.7	2020	•	•
Press Freedom Index (best 0–100 worst)	49.9	2021	•	→
Access to and affordability of justice (worst 0–1 best)	NA	NA	•	•

SDG17 – Partnerships for the Goals	Value	Year	Rating	Trend
Government spending on health and education (% of GDP)	6.5	2019	•	↗
For high-income and all OECD DAC countries: International concessional public finance, including official development assistance (% of GNI)	NA	NA	•	•
Other countries: Government revenue excluding grants (% of GDP)	NA	NA	•	•
Corporate Tax Haven Score (best 0–100 worst)	* 0.0	2019	•	•
Statistical Performance Index (worst 0–100 best)	NA	NA	•	•

5. Country Profiles

BULGARIA

Eastern Europe and Central Asia

AVERAGE PERFORMANCE BY SDG

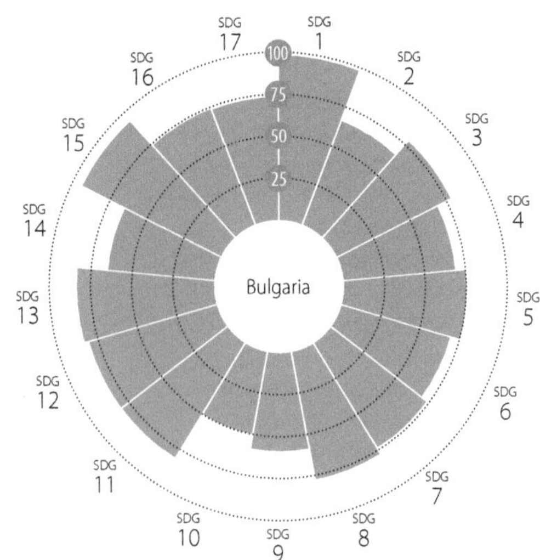

OVERALL PERFORMANCE

COUNTRY RANKING

BULGARIA

42/163

COUNTRY SCORE

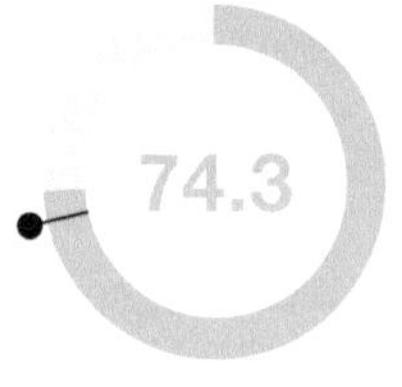

REGIONAL AVERAGE: 71.6

SDG DASHBOARDS AND TRENDS

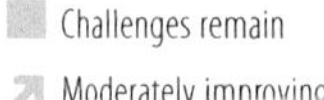

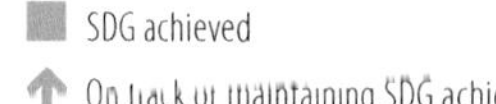

Information unavailable
Information unavailable

Note: The full title of each SDG is available here: https://sustainabledevelopment.un.org/topics/sustainabledevelopmentgoals

INTERNATIONAL SPILLOVER INDEX

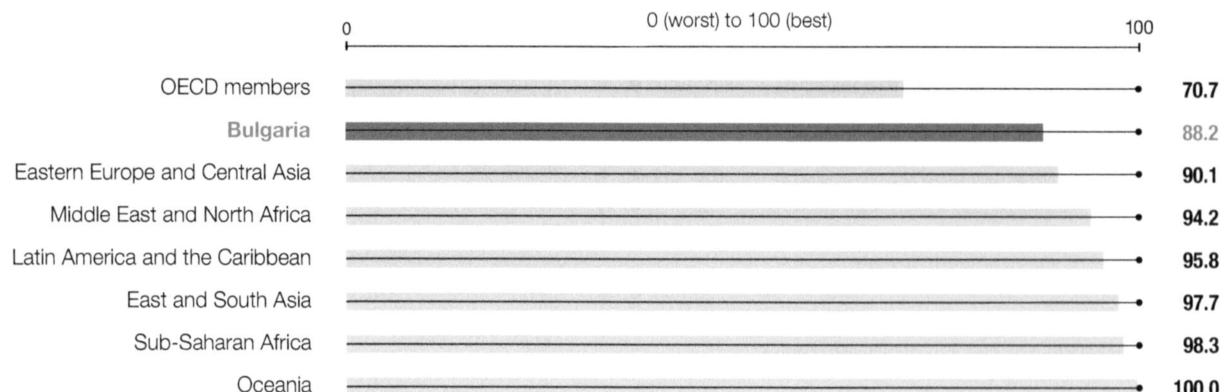

STATISTICAL PERFORMANCE INDEX

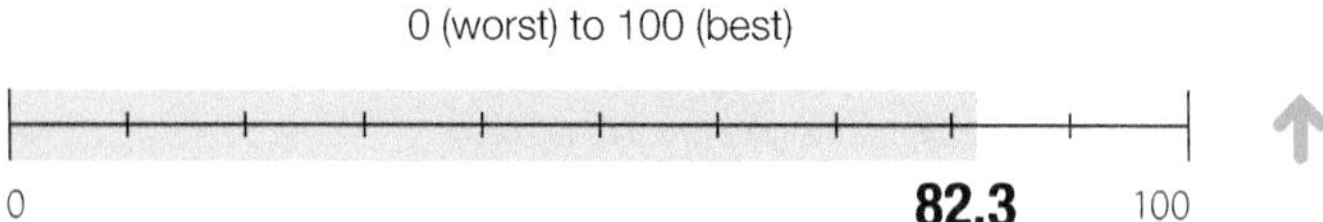

MISSING DATA IN SDG INDEX

4%

BULGARIA

Performance by Indicator

SDG1 – No Poverty	Value	Year	Rating	Trend
Poverty headcount ratio at $1.90/day (%)	0.8	2022	●	↑
Poverty headcount ratio at $3.20/day (%)	1.3	2022	●	↑
SDG2 – Zero Hunger				
Prevalence of undernourishment (%)	3.0	2019	●	↑
Prevalence of stunting in children under 5 years of age (%)	7.0	2014	●	↑
Prevalence of wasting in children under 5 years of age (%)	6.3	2014	●	↑
Prevalence of obesity, BMI ≥ 30 (% of adult population)	25.0	2016	●	↓
Human Trophic Level (best 2–3 worst)	2.4	2017	●	→
Cereal yield (tonnes per hectare of harvested land)	5.5	2018	●	↑
Sustainable Nitrogen Management Index (best 0–1.41 worst)	0.5	2015	●	↗
Exports of hazardous pesticides (tonnes per million population)	0.0	2019	●	●
SDG3 – Good Health and Well-Being				
Maternal mortality rate (per 100,000 live births)	10	2017	●	↑
Neonatal mortality rate (per 1,000 live births)	3.0	2020	●	↑
Mortality rate, under-5 (per 1,000 live births)	6.1	2020	●	↑
Incidence of tuberculosis (per 100,000 population)	19.0	2020	●	↑
New HIV infections (per 1,000 uninfected population)	1.0	2020	●	→
Age-standardized death rate due to cardiovascular disease, cancer, diabetes, or chronic respiratory disease in adults aged 30–70 years (%)	24.2	2019	●	→
Age-standardized death rate attributable to household air pollution and ambient air pollution (per 100,000 population)	62	2016	●	●
Traffic deaths (per 100,000 population)	9.2	2019	●	↑
Life expectancy at birth (years)	75.1	2019	●	→
Adolescent fertility rate (births per 1,000 females aged 15 to 19)	38.9	2018	●	→
Births attended by skilled health personnel (%)	99.8	2015	●	●
Surviving infants who received 2 WHO-recommended vaccines (%)	88	2020	●	↓
Universal health coverage (UHC) index of service coverage (worst 0–100 best)	70	2019	●	↑
Subjective well-being (average ladder score, worst 0–10 best)	5.4	2021	●	↑
SDG4 – Quality Education				
Participation rate in pre-primary organized learning (% of children aged 4 to 6)	83.2	2019	●	↓
Net primary enrollment rate (%)	85.4	2019	●	↓
Lower secondary completion rate (%)	47.0	2017	●	●
Literacy rate (% of population aged 15 to 24)	97.9	2011	●	●
SDG5 – Gender Equality				
Demand for family planning satisfied by modern methods (% of females aged 15 to 49)	NA	NA	●	●
Ratio of female-to-male mean years of education received (%)	102.7	2019	●	↑
Ratio of female-to-male labor force participation rate (%)	78.8	2020	●	↑
Seats held by women in national parliament (%)	26.7	2020	●	↗
SDG6 – Clean Water and Sanitation				
Population using at least basic drinking water services (%)	99.0	2020	●	↑
Population using at least basic sanitation services (%)	86.0	2020	●	→
Freshwater withdrawal (% of available freshwater resources)	40.1	2018	●	●
Anthropogenic wastewater that receives treatment (%)	13.9	2018	●	●
Scarce water consumption embodied in imports (m^3 H_2O eq/capita)	2269.6	2018	●	●
SDG7 – Affordable and Clean Energy				
Population with access to electricity (%)	100.0	2019	●	↑
Population with access to clean fuels and technology for cooking (%)	88.7	2016	●	●
CO_2 emissions from fuel combustion per total electricity output ($MtCO_2$/TWh)	1.0	2019	●	↑
Share of renewable energy in total primary energy supply (%)	12.9	2019	●	↗
SDG8 – Decent Work and Economic Growth				
Adjusted GDP growth (%)	1.2	2020	●	●
Victims of modern slavery (per 1,000 population)	4.5	2018	●	●
Adults with an account at a bank or other financial institution or with a mobile-money-service provider (% of population aged 15 or over)	72.2	2017	●	↑
Unemployment rate (% of total labor force)	4.9	2022	●	↑
Fundamental labor rights are effectively guaranteed (worst 0–1 best)	0.6	2020	●	↓
Fatal work-related accidents embodied in imports (per 100,000 population)	0.4	2015	●	↑

* Imputed data point

SDG9 – Industry, Innovation and Infrastructure	Value	Year	Rating	Trend
Population using the internet (%)	70.2	2020	●	↑
Mobile broadband subscriptions (per 100 population)	105.6	2019	●	↑
Logistics Performance Index: Quality of trade and transport-related infrastructure (worst 1–5 best)	2.8	2018	●	↓
The Times Higher Education Universities Ranking: Average score of top 3 universities (worst 0–100 best)	16.5	2022	●	●
Articles published in academic journals (per 1,000 population)	0.9	2020	●	↑
Expenditure on research and development (% of GDP)	0.8	2018	●	↓
SDG10 – Reduced Inequalities				
Gini coefficient	41.3	2018	●	↓
Palma ratio	1.9	2019	●	●
SDG11 – Sustainable Cities and Communities				
Proportion of urban population living in slums (%)	NA	NA	●	●
Annual mean concentration of particulate matter of less than 2.5 microns in diameter (PM2.5) ($\mu g/m^3$)	18.5	2019	●	↗
Access to improved water source, piped (% of urban population)	99.5	2020	●	↑
Satisfaction with public transport (%)	56.0	2021	●	↓
SDG12 – Responsible Consumption and Production				
Municipal solid waste (kg/capita/day)	1.1	2018	●	●
Electronic waste (kg/capita)	11.7	2019	●	●
Production-based SO_2 emissions (kg/capita)	46.3	2018	●	●
SO_2 emissions embodied in imports (kg/capita)	2.3	2018	●	●
Production-based nitrogen emissions (kg/capita)	23.0	2015	●	↓
Nitrogen emissions embodied in imports (kg/capita)	2.8	2015	●	↑
Exports of plastic waste (kg/capita)	1.7	2020	●	●
SDG13 – Climate Action				
CO_2 emissions from fossil fuel combustion and cement production (tCO_2/capita)	5.4	2020	●	↗
CO_2 emissions embodied in imports (tCO_2/capita)	0.8	2018	●	↓
CO_2 emissions embodied in fossil fuel exports (kg/capita)	23.9	2020	●	●
SDG14 – Life Below Water				
Mean area that is protected in marine sites important to biodiversity (%)	99.7	2020	●	↑
Ocean Health Index: Clean Waters score (worst 0–100 best)	42.4	2020	●	→
Fish caught from overexploited or collapsed stocks (% of total catch)	NA	NA	●	●
Fish caught by trawling or dredging (%)	62.9	2018	●	↑
Fish caught that are then discarded (%)	5.0	2018	●	↑
Marine biodiversity threats embodied in imports (per million population)	0.0	2018	●	●
SDG15 – Life on Land				
Mean area that is protected in terrestrial sites important to biodiversity (%)	96.6	2020	●	↑
Mean area that is protected in freshwater sites important to biodiversity (%)	98.7	2020	●	↑
Red List Index of species survival (worst 0–1 best)	0.9	2021	●	↑
Permanent deforestation (% of forest area, 5-year average)	0.0	2020	●	↑
Terrestrial and freshwater biodiversity threats embodied in imports (per million population)	1.1	2018	●	●
SDG16 – Peace, Justice and Strong Institutions				
Homicides (per 100,000 population)	1.0	2020	●	↑
Unsentenced detainees (% of prison population)	9.7	2019	●	↑
Population who feel safe walking alone at night in the city or area where they live (%)	65	2021	●	↑
Property Rights (worst 1–7 best)	3.9	2020	●	↑
Birth registrations with civil authority (% of children under age 5)	100.0	2020	●	●
Corruption Perception Index (worst 0–100 best)	42	2021	●	→
Children involved in child labor (% of population aged 5 to 14)	NA	NA	●	●
Exports of major conventional weapons (TIV constant million USD per 100,000 population)	0.4	2020	●	●
Press Freedom Index (best 0–100 worst)	37.3	2021	●	↓
Access to and affordability of justice (worst 0–1 best)	0.7	2020	●	↑
SDG17 – Partnerships for the Goals				
Government spending on health and education (% of GDP)	8.3	2019	●	→
For high-income and all OECD DAC countries: International concessional public finance, including official development assistance (% of GNI)	NA	NA	●	●
Other countries: Government revenue excluding grants (% of GDP)	36.0	2019	●	↑
Corporate Tax Haven Score (best 0–100 worst)	55.6	2019	●	●
Statistical Performance Index (worst 0–100 best)	82.3	2019	●	↑

BURKINA FASO

Sub-Saharan Africa

OVERALL PERFORMANCE

COUNTRY RANKING

BURKINA FASO

138/163

COUNTRY SCORE

AVERAGE PERFORMANCE BY SDG

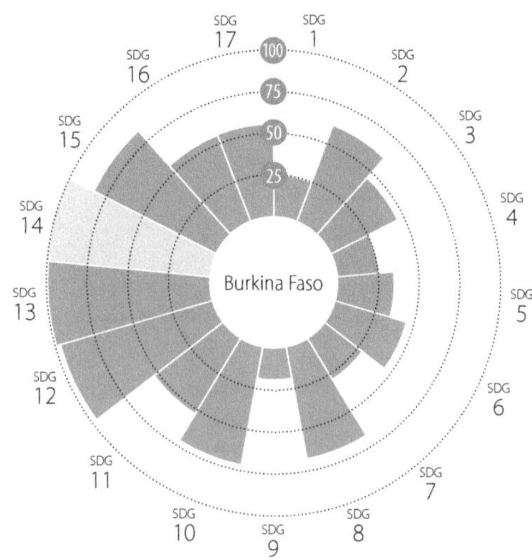

SDG DASHBOARDS AND TRENDS

Major challenges · Significant challenges · Challenges remain · SDG achieved · Information unavailable

Decreasing · Stagnating · Moderately improving · On track or maintaining SDG achievement · Information unavailable

Note: The full title of each SDG is available here: https://sustainabledevelopment.un.org/topics/sustainabledevelopmentgoals

INTERNATIONAL SPILLOVER INDEX

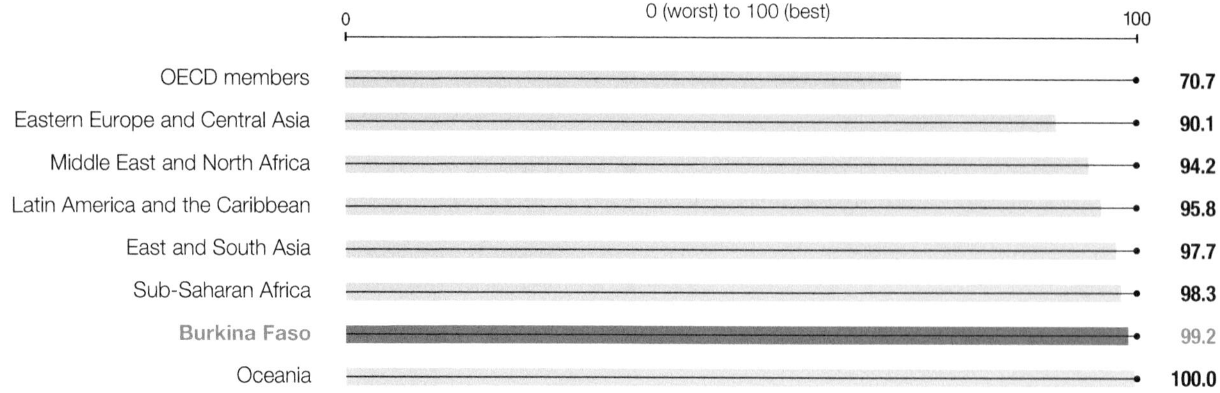

Region	Score
OECD members	70.7
Eastern Europe and Central Asia	90.1
Middle East and North Africa	94.2
Latin America and the Caribbean	95.8
East and South Asia	97.7
Sub-Saharan Africa	98.3
Burkina Faso	99.2
Oceania	100.0

STATISTICAL PERFORMANCE INDEX

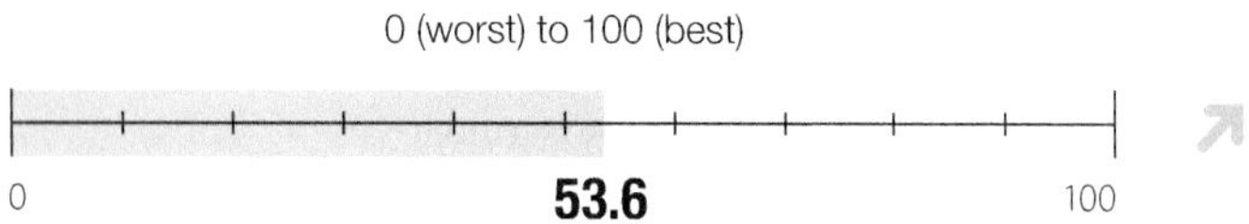

MISSING DATA IN SDG INDEX

1%

SDG1 – No Poverty	Value	Year	Rating	Trend
Poverty headcount ratio at $1.90/day (%)	36.9	2022	●	→
Poverty headcount ratio at $3.20/day (%)	70.8	2022	●	→
SDG2 – Zero Hunger				
Prevalence of undernourishment (%)	14.4	2019	●	↓
Prevalence of stunting in children under 5 years of age (%)	23.8	2019	●	→
Prevalence of wasting in children under 5 years of age (%)	8.1	2019	●	→
Prevalence of obesity, BMI ≥ 30 (% of adult population)	5.6	2016	●	↑
Human Trophic Level (best 2–3 worst)	2.1	2017	●	↑
Cereal yield (tonnes per hectare of harvested land)	1.1	2018	●	↓
Sustainable Nitrogen Management Index (best 0–1.41 worst)	0.8	2015	●	→
Exports of hazardous pesticides (tonnes per million population)	0.0	2019	●	●
SDG3 – Good Health and Well-Being				
Maternal mortality rate (per 100,000 live births)	320	2017	●	↗
Neonatal mortality rate (per 1,000 live births)	25.8	2020	●	→
Mortality rate, under-5 (per 1,000 live births)	85.0	2020	●	↗
Incidence of tuberculosis (per 100,000 population)	46.0	2020	●	→
New HIV infections (per 1,000 uninfected population)	0.1	2020	●	↑
Age-standardized death rate due to cardiovascular disease, cancer, diabetes, or chronic respiratory disease in adults aged 30–70 years (%)	23.9	2019	●	→
Age-standardized death rate attributable to household air pollution and ambient air pollution (per 100,000 population)	206	2016	●	●
Traffic deaths (per 100,000 population)	31.0	2019	●	↓
Life expectancy at birth (years)	62.7	2019	●	→
Adolescent fertility rate (births per 1,000 females aged 15 to 19)	132.3	2016	●	●
Births attended by skilled health personnel (%)	79.8	2015	●	●
Surviving infants who received 2 WHO-recommended vaccines (%)	88	2020	●	→
Universal health coverage (UHC) index of service coverage (worst 0–100 best)	43	2019	●	→
Subjective well-being (average ladder score, worst 0–10 best)	4.6	2021	●	→
SDG4 – Quality Education				
Participation rate in pre-primary organized learning (% of children aged 4 to 6)	20.7	2020	●	→
Net primary enrollment rate (%)	75.5	2020	●	↗
Lower secondary completion rate (%)	41.4	2020	●	↗
Literacy rate (% of population aged 15 to 24)	58.9	2018	●	↗
SDG5 – Gender Equality				
Demand for family planning satisfied by modern methods (% of females aged 15 to 49)	52.6	2020	●	●
Ratio of female-to-male mean years of education received (%)	47.8	2019	●	↓
Ratio of female-to-male labor force participation rate (%)	78.9	2020	●	↑
Seats held by women in national parliament (%)	6.3	2020	●	↓
SDG6 – Clean Water and Sanitation				
Population using at least basic drinking water services (%)	47.2	2020	●	↓
Population using at least basic sanitation services (%)	21.7	2020	●	→
Freshwater withdrawal (% of available freshwater resources)	7.8	2018	●	●
Anthropogenic wastewater that receives treatment (%)	0.0	2018	●	●
Scarce water consumption embodied in imports (m^3 H_2O eq/capita)	218.2	2018	●	●
SDG7 – Affordable and Clean Energy				
Population with access to electricity (%)	18.4	2019	●	→
Population with access to clean fuels and technology for cooking (%)	10.2	2019	●	→
CO_2 emissions from fuel combustion per total electricity output ($MtCO_2$/TWh)	2.1	2019	●	→
Share of renewable energy in total primary energy supply (%)	NA	NA	●	●
SDG8 – Decent Work and Economic Growth				
Adjusted GDP growth (%)	-3.4	2020	●	●
Victims of modern slavery (per 1,000 population)	4.5	2018	●	●
Adults with an account at a bank or other financial institution or with a mobile-money-service provider (% of population aged 15 or over)	43.2	2017	●	↑
Unemployment rate (% of total labor force)	4.7	2022	●	↑
Fundamental labor rights are effectively guaranteed (worst 0–1 best)	0.5	2020	●	→
Fatal work-related accidents embodied in imports (per 100,000 population)	0.0	2015	●	↑

SDG9 – Industry, Innovation and Infrastructure	Value	Year	Rating	Trend
Population using the internet (%)	22.0	2020	●	↗
Mobile broadband subscriptions (per 100 population)	31.7	2019	●	↑
Logistics Performance Index: Quality of trade and transport-related infrastructure (worst 1–5 best)	2.4	2018	●	↗
The Times Higher Education Universities Ranking: Average score of top 3 universities (worst 0–100 best)	* 0.0	2022	●	●
Articles published in academic journals (per 1,000 population)	0.0	2020	●	→
Expenditure on research and development (% of GDP)	0.6	2017	●	↑
SDG10 – Reduced Inequalities				
Gini coefficient	35.3	2014	●	●
Palma ratio	1.5	2018	●	●
SDG11 – Sustainable Cities and Communities				
Proportion of urban population living in slums (%)	56.6	2018	●	↗
Annual mean concentration of particulate matter of less than 2.5 microns in diameter (PM2.5) (μg/m^3)	45.9	2019	●	→
Access to improved water source, piped (% of urban population)	73.5	2020	●	↓
Satisfaction with public transport (%)	51.0	2021	●	↑
SDG12 – Responsible Consumption and Production				
Municipal solid waste (kg/capita/day)	0.4	2015	●	●
Electronic waste (kg/capita)	0.6	2019	●	●
Production-based SO_2 emissions (kg/capita)	0.8	2018	●	●
SO_2 emissions embodied in imports (kg/capita)	0.2	2018	●	●
Production-based nitrogen emissions (kg/capita)	16.2	2015	●	↑
Nitrogen emissions embodied in imports (kg/capita)	0.6	2015	●	↑
Exports of plastic waste (kg/capita)	0.1	2020	●	●
SDG13 – Climate Action				
CO_2 emissions from fossil fuel combustion and cement production (tCO_2/capita)	0.2	2020	●	↑
CO_2 emissions embodied in imports (tCO_2/capita)	0.1	2018	●	↑
CO_2 emissions embodied in fossil fuel exports (kg/capita)	0.0	2020	●	●
SDG14 – Life Below Water				
Mean area that is protected in marine sites important to biodiversity (%)	NA	NA	●	●
Ocean Health Index: Clean Waters score (worst 0–100 best)	NA	NA	●	●
Fish caught from overexploited or collapsed stocks (% of total catch)	NA	NA	●	●
Fish caught by trawling or dredging (%)	NA	NA	●	●
Fish caught that are then discarded (%)	NA	NA	●	●
Marine biodiversity threats embodied in imports (per million population)	0.0	2018	●	●
SDG15 – Life on Land				
Mean area that is protected in terrestrial sites important to biodiversity (%)	66.7	2020	●	→
Mean area that is protected in freshwater sites important to biodiversity (%)	50.2	2020	●	→
Red List Index of species survival (worst 0–1 best)	1.0	2021	●	↑
Permanent deforestation (% of forest area, 5-year average)	0.0	2020	●	↑
Terrestrial and freshwater biodiversity threats embodied in imports (per million population)	0.0	2018	●	●
SDG16 – Peace, Justice and Strong Institutions				
Homicides (per 100,000 population)	1.3	2017	●	↑
Unsentenced detainees (% of prison population)	42.0	2016	●	●
Population who feel safe walking alone at night in the city or area where they live (%)	49	2021	●	↓
Property Rights (worst 1–7 best)	4.0	2020	●	↓
Birth registrations with civil authority (% of children under age 5)	76.9	2020	●	●
Corruption Perception Index (worst 0–100 best)	42	2021	●	→
Children involved in child labor (% of population aged 5 to 14)	42.0	2019	●	●
Exports of major conventional weapons (TIV constant million USD per 100,000 population)	* 0.0	2020	●	●
Press Freedom Index (best 0–100 worst)	23.2	2021	●	↑
Access to and affordability of justice (worst 0–1 best)	0.4	2020	●	→
SDG17 – Partnerships for the Goals				
Government spending on health and education (% of GDP)	8.1	2019	●	↑
For high-income and all OECD DAC countries: International concessional public finance, including official development assistance (% of GNI)	NA	NA	●	●
Other countries: Government revenue excluding grants (% of GDP)	18.4	2019	●	↗
Corporate Tax Haven Score (best 0–100 worst)	* 0.0	2019	●	●
Statistical Performance Index (worst 0–100 best)	53.6	2019	●	↗

* Imputed data point

BURUNDI

Sub-Saharan Africa

OVERALL PERFORMANCE

COUNTRY RANKING

BURUNDI

141 **/163**

COUNTRY SCORE

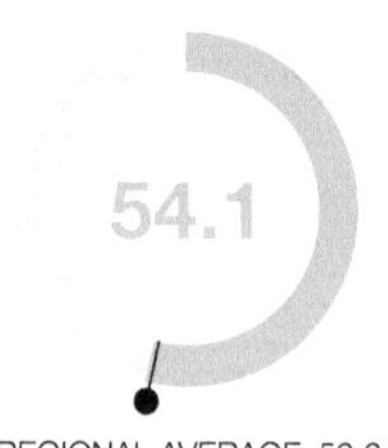

AVERAGE PERFORMANCE BY SDG

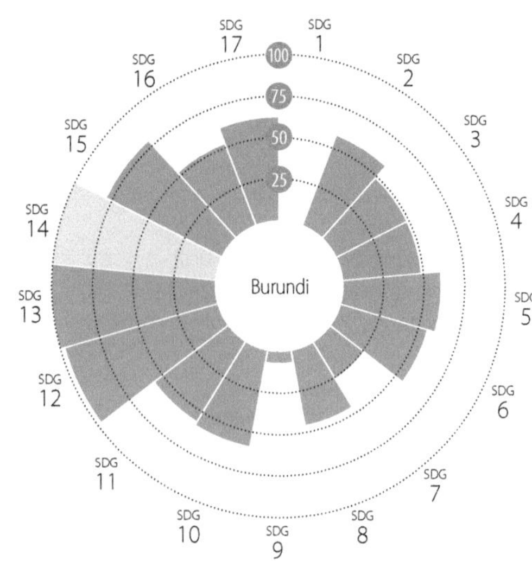

SDG DASHBOARDS AND TRENDS

Major challenges · Significant challenges · Challenges remain · SDG achieved · Information unavailable

Decreasing · Stagnating · Moderately improving · On track or maintaining SDG achievement · Information unavailable

Note: The full title of each SDG is available here: https://sustainabledevelopment.un.org/topics/sustainabledevelopmentgoals

INTERNATIONAL SPILLOVER INDEX

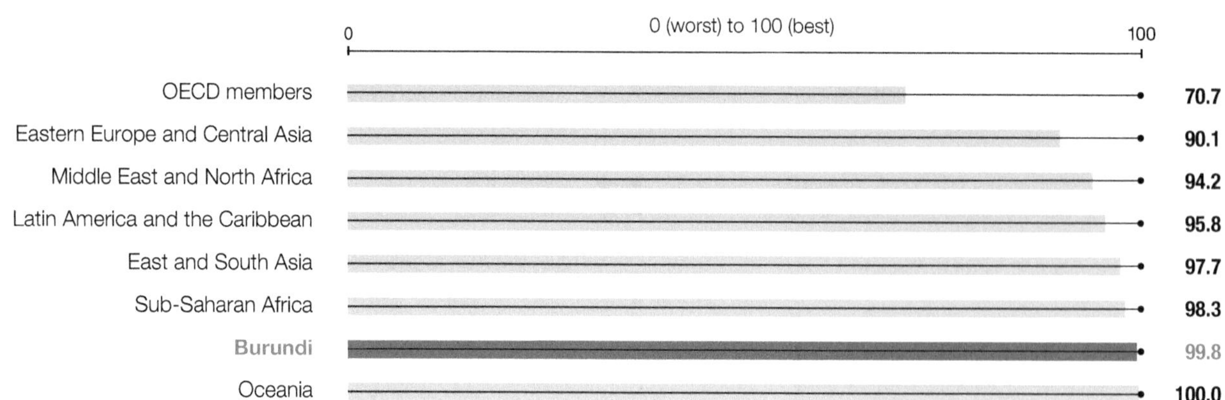

STATISTICAL PERFORMANCE INDEX

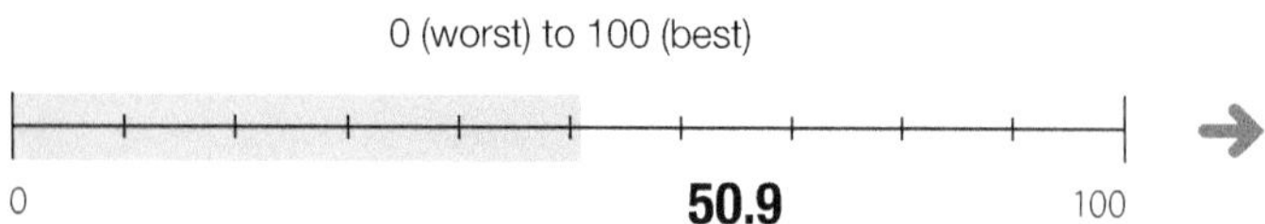

MISSING DATA IN SDG INDEX

6%

SDG1 – No Poverty	Value	Year	Rating	Trend
Poverty headcount ratio at $1.90/day (%)	74.9	2022	●	↓
Poverty headcount ratio at $3.20/day (%)	92.4	2022	●	↓
SDG2 – Zero Hunger				
Prevalence of undernourishment (%)	NA	NA	●	●
Prevalence of stunting in children under 5 years of age (%)	54.0	2019	●	→
Prevalence of wasting in children under 5 years of age (%)	4.8	2019	●	↑
Prevalence of obesity, BMI ≥ 30 (% of adult population)	5.4	2016	●	↑
Human Trophic Level (best 2–3 worst)	2.0	2007	●	●
Cereal yield (tonnes per hectare of harvested land)	1.2	2018	●	→
Sustainable Nitrogen Management Index (best 0–1.41 worst)	0.9	2015	●	↓
Exports of hazardous pesticides (tonnes per million population)	0.4	2019	●	●
SDG3 – Good Health and Well-Being				
Maternal mortality rate (per 100,000 live births)	548	2017	●	→
Neonatal mortality rate (per 1,000 live births)	20.9	2020	●	↗
Mortality rate, under-5 (per 1,000 live births)	54.4	2020	●	↗
Incidence of tuberculosis (per 100,000 population)	103.0	2020	●	↗
New HIV infections (per 1,000 uninfected population)	0.2	2020	●	↑
Age-standardized death rate due to cardiovascular disease, cancer, diabetes, or chronic respiratory disease in adults aged 30–70 years (%)	25.0	2019	●	→
Age-standardized death rate attributable to household air pollution and ambient air pollution (per 100,000 population)	180	2016	●	●
Traffic deaths (per 100,000 population)	35.5	2019	●	↓
Life expectancy at birth (years)	63.8	2019	●	→
Adolescent fertility rate (births per 1,000 females aged 15 to 19)	58.2	2015	●	●
Births attended by skilled health personnel (%)	85.1	2017	●	●
Surviving infants who received 2 WHO-recommended vaccines (%)	90	2020	●	↑
Universal health coverage (UHC) index of service coverage (worst 0–100 best)	44	2019	●	→
Subjective well-being (average ladder score, worst 0–10 best)	3.8	2018	●	●
SDG4 – Quality Education				
Participation rate in pre-primary organized learning (% of children aged 4 to 6)	49.0	2021	●	↗
Net primary enrollment rate (%)	89.9	2021	●	●
Lower secondary completion rate (%)	29.8	2019	●	↓
Literacy rate (% of population aged 15 to 24)	88.2	2017	●	●
SDG5 – Gender Equality				
Demand for family planning satisfied by modern methods (% of females aged 15 to 49)	39.6	2017	●	●
Ratio of female-to-male mean years of education received (%)	63.4	2019	●	↓
Ratio of female-to-male labor force participation rate (%)	102.5	2020	●	↑
Seats held by women in national parliament (%)	38.2	2020	●	↑
SDG6 – Clean Water and Sanitation				
Population using at least basic drinking water services (%)	62.2	2020	●	→
Population using at least basic sanitation services (%)	45.7	2020	●	↓
Freshwater withdrawal (% of available freshwater resources)	10.2	2018	●	●
Anthropogenic wastewater that receives treatment (%)	0.0	2018	●	●
Scarce water consumption embodied in imports (m^3 H_2O eq/capita)	181.0	2018	●	●
SDG7 – Affordable and Clean Energy				
Population with access to electricity (%)	11.1	2019	●	→
Population with access to clean fuels and technology for cooking (%)	0.2	2019	●	→
CO_2 emissions from fuel combustion per total electricity output ($MtCO_2$/TWh)	1.5	2019	●	↑
Share of renewable energy in total primary energy supply (%)	NA	NA	●	●
SDG8 – Decent Work and Economic Growth				
Adjusted GDP growth (%)	-8.5	2020	●	●
Victims of modern slavery (per 1,000 population)	40.0	2018	●	●
Adults with an account at a bank or other financial institution or with a mobile-money-service provider (% of population aged 15 or over)	7.1	2014	●	●
Unemployment rate (% of total labor force)	1.7	2022	●	↑
Fundamental labor rights are effectively guaranteed (worst 0–1 best)	NA	NA	●	●
Fatal work-related accidents embodied in imports (per 100,000 population)	0.0	2015	●	↑

SDG9 – Industry, Innovation and Infrastructure	Value	Year	Rating	Trend
Population using the internet (%)	9.4	2020	●	→
Mobile broadband subscriptions (per 100 population)	11.1	2019	●	→
Logistics Performance Index: Quality of trade and transport-related infrastructure (worst 1–5 best)	2.0	2018	●	↓
The Times Higher Education Universities Ranking: Average score of top 3 universities (worst 0–100 best)	* 0.0	2022	●	●
Articles published in academic journals (per 1,000 population)	0.0	2020	●	→
Expenditure on research and development (% of GDP)	0.2	2018	●	●
SDG10 – Reduced Inequalities				
Gini coefficient	38.6	2013	●	●
Palma ratio	1.7	2018	●	●
SDG11 – Sustainable Cities and Communities				
Proportion of urban population living in slums (%)	50.5	2018	●	↗
Annual mean concentration of particulate matter of less than 2.5 microns in diameter (PM2.5) (μg/m³)	37.4	2019	●	→
Access to improved water source, piped (% of urban population)	90.9	2020	●	↗
Satisfaction with public transport (%)	39.0	2018	●	●
SDG12 – Responsible Consumption and Production				
Municipal solid waste (kg/capita/day)	0.8	2002	●	●
Electronic waste (kg/capita)	0.5	2019	●	●
Production-based SO_2 emissions (kg/capita)	0.2	2018	●	●
SO_2 emissions embodied in imports (kg/capita)	0.1	2018	●	●
Production-based nitrogen emissions (kg/capita)	3.5	2015	●	↑
Nitrogen emissions embodied in imports (kg/capita)	0.2	2015	●	↑
Exports of plastic waste (kg/capita)	0.0	2020	●	●
SDG13 – Climate Action				
CO_2 emissions from fossil fuel combustion and cement production (tCO_2/capita)	0.1	2020	●	↑
CO_2 emissions embodied in imports (tCO_2/capita)	0.0	2018	●	↑
CO_2 emissions embodied in fossil fuel exports (kg/capita)	0.0	2020	●	●
SDG14 – Life Below Water				
Mean area that is protected in marine sites important to biodiversity (%)	NA	NA	●	●
Ocean Health Index: Clean Waters score (worst 0–100 best)	NA	NA	●	●
Fish caught from overexploited or collapsed stocks (% of total catch)	NA	NA	●	●
Fish caught by trawling or dredging (%)	NA	NA	●	●
Fish caught that are then discarded (%)	NA	NA	●	●
Marine biodiversity threats embodied in imports (per million population)	0.0	2018	●	●
SDG15 – Life on Land				
Mean area that is protected in terrestrial sites important to biodiversity (%)	56.8	2020	●	→
Mean area that is protected in freshwater sites important to biodiversity (%)	80.0	2020	●	→
Red List Index of species survival (worst 0–1 best)	0.9	2021	●	→
Permanent deforestation (% of forest area, 5-year average)	0.2	2020	●	↓
Terrestrial and freshwater biodiversity threats embodied in imports (per million population)	0.0	2018	●	●
SDG16 – Peace, Justice and Strong Institutions				
Homicides (per 100,000 population)	6.1	2016	●	●
Unsentenced detainees (% of prison population)	55.3	2017	●	●
Population who feel safe walking alone at night in the city or area where they live (%)	66	2018	●	●
Property Rights (worst 1–7 best)	4.1	2020	●	↑
Birth registrations with civil authority (% of children under age 5)	83.5	2020	●	●
Corruption Perception Index (worst 0–100 best)	19	2021	●	↓
Children involved in child labor (% of population aged 5 to 14)	30.9	2019	●	●
Exports of major conventional weapons (TIV constant million USD per 100,000 population)	* 0.0	2020	●	●
Press Freedom Index (best 0–100 worst)	47.6	2021	●	↗
Access to and affordability of justice (worst 0–1 best)	NA	NA	●	●
SDG17 – Partnerships for the Goals				
Government spending on health and education (% of GDP)	7.7	2019	●	↓
For high-income and all OECD DAC countries: International concessional public finance, including official development assistance (% of GNI)	NA	NA	●	●
Other countries: Government revenue excluding grants (% of GDP)	NA	NA	●	●
Corporate Tax Haven Score (best 0–100 worst)	* 0.0	2019	●	●
Statistical Performance Index (worst 0–100 best)	50.9	2019	●	→

* Imputed data point

5. Country Profiles

CABO VERDE

Sub-Saharan Africa

OVERALL PERFORMANCE

COUNTRY RANKING

Cabo Verde

NA /163

COUNTRY SCORE

REGIONAL AVERAGE: 53.6

AVERAGE PERFORMANCE BY SDG

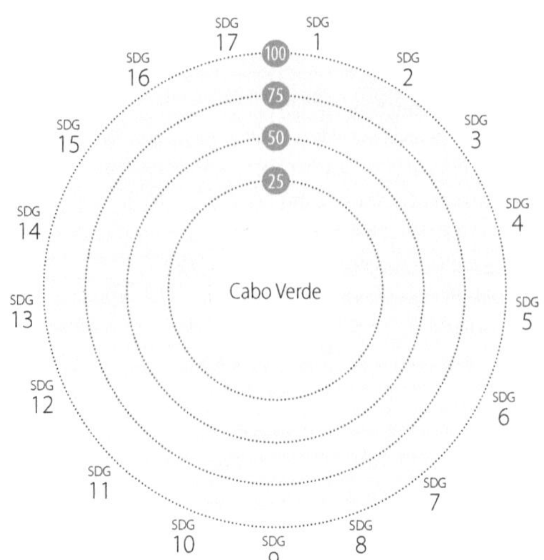

SDG DASHBOARDS AND TRENDS

Major challenges | Significant challenges | Challenges remain | SDG achieved | Information unavailable

Decreasing | Stagnating | Moderately improving | On track or maintaining SDG achievement | Information unavailable

Note: The full title of each SDG is available here: https://sustainabledevelopment.un.org/topics/sustainabledevelopmentgoals

INTERNATIONAL SPILLOVER INDEX

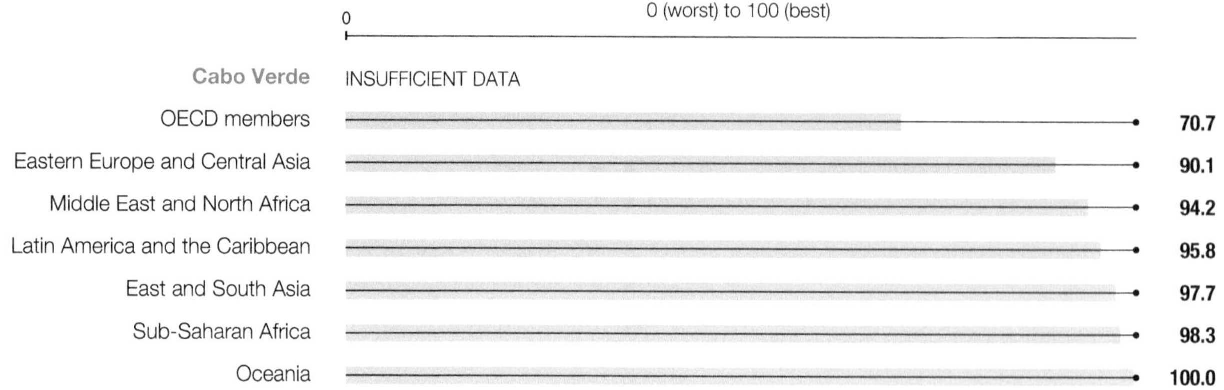

Cabo Verde	INSUFFICIENT DATA
OECD members	70.7
Eastern Europe and Central Asia	90.1
Middle East and North Africa	94.2
Latin America and the Caribbean	95.8
East and South Asia	97.7
Sub-Saharan Africa	98.3
Oceania	100.0

STATISTICAL PERFORMANCE INDEX

0 (worst) to 100 (best)

0 **54.7** 100

MISSING DATA IN SDG INDEX

21%

SDG1 – No Poverty	Value	Year	Rating	Trend
Poverty headcount ratio at $1.90/day (%)	2.1	2022	●	↑
Poverty headcount ratio at $3.20/day (%)	15.8	2022	●	→

SDG2 – Zero Hunger	Value	Year	Rating	Trend
Prevalence of undernourishment (%)		2019	●	↗
Prevalence of stunting in children under 5 years of age (%)	NA	NA	●	●
Prevalence of wasting in children under 5 years of age (%)	NA	NA	●	●
Prevalence of obesity, BMI ≥ 30 (% of adult population)	11.8	2016	●	↓
Human Trophic Level (best 2–3 worst)	2.2	2017	●	→
Cereal yield (tonnes per hectare of harvested land)	0.1	2018	●	↓
Sustainable Nitrogen Management Index (best 0–1.41 worst)	1.2	2015	●	→
Exports of hazardous pesticides (tonnes per million population)	NA	NA	●	●

SDG3 – Good Health and Well-Being	Value	Year	Rating	Trend
Maternal mortality rate (per 100,000 live births)	58	2017	●	↑
Neonatal mortality rate (per 1,000 live births)	8.5	2020	●	↑
Mortality rate, under-5 (per 1,000 live births)	14.2	2020	●	↑
Incidence of tuberculosis (per 100,000 population)	39.0	2020	●	↑
New HIV infections (per 1,000 uninfected population)	1.0	2020	●	→
Age-standardized death rate due to cardiovascular disease, cancer, diabetes, or chronic respiratory disease in adults aged 30–70 years (%)	17.4	2019	●	↓
Age-standardized death rate attributable to household air pollution and ambient air pollution (per 100,000 population)	99	2016	●	●
Traffic deaths (per 100,000 population)	26.8	2019	●	↓
Life expectancy at birth (years)	74.0	2019	●	↓
Adolescent fertility rate (births per 1,000 females aged 15 to 19)	12.0	2016	●	●
Births attended by skilled health personnel (%)	92.4	2017	●	↑
Surviving infants who received 2 WHO-recommended vaccines (%)	93	2020	●	↑
Universal health coverage (UHC) index of service coverage (worst 0–100 best)	69	2019	●	↗
Subjective well-being (average ladder score, worst 0–10 best)	NA	NA	●	●

SDG4 – Quality Education	Value	Year	Rating	Trend
Participation rate in pre-primary organized learning (% of children aged 4 to 6)	81.2	2019	●	↓
Net primary enrollment rate (%)	92.3	2019	●	→
Lower secondary completion rate (%)	71.3	2019	●	↓
Literacy rate (% of population aged 15 to 24)	98.1	2015	●	●

SDG5 – Gender Equality	Value	Year	Rating	Trend
Demand for family planning satisfied by modern methods (% of females aged 15 to 49)	73.2	2005	●	●
Ratio of female-to-male mean years of education received (%)	90.9	2019	●	→
Ratio of female-to-male labor force participation rate (%)	74.8	2020	●	↑
Seats held by women in national parliament (%)	25.0	2020	●	↗

SDG6 – Clean Water and Sanitation	Value	Year	Rating	Trend
Population using at least basic drinking water services (%)	88.8	2020	●	↗
Population using at least basic sanitation services (%)	79.1	2020	●	↑
Freshwater withdrawal (% of available freshwater resources)	8.4	2018	●	●
Anthropogenic wastewater that receives treatment (%)	20.9	2018	●	●
Scarce water consumption embodied in imports (m^3 H_2O eq/capita)	NA	NA	●	●

SDG7 – Affordable and Clean Energy	Value	Year	Rating	Trend
Population with access to electricity (%)	95.5	2019	●	↑
Population with access to clean fuels and technology for cooking (%)	78.0	2019	●	↑
CO_2 emissions from fuel combustion per total electricity output ($MtCO_2$/TWh)	1.6	2019	●	→
Share of renewable energy in total primary energy supply (%)	NA	NA	●	●

SDG8 – Decent Work and Economic Growth	Value	Year	Rating	Trend
Adjusted GDP growth (%)	-6.6	2020	●	●
Victims of modern slavery (per 1,000 population)	4.1	2018	●	●
Adults with an account at a bank or other financial institution or with a mobile-money-service provider (% of population aged 15 or over)	NA	NA	●	●
Unemployment rate (% of total labor force)	15.1	2022	●	↓
Fundamental labor rights are effectively guaranteed (worst 0–1 best)	NA	NA	●	●
Fatal work-related accidents embodied in imports (per 100,000 population)	0.2	2015	●	↑

SDG9 – Industry, Innovation and Infrastructure	Value	Year	Rating	Trend
Population using the internet (%)	64.5	2020	●	↑
Mobile broadband subscriptions (per 100 population)	76.5	2019	●	↑
Logistics Performance Index: Quality of trade and transport-related infrastructure (worst 1–5 best)	NA	NA	●	●
The Times Higher Education Universities Ranking: Average score of top 3 universities (worst 0–100 best)	* 0.0	2022	●	●
Articles published in academic journals (per 1,000 population)	0.1	2020	●	→
Expenditure on research and development (% of GDP)	0.1	2011	●	●

SDG10 – Reduced Inequalities	Value	Year	Rating	Trend
Gini coefficient	42.4	2015	●	●
Palma ratio	2.1	2018	●	●

SDG11 – Sustainable Cities and Communities	Value	Year	Rating	Trend
Proportion of urban population living in slums (%)	NA	NA	●	●
Annual mean concentration of particulate matter of less than 2.5 microns in diameter (PM2.5) (μg/m^3)	36.5	2019	●	→
Access to improved water source, piped (% of urban population)	96.6	2020	●	↑
Satisfaction with public transport (%)	NA	NA	●	●

SDG12 – Responsible Consumption and Production	Value	Year	Rating	Trend
Municipal solid waste (kg/capita/day)	0.7	2012	●	●
Electronic waste (kg/capita)	4.9	2019	●	●
Production-based SO_2 emissions (kg/capita)	NA	NA	●	●
SO_2 emissions embodied in imports (kg/capita)	NA	NA	●	●
Production-based nitrogen emissions (kg/capita)	4.5	2015	●	↑
Nitrogen emissions embodied in imports (kg/capita)	2.9	2015	●	↑
Exports of plastic waste (kg/capita)	NA	NA	●	●

SDG13 – Climate Action	Value	Year	Rating	Trend
CO_2 emissions from fossil fuel combustion and cement production (tCO_2/capita)	1.0	2020	●	↑
CO_2 emissions embodied in imports (tCO_2/capita)	NA	NA	●	●
CO_2 emissions embodied in fossil fuel exports (kg/capita)	0.0	2020	●	●

SDG14 – Life Below Water	Value	Year	Rating	Trend
Mean area that is protected in marine sites important to biodiversity (%)	14.1	2020	●	→
Ocean Health Index: Clean Waters score (worst 0–100 best)	62.4	2020	●	↗
Fish caught from overexploited or collapsed stocks (% of total catch)	0.4	2018	●	↑
Fish caught by trawling or dredging (%)	55.3	2018	●	↓
Fish caught that are then discarded (%)	6.6	2018	●	→
Marine biodiversity threats embodied in imports (per million population)	NA	NA	●	●

SDG15 – Life on Land	Value	Year	Rating	Trend
Mean area that is protected in terrestrial sites important to biodiversity (%)	12.0	2020	●	→
Mean area that is protected in freshwater sites important to biodiversity (%)	NA	NA	●	●
Red List Index of species survival (worst 0–1 best)	0.9	2021	●	↑
Permanent deforestation (% of forest area, 5-year average)	0.0	2020	●	↑
Terrestrial and freshwater biodiversity threats embodied in imports (per million population)	0.2	2018	●	●

SDG16 – Peace, Justice and Strong Institutions	Value	Year	Rating	Trend
Homicides (per 100,000 population)	6.5	2020	●	↗
Unsentenced detainees (% of prison population)	31.3	2018	●	●
Population who feel safe walking alone at night in the city or area where they live (%)	NA	NA	●	●
Property Rights (worst 1–7 best)	4.4	2020	●	↑
Birth registrations with civil authority (% of children under age 5)	91.4	2020	●	●
Corruption Perception Index (worst 0–100 best)	58	2021	●	↑
Children involved in child labor (% of population aged 5 to 14)	NA	NA	●	●
Exports of major conventional weapons (TIV constant million USD per 100,000 population)	* 0.0	2020	●	●
Press Freedom Index (best 0–100 worst)	20.1	2021	●	↑
Access to and affordability of justice (worst 0–1 best)	NA	NA	●	●

SDG17 – Partnerships for the Goals	Value	Year	Rating	Trend
Government spending on health and education (% of GDP)	8.0	2019	●	↓
For high-income and all OECD DAC countries: International concessional public finance, including official development assistance (% of GNI)	NA	NA	●	●
Other countries: Government revenue excluding grants (% of GDP)	28.8	2017	●	●
Corporate Tax Haven Score (best 0–100 worst)	* 0.0	2019	●	●
Statistical Performance Index (worst 0–100 best)	54.7	2019	●	→

* Imputed data point

5. Country Profiles

CAMBODIA

East and South Asia

OVERALL PERFORMANCE

COUNTRY RANKING

CAMBODIA

107/163

COUNTRY SCORE

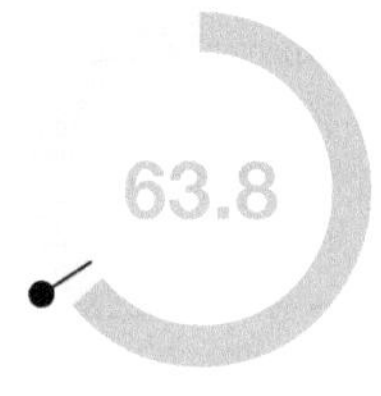

REGIONAL AVERAGE: 65.9

AVERAGE PERFORMANCE BY SDG

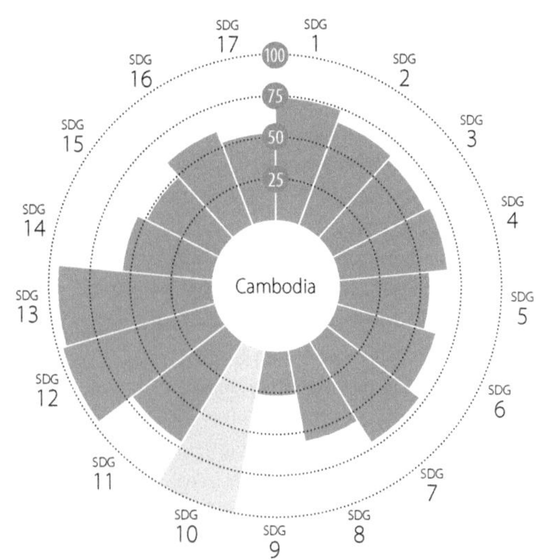

SDG DASHBOARDS AND TRENDS

Major challenges | Significant challenges | Challenges remain | SDG achieved | Information unavailable

Decreasing | Stagnating | Moderately improving | On track or maintaining SDG achievement | Information unavailable

Note: The full title of each SDG is available here: https://sustainabledevelopment.un.org/topics/sustainabledevelopmentgoals

INTERNATIONAL SPILLOVER INDEX

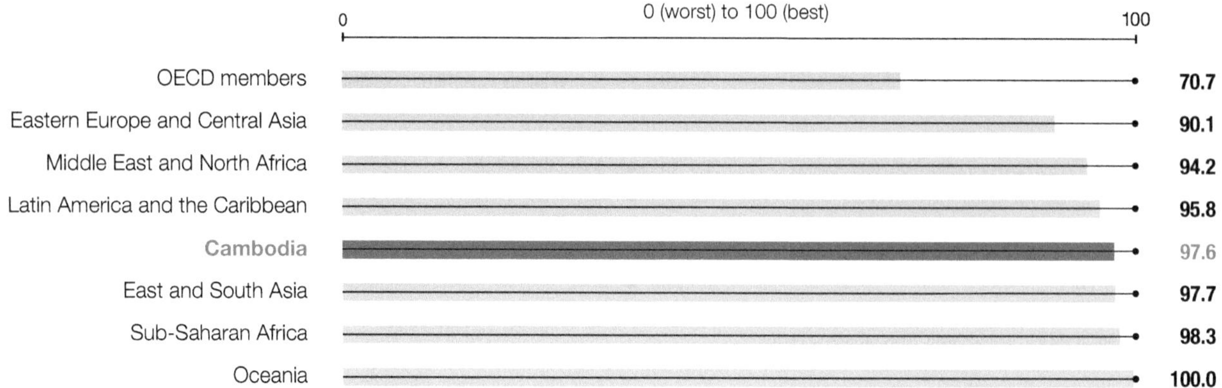

STATISTICAL PERFORMANCE INDEX

0 (worst) to 100 (best)

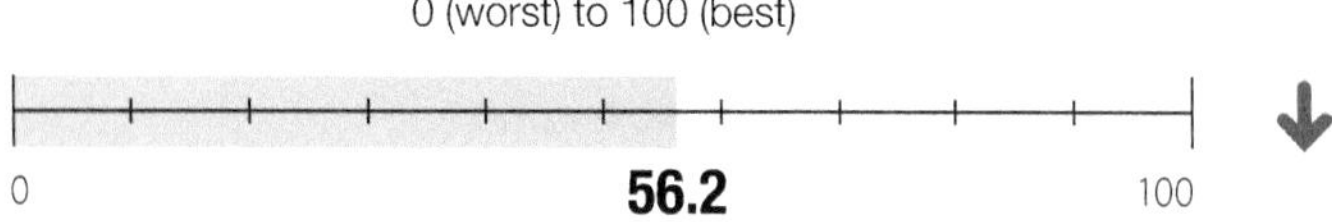

MISSING DATA IN SDG INDEX

2%

Indicator	Value	Year	Rating	Trend
SDG1 – No Poverty				
Poverty headcount ratio at \$1.90/day (%)	1.5	2022	●	↑
Poverty headcount ratio at \$3.20/day (%)	26.2	2022	●	↗
SDG2 – Zero Hunger				
Prevalence of undernourishment (%)	6.2	2019	●	↑
Prevalence of stunting in children under 5 years of age (%)	32.4	2014	●	→
Prevalence of wasting in children under 5 years of age (%)	9.7	2014	●	→
Prevalence of obesity, BMI ≥ 30 (% of adult population)	3.9	2016	●	↑
Human Trophic Level (best 2–3 worst)	2.2	2017	●	↑
Cereal yield (tonnes per hectare of harvested land)	3.6	2018	●	↑
Sustainable Nitrogen Management Index (best 0–1.41 worst)	0.6	2015	●	→
Exports of hazardous pesticides (tonnes per million population)	0.9	2019	●	●
SDG3 – Good Health and Well-Being				
Maternal mortality rate (per 100,000 live births)	160	2017	●	↑
Neonatal mortality rate (per 1,000 live births)	13.2	2020	●	↑
Mortality rate, under-5 (per 1,000 live births)	25.7	2020	●	↑
Incidence of tuberculosis (per 100,000 population)	274.0	2020	●	↗
New HIV infections (per 1,000 uninfected population)	0.1	2020	●	↑
Age-standardized death rate due to cardiovascular disease, cancer, diabetes, or chronic respiratory disease in adults aged 30–70 years (%)	22.5	2019	●	→
Age-standardized death rate attributable to household air pollution and ambient air pollution (per 100,000 population)	150	2016	●	●
Traffic deaths (per 100,000 population)	19.6	2019	●	↓
Life expectancy at birth (years)	70.1	2019	●	→
Adolescent fertility rate (births per 1,000 females aged 15 to 19)	30.0	2012	●	●
Births attended by skilled health personnel (%)	89.0	2014	●	●
Surviving infants who received 2 WHO-recommended vaccines (%)	84	2020	●	→
Universal health coverage (UHC) index of service coverage (worst 0–100 best)	61	2019	●	↗
Subjective well-being (average ladder score, worst 0–10 best)	4.6	2021	●	↗
SDG4 – Quality Education				
Participation rate in pre-primary organized learning (% of children aged 4 to 6)	70.5	2020	●	↑
Net primary enrollment rate (%)	89.2	2020	●	↓
Lower secondary completion rate (%)	58.2	2020	●	↗
Literacy rate (% of population aged 15 to 24)	92.2	2015	●	●
SDG5 – Gender Equality				
Demand for family planning satisfied by modern methods (% of females aged 15 to 49)	56.5	2014	●	●
Ratio of female-to-male mean years of education received (%)	72.4	2019	●	→
Ratio of female-to-male labor force participation rate (%)	86.0	2020	●	↑
Seats held by women in national parliament (%)	20.0	2020	●	↓
SDG6 – Clean Water and Sanitation				
Population using at least basic drinking water services (%)	71.2	2020	●	→
Population using at least basic sanitation services (%)	68.8	2020	●	↑
Freshwater withdrawal (% of available freshwater resources)	1.0	2018	●	●
Anthropogenic wastewater that receives treatment (%)	0.0	2018	●	●
Scarce water consumption embodied in imports (m^3 H_2O eq/capita)	447.8	2018	●	●
SDG7 – Affordable and Clean Energy				
Population with access to electricity (%)	93.0	2019	●	↑
Population with access to clean fuels and technology for cooking (%)	31.2	2019	●	↗
CO_2 emissions from fuel combustion per total electricity output ($MtCO_2$/TWh)	1.8	2019	●	→
Share of renewable energy in total primary energy supply (%)	47.9	2019	●	↑
SDG8 – Decent Work and Economic Growth				
Adjusted GDP growth (%)	-2.0	2020	●	●
Victims of modern slavery (per 1,000 population)	16.8	2018	●	●
Adults with an account at a bank or other financial institution or with a mobile-money-service provider (% of population aged 15 or over)	21.7	2017	●	↓
Unemployment rate (% of total labor force)	0.6	2022	●	↑
Fundamental labor rights are effectively guaranteed (worst 0–1 best)	0.5	2020	●	↓
Fatal work-related accidents embodied in imports (per 100,000 population)	0.1	2015	●	↑

Indicator	Value	Year	Rating	Trend
SDG9 – Industry, Innovation and Infrastructure				
Population using the internet (%)	32.9	2017	●	●
Mobile broadband subscriptions (per 100 population)	96.4	2019	●	↑
Logistics Performance Index: Quality of trade and transport-related infrastructure (worst 1–5 best)	2.1	2018	●	↓
The Times Higher Education Universities Ranking: Average score of top 3 universities (worst 0–100 best)	* 0.0	2022	●	●
Articles published in academic journals (per 1,000 population)	0.0	2020	●	→
Expenditure on research and development (% of GDP)	0.1	2015	●	●
SDG10 – Reduced Inequalities				
Gini coefficient	NA	NA	●	●
Palma ratio	NA	NA	●	●
SDG11 – Sustainable Cities and Communities				
Proportion of urban population living in slums (%)	45.6	2018	●	↗
Annual mean concentration of particulate matter of less than 2.5 microns in diameter (PM2.5) (μg/m^3)	23.3	2019	●	↗
Access to improved water source, piped (% of urban population)	79.6	2020	●	↑
Satisfaction with public transport (%)	69.0	2021	●	↗
SDG12 – Responsible Consumption and Production				
Municipal solid waste (kg/capita/day)	0.2	2014	●	●
Electronic waste (kg/capita)	1.1	2019	●	●
Production-based SO_2 emissions (kg/capita)	3.4	2018	●	●
SO_2 emissions embodied in imports (kg/capita)	1.4	2018	●	●
Production-based nitrogen emissions (kg/capita)	7.7	2015	●	↑
Nitrogen emissions embodied in imports (kg/capita)	0.3	2015	●	↑
Exports of plastic waste (kg/capita)	0.5	2020	●	●
SDG13 – Climate Action				
CO_2 emissions from fossil fuel combustion and cement production (tCO_2/capita)	0.9	2020	●	↑
CO_2 emissions embodied in imports (tCO_2/capita)	0.4	2018	●	↑
CO_2 emissions embodied in fossil fuel exports (kg/capita)	0.0	2020	●	●
SDG14 – Life Below Water				
Mean area that is protected in marine sites important to biodiversity (%)	51.0	2020	●	↗
Ocean Health Index: Clean Waters score (worst 0–100 best)	53.4	2020	●	→
Fish caught from overexploited or collapsed stocks (% of total catch)	46.9	2018	●	↓
Fish caught by trawling or dredging (%)	90.3	2018	●	↓
Fish caught that are then discarded (%)	0.8	2018	●	↑
Marine biodiversity threats embodied in imports (per million population)	0.0	2018	●	●
SDG15 – Life on Land				
Mean area that is protected in terrestrial sites important to biodiversity (%)	54.5	2020	●	↑
Mean area that is protected in freshwater sites important to biodiversity (%)	45.0	2020	●	↑
Red List Index of species survival (worst 0–1 best)	0.8	2021	●	↓
Permanent deforestation (% of forest area, 5-year average)	1.9	2020	●	→
Terrestrial and freshwater biodiversity threats embodied in imports (per million population)	0.0	2018	●	●
SDG16 – Peace, Justice and Strong Institutions				
Homicides (per 100,000 population)	1.8	2011	●	●
Unsentenced detainees (% of prison population)	28.7	2018	●	↑
Population who feel safe walking alone at night in the city or area where they live (%)	65	2021	●	↑
Property Rights (worst 1–7 best)	4.2	2020	●	↑
Birth registrations with civil authority (% of children under age 5)	73.3	2020	●	●
Corruption Perception Index (worst 0–100 best)	23	2021	●	→
Children involved in child labor (% of population aged 5 to 14)	12.6	2019	●	●
Exports of major conventional weapons (TIV constant million USD per 100,000 population)	0.0	2020	●	●
Press Freedom Index (best 0–100 worst)	46.8	2021	●	↓
Access to and affordability of justice (worst 0–1 best)	0.3	2020	●	↗
SDG17 – Partnerships for the Goals				
Government spending on health and education (% of GDP)	3.9	2019	●	→
For high-income and all OECD DAC countries: International concessional public finance, including official development assistance (% of GNI)	NA	NA	●	●
Other countries: Government revenue excluding grants (% of GDP)	22.8	2019	●	↑
Corporate Tax Haven Score (best 0–100 worst)	* 0.0	2019	●	●
Statistical Performance Index (worst 0–100 best)	56.2	2019	●	↓

* Imputed data point

CAMEROON

Sub-Saharan Africa

OVERALL PERFORMANCE

COUNTRY RANKING

CAMEROON

134/163

COUNTRY SCORE

AVERAGE PERFORMANCE BY SDG

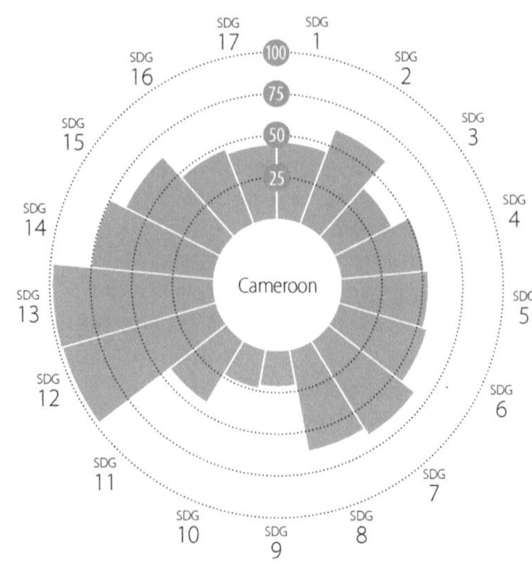

SDG DASHBOARDS AND TRENDS

Major challenges | Significant challenges | Challenges remain | SDG achieved | Information unavailable

Decreasing | Stagnating | Moderately improving | On track or maintaining SDG achievement | Information unavailable

Note: The full title of each SDG is available here: https://sustainabledevelopment.un.org/topics/sustainabledevelopmentgoals

INTERNATIONAL SPILLOVER INDEX

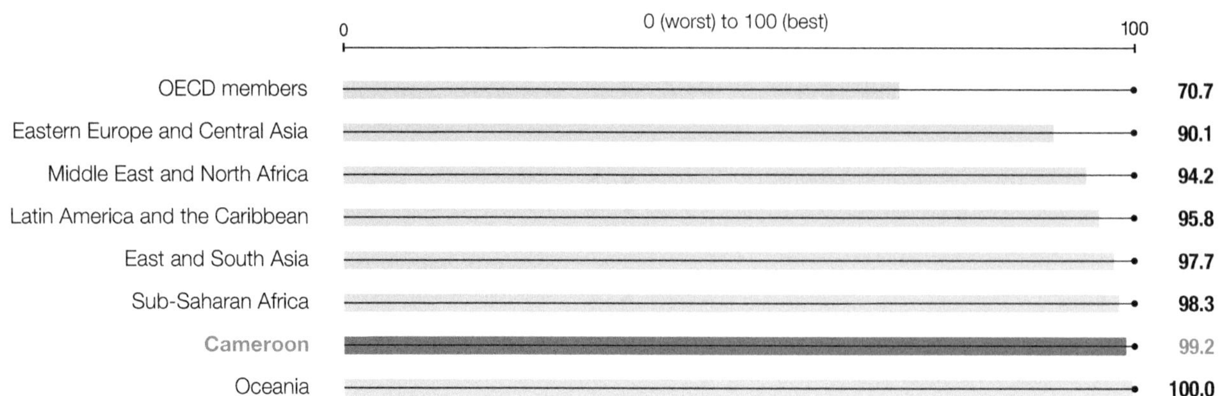

STATISTICAL PERFORMANCE INDEX

0 (worst) to 100 (best)

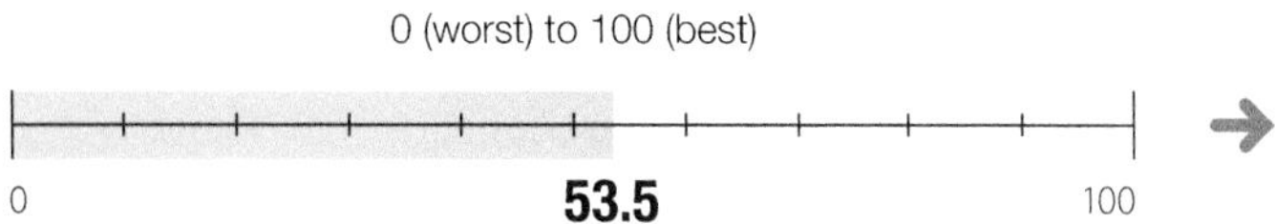

MISSING DATA IN SDG INDEX

4%

CAMEROON

Performance by Indicator

SDG1 – No Poverty	Value	Year	Rating	Trend
Poverty headcount ratio at \$1.90/day (%)	22.0	2022	●	→
Poverty headcount ratio at \$3.20/day (%)	40.4	2022	●	→
SDG2 – Zero Hunger				
Prevalence of undernourishment (%)	5.3	2019	●	↑
Prevalence of stunting in children under 5 years of age (%)	28.9	2018	●	→
Prevalence of wasting in children under 5 years of age (%)	4.3	2018	●	↑
Prevalence of obesity, BMI ≥ 30 (% of adult population)	11.4	2016	●	↓
Human Trophic Level (best 2–3 worst)	2.1	2017	●	↑
Cereal yield (tonnes per hectare of harvested land)	1.6	2018	●	→
Sustainable Nitrogen Management Index (best 0–1.41 worst)	0.8	2015	●	→
Exports of hazardous pesticides (tonnes per million population)	NA	NA	●	●
SDG3 – Good Health and Well-Being				
Maternal mortality rate (per 100,000 live births)	529	2017	●	→
Neonatal mortality rate (per 1,000 live births)	26.2	2020	●	↗
Mortality rate, under-5 (per 1,000 live births)	72.2	2020	●	↗
Incidence of tuberculosis (per 100,000 population)	174.0	2020	●	↗
New HIV infections (per 1,000 uninfected population)	0.6	2020	●	↑
Age-standardized death rate due to cardiovascular disease, cancer, diabetes, or chronic respiratory disease in adults aged 30–70 years (%)	23.9	2019	●	↗
Age-standardized death rate attributable to household air pollution and ambient air pollution (per 100,000 population)	208	2016	●	●
Traffic deaths (per 100,000 population)	30.2	2019	●	↓
Life expectancy at birth (years)	62.4	2019	●	↗
Adolescent fertility rate (births per 1,000 females aged 15 to 19)	122.2	2017	●	●
Births attended by skilled health personnel (%)	69.0	2018	●	↗
Surviving infants who received 2 WHO-recommended vaccines (%)	62	2020	●	↓
Universal health coverage (UHC) index of service coverage (worst 0–100 best)	44	2019	●	→
Subjective well-being (average ladder score, worst 0–10 best)	5.0	2021	●	→
SDG4 – Quality Education				
Participation rate in pre-primary organized learning (% of children aged 4 to 6)	43.9	2019	●	↓
Net primary enrollment rate (%)	91.7	2019	●	↓
Lower secondary completion rate (%)	47.2	2016	●	●
Literacy rate (% of population aged 15 to 24)	85.1	2018	●	●
SDG5 – Gender Equality				
Demand for family planning satisfied by modern methods (% of females aged 15 to 49)	44.9	2018	●	●
Ratio of female-to-male mean years of education received (%)	58.8	2019	●	↓
Ratio of female-to-male labor force participation rate (%)	87.1	2020	●	↑
Seats held by women in national parliament (%)	33.9	2020	●	↗
SDG6 – Clean Water and Sanitation				
Population using at least basic drinking water services (%)	65.7	2020	●	→
Population using at least basic sanitation services (%)	44.6	2020	●	→
Freshwater withdrawal (% of available freshwater resources)	1.6	2018	●	●
Anthropogenic wastewater that receives treatment (%)	0.0	2018	●	●
Scarce water consumption embodied in imports (m^3 H_2O eq/capita)	285.9	2018	●	●
SDG7 – Affordable and Clean Energy				
Population with access to electricity (%)	63.5	2019	●	→
Population with access to clean fuels and technology for cooking (%)	21.9	2019	●	→
CO_2 emissions from fuel combustion per total electricity output ($MtCO_2$/TWh)	1.0	2019	●	↑
Share of renewable energy in total primary energy supply (%)	75.7	2019	●	↑
SDG8 – Decent Work and Economic Growth				
Adjusted GDP growth (%)	-4.3	2020	●	●
Victims of modern slavery (per 1,000 population)	6.9	2018	●	●
Adults with an account at a bank or other financial institution or with a mobile-money-service provider (% of population aged 15 or over)	34.6	2017	●	↑
Unemployment rate (% of total labor force)	3.8	2022	●	↑
Fundamental labor rights are effectively guaranteed (worst 0–1 best)	0.5	2020	●	→
Fatal work-related accidents embodied in imports (per 100,000 population)	0.0	2015	●	↑

* Imputed data point

SDG9 – Industry, Innovation and Infrastructure	Value	Year	Rating	Trend
Population using the internet (%)	37.8	2020	●	↗
Mobile broadband subscriptions (per 100 population)	18.7	2019	●	↗
Logistics Performance Index: Quality of trade and transport-related infrastructure (worst 1–5 best)	2.6	2018	●	↑
The Times Higher Education Universities Ranking: Average score of top 3 universities (worst 0–100 best)	* 0.0	2022	●	●
Articles published in academic journals (per 1,000 population)	0.1	2020	●	→
Expenditure on research and development (% of GDP)	NA	NA	●	●
SDG10 – Reduced Inequalities				
Gini coefficient	46.6	2014	●	●
Palma ratio	2.7	2018	●	●
SDG11 – Sustainable Cities and Communities				
Proportion of urban population living in slums (%)	24.6	2018	●	↑
Annual mean concentration of particulate matter of less than 2.5 microns in diameter (PM2.5) (μg/m³)	80.4	2019	●	↓
Access to improved water source, piped (% of urban population)	55.3	2020	●	↓
Satisfaction with public transport (%)	45.0	2021	●	→
SDG12 – Responsible Consumption and Production				
Municipal solid waste (kg/capita/day)	0.4	2013	●	●
Electronic waste (kg/capita)	1.0	2019	●	●
Production-based SO_2 emissions (kg/capita)	1.0	2018	●	●
SO_2 emissions embodied in imports (kg/capita)	0.3	2018	●	●
Production-based nitrogen emissions (kg/capita)	7.5	2015	●	↑
Nitrogen emissions embodied in imports (kg/capita)	0.3	2015	●	↑
Exports of plastic waste (kg/capita)	0.0	2018	●	●
SDG13 – Climate Action				
CO_2 emissions from fossil fuel combustion and cement production (tCO_2/capita)	0.3	2020	●	↑
CO_2 emissions embodied in imports (tCO_2/capita)	0.1	2018	●	↑
CO_2 emissions embodied in fossil fuel exports (kg/capita)	476.9	2018	●	●
SDG14 – Life Below Water				
Mean area that is protected in marine sites important to biodiversity (%)	NA	NA	●	●
Ocean Health Index: Clean Waters score (worst 0–100 best)	36.2	2020	●	→
Fish caught from overexploited or collapsed stocks (% of total catch)	NA	NA	●	●
Fish caught by trawling or dredging (%)	9.0	2018	●	↓
Fish caught that are then discarded (%)	0.7	2018	●	↑
Marine biodiversity threats embodied in imports (per million population)	0.0	2018	●	●
SDG15 – Life on Land				
Mean area that is protected in terrestrial sites important to biodiversity (%)	35.3	2020	●	→
Mean area that is protected in freshwater sites important to biodiversity (%)	41.3	2020	●	→
Red List Index of species survival (worst 0–1 best)	0.8	2021	●	→
Permanent deforestation (% of forest area, 5-year average)	0.2	2020	●	↓
Terrestrial and freshwater biodiversity threats embodied in imports (per million population)	0.0	2018	●	●
SDG16 – Peace, Justice and Strong Institutions				
Homicides (per 100,000 population)	1.2	2016	●	●
Unsentenced detainees (% of prison population)	53.3	2017	●	●
Population who feel safe walking alone at night in the city or area where they live (%)	43	2021	●	↓
Property Rights (worst 1–7 best)	4.0	2020	●	↓
Birth registrations with civil authority (% of children under age 5)	61.9	2020	●	●
Corruption Perception Index (worst 0–100 best)	27	2021	●	→
Children involved in child labor (% of population aged 5 to 14)	38.9	2019	●	●
Exports of major conventional weapons (TIV constant million USD per 100,000 population)	* 0.0	2020	●	●
Press Freedom Index (best 0–100 worst)	43.8	2021	●	↓
Access to and affordability of justice (worst 0–1 best)	0.5	2020	●	↑
SDG17 – Partnerships for the Goals				
Government spending on health and education (% of GDP)	3.2	2019	●	→
For high-income and all OECD DAC countries: International concessional public finance, including official development assistance (% of GNI)	NA	NA	●	●
Other countries: Government revenue excluding grants (% of GDP)	15.2	2018	●	↓
Corporate Tax Haven Score (best 0–100 worst)	* 0.0	2019	●	●
Statistical Performance Index (worst 0–100 best)	53.5	2019	●	→

CANADA

OVERALL PERFORMANCE

COUNTRY RANKING

CANADA

29/163

COUNTRY SCORE

REGIONAL AVERAGE: 77.2

AVERAGE PERFORMANCE BY SDG

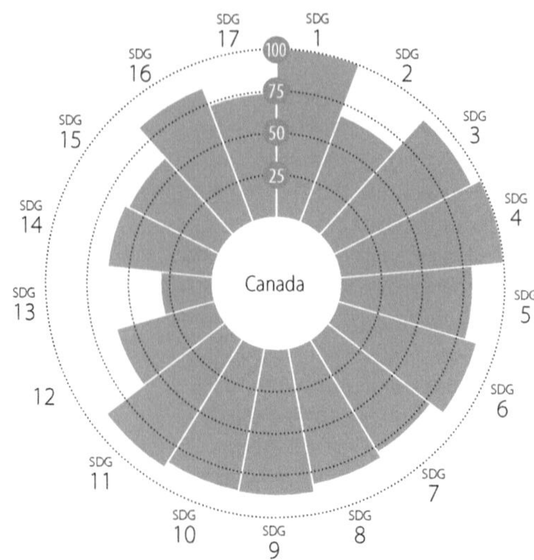

SDG DASHBOARDS AND TRENDS

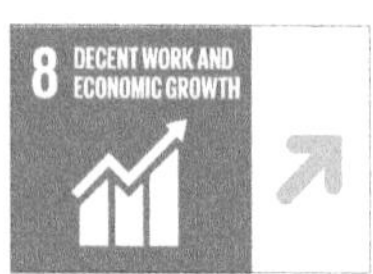

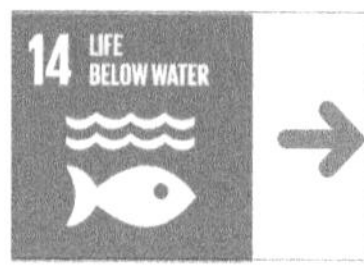

Major challenges | Significant challenges | Challenges remain | SDG achieved | Information unavailable

Decreasing | Stagnating | Moderately improving | On track or maintaining SDG achievement | Information unavailable

Note: The full title of each SDG is available here: https://sustainabledevelopment.un.org/topics/sustainabledevelopmentgoals

INTERNATIONAL SPILLOVER INDEX

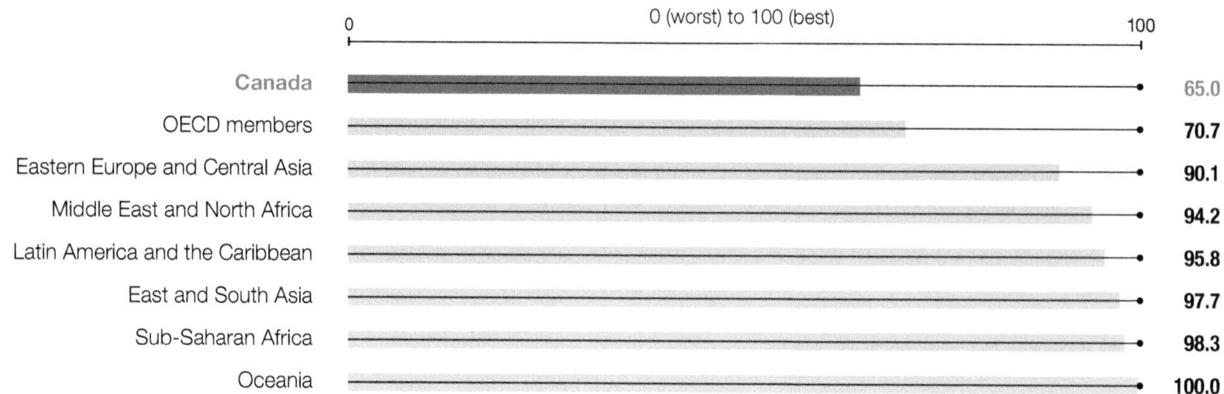

STATISTICAL PERFORMANCE INDEX

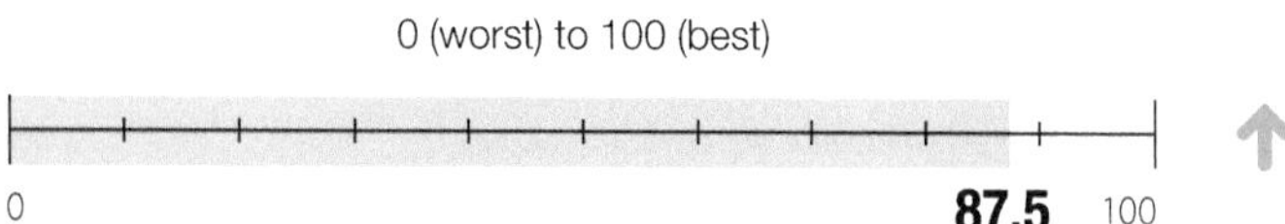

MISSING DATA IN SDG INDEX

2%

SDG1 – No Poverty	Value	Year	Rating	Trend
Poverty headcount ratio at $1.90/day (%)	0.2	2022	●	↑
Poverty headcount ratio at $3.20/day (%)	0.3	2022	●	↑
Poverty rate after taxes and transfers (%)	11.6	2019	●	↑
SDG2 – Zero Hunger				
Prevalence of undernourishment (%)	2.5	2019	●	↑
Prevalence of stunting in children under 5 years of age (%)	* 2.6	2019	●	↑
Prevalence of wasting in children under 5 years of age (%)	* 0.7	2019	●	↑
Prevalence of obesity, BMI ≥ 30 (% of adult population)	29.4	2016	●	↓
Human Trophic Level (best 2–3 worst)	2.4	2017	●	↗
Cereal yield (tonnes per hectare of harvested land)	3.9	2018	●	↑
Sustainable Nitrogen Management Index (best 0–1.41 worst)	0.5	2015	●	↓
Yield gap closure (% of potential yield)	64.0	2018	●	●
Exports of hazardous pesticides (tonnes per million population)	8.8	2019	●	●
SDG3 – Good Health and Well-Being				
Maternal mortality rate (per 100,000 live births)	10	2017	●	↑
Neonatal mortality rate (per 1,000 live births)	3.2	2020	●	↑
Mortality rate, under-5 (per 1,000 live births)	5.0	2020	●	↑
Incidence of tuberculosis (per 100,000 population)	5.9	2020	●	↑
New HIV infections (per 1,000 uninfected population)	1.0	2020	●	→
Age-standardized death rate due to cardiovascular disease, cancer, diabetes, or chronic respiratory disease in adults aged 30–70 years (%)	9.6	2019	●	↑
Age-standardized death rate attributable to household air pollution and ambient air pollution (per 100,000 population)	7	2016	●	●
Traffic deaths (per 100,000 population)	5.3	2019	●	↑
Life expectancy at birth (years)	82.2	2019	●	↑
Adolescent fertility rate (births per 1,000 females aged 15 to 19)	6.6	2018	●	↑
Births attended by skilled health personnel (%)	98.0	2018	●	↑
Surviving infants who received 2 WHO-recommended vaccines (%)	90	2020	●	↑
Universal health coverage (UHC) index of service coverage (worst 0–100 best)	89	2019	●	↑
Subjective well-being (average ladder score, worst 0–10 best)	6.9	2021	●	↑
Gap in life expectancy at birth among regions (years)	11.0	2017	●	●
Gap in self-reported health status by income (percentage points)	11.8	2019	●	↑
Daily smokers (% of population aged 15 and over)	10.3	2019	●	↑
SDG4 – Quality Education				
Participation rate in pre-primary organized learning (% of children aged 4 to 6)	* 98.8	2018	●	●
Net primary enrollment rate (%)	99.7	2019	●	↑
Lower secondary completion rate (%)	* 100.0	2019	●	↑
Literacy rate (% of population aged 15 to 24)	NA	NA	●	●
Tertiary educational attainment (% of population aged 25 to 34)	64.4	2020	●	↑
PISA score (worst 0–600 best)	516.7	2018	●	↑
Variation in science performance explained by socio-economic status (%)	6.4	2018	●	↑
Underachievers in science (% of 15-year-olds)	13.4	2018	●	↑
SDG5 – Gender Equality				
Demand for family planning satisfied by modern methods (% of females aged 15 to 49)	NA	NA	●	●
Ratio of female-to-male mean years of education received (%)	100.8	2019	●	↑
Ratio of female-to-male labor force participation rate (%)	86.7	2020	●	↑
Seats held by women in national parliament (%)	29.0	2020	●	↗
Gender wage gap (% of male median wage)	16.1	2020	●	↗
SDG6 – Clean Water and Sanitation				
Population using at least basic drinking water services (%)	99.2	2020	●	↑
Population using at least basic sanitation services (%)	99.0	2020	●	↑
Freshwater withdrawal (% of available freshwater resources)	3.7	2018	●	●
Anthropogenic wastewater that receives treatment (%)	67.4	2018	●	●
Scarce water consumption embodied in imports (m^3 H_2O eq/capita)	3231.9	2018	●	●
Population using safely managed water services (%)	99.0	2020	●	↑
Population using safely managed sanitation services (%)	84.4	2020	●	↗
SDG7 – Affordable and Clean Energy				
Population with access to electricity (%)	100.0	2019	●	↑
Population with access to clean fuels and technology for cooking (%)	100.0	2019	●	↑
CO_2 emissions from fuel combustion per total electricity output ($MtCO_2$/TWh)	0.9	2019	●	↑
Share of renewable energy in total primary energy supply (%)	16.2	2019	●	↓
SDG8 – Decent Work and Economic Growth				
Adjusted GDP growth (%)	-3.4	2020	●	●
Victims of modern slavery (per 1,000 population)	0.5	2018	●	●
Adults with an account at a bank or other financial institution or with a mobile-money-service provider (% of population aged 15 or over)	99.7	2017	●	↑
Fundamental labor rights are effectively guaranteed (worst 0–1 best)	0.7	2020	●	↑
Fatal work-related accidents embodied in imports (per 100,000 population)	1.3	2015	●	↑
Employment-to-population ratio (%)	73.2	2021	●	↑
Youth not in employment, education or training (NEET) (% of population aged 15 to 29)	13.6	2020	●	↓

SDG9 – Industry, Innovation and Infrastructure	Value	Year	Rating	Trend
Population using the internet (%)	97.0	2020	●	↑
Mobile broadband subscriptions (per 100 population)	82.7	2019	●	↑
Logistics Performance Index: Quality of trade and transport-related infrastructure (worst 1–5 best)	3.8	2018	●	↑
The Times Higher Education Universities Ranking: Average score of top 3 universities (worst 0–100 best)	78.8	2022	●	●
Articles published in academic journals (per 1,000 population)	2.9	2020	●	↑
Expenditure on research and development (% of GDP)	1.5	2019	●	↑
Researchers (per 1,000 employed population)	8.8	2018	●	↑
Triadic patent families filed (per million population)	18.5	2019	●	↑
Gap in internet access by income (percentage points)	52.4	2007	●	●
Female share of graduates from STEM fields at the tertiary level (%)	31.4	2016	●	↑
SDG10 – Reduced Inequalities				
Gini coefficient	33.3	2017	●	↗
Palma ratio	1.1	2019	●	↑
Elderly poverty rate (% of population aged 66 or over)	12.3	2019	●	↓
SDG11 – Sustainable Cities and Communities				
Proportion of urban population living in slums (%)	* 0.0	2018	●	↑
Annual mean concentration of particulate matter of less than 2.5 microns in diameter (PM2.5) (μg/m^3)	5.9	2019	●	↑
Access to improved water source, piped (% of urban population)	99.3	2020	●	↑
Satisfaction with public transport (%)	57.0	2021	●	↓
Population with rent overburden (%)	9.0	2017	●	●
SDG12 – Responsible Consumption and Production				
Electronic waste (kg/capita)	20.2	2019	●	●
Production-based SO_2 emissions (kg/capita)	24.8	2018	●	●
SO_2 emissions embodied in imports (kg/capita)	9.0	2018	●	●
Production-based nitrogen emissions (kg/capita)	38.3	2015	●	↓
Nitrogen emissions embodied in imports (kg/capita)	12.5	2015	●	↓
Exports of plastic waste (kg/capita)	4.3	2021	●	●
Non-recycled municipal solid waste (kg/capita/day)	NA	NA	●	●
SDG13 – Climate Action				
CO_2 emissions from fossil fuel combustion and cement production (tCO_2/capita)	14.2	2020	●	→
CO_2 emissions embodied in imports (tCO_2/capita)	3.3	2018	●	↑
CO_2 emissions embodied in fossil fuel exports (kg/capita)	16550.8	2021	●	●
Carbon Pricing Score at EUR60/tCO_2 (%, worst 0–100 best)	34.2	2018	●	●
SDG14 – Life Below Water				
Mean area that is protected in marine sites important to biodiversity (%)	35.6	2020	●	→
Ocean Health Index: Clean Waters score (worst 0–100 best)	94.1	2020	●	↑
Fish caught from overexploited or collapsed stocks (% of total catch)	36.3	2018	●	↑
Fish caught by trawling or dredging (%)	26.5	2018	●	↓
Fish caught that are then discarded (%)	7.2	2018	●	↓
Marine biodiversity threats embodied in imports (per million population)	0.9	2018	●	●
SDG15 – Life on Land				
Mean area that is protected in terrestrial sites important to biodiversity (%)	29.9	2020	●	→
Mean area that is protected in freshwater sites important to biodiversity (%)	22.9	2020	●	→
Red List Index of species survival (worst 0–1 best)	1.0	2021	●	↑
Permanent deforestation (% of forest area, 5-year average)	0.0	2020	●	↑
Terrestrial and freshwater biodiversity threats embodied in imports (per million population)	4.1	2018	●	●
SDG16 – Peace, Justice and Strong Institutions				
Homicides (per 100,000 population)	2.0	2020	●	→
Unsentenced detainees (% of prison population)	38.6	2017	●	●
Population who feel safe walking alone at night in the city or area where they live (%)	80	2021	●	↑
Property Rights (worst 1–7 best)	5.5	2020	●	↑
Birth registrations with civil authority (% of children under age 5)	100.0	2020	●	●
Corruption Perception Index (worst 0–100 best)	74	2021	●	↑
Children involved in child labor (% of population aged 5 to 14)	* 0.0	2019	●	●
Exports of major conventional weapons (TIV constant million USD per 100,000 population)	0.4	2020	●	●
Press Freedom Index (best 0–100 worst)	15.3	2021	●	↑
Access to and affordability of justice (worst 0–1 best)	0.6	2020	●	↗
Persons held in prison (per 100,000 population)	107.7	2017	●	↑
SDG17 – Partnerships for the Goals				
Government spending on health and education (% of GDP)	12.9	2019	●	↑
For high-income and all OECD DAC countries: International concessional public finance, including official development assistance (% of GNI)	0.3	2021	●	→
Other countries: Government revenue excluding grants (% of GDP)	NA	NA	●	●
Corporate Tax Haven Score (best 0–100 worst)	* 0.0	2019	●	●
Financial Secrecy Score (best 0–100 worst)	55.8	2020	●	●
Shifted profits of multinationals (US$ billion)	20.9	2018	●	↑
Statistical Performance Index (worst 0–100 best)	87.5	2019	●	↑

* Imputed data point

5. Country Profiles

CENTRAL AFRICAN REPUBLIC Sub-Saharan Africa

OVERALL PERFORMANCE

COUNTRY RANKING

CENTRAL AFRICAN REPUBLIC

162/163

COUNTRY SCORE

AVERAGE PERFORMANCE BY SDG

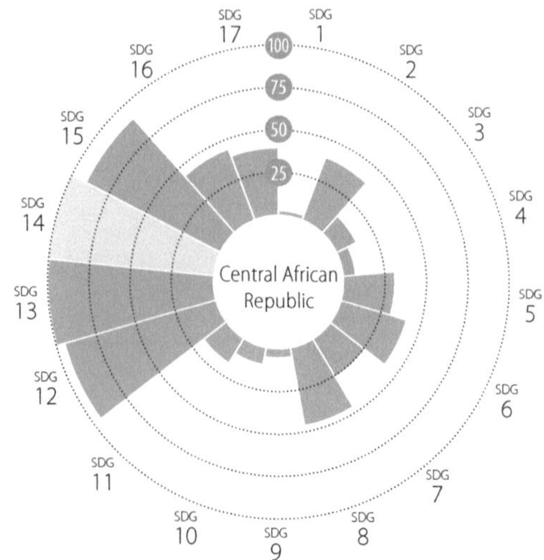

SDG DASHBOARDS AND TRENDS

Note: The full title of each SDG is available here: https://sustainabledevelopment.un.org/topics/sustainabledevelopmentgoals

INTERNATIONAL SPILLOVER INDEX

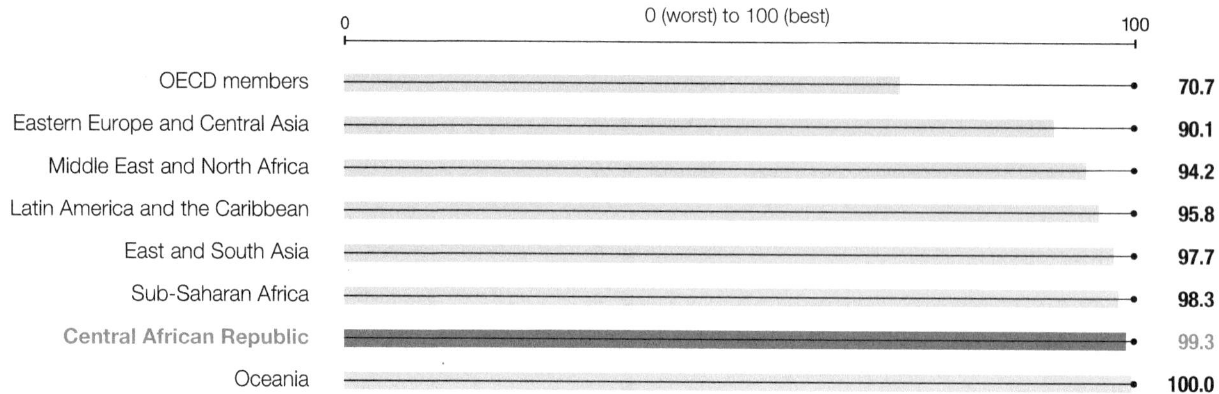

STATISTICAL PERFORMANCE INDEX

0 (worst) to 100 (best)

0 **na** 100

MISSING DATA IN SDG INDEX

10%

CENTRAL AFRICAN REPUBLIC Performance by Indicator

SDG1 – No Poverty	Value	Year	Rating	Trend
Poverty headcount ratio at \$1.90/day (%)	69.7	2022	●	→
Poverty headcount ratio at \$3.20/day (%)	85.8	2022	●	→
SDG2 – Zero Hunger				
Prevalence of undernourishment (%)	48.2	2019	●	→
Prevalence of stunting in children under 5 years of age (%)	40.2	2019	●	→
Prevalence of wasting in children under 5 years of age (%)	5.2	2019	●	→
Prevalence of obesity, BMI ≥ 30 (% of adult population)	7.5	2016	●	↑
Human Trophic Level (best 2–3 worst)	2.1	2017	●	↑
Cereal yield (tonnes per hectare of harvested land)	0.9	2018	●	→
Sustainable Nitrogen Management Index (best 0–1.41 worst)	1.0	2015	●	↓
Exports of hazardous pesticides (tonnes per million population)	NA	NA	●	●
SDG3 – Good Health and Well-Being				
Maternal mortality rate (per 100,000 live births)	829	2017	●	↗
Neonatal mortality rate (per 1,000 live births)	38.8	2020	●	→
Mortality rate, under-5 (per 1,000 live births)	103.0	2020	●	↗
Incidence of tuberculosis (per 100,000 population)	540.0	2020	●	→
New HIV infections (per 1,000 uninfected population)	1.0	2020	●	→
Age-standardized death rate due to cardiovascular disease, cancer, diabetes, or chronic respiratory disease in adults aged 30–70 years (%)	36.0	2019	●	→
Age-standardized death rate attributable to household air pollution and ambient air pollution (per 100,000 population)	212	2016	●	●
Traffic deaths (per 100,000 population)	37.7	2019	●	↓
Life expectancy at birth (years)	53.1	2019	●	→
Adolescent fertility rate (births per 1,000 females aged 15 to 19)	229.0	2009	●	●
Births attended by skilled health personnel (%)	40.0	2010	●	●
Surviving infants who received 2 WHO-recommended vaccines (%)	41	2020	●	↓
Universal health coverage (UHC) index of service coverage (worst 0–100 best)	32	2019	●	→
Subjective well-being (average ladder score, worst 0–10 best)	3.5	2017	●	●
SDG4 – Quality Education				
Participation rate in pre-primary organized learning (% of children aged 4 to 6)	6.2	2011	●	●
Net primary enrollment rate (%)	66.6	2012	●	●
Lower secondary completion rate (%)	12.2	2017	●	●
Literacy rate (% of population aged 15 to 24)	38.3	2018	●	●
SDG5 – Gender Equality				
Demand for family planning satisfied by modern methods (% of females aged 15 to 49)	27.6	2019	●	●
Ratio of female-to-male mean years of education received (%)	53.6	2019	●	→
Ratio of female-to-male labor force participation rate (%)	79.4	2020	●	↑
Seats held by women in national parliament (%)	8.6	2020	●	→
SDG6 – Clean Water and Sanitation				
Population using at least basic drinking water services (%)	37.2	2020	●	↓
Population using at least basic sanitation services (%)	14.1	2020	●	↓
Freshwater withdrawal (% of available freshwater resources)	0.3	2018	●	●
Anthropogenic wastewater that receives treatment (%)	0.0	2018	●	●
Scarce water consumption embodied in imports (m^3 H_2O eq/capita)	404.3	2018	●	●
SDG7 – Affordable and Clean Energy				
Population with access to electricity (%)	14.3	2019	●	→
Population with access to clean fuels and technology for cooking (%)	0.5	2019	●	→
CO_2 emissions from fuel combustion per total electricity output ($MtCO_2$/TWh)	1.7	2019	●	→
Share of renewable energy in total primary energy supply (%)	NA	NA	●	●
SDG8 – Decent Work and Economic Growth				
Adjusted GDP growth (%)	-5.5	2020	●	●
Victims of modern slavery (per 1,000 population)	22.3	2018	●	●
Adults with an account at a bank or other financial institution or with a mobile-money-service provider (% of population aged 15 or over)	13.7	2017	●	●
Unemployment rate (% of total labor force)	6.4	2022	●	→
Fundamental labor rights are effectively guaranteed (worst 0–1 best)	NA	NA	●	●
Fatal work-related accidents embodied in imports (per 100,000 population)	0.0	2015	●	↑

* Imputed data point

SDG9 – Industry, Innovation and Infrastructure	Value	Year	Rating	Trend
Population using the internet (%)	10.4	2020	●	→
Mobile broadband subscriptions (per 100 population)	5.0	2019	●	→
Logistics Performance Index: Quality of trade and transport-related infrastructure (worst 1–5 best)	1.9	2018	●	↓
The Times Higher Education Universities Ranking: Average score of top 3 universities (worst 0–100 best)	* 0.0	2022	●	●
Articles published in academic journals (per 1,000 population)	0.0	2020	●	→
Expenditure on research and development (% of GDP)	* 0.0	2018	●	●
SDG10 – Reduced Inequalities				
Gini coefficient	56.2	2008	●	●
Palma ratio	4.5	2018	●	●
SDG11 – Sustainable Cities and Communities				
Proportion of urban population living in slums (%)	98.5	2018	●	↓
Annual mean concentration of particulate matter of less than 2.5 microns in diameter (PM2.5) (μg/m³)	61.7	2019	●	↓
Access to improved water source, piped (% of urban population)	32.3	2020	●	↓
Satisfaction with public transport (%)	25.0	2017	●	●
SDG12 – Responsible Consumption and Production				
Municipal solid waste (kg/capita/day)	0.7	2014	●	●
Electronic waste (kg/capita)	0.5	2019	●	●
Production-based SO_2 emissions (kg/capita)	0.6	2018	●	●
SO_2 emissions embodied in imports (kg/capita)	0.2	2018	●	●
Production-based nitrogen emissions (kg/capita)	22.5	2015	●	↓
Nitrogen emissions embodied in imports (kg/capita)	0.3	2015	●	↑
Exports of plastic waste (kg/capita)	0.0	2018	●	●
SDG13 – Climate Action				
CO_2 emissions from fossil fuel combustion and cement production (tCO_2/capita)	0.0	2020	●	↑
CO_2 emissions embodied in imports (tCO_2/capita)	0.1	2018	●	↑
CO_2 emissions embodied in fossil fuel exports (kg/capita)	0.0	2020	●	●
SDG14 – Life Below Water				
Mean area that is protected in marine sites important to biodiversity (%)	NA	NA	●	●
Ocean Health Index: Clean Waters score (worst 0–100 best)	NA	NA	●	●
Fish caught from overexploited or collapsed stocks (% of total catch)	NA	NA	●	●
Fish caught by trawling or dredging (%)	NA	NA	●	●
Fish caught that are then discarded (%)	NA	NA	●	●
Marine biodiversity threats embodied in imports (per million population)	NA	NA	●	●
SDG15 – Life on Land				
Mean area that is protected in terrestrial sites important to biodiversity (%)	74.2	2020	●	→
Mean area that is protected in freshwater sites important to biodiversity (%)	94.8	2020	●	↑
Red List Index of species survival (worst 0–1 best)	0.9	2021	●	↑
Permanent deforestation (% of forest area, 5-year average)	0.1	2020	●	↑
Terrestrial and freshwater biodiversity threats embodied in imports (per million population)	0.0	2018	●	●
SDG16 – Peace, Justice and Strong Institutions				
Homicides (per 100,000 population)	NA	NA	●	●
Unsentenced detainees (% of prison population)	NA	NA	●	●
Population who feel safe walking alone at night in the city or area where they live (%)	52	2017	●	●
Property Rights (worst 1–7 best)	NA	NA	●	●
Birth registrations with civil authority (% of children under age 5)	44.8	2020	●	●
Corruption Perception Index (worst 0–100 best)	24	2021	●	→
Children involved in child labor (% of population aged 5 to 14)	30.5	2019	●	●
Exports of major conventional weapons (TIV constant million USD per 100,000 population)	* 0.0	2020	●	●
Press Freedom Index (best 0–100 worst)	41.9	2021	●	↓
Access to and affordability of justice (worst 0–1 best)	NA	NA	●	●
SDG17 – Partnerships for the Goals				
Government spending on health and education (% of GDP)	2.6	2019	●	→
For high-income and all OECD DAC countries: International concessional public finance, including official development assistance (% of GNI)	NA	NA	●	●
Other countries: Government revenue excluding grants (% of GDP)	8.8	2018	●	↗
Corporate Tax Haven Score (best 0–100 worst)	* 0.0	2019	●	●
Statistical Performance Index (worst 0–100 best)	NA	NA	●	●

5. Country Profiles

CHAD

Sub-Saharan Africa

OVERALL PERFORMANCE

COUNTRY RANKING

CHAD

161/163

COUNTRY SCORE

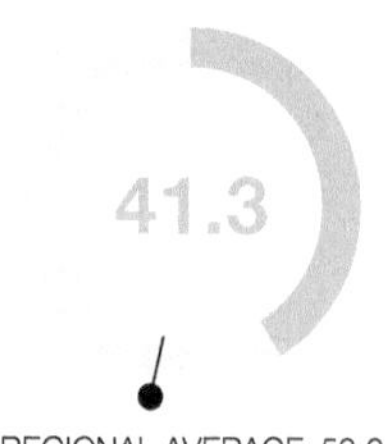

REGIONAL AVERAGE: 53.6

AVERAGE PERFORMANCE BY SDG

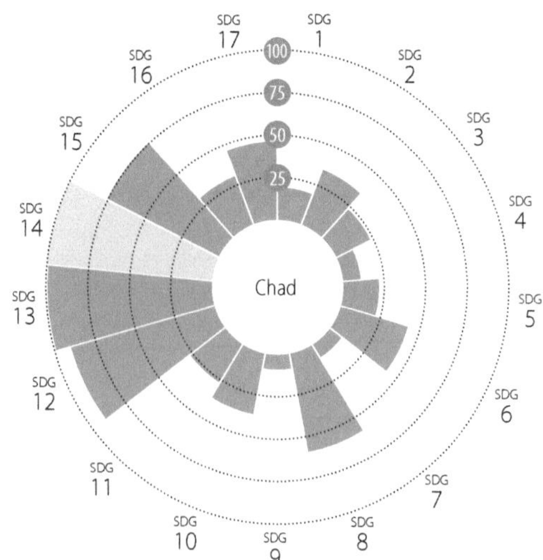

SDG DASHBOARDS AND TRENDS

Major challenges · Significant challenges · Challenges remain · SDG achieved · Information unavailable

Decreasing · Stagnating · Moderately improving · On track or maintaining SDG achievement · Information unavailable

Note: The full title of each SDG is available here: https://sustainabledevelopment.un.org/topics/sustainabledevelopmentgoals

INTERNATIONAL SPILLOVER INDEX

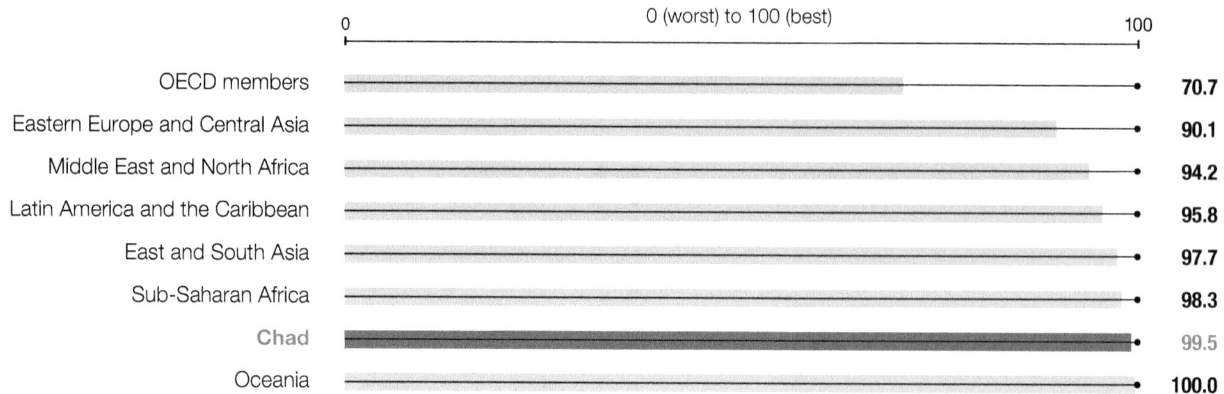

STATISTICAL PERFORMANCE INDEX

0 (worst) to 100 (best)

0 **38.5** 100

MISSING DATA IN SDG INDEX

11%

Performance by Indicator

SDG1 – No Poverty

Indicator	Value	Year	Rating	Trend
Poverty headcount ratio at \$1.90/day (%)	44.6	2022	●	↓
Poverty headcount ratio at \$3.20/day (%)	69.9	2022	●	↓

SDG2 – Zero Hunger

Indicator	Value	Year	Rating	Trend
Prevalence of undernourishment (%)	31.7	2019	●	↓
Prevalence of stunting in children under 5 years of age (%)	37.8	2019	●	→
Prevalence of wasting in children under 5 years of age (%)	13.9	2019	●	→
Prevalence of obesity, BMI ≥ 30 (% of adult population)	6.1	2016	●	↑
Human Trophic Level (best 2–3 worst)	2.3	2017	●	↓
Cereal yield (tonnes per hectare of harvested land)	0.9	2018	●	→
Sustainable Nitrogen Management Index (best 0–1.41 worst)	0.8	2015	●	→
Exports of hazardous pesticides (tonnes per million population)	NA	NA	●	●

SDG3 – Good Health and Well-Being

Indicator	Value	Year	Rating	Trend
Maternal mortality rate (per 100,000 live births)	1140	2017	●	→
Neonatal mortality rate (per 1,000 live births)	32.8	2020	●	→
Mortality rate, under-5 (per 1,000 live births)	110.0	2020	●	↗
Incidence of tuberculosis (per 100,000 population)	144.0	2020	●	→
New HIV infections (per 1,000 uninfected population)	0.2	2020	●	↑
Age-standardized death rate due to cardiovascular disease, cancer, diabetes, or chronic respiratory disease in adults aged 30–70 years (%)	22.7	2019	●	→
Age-standardized death rate attributable to household air pollution and ambient air pollution (per 100,000 population)	280	2016	●	●
Traffic deaths (per 100,000 population)	32.4	2019	●	↓
Life expectancy at birth (years)	59.6	2019	●	→
Adolescent fertility rate (births per 1,000 females aged 15 to 19)	179.4	2013	●	●
Births attended by skilled health personnel (%)	24.3	2015	●	●
Surviving infants who received 2 WHO-recommended vaccines (%)	47	2020	●	→
Universal health coverage (UHC) index of service coverage (worst 0–100 best)	28	2019	●	→
Subjective well-being (average ladder score, worst 0–10 best)	4.3	2019	●	●

SDG4 – Quality Education

Indicator	Value	Year	Rating	Trend
Participation rate in pre-primary organized learning (% of children aged 4 to 6)	13.9	2019	●	→
Net primary enrollment rate (%)	73.8	2019	●	↓
Lower secondary completion rate (%)	15.0	2018	●	→
Literacy rate (% of population aged 15 to 24)	30.8	2016	●	●

SDG5 – Gender Equality

Indicator	Value	Year	Rating	Trend
Demand for family planning satisfied by modern methods (% of females aged 15 to 49)	17.5	2019	●	●
Ratio of female-to-male mean years of education received (%)	34.2	2019	●	↓
Ratio of female-to-male labor force participation rate (%)	66.9	2020	●	↓
Seats held by women in national parliament (%)	15.4	2020	●	→

SDG6 – Clean Water and Sanitation

Indicator	Value	Year	Rating	Trend
Population using at least basic drinking water services (%)	46.2	2020	●	→
Population using at least basic sanitation services (%)	12.1	2020	●	→
Freshwater withdrawal (% of available freshwater resources)	4.3	2018	●	●
Anthropogenic wastewater that receives treatment (%)	0.0	2018	●	●
Scarce water consumption embodied in imports (m^3 H_2O eq/capita)	199.6	2018	●	●

SDG7 – Affordable and Clean Energy

Indicator	Value	Year	Rating	Trend
Population with access to electricity (%)	8.4	2019	●	→
Population with access to clean fuels and technology for cooking (%)	3.8	2019	●	→
CO_2 emissions from fuel combustion per total electricity output ($MtCO_2$/TWh)	4.4	2019	●	→
Share of renewable energy in total primary energy supply (%)	NA	NA	●	●

SDG8 – Decent Work and Economic Growth

Indicator	Value	Year	Rating	Trend
Adjusted GDP growth (%)	-7.0	2020	●	●
Victims of modern slavery (per 1,000 population)	12.0	2018	●	●
Adults with an account at a bank or other financial institution or with a mobile-money-service provider (% of population aged 15 or over)	21.8	2017	●	↗
Unemployment rate (% of total labor force)	1.8	2022	●	↑
Fundamental labor rights are effectively guaranteed (worst 0–1 best)	NA	NA	●	●
Fatal work-related accidents embodied in imports (per 100,000 population)	0.0	2015	●	↑

* Imputed data point

SDG9 – Industry, Innovation and Infrastructure

Indicator	Value	Year	Rating	Trend
Population using the internet (%)	10.4	2020	●	→
Mobile broadband subscriptions (per 100 population)	3.0	2019	●	→
Logistics Performance Index: Quality of trade and transport-related infrastructure (worst 1–5 best)	2.4	2018	●	→
The Times Higher Education Universities Ranking: Average score of top 3 universities (worst 0–100 best)	* 0.0	2022	●	●
Articles published in academic journals (per 1,000 population)	0.0	2020	●	→
Expenditure on research and development (% of GDP)	0.3	2016	●	●

SDG10 – Reduced Inequalities

Indicator	Value	Year	Rating	Trend
Gini coefficient	43.3	2011	●	●
Palma ratio	2.2	2018	●	●

SDG11 – Sustainable Cities and Communities

Indicator	Value	Year	Rating	Trend
Proportion of urban population living in slums (%)	86.6	2018	●	→
Annual mean concentration of particulate matter of less than 2.5 microns in diameter (PM2.5) (μg/m^3)	69.6	2019	●	↓
Access to improved water source, piped (% of urban population)	52.0	2020	●	↓
Satisfaction with public transport (%)	41.0	2019	●	●

SDG12 – Responsible Consumption and Production

Indicator	Value	Year	Rating	Trend
Municipal solid waste (kg/capita/day)	0.3	2010	●	●
Electronic waste (kg/capita)	0.8	2019	●	●
Production-based SO_2 emissions (kg/capita)	0.3	2018	●	●
SO_2 emissions embodied in imports (kg/capita)	0.1	2018	●	●
Production-based nitrogen emissions (kg/capita)	51.3	2015	●	↓
Nitrogen emissions embodied in imports (kg/capita)	0.1	2015	●	↑
Exports of plastic waste (kg/capita)	NA	NA	●	●

SDG13 – Climate Action

Indicator	Value	Year	Rating	Trend
CO_2 emissions from fossil fuel combustion and cement production (tCO_2/capita)	0.1	2020	●	↑
CO_2 emissions embodied in imports (tCO_2/capita)	0.1	2018	●	↑
CO_2 emissions embodied in fossil fuel exports (kg/capita)	NA	NA	●	●

SDG14 – Life Below Water

Indicator	Value	Year	Rating	Trend
Mean area that is protected in marine sites important to biodiversity (%)	NA	NA	●	●
Ocean Health Index: Clean Waters score (worst 0–100 best)	NA	NA	●	●
Fish caught from overexploited or collapsed stocks (% of total catch)	NA	NA	●	●
Fish caught by trawling or dredging (%)	NA	NA	●	●
Fish caught that are then discarded (%)	NA	NA	●	●
Marine biodiversity threats embodied in imports (per million population)	NA	NA	●	●

SDG15 – Life on Land

Indicator	Value	Year	Rating	Trend
Mean area that is protected in terrestrial sites important to biodiversity (%)	67.3	2020	●	→
Mean area that is protected in freshwater sites important to biodiversity (%)	61.4	2020	●	→
Red List Index of species survival (worst 0–1 best)	0.9	2021	●	↑
Permanent deforestation (% of forest area, 5-year average)	0.4	2020	●	↓
Terrestrial and freshwater biodiversity threats embodied in imports (per million population)	0.0	2018	●	●

SDG16 – Peace, Justice and Strong Institutions

Indicator	Value	Year	Rating	Trend
Homicides (per 100,000 population)	NA	NA	●	●
Unsentenced detainees (% of prison population)	NA	NA	●	●
Population who feel safe walking alone at night in the city or area where they live (%)	44	2019	●	●
Property Rights (worst 1–7 best)	2.9	2020	●	→
Birth registrations with civil authority (% of children under age 5)	25.7	2020	●	●
Corruption Perception Index (worst 0–100 best)	20	2021	●	↓
Children involved in child labor (% of population aged 5 to 14)	39.0	2019	●	●
Exports of major conventional weapons (TIV constant million USD per 100,000 population)	* 0.0	2020	●	●
Press Freedom Index (best 0–100 worst)	40.2	2021	●	→
Access to and affordability of justice (worst 0–1 best)	NA	NA	●	●

SDG17 – Partnerships for the Goals

Indicator	Value	Year	Rating	Trend
Government spending on health and education (% of GDP)	3.1	2019	●	↓
For high-income and all OECD DAC countries: International concessional public finance, including official development assistance (% of GNI)	NA	NA	●	●
Other countries: Government revenue excluding grants (% of GDP)	NA	NA	●	●
Corporate Tax Haven Score (best 0–100 worst)	* 0.0	2019	●	●
Statistical Performance Index (worst 0–100 best)	38.5	2019	●	↗

5. Country Profiles

CHILE

OVERALL PERFORMANCE

COUNTRY RANKING

CHILE

28/163

COUNTRY SCORE

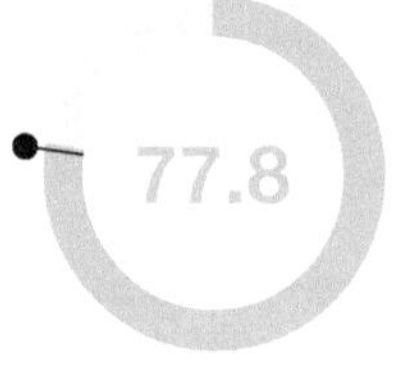

REGIONAL AVERAGE: 77.2

AVERAGE PERFORMANCE BY SDG

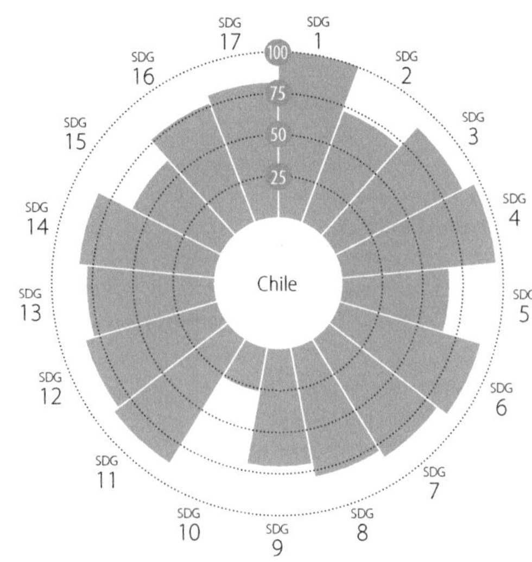

SDG DASHBOARDS AND TRENDS

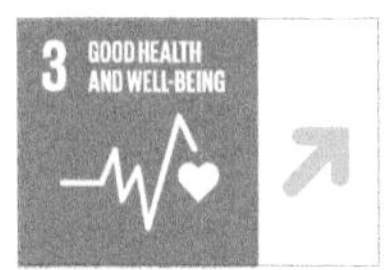

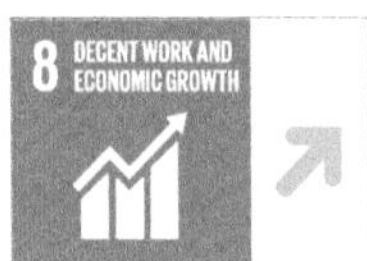

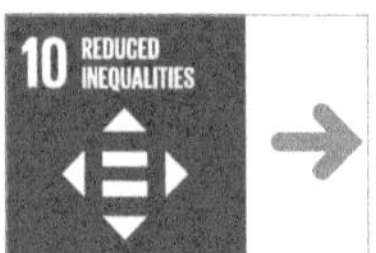

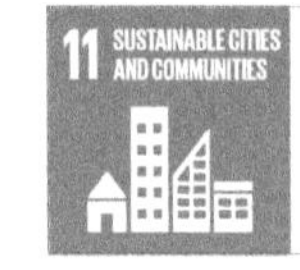

Major challenges · Significant challenges · Challenges remain · SDG achieved · Information unavailable

Decreasing · Stagnating · Moderately improving · On track or maintaining SDG achievement · Information unavailable

Note: The full title of each SDG is available here: https://sustainabledevelopment.un.org/topics/sustainabledevelopmentgoals

INTERNATIONAL SPILLOVER INDEX

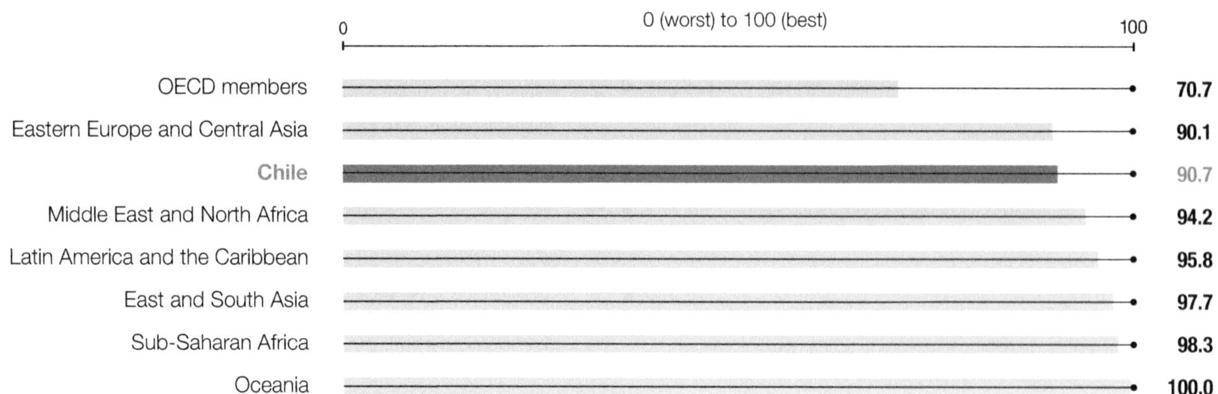

STATISTICAL PERFORMANCE INDEX

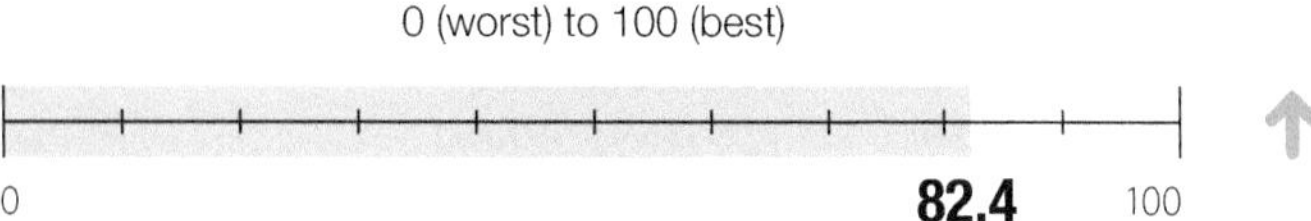

MISSING DATA IN SDG INDEX

3%

SDG1 – No Poverty	Value	Year	Rating	Trend
Poverty headcount ratio at \$1.90/day (%)	0.0	2022	●	↑
Poverty headcount ratio at \$3.20/day (%)	0.2	2022	●	↑
Poverty rate after taxes and transfers (%)	16.5	2017	●	●
SDG2 – Zero Hunger				
Prevalence of undernourishment (%)	3.4	2019	●	↑
Prevalence of stunting in children under 5 years of age (%)	1.8	2014	●	↑
Prevalence of wasting in children under 5 years of age (%)	0.3	2014	●	↑
Prevalence of obesity, BMI ≥ 30 (% of adult population)	28.0	2016	●	↓
Human Trophic Level (best 2–3 worst)	2.3	2017	●	↓
Cereal yield (tonnes per hectare of harvested land)	7.1	2018	●	↑
Sustainable Nitrogen Management Index (best 0–1.41 worst)	0.8	2015	●	→
Yield gap closure (% of potential yield)	NA	NA	●	●
Exports of hazardous pesticides (tonnes per million population)	2.0	2019	●	●
SDG3 – Good Health and Well-Being				
Maternal mortality rate (per 100,000 live births)	13	2017	●	↑
Neonatal mortality rate (per 1,000 live births)	4.4	2020	●	↑
Mortality rate, under-5 (per 1,000 live births)	6.8	2020	●	↑
Incidence of tuberculosis (per 100,000 population)	15.0	2020	●	→
New HIV infections (per 1,000 uninfected population)	0.3	2020	●	→
Age-standardized death rate due to cardiovascular disease, cancer, diabetes, or chronic respiratory disease in adults aged 30–70 years (%)	10.0	2019	●	↑
Age-standardized death rate attributable to household air pollution and ambient air pollution (per 100,000 population)	25	2016	●	●
Traffic deaths (per 100,000 population)	14.9	2019	●	↓
Life expectancy at birth (years)	80.7	2019	●	↑
Adolescent fertility rate (births per 1,000 females aged 15 to 19)	22.6	2018	●	↑
Births attended by skilled health personnel (%)	99.8	2017	●	↑
Surviving infants who received 2 WHO-recommended vaccines (%)	91	2020	●	↑
Universal health coverage (UHC) index of service coverage (worst 0–100 best)	80	2019	●	↑
Subjective well-being (average ladder score, worst 0–10 best)	6.4	2021	●	↑
Gap in life expectancy at birth among regions (years)	2.0	2016	●	●
Gap in self-reported health status by income (percentage points)	19.7	2017	●	●
Daily smokers (% of population aged 15 and over)	24.5	2016	●	●
SDG4 – Quality Education				
Participation rate in pre-primary organized learning (% of children aged 4 to 6)	95.3	2019	●	↑
Net primary enrollment rate (%)	99.5	2019	●	↑
Lower secondary completion rate (%)	94.3	2019	●	↑
Literacy rate (% of population aged 15 to 24)	99.0	2017	●	●
Tertiary educational attainment (% of population aged 25 to 34)	33.7	2017	●	●
PISA score (worst 0–600 best)	437.7	2018	●	↓
Variation in science performance explained by socio-economic status (%)	14.1	2018	●	↑
Underachievers in science (% of 15-year-olds)	35.3	2018	●	↓
SDG5 – Gender Equality				
Demand for family planning satisfied by modern methods (% of females aged 15 to 49)	NA	NA	●	●
Ratio of female-to-male mean years of education received (%)	98.1	2019	●	↑
Ratio of female-to-male labor force participation rate (%)	67.0	2020	●	→
Seats held by women in national parliament (%)	22.6	2020	●	↗
Gender wage gap (% of male median wage)	8.6	2020	●	↑
SDG6 – Clean Water and Sanitation				
Population using at least basic drinking water services (%)	100.0	2020	●	↑
Population using at least basic sanitation services (%)	100.0	2020	●	↑
Freshwater withdrawal (% of available freshwater resources)	21.6	2018	●	●
Anthropogenic wastewater that receives treatment (%)	71.9	2018	●	●
Scarce water consumption embodied in imports (m^3 H_2O eq/capita)	1142.9	2018	●	●
Population using safely managed water services (%)	98.8	2020	●	↑
Population using safely managed sanitation services (%)	78.6	2020	●	↑
SDG7 – Affordable and Clean Energy				
Population with access to electricity (%)	100.0	2019	●	↑
Population with access to clean fuels and technology for cooking (%)	100.0	2019	●	↑
CO_2 emissions from fuel combustion per total electricity output ($MtCO_2$/TWh)	1.1	2019	●	↑
Share of renewable energy in total primary energy supply (%)	27.4	2019	●	↑
SDG8 – Decent Work and Economic Growth				
Adjusted GDP growth (%)	-2.4	2020	●	●
Victims of modern slavery (per 1,000 population)	0.8	2018	●	●
Adults with an account at a bank or other financial institution or with a mobile-money-service provider (% of population aged 15 or over)	74.3	2017	●	↑
Fundamental labor rights are effectively guaranteed (worst 0–1 best)	0.7	2020	●	↑
Fatal work-related accidents embodied in imports (per 100,000 population)	0.3	2015	●	↑
Employment-to-population ratio (%)	58.5	2021	●	↓
Youth not in employment, education or training (NEET) (% of population aged 15 to 29)	18.4	2017	●	●

SDG9 – Industry, Innovation and Infrastructure	Value	Year	Rating	Trend
Population using the internet (%)	88.3	2020	●	↑
Mobile broadband subscriptions (per 100 population)	95.5	2019	●	↑
Logistics Performance Index: Quality of trade and transport-related infrastructure (worst 1–5 best)	3.2	2018	●	↑
The Times Higher Education Universities Ranking: Average score of top 3 universities (worst 0–100 best)	40.5	2022	●	●
Articles published in academic journals (per 1,000 population)	0.9	2020	●	↑
Expenditure on research and development (% of GDP)	0.4	2017	●	↓
Researchers (per 1,000 employed population)	1.1	2018	●	→
Triadic patent families filed (per million population)	0.5	2019	●	↓
Gap in internet access by income (percentage points)	7.5	2017	●	●
Female share of graduates from STEM fields at the tertiary level (%)	18.8	2017	●	→
SDG10 – Reduced Inequalities				
Gini coefficient	44.4	2017	●	→
Palma ratio	2.6	2017	●	●
Elderly poverty rate (% of population aged 66 or over)	17.6	2017	●	●
SDG11 – Sustainable Cities and Communities				
Proportion of urban population living in slums (%)	* 0.0	2018	●	↑
Annual mean concentration of particulate matter of less than 2.5 microns in diameter (PM2.5) (µg/m³)	19.4	2019	●	↗
Access to improved water source, piped (% of urban population)	99.9	2020	●	↑
Satisfaction with public transport (%)	62.0	2021	●	↑
Population with rent overburden (%)	13.9	2017	●	●
SDG12 – Responsible Consumption and Production				
Electronic waste (kg/capita)	9.9	2019	●	●
Production-based SO_2 emissions (kg/capita)	26.8	2018	●	●
SO_2 emissions embodied in imports (kg/capita)	4.7	2018	●	●
Production-based nitrogen emissions (kg/capita)	10.1	2015	●	↑
Nitrogen emissions embodied in imports (kg/capita)	4.6	2015	●	↑
Exports of plastic waste (kg/capita)	0.6	2021	●	●
Non-recycled municipal solid waste (kg/capita/day)	1.2	2018	●	↓
SDG13 – Climate Action				
CO_2 emissions from fossil fuel combustion and cement production (tCO_2/capita)	4.2	2020	●	→
CO_2 emissions embodied in imports (tCO_2/capita)	1.4	2018	●	↓
CO_2 emissions embodied in fossil fuel exports (kg/capita)	97.9	2020	●	●
Carbon Pricing Score at EUR60/tCO_2 (%, worst 0–100 best)	16.9	2018	●	→
SDG14 – Life Below Water				
Mean area that is protected in marine sites important to biodiversity (%)	29.9	2020	●	→
Ocean Health Index: Clean Waters score (worst 0–100 best)	93.8	2020	●	↑
Fish caught from overexploited or collapsed stocks (% of total catch)	NA	NA	●	●
Fish caught by trawling or dredging (%)	0.2	2018	●	↑
Fish caught that are then discarded (%)	0.3	2018	●	↑
Marine biodiversity threats embodied in imports (per million population)	0.0	2018	●	●
SDG15 – Life on Land				
Mean area that is protected in terrestrial sites important to biodiversity (%)	36.4	2020	●	→
Mean area that is protected in freshwater sites important to biodiversity (%)	40.0	2020	●	→
Red List Index of species survival (worst 0–1 best)	0.8	2021	●	↓
Permanent deforestation (% of forest area, 5-year average)	0.0	2020	●	↑
Terrestrial and freshwater biodiversity threats embodied in imports (per million population)	1.1	2018	●	●
SDG16 – Peace, Justice and Strong Institutions				
Homicides (per 100,000 population)	3.9	2019	●	→
Unsentenced detainees (% of prison population)	31.7	2019	●	↓
Population who feel safe walking alone at night in the city or area where they live (%)	43	2021	●	↓
Property Rights (worst 1–7 best)	5.4	2020	●	↑
Birth registrations with civil authority (% of children under age 5)	99.4	2020	●	●
Corruption Perception Index (worst 0–100 best)	67	2021	●	↑
Children involved in child labor (% of population aged 5 to 14)	5.9	2019	●	●
Exports of major conventional weapons (TIV constant million USD per 100,000 population)	0.0	2020	●	●
Press Freedom Index (best 0–100 worst)	27.9	2021	●	↑
Access to and affordability of justice (worst 0–1 best)	0.7	2020	●	↑
Persons held in prison (per 100,000 population)	244.1	2019	●	→
SDG17 – Partnerships for the Goals				
Government spending on health and education (% of GDP)	10.2	2019	●	↑
For high-income and all OECD DAC countries: International concessional public finance, including official development assistance (% of GNI)	NA	NA	●	●
Other countries: Government revenue excluding grants (% of GDP)	NA	NA	●	●
Corporate Tax Haven Score (best 0–100 worst)	* 0.0	2019	●	●
Financial Secrecy Score (best 0–100 worst)	55.8	2020	●	●
Shifted profits of multinationals (US\$ billion)	7.1	2018	●	↑
Statistical Performance Index (worst 0–100 best)	82.4	2019	●	↑

* Imputed data point

5. Country Profiles

CHINA

OVERALL PERFORMANCE

COUNTRY RANKING

CHINA

56/163

COUNTRY SCORE

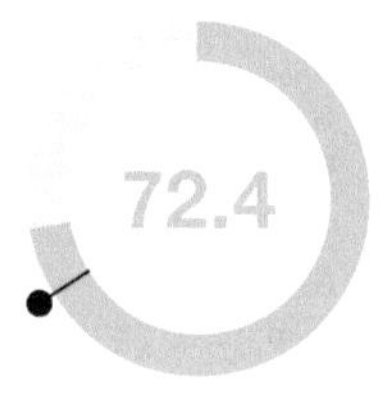

REGIONAL AVERAGE: 65.9

AVERAGE PERFORMANCE BY SDG

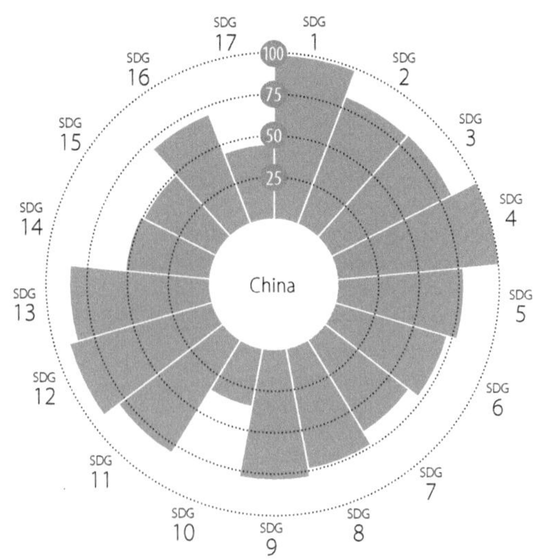

SDG DASHBOARDS AND TRENDS

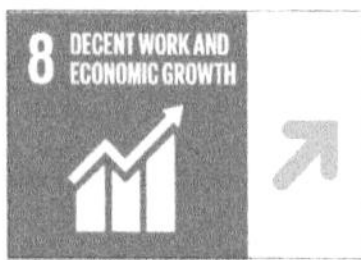

■ Major challenges ■ Significant challenges ■ Challenges remain ■ SDG achieved ■ Information unavailable

↓ Decreasing → Stagnating ↗ Moderately improving ↑ On track or maintaining SDG achievement ● Information unavailable

Note: The full title of each SDG is available here: https://sustainabledevelopment.un.org/topics/sustainabledevelopmentgoals

INTERNATIONAL SPILLOVER INDEX

STATISTICAL PERFORMANCE INDEX

0 (worst) to 100 (best)

0 **58.2** 100 ↗

MISSING DATA IN SDG INDEX

6%

Indicator	Value	Year	Rating	Trend
SDG1 – No Poverty				
Poverty headcount ratio at $1.90/day (%)	0.1	2022	●	↑
Poverty headcount ratio at $3.20/day (%)	1.3	2022	●	↑
SDG2 – Zero Hunger				
Prevalence of undernourishment (%)	2.5	2019	●	↑
Prevalence of stunting in children under 5 years of age (%)	4.8	2017	●	↑
Prevalence of wasting in children under 5 years of age (%)	1.9	2017	●	↑
Prevalence of obesity, BMI ≥ 30 (% of adult population)	6.2	2016	●	↑
Human Trophic Level (best 2–3 worst)	2.2	2017	●	↑
Cereal yield (tonnes per hectare of harvested land)	6.1	2018	●	↑
Sustainable Nitrogen Management Index (best 0–1.41 worst)	0.7	2015	●	→
Exports of hazardous pesticides (tonnes per million population)	1.9	2019	●	●
SDG3 – Good Health and Well-Being				
Maternal mortality rate (per 100,000 live births)	29	2017	●	↑
Neonatal mortality rate (per 1,000 live births)	3.5	2020	●	↑
Mortality rate, under-5 (per 1,000 live births)	7.3	2020	●	↑
Incidence of tuberculosis (per 100,000 population)	59.0	2020	●	→
New HIV infections (per 1,000 uninfected population)	1.0	2020	●	→
Age-standardized death rate due to cardiovascular disease, cancer, diabetes, or chronic respiratory disease in adults aged 30–70 years (%)	15.9	2019	●	↑
Age-standardized death rate attributable to household air pollution and ambient air pollution (per 100,000 population)	113	2016	●	●
Traffic deaths (per 100,000 population)	17.4	2019	●	→
Life expectancy at birth (years)	77.4	2019	●	↗
Adolescent fertility rate (births per 1,000 females aged 15 to 19)	9.2	2015	●	●
Births attended by skilled health personnel (%)	99.9	2016	●	●
Surviving infants who received 2 WHO-recommended vaccines (%)	99	2020	●	↑
Universal health coverage (UHC) index of service coverage (worst 0–100 best)	82	2019	●	↑
Subjective well-being (average ladder score, worst 0–10 best)	5.9	2021	●	↑
SDG4 – Quality Education				
Participation rate in pre-primary organized learning (% of children aged 4 to 6)	NA	NA	●	●
Net primary enrollment rate (%)	NA	NA	●	●
Lower secondary completion rate (%)	99.5	2011	●	●
Literacy rate (% of population aged 15 to 24)	99.8	2018	●	●
SDG5 – Gender Equality				
Demand for family planning satisfied by modern methods (% of females aged 15 to 49)	96.6	2001	●	●
Ratio of female-to-male mean years of education received (%)	91.7	2019	●	↑
Ratio of female-to-male labor force participation rate (%)	83.0	2020	●	↑
Seats held by women in national parliament (%)	24.9	2020	●	→
SDG6 – Clean Water and Sanitation				
Population using at least basic drinking water services (%)	94.3	2020	●	↑
Population using at least basic sanitation services (%)	92.4	2020	●	↑
Freshwater withdrawal (% of available freshwater resources)	43.2	2018	●	●
Anthropogenic wastewater that receives treatment (%)	9.4	2018	●	●
Scarce water consumption embodied in imports (m^3 H_2O eq/capita)	305.7	2018	●	●
SDG7 – Affordable and Clean Energy				
Population with access to electricity (%)	100.0	2019	●	↑
Population with access to clean fuels and technology for cooking (%)	64.4	2019	●	↗
CO_2 emissions from fuel combustion per total electricity output ($MtCO_2$/TWh)	1.3	2019	●	↑
Share of renewable energy in total primary energy supply (%)	9.7	2019	●	→
SDG8 – Decent Work and Economic Growth				
Adjusted GDP growth (%)	2.5	2020	●	●
Victims of modern slavery (per 1,000 population)	2.8	2018	●	●
Adults with an account at a bank or other financial institution or with a mobile-money-service provider (% of population aged 15 or over)	80.2	2017	●	↑
Unemployment rate (% of total labor force)	4.7	2022	●	↑
Fundamental labor rights are effectively guaranteed (worst 0–1 best)	0.3	2020	●	→
Fatal work-related accidents embodied in imports (per 100,000 population)	0.1	2015	●	↑
SDG9 – Industry, Innovation and Infrastructure				
Population using the internet (%)	70.4	2020	●	↑
Mobile broadband subscriptions (per 100 population)	96.7	2019	●	↑
Logistics Performance Index: Quality of trade and transport-related infrastructure (worst 1–5 best)	3.8	2018	●	↑
The Times Higher Education Universities Ranking: Average score of top 3 universities (worst 0–100 best)	81.6	2022	●	●
Articles published in academic journals (per 1,000 population)	0.5	2020	●	↑
Expenditure on research and development (% of GDP)	2.1	2018	●	↑
SDG10 – Reduced Inequalities				
Gini coefficient	38.5	2016	●	●
Palma ratio	3.9	2011	●	●
SDG11 – Sustainable Cities and Communities				
Proportion of urban population living in slums (%)	NA	NA	●	●
Annual mean concentration of particulate matter of less than 2.5 microns in diameter (PM2.5) (μg/m^3)	48.6	2019	●	↗
Access to improved water source, piped (% of urban population)	91.4	2020	●	→
Satisfaction with public transport (%)	85.0	2021	●	●
SDG12 – Responsible Consumption and Production				
Municipal solid waste (kg/capita/day)	0.8	2019	●	●
Electronic waste (kg/capita)	7.2	2019	●	●
Production-based SO_2 emissions (kg/capita)	18.0	2018	●	●
SO_2 emissions embodied in imports (kg/capita)	0.5	2018	●	●
Production-based nitrogen emissions (kg/capita)	11.1	2015	●	↑
Nitrogen emissions embodied in imports (kg/capita)	1.2	2015	●	↑
Exports of plastic waste (kg/capita)	0.0	2020	●	●
SDG13 – Climate Action				
CO_2 emissions from fossil fuel combustion and cement production (tCO_2/capita)	7.4	2020	●	→
CO_2 emissions embodied in imports (tCO_2/capita)	0.2	2018	●	↑
CO_2 emissions embodied in fossil fuel exports (kg/capita)	20.2	2020	●	●
SDG14 – Life Below Water				
Mean area that is protected in marine sites important to biodiversity (%)	7.1	2020	●	→
Ocean Health Index: Clean Waters score (worst 0–100 best)	35.1	2020	●	→
Fish caught from overexploited or collapsed stocks (% of total catch)	25.5	2018	●	↓
Fish caught by trawling or dredging (%)	51.1	2018	●	↓
Fish caught that are then discarded (%)	4.3	2018	●	↑
Marine biodiversity threats embodied in imports (per million population)	0.0	2018	●	●
SDG15 – Life on Land				
Mean area that is protected in terrestrial sites important to biodiversity (%)	10.1	2020	●	→
Mean area that is protected in freshwater sites important to biodiversity (%)	9.6	2020	●	→
Red List Index of species survival (worst 0–1 best)	0.7	2021	●	↓
Permanent deforestation (% of forest area, 5-year average)	0.0	2020	●	↑
Terrestrial and freshwater biodiversity threats embodied in imports (per million population)	0.6	2018	●	●
SDG16 – Peace, Justice and Strong Institutions				
Homicides (per 100,000 population)	0.5	2018	●	↑
Unsentenced detainees (% of prison population)	NA	NA	●	●
Population who feel safe walking alone at night in the city or area where they live (%)	94	2021	●	●
Property Rights (worst 1–7 best)	5.3	2020	●	↑
Birth registrations with civil authority (% of children under age 5)	NA	NA	●	●
Corruption Perception Index (worst 0–100 best)	45	2021	●	↗
Children involved in child labor (% of population aged 5 to 14)	NA	NA	●	●
Exports of major conventional weapons (TIV constant million USD per 100,000 population)	0.1	2020	●	●
Press Freedom Index (best 0–100 worst)	78.7	2021	●	→
Access to and affordability of justice (worst 0–1 best)	0.6	2020	●	↗
SDG17 – Partnerships for the Goals				
Government spending on health and education (% of GDP)	6.5	2019	●	↓
For high-income and all OECD DAC countries: International concessional public finance, including official development assistance (% of GNI)	NA	NA	●	●
Other countries: Government revenue excluding grants (% of GDP)	16.5	2018	●	→
Corporate Tax Haven Score (best 0–100 worst)	58.3	2019	●	●
Statistical Performance Index (worst 0–100 best)	58.2	2019	●	↗

* Imputed data point

COLOMBIA

OVERALL PERFORMANCE

COUNTRY RANKING

COLOMBIA

75/163

COUNTRY SCORE

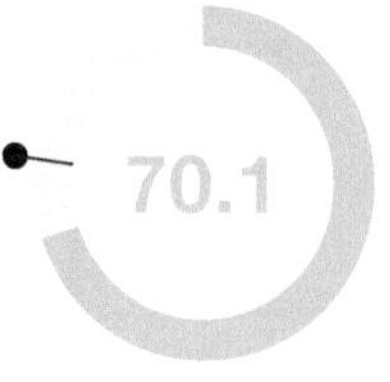

REGIONAL AVERAGE: 77.2

AVERAGE PERFORMANCE BY SDG

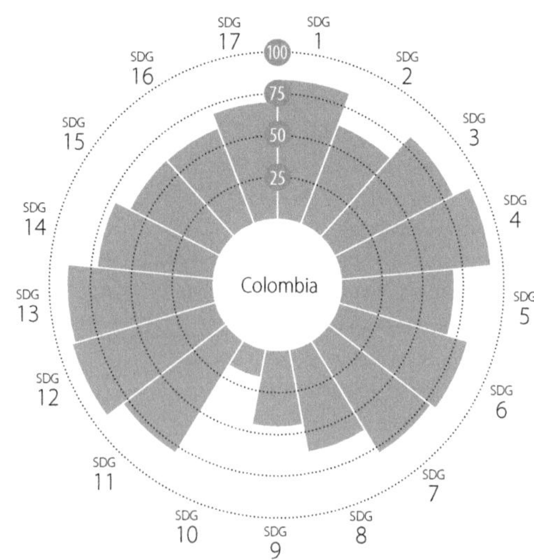

SDG DASHBOARDS AND TRENDS

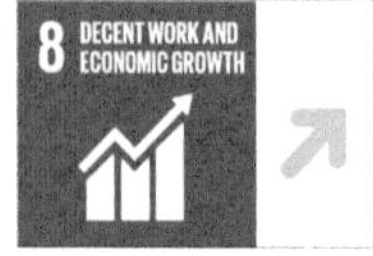

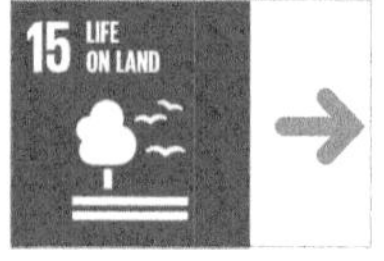

Major challenges | Significant challenges | Challenges remain | SDG achieved | Information unavailable

Decreasing | Stagnating | Moderately improving | On track or maintaining SDG achievement | Information unavailable

Note: The full title of each SDG is available here: https://sustainabledevelopment.un.org/topics/sustainabledevelopmentgoals

INTERNATIONAL SPILLOVER INDEX

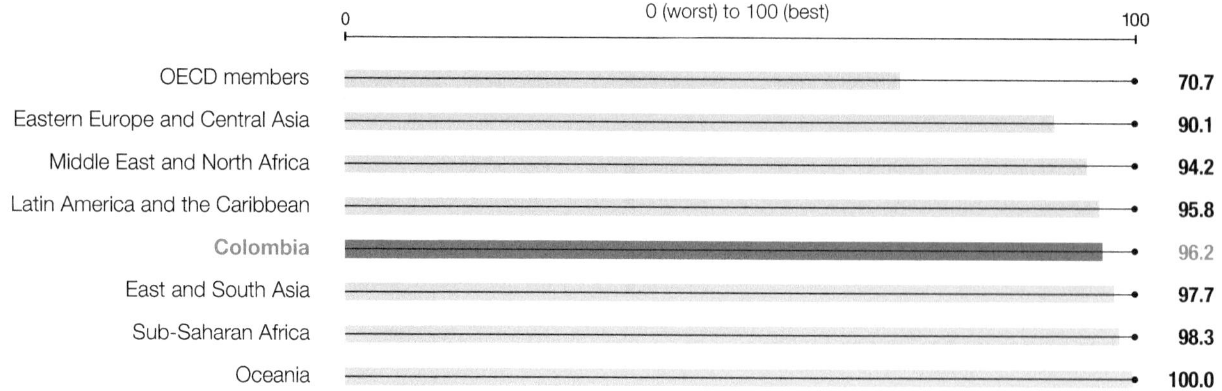

STATISTICAL PERFORMANCE INDEX

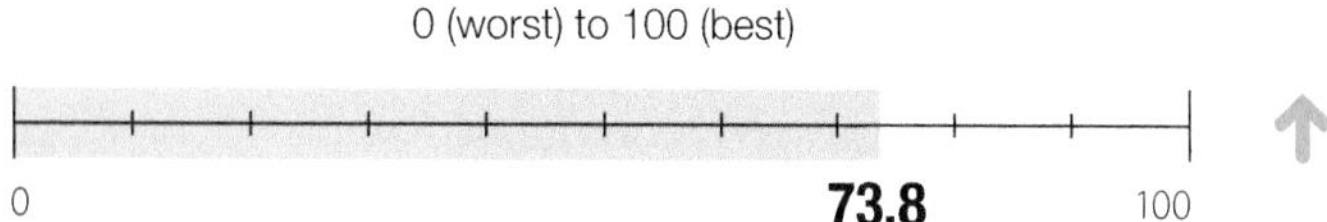

MISSING DATA IN SDG INDEX

SDG1 – No Poverty	Value	Year	Rating	Trend
Poverty headcount ratio at $1.90/day (%)	5.1	2022	●	↓
Poverty headcount ratio at $3.20/day (%)	13.9	2022	●	→
Poverty rate after taxes and transfers (%)	NA	NA	●	●
SDG2 – Zero Hunger				
Prevalence of undernourishment (%)	8.8	2019	●	↓
Prevalence of stunting in children under 5 years of age (%)	12.7	2016	●	→
Prevalence of wasting in children under 5 years of age (%)	1.6	2016	●	↑
Prevalence of obesity, BMI ≥ 30 (% of adult population)	22.3	2016	●	↓
Human Trophic Level (best 2–3 worst)	2.3	2017	●	↑
Cereal yield (tonnes per hectare of harvested land)	4.5	2018	●	↑
Sustainable Nitrogen Management Index (best 0–1.41 worst)	1.1	2015	●	↓
Yield gap closure (% of potential yield)	NA	NA	●	●
Exports of hazardous pesticides (tonnes per million population)	0.4	2019	●	●
SDG3 – Good Health and Well-Being				
Maternal mortality rate (per 100,000 live births)	83	2017	●	↗
Neonatal mortality rate (per 1,000 live births)	7.2	2020	●	↑
Mortality rate, under-5 (per 1,000 live births)	13.2	2020	●	↑
Incidence of tuberculosis (per 100,000 population)	37.0	2020	●	↓
New HIV infections (per 1,000 uninfected population)	0.2	2020	●	↑
Age-standardized death rate due to cardiovascular disease, cancer, diabetes, or chronic respiratory disease in adults aged 30–70 years (%)	9.7	2019	●	↑
Age-standardized death rate attributable to household air pollution and ambient air pollution (per 100,000 population)	37	2016	●	●
Traffic deaths (per 100,000 population)	15.4	2019	●	↗
Life expectancy at birth (years)	79.3	2019	●	↑
Adolescent fertility rate (births per 1,000 females aged 15 to 19)	57.9	2019	●	↗
Births attended by skilled health personnel (%)	99.1	2019	●	↑
Surviving infants who received 2 WHO-recommended vaccines (%)	88	2020	●	↓
Universal health coverage (UHC) index of service coverage (worst 0–100 best)	78	2019	●	↑
Subjective well-being (average ladder score, worst 0–10 best)	5.3	2021	●	↓
Gap in life expectancy at birth among regions (years)	16.0	2019	●	↓
Gap in self-reported health status by income (percentage points)	8.1	2019	●	●
Daily smokers (% of population aged 15 and over)	13.0	2013	●	●
SDG4 – Quality Education				
Participation rate in pre-primary organized learning (% of children aged 4 to 6)	99.4	2019	●	↑
Net primary enrollment rate (%)	99.1	2019	●	↑
Lower secondary completion rate (%)	78.1	2019	●	↗
Literacy rate (% of population aged 15 to 24)	99.0	2020	●	↑
Tertiary educational attainment (% of population aged 25 to 34)	30.0	2020	●	↗
PISA score (worst 0–600 best)	405.3	2018	●	↓
Variation in science performance explained by socio-economic status (%)	11.5	2018	●	↑
Underachievers in science (% of 15-year-olds)	50.4	2018	●	↓
SDG5 – Gender Equality				
Demand for family planning satisfied by modern methods (% of females aged 15 to 49)	86.6	2016	●	●
Ratio of female-to-male mean years of education received (%)	103.6	2019	●	↑
Ratio of female-to-male labor force participation rate (%)	66.2	2020	●	↓
Seats held by women in national parliament (%)	18.3	2020	●	↓
Gender wage gap (% of male median wage)	4.0	2019	●	↑
SDG6 – Clean Water and Sanitation				
Population using at least basic drinking water services (%)	97.5	2020	●	↑
Population using at least basic sanitation services (%)	93.7	2020	●	↑
Freshwater withdrawal (% of available freshwater resources)	2.0	2018	●	●
Anthropogenic wastewater that receives treatment (%)	25.6	2018	●	●
Scarce water consumption embodied in imports (m^3 H_2O eq/capita)	611.6	2018	●	●
Population using safely managed water services (%)	73.0	2020	●	→
Population using safely managed sanitation services (%)	18.3	2020	●	→
SDG7 – Affordable and Clean Energy				
Population with access to electricity (%)	99.8	2019	●	↑
Population with access to clean fuels and technology for cooking (%)	94.3	2019	●	↑
CO_2 emissions from fuel combustion per total electricity output ($MtCO_2$/TWh)	1.3	2019	●	→
Share of renewable energy in total primary energy supply (%)	22.7	2019	●	↑
SDG8 – Decent Work and Economic Growth				
Adjusted GDP growth (%)	-2.3	2020	●	●
Victims of modern slavery (per 1,000 population)	2.7	2018	●	●
Adults with an account at a bank or other financial institution or with a mobile-money-service provider (% of population aged 15 or over)	45.8	2017	●	↗
Fundamental labor rights are effectively guaranteed (worst 0–1 best)	0.5	2020	●	→
Fatal work-related accidents embodied in imports (per 100,000 population)	0.2	2015	●	↑
Employment-to-population ratio (%)	60.7	2021	●	↑
Youth not in employment, education or training (NEET) (% of population aged 15 to 29)	29.8	2020	●	↓

SDG9 – Industry, Innovation and Infrastructure	Value	Year	Rating	Trend
Population using the internet (%)	69.8	2020	●	↑
Mobile broadband subscriptions (per 100 population)	58.7	2019	●	↑
Logistics Performance Index: Quality of trade and transport-related infrastructure (worst 1–5 best)	2.7	2018	●	↑
The Times Higher Education Universities Ranking: Average score of top 3 universities (worst 0–100 best)	31.3	2022	●	●
Articles published in academic journals (per 1,000 population)	0.3	2020	●	↗
Expenditure on research and development (% of GDP)	0.2	2018	●	↓
Researchers (per 1,000 employed population)	NA	NA	●	●
Triadic patent families filed (per million population)	0.1	2019	●	→
Gap in internet access by income (percentage points)	64.3	2019	●	↓
Female share of graduates from STEM fields at the tertiary level (%)	33.4	2018	●	↑
SDG10 – Reduced Inequalities				
Gini coefficient	51.3	2019	●	↓
Palma ratio	3.3	2018	●	●
Elderly poverty rate (% of population aged 66 or over)	NA	NA	●	●
SDG11 – Sustainable Cities and Communities				
Proportion of urban population living in slums (%)	28.5	2018	●	↓
Annual mean concentration of particulate matter of less than 2.5 microns in diameter (PM2.5) (μg/m^3)	15.1	2019	●	↑
Access to improved water source, piped (% of urban population)	95.1	2020	●	↓
Satisfaction with public transport (%)	59.0	2021	●	↗
Population with rent overburden (%)	NA	NA	●	●
SDG12 – Responsible Consumption and Production				
Electronic waste (kg/capita)	6.3	2019	●	●
Production-based SO_2 emissions (kg/capita)	3.5	2018	●	●
SO_2 emissions embodied in imports (kg/capita)	1.2	2018	●	●
Production-based nitrogen emissions (kg/capita)	13.4	2015	●	↑
Nitrogen emissions embodied in imports (kg/capita)	1.9	2015	●	↑
Exports of plastic waste (kg/capita)	0.1	2020	●	●
Non-recycled municipal solid waste (kg/capita/day)	NA	NA	●	●
SDG13 – Climate Action				
CO_2 emissions from fossil fuel combustion and cement production (tCO_2/capita)	1.8	2020	●	↑
CO_2 emissions embodied in imports (tCO_2/capita)	0.4	2018	●	↑
CO_2 emissions embodied in fossil fuel exports (kg/capita)	5852.9	2020	●	●
Carbon Pricing Score at EUR60/tCO_2 (%, worst 0–100 best)	24.7	2018	●	●
SDG14 – Life Below Water				
Mean area that is protected in marine sites important to biodiversity (%)	54.8	2020	●	→
Ocean Health Index: Clean Waters score (worst 0–100 best)	63.7	2020	●	↗
Fish caught from overexploited or collapsed stocks (% of total catch)	51.1	2018	●	↓
Fish caught by trawling or dredging (%)	0.0	2018	●	↑
Fish caught that are then discarded (%)	4.1	2018	●	↑
Marine biodiversity threats embodied in imports (per million population)	0.1	2018	●	●
SDG15 – Life on Land				
Mean area that is protected in terrestrial sites important to biodiversity (%)	47.6	2020	●	→
Mean area that is protected in freshwater sites important to biodiversity (%)	50.7	2020	●	→
Red List Index of species survival (worst 0–1 best)	0.7	2021	●	↓
Permanent deforestation (% of forest area, 5-year average)	0.3	2020	●	↓
Terrestrial and freshwater biodiversity threats embodied in imports (per million population)	1.0	2018	●	●
SDG16 – Peace, Justice and Strong Institutions				
Homicides (per 100,000 population)	22.6	2020	●	↗
Unsentenced detainees (% of prison population)	33.9	2018	●	↑
Population who feel safe walking alone at night in the city or area where they live (%)	43	2021	●	↓
Property Rights (worst 1–7 best)	4.1	2020	●	↑
Birth registrations with civil authority (% of children under age 5)	96.8	2020	●	●
Corruption Perception Index (worst 0–100 best)	39	2021	●	→
Children involved in child labor (% of population aged 5 to 14)	3.6	2019	●	●
Exports of major conventional weapons (TIV constant million USD per 100,000 population)	0.0	2020	●	●
Press Freedom Index (best 0–100 worst)	43.7	2021	●	→
Access to and affordability of justice (worst 0–1 best)	0.6	2020	●	↗
Persons held in prison (per 100,000 population)	245.9	2019	●	→
SDG17 – Partnerships for the Goals				
Government spending on health and education (% of GDP)	10.0	2019	●	↑
For high-income and all OECD DAC countries: International concessional public finance, including official development assistance (% of GNI)	NA	NA	●	●
Other countries: Government revenue excluding grants (% of GDP)	24.2	2019	●	→
Corporate Tax Haven Score (best 0–100 worst)	* 0.0	2019	●	●
Financial Secrecy Score (best 0–100 worst)	56.5	2020	●	●
Shifted profits of multinationals (US$ billion)	1.9	2018	●	↑
Statistical Performance Index (worst 0–100 best)	73.8	2019	●	↑

* Imputed data point

COMOROS

Sub-Saharan Africa

AVERAGE PERFORMANCE BY SDG

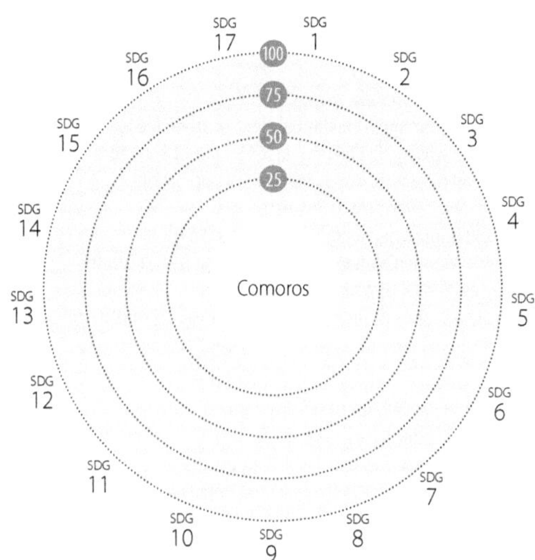

OVERALL PERFORMANCE

COUNTRY RANKING

COMOROS

NA /163

COUNTRY SCORE

na

REGIONAL AVERAGE: 53.6

SDG DASHBOARDS AND TRENDS

Major challenges · Significant challenges · Challenges remain · SDG achieved · Information unavailable

Decreasing · Stagnating · Moderately improving · On track or maintaining SDG achievement · Information unavailable

Note: The full title of each SDG is available here: https://sustainabledevelopment.un.org/topics/sustainabledevelopmentgoals

INTERNATIONAL SPILLOVER INDEX

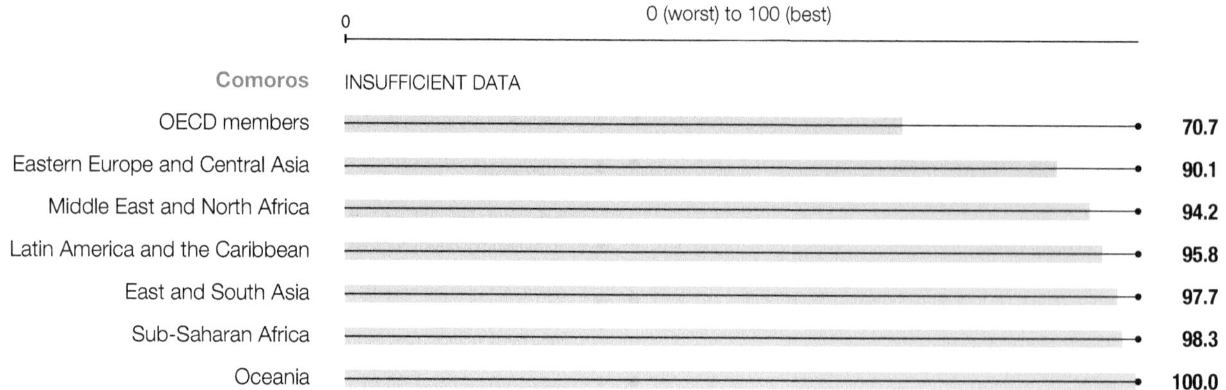

Comoros	INSUFFICIENT DATA
OECD members	70.7
Eastern Europe and Central Asia	90.1
Middle East and North Africa	94.2
Latin America and the Caribbean	95.8
East and South Asia	97.7
Sub-Saharan Africa	98.3
Oceania	100.0

STATISTICAL PERFORMANCE INDEX

0 (worst) to 100 (best)

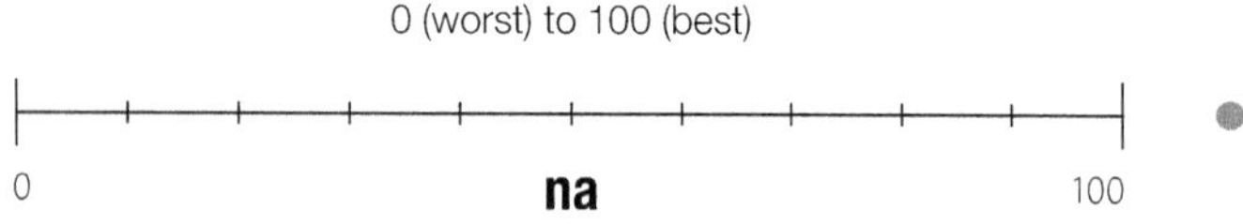

na

MISSING DATA IN SDG INDEX

23%

SDG1 – No Poverty

Indicator	Value	Year	Rating	Trend
Poverty headcount ratio at $1.90/day (%)	20.9	2022	●	→
Poverty headcount ratio at $3.20/day (%)	38.7	2022	●	→

SDG2 – Zero Hunger

Indicator	Value	Year	Rating	Trend
Prevalence of undernourishment (%)	NA	NA	●	●
Prevalence of stunting in children under 5 years of age (%)	31.1	2012	●	→
Prevalence of wasting in children under 5 years of age (%)	11.2	2012	●	→
Prevalence of obesity, BMI ≥ 30 (% of adult population)	7.8	2016	●	↑
Human Trophic Level (best 2–3 worst)	2.1	2007	●	●
Cereal yield (tonnes per hectare of harvested land)	1.4	2018	●	→
Sustainable Nitrogen Management Index (best 0–1.41 worst)	0.9	2015	●	→
Exports of hazardous pesticides (tonnes per million population)	NA	NA	●	●

SDG3 – Good Health and Well-Being

Indicator	Value	Year	Rating	Trend
Maternal mortality rate (per 100,000 live births)	273	2017	●	→
Neonatal mortality rate (per 1,000 live births)	29.0	2020	●	↗
Mortality rate, under-5 (per 1,000 live births)	61.3	2020	●	↗
Incidence of tuberculosis (per 100,000 population)	35.0	2020	●	→
New HIV infections (per 1,000 uninfected population)	0.0	2020	●	↑
Age-standardized death rate due to cardiovascular disease, cancer, diabetes, or chronic respiratory disease in adults aged 30–70 years (%)	20.6	2019	●	→
Age-standardized death rate attributable to household air pollution and ambient air pollution (per 100,000 population)	172	2016	●	●
Traffic deaths (per 100,000 population)	26.6	2019	●	→
Life expectancy at birth (years)	67.4	2019	●	→
Adolescent fertility rate (births per 1,000 females aged 15 to 19)	70.3	2011	●	●
Births attended by skilled health personnel (%)	82.2	2012	●	●
Surviving infants who received 2 WHO-recommended vaccines (%)	87	2020	●	↓
Universal health coverage (UHC) index of service coverage (worst 0–100 best)	44	2019	●	→
Subjective well-being (average ladder score, worst 0–10 best)	4.6	2019	●	●

SDG4 – Quality Education

Indicator	Value	Year	Rating	Trend
Participation rate in pre-primary organized learning (% of children aged 4 to 6)	29.9	2018	●	●
Net primary enrollment rate (%)	81.8	2018	●	●
Lower secondary completion rate (%)	43.7	2017	●	●
Literacy rate (% of population aged 15 to 24)	78.3	2018	●	●

SDG5 – Gender Equality

Indicator	Value	Year	Rating	Trend
Demand for family planning satisfied by modern methods (% of females aged 15 to 49)	28.8	2012	●	→
Ratio of female-to-male mean years of education received (%)	66.7	2019	●	→
Ratio of female-to-male labor force participation rate (%)	58.7	2020	●	→
Seats held by women in national parliament (%)	16.7	2020	●	↑

SDG6 – Clean Water and Sanitation

Indicator	Value	Year	Rating	Trend
Population using at least basic drinking water services (%)	80.2	2019	●	→
Population using at least basic sanitation services (%)	35.9	2019	●	→
Freshwater withdrawal (% of available freshwater resources)	0.8	2018	●	●
Anthropogenic wastewater that receives treatment (%)	0.1	2018	●	●
Scarce water consumption embodied in imports (m³ H_2O eq/capita)	NA	NA	●	●

SDG7 – Affordable and Clean Energy

Indicator	Value	Year	Rating	Trend
Population with access to electricity (%)	84.0	2019	●	↑
Population with access to clean fuels and technology for cooking (%)	7.5	2019	●	→
CO_2 emissions from fuel combustion per total electricity output ($MtCO_2$/TWh)	2.1	2019	●	↑
Share of renewable energy in total primary energy supply (%)	NA	NA	●	●

SDG8 – Decent Work and Economic Growth

Indicator	Value	Year	Rating	Trend
Adjusted GDP growth (%)	-5.1	2020	●	●
Victims of modern slavery (per 1,000 population)	NA	NA	●	●
Adults with an account at a bank or other financial institution or with a mobile-money-service provider (% of population aged 15 or over)	21.7	2011	●	●
Unemployment rate (% of total labor force)	9.1	2022	●	↓
Fundamental labor rights are effectively guaranteed (worst 0–1 best)	NA	NA	●	●
Fatal work-related accidents embodied in imports (per 100,000 population)	NA	NA	●	●

* Imputed data point

SDG9 – Industry, Innovation and Infrastructure

Indicator		Value	Year	Rating	Trend
Population using the internet (%)		8.5	2017	●	●
Mobile broadband subscriptions (per 100 population)		60.0	2018	●	●
Logistics Performance Index: Quality of trade and transport-related infrastructure (worst 1–5 best)		2.3	2018	●	↓
The Times Higher Education Universities Ranking: Average score of top 3 universities (worst 0–100 best)	*	0.0	2022	●	●
Articles published in academic journals (per 1,000 population)		0.0	2020	●	→
Expenditure on research and development (% of GDP)		NA	NA	●	●

SDG10 – Reduced Inequalities

Indicator	Value	Year	Rating	Trend
Gini coefficient	45.3	2014	●	●
Palma ratio	2.5	2018	●	●

SDG11 – Sustainable Cities and Communities

Indicator	Value	Year	Rating	Trend
Proportion of urban population living in slums (%)	69.6	2018	●	→
Annual mean concentration of particulate matter of less than 2.5 microns in diameter (PM2.5) (μg/m³)	20.4	2019	●	→
Access to improved water source, piped (% of urban population)	76.1	2019	●	→
Satisfaction with public transport (%)	54.0	2019	●	●

SDG12 – Responsible Consumption and Production

Indicator	Value	Year	Rating	Trend
Municipal solid waste (kg/capita/day)	0.3	2015	●	●
Electronic waste (kg/capita)	0.7	2019	●	●
Production-based SO_2 emissions (kg/capita)	NA	NA	●	●
SO_2 emissions embodied in imports (kg/capita)	NA	NA	●	●
Production-based nitrogen emissions (kg/capita)	NA	NA	●	●
Nitrogen emissions embodied in imports (kg/capita)	NA	NA	●	●
Exports of plastic waste (kg/capita)	NA	NA	●	●

SDG13 – Climate Action

Indicator	Value	Year	Rating	Trend
CO_2 emissions from fossil fuel combustion and cement production (tCO_2/capita)	0.3	2020	●	↑
CO_2 emissions embodied in imports (tCO_2/capita)	NA	NA	●	●
CO_2 emissions embodied in fossil fuel exports (kg/capita)	0.0	2018	●	●

SDG14 – Life Below Water

Indicator	Value	Year	Rating	Trend
Mean area that is protected in marine sites important to biodiversity (%)	13.0	2020	●	→
Ocean Health Index: Clean Waters score (worst 0–100 best)	38.6	2020	●	↓
Fish caught from overexploited or collapsed stocks (% of total catch)	6.6	2018	●	↑
Fish caught by trawling or dredging (%)	0.0	2018	●	↑
Fish caught that are then discarded (%)	34.9	2018	●	↓
Marine biodiversity threats embodied in imports (per million population)	NA	NA	●	●

SDG15 – Life on Land

Indicator	Value	Year	Rating	Trend
Mean area that is protected in terrestrial sites important to biodiversity (%)	55.1	2020	●	→
Mean area that is protected in freshwater sites important to biodiversity (%)	100.0	2020	●	↑
Red List Index of species survival (worst 0–1 best)	0.7	2021	●	↓
Permanent deforestation (% of forest area, 5-year average)	0.1	2020	●	↑
Terrestrial and freshwater biodiversity threats embodied in imports (per million population)	NA	NA	●	●

SDG16 – Peace, Justice and Strong Institutions

Indicator		Value	Year	Rating	Trend
Homicides (per 100,000 population)		NA	NA	●	●
Unsentenced detainees (% of prison population)		NA	NA	●	●
Population who feel safe walking alone at night in the city or area where they live (%)		67	2019	●	●
Property Rights (worst 1–7 best)		NA	NA	●	●
Birth registrations with civil authority (% of children under age 5)		87.3	2020	●	●
Corruption Perception Index (worst 0–100 best)		20	2021	●	↓
Children involved in child labor (% of population aged 5 to 14)		28.5	2019	●	●
Exports of major conventional weapons (TIV constant million USD per 100,000 population)	*	0.0	2020	●	●
Press Freedom Index (best 0–100 worst)		30.7	2021	●	↓
Access to and affordability of justice (worst 0–1 best)		NA	NA	●	●

SDG17 – Partnerships for the Goals

Indicator		Value	Year	Rating	Trend
Government spending on health and education (% of GDP)		3.4	2019	●	→
For high-income and all OECD DAC countries: International concessional public finance, including official development assistance (% of GNI)		NA	NA	●	●
Other countries: Government revenue excluding grants (% of GDP)		NA	NA	●	●
Corporate Tax Haven Score (best 0–100 worst)	*	0.0	2019	●	●
Statistical Performance Index (worst 0–100 best)		NA	NA	●	●

5. Country Profiles

CONGO, DEMOCRATIC REPUBLIC OF Sub-Saharan Africa

OVERALL PERFORMANCE

COUNTRY RANKING

CONGO, DEMOCRATIC REPUBLIC OF

157/163

COUNTRY SCORE

AVERAGE PERFORMANCE BY SDG

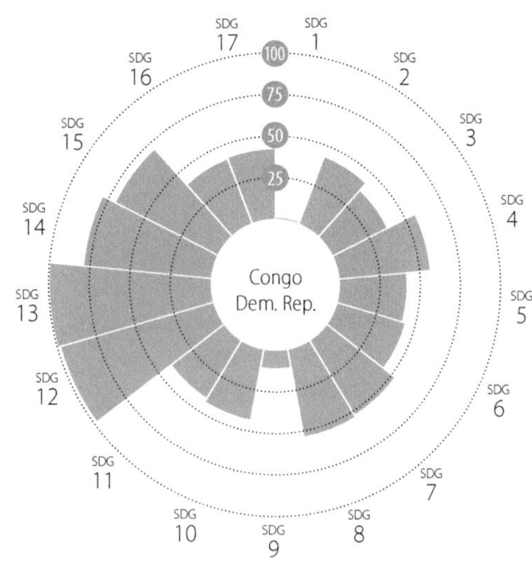

SDG DASHBOARDS AND TRENDS

Major challenges | Significant challenges | Challenges remain | SDG achieved | Information unavailable

Decreasing | Stagnating | Moderately improving | On track or maintaining SDG achievement | Information unavailable

Note: The full title of each SDG is available here: https://sustainabledevelopment.un.org/topics/sustainabledevelopmentgoals

INTERNATIONAL SPILLOVER INDEX

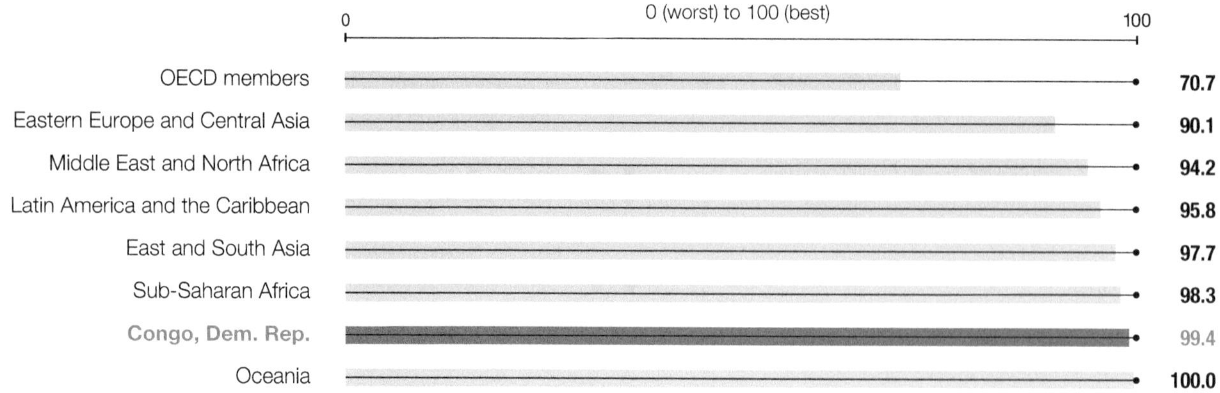

STATISTICAL PERFORMANCE INDEX

0 (worst) to 100 (best)

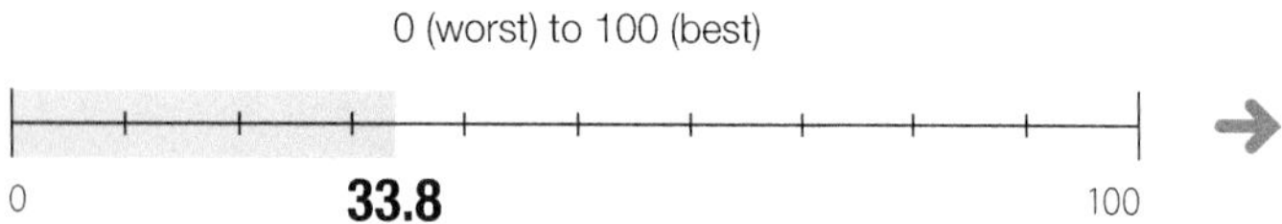

MISSING DATA IN SDG INDEX

10%

CONGO, DEMOCRATIC REPUBLIC OF

Performance by Indicator

SDG1 – No Poverty		Value	Year	Rating	Trend
Poverty headcount ratio at $1.90/day (%)		71.7	2022	●	→
Poverty headcount ratio at $3.20/day (%)		90.5	2022	●	→
SDG2 – Zero Hunger					
Prevalence of undernourishment (%)		41.7	2019	●	↓
Prevalence of stunting in children under 5 years of age (%)		41.8	2017	●	→
Prevalence of wasting in children under 5 years of age (%)		6.4	2017	●	→
Prevalence of obesity, BMI ≥ 30 (% of adult population)		6.7	2016	●	↑
Human Trophic Level (best 2–3 worst)		2.0	2007	●	●
Cereal yield (tonnes per hectare of harvested land)		0.8	2018	●	→
Sustainable Nitrogen Management Index (best 0–1.41 worst)		0.9	2015	●	↓
Exports of hazardous pesticides (tonnes per million population)		NA	NA	●	●
SDG3 – Good Health and Well-Being					
Maternal mortality rate (per 100,000 live births)		473	2017	●	→
Neonatal mortality rate (per 1,000 live births)		26.8	2020	●	→
Mortality rate, under-5 (per 1,000 live births)		81.2	2020	●	↗
Incidence of tuberculosis (per 100,000 population)		319.0	2020	●	→
New HIV infections (per 1,000 uninfected population)		0.2	2020	●	↑
Age-standardized death rate due to cardiovascular disease, cancer, diabetes, or chronic respiratory disease in adults aged 30–70 years (%)		24.1	2019	●	→
Age-standardized death rate attributable to household air pollution and ambient air pollution (per 100,000 population)		164	2016	●	●
Traffic deaths (per 100,000 population)		34.9	2019	●	↓
Life expectancy at birth (years)		62.4	2019	●	→
Adolescent fertility rate (births per 1,000 females aged 15 to 19)		109.0	2016	●	●
Births attended by skilled health personnel (%)		80.1	2014	●	●
Surviving infants who received 2 WHO-recommended vaccines (%)		57	2020	●	↓
Universal health coverage (UHC) index of service coverage (worst 0–100 best)		39	2019	●	→
Subjective well-being (average ladder score, worst 0–10 best)		4.3	2017	●	●
SDG4 – Quality Education					
Participation rate in pre-primary organized learning (% of children aged 4 to 6)		NA	NA	●	●
Net primary enrollment rate (%)		NA	NA	●	●
Lower secondary completion rate (%)		50.4	2014	●	●
Literacy rate (% of population aged 15 to 24)		85.0	2016	●	●
SDG5 – Gender Equality					
Demand for family planning satisfied by modern methods (% of females aged 15 to 49)		33.0	2018	●	→
Ratio of female-to-male mean years of education received (%)		63.1	2019	●	↗
Ratio of female-to-male labor force participation rate (%)		88.4	2020	●	↑
Seats held by women in national parliament (%)		12.8	2020	●	→
SDG6 – Clean Water and Sanitation					
Population using at least basic drinking water services (%)		46.0	2020	●	→
Population using at least basic sanitation services (%)		15.4	2020	●	↓
Freshwater withdrawal (% of available freshwater resources)		0.2	2018	●	●
Anthropogenic wastewater that receives treatment (%)		0.0	2018	●	●
Scarce water consumption embodied in imports (m^3 H_2O eq/capita)		132.7	2018	●	●
SDG7 – Affordable and Clean Energy					
Population with access to electricity (%)		19.1	2019	●	→
Population with access to clean fuels and technology for cooking (%)		4.5	2019	●	→
CO_2 emissions from fuel combustion per total electricity output ($MtCO_2$/TWh)		0.3	2019	●	↑
Share of renewable energy in total primary energy supply (%)		97.5	2019	●	↑
SDG8 – Decent Work and Economic Growth					
Adjusted GDP growth (%)		-5.4	2020	●	●
Victims of modern slavery (per 1,000 population)		13.7	2018	●	●
Adults with an account at a bank or other financial institution or with a mobile-money-service provider (% of population aged 15 or over)		25.8	2017	●	↗
Unemployment rate (% of total labor force)		5.4	2022	●	↓
Fundamental labor rights are effectively guaranteed (worst 0–1 best)		0.5	2020	●	●
Fatal work-related accidents embodied in imports (per 100,000 population)		0.0	2015	●	↑

SDG9 – Industry, Innovation and Infrastructure		Value	Year	Rating	Trend
Population using the internet (%)		13.6	2020	●	→
Mobile broadband subscriptions (per 100 population)		19.5	2019	●	↗
Logistics Performance Index: Quality of trade and transport-related infrastructure (worst 1–5 best)		2.1	2018	●	↗
The Times Higher Education Universities Ranking: Average score of top 3 universities (worst 0–100 best)	*	0.0	2022	●	●
Articles published in academic journals (per 1,000 population)		0.0	2020	●	→
Expenditure on research and development (% of GDP)		0.4	2015	●	●
SDG10 – Reduced Inequalities					
Gini coefficient		42.1	2012	●	●
Palma ratio		2.1	2018	●	●
SDG11 – Sustainable Cities and Communities					
Proportion of urban population living in slums (%)		80.4	2018	●	↓
Annual mean concentration of particulate matter of less than 2.5 microns in diameter (PM2.5) (μg/m^3)		42.8	2019	●	→
Access to improved water source, piped (% of urban population)		67.4	2020	●	→
Satisfaction with public transport (%)		41.0	2017	●	●
SDG12 – Responsible Consumption and Production					
Municipal solid waste (kg/capita/day)		0.5	2016	●	●
Electronic waste (kg/capita)		NA	NA	●	●
Production-based SO_2 emissions (kg/capita)		0.6	2018	●	●
SO_2 emissions embodied in imports (kg/capita)		0.2	2018	●	●
Production-based nitrogen emissions (kg/capita)		1.7	2015	●	↑
Nitrogen emissions embodied in imports (kg/capita)		0.3	2015	●	↑
Exports of plastic waste (kg/capita)		0.0	2020	●	●
SDG13 – Climate Action					
CO_2 emissions from fossil fuel combustion and cement production (tCO_2/capita)		0.0	2020	●	↑
CO_2 emissions embodied in imports (tCO_2/capita)		0.1	2018	●	↑
CO_2 emissions embodied in fossil fuel exports (kg/capita)		0.0	2020	●	●
SDG14 – Life Below Water					
Mean area that is protected in marine sites important to biodiversity (%)		NA	NA	●	●
Ocean Health Index: Clean Waters score (worst 0–100 best)		39.7	2020	●	↓
Fish caught from overexploited or collapsed stocks (% of total catch)		NA	NA	●	●
Fish caught by trawling or dredging (%)		0.0	2018	●	↑
Fish caught that are then discarded (%)		0.0	2018	●	↑
Marine biodiversity threats embodied in imports (per million population)		0.0	2018	●	●
SDG15 – Life on Land					
Mean area that is protected in terrestrial sites important to biodiversity (%)		52.7	2020	●	→
Mean area that is protected in freshwater sites important to biodiversity (%)		52.5	2020	●	→
Red List Index of species survival (worst 0–1 best)		0.9	2021	●	→
Permanent deforestation (% of forest area, 5-year average)		0.3	2020	●	↓
Terrestrial and freshwater biodiversity threats embodied in imports (per million population)		0.2	2018	●	●
SDG16 – Peace, Justice and Strong Institutions					
Homicides (per 100,000 population)		NA	NA	●	●
Unsentenced detainees (% of prison population)		NA	NA	●	●
Population who feel safe walking alone at night in the city or area where they live (%)		45	2017	●	●
Property Rights (worst 1–7 best)		3.2	2020	●	↓
Birth registrations with civil authority (% of children under age 5)		40.1	2020	●	●
Corruption Perception Index (worst 0–100 best)		19	2021	●	↓
Children involved in child labor (% of population aged 5 to 14)		14.7	2019	●	●
Exports of major conventional weapons (TIV constant million USD per 100,000 population)	*	0.0	2020	●	●
Press Freedom Index (best 0–100 worst)		48.6	2021	●	→
Access to and affordability of justice (worst 0–1 best)		0.4	2020	●	●
SDG17 – Partnerships for the Goals					
Government spending on health and education (% of GDP)		2.0	2019	●	↓
For high-income and all OECD DAC countries: International concessional public finance, including official development assistance (% of GNI)		NA	NA	●	●
Other countries: Government revenue excluding grants (% of GDP)		NA	NA	●	●
Corporate Tax Haven Score (best 0–100 worst)	*	0.0	2019	●	●
Statistical Performance Index (worst 0–100 best)		33.8	2019	●	→

* Imputed data point

CONGO, REPUBLIC OF

Sub-Saharan Africa

OVERALL PERFORMANCE

COUNTRY RANKING

CONGO, REPUBLIC OF

148/163

COUNTRY SCORE

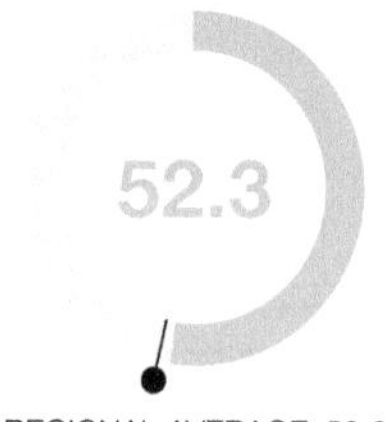

REGIONAL AVERAGE: 53.6

AVERAGE PERFORMANCE BY SDG

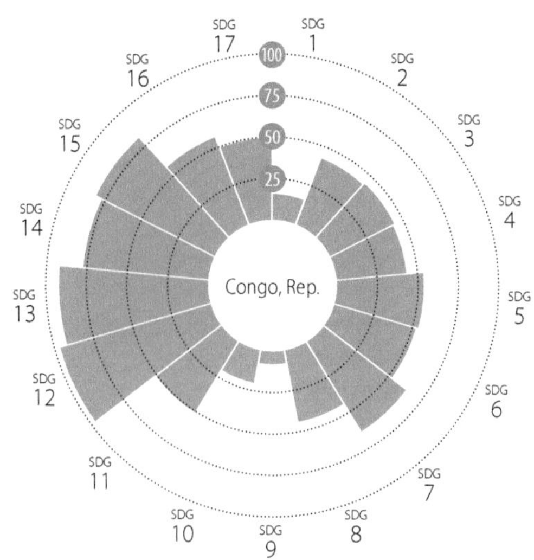

SDG DASHBOARDS AND TRENDS

Major challenges | Significant challenges | Challenges remain | SDG achieved | Information unavailable

Decreasing | Stagnating | Moderately improving | On track or maintaining SDG achievement | Information unavailable

Note: The full title of each SDG is available here: https://sustainabledevelopment.un.org/topics/sustainabledevelopmentgoals

INTERNATIONAL SPILLOVER INDEX

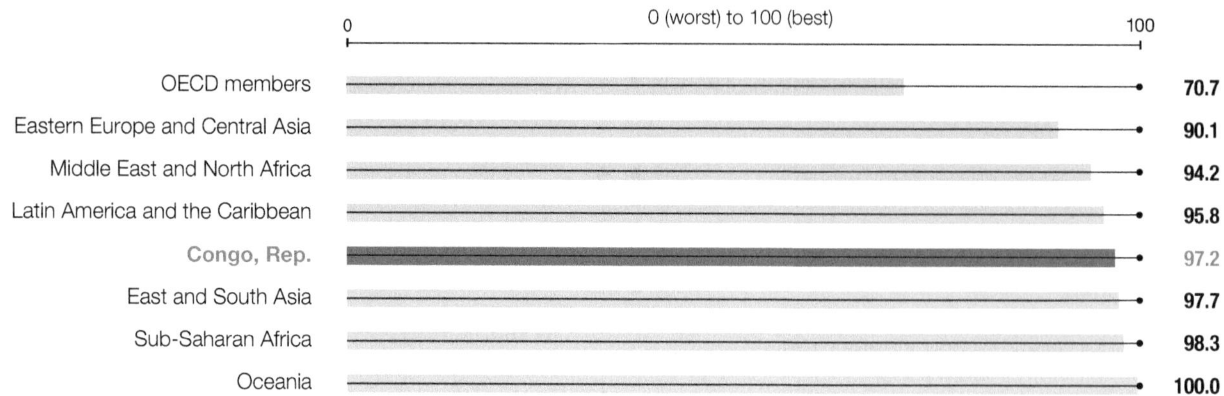

STATISTICAL PERFORMANCE INDEX

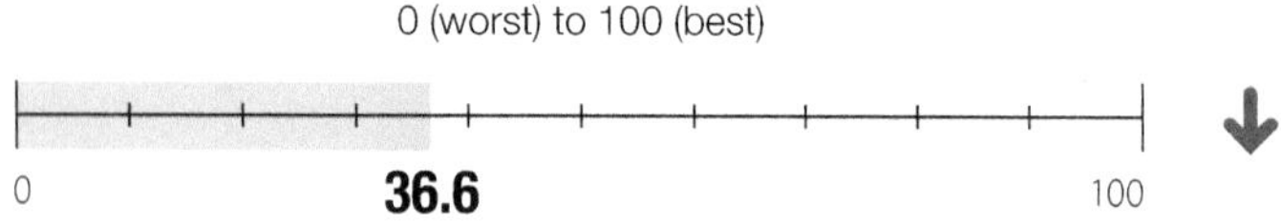

MISSING DATA IN SDG INDEX

7%

CONGO, REPUBLIC OF

Performance by Indicator

SDG1 – No Poverty

Indicator	Value	Year	Rating	Trend
Poverty headcount ratio at $1.90/day (%)	49.8	2022	●	↓
Poverty headcount ratio at $3.20/day (%)	72.6	2022	●	↓

SDG2 – Zero Hunger

Indicator	Value	Year	Rating	Trend
Prevalence of undernourishment (%)	37.7	2019	●	↓
Prevalence of stunting in children under 5 years of age (%)	21.2	2014	●	→
Prevalence of wasting in children under 5 years of age (%)	8.2	2014	●	↗
Prevalence of obesity, BMI ≥ 30 (% of adult population)	9.6	2016	●	↑
Human Trophic Level (best 2–3 worst)	2.2	2017	●	↑
Cereal yield (tonnes per hectare of harvested land)	0.8	2018	●	→
Sustainable Nitrogen Management Index (best 0–1.41 worst)	0.9	2015	●	↓
Exports of hazardous pesticides (tonnes per million population)	NA	NA	●	●

SDG3 – Good Health and Well-Being

Indicator	Value	Year	Rating	Trend
Maternal mortality rate (per 100,000 live births)	378	2017	●	↗
Neonatal mortality rate (per 1,000 live births)	18.7	2020	●	↗
Mortality rate, under-5 (per 1,000 live births)	44.6	2020	●	↗
Incidence of tuberculosis (per 100,000 population)	379.0	2020	●	→
New HIV infections (per 1,000 uninfected population)	1.9	2020	●	→
Age-standardized death rate due to cardiovascular disease, cancer, diabetes, or chronic respiratory disease in adults aged 30–70 years (%)	22.6	2019	●	↗
Age-standardized death rate attributable to household air pollution and ambient air pollution (per 100,000 population)	131	2016	●	●
Traffic deaths (per 100,000 population)	29.7	2019	●	↓
Life expectancy at birth (years)	64.7	2019	●	→
Adolescent fertility rate (births per 1,000 females aged 15 to 19)	111.3	2013	●	●
Births attended by skilled health personnel (%)	91.2	2015	●	●
Surviving infants who received 2 WHO-recommended vaccines (%)	68	2020	●	↓
Universal health coverage (UHC) index of service coverage (worst 0–100 best)	40	2019	●	→
Subjective well-being (average ladder score, worst 0–10 best)	4.9	2021	●	→

SDG4 – Quality Education

Indicator	Value	Year	Rating	Trend
Participation rate in pre-primary organized learning (% of children aged 4 to 6)	29.5	2018	●	●
Net primary enrollment rate (%)	84.4	2018	●	●
Lower secondary completion rate (%)	50.1	2012	●	●
Literacy rate (% of population aged 15 to 24)	82.1	2018	●	●

SDG5 – Gender Equality

Indicator	Value	Year	Rating	Trend
Demand for family planning satisfied by modern methods (% of females aged 15 to 49)	43.2	2015	●	↗
Ratio of female-to-male mean years of education received (%)	81.3	2019	●	↓
Ratio of female-to-male labor force participation rate (%)	95.3	2020	●	↑
Seats held by women in national parliament (%)	11.3	2020	●	→

SDG6 – Clean Water and Sanitation

Indicator	Value	Year	Rating	Trend
Population using at least basic drinking water services (%)	73.8	2020	●	→
Population using at least basic sanitation services (%)	20.5	2020	●	→
Freshwater withdrawal (% of available freshwater resources)	0.0	2018	●	●
Anthropogenic wastewater that receives treatment (%)	0.3	2018	●	●
Scarce water consumption embodied in imports (m^3 H_2O eq/capita)	1000.5	2018	●	●

SDG7 – Affordable and Clean Energy

Indicator	Value	Year	Rating	Trend
Population with access to electricity (%)	48.3	2019	●	→
Population with access to clean fuels and technology for cooking (%)	33.5	2019	●	↗
CO_2 emissions from fuel combustion per total electricity output ($MtCO_2$/TWh)	1.3	2019	●	↑
Share of renewable energy in total primary energy supply (%)	52.3	2019	●	↑

SDG8 – Decent Work and Economic Growth

Indicator	Value	Year	Rating	Trend
Adjusted GDP growth (%)	-10.9	2020	●	●
Victims of modern slavery (per 1,000 population)	8.0	2018	●	●
Adults with an account at a bank or other financial institution or with a mobile-money-service provider (% of population aged 15 or over)	26.1	2017	●	↗
Unemployment rate (% of total labor force)	22.5	2022	●	↓
Fundamental labor rights are effectively guaranteed (worst 0–1 best)	0.6	2020	●	●
Fatal work-related accidents embodied in imports (per 100,000 population)	0.1	2015	●	↑

SDG9 – Industry, Innovation and Infrastructure

Indicator	Value	Year	Rating	Trend
Population using the internet (%)	8.7	2017	●	●
Mobile broadband subscriptions (per 100 population)	5.6	2019	●	●
Logistics Performance Index: Quality of trade and transport-related infrastructure (worst 1–5 best)	2.1	2018	●	↗
The Times Higher Education Universities Ranking: Average score of top 3 universities (worst 0–100 best)	* 0.0	2022	●	●
Articles published in academic journals (per 1,000 population)	0.1	2020	●	↓
Expenditure on research and development (% of GDP)	NA	NA	●	●

SDG10 – Reduced Inequalities

Indicator	Value	Year	Rating	Trend
Gini coefficient	48.9	2011	●	●
Palma ratio	3.1	2018	●	●

SDG11 – Sustainable Cities and Communities

Indicator	Value	Year	Rating	Trend
Proportion of urban population living in slums (%)	47.3	2018	●	↓
Annual mean concentration of particulate matter of less than 2.5 microns in diameter (PM2.5) (μg/m^3)	50.1	2019	●	↓
Access to improved water source, piped (% of urban population)	72.8	2020	●	↓
Satisfaction with public transport (%)	44.0	2021	●	↓

SDG12 – Responsible Consumption and Production

Indicator	Value	Year	Rating	Trend
Municipal solid waste (kg/capita/day)	NA	NA	●	●
Electronic waste (kg/capita)	4.0	2019	●	●
Production-based SO_2 emissions (kg/capita)	1.2	2018	●	●
SO_2 emissions embodied in imports (kg/capita)	0.7	2018	●	●
Production-based nitrogen emissions (kg/capita)	2.3	2015	●	↑
Nitrogen emissions embodied in imports (kg/capita)	1.0	2015	●	↑
Exports of plastic waste (kg/capita)	0.0	2020	●	●

SDG13 – Climate Action

Indicator	Value	Year	Rating	Trend
CO_2 emissions from fossil fuel combustion and cement production (tCO_2/capita)	0.6	2020	●	↑
CO_2 emissions embodied in imports (tCO_2/capita)	0.3	2018	●	↑
CO_2 emissions embodied in fossil fuel exports (kg/capita)	6221.5	2020	●	●

SDG14 – Life Below Water

Indicator	Value	Year	Rating	Trend
Mean area that is protected in marine sites important to biodiversity (%)	65.4	2020	●	↑
Ocean Health Index: Clean Waters score (worst 0–100 best)	49.2	2020	●	→
Fish caught from overexploited or collapsed stocks (% of total catch)	NA	NA	●	●
Fish caught by trawling or dredging (%)	3.2	2018	●	↑
Fish caught that are then discarded (%)	0.9	2018	●	↑
Marine biodiversity threats embodied in imports (per million population)	0.0	2018	●	●

SDG15 – Life on Land

Indicator	Value	Year	Rating	Trend
Mean area that is protected in terrestrial sites important to biodiversity (%)	60.9	2020	●	→
Mean area that is protected in freshwater sites important to biodiversity (%)	65.7	2020	●	↑
Red List Index of species survival (worst 0–1 best)	1.0	2021	●	↑
Permanent deforestation (% of forest area, 5-year average)	0.1	2020	●	↑
Terrestrial and freshwater biodiversity threats embodied in imports (per million population)	0.3	2018	●	●

SDG16 – Peace, Justice and Strong Institutions

Indicator	Value	Year	Rating	Trend
Homicides (per 100,000 population)	NA	NA	●	●
Unsentenced detainees (% of prison population)	NA	NA	●	●
Population who feel safe walking alone at night in the city or area where they live (%)	40	2021	●	↓
Property Rights (worst 1–7 best)	NA	NA	●	●
Birth registrations with civil authority (% of children under age 5)	95.9	2020	●	●
Corruption Perception Index (worst 0–100 best)	21	2021	●	↓
Children involved in child labor (% of population aged 5 to 14)	14.1	2019	●	●
Exports of major conventional weapons (TIV constant million USD per 100,000 population)	* 0.0	2020	●	●
Press Freedom Index (best 0–100 worst)	38.8	2021	●	↓
Access to and affordability of justice (worst 0–1 best)	0.5	2020	●	●

SDG17 – Partnerships for the Goals

Indicator	Value	Year	Rating	Trend
Government spending on health and education (% of GDP)	4.7	2019	●	→
For high-income and all OECD DAC countries: International concessional public finance, including official development assistance (% of GNI)	NA	NA	●	●
Other countries: Government revenue excluding grants (% of GDP)	25.5	2018	●	↑
Corporate Tax Haven Score (best 0–100 worst)	* 0.0	2019	●	●
Statistical Performance Index (worst 0–100 best)	36.6	2019	●	↓

* Imputed data point

COSTA RICA

Latin America and the Caribbean

OVERALL PERFORMANCE

COUNTRY RANKING

COSTA RICA

47 /163

COUNTRY SCORE

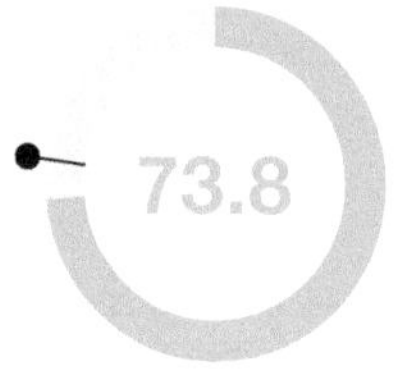

REGIONAL AVERAGE: 77.2

AVERAGE PERFORMANCE BY SDG

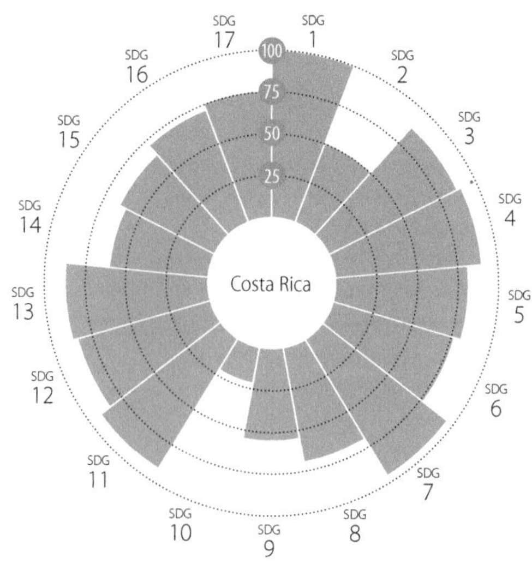

SDG DASHBOARDS AND TRENDS

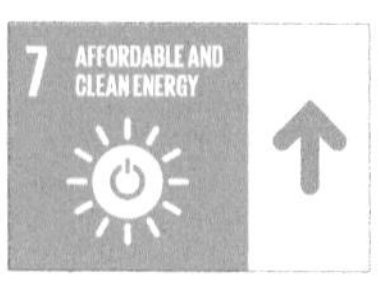

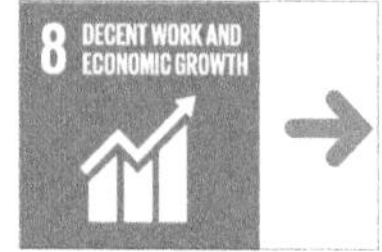

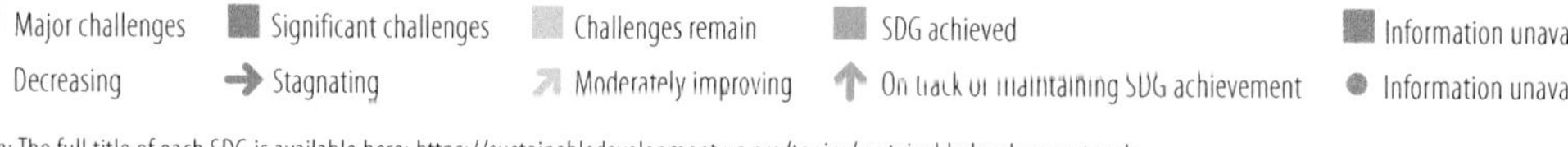

Note: The full title of each SDG is available here: https://sustainabledevelopment.un.org/topics/sustainabledevelopmentgoals

INTERNATIONAL SPILLOVER INDEX

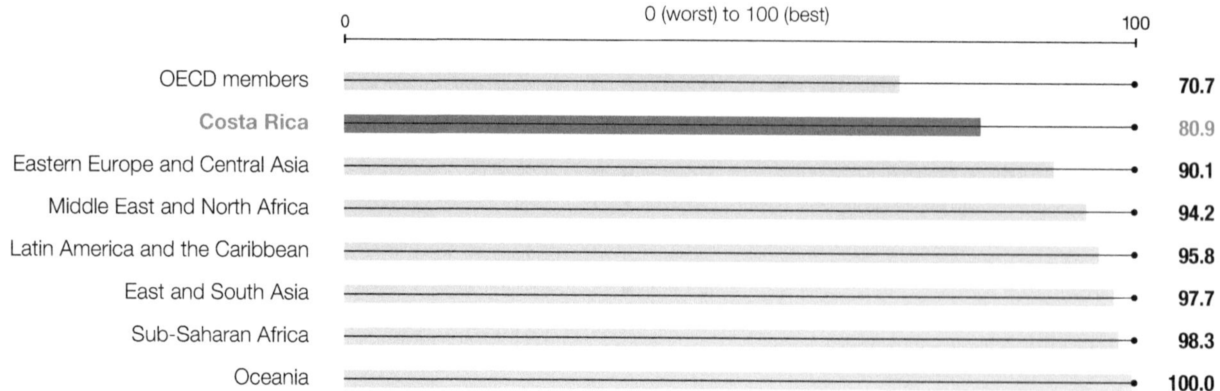

STATISTICAL PERFORMANCE INDEX

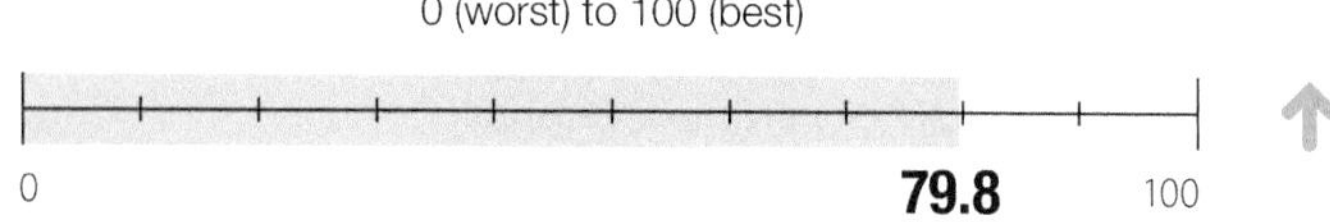

MISSING DATA IN SDG INDEX

COSTA RICA

Performance by Indicator

SDG1 – No Poverty	Value	Year	Rating	Trend
Poverty headcount ratio at \$1.90/day (%)	0.2	2022	●	↑
Poverty headcount ratio at \$3.20/day (%)	0.3	2022	●	↑
Poverty rate after taxes and transfers (%)	20.5	2020	●	→

SDG2 – Zero Hunger	Value	Year	Rating	Trend
Prevalence of undernourishment (%)	3.1	2019	●	↑
Prevalence of stunting in children under 5 years of age (%)	9.0	2018	●	↑
Prevalence of wasting in children under 5 years of age (%)	1.8	2018	●	↑
Prevalence of obesity, BMI ≥ 30 (% of adult population)	25.7	2016	●	↓
Human Trophic Level (best 2–3 worst)	2.4	2017	●	→
Cereal yield (tonnes per hectare of harvested land)	4.3	2018	●	↑
Sustainable Nitrogen Management Index (best 0–1.41 worst)	1.1	2015	●	↓
Yield gap closure (% of potential yield)	NA	NA	●	●
Exports of hazardous pesticides (tonnes per million population)	190.8	2019	●	●

SDG3 – Good Health and Well-Being	Value	Year	Rating	Trend
Maternal mortality rate (per 100,000 live births)	27	2017	●	↑
Neonatal mortality rate (per 1,000 live births)	5.6	2020	●	↑
Mortality rate, under-5 (per 1,000 live births)	7.9	2020	●	↑
Incidence of tuberculosis (per 100,000 population)	10.0	2020	●	↑
New HIV infections (per 1,000 uninfected population)	0.3	2020	●	↓
Age-standardized death rate due to cardiovascular disease, cancer, diabetes, or chronic respiratory disease in adults aged 30–70 years (%)	9.5	2019	●	↑
Age-standardized death rate attributable to household air pollution and ambient air pollution (per 100,000 population)	23	2016	●	●
Traffic deaths (per 100,000 population)	14.8	2019	●	↗
Life expectancy at birth (years)	80.9	2019	●	↑
Adolescent fertility rate (births per 1,000 females aged 15 to 19)	40.9	2019	●	↑
Births attended by skilled health personnel (%)	99.0	2018	●	↑
Surviving infants who received 2 WHO-recommended vaccines (%)	95	2020	●	↑
Universal health coverage (UHC) index of service coverage (worst 0–100 best)	78	2019	●	↑
Subjective well-being (average ladder score, worst 0–10 best)	6.4	2021	●	↑
Gap in life expectancy at birth among regions (years)	2.0	2019	●	↑
Gap in self-reported health status by income (percentage points)	NA	NA	●	●
Daily smokers (% of population aged 15 and over)	4.2	2018	●	↑

SDG4 – Quality Education	Value	Year	Rating	Trend
Participation rate in pre-primary organized learning (% of children aged 4 to 6)	98.5	2020	●	↑
Net primary enrollment rate (%)	99.9	2020	●	↑
Lower secondary completion rate (%)	69.2	2020	●	↗
Literacy rate (% of population aged 15 to 24)	99.4	2018	●	●
Tertiary educational attainment (% of population aged 25 to 34)	32.5	2020	●	●
PISA score (worst 0–600 best)	414.7	2018	●	↓
Variation in science performance explained by socio-economic status (%)	17.7	2018	●	↓
Underachievers in science (% of 15-year-olds)	47.8	2018	●	↓

SDG5 – Gender Equality	Value	Year	Rating	Trend
Demand for family planning satisfied by modern methods (% of females aged 15 to 49)	80.8	2018	●	↑
Ratio of female-to-male mean years of education received (%)	103.5	2019	●	↑
Ratio of female-to-male labor force participation rate (%)	65.4	2020	●	↗
Seats held by women in national parliament (%)	45.6	2020	●	↑
Gender wage gap (% of male median wage)	4.7	2018	●	↑

SDG6 – Clean Water and Sanitation	Value	Year	Rating	Trend
Population using at least basic drinking water services (%)	99.8	2020	●	↑
Population using at least basic sanitation services (%)	97.9	2020	●	↑
Freshwater withdrawal (% of available freshwater resources)	4.1	2018	●	●
Anthropogenic wastewater that receives treatment (%)	9.7	2018	●	●
Scarce water consumption embodied in imports (m^3 H_2O eq/capita)	2786.1	2018	●	●
Population using safely managed water services (%)	80.5	2020	●	→
Population using safely managed sanitation services (%)	30.2	2020	●	↓

SDG7 – Affordable and Clean Energy	Value	Year	Rating	Trend
Population with access to electricity (%)	99.7	2019	●	↑
Population with access to clean fuels and technology for cooking (%)	95.5	2019	●	↑
CO_2 emissions from fuel combustion per total electricity output ($MtCO_2$/TWh)	0.8	2019	●	↑
Share of renewable energy in total primary energy supply (%)	50.5	2019	●	↑

SDG8 – Decent Work and Economic Growth	Value	Year	Rating	Trend
Adjusted GDP growth (%)	-0.7	2020	●	●
Victims of modern slavery (per 1,000 population)	1.3	2018	●	●
Adults with an account at a bank or other financial institution or with a mobile-money-service provider (% of population aged 15 or over)	67.8	2017	●	↑
Fundamental labor rights are effectively guaranteed (worst 0–1 best)	0.6	2020	●	↓
Fatal work-related accidents embodied in imports (per 100,000 population)	0.5	2015	●	↑
Employment-to-population ratio (%)	57.2	2021	●	↓
Youth not in employment, education or training (NEET) (% of population aged 15 to 29)	18.8	2020	●	→

* Imputed data point

SDG9 – Industry, Innovation and Infrastructure	Value	Year	Rating	Trend
Population using the internet (%)	80.5	2020	●	↑
Mobile broadband subscriptions (per 100 population)	92.4	2019	●	↑
Logistics Performance Index: Quality of trade and transport-related infrastructure (worst 1–5 best)	2.5	2018	●	→
The Times Higher Education Universities Ranking: Average score of top 3 universities (worst 0–100 best)	39.5	2022	●	●
Articles published in academic journals (per 1,000 population)	0.3	2020	●	↗
Expenditure on research and development (% of GDP)	0.4	2018	●	↓
Researchers (per 1,000 employed population)	NA	NA	●	●
Triadic patent families filed (per million population)	0.0	2019	●	→
Gap in internet access by income (percentage points)	18.3	2020	●	●
Female share of graduates from STEM fields at the tertiary level (%)	32.2	2018	●	↑

SDG10 – Reduced Inequalities	Value	Year	Rating	Trend
Gini coefficient	48.2	2019	●	→
Palma ratio	3.1	2020	●	↓
Elderly poverty rate (% of population aged 66 or over)	17.0	2020	●	↑

SDG11 – Sustainable Cities and Communities	Value	Year	Rating	Trend
Proportion of urban population living in slums (%)	3.6	2018	●	↑
Annual mean concentration of particulate matter of less than 2.5 microns in diameter (PM2.5) (μg/m^3)	14.8	2019	●	↑
Access to improved water source, piped (% of urban population)	100.0	2020	●	↑
Satisfaction with public transport (%)	69.0	2021	●	↓
Population with rent overburden (%)	NA	NA	●	●

SDG12 – Responsible Consumption and Production	Value	Year	Rating	Trend
Electronic waste (kg/capita)	10.0	2019	●	●
Production-based SO_2 emissions (kg/capita)	4.7	2018	●	●
SO_2 emissions embodied in imports (kg/capita)	3.1	2018	●	●
Production-based nitrogen emissions (kg/capita)	13.1	2015	●	↑
Nitrogen emissions embodied in imports (kg/capita)	4.3	2015	●	↑
Exports of plastic waste (kg/capita)	2.4	2020	●	●
Non-recycled municipal solid waste (kg/capita/day)	0.7	2019	●	↑

SDG13 – Climate Action	Value	Year	Rating	Trend
CO_2 emissions from fossil fuel combustion and cement production (tCO_2/capita)	1.6	2020	●	↑
CO_2 emissions embodied in imports (tCO_2/capita)	1.0	2018	●	→
CO_2 emissions embodied in fossil fuel exports (kg/capita)	0.0	2020	●	●
Carbon Pricing Score at EUR60/tCO_2 (%, worst 0–100 best)	NA	NA	●	●

SDG14 – Life Below Water	Value	Year	Rating	Trend
Mean area that is protected in marine sites important to biodiversity (%)	48.7	2020	●	→
Ocean Health Index: Clean Waters score (worst 0–100 best)	72.8	2020	●	↗
Fish caught from overexploited or collapsed stocks (% of total catch)	36.6	2018	●	↓
Fish caught by trawling or dredging (%)	0.0	2018	●	↑
Fish caught that are then discarded (%)	45.8	2018	●	↗
Marine biodiversity threats embodied in imports (per million population)	0.2	2018	●	●

SDG15 – Life on Land	Value	Year	Rating	Trend
Mean area that is protected in terrestrial sites important to biodiversity (%)	41.1	2020	●	→
Mean area that is protected in freshwater sites important to biodiversity (%)	50.0	2020	●	→
Red List Index of species survival (worst 0–1 best)	0.8	2021	●	↓
Permanent deforestation (% of forest area, 5-year average)	0.1	2020	●	↑
Terrestrial and freshwater biodiversity threats embodied in imports (per million population)	1.6	2018	●	●

SDG16 – Peace, Justice and Strong Institutions	Value	Year	Rating	Trend
Homicides (per 100,000 population)	11.2	2020	●	→
Unsentenced detainees (% of prison population)	76.4	2019	●	↓
Population who feel safe walking alone at night in the city or area where they live (%)	53	2021	●	↗
Property Rights (worst 1–7 best)	5.1	2020	●	↑
Birth registrations with civil authority (% of children under age 5)	99.6	2020	●	●
Corruption Perception Index (worst 0–100 best)	58	2021	●	↑
Children involved in child labor (% of population aged 5 to 14)	3.8	2019	●	●
Exports of major conventional weapons (TIV constant million USD per 100,000 population)	0.0	2020	●	●
Press Freedom Index (best 0–100 worst)	8.8	2021	●	↑
Access to and affordability of justice (worst 0–1 best)	0.7	2020	●	↑
Persons held in prison (per 100,000 population)	63.2	2019	●	↑

SDG17 – Partnerships for the Goals	Value	Year	Rating	Trend
Government spending on health and education (% of GDP)	12.0	2020	●	↑
For high-income and all OECD DAC countries: International concessional public finance, including official development assistance (% of GNI)	NA	NA	●	●
Other countries: Government revenue excluding grants (% of GDP)	24.3	2019	●	→
Corporate Tax Haven Score (best 0–100 worst)	* 0.0	2019	●	●
Financial Secrecy Score (best 0–100 worst)	62.3	2020	●	●
Shifted profits of multinationals (US\$ billion)	1.7	2018	●	↑
Statistical Performance Index (worst 0–100 best)	79.8	2019	●	↑

5. Country Profiles

CÔTE D'IVOIRE

Sub-Saharan Africa

OVERALL PERFORMANCE

COUNTRY RANKING

CÔTE D'IVOIRE

127/163

COUNTRY SCORE

AVERAGE PERFORMANCE BY SDG

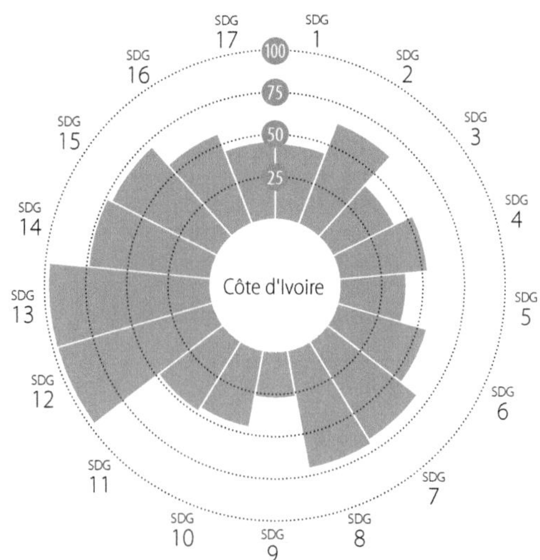

SDG DASHBOARDS AND TRENDS

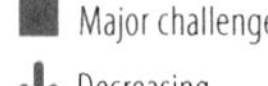

Major challenges · Significant challenges · Challenges remain · SDG achieved · Information unavailable

Decreasing · Stagnating · Moderately improving · On track or maintaining SDG achievement · Information unavailable

Note: The full title of each SDG is available here: https://sustainabledevelopment.un.org/topics/sustainabledevelopmentgoals

INTERNATIONAL SPILLOVER INDEX

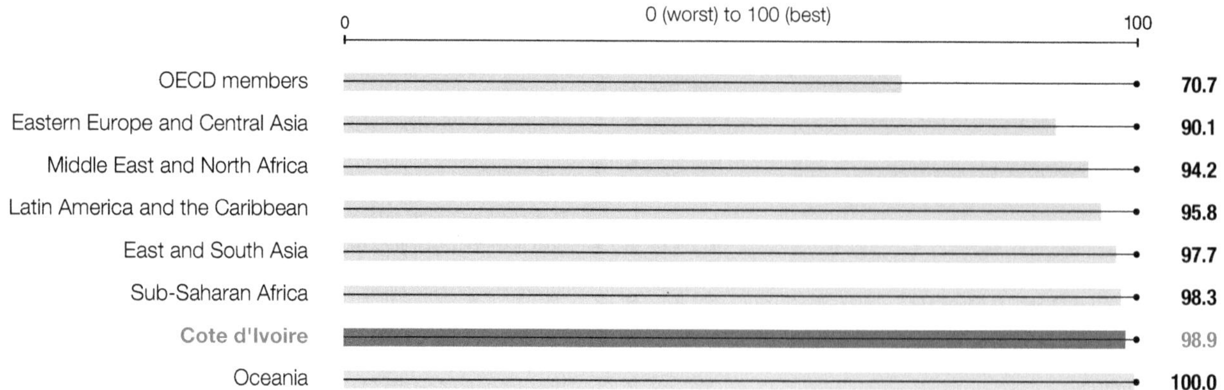

Region	Score
OECD members	70.7
Eastern Europe and Central Asia	90.1
Middle East and North Africa	94.2
Latin America and the Caribbean	95.8
East and South Asia	97.7
Sub-Saharan Africa	98.3
Cote d'Ivoire	98.9
Oceania	100.0

STATISTICAL PERFORMANCE INDEX

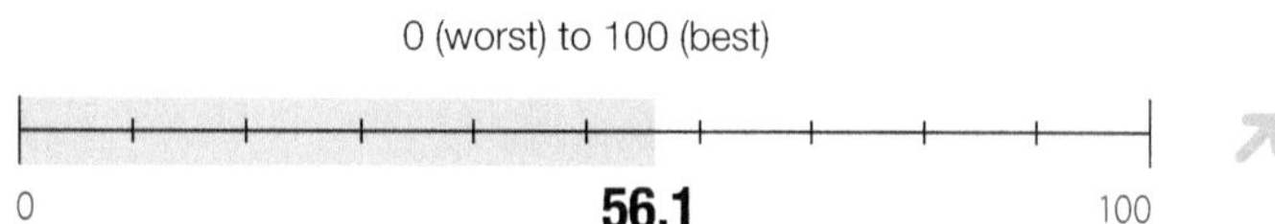

MISSING DATA IN SDG INDEX

2%

CÔTE D'IVOIRE

Performance by Indicator

SDG1 – No Poverty	Value	Year	Rating	Trend
Poverty headcount ratio at \$1.90/day (%)	20.1	2022	●	↗
Poverty headcount ratio at \$3.20/day (%)	43.4	2022	●	↗
SDG2 – Zero Hunger				
Prevalence of undernourishment (%)	14.9	2019	●	↗
Prevalence of stunting in children under 5 years of age (%)	21.6	2016	●	→
Prevalence of wasting in children under 5 years of age (%)	6.1	2016	●	→
Prevalence of obesity, BMI ≥ 30 (% of adult population)	10.3	2016	●	↓
Human Trophic Level (best 2–3 worst)	2.1	2017	●	↑
Cereal yield (tonnes per hectare of harvested land)	2.3	2018	●	↗
Sustainable Nitrogen Management Index (best 0–1.41 worst)	0.9	2015	●	→
Exports of hazardous pesticides (tonnes per million population)	2.1	2019	●	●
SDG3 – Good Health and Well-Being				
Maternal mortality rate (per 100,000 live births)	617	2017	●	↗
Neonatal mortality rate (per 1,000 live births)	33.2	2020	●	→
Mortality rate, under-5 (per 1,000 live births)	77.9	2020	●	↗
Incidence of tuberculosis (per 100,000 population)	135.0	2020	●	→
New HIV infections (per 1,000 uninfected population)	0.2	2020	●	↑
Age-standardized death rate due to cardiovascular disease, cancer, diabetes, or chronic respiratory disease in adults aged 30–70 years (%)	21.7	2019	●	↗
Age-standardized death rate attributable to household air pollution and ambient air pollution (per 100,000 population)	269	2016	●	●
Traffic deaths (per 100,000 population)	24.1	2019	●	↓
Life expectancy at birth (years)	62.9	2019	●	↗
Adolescent fertility rate (births per 1,000 females aged 15 to 19)	123.3	2015	●	●
Births attended by skilled health personnel (%)	73.6	2016	●	●
Surviving infants who received 2 WHO-recommended vaccines (%)	70	2020	●	→
Universal health coverage (UHC) index of service coverage (worst 0–100 best)	45	2019	●	→
Subjective well-being (average ladder score, worst 0–10 best)	5.1	2021	●	↑
SDG4 – Quality Education				
Participation rate in pre-primary organized learning (% of children aged 4 to 6)	24.7	2020	●	→
Net primary enrollment rate (%)	96.4	2020	●	↑
Lower secondary completion rate (%)	57.3	2020	●	↑
Literacy rate (% of population aged 15 to 24)	83.6	2019	●	↑
SDG5 – Gender Equality				
Demand for family planning satisfied by modern methods (% of females aged 15 to 49)	43.5	2018	●	→
Ratio of female-to-male mean years of education received (%)	65.6	2019	●	→
Ratio of female-to-male labor force participation rate (%)	70.9	2020	●	↑
Seats held by women in national parliament (%)	11.4	2020	●	→
SDG6 – Clean Water and Sanitation				
Population using at least basic drinking water services (%)	70.9	2020	●	↓
Population using at least basic sanitation services (%)	34.6	2020	●	→
Freshwater withdrawal (% of available freshwater resources)	5.1	2018	●	●
Anthropogenic wastewater that receives treatment (%)	0.6	2018	●	●
Scarce water consumption embodied in imports (m^3 H_2O eq/capita)	406.0	2018	●	●
SDG7 – Affordable and Clean Energy				
Population with access to electricity (%)	68.6	2019	●	↗
Population with access to clean fuels and technology for cooking (%)	30.3	2019	●	→
CO_2 emissions from fuel combustion per total electricity output ($MtCO_2$/TWh)	1.4	2019	●	→
Share of renewable energy in total primary energy supply (%)	62.7	2018	●	↑
SDG8 – Decent Work and Economic Growth				
Adjusted GDP growth (%)	-1.5	2020	●	●
Victims of modern slavery (per 1,000 population)	5.9	2018	●	●
Adults with an account at a bank or other financial institution or with a mobile-money-service provider (% of population aged 15 or over)	41.3	2017	●	↗
Unemployment rate (% of total labor force)	3.4	2022	●	↑
Fundamental labor rights are effectively guaranteed (worst 0–1 best)	0.6	2020	●	→
Fatal work-related accidents embodied in imports (per 100,000 population)	0.0	2015	●	↑

* Imputed data point

SDG9 – Industry, Innovation and Infrastructure	Value	Year	Rating	Trend
Population using the internet (%)	36.3	2019	●	↑
Mobile broadband subscriptions (per 100 population)	66.2	2019	●	↑
Logistics Performance Index: Quality of trade and transport-related infrastructure (worst 1–5 best)	2.9	2018	●	↑
The Times Higher Education Universities Ranking: Average score of top 3 universities (worst 0–100 best)	* 0.0	2022	●	●
Articles published in academic journals (per 1,000 population)	0.0	2020	●	→
Expenditure on research and development (% of GDP)	0.1	2016	●	●
SDG10 – Reduced Inequalities				
Gini coefficient	41.5	2015	●	●
Palma ratio	2.0	2018	●	●
SDG11 – Sustainable Cities and Communities				
Proportion of urban population living in slums (%)	61.1	2018	●	↓
Annual mean concentration of particulate matter of less than 2.5 microns in diameter (PM2.5) (μg/m^3)	28.3	2019	●	↓
Access to improved water source, piped (% of urban population)	59.8	2020	●	↓
Satisfaction with public transport (%)	40.0	2021	●	→
SDG12 – Responsible Consumption and Production				
Municipal solid waste (kg/capita/day)	0.6	2010	●	●
Electronic waste (kg/capita)	1.1	2019	●	●
Production-based SO_2 emissions (kg/capita)	1.1	2018	●	●
SO_2 emissions embodied in imports (kg/capita)	0.5	2018	●	●
Production-based nitrogen emissions (kg/capita)	2.0	2015	●	↑
Nitrogen emissions embodied in imports (kg/capita)	0.2	2015	●	↑
Exports of plastic waste (kg/capita)	0.0	2019	●	●
SDG13 – Climate Action				
CO_2 emissions from fossil fuel combustion and cement production (tCO_2/capita)	0.4	2020	●	↑
CO_2 emissions embodied in imports (tCO_2/capita)	0.2	2018	●	↑
CO_2 emissions embodied in fossil fuel exports (kg/capita)	205.4	2019	●	●
SDG14 – Life Below Water				
Mean area that is protected in marine sites important to biodiversity (%)	97.9	2020	●	↑
Ocean Health Index: Clean Waters score (worst 0–100 best)	40.9	2020	●	↓
Fish caught from overexploited or collapsed stocks (% of total catch)	52.1	2018	●	↓
Fish caught by trawling or dredging (%)	12.6	2018	●	↓
Fish caught that are then discarded (%)	0.7	2018	●	↑
Marine biodiversity threats embodied in imports (per million population)	0.0	2018	●	●
SDG15 – Life on Land				
Mean area that is protected in terrestrial sites important to biodiversity (%)	73.8	2020	●	→
Mean area that is protected in freshwater sites important to biodiversity (%)	80.9	2020	●	→
Red List Index of species survival (worst 0–1 best)	0.9	2021	●	↑
Permanent deforestation (% of forest area, 5-year average)	1.2	2020	●	↓
Terrestrial and freshwater biodiversity threats embodied in imports (per million population)	0.0	2018	●	●
SDG16 – Peace, Justice and Strong Institutions				
Homicides (per 100,000 population)	NA	NA	●	●
Unsentenced detainees (% of prison population)	NA	NA	●	●
Population who feel safe walking alone at night in the city or area where they live (%)	52	2021	●	↓
Property Rights (worst 1–7 best)	4.0	2020	●	↑
Birth registrations with civil authority (% of children under age 5)	71.7	2020	●	●
Corruption Perception Index (worst 0–100 best)	36	2021	●	→
Children involved in child labor (% of population aged 5 to 14)	22.1	2019	●	●
Exports of major conventional weapons (TIV constant million USD per 100,000 population)	0.0	2020	●	●
Press Freedom Index (best 0–100 worst)	28.9	2021	●	↑
Access to and affordability of justice (worst 0–1 best)	0.5	2020	●	→
SDG17 – Partnerships for the Goals				
Government spending on health and education (% of GDP)	4.7	2019	●	→
For high-income and all OECD DAC countries: International concessional public finance, including official development assistance (% of GNI)	NA	NA	●	●
Other countries: Government revenue excluding grants (% of GDP)	12.3	2019	●	→
Corporate Tax Haven Score (best 0–100 worst)	* 0.0	2019	●	●
Statistical Performance Index (worst 0–100 best)	56.1	2019	●	↗

5. Country Profiles

CROATIA

Eastern Europe and Central Asia

OVERALL PERFORMANCE

COUNTRY RANKING

CROATIA

23/163

COUNTRY SCORE

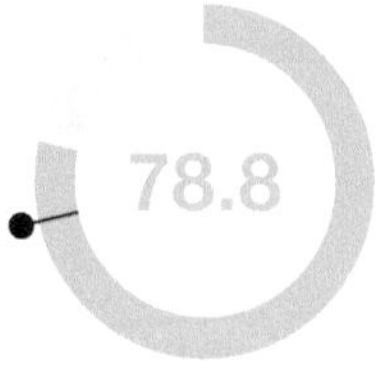

REGIONAL AVERAGE: 71.6

AVERAGE PERFORMANCE BY SDG

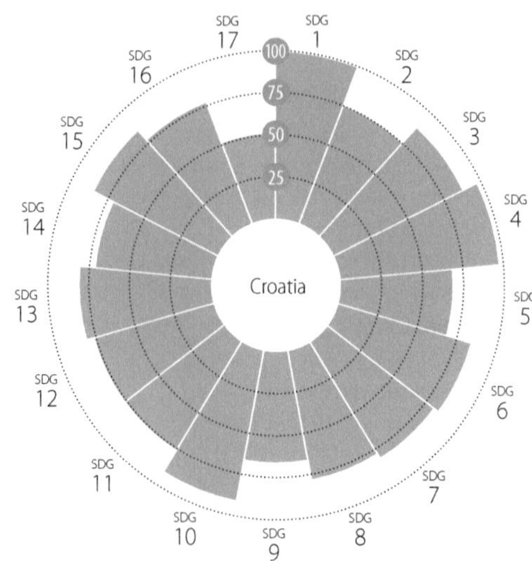

SDG DASHBOARDS AND TRENDS

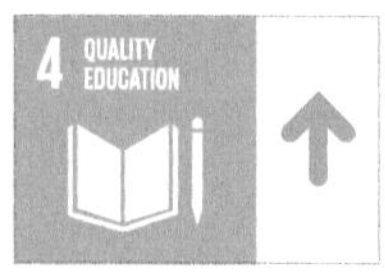

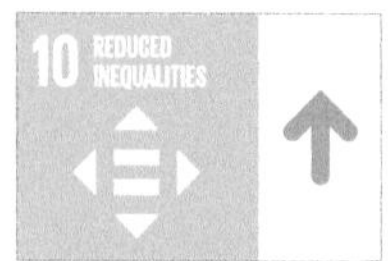

Note: The full title of each SDG is available here: https://sustainabledevelopment.un.org/topics/sustainabledevelopmentgoals

INTERNATIONAL SPILLOVER INDEX

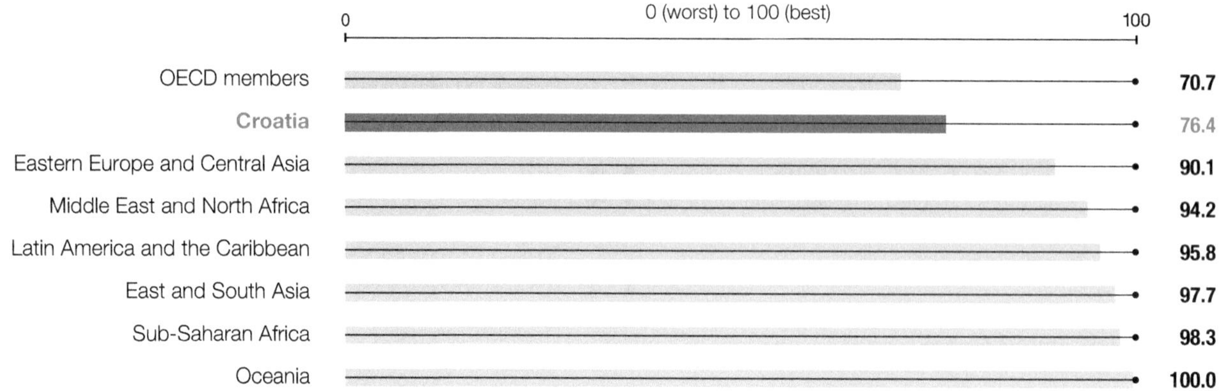

STATISTICAL PERFORMANCE INDEX

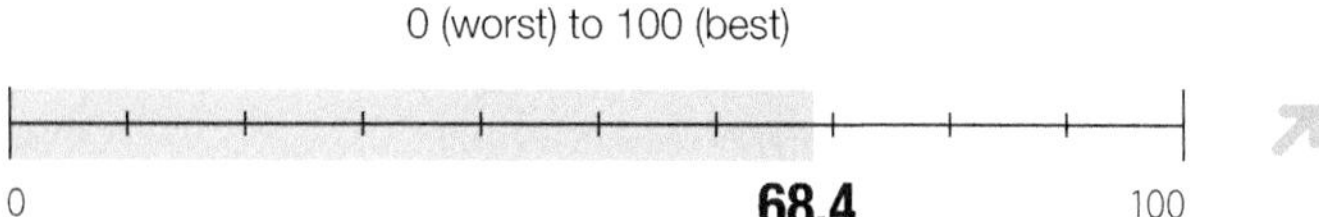

MISSING DATA IN SDG INDEX

2%

SDG1 – No Poverty	Value	Year	Rating	Trend
Poverty headcount ratio at $1.90/day (%)	0.4	2022	●	↑
Poverty headcount ratio at $3.20/day (%)	0.6	2022	●	↑
SDG2 – Zero Hunger				
Prevalence of undernourishment (%)	2.5	2019	●	↑
Prevalence of stunting in children under 5 years of age (%)	* 2.6	2019	●	↑
Prevalence of wasting in children under 5 years of age (%)	* 0.7	2019	●	↑
Prevalence of obesity, BMI ≥ 30 (% of adult population)	24.4	2016	●	↓
Human Trophic Level (best 2–3 worst)	2.4	2017	●	↑
Cereal yield (tonnes per hectare of harvested land)	7.0	2018	●	↑
Sustainable Nitrogen Management Index (best 0–1.41 worst)	0.5	2015	●	↑
Exports of hazardous pesticides (tonnes per million population)	1.1	2019	●	●
SDG3 – Good Health and Well-Being				
Maternal mortality rate (per 100,000 live births)	8	2017	●	↑
Neonatal mortality rate (per 1,000 live births)	3.0	2020	●	↑
Mortality rate, under-5 (per 1,000 live births)	4.6	2020	●	↑
Incidence of tuberculosis (per 100,000 population)	6.6	2020	●	↑
New HIV infections (per 1,000 uninfected population)	0.0	2020	●	↑
Age-standardized death rate due to cardiovascular disease, cancer, diabetes, or chronic respiratory disease in adults aged 30–70 years (%)	16.1	2019	●	↑
Age-standardized death rate attributable to household air pollution and ambient air pollution (per 100,000 population)	35	2016	●	●
Traffic deaths (per 100,000 population)	8.0	2019	●	↑
Life expectancy at birth (years)	78.6	2019	●	↑
Adolescent fertility rate (births per 1,000 females aged 15 to 19)	8.6	2018	●	↑
Births attended by skilled health personnel (%)	99.9	2017	●	↑
Surviving infants who received 2 WHO-recommended vaccines (%)	91	2020	●	↑
Universal health coverage (UHC) index of service coverage (worst 0–100 best)	73	2019	●	↗
Subjective well-being (average ladder score, worst 0–10 best)	6.3	2021	●	↑
SDG4 – Quality Education				
Participation rate in pre-primary organized learning (% of children aged 4 to 6)	95.9	2019	●	↑
Net primary enrollment rate (%)	97.8	2019	●	↑
Lower secondary completion rate (%)	101.0	2019	●	↑
Literacy rate (% of population aged 15 to 24)	99.7	2011	●	●
SDG5 – Gender Equality				
Demand for family planning satisfied by modern methods (% of females aged 15 to 49)	* 63.6	2022	●	↗
Ratio of female-to-male mean years of education received (%)	91.0	2019	●	→
Ratio of female-to-male labor force participation rate (%)	77.1	2020	●	↑
Seats held by women in national parliament (%)	31.1	2020	●	↑
SDG6 – Clean Water and Sanitation				
Population using at least basic drinking water services (%)	98.7	2007	●	●
Population using at least basic sanitation services (%)	96.6	2020	●	↑
Freshwater withdrawal (% of available freshwater resources)	1.5	2018	●	●
Anthropogenic wastewater that receives treatment (%)	51.7	2018	●	●
Scarce water consumption embodied in imports (m^3 H_2O eq/capita)	2905.6	2018	●	●
SDG7 – Affordable and Clean Energy				
Population with access to electricity (%)	100.0	2019	●	↑
Population with access to clean fuels and technology for cooking (%)	100.0	2019	●	↑
CO_2 emissions from fuel combustion per total electricity output ($MtCO_2$/TWh)	1.3	2019	●	↑
Share of renewable energy in total primary energy supply (%)	24.7	2019	●	↑
SDG8 – Decent Work and Economic Growth				
Adjusted GDP growth (%)	-1.1	2020	●	●
Victims of modern slavery (per 1,000 population)	6.0	2018	●	●
Adults with an account at a bank or other financial institution or with a mobile-money-service provider (% of population aged 15 or over)	86.1	2017	●	↑
Unemployment rate (% of total labor force)	7.2	2022	●	↑
Fundamental labor rights are effectively guaranteed (worst 0–1 best)	0.7	2020	●	↑
Fatal work-related accidents embodied in imports (per 100,000 population)	0.5	2015	●	↑

* Imputed data point

SDG9 – Industry, Innovation and Infrastructure	Value	Year	Rating	Trend
Population using the internet (%)	78.3	2020	●	↑
Mobile broadband subscriptions (per 100 population)	82.1	2019	●	↑
Logistics Performance Index: Quality of trade and transport-related infrastructure (worst 1–5 best)	3.0	2018	●	↑
The Times Higher Education Universities Ranking: Average score of top 3 universities (worst 0–100 best)	22.0	2022	●	●
Articles published in academic journals (per 1,000 population)	1.9	2020	●	↑
Expenditure on research and development (% of GDP)	1.0	2018	●	↗
SDG10 – Reduced Inequalities				
Gini coefficient	29.7	2018	●	↑
Palma ratio	1.1	2018	●	●
SDG11 – Sustainable Cities and Communities				
Proportion of urban population living in slums (%)	NA	NA	●	●
Annual mean concentration of particulate matter of less than 2.5 microns in diameter (PM2.5) (μg/m^3)	16.8	2019	●	↗
Access to improved water source, piped (% of urban population)	95.7	2007	●	●
Satisfaction with public transport (%)	48.0	2021	●	↓
SDG12 – Responsible Consumption and Production				
Municipal solid waste (kg/capita/day)	1.2	2019	●	●
Electronic waste (kg/capita)	11.9	2019	●	●
Production-based SO_2 emissions (kg/capita)	12.8	2018	●	●
SO_2 emissions embodied in imports (kg/capita)	3.2	2018	●	●
Production-based nitrogen emissions (kg/capita)	14.4	2015	●	↑
Nitrogen emissions embodied in imports (kg/capita)	4.8	2015	●	↑
Exports of plastic waste (kg/capita)	6.4	2020	●	●
SDG13 – Climate Action				
CO_2 emissions from fossil fuel combustion and cement production (tCO_2/capita)	4.1	2020	●	→
CO_2 emissions embodied in imports (tCO_2/capita)	1.2	2018	●	↓
CO_2 emissions embodied in fossil fuel exports (kg/capita)	465.6	2020	●	●
SDG14 – Life Below Water				
Mean area that is protected in marine sites important to biodiversity (%)	81.7	2020	●	→
Ocean Health Index: Clean Waters score (worst 0–100 best)	64.7	2020	●	→
Fish caught from overexploited or collapsed stocks (% of total catch)	62.0	2018	●	↑
Fish caught by trawling or dredging (%)	14.4	2018	●	↑
Fish caught that are then discarded (%)	4.3	2018	●	↑
Marine biodiversity threats embodied in imports (per million population)	0.0	2018	●	●
SDG15 – Life on Land				
Mean area that is protected in terrestrial sites important to biodiversity (%)	76.9	2020	●	→
Mean area that is protected in freshwater sites important to biodiversity (%)	84.9	2020	●	→
Red List Index of species survival (worst 0–1 best)	0.9	2021	●	→
Permanent deforestation (% of forest area, 5-year average)	0.0	2020	●	↑
Terrestrial and freshwater biodiversity threats embodied in imports (per million population)	1.4	2018	●	●
SDG16 – Peace, Justice and Strong Institutions				
Homicides (per 100,000 population)	1.0	2020	●	↑
Unsentenced detainees (% of prison population)	35.4	2019	●	↓
Population who feel safe walking alone at night in the city or area where they live (%)	84	2021	●	↑
Property Rights (worst 1–7 best)	3.8	2020	●	↑
Birth registrations with civil authority (% of children under age 5)	100.0	2020	●	●
Corruption Perception Index (worst 0–100 best)	47	2021	●	↓
Children involved in child labor (% of population aged 5 to 14)	NA	NA	●	●
Exports of major conventional weapons (TIV constant million USD per 100,000 population)	0.1	2020	●	●
Press Freedom Index (best 0–100 worst)	28.0	2021	●	↑
Access to and affordability of justice (worst 0–1 best)	0.7	2020	●	↑
SDG17 – Partnerships for the Goals				
Government spending on health and education (% of GDP)	9.6	2019	●	↓
For high-income and all OECD DAC countries: International concessional public finance, including official development assistance (% of GNI)	0.1	2021	●	●
Other countries: Government revenue excluding grants (% of GDP)	NA	NA	●	●
Corporate Tax Haven Score (best 0–100 worst)	54.5	2019	●	●
Statistical Performance Index (worst 0–100 best)	68.4	2019	●	↗

CUBA

Latin America and the Caribbean

OVERALL PERFORMANCE

COUNTRY RANKING

CUBA

40/163

COUNTRY SCORE

REGIONAL AVERAGE: 69.5

AVERAGE PERFORMANCE BY SDG

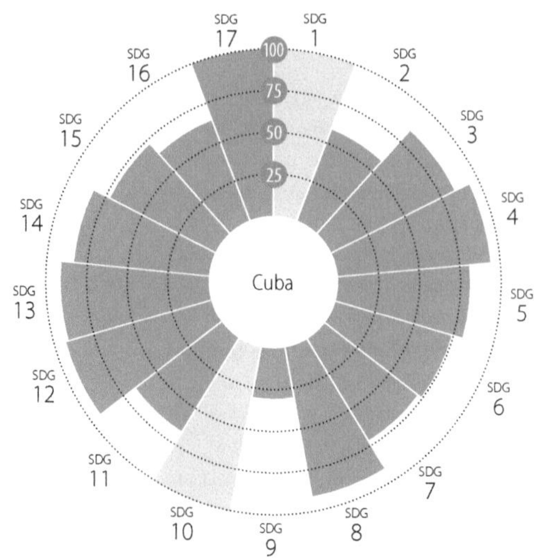

SDG DASHBOARDS AND TRENDS

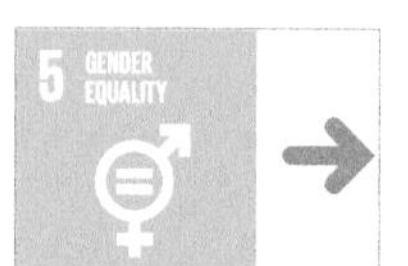

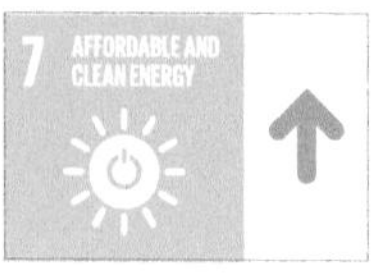

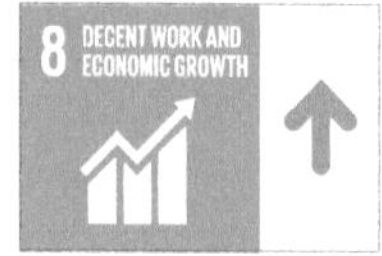

Note: The full title of each SDG is available here: https://sustainabledevelopment.un.org/topics/sustainabledevelopmentgoals

INTERNATIONAL SPILLOVER INDEX

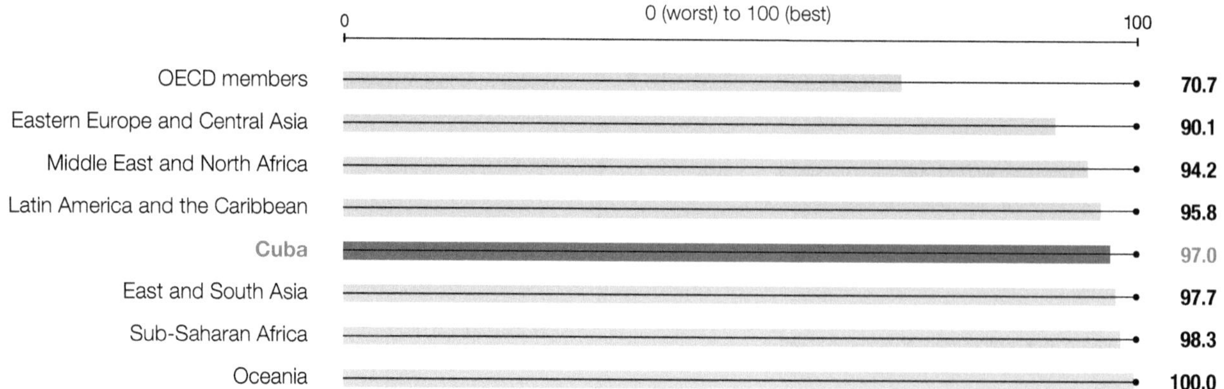

STATISTICAL PERFORMANCE INDEX

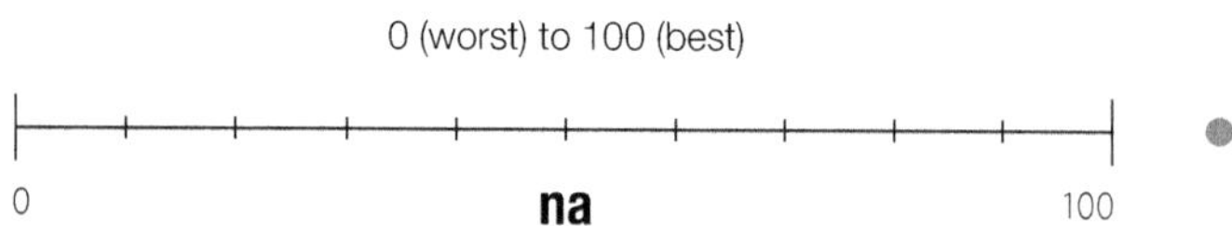

MISSING DATA IN SDG INDEX

18%

SDG1 – No Poverty

Indicator	Value	Year	Rating	Trend
Poverty headcount ratio at $1.90/day (%)	* NA	NA	●	●
Poverty headcount ratio at $3.20/day (%)	* NA	NA	●	●

SDG2 – Zero Hunger

Indicator	Value	Year	Rating	Trend
Prevalence of undernourishment (%)	2.5	2019	●	↑
Prevalence of stunting in children under 5 years of age (%)	7.1	2019	●	↑
Prevalence of wasting in children under 5 years of age (%)	2.0	2019	●	↑
Prevalence of obesity, BMI ≥ 30 (% of adult population)	24.6	2016	●	↓
Human Trophic Level (best 2–3 worst)	2.2	2017	●	→
Cereal yield (tonnes per hectare of harvested land)	2.9	2018	●	↑
Sustainable Nitrogen Management Index (best 0–1.41 worst)	1.1	2015	●	↓
Exports of hazardous pesticides (tonnes per million population)	NA	NA	●	●

SDG3 – Good Health and Well-Being

Indicator	Value	Year	Rating	Trend
Maternal mortality rate (per 100,000 live births)	36	2017	●	↑
Neonatal mortality rate (per 1,000 live births)	2.4	2020	●	↑
Mortality rate, under-5 (per 1,000 live births)	5.1	2020	●	↑
Incidence of tuberculosis (per 100,000 population)	6.3	2020	●	↑
New HIV infections (per 1,000 uninfected population)	0.2	2020	●	↑
Age-standardized death rate due to cardiovascular disease, cancer, diabetes, or chronic respiratory disease in adults aged 30–70 years (%)	16.6	2019	●	→
Age-standardized death rate attributable to household air pollution and ambient air pollution (per 100,000 population)	50	2016	●	●
Traffic deaths (per 100,000 population)	8.9	2019	●	↗
Life expectancy at birth (years)	77.8	2019	●	→
Adolescent fertility rate (births per 1,000 females aged 15 to 19)	53.3	2018	●	↓
Births attended by skilled health personnel (%)	99.9	2018	●	↑
Surviving infants who received 2 WHO-recommended vaccines (%)	98	2020	●	↑
Universal health coverage (UHC) index of service coverage (worst 0–100 best)	80	2019	●	↑
Subjective well-being (average ladder score, worst 0–10 best)	5.4	2006	●	●

SDG4 – Quality Education

Indicator	Value	Year	Rating	Trend
Participation rate in pre-primary organized learning (% of children aged 4 to 6)	95.5	2020	●	↑
Net primary enrollment rate (%)	99.8	2020	●	↑
Lower secondary completion rate (%)	86.1	2020	●	↓
Literacy rate (% of population aged 15 to 24)	99.9	2012	●	●

SDG5 – Gender Equality

Indicator	Value	Year	Rating	Trend
Demand for family planning satisfied by modern methods (% of females aged 15 to 49)	86.9	2019	●	↑
Ratio of female-to-male mean years of education received (%)	94.9	2019	●	↓
Ratio of female-to-male labor force participation rate (%)	58.6	2020	●	↓
Seats held by women in national parliament (%)	53.2	2020	●	↑

SDG6 – Clean Water and Sanitation

Indicator	Value	Year	Rating	Trend
Population using at least basic drinking water services (%)	97.0	2020	●	↑
Population using at least basic sanitation services (%)	91.4	2020	●	↗
Freshwater withdrawal (% of available freshwater resources)	23.9	2018	●	●
Anthropogenic wastewater that receives treatment (%)	3.6	2018	●	●
Scarce water consumption embodied in imports (m^3 H_2O eq/capita)	812.6	2018	●	●

SDG7 – Affordable and Clean Energy

Indicator	Value	Year	Rating	Trend
Population with access to electricity (%)	99.8	2019	●	↑
Population with access to clean fuels and technology for cooking (%)	79.4	2016	●	●
CO_2 emissions from fuel combustion per total electricity output ($MtCO_2$/TWh)	1.3	2019	●	↑
Share of renewable energy in total primary energy supply (%)	17.3	2019	●	↑

SDG8 – Decent Work and Economic Growth

Indicator	Value	Year	Rating	Trend
Adjusted GDP growth (%)	NA	NA	●	●
Victims of modern slavery (per 1,000 population)	3.8	2018	●	●
Adults with an account at a bank or other financial institution or with a mobile-money-service provider (% of population aged 15 or over)	NA	NA	●	●
Unemployment rate (% of total labor force)	2.5	2022	●	↑
Fundamental labor rights are effectively guaranteed (worst 0–1 best)	NA	NA	●	●
Fatal work-related accidents embodied in imports (per 100,000 population)	0.2	2015	●	↑

* Imputed data point

SDG9 – Industry, Innovation and Infrastructure

Indicator	Value	Year	Rating	Trend
Population using the internet (%)	74.0	2020	●	↑
Mobile broadband subscriptions (per 100 population)	25.7	2019	●	↑
Logistics Performance Index: Quality of trade and transport-related infrastructure (worst 1–5 best)	2.0	2018	●	↗
The Times Higher Education Universities Ranking: Average score of top 3 universities (worst 0–100 best)	16.5	2022	●	●
Articles published in academic journals (per 1,000 population)	0.2	2020	●	→
Expenditure on research and development (% of GDP)	0.5	2018	●	↗

SDG10 – Reduced Inequalities

Indicator	Value	Year	Rating	Trend
Gini coefficient	NA	NA	●	●
Palma ratio	NA	NA	●	●

SDG11 – Sustainable Cities and Communities

Indicator	Value	Year	Rating	Trend
Proportion of urban population living in slums (%)	6.6	2018	●	●
Annual mean concentration of particulate matter of less than 2.5 microns in diameter (PM2.5) (μg/m^3)	18.5	2019	●	↗
Access to improved water source, piped (% of urban population)	86.4	2020	●	→
Satisfaction with public transport (%)	8.0	2006	●	●

SDG12 – Responsible Consumption and Production

Indicator	Value	Year	Rating	Trend
Municipal solid waste (kg/capita/day)	0.7	2007	●	●
Electronic waste (kg/capita)	NA	NA	●	●
Production-based SO_2 emissions (kg/capita)	34.8	2018	●	●
SO_2 emissions embodied in imports (kg/capita)	0.8	2018	●	●
Production-based nitrogen emissions (kg/capita)	12.5	2015	●	↑
Nitrogen emissions embodied in imports (kg/capita)	0.9	2015	●	↑
Exports of plastic waste (kg/capita)	NA	NA	●	●

SDG13 – Climate Action

Indicator	Value	Year	Rating	Trend
CO_2 emissions from fossil fuel combustion and cement production (tCO_2/capita)	1.8	2020	●	↑
CO_2 emissions embodied in imports (tCO_2/capita)	0.3	2018	●	↑
CO_2 emissions embodied in fossil fuel exports (kg/capita)	NA	NA	●	●

SDG14 – Life Below Water

Indicator	Value	Year	Rating	Trend
Mean area that is protected in marine sites important to biodiversity (%)	70.1	2020	●	→
Ocean Health Index: Clean Waters score (worst 0–100 best)	58.3	2020	●	↓
Fish caught from overexploited or collapsed stocks (% of total catch)	5.9	2018	●	↑
Fish caught by trawling or dredging (%)	6.1	2012	●	●
Fish caught that are then discarded (%)	0.0	2018	●	↑
Marine biodiversity threats embodied in imports (per million population)	0.0	2018	●	●

SDG15 – Life on Land

Indicator	Value	Year	Rating	Trend
Mean area that is protected in terrestrial sites important to biodiversity (%)	54.5	2020	●	→
Mean area that is protected in freshwater sites important to biodiversity (%)	98.2	2020	●	↑
Red List Index of species survival (worst 0–1 best)	0.7	2021	●	↓
Permanent deforestation (% of forest area, 5-year average)	0.1	2020	●	↑
Terrestrial and freshwater biodiversity threats embodied in imports (per million population)	0.2	2018	●	●

SDG16 – Peace, Justice and Strong Institutions

Indicator	Value	Year	Rating	Trend
Homicides (per 100,000 population)	5.1	2016	●	●
Unsentenced detainees (% of prison population)	NA	NA	●	●
Population who feel safe walking alone at night in the city or area where they live (%)	51	2006	●	●
Property Rights (worst 1–7 best)	NA	NA	●	●
Birth registrations with civil authority (% of children under age 5)	99.8	2020	●	●
Corruption Perception Index (worst 0–100 best)	46	2021	●	↓
Children involved in child labor (% of population aged 5 to 14)	NA	NA	●	●
Exports of major conventional weapons (TIV constant million USD per 100,000 population)	* 0.0	2020	●	●
Press Freedom Index (best 0–100 worst)	63.9	2021	●	→
Access to and affordability of justice (worst 0–1 best)	NA	NA	●	●

SDG17 – Partnerships for the Goals

Indicator	Value	Year	Rating	Trend
Government spending on health and education (% of GDP)	23.0	2019	●	↑
For high-income and all OECD DAC countries: International concessional public finance, including official development assistance (% of GNI)	NA	NA	●	●
Other countries: Government revenue excluding grants (% of GDP)	NA	NA	●	●
Corporate Tax Haven Score (best 0–100 worst)	* 0.0	2019	●	●
Statistical Performance Index (worst 0–100 best)	NA	NA	●	●

CYPRUS

AVERAGE PERFORMANCE BY SDG

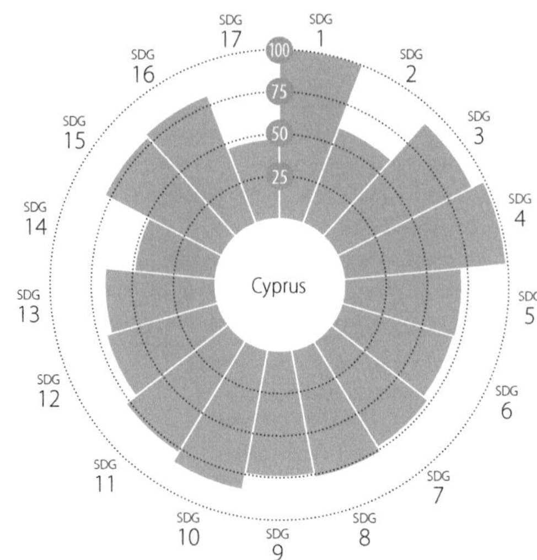

OVERALL PERFORMANCE

COUNTRY RANKING

CYPRUS

43/163

COUNTRY SCORE

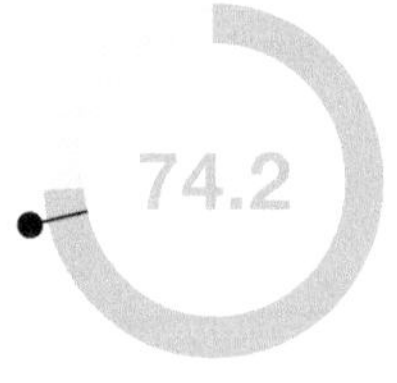

REGIONAL AVERAGE: 71.6

SDG DASHBOARDS AND TRENDS

Major challenges · Significant challenges · Challenges remain · SDG achieved · Information unavailable

Decreasing · Stagnating · Moderately improving · On track or maintaining SDG achievement · Information unavailable

Note: The full title of each SDG is available here: https://sustainabledevelopment.un.org/topics/sustainabledevelopmentgoals

INTERNATIONAL SPILLOVER INDEX

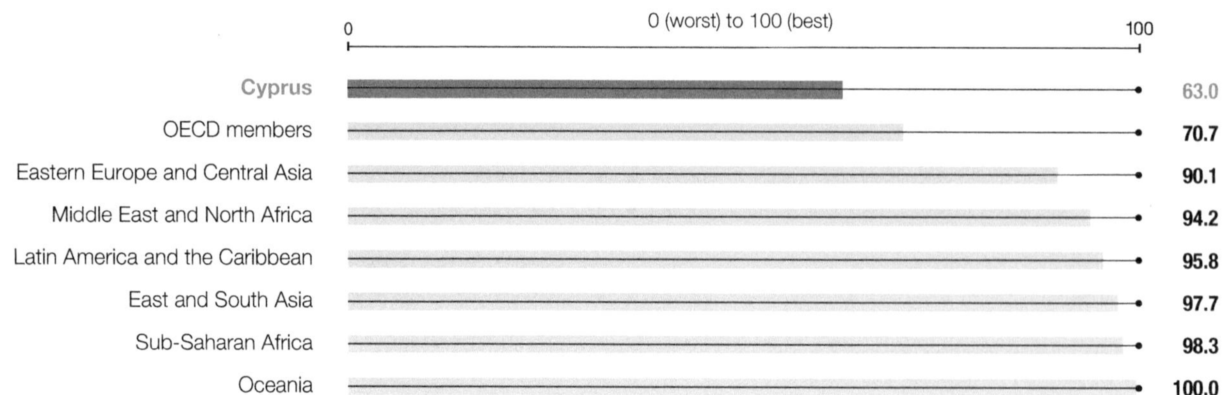

STATISTICAL PERFORMANCE INDEX

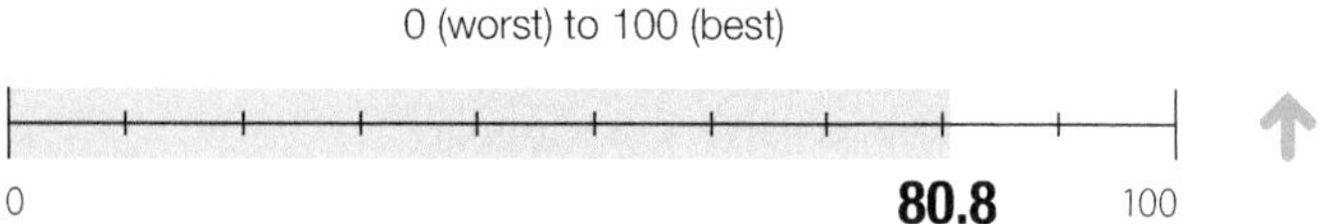

MISSING DATA IN SDG INDEX

3%

CYPRUS

SDG1 – No Poverty		Value	Year	Rating	Trend
Poverty headcount ratio at $1.90/day (%)		0.1	2022	●	↑
Poverty headcount ratio at $3.20/day (%)		0.1	2022	●	↑
SDG2 – Zero Hunger					
Prevalence of undernourishment (%)		2.5	2019	●	↑
Prevalence of stunting in children under 5 years of age (%)	*	2.6	2019	●	↑
Prevalence of wasting in children under 5 years of age (%)	*	0.7	2019	●	↑
Prevalence of obesity, BMI ≥ 30 (% of adult population)		21.8	2016	●	↓
Human Trophic Level (best 2–3 worst)		2.4	2017	●	→
Cereal yield (tonnes per hectare of harvested land)		2.0	2018	●	↓
Sustainable Nitrogen Management Index (best 0–1.41 worst)		1.1	2015	●	→
Exports of hazardous pesticides (tonnes per million population)		0.0	2019	●	●
SDG3 – Good Health and Well-Being					
Maternal mortality rate (per 100,000 live births)		6	2017	●	↑
Neonatal mortality rate (per 1,000 live births)		1.6	2020	●	↑
Mortality rate, under-5 (per 1,000 live births)		2.8	2020	●	↑
Incidence of tuberculosis (per 100,000 population)		5.7	2020	●	↑
New HIV infections (per 1,000 uninfected population)		1.0	2020	●	→
Age-standardized death rate due to cardiovascular disease, cancer, diabetes, or chronic respiratory disease in adults aged 30–70 years (%)		8.2	2019	●	↑
Age-standardized death rate attributable to household air pollution and ambient air pollution (per 100,000 population)		20	2016	●	●
Traffic deaths (per 100,000 population)		5.8	2019	●	↑
Life expectancy at birth (years)		83.1	2019	●	↑
Adolescent fertility rate (births per 1,000 females aged 15 to 19)		7.8	2018	●	↑
Births attended by skilled health personnel (%)		98.3	2018	●	↑
Surviving infants who received 2 WHO-recommended vaccines (%)		86	2019	●	↓
Universal health coverage (UHC) index of service coverage (worst 0–100 best)		79	2019	●	↑
Subjective well-being (average ladder score, worst 0–10 best)		6.3	2021	●	↑
SDG4 – Quality Education					
Participation rate in pre-primary organized learning (% of children aged 4 to 6)		98.4	2019	●	↑
Net primary enrollment rate (%)		99.5	2019	●	↑
Lower secondary completion rate (%)		98.1	2019	●	↑
Literacy rate (% of population aged 15 to 24)		99.8	2011	●	●
SDG5 – Gender Equality					
Demand for family planning satisfied by modern methods (% of females aged 15 to 49)		NA	NA	●	●
Ratio of female-to-male mean years of education received (%)		98.4	2019	●	↑
Ratio of female-to-male labor force participation rate (%)		81.7	2020	●	↑
Seats held by women in national parliament (%)		19.6	2020	●	↗
SDG6 – Clean Water and Sanitation					
Population using at least basic drinking water services (%)		99.8	2020	●	↑
Population using at least basic sanitation services (%)		99.4	2020	●	↑
Freshwater withdrawal (% of available freshwater resources)		28.3	2018	●	●
Anthropogenic wastewater that receives treatment (%)		50.0	2018	●	●
Scarce water consumption embodied in imports (m^3 H_2O eq/capita)		9197.4	2018	●	●
SDG7 – Affordable and Clean Energy					
Population with access to electricity (%)		100.0	2019	●	↑
Population with access to clean fuels and technology for cooking (%)		100.0	2019	●	↑
CO_2 emissions from fuel combustion per total electricity output ($MtCO_2$/TWh)		1.2	2019	●	↑
Share of renewable energy in total primary energy supply (%)		8.7	2019	●	→
SDG8 – Decent Work and Economic Growth					
Adjusted GDP growth (%)		-1.6	2020	●	●
Victims of modern slavery (per 1,000 population)		4.2	2018	●	●
Adults with an account at a bank or other financial institution or with a mobile-money-service provider (% of population aged 15 or over)		88.7	2017	●	↑
Unemployment rate (% of total labor force)		6.0	2022	●	↑
Fundamental labor rights are effectively guaranteed (worst 0–1 best)		0.6	2020	●	●
Fatal work-related accidents embodied in imports (per 100,000 population)		1.1	2015	●	↑

* Imputed data point

SDG9 – Industry, Innovation and Infrastructure		Value	Year	Rating	Trend
Population using the internet (%)		90.8	2020	●	↑
Mobile broadband subscriptions (per 100 population)		115.5	2019	●	↑
Logistics Performance Index: Quality of trade and transport-related infrastructure (worst 1–5 best)		2.9	2018	●	↗
The Times Higher Education Universities Ranking: Average score of top 3 universities (worst 0–100 best)		39.0	2022	●	●
Articles published in academic journals (per 1,000 population)		3.0	2020	●	↑
Expenditure on research and development (% of GDP)		0.5	2018	●	→
SDG10 – Reduced Inequalities					
Gini coefficient		32.7	2018	●	↑
Palma ratio		1.2	2018	●	●
SDG11 – Sustainable Cities and Communities					
Proportion of urban population living in slums (%)		NA	NA	●	●
Annual mean concentration of particulate matter of less than 2.5 microns in diameter (PM2.5) (μg/m³)		16.6	2019	●	↑
Access to improved water source, piped (% of urban population)		99.7	2020	●	↑
Satisfaction with public transport (%)		48.0	2021	●	↓
SDG12 – Responsible Consumption and Production					
Municipal solid waste (kg/capita/day)		1.8	2019	●	●
Electronic waste (kg/capita)		16.8	2019	●	●
Production-based SO_2 emissions (kg/capita)		17.8	2018	●	●
SO_2 emissions embodied in imports (kg/capita)		6.5	2018	●	●
Production-based nitrogen emissions (kg/capita)		6.7	2015	●	↑
Nitrogen emissions embodied in imports (kg/capita)		8.5	2015	●	→
Exports of plastic waste (kg/capita)		5.7	2020	●	●
SDG13 – Climate Action					
CO_2 emissions from fossil fuel combustion and cement production (tCO_2/capita)		5.4	2020	●	→
CO_2 emissions embodied in imports (tCO_2/capita)		2.4	2018	●	↓
CO_2 emissions embodied in fossil fuel exports (kg/capita)		0.0	2018	●	●
SDG14 – Life Below Water					
Mean area that is protected in marine sites important to biodiversity (%)		49.6	2020	●	↗
Ocean Health Index: Clean Waters score (worst 0–100 best)		58.7	2020	●	→
Fish caught from overexploited or collapsed stocks (% of total catch)		54.3	2018	●	→
Fish caught by trawling or dredging (%)		25.1	2018	●	↗
Fish caught that are then discarded (%)		23.1	2018	●	↗
Marine biodiversity threats embodied in imports (per million population)		0.3	2018	●	●
SDG15 – Life on Land					
Mean area that is protected in terrestrial sites important to biodiversity (%)		72.3	2020	●	↗
Mean area that is protected in freshwater sites important to biodiversity (%)		36.6	2020	●	→
Red List Index of species survival (worst 0–1 best)		1.0	2021	●	↑
Permanent deforestation (% of forest area, 5-year average)		0.0	2020	●	↑
Terrestrial and freshwater biodiversity threats embodied in imports (per million population)		1.3	2018	●	●
SDG16 – Peace, Justice and Strong Institutions					
Homicides (per 100,000 population)		1.2	2020	●	↑
Unsentenced detainees (% of prison population)		31.9	2019	●	↓
Population who feel safe walking alone at night in the city or area where they live (%)		73	2021	●	↑
Property Rights (worst 1–7 best)		5.0	2020	●	↑
Birth registrations with civil authority (% of children under age 5)		100.0	2020	●	●
Corruption Perception Index (worst 0–100 best)		53	2021	●	↓
Children involved in child labor (% of population aged 5 to 14)		NA	NA	●	●
Exports of major conventional weapons (TIV constant million USD per 100,000 population)	*	0.0	2020	●	●
Press Freedom Index (best 0–100 worst)		19.9	2021	●	↑
Access to and affordability of justice (worst 0–1 best)		0.7	2020	●	●
SDG17 – Partnerships for the Goals					
Government spending on health and education (% of GDP)		9.7	2019	●	↑
For high-income and all OECD DAC countries: International concessional public finance, including official development assistance (% of GNI)		0.1	2020	●	↓
Other countries: Government revenue excluding grants (% of GDP)		NA	NA	●	●
Corporate Tax Haven Score (best 0–100 worst)		71.1	2019	●	●
Statistical Performance Index (worst 0–100 best)		80.8	2019	●	↑

CZECH REPUBLIC

OECD Countries

OVERALL PERFORMANCE

COUNTRY RANKING

CZECH REPUBLIC

13 /163

COUNTRY SCORE

REGIONAL AVERAGE: 77.2

AVERAGE PERFORMANCE BY SDG

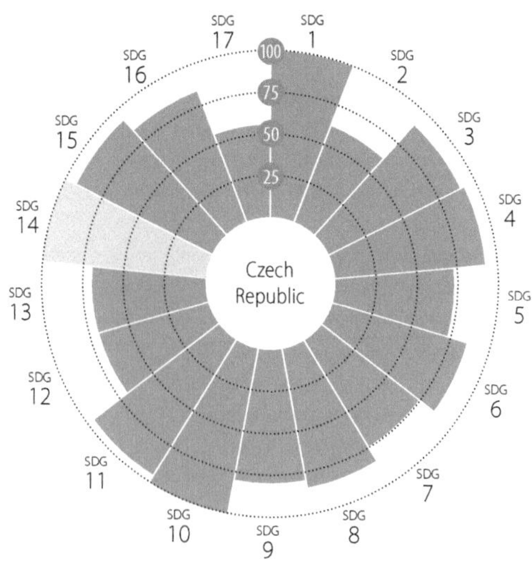

SDG DASHBOARDS AND TRENDS

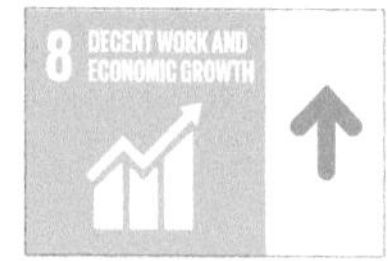

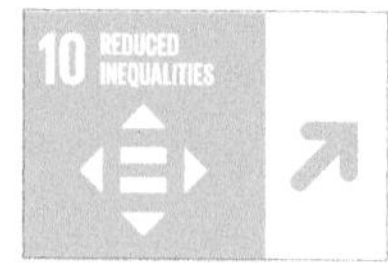

Major challenges | Significant challenges | Challenges remain | SDG achieved | Information unavailable

Decreasing | Stagnating | Moderately improving | On track or maintaining SDG achievement | Information unavailable

Note: The full title of each SDG is available here: https://sustainabledevelopment.un.org/topics/sustainabledevelopmentgoals

INTERNATIONAL SPILLOVER INDEX

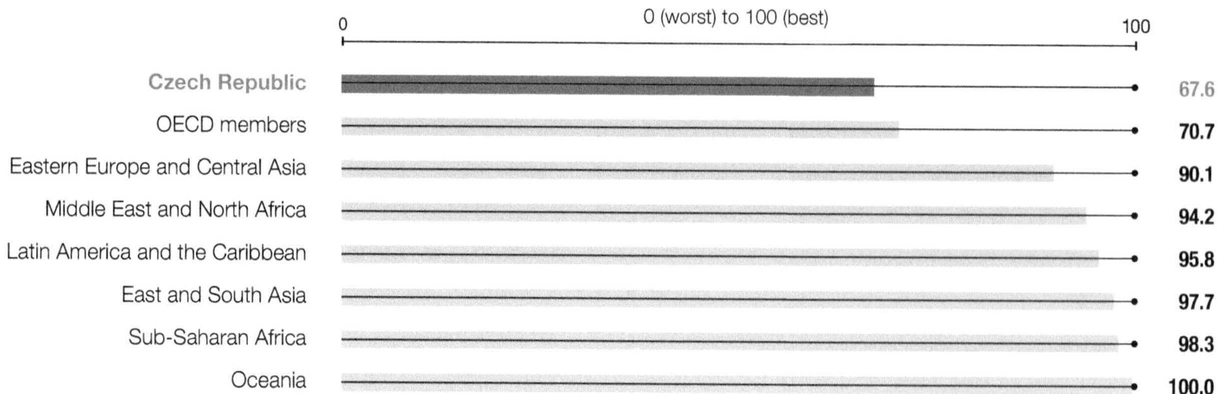

STATISTICAL PERFORMANCE INDEX

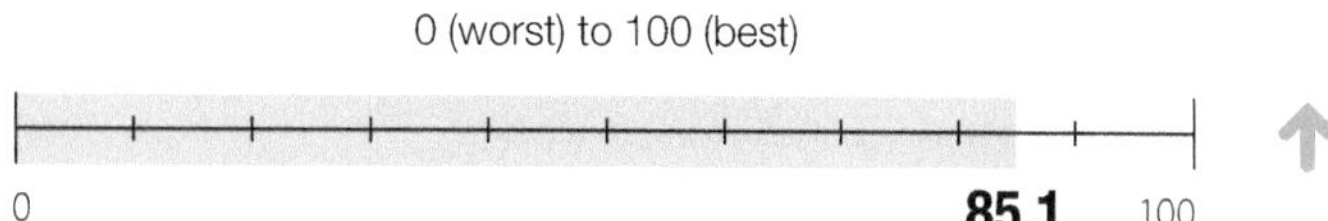

MISSING DATA IN SDG INDEX

1%

CZECH REPUBLIC

Performance by Indicator

SDG1 – No Poverty	Value	Year	Rating	Trend
Poverty headcount ratio at $1.90/day (%)	0.1	2022	●	↑
Poverty headcount ratio at $3.20/day (%)	0.1	2022	●	↑
Poverty rate after taxes and transfers (%)	5.6	2019	●	↑
SDG2 – Zero Hunger				
Prevalence of undernourishment (%)	2.5	2019	●	↑
Prevalence of stunting in children under 5 years of age (%)	2.7	2001	●	↑
Prevalence of wasting in children under 5 years of age (%)	4.6	2001	●	↑
Prevalence of obesity, BMI ≥ 30 (% of adult population)	26.0	2016	●	↓
Human Trophic Level (best 2–3 worst)	2.4	2017	●	↓
Cereal yield (tonnes per hectare of harvested land)	5.2	2018	●	↑
Sustainable Nitrogen Management Index (best 0–1.41 worst)	0.5	2015	●	↓
Yield gap closure (% of potential yield)	57.8	2018	●	●
Exports of hazardous pesticides (tonnes per million population)	115.5	2019	●	●
SDG3 – Good Health and Well-Being				
Maternal mortality rate (per 100,000 live births)	3	2017	●	↑
Neonatal mortality rate (per 1,000 live births)	1.6	2020	●	↑
Mortality rate, under-5 (per 1,000 live births)	2.9	2020	●	↑
Incidence of tuberculosis (per 100,000 population)	3.9	2020	●	↑
New HIV infections (per 1,000 uninfected population)	1.0	2020	●	→
Age-standardized death rate due to cardiovascular disease, cancer, diabetes, or chronic respiratory disease in adults aged 30–70 years (%)	14.3	2019	●	↑
Age-standardized death rate attributable to household air pollution and ambient air pollution (per 100,000 population)	30	2016	●	●
Traffic deaths (per 100,000 population)	6.0	2019	●	↑
Life expectancy at birth (years)	79.1	2019	●	↑
Adolescent fertility rate (births per 1,000 females aged 15 to 19)	10.8	2018	●	↑
Births attended by skilled health personnel (%)	99.8	2017	●	↑
Surviving infants who received 2 WHO-recommended vaccines (%)	94	2020	●	↑
Universal health coverage (UHC) index of service coverage (worst 0–100 best)	78	2019	●	↑
Subjective well-being (average ladder score, worst 0–10 best)	6.9	2021	●	↑
Gap in life expectancy at birth among regions (years)	3.7	2019	●	→
Gap in self-reported health status by income (percentage points)	44.0	2019	●	↓
Daily smokers (% of population aged 15 and over)	18.1	2019	●	↑
SDG4 – Quality Education				
Participation rate in pre-primary organized learning (% of children aged 4 to 6)	92.6	2019	●	↑
Net primary enrollment rate (%)	99.1	2019	●	↑
Lower secondary completion rate (%)	92.0	2019	●	↑
Literacy rate (% of population aged 15 to 24)	NA	NA	●	●
Tertiary educational attainment (% of population aged 25 to 34)	33.0	2020	●	↗
PISA score (worst 0–600 best)	495.3	2018	●	↑
Variation in science performance explained by socio-economic status (%)	16.9	2018	●	↑
Underachievers in science (% of 15-year-olds)	18.8	2018	●	↑
SDG5 – Gender Equality				
Demand for family planning satisfied by modern methods (% of females aged 15 to 49)	85.7	2008	●	↑
Ratio of female-to-male mean years of education received (%)	96.9	2019	●	→
Ratio of female-to-male labor force participation rate (%)	76.1	2020	●	↑
Seats held by women in national parliament (%)	22.5	2020	●	→
Gender wage gap (% of male median wage)	12.4	2020	●	↑
SDG6 – Clean Water and Sanitation				
Population using at least basic drinking water services (%)	99.9	2020	●	↑
Population using at least basic sanitation services (%)	99.1	2020	●	↑
Freshwater withdrawal (% of available freshwater resources)	24.2	2018	●	●
Anthropogenic wastewater that receives treatment (%)	60.8	2018	●	●
Scarce water consumption embodied in imports (m^3 H_2O eq/capita)	2226.9	2018	●	●
Population using safely managed water services (%)	97.9	2020	●	↑
Population using safely managed sanitation services (%)	85.2	2020	●	↑
SDG7 – Affordable and Clean Energy				
Population with access to electricity (%)	100.0	2019	●	↑
Population with access to clean fuels and technology for cooking (%)	100.0	2019	●	↑
CO_2 emissions from fuel combustion per total electricity output ($MtCO_2$/TWh)	1.2	2019	●	↗
Share of renewable energy in total primary energy supply (%)	11.0	2019	●	→
SDG8 – Decent Work and Economic Growth				
Adjusted GDP growth (%)	-0.2	2020	●	●
Victims of modern slavery (per 1,000 population)	2.9	2018	●	●
Adults with an account at a bank or other financial institution or with a mobile-money-service provider (% of population aged 15 or over)	81.0	2017	●	↑
Fundamental labor rights are effectively guaranteed (worst 0–1 best)	0.8	2020	●	↑
Fatal work-related accidents embodied in imports (per 100,000 population)	0.7	2015	●	↑
Employment-to-population ratio (%)	74.4	2020	●	↑
Youth not in employment, education or training (NEET) (% of population aged 15 to 29)	10.6	2020	●	↑

* Imputed data point

SDG9 – Industry, Innovation and Infrastructure	Value	Year	Rating	Trend
Population using the internet (%)	81.3	2020	●	↑
Mobile broadband subscriptions (per 100 population)	92.5	2019	●	↑
Logistics Performance Index: Quality of trade and transport-related infrastructure (worst 1–5 best)	3.5	2018	●	↑
The Times Higher Education Universities Ranking: Average score of top 3 universities (worst 0–100 best)	32.9	2022	●	●
Articles published in academic journals (per 1,000 population)	2.3	2020	●	↑
Expenditure on research and development (% of GDP)	1.9	2018	●	↑
Researchers (per 1,000 employed population)	7.8	2019	●	↑
Triadic patent families filed (per million population)	5.4	2019	●	→
Gap in internet access by income (percentage points)	36.1	2020	●	↑
Female share of graduates from STEM fields at the tertiary level (%)	35.6	2017	●	↑
SDG10 – Reduced Inequalities				
Gini coefficient	25.0	2018	●	↑
Palma ratio	0.8	2019	●	↑
Elderly poverty rate (% of population aged 66 or over)	8.2	2019	●	↓
SDG11 – Sustainable Cities and Communities				
Proportion of urban population living in slums (%)	* 0.0	2018	●	↑
Annual mean concentration of particulate matter of less than 2.5 microns in diameter (PM2.5) (μg/m^3)	15.3	2019	●	↑
Access to improved water source, piped (% of urban population)	99.9	2020	●	↑
Satisfaction with public transport (%)	77.0	2021	●	↑
Population with rent overburden (%)	2.2	2019	●	↑
SDG12 – Responsible Consumption and Production				
Electronic waste (kg/capita)	15.7	2019	●	●
Production-based SO_2 emissions (kg/capita)	20.3	2018	●	●
SO_2 emissions embodied in imports (kg/capita)	4.2	2018	●	●
Production-based nitrogen emissions (kg/capita)	20.0	2015	●	↑
Nitrogen emissions embodied in imports (kg/capita)	7.6	2015	●	→
Exports of plastic waste (kg/capita)	7.6	2021	●	●
Non-recycled municipal solid waste (kg/capita/day)	0.9	2019	●	↓
SDG13 – Climate Action				
CO_2 emissions from fossil fuel combustion and cement production (tCO_2/capita)	8.2	2020	●	↗
CO_2 emissions embodied in imports (tCO_2/capita)	1.6	2018	●	↓
CO_2 emissions embodied in fossil fuel exports (kg/capita)	455.4	2021	●	●
Carbon Pricing Score at EUR60/tCO_2 (%, worst 0–100 best)	30.1	2018	●	↗
SDG14 – Life Below Water				
Mean area that is protected in marine sites important to biodiversity (%)	NA	NA	●	●
Ocean Health Index: Clean Waters score (worst 0–100 best)	NA	NA	●	●
Fish caught from overexploited or collapsed stocks (% of total catch)	NA	NA	●	●
Fish caught by trawling or dredging (%)	NA	NA	●	●
Fish caught that are then discarded (%)	NA	NA	●	●
Marine biodiversity threats embodied in imports (per million population)	0.1	2018	●	●
SDG15 – Life on Land				
Mean area that is protected in terrestrial sites important to biodiversity (%)	94.7	2020	●	↑
Mean area that is protected in freshwater sites important to biodiversity (%)	92.1	2020	●	↑
Red List Index of species survival (worst 0–1 best)	1.0	2021	●	↑
Permanent deforestation (% of forest area, 5-year average)	0.0	2020	●	↑
Terrestrial and freshwater biodiversity threats embodied in imports (per million population)	1.6	2018	●	●
SDG16 – Peace, Justice and Strong Institutions				
Homicides (per 100,000 population)	0.7	2020	●	↑
Unsentenced detainees (% of prison population)	8.5	2019	●	↑
Population who feel safe walking alone at night in the city or area where they live (%)	79	2021	●	↑
Property Rights (worst 1–7 best)	4.9	2020	●	↑
Birth registrations with civil authority (% of children under age 5)	100.0	2020	●	●
Corruption Perception Index (worst 0–100 best)	54	2021	●	↓
Children involved in child labor (% of population aged 5 to 14)	* 0.0	2019	●	●
Exports of major conventional weapons (TIV constant million USD per 100,000 population)	0.7	2020	●	●
Press Freedom Index (best 0–100 worst)	23.4	2021	●	↑
Access to and affordability of justice (worst 0–1 best)	0.7	2020	●	↑
Persons held in prison (per 100,000 population)	196.9	2019	●	↓
SDG17 – Partnerships for the Goals				
Government spending on health and education (% of GDP)	10.7	2019	●	↑
For high-income and all OECD DAC countries: International concessional public finance, including official development assistance (% of GNI)	0.1	2021	●	→
Other countries: Government revenue excluding grants (% of GDP)	NA	NA	●	●
Corporate Tax Haven Score (best 0–100 worst)	58.9	2019	●	●
Financial Secrecy Score (best 0–100 worst)	55.4	2020	●	●
Shifted profits of multinationals (US$ billion)	3.0	2018	●	↑
Statistical Performance Index (worst 0–100 best)	85.1	2019	●	↑

DENMARK

OECD Countries

AVERAGE PERFORMANCE BY SDG

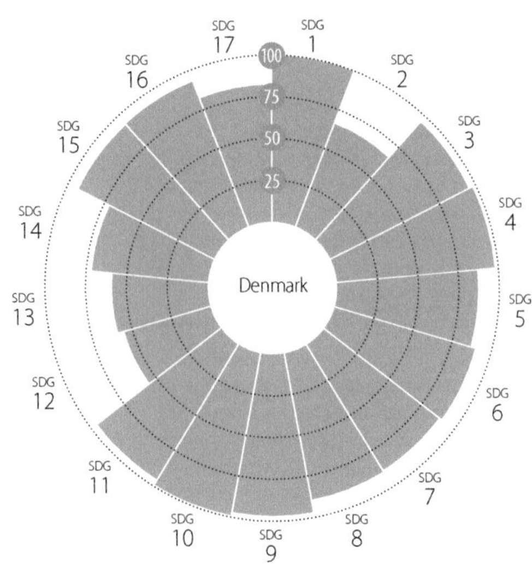

OVERALL PERFORMANCE

COUNTRY RANKING

DENMARK

2 **/163**

COUNTRY SCORE

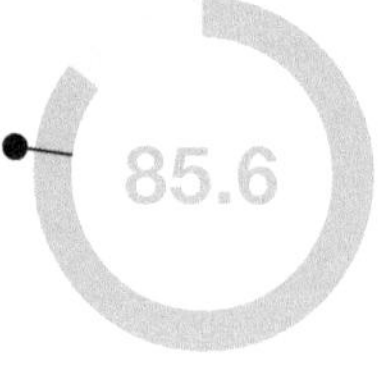

REGIONAL AVERAGE: 77.2

SDG DASHBOARDS AND TRENDS

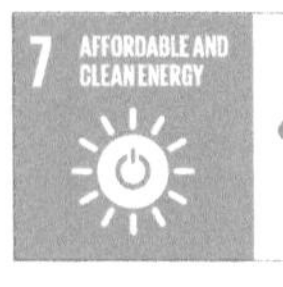

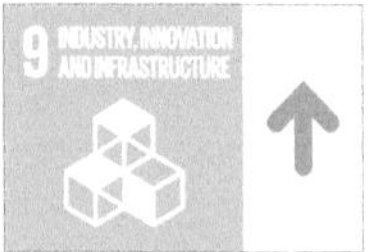

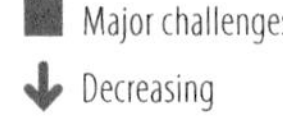
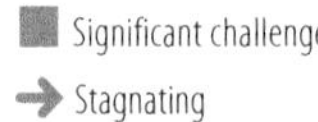

Major challenges · Significant challenges · Challenges remain · SDG achieved · Information unavailable

Decreasing · Stagnating · Moderately improving · On track or maintaining SDG achievement · Information unavailable

Note: The full title of each SDG is available here: https://sustainabledevelopment.un.org/topics/sustainabledevelopmentgoals

INTERNATIONAL SPILLOVER INDEX

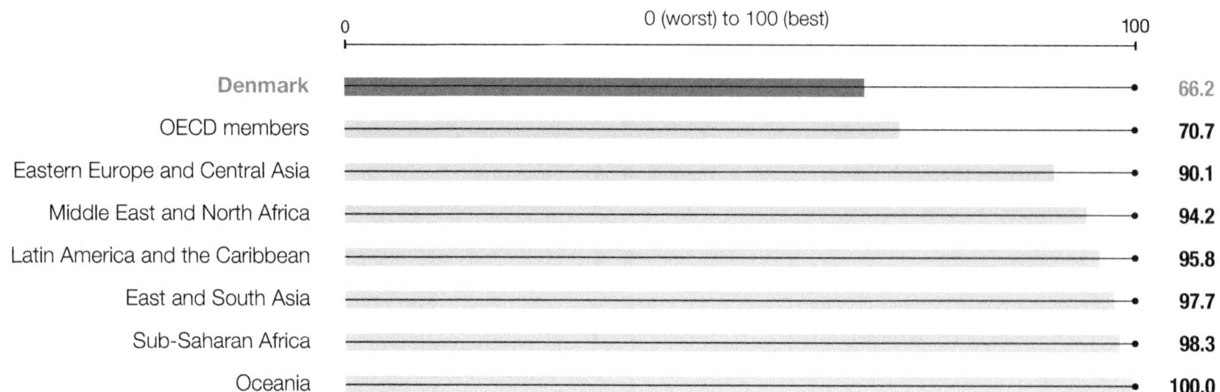

STATISTICAL PERFORMANCE INDEX

0 (worst) to 100 (best)

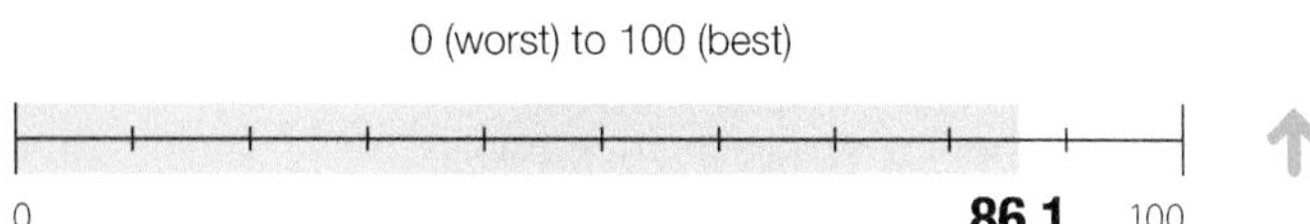

MISSING DATA IN SDG INDEX

1%

DENMARK

Performance by Indicator

SDG1 – No Poverty	Value	Year	Rating	Trend
Poverty headcount ratio at $1.90/day (%)	0.2	2022	●	↑
Poverty headcount ratio at $3.20/day (%)	0.2	2022	●	↑
Poverty rate after taxes and transfers (%)	6.4	2018	●	↑
SDG2 – Zero Hunger				
Prevalence of undernourishment (%)	2.5	2019	●	↑
Prevalence of stunting in children under 5 years of age (%)	* 2.6	2019	●	↑
Prevalence of wasting in children under 5 years of age (%)	* 0.7	2019	●	↑
Prevalence of obesity, BMI ≥ 30 (% of adult population)	19.7	2016	●	↓
Human Trophic Level (best 2–3 worst)	2.5	2017	●	↓
Cereal yield (tonnes per hectare of harvested land)	4.9	2018	●	↑
Sustainable Nitrogen Management Index (best 0–1.41 worst)	0.4	2015	●	→
Yield gap closure (% of potential yield)	74.1	2018	●	●
Exports of hazardous pesticides (tonnes per million population)	99.3	2019	●	●
SDG3 – Good Health and Well-Being				
Maternal mortality rate (per 100,000 live births)	4	2017	●	↑
Neonatal mortality rate (per 1,000 live births)	2.5	2020	●	↑
Mortality rate, under-5 (per 1,000 live births)	3.6	2020	●	↑
Incidence of tuberculosis (per 100,000 population)	4.9	2020	●	↑
New HIV infections (per 1,000 uninfected population)	0.0	2020	●	↑
Age-standardized death rate due to cardiovascular disease, cancer, diabetes, or chronic respiratory disease in adults aged 30–70 years (%)	10.8	2019	●	↑
Age-standardized death rate attributable to household air pollution and ambient air pollution (per 100,000 population)	13	2016	●	●
Traffic deaths (per 100,000 population)	3.7	2019	●	↑
Life expectancy at birth (years)	81.3	2019	●	↑
Adolescent fertility rate (births per 1,000 females aged 15 to 19)	2.0	2019	●	↑
Births attended by skilled health personnel (%)	95.3	2018	●	↓
Surviving infants who received 2 WHO-recommended vaccines (%)	94	2020	●	↑
Universal health coverage (UHC) index of service coverage (worst 0–100 best)	85	2019	●	↑
Subjective well-being (average ladder score, worst 0–10 best)	7.7	2021	●	↑
Gap in life expectancy at birth among regions (years)	2.1	2019	●	↑
Gap in self-reported health status by income (percentage points)	17.6	2020	●	↑
Daily smokers (% of population aged 15 and over)	16.9	2017	●	●
SDG4 – Quality Education				
Participation rate in pre-primary organized learning (% of children aged 4 to 6)	96.5	2019	●	↑
Net primary enrollment rate (%)	99.3	2019	●	↑
Lower secondary completion rate (%)	103.6	2019	●	↑
Literacy rate (% of population aged 15 to 24)	NA	NA	●	●
Tertiary educational attainment (% of population aged 25 to 34)	42.6	2020	●	↑
PISA score (worst 0–600 best)	501.0	2018	●	↑
Variation in science performance explained by socio-economic status (%)	11.6	2018	●	↓
Underachievers in science (% of 15-year-olds)	18.7	2018	●	↓
SDG5 – Gender Equality				
Demand for family planning satisfied by modern methods (% of females aged 15 to 49)	* 87.6	2022	●	↑
Ratio of female-to-male mean years of education received (%)	103.2	2019	●	↑
Ratio of female-to-male labor force participation rate (%)	87.0	2020	●	↑
Seats held by women in national parliament (%)	39.7	2020	●	↑
Gender wage gap (% of male median wage)	5.1	2019	●	↑
SDG6 – Clean Water and Sanitation				
Population using at least basic drinking water services (%)	100.0	2020	●	↑
Population using at least basic sanitation services (%)	99.6	2020	●	↑
Freshwater withdrawal (% of available freshwater resources)	28.9	2018	●	●
Anthropogenic wastewater that receives treatment (%)	100.0	2018	●	●
Scarce water consumption embodied in imports (m^3 H_2O eq/capita)	3552.9	2018	●	●
Population using safely managed water services (%)	96.7	2020	●	↑
Population using safely managed sanitation services (%)	91.9	2020	●	↑
SDG7 – Affordable and Clean Energy				
Population with access to electricity (%)	100.0	2019	●	↑
Population with access to clean fuels and technology for cooking (%)	100.0	2019	●	↑
CO_2 emissions from fuel combustion per total electricity output ($MtCO_2$/TWh)	0.9	2019	●	↑
Share of renewable energy in total primary energy supply (%)	35.8	2019	●	↑
SDG8 – Decent Work and Economic Growth				
Adjusted GDP growth (%)	0.8	2020	●	●
Victims of modern slavery (per 1,000 population)	1.6	2018	●	●
Adults with an account at a bank or other financial institution or with a mobile-money-service provider (% of population aged 15 or over)	99.9	2017	●	↑
Fundamental labor rights are effectively guaranteed (worst 0–1 best)	0.9	2020	●	↑
Fatal work-related accidents embodied in imports (per 100,000 population)	1.4	2015	●	↑
Employment-to-population ratio (%)	74.4	2020	●	↑
Youth not in employment, education or training (NEET) (% of population aged 15 to 29)	11.7	2020	●	→

SDG9 – Industry, Innovation and Infrastructure	Value	Year	Rating	Trend
Population using the internet (%)	96.5	2020	●	↑
Mobile broadband subscriptions (per 100 population)	138.0	2019	●	↑
Logistics Performance Index: Quality of trade and transport-related infrastructure (worst 1–5 best)	4.0	2018	●	↑
The Times Higher Education Universities Ranking: Average score of top 3 universities (worst 0–100 best)	59.7	2022	●	●
Articles published in academic journals (per 1,000 population)	5.2	2020	●	↑
Expenditure on research and development (% of GDP)	3.0	2018	●	↑
Researchers (per 1,000 employed population)	14.9	2019	●	↑
Triadic patent families filed (per million population)	56.1	2019	●	↑
Gap in internet access by income (percentage points)	9.8	2020	●	↑
Female share of graduates from STEM fields at the tertiary level (%)	34.2	2017	●	↑
SDG10 – Reduced Inequalities				
Gini coefficient	28.2	2018	●	↑
Palma ratio	0.9	2018	●	↑
Elderly poverty rate (% of population aged 66 or over)	3.6	2018	●	↑
SDG11 – Sustainable Cities and Communities				
Proportion of urban population living in slums (%)	* 0.0	2018	●	↑
Annual mean concentration of particulate matter of less than 2.5 microns in diameter (PM2.5) (μg/m^3)	9.6	2019	●	↑
Access to improved water source, piped (% of urban population)	100.0	2020	●	↑
Satisfaction with public transport (%)	73.0	2021	●	↑
Population with rent overburden (%)	16.1	2019	●	↓
SDG12 – Responsible Consumption and Production				
Electronic waste (kg/capita)	22.4	2019	●	●
Production-based SO_2 emissions (kg/capita)	11.7	2018	●	●
SO_2 emissions embodied in imports (kg/capita)	10.2	2018	●	●
Production-based nitrogen emissions (kg/capita)	31.2	2015	●	↓
Nitrogen emissions embodied in imports (kg/capita)	13.9	2015	●	↓
Exports of plastic waste (kg/capita)	7.4	2021	●	●
Non-recycled municipal solid waste (kg/capita/day)	1.1	2019	●	↗
SDG13 – Climate Action				
CO_2 emissions from fossil fuel combustion and cement production (tCO_2/capita)	4.5	2020	●	↑
CO_2 emissions embodied in imports (tCO_2/capita)	4.1	2018	●	↓
CO_2 emissions embodied in fossil fuel exports (kg/capita)	784.1	2021	●	●
Carbon Pricing Score at EUR60/tCO_2 (%, worst 0–100 best)	45.4	2018	●	↑
SDG14 – Life Below Water				
Mean area that is protected in marine sites important to biodiversity (%)	87.0	2020	●	↑
Ocean Health Index: Clean Waters score (worst 0–100 best)	52.6	2020	●	↓
Fish caught from overexploited or collapsed stocks (% of total catch)	35.7	2018	●	↓
Fish caught by trawling or dredging (%)	29.1	2018	●	↓
Fish caught that are then discarded (%)	3.6	2018	●	↑
Marine biodiversity threats embodied in imports (per million population)	0.1	2018	●	●
SDG15 – Life on Land				
Mean area that is protected in terrestrial sites important to biodiversity (%)	88.8	2020	●	↑
Mean area that is protected in freshwater sites important to biodiversity (%)	99.5	2020	●	↑
Red List Index of species survival (worst 0–1 best)	1.0	2021	●	↑
Permanent deforestation (% of forest area, 5-year average)	0.0	2020	●	↑
Terrestrial and freshwater biodiversity threats embodied in imports (per million population)	1.7	2018	●	●
SDG16 – Peace, Justice and Strong Institutions				
Homicides (per 100,000 population)	1.0	2020	●	↑
Unsentenced detainees (% of prison population)	34.5	2019	●	↓
Population who feel safe walking alone at night in the city or area where they live (%)	87	2021	●	↑
Property Rights (worst 1–7 best)	6.0	2020	●	↑
Birth registrations with civil authority (% of children under age 5)	100.0	2020	●	●
Corruption Perception Index (worst 0–100 best)	88	2021	●	↑
Children involved in child labor (% of population aged 5 to 14)	* 0.0	2019	●	●
Exports of major conventional weapons (TIV constant million USD per 100,000 population)	0.4	2020	●	●
Press Freedom Index (best 0–100 worst)	8.6	2021	●	↑
Access to and affordability of justice (worst 0–1 best)	0.8	2020	●	↑
Persons held in prison (per 100,000 population)	67.9	2019	●	↑
SDG17 – Partnerships for the Goals				
Government spending on health and education (% of GDP)	16.0	2019	●	↑
For high-income and all OECD DAC countries: International concessional public finance, including official development assistance (% of GNI)	0.7	2021	●	↑
Other countries: Government revenue excluding grants (% of GDP)	NA	NA	●	●
Corporate Tax Haven Score (best 0–100 worst)	51.7	2019	●	●
Financial Secrecy Score (best 0–100 worst)	45.3	2020	●	●
Shifted profits of multinationals (US$ billion)	6.1	2018	●	↑
Statistical Performance Index (worst 0–100 best)	86.1	2019	●	↑

* Imputed data point

5. Country Profiles

DJIBOUTI

Sub-Saharan Africa

OVERALL PERFORMANCE

COUNTRY RANKING

DJIBOUTI

155/163

COUNTRY SCORE

AVERAGE PERFORMANCE BY SDG

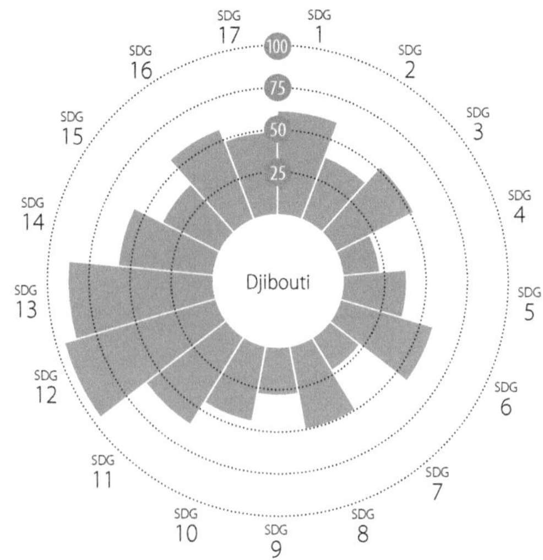

SDG DASHBOARDS AND TRENDS

Major challenges | Significant challenges | Challenges remain | SDG achieved | Information unavailable

Decreasing | Stagnating | Moderately improving | On track or maintaining SDG achievement | Information unavailable

Note: The full title of each SDG is available here: https://sustainabledevelopment.un.org/topics/sustainabledevelopmentgoals

INTERNATIONAL SPILLOVER INDEX

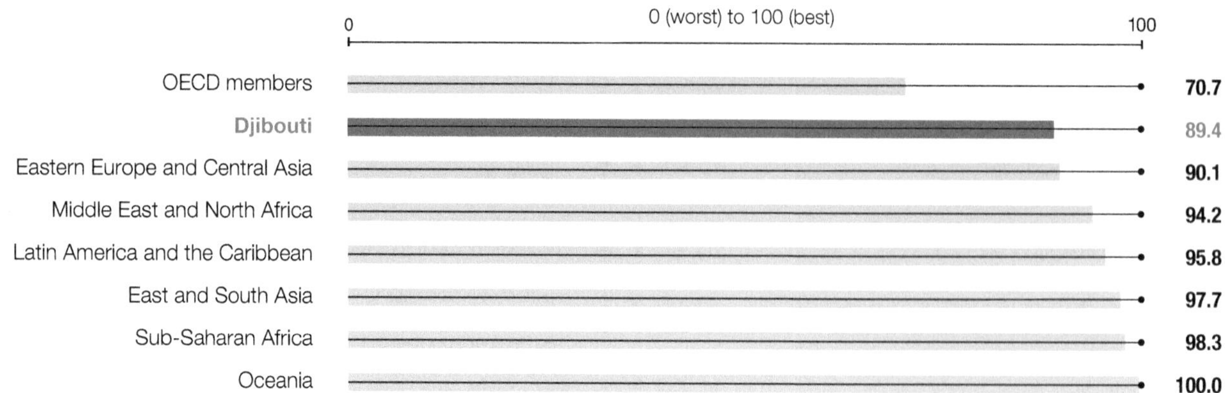

STATISTICAL PERFORMANCE INDEX

0 (worst) to 100 (best)

0 **36.6** 100

MISSING DATA IN SDG INDEX

16%

SDG1 – No Poverty	Value	Year	Rating	Trend
Poverty headcount ratio at $1.90/day (%)	12.1	2022	●	↗
Poverty headcount ratio at $3.20/day (%)	31.3	2022	●	↗
SDG2 – Zero Hunger				
Prevalence of undernourishment (%)	16.2	2019	●	→
Prevalence of stunting in children under 5 years of age (%)	33.5	2012	●	→
Prevalence of wasting in children under 5 years of age (%)	21.5	2012	●	→
Prevalence of obesity, BMI ≥ 30 (% of adult population)	13.5	2016	●	↓
Human Trophic Level (best 2–3 worst)	2.1	2017	●	↑
Cereal yield (tonnes per hectare of harvested land)	2.1	2018	●	↗
Sustainable Nitrogen Management Index (best 0–1.41 worst)	1.2	2015	●	→
Exports of hazardous pesticides (tonnes per million population)	NA	NA	●	●
SDG3 – Good Health and Well-Being				
Maternal mortality rate (per 100,000 live births)	248	2017	●	→
Neonatal mortality rate (per 1,000 live births)	30.4	2020	●	→
Mortality rate, under-5 (per 1,000 live births)	55.9	2020	●	↗
Incidence of tuberculosis (per 100,000 population)	224.0	2020	●	↑
New HIV infections (per 1,000 uninfected population)	0.1	2020	●	↑
Age-standardized death rate due to cardiovascular disease, cancer, diabetes, or chronic respiratory disease in adults aged 30–70 years (%)	22.0	2019	●	→
Age-standardized death rate attributable to household air pollution and ambient air pollution (per 100,000 population)	159	2016	●	●
Traffic deaths (per 100,000 population)	23.5	2019	●	→
Life expectancy at birth (years)	65.8	2019	●	→
Adolescent fertility rate (births per 1,000 females aged 15 to 19)	21.0	2011	●	●
Births attended by skilled health personnel (%)	87.4	2012	●	●
Surviving infants who received 2 WHO-recommended vaccines (%)	62	2020	●	↓
Universal health coverage (UHC) index of service coverage (worst 0–100 best)	48	2019	●	→
Subjective well-being (average ladder score, worst 0–10 best)	4.4	2011	●	●
SDG4 – Quality Education				
Participation rate in pre-primary organized learning (% of children aged 4 to 6)	14.9	2021	●	→
Net primary enrollment rate (%)	66.5	2021	●	→
Lower secondary completion rate (%)	49.8	2020	●	→
Literacy rate (% of population aged 15 to 24)	NA	NA	●	●
SDG5 – Gender Equality				
Demand for family planning satisfied by modern methods (% of females aged 15 to 49)	* 51.3	2022	●	↗
Ratio of female-to-male mean years of education received (%)	NA	NA	●	●
Ratio of female-to-male labor force participation rate (%)	38.8	2020	●	→
Seats held by women in national parliament (%)	26.2	2020	●	↑
SDG6 – Clean Water and Sanitation				
Population using at least basic drinking water services (%)	76.1	2020	●	→
Population using at least basic sanitation services (%)	66.7	2020	●	→
Freshwater withdrawal (% of available freshwater resources)	6.3	2018	●	●
Anthropogenic wastewater that receives treatment (%)	0.0	2018	●	●
Scarce water consumption embodied in imports (m^3 H_2O eq/capita)	3888.0	2018	●	●
SDG7 – Affordable and Clean Energy				
Population with access to electricity (%)	61.3	2019	●	→
Population with access to clean fuels and technology for cooking (%)	9.5	2019	●	→
CO_2 emissions from fuel combustion per total electricity output ($MtCO_2$/TWh)	5.8	2019	●	↓
Share of renewable energy in total primary energy supply (%)	NA	NA	●	●
SDG8 – Decent Work and Economic Growth				
Adjusted GDP growth (%)	0.1	2020	●	●
Victims of modern slavery (per 1,000 population)	7.1	2018	●	●
Adults with an account at a bank or other financial institution or with a mobile-money-service provider (% of population aged 15 or over)	12.3	2011	●	●
Unemployment rate (% of total labor force)	27.9	2022	●	↓
Fundamental labor rights are effectively guaranteed (worst 0–1 best)	NA	NA	●	●
Fatal work-related accidents embodied in imports (per 100,000 population)	0.1	2015	●	↑

* Imputed data point

SDG9 – Industry, Innovation and Infrastructure	Value	Year	Rating	Trend
Population using the internet (%)	59.0	2020	●	↑
Mobile broadband subscriptions (per 100 population)	23.6	2019	●	↗
Logistics Performance Index: Quality of trade and transport-related infrastructure (worst 1–5 best)	2.8	2018	●	↑
The Times Higher Education Universities Ranking: Average score of top 3 universities (worst 0–100 best)	* 0.0	2022	●	●
Articles published in academic journals (per 1,000 population)	0.0	2020	●	→
Expenditure on research and development (% of GDP)	NA	NA	●	●
SDG10 – Reduced Inequalities				
Gini coefficient	41.6	2017	●	●
Palma ratio	2.0	2018	●	●
SDG11 – Sustainable Cities and Communities				
Proportion of urban population living in slums (%)	65.6	2018	●	→
Annual mean concentration of particulate matter of less than 2.5 microns in diameter (PM2.5) (μg/m^3)	47.4	2019	●	↓
Access to improved water source, piped (% of urban population)	99.1	2020	●	↑
Satisfaction with public transport (%)	61.0	2011	●	●
SDG12 – Responsible Consumption and Production				
Municipal solid waste (kg/capita/day)	0.4	2002	●	●
Electronic waste (kg/capita)	1.0	2019	●	●
Production-based SO_2 emissions (kg/capita)	10.0	2018	●	●
SO_2 emissions embodied in imports (kg/capita)	2.3	2018	●	●
Production-based nitrogen emissions (kg/capita)	10.4	2015	●	↑
Nitrogen emissions embodied in imports (kg/capita)	1.3	2015	●	↑
Exports of plastic waste (kg/capita)	NA	NA	●	●
SDG13 – Climate Action				
CO_2 emissions from fossil fuel combustion and cement production (tCO_2/capita)	0.4	2020	●	↑
CO_2 emissions embodied in imports (tCO_2/capita)	1.2	2018	●	→
CO_2 emissions embodied in fossil fuel exports (kg/capita)	0.0	2020	●	●
SDG14 – Life Below Water				
Mean area that is protected in marine sites important to biodiversity (%)	0.0	2020	●	→
Ocean Health Index: Clean Waters score (worst 0–100 best)	51.7	2020	●	→
Fish caught from overexploited or collapsed stocks (% of total catch)	NA	NA	●	●
Fish caught by trawling or dredging (%)	0.0	2018	●	↑
Fish caught that are then discarded (%)	0.9	2000	●	●
Marine biodiversity threats embodied in imports (per million population)	NA	NA	●	●
SDG15 – Life on Land				
Mean area that is protected in terrestrial sites important to biodiversity (%)	0.8	2020	●	→
Mean area that is protected in freshwater sites important to biodiversity (%)	0.0	2020	●	→
Red List Index of species survival (worst 0–1 best)	0.8	2021	●	↓
Permanent deforestation (% of forest area, 5-year average)	NA	NA	●	●
Terrestrial and freshwater biodiversity threats embodied in imports (per million population)	0.0	2018	●	●
SDG16 – Peace, Justice and Strong Institutions				
Homicides (per 100,000 population)	NA	NA	●	●
Unsentenced detainees (% of prison population)	35.8	2018	●	↑
Population who feel safe walking alone at night in the city or area where they live (%)	72	2011	●	●
Property Rights (worst 1–7 best)	NA	NA	●	●
Birth registrations with civil authority (% of children under age 5)	91.7	2020	●	●
Corruption Perception Index (worst 0–100 best)	30	2021	●	↓
Children involved in child labor (% of population aged 5 to 14)	NA	NA	●	●
Exports of major conventional weapons (TIV constant million USD per 100,000 population)	* 0.0	2020	●	●
Press Freedom Index (best 0–100 worst)	78.6	2021	●	↓
Access to and affordability of justice (worst 0–1 best)	NA	NA	●	●
SDG17 – Partnerships for the Goals				
Government spending on health and education (% of GDP)	4.6	2019	●	↓
For high-income and all OECD DAC countries: International concessional public finance, including official development assistance (% of GNI)	NA	NA	●	●
Other countries: Government revenue excluding grants (% of GDP)	NA	NA	●	●
Corporate Tax Haven Score (best 0–100 worst)	* 0.0	2019	●	●
Statistical Performance Index (worst 0–100 best)	36.6	2019	●	↗

DOMINICA

Latin America and the Caribbean

OVERALL PERFORMANCE

COUNTRY RANKING

DOMINICA

NA /163

COUNTRY SCORE

REGIONAL AVERAGE: 69.5

AVERAGE PERFORMANCE BY SDG

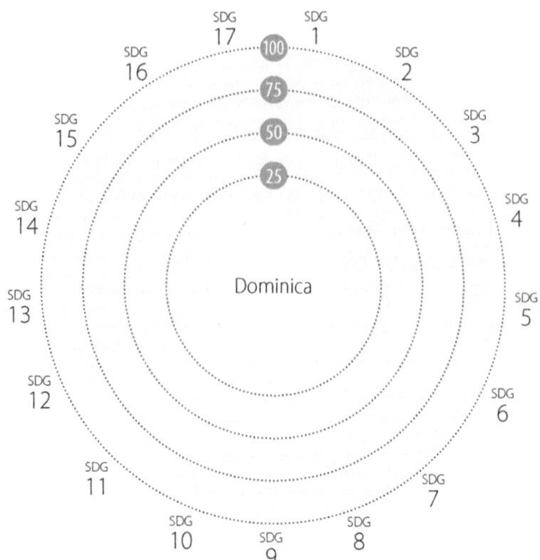

SDG DASHBOARDS AND TRENDS

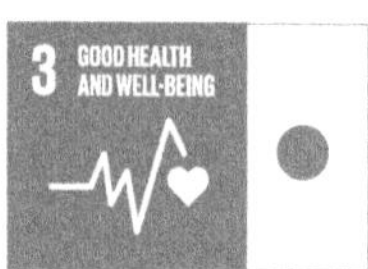

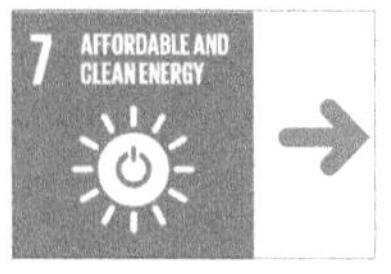

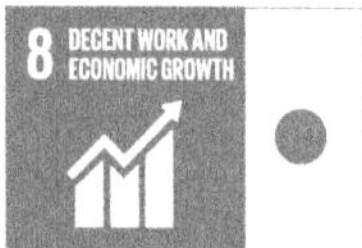

Major challenges · Significant challenges · Challenges remain · SDG achieved · Information unavailable

Decreasing · Stagnating · Moderately improving · On track or maintaining SDG achievement · Information unavailable

Note: The full title of each SDG is available here: https://sustainabledevelopment.un.org/topics/sustainabledevelopmentgoals

INTERNATIONAL SPILLOVER INDEX

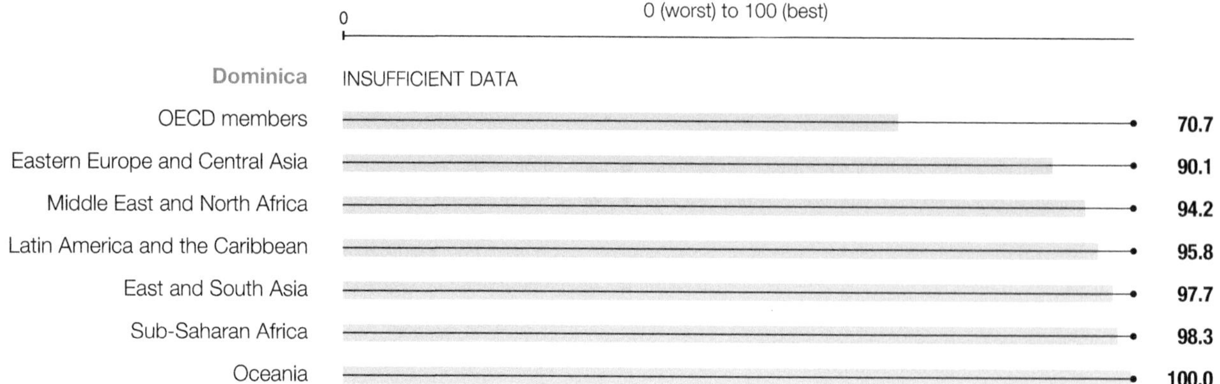

STATISTICAL PERFORMANCE INDEX

0 (worst) to 100 (best)

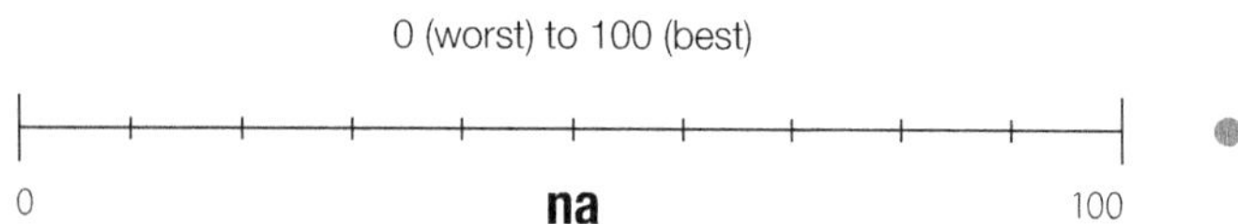

na

MISSING DATA IN SDG INDEX

50%

DOMINICA

Performance by Indicator

	Value	Year	Rating	Trend
SDG1 – No Poverty				
Poverty headcount ratio at $1.90/day (%)	NA	NA	●	●
Poverty headcount ratio at $3.20/day (%)	NA	NA	●	●
SDG2 – Zero Hunger				
Prevalence of undernourishment (%)	5.6	2019	●	↑
Prevalence of stunting in children under 5 years of age (%)	NA	NA	●	●
Prevalence of wasting in children under 5 years of age (%)	NA	NA	●	●
Prevalence of obesity, BMI ≥ 30 (% of adult population)	27.9	2016	●	↓
Human Trophic Level (best 2–3 worst)	2.2	2017	●	→
Cereal yield (tonnes per hectare of harvested land)	1.6	2018	●	→
Sustainable Nitrogen Management Index (best 0–1.41 worst)	1.1	2015	●	→
Exports of hazardous pesticides (tonnes per million population)	NA	NA	●	●
SDG3 – Good Health and Well-Being				
Maternal mortality rate (per 100,000 live births)	NA	NA	●	●
Neonatal mortality rate (per 1,000 live births)	30.0	2020	●	↓
Mortality rate, under-5 (per 1,000 live births)	35.4	2020	●	→
Incidence of tuberculosis (per 100,000 population)	47.0	2020	●	→
New HIV infections (per 1,000 uninfected population)	NA	NA	●	●
Age-standardized death rate due to cardiovascular disease, cancer, diabetes, or chronic respiratory disease in adults aged 30–70 years (%)	NA	NA	●	●
Age-standardized death rate attributable to household air pollution and ambient air pollution (per 100,000 population)	NA	NA	●	●
Traffic deaths (per 100,000 population)	NA	NA	●	●
Life expectancy at birth (years)	NA	NA	●	●
Adolescent fertility rate (births per 1,000 females aged 15 to 19)	47.1	2006	●	●
Births attended by skilled health personnel (%)	100.0	2017	●	↑
Surviving infants who received 2 WHO-recommended vaccines (%)	92	2020	●	↑
Universal health coverage (UHC) index of service coverage (worst 0–100 best)	NA	NA	●	●
Subjective well-being (average ladder score, worst 0–10 best)	NA	NA	●	●
SDG4 – Quality Education				
Participation rate in pre-primary organized learning (% of children aged 4 to 6)	96.2	2020	●	↑
Net primary enrollment rate (%)	99.1	2020	●	↑
Lower secondary completion rate (%)	90.7	2015	●	●
Literacy rate (% of population aged 15 to 24)	NA	NA	●	●
SDG5 – Gender Equality				
Demand for family planning satisfied by modern methods (% of females aged 15 to 49)	NA	NA	●	●
Ratio of female-to-male mean years of education received (%)	NA	NA	●	●
Ratio of female-to-male labor force participation rate (%)	NA	NA	●	●
Seats held by women in national parliament (%)	34.4	2020	●	↑
SDG6 – Clean Water and Sanitation				
Population using at least basic drinking water services (%)	95.4	2017	●	●
Population using at least basic sanitation services (%)	80.4	2017	●	●
Freshwater withdrawal (% of available freshwater resources)	10.0	2018	●	●
Anthropogenic wastewater that receives treatment (%)	1.0	2018	●	●
Scarce water consumption embodied in imports (m^3 H_2O eq/capita)	NA	NA	●	●
SDG7 – Affordable and Clean Energy				
Population with access to electricity (%)	100.0	2019	●	↑
Population with access to clean fuels and technology for cooking (%)	83.4	2019	●	→
CO_2 emissions from fuel combustion per total electricity output ($MtCO_2$/TWh)	1.9	2019	●	→
Share of renewable energy in total primary energy supply (%)	NA	NA	●	●
SDG8 – Decent Work and Economic Growth				
Adjusted GDP growth (%)	-5.8	2020	●	●
Victims of modern slavery (per 1,000 population)	NA	NA	●	●
Adults with an account at a bank or other financial institution or with a mobile-money-service provider (% of population aged 15 or over)	NA	NA	●	●
Unemployment rate (% of total labor force)	NA	NA	●	●
Fundamental labor rights are effectively guaranteed (worst 0–1 best)	0.6	2020	●	↓
Fatal work-related accidents embodied in imports (per 100,000 population)	NA	NA	●	●

* Imputed data point

	Value	Year	Rating	Trend
SDG9 – Industry, Innovation and Infrastructure				
Population using the internet (%)	69.6	2017	●	●
Mobile broadband subscriptions (per 100 population)	82.4	2019	●	↑
Logistics Performance Index: Quality of trade and transport-related infrastructure (worst 1–5 best)	NA	NA	●	●
The Times Higher Education Universities Ranking: Average score of top 3 universities (worst 0–100 best)	* 0.0	2022	●	●
Articles published in academic journals (per 1,000 population)	0.3	2020	●	↓
Expenditure on research and development (% of GDP)	NA	NA	●	●
SDG10 – Reduced Inequalities				
Gini coefficient	NA	NA	●	●
Palma ratio	NA	NA	●	●
SDG11 – Sustainable Cities and Communities				
Proportion of urban population living in slums (%)	NA	NA	●	●
Annual mean concentration of particulate matter of less than 2.5 microns in diameter (PM2.5) (μg/m³)	18.4	2019	●	↗
Access to improved water source, piped (% of urban population)	NA	NA	●	●
Satisfaction with public transport (%)	NA	NA	●	●
SDG12 – Responsible Consumption and Production				
Municipal solid waste (kg/capita/day)	0.5	2013	●	●
Electronic waste (kg/capita)	7.9	2019	●	●
Production-based SO_2 emissions (kg/capita)	NA	NA	●	●
SO_2 emissions embodied in imports (kg/capita)	NA	NA	●	●
Production-based nitrogen emissions (kg/capita)	NA	NA	●	●
Nitrogen emissions embodied in imports (kg/capita)	NA	NA	●	●
Exports of plastic waste (kg/capita)	NA	NA	●	●
SDG13 – Climate Action				
CO_2 emissions from fossil fuel combustion and cement production (tCO_2/capita)	1.9	2020	●	↑
CO_2 emissions embodied in imports (tCO_2/capita)	NA	NA	●	●
CO_2 emissions embodied in fossil fuel exports (kg/capita)	0.0	2020	●	●
SDG14 – Life Below Water				
Mean area that is protected in marine sites important to biodiversity (%)	0.0	2020	●	→
Ocean Health Index: Clean Waters score (worst 0–100 best)	58.9	2020	●	→
Fish caught from overexploited or collapsed stocks (% of total catch)	NA	NA	●	●
Fish caught by trawling or dredging (%)	30.4	2018	●	↑
Fish caught that are then discarded (%)	10.6	2018	●	↑
Marine biodiversity threats embodied in imports (per million population)	NA	NA	●	●
SDG15 – Life on Land				
Mean area that is protected in terrestrial sites important to biodiversity (%)	33.3	2020	●	→
Mean area that is protected in freshwater sites important to biodiversity (%)	NA	NA	●	●
Red List Index of species survival (worst 0–1 best)	0.7	2021	●	↓
Permanent deforestation (% of forest area, 5-year average)	0.1	2020	●	↑
Terrestrial and freshwater biodiversity threats embodied in imports (per million population)	NA	NA	●	●
SDG16 – Peace, Justice and Strong Institutions				
Homicides (per 100,000 population)	20.8	2020	●	↓
Unsentenced detainees (% of prison population)	58.1	2019	●	↓
Population who feel safe walking alone at night in the city or area where they live (%)	NA	NA	●	●
Property Rights (worst 1–7 best)	NA	NA	●	●
Birth registrations with civil authority (% of children under age 5)	NA	NA	●	●
Corruption Perception Index (worst 0–100 best)	55	2021	●	↓
Children involved in child labor (% of population aged 5 to 14)	NA	NA	●	●
Exports of major conventional weapons (TIV constant million USD per 100,000 population)	* 0.0	2020	●	●
Press Freedom Index (best 0–100 worst)	NA	NA	●	●
Access to and affordability of justice (worst 0–1 best)	0.8	2020	●	↑
SDG17 – Partnerships for the Goals				
Government spending on health and education (% of GDP)	8.5	2020	●	↑
For high-income and all OECD DAC countries: International concessional public finance, including official development assistance (% of GNI)	NA	NA	●	●
Other countries: Government revenue excluding grants (% of GDP)	NA	NA	●	●
Corporate Tax Haven Score (best 0–100 worst)	* 0.0	2019	●	●
Statistical Performance Index (worst 0–100 best)	NA	NA	●	●

DOMINICAN REPUBLIC Latin America and the Caribbean

OVERALL PERFORMANCE

COUNTRY RANKING

DOMINICAN REPUBLIC

68/163

COUNTRY SCORE

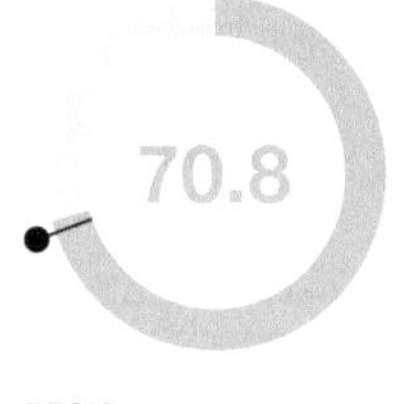

REGIONAL AVERAGE: 69.5

AVERAGE PERFORMANCE BY SDG

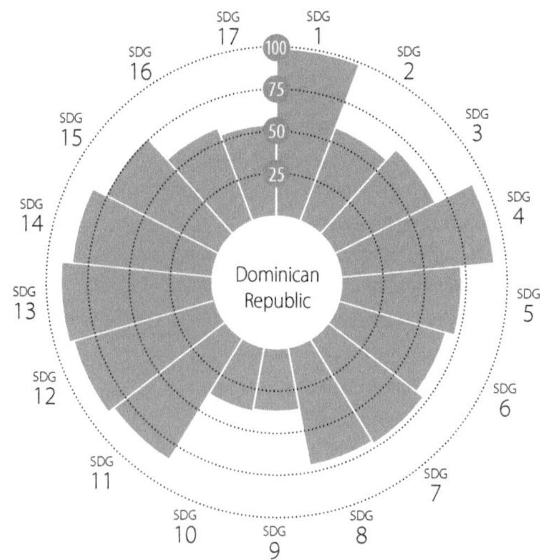

SDG DASHBOARDS AND TRENDS

Major challenges | Significant challenges | Challenges remain | SDG achieved | Information unavailable

Decreasing | Stagnating | Moderately improving | On track or maintaining SDG achievement | Information unavailable

Note: The full title of each SDG is available here: https://sustainabledevelopment.un.org/topics/sustainabledevelopmentgoals

INTERNATIONAL SPILLOVER INDEX

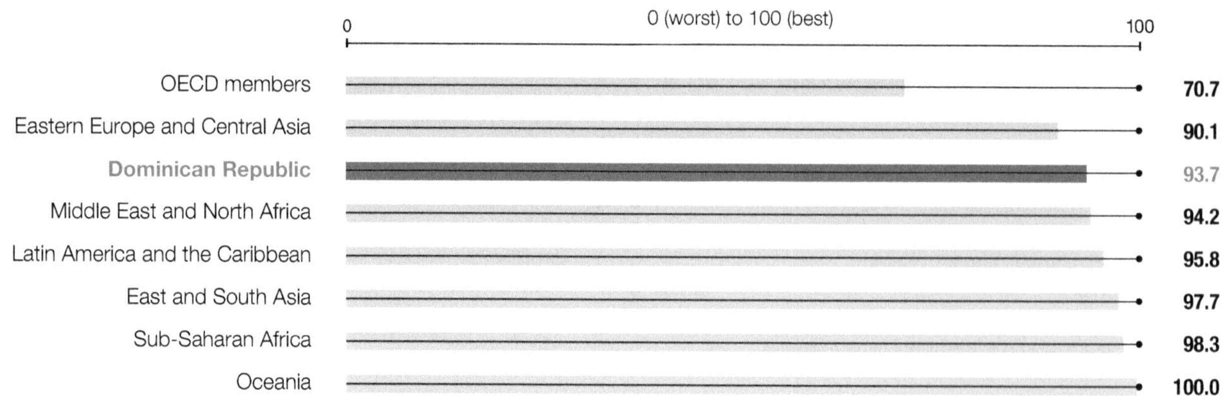

STATISTICAL PERFORMANCE INDEX

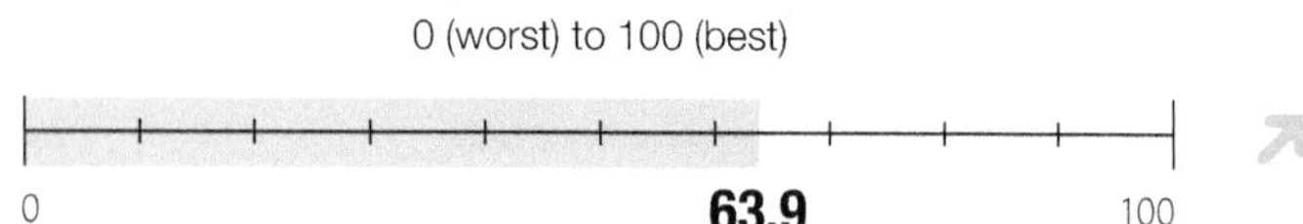

MISSING DATA IN SDG INDEX

1%

DOMINICAN REPUBLIC

SDG1 – No Poverty	Value	Year	Rating	Trend
Poverty headcount ratio at \$1.90/day (%)	0.2	2022	●	↑
Poverty headcount ratio at \$3.20/day (%)	1.5	2022	●	↑

SDG2 – Zero Hunger	Value	Year	Rating	Trend
Prevalence of undernourishment (%)	8.3	2019	●	↓
Prevalence of stunting in children under 5 years of age (%)	7.1	2013	●	↑
Prevalence of wasting in children under 5 years of age (%)	2.4	2013	●	↑
Prevalence of obesity, BMI ≥ 30 (% of adult population)	27.6	2016	●	↓
Human Trophic Level (best 2–3 worst)	2.2	2017	●	→
Cereal yield (tonnes per hectare of harvested land)	3.1	2018	●	↑
Sustainable Nitrogen Management Index (best 0–1.41 worst)	1.0	2015	●	→
Exports of hazardous pesticides (tonnes per million population)	27.7	2019	●	●

SDG3 – Good Health and Well-Being	Value	Year	Rating	Trend
Maternal mortality rate (per 100,000 live births)	95	2017	●	→
Neonatal mortality rate (per 1,000 live births)	23.4	2020	●	→
Mortality rate, under-5 (per 1,000 live births)	33.8	2020	●	→
Incidence of tuberculosis (per 100,000 population)	41.0	2020	●	↗
New HIV infections (per 1,000 uninfected population)	0.3	2020	●	→
Age-standardized death rate due to cardiovascular disease, cancer, diabetes, or chronic respiratory disease in adults aged 30–70 years (%)	19.1	2019	●	↑
Age-standardized death rate attributable to household air pollution and ambient air pollution (per 100,000 population)	43	2016	●	●
Traffic deaths (per 100,000 population)	64.6	2019	●	↓
Life expectancy at birth (years)	72.8	2019	●	→
Adolescent fertility rate (births per 1,000 females aged 15 to 19)	53.5	2019	●	●
Births attended by skilled health personnel (%)	99.8	2016	●	●
Surviving infants who received 2 WHO-recommended vaccines (%)	82	2020	●	↓
Universal health coverage (UHC) index of service coverage (worst 0–100 best)	66	2019	●	↗
Subjective well-being (average ladder score, worst 0–10 best)	6.0	2021	●	↑

SDG4 – Quality Education	Value	Year	Rating	Trend
Participation rate in pre-primary organized learning (% of children aged 4 to 6)	98.6	2020	●	↑
Net primary enrollment rate (%)	95.9	2020	●	↗
Lower secondary completion rate (%)	85.3	2020	●	↑
Literacy rate (% of population aged 15 to 24)	98.8	2016	●	●

SDG5 – Gender Equality	Value	Year	Rating	Trend
Demand for family planning satisfied by modern methods (% of females aged 15 to 49)	81.7	2014	●	↑
Ratio of female-to-male mean years of education received (%)	106.0	2019	●	↑
Ratio of female-to-male labor force participation rate (%)	64.3	2020	●	↗
Seats held by women in national parliament (%)	27.9	2020	●	↑

SDG6 – Clean Water and Sanitation	Value	Year	Rating	Trend
Population using at least basic drinking water services (%)	96.7	2020	●	↗
Population using at least basic sanitation services (%)	87.2	2020	●	↗
Freshwater withdrawal (% of available freshwater resources)	50.3	2018	●	●
Anthropogenic wastewater that receives treatment (%)	5.8	2018	●	●
Scarce water consumption embodied in imports (m^3 H_2O eq/capita)	1316.8	2018	●	●

SDG7 – Affordable and Clean Energy	Value	Year	Rating	Trend
Population with access to electricity (%)	100.0	2019	●	↑
Population with access to clean fuels and technology for cooking (%)	91.3	2019	●	↑
CO_2 emissions from fuel combustion per total electricity output ($MtCO_2$/TWh)	1.3	2019	●	→
Share of renewable energy in total primary energy supply (%)	11.0	2019	●	↓

SDG8 – Decent Work and Economic Growth	Value	Year	Rating	Trend
Adjusted GDP growth (%)	-1.5	2020	●	●
Victims of modern slavery (per 1,000 population)	4.0	2018	●	●
Adults with an account at a bank or other financial institution or with a mobile-money-service provider (% of population aged 15 or over)	56.2	2017	●	→
Unemployment rate (% of total labor force)	7.5	2022	●	→
Fundamental labor rights are effectively guaranteed (worst 0–1 best)	0.6	2020	●	↓
Fatal work-related accidents embodied in imports (per 100,000 population)	0.1	2015	●	↑

* Imputed data point

SDG9 – Industry, Innovation and Infrastructure	Value	Year	Rating	Trend
Population using the internet (%)	76.9	2020	●	↑
Mobile broadband subscriptions (per 100 population)	67.2	2019	●	↑
Logistics Performance Index: Quality of trade and transport-related infrastructure (worst 1–5 best)	2.4	2018	●	↓
The Times Higher Education Universities Ranking: Average score of top 3 universities (worst 0–100 best)	* 0.0	2022	●	●
Articles published in academic journals (per 1,000 population)	0.0	2020	●	→
Expenditure on research and development (% of GDP)	NA	NA	●	●

SDG10 – Reduced Inequalities	Value	Year	Rating	Trend
Gini coefficient	41.9	2019	●	↗
Palma ratio	2.3	2018	●	●

SDG11 – Sustainable Cities and Communities	Value	Year	Rating	Trend
Proportion of urban population living in slums (%)	14.3	2018	●	↓
Annual mean concentration of particulate matter of less than 2.5 microns in diameter (PM2.5) (μg/m^3)	12.7	2019	●	↑
Access to improved water source, piped (% of urban population)	84.1	2020	●	↓
Satisfaction with public transport (%)	67.0	2021	●	→

SDG12 – Responsible Consumption and Production	Value	Year	Rating	Trend
Municipal solid waste (kg/capita/day)	1.1	2015	●	●
Electronic waste (kg/capita)	6.4	2019	●	●
Production-based SO_2 emissions (kg/capita)	15.2	2018	●	●
SO_2 emissions embodied in imports (kg/capita)	1.4	2018	●	●
Production-based nitrogen emissions (kg/capita)	10.0	2015	●	↑
Nitrogen emissions embodied in imports (kg/capita)	1.3	2015	●	↑
Exports of plastic waste (kg/capita)	1.7	2020	●	●

SDG13 – Climate Action	Value	Year	Rating	Trend
CO_2 emissions from fossil fuel combustion and cement production (tCO_2/capita)	2.6	2020	●	→
CO_2 emissions embodied in imports (tCO_2/capita)	0.5	2018	●	↑
CO_2 emissions embodied in fossil fuel exports (kg/capita)	0.0	2020	●	●

SDG14 – Life Below Water	Value	Year	Rating	Trend
Mean area that is protected in marine sites important to biodiversity (%)	81.4	2020	●	→
Ocean Health Index: Clean Waters score (worst 0–100 best)	50.5	2020	●	→
Fish caught from overexploited or collapsed stocks (% of total catch)	2.6	2018	●	↑
Fish caught by trawling or dredging (%)	0.0	2018	●	↑
Fish caught that are then discarded (%)	0.0	2018	●	↑
Marine biodiversity threats embodied in imports (per million population)	0.1	2018	●	●

SDG15 – Life on Land	Value	Year	Rating	Trend
Mean area that is protected in terrestrial sites important to biodiversity (%)	76.9	2020	●	→
Mean area that is protected in freshwater sites important to biodiversity (%)	95.5	2020	●	↑
Red List Index of species survival (worst 0–1 best)	0.7	2021	●	↓
Permanent deforestation (% of forest area, 5-year average)	0.4	2020	●	↑
Terrestrial and freshwater biodiversity threats embodied in imports (per million population)	0.2	2018	●	●

SDG16 – Peace, Justice and Strong Institutions	Value	Year	Rating	Trend
Homicides (per 100,000 population)	8.9	2020	●	↑
Unsentenced detainees (% of prison population)	60.3	2017	●	●
Population who feel safe walking alone at night in the city or area where they live (%)	38	2021	●	→
Property Rights (worst 1–7 best)	4.2	2020	●	↑
Birth registrations with civil authority (% of children under age 5)	88.0	2020	●	●
Corruption Perception Index (worst 0–100 best)	30	2021	●	↓
Children involved in child labor (% of population aged 5 to 14)	7.0	2019	●	●
Exports of major conventional weapons (TIV constant million USD per 100,000 population)	0.0	2020	●	●
Press Freedom Index (best 0–100 worst)	25.6	2021	●	↑
Access to and affordability of justice (worst 0–1 best)	0.5	2020	●	→

SDG17 – Partnerships for the Goals	Value	Year	Rating	Trend
Government spending on health and education (% of GDP)	6.7	2019	●	↗
For high-income and all OECD DAC countries: International concessional public finance, including official development assistance (% of GNI)	NA	NA	●	●
Other countries: Government revenue excluding grants (% of GDP)	15.5	2019	●	↓
Corporate Tax Haven Score (best 0–100 worst)	* 0.0	2019	●	●
Statistical Performance Index (worst 0–100 best)	63.9	2019	●	↗

ECUADOR

Latin America and the Caribbean

OVERALL PERFORMANCE

COUNTRY RANKING

ECUADOR

63/163

COUNTRY SCORE

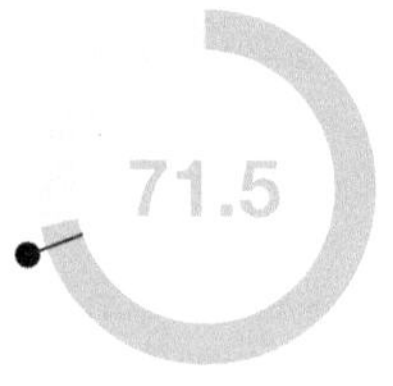

REGIONAL AVERAGE: 69.5

AVERAGE PERFORMANCE BY SDG

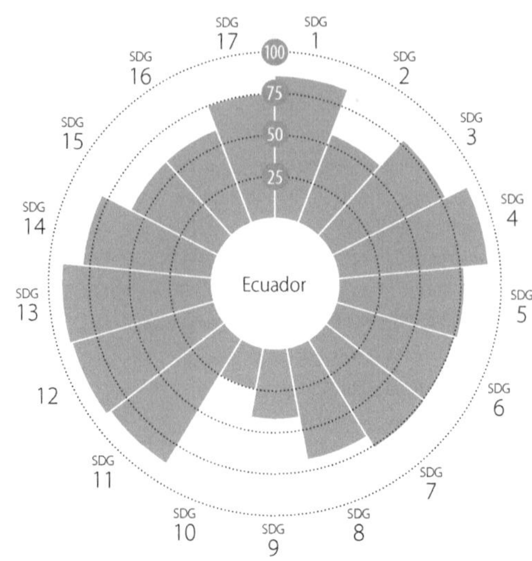

SDG DASHBOARDS AND TRENDS

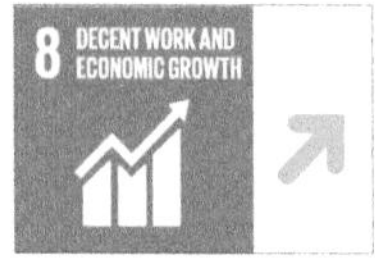

Moderately improving — On track or maintaining SDG achievement — Information unavailable — Information unavailable

Note: The full title of each SDG is available here: https://sustainabledevelopment.un.org/topics/sustainabledevelopmentgoals

INTERNATIONAL SPILLOVER INDEX

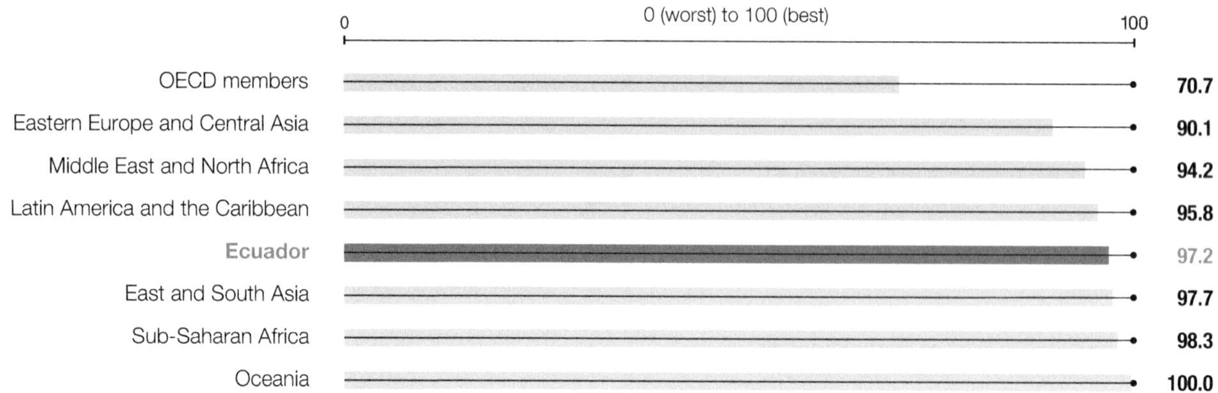

STATISTICAL PERFORMANCE INDEX

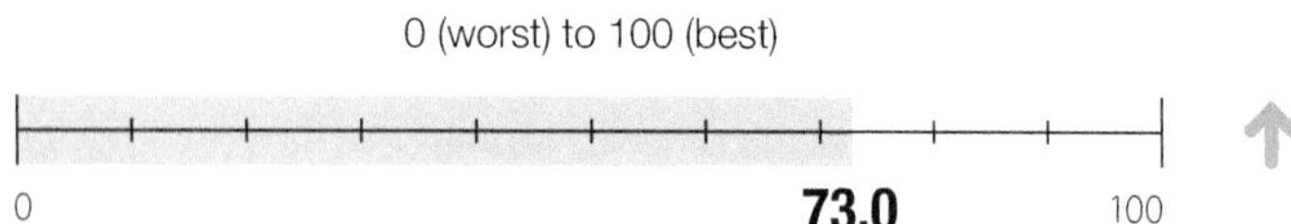

MISSING DATA IN SDG INDEX

2%

ECUADOR

Performance by Indicator

SDG1 – No Poverty	Value	Year	Rating	Trend
Poverty headcount ratio at \$1.90/day (%)	3.6	2022	●	→
Poverty headcount ratio at \$3.20/day (%)	12.4	2022	●	↓
SDG2 – Zero Hunger				
Prevalence of undernourishment (%)	12.4	2019	●	↓
Prevalence of stunting in children under 5 years of age (%)	23.0	2019	●	→
Prevalence of wasting in children under 5 years of age (%)	3.7	2019	●	↑
Prevalence of obesity, BMI ≥ 30 (% of adult population)	19.9	2016	●	↓
Human Trophic Level (best 2–3 worst)	2.3	2017	●	↗
Cereal yield (tonnes per hectare of harvested land)	3.9	2018	●	↑
Sustainable Nitrogen Management Index (best 0–1.41 worst)	1.0	2015	●	→
Exports of hazardous pesticides (tonnes per million population)	0.1	2019	●	●
SDG3 – Good Health and Well-Being				
Maternal mortality rate (per 100,000 live births)	59	2017	●	↑
Neonatal mortality rate (per 1,000 live births)	6.7	2020	●	↑
Mortality rate, under-5 (per 1,000 live births)	13.0	2020	●	↑
Incidence of tuberculosis (per 100,000 population)	48.0	2020	●	→
New HIV infections (per 1,000 uninfected population)	0.1	2020	●	↑
Age-standardized death rate due to cardiovascular disease, cancer, diabetes, or chronic respiratory disease in adults aged 30–70 years (%)	11.0	2019	●	↑
Age-standardized death rate attributable to household air pollution and ambient air pollution (per 100,000 population)	25	2016	●	●
Traffic deaths (per 100,000 population)	20.1	2019	●	↗
Life expectancy at birth (years)	78.5	2019	●	↑
Adolescent fertility rate (births per 1,000 females aged 15 to 19)	63.5	2019	●	↗
Births attended by skilled health personnel (%)	96.0	2018	●	↑
Surviving infants who received 2 WHO-recommended vaccines (%)	70	2020	●	↓
Universal health coverage (UHC) index of service coverage (worst 0–100 best)	80	2019	●	↑
Subjective well-being (average ladder score, worst 0–10 best)	5.4	2021	●	↓
SDG4 – Quality Education				
Participation rate in pre-primary organized learning (% of children aged 4 to 6)	83.7	2020	●	↓
Net primary enrollment rate (%)	98.6	2020	●	↑
Lower secondary completion rate (%)	102.3	2020	●	↑
Literacy rate (% of population aged 15 to 24)	98.8	2020	●	↑
SDG5 – Gender Equality				
Demand for family planning satisfied by modern methods (% of females aged 15 to 49)	79.4	2012	●	↑
Ratio of female-to-male mean years of education received (%)	97.8	2019	●	→
Ratio of female-to-male labor force participation rate (%)	67.0	2020	●	↑
Seats held by women in national parliament (%)	39.4	2020	●	↓
SDG6 – Clean Water and Sanitation				
Population using at least basic drinking water services (%)	95.4	2020	●	↑
Population using at least basic sanitation services (%)	91.5	2020	●	↑
Freshwater withdrawal (% of available freshwater resources)	6.8	2018	●	●
Anthropogenic wastewater that receives treatment (%)	0.0	2018	●	●
Scarce water consumption embodied in imports (m^3 H_2O eq/capita)	799.7	2018	●	●
SDG7 – Affordable and Clean Energy				
Population with access to electricity (%)	100.0	2019	●	↑
Population with access to clean fuels and technology for cooking (%)	93.9	2019	●	↑
CO_2 emissions from fuel combustion per total electricity output ($MtCO_2$/TWh)	1.3	2019	●	↑
Share of renewable energy in total primary energy supply (%)	17.5	2019	●	↑
SDG8 – Decent Work and Economic Growth				
Adjusted GDP growth (%)	-6.5	2020	●	●
Victims of modern slavery (per 1,000 population)	2.4	2018	●	●
Adults with an account at a bank or other financial institution or with a mobile-money-service provider (% of population aged 15 or over)	51.2	2017	●	↗
Unemployment rate (% of total labor force)	6.1	2022	●	↓
Fundamental labor rights are effectively guaranteed (worst 0–1 best)	0.6	2020	●	↗
Fatal work-related accidents embodied in imports (per 100,000 population)	0.1	2015	●	↑

* Imputed data point

SDG9 – Industry, Innovation and Infrastructure	Value	Year	Rating	Trend
Population using the internet (%)	64.6	2020	●	↑
Mobile broadband subscriptions (per 100 population)	53.7	2019	●	↑
Logistics Performance Index: Quality of trade and transport-related infrastructure (worst 1–5 best)	2.7	2018	●	↑
The Times Higher Education Universities Ranking: Average score of top 3 universities (worst 0–100 best)	20.8	2022	●	●
Articles published in academic journals (per 1,000 population)	0.3	2020	●	↑
Expenditure on research and development (% of GDP)	0.4	2014	●	●
SDG10 – Reduced Inequalities				
Gini coefficient	45.7	2019	●	→
Palma ratio	2.5	2018	●	●
SDG11 – Sustainable Cities and Communities				
Proportion of urban population living in slums (%)	17.1	2018	●	↑
Annual mean concentration of particulate matter of less than 2.5 microns in diameter (PM2.5) (μg/m^3)	13.7	2019	●	↑
Access to improved water source, piped (% of urban population)	100.0	2020	●	↑
Satisfaction with public transport (%)	69.0	2021	●	↑
SDG12 – Responsible Consumption and Production				
Municipal solid waste (kg/capita/day)	0.9	2015	●	●
Electronic waste (kg/capita)	5.7	2019	●	●
Production-based SO_2 emissions (kg/capita)	14.2	2018	●	●
SO_2 emissions embodied in imports (kg/capita)	0.8	2018	●	●
Production-based nitrogen emissions (kg/capita)	11.2	2015	●	↑
Nitrogen emissions embodied in imports (kg/capita)	1.3	2015	●	↑
Exports of plastic waste (kg/capita)	0.4	2020	●	●
SDG13 – Climate Action				
CO_2 emissions from fossil fuel combustion and cement production (tCO_2/capita)	1.8	2020	●	↑
CO_2 emissions embodied in imports (tCO_2/capita)	0.3	2018	●	↑
CO_2 emissions embodied in fossil fuel exports (kg/capita)	3296.8	2020	●	●
SDG14 – Life Below Water				
Mean area that is protected in marine sites important to biodiversity (%)	70.3	2020	●	→
Ocean Health Index: Clean Waters score (worst 0–100 best)	68.8	2020	●	↗
Fish caught from overexploited or collapsed stocks (% of total catch)	29.0	2018	●	↓
Fish caught by trawling or dredging (%)	0.0	2018	●	↑
Fish caught that are then discarded (%)	3.5	2018	●	↑
Marine biodiversity threats embodied in imports (per million population)	0.0	2018	●	●
SDG15 – Life on Land				
Mean area that is protected in terrestrial sites important to biodiversity (%)	29.7	2020	●	→
Mean area that is protected in freshwater sites important to biodiversity (%)	59.4	2020	●	↗
Red List Index of species survival (worst 0–1 best)	0.7	2021	●	↓
Permanent deforestation (% of forest area, 5-year average)	0.1	2020	●	↑
Terrestrial and freshwater biodiversity threats embodied in imports (per million population)	0.3	2018	●	●
SDG16 – Peace, Justice and Strong Institutions				
Homicides (per 100,000 population)	7.8	2020	●	→
Unsentenced detainees (% of prison population)	36.9	2019	●	→
Population who feel safe walking alone at night in the city or area where they live (%)	42	2021	●	↓
Property Rights (worst 1–7 best)	3.7	2020	●	↑
Birth registrations with civil authority (% of children under age 5)	82.1	2020	●	●
Corruption Perception Index (worst 0–100 best)	36	2021	●	→
Children involved in child labor (% of population aged 5 to 14)	NA	NA	●	●
Exports of major conventional weapons (TIV constant million USD per 100,000 population)	0.0	2020	●	●
Press Freedom Index (best 0–100 worst)	32.8	2021	●	→
Access to and affordability of justice (worst 0–1 best)	0.6	2020	●	↑
SDG17 – Partnerships for the Goals				
Government spending on health and education (% of GDP)	9.0	2020	●	↓
For high-income and all OECD DAC countries: International concessional public finance, including official development assistance (% of GNI)	NA	NA	●	●
Other countries: Government revenue excluding grants (% of GDP)	NA	NA	●	●
Corporate Tax Haven Score (best 0–100 worst)	* 0.0	2019	●	●
Statistical Performance Index (worst 0–100 best)	73.0	2019	●	↑

5. Country Profiles

EGYPT, ARAB REPUBLIC OF

Middle East and North Africa

OVERALL PERFORMANCE

COUNTRY RANKING

EGYPT, ARAB REPUBLIC OF

87 /163

COUNTRY SCORE

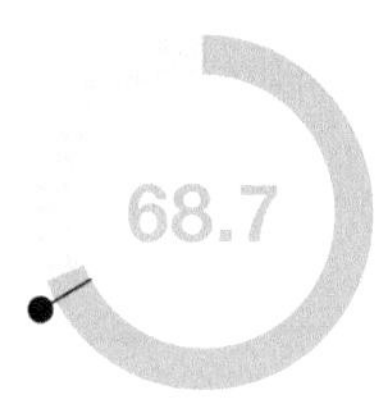

REGIONAL AVERAGE: 66.7

AVERAGE PERFORMANCE BY SDG

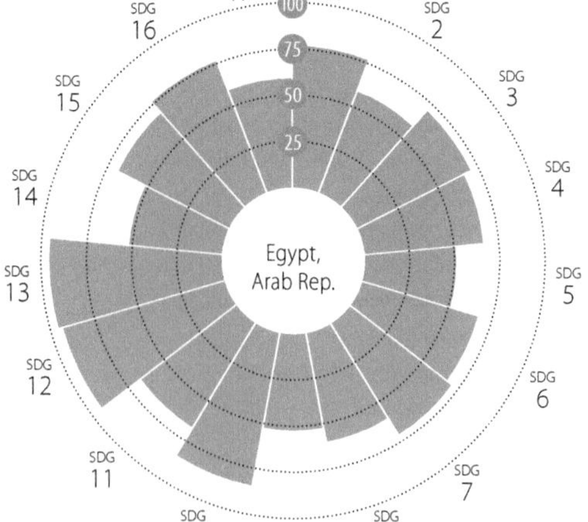

SDG DASHBOARDS AND TRENDS

Major challenges · Significant challenges · Challenges remain · SDG achieved · Information unavailable

Decreasing · Stagnating · Moderately improving · On track or maintaining SDG achievement · Information unavailable

Note: The full title of each SDG is available here: https://sustainabledevelopment.un.org/topics/sustainabledevelopmentgoals

INTERNATIONAL SPILLOVER INDEX

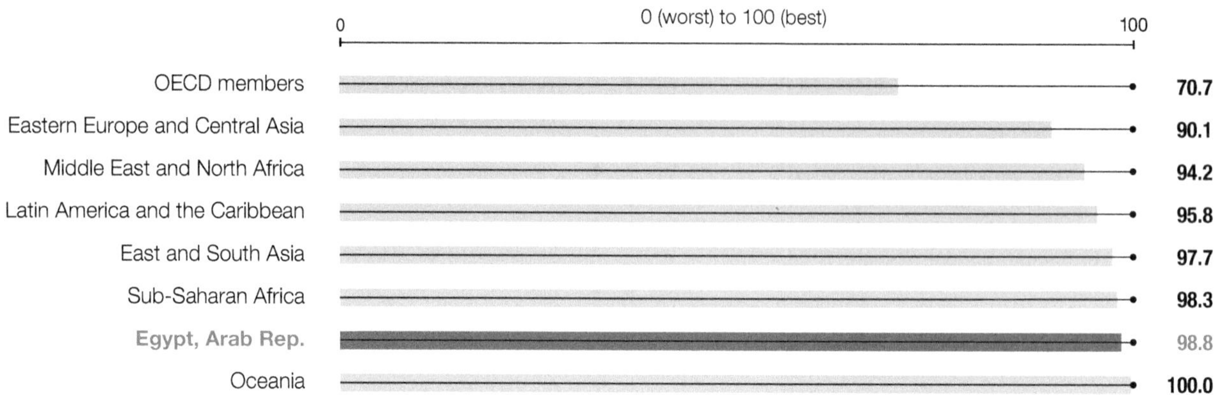

STATISTICAL PERFORMANCE INDEX

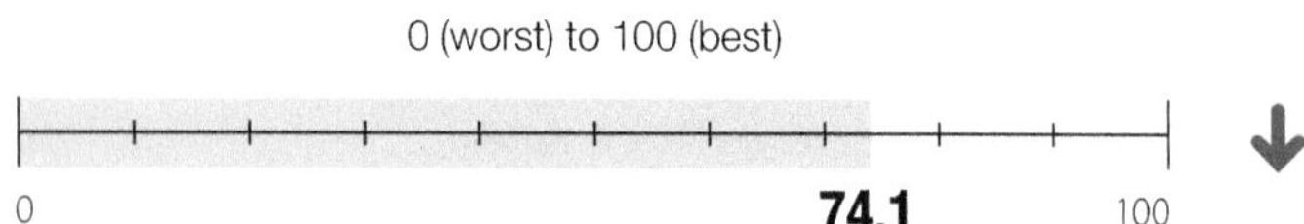

MISSING DATA IN SDG INDEX

1%

EGYPT, ARAB REPUBLIC OF

Performance by Indicator

SDG1 – No Poverty	Value	Year	Rating	Trend
Poverty headcount ratio at \$1.90/day (%)	1.9	2022	●	↑
Poverty headcount ratio at \$3.20/day (%)	22.4	2022	●	↓
SDG2 – Zero Hunger				
Prevalence of undernourishment (%)	5.4	2019	●	↑
Prevalence of stunting in children under 5 years of age (%)	22.3	2014	●	↗
Prevalence of wasting in children under 5 years of age (%)	9.5	2014	●	↗
Prevalence of obesity, BMI ≥ 30 (% of adult population)	32.0	2016	●	↓
Human Trophic Level (best 2–3 worst)	2.2	2017	●	↑
Cereal yield (tonnes per hectare of harvested land)	7.1	2018	●	↑
Sustainable Nitrogen Management Index (best 0–1.41 worst)	0.6	2015	●	↓
Exports of hazardous pesticides (tonnes per million population)	NA	NA	●	●
SDG3 – Good Health and Well-Being				
Maternal mortality rate (per 100,000 live births)	37	2017	●	↑
Neonatal mortality rate (per 1,000 live births)	10.3	2020	●	↑
Mortality rate, under-5 (per 1,000 live births)	19.5	2020	●	↑
Incidence of tuberculosis (per 100,000 population)	11.0	2020	●	↑
New HIV infections (per 1,000 uninfected population)	0.0	2020	●	↑
Age-standardized death rate due to cardiovascular disease, cancer, diabetes, or chronic respiratory disease in adults aged 30–70 years (%)	28.0	2019	●	↗
Age-standardized death rate attributable to household air pollution and ambient air pollution (per 100,000 population)	109	2016	●	●
Traffic deaths (per 100,000 population)	10.1	2019	●	↑
Life expectancy at birth (years)	71.8	2019	●	↗
Adolescent fertility rate (births per 1,000 females aged 15 to 19)	51.8	2018	●	↗
Births attended by skilled health personnel (%)	91.5	2014	●	●
Surviving infants who received 2 WHO-recommended vaccines (%)	94	2020	●	↑
Universal health coverage (UHC) index of service coverage (worst 0–100 best)	70	2019	●	↑
Subjective well-being (average ladder score, worst 0–10 best)	4.0	2021	●	↓
SDG4 – Quality Education				
Participation rate in pre-primary organized learning (% of children aged 4 to 6)	36.7	2019	●	↓
Net primary enrollment rate (%)	99.3	2019	●	↑
Lower secondary completion rate (%)	88.4	2019	●	↑
Literacy rate (% of population aged 15 to 24)	88.2	2017	●	●
SDG5 – Gender Equality				
Demand for family planning satisfied by modern methods (% of females aged 15 to 49)	80.0	2014	●	●
Ratio of female-to-male mean years of education received (%)	84.0	2019	●	↗
Ratio of female-to-male labor force participation rate (%)	23.0	2020	●	↓
Seats held by women in national parliament (%)	27.4	2020	●	↑
SDG6 – Clean Water and Sanitation				
Population using at least basic drinking water services (%)	99.4	2020	●	↑
Population using at least basic sanitation services (%)	97.3	2020	●	↑
Freshwater withdrawal (% of available freshwater resources)	116.9	2018	●	●
Anthropogenic wastewater that receives treatment (%)	42.0	2018	●	●
Scarce water consumption embodied in imports (m^3 H_2O eq/capita)	369.5	2018	●	●
SDG7 – Affordable and Clean Energy				
Population with access to electricity (%)	100.0	2019	●	↑
Population with access to clean fuels and technology for cooking (%)	99.9	2019	●	↑
CO_2 emissions from fuel combustion per total electricity output ($MtCO_2$/TWh)	1.3	2019	●	→
Share of renewable energy in total primary energy supply (%)	5.1	2019	●	↓
SDG8 – Decent Work and Economic Growth				
Adjusted GDP growth (%)	0.2	2020	●	●
Victims of modern slavery (per 1,000 population)	5.5	2018	●	●
Adults with an account at a bank or other financial institution or with a mobile-money-service provider (% of population aged 15 or over)	32.8	2017	●	↑
Unemployment rate (% of total labor force)	9.0	2022	●	↑
Fundamental labor rights are effectively guaranteed (worst 0–1 best)	0.4	2020	●	↗
Fatal work-related accidents embodied in imports (per 100,000 population)	0.1	2015	●	↑

* Imputed data point

SDG9 – Industry, Innovation and Infrastructure	Value	Year	Rating	Trend
Population using the internet (%)	71.9	2020	●	↑
Mobile broadband subscriptions (per 100 population)	59.3	2019	●	↑
Logistics Performance Index: Quality of trade and transport-related infrastructure (worst 1–5 best)	2.8	2018	●	↓
The Times Higher Education Universities Ranking: Average score of top 3 universities (worst 0–100 best)	40.5	2022	●	●
Articles published in academic journals (per 1,000 population)	0.3	2020	●	↗
Expenditure on research and development (% of GDP)	0.7	2018	●	→
SDG10 – Reduced Inequalities				
Gini coefficient	31.5	2017	●	↑
Palma ratio	1.2	2018	●	●
SDG11 – Sustainable Cities and Communities				
Proportion of urban population living in slums (%)	3.1	2018	●	↑
Annual mean concentration of particulate matter of less than 2.5 microns in diameter (PM2.5) ($\mu g/m^3$)	91.3	2019	●	↓
Access to improved water source, piped (% of urban population)	98.8	2020	●	↑
Satisfaction with public transport (%)	64.0	2021	●	↓
SDG12 – Responsible Consumption and Production				
Municipal solid waste (kg/capita/day)	0.7	2012	●	●
Electronic waste (kg/capita)	5.9	2019	●	●
Production-based SO_2 emissions (kg/capita)	8.8	2018	●	●
SO_2 emissions embodied in imports (kg/capita)	0.4	2018	●	●
Production-based nitrogen emissions (kg/capita)	7.7	2015	●	↑
Nitrogen emissions embodied in imports (kg/capita)	0.5	2015	●	↑
Exports of plastic waste (kg/capita)	0.0	2020	●	●
SDG13 – Climate Action				
CO_2 emissions from fossil fuel combustion and cement production (tCO_2/capita)	2.1	2020	●	↑
CO_2 emissions embodied in imports (tCO_2/capita)	0.1	2018	●	↑
CO_2 emissions embodied in fossil fuel exports (kg/capita)	206.5	2020	●	●
SDG14 – Life Below Water				
Mean area that is protected in marine sites important to biodiversity (%)	43.0	2020	●	→
Ocean Health Index: Clean Waters score (worst 0–100 best)	50.4	2020	●	↓
Fish caught from overexploited or collapsed stocks (% of total catch)	36.8	2018	●	↓
Fish caught by trawling or dredging (%)	41.5	2018	●	↑
Fish caught that are then discarded (%)	15.5	2018	●	↓
Marine biodiversity threats embodied in imports (per million population)	0.0	2018	●	●
SDG15 – Life on Land				
Mean area that is protected in terrestrial sites important to biodiversity (%)	38.4	2020	●	→
Mean area that is protected in freshwater sites important to biodiversity (%)	28.5	2020	●	→
Red List Index of species survival (worst 0–1 best)	0.9	2021	●	↑
Permanent deforestation (% of forest area, 5-year average)	0.0	2020	●	↑
Terrestrial and freshwater biodiversity threats embodied in imports (per million population)	0.1	2018	●	●
SDG16 – Peace, Justice and Strong Institutions				
Homicides (per 100,000 population)	2.6	2012	●	●
Unsentenced detainees (% of prison population)	9.9	2016	●	●
Population who feel safe walking alone at night in the city or area where they live (%)	88	2021	●	↑
Property Rights (worst 1–7 best)	5.2	2020	●	↑
Birth registrations with civil authority (% of children under age 5)	99.4	2020	●	●
Corruption Perception Index (worst 0–100 best)	33	2021	●	↓
Children involved in child labor (% of population aged 5 to 14)	4.8	2019	●	●
Exports of major conventional weapons (TIV constant million USD per 100,000 population)	0.0	2020	●	●
Press Freedom Index (best 0–100 worst)	56.2	2021	●	↓
Access to and affordability of justice (worst 0–1 best)	0.5	2020	●	↗
SDG17 – Partnerships for the Goals				
Government spending on health and education (% of GDP)	5.2	2019	●	↓
For high-income and all OECD DAC countries: International concessional public finance, including official development assistance (% of GNI)	NA	NA	●	●
Other countries: Government revenue excluding grants (% of GDP)	21.0	2015	●	●
Corporate Tax Haven Score (best 0–100 worst)	* 0.0	2019	●	●
Statistical Performance Index (worst 0–100 best)	74.1	2019	●	↓

5. Country Profiles

EL SALVADOR

Latin America and the Caribbean

OVERALL PERFORMANCE

COUNTRY RANKING

EL SALVADOR

79/163

COUNTRY SCORE

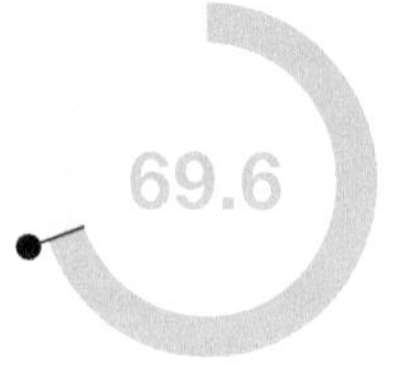

REGIONAL AVERAGE: 69.5

AVERAGE PERFORMANCE BY SDG

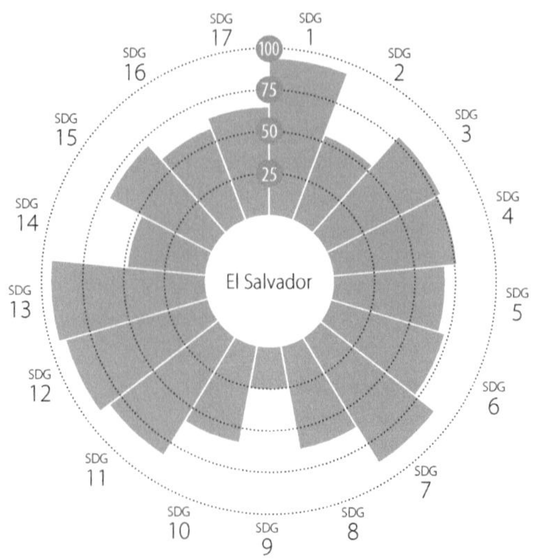

SDG DASHBOARDS AND TRENDS

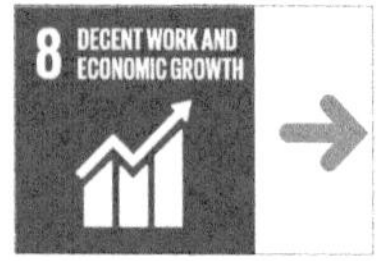

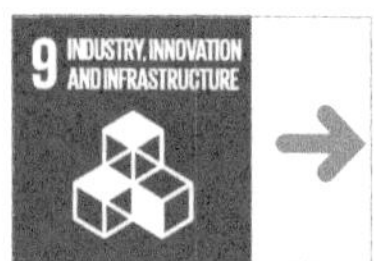

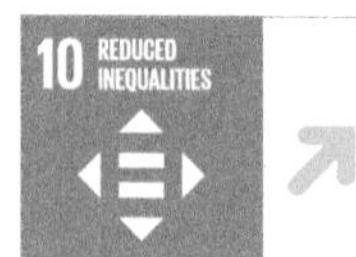

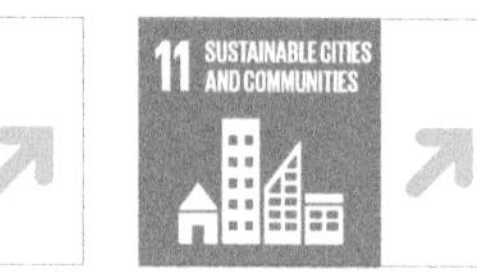

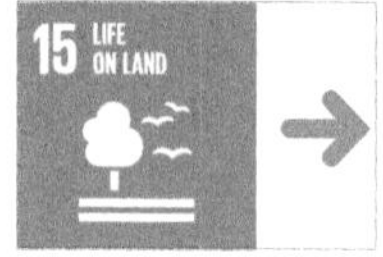

Major challenges | Significant challenges | Challenges remain | SDG achieved | Information unavailable

Decreasing | Stagnating | Moderately improving | On track or maintaining SDG achievement | Information unavailable

Note: The full title of each SDG is available here: https://sustainabledevelopment.un.org/topics/sustainabledevelopmentgoals

INTERNATIONAL SPILLOVER INDEX

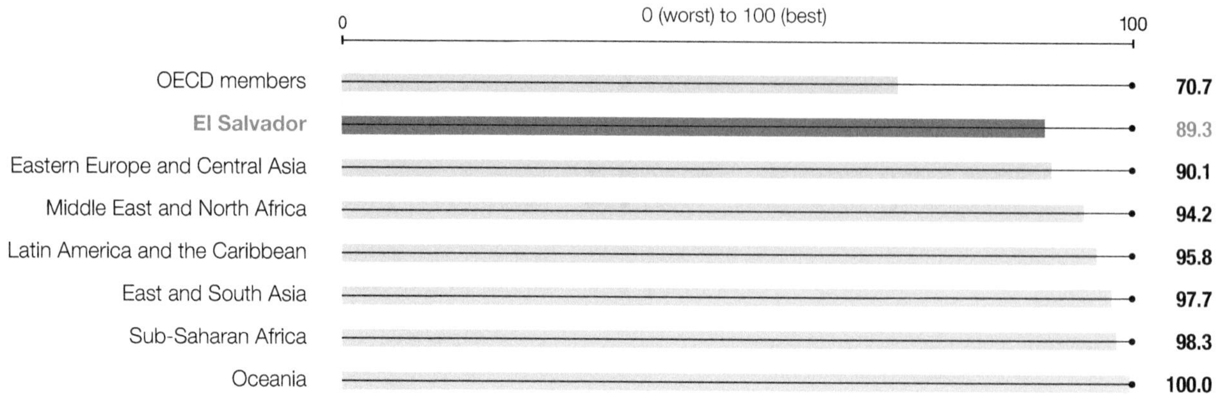

STATISTICAL PERFORMANCE INDEX

0 (worst) to 100 (best)

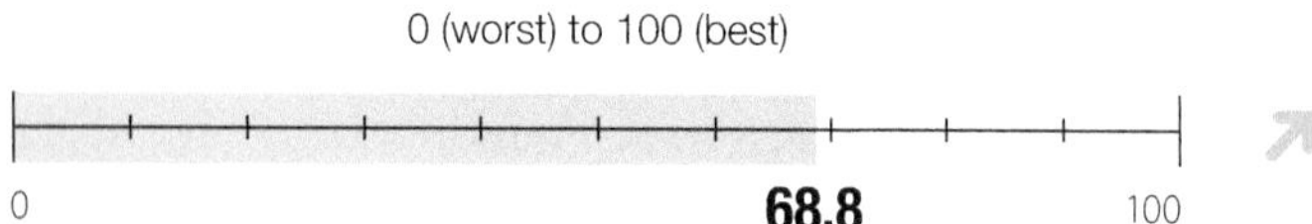

MISSING DATA IN SDG INDEX

0%

EL SALVADOR

Performance by Indicator

SDG1 – No Poverty	Value	Year	Rating	Trend
Poverty headcount ratio at \$1.90/day (%)	0.7	2022	●	↑
Poverty headcount ratio at \$3.20/day (%)	6.1	2022	●	↑
SDG2 – Zero Hunger				
Prevalence of undernourishment (%)	8.5	2019	●	↑
Prevalence of stunting in children under 5 years of age (%)	13.6	2014	●	→
Prevalence of wasting in children under 5 years of age (%)	2.1	2014	●	↑
Prevalence of obesity, BMI ≥ 30 (% of adult population)	24.6	2016	●	↓
Human Trophic Level (best 2–3 worst)	2.3	2017	●	↑
Cereal yield (tonnes per hectare of harvested land)	2.4	2018	●	↑
Sustainable Nitrogen Management Index (best 0–1.41 worst)	1.0	2015	●	→
Exports of hazardous pesticides (tonnes per million population)	81.6	2019	●	●
SDG3 – Good Health and Well-Being				
Maternal mortality rate (per 100,000 live births)	46	2017	●	↑
Neonatal mortality rate (per 1,000 live births)	6.2	2020	●	↑
Mortality rate, under-5 (per 1,000 live births)	12.9	2020	●	↑
Incidence of tuberculosis (per 100,000 population)	55.0	2020	●	→
New HIV infections (per 1,000 uninfected population)	0.1	2020	●	↑
Age-standardized death rate due to cardiovascular disease, cancer, diabetes, or chronic respiratory disease in adults aged 30–70 years (%)	10.7	2019	●	↑
Age-standardized death rate attributable to household air pollution and ambient air pollution (per 100,000 population)	42	2016	●	●
Traffic deaths (per 100,000 population)	20.9	2019	●	↓
Life expectancy at birth (years)	75.0	2019	●	↗
Adolescent fertility rate (births per 1,000 females aged 15 to 19)	69.7	2015	●	●
Births attended by skilled health personnel (%)	99.9	2018	●	↑
Surviving infants who received 2 WHO-recommended vaccines (%)	71	2020	●	↓
Universal health coverage (UHC) index of service coverage (worst 0–100 best)	76	2019	●	↑
Subjective well-being (average ladder score, worst 0–10 best)	6.4	2021	●	↑
SDG4 – Quality Education				
Participation rate in pre-primary organized learning (% of children aged 4 to 6)	80.0	2019	●	↓
Net primary enrollment rate (%)	84.2	2019	●	↓
Lower secondary completion rate (%)	77.4	2018	●	↓
Literacy rate (% of population aged 15 to 24)	98.3	2019	●	↑
SDG5 – Gender Equality				
Demand for family planning satisfied by modern methods (% of females aged 15 to 49)	80.0	2014	●	↑
Ratio of female-to-male mean years of education received (%)	90.4	2019	●	→
Ratio of female-to-male labor force participation rate (%)	59.6	2020	●	↓
Seats held by women in national parliament (%)	33.3	2020	●	→
SDG6 – Clean Water and Sanitation				
Population using at least basic drinking water services (%)	97.9	2020	●	↑
Population using at least basic sanitation services (%)	82.5	2020	●	↓
Freshwater withdrawal (% of available freshwater resources)	13.2	2018	●	●
Anthropogenic wastewater that receives treatment (%)	0.1	2018	●	●
Scarce water consumption embodied in imports (m^3 H_2O eq/capita)	1645.6	2018	●	●
SDG7 – Affordable and Clean Energy				
Population with access to electricity (%)	100.0	2019	●	↑
Population with access to clean fuels and technology for cooking (%)	89.1	2019	●	↑
CO_2 emissions from fuel combustion per total electricity output ($MtCO_2$/TWh)	1.3	2019	●	→
Share of renewable energy in total primary energy supply (%)	42.9	2019	●	↑
SDG8 – Decent Work and Economic Growth				
Adjusted GDP growth (%)	-5.0	2020	●	●
Victims of modern slavery (per 1,000 population)	2.5	2018	●	●
Adults with an account at a bank or other financial institution or with a mobile-money-service provider (% of population aged 15 or over)	30.4	2017	●	↓
Unemployment rate (% of total labor force)	5.8	2022	●	↓
Fundamental labor rights are effectively guaranteed (worst 0–1 best)	0.5	2020	●	→
Fatal work-related accidents embodied in imports (per 100,000 population)	0.4	2015	●	↑

* Imputed data point

SDG9 – Industry, Innovation and Infrastructure	Value	Year	Rating	Trend
Population using the internet (%)	54.6	2020	●	↑
Mobile broadband subscriptions (per 100 population)	60.6	2019	●	↑
Logistics Performance Index: Quality of trade and transport-related infrastructure (worst 1–5 best)	2.2	2018	●	↓
The Times Higher Education Universities Ranking: Average score of top 3 universities (worst 0–100 best)	* 0.0	2022	●	●
Articles published in academic journals (per 1,000 population)	0.0	2020	●	↓
Expenditure on research and development (% of GDP)	0.2	2018	●	→
SDG10 – Reduced Inequalities				
Gini coefficient	38.8	2019	●	↗
Palma ratio	1.7	2018	●	●
SDG11 – Sustainable Cities and Communities				
Proportion of urban population living in slums (%)	19.8	2018	●	↑
Annual mean concentration of particulate matter of less than 2.5 microns in diameter (PM2.5) (μg/m^3)	22.9	2019	●	↗
Access to improved water source, piped (% of urban population)	95.1	2020	●	↗
Satisfaction with public transport (%)	70.0	2021	●	↓
SDG12 – Responsible Consumption and Production				
Municipal solid waste (kg/capita/day)	0.7	2010	●	●
Electronic waste (kg/capita)	5.5	2019	●	●
Production-based SO_2 emissions (kg/capita)	7.4	2018	●	●
SO_2 emissions embodied in imports (kg/capita)	1.3	2018	●	●
Production-based nitrogen emissions (kg/capita)	7.8	2015	●	↑
Nitrogen emissions embodied in imports (kg/capita)	3.3	2015	●	↑
Exports of plastic waste (kg/capita)	1.4	2021	●	●
SDG13 – Climate Action				
CO_2 emissions from fossil fuel combustion and cement production (tCO_2/capita)	0.9	2020	●	↑
CO_2 emissions embodied in imports (tCO_2/capita)	0.4	2018	●	↑
CO_2 emissions embodied in fossil fuel exports (kg/capita)	0.0	2019	●	●
SDG14 – Life Below Water				
Mean area that is protected in marine sites important to biodiversity (%)	46.6	2020	●	→
Ocean Health Index: Clean Waters score (worst 0–100 best)	44.2	2020	●	↓
Fish caught from overexploited or collapsed stocks (% of total catch)	38.5	2018	●	↑
Fish caught by trawling or dredging (%)	28.6	2018	●	↓
Fish caught that are then discarded (%)	21.9	2018	●	↓
Marine biodiversity threats embodied in imports (per million population)	0.2	2018	●	●
SDG15 – Life on Land				
Mean area that is protected in terrestrial sites important to biodiversity (%)	28.0	2020	●	→
Mean area that is protected in freshwater sites important to biodiversity (%)	97.7	2020	●	↑
Red List Index of species survival (worst 0–1 best)	0.8	2021	●	↓
Permanent deforestation (% of forest area, 5-year average)	0.1	2020	●	↑
Terrestrial and freshwater biodiversity threats embodied in imports (per million population)	1.8	2018	●	●
SDG16 – Peace, Justice and Strong Institutions				
Homicides (per 100,000 population)	37.2	2019	●	↑
Unsentenced detainees (% of prison population)	29.5	2018	●	↑
Population who feel safe walking alone at night in the city or area where they live (%)	57	2021	●	↑
Property Rights (worst 1–7 best)	3.7	2020	●	↗
Birth registrations with civil authority (% of children under age 5)	89.5	2020	●	●
Corruption Perception Index (worst 0–100 best)	34	2021	●	↓
Children involved in child labor (% of population aged 5 to 14)	6.9	2019	●	●
Exports of major conventional weapons (TIV constant million USD per 100,000 population)	* 0.0	2020	●	●
Press Freedom Index (best 0–100 worst)	30.5	2021	●	↓
Access to and affordability of justice (worst 0–1 best)	0.6	2020	●	↑
SDG17 – Partnerships for the Goals				
Government spending on health and education (% of GDP)	7.9	2019	●	↓
For high-income and all OECD DAC countries: International concessional public finance, including official development assistance (% of GNI)	NA	NA	●	●
Other countries: Government revenue excluding grants (% of GDP)	24.1	2019	●	↑
Corporate Tax Haven Score (best 0–100 worst)	* 0.0	2019	●	●
Statistical Performance Index (worst 0–100 best)	68.8	2019	●	↗

5. Country Profiles

EQUATORIAL GUINEA

Sub-Saharan Africa

OVERALL PERFORMANCE

COUNTRY RANKING

COUNTRY SCORE

EQUATORIAL GUINEA

NA /163

AVERAGE PERFORMANCE BY SDG

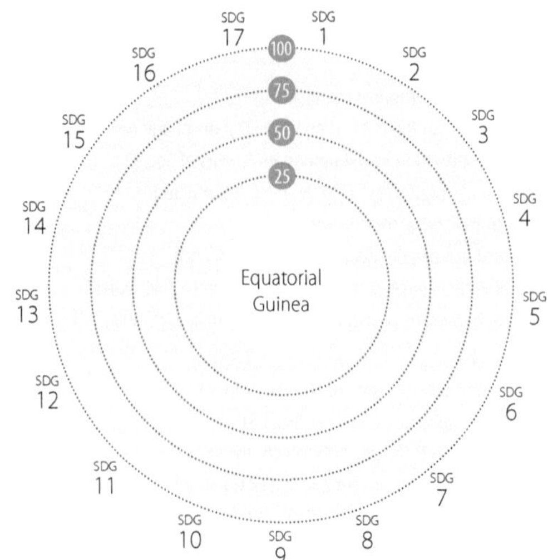

SDG DASHBOARDS AND TRENDS

Major challenges · Significant challenges · Challenges remain · SDG achieved · Information unavailable

Decreasing · Stagnating · Moderately improving · On track or maintaining SDG achievement · Information unavailable

Note: The full title of each SDG is available here: https://sustainabledevelopment.un.org/topics/sustainabledevelopmentgoals

INTERNATIONAL SPILLOVER INDEX

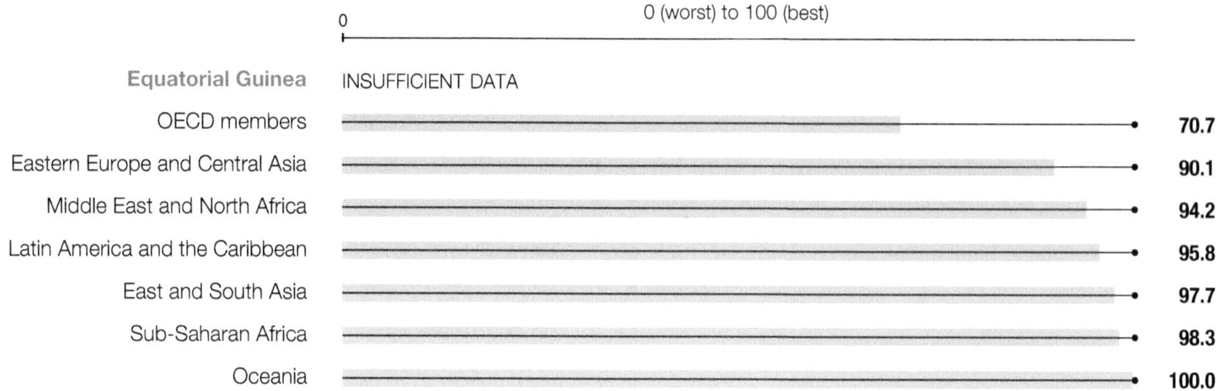

STATISTICAL PERFORMANCE INDEX

0 (worst) to 100 (best)

0 **na** 100

MISSING DATA IN SDG INDEX

31%

EQUATORIAL GUINEA

SDG1 – No Poverty		Value	Year	Rating	Trend
Poverty headcount ratio at \$1.90/day (%)	*	NA	NA	●	●
Poverty headcount ratio at \$3.20/day (%)	*	NA	NA	●	●

SDG2 – Zero Hunger	Value	Year	Rating	Trend
Prevalence of undernourishment (%)	NA	NA	●	●
Prevalence of stunting in children under 5 years of age (%)	26.2	2011	●	↗
Prevalence of wasting in children under 5 years of age (%)	3.1	2011	●	↑
Prevalence of obesity, BMI ≥ 30 (% of adult population)	8.0	2016	●	↑
Human Trophic Level (best 2–3 worst)	NA	NA	●	●
Cereal yield (tonnes per hectare of harvested land)	NA	NA	●	●
Sustainable Nitrogen Management Index (best 0–1.41 worst)	1.0	2015	●	→
Exports of hazardous pesticides (tonnes per million population)	NA	NA	●	●

SDG3 – Good Health and Well-Being	Value	Year	Rating	Trend
Maternal mortality rate (per 100,000 live births)	301	2017	●	→
Neonatal mortality rate (per 1,000 live births)	28.7	2020	●	→
Mortality rate, under-5 (per 1,000 live births)	78.5	2020	●	↗
Incidence of tuberculosis (per 100,000 population)	280.0	2020	●	↓
New HIV infections (per 1,000 uninfected population)	1.0	2020	●	→
Age-standardized death rate due to cardiovascular disease, cancer, diabetes, or chronic respiratory disease in adults aged 30–70 years (%)	22.1	2019	●	→
Age-standardized death rate attributable to household air pollution and ambient air pollution (per 100,000 population)	178	2016	●	●
Traffic deaths (per 100,000 population)	27.2	2019	●	↓
Life expectancy at birth (years)	62.2	2019	●	→
Adolescent fertility rate (births per 1,000 females aged 15 to 19)	176.0	2010	●	●
Births attended by skilled health personnel (%)	68.3	2011	●	●
Surviving infants who received 2 WHO-recommended vaccines (%)	53	2020	●	↗
Universal health coverage (UHC) index of service coverage (worst 0–100 best)	43	2019	●	→
Subjective well-being (average ladder score, worst 0–10 best)	NA	NA	●	●

SDG4 – Quality Education	Value	Year	Rating	Trend
Participation rate in pre-primary organized learning (% of children aged 4 to 6)	44.0	2015	●	●
Net primary enrollment rate (%)	44.7	2015	●	●
Lower secondary completion rate (%)	24.2	2015	●	●
Literacy rate (% of population aged 15 to 24)	98.0	2010	●	●

SDG5 – Gender Equality	Value	Year	Rating	Trend
Demand for family planning satisfied by modern methods (% of females aged 15 to 49)	20.7	2011	●	→
Ratio of female-to-male mean years of education received (%)	55.3	2019	●	→
Ratio of female-to-male labor force participation rate (%)	85.0	2020	●	↑
Seats held by women in national parliament (%)	21.0	2020	●	↓

SDG6 – Clean Water and Sanitation	Value	Year	Rating	Trend
Population using at least basic drinking water services (%)	64.7	2017	●	●
Population using at least basic sanitation services (%)	66.3	2017	●	●
Freshwater withdrawal (% of available freshwater resources)	0.2	2018	●	●
Anthropogenic wastewater that receives treatment (%)	1.3	2018	●	●
Scarce water consumption embodied in imports (m^3 H_2O eq/capita)	3523.5	2018	●	●

SDG7 – Affordable and Clean Energy	Value	Year	Rating	Trend
Population with access to electricity (%)	66.6	2019	●	→
Population with access to clean fuels and technology for cooking (%)	23.9	2019	●	→
CO_2 emissions from fuel combustion per total electricity output ($MtCO_2$/TWh)	5.2	2019	●	→
Share of renewable energy in total primary energy supply (%)	6.1	2019	●	→

SDG8 – Decent Work and Economic Growth	Value	Year	Rating	Trend
Adjusted GDP growth (%)	-10.7	2020	●	●
Victims of modern slavery (per 1,000 population)	6.4	2018	●	●
Adults with an account at a bank or other financial institution or with a mobile-money-service provider (% of population aged 15 or over)	NA	NA	●	●
Unemployment rate (% of total labor force)	8.9	2022	●	↓
Fundamental labor rights are effectively guaranteed (worst 0–1 best)	NA	NA	●	●
Fatal work-related accidents embodied in imports (per 100,000 population)	NA	NA	●	●

* Imputed data point

SDG9 – Industry, Innovation and Infrastructure		Value	Year	Rating	Trend
Population using the internet (%)		26.2	2017	●	●
Mobile broadband subscriptions (per 100 population)		0.6	2019	●	→
Logistics Performance Index: Quality of trade and transport-related infrastructure (worst 1–5 best)		1.9	2018	●	↓
The Times Higher Education Universities Ranking: Average score of top 3 universities (worst 0–100 best)	*	0.0	2022	●	●
Articles published in academic journals (per 1,000 population)		0.0	2020	●	↓
Expenditure on research and development (% of GDP)		NA	NA	●	●

SDG10 – Reduced Inequalities	Value	Year	Rating	Trend
Gini coefficient	NA	NA	●	●
Palma ratio	NA	NA	●	●

SDG11 – Sustainable Cities and Communities	Value	Year	Rating	Trend
Proportion of urban population living in slums (%)	66.1	2018	●	→
Annual mean concentration of particulate matter of less than 2.5 microns in diameter (PM2.5) (μg/m^3)	59.0	2019	●	↓
Access to improved water source, piped (% of urban population)	48.1	2017	●	●
Satisfaction with public transport (%)	NA	NA	●	●

SDG12 – Responsible Consumption and Production	Value	Year	Rating	Trend
Municipal solid waste (kg/capita/day)	0.4	2016	●	●
Electronic waste (kg/capita)	NA	NA	●	●
Production-based SO_2 emissions (kg/capita)	8.3	2018	●	●
SO_2 emissions embodied in imports (kg/capita)	1.2	2018	●	●
Production-based nitrogen emissions (kg/capita)	NA	NA	●	●
Nitrogen emissions embodied in imports (kg/capita)	NA	NA	●	●
Exports of plastic waste (kg/capita)	NA	NA	●	●

SDG13 – Climate Action	Value	Year	Rating	Trend
CO_2 emissions from fossil fuel combustion and cement production (tCO_2/capita)	7.3	2020	●	↗
CO_2 emissions embodied in imports (tCO_2/capita)	0.5	2018	●	↑
CO_2 emissions embodied in fossil fuel exports (kg/capita)	NA	NA	●	●

SDG14 – Life Below Water	Value	Year	Rating	Trend
Mean area that is protected in marine sites important to biodiversity (%)	100.0	2020	●	↑
Ocean Health Index: Clean Waters score (worst 0–100 best)	57.8	2020	●	↓
Fish caught from overexploited or collapsed stocks (% of total catch)	18.9	2018	●	↑
Fish caught by trawling or dredging (%)	28.1	2018	●	↓
Fish caught that are then discarded (%)	0.1	2018	●	↑
Marine biodiversity threats embodied in imports (per million population)	NA	NA	●	●

SDG15 – Life on Land	Value	Year	Rating	Trend
Mean area that is protected in terrestrial sites important to biodiversity (%)	100.0	2020	●	↑
Mean area that is protected in freshwater sites important to biodiversity (%)	NA	NA	●	●
Red List Index of species survival (worst 0–1 best)	0.8	2021	●	↓
Permanent deforestation (% of forest area, 5-year average)	0.1	2020	●	↑
Terrestrial and freshwater biodiversity threats embodied in imports (per million population)	NA	NA	●	●

SDG16 – Peace, Justice and Strong Institutions		Value	Year	Rating	Trend
Homicides (per 100,000 population)		NA	NA	●	●
Unsentenced detainees (% of prison population)		NA	NA	●	●
Population who feel safe walking alone at night in the city or area where they live (%)		NA	NA	●	●
Property Rights (worst 1–7 best)		NA	NA	●	●
Birth registrations with civil authority (% of children under age 5)		53.5	2020	●	●
Corruption Perception Index (worst 0–100 best)		17	2021	●	●
Children involved in child labor (% of population aged 5 to 14)		NA	NA	●	●
Exports of major conventional weapons (TIV constant million USD per 100,000 population)	*	0.0	2020	●	●
Press Freedom Index (best 0–100 worst)		55.7	2021	●	↗
Access to and affordability of justice (worst 0–1 best)		NA	NA	●	●

SDG17 – Partnerships for the Goals		Value	Year	Rating	Trend
Government spending on health and education (% of GDP)		2.9	2019	●	→
For high-income and all OECD DAC countries: International concessional public finance, including official development assistance (% of GNI)		NA	NA	●	●
Other countries: Government revenue excluding grants (% of GDP)		18.5	2019	●	↓
Corporate Tax Haven Score (best 0–100 worst)	*	0.0	2019	●	●
Statistical Performance Index (worst 0–100 best)		NA	NA	●	●

ERITREA

Sub-Saharan Africa

OVERALL PERFORMANCE

COUNTRY RANKING

ERITREA

NA /163

COUNTRY SCORE

AVERAGE PERFORMANCE BY SDG

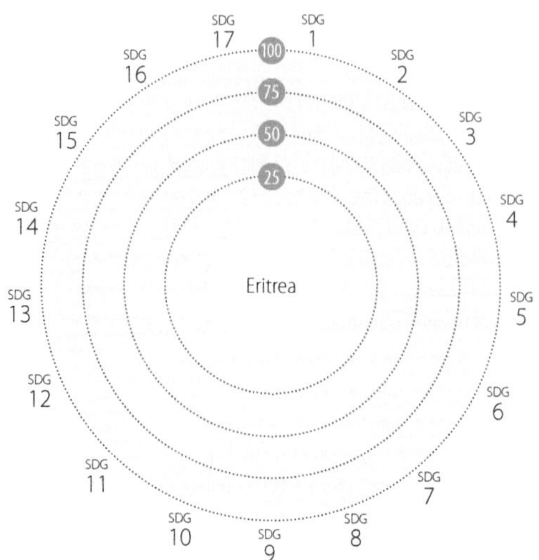

SDG DASHBOARDS AND TRENDS

Major challenges | Significant challenges | Challenges remain | SDG achieved | Information unavailable

Decreasing | Stagnating | Moderately improving | On track or maintaining SDG achievement | Information unavailable

Note: The full title of each SDG is available here: https://sustainabledevelopment.un.org/topics/sustainabledevelopmentgoals

INTERNATIONAL SPILLOVER INDEX

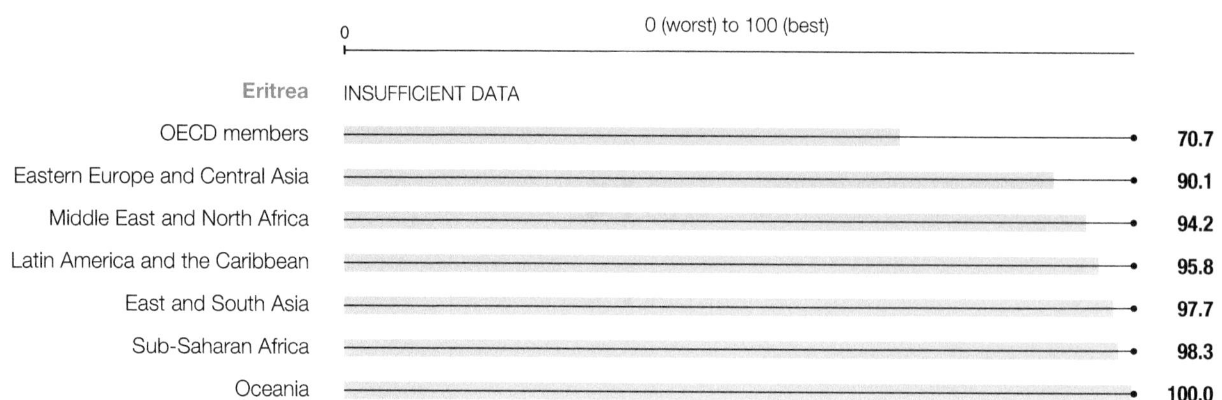

Eritrea	INSUFFICIENT DATA
OECD members	70.7
Eastern Europe and Central Asia	90.1
Middle East and North Africa	94.2
Latin America and the Caribbean	95.8
East and South Asia	97.7
Sub-Saharan Africa	98.3
Oceania	100.0

STATISTICAL PERFORMANCE INDEX

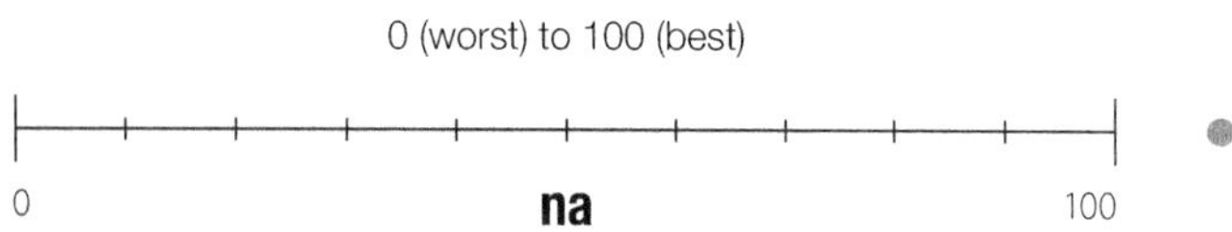

MISSING DATA IN SDG INDEX

27%

ERITREA

SDG1 – No Poverty		Value	Year	Rating	Trend
Poverty headcount ratio at $1.90/day (%)	*	NA	NA	●	●
Poverty headcount ratio at $3.20/day (%)	*	NA	NA	●	●
SDG2 – Zero Hunger					
Prevalence of undernourishment (%)		NA	NA	●	●
Prevalence of stunting in children under 5 years of age (%)		52.5	2010	●	→
Prevalence of wasting in children under 5 years of age (%)		14.6	2010	●	→
Prevalence of obesity, BMI ≥ 30 (% of adult population)		5.0	2016	●	↑
Human Trophic Level (best 2–3 worst)		2.1	2007	●	●
Cereal yield (tonnes per hectare of harvested land)		0.7	2018	●	→
Sustainable Nitrogen Management Index (best 0–1.41 worst)		1.0	2015	●	→
Exports of hazardous pesticides (tonnes per million population)		NA	NA	●	●
SDG3 – Good Health and Well-Being					
Maternal mortality rate (per 100,000 live births)		480	2017	●	↗
Neonatal mortality rate (per 1,000 live births)		17.7	2020	●	↗
Mortality rate, under-5 (per 1,000 live births)		39.3	2020	●	↗
Incidence of tuberculosis (per 100,000 population)		81.0	2020	●	↗
New HIV infections (per 1,000 uninfected population)		0.1	2020	●	↑
Age-standardized death rate due to cardiovascular disease, cancer, diabetes, or chronic respiratory disease in adults aged 30–70 years (%)		26.8	2019	●	→
Age-standardized death rate attributable to household air pollution and ambient air pollution (per 100,000 population)		174	2016	●	●
Traffic deaths (per 100,000 population)		37.9	2019	●	↓
Life expectancy at birth (years)		64.1	2019	●	→
Adolescent fertility rate (births per 1,000 females aged 15 to 19)		76.0	2008	●	●
Births attended by skilled health personnel (%)		34.1	2010	●	●
Surviving infants who received 2 WHO-recommended vaccines (%)		93	2020	●	↑
Universal health coverage (UHC) index of service coverage (worst 0–100 best)		50	2019	●	→
Subjective well-being (average ladder score, worst 0–10 best)		NA	NA	●	●
SDG4 – Quality Education					
Participation rate in pre-primary organized learning (% of children aged 4 to 6)		26.7	2018	●	●
Net primary enrollment rate (%)		52.7	2018	●	●
Lower secondary completion rate (%)		51.2	2018	●	↓
Literacy rate (% of population aged 15 to 24)		93.3	2018	●	●
SDG5 – Gender Equality					
Demand for family planning satisfied by modern methods (% of females aged 15 to 49)		21.0	2010	●	→
Ratio of female-to-male mean years of education received (%)		NA	NA	●	●
Ratio of female-to-male labor force participation rate (%)		82.3	2020	●	↑
Seats held by women in national parliament (%)		22.0	2019	●	→
SDG6 – Clean Water and Sanitation					
Population using at least basic drinking water services (%)		51.9	2016	●	●
Population using at least basic sanitation services (%)		11.9	2016	●	●
Freshwater withdrawal (% of available freshwater resources)		11.2	2018	●	●
Anthropogenic wastewater that receives treatment (%)		0.0	2018	●	●
Scarce water consumption embodied in imports (m^3 H_2O eq/capita)		486.0	2018	●	●
SDG7 – Affordable and Clean Energy					
Population with access to electricity (%)		50.4	2019	●	→
Population with access to clean fuels and technology for cooking (%)		9.3	2019	●	→
CO_2 emissions from fuel combustion per total electricity output ($MtCO_2$/TWh)		1.4	2019	●	↑
Share of renewable energy in total primary energy supply (%)		72.0	2019	●	↑
SDG8 – Decent Work and Economic Growth					
Adjusted GDP growth (%)		NA	NA	●	●
Victims of modern slavery (per 1,000 population)		93.0	2018	●	●
Adults with an account at a bank or other financial institution or with a mobile-money-service provider (% of population aged 15 or over)		NA	NA	●	●
Unemployment rate (% of total labor force)		7.9	2022	●	↓
Fundamental labor rights are effectively guaranteed (worst 0–1 best)		NA	NA	●	●
Fatal work-related accidents embodied in imports (per 100,000 population)		0.0	2015	●	↑

SDG9 – Industry, Innovation and Infrastructure		Value	Year	Rating	Trend
Population using the internet (%)		1.3	2017	●	●
Mobile broadband subscriptions (per 100 population)		0.0	2017	●	●
Logistics Performance Index: Quality of trade and transport-related infrastructure (worst 1–5 best)		1.9	2018	●	↗
The Times Higher Education Universities Ranking: Average score of top 3 universities (worst 0–100 best)	*	0.0	2022	●	●
Articles published in academic journals (per 1,000 population)		0.0	2020	●	→
Expenditure on research and development (% of GDP)	*	0.0	2018	●	●
SDG10 – Reduced Inequalities					
Gini coefficient		NA	NA	●	●
Palma ratio		NA	NA	●	●
SDG11 – Sustainable Cities and Communities					
Proportion of urban population living in slums (%)		NA	NA	●	●
Annual mean concentration of particulate matter of less than 2.5 microns in diameter (PM2.5) (μg/m³)		52.1	2019	●	↓
Access to improved water source, piped (% of urban population)		69.0	2016	●	●
Satisfaction with public transport (%)		NA	NA	●	●
SDG12 – Responsible Consumption and Production					
Municipal solid waste (kg/capita/day)		0.6	2011	●	●
Electronic waste (kg/capita)		0.6	2019	●	●
Production-based SO_2 emissions (kg/capita)		2.0	2018	●	●
SO_2 emissions embodied in imports (kg/capita)		0.0	2018	●	●
Production-based nitrogen emissions (kg/capita)		17.2	2015	●	↑
Nitrogen emissions embodied in imports (kg/capita)		0.3	2015	●	↑
Exports of plastic waste (kg/capita)		NA	NA	●	●
SDG13 – Climate Action					
CO_2 emissions from fossil fuel combustion and cement production (tCO_2/capita)		0.2	2020	●	↑
CO_2 emissions embodied in imports (tCO_2/capita)		0.0	2018	●	↑
CO_2 emissions embodied in fossil fuel exports (kg/capita)		0.0	2020	●	●
SDG14 – Life Below Water					
Mean area that is protected in marine sites important to biodiversity (%)		0.0	2020	●	→
Ocean Health Index: Clean Waters score (worst 0–100 best)		54.2	2020	●	↓
Fish caught from overexploited or collapsed stocks (% of total catch)		12.6	2018	●	↑
Fish caught by trawling or dredging (%)		0.0	2018	●	↑
Fish caught that are then discarded (%)		0.0	2018	●	↑
Marine biodiversity threats embodied in imports (per million population)		NA	NA	●	●
SDG15 – Life on Land					
Mean area that is protected in terrestrial sites important to biodiversity (%)		13.3	2020	●	→
Mean area that is protected in freshwater sites important to biodiversity (%)		0.0	2020	●	→
Red List Index of species survival (worst 0–1 best)		0.9	2021	●	↓
Permanent deforestation (% of forest area, 5-year average)		NA	NA	●	●
Terrestrial and freshwater biodiversity threats embodied in imports (per million population)		0.0	2018	●	●
SDG16 – Peace, Justice and Strong Institutions					
Homicides (per 100,000 population)		NA	NA	●	●
Unsentenced detainees (% of prison population)		NA	NA	●	●
Population who feel safe walking alone at night in the city or area where they live (%)		NA	NA	●	●
Property Rights (worst 1–7 best)		NA	NA	●	●
Birth registrations with civil authority (% of children under age 5)		NA	NA	●	●
Corruption Perception Index (worst 0–100 best)		22	2021	●	→
Children involved in child labor (% of population aged 5 to 14)		NA	NA	●	●
Exports of major conventional weapons (TIV constant million USD per 100,000 population)		0.0	2020	●	●
Press Freedom Index (best 0–100 worst)		81.5	2021	●	→
Access to and affordability of justice (worst 0–1 best)		NA	NA	●	●
SDG17 – Partnerships for the Goals					
Government spending on health and education (% of GDP)		2.9	2019	●	→
For high-income and all OECD DAC countries: International concessional public finance, including official development assistance (% of GNI)		NA	NA	●	●
Other countries: Government revenue excluding grants (% of GDP)		NA	NA	●	●
Corporate Tax Haven Score (best 0–100 worst)	*	0.0	2019	●	●
Statistical Performance Index (worst 0–100 best)		NA	NA	●	●

* Imputed data point

5. Country Profiles

ESTONIA

OECD Countries

OVERALL PERFORMANCE

COUNTRY RANKING

ESTONIA

10 /163

COUNTRY SCORE

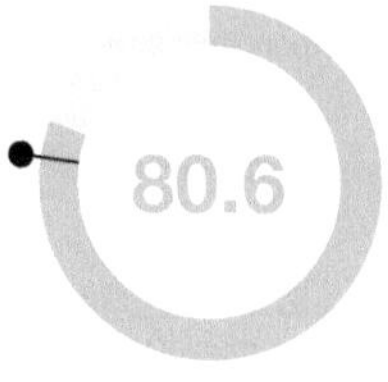

REGIONAL AVERAGE: 77.2

AVERAGE PERFORMANCE BY SDG

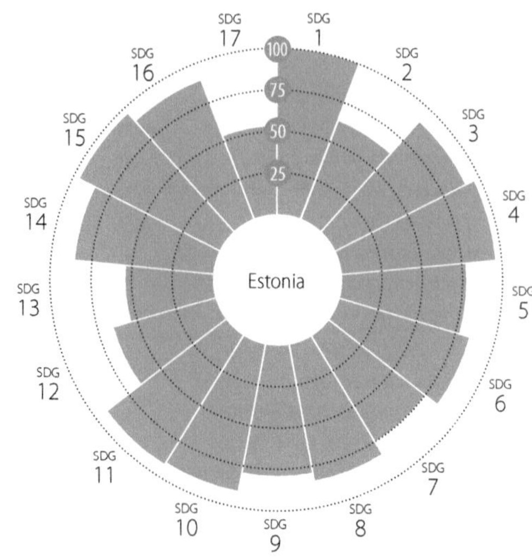

SDG DASHBOARDS AND TRENDS

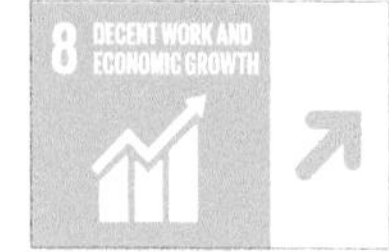

Note: The full title of each SDG is available here: https://sustainabledevelopment.un.org/topics/sustainabledevelopmentgoals

INTERNATIONAL SPILLOVER INDEX

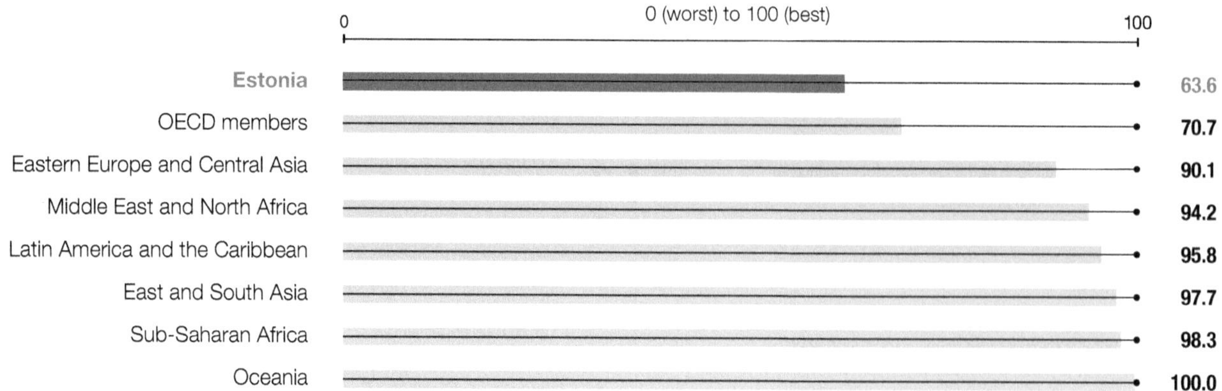

STATISTICAL PERFORMANCE INDEX

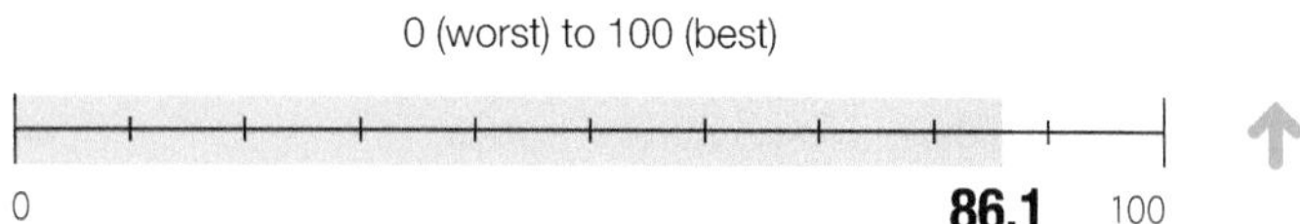

MISSING DATA IN SDG INDEX

ESTONIA

Performance by Indicator

SDG1 – No Poverty	Value	Year	Rating	Trend
Poverty headcount ratio at \$1.90/day (%)	0.0	2022	●	↑
Poverty headcount ratio at \$3.20/day (%)	0.0	2022	●	↑
Poverty rate after taxes and transfers (%)	14.9	2019	●	↗
SDG2 – Zero Hunger				
Prevalence of undernourishment (%)	2.5	2019	●	↑
Prevalence of stunting in children under 5 years of age (%)	1.2	2014	●	↑
Prevalence of wasting in children under 5 years of age (%)	1.5	2014	●	↑
Prevalence of obesity, BMI ≥ 30 (% of adult population)	21.2	2016	●	↓
Human Trophic Level (best 2–3 worst)	2.5	2017	●	↓
Cereal yield (tonnes per hectare of harvested land)	2.6	2018	●	↑
Sustainable Nitrogen Management Index (best 0–1.41 worst)	0.6	2015	●	→
Yield gap closure (% of potential yield)	40.9	2018	●	●
Exports of hazardous pesticides (tonnes per million population)	2.3	2019	●	●
SDG3 – Good Health and Well-Being				
Maternal mortality rate (per 100,000 live births)	9	2017	●	↑
Neonatal mortality rate (per 1,000 live births)	0.9	2020	●	↑
Mortality rate, under-5 (per 1,000 live births)	2.1	2020	●	↑
Incidence of tuberculosis (per 100,000 population)	10.0	2020	●	↑
New HIV infections (per 1,000 uninfected population)	0.2	2020	●	↑
Age-standardized death rate due to cardiovascular disease, cancer, diabetes, or chronic respiratory disease in adults aged 30–70 years (%)	14.9	2019	●	↑
Age-standardized death rate attributable to household air pollution and ambient air pollution (per 100,000 population)	25	2016	●	●
Traffic deaths (per 100,000 population)	4.5	2019	●	↑
Life expectancy at birth (years)	78.9	2019	●	↑
Adolescent fertility rate (births per 1,000 females aged 15 to 19)	9.6	2018	●	↑
Births attended by skilled health personnel (%)	99.1	2018	●	↑
Surviving infants who received 2 WHO-recommended vaccines (%)	91	2020	●	↑
Universal health coverage (UHC) index of service coverage (worst 0–100 best)	78	2019	●	↑
Subjective well-being (average ladder score, worst 0–10 best)	6.6	2021	●	↑
Gap in life expectancy at birth among regions (years)	4.0	2019	●	↓
Gap in self-reported health status by income (percentage points)	46.6	2020	●	↓
Daily smokers (% of population aged 15 and over)	17.9	2020	●	↑
SDG4 – Quality Education				
Participation rate in pre-primary organized learning (% of children aged 4 to 6)	93.2	2017	●	●
Net primary enrollment rate (%)	97.5	2019	●	↑
Lower secondary completion rate (%)	100.9	2019	●	↑
Literacy rate (% of population aged 15 to 24)	99.9	2011	●	●
Tertiary educational attainment (% of population aged 25 to 34)	43.1	2020	●	↑
PISA score (worst 0–600 best)	525.3	2018	●	↑
Variation in science performance explained by socio-economic status (%)	7.2	2018	●	↑
Underachievers in science (% of 15-year-olds)	8.8	2018	●	↑
SDG5 – Gender Equality				
Demand for family planning satisfied by modern methods (% of females aged 15 to 49)	* 80.1	2022	●	↑
Ratio of female-to-male mean years of education received (%)	107.1	2019	●	↑
Ratio of female-to-male labor force participation rate (%)	81.5	2020	●	↑
Seats held by women in national parliament (%)	28.7	2020	●	↗
Gender wage gap (% of male median wage)	17.3	2018	●	↑
SDG6 – Clean Water and Sanitation				
Population using at least basic drinking water services (%)	99.6	2020	●	↑
Population using at least basic sanitation services (%)	99.1	2020	●	↑
Freshwater withdrawal (% of available freshwater resources)	17.4	2018	●	●
Anthropogenic wastewater that receives treatment (%)	69.6	2018	●	●
Scarce water consumption embodied in imports (m^3 H_2O eq/capita)	4806.0	2018	●	●
Population using safely managed water services (%)	95.8	2020	●	↑
Population using safely managed sanitation services (%)	93.1	2020	●	↑
SDG7 – Affordable and Clean Energy				
Population with access to electricity (%)	100.0	2019	●	↑
Population with access to clean fuels and technology for cooking (%)	100.0	2019	●	↑
CO_2 emissions from fuel combustion per total electricity output ($MtCO_2$/TWh)	2.5	2019	●	→
Share of renewable energy in total primary energy supply (%)	22.5	2019	●	↑
SDG8 – Decent Work and Economic Growth				
Adjusted GDP growth (%)	0.8	2020	●	●
Victims of modern slavery (per 1,000 population)	3.6	2018	●	●
Adults with an account at a bank or other financial institution or with a mobile-money-service provider (% of population aged 15 or over)	98.0	2017	●	↑
Fundamental labor rights are effectively guaranteed (worst 0–1 best)	0.7	2020	●	↓
Fatal work-related accidents embodied in imports (per 100,000 population)	0.7	2015	●	↑
Employment-to-population ratio (%)	74.0	2020	●	↑
Youth not in employment, education or training (NEET) (% of population aged 15 to 29)	11.2	2020	●	↑

* Imputed data point

SDG9 – Industry, Innovation and Infrastructure	Value	Year	Rating	Trend
Population using the internet (%)	89.1	2020	●	↑
Mobile broadband subscriptions (per 100 population)	157.6	2019	●	↑
Logistics Performance Index: Quality of trade and transport-related infrastructure (worst 1–5 best)	3.1	2018	●	↑
The Times Higher Education Universities Ranking: Average score of top 3 universities (worst 0–100 best)	37.9	2022	●	●
Articles published in academic journals (per 1,000 population)	2.9	2020	●	↑
Expenditure on research and development (% of GDP)	1.4	2018	●	↓
Researchers (per 1,000 employed population)	7.7	2019	●	↑
Triadic patent families filed (per million population)	3.7	2019	●	→
Gap in internet access by income (percentage points)	28.6	2020	●	→
Female share of graduates from STEM fields at the tertiary level (%)	38.4	2017	●	↑
SDG10 – Reduced Inequalities				
Gini coefficient	30.3	2018	●	↑
Palma ratio	1.1	2019	●	↑
Elderly poverty rate (% of population aged 66 or over)	34.5	2019	●	↓
SDG11 – Sustainable Cities and Communities				
Proportion of urban population living in slums (%)	* 0.0	2018	●	↑
Annual mean concentration of particulate matter of less than 2.5 microns in diameter (PM2.5) (μg/m^3)	6.4	2019	●	↑
Access to improved water source, piped (% of urban population)	98.8	2015	●	●
Satisfaction with public transport (%)	62.0	2021	●	↓
Population with rent overburden (%)	4.6	2019	●	↑
SDG12 – Responsible Consumption and Production				
Electronic waste (kg/capita)	13.1	2019	●	●
Production-based SO_2 emissions (kg/capita)	11.7	2018	●	●
SO_2 emissions embodied in imports (kg/capita)	7.9	2018	●	●
Production-based nitrogen emissions (kg/capita)	25.4	2015	●	↓
Nitrogen emissions embodied in imports (kg/capita)	7.9	2015	●	↓
Exports of plastic waste (kg/capita)	11.4	2021	●	●
Non-recycled municipal solid waste (kg/capita/day)	0.7	2019	●	↑
SDG13 – Climate Action				
CO_2 emissions from fossil fuel combustion and cement production (tCO_2/capita)	7.9	2020	●	↑
CO_2 emissions embodied in imports (tCO_2/capita)	3.4	2018	●	↓
CO_2 emissions embodied in fossil fuel exports (kg/capita)	7.2	2020	●	●
Carbon Pricing Score at EUR60/tCO_2 (%, worst 0–100 best)	28.6	2018	●	↗
SDG14 – Life Below Water				
Mean area that is protected in marine sites important to biodiversity (%)	97.7	2020	●	↑
Ocean Health Index: Clean Waters score (worst 0–100 best)	66.2	2020	●	↓
Fish caught from overexploited or collapsed stocks (% of total catch)	1.6	2018	●	↑
Fish caught by trawling or dredging (%)	5.3	2018	●	↑
Fish caught that are then discarded (%)	5.8	2018	●	→
Marine biodiversity threats embodied in imports (per million population)	0.1	2018	●	●
SDG15 – Life on Land				
Mean area that is protected in terrestrial sites important to biodiversity (%)	94.8	2020	●	↑
Mean area that is protected in freshwater sites important to biodiversity (%)	92.9	2020	●	↑
Red List Index of species survival (worst 0–1 best)	1.0	2021	●	↑
Permanent deforestation (% of forest area, 5-year average)	0.0	2020	●	↑
Terrestrial and freshwater biodiversity threats embodied in imports (per million population)	0.3	2018	●	●
SDG16 – Peace, Justice and Strong Institutions				
Homicides (per 100,000 population)	3.2	2020	●	→
Unsentenced detainees (% of prison population)	19.8	2019	●	↑
Population who feel safe walking alone at night in the city or area where they live (%)	76	2021	●	↑
Property Rights (worst 1–7 best)	5.5	2020	●	↑
Birth registrations with civil authority (% of children under age 5)	100.0	2020	●	●
Corruption Perception Index (worst 0–100 best)	74	2021	●	↑
Children involved in child labor (% of population aged 5 to 14)	* 0.0	2019	●	●
Exports of major conventional weapons (TIV constant million USD per 100,000 population)	0.0	2020	●	●
Press Freedom Index (best 0–100 worst)	15.3	2021	●	↑
Access to and affordability of justice (worst 0–1 best)	0.7	2020	●	↑
Persons held in prison (per 100,000 population)	187.6	2019	●	↗
SDG17 – Partnerships for the Goals				
Government spending on health and education (% of GDP)	10.2	2019	●	↑
For high-income and all OECD DAC countries: International concessional public finance, including official development assistance (% of GNI)	0.2	2021	●	→
Other countries: Government revenue excluding grants (% of GDP)	NA	NA	●	●
Corporate Tax Haven Score (best 0–100 worst)	66.5	2019	●	●
Financial Secrecy Score (best 0–100 worst)	43.1	2020	●	●
Shifted profits of multinationals (US\$ billion)	0.4	2018	●	↑
Statistical Performance Index (worst 0–100 best)	86.1	2019	●	↑

ESWATINI

Sub-Saharan Africa

AVERAGE PERFORMANCE BY SDG

OVERALL PERFORMANCE

COUNTRY RANKING

ESWATINI

137/163

COUNTRY SCORE

REGIONAL AVERAGE: 53.6

SDG DASHBOARDS AND TRENDS

Major challenges | Significant challenges | Challenges remain | SDG achieved | Information unavailable

Decreasing | Stagnating | Moderately improving | On track or maintaining SDG achievement | Information unavailable

Note: The full title of each SDG is available here: https://sustainabledevelopment.un.org/topics/sustainabledevelopmentgoals

INTERNATIONAL SPILLOVER INDEX

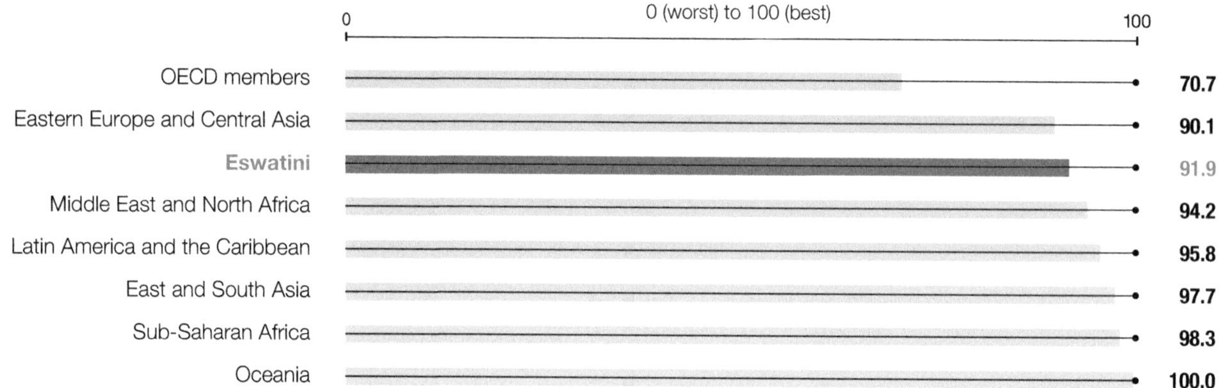

STATISTICAL PERFORMANCE INDEX

0 (worst) to 100 (best)

0 **47.2** 100

MISSING DATA IN SDG INDEX

11%

SDG1 – No Poverty

Indicator	Value	Year	Rating	Trend
Poverty headcount ratio at \$1.90/day (%)	32.2	2022	●	→
Poverty headcount ratio at \$3.20/day (%)	49.4	2022	●	→

SDG2 – Zero Hunger

Indicator	Value	Year	Rating	Trend
Prevalence of undernourishment (%)	11.6	2019	●	↗
Prevalence of stunting in children under 5 years of age (%)	25.5	2014	●	→
Prevalence of wasting in children under 5 years of age (%)	2.0	2014	●	↑
Prevalence of obesity, BMI ≥ 30 (% of adult population)	16.5	2016	●	↓
Human Trophic Level (best 2–3 worst)	4.0	2017	●	↓
Cereal yield (tonnes per hectare of harvested land)	1.2	2018	●	→
Sustainable Nitrogen Management Index (best 0–1.41 worst)	0.8	2015	●	→
Exports of hazardous pesticides (tonnes per million population)	0.0	2019	●	●

SDG3 – Good Health and Well-Being

Indicator	Value	Year	Rating	Trend
Maternal mortality rate (per 100,000 live births)	437	2017	●	↓
Neonatal mortality rate (per 1,000 live births)	20.3	2020	●	↗
Mortality rate, under-5 (per 1,000 live births)	46.6	2020	●	↗
Incidence of tuberculosis (per 100,000 population)	319.0	2020	●	↑
New HIV infections (per 1,000 uninfected population)	5.3	2020	●	↑
Age-standardized death rate due to cardiovascular disease, cancer, diabetes, or chronic respiratory disease in adults aged 30–70 years (%)	35.2	2019	●	→
Age-standardized death rate attributable to household air pollution and ambient air pollution (per 100,000 population)	137	2016	●	●
Traffic deaths (per 100,000 population)	33.5	2019	●	↓
Life expectancy at birth (years)	57.7	2019	●	↗
Adolescent fertility rate (births per 1,000 females aged 15 to 19)	87.1	2013	●	●
Births attended by skilled health personnel (%)	88.3	2014	●	●
Surviving infants who received 2 WHO-recommended vaccines (%)	76	2020	●	↓
Universal health coverage (UHC) index of service coverage (worst 0–100 best)	58	2019	●	↗
Subjective well-being (average ladder score, worst 0–10 best)	4.4	2019	●	●

SDG4 – Quality Education

Indicator	Value	Year	Rating	Trend
Participation rate in pre-primary organized learning (% of children aged 4 to 6)	18.9	2011	●	●
Net primary enrollment rate (%)	84.8	2019	●	→
Lower secondary completion rate (%)	69.8	2019	●	↑
Literacy rate (% of population aged 15 to 24)	95.5	2018	●	●

SDG5 – Gender Equality

Indicator	Value	Year	Rating	Trend
Demand for family planning satisfied by modern methods (% of females aged 15 to 49)	82.9	2014	●	↑
Ratio of female-to-male mean years of education received (%)	87.5	2019	●	↓
Ratio of female-to-male labor force participation rate (%)	84.3	2020	●	↑
Seats held by women in national parliament (%)	9.6	2020	●	→

SDG6 – Clean Water and Sanitation

Indicator	Value	Year	Rating	Trend
Population using at least basic drinking water services (%)	70.8	2020	●	→
Population using at least basic sanitation services (%)	64.3	2020	●	→
Freshwater withdrawal (% of available freshwater resources)	77.6	2018	●	●
Anthropogenic wastewater that receives treatment (%)	5.3	2018	●	●
Scarce water consumption embodied in imports (m^3 H_2O eq/capita)	NA	NA	●	●

SDG7 – Affordable and Clean Energy

Indicator	Value	Year	Rating	Trend
Population with access to electricity (%)	77.2	2019	●	↑
Population with access to clean fuels and technology for cooking (%)	54.7	2019	●	↗
CO_2 emissions from fuel combustion per total electricity output ($MtCO_2$/TWh)	1.4	2019	●	→
Share of renewable energy in total primary energy supply (%)	NA	NA	●	●

SDG8 – Decent Work and Economic Growth

Indicator	Value	Year	Rating	Trend
Adjusted GDP growth (%)	-3.1	2020	●	●
Victims of modern slavery (per 1,000 population)	8.8	2018	●	●
Adults with an account at a bank or other financial institution or with a mobile-money-service provider (% of population aged 15 or over)	28.6	2011	●	●
Unemployment rate (% of total labor force)	25.2	2022	●	↓
Fundamental labor rights are effectively guaranteed (worst 0–1 best)	NA	NA	●	●
Fatal work-related accidents embodied in imports (per 100,000 population)	0.6	2015	●	↑

* Imputed data point

SDG9 – Industry, Innovation and Infrastructure

Indicator	Value	Year	Rating	Trend
Population using the internet (%)	30.3	2017	●	●
Mobile broadband subscriptions (per 100 population)	17.4	2019	●	→
Logistics Performance Index: Quality of trade and transport-related infrastructure (worst 1–5 best)	NA	NA	●	●
The Times Higher Education Universities Ranking: Average score of top 3 universities (worst 0–100 best)	* 0.0	2022	●	●
Articles published in academic journals (per 1,000 population)	0.1	2020	●	→
Expenditure on research and development (% of GDP)	0.3	2015	●	●

SDG10 – Reduced Inequalities

Indicator	Value	Year	Rating	Trend
Gini coefficient	54.6	2016	●	●
Palma ratio	4.1	2018	●	●

SDG11 – Sustainable Cities and Communities

Indicator	Value	Year	Rating	Trend
Proportion of urban population living in slums (%)	32.7	2018	●	→
Annual mean concentration of particulate matter of less than 2.5 microns in diameter (PM2.5) (μg/m³)	16.7	2019	●	↗
Access to improved water source, piped (% of urban population)	93.1	2020	●	↗
Satisfaction with public transport (%)	64.0	2019	●	●

SDG12 – Responsible Consumption and Production

Indicator	Value	Year	Rating	Trend
Municipal solid waste (kg/capita/day)	0.5	2016	●	●
Electronic waste (kg/capita)	6.3	2019	●	●
Production-based SO_2 emissions (kg/capita)	NA	NA	●	●
SO_2 emissions embodied in imports (kg/capita)	NA	NA	●	●
Production-based nitrogen emissions (kg/capita)	17.3	2015	●	↑
Nitrogen emissions embodied in imports (kg/capita)	3.6	2015	●	↑
Exports of plastic waste (kg/capita)	0.8	2020	●	●

SDG13 – Climate Action

Indicator	Value	Year	Rating	Trend
CO_2 emissions from fossil fuel combustion and cement production (tCO_2/capita)	0.8	2020	●	↑
CO_2 emissions embodied in imports (tCO_2/capita)	NA	NA	●	●
CO_2 emissions embodied in fossil fuel exports (kg/capita)	197.7	2020	●	●

SDG14 – Life Below Water

Indicator	Value	Year	Rating	Trend
Mean area that is protected in marine sites important to biodiversity (%)	NA	NA	●	●
Ocean Health Index: Clean Waters score (worst 0–100 best)	NA	NA	●	●
Fish caught from overexploited or collapsed stocks (% of total catch)	NA	NA	●	●
Fish caught by trawling or dredging (%)	NA	NA	●	●
Fish caught that are then discarded (%)	NA	NA	●	●
Marine biodiversity threats embodied in imports (per million population)	0.5	2018	●	●

SDG15 – Life on Land

Indicator	Value	Year	Rating	Trend
Mean area that is protected in terrestrial sites important to biodiversity (%)	30.6	2020	●	→
Mean area that is protected in freshwater sites important to biodiversity (%)	NA	NA	●	●
Red List Index of species survival (worst 0–1 best)	0.8	2021	●	→
Permanent deforestation (% of forest area, 5-year average)	0.1	2020	●	↑
Terrestrial and freshwater biodiversity threats embodied in imports (per million population)	1.7	2018	●	●

SDG16 – Peace, Justice and Strong Institutions

Indicator	Value	Year	Rating	Trend
Homicides (per 100,000 population)	11.6	2017	●	↓
Unsentenced detainees (% of prison population)	32.6	2006	●	●
Population who feel safe walking alone at night in the city or area where they live (%)	45	2019	●	●
Property Rights (worst 1–7 best)	4.6	2020	●	↑
Birth registrations with civil authority (% of children under age 5)	53.5	2020	●	●
Corruption Perception Index (worst 0–100 best)	32	2021	●	↓
Children involved in child labor (% of population aged 5 to 14)	7.8	2019	●	●
Exports of major conventional weapons (TIV constant million USD per 100,000 population)	* 0.0	2020	●	●
Press Freedom Index (best 0–100 worst)	46.3	2021	●	↗
Access to and affordability of justice (worst 0–1 best)	NA	NA	●	●

SDG17 – Partnerships for the Goals

Indicator	Value	Year	Rating	Trend
Government spending on health and education (% of GDP)	8.8	2020	●	↗
For high-income and all OECD DAC countries: International concessional public finance, including official development assistance (% of GNI)	NA	NA	●	●
Other countries: Government revenue excluding grants (% of GDP)	NA	NA	●	●
Corporate Tax Haven Score (best 0–100 worst)	* 0.0	2019	●	●
Statistical Performance Index (worst 0–100 best)	47.2	2019	●	↗

ETHIOPIA

Sub-Saharan Africa

OVERALL PERFORMANCE

COUNTRY RANKING

ETHIOPIA

128/163

COUNTRY SCORE

AVERAGE PERFORMANCE BY SDG

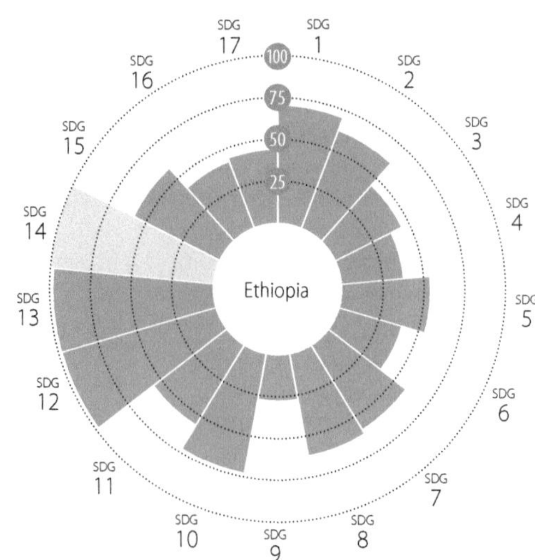

SDG DASHBOARDS AND TRENDS

Note: The full title of each SDG is available here: https://sustainabledevelopment.un.org/topics/sustainabledevelopmentgoals

INTERNATIONAL SPILLOVER INDEX

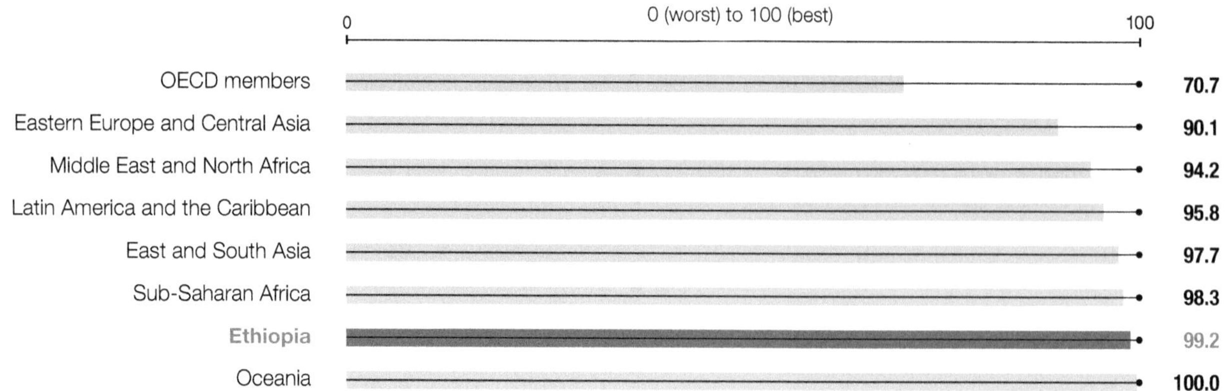

STATISTICAL PERFORMANCE INDEX

0 (worst) to 100 (best)

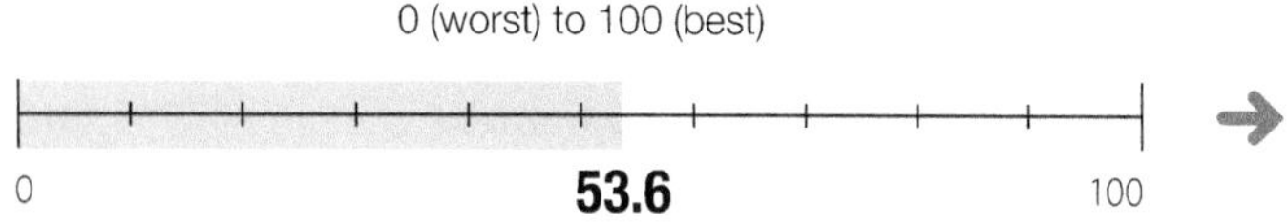

MISSING DATA IN SDG INDEX

1%

ETHIOPIA

SDG1 – No Poverty	Value	Year	Rating	Trend
Poverty headcount ratio at \$1.90/day (%)	5.8	2022	●	↑
Poverty headcount ratio at \$3.20/day (%)	26.6	2022	●	↑
SDG2 – Zero Hunger				
Prevalence of undernourishment (%)	16.2	2019	●	↓
Prevalence of stunting in children under 5 years of age (%)	36.8	2019	●	→
Prevalence of wasting in children under 5 years of age (%)	7.2	2019	●	→
Prevalence of obesity, BMI ≥ 30 (% of adult population)	4.5	2016	●	↑
Human Trophic Level (best 2–3 worst)	2.1	2017	●	↑
Cereal yield (tonnes per hectare of harvested land)	2.4	2018	●	↓
Sustainable Nitrogen Management Index (best 0–1.41 worst)	0.7	2015	●	→
Exports of hazardous pesticides (tonnes per million population)	0.0	2019	●	•
SDG3 – Good Health and Well-Being				
Maternal mortality rate (per 100,000 live births)	401	2017	●	↗
Neonatal mortality rate (per 1,000 live births)	27.0	2020	●	↗
Mortality rate, under-5 (per 1,000 live births)	48.7	2020	●	↑
Incidence of tuberculosis (per 100,000 population)	132.0	2020	●	↗
New HIV infections (per 1,000 uninfected population)	0.1	2020	●	↑
Age-standardized death rate due to cardiovascular disease, cancer, diabetes, or chronic respiratory disease in adults aged 30–70 years (%)	17.1	2019	●	↗
Age-standardized death rate attributable to household air pollution and ambient air pollution (per 100,000 population)	144	2016	●	•
Traffic deaths (per 100,000 population)	28.2	2019	●	↓
Life expectancy at birth (years)	68.7	2019	●	↗
Adolescent fertility rate (births per 1,000 females aged 15 to 19)	79.5	2014	●	•
Births attended by skilled health personnel (%)	27.7	2016	●	•
Surviving infants who received 2 WHO-recommended vaccines (%)	60	2020	●	→
Universal health coverage (UHC) index of service coverage (worst 0–100 best)	38	2019	●	→
Subjective well-being (average ladder score, worst 0–10 best)	4.5	2020	●	↓
SDG4 – Quality Education				
Participation rate in pre-primary organized learning (% of children aged 4 to 6)	43.0	2020	●	→
Net primary enrollment rate (%)	87.2	2020	●	→
Lower secondary completion rate (%)	29.5	2015	●	•
Literacy rate (% of population aged 15 to 24)	72.8	2017	●	•
SDG5 – Gender Equality				
Demand for family planning satisfied by modern methods (% of females aged 15 to 49)	63.6	2018	●	↗
Ratio of female-to-male mean years of education received (%)	39.5	2019	●	↓
Ratio of female-to-male labor force participation rate (%)	84.4	2020	●	↑
Seats held by women in national parliament (%)	38.8	2020	●	→
SDG6 – Clean Water and Sanitation				
Population using at least basic drinking water services (%)	49.6	2020	●	→
Population using at least basic sanitation services (%)	8.9	2020	●	→
Freshwater withdrawal (% of available freshwater resources)	32.3	2018	●	•
Anthropogenic wastewater that receives treatment (%)	0.0	2018	●	•
Scarce water consumption embodied in imports (m^3 H_2O eq/capita)	75.2	2018	●	•
SDG7 – Affordable and Clean Energy				
Population with access to electricity (%)	48.3	2019	●	↑
Population with access to clean fuels and technology for cooking (%)	6.6	2019	●	→
CO_2 emissions from fuel combustion per total electricity output ($MtCO_2$/TWh)	0.9	2019	●	↑
Share of renewable energy in total primary energy supply (%)	89.6	2019	●	↑
SDG8 – Decent Work and Economic Growth				
Adjusted GDP growth (%)	-0.8	2020	●	•
Victims of modern slavery (per 1,000 population)	6.2	2018	●	•
Adults with an account at a bank or other financial institution or with a mobile-money-service provider (% of population aged 15 or over)	34.8	2017	●	↑
Unemployment rate (% of total labor force)	4.0	2022	●	↑
Fundamental labor rights are effectively guaranteed (worst 0–1 best)	0.3	2020	●	→
Fatal work-related accidents embodied in imports (per 100,000 population)	0.0	2015	●	↑

SDG9 – Industry, Innovation and Infrastructure	Value	Year	Rating	Trend
Population using the internet (%)	24.0	2020	●	→
Mobile broadband subscriptions (per 100 population)	17.1	2019	●	↗
Logistics Performance Index: Quality of trade and transport-related infrastructure (worst 1–5 best)	2.1	2016	●	•
The Times Higher Education Universities Ranking: Average score of top 3 universities (worst 0–100 best)	42.5	2022	●	•
Articles published in academic journals (per 1,000 population)	0.1	2020	●	→
Expenditure on research and development (% of GDP)	0.3	2017	●	•
SDG10 – Reduced Inequalities				
Gini coefficient	35.0	2015	●	•
Palma ratio	1.5	2018	●	•
SDG11 – Sustainable Cities and Communities				
Proportion of urban population living in slums (%)	66.2	2018	●	→
Annual mean concentration of particulate matter of less than 2.5 microns in diameter (PM2.5) ($\mu g/m^3$)	39.8	2019	●	↓
Access to improved water source, piped (% of urban population)	87.9	2020	●	→
Satisfaction with public transport (%)	51.0	2020	●	↑
SDG12 – Responsible Consumption and Production				
Municipal solid waste (kg/capita/day)	0.2	2015	●	•
Electronic waste (kg/capita)	0.6	2019	●	•
Production-based SO_2 emissions (kg/capita)	0.1	2018	●	•
SO_2 emissions embodied in imports (kg/capita)	0.5	2018	●	•
Production-based nitrogen emissions (kg/capita)	13.9	2015	●	↑
Nitrogen emissions embodied in imports (kg/capita)	0.1	2015	●	↑
Exports of plastic waste (kg/capita)	0.0	2020	●	•
SDG13 – Climate Action				
CO_2 emissions from fossil fuel combustion and cement production (tCO_2/capita)	0.1	2020	●	↑
CO_2 emissions embodied in imports (tCO_2/capita)	0.2	2018	●	↑
CO_2 emissions embodied in fossil fuel exports (kg/capita)	0.0	2020	●	•
SDG14 – Life Below Water				
Mean area that is protected in marine sites important to biodiversity (%)	NA	NA	●	•
Ocean Health Index: Clean Waters score (worst 0–100 best)	NA	NA	●	•
Fish caught from overexploited or collapsed stocks (% of total catch)	NA	NA	●	•
Fish caught by trawling or dredging (%)	NA	NA	●	•
Fish caught that are then discarded (%)	NA	NA	●	•
Marine biodiversity threats embodied in imports (per million population)	0.0	2018	●	•
SDG15 – Life on Land				
Mean area that is protected in terrestrial sites important to biodiversity (%)	18.1	2020	●	→
Mean area that is protected in freshwater sites important to biodiversity (%)	16.2	2020	●	→
Red List Index of species survival (worst 0–1 best)	0.8	2021	●	→
Permanent deforestation (% of forest area, 5-year average)	0.1	2020	●	↗
Terrestrial and freshwater biodiversity threats embodied in imports (per million population)	0.0	2018	●	•
SDG16 – Peace, Justice and Strong Institutions				
Homicides (per 100,000 population)	8.8	2012	●	•
Unsentenced detainees (% of prison population)	NA	NA	●	•
Population who feel safe walking alone at night in the city or area where they live (%)	49	2020	●	↓
Property Rights (worst 1–7 best)	3.3	2020	●	↓
Birth registrations with civil authority (% of children under age 5)	2.7	2020	●	•
Corruption Perception Index (worst 0–100 best)	39	2021	●	↗
Children involved in child labor (% of population aged 5 to 14)	45.0	2019	●	•
Exports of major conventional weapons (TIV constant million USD per 100,000 population)	* 0.0	2020	●	•
Press Freedom Index (best 0–100 worst)	33.6	2021	●	↑
Access to and affordability of justice (worst 0–1 best)	0.4	2020	●	↑
SDG17 – Partnerships for the Goals				
Government spending on health and education (% of GDP)	5.8	2019	●	→
For high-income and all OECD DAC countries: International concessional public finance, including official development assistance (% of GNI)	NA	NA	●	•
Other countries: Government revenue excluding grants (% of GDP)	7.8	2019	●	↓
Corporate Tax Haven Score (best 0–100 worst)	* 0.0	2019	●	•
Statistical Performance Index (worst 0–100 best)	53.6	2019	●	→

* Imputed data point

FIJI

Oceania

OVERALL PERFORMANCE

COUNTRY RANKING

FIJI

52/163

COUNTRY SCORE

AVERAGE PERFORMANCE BY SDG

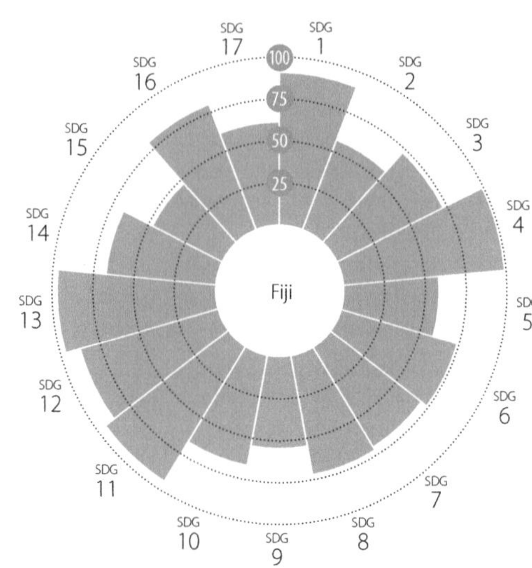

SDG DASHBOARDS AND TRENDS

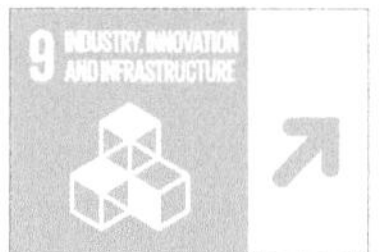

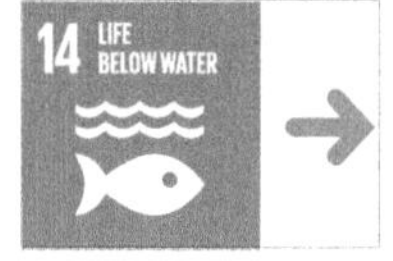

Major challenges | Significant challenges | Challenges remain | SDG achieved | Information unavailable

Decreasing | Stagnating | Moderately improving | On track or maintaining SDG achievement | Information unavailable

Note: The full title of each SDG is available here: https://sustainabledevelopment.un.org/topics/sustainabledevelopmentgoals

INTERNATIONAL SPILLOVER INDEX

STATISTICAL PERFORMANCE INDEX

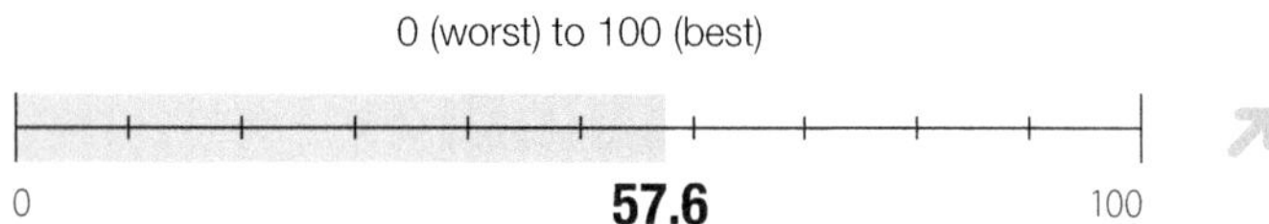

MISSING DATA IN SDG INDEX

18%

FIJI

SDG1 – No Poverty	Value	Year	Rating	Trend
Poverty headcount ratio at $1.90/day (%)	0.3	2022	●	↑
Poverty headcount ratio at $3.20/day (%)	9.5	2022	●	→
SDG2 – Zero Hunger				
Prevalence of undernourishment (%)	5.6	2019	●	↑
Prevalence of stunting in children under 5 years of age (%)	7.5	2004	●	↑
Prevalence of wasting in children under 5 years of age (%)	6.3	2004	●	→
Prevalence of obesity, BMI ≥ 30 (% of adult population)	30.2	2016	●	↓
Human Trophic Level (best 2–3 worst)	2.2	2017	●	↑
Cereal yield (tonnes per hectare of harvested land)	3.0	2018	●	↑
Sustainable Nitrogen Management Index (best 0–1.41 worst)	1.2	2015	●	↓
Exports of hazardous pesticides (tonnes per million population)	0.0	2019	●	●
SDG3 – Good Health and Well-Being				
Maternal mortality rate (per 100,000 live births)	34	2017	●	↑
Neonatal mortality rate (per 1,000 live births)	11.6	2020	●	↑
Mortality rate, under-5 (per 1,000 live births)	27.4	2020	●	↓
Incidence of tuberculosis (per 100,000 population)	66.0	2020	●	→
New HIV infections (per 1,000 uninfected population)	0.2	2020	●	↑
Age-standardized death rate due to cardiovascular disease, cancer, diabetes, or chronic respiratory disease in adults aged 30–70 years (%)	37.7	2019	●	→
Age-standardized death rate attributable to household air pollution and ambient air pollution (per 100,000 population)	99	2016	●	●
Traffic deaths (per 100,000 population)	13.5	2019	●	↓
Life expectancy at birth (years)	68.0	2019	●	→
Adolescent fertility rate (births per 1,000 females aged 15 to 19)	23.1	2016	●	●
Births attended by skilled health personnel (%)	99.8	2016	●	●
Surviving infants who received 2 WHO-recommended vaccines (%)	96	2020	●	↑
Universal health coverage (UHC) index of service coverage (worst 0–100 best)	61	2019	●	↗
Subjective well-being (average ladder score, worst 0–10 best)	NA	NA	●	●
SDG4 – Quality Education				
Participation rate in pre-primary organized learning (% of children aged 4 to 6)	99.4	2019	●	●
Net primary enrollment rate (%)	98.6	2019	●	↑
Lower secondary completion rate (%)	102.6	2016	●	●
Literacy rate (% of population aged 15 to 24)	NA	NA	●	●
SDG5 – Gender Equality				
Demand for family planning satisfied by modern methods (% of females aged 15 to 49)	* 64.9	2022	●	→
Ratio of female-to-male mean years of education received (%)	101.9	2019	●	↑
Ratio of female-to-male labor force participation rate (%)	50.4	2020	●	↓
Seats held by women in national parliament (%)	19.6	2020	●	→
SDG6 – Clean Water and Sanitation				
Population using at least basic drinking water services (%)	94.3	2020	●	→
Population using at least basic sanitation services (%)	99.2	2020	●	↑
Freshwater withdrawal (% of available freshwater resources)	0.3	2018	●	●
Anthropogenic wastewater that receives treatment (%)	3.9	2018	●	●
Scarce water consumption embodied in imports (m^3 H_2O eq/capita)	NA	NA	●	●
SDG7 – Affordable and Clean Energy				
Population with access to electricity (%)	100.0	2019	●	↑
Population with access to clean fuels and technology for cooking (%)	49.6	2019	●	↗
CO_2 emissions from fuel combustion per total electricity output ($MtCO_2$/TWh)	2.4	2019	●	→
Share of renewable energy in total primary energy supply (%)	NA	NA	●	●
SDG8 – Decent Work and Economic Growth				
Adjusted GDP growth (%)	-7.6	2020	●	●
Victims of modern slavery (per 1,000 population)	NA	NA	●	●
Adults with an account at a bank or other financial institution or with a mobile-money-service provider (% of population aged 15 or over)	NA	NA	●	●
Unemployment rate (% of total labor force)	4.9	2022	●	↑
Fundamental labor rights are effectively guaranteed (worst 0–1 best)	NA	NA	●	●
Fatal work-related accidents embodied in imports (per 100,000 population)	0.3	2015	●	↑

SDG9 – Industry, Innovation and Infrastructure	Value	Year	Rating	Trend
Population using the internet (%)	68.9	2018	●	●
Mobile broadband subscriptions (per 100 population)	72.2	2019	●	↑
Logistics Performance Index: Quality of trade and transport-related infrastructure (worst 1–5 best)	2.4	2018	●	↓
The Times Higher Education Universities Ranking: Average score of top 3 universities (worst 0–100 best)	24.8	2022	●	●
Articles published in academic journals (per 1,000 population)	0.5	2020	●	↑
Expenditure on research and development (% of GDP)	NA	NA	●	●
SDG10 – Reduced Inequalities				
Gini coefficient	36.7	2013	●	●
Palma ratio	1.6	2018	●	●
SDG11 – Sustainable Cities and Communities				
Proportion of urban population living in slums (%)	10.8	2018	●	●
Annual mean concentration of particulate matter of less than 2.5 microns in diameter (PM2.5) (μg/m^3)	10.1	2019	●	↑
Access to improved water source, piped (% of urban population)	97.3	2020	●	→
Satisfaction with public transport (%)	NA	NA	●	●
SDG12 – Responsible Consumption and Production				
Municipal solid waste (kg/capita/day)	0.6	2011	●	●
Electronic waste (kg/capita)	6.1	2019	●	●
Production-based SO_2 emissions (kg/capita)	NA	NA	●	●
SO_2 emissions embodied in imports (kg/capita)	NA	NA	●	●
Production-based nitrogen emissions (kg/capita)	14.2	2015	●	↑
Nitrogen emissions embodied in imports (kg/capita)	2.9	2015	●	↑
Exports of plastic waste (kg/capita)	0.9	2020	●	●
SDG13 – Climate Action				
CO_2 emissions from fossil fuel combustion and cement production (tCO_2/capita)	1.6	2020	●	↑
CO_2 emissions embodied in imports (tCO_2/capita)	NA	NA	●	●
CO_2 emissions embodied in fossil fuel exports (kg/capita)	0.0	2020	●	●
SDG14 – Life Below Water				
Mean area that is protected in marine sites important to biodiversity (%)	16.5	2020	●	→
Ocean Health Index: Clean Waters score (worst 0–100 best)	73.5	2020	●	→
Fish caught from overexploited or collapsed stocks (% of total catch)	9.0	2018	●	↑
Fish caught by trawling or dredging (%)	0.0	2018	●	↑
Fish caught that are then discarded (%)	11.0	2018	●	→
Marine biodiversity threats embodied in imports (per million population)	0.3	2018	●	●
SDG15 – Life on Land				
Mean area that is protected in terrestrial sites important to biodiversity (%)	11.2	2020	●	→
Mean area that is protected in freshwater sites important to biodiversity (%)	0.1	2020	●	→
Red List Index of species survival (worst 0–1 best)	0.7	2021	●	↓
Permanent deforestation (% of forest area, 5-year average)	0.0	2020	●	↑
Terrestrial and freshwater biodiversity threats embodied in imports (per million population)	0.0	2018	●	●
SDG16 – Peace, Justice and Strong Institutions				
Homicides (per 100,000 population)	2.2	2020	●	→
Unsentenced detainees (% of prison population)	25.9	2016	●	●
Population who feel safe walking alone at night in the city or area where they live (%)	NA	NA	●	●
Property Rights (worst 1–7 best)	NA	NA	●	●
Birth registrations with civil authority (% of children under age 5)	NA	NA	●	●
Corruption Perception Index (worst 0–100 best)	55	2021	●	●
Children involved in child labor (% of population aged 5 to 14)	NA	NA	●	●
Exports of major conventional weapons (TIV constant million USD per 100,000 population)	* 0.0	2020	●	●
Press Freedom Index (best 0–100 worst)	27.9	2021	●	↑
Access to and affordability of justice (worst 0–1 best)	NA	NA	●	●
SDG17 – Partnerships for the Goals				
Government spending on health and education (% of GDP)	7.6	2019	●	↗
For high-income and all OECD DAC countries: International concessional public finance, including official development assistance (% of GNI)	NA	NA	●	●
Other countries: Government revenue excluding grants (% of GDP)	24.9	2019	●	↓
Corporate Tax Haven Score (best 0–100 worst)	* 0.0	2019	●	●
Statistical Performance Index (worst 0–100 best)	57.6	2019	●	↗

* Imputed data point

5. Country Profiles

FINLAND

OECD Countries

OVERALL PERFORMANCE

COUNTRY RANKING

FINLAND

1 **/163**

COUNTRY SCORE

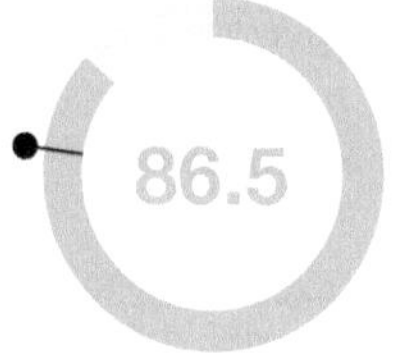

REGIONAL AVERAGE: 77.2

AVERAGE PERFORMANCE BY SDG

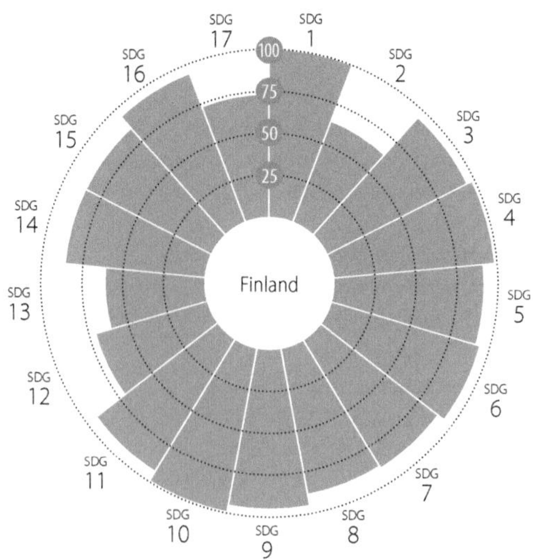

SDG DASHBOARDS AND TRENDS

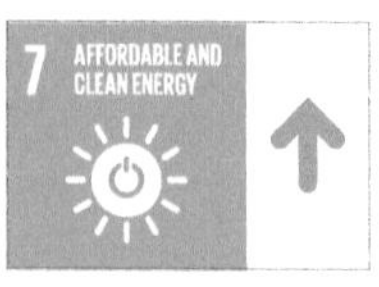

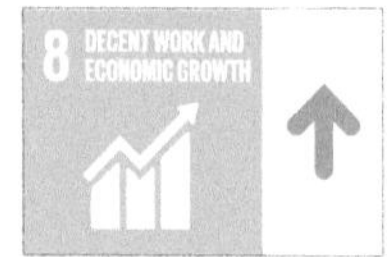

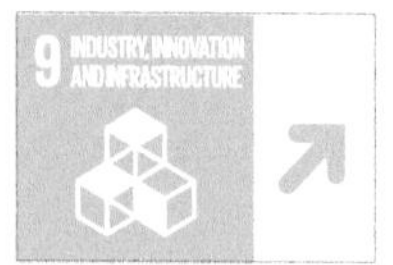

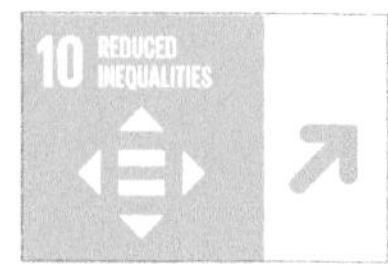

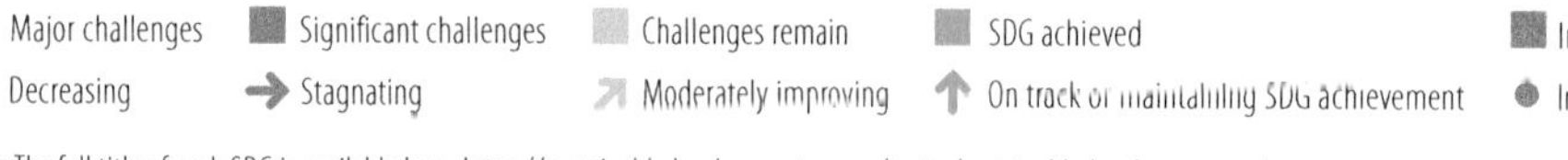

Note: The full title of each SDG is available here: https://sustainabledevelopment.un.org/topics/sustainabledevelopmentgoals

INTERNATIONAL SPILLOVER INDEX

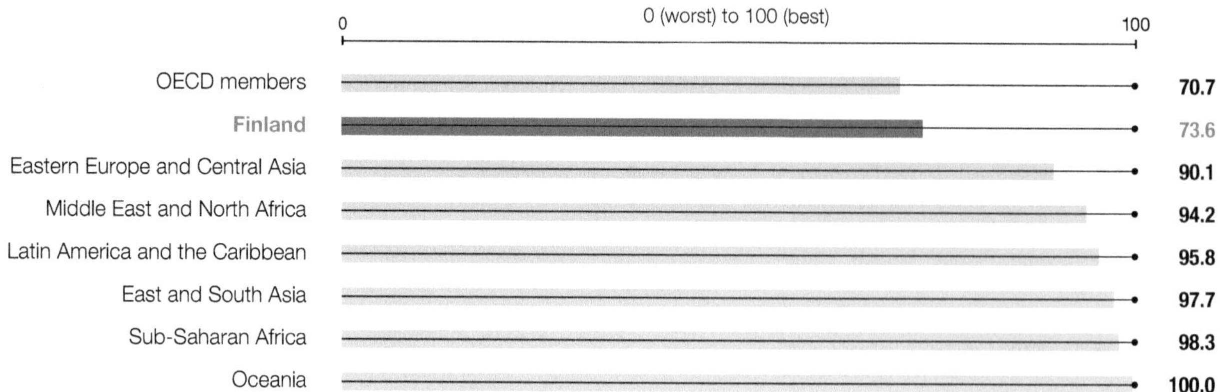

STATISTICAL PERFORMANCE INDEX

0 (worst) to 100 (best)

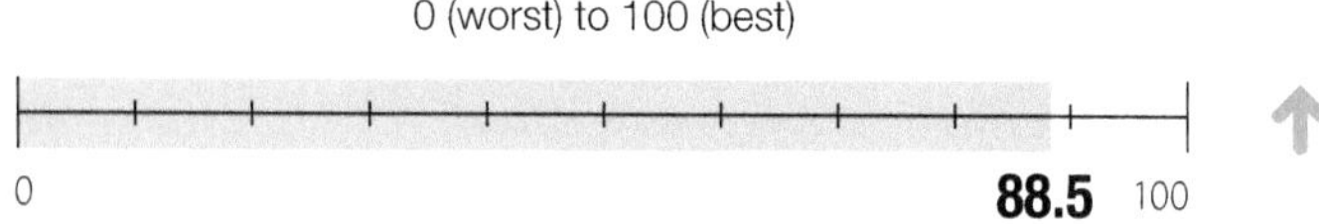

MISSING DATA IN SDG INDEX

1%

SDG1 – No Poverty

Indicator	Value	Year	Rating	Trend
Poverty headcount ratio at \$1.90/day (%)	0.1	2022	●	↑
Poverty headcount ratio at \$3.20/day (%)	0.1	2022	●	↑
Poverty rate after taxes and transfers (%)	6.5	2018	●	↑

SDG2 – Zero Hunger

Indicator	Value	Year	Rating	Trend
Prevalence of undernourishment (%)	2.5	2019	●	↑
Prevalence of stunting in children under 5 years of age (%)	* 2.6	2019	●	↑
Prevalence of wasting in children under 5 years of age (%)	* 0.7	2019	●	↑
Prevalence of obesity, BMI ≥ 30 (% of adult population)	22.2	2016	●	↓
Human Trophic Level (best 2–3 worst)	2.6	2017	●	↓
Cereal yield (tonnes per hectare of harvested land)	3.0	2018	●	↑
Sustainable Nitrogen Management Index (best 0–1.41 worst)	0.6	2015	●	↓
Yield gap closure (% of potential yield)	51.7	2018	●	●
Exports of hazardous pesticides (tonnes per million population)	1.2	2019	●	●

SDG3 – Good Health and Well-Being

Indicator	Value	Year	Rating	Trend
Maternal mortality rate (per 100,000 live births)	3	2017	●	↑
Neonatal mortality rate (per 1,000 live births)	1.4	2020	●	↑
Mortality rate, under-5 (per 1,000 live births)	2.3	2020	●	↑
Incidence of tuberculosis (per 100,000 population)	3.6	2020	●	↑
New HIV infections (per 1,000 uninfected population)	1.0	2020	●	→
Age-standardized death rate due to cardiovascular disease, cancer, diabetes, or chronic respiratory disease in adults aged 30–70 years (%)	9.6	2019	●	↑
Age-standardized death rate attributable to household air pollution and ambient air pollution (per 100,000 population)	7	2016	●	●
Traffic deaths (per 100,000 population)	3.9	2019	●	↑
Life expectancy at birth (years)	81.6	2019	●	↑
Adolescent fertility rate (births per 1,000 females aged 15 to 19)	4.3	2018	●	↑
Births attended by skilled health personnel (%)	100.0	2018	●	↑
Surviving infants who received 2 WHO-recommended vaccines (%)	91	2020	●	↑
Universal health coverage (UHC) index of service coverage (worst 0–100 best)	83	2019	●	↑
Subjective well-being (average ladder score, worst 0–10 best)	7.8	2021	●	↑
Gap in life expectancy at birth among regions (years)	4.4	2019	●	↓
Gap in self-reported health status by income (percentage points)	25.3	2020	●	→
Daily smokers (% of population aged 15 and over)	12.0	2020	●	↑

SDG4 – Quality Education

Indicator	Value	Year	Rating	Trend
Participation rate in pre-primary organized learning (% of children aged 4 to 6)	98.8	2019	●	↑
Net primary enrollment rate (%)	98.1	2019	●	↑
Lower secondary completion rate (%)	101.2	2019	●	↑
Literacy rate (% of population aged 15 to 24)	NA	NA	●	●
Tertiary educational attainment (% of population aged 25 to 34)	44.7	2020	●	↑
PISA score (worst 0–600 best)	516.3	2018	●	↑
Variation in science performance explained by socio-economic status (%)	10.5	2018	●	↑
Underachievers in science (% of 15-year-olds)	12.9	2018	●	↑

SDG5 – Gender Equality

Indicator	Value	Year	Rating	Trend
Demand for family planning satisfied by modern methods (% of females aged 15 to 49)	* 90.2	2022	●	↑
Ratio of female-to-male mean years of education received (%)	103.2	2019	●	↑
Ratio of female-to-male labor force participation rate (%)	87.7	2020	●	↑
Seats held by women in national parliament (%)	46.0	2020	●	↑
Gender wage gap (% of male median wage)	17.2	2019	●	→

SDG6 – Clean Water and Sanitation

Indicator	Value	Year	Rating	Trend
Population using at least basic drinking water services (%)	100.0	2020	●	↑
Population using at least basic sanitation services (%)	99.4	2020	●	↑
Freshwater withdrawal (% of available freshwater resources)	15.6	2018	●	●
Anthropogenic wastewater that receives treatment (%)	100.0	2018	●	●
Scarce water consumption embodied in imports (m^3 H_2O eq/capita)	3124.9	2018	●	●
Population using safely managed water services (%)	99.6	2020	●	↑
Population using safely managed sanitation services (%)	84.1	2020	●	→

SDG7 – Affordable and Clean Energy

Indicator	Value	Year	Rating	Trend
Population with access to electricity (%)	100.0	2019	●	↑
Population with access to clean fuels and technology for cooking (%)	100.0	2019	●	↑
CO_2 emissions from fuel combustion per total electricity output ($MtCO_2$/TWh)	0.6	2019	●	↑
Share of renewable energy in total primary energy supply (%)	34.9	2019	●	↑

SDG8 – Decent Work and Economic Growth

Indicator	Value	Year	Rating	Trend
Adjusted GDP growth (%)	-0.2	2020	●	●
Victims of modern slavery (per 1,000 population)	1.7	2018	●	●
Adults with an account at a bank or other financial institution or with a mobile-money-service provider (% of population aged 15 or over)	99.8	2017	●	↑
Fundamental labor rights are effectively guaranteed (worst 0–1 best)	0.9	2020	●	↑
Fatal work-related accidents embodied in imports (per 100,000 population)	0.9	2015	●	↑
Employment-to-population ratio (%)	71.2	2020	●	↑
Youth not in employment, education or training (NEET) (% of population aged 15 to 29)	10.8	2020	●	↑

* Imputed data point

SDG9 – Industry, Innovation and Infrastructure

Indicator	Value	Year	Rating	Trend
Population using the internet (%)	92.2	2020	●	↑
Mobile broadband subscriptions (per 100 population)	154.9	2019	●	↑
Logistics Performance Index: Quality of trade and transport-related infrastructure (worst 1–5 best)	4.0	2018	●	↑
The Times Higher Education Universities Ranking: Average score of top 3 universities (worst 0–100 best)	54.5	2022	●	●
Articles published in academic journals (per 1,000 population)	3.9	2020	●	↑
Expenditure on research and development (% of GDP)	2.8	2018	●	↑
Researchers (per 1,000 employed population)	15.0	2019	●	↑
Triadic patent families filed (per million population)	49.2	2019	●	↑
Gap in internet access by income (percentage points)	9.2	2020	●	↑
Female share of graduates from STEM fields at the tertiary level (%)	27.4	2017	●	→

SDG10 – Reduced Inequalities

Indicator	Value	Year	Rating	Trend
Gini coefficient	27.3	2018	●	↑
Palma ratio	1.0	2018	●	↑
Elderly poverty rate (% of population aged 66 or over)	7.2	2018	●	↓

SDG11 – Sustainable Cities and Communities

Indicator	Value	Year	Rating	Trend
Proportion of urban population living in slums (%)	* 0.0	2018	●	↑
Annual mean concentration of particulate matter of less than 2.5 microns in diameter (PM2.5) (μg/m³)	5.5	2019	●	↑
Access to improved water source, piped (% of urban population)	100.0	2020	●	↑
Satisfaction with public transport (%)	63.0	2021	●	↗
Population with rent overburden (%)	8.8	2019	●	→

SDG12 – Responsible Consumption and Production

Indicator	Value	Year	Rating	Trend
Electronic waste (kg/capita)	19.8	2019	●	●
Production-based SO_2 emissions (kg/capita)	26.6	2018	●	●
SO_2 emissions embodied in imports (kg/capita)	7.3	2018	●	●
Production-based nitrogen emissions (kg/capita)	15.9	2015	●	↑
Nitrogen emissions embodied in imports (kg/capita)	9.9	2015	●	↓
Exports of plastic waste (kg/capita)	2.2	2020	●	●
Non-recycled municipal solid waste (kg/capita/day)	0.9	2019	●	↓

SDG13 – Climate Action

Indicator	Value	Year	Rating	Trend
CO_2 emissions from fossil fuel combustion and cement production (tCO_2/capita)	7.1	2020	●	→
CO_2 emissions embodied in imports (tCO_2/capita)	2.7	2018	●	↓
CO_2 emissions embodied in fossil fuel exports (kg/capita)	0.1	2020	●	●
Carbon Pricing Score at EUR60/tCO_2 (%, worst 0–100 best)	33.5	2018	●	↓

SDG14 – Life Below Water

Indicator	Value	Year	Rating	Trend
Mean area that is protected in marine sites important to biodiversity (%)	60.7	2020	●	→
Ocean Health Index: Clean Waters score (worst 0–100 best)	70.1	2020	●	↓
Fish caught from overexploited or collapsed stocks (% of total catch)	3.1	2018	●	↑
Fish caught by trawling or dredging (%)	0.0	2018	●	↑
Fish caught that are then discarded (%)	0.2	2018	●	↑
Marine biodiversity threats embodied in imports (per million population)	0.1	2018	●	●

SDG15 – Life on Land

Indicator	Value	Year	Rating	Trend
Mean area that is protected in terrestrial sites important to biodiversity (%)	71.7	2020	●	→
Mean area that is protected in freshwater sites important to biodiversity (%)	75.8	2020	●	→
Red List Index of species survival (worst 0–1 best)	1.0	2021	●	↑
Permanent deforestation (% of forest area, 5-year average)	0.0	2020	●	↑
Terrestrial and freshwater biodiversity threats embodied in imports (per million population)	2.0	2018	●	●

SDG16 – Peace, Justice and Strong Institutions

Indicator	Value	Year	Rating	Trend
Homicides (per 100,000 population)	1.6	2020	●	↓
Unsentenced detainees (% of prison population)	21.5	2019	●	↑
Population who feel safe walking alone at night in the city or area where they live (%)	85	2021	●	↑
Property Rights (worst 1–7 best)	6.6	2020	●	↑
Birth registrations with civil authority (% of children under age 5)	100.0	2020	●	●
Corruption Perception Index (worst 0–100 best)	88	2021	●	↑
Children involved in child labor (% of population aged 5 to 14)	* 0.0	2019	●	●
Exports of major conventional weapons (TIV constant million USD per 100,000 population)	0.6	2020	●	●
Press Freedom Index (best 0–100 worst)	7.0	2021	●	↑
Access to and affordability of justice (worst 0–1 best)	0.7	2020	●	↑
Persons held in prison (per 100,000 population)	53.2	2019	●	↑

SDG17 – Partnerships for the Goals

Indicator	Value	Year	Rating	Trend
Government spending on health and education (% of GDP)	13.6	2019	●	↑
For high-income and all OECD DAC countries: International concessional public finance, including official development assistance (% of GNI)	0.5	2021	●	↓
Other countries: Government revenue excluding grants (% of GDP)	NA	NA	●	●
Corporate Tax Haven Score (best 0–100 worst)	55.0	2019	●	●
Financial Secrecy Score (best 0–100 worst)	52.1	2020	●	●
Shifted profits of multinationals (US\$ billion)	5.2	2018	●	↑
Statistical Performance Index (worst 0–100 best)	88.5	2019	●	↑

FRANCE

AVERAGE PERFORMANCE BY SDG

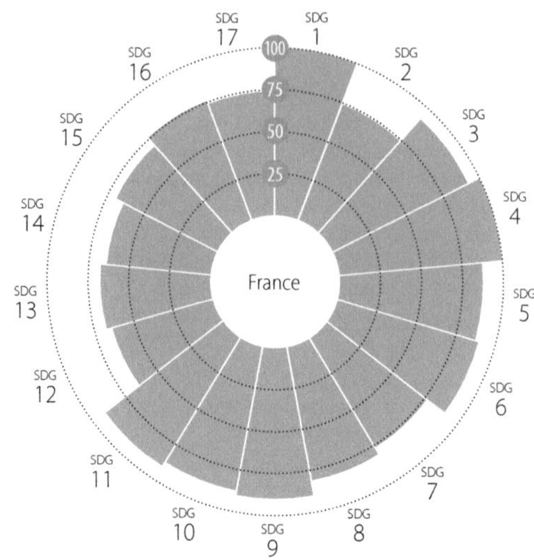

OVERALL PERFORMANCE

COUNTRY RANKING

FRANCE

7 **/163**

COUNTRY SCORE

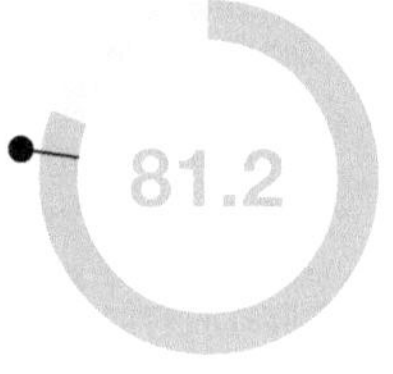

REGIONAL AVERAGE: 77.2

SDG DASHBOARDS AND TRENDS

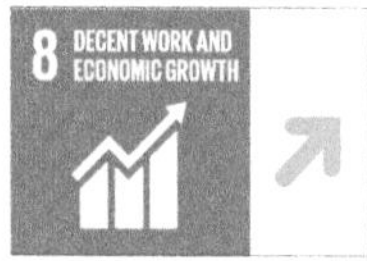

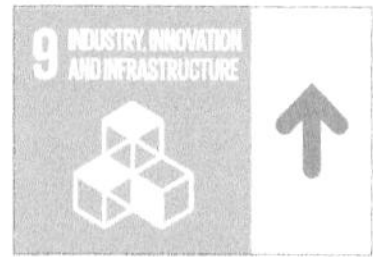

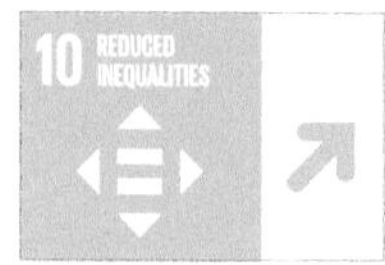

Major challenges | Significant challenges | Challenges remain | SDG achieved | Information unavailable

Decreasing | Stagnating | Moderately improving | On track or maintaining SDG achievement | Information unavailable

Note: The full title of each SDG is available here: https://sustainabledevelopment.un.org/topics/sustainabledevelopmentgoals

INTERNATIONAL SPILLOVER INDEX

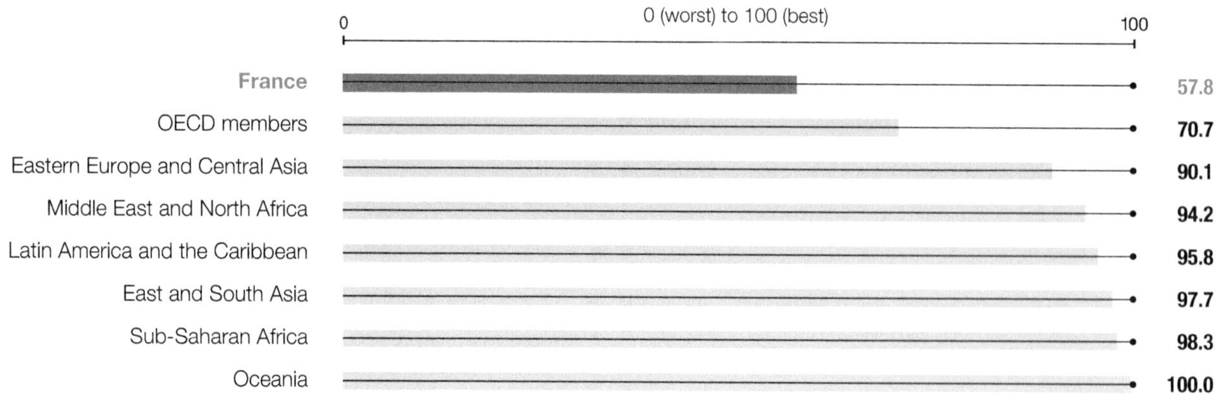

STATISTICAL PERFORMANCE INDEX

0 (worst) to 100 (best)

0 **86.3** 100

MISSING DATA IN SDG INDEX

1%

FRANCE

SDG1 – No Poverty		Value	Year	Rating	Trend
Poverty headcount ratio at $1.90/day (%)		0.2	2022	●	↑
Poverty headcount ratio at $3.20/day (%)		0.2	2022	●	↑
Poverty rate after taxes and transfers (%)		8.4	2019	●	↑
SDG2 – Zero Hunger					
Prevalence of undernourishment (%)		2.5	2019	●	↑
Prevalence of stunting in children under 5 years of age (%)	*	2.6	2019	●	↑
Prevalence of wasting in children under 5 years of age (%)	*	0.7	2019	●	↑
Prevalence of obesity, BMI ≥ 30 (% of adult population)		21.6	2016	●	↓
Human Trophic Level (best 2–3 worst)		2.5	2017	●	→
Cereal yield (tonnes per hectare of harvested land)		6.9	2018	●	↑
Sustainable Nitrogen Management Index (best 0–1.41 worst)		0.4	2015	●	↓
Yield gap closure (% of potential yield)		75.0	2018	●	●
Exports of hazardous pesticides (tonnes per million population)		5.6	2019	●	●
SDG3 – Good Health and Well-Being					
Maternal mortality rate (per 100,000 live births)		8	2017	●	↑
Neonatal mortality rate (per 1,000 live births)		2.6	2020	●	↑
Mortality rate, under-5 (per 1,000 live births)		4.4	2020	●	↑
Incidence of tuberculosis (per 100,000 population)		8.2	2020	●	↑
New HIV infections (per 1,000 uninfected population)		1.0	2020	●	→
Age-standardized death rate due to cardiovascular disease, cancer, diabetes, or chronic respiratory disease in adults aged 30–70 years (%)		10.6	2019	●	↑
Age-standardized death rate attributable to household air pollution and ambient air pollution (per 100,000 population)		10	2016	●	●
Traffic deaths (per 100,000 population)		5.1	2019	●	↑
Life expectancy at birth (years)		82.5	2019	●	↑
Adolescent fertility rate (births per 1,000 females aged 15 to 19)		8.6	2018	●	↑
Births attended by skilled health personnel (%)		98.1	2018	●	↑
Surviving infants who received 2 WHO-recommended vaccines (%)		90	2019	●	↑
Universal health coverage (UHC) index of service coverage (worst 0–100 best)		84	2019	●	↑
Subjective well-being (average ladder score, worst 0–10 best)		6.7	2021	●	↑
Gap in life expectancy at birth among regions (years)		8.7	2019	●	↓
Gap in self-reported health status by income (percentage points)		14.4	2019	●	↑
Daily smokers (% of population aged 15 and over)		24.0	2019	●	↑
SDG4 – Quality Education					
Participation rate in pre-primary organized learning (% of children aged 4 to 6)		99.9	2019	●	↑
Net primary enrollment rate (%)		100.0	2019	●	↑
Lower secondary completion rate (%)		99.5	2019	●	↑
Literacy rate (% of population aged 15 to 24)		NA	NA	●	●
Tertiary educational attainment (% of population aged 25 to 34)		49.4	2020	●	↑
PISA score (worst 0–600 best)		493.7	2018	●	↑
Variation in science performance explained by socio-economic status (%)		20.1	2018	●	→
Underachievers in science (% of 15-year-olds)		20.5	2018	●	↑
SDG5 – Gender Equality					
Demand for family planning satisfied by modern methods (% of females aged 15 to 49)		95.5	2005	●	↑
Ratio of female-to-male mean years of education received (%)		96.6	2019	●	↑
Ratio of female-to-male labor force participation rate (%)		86.1	2020	●	↑
Seats held by women in national parliament (%)		39.5	2020	●	↑
Gender wage gap (% of male median wage)		11.8	2018	●	↓
SDG6 – Clean Water and Sanitation					
Population using at least basic drinking water services (%)		100.0	2020	●	↑
Population using at least basic sanitation services (%)		98.6	2020	●	↑
Freshwater withdrawal (% of available freshwater resources)		23.6	2018	●	●
Anthropogenic wastewater that receives treatment (%)		88.0	2018	●	●
Scarce water consumption embodied in imports (m^3 H_2O eq/capita)		2875.2	2018	●	●
Population using safely managed water services (%)		99.2	2020	●	↑
Population using safely managed sanitation services (%)		78.6	2020	●	↓
SDG7 – Affordable and Clean Energy					
Population with access to electricity (%)		100.0	2019	●	↑
Population with access to clean fuels and technology for cooking (%)		100.0	2019	●	↑
CO_2 emissions from fuel combustion per total electricity output ($MtCO_2$/TWh)		0.6	2019	●	↑
Share of renewable energy in total primary energy supply (%)		10.6	2019	●	↗
SDG8 – Decent Work and Economic Growth					
Adjusted GDP growth (%)		-0.6	2020	●	●
Victims of modern slavery (per 1,000 population)		2.0	2018	●	●
Adults with an account at a bank or other financial institution or with a mobile-money-service provider (% of population aged 15 or over)		94.0	2017	●	↑
Fundamental labor rights are effectively guaranteed (worst 0–1 best)		0.8	2020	●	↑
Fatal work-related accidents embodied in imports (per 100,000 population)		1.7	2015	●	↑
Employment-to-population ratio (%)		66.1	2020	●	↑
Youth not in employment, education or training (NEET) (% of population aged 15 to 29)		15.0	2020	●	↗

SDG9 – Industry, Innovation and Infrastructure		Value	Year	Rating	Trend
Population using the internet (%)		84.8	2020	●	↑
Mobile broadband subscriptions (per 100 population)		97.0	2019	●	↑
Logistics Performance Index: Quality of trade and transport-related infrastructure (worst 1–5 best)		4.0	2018	●	↑
The Times Higher Education Universities Ranking: Average score of top 3 universities (worst 0–100 best)		67.0	2022	●	●
Articles published in academic journals (per 1,000 population)		1.7	2020	●	↑
Expenditure on research and development (% of GDP)		2.2	2018	●	↑
Researchers (per 1,000 employed population)		11.0	2019	●	↑
Triadic patent families filed (per million population)		28.5	2019	●	↑
Gap in internet access by income (percentage points)		20.7	2019	●	↑
Female share of graduates from STEM fields at the tertiary level (%)		31.8	2016	●	↑
SDG10 – Reduced Inequalities					
Gini coefficient		32.4	2018	●	↗
Palma ratio		1.1	2019	●	↗
Elderly poverty rate (% of population aged 66 or over)		4.4	2019	●	↑
SDG11 – Sustainable Cities and Communities					
Proportion of urban population living in slums (%)	*	0.0	2018	●	↑
Annual mean concentration of particulate matter of less than 2.5 microns in diameter (PM2.5) (μg/m³)		11.2	2019	●	↑
Access to improved water source, piped (% of urban population)		100.0	2020	●	↑
Satisfaction with public transport (%)		63.0	2021	●	↓
Population with rent overburden (%)		5.3	2019	●	↑
SDG12 – Responsible Consumption and Production					
Electronic waste (kg/capita)		21.0	2019	●	●
Production-based SO_2 emissions (kg/capita)		6.9	2018	●	●
SO_2 emissions embodied in imports (kg/capita)		6.1	2018	●	●
Production-based nitrogen emissions (kg/capita)		22.8	2015	●	↓
Nitrogen emissions embodied in imports (kg/capita)		12.8	2015	●	↓
Exports of plastic waste (kg/capita)		6.2	2020	●	●
Non-recycled municipal solid waste (kg/capita/day)		0.8	2019	●	↑
SDG13 – Climate Action					
CO_2 emissions from fossil fuel combustion and cement production (tCO_2/capita)		4.2	2020	●	↗
CO_2 emissions embodied in imports (tCO_2/capita)		2.5	2018	●	→
CO_2 emissions embodied in fossil fuel exports (kg/capita)		1.3	2020	●	●
Carbon Pricing Score at EUR60/tCO_2 (%, worst 0–100 best)		55.0	2018	●	↑
SDG14 – Life Below Water					
Mean area that is protected in marine sites important to biodiversity (%)		81.9	2020	●	↑
Ocean Health Index: Clean Waters score (worst 0–100 best)		49.1	2020	●	↓
Fish caught from overexploited or collapsed stocks (% of total catch)		21.0	2018	●	↑
Fish caught by trawling or dredging (%)		16.2	2018	●	↗
Fish caught that are then discarded (%)		13.2	2018	●	↑
Marine biodiversity threats embodied in imports (per million population)		0.4	2018	●	●
SDG15 – Life on Land					
Mean area that is protected in terrestrial sites important to biodiversity (%)		80.9	2020	●	↑
Mean area that is protected in freshwater sites important to biodiversity (%)		78.0	2020	●	↑
Red List Index of species survival (worst 0–1 best)		0.8	2021	●	↓
Permanent deforestation (% of forest area, 5-year average)		0.0	2020	●	↑
Terrestrial and freshwater biodiversity threats embodied in imports (per million population)		7.1	2018	●	●
SDG16 – Peace, Justice and Strong Institutions					
Homicides (per 100,000 population)		1.3	2019	●	↑
Unsentenced detainees (% of prison population)		29.8	2019	●	↑
Population who feel safe walking alone at night in the city or area where they live (%)		75	2021	●	↑
Property Rights (worst 1–7 best)		5.3	2020	●	↑
Birth registrations with civil authority (% of children under age 5)		100.0	2020	●	●
Corruption Perception Index (worst 0–100 best)		71	2021	●	↑
Children involved in child labor (% of population aged 5 to 14)	*	0.0	2019	●	●
Exports of major conventional weapons (TIV constant million USD per 100,000 population)		3.5	2020	●	●
Press Freedom Index (best 0–100 worst)		22.6	2021	●	↑
Access to and affordability of justice (worst 0–1 best)		0.7	2020	●	↑
Persons held in prison (per 100,000 population)		108.5	2019	●	→
SDG17 – Partnerships for the Goals					
Government spending on health and education (% of GDP)		13.7	2019	●	↑
For high-income and all OECD DAC countries: International concessional public finance, including official development assistance (% of GNI)		0.5	2021	●	↑
Other countries: Government revenue excluding grants (% of GDP)		NA	NA	●	●
Corporate Tax Haven Score (best 0–100 worst)		55.7	2019	●	●
Financial Secrecy Score (best 0–100 worst)		49.9	2020	●	●
Shifted profits of multinationals (US$ billion)		46.7	2018	●	↑
Statistical Performance Index (worst 0–100 best)		86.3	2019	●	↑

* Imputed data point

5. Country Profiles

GABON

OVERALL PERFORMANCE

COUNTRY RANKING

GABON

113/163

COUNTRY SCORE

AVERAGE PERFORMANCE BY SDG

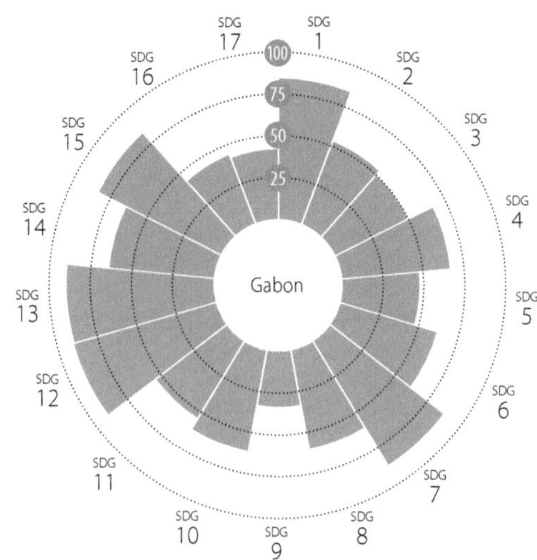

SDG DASHBOARDS AND TRENDS

Major challenges | Significant challenges | Challenges remain | SDG achieved | Information unavailable

Decreasing | Stagnating | Moderately improving | On track or maintaining SDG achievement | Information unavailable

Note: The full title of each SDG is available here: https://sustainabledevelopment.un.org/topics/sustainabledevelopmentgoals

INTERNATIONAL SPILLOVER INDEX

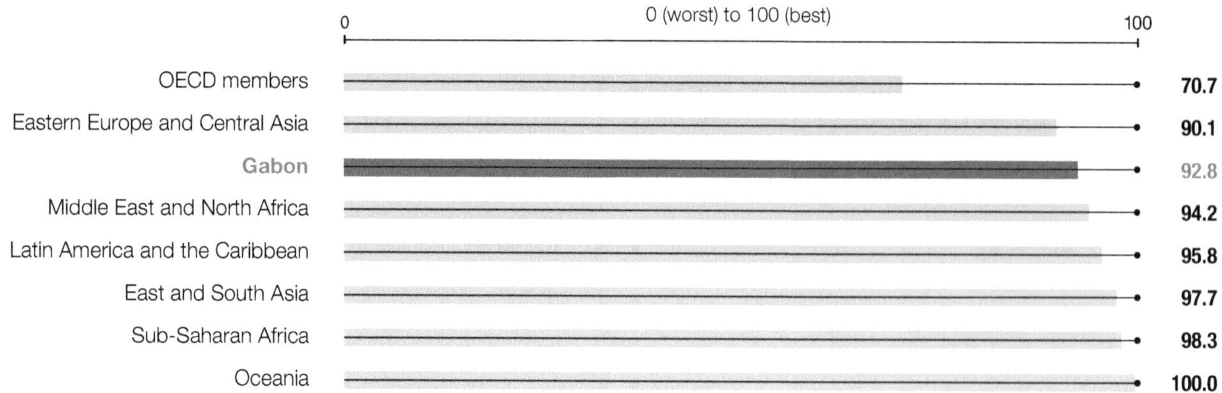

STATISTICAL PERFORMANCE INDEX

0 (worst) to 100 (best)

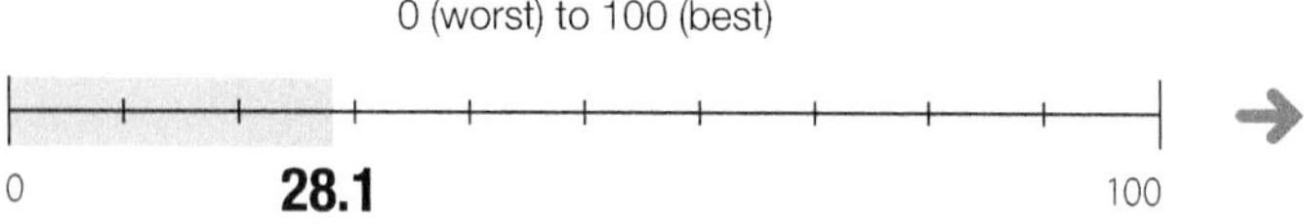

MISSING DATA IN SDG INDEX

10%

SDG1 – No Poverty	Value	Year	Rating	Trend
Poverty headcount ratio at $1.90/day (%)	3.3	2022	●	→
Poverty headcount ratio at $3.20/day (%)	14.2	2022	●	→

SDG2 – Zero Hunger	Value	Year	Rating	Trend
Prevalence of undernourishment (%)	15.7	2019	●	↓
Prevalence of stunting in children under 5 years of age (%)	17.0	2012	●	↗
Prevalence of wasting in children under 5 years of age (%)	3.4	2012	●	↑
Prevalence of obesity, BMI ≥ 30 (% of adult population)	15.0	2016	●	↓
Human Trophic Level (best 2–3 worst)	2.2	2017	●	↑
Cereal yield (tonnes per hectare of harvested land)	1.6	2018	●	→
Sustainable Nitrogen Management Index (best 0–1.41 worst)	1.0	2015	●	↓
Exports of hazardous pesticides (tonnes per million population)	NA	NA	●	●

SDG3 – Good Health and Well-Being	Value	Year	Rating	Trend
Maternal mortality rate (per 100,000 live births)	252	2017	●	→
Neonatal mortality rate (per 1,000 live births)	19.7	2020	●	↗
Mortality rate, under-5 (per 1,000 live births)	41.7	2020	●	↑
Incidence of tuberculosis (per 100,000 population)	527.0	2020	●	→
New HIV infections (per 1,000 uninfected population)	0.5	2020	●	↑
Age-standardized death rate due to cardiovascular disease, cancer, diabetes, or chronic respiratory disease in adults aged 30–70 years (%)	21.3	2019	●	↑
Age-standardized death rate attributable to household air pollution and ambient air pollution (per 100,000 population)	76	2016	●	●
Traffic deaths (per 100,000 population)	23.9	2019	●	↓
Life expectancy at birth (years)	66.5	2019	●	→
Adolescent fertility rate (births per 1,000 females aged 15 to 19)	91.0	2012	●	●
Births attended by skilled health personnel (%)	89.3	2012	●	●
Surviving infants who received 2 WHO-recommended vaccines (%)	53	2020	●	↓
Universal health coverage (UHC) index of service coverage (worst 0–100 best)	49	2019	●	↓
Subjective well-being (average ladder score, worst 0–10 best)	5.1	2021	●	↗

SDG4 – Quality Education	Value	Year	Rating	Trend
Participation rate in pre-primary organized learning (% of children aged 4 to 6)	NA	NA	●	●
Net primary enrollment rate (%)	NA	NA	●	●
Lower secondary completion rate (%)	59.3	2019	●	●
Literacy rate (% of population aged 15 to 24)	89.8	2018	●	●

SDG5 – Gender Equality	Value	Year	Rating	Trend
Demand for family planning satisfied by modern methods (% of females aged 15 to 49)	44.0	2012	●	→
Ratio of female-to-male mean years of education received (%)	81.3	2019	●	→
Ratio of female-to-male labor force participation rate (%)	68.4	2020	●	↓
Seats held by women in national parliament (%)	14.8	2020	●	→

SDG6 – Clean Water and Sanitation	Value	Year	Rating	Trend
Population using at least basic drinking water services (%)	85.3	2020	●	→
Population using at least basic sanitation services (%)	49.8	2020	●	→
Freshwater withdrawal (% of available freshwater resources)	0.5	2018	●	●
Anthropogenic wastewater that receives treatment (%)	0.0	2018	●	●
Scarce water consumption embodied in imports (m^3 H_2O eq/capita)	1536.5	2018	●	●

SDG7 – Affordable and Clean Energy	Value	Year	Rating	Trend
Population with access to electricity (%)	90.7	2019	●	↑
Population with access to clean fuels and technology for cooking (%)	87.9	2019	●	↑
CO_2 emissions from fuel combustion per total electricity output ($MtCO_2$/TWh)	1.7	2019	●	↑
Share of renewable energy in total primary energy supply (%)	80.8	2019	●	↑

SDG8 – Decent Work and Economic Growth	Value	Year	Rating	Trend
Adjusted GDP growth (%)	-3.8	2020	●	●
Victims of modern slavery (per 1,000 population)	4.8	2018	●	●
Adults with an account at a bank or other financial institution or with a mobile-money-service provider (% of population aged 15 or over)	58.6	2017	●	↑
Unemployment rate (% of total labor force)	21.8	2022	●	↓
Fundamental labor rights are effectively guaranteed (worst 0–1 best)	NA	NA	●	●
Fatal work-related accidents embodied in imports (per 100,000 population)	0.2	2015	●	↑

SDG9 – Industry, Innovation and Infrastructure	Value	Year	Rating	Trend
Population using the internet (%)	62.0	2020	●	↑
Mobile broadband subscriptions (per 100 population)	94.3	2019	●	↑
Logistics Performance Index: Quality of trade and transport-related infrastructure (worst 1–5 best)	2.1	2018	●	→
The Times Higher Education Universities Ranking: Average score of top 3 universities (worst 0–100 best)	* 0.0	2022	●	●
Articles published in academic journals (per 1,000 population)	0.1	2020	●	↓
Expenditure on research and development (% of GDP)	0.6	2009	●	●

SDG10 – Reduced Inequalities	Value	Year	Rating	Trend
Gini coefficient	38.0	2017	●	●
Palma ratio	1.6	2018	●	●

SDG11 – Sustainable Cities and Communities	Value	Year	Rating	Trend
Proportion of urban population living in slums (%)	36.5	2018	●	→
Annual mean concentration of particulate matter of less than 2.5 microns in diameter (PM2.5) (μg/m^3)	47.5	2019	●	↓
Access to improved water source, piped (% of urban population)	88.9	2020	●	↓
Satisfaction with public transport (%)	34.0	2021	●	→

SDG12 – Responsible Consumption and Production	Value	Year	Rating	Trend
Municipal solid waste (kg/capita/day)	NA	NA	●	●
Electronic waste (kg/capita)	8.7	2019	●	●
Production-based SO_2 emissions (kg/capita)	9.1	2018	●	●
SO_2 emissions embodied in imports (kg/capita)	0.8	2018	●	●
Production-based nitrogen emissions (kg/capita)	2.8	2015	●	↑
Nitrogen emissions embodied in imports (kg/capita)	3.2	2015	●	↑
Exports of plastic waste (kg/capita)	NA	NA	●	●

SDG13 – Climate Action	Value	Year	Rating	Trend
CO_2 emissions from fossil fuel combustion and cement production (tCO_2/capita)	1.9	2020	●	↑
CO_2 emissions embodied in imports (tCO_2/capita)	0.4	2018	●	↑
CO_2 emissions embodied in fossil fuel exports (kg/capita)	NA	NA	●	●

SDG14 – Life Below Water	Value	Year	Rating	Trend
Mean area that is protected in marine sites important to biodiversity (%)	63.7	2020	●	→
Ocean Health Index: Clean Waters score (worst 0–100 best)	63.7	2020	●	→
Fish caught from overexploited or collapsed stocks (% of total catch)	69.6	2018	●	↓
Fish caught by trawling or dredging (%)	41.6	2018	●	↑
Fish caught that are then discarded (%)	0.7	2018	●	↑
Marine biodiversity threats embodied in imports (per million population)	0.1	2018	●	●

SDG15 – Life on Land	Value	Year	Rating	Trend
Mean area that is protected in terrestrial sites important to biodiversity (%)	60.4	2020	●	→
Mean area that is protected in freshwater sites important to biodiversity (%)	93.6	2020	●	↑
Red List Index of species survival (worst 0–1 best)	1.0	2021	●	↑
Permanent deforestation (% of forest area, 5-year average)	0.1	2020	●	↑
Terrestrial and freshwater biodiversity threats embodied in imports (per million population)	2.5	2018	●	●

SDG16 – Peace, Justice and Strong Institutions	Value	Year	Rating	Trend
Homicides (per 100,000 population)	NA	NA	●	●
Unsentenced detainees (% of prison population)	80.2	2018	●	↓
Population who feel safe walking alone at night in the city or area where they live (%)	33	2021	●	↓
Property Rights (worst 1–7 best)	3.5	2020	●	●
Birth registrations with civil authority (% of children under age 5)	89.6	2020	●	●
Corruption Perception Index (worst 0–100 best)	31	2021	●	↓
Children involved in child labor (% of population aged 5 to 14)	19.6	2019	●	●
Exports of major conventional weapons (TIV constant million USD per 100,000 population)	* 0.0	2020	●	●
Press Freedom Index (best 0–100 worst)	38.6	2021	●	↓
Access to and affordability of justice (worst 0–1 best)	NA	NA	●	●

SDG17 – Partnerships for the Goals	Value	Year	Rating	Trend
Government spending on health and education (% of GDP)	4.4	2019	●	↓
For high-income and all OECD DAC countries: International concessional public finance, including official development assistance (% of GNI)	NA	NA	●	●
Other countries: Government revenue excluding grants (% of GDP)	19.4	2019	●	↓
Corporate Tax Haven Score (best 0–100 worst)	* 0.0	2019	●	●
Statistical Performance Index (worst 0–100 best)	28.1	2019	●	→

* Imputed data point

THE GAMBIA

Sub-Saharan Africa

OVERALL PERFORMANCE

COUNTRY RANKING

THE GAMBIA

122/163

COUNTRY SCORE

AVERAGE PERFORMANCE BY SDG

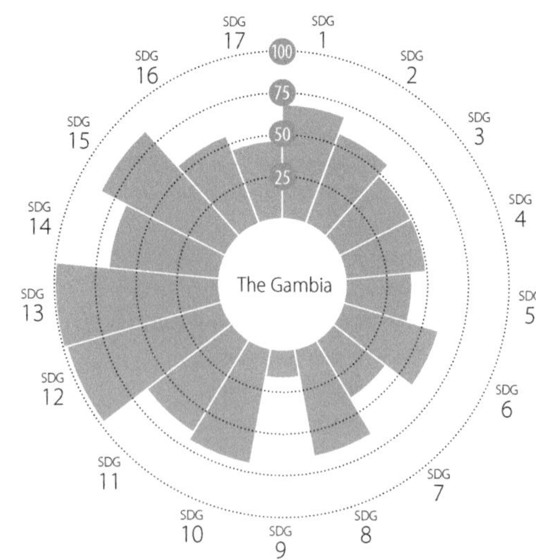

SDG DASHBOARDS AND TRENDS

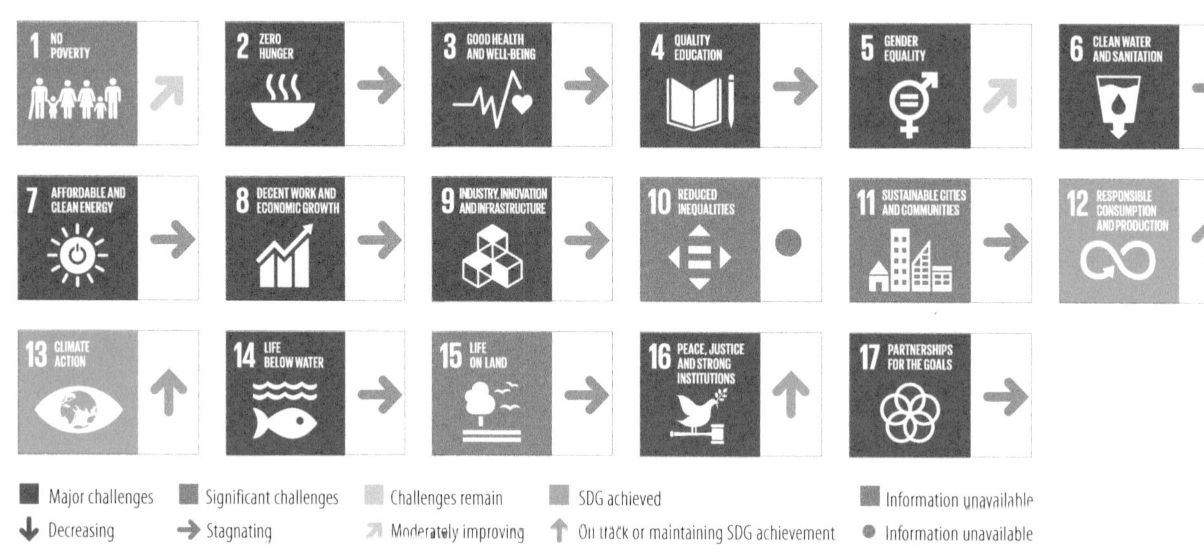

Major challenges | Significant challenges | Challenges remain | SDG achieved | Information unavailable

Decreasing | Stagnating | Moderately improving | On track or maintaining SDG achievement | Information unavailable

Note: The full title of each SDG is available here: https://sustainabledevelopment.un.org/topics/sustainabledevelopmentgoals

INTERNATIONAL SPILLOVER INDEX

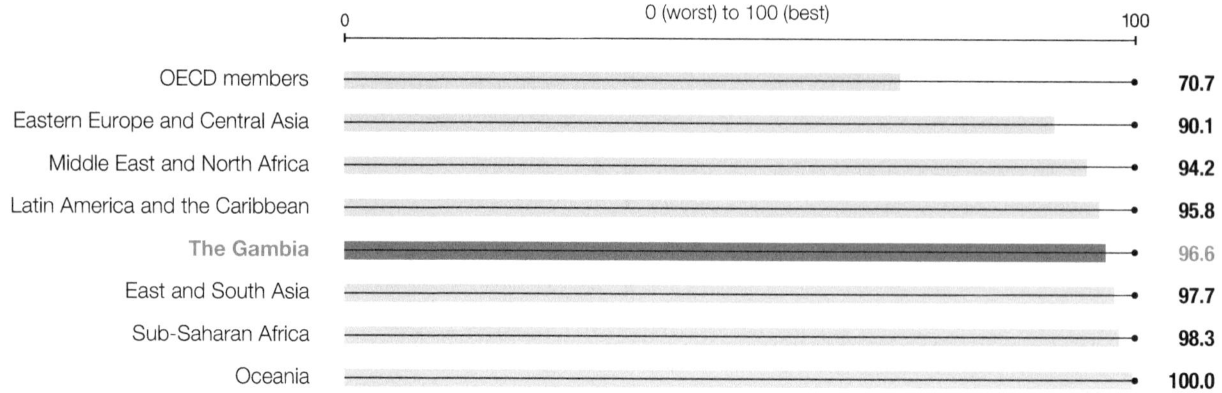

STATISTICAL PERFORMANCE INDEX

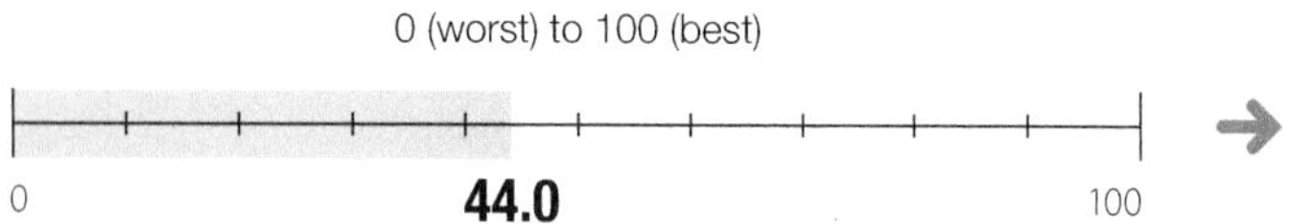

MISSING DATA IN SDG INDEX

9%

THE GAMBIA

Performance by Indicator

SDG1 – No Poverty	Value	Year	Rating	Trend
Poverty headcount ratio at \$1.90/day (%)	6.5	2022	●	↑
Poverty headcount ratio at \$3.20/day (%)	28.9	2022	●	↗

SDG2 – Zero Hunger	Value	Year	Rating	Trend
Prevalence of undernourishment (%)	13.6	2019	●	↓
Prevalence of stunting in children under 5 years of age (%)	17.5	2020	●	→
Prevalence of wasting in children under 5 years of age (%)	6.0	2018	●	→
Prevalence of obesity, BMI ≥ 30 (% of adult population)	10.3	2016	●	↓
Human Trophic Level (best 2–3 worst)	2.3	2017	●	→
Cereal yield (tonnes per hectare of harvested land)	0.8	2018	●	→
Sustainable Nitrogen Management Index (best 0–1.41 worst)	0.9	2015	●	↓
Exports of hazardous pesticides (tonnes per million population)	6.0	2019	●	●

SDG3 – Good Health and Well-Being	Value	Year	Rating	Trend
Maternal mortality rate (per 100,000 live births)	597	2017	●	→
Neonatal mortality rate (per 1,000 live births)	25.7	2020	●	↗
Mortality rate, under-5 (per 1,000 live births)	49.4	2020	●	↗
Incidence of tuberculosis (per 100,000 population)	157.0	2020	●	→
New HIV infections (per 1,000 uninfected population)	0.9	2020	●	→
Age-standardized death rate due to cardiovascular disease, cancer, diabetes, or chronic respiratory disease in adults aged 30–70 years (%)	21.1	2019	●	→
Age-standardized death rate attributable to household air pollution and ambient air pollution (per 100,000 population)	237	2016	●	●
Traffic deaths (per 100,000 population)	29.6	2019	●	↓
Life expectancy at birth (years)	65.5	2019	●	→
Adolescent fertility rate (births per 1,000 females aged 15 to 19)	67.5	2016	●	●
Births attended by skilled health personnel (%)	82.7	2018	●	●
Surviving infants who received 2 WHO-recommended vaccines (%)	85	2019	●	↓
Universal health coverage (UHC) index of service coverage (worst 0–100 best)	48	2019	●	→
Subjective well-being (average ladder score, worst 0–10 best)	5.2	2019	●	●

SDG4 – Quality Education	Value	Year	Rating	Trend
Participation rate in pre-primary organized learning (% of children aged 4 to 6)	57.8	2021	●	→
Net primary enrollment rate (%)	87.2	2020	●	↑
Lower secondary completion rate (%)	57.6	2020	●	↓
Literacy rate (% of population aged 15 to 24)	67.2	2015	●	●

SDG5 – Gender Equality	Value	Year	Rating	Trend
Demand for family planning satisfied by modern methods (% of females aged 15 to 49)	39.7	2020	●	↗
Ratio of female-to-male mean years of education received (%)	71.7	2019	●	↑
Ratio of female-to-male labor force participation rate (%)	73.1	2020	●	↑
Seats held by women in national parliament (%)	8.6	2020	●	↓

SDG6 – Clean Water and Sanitation	Value	Year	Rating	Trend
Population using at least basic drinking water services (%)	80.9	2020	●	→
Population using at least basic sanitation services (%)	46.9	2020	●	→
Freshwater withdrawal (% of available freshwater resources)	2.2	2018	●	●
Anthropogenic wastewater that receives treatment (%)	0.0	2018	●	●
Scarce water consumption embodied in imports (m^3 H_2O eq/capita)	1191.7	2018	●	●

SDG7 – Affordable and Clean Energy	Value	Year	Rating	Trend
Population with access to electricity (%)	59.9	2019	●	→
Population with access to clean fuels and technology for cooking (%)	1.4	2019	●	↓
CO_2 emissions from fuel combustion per total electricity output ($MtCO_2$/TWh)	2.2	2019	●	→
Share of renewable energy in total primary energy supply (%)	NA	NA	●	●

SDG8 – Decent Work and Economic Growth	Value	Year	Rating	Trend
Adjusted GDP growth (%)	-3.8	2020	●	●
Victims of modern slavery (per 1,000 population)	5.8	2018	●	●
Adults with an account at a bank or other financial institution or with a mobile-money-service provider (% of population aged 15 or over)	NA	NA	●	●
Unemployment rate (% of total labor force)	11.0	2022	●	↓
Fundamental labor rights are effectively guaranteed (worst 0–1 best)	0.5	2020	●	●
Fatal work-related accidents embodied in imports (per 100,000 population)	0.0	2015	●	↑

* Imputed data point

SDG9 – Industry, Innovation and Infrastructure	Value	Year	Rating	Trend
Population using the internet (%)	36.5	2020	●	↗
Mobile broadband subscriptions (per 100 population)	41.6	2019	●	↑
Logistics Performance Index: Quality of trade and transport-related infrastructure (worst 1–5 best)	1.8	2018	●	↓
The Times Higher Education Universities Ranking: Average score of top 3 universities (worst 0–100 best)	* 0.0	2022	●	●
Articles published in academic journals (per 1,000 population)	0.1	2020	●	→
Expenditure on research and development (% of GDP)	0.1	2018	●	●

SDG10 – Reduced Inequalities	Value	Year	Rating	Trend
Gini coefficient	35.9	2015	●	●
Palma ratio	1.5	2018	●	●

SDG11 – Sustainable Cities and Communities	Value	Year	Rating	Trend
Proportion of urban population living in slums (%)	24.3	2018	●	↑
Annual mean concentration of particulate matter of less than 2.5 microns in diameter (PM2.5) (μg/m^3)	35.4	2019	●	→
Access to improved water source, piped (% of urban population)	83.9	2020	●	↓
Satisfaction with public transport (%)	43.0	2019	●	●

SDG12 – Responsible Consumption and Production	Value	Year	Rating	Trend
Municipal solid waste (kg/capita/day)	0.4	2002	●	●
Electronic waste (kg/capita)	1.2	2019	●	●
Production-based SO_2 emissions (kg/capita)	1.3	2018	●	●
SO_2 emissions embodied in imports (kg/capita)	0.2	2018	●	●
Production-based nitrogen emissions (kg/capita)	5.3	2015	●	↑
Nitrogen emissions embodied in imports (kg/capita)	0.5	2015	●	↑
Exports of plastic waste (kg/capita)	NA	NA	●	●

SDG13 – Climate Action	Value	Year	Rating	Trend
CO_2 emissions from fossil fuel combustion and cement production (tCO_2/capita)	0.2	2020	●	↑
CO_2 emissions embodied in imports (tCO_2/capita)	0.1	2018	●	↑
CO_2 emissions embodied in fossil fuel exports (kg/capita)	0.0	2017	●	●

SDG14 – Life Below Water	Value	Year	Rating	Trend
Mean area that is protected in marine sites important to biodiversity (%)	40.3	2020	●	→
Ocean Health Index: Clean Waters score (worst 0–100 best)	50.3	2020	●	→
Fish caught from overexploited or collapsed stocks (% of total catch)	NA	NA	●	●
Fish caught by trawling or dredging (%)	4.2	2018	●	↑
Fish caught that are then discarded (%)	0.1	2014	●	●
Marine biodiversity threats embodied in imports (per million population)	NA	NA	●	●

SDG15 – Life on Land	Value	Year	Rating	Trend
Mean area that is protected in terrestrial sites important to biodiversity (%)	41.7	2020	●	→
Mean area that is protected in freshwater sites important to biodiversity (%)	99.0	2020	●	↑
Red List Index of species survival (worst 0–1 best)	1.0	2021	●	↑
Permanent deforestation (% of forest area, 5-year average)	0.2	2020	●	↓
Terrestrial and freshwater biodiversity threats embodied in imports (per million population)	0.0	2018	●	●

SDG16 – Peace, Justice and Strong Institutions	Value	Year	Rating	Trend
Homicides (per 100,000 population)	NA	NA	●	●
Unsentenced detainees (% of prison population)	NA	NA	●	●
Population who feel safe walking alone at night in the city or area where they live (%)	44	2019	●	●
Property Rights (worst 1–7 best)	4.5	2020	●	↑
Birth registrations with civil authority (% of children under age 5)	57.9	2020	●	●
Corruption Perception Index (worst 0–100 best)	37	2021	●	↗
Children involved in child labor (% of population aged 5 to 14)	16.9	2019	●	●
Exports of major conventional weapons (TIV constant million USD per 100,000 population)	* 0.0	2020	●	●
Press Freedom Index (best 0–100 worst)	30.8	2021	●	↑
Access to and affordability of justice (worst 0–1 best)	0.5	2020	●	●

SDG17 – Partnerships for the Goals	Value	Year	Rating	Trend
Government spending on health and education (% of GDP)	3.9	2019	●	→
For high-income and all OECD DAC countries: International concessional public finance, including official development assistance (% of GNI)	NA	NA	●	●
Other countries: Government revenue excluding grants (% of GDP)	NA	NA	●	●
Corporate Tax Haven Score (best 0–100 worst)	48.0	2019	●	●
Statistical Performance Index (worst 0–100 best)	44.0	2019	●	→

5. Country Profiles

GEORGIA

Eastern Europe and Central Asia

OVERALL PERFORMANCE

COUNTRY RANKING

GEORGIA

51 **/163**

COUNTRY SCORE

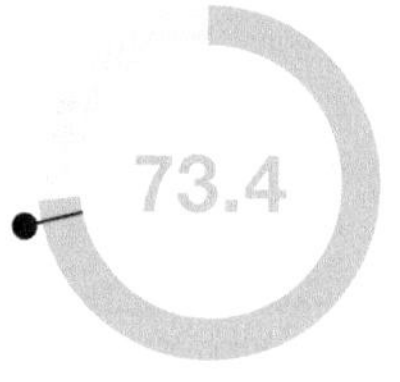

REGIONAL AVERAGE: 71.6

AVERAGE PERFORMANCE BY SDG

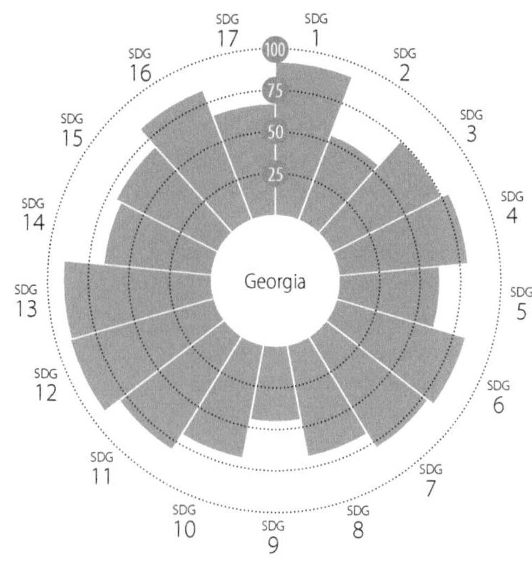

SDG DASHBOARDS AND TRENDS

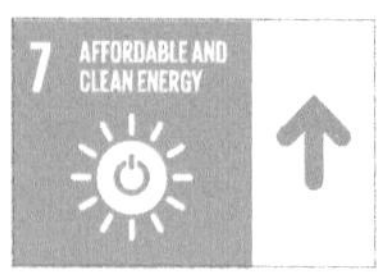

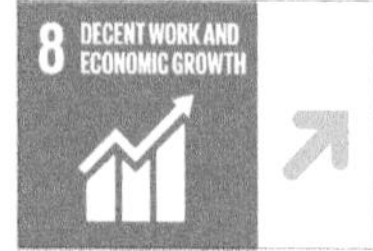

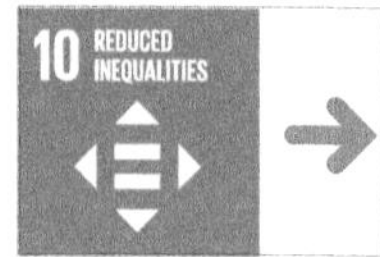

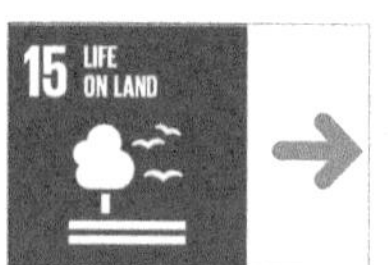

Major challenges · Significant challenges · Challenges remain · SDG achieved · Information unavailable

Decreasing · Stagnating · Moderately improving · On track or maintaining SDG achievement · Information unavailable

Note: The full title of each SDG is available here: https://sustainabledevelopment.un.org/topics/sustainabledevelopmentgoals

INTERNATIONAL SPILLOVER INDEX

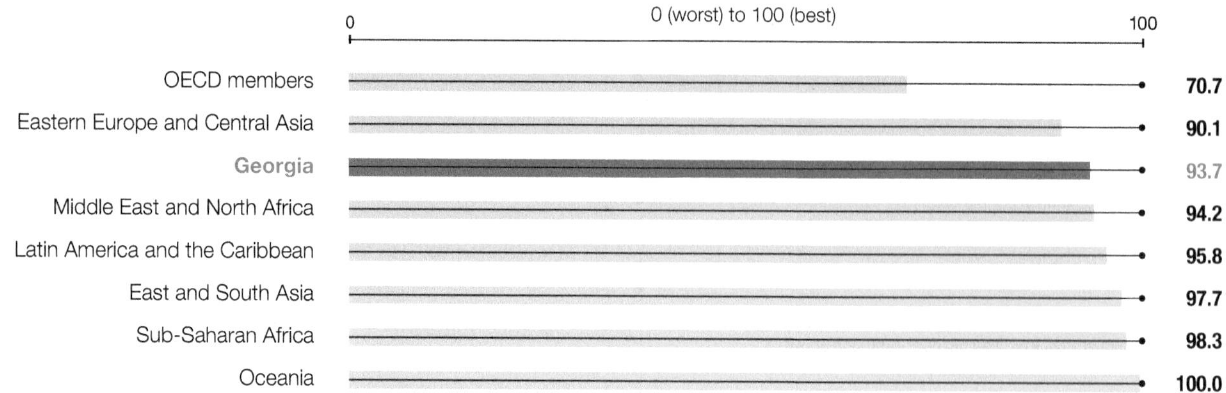

STATISTICAL PERFORMANCE INDEX

0 (worst) to 100 (best)

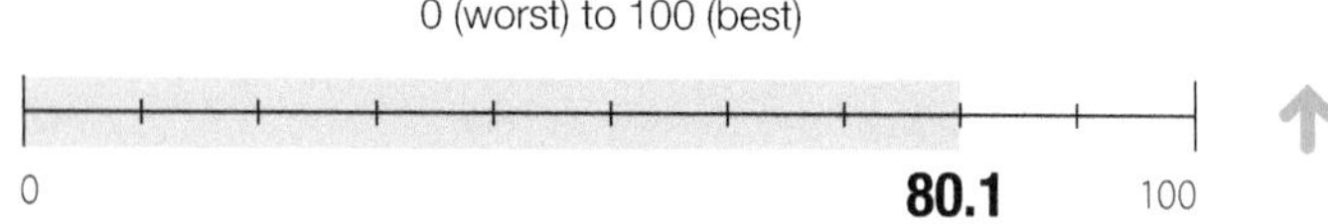

MISSING DATA IN SDG INDEX

2%

GEORGIA

SDG1 – No Poverty

Indicator	Value	Year	Rating	Trend
Poverty headcount ratio at \$1.90/day (%)	1.4	2022	●	↑
Poverty headcount ratio at \$3.20/day (%)	7.6	2022	●	↑

SDG2 – Zero Hunger

Indicator	Value	Year	Rating	Trend
Prevalence of undernourishment (%)	8.7	2019	●	→
Prevalence of stunting in children under 5 years of age (%)	5.8	2018	●	↑
Prevalence of wasting in children under 5 years of age (%)	0.6	2018	●	↑
Prevalence of obesity, BMI ≥ 30 (% of adult population)	21.7	2016	●	↓
Human Trophic Level (best 2–3 worst)	2.3	2017	●	→
Cereal yield (tonnes per hectare of harvested land)	2.5	2018	●	↑
Sustainable Nitrogen Management Index (best 0–1.41 worst)	1.1	2015	●	↓
Exports of hazardous pesticides (tonnes per million population)	NA	NA	●	●

SDG3 – Good Health and Well-Being

Indicator	Value	Year	Rating	Trend
Maternal mortality rate (per 100,000 live births)	25	2017	●	↑
Neonatal mortality rate (per 1,000 live births)	5.0	2020	●	↑
Mortality rate, under-5 (per 1,000 live births)	9.3	2020	●	↑
Incidence of tuberculosis (per 100,000 population)	70.0	2020	●	↗
New HIV infections (per 1,000 uninfected population)	0.2	2020	●	↑
Age-standardized death rate due to cardiovascular disease, cancer, diabetes, or chronic respiratory disease in adults aged 30–70 years (%)	24.9	2019	●	→
Age-standardized death rate attributable to household air pollution and ambient air pollution (per 100,000 population)	102	2016	●	●
Traffic deaths (per 100,000 population)	12.4	2019	●	↑
Life expectancy at birth (years)	73.3	2019	●	→
Adolescent fertility rate (births per 1,000 females aged 15 to 19)	29.4	2019	●	↑
Births attended by skilled health personnel (%)	99.4	2018	●	↑
Surviving infants who received 2 WHO-recommended vaccines (%)	88	2020	●	↓
Universal health coverage (UHC) index of service coverage (worst 0–100 best)	65	2019	●	→
Subjective well-being (average ladder score, worst 0–10 best)	4.9	2021	●	↑

SDG4 – Quality Education

Indicator	Value	Year	Rating	Trend
Participation rate in pre-primary organized learning (% of children aged 4 to 6)	47.8	2007	●	●
Net primary enrollment rate (%)	99.4	2020	●	↑
Lower secondary completion rate (%)	112.0	2020	●	↑
Literacy rate (% of population aged 15 to 24)	99.7	2019	●	↑

SDG5 – Gender Equality

Indicator	Value	Year	Rating	Trend
Demand for family planning satisfied by modern methods (% of females aged 15 to 49)	50.5	2018	●	→
Ratio of female-to-male mean years of education received (%)	100.8	2019	●	↑
Ratio of female-to-male labor force participation rate (%)	73.3	2020	●	↑
Seats held by women in national parliament (%)	20.7	2020	●	↗

SDG6 – Clean Water and Sanitation

Indicator	Value	Year	Rating	Trend
Population using at least basic drinking water services (%)	97.3	2020	●	↑
Population using at least basic sanitation services (%)	85.8	2020	●	↓
Freshwater withdrawal (% of available freshwater resources)	4.2	2018	●	●
Anthropogenic wastewater that receives treatment (%)	46.6	2018	●	●
Scarce water consumption embodied in imports (m^3 H_2O eq/capita)	1789.2	2018	●	●

SDG7 – Affordable and Clean Energy

Indicator	Value	Year	Rating	Trend
Population with access to electricity (%)	100.0	2019	●	↑
Population with access to clean fuels and technology for cooking (%)	88.2	2019	●	↑
CO_2 emissions from fuel combustion per total electricity output ($MtCO_2$/TWh)	0.7	2019	●	↑
Share of renewable energy in total primary energy supply (%)	20.4	2019	●	↑

SDG8 – Decent Work and Economic Growth

Indicator	Value	Year	Rating	Trend
Adjusted GDP growth (%)	-1.3	2020	●	●
Victims of modern slavery (per 1,000 population)	4.3	2018	●	●
Adults with an account at a bank or other financial institution or with a mobile-money-service provider (% of population aged 15 or over)	61.2	2017	●	↑
Unemployment rate (% of total labor force)	11.8	2022	●	↗
Fundamental labor rights are effectively guaranteed (worst 0–1 best)	0.6	2020	●	↓
Fatal work-related accidents embodied in imports (per 100,000 population)	0.3	2015	●	↑

SDG9 – Industry, Innovation and Infrastructure

Indicator	Value	Year	Rating	Trend
Population using the internet (%)	72.5	2020	●	↑
Mobile broadband subscriptions (per 100 population)	79.8	2019	●	↑
Logistics Performance Index: Quality of trade and transport-related infrastructure (worst 1–5 best)	2.4	2018	●	↓
The Times Higher Education Universities Ranking: Average score of top 3 universities (worst 0–100 best)	16.5	2022	●	●
Articles published in academic journals (per 1,000 population)	0.5	2020	●	↑
Expenditure on research and development (% of GDP)	0.3	2018	●	↓

SDG10 – Reduced Inequalities

Indicator	Value	Year	Rating	Trend
Gini coefficient	35.9	2019	●	→
Palma ratio	1.5	2018	●	●

SDG11 – Sustainable Cities and Communities

Indicator	Value	Year	Rating	Trend
Proportion of urban population living in slums (%)	34.1	2018	●	●
Annual mean concentration of particulate matter of less than 2.5 microns in diameter (PM2.5) (μg/m^3)	21.7	2019	●	↗
Access to improved water source, piped (% of urban population)	96.4	2020	●	↑
Satisfaction with public transport (%)	70.0	2021	●	→

SDG12 – Responsible Consumption and Production

Indicator	Value	Year	Rating	Trend
Municipal solid waste (kg/capita/day)	0.5	2015	●	●
Electronic waste (kg/capita)	7.3	2019	●	●
Production-based SO_2 emissions (kg/capita)	4.8	2018	●	●
SO_2 emissions embodied in imports (kg/capita)	1.5	2018	●	●
Production-based nitrogen emissions (kg/capita)	8.9	2015	●	↑
Nitrogen emissions embodied in imports (kg/capita)	3.1	2015	●	↑
Exports of plastic waste (kg/capita)	0.2	2021	●	●

SDG13 – Climate Action

Indicator	Value	Year	Rating	Trend
CO_2 emissions from fossil fuel combustion and cement production (tCO_2/capita)	2.5	2020	●	→
CO_2 emissions embodied in imports (tCO_2/capita)	0.6	2018	●	↓
CO_2 emissions embodied in fossil fuel exports (kg/capita)	14.1	2021	●	●

SDG14 – Life Below Water

Indicator	Value	Year	Rating	Trend
Mean area that is protected in marine sites important to biodiversity (%)	35.6	2020	●	→
Ocean Health Index: Clean Waters score (worst 0–100 best)	55.2	2020	●	↓
Fish caught from overexploited or collapsed stocks (% of total catch)	NA	NA	●	●
Fish caught by trawling or dredging (%)	5.3	2018	●	↑
Fish caught that are then discarded (%)	8.1	2018	●	→
Marine biodiversity threats embodied in imports (per million population)	0.0	2018	●	●

SDG15 – Life on Land

Indicator	Value	Year	Rating	Trend
Mean area that is protected in terrestrial sites important to biodiversity (%)	40.3	2020	●	→
Mean area that is protected in freshwater sites important to biodiversity (%)	38.9	2020	●	→
Red List Index of species survival (worst 0–1 best)	0.9	2021	●	→
Permanent deforestation (% of forest area, 5-year average)	0.0	2020	●	↑
Terrestrial and freshwater biodiversity threats embodied in imports (per million population)	0.7	2018	●	●

SDG16 – Peace, Justice and Strong Institutions

Indicator	Value	Year	Rating	Trend
Homicides (per 100,000 population)	1.9	2019	●	↓
Unsentenced detainees (% of prison population)	18.5	2019	●	↑
Population who feel safe walking alone at night in the city or area where they live (%)	78	2021	●	↑
Property Rights (worst 1–7 best)	5.3	2020	●	↑
Birth registrations with civil authority (% of children under age 5)	98.5	2020	●	●
Corruption Perception Index (worst 0–100 best)	55	2021	●	↗
Children involved in child labor (% of population aged 5 to 14)	1.6	2019	●	●
Exports of major conventional weapons (TIV constant million USD per 100,000 population)	0.2	2020	●	●
Press Freedom Index (best 0–100 worst)	28.6	2021	●	↑
Access to and affordability of justice (worst 0–1 best)	0.6	2020	●	↑

SDG17 – Partnerships for the Goals

Indicator	Value	Year	Rating	Trend
Government spending on health and education (% of GDP)	6.6	2020	●	↗
For high-income and all OECD DAC countries: International concessional public finance, including official development assistance (% of GNI)	NA	NA	●	●
Other countries: Government revenue excluding grants (% of GDP)	24.9	2020	●	↓
Corporate Tax Haven Score (best 0–100 worst)	* 0.0	2019	●	●
Statistical Performance Index (worst 0–100 best)	80.1	2019	●	↑

* Imputed data point

GERMANY

OECD Countries

OVERALL PERFORMANCE

COUNTRY RANKING

GERMANY

6 /163

COUNTRY SCORE

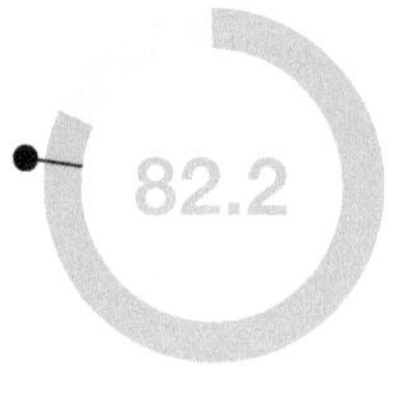

REGIONAL AVERAGE: 77.2

AVERAGE PERFORMANCE BY SDG

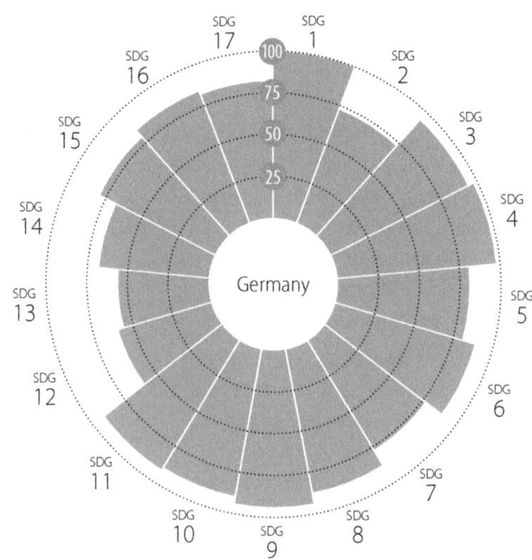

SDG DASHBOARDS AND TRENDS

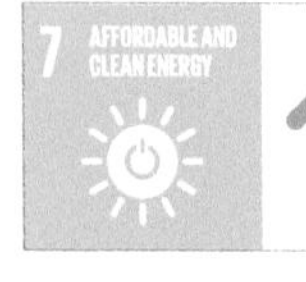

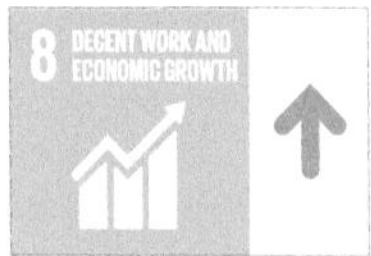

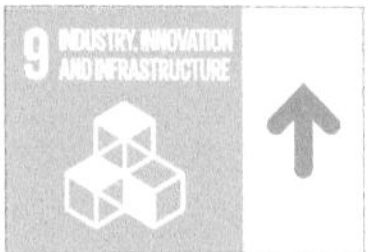

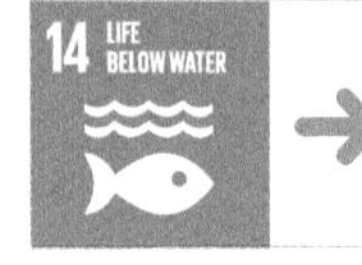

Major challenges · Significant challenges · Challenges remain · SDG achieved · Information unavailable

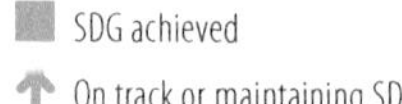

Information unavailable

Note: The full title of each SDG is available here: https://sustainabledevelopment.un.org/topics/sustainabledevelopmentgoals

INTERNATIONAL SPILLOVER INDEX

STATISTICAL PERFORMANCE INDEX

0 (worst) to 100 (best)

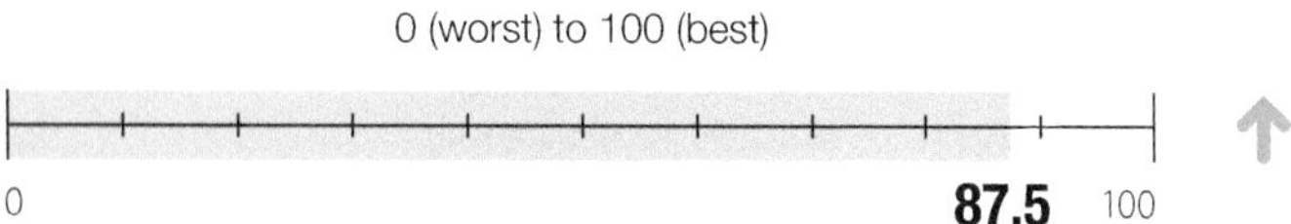

MISSING DATA IN SDG INDEX

1%

GERMANY

Performance by Indicator

SDG1 – No Poverty

Indicator	Value	Year	Rating	Trend
Poverty headcount ratio at \$1.90/day (%)	0.2	2022	●	↑
Poverty headcount ratio at \$3.20/day (%)	0.3	2022	●	↑
Poverty rate after taxes and transfers (%)	9.8	2018	●	↑

SDG2 – Zero Hunger

Indicator	Value	Year	Rating	Trend
Prevalence of undernourishment (%)	2.5	2019	●	↑
Prevalence of stunting in children under 5 years of age (%)	1.7	2016	●	↑
Prevalence of wasting in children under 5 years of age (%)	0.3	2016	●	↑
Prevalence of obesity, BMI ≥ 30 (% of adult population)	22.3	2016	●	↓
Human Trophic Level (best 2–3 worst)	2.4	2017	●	↓
Cereal yield (tonnes per hectare of harvested land)	6.2	2018	●	↑
Sustainable Nitrogen Management Index (best 0–1.41 worst)	0.5	2015	●	↓
Yield gap closure (% of potential yield)	77.2	2018	●	●
Exports of hazardous pesticides (tonnes per million population)	4.3	2019	●	●

SDG3 – Good Health and Well-Being

Indicator	Value	Year	Rating	Trend
Maternal mortality rate (per 100,000 live births)	7	2017	●	↑
Neonatal mortality rate (per 1,000 live births)	2.2	2020	●	↑
Mortality rate, under-5 (per 1,000 live births)	3.7	2020	●	↑
Incidence of tuberculosis (per 100,000 population)	5.5	2020	●	↑
New HIV infections (per 1,000 uninfected population)	0.0	2020	●	↑
Age-standardized death rate due to cardiovascular disease, cancer, diabetes, or chronic respiratory disease in adults aged 30–70 years (%)	12.1	2019	●	↑
Age-standardized death rate attributable to household air pollution and ambient air pollution (per 100,000 population)	16	2016	●	●
Traffic deaths (per 100,000 population)	3.8	2019	●	↑
Life expectancy at birth (years)	81.7	2019	●	↑
Adolescent fertility rate (births per 1,000 females aged 15 to 19)	7.2	2018	●	↑
Births attended by skilled health personnel (%)	98.8	2017	●	↑
Surviving infants who received 2 WHO-recommended vaccines (%)	93	2020	●	↑
Universal health coverage (UHC) index of service coverage (worst 0–100 best)	86	2019	●	↑
Subjective well-being (average ladder score, worst 0–10 best)	6.8	2021	●	↑
Gap in life expectancy at birth among regions (years)	5.7	2019	●	→
Gap in self-reported health status by income (percentage points)	30.9	2019	●	↓
Daily smokers (% of population aged 15 and over)	18.8	2017	●	●

SDG4 – Quality Education

Indicator	Value	Year	Rating	Trend
Participation rate in pre-primary organized learning (% of children aged 4 to 6)	97.0	2019	●	↑
Net primary enrollment rate (%)	99.0	2019	●	↑
Lower secondary completion rate (%)	* 98.9	2019	●	↑
Literacy rate (% of population aged 15 to 24)	NA	NA	●	●
Tertiary educational attainment (% of population aged 25 to 34)	34.9	2020	●	↑
PISA score (worst 0–600 best)	500.3	2018	●	↑
Variation in science performance explained by socio-economic status (%)	18.6	2018	●	↓
Underachievers in science (% of 15-year-olds)	19.6	2018	●	↓

SDG5 – Gender Equality

Indicator	Value	Year	Rating	Trend
Demand for family planning satisfied by modern methods (% of females aged 15 to 49)	* 87.7	2022	●	↑
Ratio of female-to-male mean years of education received (%)	96.5	2019	●	↑
Ratio of female-to-male labor force participation rate (%)	85.4	2020	●	↑
Seats held by women in national parliament (%)	31.2	2020	●	↓
Gender wage gap (% of male median wage)	13.9	2019	●	↗

SDG6 – Clean Water and Sanitation

Indicator	Value	Year	Rating	Trend
Population using at least basic drinking water services (%)	100.0	2020	●	↑
Population using at least basic sanitation services (%)	99.2	2020	●	↑
Freshwater withdrawal (% of available freshwater resources)	33.5	2018	●	●
Anthropogenic wastewater that receives treatment (%)	97.0	2018	●	●
Scarce water consumption embodied in imports (m^3 H_2O eq/capita)	3304.1	2018	●	●
Population using safely managed water services (%)	100.0	2020	●	↑
Population using safely managed sanitation services (%)	97.1	2020	●	↑

SDG7 – Affordable and Clean Energy

Indicator	Value	Year	Rating	Trend
Population with access to electricity (%)	100.0	2019	●	↑
Population with access to clean fuels and technology for cooking (%)	100.0	2019	●	↑
CO_2 emissions from fuel combustion per total electricity output ($MtCO_2$/TWh)	1.1	2019	●	↑
Share of renewable energy in total primary energy supply (%)	15.0	2019	●	↑

SDG8 – Decent Work and Economic Growth

Indicator	Value	Year	Rating	Trend
Adjusted GDP growth (%)	-1.0	2020	●	●
Victims of modern slavery (per 1,000 population)	2.0	2018	●	●
Adults with an account at a bank or other financial institution or with a mobile-money-service provider (% of population aged 15 or over)	99.1	2017	●	↑
Fundamental labor rights are effectively guaranteed (worst 0–1 best)	0.8	2020	●	↑
Fatal work-related accidents embodied in imports (per 100,000 population)	1.6	2015	●	↑
Employment-to-population ratio (%)	76.2	2020	●	↑
Youth not in employment, education or training (NEET) (% of population aged 15 to 29)	8.2	2019	●	↑

* Imputed data point

SDG9 – Industry, Innovation and Infrastructure

Indicator	Value	Year	Rating	Trend
Population using the internet (%)	89.8	2020	●	↑
Mobile broadband subscriptions (per 100 population)	86.5	2019	●	↑
Logistics Performance Index: Quality of trade and transport-related infrastructure (worst 1–5 best)	4.4	2018	●	↑
The Times Higher Education Universities Ranking: Average score of top 3 universities (worst 0–100 best)	75.9	2022	●	●
Articles published in academic journals (per 1,000 population)	2.1	2020	●	↑
Expenditure on research and development (% of GDP)	3.1	2018	●	↑
Researchers (per 1,000 employed population)	10.0	2019	●	↑
Triadic patent families filed (per million population)	55.3	2019	●	↑
Gap in internet access by income (percentage points)	12.4	2020	●	↑
Female share of graduates from STEM fields at the tertiary level (%)	27.6	2017	●	↑

SDG10 – Reduced Inequalities

Indicator	Value	Year	Rating	Trend
Gini coefficient	31.9	2016	●	●
Palma ratio	1.1	2018	●	↗
Elderly poverty rate (% of population aged 66 or over)	9.1	2018	●	↗

SDG11 – Sustainable Cities and Communities

Indicator	Value	Year	Rating	Trend
Proportion of urban population living in slums (%)	* 0.0	2018	●	↑
Annual mean concentration of particulate matter of less than 2.5 microns in diameter (PM2.5) (μg/m^3)	11.3	2019	●	↑
Access to improved water source, piped (% of urban population)	100.0	2020	●	↑
Satisfaction with public transport (%)	64.0	2021	●	↓
Population with rent overburden (%)	4.2	2019	●	↑

SDG12 – Responsible Consumption and Production

Indicator	Value	Year	Rating	Trend
Electronic waste (kg/capita)	19.4	2019	●	●
Production-based SO_2 emissions (kg/capita)	11.2	2018	●	●
SO_2 emissions embodied in imports (kg/capita)	7.9	2018	●	●
Production-based nitrogen emissions (kg/capita)	13.5	2015	●	↑
Nitrogen emissions embodied in imports (kg/capita)	15.9	2015	●	↓
Exports of plastic waste (kg/capita)	10.0	2020	●	●
Non-recycled municipal solid waste (kg/capita/day)	0.6	2019	●	↑

SDG13 – Climate Action

Indicator	Value	Year	Rating	Trend
CO_2 emissions from fossil fuel combustion and cement production (tCO_2/capita)	7.7	2020	●	↗
CO_2 emissions embodied in imports (tCO_2/capita)	3.0	2018	●	↓
CO_2 emissions embodied in fossil fuel exports (kg/capita)	176.2	2020	●	●
Carbon Pricing Score at EUR60/tCO_2 (%, worst 0–100 best)	40.8	2018	●	↑

SDG14 – Life Below Water

Indicator	Value	Year	Rating	Trend
Mean area that is protected in marine sites important to biodiversity (%)	77.0	2020	●	→
Ocean Health Index: Clean Waters score (worst 0–100 best)	51.0	2020	●	→
Fish caught from overexploited or collapsed stocks (% of total catch)	25.6	2018	●	↑
Fish caught by trawling or dredging (%)	18.8	2018	●	↓
Fish caught that are then discarded (%)	8.0	2018	●	↓
Marine biodiversity threats embodied in imports (per million population)	0.3	2018	●	●

SDG15 – Life on Land

Indicator	Value	Year	Rating	Trend
Mean area that is protected in terrestrial sites important to biodiversity (%)	78.7	2020	●	→
Mean area that is protected in freshwater sites important to biodiversity (%)	78.8	2020	●	→
Red List Index of species survival (worst 0–1 best)	1.0	2021	●	↑
Permanent deforestation (% of forest area, 5-year average)	0.0	2020	●	↑
Terrestrial and freshwater biodiversity threats embodied in imports (per million population)	5.7	2018	●	●

SDG16 – Peace, Justice and Strong Institutions

Indicator	Value	Year	Rating	Trend
Homicides (per 100,000 population)	0.9	2020	●	↑
Unsentenced detainees (% of prison population)	23.1	2019	●	↑
Population who feel safe walking alone at night in the city or area where they live (%)	72	2021	●	↑
Property Rights (worst 1–7 best)	5.2	2020	●	↑
Birth registrations with civil authority (% of children under age 5)	100.0	2020	●	●
Corruption Perception Index (worst 0–100 best)	80	2021	●	↑
Children involved in child labor (% of population aged 5 to 14)	* 0.0	2019	●	●
Exports of major conventional weapons (TIV constant million USD per 100,000 population)	1.8	2020	●	●
Press Freedom Index (best 0–100 worst)	15.2	2021	●	↑
Access to and affordability of justice (worst 0–1 best)	0.8	2020	●	↑
Persons held in prison (per 100,000 population)	75.6	2019	●	↑

SDG17 – Partnerships for the Goals

Indicator	Value	Year	Rating	Trend
Government spending on health and education (% of GDP)	14.1	2019	●	↑
For high-income and all OECD DAC countries: International concessional public finance, including official development assistance (% of GNI)	0.7	2021	●	↑
Other countries: Government revenue excluding grants (% of GDP)	NA	NA	●	●
Corporate Tax Haven Score (best 0–100 worst)	52.3	2019	●	●
Financial Secrecy Score (best 0–100 worst)	51.7	2020	●	●
Shifted profits of multinationals (US\$ billion)	83.2	2018	●	↑
Statistical Performance Index (worst 0–100 best)	87.5	2019	●	↑

GHANA

Sub-Saharan Africa

OVERALL PERFORMANCE

COUNTRY RANKING

GHANA

110/163

COUNTRY SCORE

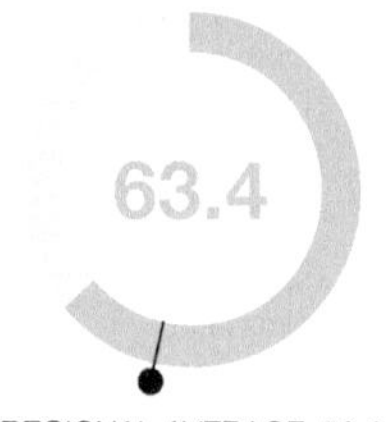

REGIONAL AVERAGE: 53.6

AVERAGE PERFORMANCE BY SDG

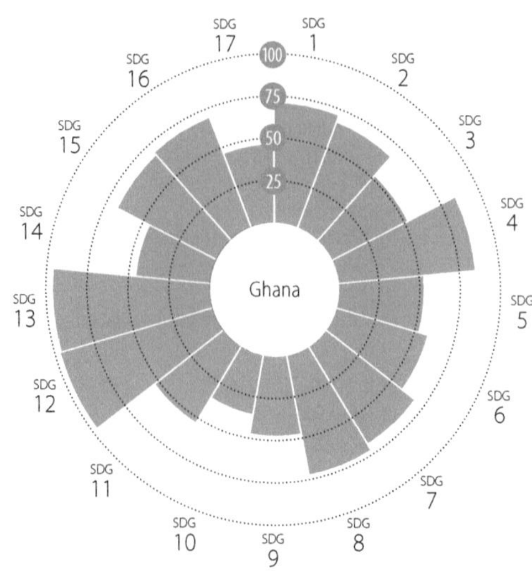

SDG DASHBOARDS AND TRENDS

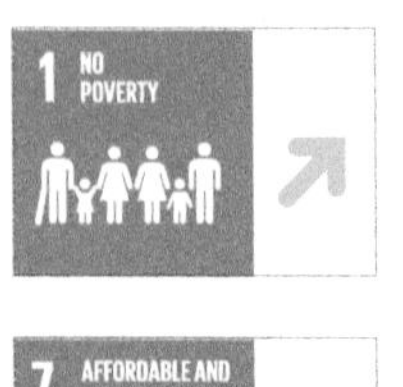

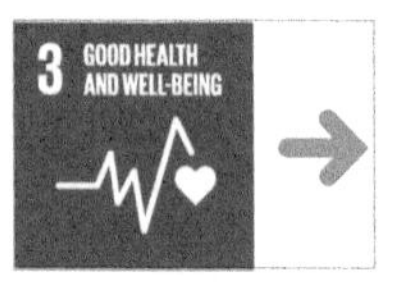

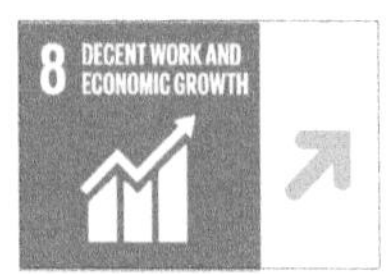

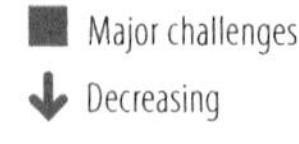

Major challenges | Significant challenges | Challenges remain | SDG achieved | Information unavailable

Decreasing | Stagnating | Moderately improving | On track or maintaining SDG achievement | Information unavailable

Note: The full title of each SDG is available here: https://sustainabledevelopment.un.org/topics/sustainabledevelopmentgoals

INTERNATIONAL SPILLOVER INDEX

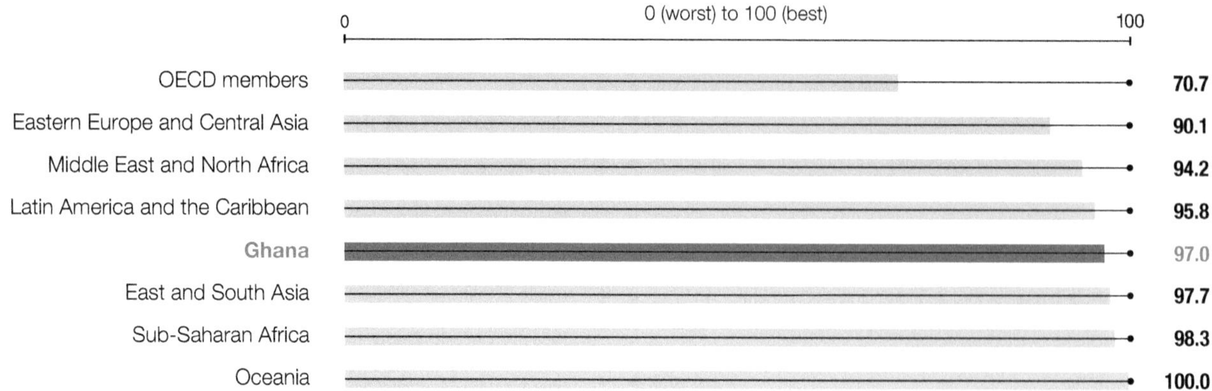

STATISTICAL PERFORMANCE INDEX

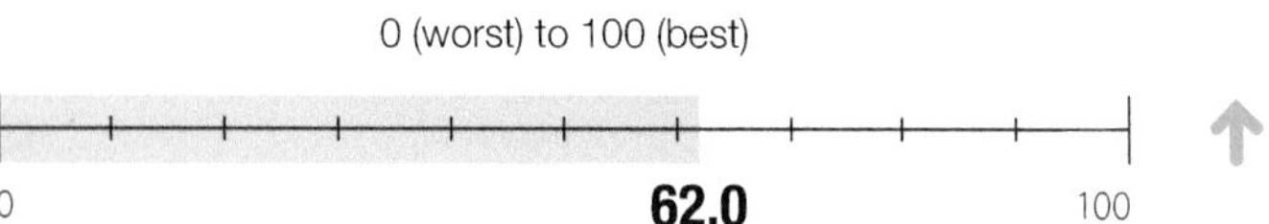

MISSING DATA IN SDG INDEX

0%

SDG1 – No Poverty	Value	Year	Rating	Trend
Poverty headcount ratio at $1.90/day (%)	9.7	2022	●	↗
Poverty headcount ratio at $3.20/day (%)	23.1	2022	●	↗
SDG2 – Zero Hunger				
Prevalence of undernourishment (%)	6.1	2019	●	↑
Prevalence of stunting in children under 5 years of age (%)	17.5	2017	●	↗
Prevalence of wasting in children under 5 years of age (%)	6.8	2017	●	→
Prevalence of obesity, BMI ≥ 30 (% of adult population)	10.9	2016	●	↓
Human Trophic Level (best 2–3 worst)	2.1	2017	●	↑
Cereal yield (tonnes per hectare of harvested land)	1.9	2018	●	→
Sustainable Nitrogen Management Index (best 0–1.41 worst)	0.8	2015	●	→
Exports of hazardous pesticides (tonnes per million population)	4.1	2019	●	●
SDG3 – Good Health and Well-Being				
Maternal mortality rate (per 100,000 live births)	308	2017	●	→
Neonatal mortality rate (per 1,000 live births)	22.9	2020	●	↗
Mortality rate, under-5 (per 1,000 live births)	44.7	2020	●	↑
Incidence of tuberculosis (per 100,000 population)	143.0	2020	●	→
New HIV infections (per 1,000 uninfected population)	0.6	2020	●	↗
Age-standardized death rate due to cardiovascular disease, cancer, diabetes, or chronic respiratory disease in adults aged 30–70 years (%)	22.5	2019	●	↗
Age-standardized death rate attributable to household air pollution and ambient air pollution (per 100,000 population)	204	2016	●	●
Traffic deaths (per 100,000 population)	25.7	2019	●	↓
Life expectancy at birth (years)	66.3	2019	●	→
Adolescent fertility rate (births per 1,000 females aged 15 to 19)	78.0	2018	●	↓
Births attended by skilled health personnel (%)	78.1	2017	●	↑
Surviving infants who received 2 WHO-recommended vaccines (%)	88	2020	●	→
Universal health coverage (UHC) index of service coverage (worst 0–100 best)	45	2019	●	→
Subjective well-being (average ladder score, worst 0–10 best)	4.4	2021	●	↗
SDG4 – Quality Education				
Participation rate in pre-primary organized learning (% of children aged 4 to 6)	93.3	2020	●	●
Net primary enrollment rate (%)	94.0	2020	●	●
Lower secondary completion rate (%)	78.2	2019	●	↗
Literacy rate (% of population aged 15 to 24)	92.5	2018	●	●
SDG5 – Gender Equality				
Demand for family planning satisfied by modern methods (% of females aged 15 to 49)	40.4	2018	●	→
Ratio of female-to-male mean years of education received (%)	81.5	2019	●	↑
Ratio of female-to-male labor force participation rate (%)	89.7	2020	●	↑
Seats held by women in national parliament (%)	13.1	2020	●	→
SDG6 – Clean Water and Sanitation				
Population using at least basic drinking water services (%)	85.8	2020	●	↗
Population using at least basic sanitation services (%)	23.7	2020	●	→
Freshwater withdrawal (% of available freshwater resources)	6.3	2018	●	●
Anthropogenic wastewater that receives treatment (%)	0.0	2018	●	●
Scarce water consumption embodied in imports (m^3 H_2O eq/capita)	472.5	2018	●	●
SDG7 – Affordable and Clean Energy				
Population with access to electricity (%)	83.5	2019	●	↑
Population with access to clean fuels and technology for cooking (%)	22.6	2019	●	→
CO_2 emissions from fuel combustion per total electricity output ($MtCO_2$/TWh)	1.0	2019	●	↑
Share of renewable energy in total primary energy supply (%)	43.3	2019	●	↑
SDG8 – Decent Work and Economic Growth				
Adjusted GDP growth (%)	-1.7	2020	●	●
Victims of modern slavery (per 1,000 population)	4.8	2018	●	●
Adults with an account at a bank or other financial institution or with a mobile-money-service provider (% of population aged 15 or over)	57.7	2017	●	↑
Unemployment rate (% of total labor force)	4.5	2022	●	↑
Fundamental labor rights are effectively guaranteed (worst 0–1 best)	0.6	2020	●	→
Fatal work-related accidents embodied in imports (per 100,000 population)	0.1	2015	●	↑

* Imputed data point

SDG9 – Industry, Innovation and Infrastructure	Value	Year	Rating	Trend
Population using the internet (%)	58.0	2020	●	↑
Mobile broadband subscriptions (per 100 population)	99.9	2019	●	↑
Logistics Performance Index: Quality of trade and transport-related infrastructure (worst 1–5 best)	2.4	2018	●	↓
The Times Higher Education Universities Ranking: Average score of top 3 universities (worst 0–100 best)	32.2	2022	●	●
Articles published in academic journals (per 1,000 population)	0.1	2020	●	→
Expenditure on research and development (% of GDP)	0.4	2010	●	●
SDG10 – Reduced Inequalities				
Gini coefficient	43.5	2016	●	●
Palma ratio	2.3	2018	●	●
SDG11 – Sustainable Cities and Communities				
Proportion of urban population living in slums (%)	29.2	2018	●	↑
Annual mean concentration of particulate matter of less than 2.5 microns in diameter (PM2.5) (μg/m^3)	40.1	2019	●	↓
Access to improved water source, piped (% of urban population)	41.1	2020	●	↓
Satisfaction with public transport (%)	51.0	2021	●	↗
SDG12 – Responsible Consumption and Production				
Municipal solid waste (kg/capita/day)	0.4	2005	●	●
Electronic waste (kg/capita)	1.8	2019	●	●
Production-based SO_2 emissions (kg/capita)	2.1	2018	●	●
SO_2 emissions embodied in imports (kg/capita)	0.8	2018	●	●
Production-based nitrogen emissions (kg/capita)	4.5	2015	●	↑
Nitrogen emissions embodied in imports (kg/capita)	0.3	2015	●	↑
Exports of plastic waste (kg/capita)	0.0	2019	●	●
SDG13 – Climate Action				
CO_2 emissions from fossil fuel combustion and cement production (tCO_2/capita)	0.5	2020	●	↑
CO_2 emissions embodied in imports (tCO_2/capita)	0.3	2018	●	↑
CO_2 emissions embodied in fossil fuel exports (kg/capita)	639.7	2019	●	●
SDG14 – Life Below Water				
Mean area that is protected in marine sites important to biodiversity (%)	19.6	2020	●	→
Ocean Health Index: Clean Waters score (worst 0–100 best)	36.3	2020	●	→
Fish caught from overexploited or collapsed stocks (% of total catch)	44.1	2018	●	↓
Fish caught by trawling or dredging (%)	7.4	2018	●	↑
Fish caught that are then discarded (%)	25.7	2018	●	↓
Marine biodiversity threats embodied in imports (per million population)	0.0	2018	●	●
SDG15 – Life on Land				
Mean area that is protected in terrestrial sites important to biodiversity (%)	68.9	2020	●	→
Mean area that is protected in freshwater sites important to biodiversity (%)	80.5	2020	●	→
Red List Index of species survival (worst 0–1 best)	0.8	2021	●	→
Permanent deforestation (% of forest area, 5-year average)	1.1	2020	●	↓
Terrestrial and freshwater biodiversity threats embodied in imports (per million population)	0.0	2018	●	●
SDG16 – Peace, Justice and Strong Institutions				
Homicides (per 100,000 population)	2.1	2017	●	→
Unsentenced detainees (% of prison population)	12.0	2017	●	●
Population who feel safe walking alone at night in the city or area where they live (%)	64	2021	●	↓
Property Rights (worst 1–7 best)	4.1	2020	●	↓
Birth registrations with civil authority (% of children under age 5)	70.6	2020	●	●
Corruption Perception Index (worst 0–100 best)	43	2021	●	↓
Children involved in child labor (% of population aged 5 to 14)	20.1	2019	●	●
Exports of major conventional weapons (TIV constant million USD per 100,000 population)	0.0	2020	●	●
Press Freedom Index (best 0–100 worst)	21.3	2021	●	↑
Access to and affordability of justice (worst 0–1 best)	0.6	2020	●	↗
SDG17 – Partnerships for the Goals				
Government spending on health and education (% of GDP)	5.4	2019	●	↓
For high-income and all OECD DAC countries: International concessional public finance, including official development assistance (% of GNI)	NA	NA	●	●
Other countries: Government revenue excluding grants (% of GDP)	14.7	2019	●	↓
Corporate Tax Haven Score (best 0–100 worst)	49.5	2019	●	●
Statistical Performance Index (worst 0–100 best)	62.0	2019	●	↑

GREECE

OECD Countries

OVERALL PERFORMANCE

COUNTRY RANKING

GREECE

32/163

COUNTRY SCORE

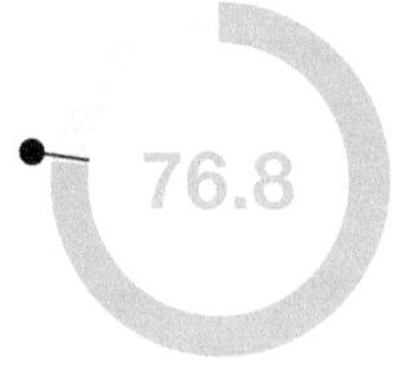

REGIONAL AVERAGE: 77.2

AVERAGE PERFORMANCE BY SDG

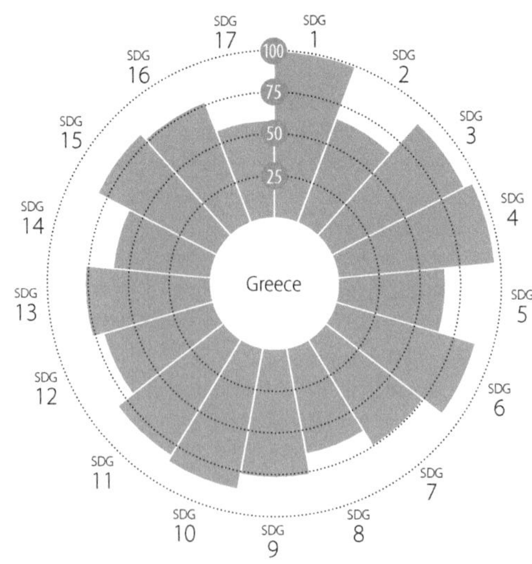

SDG DASHBOARDS AND TRENDS

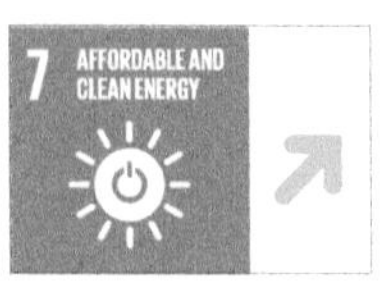

Major challenges  Significant challenges  Challenges remain  SDG achieved Information unavailable

Decreasing Stagnating Moderately improving On track or maintaining SDG achievement Information unavailable

Note: The full title of each SDG is available here: https://sustainabledevelopment.un.org/topics/sustainabledevelopmentgoals

INTERNATIONAL SPILLOVER INDEX

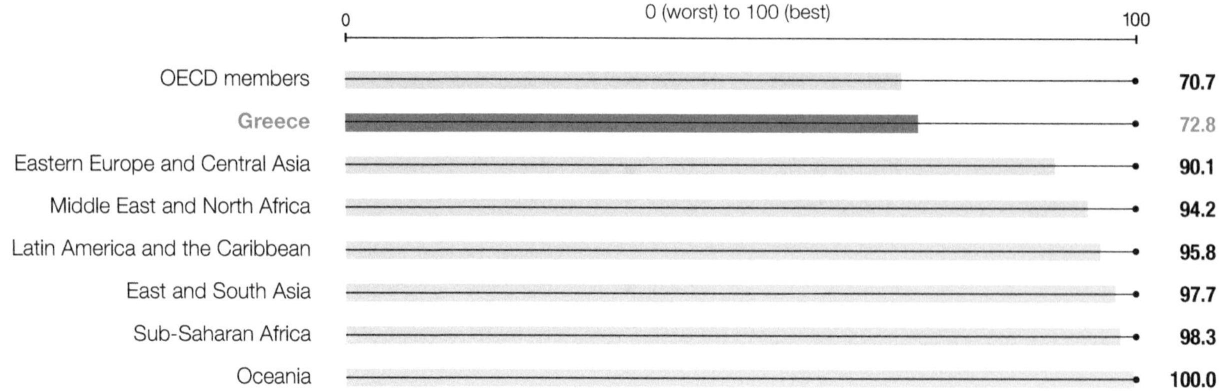

STATISTICAL PERFORMANCE INDEX

0 (worst) to 100 (best)

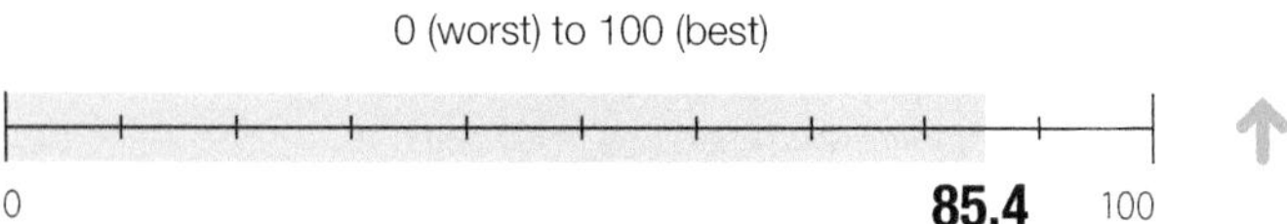

MISSING DATA IN SDG INDEX

GREECE

SDG1 – No Poverty	Value	Year	Rating	Trend
Poverty headcount ratio at \$1.90/day (%)	0.3	2022	●	↑
Poverty headcount ratio at \$3.20/day (%)	0.6	2022	●	↑
Poverty rate after taxes and transfers (%)	11.5	2019	●	↑

SDG2 – Zero Hunger	Value	Year	Rating	Trend
Prevalence of undernourishment (%)	2.5	2019	●	↑
Prevalence of stunting in children under 5 years of age (%)	1.5	2003	●	↑
Prevalence of wasting in children under 5 years of age (%)	0.6	2003	●	↑
Prevalence of obesity, BMI ≥ 30 (% of adult population)	24.9	2016	●	↓
Human Trophic Level (best 2–3 worst)	2.4	2017	●	→
Cereal yield (tonnes per hectare of harvested land)	3.8	2018	●	↑
Sustainable Nitrogen Management Index (best 0–1.41 worst)	0.6	2015	●	↓
Yield gap closure (% of potential yield)	50.6	2018	●	●
Exports of hazardous pesticides (tonnes per million population)	20.8	2019	●	●

SDG3 – Good Health and Well-Being	Value	Year	Rating	Trend
Maternal mortality rate (per 100,000 live births)	3	2017	●	↑
Neonatal mortality rate (per 1,000 live births)	2.4	2020	●	↑
Mortality rate, under-5 (per 1,000 live births)	4.1	2020	●	↑
Incidence of tuberculosis (per 100,000 population)	4.5	2020	●	↑
New HIV infections (per 1,000 uninfected population)	0.1	2020	●	↑
Age-standardized death rate due to cardiovascular disease, cancer, diabetes, or chronic respiratory disease in adults aged 30–70 years (%)	12.5	2019	●	↑
Age-standardized death rate attributable to household air pollution and ambient air pollution (per 100,000 population)	28	2016	●	●
Traffic deaths (per 100,000 population)	8.3	2019	●	↑
Life expectancy at birth (years)	81.1	2019	●	↑
Adolescent fertility rate (births per 1,000 females aged 15 to 19)	8.6	2018	●	↑
Births attended by skilled health personnel (%)	99.9	2018	●	↑
Surviving infants who received 2 WHO-recommended vaccines (%)	97	2020	●	↑
Universal health coverage (UHC) index of service coverage (worst 0–100 best)	78	2019	●	↑
Subjective well-being (average ladder score, worst 0–10 best)	6.1	2021	●	↑
Gap in life expectancy at birth among regions (years)	2.9	2019	●	↑
Gap in self-reported health status by income (percentage points)	9.5	2019	●	↑
Daily smokers (% of population aged 15 and over)	24.9	2019	●	↗

SDG4 – Quality Education	Value	Year	Rating	Trend
Participation rate in pre-primary organized learning (% of children aged 4 to 6)	96.7	2019	●	↑
Net primary enrollment rate (%)	99.1	2019	●	↑
Lower secondary completion rate (%)	93.9	2019	●	↑
Literacy rate (% of population aged 15 to 24)	99.2	2018	●	●
Tertiary educational attainment (% of population aged 25 to 34)	43.7	2020	●	↑
PISA score (worst 0–600 best)	453.3	2018	●	↓
Variation in science performance explained by socio-economic status (%)	10.9	2018	●	↑
Underachievers in science (% of 15-year-olds)	31.7	2018	●	→

SDG5 – Gender Equality	Value	Year	Rating	Trend
Demand for family planning satisfied by modern methods (% of females aged 15 to 49)	* 66.1	2022	●	↗
Ratio of female-to-male mean years of education received (%)	95.4	2019	●	↗
Ratio of female-to-male labor force participation rate (%)	73.7	2020	●	↑
Seats held by women in national parliament (%)	21.7	2020	●	→
Gender wage gap (% of male median wage)	8.9	2020	●	↓

SDG6 – Clean Water and Sanitation	Value	Year	Rating	Trend
Population using at least basic drinking water services (%)	100.0	2020	●	↑
Population using at least basic sanitation services (%)	99.0	2020	●	↑
Freshwater withdrawal (% of available freshwater resources)	20.5	2018	●	●
Anthropogenic wastewater that receives treatment (%)	81.7	2018	●	●
Scarce water consumption embodied in imports (m^3 H_2O eq/capita)	3365.4	2018	●	●
Population using safely managed water services (%)	100.0	2020	●	↑
Population using safely managed sanitation services (%)	91.7	2020	●	↑

SDG7 – Affordable and Clean Energy	Value	Year	Rating	Trend
Population with access to electricity (%)	100.0	2019	●	↑
Population with access to clean fuels and technology for cooking (%)	100.0	2019	●	↑
CO_2 emissions from fuel combustion per total electricity output ($MtCO_2$/TWh)	1.5	2019	●	→
Share of renewable energy in total primary energy supply (%)	12.8	2019	●	→

SDG8 – Decent Work and Economic Growth	Value	Year	Rating	Trend
Adjusted GDP growth (%)	-3.8	2020	●	●
Victims of modern slavery (per 1,000 population)	7.9	2018	●	●
Adults with an account at a bank or other financial institution or with a mobile-money-service provider (% of population aged 15 or over)	85.5	2017	●	↑
Fundamental labor rights are effectively guaranteed (worst 0–1 best)	0.6	2020	●	↗
Fatal work-related accidents embodied in imports (per 100,000 population)	0.9	2015	●	↑
Employment-to-population ratio (%)	53.7	2020	●	↗
Youth not in employment, education or training (NEET) (% of population aged 15 to 29)	18.7	2020	●	↑

SDG9 – Industry, Innovation and Infrastructure	Value	Year	Rating	Trend
Population using the internet (%)	78.1	2020	●	↑
Mobile broadband subscriptions (per 100 population)	87.1	2019	●	↑
Logistics Performance Index: Quality of trade and transport-related infrastructure (worst 1–5 best)	3.2	2018	●	↑
The Times Higher Education Universities Ranking: Average score of top 3 universities (worst 0–100 best)	43.3	2022	●	●
Articles published in academic journals (per 1,000 population)	1.9	2020	●	↑
Expenditure on research and development (% of GDP)	1.2	2018	●	↑
Researchers (per 1,000 employed population)	8.6	2019	●	↑
Triadic patent families filed (per million population)	1.7	2019	●	→
Gap in internet access by income (percentage points)	41.7	2020	●	→
Female share of graduates from STEM fields at the tertiary level (%)	40.1	2017	●	↑

SDG10 – Reduced Inequalities	Value	Year	Rating	Trend
Gini coefficient	32.9	2018	●	↑
Palma ratio	1.1	2019	●	↑
Elderly poverty rate (% of population aged 66 or over)	7.2	2019	●	↗

SDG11 – Sustainable Cities and Communities	Value	Year	Rating	Trend
Proportion of urban population living in slums (%)	0.0	2018	●	↑
Annual mean concentration of particulate matter of less than 2.5 microns in diameter (PM2.5) (μg/m^3)	15.4	2019	●	↑
Access to improved water source, piped (% of urban population)	100.0	2020	●	↑
Satisfaction with public transport (%)	43.0	2021	●	↓
Population with rent overburden (%)	14.2	2019	●	↑

SDG12 – Responsible Consumption and Production	Value	Year	Rating	Trend
Electronic waste (kg/capita)	16.9	2019	●	●
Production-based SO_2 emissions (kg/capita)	27.8	2018	●	●
SO_2 emissions embodied in imports (kg/capita)	5.0	2018	●	●
Production-based nitrogen emissions (kg/capita)	15.1	2015	●	↑
Nitrogen emissions embodied in imports (kg/capita)	11.8	2015	●	↓
Exports of plastic waste (kg/capita)	5.1	2020	●	●
Non-recycled municipal solid waste (kg/capita/day)	1.2	2019	●	↓

SDG13 – Climate Action	Value	Year	Rating	Trend
CO_2 emissions from fossil fuel combustion and cement production (tCO_2/capita)	5.0	2020	●	↑
CO_2 emissions embodied in imports (tCO_2/capita)	1.5	2018	●	→
CO_2 emissions embodied in fossil fuel exports (kg/capita)	40.9	2020	●	●
Carbon Pricing Score at EUR60/tCO_2 (%, worst 0–100 best)	46.8	2018	●	↑

SDG14 – Life Below Water	Value	Year	Rating	Trend
Mean area that is protected in marine sites important to biodiversity (%)	85.5	2020	●	↑
Ocean Health Index: Clean Waters score (worst 0–100 best)	58.8	2020	●	↓
Fish caught from overexploited or collapsed stocks (% of total catch)	62.5	2018	●	→
Fish caught by trawling or dredging (%)	37.3	2018	●	↓
Fish caught that are then discarded (%)	10.4	2018	●	↑
Marine biodiversity threats embodied in imports (per million population)	0.2	2018	●	●

SDG15 – Life on Land	Value	Year	Rating	Trend
Mean area that is protected in terrestrial sites important to biodiversity (%)	86.0	2020	●	↑
Mean area that is protected in freshwater sites important to biodiversity (%)	90.4	2020	●	↑
Red List Index of species survival (worst 0–1 best)	0.8	2021	●	↓
Permanent deforestation (% of forest area, 5-year average)	0.0	2020	●	↑
Terrestrial and freshwater biodiversity threats embodied in imports (per million population)	2.9	2018	●	●

SDG16 – Peace, Justice and Strong Institutions	Value	Year	Rating	Trend
Homicides (per 100,000 population)	0.8	2020	●	↑
Unsentenced detainees (% of prison population)	26.6	2019	●	↑
Population who feel safe walking alone at night in the city or area where they live (%)	65	2021	●	↗
Property Rights (worst 1–7 best)	4.2	2020	●	↑
Birth registrations with civil authority (% of children under age 5)	100.0	2020	●	●
Corruption Perception Index (worst 0–100 best)	49	2021	●	↗
Children involved in child labor (% of population aged 5 to 14)	* 0.0	2019	●	●
Exports of major conventional weapons (TIV constant million USD per 100,000 population)	0.2	2020	●	●
Press Freedom Index (best 0–100 worst)	29.0	2021	●	↑
Access to and affordability of justice (worst 0–1 best)	0.6	2020	●	↑
Persons held in prison (per 100,000 population)	104.0	2019	●	↓

SDG17 – Partnerships for the Goals	Value	Year	Rating	Trend
Government spending on health and education (% of GDP)	7.4	2019	●	↓
For high-income and all OECD DAC countries: International concessional public finance, including official development assistance (% of GNI)	0.1	2021	●	→
Other countries: Government revenue excluding grants (% of GDP)	NA	NA	●	●
Corporate Tax Haven Score (best 0–100 worst)	39.1	2019	●	●
Financial Secrecy Score (best 0–100 worst)	51.5	2020	●	●
Shifted profits of multinationals (US\$ billion)	2.2	2018	●	↑
Statistical Performance Index (worst 0–100 best)	85.4	2019	●	↑

* Imputed data point

5. Country Profiles

GRENADA

Latin America and the Caribbean

OVERALL PERFORMANCE

COUNTRY RANKING

GRENADA

NA /163

COUNTRY SCORE

na

REGIONAL AVERAGE: 69.5

AVERAGE PERFORMANCE BY SDG

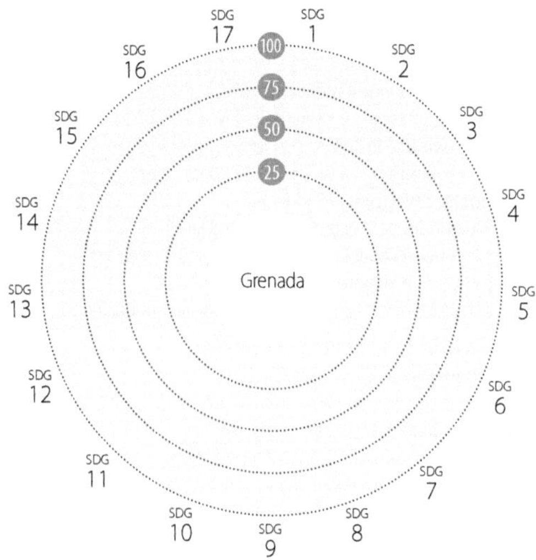

SDG DASHBOARDS AND TRENDS

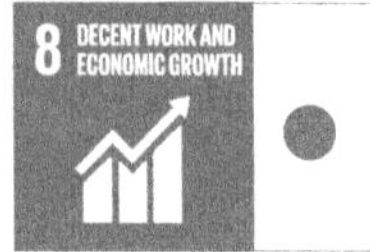

Major challenges · Significant challenges · Challenges remain · SDG achieved · Information unavailable

Decreasing · Stagnating · Moderately improving · On track or maintaining SDG achievement · Information unavailable

Note: The full title of each SDG is available here: https://sustainabledevelopment.un.org/topics/sustainabledevelopmentgoals

INTERNATIONAL SPILLOVER INDEX

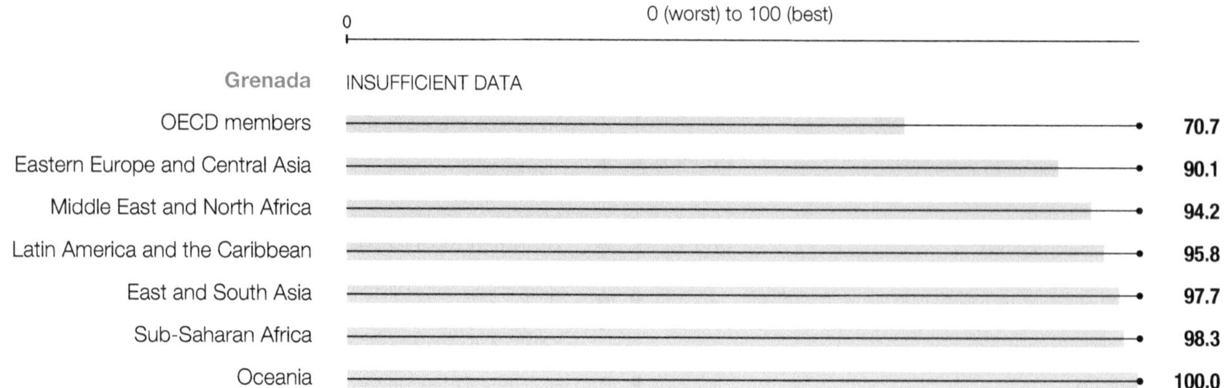

STATISTICAL PERFORMANCE INDEX

0 (worst) to 100 (best)

0 **na** 100

MISSING DATA IN SDG INDEX

41%

SDG1 – No Poverty	Value	Year	Rating	Trend
Poverty headcount ratio at $1.90/day (%)	NA	NA	●	●
Poverty headcount ratio at $3.20/day (%)	NA	NA	●	●
SDG2 – Zero Hunger				
Prevalence of undernourishment (%)	NA	NA	●	●
Prevalence of stunting in children under 5 years of age (%)	NA	NA	●	●
Prevalence of wasting in children under 5 years of age (%)	NA	NA	●	●
Prevalence of obesity, BMI ≥ 30 (% of adult population)	21.3	2016	●	↓
Human Trophic Level (best 2–3 worst)	2.3	2017	●	→
Cereal yield (tonnes per hectare of harvested land)	1.0	2018	●	→
Sustainable Nitrogen Management Index (best 0–1.41 worst)	1.0	2015	●	→
Exports of hazardous pesticides (tonnes per million population)	NA	NA	●	●
SDG3 – Good Health and Well-Being				
Maternal mortality rate (per 100,000 live births)	25	2017	●	↑
Neonatal mortality rate (per 1,000 live births)	10.9	2020	●	↑
Mortality rate, under-5 (per 1,000 live births)	16.4	2020	●	↑
Incidence of tuberculosis (per 100,000 population)	2.8	2020	●	↑
New HIV infections (per 1,000 uninfected population)	NA	NA	●	●
Age-standardized death rate due to cardiovascular disease, cancer, diabetes, or chronic respiratory disease in adults aged 30–70 years (%)	23.4	2019	●	→
Age-standardized death rate attributable to household air pollution and ambient air pollution (per 100,000 population)	45	2016	●	●
Traffic deaths (per 100,000 population)	8.0	2019	●	↑
Life expectancy at birth (years)	72.9	2019	●	→
Adolescent fertility rate (births per 1,000 females aged 15 to 19)	35.9	2014	●	●
Births attended by skilled health personnel (%)	100.0	2017	●	↑
Surviving infants who received 2 WHO-recommended vaccines (%)	72	2020	●	↓
Universal health coverage (UHC) index of service coverage (worst 0–100 best)	70	2019	●	↗
Subjective well-being (average ladder score, worst 0–10 best)	NA	NA	●	●
SDG4 – Quality Education				
Participation rate in pre-primary organized learning (% of children aged 4 to 6)	97.2	2018	●	●
Net primary enrollment rate (%)	99.2	2018	●	●
Lower secondary completion rate (%)	106.7	2018	●	↑
Literacy rate (% of population aged 15 to 24)	99.2	2014	●	●
SDG5 – Gender Equality				
Demand for family planning satisfied by modern methods (% of females aged 15 to 49)	* 77.3	2022	●	↗
Ratio of female-to-male mean years of education received (%)	NA	NA	●	●
Ratio of female-to-male labor force participation rate (%)	NA	NA	●	●
Seats held by women in national parliament (%)	46.7	2020	●	↑
SDG6 – Clean Water and Sanitation				
Population using at least basic drinking water services (%)	95.6	2017	●	●
Population using at least basic sanitation services (%)	91.5	2017	●	●
Freshwater withdrawal (% of available freshwater resources)	7.1	2018	●	●
Anthropogenic wastewater that receives treatment (%)	0.9	2018	●	●
Scarce water consumption embodied in imports (m^3 H_2O eq/capita)	NA	NA	●	●
SDG7 – Affordable and Clean Energy				
Population with access to electricity (%)	95.4	2019	●	↑
Population with access to clean fuels and technology for cooking (%)	89.1	2019	●	↑
CO_2 emissions from fuel combustion per total electricity output ($MtCO_2$/TWh)	1.4	2019	●	→
Share of renewable energy in total primary energy supply (%)	NA	NA	●	●
SDG8 – Decent Work and Economic Growth				
Adjusted GDP growth (%)	-5.8	2020	●	●
Victims of modern slavery (per 1,000 population)	NA	NA	●	●
Adults with an account at a bank or other financial institution or with a mobile-money-service provider (% of population aged 15 or over)	NA	NA	●	●
Unemployment rate (% of total labor force)	NA	NA	●	●
Fundamental labor rights are effectively guaranteed (worst 0–1 best)	0.7	2020	●	↑
Fatal work-related accidents embodied in imports (per 100,000 population)	NA	NA	●	●

SDG9 – Industry, Innovation and Infrastructure	Value	Year	Rating	Trend
Population using the internet (%)	56.9	2020	●	→
Mobile broadband subscriptions (per 100 population)	82.7	2019	●	↑
Logistics Performance Index: Quality of trade and transport-related infrastructure (worst 1–5 best)	NA	NA	●	●
The Times Higher Education Universities Ranking: Average score of top 3 universities (worst 0–100 best)	* 0.0	2022	●	●
Articles published in academic journals (per 1,000 population)	2.2	2020	●	↑
Expenditure on research and development (% of GDP)	NA	NA	●	●
SDG10 – Reduced Inequalities				
Gini coefficient	NA	NA	●	●
Palma ratio	NA	NA	●	●
SDG11 – Sustainable Cities and Communities				
Proportion of urban population living in slums (%)	NA	NA	●	●
Annual mean concentration of particulate matter of less than 2.5 microns in diameter (PM2.5) (μg/m^3)	21.4	2019	●	↗
Access to improved water source, piped (% of urban population)	NA	NA	●	●
Satisfaction with public transport (%)	NA	NA	●	●
SDG12 – Responsible Consumption and Production				
Municipal solid waste (kg/capita/day)	0.8	2012	●	●
Electronic waste (kg/capita)	8.8	2019	●	●
Production-based SO_2 emissions (kg/capita)	NA	NA	●	●
SO_2 emissions embodied in imports (kg/capita)	NA	NA	●	●
Production-based nitrogen emissions (kg/capita)	NA	NA	●	●
Nitrogen emissions embodied in imports (kg/capita)	NA	NA	●	●
Exports of plastic waste (kg/capita)	0.4	2021	●	●
SDG13 – Climate Action				
CO_2 emissions from fossil fuel combustion and cement production (tCO_2/capita)	2.6	2020	●	→
CO_2 emissions embodied in imports (tCO_2/capita)	NA	NA	●	●
CO_2 emissions embodied in fossil fuel exports (kg/capita)	0.0	2020	●	●
SDG14 – Life Below Water				
Mean area that is protected in marine sites important to biodiversity (%)	30.2	2020	●	→
Ocean Health Index: Clean Waters score (worst 0–100 best)	60.0	2020	●	→
Fish caught from overexploited or collapsed stocks (% of total catch)	NA	NA	●	●
Fish caught by trawling or dredging (%)	0.0	2018	●	↑
Fish caught that are then discarded (%)	0.5	2018	●	↑
Marine biodiversity threats embodied in imports (per million population)	NA	NA	●	●
SDG15 – Life on Land				
Mean area that is protected in terrestrial sites important to biodiversity (%)	34.5	2020	●	→
Mean area that is protected in freshwater sites important to biodiversity (%)	NA	NA	●	●
Red List Index of species survival (worst 0–1 best)	0.7	2021	●	↓
Permanent deforestation (% of forest area, 5-year average)	0.1	2020	●	→
Terrestrial and freshwater biodiversity threats embodied in imports (per million population)	NA	NA	●	●
SDG16 – Peace, Justice and Strong Institutions				
Homicides (per 100,000 population)	14.3	2019	●	↓
Unsentenced detainees (% of prison population)	10.6	2018	●	↑
Population who feel safe walking alone at night in the city or area where they live (%)	NA	NA	●	●
Property Rights (worst 1–7 best)	NA	NA	●	●
Birth registrations with civil authority (% of children under age 5)	NA	NA	●	●
Corruption Perception Index (worst 0–100 best)	53	2021	●	↓
Children involved in child labor (% of population aged 5 to 14)	NA	NA	●	●
Exports of major conventional weapons (TIV constant million USD per 100,000 population)	* 0.0	2020	●	●
Press Freedom Index (best 0–100 worst)	NA	NA	●	●
Access to and affordability of justice (worst 0–1 best)	0.6	2020	●	↓
SDG17 – Partnerships for the Goals				
Government spending on health and education (% of GDP)	5.6	2019	●	↓
For high-income and all OECD DAC countries: International concessional public finance, including official development assistance (% of GNI)	NA	NA	●	●
Other countries: Government revenue excluding grants (% of GDP)	NA	NA	●	●
Corporate Tax Haven Score (best 0–100 worst)	* 0.0	2019	●	●
Statistical Performance Index (worst 0–100 best)	NA	NA	●	●

* Imputed data point

GUATEMALA

Latin America and the Caribbean

OVERALL PERFORMANCE

COUNTRY RANKING

GUATEMALA

117/**163**

COUNTRY SCORE

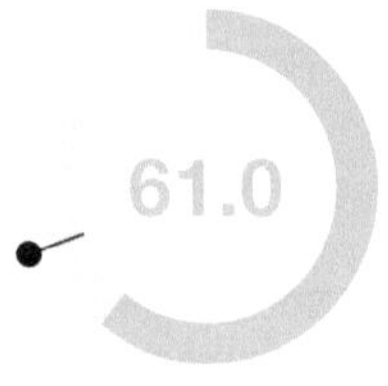

REGIONAL AVERAGE: 69.5

AVERAGE PERFORMANCE BY SDG

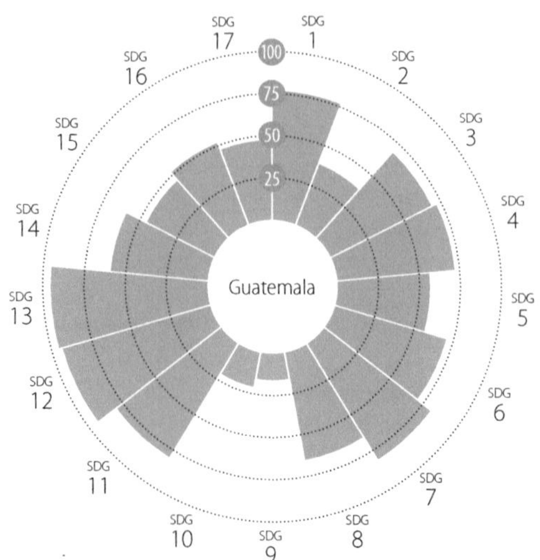

SDG DASHBOARDS AND TRENDS

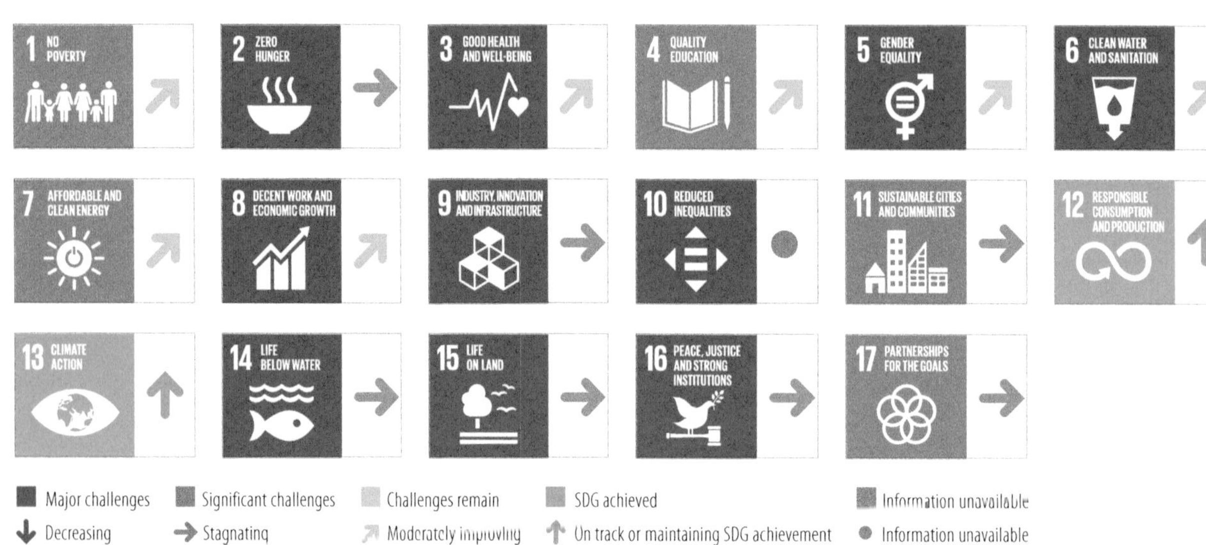

Note: The full title of each SDG is available here: https://sustainabledevelopment.un.org/topics/sustainabledevelopmentgoals

INTERNATIONAL SPILLOVER INDEX

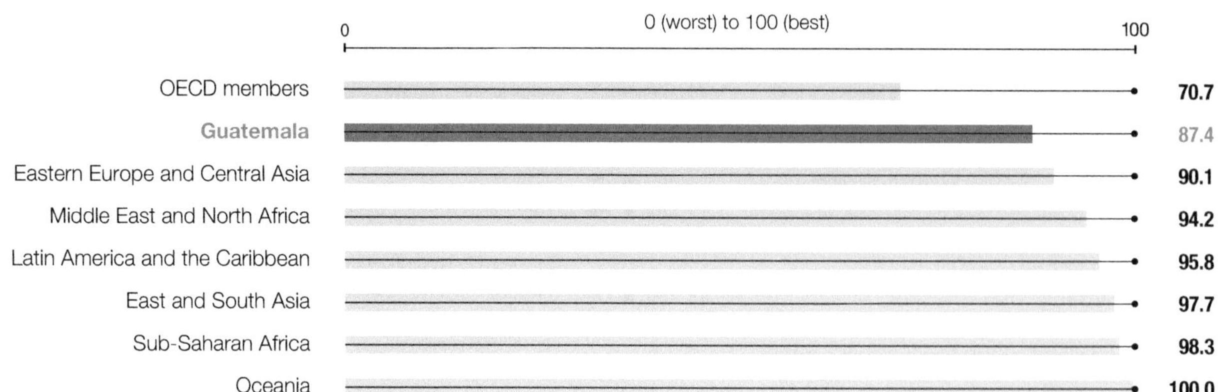

STATISTICAL PERFORMANCE INDEX

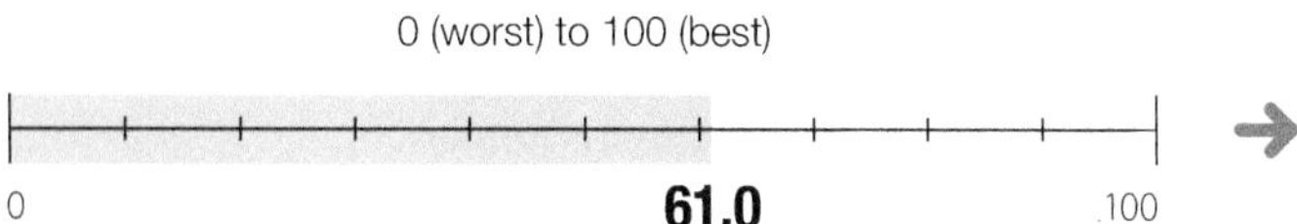

MISSING DATA IN SDG INDEX

1%

GUATEMALA

Performance by Indicator

SDG1 – No Poverty	Value	Year	Rating	Trend
Poverty headcount ratio at $1.90/day (%)	6.5	2022	●	↗
Poverty headcount ratio at $3.20/day (%)	19.5	2022	●	→

SDG2 – Zero Hunger	Value	Year	Rating	Trend
Prevalence of undernourishment (%)	16.8	2019	●	→
Prevalence of stunting in children under 5 years of age (%)	46.7	2015	●	→
Prevalence of wasting in children under 5 years of age (%)	0.8	2015	●	↑
Prevalence of obesity, BMI ≥ 30 (% of adult population)	21.2	2016	●	↓
Human Trophic Level (best 2–3 worst)	2.2	2017	●	→
Cereal yield (tonnes per hectare of harvested land)	2.2	2018	●	↗
Sustainable Nitrogen Management Index (best 0–1.41 worst)	1.0	2015	●	↓
Exports of hazardous pesticides (tonnes per million population)	431.5	2019	●	●

SDG3 – Good Health and Well-Being	Value	Year	Rating	Trend
Maternal mortality rate (per 100,000 live births)	95	2017	●	↑
Neonatal mortality rate (per 1,000 live births)	11.1	2020	●	↑
Mortality rate, under-5 (per 1,000 live births)	23.6	2020	●	↑
Incidence of tuberculosis (per 100,000 population)	27.0	2020	●	→
New HIV infections (per 1,000 uninfected population)	0.1	2020	●	↑
Age-standardized death rate due to cardiovascular disease, cancer, diabetes, or chronic respiratory disease in adults aged 30–70 years (%)	16.5	2019	●	↑
Age-standardized death rate attributable to household air pollution and ambient air pollution (per 100,000 population)	74	2016	●	●
Traffic deaths (per 100,000 population)	22.9	2019	●	↓
Life expectancy at birth (years)	72.0	2019	●	→
Adolescent fertility rate (births per 1,000 females aged 15 to 19)	77.4	2018	●	→
Births attended by skilled health personnel (%)	69.8	2016	●	●
Surviving infants who received 2 WHO-recommended vaccines (%)	83	2020	●	↑
Universal health coverage (UHC) index of service coverage (worst 0–100 best)	57	2019	●	→
Subjective well-being (average ladder score, worst 0–10 best)	6.3	2019	●	●

SDG4 – Quality Education	Value	Year	Rating	Trend
Participation rate in pre-primary organized learning (% of children aged 4 to 6)	82.5	2020	●	↗
Net primary enrollment rate (%)	89.4	2020	●	→
Lower secondary completion rate (%)	56.2	2020	●	↓
Literacy rate (% of population aged 15 to 24)	94.6	2018	●	↑

SDG5 – Gender Equality	Value	Year	Rating	Trend
Demand for family planning satisfied by modern methods (% of females aged 15 to 49)	66.1	2015	●	↗
Ratio of female-to-male mean years of education received (%)	98.5	2019	●	↑
Ratio of female-to-male labor force participation rate (%)	46.0	2020	●	→
Seats held by women in national parliament (%)	19.4	2020	●	↗

SDG6 – Clean Water and Sanitation	Value	Year	Rating	Trend
Population using at least basic drinking water services (%)	94.0	2020	●	↗
Population using at least basic sanitation services (%)	67.9	2020	●	→
Freshwater withdrawal (% of available freshwater resources)	5.7	2018	●	●
Anthropogenic wastewater that receives treatment (%)	6.8	2018	●	●
Scarce water consumption embodied in imports (m^3 H_2O eq/capita)	1125.1	2018	●	●

SDG7 – Affordable and Clean Energy	Value	Year	Rating	Trend
Population with access to electricity (%)	95.7	2019	●	↑
Population with access to clean fuels and technology for cooking (%)	48.8	2019	●	↗
CO_2 emissions from fuel combustion per total electricity output ($MtCO_2$/TWh)	1.2	2019	●	↑
Share of renewable energy in total primary energy supply (%)	62.1	2019	●	↑

SDG8 – Decent Work and Economic Growth	Value	Year	Rating	Trend
Adjusted GDP growth (%)	-2.8	2020	●	●
Victims of modern slavery (per 1,000 population)	2.9	2018	●	●
Adults with an account at a bank or other financial institution or with a mobile-money-service provider (% of population aged 15 or over)	44.1	2017	●	→
Unemployment rate (% of total labor force)	3.5	2022	●	↑
Fundamental labor rights are effectively guaranteed (worst 0–1 best)	0.4	2020	●	↓
Fatal work-related accidents embodied in imports (per 100,000 population)	0.1	2015	●	↑

SDG9 – Industry, Innovation and Infrastructure	Value	Year	Rating	Trend
Population using the internet (%)	50.0	2020	●	↑
Mobile broadband subscriptions (per 100 population)	16.5	2019	●	→
Logistics Performance Index: Quality of trade and transport-related infrastructure (worst 1–5 best)	2.2	2018	●	↓
The Times Higher Education Universities Ranking: Average score of top 3 universities (worst 0–100 best)	* 0.0	2022	●	●
Articles published in academic journals (per 1,000 population)	0.0	2020	●	→
Expenditure on research and development (% of GDP)	0.0	2018	●	↓

SDG10 – Reduced Inequalities	Value	Year	Rating	Trend
Gini coefficient	48.3	2014	●	●
Palma ratio	2.9	2018	●	●

SDG11 – Sustainable Cities and Communities	Value	Year	Rating	Trend
Proportion of urban population living in slums (%)	31.0	2018	●	→
Annual mean concentration of particulate matter of less than 2.5 microns in diameter (PM2.5) (μg/m³)	22.1	2019	●	↗
Access to improved water source, piped (% of urban population)	88.5	2020	●	↓
Satisfaction with public transport (%)	73.0	2019	●	●

SDG12 – Responsible Consumption and Production	Value	Year	Rating	Trend
Municipal solid waste (kg/capita/day)	0.5	2015	●	●
Electronic waste (kg/capita)	4.3	2019	●	●
Production-based SO_2 emissions (kg/capita)	4.8	2018	●	●
SO_2 emissions embodied in imports (kg/capita)	0.8	2018	●	●
Production-based nitrogen emissions (kg/capita)	11.1	2015	●	↑
Nitrogen emissions embodied in imports (kg/capita)	1.1	2015	●	↑
Exports of plastic waste (kg/capita)	0.5	2021	●	●

SDG13 – Climate Action	Value	Year	Rating	Trend
CO_2 emissions from fossil fuel combustion and cement production (tCO_2/capita)	1.1	2020	●	↑
CO_2 emissions embodied in imports (tCO_2/capita)	0.3	2018	●	↑
CO_2 emissions embodied in fossil fuel exports (kg/capita)	38.5	2021	●	●

SDG14 – Life Below Water	Value	Year	Rating	Trend
Mean area that is protected in marine sites important to biodiversity (%)	48.7	2020	●	↗
Ocean Health Index: Clean Waters score (worst 0–100 best)	32.0	2020	●	→
Fish caught from overexploited or collapsed stocks (% of total catch)	8.6	2018	●	↑
Fish caught by trawling or dredging (%)	24.4	2018	●	↓
Fish caught that are then discarded (%)	11.6	2018	●	↓
Marine biodiversity threats embodied in imports (per million population)	0.1	2018	●	●

SDG15 – Life on Land	Value	Year	Rating	Trend
Mean area that is protected in terrestrial sites important to biodiversity (%)	30.0	2020	●	→
Mean area that is protected in freshwater sites important to biodiversity (%)	24.8	2020	●	→
Red List Index of species survival (worst 0–1 best)	0.7	2021	●	↓
Permanent deforestation (% of forest area, 5-year average)	0.7	2020	●	↗
Terrestrial and freshwater biodiversity threats embodied in imports (per million population)	0.5	2018	●	●

SDG16 – Peace, Justice and Strong Institutions	Value	Year	Rating	Trend
Homicides (per 100,000 population)	26.0	2019	●	↗
Unsentenced detainees (% of prison population)	45.3	2019	●	↗
Population who feel safe walking alone at night in the city or area where they live (%)	56	2019	●	●
Property Rights (worst 1–7 best)	4.2	2020	●	↑
Birth registrations with civil authority (% of children under age 5)	96.4	2020	●	●
Corruption Perception Index (worst 0–100 best)	25	2021	●	↓
Children involved in child labor (% of population aged 5 to 14)	NA	NA	●	●
Exports of major conventional weapons (TIV constant million USD per 100,000 population)	* 0.0	2020	●	●
Press Freedom Index (best 0–100 worst)	38.5	2021	●	↓
Access to and affordability of justice (worst 0–1 best)	0.3	2020	●	→

SDG17 – Partnerships for the Goals	Value	Year	Rating	Trend
Government spending on health and education (% of GDP)	5.7	2020	●	→
For high-income and all OECD DAC countries: International concessional public finance, including official development assistance (% of GNI)	NA	NA	●	●
Other countries: Government revenue excluding grants (% of GDP)	11.2	2019	●	→
Corporate Tax Haven Score (best 0–100 worst)	* 0.0	2019	●	●
Statistical Performance Index (worst 0–100 best)	61.0	2019	●	→

* Imputed data point

5. Country Profiles

GUINEA

Sub-Saharan Africa

OVERALL PERFORMANCE

COUNTRY RANKING

GUINEA

152/163

COUNTRY SCORE

AVERAGE PERFORMANCE BY SDG

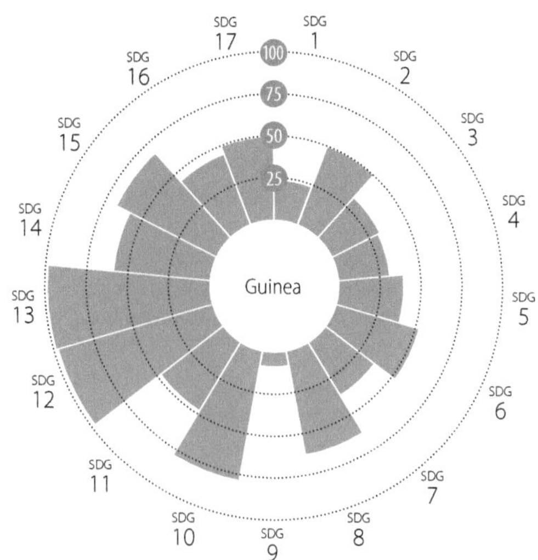

SDG DASHBOARDS AND TRENDS

Major challenges · Significant challenges · Challenges remain · SDG achieved · Information unavailable

Decreasing · Stagnating · Moderately improving · On track or maintaining SDG achievement · Information unavailable

Note: The full title of each SDG is available here: https://sustainabledevelopment.un.org/topics/sustainabledevelopmentgoals

INTERNATIONAL SPILLOVER INDEX

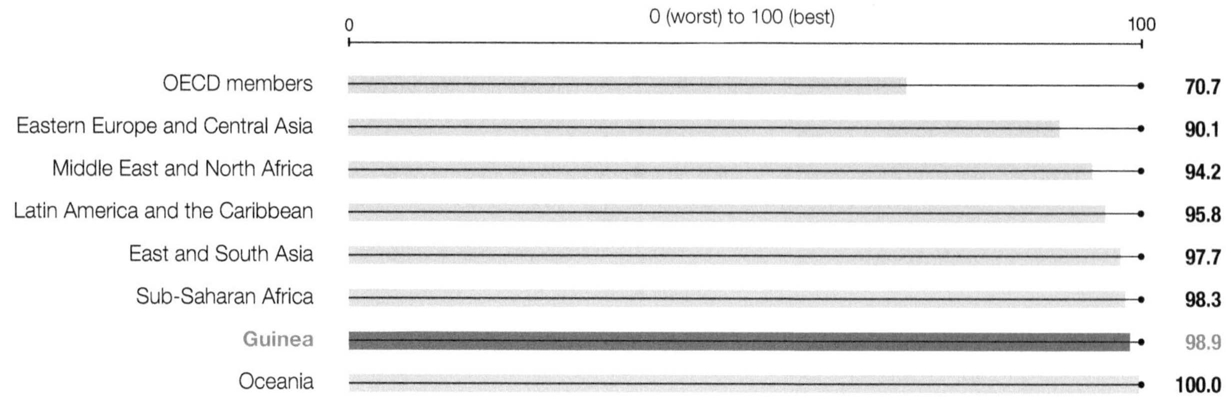

STATISTICAL PERFORMANCE INDEX

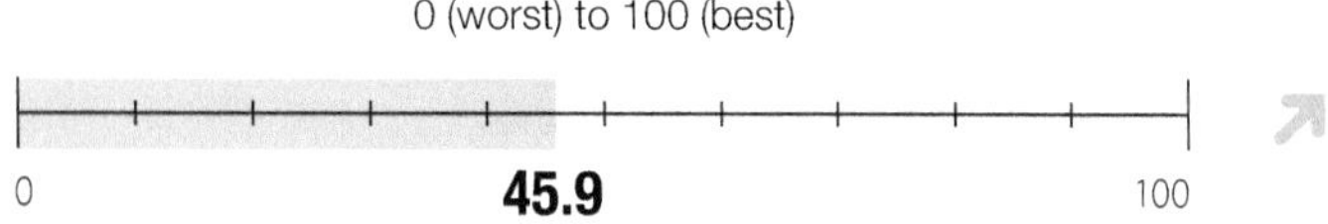

MISSING DATA IN SDG INDEX

GUINEA

Performance by Indicator

		Value	Year	Rating	Trend
SDG1 – No Poverty					
Poverty headcount ratio at $1.90/day (%)		38.7	2022	●	↓
Poverty headcount ratio at $3.20/day (%)		72.7	2022	●	↓
SDG2 – Zero Hunger					
Prevalence of undernourishment (%)		NA	NA	●	●
Prevalence of stunting in children under 5 years of age (%)		30.3	2018	●	→
Prevalence of wasting in children under 5 years of age (%)		9.2	2018	●	→
Prevalence of obesity, BMI ≥ 30 (% of adult population)		7.7	2016	●	↑
Human Trophic Level (best 2–3 worst)		2.1	2017	●	↑
Cereal yield (tonnes per hectare of harvested land)		1.2	2018	●	→
Sustainable Nitrogen Management Index (best 0–1.41 worst)		0.9	2015	●	↓
Exports of hazardous pesticides (tonnes per million population)		NA	NA	●	●
SDG3 – Good Health and Well-Being					
Maternal mortality rate (per 100,000 live births)		576	2017	●	↑
Neonatal mortality rate (per 1,000 live births)		29.9	2020	●	→
Mortality rate, under-5 (per 1,000 live births)		95.6	2020	●	→
Incidence of tuberculosis (per 100,000 population)		179.0	2020	●	↓
New HIV infections (per 1,000 uninfected population)		0.4	2020	●	↑
Age-standardized death rate due to cardiovascular disease, cancer, diabetes, or chronic respiratory disease in adults aged 30–70 years (%)		24.9	2019	●	→
Age-standardized death rate attributable to household air pollution and ambient air pollution (per 100,000 population)		243	2016	●	●
Traffic deaths (per 100,000 population)		29.7	2019	●	→
Life expectancy at birth (years)		61.0	2019	●	→
Adolescent fertility rate (births per 1,000 females aged 15 to 19)		120.0	2016	●	●
Births attended by skilled health personnel (%)		55.3	2018	●	↓
Surviving infants who received 2 WHO-recommended vaccines (%)		47	2020	●	→
Universal health coverage (UHC) index of service coverage (worst 0–100 best)		37	2019	●	→
Subjective well-being (average ladder score, worst 0–10 best)		4.9	2021	●	↑
SDG4 – Quality Education					
Participation rate in pre-primary organized learning (% of children aged 4 to 6)		47.3	2020	●	→
Net primary enrollment rate (%)		85.5	2020	●	↑
Lower secondary completion rate (%)		33.2	2020	●	↓
Literacy rate (% of population aged 15 to 24)		53.9	2018	●	↗
SDG5 – Gender Equality					
Demand for family planning satisfied by modern methods (% of females aged 15 to 49)		37.7	2018	●	→
Ratio of female-to-male mean years of education received (%)		35.7	2019	●	↓
Ratio of female-to-male labor force participation rate (%)		99.3	2020	●	↑
Seats held by women in national parliament (%)		16.7	2020	●	↓
SDG6 – Clean Water and Sanitation					
Population using at least basic drinking water services (%)		64.0	2020	●	→
Population using at least basic sanitation services (%)		29.8	2020	●	→
Freshwater withdrawal (% of available freshwater resources)		1.4	2018	●	●
Anthropogenic wastewater that receives treatment (%)		0.0	2018	●	●
Scarce water consumption embodied in imports (m^3 H_2O eq/capita)		500.6	2018	●	●
SDG7 – Affordable and Clean Energy					
Population with access to electricity (%)		42.4	2019	●	→
Population with access to clean fuels and technology for cooking (%)		1.6	2019	●	→
CO_2 emissions from fuel combustion per total electricity output ($MtCO_2$/TWh)		1.7	2019	●	↑
Share of renewable energy in total primary energy supply (%)		NA	NA	●	●
SDG8 – Decent Work and Economic Growth					
Adjusted GDP growth (%)		-1.5	2020	●	●
Victims of modern slavery (per 1,000 population)		7.8	2018	●	●
Adults with an account at a bank or other financial institution or with a mobile-money-service provider (% of population aged 15 or over)		23.5	2017	●	↑
Unemployment rate (% of total labor force)		6.2	2022	●	↓
Fundamental labor rights are effectively guaranteed (worst 0–1 best)		0.6	2020	●	●
Fatal work-related accidents embodied in imports (per 100,000 population)		0.0	2015	●	↑

		Value	Year	Rating	Trend
SDG9 – Industry, Innovation and Infrastructure					
Population using the internet (%)		26.0	2020	●	↗
Mobile broadband subscriptions (per 100 population)		23.2	2019	●	↗
Logistics Performance Index: Quality of trade and transport-related infrastructure (worst 1–5 best)		1.6	2018	●	↓
The Times Higher Education Universities Ranking: Average score of top 3 universities (worst 0–100 best)	*	0.0	2022	●	●
Articles published in academic journals (per 1,000 population)		0.0	2020	●	→
Expenditure on research and development (% of GDP)	*	0.0	2018	●	●
SDG10 – Reduced Inequalities					
Gini coefficient		33.7	2012	●	●
Palma ratio		1.3	2018	●	●
SDG11 – Sustainable Cities and Communities					
Proportion of urban population living in slums (%)		50.7	2018	●	↓
Annual mean concentration of particulate matter of less than 2.5 microns in diameter (PM2.5) (μg/m^3)		27.1	2019	●	↓
Access to improved water source, piped (% of urban population)		53.7	2020	●	↓
Satisfaction with public transport (%)		33.0	2021	●	→
SDG12 – Responsible Consumption and Production					
Municipal solid waste (kg/capita/day)		NA	NA	●	●
Electronic waste (kg/capita)		0.8	2019	●	●
Production-based SO_2 emissions (kg/capita)		1.3	2018	●	●
SO_2 emissions embodied in imports (kg/capita)		0.4	2018	●	●
Production-based nitrogen emissions (kg/capita)		12.7	2015	●	↑
Nitrogen emissions embodied in imports (kg/capita)		0.2	2015	●	↑
Exports of plastic waste (kg/capita)		NA	NA	●	●
SDG13 – Climate Action					
CO_2 emissions from fossil fuel combustion and cement production (tCO_2/capita)		0.3	2020	●	↑
CO_2 emissions embodied in imports (tCO_2/capita)		0.1	2018	●	↑
CO_2 emissions embodied in fossil fuel exports (kg/capita)		0.0	2020	●	●
SDG14 – Life Below Water					
Mean area that is protected in marine sites important to biodiversity (%)		69.3	2020	●	→
Ocean Health Index: Clean Waters score (worst 0–100 best)		44.1	2020	●	→
Fish caught from overexploited or collapsed stocks (% of total catch)		11.8	2018	●	↑
Fish caught by trawling or dredging (%)		25.4	2018	●	↓
Fish caught that are then discarded (%)		25.4	2018	●	↓
Marine biodiversity threats embodied in imports (per million population)		0.0	2018	●	●
SDG15 – Life on Land					
Mean area that is protected in terrestrial sites important to biodiversity (%)		69.8	2020	●	→
Mean area that is protected in freshwater sites important to biodiversity (%)		90.4	2020	●	↑
Red List Index of species survival (worst 0–1 best)		0.9	2021	●	→
Permanent deforestation (% of forest area, 5-year average)		1.4	2020	●	→
Terrestrial and freshwater biodiversity threats embodied in imports (per million population)		0.0	2018	●	●
SDG16 – Peace, Justice and Strong Institutions					
Homicides (per 100,000 population)		NA	NA	●	●
Unsentenced detainees (% of prison population)		65.6	2017	●	●
Population who feel safe walking alone at night in the city or area where they live (%)		48	2021	●	↓
Property Rights (worst 1–7 best)		3.7	2020	●	↓
Birth registrations with civil authority (% of children under age 5)		62.0	2020	●	●
Corruption Perception Index (worst 0–100 best)		25	2021	●	→
Children involved in child labor (% of population aged 5 to 14)		24.2	2019	●	●
Exports of major conventional weapons (TIV constant million USD per 100,000 population)	*	0.0	2020	●	●
Press Freedom Index (best 0–100 worst)		35.4	2021	●	↓
Access to and affordability of justice (worst 0–1 best)		0.5	2020	●	●
SDG17 – Partnerships for the Goals					
Government spending on health and education (% of GDP)		3.1	2020	●	→
For high-income and all OECD DAC countries: International concessional public finance, including official development assistance (% of GNI)		NA	NA	●	●
Other countries: Government revenue excluding grants (% of GDP)		NA	NA	●	●
Corporate Tax Haven Score (best 0–100 worst)	*	0.0	2019	●	●
Statistical Performance Index (worst 0–100 best)		45.9	2019	●	↗

* Imputed data point

5. Country Profiles

GUINEA-BISSAU

Sub-Saharan Africa

OVERALL PERFORMANCE

COUNTRY RANKING

GUINEA-BISSAU

NA /163

COUNTRY SCORE

AVERAGE PERFORMANCE BY SDG

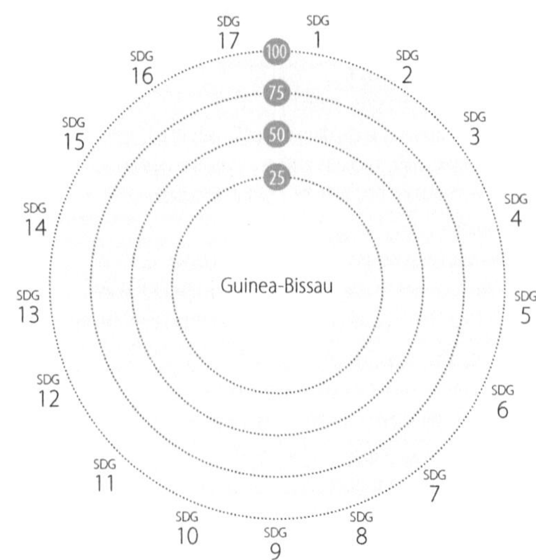

SDG DASHBOARDS AND TRENDS

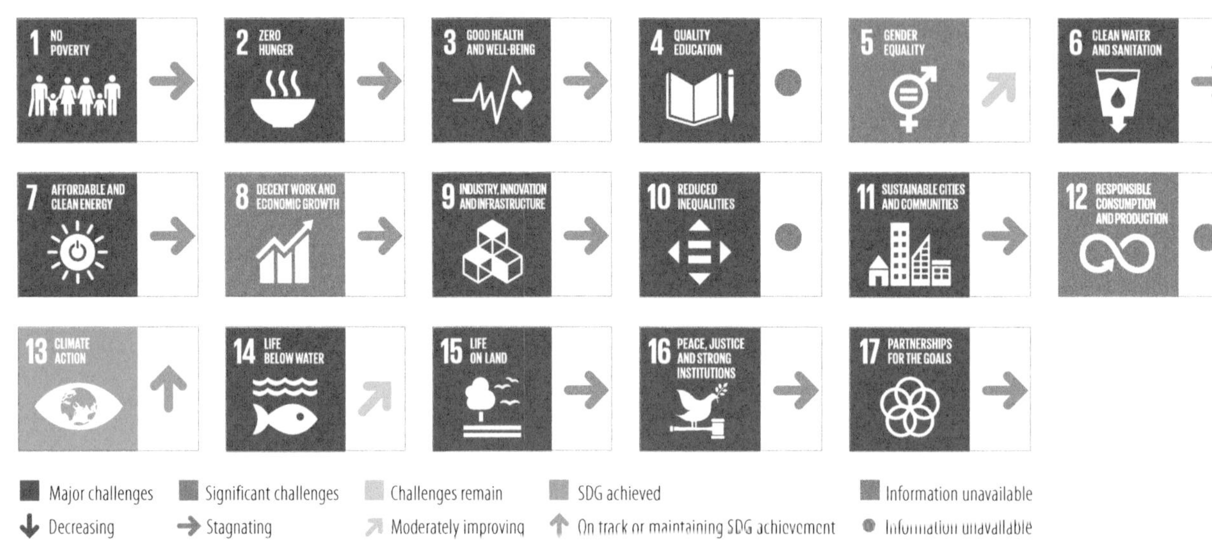

Major challenges · Significant challenges · Challenges remain · SDG achieved · Information unavailable

Decreasing · Stagnating · Moderately improving · On track or maintaining SDG achievement · Information unavailable

Note: The full title of each SDG is available here: https://sustainabledevelopment.un.org/topics/sustainabledevelopmentgoals

INTERNATIONAL SPILLOVER INDEX

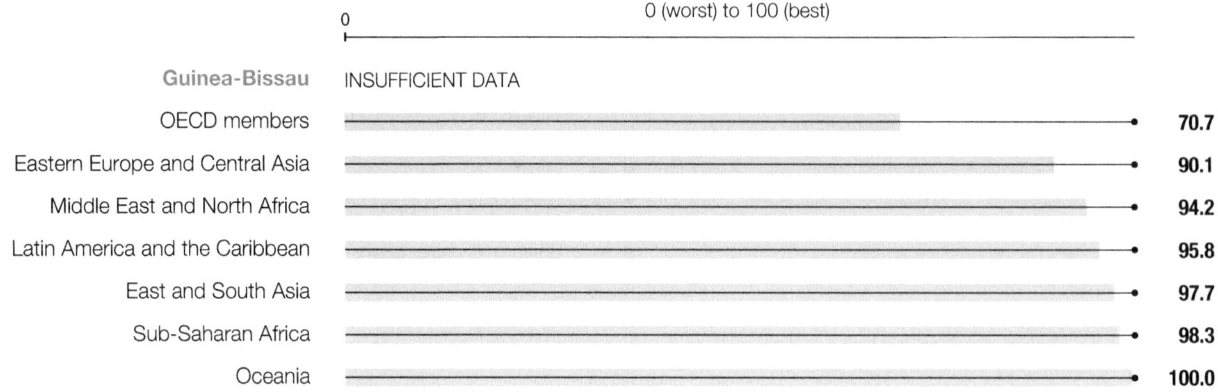

STATISTICAL PERFORMANCE INDEX

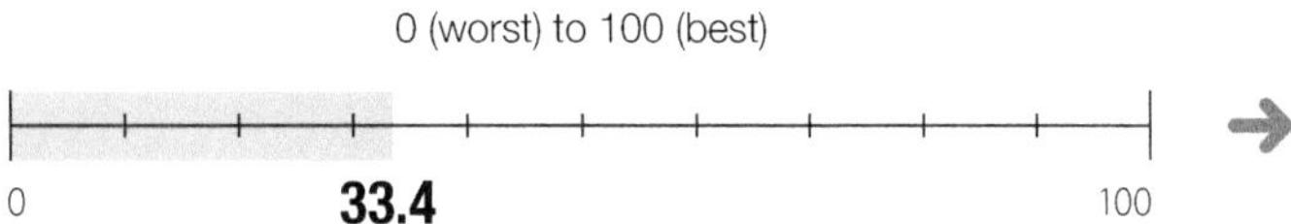

MISSING DATA IN SDG INDEX

23%

GUINEA-BISSAU

Performance by Indicator

SDG1 – No Poverty		Value	Year	Rating	Trend
Poverty headcount ratio at $1.90/day (%)		65.4	2022	●	→
Poverty headcount ratio at $3.20/day (%)		84.2	2022	●	→
SDG2 – Zero Hunger					
Prevalence of undernourishment (%)		NA	NA	●	●
Prevalence of stunting in children under 5 years of age (%)		28.1	2019	●	→
Prevalence of wasting in children under 5 years of age (%)		7.8	2019	●	→
Prevalence of obesity, BMI ≥ 30 (% of adult population)		9.5	2016	●	↑
Human Trophic Level (best 2–3 worst)		2.1	2017	●	↑
Cereal yield (tonnes per hectare of harvested land)		1.3	2018	●	↓
Sustainable Nitrogen Management Index (best 0–1.41 worst)		1.0	2015	●	↓
Exports of hazardous pesticides (tonnes per million population)		NA	NA	●	●
SDG3 – Good Health and Well-Being					
Maternal mortality rate (per 100,000 live births)		667	2017	●	→
Neonatal mortality rate (per 1,000 live births)		35.1	2020	●	→
Mortality rate, under-5 (per 1,000 live births)		76.8	2020	●	↗
Incidence of tuberculosis (per 100,000 population)		361.0	2020	●	→
New HIV infections (per 1,000 uninfected population)		0.9	2020	●	↑
Age-standardized death rate due to cardiovascular disease, cancer, diabetes, or chronic respiratory disease in adults aged 30–70 years (%)		24.9	2019	●	→
Age-standardized death rate attributable to household air pollution and ambient air pollution (per 100,000 population)		215	2016	●	●
Traffic deaths (per 100,000 population)		32.2	2019	●	↓
Life expectancy at birth (years)		60.2	2019	●	→
Adolescent fertility rate (births per 1,000 females aged 15 to 19)		84.0	2017	●	●
Births attended by skilled health personnel (%)		45.0	2014	●	●
Surviving infants who received 2 WHO-recommended vaccines (%)		72	2020	●	↓
Universal health coverage (UHC) index of service coverage (worst 0–100 best)		37	2019	●	↓
Subjective well-being (average ladder score, worst 0–10 best)		NA	NA	●	●
SDG4 – Quality Education					
Participation rate in pre-primary organized learning (% of children aged 4 to 6)		28.7	2010	●	●
Net primary enrollment rate (%)		72.7	2010	●	●
Lower secondary completion rate (%)		36.8	2010	●	●
Literacy rate (% of population aged 15 to 24)		60.4	2014	●	●
SDG5 – Gender Equality					
Demand for family planning satisfied by modern methods (% of females aged 15 to 49)		60.0	2019	●	↗
Ratio of female-to-male mean years of education received (%)		NA	NA	●	●
Ratio of female-to-male labor force participation rate (%)		81.4	2020	●	↑
Seats held by women in national parliament (%)		13.7	2020	●	→
SDG6 – Clean Water and Sanitation					
Population using at least basic drinking water services (%)		59.0	2020	●	→
Population using at least basic sanitation services (%)		18.2	2020	●	→
Freshwater withdrawal (% of available freshwater resources)		1.5	2018	●	●
Anthropogenic wastewater that receives treatment (%)		0.0	2018	●	●
Scarce water consumption embodied in imports (m^3 H_2O eq/capita)		NA	NA	●	●
SDG7 – Affordable and Clean Energy					
Population with access to electricity (%)		31.0	2019	●	↗
Population with access to clean fuels and technology for cooking (%)		1.1	2019	●	→
CO_2 emissions from fuel combustion per total electricity output ($MtCO_2$/TWh)		4.5	2019	●	→
Share of renewable energy in total primary energy supply (%)		NA	NA	●	●
SDG8 – Decent Work and Economic Growth					
Adjusted GDP growth (%)		-6.7	2020	●	●
Victims of modern slavery (per 1,000 population)		7.5	2018	●	●
Adults with an account at a bank or other financial institution or with a mobile-money-service provider (% of population aged 15 or over)		NA	NA	●	●
Unemployment rate (% of total labor force)		6.6	2022	●	→
Fundamental labor rights are effectively guaranteed (worst 0–1 best)		NA	NA	●	●
Fatal work-related accidents embodied in imports (per 100,000 population)		NA	NA	●	●

* Imputed data point

SDG9 – Industry, Innovation and Infrastructure		Value	Year	Rating	Trend
Population using the internet (%)		22.9	2020	●	↗
Mobile broadband subscriptions (per 100 population)		36.7	2019	●	↑
Logistics Performance Index: Quality of trade and transport-related infrastructure (worst 1–5 best)		1.8	2018	●	↓
The Times Higher Education Universities Ranking: Average score of top 3 universities (worst 0–100 best)	*	0.0	2022	●	●
Articles published in academic journals (per 1,000 population)		0.0	2020	●	→
Expenditure on research and development (% of GDP)	*	0.0	2018	●	●
SDG10 – Reduced Inequalities					
Gini coefficient		50.7	2010	●	●
Palma ratio		3.3	2018	●	●
SDG11 – Sustainable Cities and Communities					
Proportion of urban population living in slums (%)		78.2	2018	●	→
Annual mean concentration of particulate matter of less than 2.5 microns in diameter (PM2.5) (μg/m³)		32.2	2019	●	↓
Access to improved water source, piped (% of urban population)		55.5	2020	●	→
Satisfaction with public transport (%)		NA	NA	●	●
SDG12 – Responsible Consumption and Production					
Municipal solid waste (kg/capita/day)		0.5	2015	●	●
Electronic waste (kg/capita)		0.5	2019	●	●
Production-based SO_2 emissions (kg/capita)		NA	NA	●	●
SO_2 emissions embodied in imports (kg/capita)		NA	NA	●	●
Production-based nitrogen emissions (kg/capita)		NA	NA	●	●
Nitrogen emissions embodied in imports (kg/capita)		NA	NA	●	●
Exports of plastic waste (kg/capita)		NA	NA	●	●
SDG13 – Climate Action					
CO_2 emissions from fossil fuel combustion and cement production (tCO_2/capita)		0.1	2020	●	↑
CO_2 emissions embodied in imports (tCO_2/capita)		NA	NA	●	●
CO_2 emissions embodied in fossil fuel exports (kg/capita)		0.0	2020	●	●
SDG14 – Life Below Water					
Mean area that is protected in marine sites important to biodiversity (%)		50.7	2020	●	→
Ocean Health Index: Clean Waters score (worst 0–100 best)		56.4	2020	●	→
Fish caught from overexploited or collapsed stocks (% of total catch)		3.3	2018	●	↑
Fish caught by trawling or dredging (%)		0.0	2018	●	↑
Fish caught that are then discarded (%)		0.3	2003	●	●
Marine biodiversity threats embodied in imports (per million population)		NA	NA	●	●
SDG15 – Life on Land					
Mean area that is protected in terrestrial sites important to biodiversity (%)		59.5	2020	●	→
Mean area that is protected in freshwater sites important to biodiversity (%)		NA	NA	●	●
Red List Index of species survival (worst 0–1 best)		0.9	2021	●	↑
Permanent deforestation (% of forest area, 5-year average)		0.8	2020	●	↓
Terrestrial and freshwater biodiversity threats embodied in imports (per million population)		NA	NA	●	●
SDG16 – Peace, Justice and Strong Institutions					
Homicides (per 100,000 population)		1.2	2017	●	↑
Unsentenced detainees (% of prison population)		55.5	2017	●	●
Population who feel safe walking alone at night in the city or area where they live (%)		NA	NA	●	●
Property Rights (worst 1–7 best)		NA	NA	●	●
Birth registrations with civil authority (% of children under age 5)		46.0	2020	●	●
Corruption Perception Index (worst 0–100 best)		21	2021	●	→
Children involved in child labor (% of population aged 5 to 14)		17.2	2019	●	●
Exports of major conventional weapons (TIV constant million USD per 100,000 population)	*	0.0	2020	●	●
Press Freedom Index (best 0–100 worst)		32.7	2021	●	↓
Access to and affordability of justice (worst 0–1 best)		NA	NA	●	●
SDG17 – Partnerships for the Goals					
Government spending on health and education (% of GDP)		3.5	2019	●	→
For high-income and all OECD DAC countries: International concessional public finance, including official development assistance (% of GNI)		NA	NA	●	●
Other countries: Government revenue excluding grants (% of GDP)		12.4	2019	●	●
Corporate Tax Haven Score (best 0–100 worst)	*	0.0	2019	●	●
Statistical Performance Index (worst 0–100 best)		33.4	2019	●	→

GUYANA

Latin America and the Caribbean

OVERALL PERFORMANCE

COUNTRY RANKING

GUYANA

106/163

COUNTRY SCORE

REGIONAL AVERAGE: 69.5

AVERAGE PERFORMANCE BY SDG

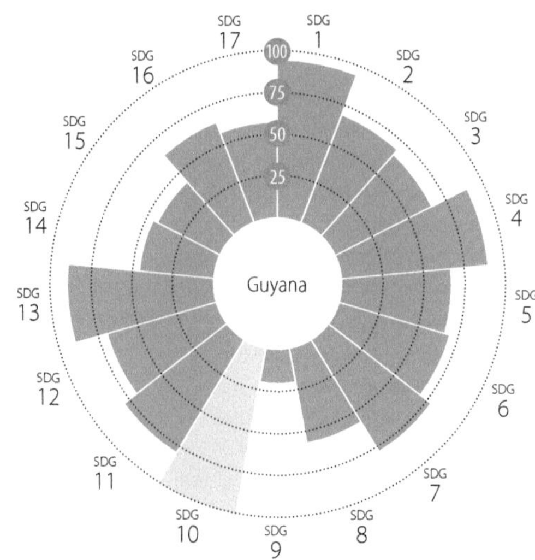

SDG DASHBOARDS AND TRENDS

Major challenges | Significant challenges | Challenges remain | SDG achieved | Information unavailable

Decreasing | Stagnating | Moderately improving | On track or maintaining SDG achievement | Information unavailable

Note: The full title of each SDG is available here: https://sustainabledevelopment.un.org/topics/sustainabledevelopmentgoals

INTERNATIONAL SPILLOVER INDEX

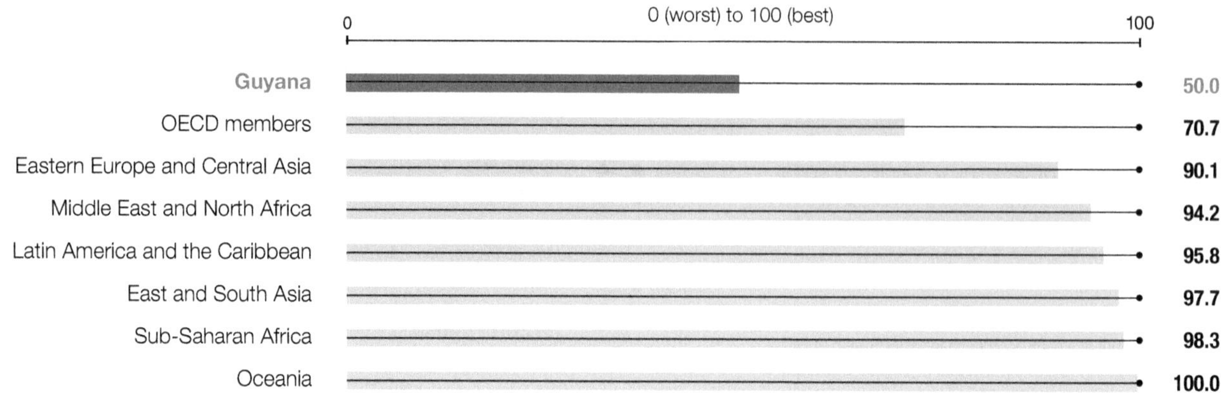

STATISTICAL PERFORMANCE INDEX

0 (worst) to 100 (best)

0 **41.5** 100

MISSING DATA IN SDG INDEX

14%

GUYANA

Performance by Indicator

Indicator	Value	Year	Rating	Trend
SDG1 – No Poverty				
Poverty headcount ratio at \$1.90/day (%)	2.4	2022	●	↑
Poverty headcount ratio at \$3.20/day (%)	4.6	2022	●	↑
SDG2 – Zero Hunger				
Prevalence of undernourishment (%)	5.2	2019	●	↑
Prevalence of stunting in children under 5 years of age (%)	11.3	2014	●	↗
Prevalence of wasting in children under 5 years of age (%)	6.4	2014	●	→
Prevalence of obesity, BMI ≥ 30 (% of adult population)	20.2	2016	●	↓
Human Trophic Level (best 2–3 worst)	2.2	2017	●	↑
Cereal yield (tonnes per hectare of harvested land)	5.7	2018	●	↑
Sustainable Nitrogen Management Index (best 0–1.41 worst)	0.7	2015	●	↓
Exports of hazardous pesticides (tonnes per million population)	0.0	2019	●	●
SDG3 – Good Health and Well-Being				
Maternal mortality rate (per 100,000 live births)	169	2017	●	→
Neonatal mortality rate (per 1,000 live births)	17.3	2020	●	↑
Mortality rate, under-5 (per 1,000 live births)	28.4	2020	●	↑
Incidence of tuberculosis (per 100,000 population)	79.0	2020	●	↗
New HIV infections (per 1,000 uninfected population)	0.4	2020	●	↗
Age-standardized death rate due to cardiovascular disease, cancer, diabetes, or chronic respiratory disease in adults aged 30–70 years (%)	29.2	2019	●	→
Age-standardized death rate attributable to household air pollution and ambient air pollution (per 100,000 population)	108	2016	●	●
Traffic deaths (per 100,000 population)	22.3	2019	●	→
Life expectancy at birth (years)	65.7	2019	●	→
Adolescent fertility rate (births per 1,000 females aged 15 to 19)	73.7	2013	●	●
Births attended by skilled health personnel (%)	95.8	2015	●	●
Surviving infants who received 2 WHO-recommended vaccines (%)	98	2020	●	↑
Universal health coverage (UHC) index of service coverage (worst 0–100 best)	74	2019	●	↗
Subjective well-being (average ladder score, worst 0–10 best)	6.0	2007	●	●
SDG4 – Quality Education				
Participation rate in pre-primary organized learning (% of children aged 4 to 6)	95.2	2012	●	●
Net primary enrollment rate (%)	98.2	2012	●	●
Lower secondary completion rate (%)	79.1	2010	●	●
Literacy rate (% of population aged 15 to 24)	96.7	2014	●	●
SDG5 – Gender Equality				
Demand for family planning satisfied by modern methods (% of females aged 15 to 49)	51.5	2014	●	↗
Ratio of female-to-male mean years of education received (%)	111.3	2019	●	↑
Ratio of female-to-male labor force participation rate (%)	62.3	2020	●	↗
Seats held by women in national parliament (%)	35.7	2020	●	↑
SDG6 – Clean Water and Sanitation				
Population using at least basic drinking water services (%)	95.6	2020	●	→
Population using at least basic sanitation services (%)	85.8	2020	●	→
Freshwater withdrawal (% of available freshwater resources)	3.3	2018	●	●
Anthropogenic wastewater that receives treatment (%)	0.0	2018	●	●
Scarce water consumption embodied in imports (m^3 H_2O eq/capita)	NA	NA	●	●
SDG7 – Affordable and Clean Energy				
Population with access to electricity (%)	92.0	2019	●	↑
Population with access to clean fuels and technology for cooking (%)	76.8	2019	●	↑
CO_2 emissions from fuel combustion per total electricity output ($MtCO_2$/TWh)	2.1	2019	●	→
Share of renewable energy in total primary energy supply (%)	NA	NA	●	●
SDG8 – Decent Work and Economic Growth				
Adjusted GDP growth (%)	13.6	2020	●	●
Victims of modern slavery (per 1,000 population)	2.6	2018	●	●
Adults with an account at a bank or other financial institution or with a mobile-money-service provider (% of population aged 15 or over)	NA	NA	●	●
Unemployment rate (% of total labor force)	14.9	2022	●	↓
Fundamental labor rights are effectively guaranteed (worst 0–1 best)	0.6	2020	●	↗
Fatal work-related accidents embodied in imports (per 100,000 population)	11.0	2015	●	↑

* Imputed data point

Indicator	Value	Year	Rating	Trend
SDG9 – Industry, Innovation and Infrastructure				
Population using the internet (%)	37.3	2017	●	●
Mobile broadband subscriptions (per 100 population)	31.7	2019	●	↑
Logistics Performance Index: Quality of trade and transport-related infrastructure (worst 1–5 best)	2.1	2018	●	↓
The Times Higher Education Universities Ranking: Average score of top 3 universities (worst 0–100 best)	* 0.0	2022	●	●
Articles published in academic journals (per 1,000 population)	0.1	2020	●	→
Expenditure on research and development (% of GDP)	NA	NA	●	●
SDG10 – Reduced Inequalities				
Gini coefficient	NA	NA	●	●
Palma ratio	NA	NA	●	●
SDG11 – Sustainable Cities and Communities				
Proportion of urban population living in slums (%)	32.5	2018	●	→
Annual mean concentration of particulate matter of less than 2.5 microns in diameter (PM2.5) (μg/m^3)	21.5	2019	●	↗
Access to improved water source, piped (% of urban population)	86.8	2020	●	→
Satisfaction with public transport (%)	72.0	2007	●	●
SDG12 – Responsible Consumption and Production				
Municipal solid waste (kg/capita/day)	0.7	2010	●	●
Electronic waste (kg/capita)	6.3	2019	●	●
Production-based SO_2 emissions (kg/capita)	NA	NA	●	●
SO_2 emissions embodied in imports (kg/capita)	NA	NA	●	●
Production-based nitrogen emissions (kg/capita)	15.5	2015	●	↑
Nitrogen emissions embodied in imports (kg/capita)	77.1	2015	●	↓
Exports of plastic waste (kg/capita)	0.0	2020	●	●
SDG13 – Climate Action				
CO_2 emissions from fossil fuel combustion and cement production (tCO_2/capita)	2.8	2020	●	→
CO_2 emissions embodied in imports (tCO_2/capita)	NA	NA	●	●
CO_2 emissions embodied in fossil fuel exports (kg/capita)	3436.6	2021	●	●
SDG14 – Life Below Water				
Mean area that is protected in marine sites important to biodiversity (%)	NA	NA	●	●
Ocean Health Index: Clean Waters score (worst 0–100 best)	75.0	2020	●	↓
Fish caught from overexploited or collapsed stocks (% of total catch)	34.5	2018	●	→
Fish caught by trawling or dredging (%)	0.0	2018	●	↑
Fish caught that are then discarded (%)	22.2	2018	●	→
Marine biodiversity threats embodied in imports (per million population)	5.4	2018	●	●
SDG15 – Life on Land				
Mean area that is protected in terrestrial sites important to biodiversity (%)	3.9	2020	●	→
Mean area that is protected in freshwater sites important to biodiversity (%)	NA	NA	●	●
Red List Index of species survival (worst 0–1 best)	0.9	2021	●	→
Permanent deforestation (% of forest area, 5-year average)	0.0	2020	●	↑
Terrestrial and freshwater biodiversity threats embodied in imports (per million population)	47.2	2018	●	●
SDG16 – Peace, Justice and Strong Institutions				
Homicides (per 100,000 population)	20.0	2020	●	↓
Unsentenced detainees (% of prison population)	35.9	2019	●	↗
Population who feel safe walking alone at night in the city or area where they live (%)	47	2007	●	●
Property Rights (worst 1–7 best)	NA	NA	●	●
Birth registrations with civil authority (% of children under age 5)	88.7	2020	●	●
Corruption Perception Index (worst 0–100 best)	39	2021	●	↗
Children involved in child labor (% of population aged 5 to 14)	10.8	2019	●	●
Exports of major conventional weapons (TIV constant million USD per 100,000 population)	* 0.0	2020	●	●
Press Freedom Index (best 0–100 worst)	25.6	2021	●	↑
Access to and affordability of justice (worst 0–1 best)	0.6	2020	●	↑
SDG17 – Partnerships for the Goals				
Government spending on health and education (% of GDP)	7.4	2019	●	↑
For high-income and all OECD DAC countries: International concessional public finance, including official development assistance (% of GNI)	NA	NA	●	●
Other countries: Government revenue excluding grants (% of GDP)	NA	NA	●	●
Corporate Tax Haven Score (best 0–100 worst)	* 0.0	2019	●	●
Statistical Performance Index (worst 0–100 best)	41.5	2019	●	↗

HAITI

Latin America and the Caribbean

OVERALL PERFORMANCE

COUNTRY RANKING

HAITI

151/163

COUNTRY SCORE

REGIONAL AVERAGE: 69.5

AVERAGE PERFORMANCE BY SDG

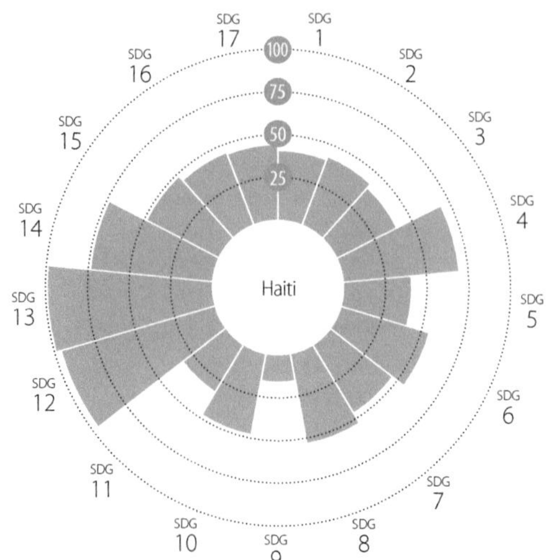

SDG DASHBOARDS AND TRENDS

Note: The full title of each SDG is available here: https://sustainabledevelopment.un.org/topics/sustainabledevelopmentgoals

INTERNATIONAL SPILLOVER INDEX

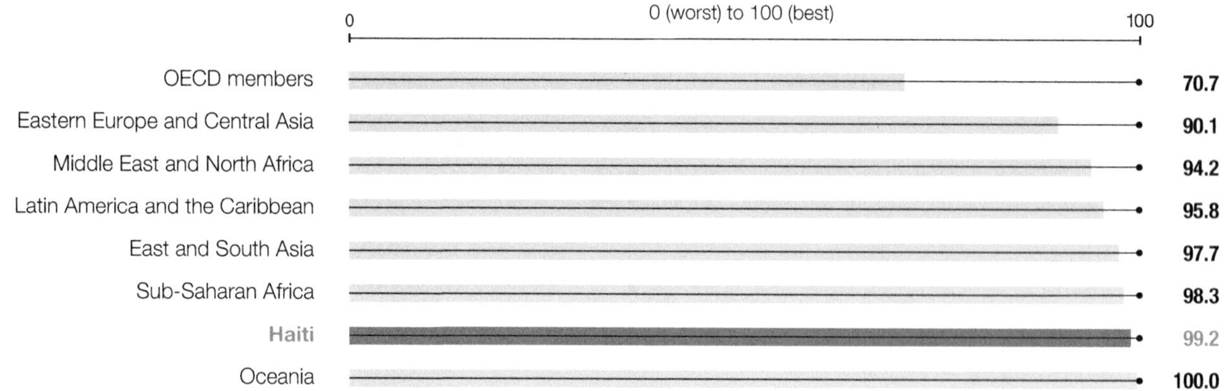

STATISTICAL PERFORMANCE INDEX

0 (worst) to 100 (best)

0 **37.5** 100

MISSING DATA IN SDG INDEX

9%

SDG1 – No Poverty	Value	Year	Rating	Trend
Poverty headcount ratio at $1.90/day (%)	21.8	2022	●	→
Poverty headcount ratio at $3.20/day (%)	46.0	2022	●	→
SDG2 – Zero Hunger				
Prevalence of undernourishment (%)	46.8	2019	●	↓
Prevalence of stunting in children under 5 years of age (%)	21.9	2017	●	→
Prevalence of wasting in children under 5 years of age (%)	3.7	2017	●	↑
Prevalence of obesity, BMI ≥ 30 (% of adult population)	22.7	2016	●	↓
Human Trophic Level (best 2–3 worst)	2.1	2017	●	↑
Cereal yield (tonnes per hectare of harvested land)	1.1	2018	●	→
Sustainable Nitrogen Management Index (best 0–1.41 worst)	0.9	2015	●	→
Exports of hazardous pesticides (tonnes per million population)	NA	NA	●	●
SDG3 – Good Health and Well-Being				
Maternal mortality rate (per 100,000 live births)	480	2017	●	→
Neonatal mortality rate (per 1,000 live births)	24.8	2020	●	→
Mortality rate, under-5 (per 1,000 live births)	60.5	2020	●	↗
Incidence of tuberculosis (per 100,000 population)	168.0	2020	●	→
New HIV infections (per 1,000 uninfected population)	0.5	2020	●	↑
Age-standardized death rate due to cardiovascular disease, cancer, diabetes, or chronic respiratory disease in adults aged 30–70 years (%)	31.3	2019	●	→
Age-standardized death rate attributable to household air pollution and ambient air pollution (per 100,000 population)	184	2016	●	●
Traffic deaths (per 100,000 population)	18.8	2019	●	↓
Life expectancy at birth (years)	64.1	2019	●	→
Adolescent fertility rate (births per 1,000 females aged 15 to 19)	54.8	2015	●	●
Births attended by skilled health personnel (%)	41.6	2017	●	●
Surviving infants who received 2 WHO-recommended vaccines (%)	51	2020	●	↓
Universal health coverage (UHC) index of service coverage (worst 0–100 best)	47	2019	●	→
Subjective well-being (average ladder score, worst 0–10 best)	3.6	2018	●	●
SDG4 – Quality Education				
Participation rate in pre-primary organized learning (% of children aged 4 to 6)	NA	NA	●	●
Net primary enrollment rate (%)	NA	NA	●	●
Lower secondary completion rate (%)	NA	NA	●	●
Literacy rate (% of population aged 15 to 24)	83.0	2016	●	●
SDG5 – Gender Equality				
Demand for family planning satisfied by modern methods (% of females aged 15 to 49)	45.4	2017	●	→
Ratio of female-to-male mean years of education received (%)	65.2	2019	●	↗
Ratio of female-to-male labor force participation rate (%)	87.5	2020	●	↑
Seats held by women in national parliament (%)	2.5	2019	●	↓
SDG6 – Clean Water and Sanitation				
Population using at least basic drinking water services (%)	66.7	2020	●	→
Population using at least basic sanitation services (%)	37.1	2020	●	→
Freshwater withdrawal (% of available freshwater resources)	13.4	2018	●	●
Anthropogenic wastewater that receives treatment (%)	0.0	2018	●	●
Scarce water consumption embodied in imports (m^3 H_2O eq/capita)	338.0	2018	●	●
SDG7 – Affordable and Clean Energy				
Population with access to electricity (%)	45.4	2019	●	→
Population with access to clean fuels and technology for cooking (%)	4.3	2019	●	→
CO_2 emissions from fuel combustion per total electricity output ($MtCO_2$/TWh)	3.5	2019	●	→
Share of renewable energy in total primary energy supply (%)	77.6	2019	●	↑
SDG8 – Decent Work and Economic Growth				
Adjusted GDP growth (%)	-6.9	2020	●	●
Victims of modern slavery (per 1,000 population)	5.6	2018	●	●
Adults with an account at a bank or other financial institution or with a mobile-money-service provider (% of population aged 15 or over)	32.6	2017	●	↑
Unemployment rate (% of total labor force)	15.4	2022	●	↓
Fundamental labor rights are effectively guaranteed (worst 0–1 best)	0.5	2020	●	●
Fatal work-related accidents embodied in imports (per 100,000 population)	0.0	2015	●	↑

* Imputed data point

SDG9 – Industry, Innovation and Infrastructure	Value	Year	Rating	Trend
Population using the internet (%)	34.5	2020	●	↗
Mobile broadband subscriptions (per 100 population)	27.2	2019	●	↑
Logistics Performance Index: Quality of trade and transport-related infrastructure (worst 1–5 best)	1.9	2018	●	↓
The Times Higher Education Universities Ranking: Average score of top 3 universities (worst 0–100 best)	* 0.0	2022	●	●
Articles published in academic journals (per 1,000 population)	0.0	2020	●	→
Expenditure on research and development (% of GDP)	NA	NA	●	●
SDG10 – Reduced Inequalities				
Gini coefficient	41.1	2012	●	●
Palma ratio	2.0	2018	●	●
SDG11 – Sustainable Cities and Communities				
Proportion of urban population living in slums (%)	77.8	2018	●	↓
Annual mean concentration of particulate matter of less than 2.5 microns in diameter (PM2.5) (μg/m³)	15.3	2019	●	↗
Access to improved water source, piped (% of urban population)	15.3	2020	●	↓
Satisfaction with public transport (%)	30.0	2018	●	●
SDG12 – Responsible Consumption and Production				
Municipal solid waste (kg/capita/day)	0.6	2015	●	●
Electronic waste (kg/capita)	NA	NA	●	●
Production-based SO_2 emissions (kg/capita)	2.0	2018	●	●
SO_2 emissions embodied in imports (kg/capita)	0.3	2018	●	●
Production-based nitrogen emissions (kg/capita)	8.6	2015	●	↑
Nitrogen emissions embodied in imports (kg/capita)	0.2	2015	●	↑
Exports of plastic waste (kg/capita)	NA	NA	●	●
SDG13 – Climate Action				
CO_2 emissions from fossil fuel combustion and cement production (tCO_2/capita)	0.3	2020	●	↑
CO_2 emissions embodied in imports (tCO_2/capita)	0.1	2018	●	↑
CO_2 emissions embodied in fossil fuel exports (kg/capita)	0.0	2020	●	●
SDG14 – Life Below Water				
Mean area that is protected in marine sites important to biodiversity (%)	29.3	2020	●	→
Ocean Health Index: Clean Waters score (worst 0–100 best)	41.9	2020	●	→
Fish caught from overexploited or collapsed stocks (% of total catch)	7.7	2018	●	↑
Fish caught by trawling or dredging (%)	0.0	2018	●	↑
Fish caught that are then discarded (%)	0.0	2018	●	↑
Marine biodiversity threats embodied in imports (per million population)	0.0	2018	●	●
SDG15 – Life on Land				
Mean area that is protected in terrestrial sites important to biodiversity (%)	29.4	2020	●	→
Mean area that is protected in freshwater sites important to biodiversity (%)	0.0	2020	●	→
Red List Index of species survival (worst 0–1 best)	0.7	2021	●	↓
Permanent deforestation (% of forest area, 5-year average)	0.3	2020	●	↑
Terrestrial and freshwater biodiversity threats embodied in imports (per million population)	0.0	2018	●	●
SDG16 – Peace, Justice and Strong Institutions				
Homicides (per 100,000 population)	6.7	2018	●	↑
Unsentenced detainees (% of prison population)	66.8	2018	●	↗
Population who feel safe walking alone at night in the city or area where they live (%)	49	2018	●	●
Property Rights (worst 1–7 best)	2.4	2020	●	↓
Birth registrations with civil authority (% of children under age 5)	84.8	2020	●	●
Corruption Perception Index (worst 0–100 best)	20	2021	●	→
Children involved in child labor (% of population aged 5 to 14)	35.5	2019	●	●
Exports of major conventional weapons (TIV constant million USD per 100,000 population)	* 0.0	2020	●	●
Press Freedom Index (best 0–100 worst)	31.1	2021	●	↓
Access to and affordability of justice (worst 0–1 best)	0.4	2020	●	●
SDG17 – Partnerships for the Goals				
Government spending on health and education (% of GDP)	2.2	2019	●	↓
For high-income and all OECD DAC countries: International concessional public finance, including official development assistance (% of GNI)	NA	NA	●	●
Other countries: Government revenue excluding grants (% of GDP)	NA	NA	●	●
Corporate Tax Haven Score (best 0–100 worst)	* 0.0	2019	●	●
Statistical Performance Index (worst 0–100 best)	37.5	2019	●	→

5. Country Profiles

HONDURAS

Latin America and the Caribbean

OVERALL PERFORMANCE

COUNTRY RANKING

HONDURAS

112 /163

COUNTRY SCORE

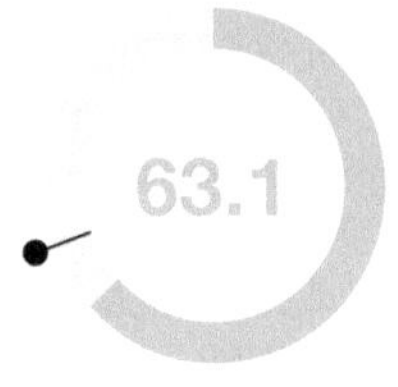

REGIONAL AVERAGE: 69.5

AVERAGE PERFORMANCE BY SDG

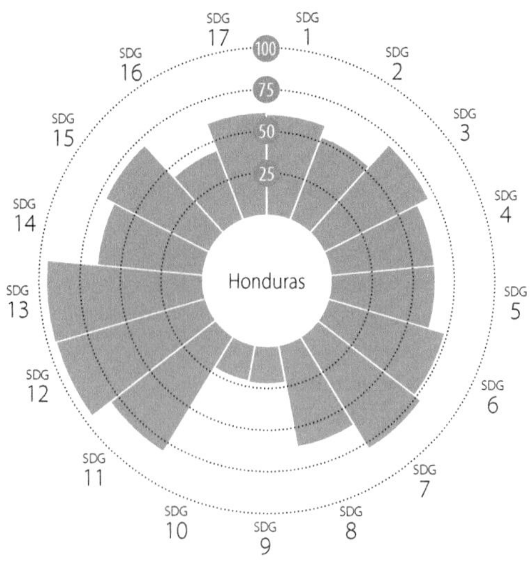

SDG DASHBOARDS AND TRENDS

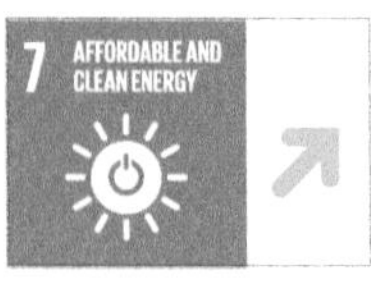
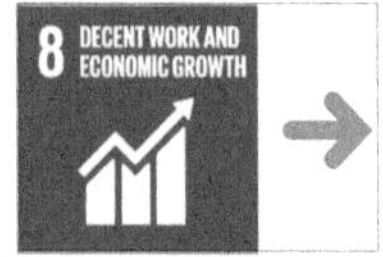

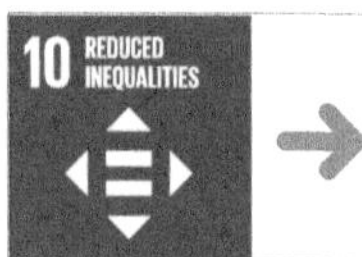

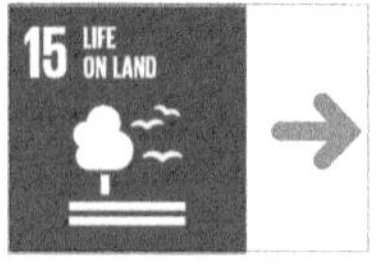

Major challenges | Significant challenges | Challenges remain | SDG achieved | Information unavailable

Decreasing | Stagnating | Moderately improving | On track or maintaining SDG achievement | Information unavailable

Note: The full title of each SDG is available here: https://sustainabledevelopment.un.org/topics/sustainabledevelopmentgoals

INTERNATIONAL SPILLOVER INDEX

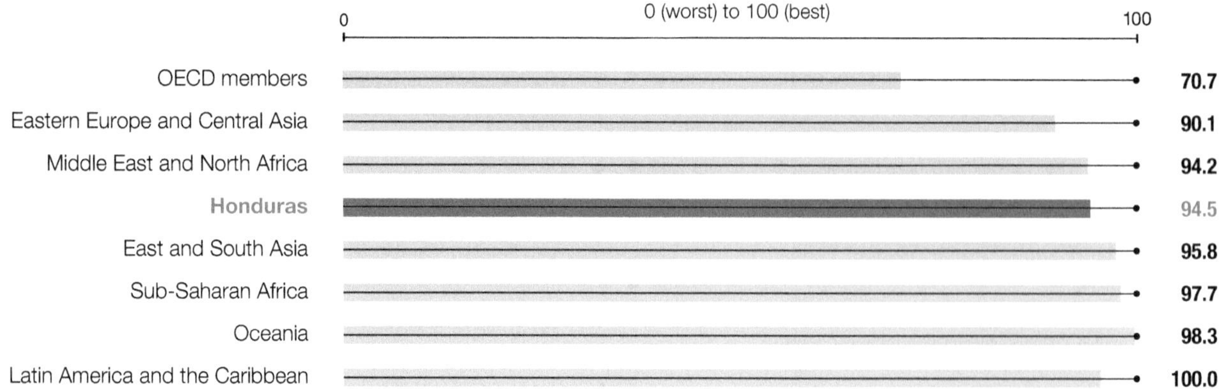

Region	Score
OECD members	70.7
Eastern Europe and Central Asia	90.1
Middle East and North Africa	94.2
Honduras	94.5
East and South Asia	95.8
Sub-Saharan Africa	97.7
Oceania	98.3
Latin America and the Caribbean	100.0

STATISTICAL PERFORMANCE INDEX

0 (worst) to 100 (best)

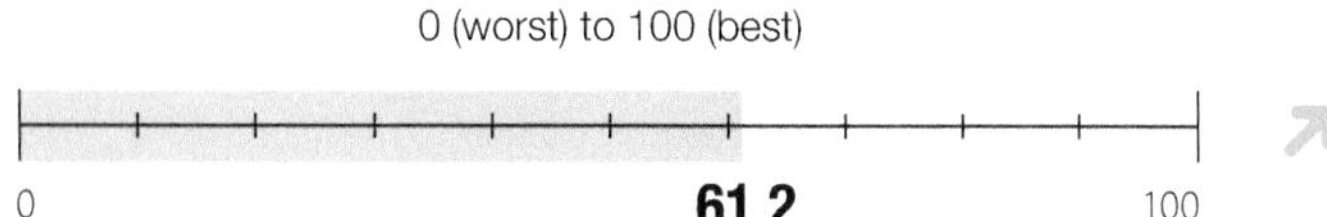

MISSING DATA IN SDG INDEX

1%

SDG1 – No Poverty	Value	Year	Rating	Trend
Poverty headcount ratio at \$1.90/day (%)	16.8	2022	●	→
Poverty headcount ratio at \$3.20/day (%)	29.5	2022	●	→
SDG2 – Zero Hunger				
Prevalence of undernourishment (%)	13.5	2019	●	↗
Prevalence of stunting in children under 5 years of age (%)	22.6	2012	●	→
Prevalence of wasting in children under 5 years of age (%)	1.4	2012	●	↑
Prevalence of obesity, BMI ≥ 30 (% of adult population)	21.4	2016	●	↓
Human Trophic Level (best 2–3 worst)	2.3	2017	●	↗
Cereal yield (tonnes per hectare of harvested land)	1.8	2018	●	→
Sustainable Nitrogen Management Index (best 0–1.41 worst)	1.0	2015	●	↓
Exports of hazardous pesticides (tonnes per million population)	31.2	2019	●	●
SDG3 – Good Health and Well-Being				
Maternal mortality rate (per 100,000 live births)	65	2017	●	↑
Neonatal mortality rate (per 1,000 live births)	8.8	2020	●	↑
Mortality rate, under-5 (per 1,000 live births)	16.2	2020	●	↑
Incidence of tuberculosis (per 100,000 population)	30.0	2020	●	↑
New HIV infections (per 1,000 uninfected population)	0.1	2020	●	↑
Age-standardized death rate due to cardiovascular disease, cancer, diabetes, or chronic respiratory disease in adults aged 30–70 years (%)	18.7	2019	●	↑
Age-standardized death rate attributable to household air pollution and ambient air pollution (per 100,000 population)	61	2016	●	●
Traffic deaths (per 100,000 population)	16.1	2019	●	↓
Life expectancy at birth (years)	71.9	2019	●	↗
Adolescent fertility rate (births per 1,000 females aged 15 to 19)	88.7	2014	●	●
Births attended by skilled health personnel (%)	74.0	2017	●	↗
Surviving infants who received 2 WHO-recommended vaccines (%)	80	2020	●	↓
Universal health coverage (UHC) index of service coverage (worst 0–100 best)	63	2019	●	↗
Subjective well-being (average ladder score, worst 0–10 best)	6.1	2021	●	↑
SDG4 – Quality Education				
Participation rate in pre-primary organized learning (% of children aged 4 to 6)	75.8	2020	●	→
Net primary enrollment rate (%)	84.0	2020	●	↗
Lower secondary completion rate (%)	43.2	2020	●	↓
Literacy rate (% of population aged 15 to 24)	96.1	2019	●	↑
SDG5 – Gender Equality				
Demand for family planning satisfied by modern methods (% of females aged 15 to 49)	76.0	2012	●	↑
Ratio of female-to-male mean years of education received (%)	101.5	2019	●	↑
Ratio of female-to-male labor force participation rate (%)	53.0	2020	●	↓
Seats held by women in national parliament (%)	21.1	2020	●	↓
SDG6 – Clean Water and Sanitation				
Population using at least basic drinking water services (%)	95.7	2020	●	↑
Population using at least basic sanitation services (%)	83.8	2020	●	↗
Freshwater withdrawal (% of available freshwater resources)	4.6	2018	●	●
Anthropogenic wastewater that receives treatment (%)	3.2	2018	●	●
Scarce water consumption embodied in imports (m^3 H_2O eq/capita)	1485.3	2018	●	●
SDG7 – Affordable and Clean Energy				
Population with access to electricity (%)	92.8	2019	●	↑
Population with access to clean fuels and technology for cooking (%)	44.9	2019	●	→
CO_2 emissions from fuel combustion per total electricity output ($MtCO_2$/TWh)	1.0	2019	●	↑
Share of renewable energy in total primary energy supply (%)	47.5	2019	●	↑
SDG8 – Decent Work and Economic Growth				
Adjusted GDP growth (%)	-6.3	2020	●	●
Victims of modern slavery (per 1,000 population)	3.4	2018	●	●
Adults with an account at a bank or other financial institution or with a mobile-money-service provider (% of population aged 15 or over)	45.3	2017	●	↑
Unemployment rate (% of total labor force)	8.4	2022	●	↓
Fundamental labor rights are effectively guaranteed (worst 0–1 best)	0.5	2020	●	↓
Fatal work-related accidents embodied in imports (per 100,000 population)	0.2	2015	●	↑

* Imputed data point

SDG9 – Industry, Innovation and Infrastructure	Value	Year	Rating	Trend
Population using the internet (%)	42.1	2020	●	↗
Mobile broadband subscriptions (per 100 population)	45.1	2019	●	↑
Logistics Performance Index: Quality of trade and transport-related infrastructure (worst 1–5 best)	2.5	2018	●	↑
The Times Higher Education Universities Ranking: Average score of top 3 universities (worst 0–100 best)	* 0.0	2022	●	●
Articles published in academic journals (per 1,000 population)	0.0	2020	●	→
Expenditure on research and development (% of GDP)	0.0	2017	●	→
SDG10 – Reduced Inequalities				
Gini coefficient	48.2	2019	●	→
Palma ratio	3.8	2018	●	●
SDG11 – Sustainable Cities and Communities				
Proportion of urban population living in slums (%)	40.5	2018	●	↓
Annual mean concentration of particulate matter of less than 2.5 microns in diameter (PM2.5) (μg/m³)	18.8	2019	●	↑
Access to improved water source, piped (% of urban population)	96.7	2020	●	↑
Satisfaction with public transport (%)	73.0	2021	●	↑
SDG12 – Responsible Consumption and Production				
Municipal solid waste (kg/capita/day)	0.6	2016	●	●
Electronic waste (kg/capita)	2.6	2019	●	●
Production-based SO_2 emissions (kg/capita)	8.8	2018	●	●
SO_2 emissions embodied in imports (kg/capita)	0.9	2018	●	●
Production-based nitrogen emissions (kg/capita)	6.7	2015	●	↑
Nitrogen emissions embodied in imports (kg/capita)	1.5	2015	●	↑
Exports of plastic waste (kg/capita)	0.3	2019	●	●
SDG13 – Climate Action				
CO_2 emissions from fossil fuel combustion and cement production (tCO_2/capita)	1.0	2020	●	↑
CO_2 emissions embodied in imports (tCO_2/capita)	0.3	2018	●	↑
CO_2 emissions embodied in fossil fuel exports (kg/capita)	0.0	2019	●	●
SDG14 – Life Below Water				
Mean area that is protected in marine sites important to biodiversity (%)	41.0	2020	●	→
Ocean Health Index: Clean Waters score (worst 0–100 best)	59.2	2020	●	↓
Fish caught from overexploited or collapsed stocks (% of total catch)	13.6	2018	●	↑
Fish caught by trawling or dredging (%)	0.7	2006	●	●
Fish caught that are then discarded (%)	15.4	2018	●	↓
Marine biodiversity threats embodied in imports (per million population)	0.1	2018	●	●
SDG15 – Life on Land				
Mean area that is protected in terrestrial sites important to biodiversity (%)	72.3	2020	●	→
Mean area that is protected in freshwater sites important to biodiversity (%)	99.4	2020	●	↑
Red List Index of species survival (worst 0–1 best)	0.7	2021	●	↓
Permanent deforestation (% of forest area, 5-year average)	0.8	2020	●	↑
Terrestrial and freshwater biodiversity threats embodied in imports (per million population)	0.6	2018	●	●
SDG16 – Peace, Justice and Strong Institutions				
Homicides (per 100,000 population)	36.3	2020	●	↑
Unsentenced detainees (% of prison population)	54.1	2018	●	→
Population who feel safe walking alone at night in the city or area where they live (%)	53	2021	●	↗
Property Rights (worst 1–7 best)	3.3	2020	●	↓
Birth registrations with civil authority (% of children under age 5)	93.6	2020	●	●
Corruption Perception Index (worst 0–100 best)	23	2021	●	↓
Children involved in child labor (% of population aged 5 to 14)	NA	NA	●	●
Exports of major conventional weapons (TIV constant million USD per 100,000 population)	* 0.0	2020	●	●
Press Freedom Index (best 0–100 worst)	49.4	2021	●	↓
Access to and affordability of justice (worst 0–1 best)	0.5	2020	●	→
SDG17 – Partnerships for the Goals				
Government spending on health and education (% of GDP)	7.8	2019	●	↓
For high-income and all OECD DAC countries: International concessional public finance, including official development assistance (% of GNI)	NA	NA	●	●
Other countries: Government revenue excluding grants (% of GDP)	23.4	2015	●	●
Corporate Tax Haven Score (best 0–100 worst)	* 0.0	2019	●	●
Statistical Performance Index (worst 0–100 best)	61.2	2019	●	↗

HUNGARY

OECD Countries

OVERALL PERFORMANCE

COUNTRY RANKING

HUNGARY

21 /163

COUNTRY SCORE

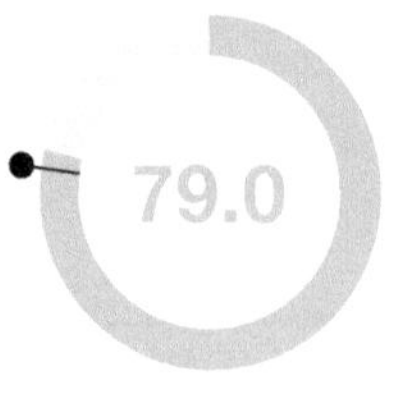

REGIONAL AVERAGE: 77.2

AVERAGE PERFORMANCE BY SDG

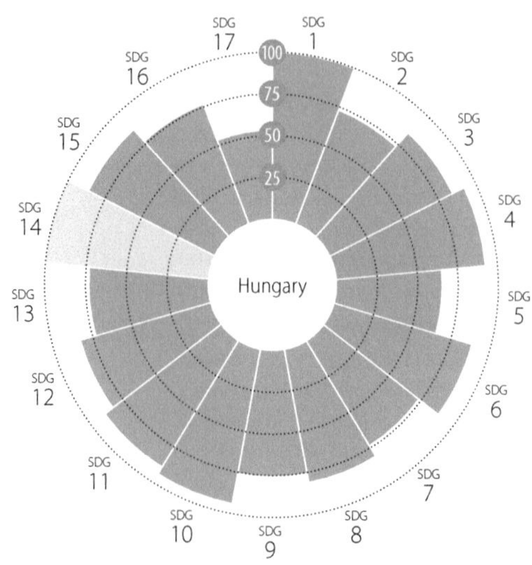

SDG DASHBOARDS AND TRENDS

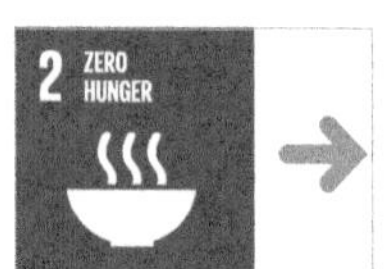

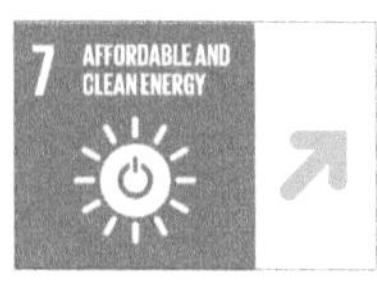

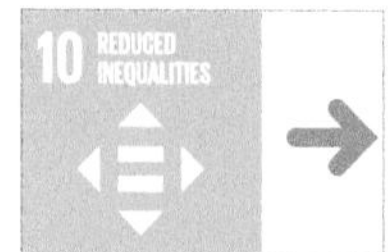

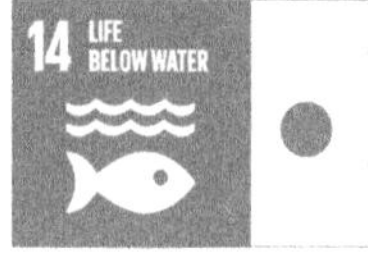

Major challenges | Significant challenges | Challenges remain | SDG achieved | Information unavailable

Decreasing | Stagnating | Moderately improving | On track or maintaining SDG achievement | Information unavailable

Note: The full title of each SDG is available here: https://sustainabledevelopment.un.org/topics/sustainabledevelopmentgoals

INTERNATIONAL SPILLOVER INDEX

STATISTICAL PERFORMANCE INDEX

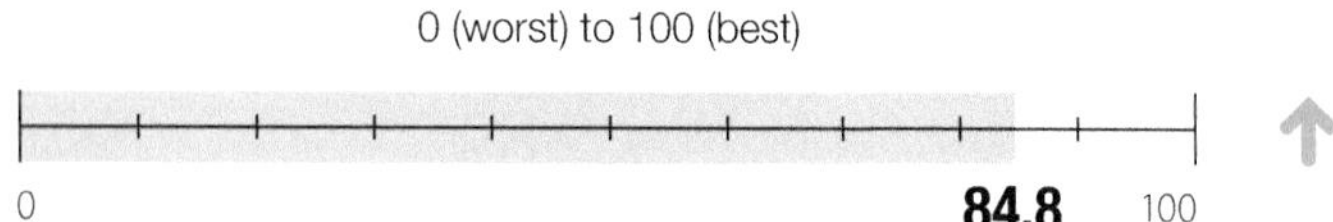

MISSING DATA IN SDG INDEX

0%

HUNGARY

Performance by Indicator

SDG1 – No Poverty

Indicator		Value	Year	Rating	Trend
Poverty headcount ratio at \$1.90/day (%)		0.4	2022	●	↑
Poverty headcount ratio at \$3.20/day (%)		0.6	2022	●	↑
Poverty rate after taxes and transfers (%)		9.2	2019	●	↑

SDG2 – Zero Hunger

Indicator		Value	Year	Rating	Trend
Prevalence of undernourishment (%)		2.5	2019	●	↑
Prevalence of stunting in children under 5 years of age (%)	*	2.6	2019	●	↑
Prevalence of wasting in children under 5 years of age (%)	*	0.7	2019	●	↑
Prevalence of obesity, BMI ≥ 30 (% of adult population)		26.4	2016	●	↓
Human Trophic Level (best 2–3 worst)		2.4	2017	●	↓
Cereal yield (tonnes per hectare of harvested land)		6.3	2018	●	↑
Sustainable Nitrogen Management Index (best 0–1.41 worst)		0.4	2015	●	→
Yield gap closure (% of potential yield)		64.1	2018	●	●
Exports of hazardous pesticides (tonnes per million population)		4.7	2019	●	●

SDG3 – Good Health and Well-Being

Indicator		Value	Year	Rating	Trend
Maternal mortality rate (per 100,000 live births)		12	2017	●	↑
Neonatal mortality rate (per 1,000 live births)		2.1	2020	●	↑
Mortality rate, under-5 (per 1,000 live births)		4.0	2020	●	↑
Incidence of tuberculosis (per 100,000 population)		4.6	2020	●	↑
New HIV infections (per 1,000 uninfected population)		1.0	2020	●	→
Age-standardized death rate due to cardiovascular disease, cancer, diabetes, or chronic respiratory disease in adults aged 30–70 years (%)		22.1	2019	●	→
Age-standardized death rate attributable to household air pollution and ambient air pollution (per 100,000 population)		39	2016	●	●
Traffic deaths (per 100,000 population)		7.7	2019	●	↑
Life expectancy at birth (years)		76.4	2019	●	↗
Adolescent fertility rate (births per 1,000 females aged 15 to 19)		22.0	2018	●	↑
Births attended by skilled health personnel (%)		99.7	2017	●	↑
Surviving infants who received 2 WHO-recommended vaccines (%)		99	2020	●	↑
Universal health coverage (UHC) index of service coverage (worst 0–100 best)		73	2019	●	↑
Subjective well-being (average ladder score, worst 0–10 best)		6.2	2021	●	↑
Gap in life expectancy at birth among regions (years)		4.2	2019	●	↓
Gap in self-reported health status by income (percentage points)		24.2	2020	●	↓
Daily smokers (% of population aged 15 and over)		24.9	2019	●	→

SDG4 – Quality Education

Indicator		Value	Year	Rating	Trend
Participation rate in pre-primary organized learning (% of children aged 4 to 6)		93.2	2019	●	↑
Net primary enrollment rate (%)		94.5	2019	●	↓
Lower secondary completion rate (%)		93.7	2019	●	↑
Literacy rate (% of population aged 15 to 24)		98.8	2014	●	●
Tertiary educational attainment (% of population aged 25 to 34)		30.7	2020	●	↓
PISA score (worst 0–600 best)		479.3	2018	●	↑
Variation in science performance explained by socio-economic status (%)		21.2	2018	●	→
Underachievers in science (% of 15-year-olds)		24.1	2018	●	↗

SDG5 – Gender Equality

Indicator		Value	Year	Rating	Trend
Demand for family planning satisfied by modern methods (% of females aged 15 to 49)	*	79.9	2022	●	↑
Ratio of female-to-male mean years of education received (%)		96.7	2019	●	↑
Ratio of female-to-male labor force participation rate (%)		73.2	2020	●	↑
Seats held by women in national parliament (%)		12.1	2020	●	→
Gender wage gap (% of male median wage)		9.9	2020	●	→

SDG6 – Clean Water and Sanitation

Indicator		Value	Year	Rating	Trend
Population using at least basic drinking water services (%)		100.0	2020	●	↑
Population using at least basic sanitation services (%)		98.0	2020	●	↑
Freshwater withdrawal (% of available freshwater resources)		7.7	2018	●	●
Anthropogenic wastewater that receives treatment (%)		53.8	2018	●	●
Scarce water consumption embodied in imports (m^3 H_2O eq/capita)		1437.2	2018	●	●
Population using safely managed water services (%)		92.6	2020	●	→
Population using safely managed sanitation services (%)		87.8	2020	●	↑

SDG7 – Affordable and Clean Energy

Indicator		Value	Year	Rating	Trend
Population with access to electricity (%)		100.0	2019	●	↑
Population with access to clean fuels and technology for cooking (%)		100.0	2019	●	↑
CO_2 emissions from fuel combustion per total electricity output ($MtCO_2$/TWh)		1.5	2019	●	→
Share of renewable energy in total primary energy supply (%)		10.6	2019	●	↓

SDG8 – Decent Work and Economic Growth

Indicator		Value	Year	Rating	Trend
Adjusted GDP growth (%)		0.9	2020	●	●
Victims of modern slavery (per 1,000 population)		3.7	2018	●	●
Adults with an account at a bank or other financial institution or with a mobile-money-service provider (% of population aged 15 or over)		74.9	2017	●	↑
Fundamental labor rights are effectively guaranteed (worst 0–1 best)		0.7	2020	●	↓
Fatal work-related accidents embodied in imports (per 100,000 population)		0.4	2015	●	↑
Employment-to-population ratio (%)		72.0	2020	●	↑
Youth not in employment, education or training (NEET) (% of population aged 15 to 29)		14.3	2020	●	↗

* Imputed data point

SDG9 – Industry, Innovation and Infrastructure

Indicator		Value	Year	Rating	Trend
Population using the internet (%)		84.8	2020	●	↑
Mobile broadband subscriptions (per 100 population)		71.9	2019	●	↑
Logistics Performance Index: Quality of trade and transport-related infrastructure (worst 1–5 best)		3.3	2018	●	↑
The Times Higher Education Universities Ranking: Average score of top 3 universities (worst 0–100 best)		37.9	2022	●	●
Articles published in academic journals (per 1,000 population)		1.3	2020	●	↑
Expenditure on research and development (% of GDP)		1.5	2018	●	↑
Researchers (per 1,000 employed population)		8.3	2019	●	↑
Triadic patent families filed (per million population)		5.0	2019	●	→
Gap in internet access by income (percentage points)		38.3	2020	●	↑
Female share of graduates from STEM fields at the tertiary level (%)		31.7	2017	●	↑

SDG10 – Reduced Inequalities

Indicator		Value	Year	Rating	Trend
Gini coefficient		29.6	2018	●	↑
Palma ratio		1.0	2019	●	→
Elderly poverty rate (% of population aged 66 or over)		13.2	2019	●	↓

SDG11 – Sustainable Cities and Communities

Indicator		Value	Year	Rating	Trend
Proportion of urban population living in slums (%)		0.0	2018	●	↑
Annual mean concentration of particulate matter of less than 2.5 microns in diameter (PM2.5) (μg/m³)		15.1	2019	●	↑
Access to improved water source, piped (% of urban population)		100.0	2020	●	↑
Satisfaction with public transport (%)		61.0	2021	●	→
Population with rent overburden (%)		8.2	2019	●	↓

SDG12 – Responsible Consumption and Production

Indicator		Value	Year	Rating	Trend
Electronic waste (kg/capita)		13.6	2019	●	●
Production-based SO_2 emissions (kg/capita)		12.0	2018	●	●
SO_2 emissions embodied in imports (kg/capita)		3.2	2018	●	●
Production-based nitrogen emissions (kg/capita)		20.5	2015	●	↓
Nitrogen emissions embodied in imports (kg/capita)		3.3	2015	●	↑
Exports of plastic waste (kg/capita)		0.0	2020	●	●
Non-recycled municipal solid waste (kg/capita/day)		0.7	2019	●	↑

SDG13 – Climate Action

Indicator		Value	Year	Rating	Trend
CO_2 emissions from fossil fuel combustion and cement production (tCO_2/capita)		5.0	2020	●	↓
CO_2 emissions embodied in imports (tCO_2/capita)		1.8	2018	●	↓
CO_2 emissions embodied in fossil fuel exports (kg/capita)		437.3	2020	●	●
Carbon Pricing Score at EUR60/tCO_2 (%, worst 0–100 best)		35.0	2018	●	↗

SDG14 – Life Below Water

Indicator		Value	Year	Rating	Trend
Mean area that is protected in marine sites important to biodiversity (%)		NA	NA	●	●
Ocean Health Index: Clean Waters score (worst 0–100 best)		NA	NA	●	●
Fish caught from overexploited or collapsed stocks (% of total catch)		NA	NA	●	●
Fish caught by trawling or dredging (%)		NA	NA	●	●
Fish caught that are then discarded (%)		NA	NA	●	●
Marine biodiversity threats embodied in imports (per million population)		0.0	2018	●	●

SDG15 – Life on Land

Indicator		Value	Year	Rating	Trend
Mean area that is protected in terrestrial sites important to biodiversity (%)		82.8	2020	●	→
Mean area that is protected in freshwater sites important to biodiversity (%)		84.8	2020	●	→
Red List Index of species survival (worst 0–1 best)		0.9	2021	●	→
Permanent deforestation (% of forest area, 5-year average)		0.0	2020	●	↑
Terrestrial and freshwater biodiversity threats embodied in imports (per million population)		0.4	2018	●	●

SDG16 – Peace, Justice and Strong Institutions

Indicator		Value	Year	Rating	Trend
Homicides (per 100,000 population)		0.8	2020	●	↑
Unsentenced detainees (% of prison population)		16.5	2019	●	↑
Population who feel safe walking alone at night in the city or area where they live (%)		72	2021	●	↑
Property Rights (worst 1–7 best)		3.9	2020	●	↑
Birth registrations with civil authority (% of children under age 5)		100.0	2020	●	●
Corruption Perception Index (worst 0–100 best)		43	2021	●	↓
Children involved in child labor (% of population aged 5 to 14)	*	0.0	2019	●	●
Exports of major conventional weapons (TIV constant million USD per 100,000 population)		0.0	2020	●	●
Press Freedom Index (best 0–100 worst)		31.8	2021	●	↓
Access to and affordability of justice (worst 0–1 best)		0.5	2020	●	→
Persons held in prison (per 100,000 population)		172.1	2019	●	→

SDG17 – Partnerships for the Goals

Indicator		Value	Year	Rating	Trend
Government spending on health and education (% of GDP)		8.9	2019	●	↓
For high-income and all OECD DAC countries: International concessional public finance, including official development assistance (% of GNI)		0.3	2021	●	↗
Other countries: Government revenue excluding grants (% of GDP)		NA	NA	●	●
Corporate Tax Haven Score (best 0–100 worst)		69.1	2019	●	●
Financial Secrecy Score (best 0–100 worst)		53.8	2020	●	●
Shifted profits of multinationals (US\$ billion)		6.3	2018	●	↑
Statistical Performance Index (worst 0–100 best)		84.8	2019	●	↑

5. Country Profiles

ICELAND

OECD Countries

OVERALL PERFORMANCE

COUNTRY RANKING

ICELAND

22/163

COUNTRY SCORE

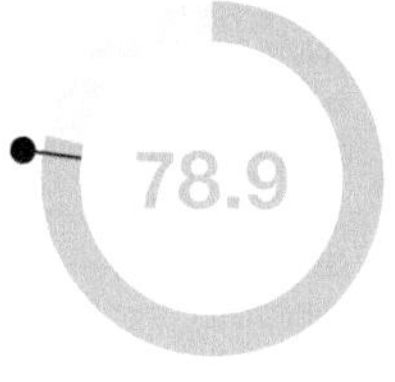

REGIONAL AVERAGE: 77.2

AVERAGE PERFORMANCE BY SDG

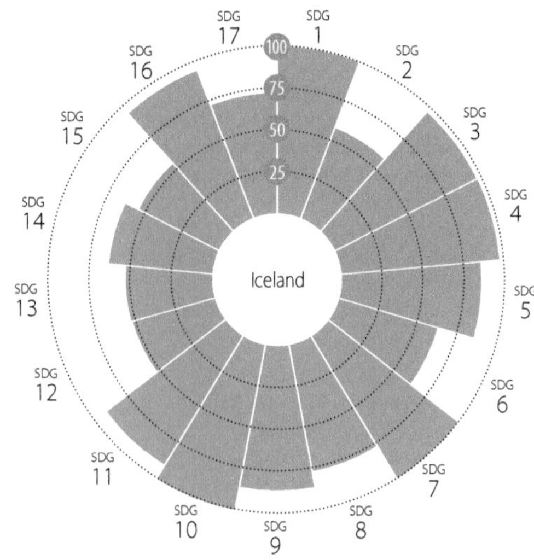

SDG DASHBOARDS AND TRENDS

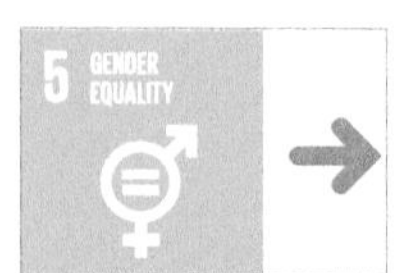

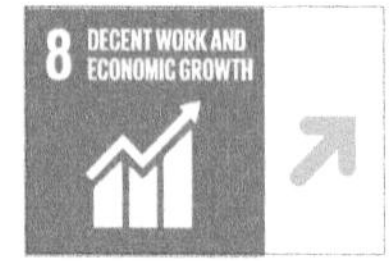

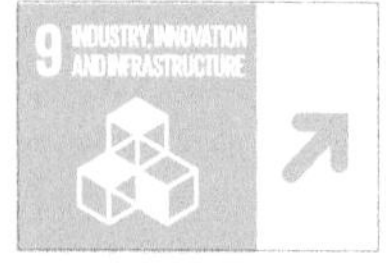

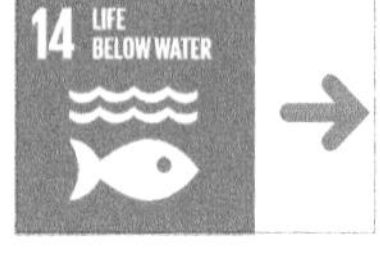

Major challenges | Significant challenges | Challenges remain | SDG achieved | Information unavailable

Decreasing | Stagnating | Moderately improving | On track or maintaining SDG achievement | Information unavailable

Note: The full title of each SDG is available here: https://sustainabledevelopment.un.org/topics/sustainabledevelopmentgoals

INTERNATIONAL SPILLOVER INDEX

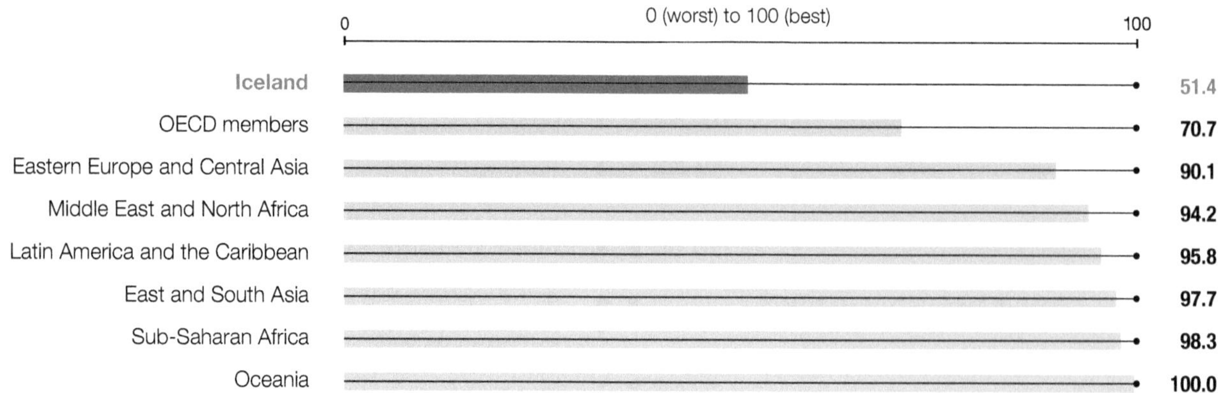

STATISTICAL PERFORMANCE INDEX

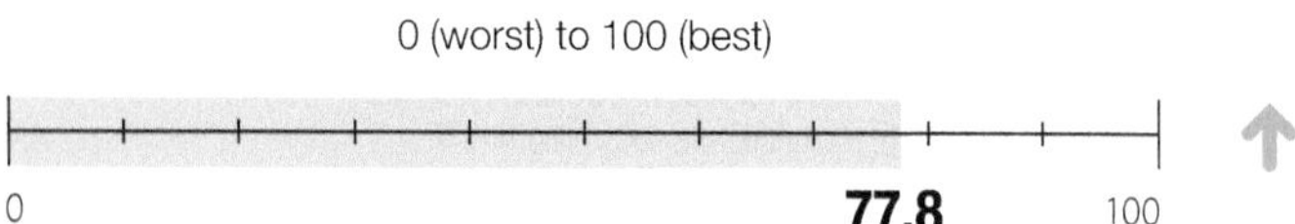

MISSING DATA IN SDG INDEX

9%

ICELAND

Performance by Indicator

SDG1 – No Poverty		Value	Year	Rating	Trend
Poverty headcount ratio at \$1.90/day (%)		0.1	2022	●	↑
Poverty headcount ratio at \$3.20/day (%)		0.1	2022	●	↑
Poverty rate after taxes and transfers (%)		4.9	2017	●	●
SDG2 – Zero Hunger					
Prevalence of undernourishment (%)		2.5	2019	●	↑
Prevalence of stunting in children under 5 years of age (%)	*	2.6	2019	●	↑
Prevalence of wasting in children under 5 years of age (%)	*	0.7	2019	●	↑
Prevalence of obesity, BMI ≥ 30 (% of adult population)		21.9	2016	●	↓
Human Trophic Level (best 2–3 worst)		2.6	2017	●	→
Cereal yield (tonnes per hectare of harvested land)		2.6	2018	●	↑
Sustainable Nitrogen Management Index (best 0–1.41 worst)		0.6	2015	●	→
Yield gap closure (% of potential yield)		NA	NA	●	●
Exports of hazardous pesticides (tonnes per million population)		NA	NA	●	●
SDG3 – Good Health and Well-Being					
Maternal mortality rate (per 100,000 live births)		4	2017	●	↑
Neonatal mortality rate (per 1,000 live births)		1.0	2020	●	↑
Mortality rate, under-5 (per 1,000 live births)		1.9	2020	●	↑
Incidence of tuberculosis (per 100,000 population)		2.8	2020	●	↑
New HIV infections (per 1,000 uninfected population)		0.0	2020	●	↑
Age-standardized death rate due to cardiovascular disease, cancer, diabetes, or chronic respiratory disease in adults aged 30–70 years (%)		8.7	2019	●	↑
Age-standardized death rate attributable to household air pollution and ambient air pollution (per 100,000 population)		9	2016	●	●
Traffic deaths (per 100,000 population)		2.1	2019	●	↑
Life expectancy at birth (years)		82.3	2019	●	↑
Adolescent fertility rate (births per 1,000 females aged 15 to 19)		5.3	2018	●	↑
Births attended by skilled health personnel (%)		98.2	2018	●	↑
Surviving infants who received 2 WHO-recommended vaccines (%)		93	2020	●	↑
Universal health coverage (UHC) index of service coverage (worst 0–100 best)		87	2019	●	↑
Subjective well-being (average ladder score, worst 0–10 best)		7.6	2021	●	↑
Gap in life expectancy at birth among regions (years)		0.6	2019	●	↑
Gap in self-reported health status by income (percentage points)		20.1	2018	●	↓
Daily smokers (% of population aged 15 and over)		7.3	2020	●	↑
SDG4 – Quality Education					
Participation rate in pre-primary organized learning (% of children aged 4 to 6)		95.0	2019	●	↑
Net primary enrollment rate (%)		99.8	2019	●	↑
Lower secondary completion rate (%)		101.0	2019	●	↑
Literacy rate (% of population aged 15 to 24)		NA	NA	●	●
Tertiary educational attainment (% of population aged 25 to 34)		38.3	2020	●	↗
PISA score (worst 0–600 best)		481.3	2018	●	→
Variation in science performance explained by socio-economic status (%)		8.9	2018	●	↑
Underachievers in science (% of 15-year-olds)		25.0	2018	●	→
SDG5 – Gender Equality					
Demand for family planning satisfied by modern methods (% of females aged 15 to 49)		NA	NA	●	●
Ratio of female-to-male mean years of education received (%)		96.9	2019	●	→
Ratio of female-to-male labor force participation rate (%)		89.0	2020	●	↑
Seats held by women in national parliament (%)		38.1	2020	●	↓
Gender wage gap (% of male median wage)		12.9	2018	●	↗
SDG6 – Clean Water and Sanitation					
Population using at least basic drinking water services (%)		100.0	2020	●	↑
Population using at least basic sanitation services (%)		98.8	2020	●	↑
Freshwater withdrawal (% of available freshwater resources)		0.4	2018	●	●
Anthropogenic wastewater that receives treatment (%)		15.5	2018	●	●
Scarce water consumption embodied in imports (m^3 H_2O eq/capita)		15785.4	2018	●	●
Population using safely managed water services (%)		100.0	2020	●	↑
Population using safely managed sanitation services (%)		83.7	2020	●	↑
SDG7 – Affordable and Clean Energy					
Population with access to electricity (%)		100.0	2019	●	↑
Population with access to clean fuels and technology for cooking (%)		100.0	2019	●	↑
CO_2 emissions from fuel combustion per total electricity output ($MtCO_2$/TWh)		0.1	2019	●	↑
Share of renewable energy in total primary energy supply (%)		88.9	2019	●	↑
SDG8 – Decent Work and Economic Growth					
Adjusted GDP growth (%)		-3.2	2020	●	●
Victims of modern slavery (per 1,000 population)		2.1	2018	●	●
Adults with an account at a bank or other financial institution or with a mobile-money-service provider (% of population aged 15 or over)		NA	NA	●	●
Fundamental labor rights are effectively guaranteed (worst 0–1 best)		NA	NA	●	●
Fatal work-related accidents embodied in imports (per 100,000 population)		1.8	2015	●	↗
Employment-to-population ratio (%)		80.3	2020	●	↑
Youth not in employment, education or training (NEET) (% of population aged 15 to 29)		9.4	2020	●	↑

* Imputed data point

SDG9 – Industry, Innovation and Infrastructure		Value	Year	Rating	Trend
Population using the internet (%)		99.0	2020	●	↑
Mobile broadband subscriptions (per 100 population)		123.2	2019	●	↑
Logistics Performance Index: Quality of trade and transport-related infrastructure (worst 1–5 best)		3.2	2018	●	↑
The Times Higher Education Universities Ranking: Average score of top 3 universities (worst 0–100 best)		44.8	2022	●	●
Articles published in academic journals (per 1,000 population)		5.1	2020	●	↑
Expenditure on research and development (% of GDP)		2.0	2018	●	↑
Researchers (per 1,000 employed population)		10.4	2017	●	●
Triadic patent families filed (per million population)		8.8	2019	●	↓
Gap in internet access by income (percentage points)		4.9	2017	●	●
Female share of graduates from STEM fields at the tertiary level (%)		35.2	2012	●	●
SDG10 – Reduced Inequalities					
Gini coefficient		26.1	2017	●	↑
Palma ratio		0.9	2017	●	●
Elderly poverty rate (% of population aged 66 or over)		3.1	2017	●	●
SDG11 – Sustainable Cities and Communities					
Proportion of urban population living in slums (%)	*	0.0	2018	●	↑
Annual mean concentration of particulate matter of less than 2.5 microns in diameter (PM2.5) (μg/m³)		6.1	2019	●	↑
Access to improved water source, piped (% of urban population)		100.0	2020	●	↑
Satisfaction with public transport (%)		59.0	2021	●	→
Population with rent overburden (%)		16.2	2018	●	↑
SDG12 – Responsible Consumption and Production					
Electronic waste (kg/capita)		21.4	2019	●	●
Production-based SO_2 emissions (kg/capita)		29.4	2018	●	●
SO_2 emissions embodied in imports (kg/capita)		13.1	2018	●	●
Production-based nitrogen emissions (kg/capita)		23.0	2015	●	↑
Nitrogen emissions embodied in imports (kg/capita)		12.7	2015	●	↓
Exports of plastic waste (kg/capita)		23.5	2021	●	●
Non-recycled municipal solid waste (kg/capita/day)		1.4	2017	●	●
SDG13 – Climate Action					
CO_2 emissions from fossil fuel combustion and cement production (tCO_2/capita)		8.6	2020	●	↗
CO_2 emissions embodied in imports (tCO_2/capita)		5.6	2018	●	↓
CO_2 emissions embodied in fossil fuel exports (kg/capita)		0.0	2017	●	●
Carbon Pricing Score at EUR60/tCO_2 (%, worst 0–100 best)		57.0	2018	●	↑
SDG14 – Life Below Water					
Mean area that is protected in marine sites important to biodiversity (%)		15.2	2020	●	→
Ocean Health Index: Clean Waters score (worst 0–100 best)		79.5	2020	●	↓
Fish caught from overexploited or collapsed stocks (% of total catch)		27.1	2018	●	↑
Fish caught by trawling or dredging (%)		26.0	2018	●	↓
Fish caught that are then discarded (%)		2.8	2018	●	↑
Marine biodiversity threats embodied in imports (per million population)		NA	NA	●	●
SDG15 – Life on Land					
Mean area that is protected in terrestrial sites important to biodiversity (%)		19.1	2020	●	→
Mean area that is protected in freshwater sites important to biodiversity (%)		35.9	2020	●	→
Red List Index of species survival (worst 0–1 best)		0.9	2021	●	↓
Permanent deforestation (% of forest area, 5-year average)		NA	NA	●	●
Terrestrial and freshwater biodiversity threats embodied in imports (per million population)		0.4	2018	●	●
SDG16 – Peace, Justice and Strong Institutions					
Homicides (per 100,000 population)		1.5	2020	●	↑
Unsentenced detainees (% of prison population)		7.4	2018	●	↑
Population who feel safe walking alone at night in the city or area where they live (%)		85	2021	●	↑
Property Rights (worst 1–7 best)		5.9	2020	●	↑
Birth registrations with civil authority (% of children under age 5)		100.0	2020	●	●
Corruption Perception Index (worst 0–100 best)		74	2021	●	↑
Children involved in child labor (% of population aged 5 to 14)	*	0.0	2019	●	●
Exports of major conventional weapons (TIV constant million USD per 100,000 population)	*	0.0	2020	●	●
Press Freedom Index (best 0–100 worst)		15.4	2021	●	↑
Access to and affordability of justice (worst 0–1 best)		NA	NA	●	●
Persons held in prison (per 100,000 population)		40.4	2018	●	↑
SDG17 – Partnerships for the Goals					
Government spending on health and education (% of GDP)		14.7	2019	●	↑
For high-income and all OECD DAC countries: International concessional public finance, including official development assistance (% of GNI)		0.3	2021	●	→
Other countries: Government revenue excluding grants (% of GDP)		NA	NA	●	●
Corporate Tax Haven Score (best 0–100 worst)	*	0.0	2019	●	●
Financial Secrecy Score (best 0–100 worst)		57.4	2020	●	●
Shifted profits of multinationals (US\$ billion)		0.6	2018	●	↑
Statistical Performance Index (worst 0–100 best)		77.8	2019	●	↑

5. Country Profiles

OVERALL PERFORMANCE

COUNTRY RANKING

INDIA

121/163

COUNTRY SCORE

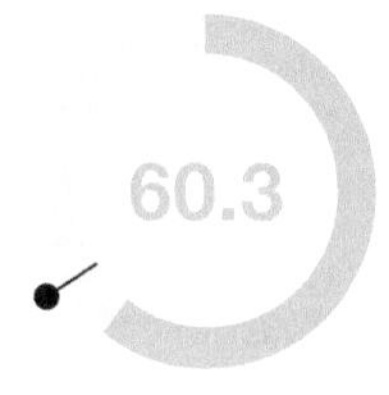

REGIONAL AVERAGE: 65.9

AVERAGE PERFORMANCE BY SDG

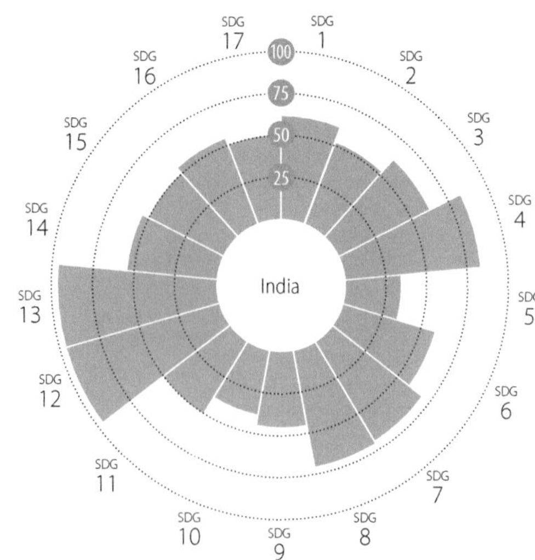

SDG DASHBOARDS AND TRENDS

Major challenges | Significant challenges | Challenges remain | SDG achieved | Information unavailable

Decreasing | Stagnating | Moderately improving | On track or maintaining SDG achievement | Information unavailable

Note: The full title of each SDG is available here: https://sustainabledevelopment.un.org/topics/sustainabledevelopmentgoals

INTERNATIONAL SPILLOVER INDEX

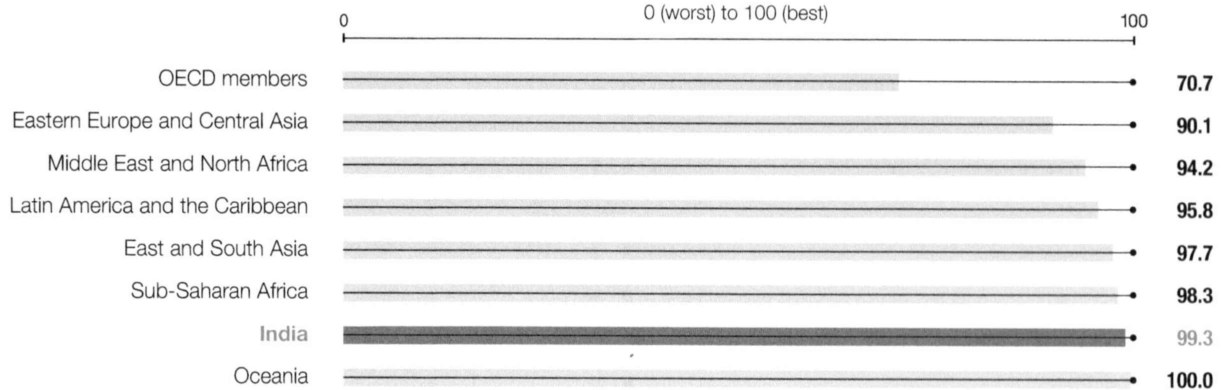

STATISTICAL PERFORMANCE INDEX

0 (worst) to 100 (best)

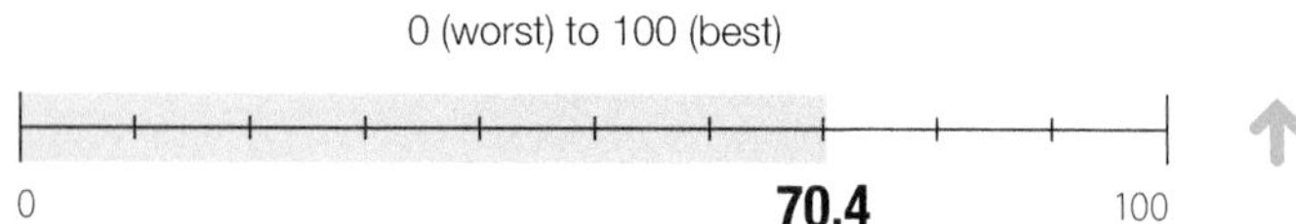

MISSING DATA IN SDG INDEX

1%

INDIA

Performance by Indicator

SDG1 – No Poverty	Value	Year	Rating	Trend
Poverty headcount ratio at \$1.90/day (%)	5.9	2022	●	↑
Poverty headcount ratio at \$3.20/day (%)	35.7	2022	●	↗
SDG2 – Zero Hunger				
Prevalence of undernourishment (%)	15.3	2019	●	↓
Prevalence of stunting in children under 5 years of age (%)	34.7	2017	●	→
Prevalence of wasting in children under 5 years of age (%)	17.3	2017	●	→
Prevalence of obesity, BMI ≥ 30 (% of adult population)	3.9	2016	●	↑
Human Trophic Level (best 2–3 worst)	2.2	2017	●	→
Cereal yield (tonnes per hectare of harvested land)	3.2	2018	●	↑
Sustainable Nitrogen Management Index (best 0–1.41 worst)	0.9	2015	●	→
Exports of hazardous pesticides (tonnes per million population)	0.5	2019	●	●
SDG3 – Good Health and Well-Being				
Maternal mortality rate (per 100,000 live births)	145	2017	●	↑
Neonatal mortality rate (per 1,000 live births)	20.3	2020	●	↑
Mortality rate, under-5 (per 1,000 live births)	32.6	2020	●	↑
Incidence of tuberculosis (per 100,000 population)	188.0	2020	●	→
New HIV infections (per 1,000 uninfected population)	0.0	2020	●	↑
Age-standardized death rate due to cardiovascular disease, cancer, diabetes, or chronic respiratory disease in adults aged 30–70 years (%)	21.9	2019	●	→
Age-standardized death rate attributable to household air pollution and ambient air pollution (per 100,000 population)	184	2016	●	●
Traffic deaths (per 100,000 population)	15.6	2019	●	→
Life expectancy at birth (years)	70.8	2019	●	↗
Adolescent fertility rate (births per 1,000 females aged 15 to 19)	12.2	2018	●	↑
Births attended by skilled health personnel (%)	81.4	2016	●	●
Surviving infants who received 2 WHO-recommended vaccines (%)	85	2020	●	→
Universal health coverage (UHC) index of service coverage (worst 0–100 best)	61	2019	●	↗
Subjective well-being (average ladder score, worst 0–10 best)	3.6	2021	●	↓
SDG4 – Quality Education				
Participation rate in pre-primary organized learning (% of children aged 4 to 6)	85.2	2020	●	●
Net primary enrollment rate (%)	94.6	2020	●	●
Lower secondary completion rate (%)	84.6	2020	●	→
Literacy rate (% of population aged 15 to 24)	91.7	2018	●	●
SDG5 – Gender Equality				
Demand for family planning satisfied by modern methods (% of females aged 15 to 49)	72.8	2016	●	↗
Ratio of female-to-male mean years of education received (%)	62.1	2019	●	→
Ratio of female-to-male labor force participation rate (%)	26.8	2020	●	↓
Seats held by women in national parliament (%)	14.4	2020	●	→
SDG6 – Clean Water and Sanitation				
Population using at least basic drinking water services (%)	90.5	2020	●	↗
Population using at least basic sanitation services (%)	71.3	2020	●	↑
Freshwater withdrawal (% of available freshwater resources)	66.5	2018	●	●
Anthropogenic wastewater that receives treatment (%)	2.2	2018	●	●
Scarce water consumption embodied in imports (m^3 H_2O eq/capita)	97.4	2018	●	●
SDG7 – Affordable and Clean Energy				
Population with access to electricity (%)	97.8	2019	●	↑
Population with access to clean fuels and technology for cooking (%)	64.2	2019	●	↑
CO_2 emissions from fuel combustion per total electricity output ($MtCO_2$/TWh)	1.7	2019	●	→
Share of renewable energy in total primary energy supply (%)	23.1	2019	●	↑
SDG8 – Decent Work and Economic Growth				
Adjusted GDP growth (%)	-3.6	2020	●	●
Victims of modern slavery (per 1,000 population)	6.1	2018	●	●
Adults with an account at a bank or other financial institution or with a mobile-money-service provider (% of population aged 15 or over)	79.9	2017	●	↑
Unemployment rate (% of total labor force)	5.4	2022	●	→
Fundamental labor rights are effectively guaranteed (worst 0–1 best)	0.5	2020	●	↑
Fatal work-related accidents embodied in imports (per 100,000 population)	0.1	2015	●	↑

* Imputed data point

SDG9 – Industry, Innovation and Infrastructure	Value	Year	Rating	Trend
Population using the internet (%)	43.0	2020	●	↑
Mobile broadband subscriptions (per 100 population)	47.0	2019	●	↑
Logistics Performance Index: Quality of trade and transport-related infrastructure (worst 1–5 best)	2.9	2018	●	↗
The Times Higher Education Universities Ranking: Average score of top 3 universities (worst 0–100 best)	45.7	2022	●	●
Articles published in academic journals (per 1,000 population)	0.1	2020	●	→
Expenditure on research and development (% of GDP)	0.7	2018	●	↓
SDG10 – Reduced Inequalities				
Gini coefficient	35.7	2011	●	●
Palma ratio	3.1	2011	●	●
SDG11 – Sustainable Cities and Communities				
Proportion of urban population living in slums (%)	34.8	2018	●	↓
Annual mean concentration of particulate matter of less than 2.5 microns in diameter (PM2.5) (μg/m³)	90.6	2019	●	↓
Access to improved water source, piped (% of urban population)	65.9	2020	●	↓
Satisfaction with public transport (%)	68.0	2021	●	→
SDG12 – Responsible Consumption and Production				
Municipal solid waste (kg/capita/day)	0.4	2018	●	●
Electronic waste (kg/capita)	2.4	2019	●	●
Production-based SO_2 emissions (kg/capita)	7.6	2018	●	●
SO_2 emissions embodied in imports (kg/capita)	0.2	2018	●	●
Production-based nitrogen emissions (kg/capita)	8.0	2015	●	↑
Nitrogen emissions embodied in imports (kg/capita)	0.4	2015	●	↑
Exports of plastic waste (kg/capita)	0.0	2021	●	●
SDG13 – Climate Action				
CO_2 emissions from fossil fuel combustion and cement production (tCO_2/capita)	1.8	2020	●	↑
CO_2 emissions embodied in imports (tCO_2/capita)	0.1	2018	●	↑
CO_2 emissions embodied in fossil fuel exports (kg/capita)	1.4	2020	●	●
SDG14 – Life Below Water				
Mean area that is protected in marine sites important to biodiversity (%)	19.2	2020	●	→
Ocean Health Index: Clean Waters score (worst 0–100 best)	29.5	2020	●	→
Fish caught from overexploited or collapsed stocks (% of total catch)	7.4	2018	●	↑
Fish caught by trawling or dredging (%)	54.9	2018	●	↓
Fish caught that are then discarded (%)	4.9	2018	●	↑
Marine biodiversity threats embodied in imports (per million population)	0.0	2018	●	●
SDG15 – Life on Land				
Mean area that is protected in terrestrial sites important to biodiversity (%)	20.7	2020	●	→
Mean area that is protected in freshwater sites important to biodiversity (%)	18.9	2020	●	→
Red List Index of species survival (worst 0–1 best)	0.7	2021	●	↓
Permanent deforestation (% of forest area, 5-year average)	0.0	2020	●	↑
Terrestrial and freshwater biodiversity threats embodied in imports (per million population)	0.1	2018	●	●
SDG16 – Peace, Justice and Strong Institutions				
Homicides (per 100,000 population)	3.0	2020	●	↗
Unsentenced detainees (% of prison population)	69.1	2019	●	↓
Population who feel safe walking alone at night in the city or area where they live (%)	62	2021	●	↓
Property Rights (worst 1–7 best)	3.7	2020	●	↓
Birth registrations with civil authority (% of children under age 5)	79.7	2020	●	●
Corruption Perception Index (worst 0–100 best)	40	2021	●	→
Children involved in child labor (% of population aged 5 to 14)	NA	NA	●	●
Exports of major conventional weapons (TIV constant million USD per 100,000 population)	0.0	2020	●	●
Press Freedom Index (best 0–100 worst)	46.6	2021	●	↓
Access to and affordability of justice (worst 0–1 best)	0.4	2020	●	↗
SDG17 – Partnerships for the Goals				
Government spending on health and education (% of GDP)	4.4	2019	●	→
For high-income and all OECD DAC countries: International concessional public finance, including official development assistance (% of GNI)	NA	NA	●	●
Other countries: Government revenue excluding grants (% of GDP)	13.2	2018	●	→
Corporate Tax Haven Score (best 0–100 worst)	* 0.0	2019	●	●
Statistical Performance Index (worst 0–100 best)	70.4	2019	●	↑

5. Country Profiles

INDONESIA

East and South Asia

OVERALL PERFORMANCE

COUNTRY RANKING

INDONESIA

82/163

COUNTRY SCORE

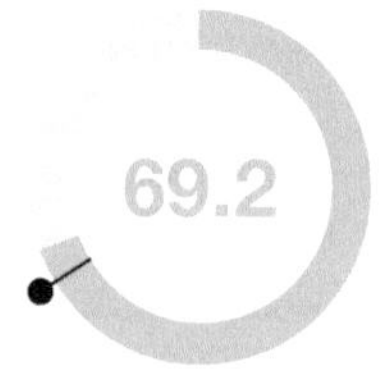

REGIONAL AVERAGE: 65.9

AVERAGE PERFORMANCE BY SDG

SDG DASHBOARDS AND TRENDS

Major challenges | Significant challenges | Challenges remain | SDG achieved | Information unavailable

Decreasing | Stagnating | Moderately improving | On track or maintaining SDG achievement | Information unavailable

Note: The full title of each SDG is available here: https://sustainabledevelopment.un.org/topics/sustainabledevelopmentgoals

INTERNATIONAL SPILLOVER INDEX

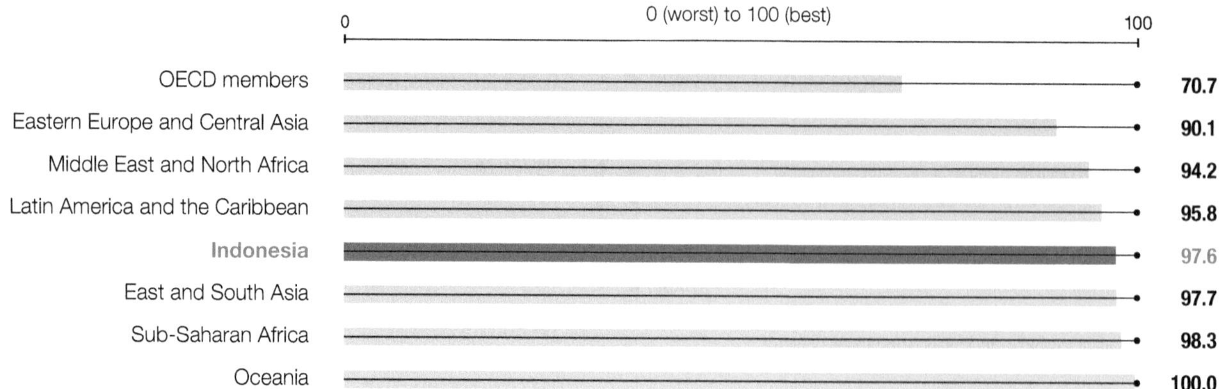

STATISTICAL PERFORMANCE INDEX

0 (worst) to 100 (best)

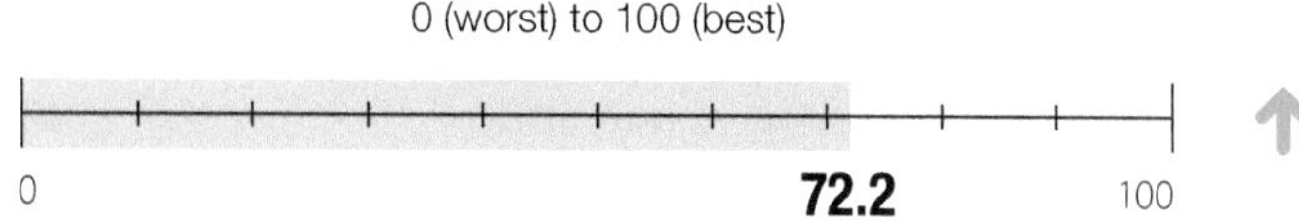

MISSING DATA IN SDG INDEX

1%

SDG1 – No Poverty	Value	Year	Rating	Trend
Poverty headcount ratio at $1.90/day (%)	1.8	2022	●	↑
Poverty headcount ratio at $3.20/day (%)	19.0	2022	●	↗

SDG2 – Zero Hunger	Value	Year	Rating	Trend
Prevalence of undernourishment (%)	6.5	2019	●	↑
Prevalence of stunting in children under 5 years of age (%)	30.8	2018	●	→
Prevalence of wasting in children under 5 years of age (%)	10.2	2018	●	→
Prevalence of obesity, BMI ≥ 30 (% of adult population)	6.9	2016	●	↑
Human Trophic Level (best 2–3 worst)	2.2	2017	●	↑
Cereal yield (tonnes per hectare of harvested land)	5.2	2018	●	↑
Sustainable Nitrogen Management Index (best 0–1.41 worst)	0.7	2015	●	→
Exports of hazardous pesticides (tonnes per million population)	15.9	2019	●	●

SDG3 – Good Health and Well-Being	Value	Year	Rating	Trend
Maternal mortality rate (per 100,000 live births)	177	2017	●	↗
Neonatal mortality rate (per 1,000 live births)	11.7	2020	●	↑
Mortality rate, under-5 (per 1,000 live births)	23.0	2020	●	↑
Incidence of tuberculosis (per 100,000 population)	301.0	2020	●	→
New HIV infections (per 1,000 uninfected population)	0.1	2020	●	↑
Age-standardized death rate due to cardiovascular disease, cancer, diabetes, or chronic respiratory disease in adults aged 30–70 years (%)	24.8	2019	●	→
Age-standardized death rate attributable to household air pollution and ambient air pollution (per 100,000 population)	112	2016	●	●
Traffic deaths (per 100,000 population)	11.3	2019	●	↗
Life expectancy at birth (years)	71.3	2019	●	→
Adolescent fertility rate (births per 1,000 females aged 15 to 19)	36.0	2016	●	●
Births attended by skilled health personnel (%)	94.7	2019	●	↑
Surviving infants who received 2 WHO-recommended vaccines (%)	76	2020	●	↓
Universal health coverage (UHC) index of service coverage (worst 0–100 best)	59	2019	●	↑
Subjective well-being (average ladder score, worst 0–10 best)	5.4	2021	●	↑

SDG4 – Quality Education	Value	Year	Rating	Trend
Participation rate in pre-primary organized learning (% of children aged 4 to 6)	95.8	2018	●	●
Net primary enrollment rate (%)	94.4	2018	●	●
Lower secondary completion rate (%)	90.0	2017	●	●
Literacy rate (% of population aged 15 to 24)	99.8	2020	●	↑

SDG5 – Gender Equality	Value	Year	Rating	Trend
Demand for family planning satisfied by modern methods (% of females aged 15 to 49)	77.0	2017	●	↑
Ratio of female-to-male mean years of education received (%)	90.7	2019	●	↗
Ratio of female-to-male labor force participation rate (%)	65.2	2020	●	↑
Seats held by women in national parliament (%)	20.3	2020	●	→

SDG6 – Clean Water and Sanitation	Value	Year	Rating	Trend
Population using at least basic drinking water services (%)	92.4	2020	●	↑
Population using at least basic sanitation services (%)	86.5	2020	●	↑
Freshwater withdrawal (% of available freshwater resources)	29.7	2018	●	●
Anthropogenic wastewater that receives treatment (%)	0.0	2018	●	●
Scarce water consumption embodied in imports (m^3 H_2O eq/capita)	351.0	2018	●	●

SDG7 – Affordable and Clean Energy	Value	Year	Rating	Trend
Population with access to electricity (%)	98.9	2019	●	↑
Population with access to clean fuels and technology for cooking (%)	82.4	2019	●	↑
CO_2 emissions from fuel combustion per total electricity output ($MtCO_2$/TWh)	2.1	2019	●	→
Share of renewable energy in total primary energy supply (%)	23.9	2019	●	↑

SDG8 – Decent Work and Economic Growth	Value	Year	Rating	Trend
Adjusted GDP growth (%)	-1.1	2020	●	●
Victims of modern slavery (per 1,000 population)	4.7	2018	●	●
Adults with an account at a bank or other financial institution or with a mobile-money-service provider (% of population aged 15 or over)	48.9	2017	●	↑
Unemployment rate (% of total labor force)	4.4	2022	●	↑
Fundamental labor rights are effectively guaranteed (worst 0–1 best)	0.6	2020	●	↗
Fatal work-related accidents embodied in imports (per 100,000 population)	0.1	2015	●	↑

SDG9 – Industry, Innovation and Infrastructure	Value	Year	Rating	Trend
Population using the internet (%)	53.7	2020	●	↑
Mobile broadband subscriptions (per 100 population)	81.2	2019	●	↑
Logistics Performance Index: Quality of trade and transport-related infrastructure (worst 1–5 best)	2.9	2018	●	→
The Times Higher Education Universities Ranking: Average score of top 3 universities (worst 0–100 best)	26.4	2022	●	●
Articles published in academic journals (per 1,000 population)	0.2	2020	●	↗
Expenditure on research and development (% of GDP)	0.2	2018	●	↓

SDG10 – Reduced Inequalities	Value	Year	Rating	Trend
Gini coefficient	38.2	2019	●	↗
Palma ratio	1.8	2018	●	●

SDG11 – Sustainable Cities and Communities	Value	Year	Rating	Trend
Proportion of urban population living in slums (%)	30.4	2018	●	↓
Annual mean concentration of particulate matter of less than 2.5 microns in diameter (PM2.5) (μg/m^3)	16.2	2019	●	→
Access to improved water source, piped (% of urban population)	44.6	2020	●	→
Satisfaction with public transport (%)	78.0	2021	●	↑

SDG12 – Responsible Consumption and Production	Value	Year	Rating	Trend
Municipal solid waste (kg/capita/day)	0.7	2016	●	●
Electronic waste (kg/capita)	6.1	2019	●	●
Production-based SO_2 emissions (kg/capita)	8.0	2018	●	●
SO_2 emissions embodied in imports (kg/capita)	0.5	2018	●	●
Production-based nitrogen emissions (kg/capita)	7.3	2015	●	↑
Nitrogen emissions embodied in imports (kg/capita)	1.0	2015	●	↑
Exports of plastic waste (kg/capita)	0.4	2020	●	●

SDG13 – Climate Action	Value	Year	Rating	Trend
CO_2 emissions from fossil fuel combustion and cement production (tCO_2/capita)	2.2	2020	●	→
CO_2 emissions embodied in imports (tCO_2/capita)	0.2	2018	●	↑
CO_2 emissions embodied in fossil fuel exports (kg/capita)	3121.1	2020	●	●

SDG14 – Life Below Water	Value	Year	Rating	Trend
Mean area that is protected in marine sites important to biodiversity (%)	25.5	2020	●	→
Ocean Health Index: Clean Waters score (worst 0–100 best)	58.2	2020	●	→
Fish caught from overexploited or collapsed stocks (% of total catch)	16.7	2018	●	↑
Fish caught by trawling or dredging (%)	38.3	2018	●	→
Fish caught that are then discarded (%)	4.4	2018	●	↑
Marine biodiversity threats embodied in imports (per million population)	0.0	2018	●	●

SDG15 – Life on Land	Value	Year	Rating	Trend
Mean area that is protected in terrestrial sites important to biodiversity (%)	25.9	2020	●	→
Mean area that is protected in freshwater sites important to biodiversity (%)	39.0	2020	●	→
Red List Index of species survival (worst 0–1 best)	0.8	2021	●	↓
Permanent deforestation (% of forest area, 5-year average)	0.7	2020	●	↑
Terrestrial and freshwater biodiversity threats embodied in imports (per million population)	0.2	2018	●	●

SDG16 – Peace, Justice and Strong Institutions	Value	Year	Rating	Trend
Homicides (per 100,000 population)	0.6	2004	●	●
Unsentenced detainees (% of prison population)	30.2	2017	●	●
Population who feel safe walking alone at night in the city or area where they live (%)	84	2021	●	↑
Property Rights (worst 1–7 best)	4.8	2020	●	↑
Birth registrations with civil authority (% of children under age 5)	74.4	2020	●	●
Corruption Perception Index (worst 0–100 best)	38	2021	●	→
Children involved in child labor (% of population aged 5 to 14)	NA	NA	●	●
Exports of major conventional weapons (TIV constant million USD per 100,000 population)	0.0	2020	●	●
Press Freedom Index (best 0–100 worst)	37.4	2021	●	↗
Access to and affordability of justice (worst 0–1 best)	0.5	2020	●	↓

SDG17 – Partnerships for the Goals	Value	Year	Rating	Trend
Government spending on health and education (% of GDP)	4.3	2019	●	↓
For high-income and all OECD DAC countries: International concessional public finance, including official development assistance (% of GNI)	NA	NA	●	●
Other countries: Government revenue excluding grants (% of GDP)	12.3	2019	●	↓
Corporate Tax Haven Score (best 0–100 worst)	* 0.0	2019	●	●
Statistical Performance Index (worst 0–100 best)	72.2	2019	●	↑

* Imputed data point

IRAN, ISLAMIC REPUBLIC OF

Middle East and North Africa

OVERALL PERFORMANCE

COUNTRY RANKING

IRAN, ISLAMIC REPUBLIC OF

88/163

COUNTRY SCORE

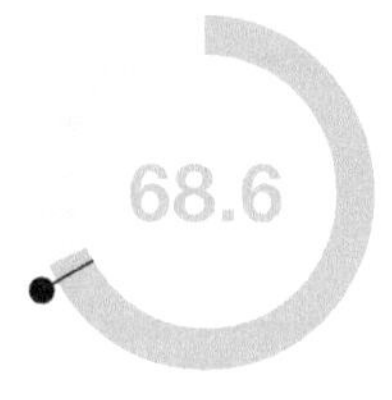

REGIONAL AVERAGE: 66.7

AVERAGE PERFORMANCE BY SDG

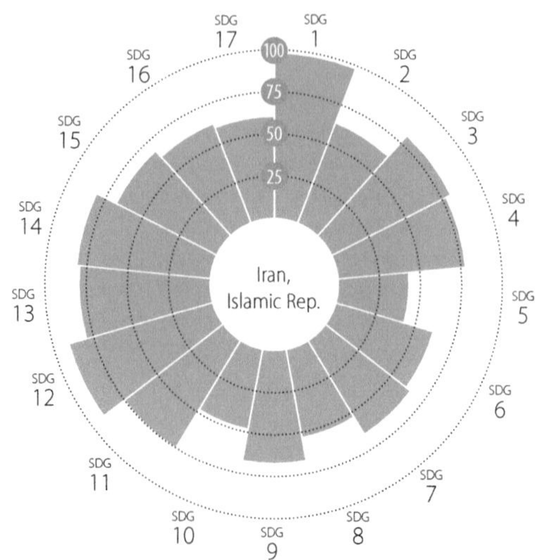

SDG DASHBOARDS AND TRENDS

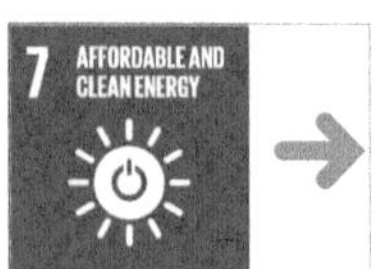

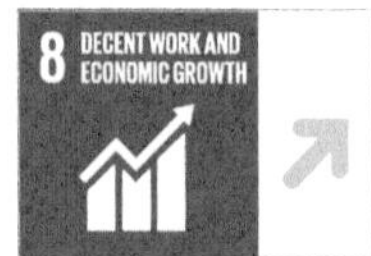

Information unavailable
Information unavailable

Note: The full title of each SDG is available here: https://sustainabledevelopment.un.org/topics/sustainabledevelopmentgoals

INTERNATIONAL SPILLOVER INDEX

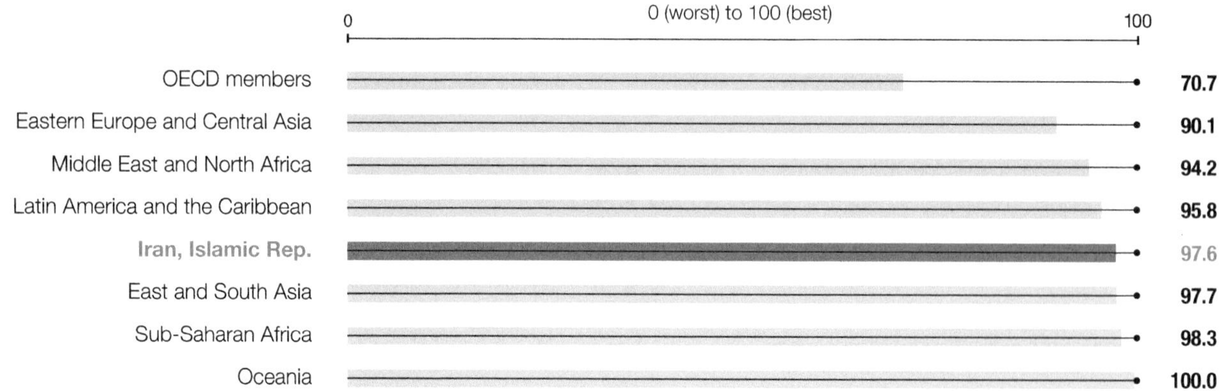

STATISTICAL PERFORMANCE INDEX

0 (worst) to 100 (best)

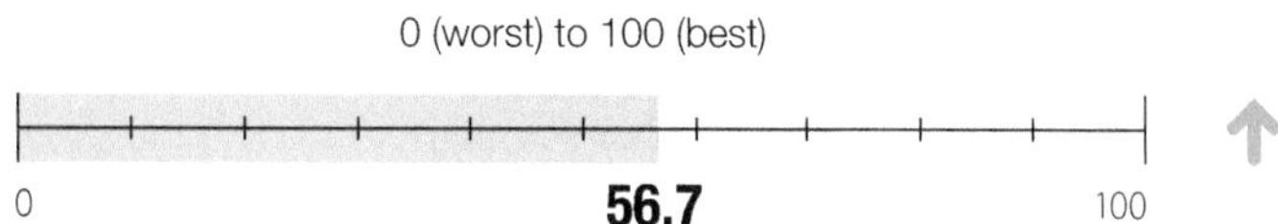

MISSING DATA IN SDG INDEX

2%

IRAN, ISLAMIC REPUBLIC OF Performance by Indicator

SDG1 – No Poverty	Value	Year	Rating	Trend
Poverty headcount ratio at $1.90/day (%)	0.1	2022	●	↑
Poverty headcount ratio at $3.20/day (%)	2.6	2022	●	→
SDG2 – Zero Hunger				
Prevalence of undernourishment (%)	5.5	2019	●	↑
Prevalence of stunting in children under 5 years of age (%)	6.8	2010	●	↑
Prevalence of wasting in children under 5 years of age (%)	4.0	2010	●	↑
Prevalence of obesity, BMI ≥ 30 (% of adult population)	25.8	2016	●	↓
Human Trophic Level (best 2–3 worst)	2.2	2017	●	↑
Cereal yield (tonnes per hectare of harvested land)	2.3	2018	●	↑
Sustainable Nitrogen Management Index (best 0–1.41 worst)	0.8	2015	●	→
Exports of hazardous pesticides (tonnes per million population)	0.0	2019	●	●
SDG3 – Good Health and Well-Being				
Maternal mortality rate (per 100,000 live births)	16	2017	●	↑
Neonatal mortality rate (per 1,000 live births)	8.3	2020	●	↑
Mortality rate, under-5 (per 1,000 live births)	12.9	2020	●	↑
Incidence of tuberculosis (per 100,000 population)	13.0	2020	●	↑
New HIV infections (per 1,000 uninfected population)	0.0	2020	●	↑
Age-standardized death rate due to cardiovascular disease, cancer, diabetes, or chronic respiratory disease in adults aged 30–70 years (%)	14.8	2019	●	↑
Age-standardized death rate attributable to household air pollution and ambient air pollution (per 100,000 population)	51	2016	●	●
Traffic deaths (per 100,000 population)	21.5	2019	●	→
Life expectancy at birth (years)	77.4	2019	●	↗
Adolescent fertility rate (births per 1,000 females aged 15 to 19)	31.1	2018	●	↑
Births attended by skilled health personnel (%)	99.0	2014	●	●
Surviving infants who received 2 WHO-recommended vaccines (%)	99	2020	●	↑
Universal health coverage (UHC) index of service coverage (worst 0–100 best)	77	2019	●	↑
Subjective well-being (average ladder score, worst 0–10 best)	4.8	2021	●	→
SDG4 – Quality Education				
Participation rate in pre-primary organized learning (% of children aged 4 to 6)	50.8	2016	●	●
Net primary enrollment rate (%)	99.8	2017	●	●
Lower secondary completion rate (%)	90.2	2017	●	●
Literacy rate (% of population aged 15 to 24)	98.1	2016	●	●
SDG5 – Gender Equality				
Demand for family planning satisfied by modern methods (% of females aged 15 to 49)	68.6	2011	●	↗
Ratio of female-to-male mean years of education received (%)	99.0	2019	●	↑
Ratio of female-to-male labor force participation rate (%)	20.4	2020	●	↓
Seats held by women in national parliament (%)	5.6	2020	●	→
SDG6 – Clean Water and Sanitation				
Population using at least basic drinking water services (%)	97.5	2020	●	↑
Population using at least basic sanitation services (%)	90.3	2020	●	↗
Freshwater withdrawal (% of available freshwater resources)	81.3	2018	●	●
Anthropogenic wastewater that receives treatment (%)	3.7	2018	●	●
Scarce water consumption embodied in imports (m^3 H_2O eq/capita)	664.9	2018	●	●
SDG7 – Affordable and Clean Energy				
Population with access to electricity (%)	100.0	2019	●	↑
Population with access to clean fuels and technology for cooking (%)	96.5	2019	●	↑
CO_2 emissions from fuel combustion per total electricity output ($MtCO_2$/TWh)	2.3	2019	●	→
Share of renewable energy in total primary energy supply (%)	0.7	2019	●	↓
SDG8 – Decent Work and Economic Growth				
Adjusted GDP growth (%)	-6.9	2020	●	●
Victims of modern slavery (per 1,000 population)	16.2	2018	●	●
Adults with an account at a bank or other financial institution or with a mobile-money-service provider (% of population aged 15 or over)	94.0	2017	●	↑
Unemployment rate (% of total labor force)	11.1	2022	●	→
Fundamental labor rights are effectively guaranteed (worst 0–1 best)	0.2	2020	●	→
Fatal work-related accidents embodied in imports (per 100,000 population)	0.2	2015	●	↑

SDG9 – Industry, Innovation and Infrastructure	Value	Year	Rating	Trend
Population using the internet (%)	84.1	2020	●	↑
Mobile broadband subscriptions (per 100 population)	80.2	2019	●	↑
Logistics Performance Index: Quality of trade and transport-related infrastructure (worst 1–5 best)	2.8	2018	●	●
The Times Higher Education Universities Ranking: Average score of top 3 universities (worst 0–100 best)	45.1	2022	●	●
Articles published in academic journals (per 1,000 population)	0.8	2020	●	↑
Expenditure on research and development (% of GDP)	0.8	2017	●	↑
SDG10 – Reduced Inequalities				
Gini coefficient	42.0	2018	●	↓
Palma ratio	1.9	2018	●	●
SDG11 – Sustainable Cities and Communities				
Proportion of urban population living in slums (%)	23.9	2018	●	●
Annual mean concentration of particulate matter of less than 2.5 microns in diameter (PM2.5) (μg/m^3)	39.2	2019	●	→
Access to improved water source, piped (% of urban population)	99.5	2020	●	↑
Satisfaction with public transport (%)	61.0	2021	●	↓
SDG12 – Responsible Consumption and Production				
Municipal solid waste (kg/capita/day)	0.6	2017	●	●
Electronic waste (kg/capita)	9.5	2019	●	●
Production-based SO_2 emissions (kg/capita)	11.1	2018	●	●
SO_2 emissions embodied in imports (kg/capita)	0.8	2018	●	●
Production-based nitrogen emissions (kg/capita)	9.5	2015	●	↑
Nitrogen emissions embodied in imports (kg/capita)	1.1	2015	●	↑
Exports of plastic waste (kg/capita)	0.2	2018	●	●
SDG13 – Climate Action				
CO_2 emissions from fossil fuel combustion and cement production (tCO_2/capita)	8.9	2020	●	↓
CO_2 emissions embodied in imports (tCO_2/capita)	0.3	2018	●	↑
CO_2 emissions embodied in fossil fuel exports (kg/capita)	4726.6	2018	●	●
SDG14 – Life Below Water				
Mean area that is protected in marine sites important to biodiversity (%)	68.0	2020	●	→
Ocean Health Index: Clean Waters score (worst 0–100 best)	66.1	2020	●	↓
Fish caught from overexploited or collapsed stocks (% of total catch)	14.4	2018	●	↑
Fish caught by trawling or dredging (%)	1.4	2018	●	↑
Fish caught that are then discarded (%)	3.8	2018	●	↑
Marine biodiversity threats embodied in imports (per million population)	0.0	2018	●	●
SDG15 – Life on Land				
Mean area that is protected in terrestrial sites important to biodiversity (%)	43.6	2020	●	→
Mean area that is protected in freshwater sites important to biodiversity (%)	36.7	2020	●	→
Red List Index of species survival (worst 0–1 best)	0.8	2021	●	↓
Permanent deforestation (% of forest area, 5-year average)	0.0	2020	●	↑
Terrestrial and freshwater biodiversity threats embodied in imports (per million population)	0.2	2018	●	●
SDG16 – Peace, Justice and Strong Institutions				
Homicides (per 100,000 population)	2.2	2018	●	↑
Unsentenced detainees (% of prison population)	NA	NA	●	●
Population who feel safe walking alone at night in the city or area where they live (%)	75	2021	●	↑
Property Rights (worst 1–7 best)	3.5	2020	●	↓
Birth registrations with civil authority (% of children under age 5)	98.6	2020	●	●
Corruption Perception Index (worst 0–100 best)	25	2021	●	↓
Children involved in child labor (% of population aged 5 to 14)	NA	NA	●	●
Exports of major conventional weapons (TIV constant million USD per 100,000 population)	0.0	2020	●	●
Press Freedom Index (best 0–100 worst)	72.7	2021	●	↓
Access to and affordability of justice (worst 0–1 best)	0.6	2020	●	↑
SDG17 – Partnerships for the Goals				
Government spending on health and education (% of GDP)	7.0	2019	●	→
For high-income and all OECD DAC countries: International concessional public finance, including official development assistance (% of GNI)	NA	NA	●	●
Other countries: Government revenue excluding grants (% of GDP)	25.4	2009	●	●
Corporate Tax Haven Score (best 0–100 worst)	* 0.0	2019	●	●
Statistical Performance Index (worst 0–100 best)	56.7	2019	●	↑

* Imputed data point

IRAQ

Middle East and North Africa

OVERALL PERFORMANCE

COUNTRY RANKING

IRAQ

115/163

COUNTRY SCORE

REGIONAL AVERAGE: 66.7

AVERAGE PERFORMANCE BY SDG

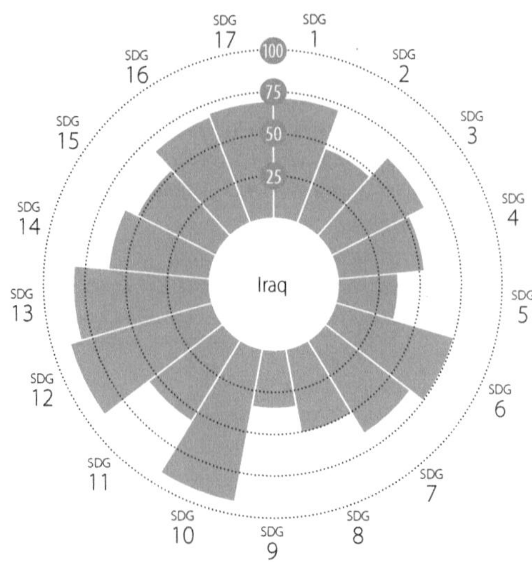

SDG DASHBOARDS AND TRENDS

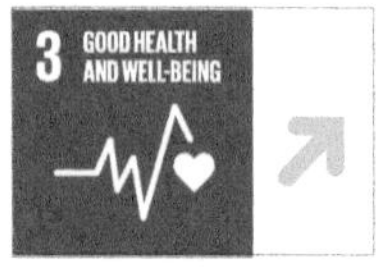

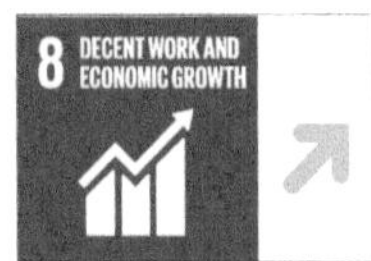

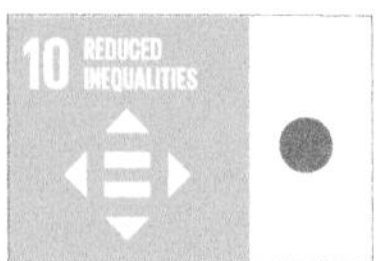

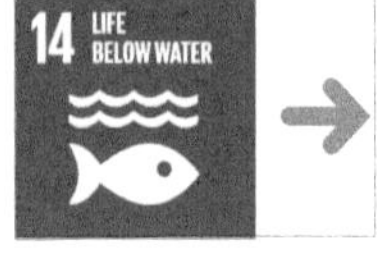

Note: The full title of each SDG is available here: https://sustainabledevelopment.un.org/topics/sustainabledevelopmentgoals

INTERNATIONAL SPILLOVER INDEX

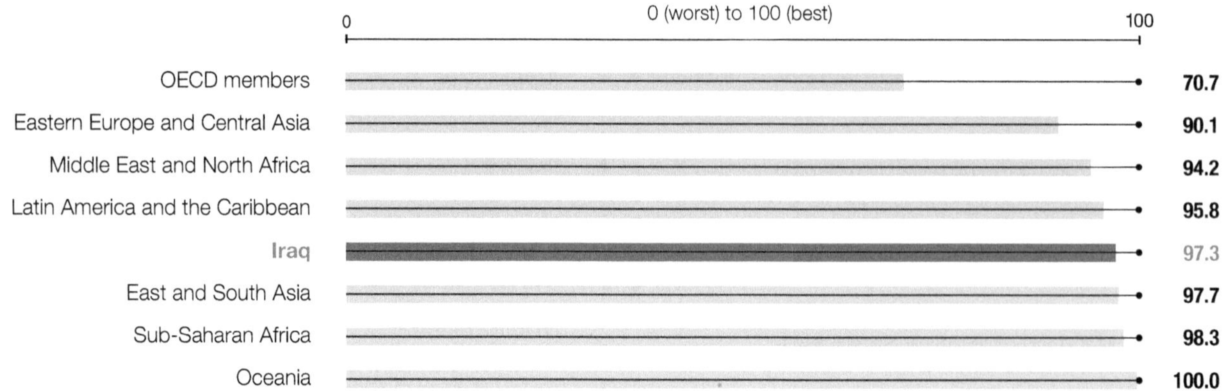

STATISTICAL PERFORMANCE INDEX

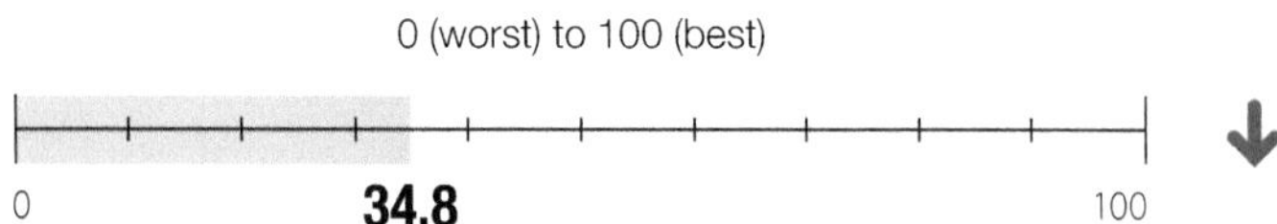

MISSING DATA IN SDG INDEX

11%

SDG1 – No Poverty	Value	Year	Rating	Trend
Poverty headcount ratio at $1.90/day (%)	4.0	2022	●	↓
Poverty headcount ratio at $3.20/day (%)	26.6	2022	●	↓
SDG2 – Zero Hunger				
Prevalence of undernourishment (%)	37.5	2019	●	→
Prevalence of stunting in children under 5 years of age (%)	12.6	2018	●	↗
Prevalence of wasting in children under 5 years of age (%)	3.0	2018	●	↑
Prevalence of obesity, BMI ≥ 30 (% of adult population)	30.4	2016	●	↓
Human Trophic Level (best 2–3 worst)	2.1	2017	●	↑
Cereal yield (tonnes per hectare of harvested land)	2.6	2018	●	↑
Sustainable Nitrogen Management Index (best 0–1.41 worst)	0.8	2015	●	↗
Exports of hazardous pesticides (tonnes per million population)	NA	NA	●	●
SDG3 – Good Health and Well-Being				
Maternal mortality rate (per 100,000 live births)	79	2017	●	↑
Neonatal mortality rate (per 1,000 live births)	14.4	2020	●	↑
Mortality rate, under-5 (per 1,000 live births)	25.2	2020	●	↑
Incidence of tuberculosis (per 100,000 population)	27.0	2020	●	↑
New HIV infections (per 1,000 uninfected population)	1.0	2020	●	→
Age-standardized death rate due to cardiovascular disease, cancer, diabetes, or chronic respiratory disease in adults aged 30–70 years (%)	23.6	2019	●	→
Age-standardized death rate attributable to household air pollution and ambient air pollution (per 100,000 population)	75	2016	●	●
Traffic deaths (per 100,000 population)	27.3	2019	●	↓
Life expectancy at birth (years)	72.4	2019	●	↗
Adolescent fertility rate (births per 1,000 females aged 15 to 19)	70.0	2016	●	●
Births attended by skilled health personnel (%)	95.6	2018	●	●
Surviving infants who received 2 WHO-recommended vaccines (%)	74	2020	●	↗
Universal health coverage (UHC) index of service coverage (worst 0–100 best)	55	2019	●	↗
Subjective well-being (average ladder score, worst 0–10 best)	5.1	2021	●	↑
SDG4 – Quality Education				
Participation rate in pre-primary organized learning (% of children aged 4 to 6)	17.7	2007	●	●
Net primary enrollment rate (%)	92.8	2007	●	●
Lower secondary completion rate (%)	48.4	2007	●	●
Literacy rate (% of population aged 15 to 24)	93.5	2017	●	●
SDG5 – Gender Equality				
Demand for family planning satisfied by modern methods (% of females aged 15 to 49)	53.7	2018	●	→
Ratio of female-to-male mean years of education received (%)	69.8	2019	●	→
Ratio of female-to-male labor force participation rate (%)	15.5	2020	●	↓
Seats held by women in national parliament (%)	26.4	2020	●	↓
SDG6 – Clean Water and Sanitation				
Population using at least basic drinking water services (%)	98.4	2020	●	↑
Population using at least basic sanitation services (%)	100.0	2020	●	↑
Freshwater withdrawal (% of available freshwater resources)	47.1	2018	●	●
Anthropogenic wastewater that receives treatment (%)	19.5	2018	●	●
Scarce water consumption embodied in imports (m^3 H_2O eq/capita)	909.9	2018	●	●
SDG7 – Affordable and Clean Energy				
Population with access to electricity (%)	100.0	2019	●	↑
Population with access to clean fuels and technology for cooking (%)	99.0	2019	●	↑
CO_2 emissions from fuel combustion per total electricity output ($MtCO_2$/TWh)	2.5	2019	●	→
Share of renewable energy in total primary energy supply (%)	0.4	2019	●	↓
SDG8 – Decent Work and Economic Growth				
Adjusted GDP growth (%)	-7.8	2020	●	●
Victims of modern slavery (per 1,000 population) *	NA	NA	●	●
Adults with an account at a bank or other financial institution or with a mobile-money-service provider (% of population aged 15 or over)	22.7	2017	●	↗
Unemployment rate (% of total labor force)	13.3	2022	●	↓
Fundamental labor rights are effectively guaranteed (worst 0–1 best)	NA	NA	●	●
Fatal work-related accidents embodied in imports (per 100,000 population)	0.1	2015	●	↑

SDG9 – Industry, Innovation and Infrastructure	Value	Year	Rating	Trend
Population using the internet (%)	60.0	2019	●	↑
Mobile broadband subscriptions (per 100 population)	42.1	2019	●	↑
Logistics Performance Index: Quality of trade and transport-related infrastructure (worst 1–5 best)	2.0	2018	●	↓
The Times Higher Education Universities Ranking: Average score of top 3 universities (worst 0–100 best)	20.8	2022	●	●
Articles published in academic journals (per 1,000 population)	0.5	2020	●	↑
Expenditure on research and development (% of GDP)	0.0	2018	●	→
SDG10 – Reduced Inequalities				
Gini coefficient	29.5	2012	●	●
Palma ratio	1.1	2018	●	●
SDG11 – Sustainable Cities and Communities				
Proportion of urban population living in slums (%)	46.4	2018	●	→
Annual mean concentration of particulate matter of less than 2.5 microns in diameter (PM2.5) (μg/m^3)	61.9	2019	●	→
Access to improved water source, piped (% of urban population)	88.2	2020	●	↓
Satisfaction with public transport (%)	55.0	2021	●	→
SDG12 – Responsible Consumption and Production				
Municipal solid waste (kg/capita/day)	1.0	2015	●	●
Electronic waste (kg/capita)	7.1	2019	●	●
Production-based SO_2 emissions (kg/capita)	33.5	2018	●	●
SO_2 emissions embodied in imports (kg/capita)	1.0	2018	●	●
Production-based nitrogen emissions (kg/capita)	4.2	2015	●	↑
Nitrogen emissions embodied in imports (kg/capita)	0.4	2015	●	↑
Exports of plastic waste (kg/capita)	NA	NA	●	●
SDG13 – Climate Action				
CO_2 emissions from fossil fuel combustion and cement production (tCO_2/capita)	5.2	2020	●	→
CO_2 emissions embodied in imports (tCO_2/capita)	0.3	2018	●	↑
CO_2 emissions embodied in fossil fuel exports (kg/capita)	NA	NA	●	●
SDG14 – Life Below Water				
Mean area that is protected in marine sites important to biodiversity (%)	0.0	2020	●	→
Ocean Health Index: Clean Waters score (worst 0–100 best)	45.0	2020	●	↓
Fish caught from overexploited or collapsed stocks (% of total catch)	NA	NA	●	●
Fish caught by trawling or dredging (%)	7.4	2018	●	↓
Fish caught that are then discarded (%)	2.6	2018	●	↑
Marine biodiversity threats embodied in imports (per million population)	0.0	2018	●	●
SDG15 – Life on Land				
Mean area that is protected in terrestrial sites important to biodiversity (%)	5.6	2020	●	→
Mean area that is protected in freshwater sites important to biodiversity (%)	8.1	2020	●	→
Red List Index of species survival (worst 0–1 best)	0.8	2021	●	↓
Permanent deforestation (% of forest area, 5-year average)	0.0	2020	●	↑
Terrestrial and freshwater biodiversity threats embodied in imports (per million population)	0.0	2018	●	●
SDG16 – Peace, Justice and Strong Institutions				
Homicides (per 100,000 population)	NA	NA	●	●
Unsentenced detainees (% of prison population)	24.7	2013	●	●
Population who feel safe walking alone at night in the city or area where they live (%)	68	2021	●	↑
Property Rights (worst 1–7 best)	NA	NA	●	●
Birth registrations with civil authority (% of children under age 5)	98.8	2020	●	●
Corruption Perception Index (worst 0–100 best)	23	2021	●	→
Children involved in child labor (% of population aged 5 to 14)	4.5	2019	●	●
Exports of major conventional weapons (TIV constant million USD per 100,000 population) *	0.0	2020	●	●
Press Freedom Index (best 0–100 worst)	55.6	2021	●	↓
Access to and affordability of justice (worst 0–1 best)	NA	NA	●	●
SDG17 – Partnerships for the Goals				
Government spending on health and education (% of GDP)	NA	NA	●	●
For high-income and all OECD DAC countries: International concessional public finance, including official development assistance (% of GNI)	NA	NA	●	●
Other countries: Government revenue excluding grants (% of GDP)	38.4	2019	●	↑
Corporate Tax Haven Score (best 0–100 worst) *	0.0	2019	●	●
Statistical Performance Index (worst 0–100 best)	34.8	2019	●	↓

* Imputed data point

IRELAND

OVERALL PERFORMANCE

COUNTRY RANKING

IRELAND

9 /163

COUNTRY SCORE

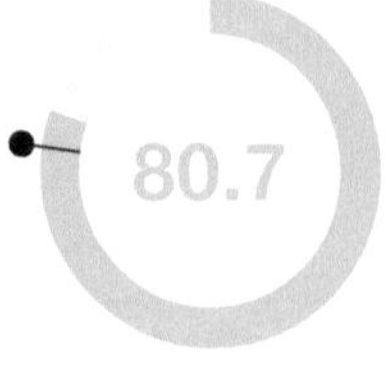

REGIONAL AVERAGE: 77.2

AVERAGE PERFORMANCE BY SDG

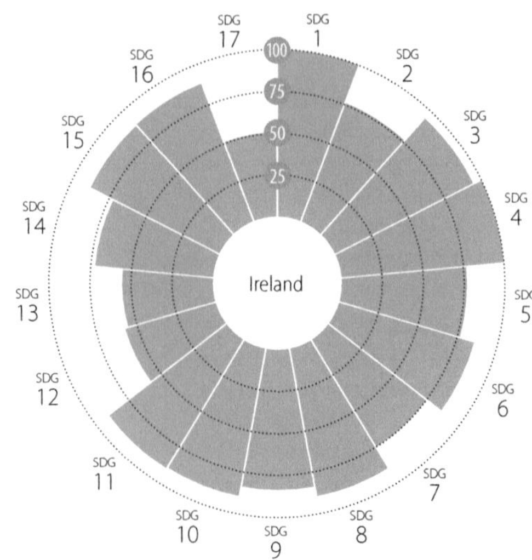

SDG DASHBOARDS AND TRENDS

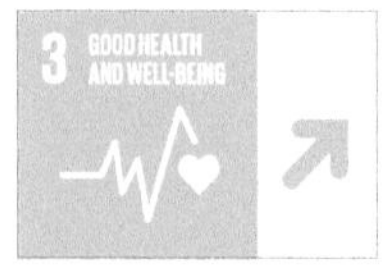

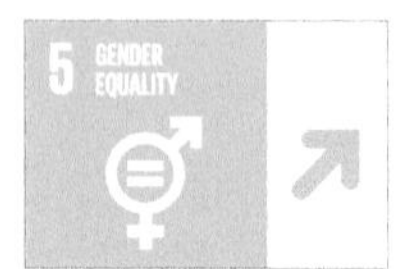

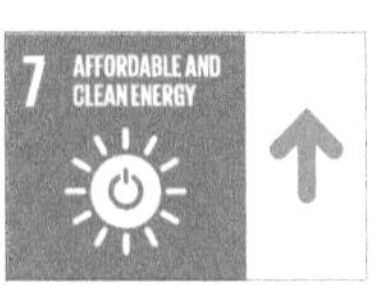

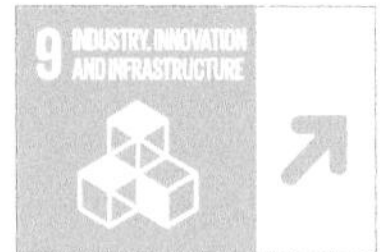

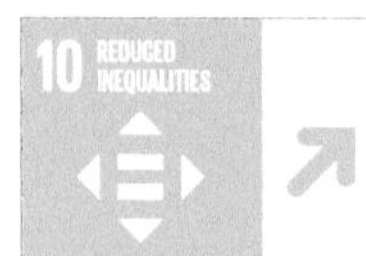

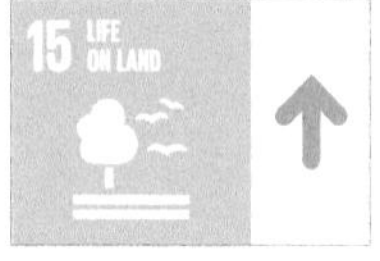

Information unavailable
Information unavailable

Note: The full title of each SDG is available here: https://sustainabledevelopment.un.org/topics/sustainabledevelopmentgoals

INTERNATIONAL SPILLOVER INDEX

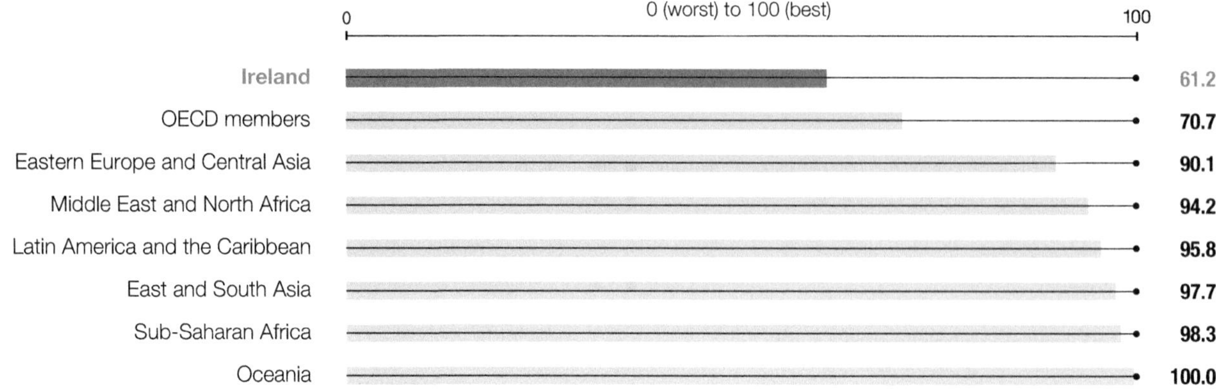

STATISTICAL PERFORMANCE INDEX

0 (worst) to 100 (best)

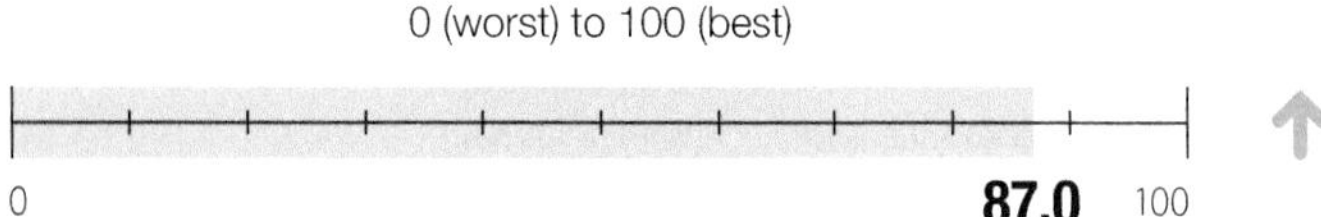

MISSING DATA IN SDG INDEX

1%

SDG1 – No Poverty	Value	Year	Rating	Trend
Poverty headcount ratio at \$1.90/day (%)	0.1	2022	●	↑
Poverty headcount ratio at \$3.20/day (%)	0.1	2022	●	↑
Poverty rate after taxes and transfers (%)	7.4	2018	●	↑

SDG2 – Zero Hunger	Value	Year	Rating	Trend
Prevalence of undernourishment (%)	2.5	2019	●	↑
Prevalence of stunting in children under 5 years of age (%)	* 2.6	2019	●	↑
Prevalence of wasting in children under 5 years of age (%)	* 0.7	2019	●	↑
Prevalence of obesity, BMI ≥ 30 (% of adult population)	25.3	2016	●	↓
Human Trophic Level (best 2–3 worst)	2.4	2017	●	↗
Cereal yield (tonnes per hectare of harvested land)	7.1	2018	●	↑
Sustainable Nitrogen Management Index (best 0–1.41 worst)	0.0	2015	●	↑
Yield gap closure (% of potential yield)	74.6	2018	●	●
Exports of hazardous pesticides (tonnes per million population)	52.8	2019	●	●

SDG3 – Good Health and Well-Being	Value	Year	Rating	Trend
Maternal mortality rate (per 100,000 live births)	5	2017	●	↑
Neonatal mortality rate (per 1,000 live births)	2.0	2020	●	↑
Mortality rate, under-5 (per 1,000 live births)	3.0	2020	●	↑
Incidence of tuberculosis (per 100,000 population)	5.3	2020	●	↑
New HIV infections (per 1,000 uninfected population)	0.1	2020	●	↑
Age-standardized death rate due to cardiovascular disease, cancer, diabetes, or chronic respiratory disease in adults aged 30–70 years (%)	9.7	2019	●	↑
Age-standardized death rate attributable to household air pollution and ambient air pollution (per 100,000 population)	12	2016	●	●
Traffic deaths (per 100,000 population)	3.1	2019	●	↑
Life expectancy at birth (years)	81.8	2019	●	↑
Adolescent fertility rate (births per 1,000 females aged 15 to 19)	6.2	2018	●	↑
Births attended by skilled health personnel (%)	99.7	2016	●	●
Surviving infants who received 2 WHO-recommended vaccines (%)	92	2020	●	↑
Universal health coverage (UHC) index of service coverage (worst 0–100 best)	83	2019	●	↑
Subjective well-being (average ladder score, worst 0–10 best)	6.8	2021	●	↑
Gap in life expectancy at birth among regions (years)	NA	NA	●	●
Gap in self-reported health status by income (percentage points)	21.3	2019	●	↓
Daily smokers (% of population aged 15 and over)	14.0	2019	●	↑

SDG4 – Quality Education	Value	Year	Rating	Trend
Participation rate in pre-primary organized learning (% of children aged 4 to 6)	99.9	2019	●	↑
Net primary enrollment rate (%)	99.9	2019	●	↑
Lower secondary completion rate (%)	101.2	2019	●	↑
Literacy rate (% of population aged 15 to 24)	NA	NA	●	●
Tertiary educational attainment (% of population aged 25 to 34)	58.4	2020	●	↑
PISA score (worst 0–600 best)	504.7	2018	●	↑
Variation in science performance explained by socio-economic status (%)	11.1	2018	●	↑
Underachievers in science (% of 15-year-olds)	17.0	2018	●	↓

SDG5 – Gender Equality	Value	Year	Rating	Trend
Demand for family planning satisfied by modern methods (% of females aged 15 to 49)	* 87.8	2022	●	↑
Ratio of female-to-male mean years of education received (%)	104.0	2019	●	↑
Ratio of female-to-male labor force participation rate (%)	81.8	2020	●	↑
Seats held by women in national parliament (%)	22.5	2020	●	↗
Gender wage gap (% of male median wage)	5.2	2019	●	↑

SDG6 – Clean Water and Sanitation	Value	Year	Rating	Trend
Population using at least basic drinking water services (%)	97.4	2020	●	→
Population using at least basic sanitation services (%)	91.3	2020	●	→
Freshwater withdrawal (% of available freshwater resources)	6.9	2018	●	●
Anthropogenic wastewater that receives treatment (%)	89.7	2018	●	●
Scarce water consumption embodied in imports (m^3 H_2O eq/capita)	5285.6	2018	●	●
Population using safely managed water services (%)	97.3	2020	●	↑
Population using safely managed sanitation services (%)	82.9	2020	●	↑

SDG7 – Affordable and Clean Energy	Value	Year	Rating	Trend
Population with access to electricity (%)	100.0	2019	●	↑
Population with access to clean fuels and technology for cooking (%)	100.0	2019	●	↑
CO_2 emissions from fuel combustion per total electricity output ($MtCO_2$/TWh)	1.1	2019	●	↑
Share of renewable energy in total primary energy supply (%)	11.5	2019	●	↑

SDG8 – Decent Work and Economic Growth	Value	Year	Rating	Trend
Adjusted GDP growth (%)	4.7	2020	●	●
Victims of modern slavery (per 1,000 population)	1.7	2018	●	●
Adults with an account at a bank or other financial institution or with a mobile-money-service provider (% of population aged 15 or over)	95.3	2017	●	↑
Fundamental labor rights are effectively guaranteed (worst 0–1 best)	0.8	2020	●	●
Fatal work-related accidents embodied in imports (per 100,000 population)	1.4	2015	●	↑
Employment-to-population ratio (%)	66.6	2020	●	↑
Youth not in employment, education or training (NEET) (% of population aged 15 to 29)	11.0	2020	●	↑

* Imputed data point

SDG9 – Industry, Innovation and Infrastructure	Value	Year	Rating	Trend
Population using the internet (%)	92.0	2020	●	↑
Mobile broadband subscriptions (per 100 population)	105.3	2019	●	↑
Logistics Performance Index: Quality of trade and transport-related infrastructure (worst 1–5 best)	3.3	2018	●	↑
The Times Higher Education Universities Ranking: Average score of top 3 universities (worst 0–100 best)	54.0	2022	●	●
Articles published in academic journals (per 1,000 population)	3.4	2020	●	↑
Expenditure on research and development (% of GDP)	1.1	2018	●	↓
Researchers (per 1,000 employed population)	11.4	2019	●	↑
Triadic patent families filed (per million population)	22.6	2019	●	↑
Gap in internet access by income (percentage points)	18.1	2020	●	●
Female share of graduates from STEM fields at the tertiary level (%)	29.0	2016	●	↑

SDG10 – Reduced Inequalities	Value	Year	Rating	Trend
Gini coefficient	31.4	2017	●	↑
Palma ratio	1.1	2018	●	↑
Elderly poverty rate (% of population aged 66 or over)	7.4	2018	●	↓

SDG11 – Sustainable Cities and Communities	Value	Year	Rating	Trend
Proportion of urban population living in slums (%)	0.0	2018	●	↑
Annual mean concentration of particulate matter of less than 2.5 microns in diameter (PM2.5) (μg/m³)	7.8	2019	●	↑
Access to improved water source, piped (% of urban population)	97.0	2020	●	↓
Satisfaction with public transport (%)	61.0	2021	●	→
Population with rent overburden (%)	5.6	2018	●	↑

SDG12 – Responsible Consumption and Production	Value	Year	Rating	Trend
Electronic waste (kg/capita)	18.7	2019	●	●
Production-based SO_2 emissions (kg/capita)	18.1	2018	●	●
SO_2 emissions embodied in imports (kg/capita)	13.6	2018	●	●
Production-based nitrogen emissions (kg/capita)	57.3	2015	●	↓
Nitrogen emissions embodied in imports (kg/capita)	13.6	2015	●	↓
Exports of plastic waste (kg/capita)	4.8	2020	●	●
Non-recycled municipal solid waste (kg/capita/day)	1.0	2018	●	↓

SDG13 – Climate Action	Value	Year	Rating	Trend
CO_2 emissions from fossil fuel combustion and cement production (tCO_2/capita)	6.8	2020	●	↗
CO_2 emissions embodied in imports (tCO_2/capita)	5.2	2018	●	↓
CO_2 emissions embodied in fossil fuel exports (kg/capita)	29.2	2020	●	●
Carbon Pricing Score at EUR60/tCO_2 (%, worst 0–100 best)	52.7	2018	●	↑

SDG14 – Life Below Water	Value	Year	Rating	Trend
Mean area that is protected in marine sites important to biodiversity (%)	81.9	2020	●	↑
Ocean Health Index: Clean Waters score (worst 0–100 best)	61.5	2020	●	→
Fish caught from overexploited or collapsed stocks (% of total catch)	25.2	2018	●	↑
Fish caught by trawling or dredging (%)	8.6	2018	●	↓
Fish caught that are then discarded (%)	10.6	2018	●	→
Marine biodiversity threats embodied in imports (per million population)	0.1	2018	●	●

SDG15 – Life on Land	Value	Year	Rating	Trend
Mean area that is protected in terrestrial sites important to biodiversity (%)	80.7	2020	●	↑
Mean area that is protected in freshwater sites important to biodiversity (%)	98.6	2020	●	↑
Red List Index of species survival (worst 0–1 best)	0.9	2021	●	↑
Permanent deforestation (% of forest area, 5-year average)	0.0	2020	●	↑
Terrestrial and freshwater biodiversity threats embodied in imports (per million population)	1.7	2018	●	●

SDG16 – Peace, Justice and Strong Institutions	Value	Year	Rating	Trend
Homicides (per 100,000 population)	0.7	2020	●	↑
Unsentenced detainees (% of prison population)	20.1	2019	●	↑
Population who feel safe walking alone at night in the city or area where they live (%)	70	2021	●	↑
Property Rights (worst 1–7 best)	5.6	2020	●	↑
Birth registrations with civil authority (% of children under age 5)	100.0	2020	●	●
Corruption Perception Index (worst 0–100 best)	74	2021	●	↑
Children involved in child labor (% of population aged 5 to 14)	* 0.0	2019	●	●
Exports of major conventional weapons (TIV constant million USD per 100,000 population)	0.0	2020	●	●
Press Freedom Index (best 0–100 worst)	11.9	2021	●	↑
Access to and affordability of justice (worst 0–1 best)	0.6	2020	●	●
Persons held in prison (per 100,000 population)	82.3	2019	●	↑

SDG17 – Partnerships for the Goals	Value	Year	Rating	Trend
Government spending on health and education (% of GDP)	8.4	2019	●	↓
For high-income and all OECD DAC countries: International concessional public finance, including official development assistance (% of GNI)	0.3	2021	●	↓
Other countries: Government revenue excluding grants (% of GDP)	NA	NA	●	●
Corporate Tax Haven Score (best 0–100 worst)	75.7	2019	●	●
Financial Secrecy Score (best 0–100 worst)	48.2	2020	●	●
Shifted profits of multinationals (US\$ billion)	-126.4	2018	●	↓
Statistical Performance Index (worst 0–100 best)	87.0	2019	●	↑

ISRAEL

OVERALL PERFORMANCE

COUNTRY RANKING

ISRAEL

49/163

COUNTRY SCORE

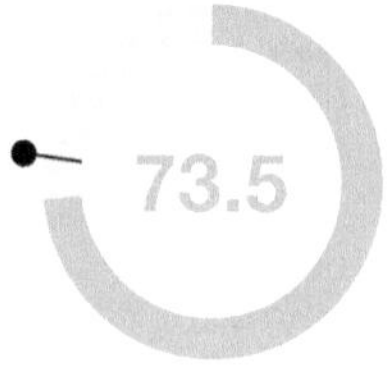

REGIONAL AVERAGE: 77.2

AVERAGE PERFORMANCE BY SDG

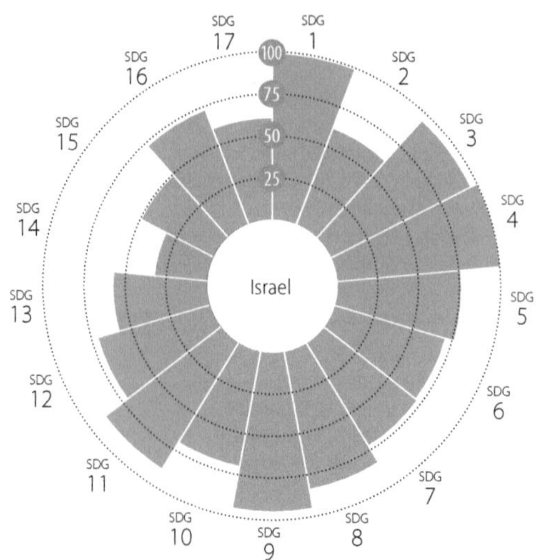

SDG DASHBOARDS AND TRENDS

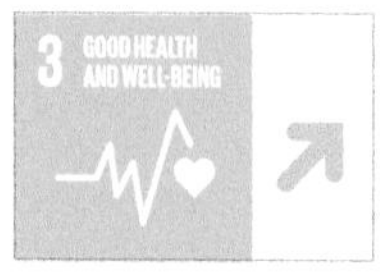

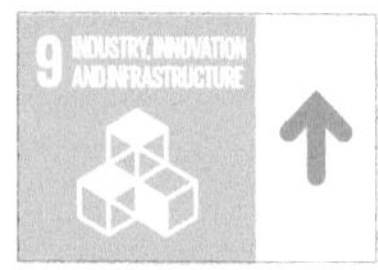

Major challenges · Significant challenges · Challenges remain · SDG achieved · Information unavailable

Decreasing · Stagnating · Moderately improving · On track or maintaining SDG achievement · Information unavailable

Note: The full title of each SDG is available here: https://sustainabledevelopment.un.org/topics/sustainabledevelopmentgoals

INTERNATIONAL SPILLOVER INDEX

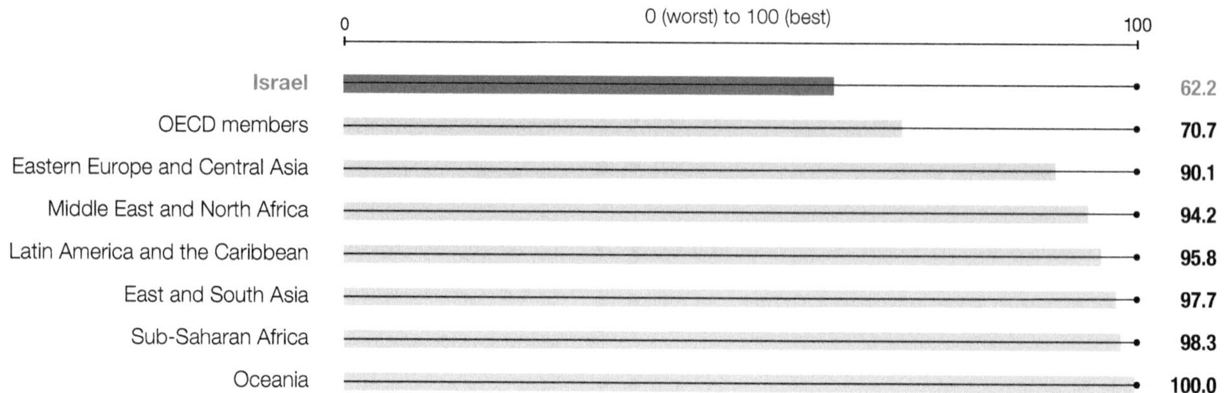

STATISTICAL PERFORMANCE INDEX

0 (worst) to 100 (best)

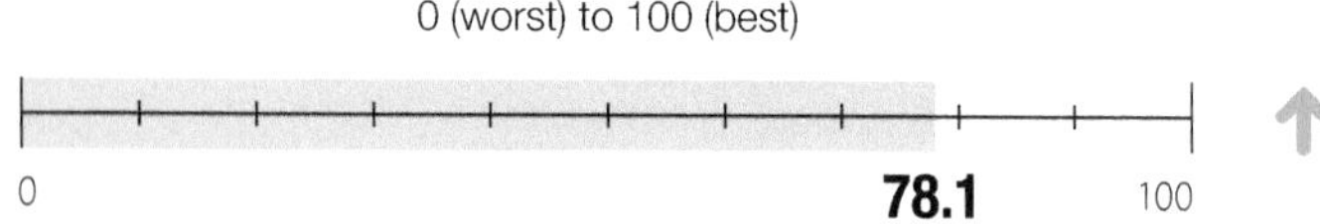

MISSING DATA IN SDG INDEX

5%

ISRAEL

SDG1 – No Poverty

Indicator		Value	Year	Rating	Trend
Poverty headcount ratio at $1.90/day (%)		0.2	2022	●	↑
Poverty headcount ratio at $3.20/day (%)		0.6	2022	●	↑
Poverty rate after taxes and transfers (%)		16.9	2018	●	↑

SDG2 – Zero Hunger

Indicator		Value	Year	Rating	Trend
Prevalence of undernourishment (%)		2.5	2019	●	↑
Prevalence of stunting in children under 5 years of age (%)	*	2.6	2019	●	↑
Prevalence of wasting in children under 5 years of age (%)	*	0.7	2019	●	↑
Prevalence of obesity, BMI ≥ 30 (% of adult population)		26.1	2016	●	↓
Human Trophic Level (best 2–3 worst)		2.4	2017	●	↓
Cereal yield (tonnes per hectare of harvested land)		3.0	2018	●	↑
Sustainable Nitrogen Management Index (best 0–1.41 worst)		0.9	2015	●	→
Yield gap closure (% of potential yield)		NA	NA	●	●
Exports of hazardous pesticides (tonnes per million population)		2.4	2019	●	●

SDG3 – Good Health and Well-Being

Indicator		Value	Year	Rating	Trend
Maternal mortality rate (per 100,000 live births)		3	2017	●	↑
Neonatal mortality rate (per 1,000 live births)		1.9	2020	●	↑
Mortality rate, under-5 (per 1,000 live births)		3.6	2020	●	↑
Incidence of tuberculosis (per 100,000 population)		2.1	2020	●	↑
New HIV infections (per 1,000 uninfected population)		1.0	2020	●	→
Age-standardized death rate due to cardiovascular disease, cancer, diabetes, or chronic respiratory disease in adults aged 30–70 years (%)		8.8	2019	●	↑
Age-standardized death rate attributable to household air pollution and ambient air pollution (per 100,000 population)		15	2016	●	●
Traffic deaths (per 100,000 population)		3.9	2019	●	↑
Life expectancy at birth (years)		82.6	2019	●	↑
Adolescent fertility rate (births per 1,000 females aged 15 to 19)		8.2	2018	●	↑
Births attended by skilled health personnel (%)		NA	NA	●	●
Surviving infants who received 2 WHO-recommended vaccines (%)		98	2020	●	↑
Universal health coverage (UHC) index of service coverage (worst 0–100 best)		84	2019	●	↑
Subjective well-being (average ladder score, worst 0–10 best)		7.6	2021	●	↑
Gap in life expectancy at birth among regions (years)		2.6	2019	●	↑
Gap in self-reported health status by income (percentage points)		9.5	2019	●	↑
Daily smokers (% of population aged 15 and over)		16.4	2019	●	↑

SDG4 – Quality Education

Indicator		Value	Year	Rating	Trend
Participation rate in pre-primary organized learning (% of children aged 4 to 6)		99.8	2019	●	↑
Net primary enrollment rate (%)		99.5	2019	●	↑
Lower secondary completion rate (%)		103.2	2019	●	↑
Literacy rate (% of population aged 15 to 24)		NA	NA	●	●
Tertiary educational attainment (% of population aged 25 to 34)		47.3	2020	●	↑
PISA score (worst 0–600 best)		465.0	2018	●	↓
Variation in science performance explained by socio-economic status (%)		13.6	2018	●	↓
Underachievers in science (% of 15-year-olds)		33.1	2018	●	↓

SDG5 – Gender Equality

Indicator		Value	Year	Rating	Trend
Demand for family planning satisfied by modern methods (% of females aged 15 to 49)	*	68.4	2022	●	→
Ratio of female-to-male mean years of education received (%)		100.8	2019	●	↑
Ratio of female-to-male labor force participation rate (%)		88.8	2020	●	↑
Seats held by women in national parliament (%)		27.5	2020	●	→
Gender wage gap (% of male median wage)		22.7	2018	●	↓

SDG6 – Clean Water and Sanitation

Indicator		Value	Year	Rating	Trend
Population using at least basic drinking water services (%)		100.0	2020	●	↑
Population using at least basic sanitation services (%)		99.9	2020	●	↑
Freshwater withdrawal (% of available freshwater resources)		95.9	2018	●	●
Anthropogenic wastewater that receives treatment (%)		81.7	2018	●	●
Scarce water consumption embodied in imports (m^3 H_2O eq/capita)		4173.6	2018	●	●
Population using safely managed water services (%)		99.3	2020	●	↑
Population using safely managed sanitation services (%)		95.0	2020	●	↑

SDG7 – Affordable and Clean Energy

Indicator		Value	Year	Rating	Trend
Population with access to electricity (%)		100.0	2019	●	↑
Population with access to clean fuels and technology for cooking (%)		100.0	2019	●	↑
CO_2 emissions from fuel combustion per total electricity output ($MtCO_2$/TWh)		1.0	2019	●	↑
Share of renewable energy in total primary energy supply (%)		3.2	2019	●	→

SDG8 – Decent Work and Economic Growth

Indicator		Value	Year	Rating	Trend
Adjusted GDP growth (%)		-2.2	2020	●	●
Victims of modern slavery (per 1,000 population)		3.9	2018	●	●
Adults with an account at a bank or other financial institution or with a mobile-money-service provider (% of population aged 15 or over)		92.8	2017	●	↑
Fundamental labor rights are effectively guaranteed (worst 0–1 best)		NA	NA	●	●
Fatal work-related accidents embodied in imports (per 100,000 population)		0.6	2015	●	↑
Employment-to-population ratio (%)		66.6	2021	●	↑
Youth not in employment, education or training (NEET) (% of population aged 15 to 29)		14.0	2020	●	→

* Imputed data point

SDG9 – Industry, Innovation and Infrastructure

Indicator		Value	Year	Rating	Trend
Population using the internet (%)		90.1	2020	●	↑
Mobile broadband subscriptions (per 100 population)		115.0	2019	●	↑
Logistics Performance Index: Quality of trade and transport-related infrastructure (worst 1–5 best)		3.3	2018	●	↑
The Times Higher Education Universities Ranking: Average score of top 3 universities (worst 0–100 best)		47.2	2022	●	●
Articles published in academic journals (per 1,000 population)		2.6	2020	●	↑
Expenditure on research and development (% of GDP)		4.9	2018	●	↑
Researchers (per 1,000 employed population)		NA	NA	●	●
Triadic patent families filed (per million population)		60.7	2019	●	↑
Gap in internet access by income (percentage points)		39.9	2018	●	●
Female share of graduates from STEM fields at the tertiary level (%)		NA	NA	●	●

SDG10 – Reduced Inequalities

Indicator		Value	Year	Rating	Trend
Gini coefficient		39.0	2016	●	●
Palma ratio		1.4	2018	●	↑
Elderly poverty rate (% of population aged 66 or over)		20.6	2018	●	→

SDG11 – Sustainable Cities and Communities

Indicator		Value	Year	Rating	Trend
Proportion of urban population living in slums (%)	*	0.0	2018	●	↑
Annual mean concentration of particulate matter of less than 2.5 microns in diameter (PM2.5) (μg/m^3)		18.5	2019	●	↗
Access to improved water source, piped (% of urban population)		100.0	2020	●	↑
Satisfaction with public transport (%)		62.0	2021	●	→
Population with rent overburden (%)		NA	NA	●	●

SDG12 – Responsible Consumption and Production

Indicator		Value	Year	Rating	Trend
Electronic waste (kg/capita)		14.5	2019	●	●
Production-based SO_2 emissions (kg/capita)		14.8	2018	●	●
SO_2 emissions embodied in imports (kg/capita)		7.1	2018	●	●
Production-based nitrogen emissions (kg/capita)		4.4	2015	●	↑
Nitrogen emissions embodied in imports (kg/capita)		21.2	2015	●	↓
Exports of plastic waste (kg/capita)		2.1	2020	●	●
Non-recycled municipal solid waste (kg/capita/day)		1.5	2019	●	↓

SDG13 – Climate Action

Indicator		Value	Year	Rating	Trend
CO_2 emissions from fossil fuel combustion and cement production (tCO_2/capita)		6.5	2020	●	↗
CO_2 emissions embodied in imports (tCO_2/capita)		3.0	2018	●	↗
CO_2 emissions embodied in fossil fuel exports (kg/capita)		34.1	2019	●	●
Carbon Pricing Score at EUR60/tCO_2 (%, worst 0–100 best)		35.5	2018	●	↗

SDG14 – Life Below Water

Indicator		Value	Year	Rating	Trend
Mean area that is protected in marine sites important to biodiversity (%)		14.8	2020	●	→
Ocean Health Index: Clean Waters score (worst 0–100 best)		30.2	2020	●	→
Fish caught from overexploited or collapsed stocks (% of total catch)		NA	NA	●	●
Fish caught by trawling or dredging (%)		48.7	2018	●	↗
Fish caught that are then discarded (%)		23.9	2018	●	→
Marine biodiversity threats embodied in imports (per million population)		0.0	2018	●	●

SDG15 – Life on Land

Indicator		Value	Year	Rating	Trend
Mean area that is protected in terrestrial sites important to biodiversity (%)		17.1	2020	●	→
Mean area that is protected in freshwater sites important to biodiversity (%)		22.7	2020	●	→
Red List Index of species survival (worst 0–1 best)		0.7	2021	●	↓
Permanent deforestation (% of forest area, 5-year average)		0.0	2020	●	↑
Terrestrial and freshwater biodiversity threats embodied in imports (per million population)		2.1	2018	●	●

SDG16 – Peace, Justice and Strong Institutions

Indicator		Value	Year	Rating	Trend
Homicides (per 100,000 population)		1.5	2019	●	↑
Unsentenced detainees (% of prison population)		25.7	2016	●	●
Population who feel safe walking alone at night in the city or area where they live (%)		77	2021	●	↑
Property Rights (worst 1–7 best)		5.6	2020	●	↑
Birth registrations with civil authority (% of children under age 5)		100.0	2020	●	●
Corruption Perception Index (worst 0–100 best)		59	2021	●	↓
Children involved in child labor (% of population aged 5 to 14)	*	0.0	2019	●	●
Exports of major conventional weapons (TIV constant million USD per 100,000 population)		9.6	2020	●	●
Press Freedom Index (best 0–100 worst)		30.9	2021	●	↑
Access to and affordability of justice (worst 0–1 best)		NA	NA	●	●
Persons held in prison (per 100,000 population)		231.2	2018	●	↗

SDG17 – Partnerships for the Goals

Indicator		Value	Year	Rating	Trend
Government spending on health and education (% of GDP)		11.0	2019	●	↑
For high-income and all OECD DAC countries: International concessional public finance, including official development assistance (% of GNI)		0.1	2021	●	→
Other countries: Government revenue excluding grants (% of GDP)		NA	NA	●	●
Corporate Tax Haven Score (best 0–100 worst)	*	0.0	2019	●	●
Financial Secrecy Score (best 0–100 worst)		58.7	2020	●	●
Shifted profits of multinationals (US$ billion)		4.1	2018	●	↑
Statistical Performance Index (worst 0–100 best)		78.1	2019	●	↑

OVERALL PERFORMANCE

COUNTRY RANKING

ITALY

25/163

COUNTRY SCORE

REGIONAL AVERAGE: 77.2

AVERAGE PERFORMANCE BY SDG

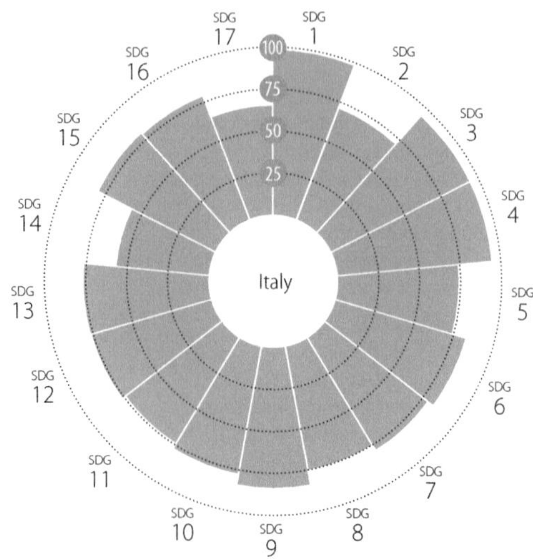

SDG DASHBOARDS AND TRENDS

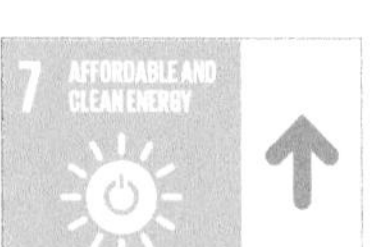

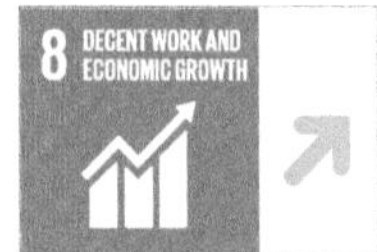

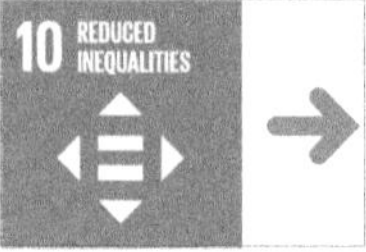

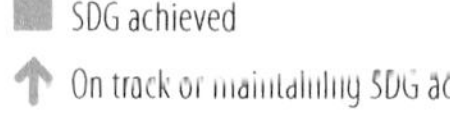

Information unavailable
Information unavailable

Note: The full title of each SDG is available here: https://sustainabledevelopment.un.org/topics/sustainabledevelopmentgoals

INTERNATIONAL SPILLOVER INDEX

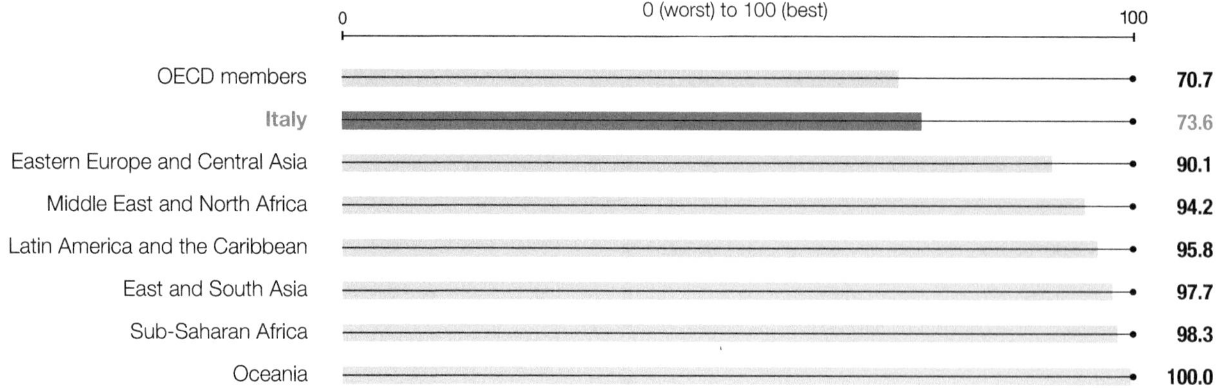

STATISTICAL PERFORMANCE INDEX

0 (worst) to 100 (best)

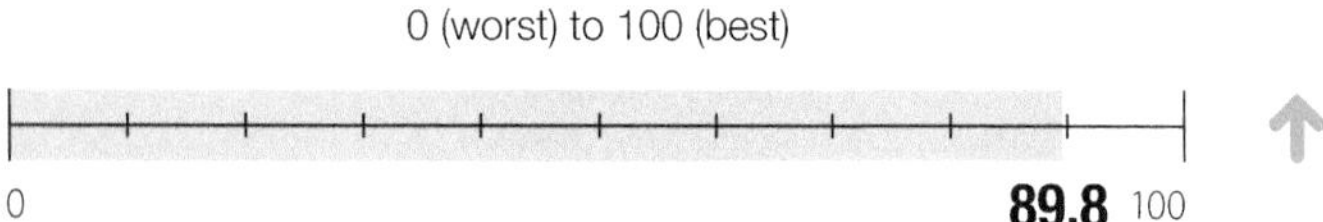

MISSING DATA IN SDG INDEX

1%

ITALY

Performance by Indicator

SDG1 – No Poverty

Indicator		Value	Year	Rating	Trend
Poverty headcount ratio at $1.90/day (%)		1.0	2022	●	↑
Poverty headcount ratio at $3.20/day (%)		1.3	2022	●	↑
Poverty rate after taxes and transfers (%)		14.2	2018	●	→

SDG2 – Zero Hunger

Indicator		Value	Year	Rating	Trend
Prevalence of undernourishment (%)		2.5	2019	●	↑
Prevalence of stunting in children under 5 years of age (%)	*	2.6	2019	●	↑
Prevalence of wasting in children under 5 years of age (%)	*	0.7	2019	●	↑
Prevalence of obesity, BMI ≥ 30 (% of adult population)		19.9	2016	●	↓
Human Trophic Level (best 2–3 worst)		2.4	2017	●	→
Cereal yield (tonnes per hectare of harvested land)		5.3	2018	●	↑
Sustainable Nitrogen Management Index (best 0–1.41 worst)		0.6	2015	●	→
Yield gap closure (% of potential yield)		58.9	2018	●	●
Exports of hazardous pesticides (tonnes per million population)		4.5	2019	●	●

SDG3 – Good Health and Well-Being

Indicator		Value	Year	Rating	Trend
Maternal mortality rate (per 100,000 live births)		2	2017	●	↑
Neonatal mortality rate (per 1,000 live births)		1.7	2020	●	↑
Mortality rate, under-5 (per 1,000 live births)		2.9	2020	●	↑
Incidence of tuberculosis (per 100,000 population)		6.6	2020	●	↑
New HIV infections (per 1,000 uninfected population)		0.0	2020	●	↑
Age-standardized death rate due to cardiovascular disease, cancer, diabetes, or chronic respiratory disease in adults aged 30–70 years (%)		9.0	2019	●	↑
Age-standardized death rate attributable to household air pollution and ambient air pollution (per 100,000 population)		15	2016	●	●
Traffic deaths (per 100,000 population)		5.3	2019	●	↑
Life expectancy at birth (years)		83.0	2019	●	↑
Adolescent fertility rate (births per 1,000 females aged 15 to 19)		4.1	2018	●	↑
Births attended by skilled health personnel (%)		99.9	2016	●	●
Surviving infants who received 2 WHO-recommended vaccines (%)		92	2020	●	↑
Universal health coverage (UHC) index of service coverage (worst 0–100 best)		83	2019	●	↑
Subjective well-being (average ladder score, worst 0–10 best)		6.5	2021	●	↑
Gap in life expectancy at birth among regions (years)		2.8	2019	●	↑
Gap in self-reported health status by income (percentage points)		9.3	2019	●	↑
Daily smokers (% of population aged 15 and over)		18.6	2019	●	↑

SDG4 – Quality Education

Indicator		Value	Year	Rating	Trend
Participation rate in pre-primary organized learning (% of children aged 4 to 6)		91.5	2019	●	↑
Net primary enrollment rate (%)		96.5	2019	●	↓
Lower secondary completion rate (%)		97.5	2019	●	↑
Literacy rate (% of population aged 15 to 24)		99.9	2018	●	●
Tertiary educational attainment (% of population aged 25 to 34)		28.9	2020	●	↗
PISA score (worst 0–600 best)		477.0	2018	●	↓
Variation in science performance explained by socio-economic status (%)		8.5	2018	●	↑
Underachievers in science (% of 15-year-olds)		25.9	2018	●	↓

SDG5 – Gender Equality

Indicator		Value	Year	Rating	Trend
Demand for family planning satisfied by modern methods (% of females aged 15 to 49)	*	74.4	2022	●	↗
Ratio of female-to-male mean years of education received (%)		96.2	2019	●	→
Ratio of female-to-male labor force participation rate (%)		68.9	2020	●	↑
Seats held by women in national parliament (%)		35.7	2020	●	↑
Gender wage gap (% of male median wage)		7.6	2019	●	↑

SDG6 – Clean Water and Sanitation

Indicator		Value	Year	Rating	Trend
Population using at least basic drinking water services (%)		99.9	2020	●	↑
Population using at least basic sanitation services (%)		99.9	2020	●	↑
Freshwater withdrawal (% of available freshwater resources)		30.0	2018	●	●
Anthropogenic wastewater that receives treatment (%)		58.8	2018	●	●
Scarce water consumption embodied in imports (m^3 H_2O eq/capita)		3058.6	2018	●	●
Population using safely managed water services (%)		95.8	2020	●	↑
Population using safely managed sanitation services (%)		95.8	2020	●	↑

SDG7 – Affordable and Clean Energy

Indicator		Value	Year	Rating	Trend
Population with access to electricity (%)		100.0	2019	●	↑
Population with access to clean fuels and technology for cooking (%)		100.0	2019	●	↑
CO_2 emissions from fuel combustion per total electricity output ($MtCO_2$/TWh)		1.1	2019	●	↑
Share of renewable energy in total primary energy supply (%)		18.1	2019	●	↑

SDG8 – Decent Work and Economic Growth

Indicator		Value	Year	Rating	Trend
Adjusted GDP growth (%)		-2.3	2020	●	●
Victims of modern slavery (per 1,000 population)		2.4	2018	●	●
Adults with an account at a bank or other financial institution or with a mobile-money-service provider (% of population aged 15 or over)		93.8	2017	●	↑
Fundamental labor rights are effectively guaranteed (worst 0–1 best)		0.6	2020	●	→
Fatal work-related accidents embodied in imports (per 100,000 population)		0.8	2015	●	↑
Employment-to-population ratio (%)		57.5	2020	●	↑
Youth not in employment, education or training (NEET) (% of population aged 15 to 29)		23.5	2020	●	↗

* Imputed data point

SDG9 – Industry, Innovation and Infrastructure

Indicator		Value	Year	Rating	Trend
Population using the internet (%)		70.5	2020	●	↑
Mobile broadband subscriptions (per 100 population)		92.2	2019	●	↑
Logistics Performance Index: Quality of trade and transport-related infrastructure (worst 1–5 best)		3.9	2018	●	↑
The Times Higher Education Universities Ranking: Average score of top 3 universities (worst 0–100 best)		54.6	2022	●	●
Articles published in academic journals (per 1,000 population)		2.1	2020	●	↑
Expenditure on research and development (% of GDP)		1.4	2018	●	↑
Researchers (per 1,000 employed population)		6.3	2019	●	↑
Triadic patent families filed (per million population)		15.6	2019	●	↑
Gap in internet access by income (percentage points)		47.4	2013	●	●
Female share of graduates from STEM fields at the tertiary level (%)		39.5	2016	●	↑

SDG10 – Reduced Inequalities

Indicator		Value	Year	Rating	Trend
Gini coefficient		35.9	2017	●	↓
Palma ratio		1.3	2018	●	→
Elderly poverty rate (% of population aged 66 or over)		11.3	2018	●	↓

SDG11 – Sustainable Cities and Communities

Indicator		Value	Year	Rating	Trend
Proportion of urban population living in slums (%)		0.0	2018	●	↑
Annual mean concentration of particulate matter of less than 2.5 microns in diameter (PM2.5) (μg/m³)		15.8	2019	●	↗
Access to improved water source, piped (% of urban population)		NA	NA	●	●
Satisfaction with public transport (%)		41.0	2021	●	→
Population with rent overburden (%)		8.4	2018	●	↑

SDG12 – Responsible Consumption and Production

Indicator		Value	Year	Rating	Trend
Electronic waste (kg/capita)		17.5	2019	●	●
Production-based SO_2 emissions (kg/capita)		7.7	2018	●	●
SO_2 emissions embodied in imports (kg/capita)		4.0	2018	●	●
Production-based nitrogen emissions (kg/capita)		8.0	2015	●	↑
Nitrogen emissions embodied in imports (kg/capita)		10.7	2015	●	↓
Exports of plastic waste (kg/capita)		1.7	2020	●	●
Non-recycled municipal solid waste (kg/capita/day)		0.6	2019	●	↑

SDG13 – Climate Action

Indicator		Value	Year	Rating	Trend
CO_2 emissions from fossil fuel combustion and cement production (tCO_2/capita)		5.0	2020	●	↗
CO_2 emissions embodied in imports (tCO_2/capita)		1.5	2018	●	→
CO_2 emissions embodied in fossil fuel exports (kg/capita)		33.9	2020	●	●
Carbon Pricing Score at EUR60/tCO_2 (%, worst 0–100 best)		50.9	2018	●	↗

SDG14 – Life Below Water

Indicator		Value	Year	Rating	Trend
Mean area that is protected in marine sites important to biodiversity (%)		76.0	2020	●	↑
Ocean Health Index: Clean Waters score (worst 0–100 best)		50.0	2020	●	↓
Fish caught from overexploited or collapsed stocks (% of total catch)		52.3	2018	●	↓
Fish caught by trawling or dredging (%)		46.4	2018	●	↓
Fish caught that are then discarded (%)		8.4	2018	●	↓
Marine biodiversity threats embodied in imports (per million population)		0.3	2018	●	●

SDG15 – Life on Land

Indicator		Value	Year	Rating	Trend
Mean area that is protected in terrestrial sites important to biodiversity (%)		75.7	2020	●	↗
Mean area that is protected in freshwater sites important to biodiversity (%)		85.2	2020	●	↑
Red List Index of species survival (worst 0–1 best)		0.9	2021	●	→
Permanent deforestation (% of forest area, 5-year average)		0.0	2020	●	↑
Terrestrial and freshwater biodiversity threats embodied in imports (per million population)		3.5	2018	●	●

SDG16 – Peace, Justice and Strong Institutions

Indicator		Value	Year	Rating	Trend
Homicides (per 100,000 population)		0.5	2020	●	↑
Unsentenced detainees (% of prison population)		17.4	2019	●	↑
Population who feel safe walking alone at night in the city or area where they live (%)		69	2021	●	↑
Property Rights (worst 1–7 best)		4.6	2020	●	↑
Birth registrations with civil authority (% of children under age 5)		100.0	2020	●	●
Corruption Perception Index (worst 0–100 best)		56	2021	●	↑
Children involved in child labor (% of population aged 5 to 14)	*	0.0	2019	●	●
Exports of major conventional weapons (TIV constant million USD per 100,000 population)		1.0	2020	●	●
Press Freedom Index (best 0–100 worst)		23.4	2021	●	↑
Access to and affordability of justice (worst 0–1 best)		0.6	2020	●	↑
Persons held in prison (per 100,000 population)		102.8	2019	●	↓

SDG17 – Partnerships for the Goals

Indicator		Value	Year	Rating	Trend
Government spending on health and education (% of GDP)		10.7	2019	●	↑
For high-income and all OECD DAC countries: International concessional public finance, including official development assistance (% of GNI)		0.3	2021	●	→
Other countries: Government revenue excluding grants (% of GDP)		NA	NA	●	●
Corporate Tax Haven Score (best 0–100 worst)		50.5	2019	●	●
Financial Secrecy Score (best 0–100 worst)		50.4	2020	●	●
Shifted profits of multinationals (US$ billion)		31.7	2018	●	↑
Statistical Performance Index (worst 0–100 best)		89.8	2019	●	↑

JAMAICA

Latin America and the Caribbean

OVERALL PERFORMANCE

COUNTRY RANKING

JAMAICA

83/163

COUNTRY SCORE

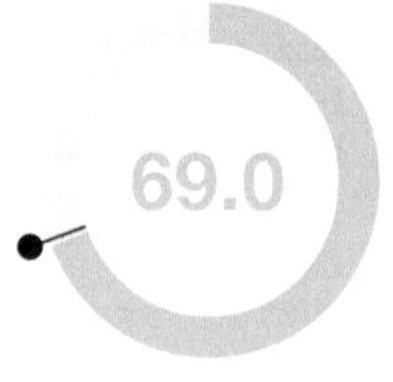

REGIONAL AVERAGE: 69.5

AVERAGE PERFORMANCE BY SDG

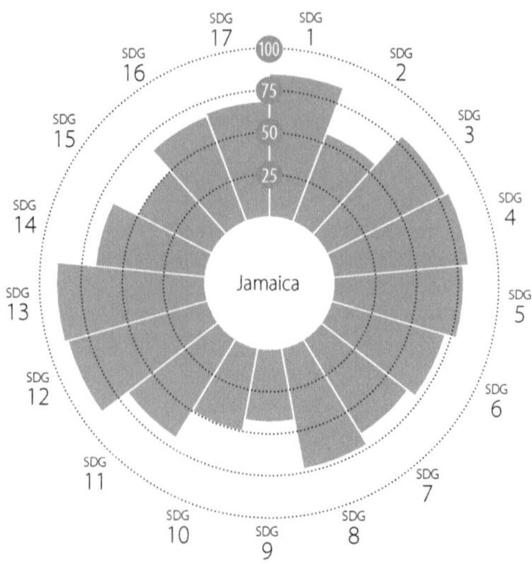

SDG DASHBOARDS AND TRENDS

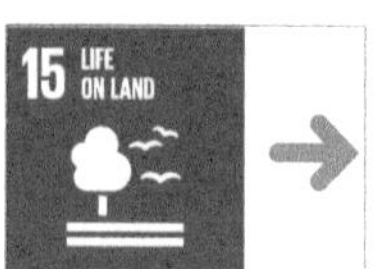

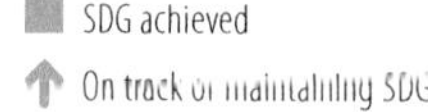

Major challenges · Significant challenges · Challenges remain · SDG achieved · Information unavailable

Decreasing · Stagnating · Moderately improving · On track or maintaining SDG achievement · Information unavailable

Note: The full title of each SDG is available here: https://sustainabledevelopment.un.org/topics/sustainabledevelopmentgoals

INTERNATIONAL SPILLOVER INDEX

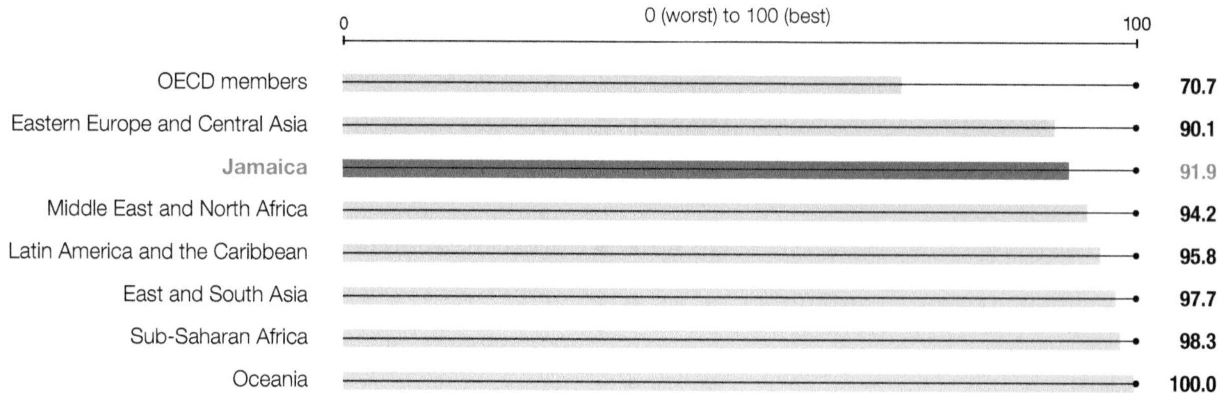

STATISTICAL PERFORMANCE INDEX

0 (worst) to 100 (best)

0 — **54.6** — 100

MISSING DATA IN SDG INDEX

1%

SDG1 – No Poverty	Value	Year	Rating	Trend
Poverty headcount ratio at $1.90/day (%)	1.7	2022	●	↑
Poverty headcount ratio at $3.20/day (%)	15.0	2022	●	↓
SDG2 – Zero Hunger				
Prevalence of undernourishment (%)	7.7	2019	●	↑
Prevalence of stunting in children under 5 years of age (%)	9.3	2016	●	↑
Prevalence of wasting in children under 5 years of age (%)	3.3	2016	●	↑
Prevalence of obesity, BMI ≥ 30 (% of adult population)	24.7	2016	●	↓
Human Trophic Level (best 2–3 worst)	2.3	2017	●	→
Cereal yield (tonnes per hectare of harvested land)	1.1	2018	●	→
Sustainable Nitrogen Management Index (best 0–1.41 worst)	1.1	2015	●	→
Exports of hazardous pesticides (tonnes per million population)	0.0	2019	●	●
SDG3 – Good Health and Well-Being				
Maternal mortality rate (per 100,000 live births)	80	2017	●	→
Neonatal mortality rate (per 1,000 live births)	9.3	2020	●	↑
Mortality rate, under-5 (per 1,000 live births)	13.3	2020	●	↑
Incidence of tuberculosis (per 100,000 population)	2.4	2020	●	↑
New HIV infections (per 1,000 uninfected population)	0.5	2020	●	↗
Age-standardized death rate due to cardiovascular disease, cancer, diabetes, or chronic respiratory disease in adults aged 30–70 years (%)	16.9	2019	●	→
Age-standardized death rate attributable to household air pollution and ambient air pollution (per 100,000 population)	25	2016	●	●
Traffic deaths (per 100,000 population)	15.1	2019	●	↓
Life expectancy at birth (years)	76.0	2019	●	→
Adolescent fertility rate (births per 1,000 females aged 15 to 19)	51.7	2017	●	●
Births attended by skilled health personnel (%)	99.7	2016	●	●
Surviving infants who received 2 WHO-recommended vaccines (%)	93	2020	●	↑
Universal health coverage (UHC) index of service coverage (worst 0–100 best)	70	2019	●	↗
Subjective well-being (average ladder score, worst 0–10 best)	5.8	2021	●	↑
SDG4 – Quality Education				
Participation rate in pre-primary organized learning (% of children aged 4 to 6)	85.9	2020	●	↓
Net primary enrollment rate (%)	88.0	2007	●	●
Lower secondary completion rate (%)	82.7	2020	●	↓
Literacy rate (% of population aged 15 to 24)	96.3	2014	●	●
SDG5 – Gender Equality				
Demand for family planning satisfied by modern methods (% of females aged 15 to 49)	82.9	2009	●	↑
Ratio of female-to-male mean years of education received (%)	109.7	2019	●	↑
Ratio of female-to-male labor force participation rate (%)	80.4	2020	●	↑
Seats held by women in national parliament (%)	28.6	2020	●	↑
SDG6 – Clean Water and Sanitation				
Population using at least basic drinking water services (%)	91.0	2020	●	→
Population using at least basic sanitation services (%)	86.6	2020	●	→
Freshwater withdrawal (% of available freshwater resources)	12.5	2018	●	●
Anthropogenic wastewater that receives treatment (%)	3.0	2018	●	●
Scarce water consumption embodied in imports (m^3 H_2O eq/capita)	2255.6	2018	●	●
SDG7 – Affordable and Clean Energy				
Population with access to electricity (%)	99.4	2019	●	↑
Population with access to clean fuels and technology for cooking (%)	83.2	2019	●	↓
CO_2 emissions from fuel combustion per total electricity output ($MtCO_2$/TWh)	1.9	2019	●	→
Share of renewable energy in total primary energy supply (%)	8.0	2019	●	↓
SDG8 – Decent Work and Economic Growth				
Adjusted GDP growth (%)	-5.9	2020	●	●
Victims of modern slavery (per 1,000 population)	2.6	2018	●	●
Adults with an account at a bank or other financial institution or with a mobile-money-service provider (% of population aged 15 or over)	78.5	2014	●	●
Unemployment rate (% of total labor force)	8.3	2022	●	↑
Fundamental labor rights are effectively guaranteed (worst 0–1 best)	0.6	2020	●	↗
Fatal work-related accidents embodied in imports (per 100,000 population)	0.2	2015	●	↑

SDG9 – Industry, Innovation and Infrastructure	Value	Year	Rating	Trend
Population using the internet (%)	68.2	2018	●	●
Mobile broadband subscriptions (per 100 population)	55.3	2019	●	↗
Logistics Performance Index: Quality of trade and transport-related infrastructure (worst 1–5 best)	2.3	2018	●	↓
The Times Higher Education Universities Ranking: Average score of top 3 universities (worst 0–100 best)	42.5	2022	●	●
Articles published in academic journals (per 1,000 population)	0.2	2020	●	→
Expenditure on research and development (% of GDP)	0.1	2002	●	●
SDG10 – Reduced Inequalities				
Gini coefficient	45.5	2004	●	●
Palma ratio	NA	NA	●	●
SDG11 – Sustainable Cities and Communities				
Proportion of urban population living in slums (%)	59.6	2018	●	→
Annual mean concentration of particulate matter of less than 2.5 microns in diameter (PM2.5) (μg/m^3)	12.7	2019	●	↑
Access to improved water source, piped (% of urban population)	91.1	2020	●	→
Satisfaction with public transport (%)	56.0	2021	●	↓
SDG12 – Responsible Consumption and Production				
Municipal solid waste (kg/capita/day)	1.0	2016	●	●
Electronic waste (kg/capita)	6.2	2019	●	●
Production-based SO_2 emissions (kg/capita)	21.1	2018	●	●
SO_2 emissions embodied in imports (kg/capita)	1.5	2018	●	●
Production-based nitrogen emissions (kg/capita)	6.0	2015	●	↑
Nitrogen emissions embodied in imports (kg/capita)	2.3	2015	●	↑
Exports of plastic waste (kg/capita)	2.2	2020	●	●
SDG13 – Climate Action				
CO_2 emissions from fossil fuel combustion and cement production (tCO_2/capita)	2.5	2020	●	↑
CO_2 emissions embodied in imports (tCO_2/capita)	0.6	2018	●	↗
CO_2 emissions embodied in fossil fuel exports (kg/capita)	0.0	2020	●	●
SDG14 – Life Below Water				
Mean area that is protected in marine sites important to biodiversity (%)	26.6	2020	●	→
Ocean Health Index: Clean Waters score (worst 0–100 best)	44.9	2020	●	→
Fish caught from overexploited or collapsed stocks (% of total catch)	33.1	2018	●	↑
Fish caught by trawling or dredging (%)	0.0	2018	●	↑
Fish caught that are then discarded (%)	0.6	2018	●	↑
Marine biodiversity threats embodied in imports (per million population)	0.2	2018	●	●
SDG15 – Life on Land				
Mean area that is protected in terrestrial sites important to biodiversity (%)	21.9	2020	●	→
Mean area that is protected in freshwater sites important to biodiversity (%)	27.8	2020	●	→
Red List Index of species survival (worst 0–1 best)	0.7	2021	●	↓
Permanent deforestation (% of forest area, 5-year average)	0.1	2020	●	→
Terrestrial and freshwater biodiversity threats embodied in imports (per million population)	0.6	2018	●	●
SDG16 – Peace, Justice and Strong Institutions				
Homicides (per 100,000 population)	44.7	2020	●	↓
Unsentenced detainees (% of prison population)	27.6	2019	●	↑
Population who feel safe walking alone at night in the city or area where they live (%)	60	2021	●	↓
Property Rights (worst 1–7 best)	4.4	2020	●	↓
Birth registrations with civil authority (% of children under age 5)	98.0	2020	●	●
Corruption Perception Index (worst 0–100 best)	44	2021	●	→
Children involved in child labor (% of population aged 5 to 14)	2.9	2019	●	●
Exports of major conventional weapons (TIV constant million USD per 100,000 population)	* 0.0	2020	●	●
Press Freedom Index (best 0–100 worst)	10.0	2021	●	↑
Access to and affordability of justice (worst 0–1 best)	0.5	2020	●	↓
SDG17 – Partnerships for the Goals				
Government spending on health and education (% of GDP)	9.4	2020	●	↑
For high-income and all OECD DAC countries: International concessional public finance, including official development assistance (% of GNI)	NA	NA	●	●
Other countries: Government revenue excluding grants (% of GDP)	30.8	2019	●	↑
Corporate Tax Haven Score (best 0–100 worst)	* 0.0	2019	●	●
Statistical Performance Index (worst 0–100 best)	54.6	2019	●	↗

* Imputed data point

JAPAN

OECD Countries

OVERALL PERFORMANCE

COUNTRY RANKING

JAPAN

19 /163

COUNTRY SCORE

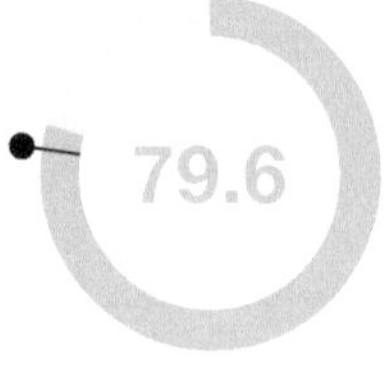

REGIONAL AVERAGE: 77.2

AVERAGE PERFORMANCE BY SDG

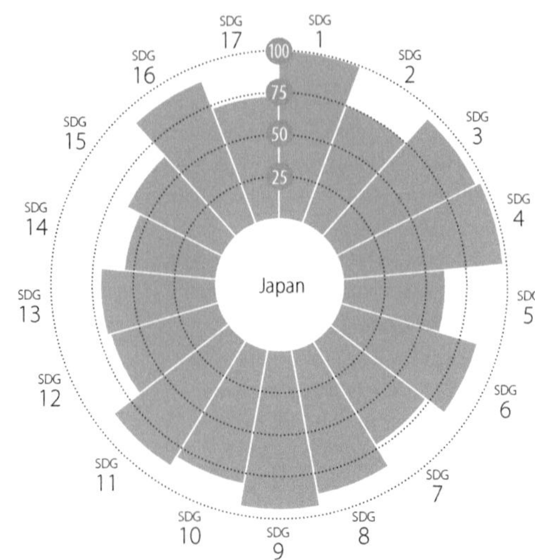

SDG DASHBOARDS AND TRENDS

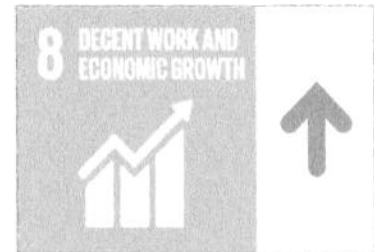

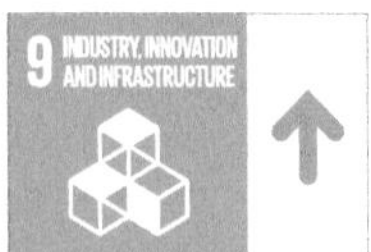

Major challenges — Significant challenges — Challenges remain — SDG achieved — Information unavailable

Decreasing — Stagnating — Moderately improving — On track or maintaining SDG achievement — Information unavailable

Note: The full title of each SDG is available here: https://sustainabledevelopment.un.org/topics/sustainabledevelopmentgoals

INTERNATIONAL SPILLOVER INDEX

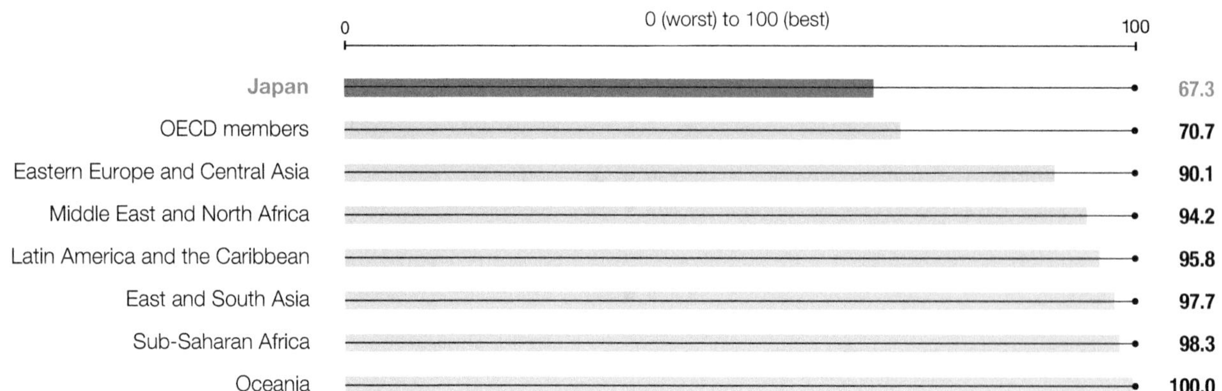

STATISTICAL PERFORMANCE INDEX

0 (worst) to 100 (best)

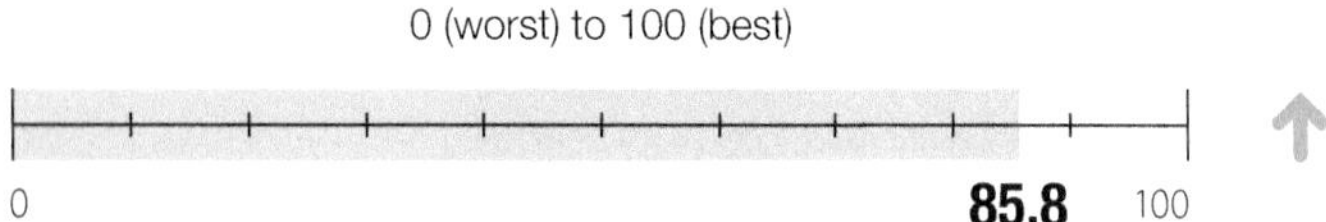

MISSING DATA IN SDG INDEX

3%

JAPAN

Performance by Indicator

SDG1 – No Poverty

Indicator	Value	Year	Rating	Trend
Poverty headcount ratio at $1.90/day (%)	0.4	2022	●	↑
Poverty headcount ratio at $3.20/day (%)	0.5	2022	●	↑
Poverty rate after taxes and transfers (%)	15.7	2018	●	●

SDG2 – Zero Hunger

Indicator	Value	Year	Rating	Trend
Prevalence of undernourishment (%)	2.5	2019	●	↑
Prevalence of stunting in children under 5 years of age (%)	7.1	2010	●	↑
Prevalence of wasting in children under 5 years of age (%)	2.3	2010	●	↑
Prevalence of obesity, BMI $\geq$ 30 (% of adult population)	4.3	2016	●	↑
Human Trophic Level (best 2–3 worst)	2.4	2017	●	→
Cereal yield (tonnes per hectare of harvested land)	5.9	2018	●	↑
Sustainable Nitrogen Management Index (best 0–1.41 worst)	0.6	2015	●	↓
Yield gap closure (% of potential yield)	NA	NA	●	●
Exports of hazardous pesticides (tonnes per million population)	36.1	2019	●	●

SDG3 – Good Health and Well-Being

Indicator	Value	Year	Rating	Trend
Maternal mortality rate (per 100,000 live births)	5	2017	●	↑
Neonatal mortality rate (per 1,000 live births)	0.8	2020	●	↑
Mortality rate, under-5 (per 1,000 live births)	2.5	2020	●	↑
Incidence of tuberculosis (per 100,000 population)	12.0	2020	●	↑
New HIV infections (per 1,000 uninfected population)	0.0	2020	●	↑
Age-standardized death rate due to cardiovascular disease, cancer, diabetes, or chronic respiratory disease in adults aged 30–70 years (%)	8.3	2019	●	↑
Age-standardized death rate attributable to household air pollution and ambient air pollution (per 100,000 population)	12	2016	●	●
Traffic deaths (per 100,000 population)	3.6	2019	●	↑
Life expectancy at birth (years)	84.3	2019	●	↑
Adolescent fertility rate (births per 1,000 females aged 15 to 19)	3.1	2018	●	↑
Births attended by skilled health personnel (%)	99.9	2018	●	↑
Surviving infants who received 2 WHO-recommended vaccines (%)	96	2020	●	↑
Universal health coverage (UHC) index of service coverage (worst 0–100 best)	85	2019	●	↑
Subjective well-being (average ladder score, worst 0–10 best)	6.1	2021	●	↑
Gap in life expectancy at birth among regions (years)	2.3	2015	●	●
Gap in self-reported health status by income (percentage points)	12.3	2019	●	↑
Daily smokers (% of population aged 15 and over)	16.7	2019	●	↑

SDG4 – Quality Education

Indicator	Value	Year	Rating	Trend
Participation rate in pre-primary organized learning (% of children aged 4 to 6)	NA	NA	●	●
Net primary enrollment rate (%)	97.8	2019	●	↑
Lower secondary completion rate (%)	* 100.0	2019	●	↑
Literacy rate (% of population aged 15 to 24)	NA	NA	●	●
Tertiary educational attainment (% of population aged 25 to 34)	61.5	2019	●	↑
PISA score (worst 0–600 best)	520.0	2018	●	↑
Variation in science performance explained by socio-economic status (%)	7.7	2018	●	↑
Underachievers in science (% of 15-year-olds)	10.8	2018	●	↑

SDG5 – Gender Equality

Indicator	Value	Year	Rating	Trend
Demand for family planning satisfied by modern methods (% of females aged 15 to 49)	* 67.9	2022	●	↗
Ratio of female-to-male mean years of education received (%)	104.0	2019	●	↑
Ratio of female-to-male labor force participation rate (%)	74.5	2020	●	↑
Seats held by women in national parliament (%)	9.9	2020	●	→
Gender wage gap (% of male median wage)	22.5	2020	●	↗

SDG6 – Clean Water and Sanitation

Indicator	Value	Year	Rating	Trend
Population using at least basic drinking water services (%)	99.1	2020	●	↑
Population using at least basic sanitation services (%)	99.9	2020	●	↑
Freshwater withdrawal (% of available freshwater resources)	36.5	2018	●	●
Anthropogenic wastewater that receives treatment (%)	75.3	2018	●	●
Scarce water consumption embodied in imports (m^3 H_2O eq/capita)	1937.4	2018	●	●
Population using safely managed water services (%)	98.6	2020	●	↑
Population using safely managed sanitation services (%)	81.4	2020	●	↗

SDG7 – Affordable and Clean Energy

Indicator	Value	Year	Rating	Trend
Population with access to electricity (%)	100.0	2019	●	↑
Population with access to clean fuels and technology for cooking (%)	100.0	2019	●	↑
CO_2 emissions from fuel combustion per total electricity output ($MtCO_2$/TWh)	1.1	2019	●	↑
Share of renewable energy in total primary energy supply (%)	6.3	2019	●	→

SDG8 – Decent Work and Economic Growth

Indicator	Value	Year	Rating	Trend
Adjusted GDP growth (%)	-1.7	2020	●	●
Victims of modern slavery (per 1,000 population)	0.3	2018	●	●
Adults with an account at a bank or other financial institution or with a mobile-money-service provider (% of population aged 15 or over)	98.2	2017	●	↑
Fundamental labor rights are effectively guaranteed (worst 0–1 best)	0.8	2020	●	↑
Fatal work-related accidents embodied in imports (per 100,000 population)	1.0	2015	●	↑
Employment-to-population ratio (%)	77.8	2021	●	↑
Youth not in employment, education or training (NEET) (% of population aged 15 to 29)	9.8	2014	●	●

SDG9 – Industry, Innovation and Infrastructure

Indicator	Value	Year	Rating	Trend
Population using the internet (%)	90.2	2020	●	↑
Mobile broadband subscriptions (per 100 population)	203.0	2019	●	↑
Logistics Performance Index: Quality of trade and transport-related infrastructure (worst 1–5 best)	4.2	2018	●	↑
The Times Higher Education Universities Ranking: Average score of top 3 universities (worst 0–100 best)	65.9	2022	●	●
Articles published in academic journals (per 1,000 population)	1.0	2020	●	↑
Expenditure on research and development (% of GDP)	3.3	2018	●	↑
Researchers (per 1,000 employed population)	9.8	2019	●	↑
Triadic patent families filed (per million population)	139.5	2019	●	↑
Gap in internet access by income (percentage points)	NA	NA	●	●
Female share of graduates from STEM fields at the tertiary level (%)	NA	NA	●	●

SDG10 – Reduced Inequalities

Indicator	Value	Year	Rating	Trend
Gini coefficient	32.9	2013	●	●
Palma ratio	1.3	2018	●	●
Elderly poverty rate (% of population aged 66 or over)	20.0	2018	●	●

SDG11 – Sustainable Cities and Communities

Indicator	Value	Year	Rating	Trend
Proportion of urban population living in slums (%)	* 0.0	2018	●	↑
Annual mean concentration of particulate matter of less than 2.5 microns in diameter (PM2.5) (μg/m³)	11.0	2019	●	↑
Access to improved water source, piped (% of urban population)	NA	NA	●	●
Satisfaction with public transport (%)	62.0	2021	●	↑
Population with rent overburden (%)	9.0	2018	●	↓

SDG12 – Responsible Consumption and Production

Indicator	Value	Year	Rating	Trend
Electronic waste (kg/capita)	20.4	2019	●	●
Production-based SO_2 emissions (kg/capita)	12.3	2018	●	●
SO_2 emissions embodied in imports (kg/capita)	5.3	2018	●	●
Production-based nitrogen emissions (kg/capita)	2.0	2015	●	↑
Nitrogen emissions embodied in imports (kg/capita)	14.1	2015	●	↓
Exports of plastic waste (kg/capita)	8.2	2021	●	●
Non-recycled municipal solid waste (kg/capita/day)	0.7	2018	●	↑

SDG13 – Climate Action

Indicator	Value	Year	Rating	Trend
CO_2 emissions from fossil fuel combustion and cement production (tCO_2/capita)	8.2	2020	●	↗
CO_2 emissions embodied in imports (tCO_2/capita)	1.7	2018	●	↗
CO_2 emissions embodied in fossil fuel exports (kg/capita)	0.4	2021	●	●
Carbon Pricing Score at EUR60/tCO_2 (%, worst 0–100 best)	24.1	2018	●	→

SDG14 – Life Below Water

Indicator	Value	Year	Rating	Trend
Mean area that is protected in marine sites important to biodiversity (%)	67.1	2020	●	→
Ocean Health Index: Clean Waters score (worst 0–100 best)	59.4	2020	●	↓
Fish caught from overexploited or collapsed stocks (% of total catch)	60.9	2018	●	↓
Fish caught by trawling or dredging (%)	10.4	2018	●	↑
Fish caught that are then discarded (%)	10.3	2018	●	↗
Marine biodiversity threats embodied in imports (per million population)	1.0	2018	●	●

SDG15 – Life on Land

Indicator	Value	Year	Rating	Trend
Mean area that is protected in terrestrial sites important to biodiversity (%)	65.1	2020	●	→
Mean area that is protected in freshwater sites important to biodiversity (%)	64.4	2020	●	→
Red List Index of species survival (worst 0–1 best)	0.8	2021	●	↓
Permanent deforestation (% of forest area, 5-year average)	0.0	2020	●	↑
Terrestrial and freshwater biodiversity threats embodied in imports (per million population)	5.1	2018	●	●

SDG16 – Peace, Justice and Strong Institutions

Indicator	Value	Year	Rating	Trend
Homicides (per 100,000 population)	0.3	2019	●	↑
Unsentenced detainees (% of prison population)	12.4	2019	●	↑
Population who feel safe walking alone at night in the city or area where they live (%)	76	2021	●	↑
Property Rights (worst 1–7 best)	6.2	2020	●	↑
Birth registrations with civil authority (% of children under age 5)	100.0	2020	●	●
Corruption Perception Index (worst 0–100 best)	73	2021	●	↑
Children involved in child labor (% of population aged 5 to 14)	* 0.0	2019	●	●
Exports of major conventional weapons (TIV constant million USD per 100,000 population)	0.0	2020	●	●
Press Freedom Index (best 0–100 worst)	28.9	2021	●	↑
Access to and affordability of justice (worst 0–1 best)	0.7	2020	●	↑
Persons held in prison (per 100,000 population)	38.2	2019	●	↑

SDG17 – Partnerships for the Goals

Indicator	Value	Year	Rating	Trend
Government spending on health and education (% of GDP)	12.4	2019	●	↑
For high-income and all OECD DAC countries: International concessional public finance, including official development assistance (% of GNI)	0.3	2021	●	↗
Other countries: Government revenue excluding grants (% of GDP)	NA	NA	●	●
Corporate Tax Haven Score (best 0–100 worst)	* 0.0	2019	●	●
Financial Secrecy Score (best 0–100 worst)	62.9	2020	●	●
Shifted profits of multinationals (US$ billion)	17.3	2018	●	↑
Statistical Performance Index (worst 0–100 best)	85.8	2019	●	↑

* Imputed data point

JORDAN

Middle East and North Africa

OVERALL PERFORMANCE

COUNTRY RANKING

JORDAN

80/163

COUNTRY SCORE

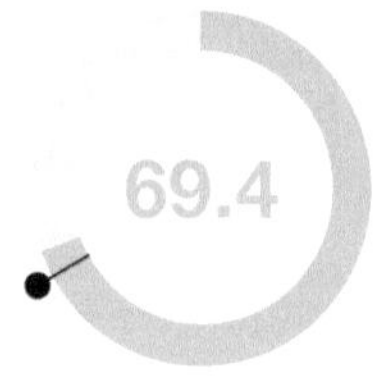

REGIONAL AVERAGE: 66.7

AVERAGE PERFORMANCE BY SDG

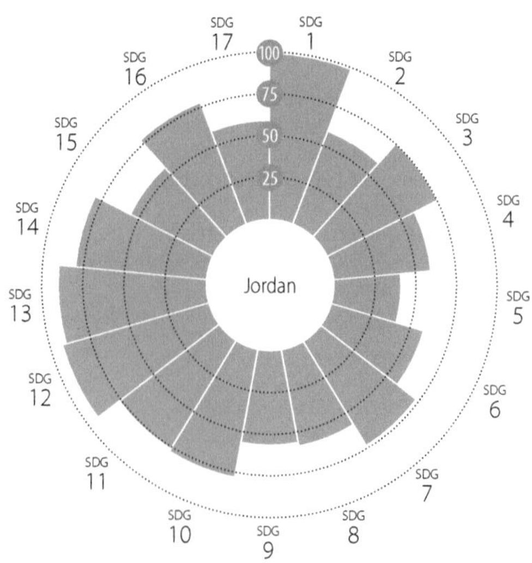

SDG DASHBOARDS AND TRENDS

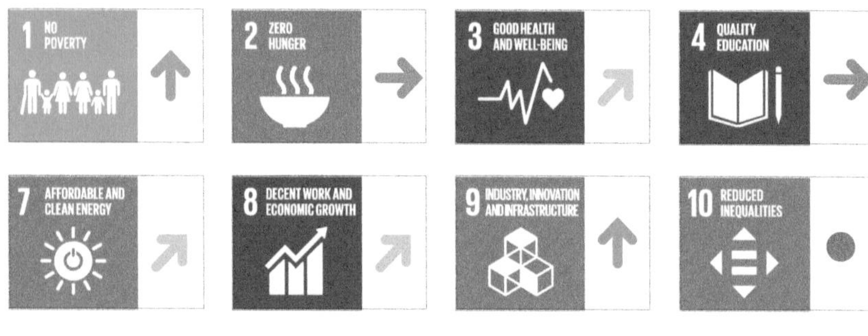

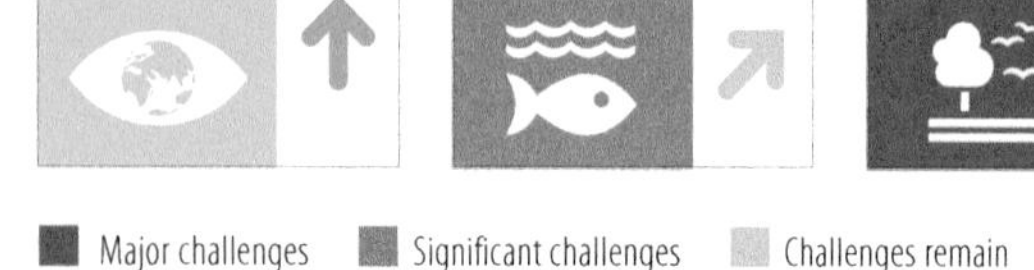

Major challenges | Significant challenges | Challenges remain | SDG achieved | Information unavailable

Decreasing | Stagnating | Moderately improving | On track or maintaining SDG achievement | Information unavailable

Note: The full title of each SDG is available here: https://sustainabledevelopment.un.org/topics/sustainabledevelopmentgoals

INTERNATIONAL SPILLOVER INDEX

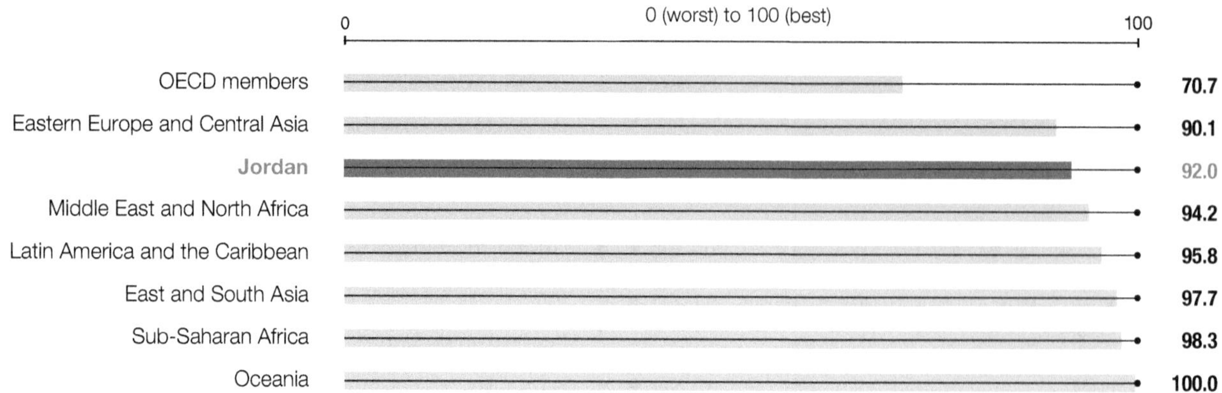

STATISTICAL PERFORMANCE INDEX

0 (worst) to 100 (best)

0 **62.0** 100

MISSING DATA IN SDG INDEX

3%

JORDAN

Performance by Indicator

SDG1 – No Poverty	Value	Year	Rating	Trend
Poverty headcount ratio at $1.90/day (%)	0.0	2022	●	↑
Poverty headcount ratio at $3.20/day (%)	1.1	2022	●	↑
SDG2 – Zero Hunger				
Prevalence of undernourishment (%)	9.5	2019	●	↓
Prevalence of stunting in children under 5 years of age (%)	7.8	2012	●	↗
Prevalence of wasting in children under 5 years of age (%)	2.4	2012	●	↑
Prevalence of obesity, BMI ≥ 30 (% of adult population)	35.5	2016	●	↓
Human Trophic Level (best 2–3 worst)	2.2	2017	●	↑
Cereal yield (tonnes per hectare of harvested land)	1.5	2018	●	↓
Sustainable Nitrogen Management Index (best 0–1.41 worst)	0.6	2015	●	↑
Exports of hazardous pesticides (tonnes per million population)	1.1	2019	●	●
SDG3 – Good Health and Well-Being				
Maternal mortality rate (per 100,000 live births)	46	2017	●	↑
Neonatal mortality rate (per 1,000 live births)	8.8	2020	●	↑
Mortality rate, under-5 (per 1,000 live births)	15.0	2020	●	↑
Incidence of tuberculosis (per 100,000 population)	4.7	2020	●	↑
New HIV infections (per 1,000 uninfected population)	0.0	2020	●	↑
Age-standardized death rate due to cardiovascular disease, cancer, diabetes, or chronic respiratory disease in adults aged 30–70 years (%)	15.3	2019	●	↓
Age-standardized death rate attributable to household air pollution and ambient air pollution (per 100,000 population)	51	2016	●	●
Traffic deaths (per 100,000 population)	17.0	2019	●	↑
Life expectancy at birth (years)	77.9	2019	●	→
Adolescent fertility rate (births per 1,000 females aged 15 to 19)	27.0	2016	●	●
Births attended by skilled health personnel (%)	99.7	2018	●	●
Surviving infants who received 2 WHO-recommended vaccines (%)	76	2020	●	↓
Universal health coverage (UHC) index of service coverage (worst 0–100 best)	60	2019	●	→
Subjective well-being (average ladder score, worst 0–10 best)	3.9	2021	●	↓
SDG4 – Quality Education				
Participation rate in pre-primary organized learning (% of children aged 4 to 6)	49.6	2020	●	●
Net primary enrollment rate (%)	79.9	2020	●	↗
Lower secondary completion rate (%)	66.4	2020	●	↓
Literacy rate (% of population aged 15 to 24)	99.3	2018	●	●
SDG5 – Gender Equality				
Demand for family planning satisfied by modern methods (% of females aged 15 to 49)	56.7	2018	●	↓
Ratio of female-to-male mean years of education received (%)	96.3	2019	●	↑
Ratio of female-to-male labor force participation rate (%)	21.6	2020	●	↓
Seats held by women in national parliament (%)	11.5	2020	●	↓
SDG6 – Clean Water and Sanitation				
Population using at least basic drinking water services (%)	98.9	2020	●	↑
Population using at least basic sanitation services (%)	97.1	2020	●	↑
Freshwater withdrawal (% of available freshwater resources)	100.1	2018	●	●
Anthropogenic wastewater that receives treatment (%)	18.6	2018	●	●
Scarce water consumption embodied in imports (m^3 H_2O eq/capita)	2627.2	2018	●	●
SDG7 – Affordable and Clean Energy				
Population with access to electricity (%)	100.0	2019	●	↑
Population with access to clean fuels and technology for cooking (%)	99.9	2019	●	↑
CO_2 emissions from fuel combustion per total electricity output ($MtCO_2$/TWh)	1.0	2019	●	↑
Share of renewable energy in total primary energy supply (%)	6.2	2019	●	↗
SDG8 – Decent Work and Economic Growth				
Adjusted GDP growth (%)	-3.4	2020	●	●
Victims of modern slavery (per 1,000 population)	1.8	2018	●	●
Adults with an account at a bank or other financial institution or with a mobile-money-service provider (% of population aged 15 or over)	42.5	2017	●	↑
Unemployment rate (% of total labor force)	18.8	2022	●	↓
Fundamental labor rights are effectively guaranteed (worst 0–1 best)	0.5	2020	●	→
Fatal work-related accidents embodied in imports (per 100,000 population)	0.3	2015	●	↑

SDG9 – Industry, Innovation and Infrastructure	Value	Year	Rating	Trend
Population using the internet (%)	66.1	2018	●	●
Mobile broadband subscriptions (per 100 population)	77.0	2019	●	↑
Logistics Performance Index: Quality of trade and transport-related infrastructure (worst 1–5 best)	2.7	2018	●	↑
The Times Higher Education Universities Ranking: Average score of top 3 universities (worst 0–100 best)	33.9	2022	●	●
Articles published in academic journals (per 1,000 population)	0.6	2020	●	↑
Expenditure on research and development (% of GDP)	0.7	2016	●	●
SDG10 – Reduced Inequalities				
Gini coefficient	33.7	2010	●	●
Palma ratio	1.4	2018	●	●
SDG11 – Sustainable Cities and Communities				
Proportion of urban population living in slums (%)	20.7	2018	●	↓
Annual mean concentration of particulate matter of less than 2.5 microns in diameter (PM2.5) (μg/m³)	33.5	2019	●	→
Access to improved water source, piped (% of urban population)	89.9	2020	●	→
Satisfaction with public transport (%)	63.0	2021	●	→
SDG12 – Responsible Consumption and Production				
Municipal solid waste (kg/capita/day)	0.8	2013	●	●
Electronic waste (kg/capita)	5.4	2019	●	●
Production-based SO_2 emissions (kg/capita)	15.2	2018	●	●
SO_2 emissions embodied in imports (kg/capita)	2.2	2018	●	●
Production-based nitrogen emissions (kg/capita)	2.5	2015	●	↑
Nitrogen emissions embodied in imports (kg/capita)	2.6	2015	●	↑
Exports of plastic waste (kg/capita)	0.1	2020	●	●
SDG13 – Climate Action				
CO_2 emissions from fossil fuel combustion and cement production (tCO_2/capita)	2.5	2020	●	↑
CO_2 emissions embodied in imports (tCO_2/capita)	0.6	2018	●	↑
CO_2 emissions embodied in fossil fuel exports (kg/capita)	1.0	2020	●	●
SDG14 – Life Below Water				
Mean area that is protected in marine sites important to biodiversity (%)	NA	NA	●	●
Ocean Health Index: Clean Waters score (worst 0–100 best)	47.3	2020	●	↓
Fish caught from overexploited or collapsed stocks (% of total catch)	NA	NA	●	●
Fish caught by trawling or dredging (%)	0.0	2018	●	↑
Fish caught that are then discarded (%)	0.0	2018	●	↑
Marine biodiversity threats embodied in imports (per million population)	0.2	2018	●	●
SDG15 – Life on Land				
Mean area that is protected in terrestrial sites important to biodiversity (%)	12.9	2020	●	→
Mean area that is protected in freshwater sites important to biodiversity (%)	18.7	2020	●	→
Red List Index of species survival (worst 0–1 best)	1.0	2021	●	↑
Permanent deforestation (% of forest area, 5-year average)	NA	NA	●	●
Terrestrial and freshwater biodiversity threats embodied in imports (per million population)	0.2	2018	●	●
SDG16 – Peace, Justice and Strong Institutions				
Homicides (per 100,000 population)	1.0	2020	●	↑
Unsentenced detainees (% of prison population)	39.0	2015	●	●
Population who feel safe walking alone at night in the city or area where they live (%)	87	2021	●	↑
Property Rights (worst 1–7 best)	5.1	2020	●	↑
Birth registrations with civil authority (% of children under age 5)	98.0	2020	●	●
Corruption Perception Index (worst 0–100 best)	49	2021	●	↓
Children involved in child labor (% of population aged 5 to 14)	1.7	2019	●	●
Exports of major conventional weapons (TIV constant million USD per 100,000 population)	0.4	2020	●	●
Press Freedom Index (best 0–100 worst)	42.9	2021	●	→
Access to and affordability of justice (worst 0–1 best)	0.6	2020	●	↑
SDG17 – Partnerships for the Goals				
Government spending on health and education (% of GDP)	6.9	2019	●	↓
For high-income and all OECD DAC countries: International concessional public finance, including official development assistance (% of GNI)	NA	NA	●	●
Other countries: Government revenue excluding grants (% of GDP)	22.0	2019	●	→
Corporate Tax Haven Score (best 0–100 worst)	* 0.0	2019	●	●
Statistical Performance Index (worst 0–100 best)	62.0	2019	●	↗

* Imputed data point

5. Country Profiles

KAZAKHSTAN

Eastern Europe and Central Asia

OVERALL PERFORMANCE

COUNTRY RANKING

KAZAKHSTAN

65/163

COUNTRY SCORE

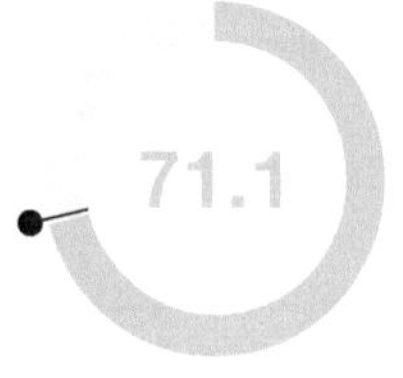

REGIONAL AVERAGE: 71.6

AVERAGE PERFORMANCE BY SDG

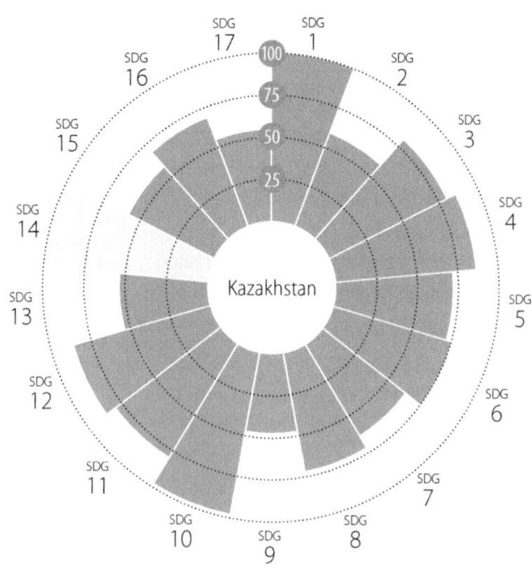

SDG DASHBOARDS AND TRENDS

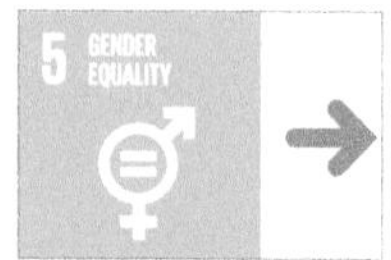

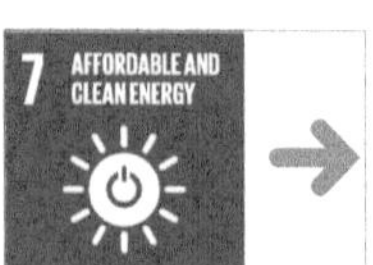

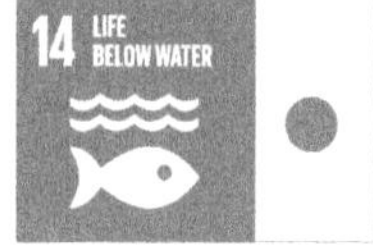

Major challenges · Significant challenges · Challenges remain · SDG achieved · Information unavailable

Decreasing · Stagnating · Moderately improving · On track or maintaining SDG achievement · Information unavailable

Note: The full title of each SDG is available here: https://sustainabledevelopment.un.org/topics/sustainabledevelopmentgoals

INTERNATIONAL SPILLOVER INDEX

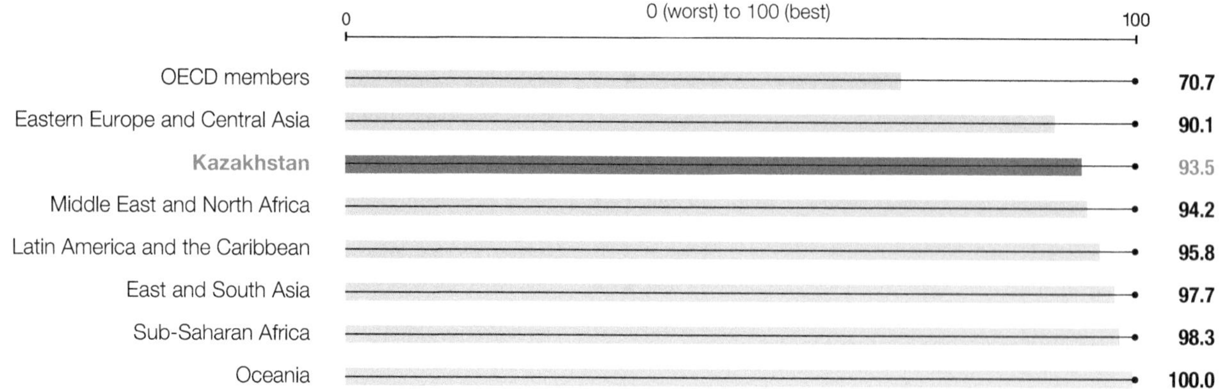

Region	Score
OECD members	70.7
Eastern Europe and Central Asia	90.1
Kazakhstan	93.5
Middle East and North Africa	94.2
Latin America and the Caribbean	95.8
East and South Asia	97.7
Sub-Saharan Africa	98.3
Oceania	100.0

STATISTICAL PERFORMANCE INDEX

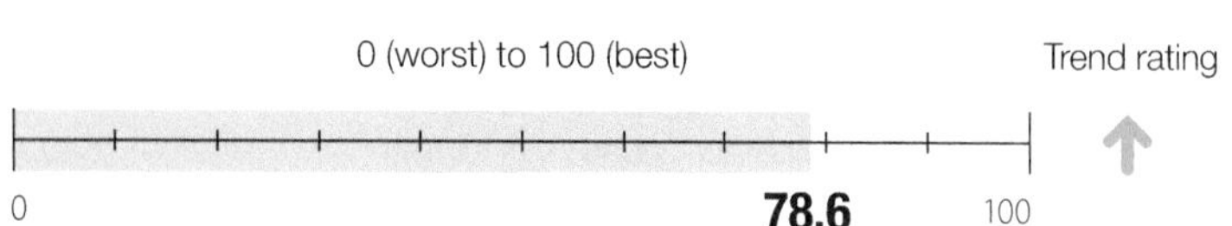

MISSING DATA IN SDG INDEX

1%

SDG1 – No Poverty	Value	Year	Rating	Trend
Poverty headcount ratio at $1.90/day (%)	0.0	2022	●	↑
Poverty headcount ratio at $3.20/day (%)	0.0	2022	●	↑
SDG2 – Zero Hunger				
Prevalence of undernourishment (%)	2.5	2019	●	↑
Prevalence of stunting in children under 5 years of age (%)	8.0	2015	●	↗
Prevalence of wasting in children under 5 years of age (%)	3.1	2015	●	↑
Prevalence of obesity, BMI ≥ 30 (% of adult population)	21.0	2016	●	↓
Human Trophic Level (best 2–3 worst)	2.4	2017	●	↓
Cereal yield (tonnes per hectare of harvested land)	1.4	2018	●	→
Sustainable Nitrogen Management Index (best 0–1.41 worst)	0.8	2015	●	→
Exports of hazardous pesticides (tonnes per million population)	0.3	2019	●	●
SDG3 – Good Health and Well-Being				
Maternal mortality rate (per 100,000 live births)	10	2017	●	↑
Neonatal mortality rate (per 1,000 live births)	4.8	2020	●	↑
Mortality rate, under-5 (per 1,000 live births)	10.0	2020	●	↑
Incidence of tuberculosis (per 100,000 population)	69.0	2020	●	↗
New HIV infections (per 1,000 uninfected population)	0.2	2020	●	↑
Age-standardized death rate due to cardiovascular disease, cancer, diabetes, or chronic respiratory disease in adults aged 30–70 years (%)	22.4	2019	●	↑
Age-standardized death rate attributable to household air pollution and ambient air pollution (per 100,000 population)	63	2016	●	●
Traffic deaths (per 100,000 population)	12.7	2019	●	↑
Life expectancy at birth (years)	74.0	2019	●	↗
Adolescent fertility rate (births per 1,000 females aged 15 to 19)	23.2	2019	●	↑
Births attended by skilled health personnel (%)	99.9	2018	●	↑
Surviving infants who received 2 WHO-recommended vaccines (%)	88	2020	●	↓
Universal health coverage (UHC) index of service coverage (worst 0–100 best)	76	2019	●	↑
Subjective well-being (average ladder score, worst 0–10 best)	6.3	2021	●	↑
SDG4 – Quality Education				
Participation rate in pre-primary organized learning (% of children aged 4 to 6)	77.7	2020	●	↓
Net primary enrollment rate (%)	90.4	2020	●	↓
Lower secondary completion rate (%)	104.0	2020	●	↑
Literacy rate (% of population aged 15 to 24)	99.9	2018	●	●
SDG5 – Gender Equality				
Demand for family planning satisfied by modern methods (% of females aged 15 to 49)	73.2	2018	●	→
Ratio of female-to-male mean years of education received (%)	91.6	2019	●	↓
Ratio of female-to-male labor force participation rate (%)	84.4	2020	●	↑
Seats held by women in national parliament (%)	27.1	2020	●	→
SDG6 – Clean Water and Sanitation				
Population using at least basic drinking water services (%)	95.4	2020	●	→
Population using at least basic sanitation services (%)	97.9	2020	●	↑
Freshwater withdrawal (% of available freshwater resources)	32.7	2018	●	●
Anthropogenic wastewater that receives treatment (%)	28.6	2018	●	●
Scarce water consumption embodied in imports (m^3 H_2O eq/capita)	2267.8	2018	●	●
SDG7 – Affordable and Clean Energy				
Population with access to electricity (%)	100.0	2019	●	↑
Population with access to clean fuels and technology for cooking (%)	97.6	2019	●	↑
CO_2 emissions from fuel combustion per total electricity output ($MtCO_2$/TWh)	2.7	2019	●	→
Share of renewable energy in total primary energy supply (%)	1.5	2019	●	↓
SDG8 – Decent Work and Economic Growth				
Adjusted GDP growth (%)	-0.7	2020	●	●
Victims of modern slavery (per 1,000 population)	4.2	2018	●	●
Adults with an account at a bank or other financial institution or with a mobile-money-service provider (% of population aged 15 or over)	58.7	2017	●	↗
Unemployment rate (% of total labor force)	4.9	2022	●	↑
Fundamental labor rights are effectively guaranteed (worst 0–1 best)	0.5	2020	●	→
Fatal work-related accidents embodied in imports (per 100,000 population)	0.2	2015	●	↑

* Imputed data point

SDG9 – Industry, Innovation and Infrastructure	Value	Year	Rating	Trend
Population using the internet (%)	85.9	2020	●	↑
Mobile broadband subscriptions (per 100 population)	90.3	2019	●	↑
Logistics Performance Index: Quality of trade and transport-related infrastructure (worst 1–5 best)	2.5	2018	●	↑
The Times Higher Education Universities Ranking: Average score of top 3 universities (worst 0–100 best)	16.5	2022	●	●
Articles published in academic journals (per 1,000 population)	0.3	2020	●	↗
Expenditure on research and development (% of GDP)	0.1	2018	●	↓
SDG10 – Reduced Inequalities				
Gini coefficient	27.8	2018	●	↑
Palma ratio	1.0	2018	●	●
SDG11 – Sustainable Cities and Communities				
Proportion of urban population living in slums (%)	10.5	2018	●	●
Annual mean concentration of particulate matter of less than 2.5 microns in diameter (PM2.5) ($\mu g/m^3$)	13.6	2019	●	↗
Access to improved water source, piped (% of urban population)	94.0	2020	●	→
Satisfaction with public transport (%)	47.0	2021	●	↓
SDG12 – Responsible Consumption and Production				
Municipal solid waste (kg/capita/day)	0.8	2012	●	●
Electronic waste (kg/capita)	9.2	2019	●	●
Production-based SO_2 emissions (kg/capita)	68.2	2018	●	●
SO_2 emissions embodied in imports (kg/capita)	2.3	2018	●	●
Production-based nitrogen emissions (kg/capita)	17.9	2015	●	↑
Nitrogen emissions embodied in imports (kg/capita)	2.8	2015	●	↑
Exports of plastic waste (kg/capita)	0.3	2020	●	●
SDG13 – Climate Action				
CO_2 emissions from fossil fuel combustion and cement production (tCO_2/capita)	15.5	2020	●	→
CO_2 emissions embodied in imports (tCO_2/capita)	0.9	2018	●	↑
CO_2 emissions embodied in fossil fuel exports (kg/capita)	16273.1	2020	●	●
SDG14 – Life Below Water				
Mean area that is protected in marine sites important to biodiversity (%)	NA	NA	●	●
Ocean Health Index: Clean Waters score (worst 0–100 best)	NA	NA	●	●
Fish caught from overexploited or collapsed stocks (% of total catch)	NA	NA	●	●
Fish caught by trawling or dredging (%)	NA	NA	●	●
Fish caught that are then discarded (%)	NA	NA	●	●
Marine biodiversity threats embodied in imports (per million population)	0.0	2018	●	●
SDG15 – Life on Land				
Mean area that is protected in terrestrial sites important to biodiversity (%)	13.1	2020	●	→
Mean area that is protected in freshwater sites important to biodiversity (%)	10.0	2020	●	→
Red List Index of species survival (worst 0–1 best)	0.9	2021	●	→
Permanent deforestation (% of forest area, 5-year average)	0.0	2020	●	↑
Terrestrial and freshwater biodiversity threats embodied in imports (per million population)	0.3	2018	●	●
SDG16 – Peace, Justice and Strong Institutions				
Homicides (per 100,000 population)	3.2	2020	●	↑
Unsentenced detainees (% of prison population)	11.3	2017	●	●
Population who feel safe walking alone at night in the city or area where they live (%)	60	2021	●	↓
Property Rights (worst 1–7 best)	3.9	2020	●	↓
Birth registrations with civil authority (% of children under age 5)	99.7	2020	●	●
Corruption Perception Index (worst 0–100 best)	37	2021	●	↗
Children involved in child labor (% of population aged 5 to 14)	NA	NA	●	●
Exports of major conventional weapons (TIV constant million USD per 100,000 population)	0.0	2020	●	●
Press Freedom Index (best 0–100 worst)	50.3	2021	●	→
Access to and affordability of justice (worst 0–1 best)	0.6	2020	●	↑
SDG17 – Partnerships for the Goals				
Government spending on health and education (% of GDP)	4.5	2019	●	↓
For high-income and all OECD DAC countries: International concessional public finance, including official development assistance (% of GNI)	NA	NA	●	●
Other countries: Government revenue excluding grants (% of GDP)	14.9	2019	●	→
Corporate Tax Haven Score (best 0–100 worst)	* 0.0	2019	●	●
Statistical Performance Index (worst 0–100 best)	78.6	2019	●	↑

KENYA

Sub-Saharan Africa

OVERALL PERFORMANCE

COUNTRY RANKING

KENYA

118/163

COUNTRY SCORE

AVERAGE PERFORMANCE BY SDG

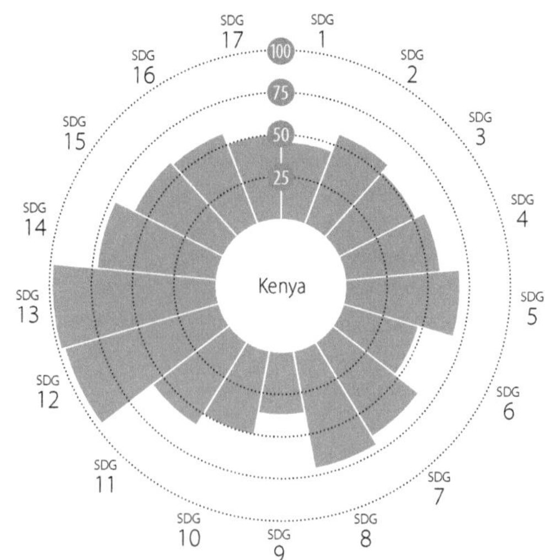

SDG DASHBOARDS AND TRENDS

Note: The full title of each SDG is available here: https://sustainabledevelopment.un.org/topics/sustainabledevelopmentgoals

INTERNATIONAL SPILLOVER INDEX

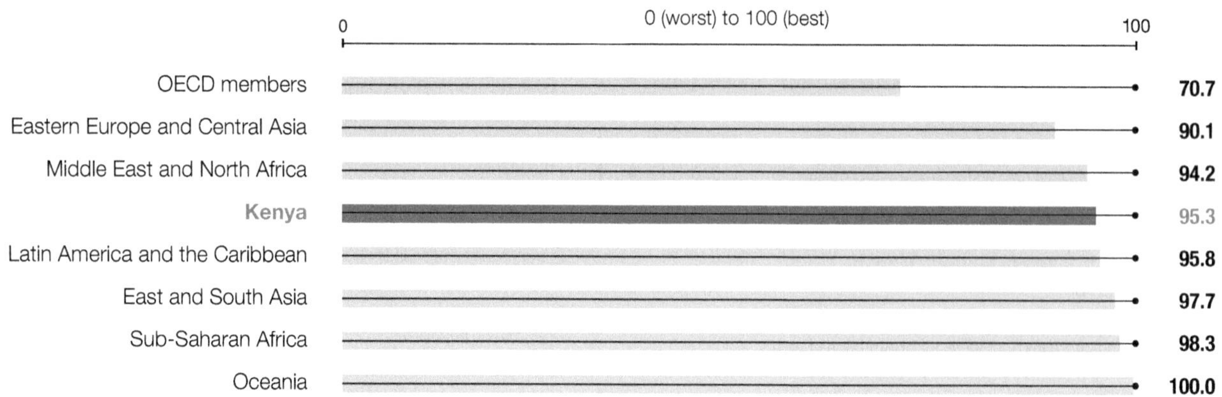

STATISTICAL PERFORMANCE INDEX

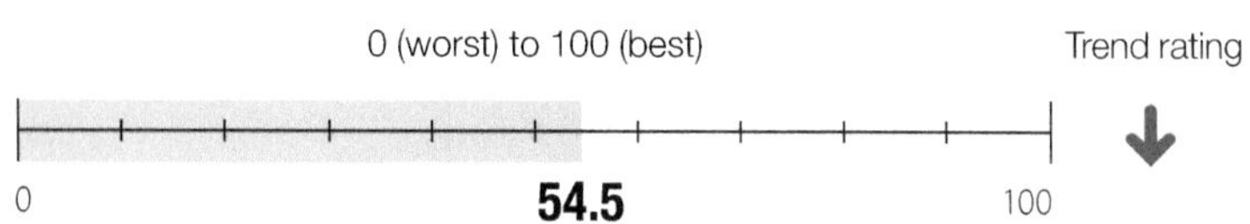

MISSING DATA IN SDG INDEX

1%

KENYA

Performance by Indicator

SDG1 – No Poverty	Value	Year	Rating	Trend
Poverty headcount ratio at $1.90/day (%)	17.4	2022	●	→
Poverty headcount ratio at $3.20/day (%)	43.8	2022	●	→
SDG2 – Zero Hunger				
Prevalence of undernourishment (%)	24.8	2019	●	↓
Prevalence of stunting in children under 5 years of age (%)	26.2	2014	●	→
Prevalence of wasting in children under 5 years of age (%)	4.2	2014	●	↑
Prevalence of obesity, BMI ≥ 30 (% of adult population)	7.1	2016	●	↑
Human Trophic Level (best 2–3 worst)	2.2	2017	●	→
Cereal yield (tonnes per hectare of harvested land)	1.8	2018	●	→
Sustainable Nitrogen Management Index (best 0–1.41 worst)	0.9	2015	●	→
Exports of hazardous pesticides (tonnes per million population)	1.0	2019	●	●
SDG3 – Good Health and Well-Being				
Maternal mortality rate (per 100,000 live births)	342	2017	●	→
Neonatal mortality rate (per 1,000 live births)	20.5	2020	●	↗
Mortality rate, under-5 (per 1,000 live births)	41.9	2020	●	↗
Incidence of tuberculosis (per 100,000 population)	259.0	2020	●	↗
New HIV infections (per 1,000 uninfected population)	0.7	2020	●	↑
Age-standardized death rate due to cardiovascular disease, cancer, diabetes, or chronic respiratory disease in adults aged 30–70 years (%)	21.0	2019	●	→
Age-standardized death rate attributable to household air pollution and ambient air pollution (per 100,000 population)	78	2016	●	●
Traffic deaths (per 100,000 population)	28.3	2019	●	↓
Life expectancy at birth (years)	66.1	2019	●	→
Adolescent fertility rate (births per 1,000 females aged 15 to 19)	96.0	2014	●	●
Births attended by skilled health personnel (%)	61.8	2014	●	●
Surviving infants who received 2 WHO-recommended vaccines (%)	88	2020	●	→
Universal health coverage (UHC) index of service coverage (worst 0–100 best)	56	2019	●	↗
Subjective well-being (average ladder score, worst 0–10 best)	4.5	2021	●	→
SDG4 – Quality Education				
Participation rate in pre-primary organized learning (% of children aged 4 to 6)	46.3	2009	●	●
Net primary enrollment rate (%)	81.2	2012	●	●
Lower secondary completion rate (%)	79.2	2016	●	●
Literacy rate (% of population aged 15 to 24)	87.8	2018	●	↗
SDG5 – Gender Equality				
Demand for family planning satisfied by modern methods (% of females aged 15 to 49)	74.4	2019	●	→
Ratio of female-to-male mean years of education received (%)	83.3	2019	●	↗
Ratio of female-to-male labor force participation rate (%)	94.0	2020	●	↑
Seats held by women in national parliament (%)	21.8	2020	●	→
SDG6 – Clean Water and Sanitation				
Population using at least basic drinking water services (%)	61.6	2020	●	→
Population using at least basic sanitation services (%)	32.7	2020	●	→
Freshwater withdrawal (% of available freshwater resources)	33.2	2018	●	●
Anthropogenic wastewater that receives treatment (%)	0.5	2018	●	●
Scarce water consumption embodied in imports (m^3 H_2O eq/capita)	590.7	2018	●	●
SDG7 – Affordable and Clean Energy				
Population with access to electricity (%)	69.7	2019	●	↑
Population with access to clean fuels and technology for cooking (%)	17.0	2019	●	→
CO_2 emissions from fuel combustion per total electricity output ($MtCO_2$/TWh)	1.4	2019	●	→
Share of renewable energy in total primary energy supply (%)	78.2	2019	●	↑
SDG8 – Decent Work and Economic Growth				
Adjusted GDP growth (%)	-3.0	2020	●	●
Victims of modern slavery (per 1,000 population)	6.9	2018	●	●
Adults with an account at a bank or other financial institution or with a mobile-money-service provider (% of population aged 15 or over)	81.6	2017	●	↑
Unemployment rate (% of total labor force)	5.5	2022	●	↓
Fundamental labor rights are effectively guaranteed (worst 0–1 best)	0.5	2020	●	↓
Fatal work-related accidents embodied in imports (per 100,000 population)	0.6	2015	●	↑

* Imputed data point

SDG9 – Industry, Innovation and Infrastructure	Value	Year	Rating	Trend
Population using the internet (%)	29.5	2020	●	↗
Mobile broadband subscriptions (per 100 population)	41.1	2019	●	↑
Logistics Performance Index: Quality of trade and transport-related infrastructure (worst 1–5 best)	2.6	2018	●	↑
The Times Higher Education Universities Ranking: Average score of top 3 universities (worst 0–100 best)	39.5	2022	●	●
Articles published in academic journals (per 1,000 population)	0.1	2020	●	→
Expenditure on research and development (% of GDP)	0.8	2010	●	●
SDG10 – Reduced Inequalities				
Gini coefficient	40.8	2015	●	●
Palma ratio	1.9	2018	●	●
SDG11 – Sustainable Cities and Communities				
Proportion of urban population living in slums (%)	46.1	2018	●	↗
Annual mean concentration of particulate matter of less than 2.5 microns in diameter (PM2.5) (μg/m^3)	28.4	2019	●	↓
Access to improved water source, piped (% of urban population)	60.2	2020	●	↓
Satisfaction with public transport (%)	52.0	2021	●	→
SDG12 – Responsible Consumption and Production				
Municipal solid waste (kg/capita/day)	0.4	2010	●	●
Electronic waste (kg/capita)	1.0	2019	●	●
Production-based SO_2 emissions (kg/capita)	1.2	2018	●	●
SO_2 emissions embodied in imports (kg/capita)	0.4	2018	●	●
Production-based nitrogen emissions (kg/capita)	12.4	2015	●	↑
Nitrogen emissions embodied in imports (kg/capita)	2.2	2015	●	↑
Exports of plastic waste (kg/capita)	0.1	2020	●	●
SDG13 – Climate Action				
CO_2 emissions from fossil fuel combustion and cement production (tCO_2/capita)	0.3	2020	●	↑
CO_2 emissions embodied in imports (tCO_2/capita)	0.1	2018	●	↑
CO_2 emissions embodied in fossil fuel exports (kg/capita)	0.0	2020	●	●
SDG14 – Life Below Water				
Mean area that is protected in marine sites important to biodiversity (%)	43.1	2020	●	→
Ocean Health Index: Clean Waters score (worst 0–100 best)	47.0	2020	●	↓
Fish caught from overexploited or collapsed stocks (% of total catch)	22.2	2018	●	↑
Fish caught by trawling or dredging (%)	0.0	2018	●	↑
Fish caught that are then discarded (%)	2.8	2018	●	↑
Marine biodiversity threats embodied in imports (per million population)	0.0	2018	●	●
SDG15 – Life on Land				
Mean area that is protected in terrestrial sites important to biodiversity (%)	34.2	2020	●	→
Mean area that is protected in freshwater sites important to biodiversity (%)	36.9	2020	●	→
Red List Index of species survival (worst 0–1 best)	0.8	2021	●	↓
Permanent deforestation (% of forest area, 5-year average)	0.3	2020	●	→
Terrestrial and freshwater biodiversity threats embodied in imports (per million population)	0.7	2018	●	●
SDG16 – Peace, Justice and Strong Institutions				
Homicides (per 100,000 population)	4.0	2020	●	↗
Unsentenced detainees (% of prison population)	44.6	2019	●	↓
Population who feel safe walking alone at night in the city or area where they live (%)	49	2021	●	↓
Property Rights (worst 1–7 best)	4.1	2020	●	↓
Birth registrations with civil authority (% of children under age 5)	66.9	2020	●	●
Corruption Perception Index (worst 0–100 best)	30	2021	●	→
Children involved in child labor (% of population aged 5 to 14)	NA	NA	●	●
Exports of major conventional weapons (TIV constant million USD per 100,000 population) *	0.0	2020	●	●
Press Freedom Index (best 0–100 worst)	33.7	2021	●	↓
Access to and affordability of justice (worst 0–1 best)	0.5	2020	●	↗
SDG17 – Partnerships for the Goals				
Government spending on health and education (% of GDP)	7.2	2020	●	↓
For high-income and all OECD DAC countries: International concessional public finance, including official development assistance (% of GNI)	NA	NA	●	●
Other countries: Government revenue excluding grants (% of GDP)	19.1	2019	●	↓
Corporate Tax Haven Score (best 0–100 worst)	50.8	2019	●	●
Statistical Performance Index (worst 0–100 best)	54.5	2019	●	↓

KIRIBATI

Oceania

OVERALL PERFORMANCE

COUNTRY RANKING

KIRIBATI

NA /163

COUNTRY SCORE

AVERAGE PERFORMANCE BY SDG

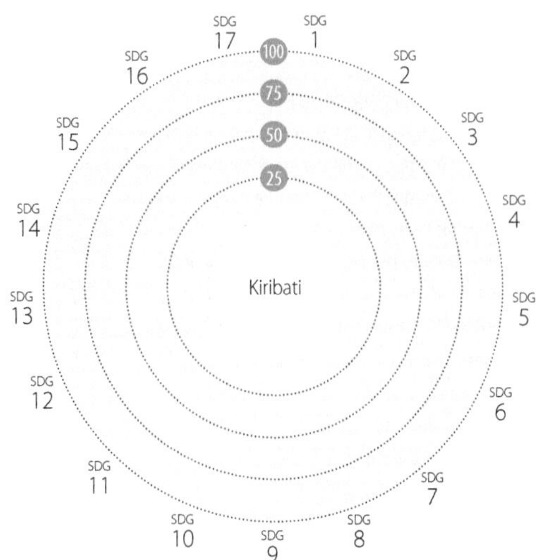

SDG DASHBOARDS AND TRENDS

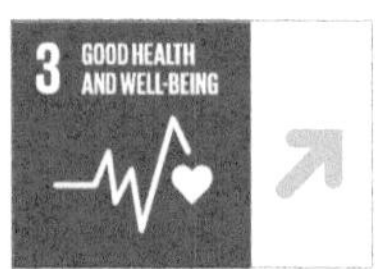

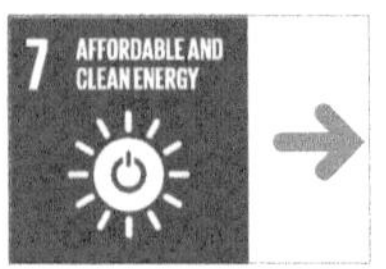
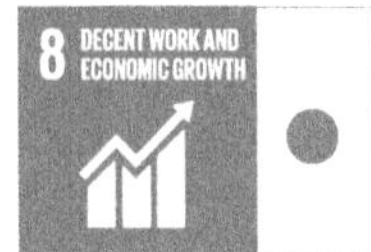

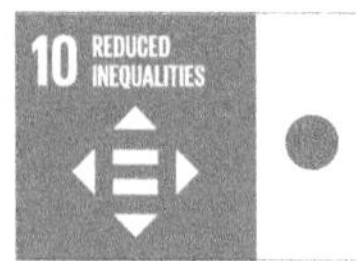

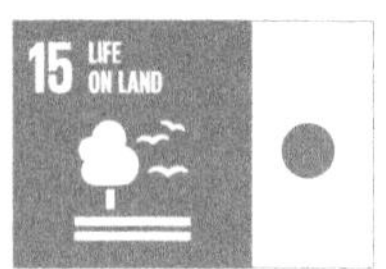

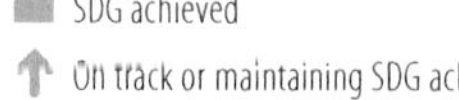

Major challenges | Significant challenges | Challenges remain | SDG achieved | Information unavailable

Decreasing | Stagnating | Moderately improving | On track or maintaining SDG achievement | Information unavailable

Note: The full title of each SDG is available here: https://sustainabledevelopment.un.org/topics/sustainabledevelopmentgoals

INTERNATIONAL SPILLOVER INDEX

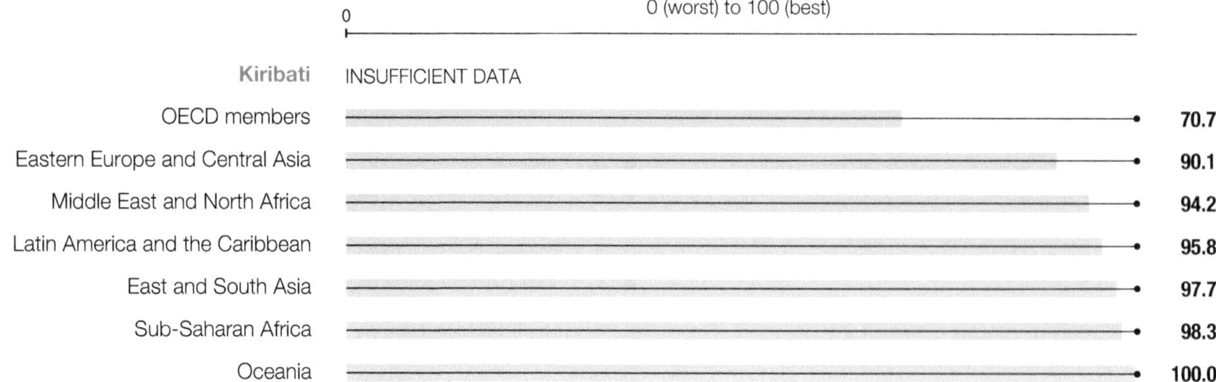

STATISTICAL PERFORMANCE INDEX

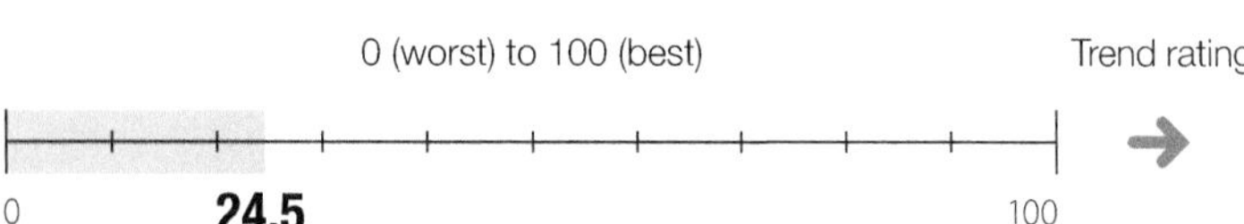

MISSING DATA IN SDG INDEX

39%

SDG1 – No Poverty

Indicator	Value	Year	Rating	Trend
Poverty headcount ratio at $1.90/day (%)	NA	NA	●	●
Poverty headcount ratio at $3.20/day (%)	NA	NA	●	●

SDG2 – Zero Hunger

Indicator	Value	Year	Rating	Trend
Prevalence of undernourishment (%)	4.1	2019	●	↑
Prevalence of stunting in children under 5 years of age (%)	15.2	2018	●	→
Prevalence of wasting in children under 5 years of age (%)	3.5	2018	●	↑
Prevalence of obesity, BMI ≥ 30 (% of adult population)	46.0	2016	●	↓
Human Trophic Level (best 2–3 worst)	2.3	2017	●	→
Cereal yield (tonnes per hectare of harvested land)	NA	NA	●	●
Sustainable Nitrogen Management Index (best 0–1.41 worst)	1.0	2015	●	↓
Exports of hazardous pesticides (tonnes per million population)	NA	NA	●	●

SDG3 – Good Health and Well-Being

Indicator	Value	Year	Rating	Trend
Maternal mortality rate (per 100,000 live births)	92	2017	●	↑
Neonatal mortality rate (per 1,000 live births)	21.3	2020	●	↗
Mortality rate, under-5 (per 1,000 live births)	49.6	2020	●	↗
Incidence of tuberculosis (per 100,000 population)	425.0	2020	●	↗
New HIV infections (per 1,000 uninfected population)	NA	NA	●	●
Age-standardized death rate due to cardiovascular disease, cancer, diabetes, or chronic respiratory disease in adults aged 30–70 years (%)	50.9	2019	●	→
Age-standardized death rate attributable to household air pollution and ambient air pollution (per 100,000 population)	140	2016	●	●
Traffic deaths (per 100,000 population)	1.9	2019	●	↑
Life expectancy at birth (years)	59.4	2019	●	→
Adolescent fertility rate (births per 1,000 females aged 15 to 19)	50.6	2017	●	●
Births attended by skilled health personnel (%)	98.3	2010	●	●
Surviving infants who received 2 WHO-recommended vaccines (%)	82	2020	●	↑
Universal health coverage (UHC) index of service coverage (worst 0–100 best)	51	2019	●	→
Subjective well-being (average ladder score, worst 0–10 best)	NA	NA	●	●

SDG4 – Quality Education

Indicator	Value	Year	Rating	Trend
Participation rate in pre-primary organized learning (% of children aged 4 to 6)	97.7	2020	●	●
Net primary enrollment rate (%)	96.7	2020	●	↓
Lower secondary completion rate (%)	99.9	2020	●	↑
Literacy rate (% of population aged 15 to 24)	NA	NA	●	●

SDG5 – Gender Equality

Indicator	Value	Year	Rating	Trend
Demand for family planning satisfied by modern methods (% of females aged 15 to 49)	53.1	2019	●	→
Ratio of female-to-male mean years of education received (%)	NA	NA	●	●
Ratio of female-to-male labor force participation rate (%)	NA	NA	●	●
Seats held by women in national parliament (%)	8.9	2020	●	→

SDG6 – Clean Water and Sanitation

Indicator	Value	Year	Rating	Trend
Population using at least basic drinking water services (%)	78.0	2020	●	↗
Population using at least basic sanitation services (%)	45.6	2020	●	→
Freshwater withdrawal (% of available freshwater resources)	NA	NA	●	●
Anthropogenic wastewater that receives treatment (%)	0.0	2018	●	●
Scarce water consumption embodied in imports (m^3 H_2O eq/capita)	NA	NA	●	●

SDG7 – Affordable and Clean Energy

Indicator	Value	Year	Rating	Trend
Population with access to electricity (%)	100.0	2019	●	↑
Population with access to clean fuels and technology for cooking (%)	10.2	2019	●	→
CO_2 emissions from fuel combustion per total electricity output ($MtCO_2$/TWh)	3.2	2019	●	→
Share of renewable energy in total primary energy supply (%)	NA	NA	●	●

SDG8 – Decent Work and Economic Growth

Indicator	Value	Year	Rating	Trend
Adjusted GDP growth (%)	-4.7	2020	●	●
Victims of modern slavery (per 1,000 population)	NA	NA	●	●
Adults with an account at a bank or other financial institution or with a mobile-money-service provider (% of population aged 15 or over)	NA	NA	●	●
Unemployment rate (% of total labor force)	NA	NA	●	●
Fundamental labor rights are effectively guaranteed (worst 0–1 best)	NA	NA	●	●
Fatal work-related accidents embodied in imports (per 100,000 population)	NA	NA	●	●

* Imputed data point

SDG9 – Industry, Innovation and Infrastructure

Indicator	Value	Year	Rating	Trend
Population using the internet (%)	38.0	2020	●	↑
Mobile broadband subscriptions (per 100 population)	39.1	2019	●	●
Logistics Performance Index: Quality of trade and transport-related infrastructure (worst 1–5 best)	NA	NA	●	●
The Times Higher Education Universities Ranking: Average score of top 3 universities (worst 0–100 best)	* 0.0	2022	●	●
Articles published in academic journals (per 1,000 population)	0.1	2020	●	→
Expenditure on research and development (% of GDP)	NA	NA	●	●

SDG10 – Reduced Inequalities

Indicator	Value	Year	Rating	Trend
Gini coefficient	37.0	2006	●	●
Palma ratio	NA	NA	●	●

SDG11 – Sustainable Cities and Communities

Indicator	Value	Year	Rating	Trend
Proportion of urban population living in slums (%)	NA	NA	●	●
Annual mean concentration of particulate matter of less than 2.5 microns in diameter (PM2.5) (μg/m^3)	10.0	2019	●	↑
Access to improved water source, piped (% of urban population)	62.4	2020	●	→
Satisfaction with public transport (%)	NA	NA	●	●

SDG12 – Responsible Consumption and Production

Indicator	Value	Year	Rating	Trend
Municipal solid waste (kg/capita/day)	0.9	2016	●	●
Electronic waste (kg/capita)	0.9	2019	●	●
Production-based SO_2 emissions (kg/capita)	NA	NA	●	●
SO_2 emissions embodied in imports (kg/capita)	NA	NA	●	●
Production-based nitrogen emissions (kg/capita)	NA	NA	●	●
Nitrogen emissions embodied in imports (kg/capita)	NA	NA	●	●
Exports of plastic waste (kg/capita)	0.0	2017	●	●

SDG13 – Climate Action

Indicator	Value	Year	Rating	Trend
CO_2 emissions from fossil fuel combustion and cement production (tCO_2/capita)	0.6	2020	●	↑
CO_2 emissions embodied in imports (tCO_2/capita)	NA	NA	●	●
CO_2 emissions embodied in fossil fuel exports (kg/capita)	0.0	2020	●	●

SDG14 – Life Below Water

Indicator	Value	Year	Rating	Trend
Mean area that is protected in marine sites important to biodiversity (%)	32.9	2020	●	→
Ocean Health Index: Clean Waters score (worst 0–100 best)	NA	NA	●	●
Fish caught from overexploited or collapsed stocks (% of total catch)	14.2	2018	●	↑
Fish caught by trawling or dredging (%)	0.0	2018	●	↑
Fish caught that are then discarded (%)	1.8	2018	●	↑
Marine biodiversity threats embodied in imports (per million population)	NA	NA	●	●

SDG15 – Life on Land

Indicator	Value	Year	Rating	Trend
Mean area that is protected in terrestrial sites important to biodiversity (%)	40.0	2020	●	→
Mean area that is protected in freshwater sites important to biodiversity (%)	NA	NA	●	●
Red List Index of species survival (worst 0–1 best)	0.8	2021	●	↓
Permanent deforestation (% of forest area, 5-year average)	NA	NA	●	●
Terrestrial and freshwater biodiversity threats embodied in imports (per million population)	NA	NA	●	●

SDG16 – Peace, Justice and Strong Institutions

Indicator	Value	Year	Rating	Trend
Homicides (per 100,000 population)	7.5	2012	●	●
Unsentenced detainees (% of prison population)	4.7	2016	●	●
Population who feel safe walking alone at night in the city or area where they live (%)	NA	NA	●	●
Property Rights (worst 1–7 best)	NA	NA	●	●
Birth registrations with civil authority (% of children under age 5)	91.6	2020	●	●
Corruption Perception Index (worst 0–100 best)	NA	NA	●	●
Children involved in child labor (% of population aged 5 to 14)	16.5	2019	●	●
Exports of major conventional weapons (TIV constant million USD per 100,000 population)	* 0.0	2020	●	●
Press Freedom Index (best 0–100 worst)	NA	NA	●	●
Access to and affordability of justice (worst 0–1 best)	NA	NA	●	●

SDG17 – Partnerships for the Goals

Indicator	Value	Year	Rating	Trend
Government spending on health and education (% of GDP)	20.8	2019	●	↑
For high-income and all OECD DAC countries: International concessional public finance, including official development assistance (% of GNI)	NA	NA	●	●
Other countries: Government revenue excluding grants (% of GDP)	118.6	2019	●	↑
Corporate Tax Haven Score (best 0–100 worst)	* 0.0	2019	●	●
Statistical Performance Index (worst 0–100 best)	24.5	2019	●	→

KOREA, DEMOCRATIC REPUBLIC OF East and South Asia

OVERALL PERFORMANCE

COUNTRY RANKING

KOREA, DEMOCRATIC REPUBLIC OF

NA /163

COUNTRY SCORE

REGIONAL AVERAGE: 65.9

AVERAGE PERFORMANCE BY SDG

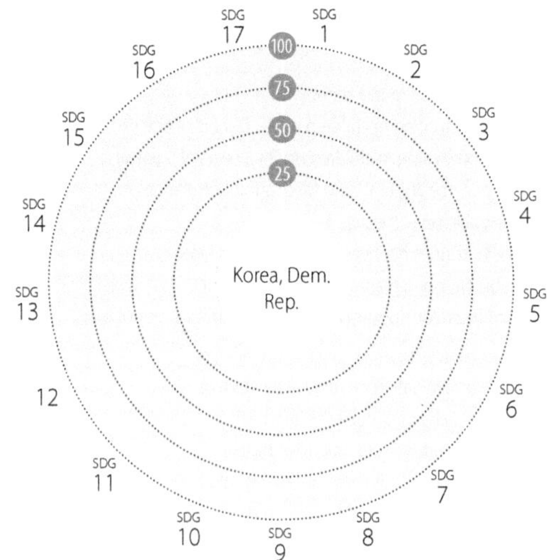

SDG DASHBOARDS AND TRENDS

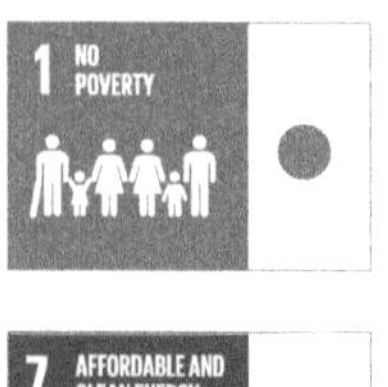

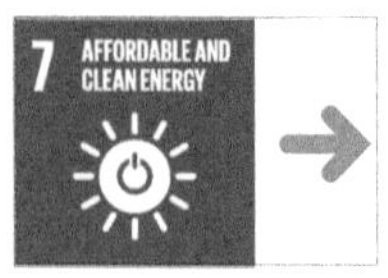

Information unavailable

Information unavailable

Note: The full title of each SDG is available here: https://sustainabledevelopment.un.org/topics/sustainabledevelopmentgoals

INTERNATIONAL SPILLOVER INDEX

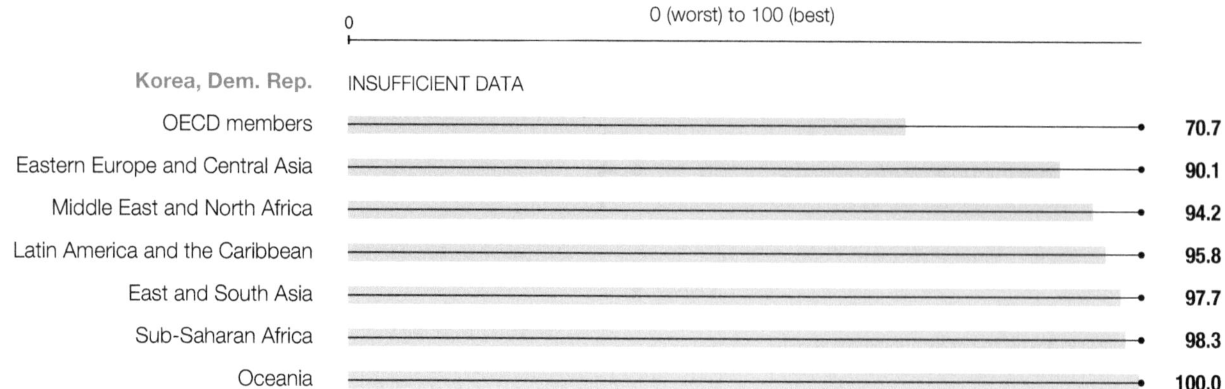

STATISTICAL PERFORMANCE INDEX

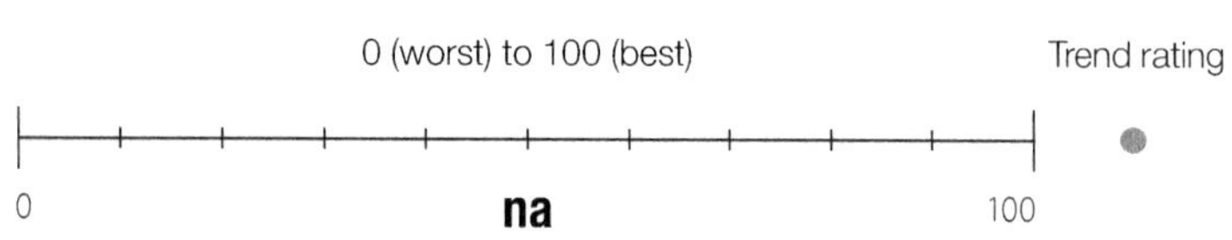

Trend rating

MISSING DATA IN SDG INDEX

31%

KOREA, DEMOCRATIC REPUBLIC OF Performance by Indicator

SDG1 – No Poverty		Value	Year	Rating	Trend
Poverty headcount ratio at $1.90/day (%)	*	NA	NA	●	●
Poverty headcount ratio at $3.20/day (%)	*	NA	NA	●	●
SDG2 – Zero Hunger					
Prevalence of undernourishment (%)		42.4	2019	●	↓
Prevalence of stunting in children under 5 years of age (%)		19.1	2017	●	→
Prevalence of wasting in children under 5 years of age (%)		2.5	2017	●	↑
Prevalence of obesity, BMI ≥ 30 (% of adult population)		6.8	2016	●	↑
Human Trophic Level (best 2–3 worst)		2.1	2017	●	↑
Cereal yield (tonnes per hectare of harvested land)		3.6	2018	●	↑
Sustainable Nitrogen Management Index (best 0–1.41 worst)		0.5	2015	●	→
Exports of hazardous pesticides (tonnes per million population)		NA	NA	●	●
SDG3 – Good Health and Well-Being					
Maternal mortality rate (per 100,000 live births)		89	2017	●	↗
Neonatal mortality rate (per 1,000 live births)		8.9	2020	●	↑
Mortality rate, under-5 (per 1,000 live births)		16.5	2020	●	↑
Incidence of tuberculosis (per 100,000 population)		523.0	2020	●	↓
New HIV infections (per 1,000 uninfected population)		1.0	2020	●	→
Age-standardized death rate due to cardiovascular disease, cancer, diabetes, or chronic respiratory disease in adults aged 30–70 years (%)		23.9	2019	●	↗
Age-standardized death rate attributable to household air pollution and ambient air pollution (per 100,000 population)		207	2016	●	●
Traffic deaths (per 100,000 population)		24.2	2019	●	↓
Life expectancy at birth (years)		72.6	2019	●	→
Adolescent fertility rate (births per 1,000 females aged 15 to 19)		1.0	2017	●	●
Births attended by skilled health personnel (%)		99.5	2017	●	●
Surviving infants who received 2 WHO-recommended vaccines (%)		97	2020	●	↑
Universal health coverage (UHC) index of service coverage (worst 0–100 best)		68	2019	●	↑
Subjective well-being (average ladder score, worst 0–10 best)		NA	NA	●	●
SDG4 – Quality Education					
Participation rate in pre-primary organized learning (% of children aged 4 to 6)		NA	NA	●	●
Net primary enrollment rate (%)		97.8	2009	●	●
Lower secondary completion rate (%)		NA	NA	●	●
Literacy rate (% of population aged 15 to 24)		100.0	2008	●	●
SDG5 – Gender Equality					
Demand for family planning satisfied by modern methods (% of females aged 15 to 49)		89.6	2017	●	↑
Ratio of female-to-male mean years of education received (%)		NA	NA	●	●
Ratio of female-to-male labor force participation rate (%)		90.0	2020	●	↑
Seats held by women in national parliament (%)		17.6	2020	●	→
SDG6 – Clean Water and Sanitation					
Population using at least basic drinking water services (%)		93.8	2020	●	→
Population using at least basic sanitation services (%)		84.7	2020	●	↗
Freshwater withdrawal (% of available freshwater resources)		27.7	2018	●	●
Anthropogenic wastewater that receives treatment (%)		0.0	2018	●	●
Scarce water consumption embodied in imports (m^3 H_2O eq/capita)		41.3	2018	●	●
SDG7 – Affordable and Clean Energy					
Population with access to electricity (%)		49.4	2019	●	↗
Population with access to clean fuels and technology for cooking (%)		10.8	2019	●	→
CO_2 emissions from fuel combustion per total electricity output ($MtCO_2$/TWh)		1.7	2019	●	→
Share of renewable energy in total primary energy supply (%)		NA	NA	●	●
SDG8 – Decent Work and Economic Growth					
Adjusted GDP growth (%)		NA	NA	●	●
Victims of modern slavery (per 1,000 population)		104.6	2018	●	●
Adults with an account at a bank or other financial institution or with a mobile-money-service provider (% of population aged 15 or over)		NA	NA	●	●
Unemployment rate (% of total labor force)		2.2	2022	●	↑
Fundamental labor rights are effectively guaranteed (worst 0–1 best)		NA	NA	●	●
Fatal work-related accidents embodied in imports (per 100,000 population)		0.0	2015	●	↑

* Imputed data point

SDG9 – Industry, Innovation and Infrastructure		Value	Year	Rating	Trend
Population using the internet (%)		0.0	2012	●	●
Mobile broadband subscriptions (per 100 population)		16.6	2019	●	→
Logistics Performance Index: Quality of trade and transport-related infrastructure (worst 1–5 best)		NA	NA	●	●
The Times Higher Education Universities Ranking: Average score of top 3 universities (worst 0–100 best)	*	0.0	2022	●	●
Articles published in academic journals (per 1,000 population)		0.0	2020	●	→
Expenditure on research and development (% of GDP)	*	0.0	2018	●	●
SDG10 – Reduced Inequalities					
Gini coefficient		NA	NA	●	●
Palma ratio		NA	NA	●	●
SDG11 – Sustainable Cities and Communities					
Proportion of urban population living in slums (%)		NA	NA	●	●
Annual mean concentration of particulate matter of less than 2.5 microns in diameter (PM2.5) (μg/m^3)		29.8	2019	●	↑
Access to improved water source, piped (% of urban population)		73.6	2020	●	↓
Satisfaction with public transport (%)		NA	NA	●	●
SDG12 – Responsible Consumption and Production					
Municipal solid waste (kg/capita/day)		NA	NA	●	●
Electronic waste (kg/capita)		NA	NA	●	●
Production-based SO_2 emissions (kg/capita)		3.9	2018	●	●
SO_2 emissions embodied in imports (kg/capita)		0.0	2018	●	●
Production-based nitrogen emissions (kg/capita)		3.9	2015	●	↑
Nitrogen emissions embodied in imports (kg/capita)		0.1	2015	●	↑
Exports of plastic waste (kg/capita)		NA	NA	●	●
SDG13 – Climate Action					
CO_2 emissions from fossil fuel combustion and cement production (tCO_2/capita)		1.1	2020	●	↑
CO_2 emissions embodied in imports (tCO_2/capita)		0.0	2018	●	↑
CO_2 emissions embodied in fossil fuel exports (kg/capita)		NA	NA	●	●
SDG14 – Life Below Water					
Mean area that is protected in marine sites important to biodiversity (%)		0.0	2020	●	→
Ocean Health Index: Clean Waters score (worst 0–100 best)		53.8	2020	●	→
Fish caught from overexploited or collapsed stocks (% of total catch)		35.3	2018	●	↓
Fish caught by trawling or dredging (%)		31.2	2018	●	↓
Fish caught that are then discarded (%)		0.5	2018	●	↑
Marine biodiversity threats embodied in imports (per million population)		NA	NA	●	●
SDG15 – Life on Land					
Mean area that is protected in terrestrial sites important to biodiversity (%)		0.0	2020	●	→
Mean area that is protected in freshwater sites important to biodiversity (%)		0.0	2020	●	→
Red List Index of species survival (worst 0–1 best)		0.9	2021	●	↑
Permanent deforestation (% of forest area, 5-year average)		0.0	2020	●	↑
Terrestrial and freshwater biodiversity threats embodied in imports (per million population)		0.0	2018	●	●
SDG16 – Peace, Justice and Strong Institutions					
Homicides (per 100,000 population)		NA	NA	●	●
Unsentenced detainees (% of prison population)		NA	NA	●	●
Population who feel safe walking alone at night in the city or area where they live (%)		NA	NA	●	●
Property Rights (worst 1–7 best)		NA	NA	●	●
Birth registrations with civil authority (% of children under age 5)		100.0	2020	●	●
Corruption Perception Index (worst 0–100 best)		16	2021	●	→
Children involved in child labor (% of population aged 5 to 14)		4.3	2019	●	●
Exports of major conventional weapons (TIV constant million USD per 100,000 population)		0.0	2020	●	●
Press Freedom Index (best 0–100 worst)		81.3	2021	●	→
Access to and affordability of justice (worst 0–1 best)		NA	NA	●	●
SDG17 – Partnerships for the Goals					
Government spending on health and education (% of GDP)		NA	NA	●	●
For high-income and all OECD DAC countries: International concessional public finance, including official development assistance (% of GNI)		NA	NA	●	●
Other countries: Government revenue excluding grants (% of GDP)		NA	NA	●	●
Corporate Tax Haven Score (best 0–100 worst)	*	0.0	2019	●	●
Statistical Performance Index (worst 0–100 best)		NA	NA	●	●

5. Country Profiles

KOREA, REPUBLIC OF

OECD Countries

OVERALL PERFORMANCE

COUNTRY RANKING

KOREA, REPUBLIC OF

27 /163

COUNTRY SCORE

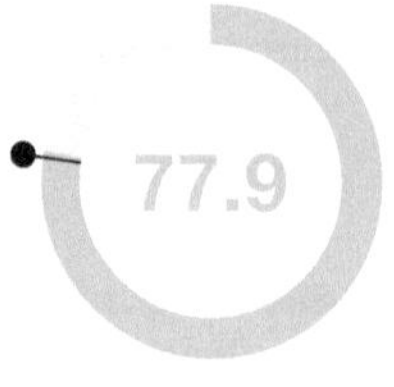

REGIONAL AVERAGE: 77.2

AVERAGE PERFORMANCE BY SDG

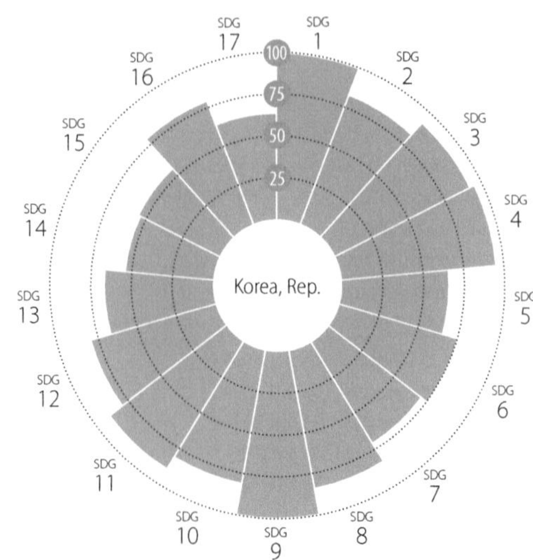

SDG DASHBOARDS AND TRENDS

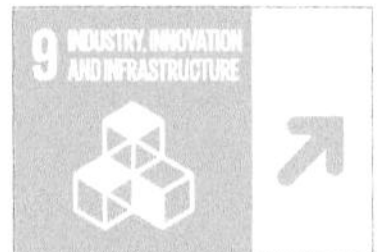

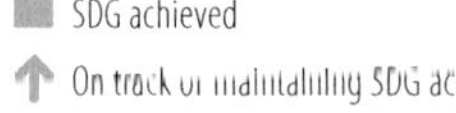

Information unavailable
Information unavailable

Note: The full title of each SDG is available here: https://sustainabledevelopment.un.org/topics/sustainabledevelopmentgoals

INTERNATIONAL SPILLOVER INDEX

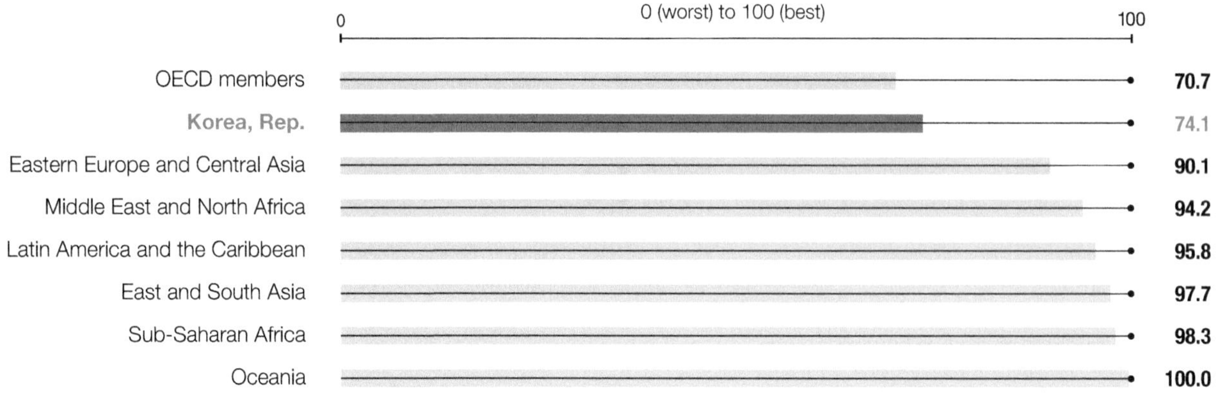

STATISTICAL PERFORMANCE INDEX

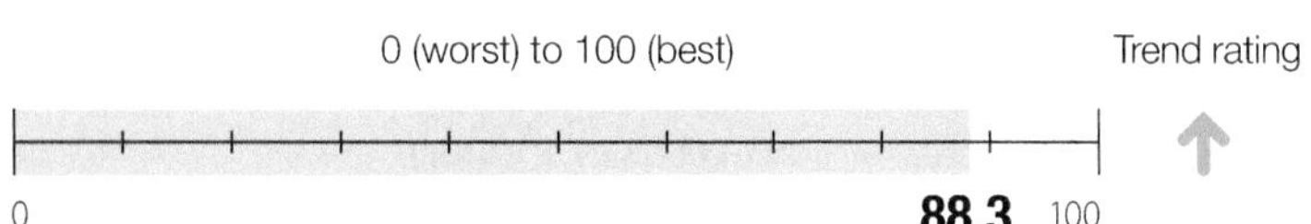

MISSING DATA IN SDG INDEX

2%

KOREA, REPUBLIC OF

Performance by Indicator

SDG1 – No Poverty	Value	Year	Rating	Trend
Poverty headcount ratio at \$1.90/day (%)	0.4	2022	●	↑
Poverty headcount ratio at \$3.20/day (%)	0.5	2022	●	↑
Poverty rate after taxes and transfers (%)	16.7	2018	●	↗
SDG2 – Zero Hunger				
Prevalence of undernourishment (%)	2.5	2019	●	↑
Prevalence of stunting in children under 5 years of age (%)	2.5	2009	●	↑
Prevalence of wasting in children under 5 years of age (%)	1.2	2009	●	↑
Prevalence of obesity, BMI ≥ 30 (% of adult population)	4.7	2016	●	↑
Human Trophic Level (best 2–3 worst)	2.3	2017	●	↓
Cereal yield (tonnes per hectare of harvested land)	6.6	2018	●	↑
Sustainable Nitrogen Management Index (best 0–1.41 worst)	0.6	2015	●	↓
Yield gap closure (% of potential yield)	NA	NA	●	●
Exports of hazardous pesticides (tonnes per million population)	1.8	2019	●	●
SDG3 – Good Health and Well-Being				
Maternal mortality rate (per 100,000 live births)	11	2017	●	↑
Neonatal mortality rate (per 1,000 live births)	1.5	2020	●	↑
Mortality rate, under-5 (per 1,000 live births)	3.0	2020	●	↑
Incidence of tuberculosis (per 100,000 population)	49.0	2020	●	↑
New HIV infections (per 1,000 uninfected population)	1.0	2020	●	→
Age-standardized death rate due to cardiovascular disease, cancer, diabetes, or chronic respiratory disease in adults aged 30–70 years (%)	7.3	2019	●	↑
Age-standardized death rate attributable to household air pollution and ambient air pollution (per 100,000 population)	20	2016	●	●
Traffic deaths (per 100,000 population)	8.6	2019	●	↑
Life expectancy at birth (years)	83.3	2019	●	↑
Adolescent fertility rate (births per 1,000 females aged 15 to 19)	0.9	2018	●	↑
Births attended by skilled health personnel (%)	100.0	2015	●	●
Surviving infants who received 2 WHO-recommended vaccines (%)	98	2019	●	↑
Universal health coverage (UHC) index of service coverage (worst 0–100 best)	87	2019	●	↑
Subjective well-being (average ladder score, worst 0–10 best)	6.1	2021	●	↑
Gap in life expectancy at birth among regions (years)	2.2	2017	●	●
Gap in self-reported health status by income (percentage points)	13.8	2019	●	↑
Daily smokers (% of population aged 15 and over)	16.4	2019	●	↑
SDG4 – Quality Education				
Participation rate in pre-primary organized learning (% of children aged 4 to 6)	89.3	2019	●	↓
Net primary enrollment rate (%)	100.0	2019	●	↑
Lower secondary completion rate (%)	96.7	2019	●	↑
Literacy rate (% of population aged 15 to 24)	100.0	2008	●	●
Tertiary educational attainment (% of population aged 25 to 34)	69.8	2020	●	↑
PISA score (worst 0–600 best)	519.7	2018	●	↑
Variation in science performance explained by socio-economic status (%)	8.0	2018	●	↑
Underachievers in science (% of 15-year-olds)	14.2	2018	●	↑
SDG5 – Gender Equality				
Demand for family planning satisfied by modern methods (% of females aged 15 to 49)	* 82.3	2022	●	↑
Ratio of female-to-male mean years of education received (%)	88.4	2019	●	→
Ratio of female-to-male labor force participation rate (%)	73.1	2020	●	↑
Seats held by women in national parliament (%)	19.0	2020	●	→
Gender wage gap (% of male median wage)	31.5	2020	●	↗
SDG6 – Clean Water and Sanitation				
Population using at least basic drinking water services (%)	99.9	2020	●	↑
Population using at least basic sanitation services (%)	99.9	2020	●	↑
Freshwater withdrawal (% of available freshwater resources)	85.2	2018	●	●
Anthropogenic wastewater that receives treatment (%)	76.8	2018	●	●
Scarce water consumption embodied in imports (m^3 H_2O eq/capita)	2208.0	2018	●	●
Population using safely managed water services (%)	99.2	2020	●	↑
Population using safely managed sanitation services (%)	99.9	2020	●	↑
SDG7 – Affordable and Clean Energy				
Population with access to electricity (%)	100.0	2019	●	↑
Population with access to clean fuels and technology for cooking (%)	100.0	2019	●	↑
CO_2 emissions from fuel combustion per total electricity output ($MtCO_2$/TWh)	1.1	2019	●	↑
Share of renewable energy in total primary energy supply (%)	2.0	2019	●	→
SDG8 – Decent Work and Economic Growth				
Adjusted GDP growth (%)	0.9	2020	●	●
Victims of modern slavery (per 1,000 population)	1.9	2018	●	●
Adults with an account at a bank or other financial institution or with a mobile-money-service provider (% of population aged 15 or over)	94.9	2017	●	↑
Fundamental labor rights are effectively guaranteed (worst 0–1 best)	0.6	2020	●	↓
Fatal work-related accidents embodied in imports (per 100,000 population)	0.9	2015	●	↑
Employment-to-population ratio (%)	66.5	2021	●	↑
Youth not in employment, education or training (NEET) (% of population aged 15 to 29)	NA	NA	●	●

* Imputed data point

SDG9 – Industry, Innovation and Infrastructure	Value	Year	Rating	Trend
Population using the internet (%)	96.5	2020	●	↑
Mobile broadband subscriptions (per 100 population)	114.9	2019	●	↑
Logistics Performance Index: Quality of trade and transport-related infrastructure (worst 1–5 best)	3.7	2018	●	↑
The Times Higher Education Universities Ranking: Average score of top 3 universities (worst 0–100 best)	64.1	2022	●	●
Articles published in academic journals (per 1,000 population)	1.8	2020	●	↑
Expenditure on research and development (% of GDP)	4.5	2018	●	↑
Researchers (per 1,000 employed population)	15.9	2019	●	↑
Triadic patent families filed (per million population)	49.9	2019	●	↑
Gap in internet access by income (percentage points)	0.8	2020	●	↑
Female share of graduates from STEM fields at the tertiary level (%)	25.2	2017	●	↓
SDG10 – Reduced Inequalities				
Gini coefficient	31.4	2016	●	●
Palma ratio	1.4	2018	●	↗
Elderly poverty rate (% of population aged 66 or over)	43.4	2018	●	→
SDG11 – Sustainable Cities and Communities				
Proportion of urban population living in slums (%)	* 0.0	2018	●	↑
Annual mean concentration of particulate matter of less than 2.5 microns in diameter (PM2.5) (μg/m³)	23.8	2019	●	↗
Access to improved water source, piped (% of urban population)	NA	NA	●	●
Satisfaction with public transport (%)	75.0	2021	●	↑
Population with rent overburden (%)	3.1	2012	●	●
SDG12 – Responsible Consumption and Production				
Electronic waste (kg/capita)	15.8	2019	●	●
Production-based SO_2 emissions (kg/capita)	21.4	2018	●	●
SO_2 emissions embodied in imports (kg/capita)	4.1	2018	●	●
Production-based nitrogen emissions (kg/capita)	3.5	2015	●	↑
Nitrogen emissions embodied in imports (kg/capita)	9.3	2015	●	→
Exports of plastic waste (kg/capita)	1.6	2020	●	●
Non-recycled municipal solid waste (kg/capita/day)	0.4	2018	●	↑
SDG13 – Climate Action				
CO_2 emissions from fossil fuel combustion and cement production (tCO_2/capita)	11.7	2020	●	→
CO_2 emissions embodied in imports (tCO_2/capita)	1.4	2018	●	↓
CO_2 emissions embodied in fossil fuel exports (kg/capita)	1.4	2020	●	●
Carbon Pricing Score at EUR60/tCO_2 (%, worst 0–100 best)	49.2	2018	●	↑
SDG14 – Life Below Water				
Mean area that is protected in marine sites important to biodiversity (%)	38.7	2020	●	→
Ocean Health Index: Clean Waters score (worst 0–100 best)	60.0	2020	●	↓
Fish caught from overexploited or collapsed stocks (% of total catch)	42.2	2018	●	↓
Fish caught by trawling or dredging (%)	33.7	2018	●	↓
Fish caught that are then discarded (%)	11.7	2018	●	→
Marine biodiversity threats embodied in imports (per million population)	0.4	2018	●	●
SDG15 – Life on Land				
Mean area that is protected in terrestrial sites important to biodiversity (%)	37.6	2020	●	→
Mean area that is protected in freshwater sites important to biodiversity (%)	36.8	2020	●	→
Red List Index of species survival (worst 0–1 best)	0.7	2021	●	↓
Permanent deforestation (% of forest area, 5-year average)	0.0	2020	●	↑
Terrestrial and freshwater biodiversity threats embodied in imports (per million population)	2.5	2018	●	●
SDG16 – Peace, Justice and Strong Institutions				
Homicides (per 100,000 population)	0.6	2020	●	↑
Unsentenced detainees (% of prison population)	34.9	2018	●	↗
Population who feel safe walking alone at night in the city or area where they live (%)	82	2021	●	↑
Property Rights (worst 1–7 best)	5.2	2020	●	↑
Birth registrations with civil authority (% of children under age 5)	NA	NA	●	●
Corruption Perception Index (worst 0–100 best)	62	2021	●	↑
Children involved in child labor (% of population aged 5 to 14)	* 0.0	2019	●	●
Exports of major conventional weapons (TIV constant million USD per 100,000 population)	1.5	2020	●	●
Press Freedom Index (best 0–100 worst)	23.4	2021	●	↑
Access to and affordability of justice (worst 0–1 best)	0.7	2020	●	↑
Persons held in prison (per 100,000 population)	105.6	2019	●	↗
SDG17 – Partnerships for the Goals				
Government spending on health and education (% of GDP)	9.3	2019	●	↑
For high-income and all OECD DAC countries: International concessional public finance, including official development assistance (% of GNI)	0.2	2021	●	→
Other countries: Government revenue excluding grants (% of GDP)	NA	NA	●	●
Corporate Tax Haven Score (best 0–100 worst)	* 0.0	2019	●	●
Financial Secrecy Score (best 0–100 worst)	61.6	2020	●	●
Shifted profits of multinationals (US\$ billion)	8.4	2018	●	↑
Statistical Performance Index (worst 0–100 best)	88.3	2019	●	↑

5. Country Profiles

KUWAIT

Middle East and North Africa

AVERAGE PERFORMANCE BY SDG

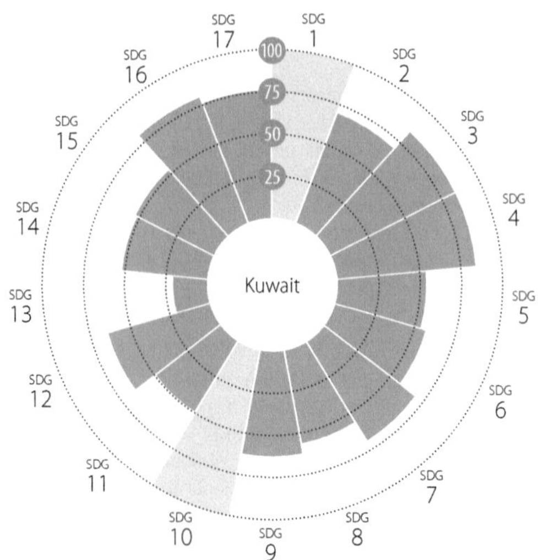

OVERALL PERFORMANCE

COUNTRY RANKING

KUWAIT

101/163

COUNTRY SCORE

REGIONAL AVERAGE: 66.7

SDG DASHBOARDS AND TRENDS

Major challenges | Significant challenges | Challenges remain | SDG achieved | Information unavailable

Decreasing | Stagnating | Moderately improving | On track or maintaining SDG achievement | Information unavailable

Note: The full title of each SDG is available here: https://sustainabledevelopment.un.org/topics/sustainabledevelopmentgoals

INTERNATIONAL SPILLOVER INDEX

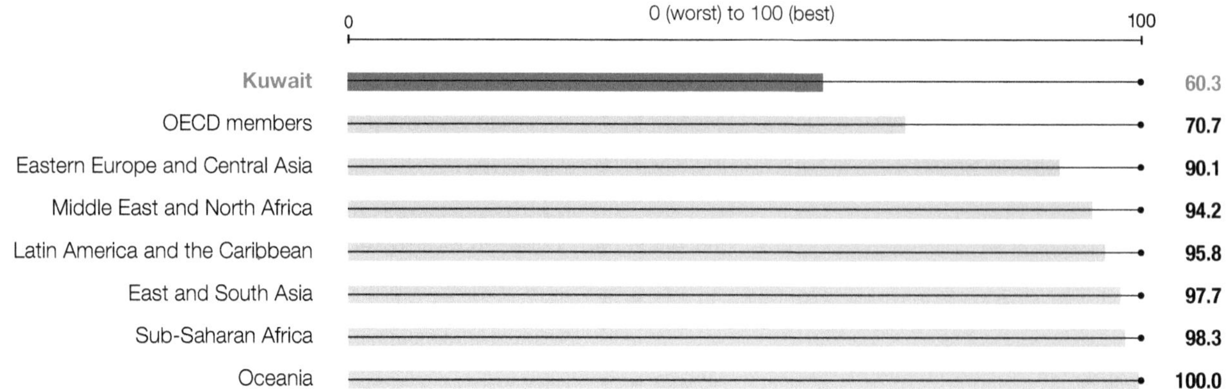

STATISTICAL PERFORMANCE INDEX

0 (worst) to 100 (best)

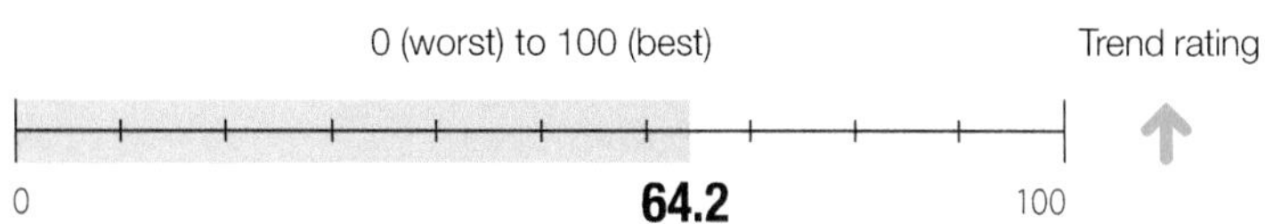

Trend rating

MISSING DATA IN SDG INDEX

16%

SDG1 – No Poverty	Value	Year	Rating	Trend
Poverty headcount ratio at \$1.90/day (%)	* NA	NA	●	●
Poverty headcount ratio at \$3.20/day (%)	* NA	NA	●	●

SDG2 – Zero Hunger	Value	Year	Rating	Trend
Prevalence of undernourishment (%)	2.5	2019	●	↑
Prevalence of stunting in children under 5 years of age (%)	6.4	2017	●	↑
Prevalence of wasting in children under 5 years of age (%)	2.5	2017	●	↑
Prevalence of obesity, BMI ≥ 30 (% of adult population)	37.9	2016	●	↓
Human Trophic Level (best 2–3 worst)	2.2	2017	●	↓
Cereal yield (tonnes per hectare of harvested land)	10.5	2018	●	↑
Sustainable Nitrogen Management Index (best 0–1.41 worst)	0.7	2015	●	↓
Exports of hazardous pesticides (tonnes per million population)	2.6	2019	●	●

SDG3 – Good Health and Well-Being	Value	Year	Rating	Trend
Maternal mortality rate (per 100,000 live births)	12	2017	●	↑
Neonatal mortality rate (per 1,000 live births)	5.0	2020	●	↑
Mortality rate, under-5 (per 1,000 live births)	8.9	2020	●	↑
Incidence of tuberculosis (per 100,000 population)	19.0	2020	●	↗
New HIV infections (per 1,000 uninfected population)	1.0	2020	●	→
Age-standardized death rate due to cardiovascular disease, cancer, diabetes, or chronic respiratory disease in adults aged 30–70 years (%)	11.9	2019	●	↑
Age-standardized death rate attributable to household air pollution and ambient air pollution (per 100,000 population)	104	2016	●	●
Traffic deaths (per 100,000 population)	15.4	2019	●	↑
Life expectancy at birth (years)	81.0	2019	●	↑
Adolescent fertility rate (births per 1,000 females aged 15 to 19)	5.0	2018	●	↑
Births attended by skilled health personnel (%)	99.9	2016	●	●
Surviving infants who received 2 WHO-recommended vaccines (%)	91	2019	●	↑
Universal health coverage (UHC) index of service coverage (worst 0–100 best)	70	2019	●	↗
Subjective well-being (average ladder score, worst 0–10 best)	6.1	2019	●	●

SDG4 – Quality Education	Value	Year	Rating	Trend
Participation rate in pre-primary organized learning (% of children aged 4 to 6)	69.3	2020	●	↓
Net primary enrollment rate (%)	97.3	2016	●	●
Lower secondary completion rate (%)	92.2	2020	●	↑
Literacy rate (% of population aged 15 to 24)	99.3	2020	●	↑

SDG5 – Gender Equality	Value	Year	Rating	Trend
Demand for family planning satisfied by modern methods (% of females aged 15 to 49)	* 67.0	2022	●	→
Ratio of female-to-male mean years of education received (%)	117.6	2019	●	↑
Ratio of female-to-male labor force participation rate (%)	55.9	2020	●	↓
Seats held by women in national parliament (%)	6.3	2020	●	→

SDG6 – Clean Water and Sanitation	Value	Year	Rating	Trend
Population using at least basic drinking water services (%)	100.0	2020	●	↑
Population using at least basic sanitation services (%)	100.0	2020	●	↑
Freshwater withdrawal (% of available freshwater resources)	3850.5	2018	●	●
Anthropogenic wastewater that receives treatment (%)	43.1	2018	●	●
Scarce water consumption embodied in imports (m^3 H_2O eq/capita)	6422.3	2018	●	●

SDG7 – Affordable and Clean Energy	Value	Year	Rating	Trend
Population with access to electricity (%)	100.0	2019	●	↑
Population with access to clean fuels and technology for cooking (%)	100.0	2019	●	↑
CO_2 emissions from fuel combustion per total electricity output ($MtCO_2$/TWh)	1.5	2019	●	→
Share of renewable energy in total primary energy supply (%)	0.1	2019	●	→

SDG8 – Decent Work and Economic Growth	Value	Year	Rating	Trend
Adjusted GDP growth (%)	-4.5	2020	●	●
Victims of modern slavery (per 1,000 population)	* NA	NA	●	●
Adults with an account at a bank or other financial institution or with a mobile-money-service provider (% of population aged 15 or over)	79.8	2017	●	↑
Unemployment rate (% of total labor force)	3.4	2022	●	↑
Fundamental labor rights are effectively guaranteed (worst 0–1 best)	NA	NA	●	●
Fatal work-related accidents embodied in imports (per 100,000 population)	5.7	2015	●	↗

SDG9 – Industry, Innovation and Infrastructure	Value	Year	Rating	Trend
Population using the internet (%)	99.1	2020	●	↑
Mobile broadband subscriptions (per 100 population)	132.7	2019	●	↑
Logistics Performance Index: Quality of trade and transport-related infrastructure (worst 1–5 best)	3.0	2018	●	↑
The Times Higher Education Universities Ranking: Average score of top 3 universities (worst 0–100 best)	29.6	2022	●	●
Articles published in academic journals (per 1,000 population)	0.5	2020	●	↑
Expenditure on research and development (% of GDP)	0.1	2018	●	↓

SDG10 – Reduced Inequalities	Value	Year	Rating	Trend
Gini coefficient	NA	NA	●	●
Palma ratio	NA	NA	●	●

SDG11 – Sustainable Cities and Communities	Value	Year	Rating	Trend
Proportion of urban population living in slums (%)	NA	NA	●	●
Annual mean concentration of particulate matter of less than 2.5 microns in diameter (PM2.5) (μg/m^3)	60.7	2019	●	→
Access to improved water source, piped (% of urban population)	NA	NA	●	●
Satisfaction with public transport (%)	61.0	2019	●	●

SDG12 – Responsible Consumption and Production	Value	Year	Rating	Trend
Municipal solid waste (kg/capita/day)	1.6	2010	●	●
Electronic waste (kg/capita)	15.8	2019	●	●
Production-based SO_2 emissions (kg/capita)	155.0	2018	●	●
SO_2 emissions embodied in imports (kg/capita)	8.1	2018	●	●
Production-based nitrogen emissions (kg/capita)	2.9	2015	●	↑
Nitrogen emissions embodied in imports (kg/capita)	31.9	2015	●	↓
Exports of plastic waste (kg/capita)	2.0	2020	●	●

SDG13 – Climate Action	Value	Year	Rating	Trend
CO_2 emissions from fossil fuel combustion and cement production (tCO_2/capita)	20.8	2020	●	→
CO_2 emissions embodied in imports (tCO_2/capita)	3.1	2018	●	↗
CO_2 emissions embodied in fossil fuel exports (kg/capita)	18618.3	2020	●	●

SDG14 – Life Below Water	Value	Year	Rating	Trend
Mean area that is protected in marine sites important to biodiversity (%)	32.1	2020	●	↗
Ocean Health Index: Clean Waters score (worst 0–100 best)	59.8	2020	●	↓
Fish caught from overexploited or collapsed stocks (% of total catch)	NA	NA	●	●
Fish caught by trawling or dredging (%)	0.0	2018	●	↑
Fish caught that are then discarded (%)	78.4	2018	●	→
Marine biodiversity threats embodied in imports (per million population)	0.4	2018	●	●

SDG15 – Life on Land	Value	Year	Rating	Trend
Mean area that is protected in terrestrial sites important to biodiversity (%)	51.7	2020	●	↗
Mean area that is protected in freshwater sites important to biodiversity (%)	NA	NA	●	●
Red List Index of species survival (worst 0–1 best)	0.8	2021	●	↓
Permanent deforestation (% of forest area, 5-year average)	NA	NA	●	●
Terrestrial and freshwater biodiversity threats embodied in imports (per million population)	5.2	2018	●	●

SDG16 – Peace, Justice and Strong Institutions	Value	Year	Rating	Trend
Homicides (per 100,000 population)	1.8	2012	●	●
Unsentenced detainees (% of prison population)	5.6	2016	●	●
Population who feel safe walking alone at night in the city or area where they live (%)	90	2019	●	●
Property Rights (worst 1–7 best)	4.7	2020	●	↑
Birth registrations with civil authority (% of children under age 5)	NA	NA	●	●
Corruption Perception Index (worst 0–100 best)	43	2021	●	↓
Children involved in child labor (% of population aged 5 to 14)	NA	NA	●	●
Exports of major conventional weapons (TIV constant million USD per 100,000 population)	* 0.0	2020	●	●
Press Freedom Index (best 0–100 worst)	34.4	2021	●	↓
Access to and affordability of justice (worst 0–1 best)	NA	NA	●	●

SDG17 – Partnerships for the Goals	Value	Year	Rating	Trend
Government spending on health and education (% of GDP)	11.3	2020	●	↑
For high-income and all OECD DAC countries: International concessional public finance, including official development assistance (% of GNI)	NA	NA	●	●
Other countries: Government revenue excluding grants (% of GDP)	NA	NA	●	●
Corporate Tax Haven Score (best 0–100 worst)	* 0.0	2019	●	●
Statistical Performance Index (worst 0–100 best)	64.2	2019	●	↑

* Imputed data point

5. Country Profiles

KYRGYZ REPUBLIC

Eastern Europe and Central Asia

OVERALL PERFORMANCE

COUNTRY RANKING

KYRGYZ REPUBLIC

48/163

COUNTRY SCORE

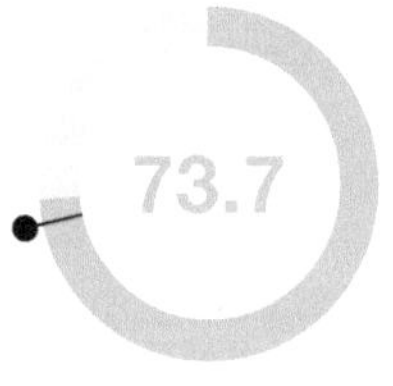

REGIONAL AVERAGE: 71.6

AVERAGE PERFORMANCE BY SDG

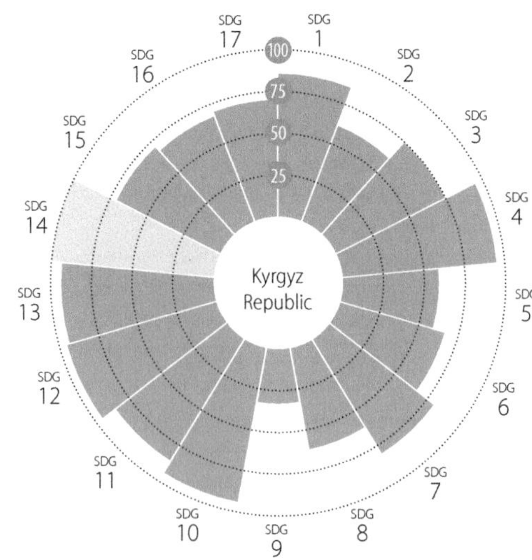

SDG DASHBOARDS AND TRENDS

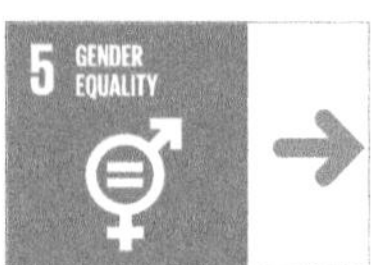

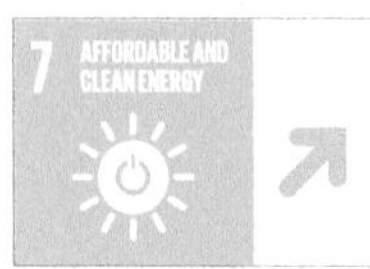

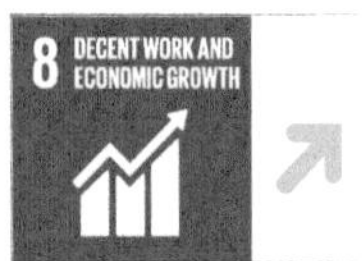

Major challenges · Significant challenges · Challenges remain · SDG achieved · Information unavailable

Decreasing · Stagnating · Moderately improving · On track or maintaining SDG achievement · Information unavailable

Note: The full title of each SDG is available here: https://sustainabledevelopment.un.org/topics/sustainabledevelopmentgoals

INTERNATIONAL SPILLOVER INDEX

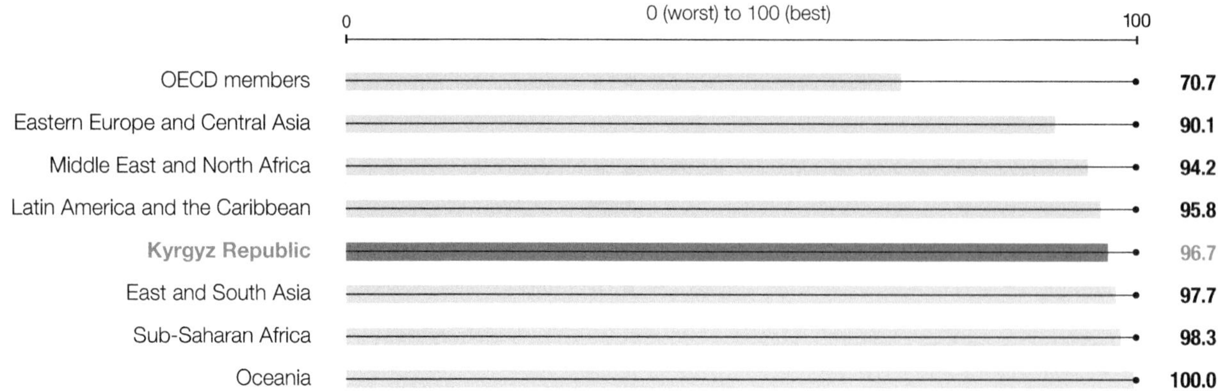

STATISTICAL PERFORMANCE INDEX

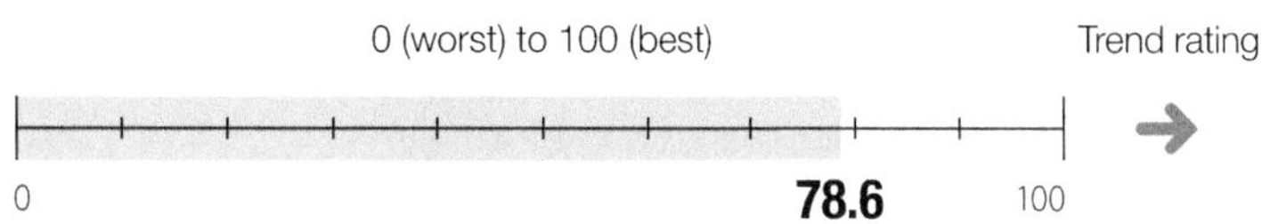

MISSING DATA IN SDG INDEX

1%

KYRGYZ REPUBLIC

Performance by Indicator

Indicator	Value	Year	Rating	Trend
SDG1 – No Poverty				
Poverty headcount ratio at $1.90/day (%)	0.9	2022	●	↑
Poverty headcount ratio at $3.20/day (%)	14.1	2022	●	↗
SDG2 – Zero Hunger				
Prevalence of undernourishment (%)	7.2	2019	●	↑
Prevalence of stunting in children under 5 years of age (%)	11.8	2018	●	→
Prevalence of wasting in children under 5 years of age (%)	2.0	2018	●	↑
Prevalence of obesity, BMI ≥ 30 (% of adult population)	16.6	2016	●	↓
Human Trophic Level (best 2–3 worst)	2.3	2017	●	↗
Cereal yield (tonnes per hectare of harvested land)	3.2	2018	●	↑
Sustainable Nitrogen Management Index (best 0–1.41 worst)	0.6	2015	●	↓
Exports of hazardous pesticides (tonnes per million population)	NA	NA	●	●
SDG3 – Good Health and Well-Being				
Maternal mortality rate (per 100,000 live births)	60	2017	●	↑
Neonatal mortality rate (per 1,000 live births)	11.7	2020	●	↑
Mortality rate, under-5 (per 1,000 live births)	17.5	2020	●	↑
Incidence of tuberculosis (per 100,000 population)	105.0	2020	●	↗
New HIV infections (per 1,000 uninfected population)	0.1	2020	●	↑
Age-standardized death rate due to cardiovascular disease, cancer, diabetes, or chronic respiratory disease in adults aged 30–70 years (%)	20.3	2019	●	↑
Age-standardized death rate attributable to household air pollution and ambient air pollution (per 100,000 population)	111	2016	●	●
Traffic deaths (per 100,000 population)	12.7	2019	●	↑
Life expectancy at birth (years)	74.2	2019	●	↑
Adolescent fertility rate (births per 1,000 females aged 15 to 19)	37.7	2019	●	↗
Births attended by skilled health personnel (%)	99.8	2018	●	↑
Surviving infants who received 2 WHO-recommended vaccines (%)	87	2020	●	↓
Universal health coverage (UHC) index of service coverage (worst 0–100 best)	70	2019	●	→
Subjective well-being (average ladder score, worst 0–10 best)	5.6	2021	●	↑
SDG4 – Quality Education				
Participation rate in pre-primary organized learning (% of children aged 4 to 6)	87.1	2020	●	↑
Net primary enrollment rate (%)	99.9	2020	●	↑
Lower secondary completion rate (%)	103.9	2020	●	↑
Literacy rate (% of population aged 15 to 24)	99.8	2018	●	●
SDG5 – Gender Equality				
Demand for family planning satisfied by modern methods (% of females aged 15 to 49)	64.6	2018	●	→
Ratio of female-to-male mean years of education received (%)	101.8	2019	●	↑
Ratio of female-to-male labor force participation rate (%)	58.5	2020	●	↓
Seats held by women in national parliament (%)	16.5	2020	●	↓
SDG6 – Clean Water and Sanitation				
Population using at least basic drinking water services (%)	91.7	2020	●	↑
Population using at least basic sanitation services (%)	97.9	2020	●	↑
Freshwater withdrawal (% of available freshwater resources)	50.0	2018	●	●
Anthropogenic wastewater that receives treatment (%)	0.2	2018	●	●
Scarce water consumption embodied in imports (m^3 H_2O eq/capita)	1060.6	2018	●	●
SDG7 – Affordable and Clean Energy				
Population with access to electricity (%)	99.9	2019	●	↑
Population with access to clean fuels and technology for cooking (%)	76.7	2019	●	→
CO_2 emissions from fuel combustion per total electricity output ($MtCO_2$/TWh)	0.7	2019	●	↑
Share of renewable energy in total primary energy supply (%)	29.7	2019	●	↑
SDG8 – Decent Work and Economic Growth				
Adjusted GDP growth (%)	-6.2	2020	●	●
Victims of modern slavery (per 1,000 population)	4.1	2018	●	●
Adults with an account at a bank or other financial institution or with a mobile-money-service provider (% of population aged 15 or over)	39.9	2017	●	↑
Unemployment rate (% of total labor force)	8.8	2022	●	↓
Fundamental labor rights are effectively guaranteed (worst 0–1 best)	0.5	2020	●	↓
Fatal work-related accidents embodied in imports (per 100,000 population)	0.1	2015	●	↑

Indicator	Value	Year	Rating	Trend
SDG9 – Industry, Innovation and Infrastructure				
Population using the internet (%)	51.0	2019	●	↑
Mobile broadband subscriptions (per 100 population)	122.9	2019	●	↑
Logistics Performance Index: Quality of trade and transport-related infrastructure (worst 1–5 best)	2.4	2018	●	↑
The Times Higher Education Universities Ranking: Average score of top 3 universities (worst 0–100 best)	* 0.0	2022	●	●
Articles published in academic journals (per 1,000 population)	0.1	2020	●	→
Expenditure on research and development (% of GDP)	0.1	2018	●	↓
SDG10 – Reduced Inequalities				
Gini coefficient	29.7	2019	●	↑
Palma ratio	1.0	2018	●	●
SDG11 – Sustainable Cities and Communities				
Proportion of urban population living in slums (%)	8.5	2018	●	●
Annual mean concentration of particulate matter of less than 2.5 microns in diameter (PM2.5) (μg/m^3)	19.8	2019	●	↗
Access to improved water source, piped (% of urban population)	100.0	2020	●	↑
Satisfaction with public transport (%)	62.0	2021	●	↓
SDG12 – Responsible Consumption and Production				
Municipal solid waste (kg/capita/day)	0.5	2015	●	●
Electronic waste (kg/capita)	1.5	2019	●	●
Production-based SO_2 emissions (kg/capita)	7.5	2018	●	●
SO_2 emissions embodied in imports (kg/capita)	1.3	2018	●	●
Production-based nitrogen emissions (kg/capita)	10.7	2015	●	↑
Nitrogen emissions embodied in imports (kg/capita)	1.1	2015	●	↑
Exports of plastic waste (kg/capita)	0.2	2021	●	●
SDG13 – Climate Action				
CO_2 emissions from fossil fuel combustion and cement production (tCO_2/capita)	1.8	2020	●	↑
CO_2 emissions embodied in imports (tCO_2/capita)	0.4	2018	●	↑
CO_2 emissions embodied in fossil fuel exports (kg/capita)	218.7	2021	●	●
SDG14 – Life Below Water				
Mean area that is protected in marine sites important to biodiversity (%)	NA	NA	●	●
Ocean Health Index: Clean Waters score (worst 0–100 best)	NA	NA	●	●
Fish caught from overexploited or collapsed stocks (% of total catch)	NA	NA	●	●
Fish caught by trawling or dredging (%)	NA	NA	●	●
Fish caught that are then discarded (%)	NA	NA	●	●
Marine biodiversity threats embodied in imports (per million population)	0.0	2018	●	●
SDG15 – Life on Land				
Mean area that is protected in terrestrial sites important to biodiversity (%)	23.6	2020	●	→
Mean area that is protected in freshwater sites important to biodiversity (%)	35.4	2020	●	→
Red List Index of species survival (worst 0–1 best)	1.0	2021	●	↑
Permanent deforestation (% of forest area, 5-year average)	0.0	2020	●	↑
Terrestrial and freshwater biodiversity threats embodied in imports (per million population)	0.0	2018	●	●
SDG16 – Peace, Justice and Strong Institutions				
Homicides (per 100,000 population)	2.2	2018	●	↑
Unsentenced detainees (% of prison population)	14.5	2018	●	↑
Population who feel safe walking alone at night in the city or area where they live (%)	67	2021	●	↑
Property Rights (worst 1–7 best)	3.5	2020	●	→
Birth registrations with civil authority (% of children under age 5)	98.9	2020	●	●
Corruption Perception Index (worst 0–100 best)	27	2021	●	↓
Children involved in child labor (% of population aged 5 to 14)	22.3	2019	●	●
Exports of major conventional weapons (TIV constant million USD per 100,000 population)	0.1	2020	●	●
Press Freedom Index (best 0–100 worst)	30.4	2021	●	→
Access to and affordability of justice (worst 0–1 best)	0.6	2020	●	↓
SDG17 – Partnerships for the Goals				
Government spending on health and education (% of GDP)	7.7	2019	●	↓
For high-income and all OECD DAC countries: International concessional public finance, including official development assistance (% of GNI)	NA	NA	●	●
Other countries: Government revenue excluding grants (% of GDP)	27.3	2019	●	↓
Corporate Tax Haven Score (best 0–100 worst)	* 0.0	2019	●	●
Statistical Performance Index (worst 0–100 best)	78.6	2019	●	→

* Imputed data point

LAO PEOPLE'S DEMOCRATIC REPUBLIC

East and South Asia

OVERALL PERFORMANCE

COUNTRY RANKING

LAO PDR

111 /163

COUNTRY SCORE

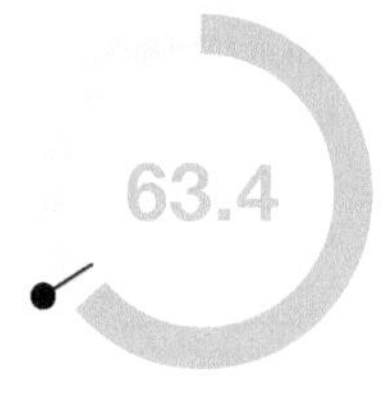

REGIONAL AVERAGE: 65.9

AVERAGE PERFORMANCE BY SDG

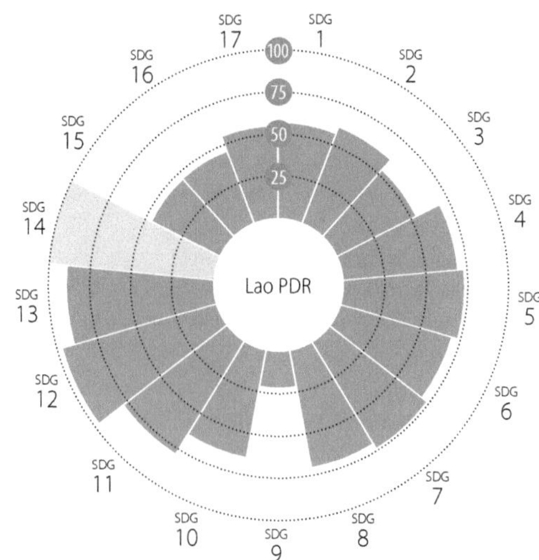

SDG DASHBOARDS AND TRENDS

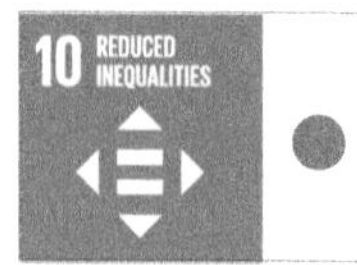

Information unavailable
Information unavailable

Note: The full title of each SDG is available here: https://sustainabledevelopment.un.org/topics/sustainabledevelopmentgoals

INTERNATIONAL SPILLOVER INDEX

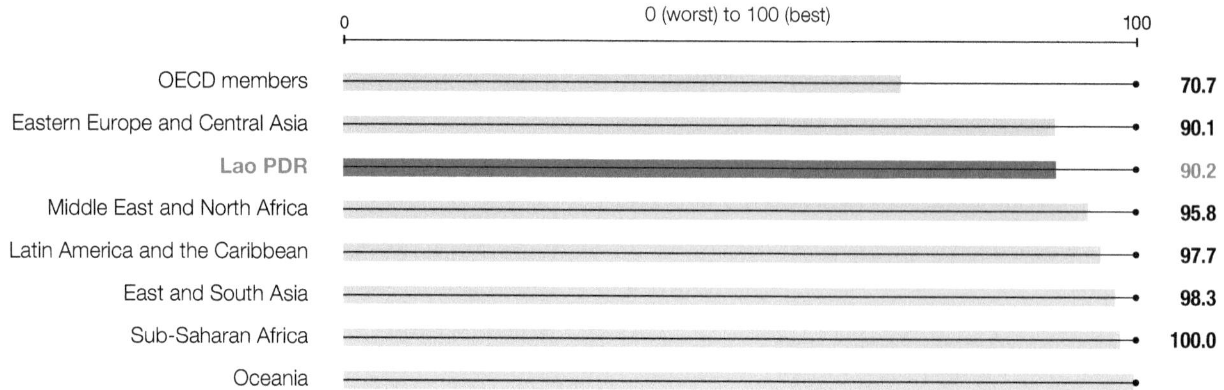

STATISTICAL PERFORMANCE INDEX

0 (worst) to 100 (best)

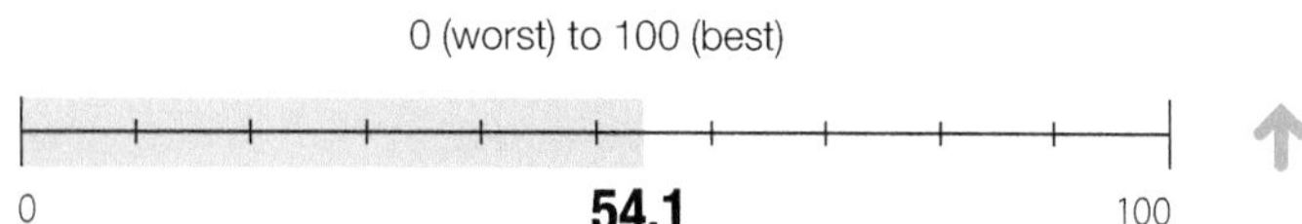

MISSING DATA IN SDG INDEX

6%

SDG1 – No Poverty	Value	Year	Rating	Trend
Poverty headcount ratio at $1.90/day (%)	10.6	2022	●	↗
Poverty headcount ratio at $3.20/day (%)	36.6	2022	●	→
SDG2 – Zero Hunger				
Prevalence of undernourishment (%)	5.3	2019	●	↑
Prevalence of stunting in children under 5 years of age (%)	33.1	2017	●	→
Prevalence of wasting in children under 5 years of age (%)	9.0	2017	●	→
Prevalence of obesity, BMI ≥ 30 (% of adult population)	5.3	2016	●	↑
Human Trophic Level (best 2–3 worst)	2.1	2017	●	↑
Cereal yield (tonnes per hectare of harvested land)	4.5	2018	●	↑
Sustainable Nitrogen Management Index (best 0–1.41 worst)	0.4	2015	●	→
Exports of hazardous pesticides (tonnes per million population)	205.8	2019	●	●
SDG3 – Good Health and Well-Being				
Maternal mortality rate (per 100,000 live births)	185	2017	●	↑
Neonatal mortality rate (per 1,000 live births)	21.7	2020	●	↗
Mortality rate, under-5 (per 1,000 live births)	44.1	2020	●	↑
Incidence of tuberculosis (per 100,000 population)	149.0	2020	●	↗
New HIV infections (per 1,000 uninfected population)	0.1	2020	●	↑
Age-standardized death rate due to cardiovascular disease, cancer, diabetes, or chronic respiratory disease in adults aged 30–70 years (%)	26.8	2019	●	→
Age-standardized death rate attributable to household air pollution and ambient air pollution (per 100,000 population)	188	2016	●	●
Traffic deaths (per 100,000 population)	17.9	2019	●	↓
Life expectancy at birth (years)	68.5	2019	●	→
Adolescent fertility rate (births per 1,000 females aged 15 to 19)	83.4	2016	●	●
Births attended by skilled health personnel (%)	64.4	2017	●	●
Surviving infants who received 2 WHO-recommended vaccines (%)	79	2020	●	↓
Universal health coverage (UHC) index of service coverage (worst 0–100 best)	50	2019	●	↗
Subjective well-being (average ladder score, worst 0–10 best)	4.9	2021	●	●
SDG4 – Quality Education				
Participation rate in pre-primary organized learning (% of children aged 4 to 6)	70.5	2020	●	↑
Net primary enrollment rate (%)	91.8	2020	●	↓
Lower secondary completion rate (%)	62.0	2020	●	↓
Literacy rate (% of population aged 15 to 24)	92.5	2015	●	●
SDG5 – Gender Equality				
Demand for family planning satisfied by modern methods (% of females aged 15 to 49)	72.3	2017	●	↗
Ratio of female-to-male mean years of education received (%)	86.0	2019	●	↑
Ratio of female-to-male labor force participation rate (%)	96.2	2020	●	↑
Seats held by women in national parliament (%)	27.5	2020	●	↗
SDG6 – Clean Water and Sanitation				
Population using at least basic drinking water services (%)	85.2	2020	●	↑
Population using at least basic sanitation services (%)	79.5	2020	●	↑
Freshwater withdrawal (% of available freshwater resources)	4.8	2018	●	●
Anthropogenic wastewater that receives treatment (%)	0.0	2018	●	●
Scarce water consumption embodied in imports (m^3 H_2O eq/capita)	843.9	2018	●	●
SDG7 – Affordable and Clean Energy				
Population with access to electricity (%)	100.0	2019	●	↑
Population with access to clean fuels and technology for cooking (%)	7.9	2019	●	→
CO_2 emissions from fuel combustion per total electricity output ($MtCO_2$/TWh)	0.8	2019	●	↑
Share of renewable energy in total primary energy supply (%)	58.4	2019	●	↑
SDG8 – Decent Work and Economic Growth				
Adjusted GDP growth (%)	-0.7	2020	●	●
Victims of modern slavery (per 1,000 population)	9.4	2018	●	●
Adults with an account at a bank or other financial institution or with a mobile-money-service provider (% of population aged 15 or over)	29.1	2017	●	●
Unemployment rate (% of total labor force)	1.3	2022	●	↑
Fundamental labor rights are effectively guaranteed (worst 0–1 best)	NA	NA	●	●
Fatal work-related accidents embodied in imports (per 100,000 population)	0.0	2015	●	↑

* Imputed data point

SDG9 – Industry, Innovation and Infrastructure	Value	Year	Rating	Trend
Population using the internet (%)	33.8	2020	●	↗
Mobile broadband subscriptions (per 100 population)	48.6	2019	●	↑
Logistics Performance Index: Quality of trade and transport-related infrastructure (worst 1–5 best)	2.4	2018	●	↑
The Times Higher Education Universities Ranking: Average score of top 3 universities (worst 0–100 best)	* 0.0	2022	●	●
Articles published in academic journals (per 1,000 population)	0.0	2020	●	→
Expenditure on research and development (% of GDP)	0.0	2002	●	●
SDG10 – Reduced Inequalities				
Gini coefficient	38.8	2018	●	●
Palma ratio	1.6	2018	●	●
SDG11 – Sustainable Cities and Communities				
Proportion of urban population living in slums (%)	18.5	2018	●	↑
Annual mean concentration of particulate matter of less than 2.5 microns in diameter (PM2.5) (μg/m^3)	23.1	2019	●	↗
Access to improved water source, piped (% of urban population)	62.2	2020	●	→
Satisfaction with public transport (%)	77.0	2021	●	●
SDG12 – Responsible Consumption and Production				
Municipal solid waste (kg/capita/day)	0.1	2015	●	●
Electronic waste (kg/capita)	2.5	2019	●	●
Production-based SO_2 emissions (kg/capita)	2.6	2018	●	●
SO_2 emissions embodied in imports (kg/capita)	1.0	2018	●	●
Production-based nitrogen emissions (kg/capita)	12.5	2015	●	↑
Nitrogen emissions embodied in imports (kg/capita)	0.3	2015	●	↑
Exports of plastic waste (kg/capita)	0.3	2020	●	●
SDG13 – Climate Action				
CO_2 emissions from fossil fuel combustion and cement production (tCO_2/capita)	4.7	2020	●	↓
CO_2 emissions embodied in imports (tCO_2/capita)	0.4	2018	●	↑
CO_2 emissions embodied in fossil fuel exports (kg/capita)	60.7	2020	●	●
SDG14 – Life Below Water				
Mean area that is protected in marine sites important to biodiversity (%)	NA	NA	●	●
Ocean Health Index: Clean Waters score (worst 0–100 best)	NA	NA	●	●
Fish caught from overexploited or collapsed stocks (% of total catch)	NA	NA	●	●
Fish caught by trawling or dredging (%)	NA	NA	●	●
Fish caught that are then discarded (%)	NA	NA	●	●
Marine biodiversity threats embodied in imports (per million population)	0.0	2018	●	●
SDG15 – Life on Land				
Mean area that is protected in terrestrial sites important to biodiversity (%)	44.0	2020	●	→
Mean area that is protected in freshwater sites important to biodiversity (%)	29.9	2020	●	→
Red List Index of species survival (worst 0–1 best)	0.8	2021	●	↓
Permanent deforestation (% of forest area, 5-year average)	1.5	2020	●	↓
Terrestrial and freshwater biodiversity threats embodied in imports (per million population)	0.0	2018	●	●
SDG16 – Peace, Justice and Strong Institutions				
Homicides (per 100,000 population)	NA	NA	●	●
Unsentenced detainees (% of prison population)	NA	NA	●	●
Population who feel safe walking alone at night in the city or area where they live (%)	61	2021	●	●
Property Rights (worst 1–7 best)	3.9	2020	●	→
Birth registrations with civil authority (% of children under age 5)	73.0	2020	●	●
Corruption Perception Index (worst 0–100 best)	30	2021	●	→
Children involved in child labor (% of population aged 5 to 14)	28.2	2019	●	●
Exports of major conventional weapons (TIV constant million USD per 100,000 population)	* 0.0	2020	●	●
Press Freedom Index (best 0–100 worst)	70.6	2021	●	→
Access to and affordability of justice (worst 0–1 best)	NA	NA	●	●
SDG17 – Partnerships for the Goals				
Government spending on health and education (% of GDP)	3.9	2019	●	→
For high-income and all OECD DAC countries: International concessional public finance, including official development assistance (% of GNI)	NA	NA	●	●
Other countries: Government revenue excluding grants (% of GDP)	NA	NA	●	●
Corporate Tax Haven Score (best 0–100 worst)	* 0.0	2019	●	●
Statistical Performance Index (worst 0–100 best)	54.1	2019	●	↑

LATVIA

OVERALL PERFORMANCE

COUNTRY RANKING

LATVIA

14 /163

COUNTRY SCORE

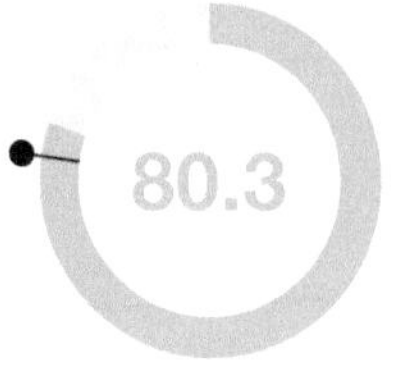

REGIONAL AVERAGE: 77.2

AVERAGE PERFORMANCE BY SDG

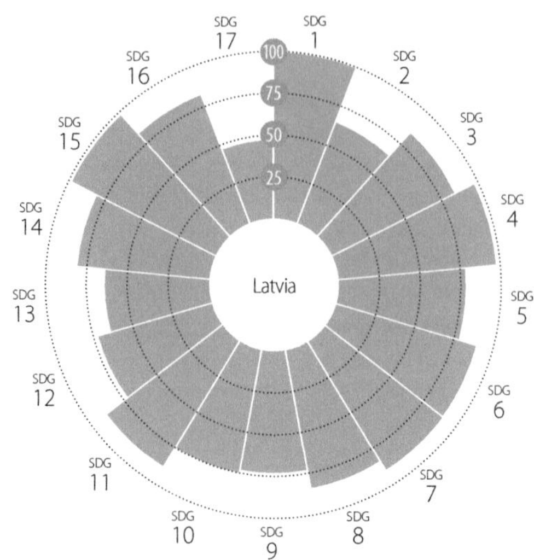

SDG DASHBOARDS AND TRENDS

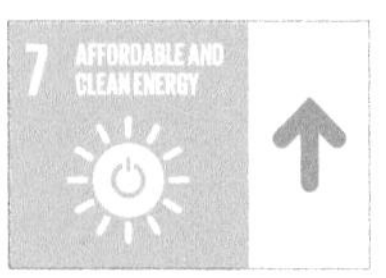

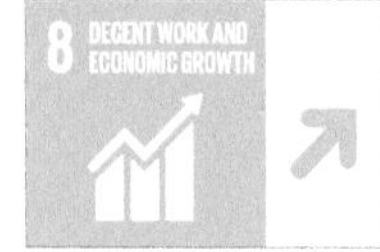

Major challenges | Significant challenges | Challenges remain | SDG achieved | Information unavailable

Decreasing | Stagnating | Moderately improving | On track or maintaining SDG achievement | Information unavailable

Note: The full title of each SDG is available here: https://sustainabledevelopment.un.org/topics/sustainabledevelopmentgoals

INTERNATIONAL SPILLOVER INDEX

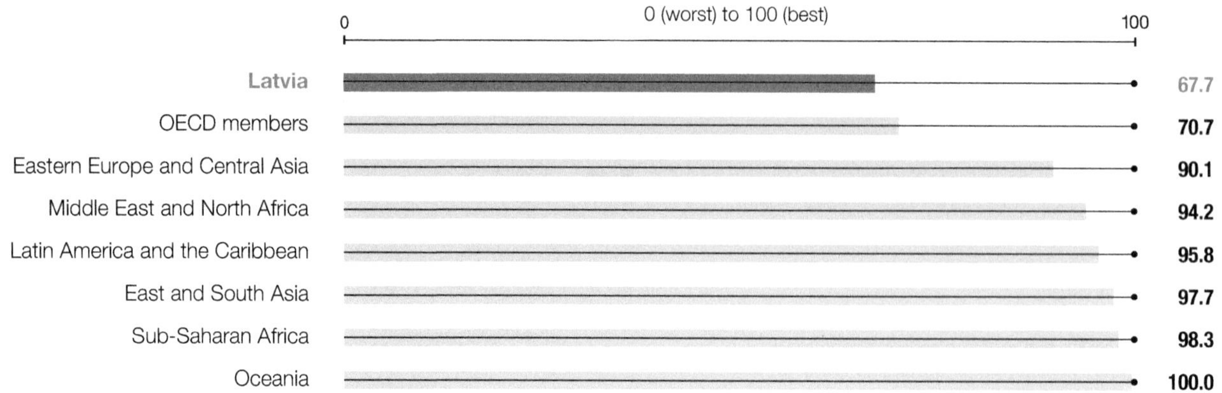

	Score
Latvia	67.7
OECD members	70.7
Eastern Europe and Central Asia	90.1
Middle East and North Africa	94.2
Latin America and the Caribbean	95.8
East and South Asia	97.7
Sub-Saharan Africa	98.3
Oceania	100.0

STATISTICAL PERFORMANCE INDEX

0 (worst) to 100 (best)

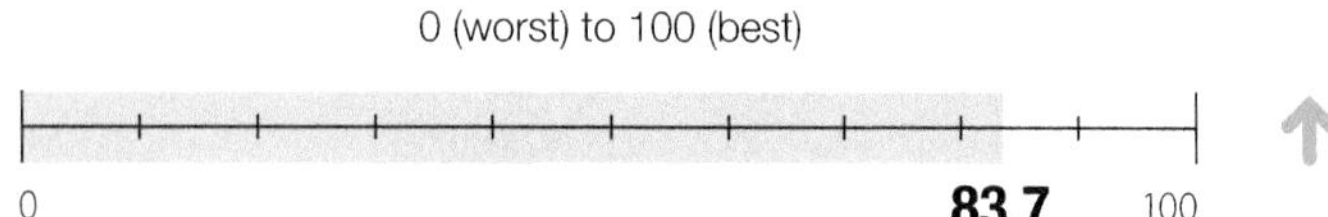

MISSING DATA IN SDG INDEX

0%

LATVIA

Performance by Indicator

SDG1 – No Poverty	Value	Year	Rating	Trend
Poverty headcount ratio at $1.90/day (%)	0.3	2022	●	↑
Poverty headcount ratio at $3.20/day (%)	0.5	2022	●	↑
Poverty rate after taxes and transfers (%)	16.2	2019	●	→
SDG2 – Zero Hunger				
Prevalence of undernourishment (%)	2.5	2019	●	↑
Prevalence of stunting in children under 5 years of age (%)	* 2.6	2019	●	↑
Prevalence of wasting in children under 5 years of age (%)	* 0.7	2019	●	↑
Prevalence of obesity, BMI ≥ 30 (% of adult population)	23.6	2016	●	↓
Human Trophic Level (best 2–3 worst)	2.4	2017	●	↓
Cereal yield (tonnes per hectare of harvested land)	3.0	2018	●	↑
Sustainable Nitrogen Management Index (best 0–1.41 worst)	0.6	2015	●	→
Yield gap closure (% of potential yield)	43.9	2018	●	●
Exports of hazardous pesticides (tonnes per million population)	22.1	2019	●	●
SDG3 – Good Health and Well-Being				
Maternal mortality rate (per 100,000 live births)	19	2017	●	↑
Neonatal mortality rate (per 1,000 live births)	2.3	2020	●	↑
Mortality rate, under-5 (per 1,000 live births)	4.0	2020	●	↑
Incidence of tuberculosis (per 100,000 population)	23.0	2020	●	↑
New HIV infections (per 1,000 uninfected population)	1.0	2020	●	→
Age-standardized death rate due to cardiovascular disease, cancer, diabetes, or chronic respiratory disease in adults aged 30–70 years (%)	21.6	2019	●	→
Age-standardized death rate attributable to household air pollution and ambient air pollution (per 100,000 population)	41	2016	●	●
Traffic deaths (per 100,000 population)	8.1	2019	●	↑
Life expectancy at birth (years)	75.4	2019	●	→
Adolescent fertility rate (births per 1,000 females aged 15 to 19)	12.1	2018	●	↑
Births attended by skilled health personnel (%)	99.9	2017	●	↑
Surviving infants who received 2 WHO-recommended vaccines (%)	99	2020	●	↑
Universal health coverage (UHC) index of service coverage (worst 0–100 best)	72	2019	●	↑
Subjective well-being (average ladder score, worst 0–10 best)	6.4	2021	●	↑
Gap in life expectancy at birth among regions (years)	3.5	2019	●	→
Gap in self-reported health status by income (percentage points)	44.3	2019	●	↓
Daily smokers (% of population aged 15 and over)	22.6	2019	●	↗
SDG4 – Quality Education				
Participation rate in pre-primary organized learning (% of children aged 4 to 6)	97.8	2019	●	↑
Net primary enrollment rate (%)	98.8	2019	●	↑
Lower secondary completion rate (%)	96.9	2019	●	↑
Literacy rate (% of population aged 15 to 24)	99.8	2018	●	●
Tertiary educational attainment (% of population aged 25 to 34)	44.2	2020	●	↑
PISA score (worst 0–600 best)	487.3	2018	●	↗
Variation in science performance explained by socio-economic status (%)	8.4	2018	●	↑
Underachievers in science (% of 15-year-olds)	18.5	2018	●	↓
SDG5 – Gender Equality				
Demand for family planning satisfied by modern methods (% of females aged 15 to 49)	* 80.6	2022	●	↑
Ratio of female-to-male mean years of education received (%)	106.3	2019	●	↑
Ratio of female-to-male labor force participation rate (%)	81.7	2020	●	↑
Seats held by women in national parliament (%)	30.0	2020	●	↑
Gender wage gap (% of male median wage)	20.3	2018	●	→
SDG6 – Clean Water and Sanitation				
Population using at least basic drinking water services (%)	98.8	2020	●	↑
Population using at least basic sanitation services (%)	92.4	2020	●	↗
Freshwater withdrawal (% of available freshwater resources)	1.1	2018	●	●
Anthropogenic wastewater that receives treatment (%)	90.7	2018	●	●
Scarce water consumption embodied in imports (m^3 H_2O eq/capita)	3666.4	2018	●	●
Population using safely managed water services (%)	96.3	2020	●	↑
Population using safely managed sanitation services (%)	83.4	2020	●	↑
SDG7 – Affordable and Clean Energy				
Population with access to electricity (%)	100.0	2019	●	↑
Population with access to clean fuels and technology for cooking (%)	100.0	2019	●	↑
CO_2 emissions from fuel combustion per total electricity output ($MtCO_2$/TWh)	1.1	2019	●	↑
Share of renewable energy in total primary energy supply (%)	40.6	2019	●	↑
SDG8 – Decent Work and Economic Growth				
Adjusted GDP growth (%)	0.1	2020	●	●
Victims of modern slavery (per 1,000 population)	3.9	2018	●	●
Adults with an account at a bank or other financial institution or with a mobile-money-service provider (% of population aged 15 or over)	93.2	2017	●	↑
Fundamental labor rights are effectively guaranteed (worst 0–1 best)	0.8	2020	●	●
Fatal work-related accidents embodied in imports (per 100,000 population)	0.5	2015	●	↑
Employment-to-population ratio (%)	71.5	2020	●	↑
Youth not in employment, education or training (NEET) (% of population aged 15 to 29)	13.6	2020	●	↓

* Imputed data point

SDG9 – Industry, Innovation and Infrastructure	Value	Year	Rating	Trend
Population using the internet (%)	88.9	2020	●	↑
Mobile broadband subscriptions (per 100 population)	132.8	2019	●	↑
Logistics Performance Index: Quality of trade and transport-related infrastructure (worst 1–5 best)	3.0	2018	●	↓
The Times Higher Education Universities Ranking: Average score of top 3 universities (worst 0–100 best)	33.1	2022	●	●
Articles published in academic journals (per 1,000 population)	1.3	2020	●	↑
Expenditure on research and development (% of GDP)	0.6	2018	●	→
Researchers (per 1,000 employed population)	4.0	2019	●	↓
Triadic patent families filed (per million population)	3.8	2019	●	→
Gap in internet access by income (percentage points)	22.3	2020	●	↑
Female share of graduates from STEM fields at the tertiary level (%)	31.1	2017	●	↑
SDG10 – Reduced Inequalities				
Gini coefficient	35.1	2018	●	↓
Palma ratio	1.4	2019	●	→
Elderly poverty rate (% of population aged 66 or over)	33.8	2019	●	↓
SDG11 – Sustainable Cities and Communities				
Proportion of urban population living in slums (%)	* 0.0	2018	●	↑
Annual mean concentration of particulate matter of less than 2.5 microns in diameter (PM2.5) (μg/m³)	12.7	2019	●	↑
Access to improved water source, piped (% of urban population)	98.0	2020	●	↑
Satisfaction with public transport (%)	59.0	2021	●	↓
Population with rent overburden (%)	1.8	2019	●	↑
SDG12 – Responsible Consumption and Production				
Electronic waste (kg/capita)	10.6	2019	●	●
Production-based SO_2 emissions (kg/capita)	8.4	2018	●	●
SO_2 emissions embodied in imports (kg/capita)	4.7	2018	●	●
Production-based nitrogen emissions (kg/capita)	25.5	2015	●	↓
Nitrogen emissions embodied in imports (kg/capita)	7.8	2015	●	↓
Exports of plastic waste (kg/capita)	7.8	2021	●	●
Non-recycled municipal solid waste (kg/capita/day)	0.7	2019	●	↑
SDG13 – Climate Action				
CO_2 emissions from fossil fuel combustion and cement production (tCO_2/capita)	3.6	2020	●	→
CO_2 emissions embodied in imports (tCO_2/capita)	3.0	2018	●	↓
CO_2 emissions embodied in fossil fuel exports (kg/capita)	13.2	2021	●	●
Carbon Pricing Score at EUR60/tCO_2 (%, worst 0–100 best)	29.2	2018	●	→
SDG14 – Life Below Water				
Mean area that is protected in marine sites important to biodiversity (%)	96.2	2020	●	↑
Ocean Health Index: Clean Waters score (worst 0–100 best)	53.7	2020	●	→
Fish caught from overexploited or collapsed stocks (% of total catch)	5.3	2018	●	↑
Fish caught by trawling or dredging (%)	0.2	2017	●	↑
Fish caught that are then discarded (%)	8.4	2018	●	↗
Marine biodiversity threats embodied in imports (per million population)	0.0	2018	●	●
SDG15 – Life on Land				
Mean area that is protected in terrestrial sites important to biodiversity (%)	97.2	2020	●	↑
Mean area that is protected in freshwater sites important to biodiversity (%)	97.5	2020	●	↑
Red List Index of species survival (worst 0–1 best)	1.0	2021	●	↑
Permanent deforestation (% of forest area, 5-year average)	0.0	2020	●	↑
Terrestrial and freshwater biodiversity threats embodied in imports (per million population)	0.2	2018	●	●
SDG16 – Peace, Justice and Strong Institutions				
Homicides (per 100,000 population)	2.6	2020	●	↑
Unsentenced detainees (% of prison population)	27.8	2019	●	↑
Population who feel safe walking alone at night in the city or area where they live (%)	78	2021	●	↑
Property Rights (worst 1–7 best)	4.5	2020	●	↑
Birth registrations with civil authority (% of children under age 5)	100.0	2020	●	●
Corruption Perception Index (worst 0–100 best)	59	2021	●	↑
Children involved in child labor (% of population aged 5 to 14)	* 0.0	2019	●	●
Exports of major conventional weapons (TIV constant million USD per 100,000 population)	* 0.0	2020	●	●
Press Freedom Index (best 0–100 worst)	19.3	2021	●	↑
Access to and affordability of justice (worst 0–1 best)	0.6	2020	●	●
Persons held in prison (per 100,000 population)	179.0	2019	●	↑
SDG17 – Partnerships for the Goals				
Government spending on health and education (% of GDP)	8.2	2019	●	↓
For high-income and all OECD DAC countries: International concessional public finance, including official development assistance (% of GNI)	0.1	2021	●	→
Other countries: Government revenue excluding grants (% of GDP)	NA	NA	●	●
Corporate Tax Haven Score (best 0–100 worst)	68.1	2019	●	●
Financial Secrecy Score (best 0–100 worst)	59.1	2020	●	●
Shifted profits of multinationals (US$ billion)	0.4	2018	●	↑
Statistical Performance Index (worst 0–100 best)	83.7	2019	●	↑

5. Country Profiles

LEBANON

Middle East and North Africa

OVERALL PERFORMANCE

COUNTRY RANKING

LEBANON

97 **/163**

COUNTRY SCORE

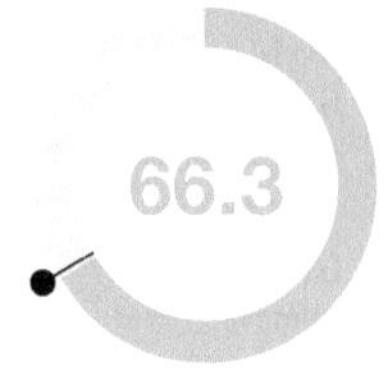

REGIONAL AVERAGE: 66.7

AVERAGE PERFORMANCE BY SDG

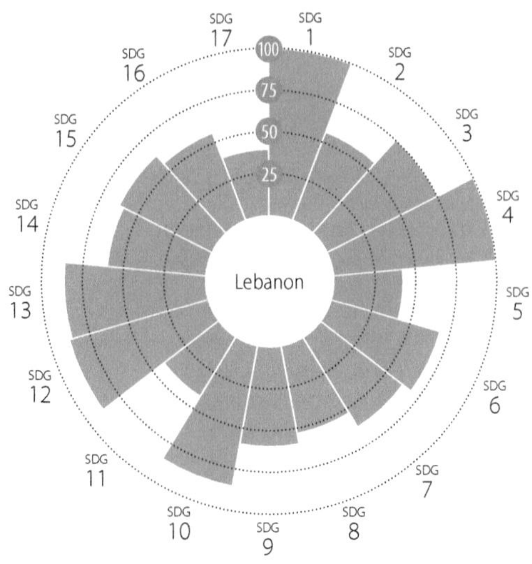

SDG DASHBOARDS AND TRENDS

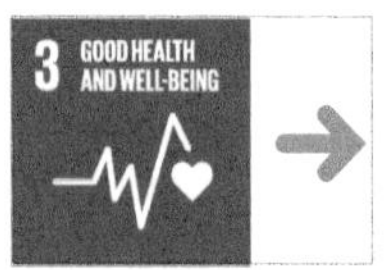

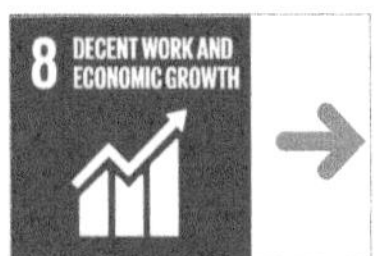

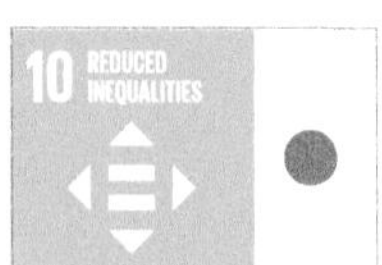

Major challenges · Significant challenges · Challenges remain · SDG achieved · Information unavailable

Decreasing · Stagnating · Moderately improving · On track or maintaining SDG achievement · Information unavailable

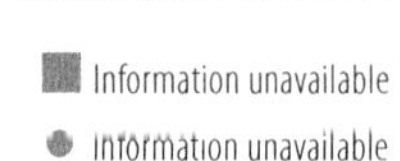

Note: The full title of each SDG is available here: https://sustainabledevelopment.un.org/topics/sustainabledevelopmentgoals

INTERNATIONAL SPILLOVER INDEX

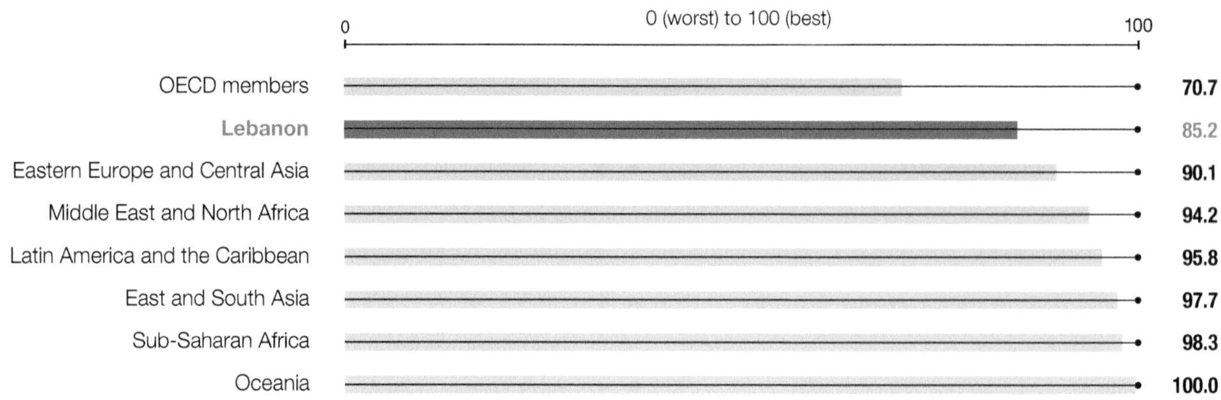

STATISTICAL PERFORMANCE INDEX

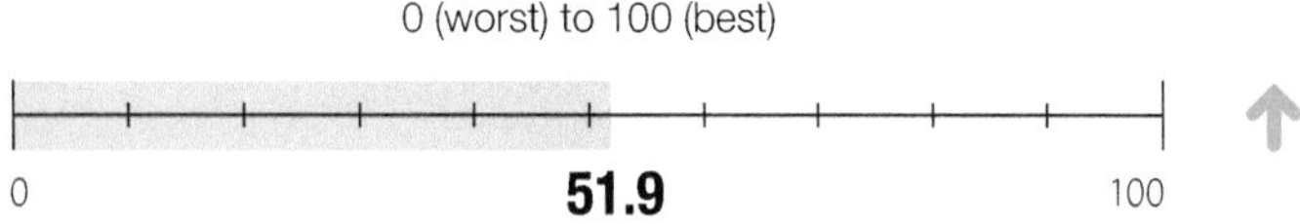

MISSING DATA IN SDG INDEX

10%

SDG1 – No Poverty	Value	Year	Rating	Trend
Poverty headcount ratio at \$1.90/day (%)	0.1	2022	●	↑
Poverty headcount ratio at \$3.20/day (%)	0.4	2022	●	↑

SDG2 – Zero Hunger	Value	Year	Rating	Trend
Prevalence of undernourishment (%)	9.3	2019	●	↓
Prevalence of stunting in children under 5 years of age (%)	16.5	2004	●	→
Prevalence of wasting in children under 5 years of age (%)	6.6	2004	●	→
Prevalence of obesity, BMI ≥ 30 (% of adult population)	32.0	2016	●	↓
Human Trophic Level (best 2–3 worst)	2.2	2017	●	↑
Cereal yield (tonnes per hectare of harvested land)	3.2	2018	●	↑
Sustainable Nitrogen Management Index (best 0–1.41 worst)	0.9	2015	●	↓
Exports of hazardous pesticides (tonnes per million population)	0.1	2019	●	●

SDG3 – Good Health and Well-Being	Value	Year	Rating	Trend
Maternal mortality rate (per 100,000 live births)	29	2017	●	↑
Neonatal mortality rate (per 1,000 live births)	4.0	2020	●	↑
Mortality rate, under-5 (per 1,000 live births)	7.0	2020	●	↑
Incidence of tuberculosis (per 100,000 population)	13.0	2020	●	→
New HIV infections (per 1,000 uninfected population)	0.0	2020	●	↑
Age-standardized death rate due to cardiovascular disease, cancer, diabetes, or chronic respiratory disease in adults aged 30–70 years (%)	19.9	2019	●	→
Age-standardized death rate attributable to household air pollution and ambient air pollution (per 100,000 population)	51	2016	●	●
Traffic deaths (per 100,000 population)	16.4	2019	●	↓
Life expectancy at birth (years)	76.4	2019	●	→
Adolescent fertility rate (births per 1,000 females aged 15 to 19)	11.7	2019	●	●
Births attended by skilled health personnel (%)	98.2	2004	●	●
Surviving infants who received 2 WHO-recommended vaccines (%)	71	2020	●	↓
Universal health coverage (UHC) index of service coverage (worst 0–100 best)	72	2019	●	↑
Subjective well-being (average ladder score, worst 0–10 best)	2.2	2021	●	↓

SDG4 – Quality Education	Value	Year	Rating	Trend
Participation rate in pre-primary organized learning (% of children aged 4 to 6)	NA	NA	●	●
Net primary enrollment rate (%)	NA	NA	●	●
Lower secondary completion rate (%)	NA	NA	●	●
Literacy rate (% of population aged 15 to 24)	99.8	2018	●	●

SDG5 – Gender Equality	Value	Year	Rating	Trend
Demand for family planning satisfied by modern methods (% of females aged 15 to 49)	* 62.2	2022	●	→
Ratio of female-to-male mean years of education received (%)	95.5	2019	●	→
Ratio of female-to-male labor force participation rate (%)	32.2	2020	●	↓
Seats held by women in national parliament (%)	4.7	2020	●	→

SDG6 – Clean Water and Sanitation	Value	Year	Rating	Trend
Population using at least basic drinking water services (%)	92.6	2020	●	↗
Population using at least basic sanitation services (%)	99.2	2020	●	↑
Freshwater withdrawal (% of available freshwater resources)	58.8	2018	●	●
Anthropogenic wastewater that receives treatment (%)	38.2	2018	●	●
Scarce water consumption embodied in imports (m^3 H_2O eq/capita)	3351.5	2018	●	●

SDG7 – Affordable and Clean Energy	Value	Year	Rating	Trend
Population with access to electricity (%)	100.0	2019	●	↑
Population with access to clean fuels and technology for cooking (%)	NA	NA	●	●
CO_2 emissions from fuel combustion per total electricity output ($MtCO_2$/TWh)	0.9	2019	●	↑
Share of renewable energy in total primary energy supply (%)	3.5	2019	●	→

SDG8 – Decent Work and Economic Growth	Value	Year	Rating	Trend
Adjusted GDP growth (%)	-12.8	2020	●	●
Victims of modern slavery (per 1,000 population)	1.7	2018	●	●
Adults with an account at a bank or other financial institution or with a mobile-money-service provider (% of population aged 15 or over)	44.8	2017	●	↓
Unemployment rate (% of total labor force)	14.2	2022	●	↓
Fundamental labor rights are effectively guaranteed (worst 0–1 best)	0.5	2020	●	↓
Fatal work-related accidents embodied in imports (per 100,000 population)	0.6	2015	●	↑

* Imputed data point

SDG9 – Industry, Innovation and Infrastructure	Value	Year	Rating	Trend
Population using the internet (%)	84.1	2020	●	↑
Mobile broadband subscriptions (per 100 population)	42.8	2019	●	↓
Logistics Performance Index: Quality of trade and transport-related infrastructure (worst 1–5 best)	2.6	2018	●	↗
The Times Higher Education Universities Ranking: Average score of top 3 universities (worst 0–100 best)	33.8	2022	●	●
Articles published in academic journals (per 1,000 population)	0.6	2020	●	↑
Expenditure on research and development (% of GDP)	NA	NA	●	●

SDG10 – Reduced Inequalities	Value	Year	Rating	Trend
Gini coefficient	31.8	2011	●	●
Palma ratio	1.2	2018	●	●

SDG11 – Sustainable Cities and Communities	Value	Year	Rating	Trend
Proportion of urban population living in slums (%)	NA	NA	●	●
Annual mean concentration of particulate matter of less than 2.5 microns in diameter (PM2.5) (μg/m^3)	30.6	2019	●	→
Access to improved water source, piped (% of urban population)	NA	NA	●	●
Satisfaction with public transport (%)	28.0	2021	●	↓

SDG12 – Responsible Consumption and Production	Value	Year	Rating	Trend
Municipal solid waste (kg/capita/day)	0.9	2014	●	●
Electronic waste (kg/capita)	8.2	2019	●	●
Production-based SO_2 emissions (kg/capita)	30.1	2018	●	●
SO_2 emissions embodied in imports (kg/capita)	2.4	2018	●	●
Production-based nitrogen emissions (kg/capita)	3.2	2015	●	↑
Nitrogen emissions embodied in imports (kg/capita)	4.4	2015	●	↑
Exports of plastic waste (kg/capita)	1.0	2020	●	●

SDG13 – Climate Action	Value	Year	Rating	Trend
CO_2 emissions from fossil fuel combustion and cement production (tCO_2/capita)	3.8	2020	●	→
CO_2 emissions embodied in imports (tCO_2/capita)	0.8	2018	●	↑
CO_2 emissions embodied in fossil fuel exports (kg/capita)	0.0	2020	●	●

SDG14 – Life Below Water	Value	Year	Rating	Trend
Mean area that is protected in marine sites important to biodiversity (%)	12.6	2020	●	→
Ocean Health Index: Clean Waters score (worst 0–100 best)	33.1	2020	●	→
Fish caught from overexploited or collapsed stocks (% of total catch)	NA	NA	●	●
Fish caught by trawling or dredging (%)	9.0	2008	●	●
Fish caught that are then discarded (%)	0.4	2018	●	↑
Marine biodiversity threats embodied in imports (per million population)	0.2	2018	●	●

SDG15 – Life on Land	Value	Year	Rating	Trend
Mean area that is protected in terrestrial sites important to biodiversity (%)	12.3	2020	●	→
Mean area that is protected in freshwater sites important to biodiversity (%)	21.1	2020	●	→
Red List Index of species survival (worst 0–1 best)	0.9	2021	●	↑
Permanent deforestation (% of forest area, 5-year average)	0.0	2020	●	↑
Terrestrial and freshwater biodiversity threats embodied in imports (per million population)	0.6	2018	●	●

SDG16 – Peace, Justice and Strong Institutions	Value	Year	Rating	Trend
Homicides (per 100,000 population)	1.9	2020	●	↑
Unsentenced detainees (% of prison population)	91.9	2019	●	↓
Population who feel safe walking alone at night in the city or area where they live (%)	47	2021	●	↓
Property Rights (worst 1–7 best)	3.8	2020	●	↓
Birth registrations with civil authority (% of children under age 5)	99.5	2020	●	●
Corruption Perception Index (worst 0–100 best)	24	2021	●	↓
Children involved in child labor (% of population aged 5 to 14)	NA	NA	●	●
Exports of major conventional weapons (TIV constant million USD per 100,000 population)	0.0	2020	●	●
Press Freedom Index (best 0–100 worst)	34.9	2021	●	↓
Access to and affordability of justice (worst 0–1 best)	0.5	2020	●	↗

SDG17 – Partnerships for the Goals	Value	Year	Rating	Trend
Government spending on health and education (% of GDP)	6.8	2019	●	↑
For high-income and all OECD DAC countries: International concessional public finance, including official development assistance (% of GNI)	NA	NA	●	●
Other countries: Government revenue excluding grants (% of GDP)	19.2	2019	●	↗
Corporate Tax Haven Score (best 0–100 worst)	72.8	2019	●	●
Statistical Performance Index (worst 0–100 best)	51.9	2019	●	↑

LESOTHO

Sub-Saharan Africa

OVERALL PERFORMANCE

COUNTRY RANKING

LESOTHO

135/163

COUNTRY SCORE

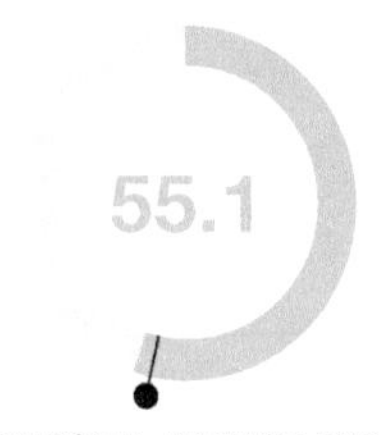

REGIONAL AVERAGE: 53.6

AVERAGE PERFORMANCE BY SDG

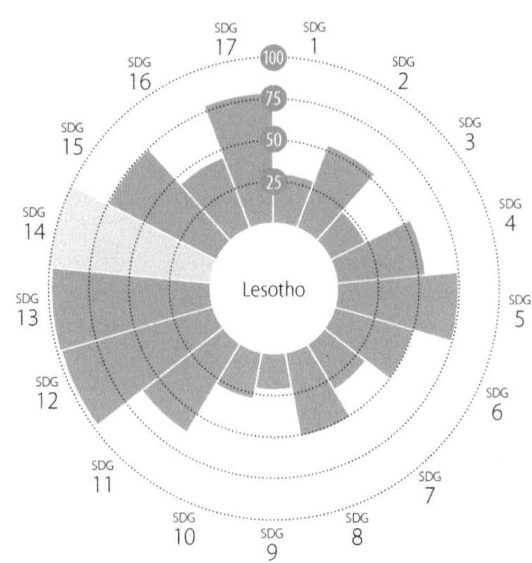

SDG DASHBOARDS AND TRENDS

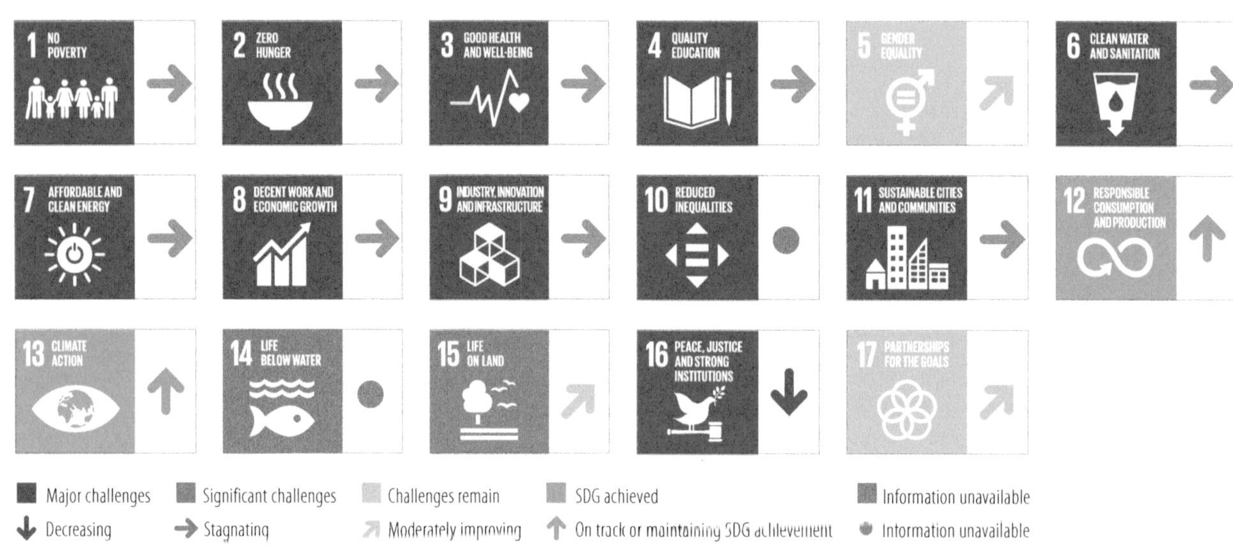

Major challenges | Significant challenges | Challenges remain | SDG achieved | Information unavailable

Decreasing | Stagnating | Moderately improving | On track or maintaining SDG achievement | Information unavailable

Note: The full title of each SDG is available here: https://sustainabledevelopment.un.org/topics/sustainabledevelopmentgoals

INTERNATIONAL SPILLOVER INDEX

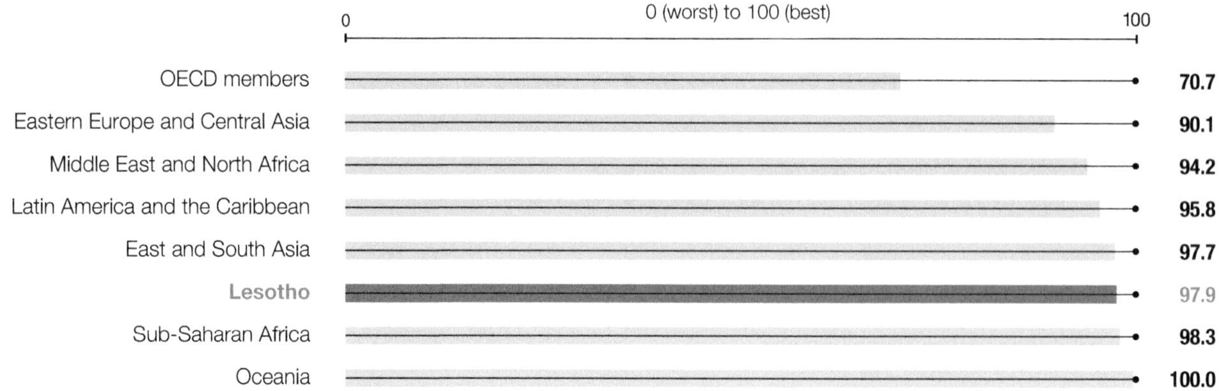

STATISTICAL PERFORMANCE INDEX

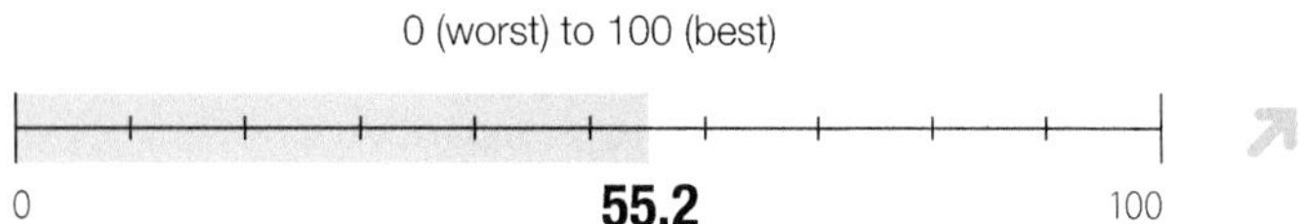

MISSING DATA IN SDG INDEX

9%

LESOTHO

Performance by Indicator

SDG1 – No Poverty	Value	Year	Rating	Trend
Poverty headcount ratio at \$1.90/day (%)	30.1	2022	●	→
Poverty headcount ratio at \$3.20/day (%)	51.2	2022	●	→
SDG2 – Zero Hunger				
Prevalence of undernourishment (%)	23.5	2019	●	↑
Prevalence of stunting in children under 5 years of age (%)	34.6	2018	●	→
Prevalence of wasting in children under 5 years of age (%)	2.1	2018	●	↑
Prevalence of obesity, BMI ≥ 30 (% of adult population)	16.6	2016	●	↓
Human Trophic Level (best 2–3 worst)	2.1	2017	●	↑
Cereal yield (tonnes per hectare of harvested land)	0.8	2018	●	→
Sustainable Nitrogen Management Index (best 0–1.41 worst)	1.0	2015	●	→
Exports of hazardous pesticides (tonnes per million population)	0.2	2019	●	●
SDG3 – Good Health and Well-Being				
Maternal mortality rate (per 100,000 live births)	544	2017	●	→
Neonatal mortality rate (per 1,000 live births)	44.3	2020	●	→
Mortality rate, under-5 (per 1,000 live births)	89.5	2020	●	→
Incidence of tuberculosis (per 100,000 population)	650.0	2020	●	↗
New HIV infections (per 1,000 uninfected population)	4.9	2020	●	↑
Age-standardized death rate due to cardiovascular disease, cancer, diabetes, or chronic respiratory disease in adults aged 30–70 years (%)	42.7	2019	●	↗
Age-standardized death rate attributable to household air pollution and ambient air pollution (per 100,000 population)	178	2016	●	●
Traffic deaths (per 100,000 population)	31.9	2019	●	↓
Life expectancy at birth (years)	50.8	2019	●	→
Adolescent fertility rate (births per 1,000 females aged 15 to 19)	90.8	2017	●	●
Births attended by skilled health personnel (%)	86.6	2018	●	↑
Surviving infants who received 2 WHO-recommended vaccines (%)	75	2020	●	↓
Universal health coverage (UHC) index of service coverage (worst 0–100 best)	48	2019	●	→
Subjective well-being (average ladder score, worst 0–10 best)	3.5	2019	●	●
SDG4 – Quality Education				
Participation rate in pre-primary organized learning (% of children aged 4 to 6)	39.9	2018	●	●
Net primary enrollment rate (%)	97.6	2017	●	●
Lower secondary completion rate (%)	50.0	2018	●	→
Literacy rate (% of population aged 15 to 24)	86.6	2014	●	●
SDG5 – Gender Equality				
Demand for family planning satisfied by modern methods (% of females aged 15 to 49)	82.8	2018	●	↑
Ratio of female-to-male mean years of education received (%)	124.1	2019	●	↑
Ratio of female-to-male labor force participation rate (%)	78.1	2020	●	↑
Seats held by women in national parliament (%)	23.3	2020	●	↓
SDG6 – Clean Water and Sanitation				
Population using at least basic drinking water services (%)	72.2	2020	●	→
Population using at least basic sanitation services (%)	50.3	2020	●	↗
Freshwater withdrawal (% of available freshwater resources)	2.6	2018	●	●
Anthropogenic wastewater that receives treatment (%)	0.3	2018	●	●
Scarce water consumption embodied in imports (m^3 H_2O eq/capita)	NA	NA	●	●
SDG7 – Affordable and Clean Energy				
Population with access to electricity (%)	44.6	2019	●	↗
Population with access to clean fuels and technology for cooking (%)	39.4	2019	●	→
CO_2 emissions from fuel combustion per total electricity output ($MtCO_2$/TWh)	4.9	2019	●	→
Share of renewable energy in total primary energy supply (%)	NA	NA	●	●
SDG8 – Decent Work and Economic Growth				
Adjusted GDP growth (%)	-9.5	2020	●	●
Victims of modern slavery (per 1,000 population)	4.2	2018	●	●
Adults with an account at a bank or other financial institution or with a mobile-money-service provider (% of population aged 15 or over)	45.6	2017	●	●
Unemployment rate (% of total labor force)	23.9	2022	●	↓
Fundamental labor rights are effectively guaranteed (worst 0–1 best)	NA	NA	●	●
Fatal work-related accidents embodied in imports (per 100,000 population)	0.3	2015	●	↑

SDG9 – Industry, Innovation and Infrastructure	Value	Year	Rating	Trend
Population using the internet (%)	43.0	2020	●	↗
Mobile broadband subscriptions (per 100 population)	61.9	2019	●	↑
Logistics Performance Index: Quality of trade and transport-related infrastructure (worst 1–5 best)	2.0	2018	●	↓
The Times Higher Education Universities Ranking: Average score of top 3 universities (worst 0–100 best)	* 0.0	2022	●	●
Articles published in academic journals (per 1,000 population)	0.0	2020	●	→
Expenditure on research and development (% of GDP)	0.1	2015	●	●
SDG10 – Reduced Inequalities				
Gini coefficient	44.9	2017	●	●
Palma ratio	2.4	2018	●	●
SDG11 – Sustainable Cities and Communities				
Proportion of urban population living in slums (%)	61.9	2018	●	↓
Annual mean concentration of particulate matter of less than 2.5 microns in diameter (PM2.5) (μg/m^3)	26.6	2019	●	↗
Access to improved water source, piped (% of urban population)	91.3	2020	●	↗
Satisfaction with public transport (%)	52.0	2019	●	●
SDG12 – Responsible Consumption and Production				
Municipal solid waste (kg/capita/day)	0.1	2006	●	●
Electronic waste (kg/capita)	1.1	2019	●	●
Production-based SO_2 emissions (kg/capita)	NA	NA	●	●
SO_2 emissions embodied in imports (kg/capita)	NA	NA	●	●
Production-based nitrogen emissions (kg/capita)	9.6	2015	●	↑
Nitrogen emissions embodied in imports (kg/capita)	2.3	2015	●	↑
Exports of plastic waste (kg/capita)	0.0	2020	●	●
SDG13 – Climate Action				
CO_2 emissions from fossil fuel combustion and cement production (tCO_2/capita)	1.0	2020	●	↑
CO_2 emissions embodied in imports (tCO_2/capita)	NA	NA	●	●
CO_2 emissions embodied in fossil fuel exports (kg/capita)	0.0	2020	●	●
SDG14 – Life Below Water				
Mean area that is protected in marine sites important to biodiversity (%)	NA	NA	●	●
Ocean Health Index: Clean Waters score (worst 0–100 best)	NA	NA	●	●
Fish caught from overexploited or collapsed stocks (% of total catch)	NA	NA	●	●
Fish caught by trawling or dredging (%)	NA	NA	●	●
Fish caught that are then discarded (%)	NA	NA	●	●
Marine biodiversity threats embodied in imports (per million population)	0.0	2018	●	●
SDG15 – Life on Land				
Mean area that is protected in terrestrial sites important to biodiversity (%)	16.5	2020	●	→
Mean area that is protected in freshwater sites important to biodiversity (%)	NA	NA	●	●
Red List Index of species survival (worst 0–1 best)	0.9	2021	●	↑
Permanent deforestation (% of forest area, 5-year average)	0.0	2020	●	↑
Terrestrial and freshwater biodiversity threats embodied in imports (per million population)	0.5	2018	●	●
SDG16 – Peace, Justice and Strong Institutions				
Homicides (per 100,000 population)	43.6	2015	●	●
Unsentenced detainees (% of prison population)	19.5	2016	●	●
Population who feel safe walking alone at night in the city or area where they live (%)	34	2019	●	●
Property Rights (worst 1–7 best)	3.2	2020	●	↓
Birth registrations with civil authority (% of children under age 5)	44.5	2020	●	●
Corruption Perception Index (worst 0–100 best)	38	2021	●	↓
Children involved in child labor (% of population aged 5 to 14)	13.9	2019	●	●
Exports of major conventional weapons (TIV constant million USD per 100,000 population)	* 0.0	2020	●	●
Press Freedom Index (best 0–100 worst)	31.6	2021	●	↓
Access to and affordability of justice (worst 0–1 best)	NA	NA	●	●
SDG17 – Partnerships for the Goals				
Government spending on health and education (% of GDP)	12.3	2020	●	↑
For high-income and all OECD DAC countries: International concessional public finance, including official development assistance (% of GNI)	NA	NA	●	●
Other countries: Government revenue excluding grants (% of GDP)	37.2	2019	●	↑
Corporate Tax Haven Score (best 0–100 worst)	* 0.0	2019	●	●
Statistical Performance Index (worst 0–100 best)	55.2	2019	●	↗

* Imputed data point

5. Country Profiles

LIBERIA

Sub-Saharan Africa

OVERALL PERFORMANCE

COUNTRY RANKING

LIBERIA

158 /163

COUNTRY SCORE

REGIONAL AVERAGE: 53.6

AVERAGE PERFORMANCE BY SDG

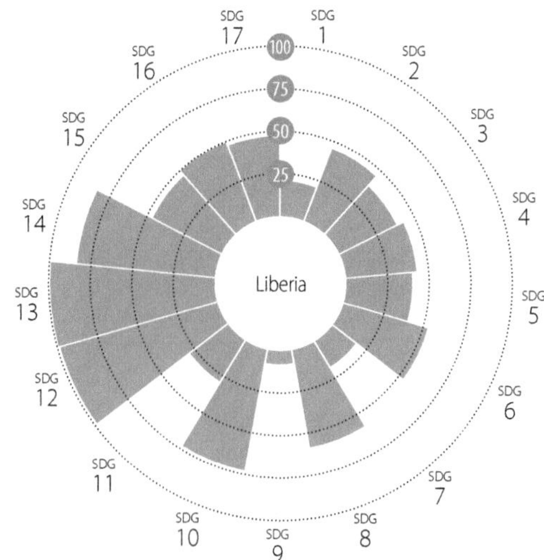

SDG DASHBOARDS AND TRENDS

Major challenges | Significant challenges | Challenges remain | SDG achieved | Information unavailable

Decreasing | Stagnating | Moderately improving | On track or maintaining SDG achievement | Information unavailable

Note: The full title of each SDG is available here: https://sustainabledevelopment.un.org/topics/sustainabledevelopmentgoals

INTERNATIONAL SPILLOVER INDEX

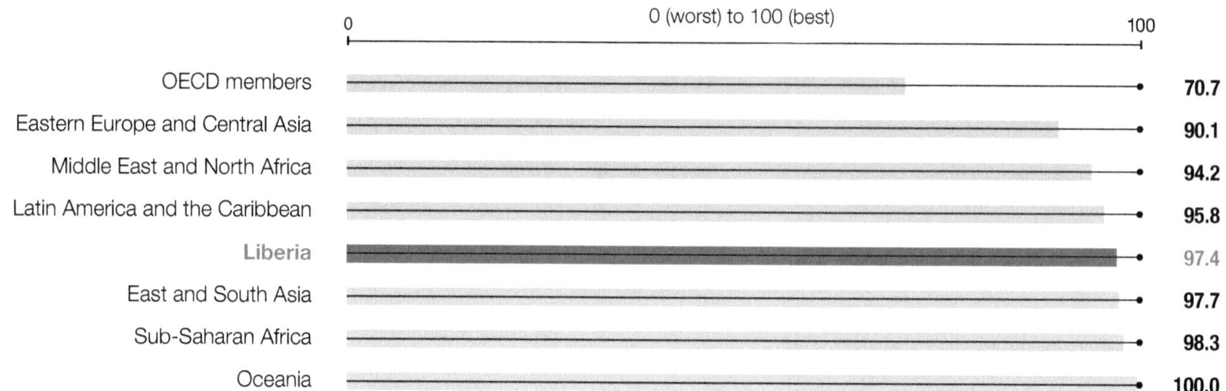

STATISTICAL PERFORMANCE INDEX

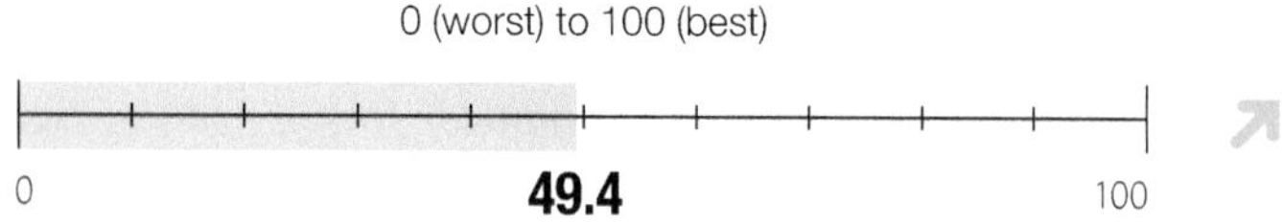

MISSING DATA IN SDG INDEX

5%

SDG1 – No Poverty	Value	Year	Rating	Trend
Poverty headcount ratio at \$1.90/day (%)	41.8	2022	●	↓
Poverty headcount ratio at \$3.20/day (%)	73.1	2022	●	→
SDG2 – Zero Hunger				
Prevalence of undernourishment (%)	38.9	2019	●	↓
Prevalence of stunting in children under 5 years of age (%)	29.8	2019	●	→
Prevalence of wasting in children under 5 years of age (%)	3.4	2019	●	↑
Prevalence of obesity, BMI ≥ 30 (% of adult population)	9.9	2016	●	↑
Human Trophic Level (best 2–3 worst)	2.1	2017	●	↑
Cereal yield (tonnes per hectare of harvested land)	1.1	2018	●	↓
Sustainable Nitrogen Management Index (best 0–1.41 worst)	1.0	2015	●	↓
Exports of hazardous pesticides (tonnes per million population)	NA	NA	●	●
SDG3 – Good Health and Well-Being				
Maternal mortality rate (per 100,000 live births)	661	2017	●	→
Neonatal mortality rate (per 1,000 live births)	30.6	2020	●	→
Mortality rate, under-5 (per 1,000 live births)	78.3	2020	●	→
Incidence of tuberculosis (per 100,000 population)	314.0	2020	●	↓
New HIV infections (per 1,000 uninfected population)	0.3	2020	●	↑
Age-standardized death rate due to cardiovascular disease, cancer, diabetes, or chronic respiratory disease in adults aged 30–70 years (%)	17.8	2019	●	→
Age-standardized death rate attributable to household air pollution and ambient air pollution (per 100,000 population)	170	2016	●	●
Traffic deaths (per 100,000 population)	38.9	2019	●	↓
Life expectancy at birth (years)	64.1	2019	●	↗
Adolescent fertility rate (births per 1,000 females aged 15 to 19)	128.0	2018	●	↗
Births attended by skilled health personnel (%)	84.4	2020	●	●
Surviving infants who received 2 WHO-recommended vaccines (%)	61	2020	●	↓
Universal health coverage (UHC) index of service coverage (worst 0–100 best)	42	2019	●	→
Subjective well-being (average ladder score, worst 0–10 best)	5.1	2019	●	●
SDG4 – Quality Education				
Participation rate in pre-primary organized learning (% of children aged 4 to 6)	78.8	2017	●	●
Net primary enrollment rate (%)	78.6	2017	●	●
Lower secondary completion rate (%)	44.2	2017	●	●
Literacy rate (% of population aged 15 to 24)	55.4	2017	●	●
SDG5 – Gender Equality				
Demand for family planning satisfied by modern methods (% of females aged 15 to 49)	41.0	2020	●	→
Ratio of female-to-male mean years of education received (%)	56.5	2019	●	↗
Ratio of female-to-male labor force participation rate (%)	86.8	2020	●	↑
Seats held by women in national parliament (%)	12.3	2020	●	→
SDG6 – Clean Water and Sanitation				
Population using at least basic drinking water services (%)	75.3	2020	●	→
Population using at least basic sanitation services (%)	18.2	2020	●	→
Freshwater withdrawal (% of available freshwater resources)	0.3	2018	●	●
Anthropogenic wastewater that receives treatment (%)	0.0	2018	●	●
Scarce water consumption embodied in imports (m^3 H_2O eq/capita)	441.5	2018	●	●
SDG7 – Affordable and Clean Energy				
Population with access to electricity (%)	27.6	2019	●	↗
Population with access to clean fuels and technology for cooking (%)	0.2	2019	●	→
CO_2 emissions from fuel combustion per total electricity output ($MtCO_2$/TWh)	4.0	2019	●	→
Share of renewable energy in total primary energy supply (%)	NA	NA	●	●
SDG8 – Decent Work and Economic Growth				
Adjusted GDP growth (%)	-9.5	2020	●	●
Victims of modern slavery (per 1,000 population)	7.4	2018	●	●
Adults with an account at a bank or other financial institution or with a mobile-money-service provider (% of population aged 15 or over)	35.7	2017	●	●
Unemployment rate (% of total labor force)	3.9	2022	●	↑
Fundamental labor rights are effectively guaranteed (worst 0–1 best)	0.5	2020	●	→
Fatal work-related accidents embodied in imports (per 100,000 population)	0.0	2015	●	↑

* Imputed data point

SDG9 – Industry, Innovation and Infrastructure	Value	Year	Rating	Trend
Population using the internet (%)	25.6	2020	●	↗
Mobile broadband subscriptions (per 100 population)	8.1	2019	●	→
Logistics Performance Index: Quality of trade and transport-related infrastructure (worst 1–5 best)	1.9	2018	●	↓
The Times Higher Education Universities Ranking: Average score of top 3 universities (worst 0–100 best)	* 0.0	2022	●	●
Articles published in academic journals (per 1,000 population)	0.0	2020	●	→
Expenditure on research and development (% of GDP)	* 0.0	2018	●	●
SDG10 – Reduced Inequalities				
Gini coefficient	35.3	2016	●	●
Palma ratio	1.4	2018	●	●
SDG11 – Sustainable Cities and Communities				
Proportion of urban population living in slums (%)	66.6	2018	●	↓
Annual mean concentration of particulate matter of less than 2.5 microns in diameter (PM2.5) (μg/m³)	18.8	2019	●	→
Access to improved water source, piped (% of urban population)	8.3	2020	●	↓
Satisfaction with public transport (%)	16.0	2019	●	●
SDG12 – Responsible Consumption and Production				
Municipal solid waste (kg/capita/day)	0.4	2007	●	●
Electronic waste (kg/capita)	NA	NA	●	●
Production-based SO_2 emissions (kg/capita)	1.1	2018	●	●
SO_2 emissions embodied in imports (kg/capita)	0.3	2018	●	●
Production-based nitrogen emissions (kg/capita)	2.2	2015	●	↑
Nitrogen emissions embodied in imports (kg/capita)	0.3	2015	●	↑
Exports of plastic waste (kg/capita)	NA	NA	●	●
SDG13 – Climate Action				
CO_2 emissions from fossil fuel combustion and cement production (tCO_2/capita)	0.2	2020	●	↑
CO_2 emissions embodied in imports (tCO_2/capita)	0.1	2018	●	↑
CO_2 emissions embodied in fossil fuel exports (kg/capita)	0.0	2020	●	●
SDG14 – Life Below Water				
Mean area that is protected in marine sites important to biodiversity (%)	96.7	2020	●	↑
Ocean Health Index: Clean Waters score (worst 0–100 best)	49.8	2020	●	→
Fish caught from overexploited or collapsed stocks (% of total catch)	20.2	2018	●	↑
Fish caught by trawling or dredging (%)	6.0	2005	●	●
Fish caught that are then discarded (%)	0.0	2018	●	↑
Marine biodiversity threats embodied in imports (per million population)	0.0	2018	●	●
SDG15 – Life on Land				
Mean area that is protected in terrestrial sites important to biodiversity (%)	15.8	2020	●	→
Mean area that is protected in freshwater sites important to biodiversity (%)	24.3	2020	●	→
Red List Index of species survival (worst 0–1 best)	0.9	2021	●	↑
Permanent deforestation (% of forest area, 5-year average)	1.3	2020	●	↓
Terrestrial and freshwater biodiversity threats embodied in imports (per million population)	0.0	2018	●	●
SDG16 – Peace, Justice and Strong Institutions				
Homicides (per 100,000 population)	3.3	2012	●	●
Unsentenced detainees (% of prison population)	63.0	2017	●	●
Population who feel safe walking alone at night in the city or area where they live (%)	33	2019	●	●
Property Rights (worst 1–7 best)	4.6	2020	●	●
Birth registrations with civil authority (% of children under age 5)	24.6	2020	●	●
Corruption Perception Index (worst 0–100 best)	29	2021	●	↓
Children involved in child labor (% of population aged 5 to 14)	14.0	2019	●	●
Exports of major conventional weapons (TIV constant million USD per 100,000 population)	* 0.0	2020	●	●
Press Freedom Index (best 0–100 worst)	33.4	2021	●	↓
Access to and affordability of justice (worst 0–1 best)	0.5	2020	●	↑
SDG17 – Partnerships for the Goals				
Government spending on health and education (% of GDP)	3.7	2020	●	→
For high-income and all OECD DAC countries: International concessional public finance, including official development assistance (% of GNI)	NA	NA	●	●
Other countries: Government revenue excluding grants (% of GDP)	NA	NA	●	●
Corporate Tax Haven Score (best 0–100 worst)	49.0	2019	●	●
Statistical Performance Index (worst 0–100 best)	49.4	2019	●	↗

LIBYA

Middle East and North Africa

OVERALL PERFORMANCE

COUNTRY RANKING

LIBYA

NA /163

COUNTRY SCORE

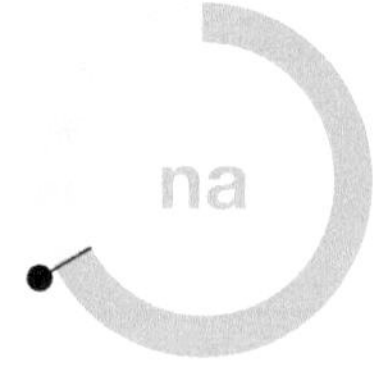

REGIONAL AVERAGE: 66.7

AVERAGE PERFORMANCE BY SDG

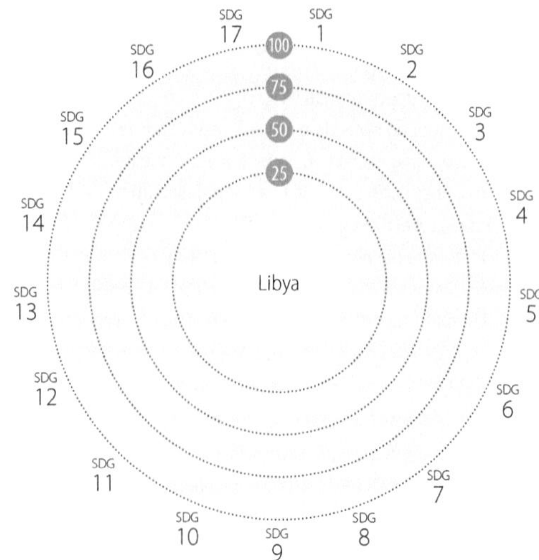

SDG DASHBOARDS AND TRENDS

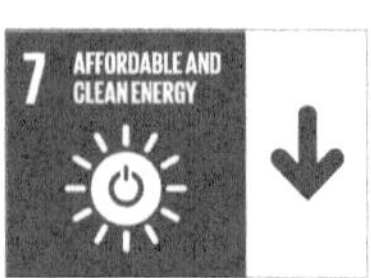

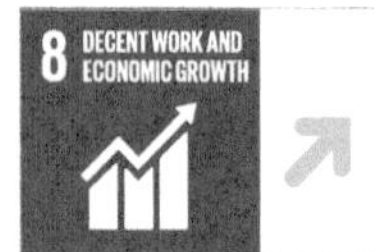

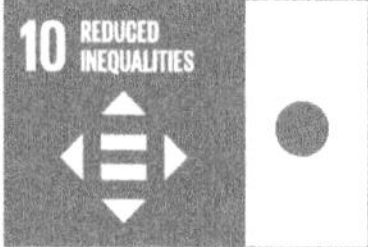

Major challenges | Significant challenges | Challenges remain | SDG achieved | Information unavailable

Decreasing | Stagnating | Moderately improving | On track or maintaining SDG achievement | Information unavailable

Note: The full title of each SDG is available here: https://sustainabledevelopment.un.org/topics/sustainabledevelopmentgoals

INTERNATIONAL SPILLOVER INDEX

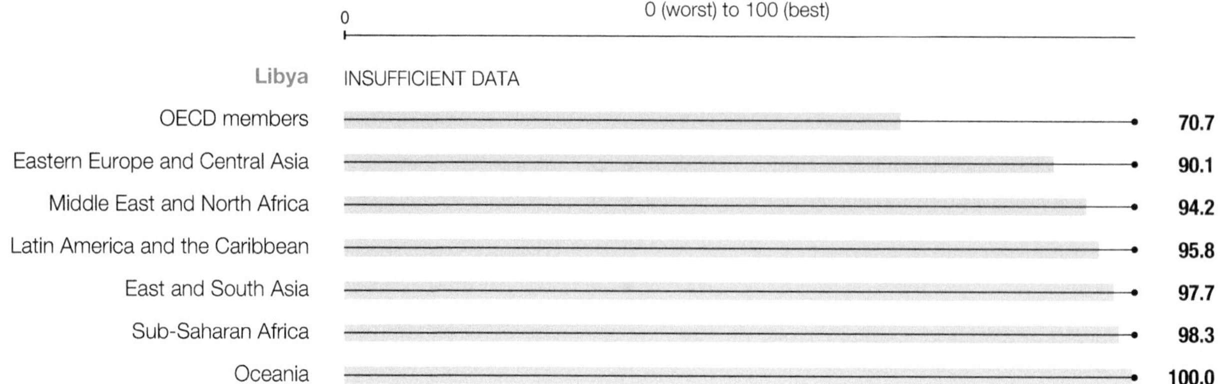

STATISTICAL PERFORMANCE INDEX

0 (worst) to 100 (best)

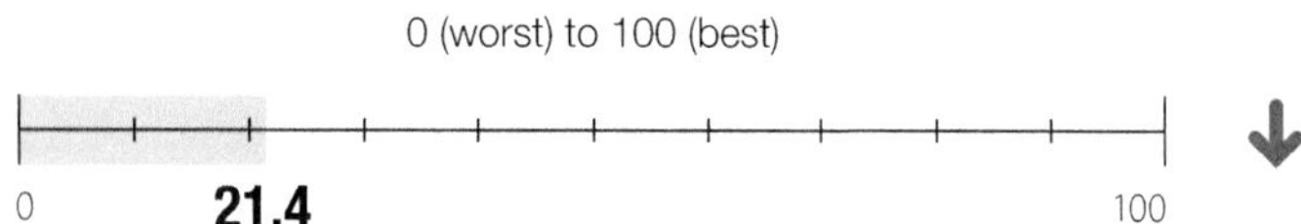

MISSING DATA IN SDG INDEX

24%

Performance by Indicator

SDG1 – No Poverty	Value	Year	Rating	Trend
Poverty headcount ratio at $1.90/day (%)	* NA	NA	●	●
Poverty headcount ratio at $3.20/day (%)	* NA	NA	●	●
SDG2 – Zero Hunger				
Prevalence of undernourishment (%)	NA	NA	●	●
Prevalence of stunting in children under 5 years of age (%)	38.1	2014	●	↓
Prevalence of wasting in children under 5 years of age (%)	10.2	2014	●	→
Prevalence of obesity, BMI ≥ 30 (% of adult population)	32.5	2016	●	↓
Human Trophic Level (best 2–3 worst)	2.2	2007	●	●
Cereal yield (tonnes per hectare of harvested land)	0.7	2018	●	↓
Sustainable Nitrogen Management Index (best 0–1.41 worst)	0.9	2015	●	→
Exports of hazardous pesticides (tonnes per million population)	NA	NA	●	●
SDG3 – Good Health and Well-Being				
Maternal mortality rate (per 100,000 live births)	72	2017	●	↓
Neonatal mortality rate (per 1,000 live births)	6.0	2020	●	↑
Mortality rate, under-5 (per 1,000 live births)	11.1	2020	●	↑
Incidence of tuberculosis (per 100,000 population)	59.0	2020	●	→
New HIV infections (per 1,000 uninfected population)	0.1	2020	●	↑
Age-standardized death rate due to cardiovascular disease, cancer, diabetes, or chronic respiratory disease in adults aged 30–70 years (%)	18.6	2019	●	→
Age-standardized death rate attributable to household air pollution and ambient air pollution (per 100,000 population)	72	2016	●	●
Traffic deaths (per 100,000 population)	21.3	2019	●	↗
Life expectancy at birth (years)	75.8	2019	●	↗
Adolescent fertility rate (births per 1,000 females aged 15 to 19)	10.9	2013	●	●
Births attended by skilled health personnel (%)	99.9	2013	●	●
Surviving infants who received 2 WHO-recommended vaccines (%)	73	2020	●	↓
Universal health coverage (UHC) index of service coverage (worst 0–100 best)	60	2019	●	→
Subjective well-being (average ladder score, worst 0–10 best)	5.3	2019	●	●
SDG4 – Quality Education				
Participation rate in pre-primary organized learning (% of children aged 4 to 6)	NA	NA	●	●
Net primary enrollment rate (%)	NA	NA	●	●
Lower secondary completion rate (%)	NA	NA	●	●
Literacy rate (% of population aged 15 to 24)	99.6	2004	●	●
SDG5 – Gender Equality				
Demand for family planning satisfied by modern methods (% of females aged 15 to 49)	24.0	2014	●	→
Ratio of female-to-male mean years of education received (%)	118.1	2019	●	↑
Ratio of female-to-male labor force participation rate (%)	56.0	2020	●	→
Seats held by women in national parliament (%)	16.0	2020	●	→
SDG6 – Clean Water and Sanitation				
Population using at least basic drinking water services (%)	99.9	2020	●	↑
Population using at least basic sanitation services (%)	92.1	2020	●	→
Freshwater withdrawal (% of available freshwater resources)	817.1	2018	●	●
Anthropogenic wastewater that receives treatment (%)	9.6	2018	●	●
Scarce water consumption embodied in imports (m^3 H_2O eq/capita)	NA	NA	●	●
SDG7 – Affordable and Clean Energy				
Population with access to electricity (%)	68.5	2019	●	↓
Population with access to clean fuels and technology for cooking (%)	NA	NA	●	●
CO_2 emissions from fuel combustion per total electricity output ($MtCO_2/TWh$)	1.5	2019	●	→
Share of renewable energy in total primary energy supply (%)	2.8	2019	●	↓
SDG8 – Decent Work and Economic Growth				
Adjusted GDP growth (%)	-10.6	2020	●	●
Victims of modern slavery (per 1,000 population)	* NA	NA	●	●
Adults with an account at a bank or other financial institution or with a mobile-money-service provider (% of population aged 15 or over)	65.7	2017	●	●
Unemployment rate (% of total labor force)	19.5	2022	●	→
Fundamental labor rights are effectively guaranteed (worst 0–1 best)	NA	NA	●	●
Fatal work-related accidents embodied in imports (per 100,000 population)	0.1	2015	●	↑

* Imputed data point

SDG9 – Industry, Innovation and Infrastructure	Value	Year	Rating	Trend
Population using the internet (%)	17.8	2014	●	●
Mobile broadband subscriptions (per 100 population)	21.4	2019	●	↓
Logistics Performance Index: Quality of trade and transport-related infrastructure (worst 1–5 best)	2.2	2018	●	↓
The Times Higher Education Universities Ranking: Average score of top 3 universities (worst 0–100 best)	* 0.0	2022	●	●
Articles published in academic journals (per 1,000 population)	0.1	2020	●	→
Expenditure on research and development (% of GDP)	NA	NA	●	●
SDG10 – Reduced Inequalities				
Gini coefficient	NA	NA	●	●
Palma ratio	NA	NA	●	●
SDG11 – Sustainable Cities and Communities				
Proportion of urban population living in slums (%)	NA	NA	●	●
Annual mean concentration of particulate matter of less than 2.5 microns in diameter (PM2.5) (μg/m^3)	55.5	2019	●	↓
Access to improved water source, piped (% of urban population)	NA	NA	●	●
Satisfaction with public transport (%)	43.0	2019	●	●
SDG12 – Responsible Consumption and Production				
Municipal solid waste (kg/capita/day)	0.9	2011	●	●
Electronic waste (kg/capita)	11.5	2019	●	●
Production-based SO_2 emissions (kg/capita)	27.7	2018	●	●
SO_2 emissions embodied in imports (kg/capita)	1.5	2018	●	●
Production-based nitrogen emissions (kg/capita)	8.9	2015	●	↑
Nitrogen emissions embodied in imports (kg/capita)	2.0	2015	●	↑
Exports of plastic waste (kg/capita)	0.5	2018	●	●
SDG13 – Climate Action				
CO_2 emissions from fossil fuel combustion and cement production (tCO_2/capita)	7.4	2020	●	↗
CO_2 emissions embodied in imports (tCO_2/capita)	0.6	2018	●	↓
CO_2 emissions embodied in fossil fuel exports (kg/capita)	20233.9	2018	●	●
SDG14 – Life Below Water				
Mean area that is protected in marine sites important to biodiversity (%)	0.0	2020	●	→
Ocean Health Index: Clean Waters score (worst 0–100 best)	55.6	2020	●	↓
Fish caught from overexploited or collapsed stocks (% of total catch)	20.0	2018	●	↑
Fish caught by trawling or dredging (%)	21.6	2018	●	↓
Fish caught that are then discarded (%)	31.6	2018	●	↓
Marine biodiversity threats embodied in imports (per million population)	0.0	2018	●	●
SDG15 – Life on Land				
Mean area that is protected in terrestrial sites important to biodiversity (%)	0.0	2020	●	→
Mean area that is protected in freshwater sites important to biodiversity (%)	NA	NA	●	●
Red List Index of species survival (worst 0–1 best)	1.0	2021	●	↑
Permanent deforestation (% of forest area, 5-year average)	0.0	2020	●	↑
Terrestrial and freshwater biodiversity threats embodied in imports (per million population)	0.1	2018	●	●
SDG16 – Peace, Justice and Strong Institutions				
Homicides (per 100,000 population)	NA	NA	●	●
Unsentenced detainees (% of prison population)	90.0	2016	●	●
Population who feel safe walking alone at night in the city or area where they live (%)	58	2019	●	●
Property Rights (worst 1–7 best)	NA	NA	●	●
Birth registrations with civil authority (% of children under age 5)	NA	NA	●	●
Corruption Perception Index (worst 0–100 best)	17	2021	●	→
Children involved in child labor (% of population aged 5 to 14)	NA	NA	●	●
Exports of major conventional weapons (TIV constant million USD per 100,000 population)	0.0	2020	●	●
Press Freedom Index (best 0–100 worst)	55.7	2021	●	→
Access to and affordability of justice (worst 0–1 best)	NA	NA	●	●
SDG17 – Partnerships for the Goals				
Government spending on health and education (% of GDP)	6.1	2011	●	●
For high-income and all OECD DAC countries: International concessional public finance, including official development assistance (% of GNI)	NA	NA	●	●
Other countries: Government revenue excluding grants (% of GDP)	NA	NA	●	●
Corporate Tax Haven Score (best 0–100 worst)	* 0.0	2019	●	●
Statistical Performance Index (worst 0–100 best)	21.4	2019	●	↓

LIECHTENSTEIN

Western Europe

AVERAGE PERFORMANCE BY SDG

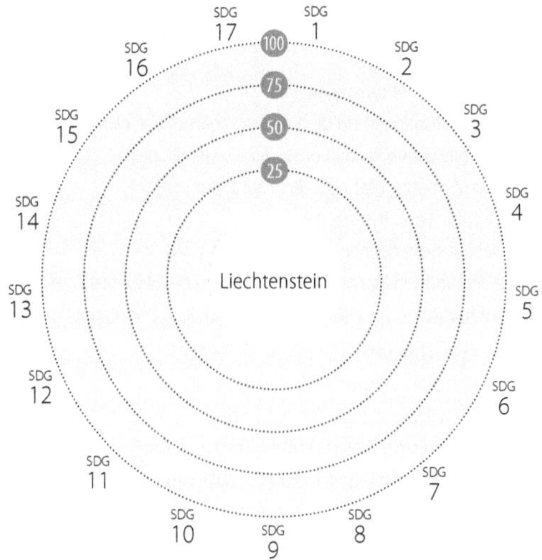

OVERALL PERFORMANCE

COUNTRY RANKING

LIECHTENSTEIN

NA /163

COUNTRY SCORE

na

REGIONAL AVERAGE: 71.6

SDG DASHBOARDS AND TRENDS

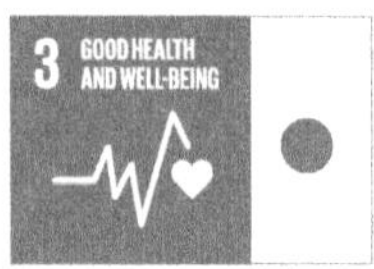

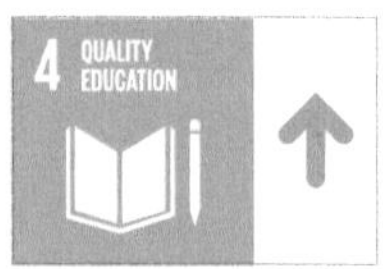

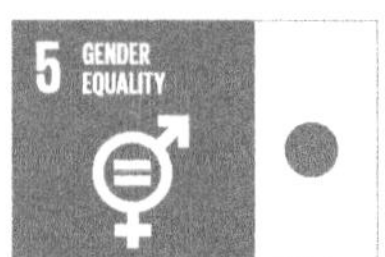

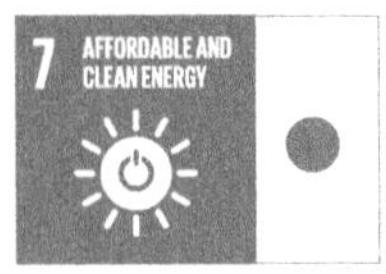

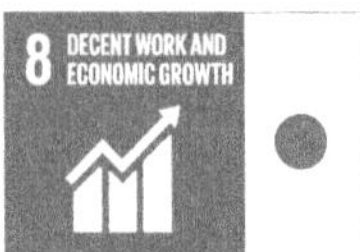

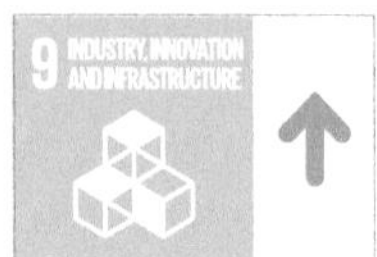

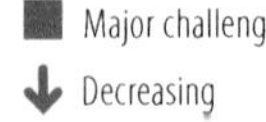

Major challenges | Significant challenges | Challenges remain | SDG achieved | Information unavailable

Decreasing | Stagnating | Moderately improving | On track or maintaining SDG achievement | Information unavailable

Note: The full title of each SDG is available here: https://sustainabledevelopment.un.org/topics/sustainabledevelopmentgoals

INTERNATIONAL SPILLOVER INDEX

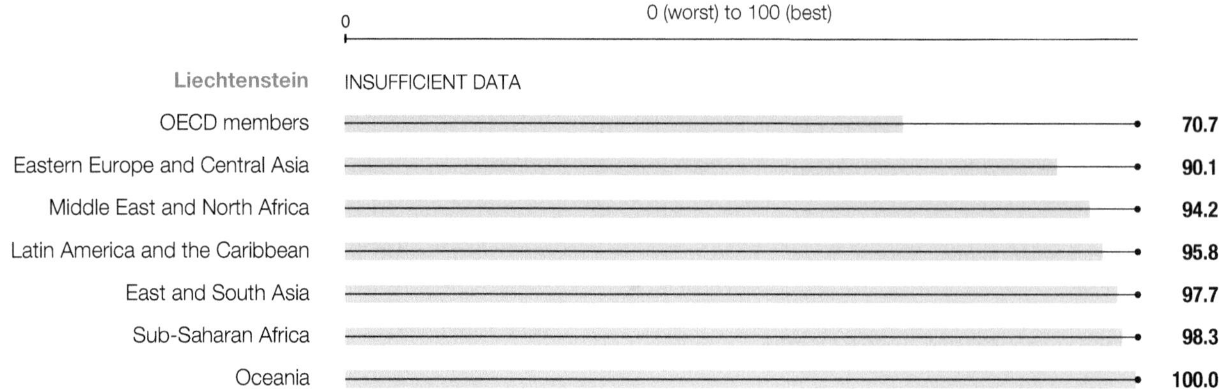

STATISTICAL PERFORMANCE INDEX

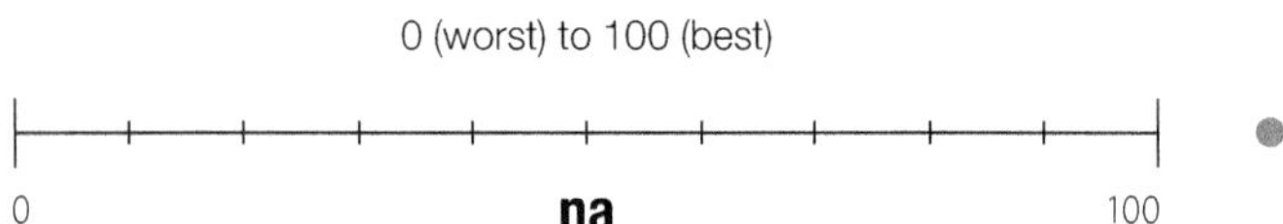

MISSING DATA IN SDG INDEX

66%

LIECHTENSTEIN

Performance by Indicator

SDG1 – No Poverty		Value	Year	Rating	Trend
Poverty headcount ratio at $1.90/day (%)		NA	NA	●	●
Poverty headcount ratio at $3.20/day (%)		NA	NA	●	●
SDG2 – Zero Hunger					
Prevalence of undernourishment (%)	*	1.2	2019	●	●
Prevalence of stunting in children under 5 years of age (%)	*	2.6	2019	●	●
Prevalence of wasting in children under 5 years of age (%)	*	0.7	2019	●	●
Prevalence of obesity, BMI ≥ 30 (% of adult population)		NA	NA	●	●
Human Trophic Level (best 2–3 worst)		NA	NA	●	●
Cereal yield (tonnes per hectare of harvested land)		NA	NA	●	●
Sustainable Nitrogen Management Index (best 0–1.41 worst)		NA	NA	●	●
Exports of hazardous pesticides (tonnes per million population)		NA	NA	●	●
SDG3 – Good Health and Well-Being					
Maternal mortality rate (per 100,000 live births)		NA	NA	●	●
Neonatal mortality rate (per 1,000 live births)		NA	NA	●	●
Mortality rate, under-5 (per 1,000 live births)		NA	NA	●	●
Incidence of tuberculosis (per 100,000 population)		NA	NA	●	●
New HIV infections (per 1,000 uninfected population)		NA	NA	●	●
Age-standardized death rate due to cardiovascular disease, cancer, diabetes, or chronic respiratory disease in adults aged 30–70 years (%)		NA	NA	●	●
Age-standardized death rate attributable to household air pollution and ambient air pollution (per 100,000 population)		NA	NA	●	●
Traffic deaths (per 100,000 population)		NA	NA	●	●
Life expectancy at birth (years)		NA	NA	●	●
Adolescent fertility rate (births per 1,000 females aged 15 to 19)		NA	NA	●	●
Births attended by skilled health personnel (%)		NA	NA	●	●
Surviving infants who received 2 WHO-recommended vaccines (%)		NA	NA	●	●
Universal health coverage (UHC) index of service coverage (worst 0–100 best)		NA	NA	●	●
Subjective well-being (average ladder score, worst 0–10 best)		NA	NA	●	●
SDG4 – Quality Education					
Participation rate in pre-primary organized learning (% of children aged 4 to 6)		97.1	2019	●	↑
Net primary enrollment rate (%)		99.9	2019	●	↑
Lower secondary completion rate (%)		102.6	2019	●	↑
Literacy rate (% of population aged 15 to 24)		NA	NA	●	●
SDG5 – Gender Equality					
Demand for family planning satisfied by modern methods (% of females aged 15 to 49)		NA	NA	●	●
Ratio of female-to-male mean years of education received (%)		NA	NA	●	●
Ratio of female-to-male labor force participation rate (%)		NA	NA	●	●
Seats held by women in national parliament (%)		12.0	2020	●	↓
SDG6 – Clean Water and Sanitation					
Population using at least basic drinking water services (%)		100.0	2020	●	↑
Population using at least basic sanitation services (%)		100.0	2020	●	↑
Freshwater withdrawal (% of available freshwater resources)		NA	NA	●	●
Anthropogenic wastewater that receives treatment (%)		NA	NA	●	●
Scarce water consumption embodied in imports (m^3 H_2O eq/capita)		NA	NA	●	●
SDG7 – Affordable and Clean Energy					
Population with access to electricity (%)		100.0	2019	●	↑
Population with access to clean fuels and technology for cooking (%)		NA	NA	●	●
CO_2 emissions from fuel combustion per total electricity output ($MtCO_2$/TWh)		NA	NA	●	●
Share of renewable energy in total primary energy supply (%)		NA	NA	●	●
SDG8 – Decent Work and Economic Growth					
Adjusted GDP growth (%)		NA	NA	●	●
Victims of modern slavery (per 1,000 population)		NA	NA	●	●
Adults with an account at a bank or other financial institution or with a mobile-money-service provider (% of population aged 15 or over)		NA	NA	●	●
Unemployment rate (% of total labor force)		NA	NA	●	●
Fundamental labor rights are effectively guaranteed (worst 0–1 best)		NA	NA	●	●
Fatal work-related accidents embodied in imports (per 100,000 population)		1.3	2015	●	↑

* Imputed data point

SDG9 – Industry, Innovation and Infrastructure		Value	Year	Rating	Trend
Population using the internet (%)		99.5	2017	●	●
Mobile broadband subscriptions (per 100 population)		125.6	2019	●	↑
Logistics Performance Index: Quality of trade and transport-related infrastructure (worst 1–5 best)		NA	NA	●	●
The Times Higher Education Universities Ranking: Average score of top 3 universities (worst 0–100 best)	*	0.0	2022	●	●
Articles published in academic journals (per 1,000 population)		3.3	2020	●	↑
Expenditure on research and development (% of GDP)		NA	NA	●	●
SDG10 – Reduced Inequalities					
Gini coefficient		NA	NA	●	●
Palma ratio		NA	NA	●	●
SDG11 – Sustainable Cities and Communities					
Proportion of urban population living in slums (%)		NA	NA	●	●
Annual mean concentration of particulate matter of less than 2.5 microns in diameter (PM2.5) ($\mu g/m^3$)		NA	NA	●	●
Access to improved water source, piped (% of urban population)		NA	NA	●	●
Satisfaction with public transport (%)		NA	NA	●	●
SDG12 – Responsible Consumption and Production					
Municipal solid waste (kg/capita/day)		2.4	2015	●	●
Electronic waste (kg/capita)		NA	NA	●	●
Production-based SO_2 emissions (kg/capita)		NA	NA	●	●
SO_2 emissions embodied in imports (kg/capita)		NA	NA	●	●
Production-based nitrogen emissions (kg/capita)		3.8	2015	●	↑
Nitrogen emissions embodied in imports (kg/capita)		28.9	2015	●	↓
Exports of plastic waste (kg/capita)		NA	NA	●	●
SDG13 – Climate Action					
CO_2 emissions from fossil fuel combustion and cement production (tCO_2/capita)		3.7	2020	●	↗
CO_2 emissions embodied in imports (tCO_2/capita)		NA	NA	●	●
CO_2 emissions embodied in fossil fuel exports (kg/capita)		NA	NA	●	●
SDG14 – Life Below Water					
Mean area that is protected in marine sites important to biodiversity (%)		NA	NA	●	●
Ocean Health Index: Clean Waters score (worst 0–100 best)		NA	NA	●	●
Fish caught from overexploited or collapsed stocks (% of total catch)		NA	NA	●	●
Fish caught by trawling or dredging (%)		NA	NA	●	●
Fish caught that are then discarded (%)		NA	NA	●	●
Marine biodiversity threats embodied in imports (per million population)		NA	NA	●	●
SDG15 – Life on Land					
Mean area that is protected in terrestrial sites important to biodiversity (%)		80.8	2020	●	→
Mean area that is protected in freshwater sites important to biodiversity (%)		NA	NA	●	●
Red List Index of species survival (worst 0–1 best)		1.0	2021	●	↑
Permanent deforestation (% of forest area, 5-year average)		0.0	2020	●	↑
Terrestrial and freshwater biodiversity threats embodied in imports (per million population)		0.4	2018	●	●
SDG16 – Peace, Justice and Strong Institutions					
Homicides (per 100,000 population)		2.6	2019	●	↓
Unsentenced detainees (% of prison population)		39.7	2019	●	↑
Population who feel safe walking alone at night in the city or area where they live (%)		NA	NA	●	●
Property Rights (worst 1–7 best)		NA	NA	●	●
Birth registrations with civil authority (% of children under age 5)		100.0	2020	●	●
Corruption Perception Index (worst 0–100 best)		NA	NA	●	●
Children involved in child labor (% of population aged 5 to 14)		NA	NA	●	●
Exports of major conventional weapons (TIV constant million USD per 100,000 population)	*	0.0	2020	●	●
Press Freedom Index (best 0–100 worst)		19.5	2021	●	↑
Access to and affordability of justice (worst 0–1 best)		NA	NA	●	●
SDG17 – Partnerships for the Goals					
Government spending on health and education (% of GDP)		NA	NA	●	●
For high-income and all OECD DAC countries: International concessional public finance, including official development assistance (% of GNI)		0.4	2018	●	●
Other countries: Government revenue excluding grants (% of GDP)		NA	NA	●	●
Corporate Tax Haven Score (best 0–100 worst)		69.5	2019	●	●
Statistical Performance Index (worst 0–100 best)		NA	NA	●	●

LITHUANIA

OECD Countries

OVERALL PERFORMANCE

COUNTRY RANKING

LITHUANIA

39/163

COUNTRY SCORE

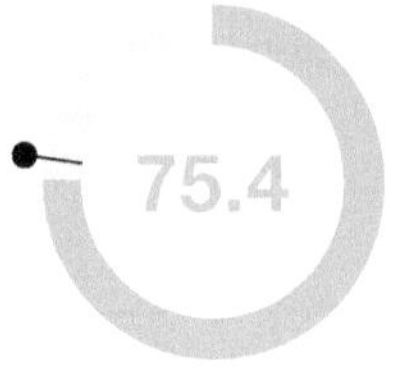

REGIONAL AVERAGE: 77.2

AVERAGE PERFORMANCE BY SDG

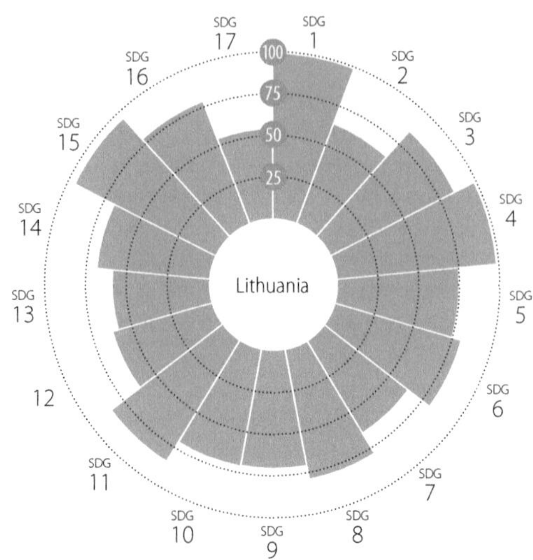

SDG DASHBOARDS AND TRENDS

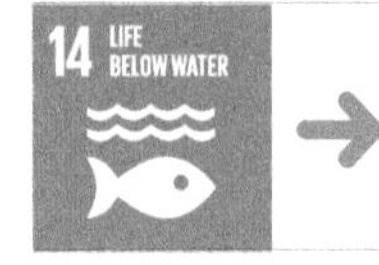

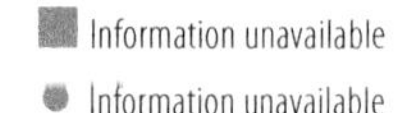

Major challenges | Significant challenges | Challenges remain | SDG achieved | Information unavailable

Decreasing | Stagnating | Moderately improving | On track or maintaining SDG achievement | Information unavailable

Note: The full title of each SDG is available here: https://sustainabledevelopment.un.org/topics/sustainabledevelopmentgoals

INTERNATIONAL SPILLOVER INDEX

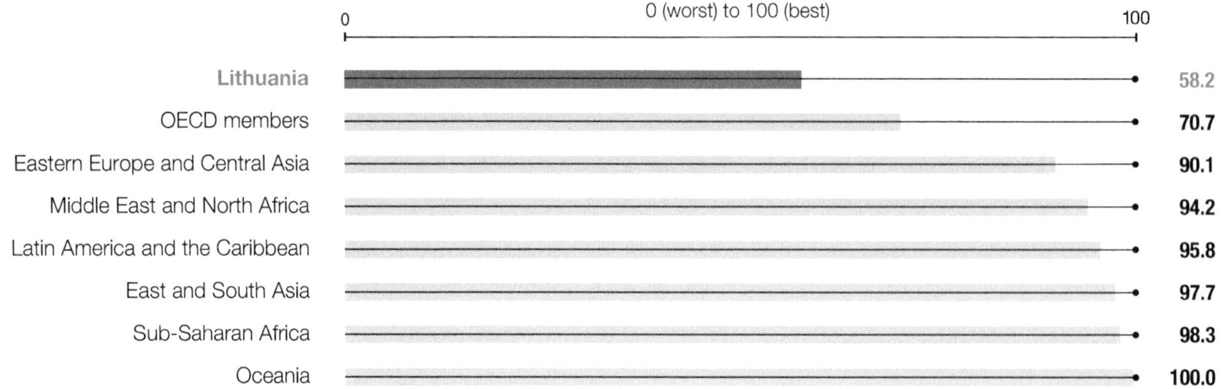

STATISTICAL PERFORMANCE INDEX

0 (worst) to 100 (best)

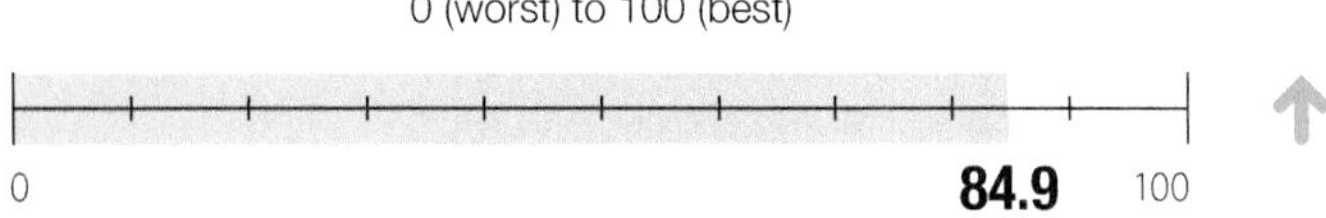

MISSING DATA IN SDG INDEX

1%

SDG1 – No Poverty	Value	Year	Rating	Trend
Poverty headcount ratio at $1.90/day (%)	0.5	2022	●	↑
Poverty headcount ratio at $3.20/day (%)	0.7	2022	●	↑
Poverty rate after taxes and transfers (%)	15.4	2019	●	↗

SDG2 – Zero Hunger	Value	Year	Rating	Trend
Prevalence of undernourishment (%)	2.5	2019	●	↑
Prevalence of stunting in children under 5 years of age (%)	* 2.6	2019	●	↑
Prevalence of wasting in children under 5 years of age (%)	* 0.7	2019	●	↑
Prevalence of obesity, BMI ≥ 30 (% of adult population)	26.3	2016	●	↓
Human Trophic Level (best 2–3 worst)	2.5	2017	●	↓
Cereal yield (tonnes per hectare of harvested land)	3.2	2018	●	↑
Sustainable Nitrogen Management Index (best 0–1.41 worst)	0.5	2015	●	↓
Yield gap closure (% of potential yield)	45.6	2018	●	●
Exports of hazardous pesticides (tonnes per million population)	12.0	2019	●	●

SDG3 – Good Health and Well-Being	Value	Year	Rating	Trend
Maternal mortality rate (per 100,000 live births)	8	2017	●	↑
Neonatal mortality rate (per 1,000 live births)	1.9	2020	●	↑
Mortality rate, under-5 (per 1,000 live births)	3.3	2020	●	↑
Incidence of tuberculosis (per 100,000 population)	29.0	2020	●	↑
New HIV infections (per 1,000 uninfected population)	1.0	2020	●	→
Age-standardized death rate due to cardiovascular disease, cancer, diabetes, or chronic respiratory disease in adults aged 30–70 years (%)	19.3	2019	●	↑
Age-standardized death rate attributable to household air pollution and ambient air pollution (per 100,000 population)	34	2016	●	●
Traffic deaths (per 100,000 population)	8.1	2019	●	↑
Life expectancy at birth (years)	76.0	2019	●	↑
Adolescent fertility rate (births per 1,000 females aged 15 to 19)	11.2	2018	●	↑
Births attended by skilled health personnel (%)	100.0	2014	●	●
Surviving infants who received 2 WHO-recommended vaccines (%)	90	2020	●	↑
Universal health coverage (UHC) index of service coverage (worst 0–100 best)	70	2019	●	↑
Subjective well-being (average ladder score, worst 0–10 best)	6.9	2021	●	↑
Gap in life expectancy at birth among regions (years)	2.9	2019	●	↑
Gap in self-reported health status by income (percentage points)	40.7	2019	●	↓
Daily smokers (% of population aged 15 and over)	18.9	2019	●	↑

SDG4 – Quality Education	Value	Year	Rating	Trend
Participation rate in pre-primary organized learning (% of children aged 4 to 6)	96.2	2019	●	↑
Net primary enrollment rate (%)	99.9	2019	●	↑
Lower secondary completion rate (%)	100.4	2019	●	↑
Literacy rate (% of population aged 15 to 24)	99.9	2011	●	●
Tertiary educational attainment (% of population aged 25 to 34)	56.2	2020	●	↑
PISA score (worst 0–600 best)	479.7	2018	●	↑
Variation in science performance explained by socio-economic status (%)	12.5	2018	●	↓
Underachievers in science (% of 15-year-olds)	22.2	2018	●	↑

SDG5 – Gender Equality	Value	Year	Rating	Trend
Demand for family planning satisfied by modern methods (% of females aged 15 to 49)	* 71.9	2022	●	↗
Ratio of female-to-male mean years of education received (%)	100.8	2019	●	↑
Ratio of female-to-male labor force participation rate (%)	83.3	2020	●	↑
Seats held by women in national parliament (%)	27.0	2020	●	↗
Gender wage gap (% of male median wage)	11.7	2018	●	↗

SDG6 – Clean Water and Sanitation	Value	Year	Rating	Trend
Population using at least basic drinking water services (%)	98.0	2020	●	↑
Population using at least basic sanitation services (%)	93.9	2020	●	↑
Freshwater withdrawal (% of available freshwater resources)	1.8	2018	●	●
Anthropogenic wastewater that receives treatment (%)	51.4	2018	●	●
Scarce water consumption embodied in imports (m^3 H_2O eq/capita)	4422.0	2018	●	●
Population using safely managed water services (%)	94.9	2020	●	↑
Population using safely managed sanitation services (%)	93.9	2020	●	↑

SDG7 – Affordable and Clean Energy	Value	Year	Rating	Trend
Population with access to electricity (%)	100.0	2019	●	↑
Population with access to clean fuels and technology for cooking (%)	100.0	2019	●	↑
CO_2 emissions from fuel combustion per total electricity output ($MtCO_2$/TWh)	4.8	2019	●	↓
Share of renewable energy in total primary energy supply (%)	20.5	2019	●	↑

SDG8 – Decent Work and Economic Growth	Value	Year	Rating	Trend
Adjusted GDP growth (%)	2.1	2020	●	●
Victims of modern slavery (per 1,000 population)	5.8	2018	●	●
Adults with an account at a bank or other financial institution or with a mobile-money-service provider (% of population aged 15 or over)	82.9	2017	●	↑
Fundamental labor rights are effectively guaranteed (worst 0–1 best)	0.7	2020	●	●
Fatal work-related accidents embodied in imports (per 100,000 population)	0.7	2015	●	↑
Employment-to-population ratio (%)	71.6	2020	●	↑
Youth not in employment, education or training (NEET) (% of population aged 15 to 29)	12.5	2020	●	↗

SDG9 – Industry, Innovation and Infrastructure	Value	Year	Rating	Trend
Population using the internet (%)	83.1	2020	●	↑
Mobile broadband subscriptions (per 100 population)	105.7	2019	●	↑
Logistics Performance Index: Quality of trade and transport-related infrastructure (worst 1–5 best)	2.7	2018	●	↓
The Times Higher Education Universities Ranking: Average score of top 3 universities (worst 0–100 best)	29.8	2022	●	●
Articles published in academic journals (per 1,000 population)	1.7	2020	●	↑
Expenditure on research and development (% of GDP)	0.9	2018	●	↓
Researchers (per 1,000 employed population)	6.9	2019	●	↑
Triadic patent families filed (per million population)	3.0	2019	●	→
Gap in internet access by income (percentage points)	42.6	2020	●	↗
Female share of graduates from STEM fields at the tertiary level (%)	29.6	2017	●	↓

SDG10 – Reduced Inequalities	Value	Year	Rating	Trend
Gini coefficient	35.7	2018	●	↑
Palma ratio	1.5	2019	●	↗
Elderly poverty rate (% of population aged 66 or over)	28.7	2019	●	↓

SDG11 – Sustainable Cities and Communities	Value	Year	Rating	Trend
Proportion of urban population living in slums (%)	* 0.0	2018	●	↑
Annual mean concentration of particulate matter of less than 2.5 microns in diameter (PM2.5) (μg/m^3)	11.2	2019	●	↑
Access to improved water source, piped (% of urban population)	100.0	2020	●	↑
Satisfaction with public transport (%)	47.0	2021	●	↓
Population with rent overburden (%)	2.7	2019	●	↑

SDG12 – Responsible Consumption and Production	Value	Year	Rating	Trend
Electronic waste (kg/capita)	12.3	2019	●	●
Production-based SO_2 emissions (kg/capita)	8.5	2018	●	●
SO_2 emissions embodied in imports (kg/capita)	7.4	2018	●	●
Production-based nitrogen emissions (kg/capita)	34.7	2015	●	↓
Nitrogen emissions embodied in imports (kg/capita)	9.6	2015	●	↓
Exports of plastic waste (kg/capita)	12.1	2021	●	●
Non-recycled municipal solid waste (kg/capita/day)	0.6	2019	●	↑

SDG13 – Climate Action	Value	Year	Rating	Trend
CO_2 emissions from fossil fuel combustion and cement production (tCO_2/capita)	5.1	2020	●	↓
CO_2 emissions embodied in imports (tCO_2/capita)	8.6	2018	●	↓
CO_2 emissions embodied in fossil fuel exports (kg/capita)	41.8	2021	●	●
Carbon Pricing Score at EUR60/tCO_2 (%, worst 0–100 best)	45.0	2018	●	●

SDG14 – Life Below Water	Value	Year	Rating	Trend
Mean area that is protected in marine sites important to biodiversity (%)	83.4	2020	●	→
Ocean Health Index: Clean Waters score (worst 0–100 best)	45.2	2020	●	→
Fish caught from overexploited or collapsed stocks (% of total catch)	NA	NA	●	●
Fish caught by trawling or dredging (%)	34.9	2018	●	↓
Fish caught that are then discarded (%)	4.4	2018	●	↑
Marine biodiversity threats embodied in imports (per million population)	0.1	2018	●	●

SDG15 – Life on Land	Value	Year	Rating	Trend
Mean area that is protected in terrestrial sites important to biodiversity (%)	90.9	2020	●	↑
Mean area that is protected in freshwater sites important to biodiversity (%)	95.2	2020	●	↑
Red List Index of species survival (worst 0–1 best)	1.0	2021	●	↑
Permanent deforestation (% of forest area, 5-year average)	0.0	2020	●	↑
Terrestrial and freshwater biodiversity threats embodied in imports (per million population)	0.8	2018	●	●

SDG16 – Peace, Justice and Strong Institutions	Value	Year	Rating	Trend
Homicides (per 100,000 population)	3.7	2020	●	↑
Unsentenced detainees (% of prison population)	11.8	2019	●	↑
Population who feel safe walking alone at night in the city or area where they live (%)	64	2021	●	↑
Property Rights (worst 1–7 best)	5.0	2020	●	↑
Birth registrations with civil authority (% of children under age 5)	100.0	2020	●	●
Corruption Perception Index (worst 0–100 best)	61	2021	●	↑
Children involved in child labor (% of population aged 5 to 14)	* 0.0	2019	●	●
Exports of major conventional weapons (TIV constant million USD per 100,000 population)	2.2	2020	●	●
Press Freedom Index (best 0–100 worst)	20.2	2021	●	↑
Access to and affordability of justice (worst 0–1 best)	0.7	2020	●	●
Persons held in prison (per 100,000 population)	222.4	2019	●	↗

SDG17 – Partnerships for the Goals	Value	Year	Rating	Trend
Government spending on health and education (% of GDP)	8.5	2019	●	↓
For high-income and all OECD DAC countries: International concessional public finance, including official development assistance (% of GNI)	0.1	2021	●	→
Other countries: Government revenue excluding grants (% of GDP)	NA	NA	●	●
Corporate Tax Haven Score (best 0–100 worst)	54.8	2019	●	●
Financial Secrecy Score (best 0–100 worst)	50.3	2020	●	●
Shifted profits of multinationals (US$ billion)	NA	NA	●	●
Statistical Performance Index (worst 0–100 best)	84.9	2019	●	↑

* Imputed data point

LUXEMBOURG

OECD Countries

OVERALL PERFORMANCE

COUNTRY RANKING

LUXEMBOURG

36/163

COUNTRY SCORE

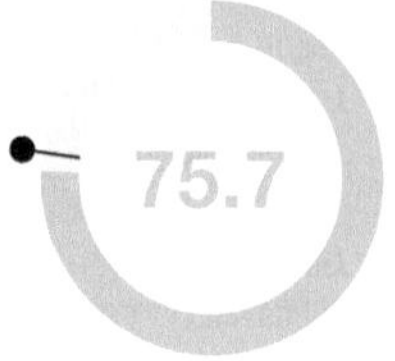

REGIONAL AVERAGE: 77.2

AVERAGE PERFORMANCE BY SDG

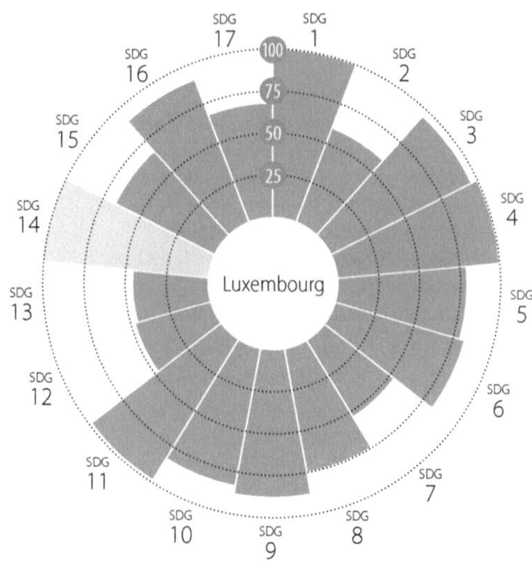

SDG DASHBOARDS AND TRENDS

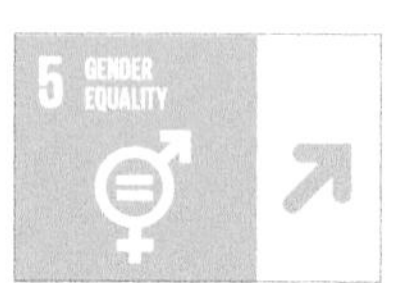

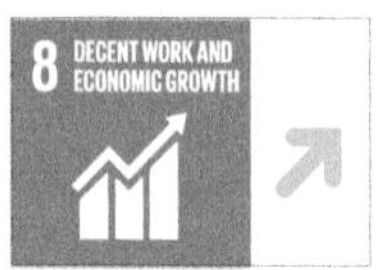

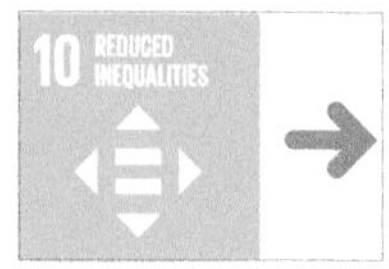

Major challenges · Significant challenges · Challenges remain · SDG achieved · Information unavailable

Decreasing · Stagnating · Moderately improving · On track or maintaining SDG achievement · Information unavailable

Note: The full title of each SDG is available here: https://sustainabledevelopment.un.org/topics/sustainabledevelopmentgoals

INTERNATIONAL SPILLOVER INDEX

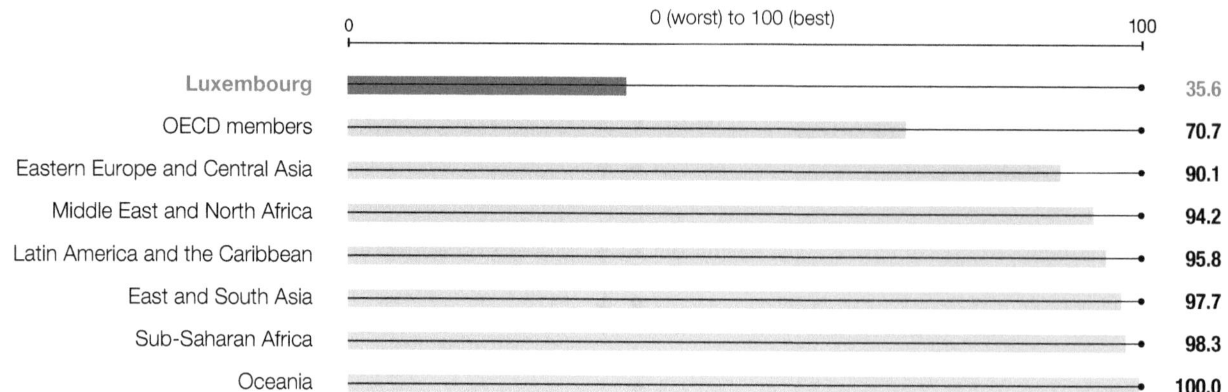

STATISTICAL PERFORMANCE INDEX

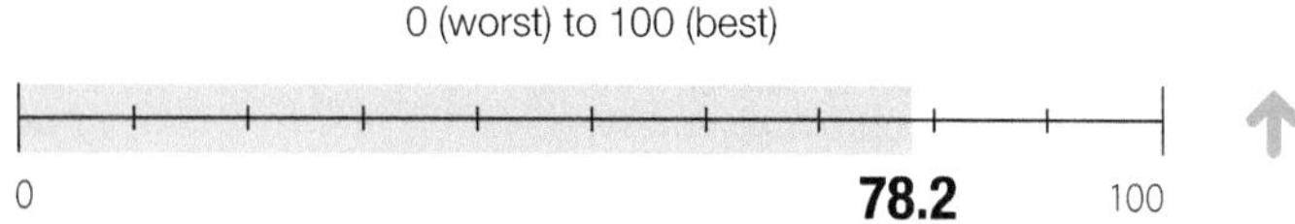

MISSING DATA IN SDG INDEX

2%

SDG1 – No Poverty	Value	Year	Rating	Trend
Poverty headcount ratio at \$1.90/day (%)	0.3	2022	●	↑
Poverty headcount ratio at \$3.20/day (%)	0.3	2022	●	↑
Poverty rate after taxes and transfers (%)	10.5	2019	●	↑
SDG2 – Zero Hunger				
Prevalence of undernourishment (%)	2.5	2019	●	↑
Prevalence of stunting in children under 5 years of age (%)	* 2.6	2019	●	↑
Prevalence of wasting in children under 5 years of age (%)	* 0.7	2019	●	↑
Prevalence of obesity, BMI ≥ 30 (% of adult population)	22.6	2016	●	↓
Human Trophic Level (best 2–3 worst)	2.3	2017	●	→
Cereal yield (tonnes per hectare of harvested land)	5.9	2018	●	↑
Sustainable Nitrogen Management Index (best 0–1.41 worst)	0.7	2015	●	↓
Yield gap closure (% of potential yield)	65.0	2018	●	●
Exports of hazardous pesticides (tonnes per million population)	257.9	2019	●	●
SDG3 – Good Health and Well-Being				
Maternal mortality rate (per 100,000 live births)	5	2017	●	↑
Neonatal mortality rate (per 1,000 live births)	1.7	2020	●	↑
Mortality rate, under-5 (per 1,000 live births)	2.8	2020	●	↑
Incidence of tuberculosis (per 100,000 population)	5.9	2020	●	↑
New HIV infections (per 1,000 uninfected population)	1.0	2020	●	→
Age-standardized death rate due to cardiovascular disease, cancer, diabetes, or chronic respiratory disease in adults aged 30–70 years (%)	9.8	2019	●	↑
Age-standardized death rate attributable to household air pollution and ambient air pollution (per 100,000 population)	12	2016	●	●
Traffic deaths (per 100,000 population)	4.1	2019	●	↑
Life expectancy at birth (years)	82.4	2019	●	↑
Adolescent fertility rate (births per 1,000 females aged 15 to 19)	4.6	2018	●	↑
Births attended by skilled health personnel (%)	99.9	2009	●	●
Surviving infants who received 2 WHO-recommended vaccines (%)	99	2020	●	↑
Universal health coverage (UHC) index of service coverage (worst 0–100 best)	86	2019	●	↑
Subjective well-being (average ladder score, worst 0–10 best)	7.4	2019	●	●
Gap in life expectancy at birth among regions (years)	0.0	2019	●	↑
Gap in self-reported health status by income (percentage points)	11.0	2019	●	↑
Daily smokers (% of population aged 15 and over)	16.9	2020	●	↑
SDG4 – Quality Education				
Participation rate in pre-primary organized learning (% of children aged 4 to 6)	99.8	2019	●	↑
Net primary enrollment rate (%)	99.4	2019	●	↑
Lower secondary completion rate (%)	116.7	2019	●	↑
Literacy rate (% of population aged 15 to 24)	NA	NA	●	●
Tertiary educational attainment (% of population aged 25 to 34)	58.2	2020	●	↑
PISA score (worst 0–600 best)	476.7	2018	●	↓
Variation in science performance explained by socio-economic status (%)	20.9	2018	●	↓
Underachievers in science (% of 15-year-olds)	26.8	2018	●	↓
SDG5 – Gender Equality				
Demand for family planning satisfied by modern methods (% of females aged 15 to 49)	NA	NA	●	●
Ratio of female-to-male mean years of education received (%)	95.2	2019	●	↗
Ratio of female-to-male labor force participation rate (%)	88.3	2020	●	↑
Seats held by women in national parliament (%)	30.0	2020	●	→
Gender wage gap (% of male median wage)	3.4	2014	●	●
SDG6 – Clean Water and Sanitation				
Population using at least basic drinking water services (%)	99.9	2020	●	↑
Population using at least basic sanitation services (%)	97.6	2020	●	↑
Freshwater withdrawal (% of available freshwater resources)	4.3	2018	●	●
Anthropogenic wastewater that receives treatment (%)	98.5	2018	●	●
Scarce water consumption embodied in imports (m^3 H_2O eq/capita)	9563.0	2018	●	●
Population using safely managed water services (%)	99.5	2020	●	↑
Population using safely managed sanitation services (%)	96.8	2020	●	↑
SDG7 – Affordable and Clean Energy				
Population with access to electricity (%)	100.0	2019	●	↑
Population with access to clean fuels and technology for cooking (%)	100.0	2019	●	↑
CO_2 emissions from fuel combustion per total electricity output ($MtCO_2$/TWh)	13.2	2019	●	↓
Share of renewable energy in total primary energy supply (%)	8.1	2019	●	↗
SDG8 – Decent Work and Economic Growth				
Adjusted GDP growth (%)	-0.2	2020	●	●
Victims of modern slavery (per 1,000 population)	1.5	2018	●	●
Adults with an account at a bank or other financial institution or with a mobile-money-service provider (% of population aged 15 or over)	98.8	2017	●	↑
Fundamental labor rights are effectively guaranteed (worst 0–1 best)	0.8	2020	●	●
Fatal work-related accidents embodied in imports (per 100,000 population)	5.6	2015	●	↗
Employment-to-population ratio (%)	67.3	2020	●	↑
Youth not in employment, education or training (NEET) (% of population aged 15 to 29)	7.9	2020	●	↑

* Imputed data point

SDG9 – Industry, Innovation and Infrastructure	Value	Year	Rating	Trend
Population using the internet (%)	98.8	2020	●	↑
Mobile broadband subscriptions (per 100 population)	121.8	2019	●	↑
Logistics Performance Index: Quality of trade and transport-related infrastructure (worst 1–5 best)	3.6	2018	●	↑
The Times Higher Education Universities Ranking: Average score of top 3 universities (worst 0–100 best)	49.2	2022	●	●
Articles published in academic journals (per 1,000 population)	3.6	2020	●	↑
Expenditure on research and development (% of GDP)	1.2	2018	●	↓
Researchers (per 1,000 employed population)	6.3	2019	●	↓
Triadic patent families filed (per million population)	62.2	2019	●	↑
Gap in internet access by income (percentage points)	10.5	2020	●	↓
Female share of graduates from STEM fields at the tertiary level (%)	27.6	2016	●	↓
SDG10 – Reduced Inequalities				
Gini coefficient	35.4	2018	●	↓
Palma ratio	1.1	2019	●	→
Elderly poverty rate (% of population aged 66 or over)	5.2	2019	●	↑
SDG11 – Sustainable Cities and Communities				
Proportion of urban population living in slums (%)	* 0.0	2018	●	↑
Annual mean concentration of particulate matter of less than 2.5 microns in diameter (PM2.5) (μg/m³)	9.5	2019	●	↑
Access to improved water source, piped (% of urban population)	100.0	2020	●	↑
Satisfaction with public transport (%)	79.0	2019	●	●
Population with rent overburden (%)	11.7	2018	●	↑
SDG12 – Responsible Consumption and Production				
Electronic waste (kg/capita)	18.9	2019	●	●
Production-based SO_2 emissions (kg/capita)	17.4	2018	●	●
SO_2 emissions embodied in imports (kg/capita)	7.7	2018	●	●
Production-based nitrogen emissions (kg/capita)	7.9	2015	●	↑
Nitrogen emissions embodied in imports (kg/capita)	55.5	2015	●	↓
Exports of plastic waste (kg/capita)	18.3	2021	●	●
Non-recycled municipal solid waste (kg/capita/day)	1.1	2019	●	↓
SDG13 – Climate Action				
CO_2 emissions from fossil fuel combustion and cement production (tCO_2/capita)	13.1	2020	●	↗
CO_2 emissions embodied in imports (tCO_2/capita)	3.9	2018	●	↗
CO_2 emissions embodied in fossil fuel exports (kg/capita)	0.0	2020	●	●
Carbon Pricing Score at EUR60/tCO_2 (%, worst 0–100 best)	68.7	2018	●	↑
SDG14 – Life Below Water				
Mean area that is protected in marine sites important to biodiversity (%)	NA	NA	●	●
Ocean Health Index: Clean Waters score (worst 0–100 best)	NA	NA	●	●
Fish caught from overexploited or collapsed stocks (% of total catch)	NA	NA	●	●
Fish caught by trawling or dredging (%)	NA	NA	●	●
Fish caught that are then discarded (%)	NA	NA	●	●
Marine biodiversity threats embodied in imports (per million population)	0.7	2018	●	●
SDG15 – Life on Land				
Mean area that is protected in terrestrial sites important to biodiversity (%)	82.4	2020	●	↑
Mean area that is protected in freshwater sites important to biodiversity (%)	37.1	2020	●	→
Red List Index of species survival (worst 0–1 best)	1.0	2021	●	↑
Permanent deforestation (% of forest area, 5-year average)	0.1	2020	●	↓
Terrestrial and freshwater biodiversity threats embodied in imports (per million population)	7.9	2018	●	●
SDG16 – Peace, Justice and Strong Institutions				
Homicides (per 100,000 population)	0.2	2020	●	↑
Unsentenced detainees (% of prison population)	49.8	2019	●	↓
Population who feel safe walking alone at night in the city or area where they live (%)	87	2019	●	●
Property Rights (worst 1–7 best)	6.2	2020	●	↑
Birth registrations with civil authority (% of children under age 5)	100.0	2020	●	●
Corruption Perception Index (worst 0–100 best)	81	2021	●	↑
Children involved in child labor (% of population aged 5 to 14)	* 0.0	2019	●	●
Exports of major conventional weapons (TIV constant million USD per 100,000 population)	0.0	2020	●	●
Press Freedom Index (best 0–100 worst)	17.6	2021	●	↑
Access to and affordability of justice (worst 0–1 best)	0.7	2020	●	●
Persons held in prison (per 100,000 population)	87.1	2019	●	↑
SDG17 – Partnerships for the Goals				
Government spending on health and education (% of GDP)	8.3	2019	●	↓
For high-income and all OECD DAC countries: International concessional public finance, including official development assistance (% of GNI)	1.0	2021	●	↑
Other countries: Government revenue excluding grants (% of GDP)	NA	NA	●	●
Corporate Tax Haven Score (best 0–100 worst)	72.4	2019	●	●
Financial Secrecy Score (best 0–100 worst)	55.5	2020	●	●
Shifted profits of multinationals (US\$ billion)	-56.7	2018	●	↓
Statistical Performance Index (worst 0–100 best)	78.2	2019	●	↑

MADAGASCAR

Sub-Saharan Africa

OVERALL PERFORMANCE

COUNTRY RANKING

MADAGASCAR

156/163

COUNTRY SCORE

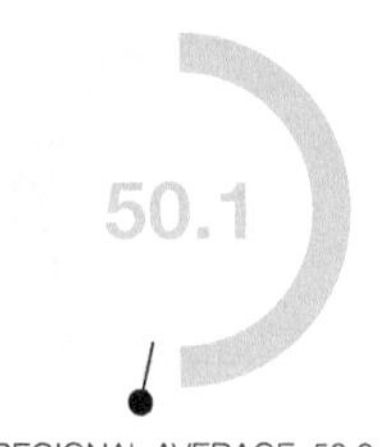

AVERAGE PERFORMANCE BY SDG

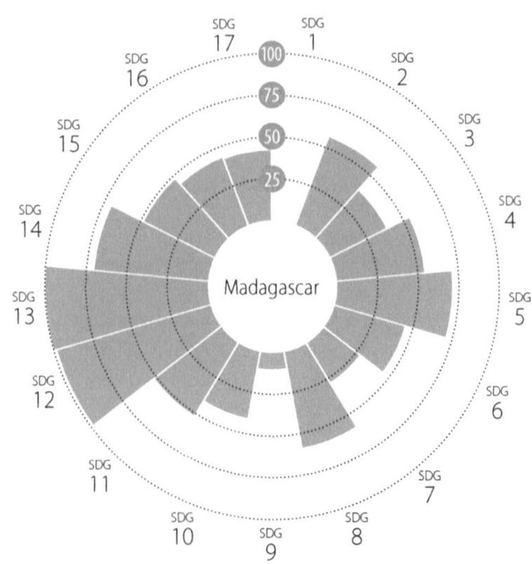

SDG DASHBOARDS AND TRENDS

Major challenges | Significant challenges | Challenges remain | SDG achieved | Information unavailable

Decreasing | Stagnating | Moderately improving | On track or maintaining SDG achievement | Information unavailable

Note: The full title of each SDG is available here: https://sustainabledevelopment.un.org/topics/sustainabledevelopmentgoals

INTERNATIONAL SPILLOVER INDEX

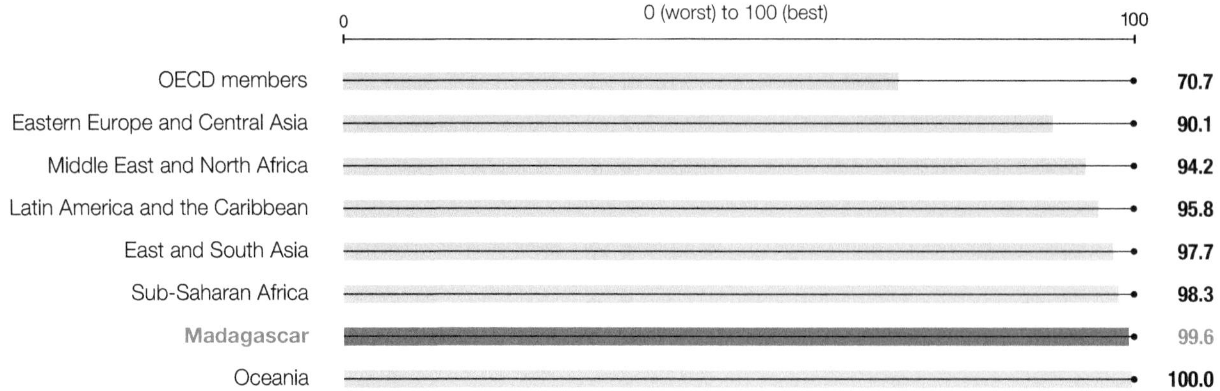

STATISTICAL PERFORMANCE INDEX

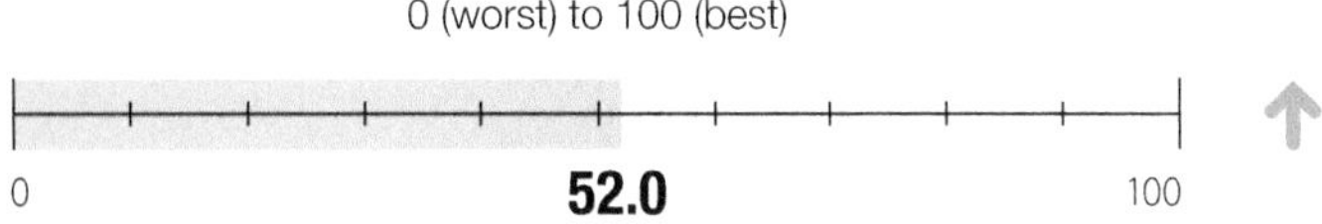

MISSING DATA IN SDG INDEX

2%

SDG1 – No Poverty	Value	Year	Rating	Trend
Poverty headcount ratio at $1.90/day (%)	76.4	2022	●	→
Poverty headcount ratio at $3.20/day (%)	92.2	2022	●	→
SDG2 – Zero Hunger				
Prevalence of undernourishment (%)	43.2	2019	●	↓
Prevalence of stunting in children under 5 years of age (%)	41.6	2018	●	→
Prevalence of wasting in children under 5 years of age (%)	6.4	2018	●	→
Prevalence of obesity, BMI ≥ 30 (% of adult population)	5.3	2016	●	↑
Human Trophic Level (best 2–3 worst)	2.1	2017	●	↑
Cereal yield (tonnes per hectare of harvested land)	4.0	2018	●	↑
Sustainable Nitrogen Management Index (best 0–1.41 worst)	0.7	2015	●	→
Exports of hazardous pesticides (tonnes per million population)	0.0	2019	●	●
SDG3 – Good Health and Well-Being				
Maternal mortality rate (per 100,000 live births)	335	2017	●	↗
Neonatal mortality rate (per 1,000 live births)	20.3	2020	●	↗
Mortality rate, under-5 (per 1,000 live births)	50.2	2020	●	↗
Incidence of tuberculosis (per 100,000 population)	238.0	2020	●	↓
New HIV infections (per 1,000 uninfected population)	0.2	2020	●	↓
Age-standardized death rate due to cardiovascular disease, cancer, diabetes, or chronic respiratory disease in adults aged 30–70 years (%)	26.0	2019	●	→
Age-standardized death rate attributable to household air pollution and ambient air pollution (per 100,000 population)	160	2016	●	●
Traffic deaths (per 100,000 population)	29.2	2019	●	↓
Life expectancy at birth (years)	65.4	2019	●	→
Adolescent fertility rate (births per 1,000 females aged 15 to 19)	150.8	2017	●	●
Births attended by skilled health personnel (%)	46.0	2018	●	●
Surviving infants who received 2 WHO-recommended vaccines (%)	59	2020	●	↓
Universal health coverage (UHC) index of service coverage (worst 0–100 best)	35	2019	●	→
Subjective well-being (average ladder score, worst 0–10 best)	4.3	2019	●	●
SDG4 – Quality Education				
Participation rate in pre-primary organized learning (% of children aged 4 to 6)	59.3	2019	●	●
Net primary enrollment rate (%)	97.7	2019	●	●
Lower secondary completion rate (%)	35.5	2019	●	↓
Literacy rate (% of population aged 15 to 24)	79.9	2018	●	●
SDG5 – Gender Equality				
Demand for family planning satisfied by modern methods (% of females aged 15 to 49)	65.9	2018	●	↗
Ratio of female-to-male mean years of education received (%)	110.3	2019	●	↑
Ratio of female-to-male labor force participation rate (%)	92.7	2020	●	↑
Seats held by women in national parliament (%)	17.9	2020	●	↓
SDG6 – Clean Water and Sanitation				
Population using at least basic drinking water services (%)	53.4	2020	●	→
Population using at least basic sanitation services (%)	12.3	2020	●	→
Freshwater withdrawal (% of available freshwater resources)	11.3	2018	●	●
Anthropogenic wastewater that receives treatment (%)	0.0	2018	●	●
Scarce water consumption embodied in imports (m^3 H_2O eq/capita)	195.0	2018	●	●
SDG7 – Affordable and Clean Energy				
Population with access to electricity (%)	26.9	2019	●	→
Population with access to clean fuels and technology for cooking (%)	0.9	2019	●	→
CO_2 emissions from fuel combustion per total electricity output ($MtCO_2$/TWh)	2.2	2019	●	→
Share of renewable energy in total primary energy supply (%)	NA	NA	●	●
SDG8 – Decent Work and Economic Growth				
Adjusted GDP growth (%)	-8.2	2020	●	●
Victims of modern slavery (per 1,000 population)	7.5	2018	●	●
Adults with an account at a bank or other financial institution or with a mobile-money-service provider (% of population aged 15 or over)	17.9	2017	●	↗
Unemployment rate (% of total labor force)	2.4	2022	●	↑
Fundamental labor rights are effectively guaranteed (worst 0–1 best)	0.6	2020	●	↓
Fatal work-related accidents embodied in imports (per 100,000 population)	0.0	2015	●	↑

* Imputed data point

SDG9 – Industry, Innovation and Infrastructure	Value	Year	Rating	Trend
Population using the internet (%)	15.0	2018	●	●
Mobile broadband subscriptions (per 100 population)	18.8	2019	●	↗
Logistics Performance Index: Quality of trade and transport-related infrastructure (worst 1–5 best)	2.2	2018	●	→
The Times Higher Education Universities Ranking: Average score of top 3 universities (worst 0–100 best)	* 0.0	2022	●	●
Articles published in academic journals (per 1,000 population)	0.0	2020	●	→
Expenditure on research and development (% of GDP)	0.0	2017	●	→
SDG10 – Reduced Inequalities				
Gini coefficient	42.6	2012	●	●
Palma ratio	2.1	2018	●	●
SDG11 – Sustainable Cities and Communities				
Proportion of urban population living in slums (%)	73.3	2018	●	→
Annual mean concentration of particulate matter of less than 2.5 microns in diameter (PM2.5) (μg/m^3)	22.3	2019	●	→
Access to improved water source, piped (% of urban population)	65.0	2020	●	→
Satisfaction with public transport (%)	47.0	2019	●	●
SDG12 – Responsible Consumption and Production				
Municipal solid waste (kg/capita/day)	0.4	2016	●	●
Electronic waste (kg/capita)	0.6	2019	●	●
Production-based SO_2 emissions (kg/capita)	1.0	2018	●	●
SO_2 emissions embodied in imports (kg/capita)	0.2	2018	●	●
Production-based nitrogen emissions (kg/capita)	8.2	2015	●	↑
Nitrogen emissions embodied in imports (kg/capita)	0.1	2015	●	↑
Exports of plastic waste (kg/capita)	0.0	2019	●	●
SDG13 – Climate Action				
CO_2 emissions from fossil fuel combustion and cement production (tCO_2/capita)	0.1	2020	●	↑
CO_2 emissions embodied in imports (tCO_2/capita)	0.1	2018	●	↑
CO_2 emissions embodied in fossil fuel exports (kg/capita)	0.0	2019	●	●
SDG14 – Life Below Water				
Mean area that is protected in marine sites important to biodiversity (%)	20.3	2020	●	→
Ocean Health Index: Clean Waters score (worst 0–100 best)	58.0	2020	●	↓
Fish caught from overexploited or collapsed stocks (% of total catch)	8.1	2018	●	↑
Fish caught by trawling or dredging (%)	0.7	2018	●	↑
Fish caught that are then discarded (%)	6.8	2018	●	↓
Marine biodiversity threats embodied in imports (per million population)	0.0	2018	●	●
SDG15 – Life on Land				
Mean area that is protected in terrestrial sites important to biodiversity (%)	27.2	2020	●	→
Mean area that is protected in freshwater sites important to biodiversity (%)	49.3	2020	●	→
Red List Index of species survival (worst 0–1 best)	0.7	2021	●	↓
Permanent deforestation (% of forest area, 5-year average)	1.1	2020	●	↑
Terrestrial and freshwater biodiversity threats embodied in imports (per million population)	0.0	2018	●	●
SDG16 – Peace, Justice and Strong Institutions				
Homicides (per 100,000 population)	NA	NA	●	●
Unsentenced detainees (% of prison population)	56.4	2018	●	↓
Population who feel safe walking alone at night in the city or area where they live (%)	43	2019	●	●
Property Rights (worst 1–7 best)	3.2	2020	●	●
Birth registrations with civil authority (% of children under age 5)	78.6	2020	●	●
Corruption Perception Index (worst 0–100 best)	26	2021	●	↓
Children involved in child labor (% of population aged 5 to 14)	36.7	2019	●	●
Exports of major conventional weapons (TIV constant million USD per 100,000 population)	* 0.0	2020	●	●
Press Freedom Index (best 0–100 worst)	28.2	2021	●	↑
Access to and affordability of justice (worst 0–1 best)	0.4	2020	●	↗
SDG17 – Partnerships for the Goals				
Government spending on health and education (% of GDP)	4.1	2019	●	↓
For high-income and all OECD DAC countries: International concessional public finance, including official development assistance (% of GNI)	NA	NA	●	●
Other countries: Government revenue excluding grants (% of GDP)	11.6	2019	●	→
Corporate Tax Haven Score (best 0–100 worst)	* 0.0	2019	●	●
Statistical Performance Index (worst 0–100 best)	52.0	2019	●	↑

5. Country Profiles

MALAWI

Sub-Saharan Africa

OVERALL PERFORMANCE

COUNTRY RANKING

MALAWI

145/163

COUNTRY SCORE

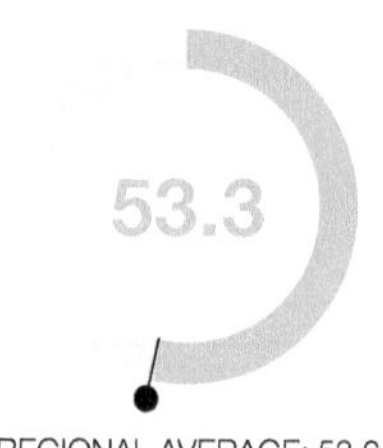

AVERAGE PERFORMANCE BY SDG

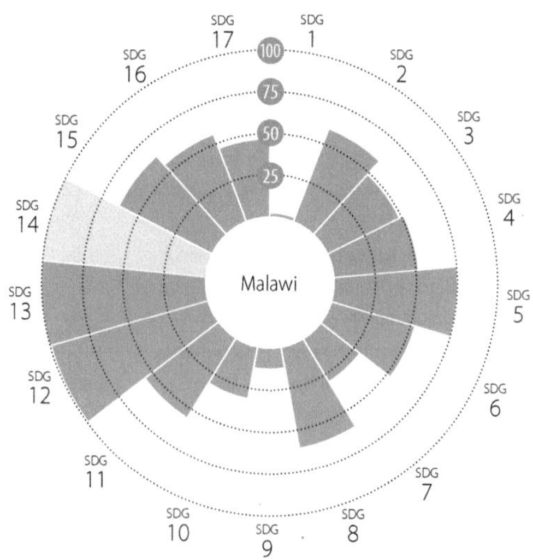

SDG DASHBOARDS AND TRENDS

Major challenges | Significant challenges | Challenges remain | SDG achieved | Information unavailable

Decreasing | Stagnating | Moderately improving | On track or maintaining SDG achievement | Information unavailable

Note: The full title of each SDG is available here: https://sustainabledevelopment.un.org/topics/sustainabledevelopmentgoals

INTERNATIONAL SPILLOVER INDEX

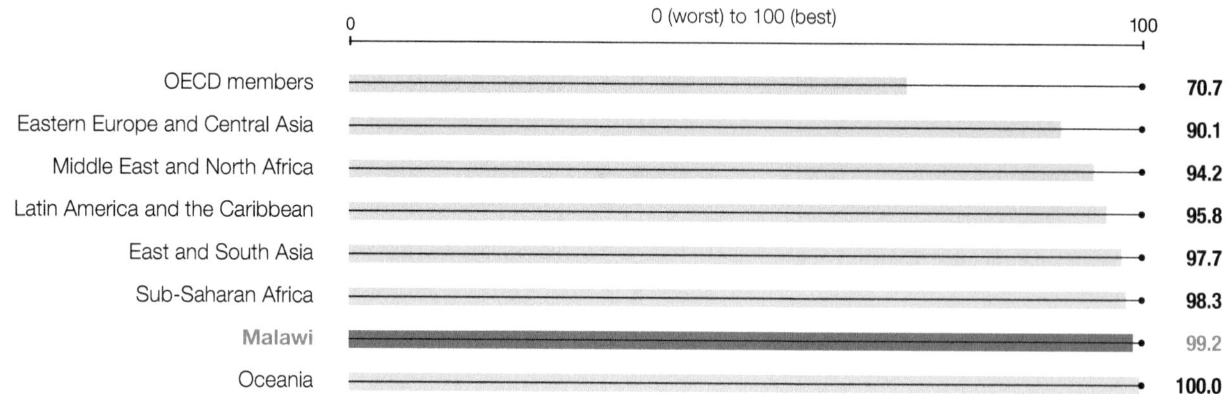

STATISTICAL PERFORMANCE INDEX

0 (worst) to 100 (best)

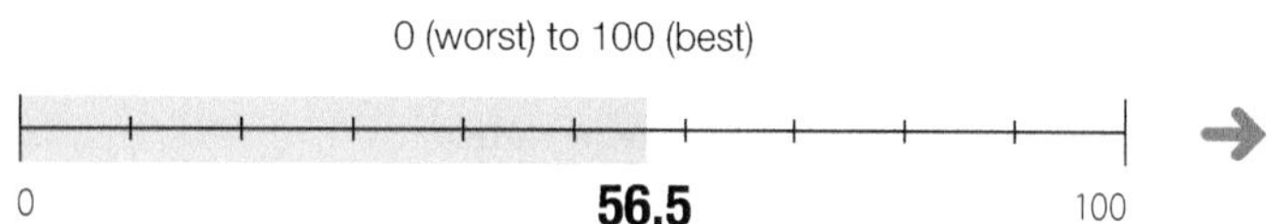

MISSING DATA IN SDG INDEX

3%

MALAWI

Performance by Indicator

SDG1 – No Poverty		Value	Year	Rating	Trend
Poverty headcount ratio at \$1.90/day (%)		69.7	2022	●	→
Poverty headcount ratio at \$3.20/day (%)		88.7	2022	●	→
SDG2 – Zero Hunger					
Prevalence of undernourishment (%)		17.3	2019	●	↓
Prevalence of stunting in children under 5 years of age (%)		40.9	2019	●	→
Prevalence of wasting in children under 5 years of age (%)		0.6	2019	●	↑
Prevalence of obesity, BMI ≥ 30 (% of adult population)		5.8	2016	●	↑
Human Trophic Level (best 2–3 worst)		2.1	2017	●	↑
Cereal yield (tonnes per hectare of harvested land)		1.5	2018	●	↓
Sustainable Nitrogen Management Index (best 0–1.41 worst)		0.7	2015	●	→
Exports of hazardous pesticides (tonnes per million population)		NA	NA	●	●
SDG3 – Good Health and Well-Being					
Maternal mortality rate (per 100,000 live births)		349	2017	●	↗
Neonatal mortality rate (per 1,000 live births)		19.1	2020	●	↑
Mortality rate, under-5 (per 1,000 live births)		38.6	2020	●	↑
Incidence of tuberculosis (per 100,000 population)		141.0	2020	●	↗
New HIV infections (per 1,000 uninfected population)		1.2	2020	●	↑
Age-standardized death rate due to cardiovascular disease, cancer, diabetes, or chronic respiratory disease in adults aged 30–70 years (%)		22.6	2019	●	↗
Age-standardized death rate attributable to household air pollution and ambient air pollution (per 100,000 population)		115	2016	●	●
Traffic deaths (per 100,000 population)		33.4	2019	●	↓
Life expectancy at birth (years)		65.6	2019	●	↗
Adolescent fertility rate (births per 1,000 females aged 15 to 19)		137.6	2015	●	●
Births attended by skilled health personnel (%)		89.8	2016	●	●
Surviving infants who received 2 WHO-recommended vaccines (%)		90	2020	●	↑
Universal health coverage (UHC) index of service coverage (worst 0–100 best)		48	2019	●	↗
Subjective well-being (average ladder score, worst 0–10 best)		3.6	2021	●	↓
SDG4 – Quality Education					
Participation rate in pre-primary organized learning (% of children aged 4 to 6)		NA	NA	●	●
Net primary enrollment rate (%)		98.1	2019	●	↑
Lower secondary completion rate (%)		24.0	2015	●	●
Literacy rate (% of population aged 15 to 24)		72.9	2015	●	●
SDG5 – Gender Equality					
Demand for family planning satisfied by modern methods (% of females aged 15 to 49)		73.9	2016	●	↑
Ratio of female-to-male mean years of education received (%)		132.7	2019	●	↑
Ratio of female-to-male labor force participation rate (%)		89.0	2020	●	↑
Seats held by women in national parliament (%)		22.9	2020	●	↗
SDG6 – Clean Water and Sanitation					
Population using at least basic drinking water services (%)		70.0	2020	●	→
Population using at least basic sanitation services (%)		26.6	2020	●	→
Freshwater withdrawal (% of available freshwater resources)		17.5	2018	●	●
Anthropogenic wastewater that receives treatment (%)		0.0	2018	●	●
Scarce water consumption embodied in imports (m^3 H_2O eq/capita)		171.2	2018	●	●
SDG7 – Affordable and Clean Energy					
Population with access to electricity (%)		11.2	2019	●	→
Population with access to clean fuels and technology for cooking (%)		1.9	2019	●	↓
CO_2 emissions from fuel combustion per total electricity output ($MtCO_2$/TWh)		0.9	2019	●	↑
Share of renewable energy in total primary energy supply (%)		NA	NA	●	●
SDG8 – Decent Work and Economic Growth					
Adjusted GDP growth (%)		-4.8	2020	●	●
Victims of modern slavery (per 1,000 population)		7.5	2018	●	●
Adults with an account at a bank or other financial institution or with a mobile-money-service provider (% of population aged 15 or over)		33.7	2017	●	↑
Unemployment rate (% of total labor force)		7.0	2022	●	↓
Fundamental labor rights are effectively guaranteed (worst 0–1 best)		0.5	2020	●	↑
Fatal work-related accidents embodied in imports (per 100,000 population)		0.1	2015	●	↑

SDG9 – Industry, Innovation and Infrastructure		Value	Year	Rating	Trend
Population using the internet (%)		9.9	2019	●	→
Mobile broadband subscriptions (per 100 population)		31.8	2019	●	↗
Logistics Performance Index: Quality of trade and transport-related infrastructure (worst 1–5 best)		2.2	2018	●	↓
The Times Higher Education Universities Ranking: Average score of top 3 universities (worst 0–100 best)	*	0.0	2022	●	●
Articles published in academic journals (per 1,000 population)		0.1	2020	●	→
Expenditure on research and development (% of GDP)	*	0.0	2018	●	●
SDG10 – Reduced Inequalities					
Gini coefficient		44.7	2016	●	●
Palma ratio		2.4	2018	●	●
SDG11 – Sustainable Cities and Communities					
Proportion of urban population living in slums (%)		66.9	2018	●	↓
Annual mean concentration of particulate matter of less than 2.5 microns in diameter (PM2.5) ($\mu g/m^3$)		23.0	2019	●	→
Access to improved water source, piped (% of urban population)		80.7	2020	●	→
Satisfaction with public transport (%)		43.0	2021	●	→
SDG12 – Responsible Consumption and Production					
Municipal solid waste (kg/capita/day)		0.2	2013	●	●
Electronic waste (kg/capita)		0.5	2019	●	●
Production-based SO_2 emissions (kg/capita)		0.6	2018	●	●
SO_2 emissions embodied in imports (kg/capita)		0.1	2018	●	●
Production-based nitrogen emissions (kg/capita)		6.1	2015	●	↑
Nitrogen emissions embodied in imports (kg/capita)		0.3	2015	●	↑
Exports of plastic waste (kg/capita)		0.0	2020	●	●
SDG13 – Climate Action					
CO_2 emissions from fossil fuel combustion and cement production (tCO_2/capita)		0.1	2020	●	↑
CO_2 emissions embodied in imports (tCO_2/capita)		0.0	2018	●	↑
CO_2 emissions embodied in fossil fuel exports (kg/capita)		0.5	2020	●	●
SDG14 – Life Below Water					
Mean area that is protected in marine sites important to biodiversity (%)		NA	NA	●	●
Ocean Health Index: Clean Waters score (worst 0–100 best)		NA	NA	●	●
Fish caught from overexploited or collapsed stocks (% of total catch)		NA	NA	●	●
Fish caught by trawling or dredging (%)		NA	NA	●	●
Fish caught that are then discarded (%)		NA	NA	●	●
Marine biodiversity threats embodied in imports (per million population)		0.0	2018	●	●
SDG15 – Life on Land					
Mean area that is protected in terrestrial sites important to biodiversity (%)		70.8	2020	●	→
Mean area that is protected in freshwater sites important to biodiversity (%)		25.8	2020	●	→
Red List Index of species survival (worst 0–1 best)		0.8	2021	●	→
Permanent deforestation (% of forest area, 5-year average)		0.5	2020	●	↓
Terrestrial and freshwater biodiversity threats embodied in imports (per million population)		0.3	2018	●	●
SDG16 – Peace, Justice and Strong Institutions					
Homicides (per 100,000 population)		1.8	2012	●	●
Unsentenced detainees (% of prison population)		17.9	2018	●	↑
Population who feel safe walking alone at night in the city or area where they live (%)		43	2021	●	→
Property Rights (worst 1–7 best)		4.2	2020	●	↑
Birth registrations with civil authority (% of children under age 5)		5.6	2020	●	●
Corruption Perception Index (worst 0–100 best)		35	2021	●	→
Children involved in child labor (% of population aged 5 to 14)		19.4	2019	●	●
Exports of major conventional weapons (TIV constant million USD per 100,000 population)		0.0	2020	●	●
Press Freedom Index (best 0–100 worst)		28.8	2021	●	↑
Access to and affordability of justice (worst 0–1 best)		0.5	2020	●	↓
SDG17 – Partnerships for the Goals					
Government spending on health and education (% of GDP)		5.3	2020	●	↓
For high-income and all OECD DAC countries: International concessional public finance, including official development assistance (% of GNI)		NA	NA	●	●
Other countries: Government revenue excluding grants (% of GDP)		12.5	2020	●	↓
Corporate Tax Haven Score (best 0–100 worst)	*	0.0	2019	●	●
Statistical Performance Index (worst 0–100 best)		56.5	2019	●	→

* Imputed data point

5. Country Profiles

MALAYSIA

East and South Asia

OVERALL PERFORMANCE

COUNTRY RANKING

MALAYSIA

72/163

COUNTRY SCORE

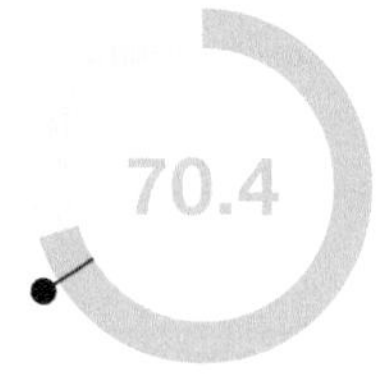

REGIONAL AVERAGE: 65.9

AVERAGE PERFORMANCE BY SDG

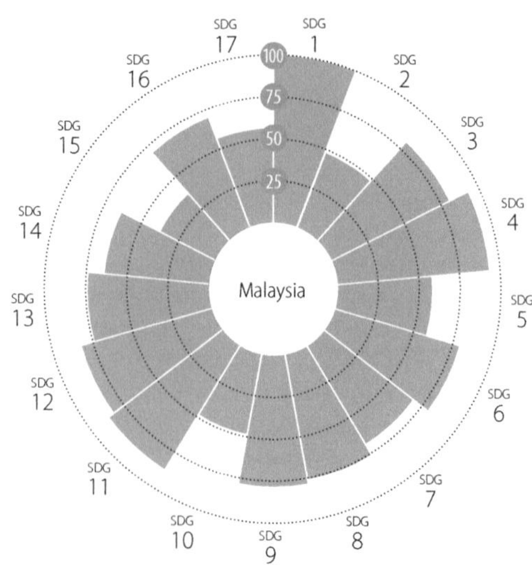

SDG DASHBOARDS AND TRENDS

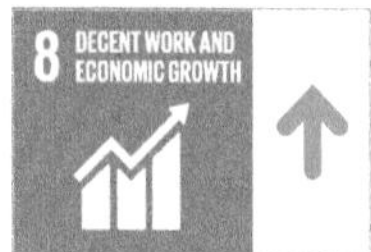

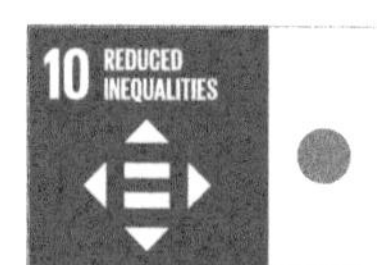

Major challenges · Significant challenges · Challenges remain · SDG achieved · Information unavailable

Decreasing · Stagnating · Moderately improving · On track or maintaining SDG achievement · Information unavailable

Note: The full title of each SDG is available here: https://sustainabledevelopment.un.org/topics/sustainabledevelopmentgoals

INTERNATIONAL SPILLOVER INDEX

STATISTICAL PERFORMANCE INDEX

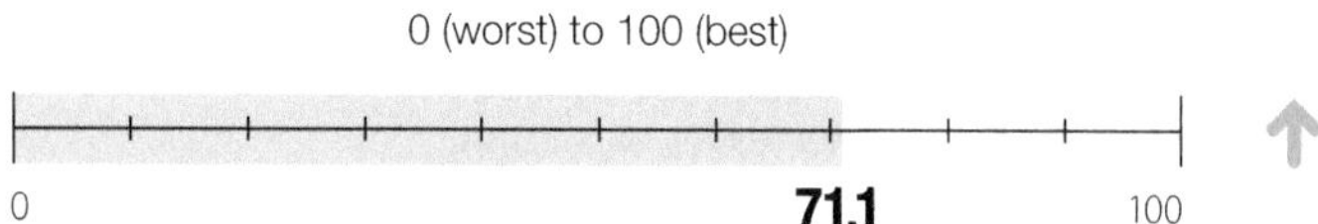

MISSING DATA IN SDG INDEX

3%

MALAYSIA

SDG1 – No Poverty

Indicator	Value	Year	Rating	Trend
Poverty headcount ratio at $1.90/day (%)	0.0	2022	●	↑
Poverty headcount ratio at $3.20/day (%)	0.0	2022	●	↑

SDG2 – Zero Hunger

Indicator	Value	Year	Rating	Trend
Prevalence of undernourishment (%)	3.2	2019	●	↑
Prevalence of stunting in children under 5 years of age (%)	21.8	2019	●	→
Prevalence of wasting in children under 5 years of age (%)	9.7	2019	●	→
Prevalence of obesity, BMI ≥ 30 (% of adult population)	15.6	2016	●	↓
Human Trophic Level (best 2–3 worst)	2.4	2017	●	→
Cereal yield (tonnes per hectare of harvested land)	4.1	2018	●	↑
Sustainable Nitrogen Management Index (best 0–1.41 worst)	0.5	2015	●	↑
Exports of hazardous pesticides (tonnes per million population)	515.9	2019	●	●

SDG3 – Good Health and Well-Being

Indicator	Value	Year	Rating	Trend
Maternal mortality rate (per 100,000 live births)	29	2017	●	↑
Neonatal mortality rate (per 1,000 live births)	4.6	2020	●	↑
Mortality rate, under-5 (per 1,000 live births)	8.6	2020	●	↑
Incidence of tuberculosis (per 100,000 population)	92.0	2020	●	→
New HIV infections (per 1,000 uninfected population)	0.2	2020	●	↑
Age-standardized death rate due to cardiovascular disease, cancer, diabetes, or chronic respiratory disease in adults aged 30–70 years (%)	18.5	2019	●	→
Age-standardized death rate attributable to household air pollution and ambient air pollution (per 100,000 population)	47	2016	●	●
Traffic deaths (per 100,000 population)	22.5	2019	●	→
Life expectancy at birth (years)	74.7	2019	●	↓
Adolescent fertility rate (births per 1,000 females aged 15 to 19)	8.8	2018	●	↑
Births attended by skilled health personnel (%)	99.6	2017	●	↑
Surviving infants who received 2 WHO-recommended vaccines (%)	95	2020	●	↑
Universal health coverage (UHC) index of service coverage (worst 0–100 best)	76	2019	●	↑
Subjective well-being (average ladder score, worst 0–10 best)	6.0	2021	●	↑

SDG4 – Quality Education

Indicator	Value	Year	Rating	Trend
Participation rate in pre-primary organized learning (% of children aged 4 to 6)	99.3	2015	●	●
Net primary enrollment rate (%)	98.6	2019	●	↑
Lower secondary completion rate (%)	84.9	2019	●	→
Literacy rate (% of population aged 15 to 24)	96.8	2019	●	↑

SDG5 – Gender Equality

Indicator	Value	Year	Rating	Trend
Demand for family planning satisfied by modern methods (% of females aged 15 to 49)	* 57.4	2022	●	→
Ratio of female-to-male mean years of education received (%)	98.1	2019	●	↑
Ratio of female-to-male labor force participation rate (%)	66.3	2020	●	↗
Seats held by women in national parliament (%)	14.9	2020	●	→

SDG6 – Clean Water and Sanitation

Indicator	Value	Year	Rating	Trend
Population using at least basic drinking water services (%)	97.1	2020	●	→
Population using at least basic sanitation services (%)	99.6	2018	●	●
Freshwater withdrawal (% of available freshwater resources)	3.4	2018	●	●
Anthropogenic wastewater that receives treatment (%)	12.4	2018	●	●
Scarce water consumption embodied in imports (m^3 H_2O eq/capita)	1560.0	2018	●	●

SDG7 – Affordable and Clean Energy

Indicator	Value	Year	Rating	Trend
Population with access to electricity (%)	100.0	2019	●	↑
Population with access to clean fuels and technology for cooking (%)	96.1	2019	●	↑
CO_2 emissions from fuel combustion per total electricity output ($MtCO_2$/TWh)	1.6	2019	●	→
Share of renewable energy in total primary energy supply (%)	3.5	2019	●	→

SDG8 – Decent Work and Economic Growth

Indicator	Value	Year	Rating	Trend
Adjusted GDP growth (%)	-1.6	2020	●	●
Victims of modern slavery (per 1,000 population)	6.9	2018	●	●
Adults with an account at a bank or other financial institution or with a mobile-money-service provider (% of population aged 15 or over)	85.3	2017	●	↑
Unemployment rate (% of total labor force)	4.2	2022	●	↑
Fundamental labor rights are effectively guaranteed (worst 0–1 best)	0.6	2020	●	↑
Fatal work-related accidents embodied in imports (per 100,000 population)	0.9	2015	●	↑

* Imputed data point

SDG9 – Industry, Innovation and Infrastructure

Indicator	Value	Year	Rating	Trend
Population using the internet (%)	89.6	2020	●	↑
Mobile broadband subscriptions (per 100 population)	126.5	2019	●	↑
Logistics Performance Index: Quality of trade and transport-related infrastructure (worst 1–5 best)	3.1	2018	●	↑
The Times Higher Education Universities Ranking: Average score of top 3 universities (worst 0–100 best)	40.5	2022	●	●
Articles published in academic journals (per 1,000 population)	1.1	2020	●	↑
Expenditure on research and development (% of GDP)	1.0	2018	●	↓

SDG10 – Reduced Inequalities

Indicator	Value	Year	Rating	Trend
Gini coefficient	41.1	2015	●	●
Palma ratio	2.0	2018	●	●

SDG11 – Sustainable Cities and Communities

Indicator	Value	Year	Rating	Trend
Proportion of urban population living in slums (%)	NA	NA	●	●
Annual mean concentration of particulate matter of less than 2.5 microns in diameter (PM2.5) (μg/m^3)	14.8	2019	●	↑
Access to improved water source, piped (% of urban population)	99.0	2020	●	↑
Satisfaction with public transport (%)	64.0	2021	●	↓

SDG12 – Responsible Consumption and Production

Indicator	Value	Year	Rating	Trend
Municipal solid waste (kg/capita/day)	1.2	2014	●	●
Electronic waste (kg/capita)	11.1	2019	●	●
Production-based SO_2 emissions (kg/capita)	17.3	2018	●	●
SO_2 emissions embodied in imports (kg/capita)	2.4	2018	●	●
Production-based nitrogen emissions (kg/capita)	7.1	2015	●	↑
Nitrogen emissions embodied in imports (kg/capita)	7.9	2015	●	→
Exports of plastic waste (kg/capita)	1.7	2020	●	●

SDG13 – Climate Action

Indicator	Value	Year	Rating	Trend
CO_2 emissions from fossil fuel combustion and cement production (tCO_2/capita)	8.4	2020	●	→
CO_2 emissions embodied in imports (tCO_2/capita)	0.9	2018	●	→
CO_2 emissions embodied in fossil fuel exports (kg/capita)	3602.8	2020	●	●

SDG14 – Life Below Water

Indicator	Value	Year	Rating	Trend
Mean area that is protected in marine sites important to biodiversity (%)	13.7	2020	●	→
Ocean Health Index: Clean Waters score (worst 0–100 best)	57.7	2020	●	↓
Fish caught from overexploited or collapsed stocks (% of total catch)	23.3	2018	●	↑
Fish caught by trawling or dredging (%)	28.1	2018	●	→
Fish caught that are then discarded (%)	0.7	2018	●	↑
Marine biodiversity threats embodied in imports (per million population)	0.2	2018	●	●

SDG15 – Life on Land

Indicator	Value	Year	Rating	Trend
Mean area that is protected in terrestrial sites important to biodiversity (%)	28.5	2020	●	→
Mean area that is protected in freshwater sites important to biodiversity (%)	50.0	2020	●	→
Red List Index of species survival (worst 0–1 best)	0.7	2021	●	↓
Permanent deforestation (% of forest area, 5-year average)	1.4	2020	●	↑
Terrestrial and freshwater biodiversity threats embodied in imports (per million population)	2.1	2018	●	●

SDG16 – Peace, Justice and Strong Institutions

Indicator	Value	Year	Rating	Trend
Homicides (per 100,000 population)	2.1	2013	●	●
Unsentenced detainees (% of prison population)	26.7	2018	●	↑
Population who feel safe walking alone at night in the city or area where they live (%)	60	2021	●	↑
Property Rights (worst 1–7 best)	5.3	2020	●	↑
Birth registrations with civil authority (% of children under age 5)	NA	NA	●	●
Corruption Perception Index (worst 0–100 best)	48	2021	●	↓
Children involved in child labor (% of population aged 5 to 14)	NA	NA	●	●
Exports of major conventional weapons (TIV constant million USD per 100,000 population)	0.0	2020	●	●
Press Freedom Index (best 0–100 worst)	39.5	2021	●	↑
Access to and affordability of justice (worst 0–1 best)	0.6	2020	●	↑

SDG17 – Partnerships for the Goals

Indicator	Value	Year	Rating	Trend
Government spending on health and education (% of GDP)	6.2	2019	●	↓
For high-income and all OECD DAC countries: International concessional public finance, including official development assistance (% of GNI)	NA	NA	●	●
Other countries: Government revenue excluding grants (% of GDP)	17.5	2019	●	↓
Corporate Tax Haven Score (best 0–100 worst)	* 0.0	2019	●	●
Statistical Performance Index (worst 0–100 best)	71.1	2019	●	↑

MALDIVES

East and South Asia

OVERALL PERFORMANCE

COUNTRY RANKING

MALDIVES

67/163

COUNTRY SCORE

REGIONAL AVERAGE: 65.9

AVERAGE PERFORMANCE BY SDG

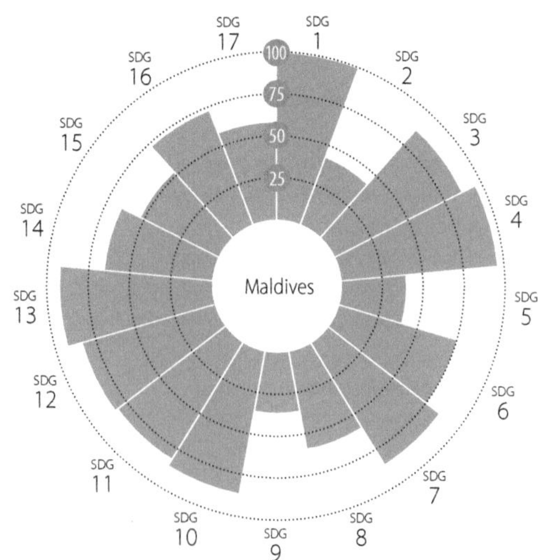

SDG DASHBOARDS AND TRENDS

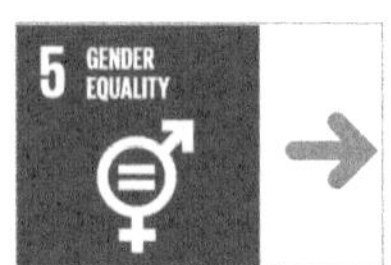

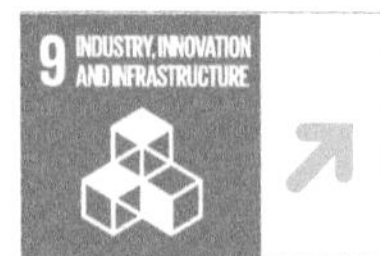

Major challenges | Significant challenges | Challenges remain | SDG achieved | Information unavailable

Decreasing | Stagnating | Moderately improving | On track or maintaining SDG achievement | Information unavailable

Note: The full title of each SDG is available here: https://sustainabledevelopment.un.org/topics/sustainabledevelopmentgoals

INTERNATIONAL SPILLOVER INDEX

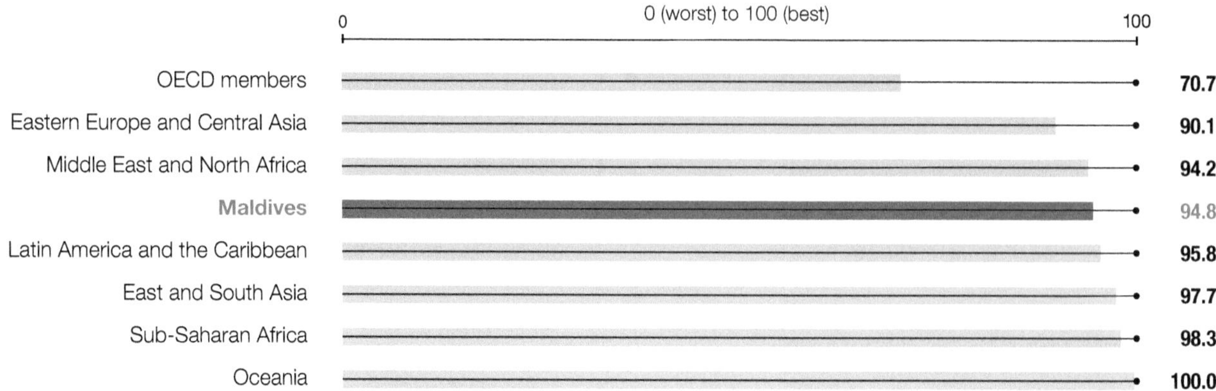

STATISTICAL PERFORMANCE INDEX

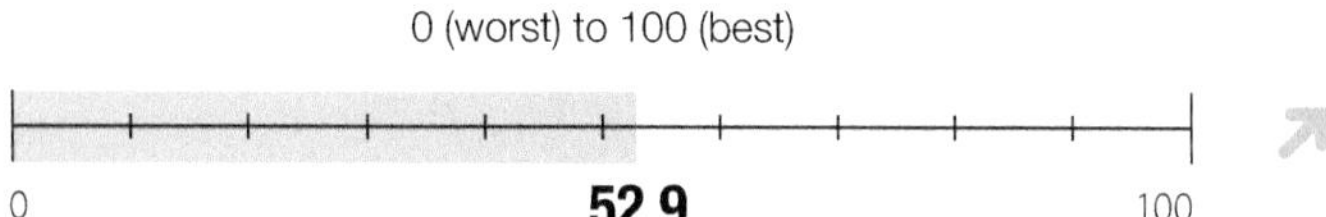

MISSING DATA IN SDG INDEX

18%

SDG1 – No Poverty

Indicator	Value	Year	Rating	Trend
Poverty headcount ratio at $1.90/day (%)	0.1	2022	●	↑
Poverty headcount ratio at $3.20/day (%)	0.3	2022	●	↑

SDG2 – Zero Hunger

Indicator	Value	Year	Rating	Trend
Prevalence of undernourishment (%)	NA	NA	●	●
Prevalence of stunting in children under 5 years of age (%)	15.3	2017	●	→
Prevalence of wasting in children under 5 years of age (%)	9.1	2017	●	→
Prevalence of obesity, BMI ≥ 30 (% of adult population)	8.6	2016	●	↑
Human Trophic Level (best 2–3 worst)	2.4	2017	●	↑
Cereal yield (tonnes per hectare of harvested land)	2.7	2018	●	↑
Sustainable Nitrogen Management Index (best 0–1.41 worst)	1.1	2015	●	↓
Exports of hazardous pesticides (tonnes per million population)	NA	NA	●	●

SDG3 – Good Health and Well-Being

Indicator	Value	Year	Rating	Trend
Maternal mortality rate (per 100,000 live births)	53	2017	●	↑
Neonatal mortality rate (per 1,000 live births)	4.1	2020	●	↑
Mortality rate, under-5 (per 1,000 live births)	6.5	2020	●	↑
Incidence of tuberculosis (per 100,000 population)	37.0	2020	●	→
New HIV infections (per 1,000 uninfected population)	1.0	2020	●	→
Age-standardized death rate due to cardiovascular disease, cancer, diabetes, or chronic respiratory disease in adults aged 30–70 years (%)	11.6	2019	●	↑
Age-standardized death rate attributable to household air pollution and ambient air pollution (per 100,000 population)	26	2016	●	●
Traffic deaths (per 100,000 population)	1.6	2019	●	↑
Life expectancy at birth (years)	79.6	2019	●	↑
Adolescent fertility rate (births per 1,000 females aged 15 to 19)	8.9	2017	●	●
Births attended by skilled health personnel (%)	99.5	2017	●	↑
Surviving infants who received 2 WHO-recommended vaccines (%)	99	2020	●	↑
Universal health coverage (UHC) index of service coverage (worst 0–100 best)	69	2019	●	→
Subjective well-being (average ladder score, worst 0–10 best)	5.2	2017	●	●

SDG4 – Quality Education

Indicator	Value	Year	Rating	Trend
Participation rate in pre-primary organized learning (% of children aged 4 to 6)	93.2	2019	●	↑
Net primary enrollment rate (%)	98.0	2019	●	↑
Lower secondary completion rate (%)	111.2	2019	●	↑
Literacy rate (% of population aged 15 to 24)	98.8	2016	●	●

SDG5 – Gender Equality

Indicator	Value	Year	Rating	Trend
Demand for family planning satisfied by modern methods (% of females aged 15 to 49)	29.2	2017	●	→
Ratio of female-to-male mean years of education received (%)	100.0	2019	●	↑
Ratio of female-to-male labor force participation rate (%)	50.7	2020	●	↓
Seats held by women in national parliament (%)	4.6	2020	●	↓

SDG6 – Clean Water and Sanitation

Indicator	Value	Year	Rating	Trend
Population using at least basic drinking water services (%)	99.5	2020	●	↑
Population using at least basic sanitation services (%)	99.2	2020	●	↑
Freshwater withdrawal (% of available freshwater resources)	15.7	2018	●	●
Anthropogenic wastewater that receives treatment (%)	4.6	2018	●	●
Scarce water consumption embodied in imports (m^3 H_2O eq/capita)	NA	NA	●	●

SDG7 – Affordable and Clean Energy

Indicator	Value	Year	Rating	Trend
Population with access to electricity (%)	100.0	2019	●	↑
Population with access to clean fuels and technology for cooking (%)	99.1	2019	●	↑
CO_2 emissions from fuel combustion per total electricity output ($MtCO_2$/TWh)	2.6	2019	●	→
Share of renewable energy in total primary energy supply (%)	NA	NA	●	●

SDG8 – Decent Work and Economic Growth

Indicator	Value	Year	Rating	Trend
Adjusted GDP growth (%)	-13.1	2020	●	●
Victims of modern slavery (per 1,000 population)	NA	NA	●	●
Adults with an account at a bank or other financial institution or with a mobile-money-service provider (% of population aged 15 or over)	NA	NA	●	●
Unemployment rate (% of total labor force)	5.2	2022	●	↑
Fundamental labor rights are effectively guaranteed (worst 0–1 best)	NA	NA	●	●
Fatal work-related accidents embodied in imports (per 100,000 population)	0.9	2015	●	↑

* Imputed data point

SDG9 – Industry, Innovation and Infrastructure

Indicator	Value	Year	Rating	Trend
Population using the internet (%)	62.9	2020	●	↗
Mobile broadband subscriptions (per 100 population)	50.6	2019	●	→
Logistics Performance Index: Quality of trade and transport-related infrastructure (worst 1–5 best)	2.7	2018	●	↑
The Times Higher Education Universities Ranking: Average score of top 3 universities (worst 0–100 best)	* 0.0	2022	●	●
Articles published in academic journals (per 1,000 population)	0.2	2020	●	↗
Expenditure on research and development (% of GDP)	NA	NA	●	●

SDG10 – Reduced Inequalities

Indicator	Value	Year	Rating	Trend
Gini coefficient	31.3	2016	●	●
Palma ratio	1.2	2018	●	●

SDG11 – Sustainable Cities and Communities

Indicator	Value	Year	Rating	Trend
Proportion of urban population living in slums (%)	32.1	2018	●	●
Annual mean concentration of particulate matter of less than 2.5 microns in diameter (PM2.5) (μg/m^3)	6.8	2019	●	↑
Access to improved water source, piped (% of urban population)	99.0	2020	●	↑
Satisfaction with public transport (%)	59.0	2017	●	●

SDG12 – Responsible Consumption and Production

Indicator	Value	Year	Rating	Trend
Municipal solid waste (kg/capita/day)	1.3	2015	●	●
Electronic waste (kg/capita)	9.1	2019	●	●
Production-based SO_2 emissions (kg/capita)	NA	NA	●	●
SO_2 emissions embodied in imports (kg/capita)	NA	NA	●	●
Production-based nitrogen emissions (kg/capita)	0.0	2015	●	↑
Nitrogen emissions embodied in imports (kg/capita)	4.8	2015	●	↑
Exports of plastic waste (kg/capita)	0.5	2019	●	●

SDG13 – Climate Action

Indicator	Value	Year	Rating	Trend
CO_2 emissions from fossil fuel combustion and cement production (tCO_2/capita)	3.3	2020	●	→
CO_2 emissions embodied in imports (tCO_2/capita)	NA	NA	●	●
CO_2 emissions embodied in fossil fuel exports (kg/capita)	0.0	2020	●	●

SDG14 – Life Below Water

Indicator	Value	Year	Rating	Trend
Mean area that is protected in marine sites important to biodiversity (%)	0.0	2020	●	→
Ocean Health Index: Clean Waters score (worst 0–100 best)	58.7	2020	●	↑
Fish caught from overexploited or collapsed stocks (% of total catch)	43.4	2018	●	↑
Fish caught by trawling or dredging (%)	0.0	2018	●	↑
Fish caught that are then discarded (%)	0.1	2018	●	↑
Marine biodiversity threats embodied in imports (per million population)	0.1	2018	●	●

SDG15 – Life on Land

Indicator	Value	Year	Rating	Trend
Mean area that is protected in terrestrial sites important to biodiversity (%)	0.0	2020	●	→
Mean area that is protected in freshwater sites important to biodiversity (%)	NA	NA	●	●
Red List Index of species survival (worst 0–1 best)	0.8	2021	●	↓
Permanent deforestation (% of forest area, 5-year average)	NA	NA	●	●
Terrestrial and freshwater biodiversity threats embodied in imports (per million population)	0.3	2018	●	●

SDG16 – Peace, Justice and Strong Institutions

Indicator	Value	Year	Rating	Trend
Homicides (per 100,000 population)	0.6	2019	●	↑
Unsentenced detainees (% of prison population)	NA	NA	●	●
Population who feel safe walking alone at night in the city or area where they live (%)	50	2017	●	●
Property Rights (worst 1–7 best)	NA	NA	●	●
Birth registrations with civil authority (% of children under age 5)	98.8	2020	●	●
Corruption Perception Index (worst 0–100 best)	40	2021	●	→
Children involved in child labor (% of population aged 5 to 14)	NA	NA	●	●
Exports of major conventional weapons (TIV constant million USD per 100,000 population)	* 0.0	2020	●	●
Press Freedom Index (best 0–100 worst)	29.1	2021	●	↑
Access to and affordability of justice (worst 0–1 best)	NA	NA	●	●

SDG17 – Partnerships for the Goals

Indicator	Value	Year	Rating	Trend
Government spending on health and education (% of GDP)	10.5	2019	●	↑
For high-income and all OECD DAC countries: International concessional public finance, including official development assistance (% of GNI)	NA	NA	●	●
Other countries: Government revenue excluding grants (% of GDP)	17.7	2009	●	●
Corporate Tax Haven Score (best 0–100 worst)	* 0.0	2019	●	●
Statistical Performance Index (worst 0–100 best)	52.9	2019	●	↗

5. Country Profiles

MALI

OVERALL PERFORMANCE

COUNTRY RANKING

MALI

142/163

COUNTRY SCORE

AVERAGE PERFORMANCE BY SDG

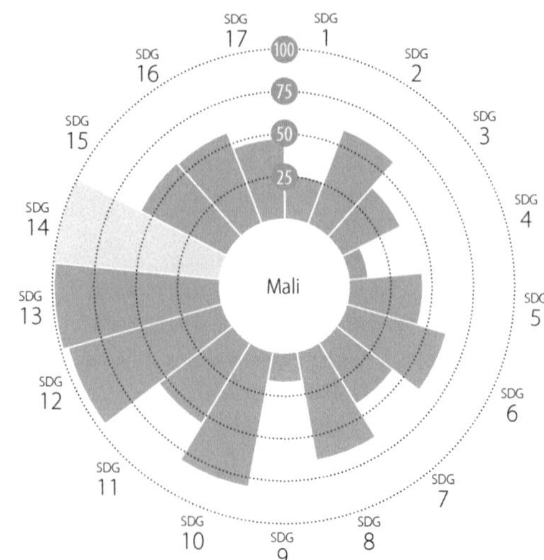

SDG DASHBOARDS AND TRENDS

Note: The full title of each SDG is available here: https://sustainabledevelopment.un.org/topics/sustainabledevelopmentgoals

INTERNATIONAL SPILLOVER INDEX

STATISTICAL PERFORMANCE INDEX

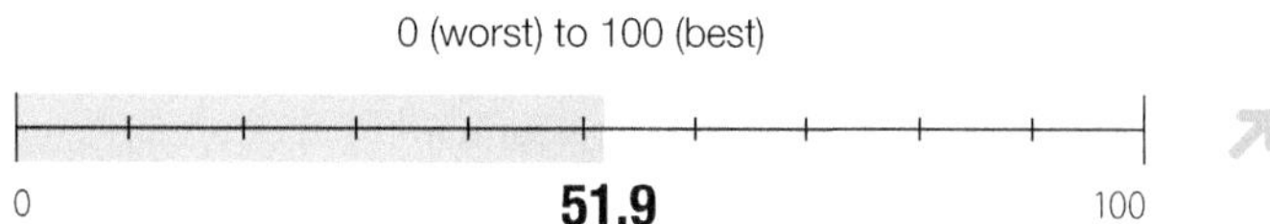

MISSING DATA IN SDG INDEX

3%

Performance by Indicator

SDG1 – No Poverty	Value	Year	Rating	Trend
Poverty headcount ratio at $1.90/day (%)	36.3	2022	●	→
Poverty headcount ratio at $3.20/day (%)	68.8	2022	●	→

SDG2 – Zero Hunger	Value	Year	Rating	Trend
Prevalence of undernourishment (%)	10.4	2019	●	↓
Prevalence of stunting in children under 5 years of age (%)	26.4	2019	●	→
Prevalence of wasting in children under 5 years of age (%)	9.3	2019	●	→
Prevalence of obesity, BMI ≥ 30 (% of adult population)	8.6	2016	●	↑
Human Trophic Level (best 2–3 worst)	2.2	2017	●	↑
Cereal yield (tonnes per hectare of harvested land)	1.8	2018	●	↑
Sustainable Nitrogen Management Index (best 0–1.41 worst)	0.8	2015	●	→
Exports of hazardous pesticides (tonnes per million population)	0.5	2019	●	●

SDG3 – Good Health and Well-Being	Value	Year	Rating	Trend
Maternal mortality rate (per 100,000 live births)	562	2017	●	↗
Neonatal mortality rate (per 1,000 live births)	31.6	2020	●	→
Mortality rate, under-5 (per 1,000 live births)	91.0	2020	●	↗
Incidence of tuberculosis (per 100,000 population)	52.0	2020	●	→
New HIV infections (per 1,000 uninfected population)	0.3	2020	●	↑
Age-standardized death rate due to cardiovascular disease, cancer, diabetes, or chronic respiratory disease in adults aged 30–70 years (%)	22.3	2019	●	→
Age-standardized death rate attributable to household air pollution and ambient air pollution (per 100,000 population)	209	2016	●	●
Traffic deaths (per 100,000 population)	22.7	2019	●	→
Life expectancy at birth (years)	62.8	2019	●	→
Adolescent fertility rate (births per 1,000 females aged 15 to 19)	164.0	2017	●	●
Births attended by skilled health personnel (%)	67.3	2018	●	↑
Surviving infants who received 2 WHO-recommended vaccines (%)	62	2020	●	↓
Universal health coverage (UHC) index of service coverage (worst 0–100 best)	42	2019	●	→
Subjective well-being (average ladder score, worst 0–10 best)	4.1	2021	●	↓

SDG4 – Quality Education	Value	Year	Rating	Trend
Participation rate in pre-primary organized learning (% of children aged 4 to 6)	44.8	2018	●	●
Net primary enrollment rate (%)	59.0	2018	●	●
Lower secondary completion rate (%)	29.7	2017	●	●
Literacy rate (% of population aged 15 to 24)	46.2	2020	●	↓

SDG5 – Gender Equality	Value	Year	Rating	Trend
Demand for family planning satisfied by modern methods (% of females aged 15 to 49)	41.2	2018	●	→
Ratio of female-to-male mean years of education received (%)	56.7	2019	●	→
Ratio of female-to-male labor force participation rate (%)	72.5	2020	●	↑
Seats held by women in national parliament (%)	27.9	2020	●	↑

SDG6 – Clean Water and Sanitation	Value	Year	Rating	Trend
Population using at least basic drinking water services (%)	82.5	2020	●	↑
Population using at least basic sanitation services (%)	45.4	2020	●	→
Freshwater withdrawal (% of available freshwater resources)	8.0	2018	●	●
Anthropogenic wastewater that receives treatment (%)	0.0	2018	●	●
Scarce water consumption embodied in imports (m^3 H_2O eq/capita)	305.7	2018	●	●

SDG7 – Affordable and Clean Energy	Value	Year	Rating	Trend
Population with access to electricity (%)	48.0	2019	●	↗
Population with access to clean fuels and technology for cooking (%)	0.9	2019	●	→
CO_2 emissions from fuel combustion per total electricity output ($MtCO_2$/TWh)	1.0	2019	●	↑
Share of renewable energy in total primary energy supply (%)	NA	NA	●	●

SDG8 – Decent Work and Economic Growth	Value	Year	Rating	Trend
Adjusted GDP growth (%)	-5.3	2020	●	●
Victims of modern slavery (per 1,000 population)	3.6	2018	●	●
Adults with an account at a bank or other financial institution or with a mobile-money-service provider (% of population aged 15 or over)	35.4	2017	●	↑
Unemployment rate (% of total labor force)	7.5	2022	●	→
Fundamental labor rights are effectively guaranteed (worst 0–1 best)	0.6	2020	●	●
Fatal work-related accidents embodied in imports (per 100,000 population)	0.0	2015	●	↑

SDG9 – Industry, Innovation and Infrastructure	Value	Year	Rating	Trend
Population using the internet (%)	27.4	2020	●	↗
Mobile broadband subscriptions (per 100 population)	35.1	2019	●	↑
Logistics Performance Index: Quality of trade and transport-related infrastructure (worst 1–5 best)	2.3	2018	●	↗
The Times Higher Education Universities Ranking: Average score of top 3 universities (worst 0–100 best)	* 0.0	2022	●	●
Articles published in academic journals (per 1,000 population)	0.0	2020	●	→
Expenditure on research and development (% of GDP)	0.3	2017	●	↓

SDG10 – Reduced Inequalities	Value	Year	Rating	Trend
Gini coefficient	33.0	2009	●	●
Palma ratio	1.3	2018	●	●

SDG11 – Sustainable Cities and Communities	Value	Year	Rating	Trend
Proportion of urban population living in slums (%)	46.0	2018	●	↗
Annual mean concentration of particulate matter of less than 2.5 microns in diameter (PM2.5) (μg/m³)	39.4	2019	●	→
Access to improved water source, piped (% of urban population)	84.6	2020	●	↗
Satisfaction with public transport (%)	40.0	2021	●	→

SDG12 – Responsible Consumption and Production	Value	Year	Rating	Trend
Municipal solid waste (kg/capita/day)	0.3	2012	●	●
Electronic waste (kg/capita)	0.8	2019	●	●
Production-based SO_2 emissions (kg/capita)	0.3	2018	●	●
SO_2 emissions embodied in imports (kg/capita)	0.2	2018	●	●
Production-based nitrogen emissions (kg/capita)	21.4	2015	●	↓
Nitrogen emissions embodied in imports (kg/capita)	0.2	2015	●	↑
Exports of plastic waste (kg/capita)	0.1	2019	●	●

SDG13 – Climate Action	Value	Year	Rating	Trend
CO_2 emissions from fossil fuel combustion and cement production (tCO_2/capita)	0.2	2020	●	↑
CO_2 emissions embodied in imports (tCO_2/capita)	0.1	2018	●	↑
CO_2 emissions embodied in fossil fuel exports (kg/capita)	0.0	2018	●	●

SDG14 – Life Below Water	Value	Year	Rating	Trend
Mean area that is protected in marine sites important to biodiversity (%)	NA	NA	●	●
Ocean Health Index: Clean Waters score (worst 0–100 best)	NA	NA	●	●
Fish caught from overexploited or collapsed stocks (% of total catch)	NA	NA	●	●
Fish caught by trawling or dredging (%)	NA	NA	●	●
Fish caught that are then discarded (%)	NA	NA	●	●
Marine biodiversity threats embodied in imports (per million population)	0.0	2018	●	●

SDG15 – Life on Land	Value	Year	Rating	Trend
Mean area that is protected in terrestrial sites important to biodiversity (%)	8.1	2020	●	→
Mean area that is protected in freshwater sites important to biodiversity (%)	0.0	2020	●	→
Red List Index of species survival (worst 0–1 best)	1.0	2021	●	↑
Permanent deforestation (% of forest area, 5-year average)	0.2	2020	●	↗
Terrestrial and freshwater biodiversity threats embodied in imports (per million population)	0.0	2018	●	●

SDG16 – Peace, Justice and Strong Institutions	Value	Year	Rating	Trend
Homicides (per 100,000 population)	NA	NA	●	●
Unsentenced detainees (% of prison population)	NA	NA	●	●
Population who feel safe walking alone at night in the city or area where they live (%)	51	2021	●	↓
Property Rights (worst 1–7 best)	3.6	2020	●	↓
Birth registrations with civil authority (% of children under age 5)	86.7	2020	●	●
Corruption Perception Index (worst 0–100 best)	29	2021	●	↓
Children involved in child labor (% of population aged 5 to 14)	13.2	2019	●	●
Exports of major conventional weapons (TIV constant million USD per 100,000 population)	* 0.0	2020	●	●
Press Freedom Index (best 0–100 worst)	33.5	2021	●	↑
Access to and affordability of justice (worst 0–1 best)	0.4	2020	●	●

SDG17 – Partnerships for the Goals	Value	Year	Rating	Trend
Government spending on health and education (% of GDP)	4.7	2019	●	→
For high-income and all OECD DAC countries: International concessional public finance, including official development assistance (% of GNI)	NA	NA	●	●
Other countries: Government revenue excluding grants (% of GDP)	15.4	2019	●	→
Corporate Tax Haven Score (best 0–100 worst)	* 0.0	2019	●	●
Statistical Performance Index (worst 0–100 best)	51.9	2019	●	↗

* Imputed data point

5. Country Profiles

MALTA

Eastern Europe and Central Asia

AVERAGE PERFORMANCE BY SDG

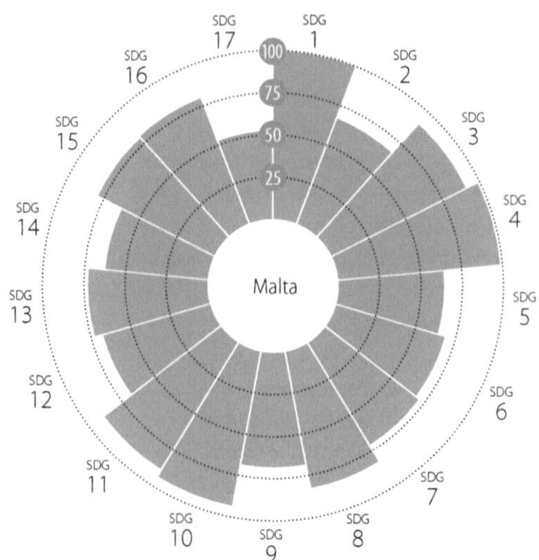

OVERALL PERFORMANCE

COUNTRY RANKING

MALTA

33/163

COUNTRY SCORE

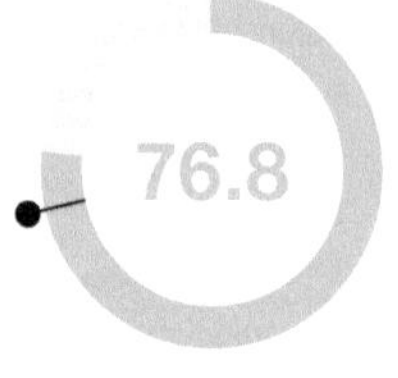

REGIONAL AVERAGE: 71.6

SDG DASHBOARDS AND TRENDS

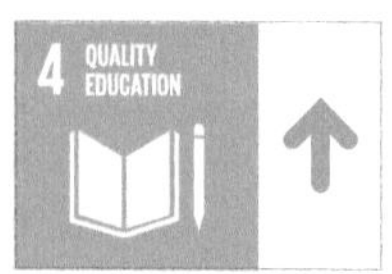

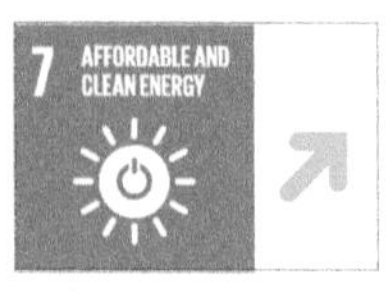

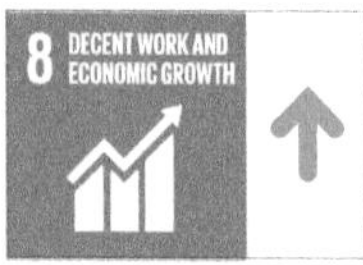

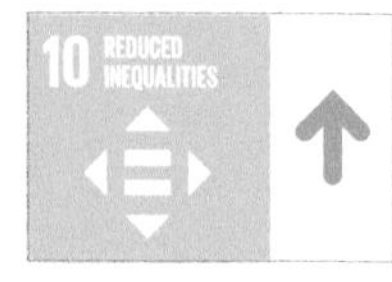

Major challenges | Significant challenges | Challenges remain | SDG achieved | Information unavailable

Decreasing | Stagnating | Moderately improving | On track or maintaining SDG achievement | Information unavailable

Note: The full title of each SDG is available here: https://sustainabledevelopment.un.org/topics/sustainabledevelopmentgoals

INTERNATIONAL SPILLOVER INDEX

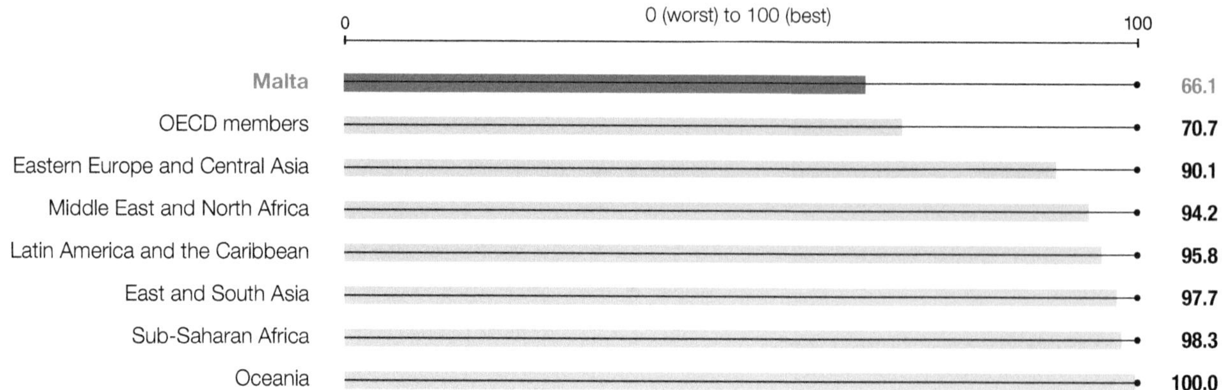

STATISTICAL PERFORMANCE INDEX

0 (worst) to 100 (best)

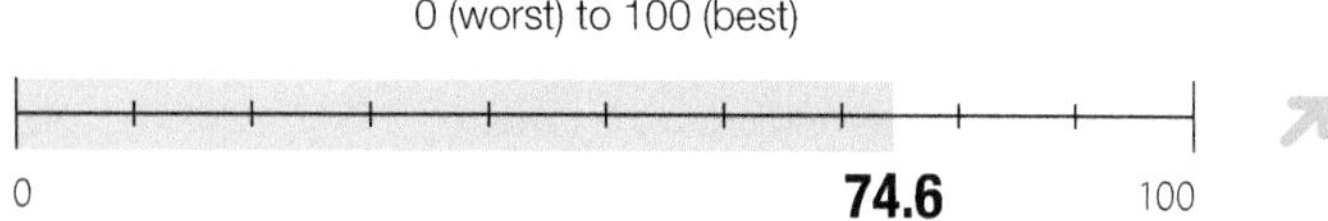

MISSING DATA IN SDG INDEX

5%

SDG1 – No Poverty	Value	Year	Rating	Trend
Poverty headcount ratio at $1.90/day (%)	0.1	2022	●	↑
Poverty headcount ratio at $3.20/day (%)	0.1	2022	●	↑
SDG2 – Zero Hunger				
Prevalence of undernourishment (%)	2.5	2019	●	↑
Prevalence of stunting in children under 5 years of age (%)	* 2.6	2019	●	↑
Prevalence of wasting in children under 5 years of age (%)	* 0.7	2019	●	↑
Prevalence of obesity, BMI ≥ 30 (% of adult population)	28.9	2016	●	↓
Human Trophic Level (best 2–3 worst)	2.3	2017	●	→
Cereal yield (tonnes per hectare of harvested land)	4.9	2018	●	↑
Sustainable Nitrogen Management Index (best 0–1.41 worst)	0.9	2015	●	↓
Exports of hazardous pesticides (tonnes per million population)	0.0	2019	●	●
SDG3 – Good Health and Well-Being				
Maternal mortality rate (per 100,000 live births)	6	2017	●	↑
Neonatal mortality rate (per 1,000 live births)	4.3	2020	●	↑
Mortality rate, under-5 (per 1,000 live births)	6.5	2020	●	↑
Incidence of tuberculosis (per 100,000 population)	36.0	2020	●	↓
New HIV infections (per 1,000 uninfected population)	1.0	2020	●	→
Age-standardized death rate due to cardiovascular disease, cancer, diabetes, or chronic respiratory disease in adults aged 30–70 years (%)	10.5	2019	●	↑
Age-standardized death rate attributable to household air pollution and ambient air pollution (per 100,000 population)	20	2016	●	●
Traffic deaths (per 100,000 population)	4.1	2019	●	↑
Life expectancy at birth (years)	81.9	2019	●	↑
Adolescent fertility rate (births per 1,000 females aged 15 to 19)	12.1	2018	●	↑
Births attended by skilled health personnel (%)	99.7	2017	●	↑
Surviving infants who received 2 WHO-recommended vaccines (%)	95	2020	●	↑
Universal health coverage (UHC) index of service coverage (worst 0–100 best)	81	2019	●	↑
Subjective well-being (average ladder score, worst 0–10 best)	6.4	2021	●	↑
SDG4 – Quality Education				
Participation rate in pre-primary organized learning (% of children aged 4 to 6)	97.5	2019	●	↑
Net primary enrollment rate (%)	99.5	2019	●	↑
Lower secondary completion rate (%)	104.0	2019	●	↑
Literacy rate (% of population aged 15 to 24)	99.3	2018	●	●
SDG5 – Gender Equality				
Demand for family planning satisfied by modern methods (% of females aged 15 to 49)	* 75.2	2022	●	↗
Ratio of female-to-male mean years of education received (%)	95.7	2019	●	↑
Ratio of female-to-male labor force participation rate (%)	74.4	2020	●	↑
Seats held by women in national parliament (%)	13.4	2020	●	→
SDG6 – Clean Water and Sanitation				
Population using at least basic drinking water services (%)	100.0	2020	●	↑
Population using at least basic sanitation services (%)	100.0	2020	●	↑
Freshwater withdrawal (% of available freshwater resources)	81.7	2018	●	●
Anthropogenic wastewater that receives treatment (%)	* 100.0	2018	●	●
Scarce water consumption embodied in imports (m^3 H_2O eq/capita)	8655.6	2018	●	●
SDG7 – Affordable and Clean Energy				
Population with access to electricity (%)	100.0	2019	●	↑
Population with access to clean fuels and technology for cooking (%)	100.0	2019	●	↑
CO_2 emissions from fuel combustion per total electricity output ($MtCO_2$/TWh)	1.2	2019	●	↑
Share of renewable energy in total primary energy supply (%)	5.2	2019	●	→
SDG8 – Decent Work and Economic Growth				
Adjusted GDP growth (%)	-3.1	2020	●	●
Victims of modern slavery (per 1,000 population)	NA	NA	●	●
Adults with an account at a bank or other financial institution or with a mobile-money-service provider (% of population aged 15 or over)	97.4	2017	●	↑
Unemployment rate (% of total labor force)	3.1	2022	●	↑
Fundamental labor rights are effectively guaranteed (worst 0–1 best)	0.8	2020	●	●
Fatal work-related accidents embodied in imports (per 100,000 population)	1.2	2015	●	↑

* Imputed data point

SDG9 – Industry, Innovation and Infrastructure	Value	Year	Rating	Trend
Population using the internet (%)	86.9	2020	●	↑
Mobile broadband subscriptions (per 100 population)	88.0	2019	●	↑
Logistics Performance Index: Quality of trade and transport-related infrastructure (worst 1–5 best)	2.9	2018	●	↓
The Times Higher Education Universities Ranking: Average score of top 3 universities (worst 0–100 best)	29.6	2022	●	●
Articles published in academic journals (per 1,000 population)	2.3	2020	●	↑
Expenditure on research and development (% of GDP)	0.6	2018	●	↓
SDG10 – Reduced Inequalities				
Gini coefficient	28.7	2018	●	↑
Palma ratio	1.1	2018	●	●
SDG11 – Sustainable Cities and Communities				
Proportion of urban population living in slums (%)	NA	NA	●	●
Annual mean concentration of particulate matter of less than 2.5 microns in diameter (PM2.5) (μg/m^3)	13.3	2019	●	↑
Access to improved water source, piped (% of urban population)	100.0	2020	●	↑
Satisfaction with public transport (%)	67.0	2021	●	↑
SDG12 – Responsible Consumption and Production				
Municipal solid waste (kg/capita/day)	2.2	2019	●	●
Electronic waste (kg/capita)	14.5	2019	●	●
Production-based SO_2 emissions (kg/capita)	17.9	2018	●	●
SO_2 emissions embodied in imports (kg/capita)	4.7	2018	●	●
Production-based nitrogen emissions (kg/capita)	1.7	2015	●	↑
Nitrogen emissions embodied in imports (kg/capita)	14.8	2015	●	→
Exports of plastic waste (kg/capita)	6.8	2020	●	●
SDG13 – Climate Action				
CO_2 emissions from fossil fuel combustion and cement production (tCO_2/capita)	3.6	2020	●	↗
CO_2 emissions embodied in imports (tCO_2/capita)	2.1	2018	●	↑
CO_2 emissions embodied in fossil fuel exports (kg/capita)	0.0	2019	●	●
SDG14 – Life Below Water				
Mean area that is protected in marine sites important to biodiversity (%)	89.5	2020	●	↑
Ocean Health Index: Clean Waters score (worst 0–100 best)	41.2	2020	●	↓
Fish caught from overexploited or collapsed stocks (% of total catch)	18.9	2018	●	↑
Fish caught by trawling or dredging (%)	89.6	2018	●	→
Fish caught that are then discarded (%)	1.6	2018	●	↑
Marine biodiversity threats embodied in imports (per million population)	0.1	2018	●	●
SDG15 – Life on Land				
Mean area that is protected in terrestrial sites important to biodiversity (%)	79.5	2020	●	→
Mean area that is protected in freshwater sites important to biodiversity (%)	NA	NA	●	●
Red List Index of species survival (worst 0–1 best)	0.9	2021	●	→
Permanent deforestation (% of forest area, 5-year average)	NA	NA	●	●
Terrestrial and freshwater biodiversity threats embodied in imports (per million population)	1.1	2018	●	●
SDG16 – Peace, Justice and Strong Institutions				
Homicides (per 100,000 population)	1.6	2020	●	↓
Unsentenced detainees (% of prison population)	32.5	2019	●	↓
Population who feel safe walking alone at night in the city or area where they live (%)	77	2021	●	↑
Property Rights (worst 1–7 best)	5.2	2020	●	↑
Birth registrations with civil authority (% of children under age 5)	100.0	2020	●	●
Corruption Perception Index (worst 0–100 best)	54	2021	●	↓
Children involved in child labor (% of population aged 5 to 14)	NA	NA	●	●
Exports of major conventional weapons (TIV constant million USD per 100,000 population)	0.0	2020	●	●
Press Freedom Index (best 0–100 worst)	30.5	2021	●	↓
Access to and affordability of justice (worst 0–1 best)	0.7	2020	●	●
SDG17 – Partnerships for the Goals				
Government spending on health and education (% of GDP)	9.8	2019	●	↓
For high-income and all OECD DAC countries: International concessional public finance, including official development assistance (% of GNI)	0.4	2020	●	↑
Other countries: Government revenue excluding grants (% of GDP)	NA	NA	●	●
Corporate Tax Haven Score (best 0–100 worst)	73.5	2019	●	●
Statistical Performance Index (worst 0–100 best)	74.6	2019	●	↗

5. Country Profiles

MARSHALL ISLANDS

Oceania

OVERALL PERFORMANCE

COUNTRY RANKING

MARSHALL ISLANDS

NA /163

COUNTRY SCORE

REGIONAL AVERAGE: 52.3

AVERAGE PERFORMANCE BY SDG

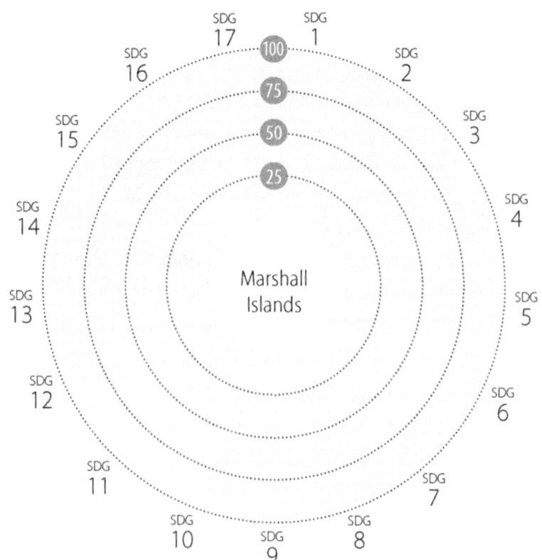

SDG DASHBOARDS AND TRENDS

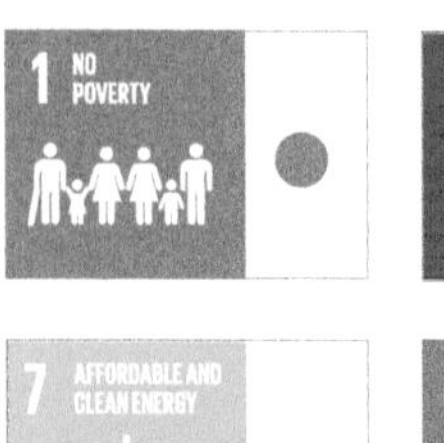

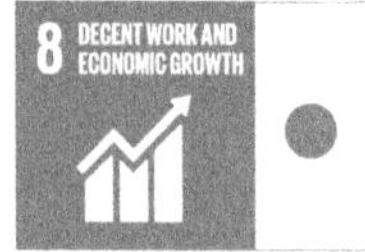

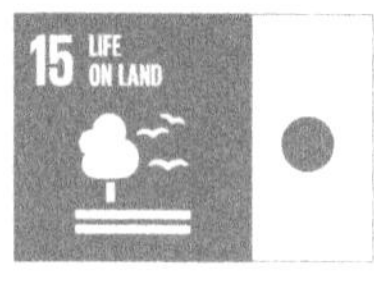

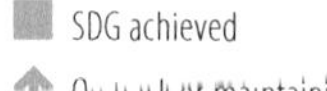

Major challenges · Significant challenges · Challenges remain · SDG achieved · Information unavailable

Decreasing · Stagnating · Moderately improving · On track or maintaining SDG achievement · Information unavailable

Note: The full title of each SDG is available here: https://sustainabledevelopment.un.org/topics/sustainabledevelopmentgoals

INTERNATIONAL SPILLOVER INDEX

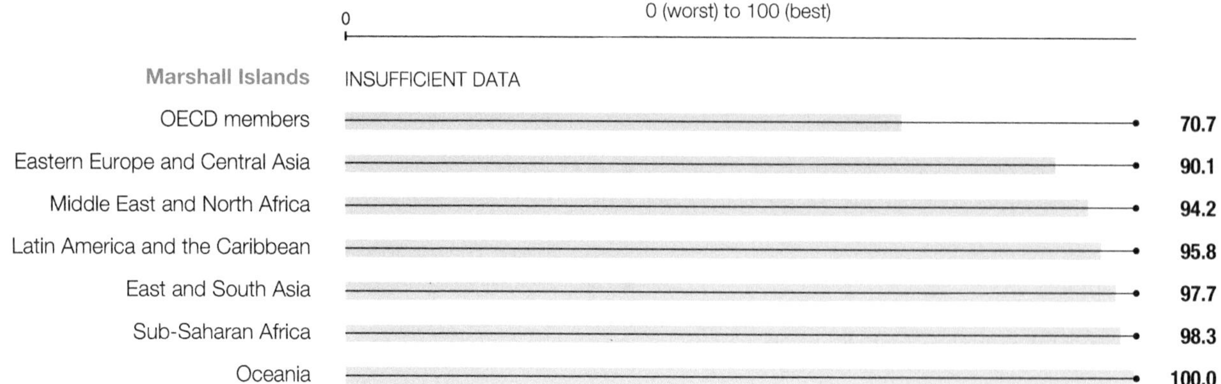

STATISTICAL PERFORMANCE INDEX

0 (worst) to 100 (best)

0 **20.9** 100

MISSING DATA IN SDG INDEX

55%

MARSHALL ISLANDS

SDG1 – No Poverty	Value	Year	Rating	Trend
Poverty headcount ratio at $1.90/day (%)	NA	NA	●	●
Poverty headcount ratio at $3.20/day (%)	NA	NA	●	●

SDG2 – Zero Hunger	Value	Year	Rating	Trend
Prevalence of undernourishment (%)	NA	NA	●	●
Prevalence of stunting in children under 5 years of age (%)	34.8	2017	●	●
Prevalence of wasting in children under 5 years of age (%)	3.5	2017	●	●
Prevalence of obesity, BMI ≥ 30 (% of adult population)	52.9	2016	●	↓
Human Trophic Level (best 2–3 worst)	NA	NA	●	●
Cereal yield (tonnes per hectare of harvested land)	NA	NA	●	●
Sustainable Nitrogen Management Index (best 0–1.41 worst)	1.3	2015	●	↓
Exports of hazardous pesticides (tonnes per million population)	NA	NA	●	●

SDG3 – Good Health and Well-Being	Value	Year	Rating	Trend
Maternal mortality rate (per 100,000 live births)	NA	NA	●	●
Neonatal mortality rate (per 1,000 live births)	14.2	2020	●	↑
Mortality rate, under-5 (per 1,000 live births)	30.7	2020	●	↑
Incidence of tuberculosis (per 100,000 population)	483.0	2020	●	↓
New HIV infections (per 1,000 uninfected population)	NA	NA	●	●
Age-standardized death rate due to cardiovascular disease, cancer, diabetes, or chronic respiratory disease in adults aged 30–70 years (%)	NA	NA	●	●
Age-standardized death rate attributable to household air pollution and ambient air pollution (per 100,000 population)	NA	NA	●	●
Traffic deaths (per 100,000 population)	NA	NA	●	●
Life expectancy at birth (years)	NA	NA	●	●
Adolescent fertility rate (births per 1,000 females aged 15 to 19)	84.5	2011	●	●
Births attended by skilled health personnel (%)	92.4	2017	●	●
Surviving infants who received 2 WHO-recommended vaccines (%)	79	2019	●	↗
Universal health coverage (UHC) index of service coverage (worst 0–100 best)	NA	NA	●	●
Subjective well-being (average ladder score, worst 0–10 best)	NA	NA	●	●

SDG4 – Quality Education	Value	Year	Rating	Trend
Participation rate in pre-primary organized learning (% of children aged 4 to 6)	60.5	2020	●	↓
Net primary enrollment rate (%)	70.2	2020	●	↓
Lower secondary completion rate (%)	97.7	2020	●	●
Literacy rate (% of population aged 15 to 24)	98.5	2011	●	●

SDG5 – Gender Equality	Value	Year	Rating	Trend
Demand for family planning satisfied by modern methods (% of females aged 15 to 49)	80.5	2007	●	●
Ratio of female-to-male mean years of education received (%)	96.4	2019	●	→
Ratio of female-to-male labor force participation rate (%)	NA	NA	●	●
Seats held by women in national parliament (%)	6.1	2020	●	↓

SDG6 – Clean Water and Sanitation	Value	Year	Rating	Trend
Population using at least basic drinking water services (%)	88.6	2020	●	→
Population using at least basic sanitation services (%)	84.2	2020	●	→
Freshwater withdrawal (% of available freshwater resources)	NA	NA	●	●
Anthropogenic wastewater that receives treatment (%)	0.0	2018	●	●
Scarce water consumption embodied in imports (m^3 H_2O eq/capita)	NA	NA	●	●

SDG7 – Affordable and Clean Energy	Value	Year	Rating	Trend
Population with access to electricity (%)	97.4	2019	●	↑
Population with access to clean fuels and technology for cooking (%)	65.1	2019	●	→
CO_2 emissions from fuel combustion per total electricity output ($MtCO_2$/TWh)	NA	NA	●	●
Share of renewable energy in total primary energy supply (%)	NA	NA	●	●

SDG8 – Decent Work and Economic Growth	Value	Year	Rating	Trend
Adjusted GDP growth (%)	-2.3	2020	●	●
Victims of modern slavery (per 1,000 population)	NA	NA	●	●
Adults with an account at a bank or other financial institution or with a mobile-money-service provider (% of population aged 15 or over)	NA	NA	●	●
Unemployment rate (% of total labor force)	NA	NA	●	●
Fundamental labor rights are effectively guaranteed (worst 0–1 best)	NA	NA	●	●
Fatal work-related accidents embodied in imports (per 100,000 population)	NA	NA	●	●

SDG9 – Industry, Innovation and Infrastructure	Value	Year	Rating	Trend
Population using the internet (%)	38.7	2017	●	●
Mobile broadband subscriptions (per 100 population)	0.0	2017	●	●
Logistics Performance Index: Quality of trade and transport-related infrastructure (worst 1–5 best)	NA	NA	●	●
The Times Higher Education Universities Ranking: Average score of top 3 universities (worst 0–100 best) *	0.0	2022	●	●
Articles published in academic journals (per 1,000 population)	0.1	2020	●	↓
Expenditure on research and development (% of GDP)	NA	NA	●	●

SDG10 – Reduced Inequalities	Value	Year	Rating	Trend
Gini coefficient	NA	NA	●	●
Palma ratio	NA	NA	●	●

SDG11 – Sustainable Cities and Communities	Value	Year	Rating	Trend
Proportion of urban population living in slums (%)	NA	NA	●	●
Annual mean concentration of particulate matter of less than 2.5 microns in diameter (PM2.5) (μg/m^3)	NA	NA	●	●
Access to improved water source, piped (% of urban population)	35.7	2020	●	→
Satisfaction with public transport (%)	NA	NA	●	●

SDG12 – Responsible Consumption and Production	Value	Year	Rating	Trend
Municipal solid waste (kg/capita/day)	0.4	2013	●	●
Electronic waste (kg/capita)	NA	NA	●	●
Production-based SO_2 emissions (kg/capita)	NA	NA	●	●
SO_2 emissions embodied in imports (kg/capita)	NA	NA	●	●
Production-based nitrogen emissions (kg/capita)	NA	NA	●	●
Nitrogen emissions embodied in imports (kg/capita)	NA	NA	●	●
Exports of plastic waste (kg/capita)	NA	NA	●	●

SDG13 – Climate Action	Value	Year	Rating	Trend
CO_2 emissions from fossil fuel combustion and cement production (tCO_2/capita)	NA	NA	●	●
CO_2 emissions embodied in imports (tCO_2/capita)	NA	NA	●	●
CO_2 emissions embodied in fossil fuel exports (kg/capita)	NA	NA	●	●

SDG14 – Life Below Water	Value	Year	Rating	Trend
Mean area that is protected in marine sites important to biodiversity (%)	7.8	2020	●	→
Ocean Health Index: Clean Waters score (worst 0–100 best)	36.6	2020	●	→
Fish caught from overexploited or collapsed stocks (% of total catch)	2.3	2018	●	↑
Fish caught by trawling or dredging (%)	0.0	2018	●	↑
Fish caught that are then discarded (%)	0.0	2018	●	↑
Marine biodiversity threats embodied in imports (per million population)	NA	NA	●	●

SDG15 – Life on Land	Value	Year	Rating	Trend
Mean area that is protected in terrestrial sites important to biodiversity (%)	10.1	2020	●	→
Mean area that is protected in freshwater sites important to biodiversity (%)	NA	NA	●	●
Red List Index of species survival (worst 0–1 best)	0.8	2021	●	↓
Permanent deforestation (% of forest area, 5-year average)	NA	NA	●	●
Terrestrial and freshwater biodiversity threats embodied in imports (per million population)	NA	NA	●	●

SDG16 – Peace, Justice and Strong Institutions	Value	Year	Rating	Trend
Homicides (per 100,000 population)	NA	NA	●	●
Unsentenced detainees (% of prison population)	NA	NA	●	●
Population who feel safe walking alone at night in the city or area where they live (%)	NA	NA	●	●
Property Rights (worst 1–7 best)	NA	NA	●	●
Birth registrations with civil authority (% of children under age 5)	83.8	2020	●	●
Corruption Perception Index (worst 0–100 best)	NA	NA	●	●
Children involved in child labor (% of population aged 5 to 14)	NA	NA	●	●
Exports of major conventional weapons (TIV constant million USD per 100,000 population) *	0.0	2020	●	●
Press Freedom Index (best 0–100 worst)	NA	NA	●	●
Access to and affordability of justice (worst 0–1 best)	NA	NA	●	●

SDG17 – Partnerships for the Goals	Value	Year	Rating	Trend
Government spending on health and education (% of GDP)	16.3	2019	●	↑
For high-income and all OECD DAC countries: International concessional public finance, including official development assistance (% of GNI)	NA	NA	●	●
Other countries: Government revenue excluding grants (% of GDP)	32.8	2019	●	↑
Corporate Tax Haven Score (best 0–100 worst) *	0.0	2019	●	●
Statistical Performance Index (worst 0–100 best)	20.9	2019	●	↗

* Imputed data point

MAURITANIA

Sub-Saharan Africa

OVERALL PERFORMANCE

COUNTRY RANKING

MAURITANIA

132 /163

COUNTRY SCORE

AVERAGE PERFORMANCE BY SDG

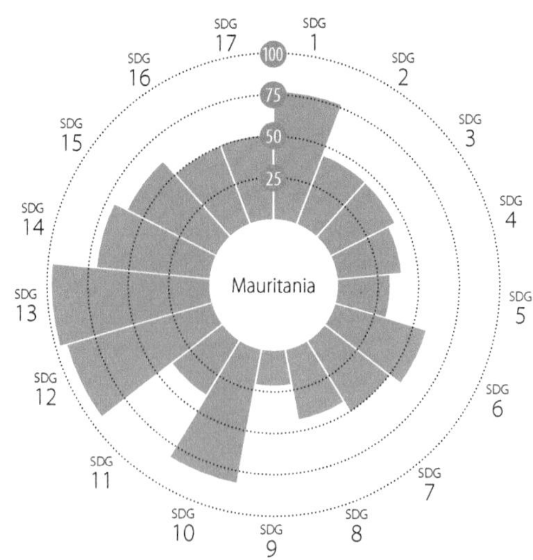

SDG DASHBOARDS AND TRENDS

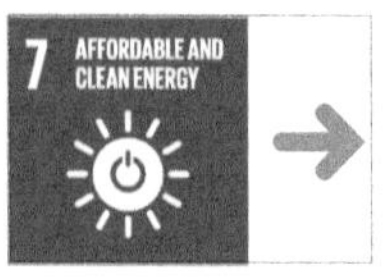
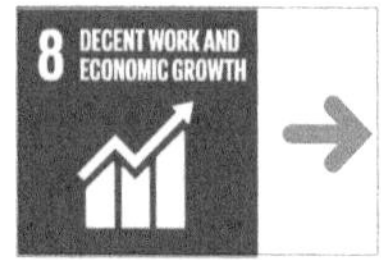

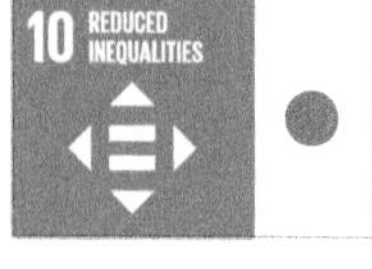

Major challenges | Significant challenges | Challenges remain | SDG achieved | Information unavailable

Decreasing | Stagnating | Moderately improving | On track or maintaining SDG achievement | Information unavailable

Note: The full title of each SDG is available here: https://sustainabledevelopment.un.org/topics/sustainabledevelopmentgoals

INTERNATIONAL SPILLOVER INDEX

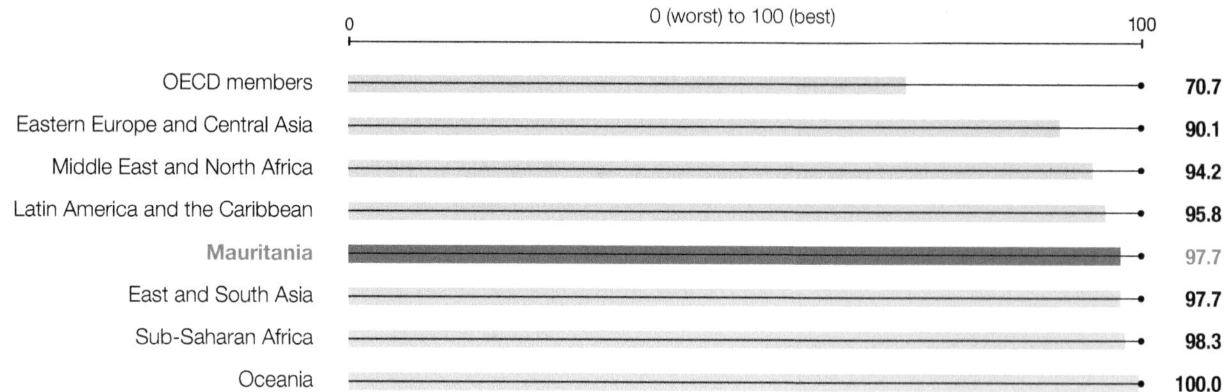

STATISTICAL PERFORMANCE INDEX

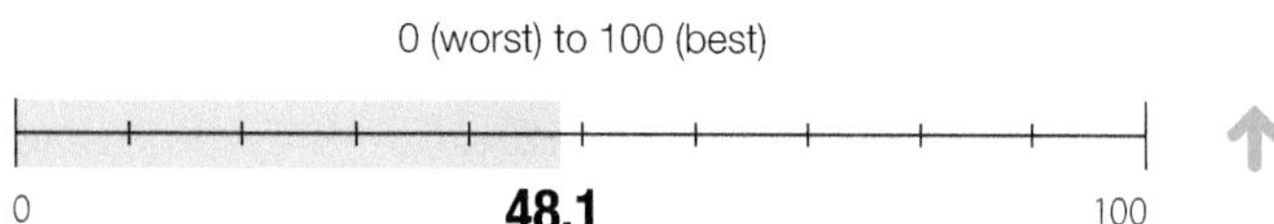

MISSING DATA IN SDG INDEX

6%

SDG1 – No Poverty	Value	Year	Rating	Trend
Poverty headcount ratio at \$1.90/day (%)	4.5	2022	●	↗
Poverty headcount ratio at \$3.20/day (%)	20.8	2022	●	→
SDG2 – Zero Hunger				
Prevalence of undernourishment (%)	9.1	2019	●	→
Prevalence of stunting in children under 5 years of age (%)	22.8	2018	●	→
Prevalence of wasting in children under 5 years of age (%)	11.5	2018	●	→
Prevalence of obesity, BMI ≥ 30 (% of adult population)	12.7	2016	●	↓
Human Trophic Level (best 2–3 worst)	2.3	2017	●	→
Cereal yield (tonnes per hectare of harvested land)	1.3	2018	●	↓
Sustainable Nitrogen Management Index (best 0–1.41 worst)	0.9	2015	●	→
Exports of hazardous pesticides (tonnes per million population)	NA	NA	●	●
SDG3 – Good Health and Well-Being				
Maternal mortality rate (per 100,000 live births)	766	2017	●	→
Neonatal mortality rate (per 1,000 live births)	31.2	2020	●	→
Mortality rate, under-5 (per 1,000 live births)	70.7	2020	●	↗
Incidence of tuberculosis (per 100,000 population)	87.0	2020	●	↗
New HIV infections (per 1,000 uninfected population)	1.0	2020	●	→
Age-standardized death rate due to cardiovascular disease, cancer, diabetes, or chronic respiratory disease in adults aged 30–70 years (%)	16.1	2019	●	→
Age-standardized death rate attributable to household air pollution and ambient air pollution (per 100,000 population)	169	2016	●	●
Traffic deaths (per 100,000 population)	25.6	2019	●	→
Life expectancy at birth (years)	68.4	2019	●	→
Adolescent fertility rate (births per 1,000 females aged 15 to 19)	84.0	2014	●	●
Births attended by skilled health personnel (%)	69.3	2015	●	●
Surviving infants who received 2 WHO-recommended vaccines (%)	71	2020	●	→
Universal health coverage (UHC) index of service coverage (worst 0–100 best)	40	2019	●	→
Subjective well-being (average ladder score, worst 0–10 best)	4.2	2019	●	●
SDG4 – Quality Education				
Participation rate in pre-primary organized learning (% of children aged 4 to 6)	NA	NA	●	●
Net primary enrollment rate (%)	76.9	2019	●	↗
Lower secondary completion rate (%)	45.9	2019	●	↗
Literacy rate (% of population aged 15 to 24)	63.9	2017	●	●
SDG5 – Gender Equality				
Demand for family planning satisfied by modern methods (% of females aged 15 to 49)	30.4	2015	●	→
Ratio of female-to-male mean years of education received (%)	67.9	2019	●	↗
Ratio of female-to-male labor force participation rate (%)	44.1	2020	●	↓
Seats held by women in national parliament (%)	20.3	2020	●	↓
SDG6 – Clean Water and Sanitation				
Population using at least basic drinking water services (%)	71.7	2020	●	→
Population using at least basic sanitation services (%)	49.8	2020	●	→
Freshwater withdrawal (% of available freshwater resources)	13.3	2018	●	●
Anthropogenic wastewater that receives treatment (%)	0.0	2018	●	●
Scarce water consumption embodied in imports (m^3 H_2O eq/capita)	709.4	2018	●	●
SDG7 – Affordable and Clean Energy				
Population with access to electricity (%)	45.8	2019	●	→
Population with access to clean fuels and technology for cooking (%)	43.4	2019	●	↓
CO_2 emissions from fuel combustion per total electricity output ($MtCO_2$/TWh)	1.9	2019	●	↑
Share of renewable energy in total primary energy supply (%)	NA	NA	●	●
SDG8 – Decent Work and Economic Growth				
Adjusted GDP growth (%)	-3.8	2020	●	●
Victims of modern slavery (per 1,000 population)	21.4	2018	●	●
Adults with an account at a bank or other financial institution or with a mobile-money-service provider (% of population aged 15 or over)	20.9	2017	●	↓
Unemployment rate (% of total labor force)	11.2	2022	●	↓
Fundamental labor rights are effectively guaranteed (worst 0–1 best)	0.5	2020	●	●
Fatal work-related accidents embodied in imports (per 100,000 population)	0.1	2015	●	↑

SDG9 – Industry, Innovation and Infrastructure	Value	Year	Rating	Trend
Population using the internet (%)	40.8	2020	●	↑
Mobile broadband subscriptions (per 100 population)	55.5	2019	●	↑
Logistics Performance Index: Quality of trade and transport-related infrastructure (worst 1–5 best)	2.3	2018	●	↓
The Times Higher Education Universities Ranking: Average score of top 3 universities (worst 0–100 best) *	0.0	2022	●	●
Articles published in academic journals (per 1,000 population)	0.0	2020	●	→
Expenditure on research and development (% of GDP)	0.0	2018	●	●
SDG10 – Reduced Inequalities				
Gini coefficient	32.6	2014	●	●
Palma ratio	1.3	2018	●	●
SDG11 – Sustainable Cities and Communities				
Proportion of urban population living in slums (%)	79.5	2018	●	→
Annual mean concentration of particulate matter of less than 2.5 microns in diameter (PM2.5) (μg/m³)	50.4	2019	●	→
Access to improved water source, piped (% of urban population)	65.5	2020	●	→
Satisfaction with public transport (%)	42.0	2019	●	●
SDG12 – Responsible Consumption and Production				
Municipal solid waste (kg/capita/day)	0.4	2009	●	●
Electronic waste (kg/capita)	1.4	2019	●	●
Production-based SO_2 emissions (kg/capita)	3.0	2018	●	●
SO_2 emissions embodied in imports (kg/capita)	0.5	2018	●	●
Production-based nitrogen emissions (kg/capita)	32.7	2015	●	↓
Nitrogen emissions embodied in imports (kg/capita)	0.9	2015	●	↑
Exports of plastic waste (kg/capita)	0.4	2020	●	●
SDG13 – Climate Action				
CO_2 emissions from fossil fuel combustion and cement production (tCO_2/capita)	0.7	2020	●	↑
CO_2 emissions embodied in imports (tCO_2/capita)	0.2	2018	●	↑
CO_2 emissions embodied in fossil fuel exports (kg/capita)	0.0	2020	●	●
SDG14 – Life Below Water				
Mean area that is protected in marine sites important to biodiversity (%)	37.2	2020	●	→
Ocean Health Index: Clean Waters score (worst 0–100 best)	61.2	2020	●	↓
Fish caught from overexploited or collapsed stocks (% of total catch)	17.6	2018	●	↑
Fish caught by trawling or dredging (%)	6.5	2018	●	↑
Fish caught that are then discarded (%)	7.3	2018	●	↓
Marine biodiversity threats embodied in imports (per million population)	0.1	2018	●	●
SDG15 – Life on Land				
Mean area that is protected in terrestrial sites important to biodiversity (%)	11.2	2020	●	→
Mean area that is protected in freshwater sites important to biodiversity (%)	0.0	2020	●	→
Red List Index of species survival (worst 0–1 best)	1.0	2021	●	↑
Permanent deforestation (% of forest area, 5-year average)	0.0	2020	●	↑
Terrestrial and freshwater biodiversity threats embodied in imports (per million population)	0.1	2018	●	●
SDG16 – Peace, Justice and Strong Institutions				
Homicides (per 100,000 population)	NA	NA	●	●
Unsentenced detainees (% of prison population)	NA	NA	●	●
Population who feel safe walking alone at night in the city or area where they live (%)	51	2019	●	●
Property Rights (worst 1–7 best)	2.8	2020	●	→
Birth registrations with civil authority (% of children under age 5)	65.6	2020	●	●
Corruption Perception Index (worst 0–100 best)	28	2021	●	↓
Children involved in child labor (% of population aged 5 to 14)	14.0	2019	●	●
Exports of major conventional weapons (TIV constant million USD per 100,000 population) *	0.0	2020	●	●
Press Freedom Index (best 0–100 worst)	32.3	2021	●	↓
Access to and affordability of justice (worst 0–1 best)	0.4	2020	●	●
SDG17 – Partnerships for the Goals				
Government spending on health and education (% of GDP)	3.1	2020	●	↓
For high-income and all OECD DAC countries: International concessional public finance, including official development assistance (% of GNI)	NA	NA	●	●
Other countries: Government revenue excluding grants (% of GDP)	NA	NA	●	●
Corporate Tax Haven Score (best 0–100 worst) *	0.0	2019	●	●
Statistical Performance Index (worst 0–100 best)	48.1	2019	●	↑

* Imputed data point

MAURITIUS

Sub-Saharan Africa

OVERALL PERFORMANCE

COUNTRY RANKING

MAURITIUS

89/163

COUNTRY SCORE

REGIONAL AVERAGE: 53.6

AVERAGE PERFORMANCE BY SDG

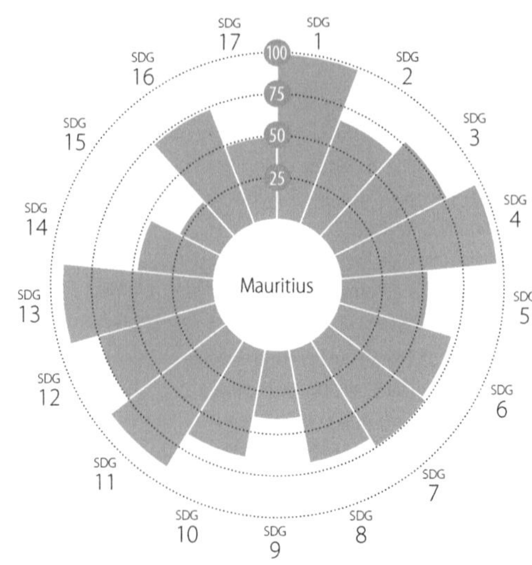

SDG DASHBOARDS AND TRENDS

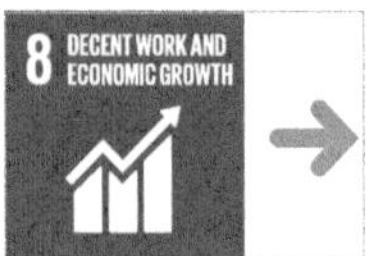

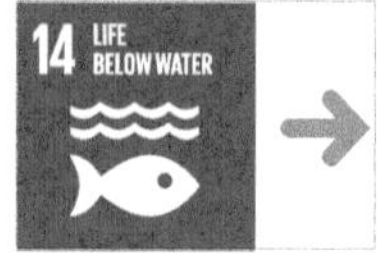

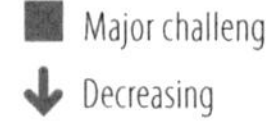

Information unavailable

Information unavailable

Note: The full title of each SDG is available here: https://sustainabledevelopment.un.org/topics/sustainabledevelopmentgoals

INTERNATIONAL SPILLOVER INDEX

STATISTICAL PERFORMANCE INDEX

0 (worst) to 100 (best)

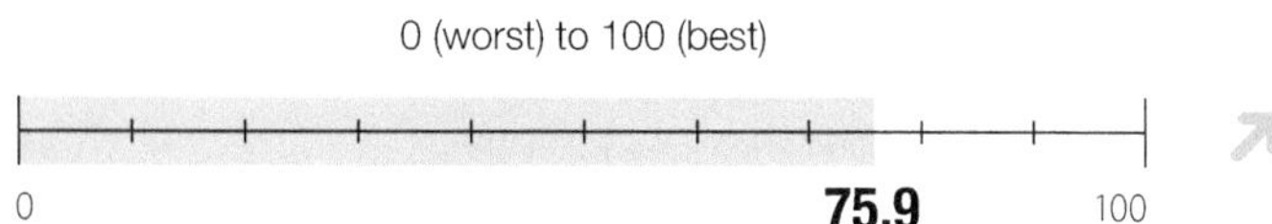

MISSING DATA IN SDG INDEX

11%

MAURITIUS

SDG1 – No Poverty

Indicator	Value	Year	Rating	Trend
Poverty headcount ratio at \$1.90/day (%)	0.3	2022	●	↑
Poverty headcount ratio at \$3.20/day (%)	1.7	2022	●	↑

SDG2 – Zero Hunger

Indicator	Value	Year	Rating	Trend
Prevalence of undernourishment (%)	6.2	2019	●	↑
Prevalence of stunting in children under 5 years of age (%)	NA	NA	●	●
Prevalence of wasting in children under 5 years of age (%)	NA	NA	●	●
Prevalence of obesity, BMI ≥ 30 (% of adult population)	10.8	2016	●	↓
Human Trophic Level (best 2–3 worst)	2.2	2017	●	↑
Cereal yield (tonnes per hectare of harvested land)	5.3	2018	●	↑
Sustainable Nitrogen Management Index (best 0–1.41 worst)	1.1	2015	●	→
Exports of hazardous pesticides (tonnes per million population)	0.0	2019	●	●

SDG3 – Good Health and Well-Being

Indicator	Value	Year	Rating	Trend
Maternal mortality rate (per 100,000 live births)	61	2017	●	↑
Neonatal mortality rate (per 1,000 live births)	10.5	2020	●	↑
Mortality rate, under-5 (per 1,000 live births)	16.5	2020	●	↑
Incidence of tuberculosis (per 100,000 population)	12.0	2020	●	↑
New HIV infections (per 1,000 uninfected population)	0.8	2020	●	→
Age-standardized death rate due to cardiovascular disease, cancer, diabetes, or chronic respiratory disease in adults aged 30–70 years (%)	23.2	2019	●	→
Age-standardized death rate attributable to household air pollution and ambient air pollution (per 100,000 population)	38	2016	●	●
Traffic deaths (per 100,000 population)	12.2	2019	●	↑
Life expectancy at birth (years)	74.1	2019	●	↓
Adolescent fertility rate (births per 1,000 females aged 15 to 19)	23.2	2019	●	↑
Births attended by skilled health personnel (%)	99.8	2017	●	↑
Surviving infants who received 2 WHO-recommended vaccines (%)	89	2020	●	↓
Universal health coverage (UHC) index of service coverage (worst 0–100 best)	65	2019	●	→
Subjective well-being (average ladder score, worst 0–10 best)	5.9	2021	●	↑

SDG4 – Quality Education

Indicator	Value	Year	Rating	Trend
Participation rate in pre-primary organized learning (% of children aged 4 to 6)	90.8	2021	●	↑
Net primary enrollment rate (%)	99.7	2021	●	↑
Lower secondary completion rate (%)	102.6	2020	●	↑
Literacy rate (% of population aged 15 to 24)	99.0	2018	●	●

SDG5 – Gender Equality

Indicator	Value	Year	Rating	Trend
Demand for family planning satisfied by modern methods (% of females aged 15 to 49)	40.8	2014	●	↗
Ratio of female-to-male mean years of education received (%)	96.9	2019	●	↑
Ratio of female-to-male labor force participation rate (%)	61.3	2020	●	↓
Seats held by women in national parliament (%)	20.0	2020	●	↗

SDG6 – Clean Water and Sanitation

Indicator	Value	Year	Rating	Trend
Population using at least basic drinking water services (%)	99.9	2020	●	↑
Population using at least basic sanitation services (%)	95.5	2017	●	●
Freshwater withdrawal (% of available freshwater resources)	21.5	2018	●	●
Anthropogenic wastewater that receives treatment (%)	2.5	2018	●	●
Scarce water consumption embodied in imports (m^3 H_2O eq/capita)	NA	NA	●	●

SDG7 – Affordable and Clean Energy

Indicator	Value	Year	Rating	Trend
Population with access to electricity (%)	100.0	2019	●	↑
Population with access to clean fuels and technology for cooking (%)	100.0	2019	●	↑
CO_2 emissions from fuel combustion per total electricity output ($MtCO_2$/TWh)	1.5	2019	●	→
Share of renewable energy in total primary energy supply (%)	14.2	2019	●	↓

SDG8 – Decent Work and Economic Growth

Indicator	Value	Year	Rating	Trend
Adjusted GDP growth (%)	-4.8	2020	●	●
Victims of modern slavery (per 1,000 population)	1.0	2018	●	●
Adults with an account at a bank or other financial institution or with a mobile-money-service provider (% of population aged 15 or over)	89.8	2017	●	↑
Unemployment rate (% of total labor force)	6.9	2022	●	→
Fundamental labor rights are effectively guaranteed (worst 0–1 best)	0.6	2020	●	●
Fatal work-related accidents embodied in imports (per 100,000 population)	3.3	2015	●	↓

* Imputed data point

SDG9 – Industry, Innovation and Infrastructure

Indicator	Value	Year	Rating	Trend
Population using the internet (%)	64.9	2020	●	↑
Mobile broadband subscriptions (per 100 population)	87.4	2019	●	↑
Logistics Performance Index: Quality of trade and transport-related infrastructure (worst 1–5 best)	2.8	2018	●	↑
The Times Higher Education Universities Ranking: Average score of top 3 universities (worst 0–100 best)	* 0.0	2022	●	●
Articles published in academic journals (per 1,000 population)	0.4	2020	●	↑
Expenditure on research and development (% of GDP)	0.3	2018	●	●

SDG10 – Reduced Inequalities

Indicator	Value	Year	Rating	Trend
Gini coefficient	36.8	2017	●	●
Palma ratio	1.6	2018	●	●

SDG11 – Sustainable Cities and Communities

Indicator	Value	Year	Rating	Trend
Proportion of urban population living in slums (%)	NA	NA	●	●
Annual mean concentration of particulate matter of less than 2.5 microns in diameter (PM2.5) (μg/m³)	14.2	2019	●	→
Access to improved water source, piped (% of urban population)	99.9	2020	●	↑
Satisfaction with public transport (%)	68.0	2021	●	↗

SDG12 – Responsible Consumption and Production

Indicator	Value	Year	Rating	Trend
Municipal solid waste (kg/capita/day)	1.0	2016	●	●
Electronic waste (kg/capita)	10.1	2019	●	●
Production-based SO_2 emissions (kg/capita)	NA	NA	●	●
SO_2 emissions embodied in imports (kg/capita)	NA	NA	●	●
Production-based nitrogen emissions (kg/capita)	8.7	2015	●	↑
Nitrogen emissions embodied in imports (kg/capita)	18.8	2015	●	→
Exports of plastic waste (kg/capita)	1.3	2021	●	●

SDG13 – Climate Action

Indicator	Value	Year	Rating	Trend
CO_2 emissions from fossil fuel combustion and cement production (tCO_2/capita)	3.1	2020	●	→
CO_2 emissions embodied in imports (tCO_2/capita)	NA	NA	●	●
CO_2 emissions embodied in fossil fuel exports (kg/capita)	0.0	2020	●	●

SDG14 – Life Below Water

Indicator	Value	Year	Rating	Trend
Mean area that is protected in marine sites important to biodiversity (%)	11.1	2020	●	→
Ocean Health Index: Clean Waters score (worst 0–100 best)	65.2	2020	●	↓
Fish caught from overexploited or collapsed stocks (% of total catch)	71.9	2018	●	↓
Fish caught by trawling or dredging (%)	1.2	2018	●	↑
Fish caught that are then discarded (%)	2.5	2018	●	↑
Marine biodiversity threats embodied in imports (per million population)	1.8	2018	●	●

SDG15 – Life on Land

Indicator	Value	Year	Rating	Trend
Mean area that is protected in terrestrial sites important to biodiversity (%)	9.6	2020	●	→
Mean area that is protected in freshwater sites important to biodiversity (%)	NA	NA	●	●
Red List Index of species survival (worst 0–1 best)	0.4	2021	●	↓
Permanent deforestation (% of forest area, 5-year average)	0.0	2020	●	↑
Terrestrial and freshwater biodiversity threats embodied in imports (per million population)	22.1	2018	●	●

SDG16 – Peace, Justice and Strong Institutions

Indicator	Value	Year	Rating	Trend
Homicides (per 100,000 population)	2.9	2018	●	→
Unsentenced detainees (% of prison population)	43.5	2018	●	↓
Population who feel safe walking alone at night in the city or area where they live (%)	68	2021	●	↑
Property Rights (worst 1–7 best)	5.4	2020	●	↑
Birth registrations with civil authority (% of children under age 5)	NA	NA	●	●
Corruption Perception Index (worst 0–100 best)	54	2021	●	→
Children involved in child labor (% of population aged 5 to 14)	NA	NA	●	●
Exports of major conventional weapons (TIV constant million USD per 100,000 population)	* 0.0	2020	●	●
Press Freedom Index (best 0–100 worst)	28.7	2021	●	↑
Access to and affordability of justice (worst 0–1 best)	0.6	2020	●	●

SDG17 – Partnerships for the Goals

Indicator	Value	Year	Rating	Trend
Government spending on health and education (% of GDP)	7.5	2020	●	→
For high-income and all OECD DAC countries: International concessional public finance, including official development assistance (% of GNI)	NA	NA	●	●
Other countries: Government revenue excluding grants (% of GDP)	23.0	2019	●	↑
Corporate Tax Haven Score (best 0–100 worst)	79.8	2019	●	●
Statistical Performance Index (worst 0–100 best)	75.9	2019	●	↗

MEXICO

OECD Countries

OVERALL PERFORMANCE

COUNTRY RANKING

MEXICO

74 **/163**

COUNTRY SCORE

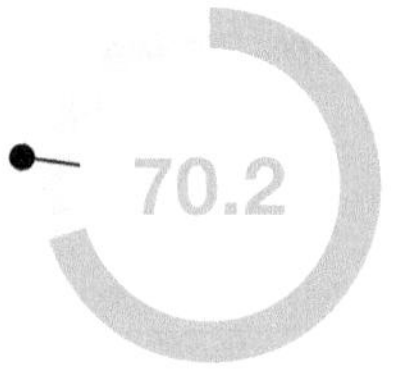

REGIONAL AVERAGE: 77.2

AVERAGE PERFORMANCE BY SDG

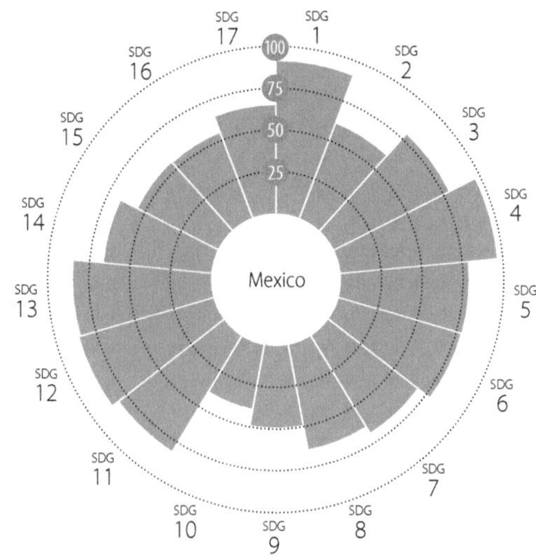

SDG DASHBOARDS AND TRENDS

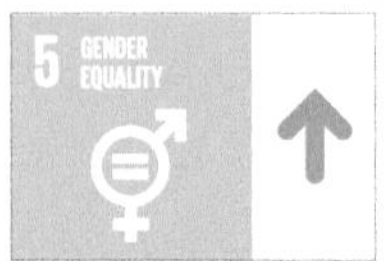

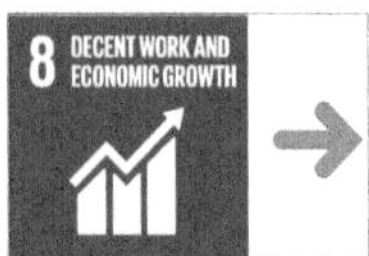

Major challenges · Significant challenges · Challenges remain · SDG achieved · Information unavailable

Decreasing · Stagnating · Moderately improving · On track or maintaining SDG achievement · Information unavailable

Note: The full title of each SDG is available here: https://sustainabledevelopment.un.org/topics/sustainabledevelopmentgoals

INTERNATIONAL SPILLOVER INDEX

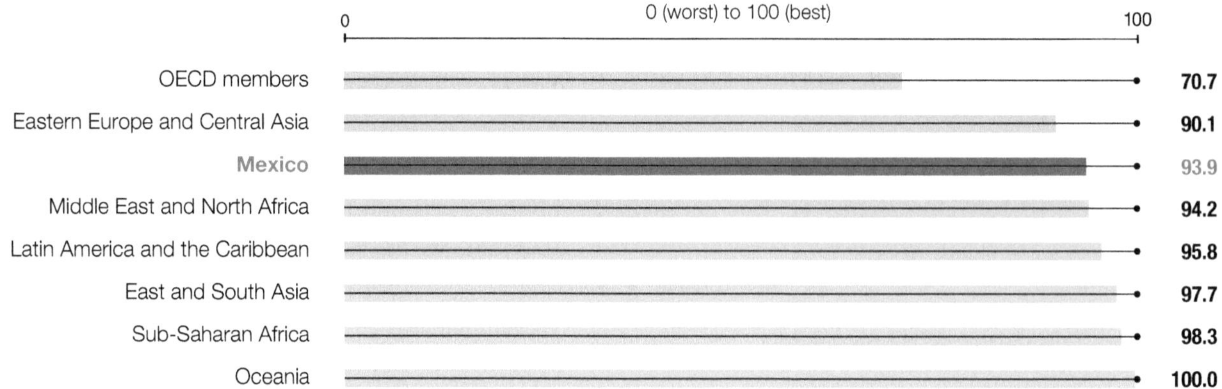

STATISTICAL PERFORMANCE INDEX

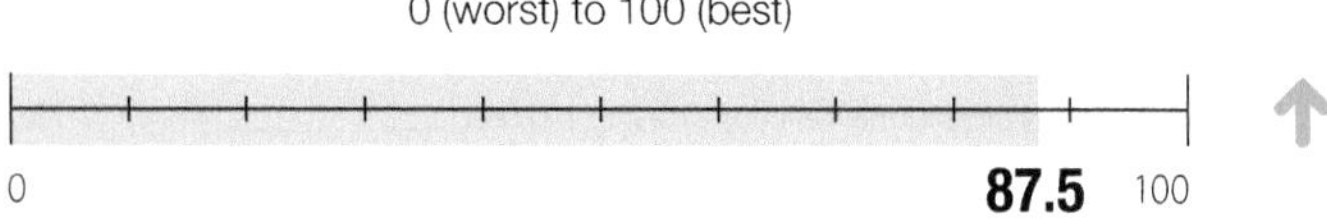

MISSING DATA IN SDG INDEX

0%

MEXICO

Performance by Indicator

SDG1 – No Poverty	Value	Year	Rating	Trend
Poverty headcount ratio at $1.90/day (%)	1.5	2022	●	↑
Poverty headcount ratio at $3.20/day (%)	8.4	2022	●	↗
Poverty rate after taxes and transfers (%)	15.9	2018	●	↗

SDG2 – Zero Hunger	Value	Year	Rating	Trend
Prevalence of undernourishment (%)	7.2	2019	●	↑
Prevalence of stunting in children under 5 years of age (%)	14.1	2019	●	↗
Prevalence of wasting in children under 5 years of age (%)	1.4	2019	●	↑
Prevalence of obesity, BMI ≥ 30 (% of adult population)	28.9	2016	●	↓
Human Trophic Level (best 2–3 worst)	2.3	2017	●	→
Cereal yield (tonnes per hectare of harvested land)	3.8	2018	●	↑
Sustainable Nitrogen Management Index (best 0–1.41 worst)	0.8	2015	●	↓
Yield gap closure (% of potential yield)	NA	NA	●	●
Exports of hazardous pesticides (tonnes per million population)	0.2	2019	●	●

SDG3 – Good Health and Well-Being	Value	Year	Rating	Trend
Maternal mortality rate (per 100,000 live births)	33	2017	●	↑
Neonatal mortality rate (per 1,000 live births)	8.4	2020	●	↑
Mortality rate, under-5 (per 1,000 live births)	13.7	2020	●	↑
Incidence of tuberculosis (per 100,000 population)	24.0	2020	●	↓
New HIV infections (per 1,000 uninfected population)	0.2	2020	●	↑
Age-standardized death rate due to cardiovascular disease, cancer, diabetes, or chronic respiratory disease in adults aged 30–70 years (%)	15.6	2019	●	→
Age-standardized death rate attributable to household air pollution and ambient air pollution (per 100,000 population)	37	2016	●	●
Traffic deaths (per 100,000 population)	12.8	2019	●	↗
Life expectancy at birth (years)	76.0	2019	●	→
Adolescent fertility rate (births per 1,000 females aged 15 to 19)	62.0	2017	●	●
Births attended by skilled health personnel (%)	96.4	2016	●	●
Surviving infants who received 2 WHO-recommended vaccines (%)	74	2020	●	↓
Universal health coverage (UHC) index of service coverage (worst 0–100 best)	74	2019	●	↗
Subjective well-being (average ladder score, worst 0–10 best)	6.0	2021	●	↑
Gap in life expectancy at birth among regions (years)	3.7	2016	●	●
Gap in self-reported health status by income (percentage points)	NA	NA	●	●
Daily smokers (% of population aged 15 and over)	7.6	2017	●	●

SDG4 – Quality Education	Value	Year	Rating	Trend
Participation rate in pre-primary organized learning (% of children aged 4 to 6)	99.1	2019	●	↑
Net primary enrollment rate (%)	99.2	2019	●	↑
Lower secondary completion rate (%)	90.7	2019	●	↑
Literacy rate (% of population aged 15 to 24)	99.1	2020	●	↑
Tertiary educational attainment (% of population aged 25 to 34)	25.3	2020	●	↗
PISA score (worst 0–600 best)	416.0	2018	●	→
Variation in science performance explained by socio-economic status (%)	12.1	2018	●	↓
Underachievers in science (% of 15-year-olds)	46.8	2018	●	→

SDG5 – Gender Equality	Value	Year	Rating	Trend
Demand for family planning satisfied by modern methods (% of females aged 15 to 49)	79.8	2015	●	↑
Ratio of female-to-male mean years of education received (%)	96.6	2019	●	↑
Ratio of female-to-male labor force participation rate (%)	57.2	2020	●	→
Seats held by women in national parliament (%)	48.2	2020	●	↑
Gender wage gap (% of male median wage)	9.6	2020	●	↑

SDG6 – Clean Water and Sanitation	Value	Year	Rating	Trend
Population using at least basic drinking water services (%)	99.7	2020	●	↑
Population using at least basic sanitation services (%)	92.4	2020	●	↑
Freshwater withdrawal (% of available freshwater resources)	33.3	2018	●	●
Anthropogenic wastewater that receives treatment (%)	31.6	2018	●	●
Scarce water consumption embodied in imports (m^3 H_2O eq/capita)	1348.1	2018	●	●
Population using safely managed water services (%)	43.0	2020	●	→
Population using safely managed sanitation services (%)	57.3	2020	●	↗

SDG7 – Affordable and Clean Energy	Value	Year	Rating	Trend
Population with access to electricity (%)	100.0	2019	●	↑
Population with access to clean fuels and technology for cooking (%)	84.8	2019	●	↑
CO_2 emissions from fuel combustion per total electricity output ($MtCO_2$/TWh)	1.3	2019	●	↑
Share of renewable energy in total primary energy supply (%)	8.6	2019	●	→

SDG8 – Decent Work and Economic Growth	Value	Year	Rating	Trend
Adjusted GDP growth (%)	-5.8	2020	●	●
Victims of modern slavery (per 1,000 population)	2.7	2018	●	●
Adults with an account at a bank or other financial institution or with a mobile-money-service provider (% of population aged 15 or over)	36.9	2017	●	↓
Fundamental labor rights are effectively guaranteed (worst 0–1 best)	0.5	2020	●	→
Fatal work-related accidents embodied in imports (per 100,000 population)	0.2	2015	●	↑
Employment-to-population ratio (%)	61.0	2021	●	↑
Youth not in employment, education or training (NEET) (% of population aged 15 to 29)	22.1	2020	●	↓

SDG9 – Industry, Innovation and Infrastructure	Value	Year	Rating	Trend
Population using the internet (%)	72.0	2020	●	↑
Mobile broadband subscriptions (per 100 population)	76.4	2019	●	↑
Logistics Performance Index: Quality of trade and transport-related infrastructure (worst 1–5 best)	2.8	2018	●	↓
The Times Higher Education Universities Ranking: Average score of top 3 universities (worst 0–100 best)	31.4	2022	●	●
Articles published in academic journals (per 1,000 population)	0.2	2020	●	→
Expenditure on research and development (% of GDP)	0.3	2018	●	↓
Researchers (per 1,000 employed population)	1.2	2020	●	→
Triadic patent families filed (per million population)	0.2	2019	●	↓
Gap in internet access by income (percentage points)	59.8	2012	●	●
Female share of graduates from STEM fields at the tertiary level (%)	30.6	2017	●	↑

SDG10 – Reduced Inequalities	Value	Year	Rating	Trend
Gini coefficient	45.4	2018	●	→
Palma ratio	2.0	2018	●	↑
Elderly poverty rate (% of population aged 66 or over)	26.6	2018	●	↓

SDG11 – Sustainable Cities and Communities	Value	Year	Rating	Trend
Proportion of urban population living in slums (%)	15.1	2018	●	↓
Annual mean concentration of particulate matter of less than 2.5 microns in diameter (PM2.5) (μg/m^3)	19.0	2019	●	↗
Access to improved water source, piped (% of urban population)	99.1	2020	●	↑
Satisfaction with public transport (%)	57.0	2021	●	→
Population with rent overburden (%)	4.1	2018	●	↑

SDG12 – Responsible Consumption and Production	Value	Year	Rating	Trend
Electronic waste (kg/capita)	9.7	2019	●	●
Production-based SO_2 emissions (kg/capita)	9.7	2018	●	●
SO_2 emissions embodied in imports (kg/capita)	2.4	2018	●	●
Production-based nitrogen emissions (kg/capita)	12.1	2015	●	↑
Nitrogen emissions embodied in imports (kg/capita)	3.1	2015	●	↑
Exports of plastic waste (kg/capita)	0.0	2021	●	●
Non-recycled municipal solid waste (kg/capita/day)	0.9	2012	●	●

SDG13 – Climate Action	Value	Year	Rating	Trend
CO_2 emissions from fossil fuel combustion and cement production (tCO_2/capita)	2.8	2020	●	↑
CO_2 emissions embodied in imports (tCO_2/capita)	0.9	2018	●	↗
CO_2 emissions embodied in fossil fuel exports (kg/capita)	1315.7	2021	●	●
Carbon Pricing Score at EUR60/tCO_2 (%, worst 0–100 best)	30.4	2018	●	↓

SDG14 – Life Below Water	Value	Year	Rating	Trend
Mean area that is protected in marine sites important to biodiversity (%)	61.9	2020	●	→
Ocean Health Index: Clean Waters score (worst 0–100 best)	64.5	2020	●	→
Fish caught from overexploited or collapsed stocks (% of total catch)	17.3	2018	●	↑
Fish caught by trawling or dredging (%)	15.3	2018	●	↓
Fish caught that are then discarded (%)	15.3	2018	●	↑
Marine biodiversity threats embodied in imports (per million population)	0.0	2018	●	●

SDG15 – Life on Land	Value	Year	Rating	Trend
Mean area that is protected in terrestrial sites important to biodiversity (%)	36.2	2020	●	→
Mean area that is protected in freshwater sites important to biodiversity (%)	50.0	2020	●	→
Red List Index of species survival (worst 0–1 best)	0.7	2021	●	↓
Permanent deforestation (% of forest area, 5-year average)	0.3	2020	●	↓
Terrestrial and freshwater biodiversity threats embodied in imports (per million population)	0.7	2018	●	●

SDG16 – Peace, Justice and Strong Institutions	Value	Year	Rating	Trend
Homicides (per 100,000 population)	28.4	2020	●	↓
Unsentenced detainees (% of prison population)	35.7	2019	●	↓
Population who feel safe walking alone at night in the city or area where they live (%)	46	2021	●	→
Property Rights (worst 1–7 best)	3.9	2020	●	↓
Birth registrations with civil authority (% of children under age 5)	95.0	2020	●	●
Corruption Perception Index (worst 0–100 best)	31	2021	●	→
Children involved in child labor (% of population aged 5 to 14)	4.7	2019	●	●
Exports of major conventional weapons (TIV constant million USD per 100,000 population)	0.0	2020	●	●
Press Freedom Index (best 0–100 worst)	46.7	2021	●	→
Access to and affordability of justice (worst 0–1 best)	0.4	2020	●	↓
Persons held in prison (per 100,000 population)	155.8	2019	●	→

SDG17 – Partnerships for the Goals	Value	Year	Rating	Trend
Government spending on health and education (% of GDP)	6.9	2019	●	↓
For high-income and all OECD DAC countries: International concessional public finance, including official development assistance (% of GNI)	NA	NA	●	●
Other countries: Government revenue excluding grants (% of GDP)	18.6	2019	●	↓
Corporate Tax Haven Score (best 0–100 worst)	* 0.0	2019	●	●
Financial Secrecy Score (best 0–100 worst)	52.8	2020	●	●
Shifted profits of multinationals (US$ billion)	16.7	2018	●	↑
Statistical Performance Index (worst 0–100 best)	87.5	2019	●	↑

* Imputed data point

MICRONESIA, FEDERATED STATES OF Oceania

OVERALL PERFORMANCE

COUNTRY RANKING

MICRONESIA, FEDERATED STATES OF

NA /163

COUNTRY SCORE

na

AVERAGE PERFORMANCE BY SDG

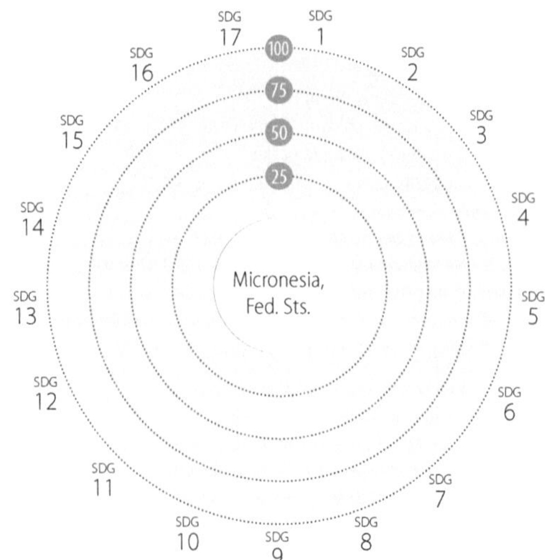

SDG DASHBOARDS AND TRENDS

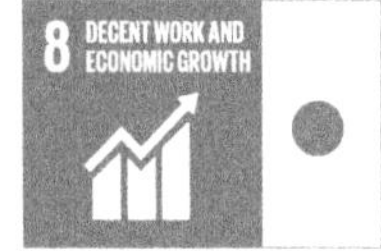

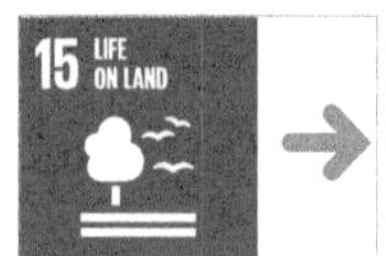

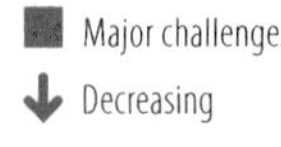

Major challenges | Significant challenges | Challenges remain | SDG achieved | Information unavailable

Decreasing | Stagnating | Moderately improving | On track or maintaining SDG achievement | Information unavailable

Note: The full title of each SDG is available here: https://sustainabledevelopment.un.org/topics/sustainabledevelopmentgoals

INTERNATIONAL SPILLOVER INDEX

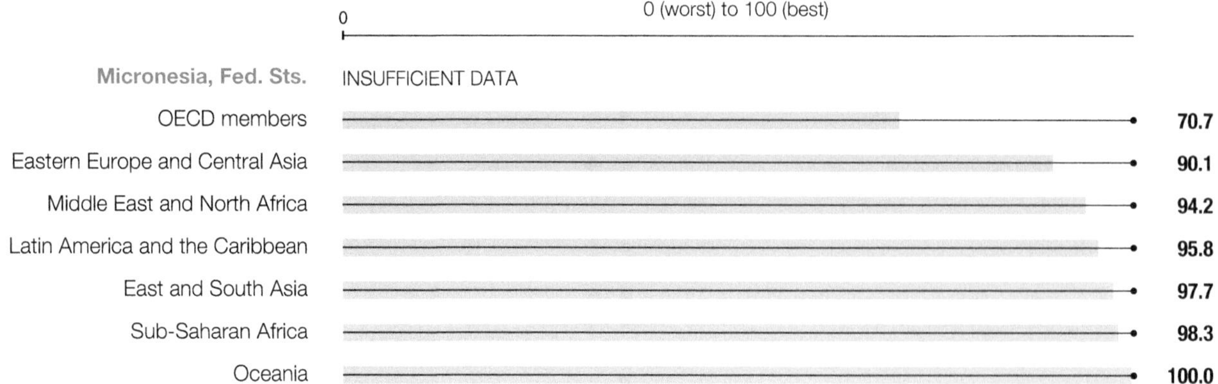

STATISTICAL PERFORMANCE INDEX

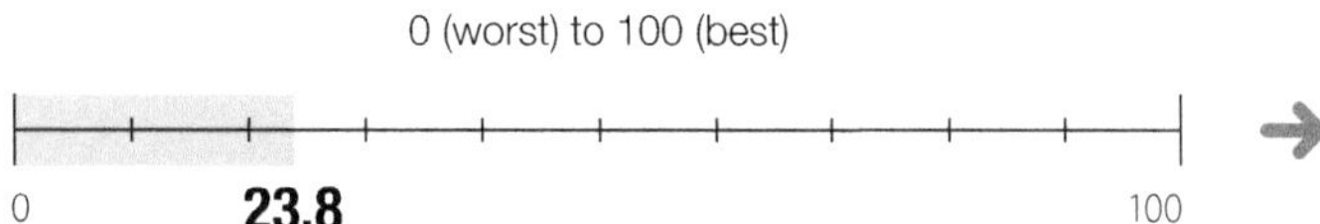

MISSING DATA IN SDG INDEX

47%

MICRONESIA, FEDERATED STATES OF

Performance by Indicator

SDG1 – No Poverty	Value	Year	Rating	Trend
Poverty headcount ratio at \$1.90/day (%)	NA	NA	●	●
Poverty headcount ratio at \$3.20/day (%)	NA	NA	●	●
SDG2 – Zero Hunger				
Prevalence of undernourishment (%)	NA	NA	●	●
Prevalence of stunting in children under 5 years of age (%)	NA	NA	●	●
Prevalence of wasting in children under 5 years of age (%)	NA	NA	●	●
Prevalence of obesity, BMI ≥ 30 (% of adult population)	45.8	2016	●	↓
Human Trophic Level (best 2–3 worst)	NA	NA	●	●
Cereal yield (tonnes per hectare of harvested land)	1.8	2018	●	↗
Sustainable Nitrogen Management Index (best 0–1.41 worst)	1.1	2015	●	→
Exports of hazardous pesticides (tonnes per million population)	NA	NA	●	●
SDG3 – Good Health and Well-Being				
Maternal mortality rate (per 100,000 live births)	88	2017	●	↑
Neonatal mortality rate (per 1,000 live births)	12.9	2020	●	↑
Mortality rate, under-5 (per 1,000 live births)	24.7	2020	●	↑
Incidence of tuberculosis (per 100,000 population)	75.0	2020	●	↑
New HIV infections (per 1,000 uninfected population)	NA	NA	●	●
Age-standardized death rate due to cardiovascular disease, cancer, diabetes, or chronic respiratory disease in adults aged 30–70 years (%)	46.3	2019	●	↓
Age-standardized death rate attributable to household air pollution and ambient air pollution (per 100,000 population)	152	2016	●	●
Traffic deaths (per 100,000 population)	0.2	2019	●	↑
Life expectancy at birth (years)	63.0	2019	●	→
Adolescent fertility rate (births per 1,000 females aged 15 to 19)	44.0	2009	●	●
Births attended by skilled health personnel (%)	100.0	2009	●	●
Surviving infants who received 2 WHO-recommended vaccines (%)	79	2020	●	↑
Universal health coverage (UHC) index of service coverage (worst 0–100 best)	48	2019	●	→
Subjective well-being (average ladder score, worst 0–10 best)	NA	NA	●	●
SDG4 – Quality Education				
Participation rate in pre-primary organized learning (% of children aged 4 to 6)	68.0	2019	●	↓
Net primary enrollment rate (%)	83.3	2020	●	↓
Lower secondary completion rate (%)	79.5	2019	●	↓
Literacy rate (% of population aged 15 to 24)	NA	NA	●	●
SDG5 – Gender Equality				
Demand for family planning satisfied by modern methods (% of females aged 15 to 49)	NA	NA	●	●
Ratio of female-to-male mean years of education received (%)	NA	NA	●	●
Ratio of female-to-male labor force participation rate (%)	NA	NA	●	●
Seats held by women in national parliament (%)	0.0	2020	●	→
SDG6 – Clean Water and Sanitation				
Population using at least basic drinking water services (%)	88.3	2019	●	→
Population using at least basic sanitation services (%)	88.3	2019	●	→
Freshwater withdrawal (% of available freshwater resources)	NA	NA	●	●
Anthropogenic wastewater that receives treatment (%)	0.1	2018	●	●
Scarce water consumption embodied in imports (m^3 H_2O eq/capita)	NA	NA	●	●
SDG7 – Affordable and Clean Energy				
Population with access to electricity (%)	82.1	2019	●	↑
Population with access to clean fuels and technology for cooking (%)	12.5	2019	●	→
CO_2 emissions from fuel combustion per total electricity output ($MtCO_2$/TWh)	NA	NA	●	●
Share of renewable energy in total primary energy supply (%)	NA	NA	●	●
SDG8 – Decent Work and Economic Growth				
Adjusted GDP growth (%)	-5.6	2020	●	●
Victims of modern slavery (per 1,000 population)	NA	NA	●	●
Adults with an account at a bank or other financial institution or with a mobile-money-service provider (% of population aged 15 or over)	NA	NA	●	●
Unemployment rate (% of total labor force)	NA	NA	●	●
Fundamental labor rights are effectively guaranteed (worst 0–1 best)	NA	NA	●	●
Fatal work-related accidents embodied in imports (per 100,000 population)	NA	NA	●	●

* Imputed data point

SDG9 – Industry, Innovation and Infrastructure	Value	Year	Rating	Trend
Population using the internet (%)	35.3	2017	●	●
Mobile broadband subscriptions (per 100 population)	0.0	2017	●	●
Logistics Performance Index: Quality of trade and transport-related infrastructure (worst 1–5 best)	NA	NA	●	●
The Times Higher Education Universities Ranking: Average score of top 3 universities (worst 0–100 best)	* 0.0	2022	●	●
Articles published in academic journals (per 1,000 population)	0.3	2020	●	↗
Expenditure on research and development (% of GDP)	NA	NA	●	●
SDG10 – Reduced Inequalities				
Gini coefficient	40.1	2013	●	●
Palma ratio	1.8	2018	●	●
SDG11 – Sustainable Cities and Communities				
Proportion of urban population living in slums (%)	NA	NA	●	●
Annual mean concentration of particulate matter of less than 2.5 microns in diameter (PM2.5) (μg/m³)	10.7	2019	●	↑
Access to improved water source, piped (% of urban population)	NA	NA	●	●
Satisfaction with public transport (%)	NA	NA	●	●
SDG12 – Responsible Consumption and Production				
Municipal solid waste (kg/capita/day)	0.6	2016	●	●
Electronic waste (kg/capita)	1.9	2019	●	●
Production-based SO_2 emissions (kg/capita)	NA	NA	●	●
SO_2 emissions embodied in imports (kg/capita)	NA	NA	●	●
Production-based nitrogen emissions (kg/capita)	NA	NA	●	●
Nitrogen emissions embodied in imports (kg/capita)	NA	NA	●	●
Exports of plastic waste (kg/capita)	NA	NA	●	●
SDG13 – Climate Action				
CO_2 emissions from fossil fuel combustion and cement production (tCO_2/capita)	1.3	2020	●	↑
CO_2 emissions embodied in imports (tCO_2/capita)	NA	NA	●	●
CO_2 emissions embodied in fossil fuel exports (kg/capita)	0.0	2020	●	●
SDG14 – Life Below Water				
Mean area that is protected in marine sites important to biodiversity (%)	1.6	2020	●	→
Ocean Health Index: Clean Waters score (worst 0–100 best)	63.6	2020	●	↗
Fish caught from overexploited or collapsed stocks (% of total catch)	97.2	2018	●	↓
Fish caught by trawling or dredging (%)	0.0	2018	●	↑
Fish caught that are then discarded (%)	3.4	2018	●	↑
Marine biodiversity threats embodied in imports (per million population)	NA	NA	●	●
SDG15 – Life on Land				
Mean area that is protected in terrestrial sites important to biodiversity (%)	0.0	2020	●	→
Mean area that is protected in freshwater sites important to biodiversity (%)	NA	NA	●	●
Red List Index of species survival (worst 0–1 best)	0.6	2021	●	↓
Permanent deforestation (% of forest area, 5-year average)	0.0	2020	●	↑
Terrestrial and freshwater biodiversity threats embodied in imports (per million population)	NA	NA	●	●
SDG16 – Peace, Justice and Strong Institutions				
Homicides (per 100,000 population)	0.9	2019	●	●
Unsentenced detainees (% of prison population)	NA	NA	●	●
Population who feel safe walking alone at night in the city or area where they live (%)	NA	NA	●	●
Property Rights (worst 1–7 best)	NA	NA	●	●
Birth registrations with civil authority (% of children under age 5)	NA	NA	●	●
Corruption Perception Index (worst 0–100 best)	NA	NA	●	●
Children involved in child labor (% of population aged 5 to 14)	NA	NA	●	●
Exports of major conventional weapons (TIV constant million USD per 100,000 population)	* 0.0	2020	●	●
Press Freedom Index (best 0–100 worst)	NA	NA	●	●
Access to and affordability of justice (worst 0–1 best)	NA	NA	●	●
SDG17 – Partnerships for the Goals				
Government spending on health and education (% of GDP)	12.9	2019	●	↑
For high-income and all OECD DAC countries: International concessional public finance, including official development assistance (% of GNI)	NA	NA	●	●
Other countries: Government revenue excluding grants (% of GDP)	38.7	2019	●	↑
Corporate Tax Haven Score (best 0–100 worst)	* 0.0	2019	●	●
Statistical Performance Index (worst 0–100 best)	23.8	2019	●	→

MOLDOVA

Eastern Europe and Central Asia

OVERALL PERFORMANCE

COUNTRY RANKING

MOLDOVA

46/163

COUNTRY SCORE

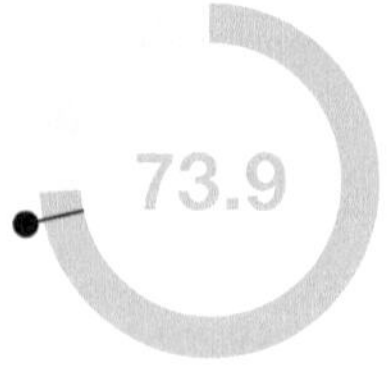

REGIONAL AVERAGE: 71.6

AVERAGE PERFORMANCE BY SDG

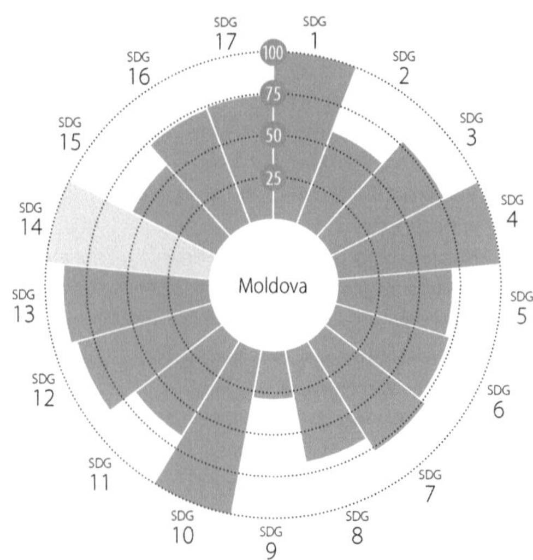

SDG DASHBOARDS AND TRENDS

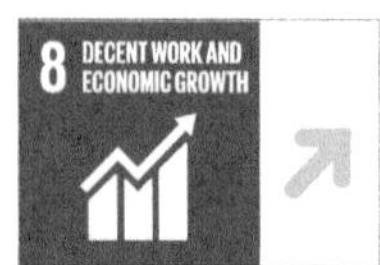

 Major challenges
 Significant challenges
 Challenges remain
 SDG achieved
Information unavailable

Decreasing · Stagnating · Moderately improving · On track or maintaining SDG achievement · Information unavailable

Note: The full title of each SDG is available here: https://sustainabledevelopment.un.org/topics/sustainabledevelopmentgoals

INTERNATIONAL SPILLOVER INDEX

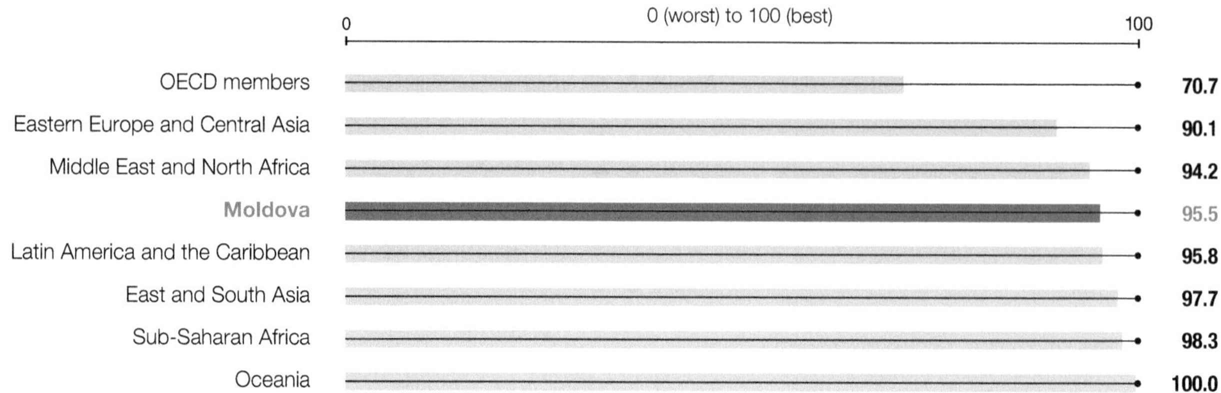

STATISTICAL PERFORMANCE INDEX

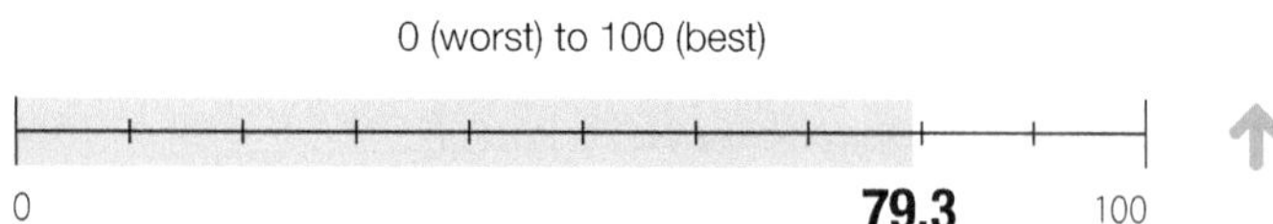

MISSING DATA IN SDG INDEX

3%

MOLDOVA

Performance by Indicator

SDG1 – No Poverty

	Value	Year	Rating	Trend
Poverty headcount ratio at \$1.90/day (%)	0.1	2022	●	↑
Poverty headcount ratio at \$3.20/day (%)	0.4	2022	●	↑

SDG2 – Zero Hunger

	Value	Year	Rating	Trend
Prevalence of undernourishment (%)	NA	NA	●	●
Prevalence of stunting in children under 5 years of age (%)	6.4	2012	●	↑
Prevalence of wasting in children under 5 years of age (%)	1.9	2012	●	↑
Prevalence of obesity, BMI ≥ 30 (% of adult population)	18.9	2016	●	↓
Human Trophic Level (best 2–3 worst)	2.4	2017	●	→
Cereal yield (tonnes per hectare of harvested land)	3.7	2018	●	↑
Sustainable Nitrogen Management Index (best 0–1.41 worst)	0.6	2015	●	↓
Exports of hazardous pesticides (tonnes per million population)	NA	NA	●	●

SDG3 – Good Health and Well-Being

	Value	Year	Rating	Trend
Maternal mortality rate (per 100,000 live births)	19	2017	●	↑
Neonatal mortality rate (per 1,000 live births)	10.6	2020	●	↑
Mortality rate, under-5 (per 1,000 live births)	14.5	2020	●	↑
Incidence of tuberculosis (per 100,000 population)	74.0	2020	●	↗
New HIV infections (per 1,000 uninfected population)	0.2	2020	●	↑
Age-standardized death rate due to cardiovascular disease, cancer, diabetes, or chronic respiratory disease in adults aged 30–70 years (%)	24.1	2019	●	↗
Age-standardized death rate attributable to household air pollution and ambient air pollution (per 100,000 population)	78	2016	●	●
Traffic deaths (per 100,000 population)	7.3	2019	●	↑
Life expectancy at birth (years)	73.3	2019	●	↗
Adolescent fertility rate (births per 1,000 females aged 15 to 19)	21.4	2018	●	↑
Births attended by skilled health personnel (%)	99.7	2018	●	↑
Surviving infants who received 2 WHO-recommended vaccines (%)	84	2020	●	↓
Universal health coverage (UHC) index of service coverage (worst 0–100 best)	67	2019	●	↗
Subjective well-being (average ladder score, worst 0–10 best)	6.0	2021	●	↑

SDG4 – Quality Education

	Value	Year	Rating	Trend
Participation rate in pre-primary organized learning (% of children aged 4 to 6)	99.7	2020	●	↑
Net primary enrollment rate (%)	99.2	2020	●	↑
Lower secondary completion rate (%)	106.7	2020	●	↑
Literacy rate (% of population aged 15 to 24)	99.8	2014	●	●

SDG5 – Gender Equality

	Value	Year	Rating	Trend
Demand for family planning satisfied by modern methods (% of females aged 15 to 49)	63.9	2020	●	→
Ratio of female-to-male mean years of education received (%)	101.7	2019	●	↑
Ratio of female-to-male labor force participation rate (%)	80.2	2020	●	↑
Seats held by women in national parliament (%)	24.8	2020	●	→

SDG6 – Clean Water and Sanitation

	Value	Year	Rating	Trend
Population using at least basic drinking water services (%)	90.6	2020	●	↗
Population using at least basic sanitation services (%)	78.7	2020	●	→
Freshwater withdrawal (% of available freshwater resources)	12.4	2018	●	●
Anthropogenic wastewater that receives treatment (%)	9.0	2018	●	●
Scarce water consumption embodied in imports (m^3 H_2O eq/capita)	1055.4	2018	●	●

SDG7 – Affordable and Clean Energy

	Value	Year	Rating	Trend
Population with access to electricity (%)	100.0	2019	●	↑
Population with access to clean fuels and technology for cooking (%)	95.7	2019	●	↑
CO_2 emissions from fuel combustion per total electricity output ($MtCO_2$/TWh)	1.0	2019	●	↓
Share of renewable energy in total primary energy supply (%)	17.0	2019	●	↓

SDG8 – Decent Work and Economic Growth

	Value	Year	Rating	Trend
Adjusted GDP growth (%)	-0.6	2020	●	●
Victims of modern slavery (per 1,000 population)	5.5	2018	●	●
Adults with an account at a bank or other financial institution or with a mobile-money-service provider (% of population aged 15 or over)	43.8	2017	●	↑
Unemployment rate (% of total labor force)	3.7	2022	●	↑
Fundamental labor rights are effectively guaranteed (worst 0–1 best)	0.5	2020	●	↓
Fatal work-related accidents embodied in imports (per 100,000 population)	0.0	2015	●	↑

* Imputed data point

SDG9 – Industry, Innovation and Infrastructure

	Value	Year	Rating	Trend
Population using the internet (%)	76.1	2017	●	●
Mobile broadband subscriptions (per 100 population)	58.9	2019	●	↑
Logistics Performance Index: Quality of trade and transport-related infrastructure (worst 1–5 best)	2.0	2018	●	↓
The Times Higher Education Universities Ranking: Average score of top 3 universities (worst 0–100 best)	* 0.0	2022	●	●
Articles published in academic journals (per 1,000 population)	0.1	2020	●	→
Expenditure on research and development (% of GDP)	0.3	2018	●	↓

SDG10 – Reduced Inequalities

	Value	Year	Rating	Trend
Gini coefficient	25.7	2018	●	↑
Palma ratio	0.9	2018	●	●

SDG11 – Sustainable Cities and Communities

	Value	Year	Rating	Trend
Proportion of urban population living in slums (%)	70.4	2018	●	●
Annual mean concentration of particulate matter of less than 2.5 microns in diameter (PM2.5) (μg/m^3)	15.8	2019	●	↗
Access to improved water source, piped (% of urban population)	93.0	2020	●	↑
Satisfaction with public transport (%)	60.0	2021	●	↑

SDG12 – Responsible Consumption and Production

	Value	Year	Rating	Trend
Municipal solid waste (kg/capita/day)	2.7	2015	●	●
Electronic waste (kg/capita)	4.0	2019	●	●
Production-based SO_2 emissions (kg/capita)	1.1	2018	●	●
SO_2 emissions embodied in imports (kg/capita)	2.2	2018	●	●
Production-based nitrogen emissions (kg/capita)	8.4	2015	●	↑
Nitrogen emissions embodied in imports (kg/capita)	0.1	2015	●	↑
Exports of plastic waste (kg/capita)	0.1	2020	●	●

SDG13 – Climate Action

	Value	Year	Rating	Trend
CO_2 emissions from fossil fuel combustion and cement production (tCO_2/capita)	1.3	2020	●	↑
CO_2 emissions embodied in imports (tCO_2/capita)	0.9	2018	●	↓
CO_2 emissions embodied in fossil fuel exports (kg/capita)	0.0	2020	●	●

SDG14 – Life Below Water

	Value	Year	Rating	Trend
Mean area that is protected in marine sites important to biodiversity (%)	NA	NA	●	●
Ocean Health Index: Clean Waters score (worst 0–100 best)	NA	NA	●	●
Fish caught from overexploited or collapsed stocks (% of total catch)	NA	NA	●	●
Fish caught by trawling or dredging (%)	NA	NA	●	●
Fish caught that are then discarded (%)	NA	NA	●	●
Marine biodiversity threats embodied in imports (per million population)	0.0	2018	●	●

SDG15 – Life on Land

	Value	Year	Rating	Trend
Mean area that is protected in terrestrial sites important to biodiversity (%)	0.0	2020	●	→
Mean area that is protected in freshwater sites important to biodiversity (%)	0.0	2020	●	→
Red List Index of species survival (worst 0–1 best)	0.9	2021	●	↑
Permanent deforestation (% of forest area, 5-year average)	0.0	2020	●	↑
Terrestrial and freshwater biodiversity threats embodied in imports (per million population)	0.0	2018	●	●

SDG16 – Peace, Justice and Strong Institutions

	Value	Year	Rating	Trend
Homicides (per 100,000 population)	3.9	2019	●	↗
Unsentenced detainees (% of prison population)	7.1	2019	●	↑
Population who feel safe walking alone at night in the city or area where they live (%)	69	2021	●	↑
Property Rights (worst 1–7 best)	3.9	2020	●	↑
Birth registrations with civil authority (% of children under age 5)	99.6	2020	●	●
Corruption Perception Index (worst 0–100 best)	36	2021	●	→
Children involved in child labor (% of population aged 5 to 14)	NA	NA	●	●
Exports of major conventional weapons (TIV constant million USD per 100,000 population)	0.0	2020	●	●
Press Freedom Index (best 0–100 worst)	31.6	2021	●	↓
Access to and affordability of justice (worst 0–1 best)	0.5	2020	●	↗

SDG17 – Partnerships for the Goals

	Value	Year	Rating	Trend
Government spending on health and education (% of GDP)	9.9	2019	●	↑
For high-income and all OECD DAC countries: International concessional public finance, including official development assistance (% of GNI)	NA	NA	●	●
Other countries: Government revenue excluding grants (% of GDP)	27.1	2019	●	↗
Corporate Tax Haven Score (best 0–100 worst)	* 0.0	2019	●	●
Statistical Performance Index (worst 0–100 best)	79.3	2019	●	↑

MONACO

Western Europe

AVERAGE PERFORMANCE BY SDG

SDG 17, SDG 1, SDG 2, SDG 3, SDG 4, SDG 5, SDG 6, SDG 7, SDG 8, SDG 9, SDG 10, SDG 11, SDG 12, SDG 13, SDG 14, SDG 15, SDG 16

100, 75, 50, 25

Monaco

OVERALL PERFORMANCE

COUNTRY RANKING

MONACO

NA **/163**

COUNTRY SCORE

na

REGIONAL AVERAGE: 71.6

SDG DASHBOARDS AND TRENDS

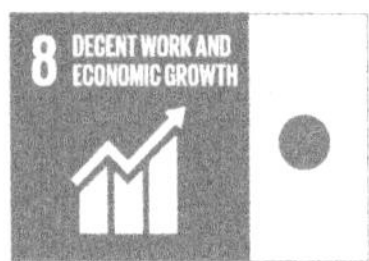

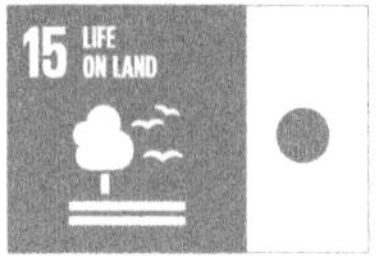

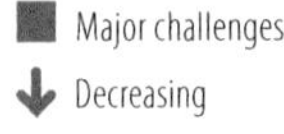

Major challenges · Significant challenges · Challenges remain · SDG achieved · Information unavailable

Decreasing · Stagnating · Moderately improving · On track or maintaining SDG achievement · Information unavailable

Note: The full title of each SDG is available here: https://sustainabledevelopment.un.org/topics/sustainabledevelopmentgoals

INTERNATIONAL SPILLOVER INDEX

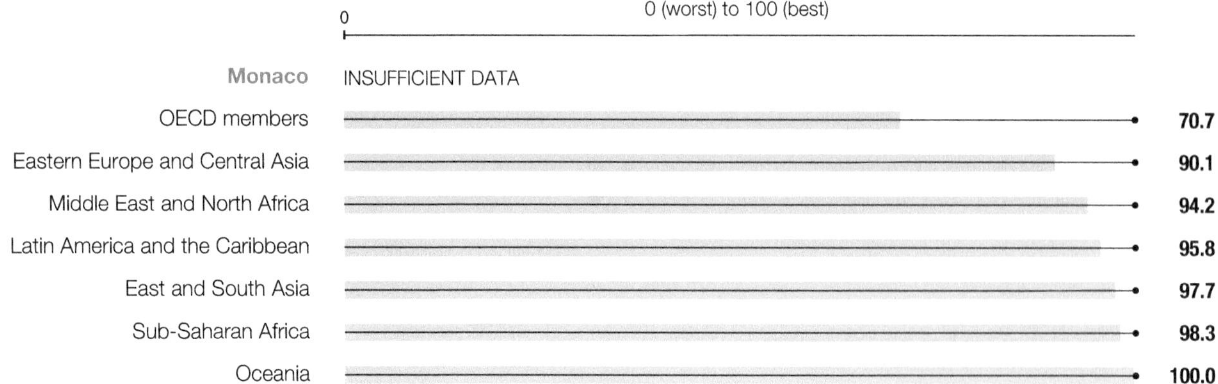

STATISTICAL PERFORMANCE INDEX

0 (worst) to 100 (best)

0 **na** 100

MISSING DATA IN SDG INDEX

63%

MONACO

Performance by Indicator

SDG1 – No Poverty	Value	Year	Rating	Trend
Poverty headcount ratio at $1.90/day (%)	NA	NA	●	●
Poverty headcount ratio at $3.20/day (%)	NA	NA	●	●

SDG2 – Zero Hunger	Value	Year	Rating	Trend
Prevalence of undernourishment (%)	* 1.2	2019	●	●
Prevalence of stunting in children under 5 years of age (%)	* 2.6	2019	●	↑
Prevalence of wasting in children under 5 years of age (%)	* 0.7	2019	●	↑
Prevalence of obesity, BMI ≥ 30 (% of adult population)	NA	NA	●	●
Human Trophic Level (best 2–3 worst)	NA	NA	●	●
Cereal yield (tonnes per hectare of harvested land)	NA	NA	●	●
Sustainable Nitrogen Management Index (best 0–1.41 worst)	NA	NA	●	●
Exports of hazardous pesticides (tonnes per million population)	NA	NA	●	●

SDG3 – Good Health and Well-Being	Value	Year	Rating	Trend
Maternal mortality rate (per 100,000 live births)	NA	NA	●	●
Neonatal mortality rate (per 1,000 live births)	1.6	2020	●	↑
Mortality rate, under-5 (per 1,000 live births)	3.0	2020	●	↑
Incidence of tuberculosis (per 100,000 population)	0.0	2020	●	↑
New HIV infections (per 1,000 uninfected population)	NA	NA	●	●
Age-standardized death rate due to cardiovascular disease, cancer, diabetes, or chronic respiratory disease in adults aged 30–70 years (%)	NA	NA	●	●
Age-standardized death rate attributable to household air pollution and ambient air pollution (per 100,000 population)	NA	NA	●	●
Traffic deaths (per 100,000 population)	NA	NA	●	●
Life expectancy at birth (years)	NA	NA	●	●
Adolescent fertility rate (births per 1,000 females aged 15 to 19)	NA	NA	●	●
Births attended by skilled health personnel (%)	NA	NA	●	●
Surviving infants who received 2 WHO-recommended vaccines (%)	88	2019	●	→
Universal health coverage (UHC) index of service coverage (worst 0–100 best)	NA	NA	●	●
Subjective well-being (average ladder score, worst 0–10 best)	NA	NA	●	●

SDG4 – Quality Education	Value	Year	Rating	Trend
Participation rate in pre-primary organized learning (% of children aged 4 to 6)	NA	NA	●	●
Net primary enrollment rate (%)	NA	NA	●	●
Lower secondary completion rate (%)	NA	NA	●	●
Literacy rate (% of population aged 15 to 24)	NA	NA	●	●

SDG5 – Gender Equality	Value	Year	Rating	Trend
Demand for family planning satisfied by modern methods (% of females aged 15 to 49)	NA	NA	●	●
Ratio of female-to-male mean years of education received (%)	NA	NA	●	●
Ratio of female-to-male labor force participation rate (%)	NA	NA	●	●
Seats held by women in national parliament (%)	33.3	2020	●	↑

SDG6 – Clean Water and Sanitation	Value	Year	Rating	Trend
Population using at least basic drinking water services (%)	100.0	2020	●	↑
Population using at least basic sanitation services (%)	100.0	2020	●	↑
Freshwater withdrawal (% of available freshwater resources)	NA	NA	●	●
Anthropogenic wastewater that receives treatment (%)	100.0	2018	●	●
Scarce water consumption embodied in imports (m^3 H_2O eq/capita)	NA	NA	●	●

SDG7 – Affordable and Clean Energy	Value	Year	Rating	Trend
Population with access to electricity (%)	100.0	2019	●	↑
Population with access to clean fuels and technology for cooking (%)	100.0	2019	●	↑
CO_2 emissions from fuel combustion per total electricity output ($MtCO_2$/TWh)	NA	NA	●	●
Share of renewable energy in total primary energy supply (%)	NA	NA	●	●

SDG8 – Decent Work and Economic Growth	Value	Year	Rating	Trend
Adjusted GDP growth (%)	NA	NA	●	●
Victims of modern slavery (per 1,000 population)	NA	NA	●	●
Adults with an account at a bank or other financial institution or with a mobile-money-service provider (% of population aged 15 or over)	NA	NA	●	●
Unemployment rate (% of total labor force)	NA	NA	●	●
Fundamental labor rights are effectively guaranteed (worst 0–1 best)	NA	NA	●	●
Fatal work-related accidents embodied in imports (per 100,000 population)	1.5	2015	●	↑

* Imputed data point

SDG9 – Industry, Innovation and Infrastructure	Value	Year	Rating	Trend
Population using the internet (%)	97.1	2017	●	●
Mobile broadband subscriptions (per 100 population)	86.4	2019	●	↑
Logistics Performance Index: Quality of trade and transport-related infrastructure (worst 1–5 best)	NA	NA	●	●
The Times Higher Education Universities Ranking: Average score of top 3 universities (worst 0–100 best)	* 0.0	2022	●	●
Articles published in academic journals (per 1,000 population)	5.9	2020	●	↑
Expenditure on research and development (% of GDP)	0.0	2005	●	●

SDG10 – Reduced Inequalities	Value	Year	Rating	Trend
Gini coefficient	NA	NA	●	●
Palma ratio	NA	NA	●	●

SDG11 – Sustainable Cities and Communities	Value	Year	Rating	Trend
Proportion of urban population living in slums (%)	NA	NA	●	●
Annual mean concentration of particulate matter of less than 2.5 microns in diameter (PM2.5) (μg/m^3)	11.8	2019	●	↑
Access to improved water source, piped (% of urban population)	100.0	2020	●	↑
Satisfaction with public transport (%)	NA	NA	●	●

SDG12 – Responsible Consumption and Production	Value	Year	Rating	Trend
Municipal solid waste (kg/capita/day)	3.5	2012	●	●
Electronic waste (kg/capita)	NA	NA	●	●
Production-based SO_2 emissions (kg/capita)	NA	NA	●	●
SO_2 emissions embodied in imports (kg/capita)	NA	NA	●	●
Production-based nitrogen emissions (kg/capita)	0.0	2015	●	↑
Nitrogen emissions embodied in imports (kg/capita)	35.7	2015	●	↓
Exports of plastic waste (kg/capita)	NA	NA	●	●

SDG13 – Climate Action	Value	Year	Rating	Trend
CO_2 emissions from fossil fuel combustion and cement production (tCO_2/capita)	NA	NA	●	●
CO_2 emissions embodied in imports (tCO_2/capita)	NA	NA	●	●
CO_2 emissions embodied in fossil fuel exports (kg/capita)	NA	NA	●	●

SDG14 – Life Below Water	Value	Year	Rating	Trend
Mean area that is protected in marine sites important to biodiversity (%)	NA	NA	●	●
Ocean Health Index: Clean Waters score (worst 0–100 best)	19.6	2020	●	↓
Fish caught from overexploited or collapsed stocks (% of total catch)	NA	NA	●	●
Fish caught by trawling or dredging (%)	0.0	2018	●	↑
Fish caught that are then discarded (%)	0.0	2018	●	↑
Marine biodiversity threats embodied in imports (per million population)	NA	NA	●	●

SDG15 – Life on Land	Value	Year	Rating	Trend
Mean area that is protected in terrestrial sites important to biodiversity (%)	NA	NA	●	●
Mean area that is protected in freshwater sites important to biodiversity (%)	NA	NA	●	●
Red List Index of species survival (worst 0–1 best)	0.8	2021	●	↓
Permanent deforestation (% of forest area, 5-year average)	NA	NA	●	●
Terrestrial and freshwater biodiversity threats embodied in imports (per million population)	0.4	2018	●	●

SDG16 – Peace, Justice and Strong Institutions	Value	Year	Rating	Trend
Homicides (per 100,000 population)	0.0	2008	●	●
Unsentenced detainees (% of prison population)	35.5	2016	●	●
Population who feel safe walking alone at night in the city or area where they live (%)	NA	NA	●	●
Property Rights (worst 1–7 best)	NA	NA	●	●
Birth registrations with civil authority (% of children under age 5)	100.0	2020	●	●
Corruption Perception Index (worst 0–100 best)	NA	NA	●	●
Children involved in child labor (% of population aged 5 to 14)	NA	NA	●	●
Exports of major conventional weapons (TIV constant million USD per 100,000 population)	* 0.0	2020	●	●
Press Freedom Index (best 0–100 worst)	NA	NA	●	●
Access to and affordability of justice (worst 0–1 best)	NA	NA	●	●

SDG17 – Partnerships for the Goals	Value	Year	Rating	Trend
Government spending on health and education (% of GDP)	2.4	2019	●	↓
For high-income and all OECD DAC countries: International concessional public finance, including official development assistance (% of GNI)	NA	NA	●	●
Other countries: Government revenue excluding grants (% of GDP)	NA	NA	●	●
Corporate Tax Haven Score (best 0–100 worst)	67.6	2019	●	●
Statistical Performance Index (worst 0–100 best)	NA	NA	●	●

5. Country Profiles

MONGOLIA

East and South Asia

OVERALL PERFORMANCE

COUNTRY RANKING

MONGOLIA

109/163

COUNTRY SCORE

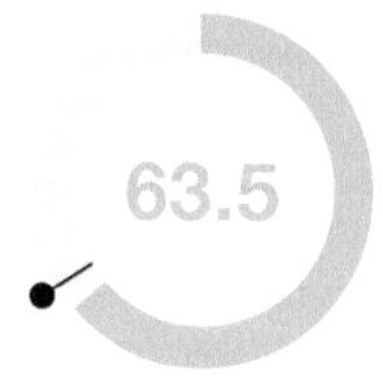

REGIONAL AVERAGE: 65.9

AVERAGE PERFORMANCE BY SDG

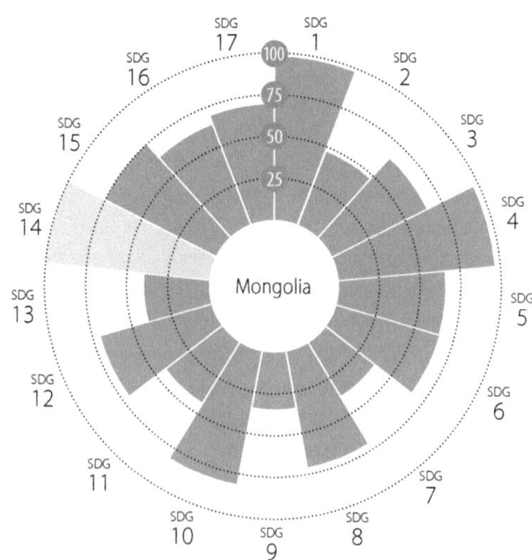

SDG DASHBOARDS AND TRENDS

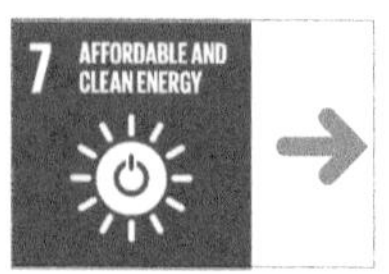
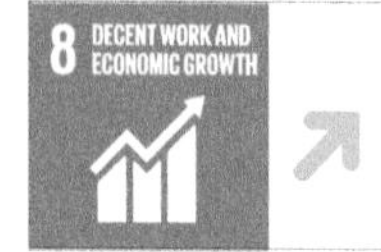

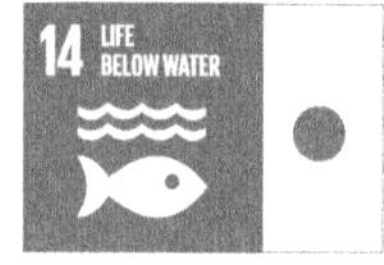

Major challenges | Significant challenges | Challenges remain | SDG achieved | Information unavailable

Decreasing | Stagnating | Moderately improving | On track or maintaining SDG achievement | Information unavailable

Note: The full title of each SDG is available here: https://sustainabledevelopment.un.org/topics/sustainabledevelopmentgoals

INTERNATIONAL SPILLOVER INDEX

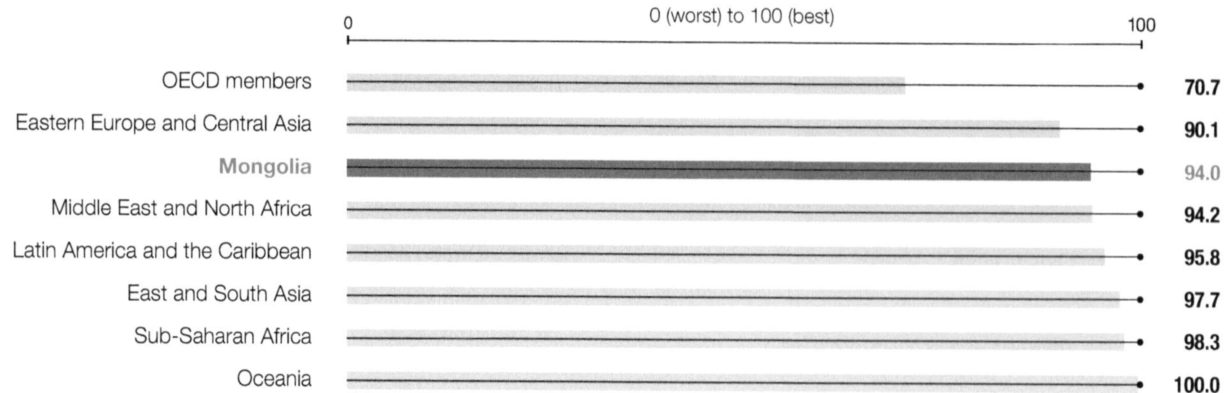

STATISTICAL PERFORMANCE INDEX

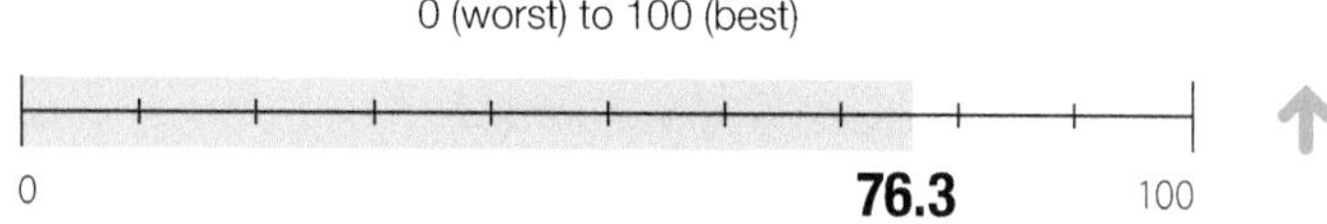

MISSING DATA IN SDG INDEX

1%

MONGOLIA

Performance by Indicator

SDG1 – No Poverty	Value	Year	Rating	Trend
Poverty headcount ratio at $1.90/day (%)	0.2	2022	●	↑
Poverty headcount ratio at $3.20/day (%)	2.3	2022	●	↑

SDG2 – Zero Hunger	Value	Year	Rating	Trend
Prevalence of undernourishment (%)	4.3	2019	●	↑
Prevalence of stunting in children under 5 years of age (%)	9.4	2018	●	→
Prevalence of wasting in children under 5 years of age (%)	0.9	2018	●	↑
Prevalence of obesity, BMI ≥ 30 (% of adult population)	20.6	2016	●	↓
Human Trophic Level (best 2–3 worst)	2.5	2017	●	↓
Cereal yield (tonnes per hectare of harvested land)	1.2	2018	●	↑
Sustainable Nitrogen Management Index (best 0–1.41 worst)	1.1	2015	●	↓
Exports of hazardous pesticides (tonnes per million population)	NA	NA	●	●

SDG3 – Good Health and Well-Being	Value	Year	Rating	Trend
Maternal mortality rate (per 100,000 live births)	45	2017	●	↑
Neonatal mortality rate (per 1,000 live births)	7.9	2020	●	↑
Mortality rate, under-5 (per 1,000 live births)	15.4	2020	●	↑
Incidence of tuberculosis (per 100,000 population)	437.0	2020	●	↓
New HIV infections (per 1,000 uninfected population)	0.0	2020	●	↑
Age-standardized death rate due to cardiovascular disease, cancer, diabetes, or chronic respiratory disease in adults aged 30–70 years (%)	35.0	2019	●	→
Age-standardized death rate attributable to household air pollution and ambient air pollution (per 100,000 population)	156	2016	●	●
Traffic deaths (per 100,000 population)	21.0	2019	●	↓
Life expectancy at birth (years)	68.1	2019	●	→
Adolescent fertility rate (births per 1,000 females aged 15 to 19)	30.5	2019	●	→
Births attended by skilled health personnel (%)	99.3	2018	●	↑
Surviving infants who received 2 WHO-recommended vaccines (%)	96	2020	●	↑
Universal health coverage (UHC) index of service coverage (worst 0–100 best)	63	2019	●	→
Subjective well-being (average ladder score, worst 0–10 best)	5.7	2021	●	↑

SDG4 – Quality Education	Value	Year	Rating	Trend
Participation rate in pre-primary organized learning (% of children aged 4 to 6)	96.1	2019	●	↑
Net primary enrollment rate (%)	99.4	2019	●	↑
Lower secondary completion rate (%)	94.8	2019	●	●
Literacy rate (% of population aged 15 to 24)	99.1	2020	●	●

SDG5 – Gender Equality	Value	Year	Rating	Trend
Demand for family planning satisfied by modern methods (% of females aged 15 to 49)	63.6	2018	●	→
Ratio of female-to-male mean years of education received (%)	110.3	2019	●	↑
Ratio of female-to-male labor force participation rate (%)	77.6	2020	●	↑
Seats held by women in national parliament (%)	17.3	2020	●	→

SDG6 – Clean Water and Sanitation	Value	Year	Rating	Trend
Population using at least basic drinking water services (%)	85.5	2020	●	↗
Population using at least basic sanitation services (%)	67.7	2020	●	↗
Freshwater withdrawal (% of available freshwater resources)	3.4	2018	●	●
Anthropogenic wastewater that receives treatment (%)	3.3	2018	●	●
Scarce water consumption embodied in imports (m^3 H_2O eq/capita)	1823.8	2018	●	●

SDG7 – Affordable and Clean Energy	Value	Year	Rating	Trend
Population with access to electricity (%)	99.1	2019	●	↑
Population with access to clean fuels and technology for cooking (%)	51.6	2019	●	↗
CO_2 emissions from fuel combustion per total electricity output ($MtCO_2$/TWh)	7.6	2019	●	↓
Share of renewable energy in total primary energy supply (%)	3.0	2019	●	↓

SDG8 – Decent Work and Economic Growth	Value	Year	Rating	Trend
Adjusted GDP growth (%)	-1.5	2020	●	●
Victims of modern slavery (per 1,000 population)	12.3	2018	●	●
Adults with an account at a bank or other financial institution or with a mobile-money-service provider (% of population aged 15 or over)	93.0	2017	●	↑
Unemployment rate (% of total labor force)	6.2	2022	●	↓
Fundamental labor rights are effectively guaranteed (worst 0–1 best)	0.5	2020	●	↗
Fatal work-related accidents embodied in imports (per 100,000 population)	0.3	2015	●	↑

* Imputed data point

SDG9 – Industry, Innovation and Infrastructure	Value	Year	Rating	Trend
Population using the internet (%)	62.5	2020	●	↑
Mobile broadband subscriptions (per 100 population)	111.8	2019	●	↑
Logistics Performance Index: Quality of trade and transport-related infrastructure (worst 1–5 best)	2.1	2018	●	↓
The Times Higher Education Universities Ranking: Average score of top 3 universities (worst 0–100 best)	* 0.0	2022	●	●
Articles published in academic journals (per 1,000 population)	0.2	2020	●	→
Expenditure on research and development (% of GDP)	0.1	2018	●	↓

SDG10 – Reduced Inequalities	Value	Year	Rating	Trend
Gini coefficient	32.7	2018	●	↓
Palma ratio	1.3	2018	●	●

SDG11 – Sustainable Cities and Communities	Value	Year	Rating	Trend
Proportion of urban population living in slums (%)	37.1	2018	●	↗
Annual mean concentration of particulate matter of less than 2.5 microns in diameter (PM2.5) (μg/m^3)	38.6	2019	●	→
Access to improved water source, piped (% of urban population)	34.8	2020	●	↓
Satisfaction with public transport (%)	34.0	2021	●	↓

SDG12 – Responsible Consumption and Production	Value	Year	Rating	Trend
Municipal solid waste (kg/capita/day)	2.6	2016	●	●
Electronic waste (kg/capita)	5.2	2019	●	●
Production-based SO_2 emissions (kg/capita)	19.8	2018	●	●
SO_2 emissions embodied in imports (kg/capita)	2.0	2018	●	●
Production-based nitrogen emissions (kg/capita)	103.8	2015	●	↓
Nitrogen emissions embodied in imports (kg/capita)	1.2	2015	●	↑
Exports of plastic waste (kg/capita)	0.7	2019	●	●

SDG13 – Climate Action	Value	Year	Rating	Trend
CO_2 emissions from fossil fuel combustion and cement production (tCO_2/capita)	27.0	2020	●	↓
CO_2 emissions embodied in imports (tCO_2/capita)	0.8	2018	●	↓
CO_2 emissions embodied in fossil fuel exports (kg/capita)	25479.1	2020	●	●

SDG14 – Life Below Water	Value	Year	Rating	Trend
Mean area that is protected in marine sites important to biodiversity (%)	NA	NA	●	●
Ocean Health Index: Clean Waters score (worst 0–100 best)	NA	NA	●	●
Fish caught from overexploited or collapsed stocks (% of total catch)	NA	NA	●	●
Fish caught by trawling or dredging (%)	NA	NA	●	●
Fish caught that are then discarded (%)	NA	NA	●	●
Marine biodiversity threats embodied in imports (per million population)	0.0	2018	●	●

SDG15 – Life on Land	Value	Year	Rating	Trend
Mean area that is protected in terrestrial sites important to biodiversity (%)	45.0	2020	●	→
Mean area that is protected in freshwater sites important to biodiversity (%)	41.4	2020	●	→
Red List Index of species survival (worst 0–1 best)	1.0	2021	●	↑
Permanent deforestation (% of forest area, 5-year average)	0.0	2020	●	↑
Terrestrial and freshwater biodiversity threats embodied in imports (per million population)	0.0	2018	●	●

SDG16 – Peace, Justice and Strong Institutions	Value	Year	Rating	Trend
Homicides (per 100,000 population)	6.0	2020	●	↗
Unsentenced detainees (% of prison population)	25.4	2019	●	↑
Population who feel safe walking alone at night in the city or area where they live (%)	46	2021	●	↓
Property Rights (worst 1–7 best)	3.6	2020	●	↓
Birth registrations with civil authority (% of children under age 5)	99.6	2020	●	●
Corruption Perception Index (worst 0–100 best)	35	2021	●	↓
Children involved in child labor (% of population aged 5 to 14)	14.7	2019	●	●
Exports of major conventional weapons (TIV constant million USD per 100,000 population)	* 0.0	2020	●	●
Press Freedom Index (best 0–100 worst)	29.0	2021	●	↑
Access to and affordability of justice (worst 0–1 best)	0.5	2020	●	↑

SDG17 – Partnerships for the Goals	Value	Year	Rating	Trend
Government spending on health and education (% of GDP)	7.1	2019	●	↗
For high-income and all OECD DAC countries: International concessional public finance, including official development assistance (% of GNI)	NA	NA	●	●
Other countries: Government revenue excluding grants (% of GDP)	28.5	2018	●	↑
Corporate Tax Haven Score (best 0–100 worst)	* 0.0	2019	●	●
Statistical Performance Index (worst 0–100 best)	76.3	2019	●	↑

5. Country Profiles

MONTENEGRO

Eastern Europe and Central Asia

AVERAGE PERFORMANCE BY SDG

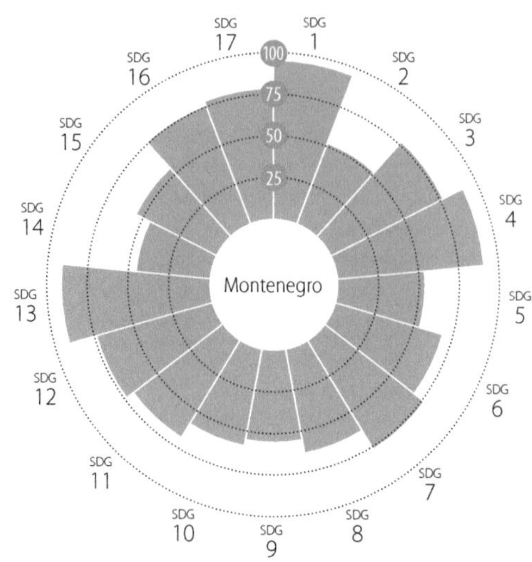

OVERALL PERFORMANCE

COUNTRY RANKING

MONTENEGRO

86/163

COUNTRY SCORE

REGIONAL AVERAGE: 71.6

SDG DASHBOARDS AND TRENDS

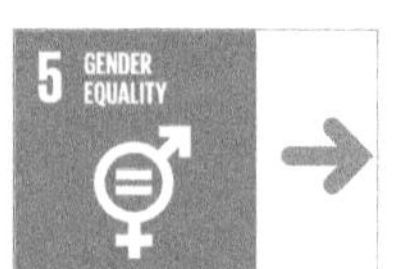

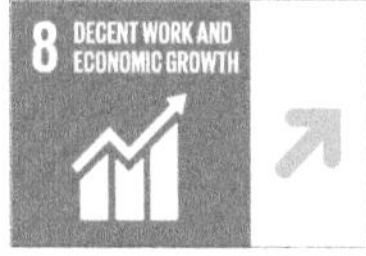

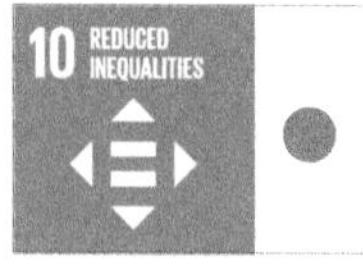

Note: The full title of each SDG is available here: https://sustainabledevelopment.un.org/topics/sustainabledevelopmentgoals

INTERNATIONAL SPILLOVER INDEX

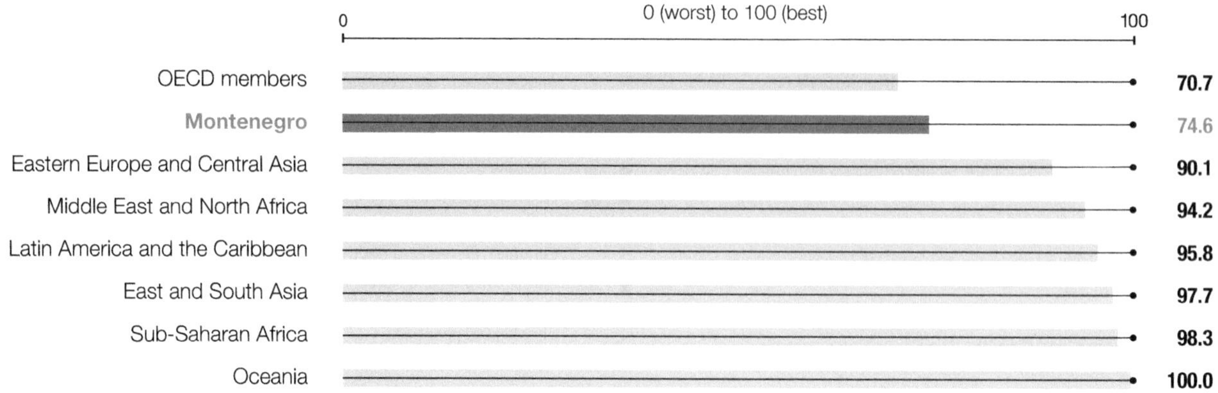

STATISTICAL PERFORMANCE INDEX

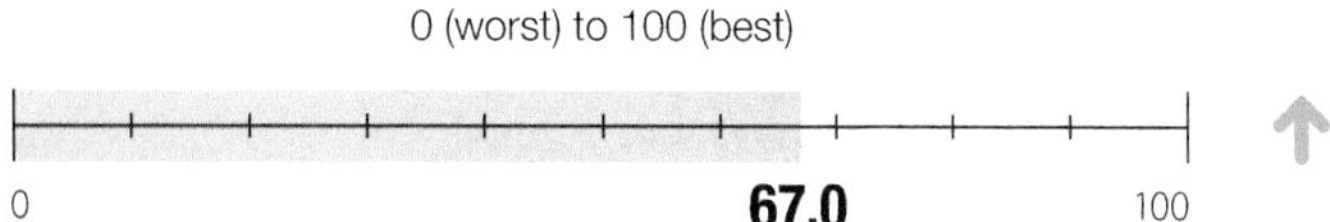

MISSING DATA IN SDG INDEX

12%

SDG1 – No Poverty	Value	Year	Rating	Trend
Poverty headcount ratio at $1.90/day (%)	1.8	2022	●	↑
Poverty headcount ratio at $3.20/day (%)	4.1	2022	●	↑

SDG2 – Zero Hunger	Value	Year	Rating	Trend
Prevalence of undernourishment (%)	2.5	2019	●	↑
Prevalence of stunting in children under 5 years of age (%)	7.2	2018	●	↑
Prevalence of wasting in children under 5 years of age (%)	2.2	2018	●	↑
Prevalence of obesity, BMI ≥ 30 (% of adult population)	23.3	2016	●	↓
Human Trophic Level (best 2–3 worst)	2.5	2017	●	→
Cereal yield (tonnes per hectare of harvested land)	3.3	2018	●	↑
Sustainable Nitrogen Management Index (best 0–1.41 worst)	1.1	2015	●	↓
Exports of hazardous pesticides (tonnes per million population)	NA	NA	●	●

SDG3 – Good Health and Well-Being	Value	Year	Rating	Trend
Maternal mortality rate (per 100,000 live births)	6	2017	●	↑
Neonatal mortality rate (per 1,000 live births)	1.1	2020	●	↑
Mortality rate, under-5 (per 1,000 live births)	2.4	2020	●	↑
Incidence of tuberculosis (per 100,000 population)	16.0	2020	●	→
New HIV infections (per 1,000 uninfected population)	0.0	2020	●	↑
Age-standardized death rate due to cardiovascular disease, cancer, diabetes, or chronic respiratory disease in adults aged 30–70 years (%)	22.3	2019	●	→
Age-standardized death rate attributable to household air pollution and ambient air pollution (per 100,000 population)	79	2016	●	●
Traffic deaths (per 100,000 population)	7.6	2019	●	↑
Life expectancy at birth (years)	75.9	2019	●	→
Adolescent fertility rate (births per 1,000 females aged 15 to 19)	10.0	2018	●	↑
Births attended by skilled health personnel (%)	98.8	2018	●	●
Surviving infants who received 2 WHO-recommended vaccines (%)	24	2020	●	↓
Universal health coverage (UHC) index of service coverage (worst 0–100 best)	67	2019	●	↗
Subjective well-being (average ladder score, worst 0–10 best)	5.7	2020	●	↑

SDG4 – Quality Education	Value	Year	Rating	Trend
Participation rate in pre-primary organized learning (% of children aged 4 to 6)	83.8	2020	●	↑
Net primary enrollment rate (%)	99.9	2020	●	↑
Lower secondary completion rate (%)	89.7	2020	●	↓
Literacy rate (% of population aged 15 to 24)	99.1	2018	●	●

SDG5 – Gender Equality	Value	Year	Rating	Trend
Demand for family planning satisfied by modern methods (% of females aged 15 to 49)	32.9	2018	●	→
Ratio of female-to-male mean years of education received (%)	88.6	2019	●	↓
Ratio of female-to-male labor force participation rate (%)	76.6	2020	●	↑
Seats held by women in national parliament (%)	22.2	2020	●	↗

SDG6 – Clean Water and Sanitation	Value	Year	Rating	Trend
Population using at least basic drinking water services (%)	98.9	2020	●	↑
Population using at least basic sanitation services (%)	97.8	2020	●	↑
Freshwater withdrawal (% of available freshwater resources)	NA	NA	●	●
Anthropogenic wastewater that receives treatment (%)	8.4	2018	●	●
Scarce water consumption embodied in imports (m^3 H_2O eq/capita)	NA	NA	●	●

SDG7 – Affordable and Clean Energy	Value	Year	Rating	Trend
Population with access to electricity (%)	100.0	2019	●	↑
Population with access to clean fuels and technology for cooking (%)	62.2	2019	●	→
CO_2 emissions from fuel combustion per total electricity output ($MtCO_2$/TWh)	0.7	2019	●	↑
Share of renewable energy in total primary energy supply (%)	28.7	2019	●	↑

SDG8 – Decent Work and Economic Growth	Value	Year	Rating	Trend
Adjusted GDP growth (%)	-3.0	2020	●	●
Victims of modern slavery (per 1,000 population)	5.9	2018	●	●
Adults with an account at a bank or other financial institution or with a mobile-money-service provider (% of population aged 15 or over)	68.4	2017	●	↑
Unemployment rate (% of total labor force)	16.7	2022	●	→
Fundamental labor rights are effectively guaranteed (worst 0–1 best)	NA	NA	●	●
Fatal work-related accidents embodied in imports (per 100,000 population)	1.3	2015	●	↑

SDG9 – Industry, Innovation and Infrastructure	Value	Year	Rating	Trend
Population using the internet (%)	77.6	2020	●	↑
Mobile broadband subscriptions (per 100 population)	80.5	2019	●	↑
Logistics Performance Index: Quality of trade and transport-related infrastructure (worst 1–5 best)	2.6	2018	●	↓
The Times Higher Education Universities Ranking: Average score of top 3 universities (worst 0–100 best)	16.5	2022	●	●
Articles published in academic journals (per 1,000 population)	1.0	2020	●	↑
Expenditure on research and development (% of GDP)	0.4	2018	●	↓

SDG10 – Reduced Inequalities	Value	Year	Rating	Trend
Gini coefficient	38.5	2016	●	●
Palma ratio	1.7	2018	●	●

SDG11 – Sustainable Cities and Communities	Value	Year	Rating	Trend
Proportion of urban population living in slums (%)	27.1	2018	●	●
Annual mean concentration of particulate matter of less than 2.5 microns in diameter (PM2.5) (μg/m^3)	19.6	2019	●	↗
Access to improved water source, piped (% of urban population)	96.2	2020	●	→
Satisfaction with public transport (%)	35.0	2020	●	↓

SDG12 – Responsible Consumption and Production	Value	Year	Rating	Trend
Municipal solid waste (kg/capita/day)	1.4	2018	●	●
Electronic waste (kg/capita)	10.7	2019	●	●
Production-based SO_2 emissions (kg/capita)	NA	NA	●	●
SO_2 emissions embodied in imports (kg/capita)	NA	NA	●	●
Production-based nitrogen emissions (kg/capita)	5.5	2015	●	↑
Nitrogen emissions embodied in imports (kg/capita)	19.5	2015	●	↓
Exports of plastic waste (kg/capita)	0.6	2021	●	●

SDG13 – Climate Action	Value	Year	Rating	Trend
CO_2 emissions from fossil fuel combustion and cement production (tCO_2/capita)	3.7	2020	●	→
CO_2 emissions embodied in imports (tCO_2/capita)	NA	NA	●	●
CO_2 emissions embodied in fossil fuel exports (kg/capita)	190.2	2020	●	●

SDG14 – Life Below Water	Value	Year	Rating	Trend
Mean area that is protected in marine sites important to biodiversity (%)	17.8	2020	●	↗
Ocean Health Index: Clean Waters score (worst 0–100 best)	61.5	2020	●	→
Fish caught from overexploited or collapsed stocks (% of total catch)	NA	NA	●	●
Fish caught by trawling or dredging (%)	28.6	2018	●	↑
Fish caught that are then discarded (%)	10.7	2018	●	→
Marine biodiversity threats embodied in imports (per million population)	1.1	2018	●	●

SDG15 – Life on Land	Value	Year	Rating	Trend
Mean area that is protected in terrestrial sites important to biodiversity (%)	25.9	2020	●	→
Mean area that is protected in freshwater sites important to biodiversity (%)	49.2	2020	●	→
Red List Index of species survival (worst 0–1 best)	0.8	2021	●	↓
Permanent deforestation (% of forest area, 5-year average)	0.0	2020	●	↑
Terrestrial and freshwater biodiversity threats embodied in imports (per million population)	5.3	2018	●	●

SDG16 – Peace, Justice and Strong Institutions	Value	Year	Rating	Trend
Homicides (per 100,000 population)	2.9	2020	●	→
Unsentenced detainees (% of prison population)	33.7	2019	●	↓
Population who feel safe walking alone at night in the city or area where they live (%)	83	2020	●	↑
Property Rights (worst 1–7 best)	4.4	2020	●	↑
Birth registrations with civil authority (% of children under age 5)	99.4	2020	●	●
Corruption Perception Index (worst 0–100 best)	46	2021	●	→
Children involved in child labor (% of population aged 5 to 14)	7.7	2019	●	●
Exports of major conventional weapons (TIV constant million USD per 100,000 population)	0.0	2020	●	●
Press Freedom Index (best 0–100 worst)	34.3	2021	●	→
Access to and affordability of justice (worst 0–1 best)	NA	NA	●	●

SDG17 – Partnerships for the Goals	Value	Year	Rating	Trend
Government spending on health and education (% of GDP)	NA	NA	●	●
For high-income and all OECD DAC countries: International concessional public finance, including official development assistance (% of GNI)	NA	NA	●	●
Other countries: Government revenue excluding grants (% of GDP)	NA	NA	●	●
Corporate Tax Haven Score (best 0–100 worst)	* 0.0	2019	●	●
Statistical Performance Index (worst 0–100 best)	67.0	2019	●	↑

* Imputed data point

MOROCCO

Middle East and North Africa

OVERALL PERFORMANCE

COUNTRY RANKING

MOROCCO

84/163

COUNTRY SCORE

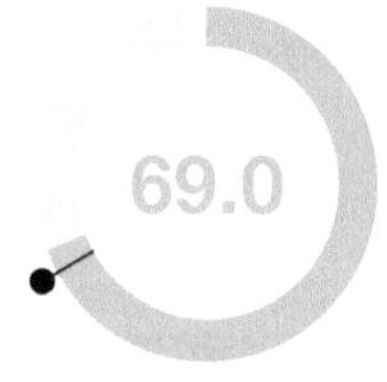

REGIONAL AVERAGE: 66.7

AVERAGE PERFORMANCE BY SDG

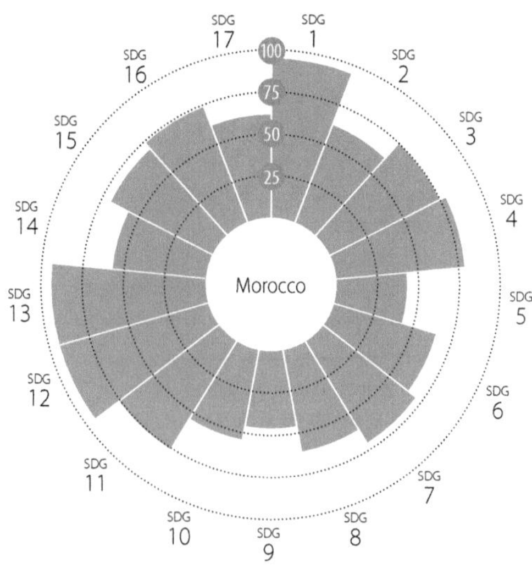

SDG DASHBOARDS AND TRENDS

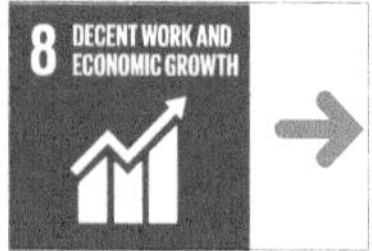

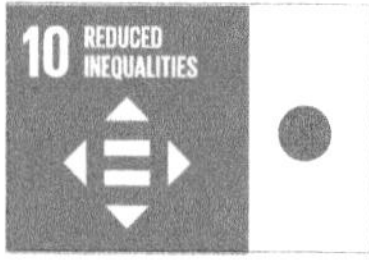

Major challenges · Significant challenges · Challenges remain · SDG achieved · Information unavailable

Decreasing · Stagnating · Moderately improving · On track or maintaining SDG achievement

Note: The full title of each SDG is available here: https://sustainabledevelopment.un.org/topics/sustainabledevelopmentgoals

INTERNATIONAL SPILLOVER INDEX

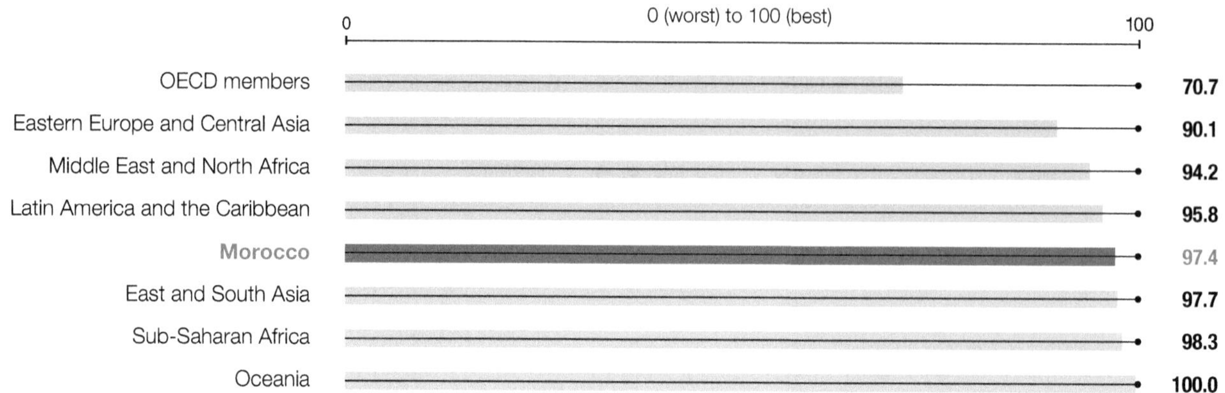

STATISTICAL PERFORMANCE INDEX

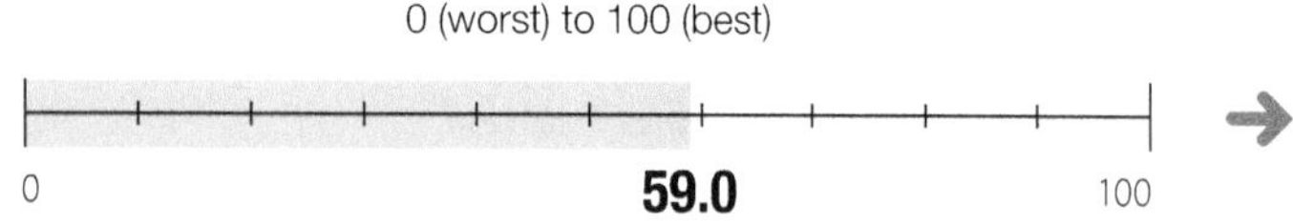

MISSING DATA IN SDG INDEX

1%

MOROCCO

Performance by Indicator

SDG1 – No Poverty	Value	Year	Rating	Trend
Poverty headcount ratio at $1.90/day (%)	0.2	2022	●	↑
Poverty headcount ratio at $3.20/day (%)	5.2	2022	●	↗
SDG2 – Zero Hunger				
Prevalence of undernourishment (%)	4.2	2019	●	↑
Prevalence of stunting in children under 5 years of age (%)	15.1	2017	●	↗
Prevalence of wasting in children under 5 years of age (%)	2.6	2017	●	↑
Prevalence of obesity, BMI ≥ 30 (% of adult population)	26.1	2016	●	↓
Human Trophic Level (best 2–3 worst)	2.2	2017	●	↑
Cereal yield (tonnes per hectare of harvested land)	2.3	2018	●	↑
Sustainable Nitrogen Management Index (best 0–1.41 worst)	0.8	2015	●	→
Exports of hazardous pesticides (tonnes per million population)	1.0	2019	●	●
SDG3 – Good Health and Well-Being				
Maternal mortality rate (per 100,000 live births)	70	2017	●	↑
Neonatal mortality rate (per 1,000 live births)	11.5	2020	●	↑
Mortality rate, under-5 (per 1,000 live births)	18.7	2020	●	↑
Incidence of tuberculosis (per 100,000 population)	98.0	2020	●	→
New HIV infections (per 1,000 uninfected population)	0.0	2020	●	↑
Age-standardized death rate due to cardiovascular disease, cancer, diabetes, or chronic respiratory disease in adults aged 30–70 years (%)	24.1	2019	●	→
Age-standardized death rate attributable to household air pollution and ambient air pollution (per 100,000 population)	49	2016	●	●
Traffic deaths (per 100,000 population)	17.0	2019	●	↗
Life expectancy at birth (years)	73.0	2019	●	→
Adolescent fertility rate (births per 1,000 females aged 15 to 19)	19.0	2017	●	●
Births attended by skilled health personnel (%)	86.6	2018	●	●
Surviving infants who received 2 WHO-recommended vaccines (%)	99	2019	●	↑
Universal health coverage (UHC) index of service coverage (worst 0–100 best)	73	2019	●	↑
Subjective well-being (average ladder score, worst 0–10 best)	5.3	2021	●	→
SDG4 – Quality Education				
Participation rate in pre-primary organized learning (% of children aged 4 to 6)	72.9	2020	●	↑
Net primary enrollment rate (%)	99.6	2020	●	↑
Lower secondary completion rate (%)	67.9	2020	●	↓
Literacy rate (% of population aged 15 to 24)	97.7	2018	●	●
SDG5 – Gender Equality				
Demand for family planning satisfied by modern methods (% of females aged 15 to 49)	72.0	2018	●	→
Ratio of female-to-male mean years of education received (%)	71.2	2019	●	↑
Ratio of female-to-male labor force participation rate (%)	33.2	2020	●	↓
Seats held by women in national parliament (%)	20.5	2020	●	→
SDG6 – Clean Water and Sanitation				
Population using at least basic drinking water services (%)	90.4	2020	●	↑
Population using at least basic sanitation services (%)	87.3	2020	●	↑
Freshwater withdrawal (% of available freshwater resources)	50.8	2018	●	●
Anthropogenic wastewater that receives treatment (%)	5.4	2018	●	●
Scarce water consumption embodied in imports (m^3 H_2O eq/capita)	1062.6	2018	●	●
SDG7 – Affordable and Clean Energy				
Population with access to electricity (%)	99.6	2019	●	↑
Population with access to clean fuels and technology for cooking (%)	98.1	2019	●	↑
CO_2 emissions from fuel combustion per total electricity output ($MtCO_2$/TWh)	1.7	2019	●	↗
Share of renewable energy in total primary energy supply (%)	9.4	2019	●	→
SDG8 – Decent Work and Economic Growth				
Adjusted GDP growth (%)	-4.8	2020	●	●
Victims of modern slavery (per 1,000 population)	2.4	2018	●	●
Adults with an account at a bank or other financial institution or with a mobile-money-service provider (% of population aged 15 or over)	28.6	2017	●	●
Unemployment rate (% of total labor force)	11.2	2022	●	↓
Fundamental labor rights are effectively guaranteed (worst 0–1 best)	0.6	2020	●	↓
Fatal work-related accidents embodied in imports (per 100,000 population)	0.1	2015	●	↑

SDG9 – Industry, Innovation and Infrastructure	Value	Year	Rating	Trend
Population using the internet (%)	84.1	2020	●	↑
Mobile broadband subscriptions (per 100 population)	64.9	2019	●	↑
Logistics Performance Index: Quality of trade and transport-related infrastructure (worst 1–5 best)	2.4	2018	●	●
The Times Higher Education Universities Ranking: Average score of top 3 universities (worst 0–100 best)	23.6	2022	●	●
Articles published in academic journals (per 1,000 population)	0.3	2020	●	↗
Expenditure on research and development (% of GDP)	0.7	2010	●	●
SDG10 – Reduced Inequalities				
Gini coefficient	39.5	2013	●	●
Palma ratio	1.8	2018	●	●
SDG11 – Sustainable Cities and Communities				
Proportion of urban population living in slums (%)	9.0	2018	●	↑
Annual mean concentration of particulate matter of less than 2.5 microns in diameter (PM2.5) (μg/m^3)	33.4	2019	●	↓
Access to improved water source, piped (% of urban population)	92.6	2020	●	→
Satisfaction with public transport (%)	54.0	2021	●	↓
SDG12 – Responsible Consumption and Production				
Municipal solid waste (kg/capita/day)	0.5	2014	●	●
Electronic waste (kg/capita)	4.6	2019	●	●
Production-based SO_2 emissions (kg/capita)	9.2	2018	●	●
SO_2 emissions embodied in imports (kg/capita)	0.8	2018	●	●
Production-based nitrogen emissions (kg/capita)	9.8	2015	●	↑
Nitrogen emissions embodied in imports (kg/capita)	0.6	2015	●	↑
Exports of plastic waste (kg/capita)	0.1	2020	●	●
SDG13 – Climate Action				
CO_2 emissions from fossil fuel combustion and cement production (tCO_2/capita)	1.7	2020	●	↑
CO_2 emissions embodied in imports (tCO_2/capita)	0.3	2018	●	↑
CO_2 emissions embodied in fossil fuel exports (kg/capita)	0.0	2020	●	●
SDG14 – Life Below Water				
Mean area that is protected in marine sites important to biodiversity (%)	43.3	2020	●	→
Ocean Health Index: Clean Waters score (worst 0–100 best)	55.3	2020	●	↓
Fish caught from overexploited or collapsed stocks (% of total catch)	10.6	2018	●	↑
Fish caught by trawling or dredging (%)	71.2	2018	●	↓
Fish caught that are then discarded (%)	9.7	2018	●	→
Marine biodiversity threats embodied in imports (per million population)	0.0	2018	●	●
SDG15 – Life on Land				
Mean area that is protected in terrestrial sites important to biodiversity (%)	38.5	2020	●	→
Mean area that is protected in freshwater sites important to biodiversity (%)	54.3	2020	●	→
Red List Index of species survival (worst 0–1 best)	0.9	2021	●	→
Permanent deforestation (% of forest area, 5-year average)	0.2	2020	●	↓
Terrestrial and freshwater biodiversity threats embodied in imports (per million population)	0.1	2018	●	●
SDG16 – Peace, Justice and Strong Institutions				
Homicides (per 100,000 population)	1.3	2020	●	↑
Unsentenced detainees (% of prison population)	14.5	2019	●	↑
Population who feel safe walking alone at night in the city or area where they live (%)	65	2021	●	↓
Property Rights (worst 1–7 best)	5.3	2020	●	↑
Birth registrations with civil authority (% of children under age 5)	96.9	2020	●	●
Corruption Perception Index (worst 0–100 best)	39	2021	●	→
Children involved in child labor (% of population aged 5 to 14)	NA	NA	●	●
Exports of major conventional weapons (TIV constant million USD per 100,000 population)	* 0.0	2020	●	●
Press Freedom Index (best 0–100 worst)	43.9	2021	●	↓
Access to and affordability of justice (worst 0–1 best)	0.5	2020	●	↑
SDG17 – Partnerships for the Goals				
Government spending on health and education (% of GDP)	7.4	2019	●	→
For high-income and all OECD DAC countries: International concessional public finance, including official development assistance (% of GNI)	NA	NA	●	●
Other countries: Government revenue excluding grants (% of GDP)	25.5	2019	●	↓
Corporate Tax Haven Score (best 0–100 worst)	* 0.0	2019	●	●
Statistical Performance Index (worst 0–100 best)	59.0	2019	●	→

* Imputed data point

5. Country Profiles

MOZAMBIQUE

Sub-Saharan Africa

OVERALL PERFORMANCE

COUNTRY RANKING

MOZAMBIQUE

143/163

COUNTRY SCORE

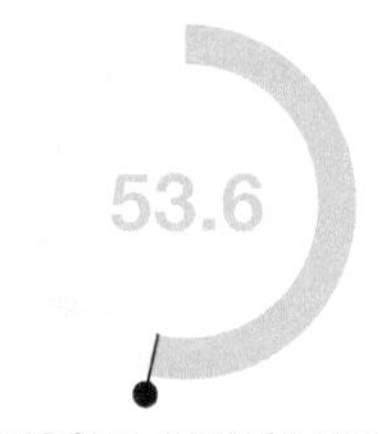

AVERAGE PERFORMANCE BY SDG

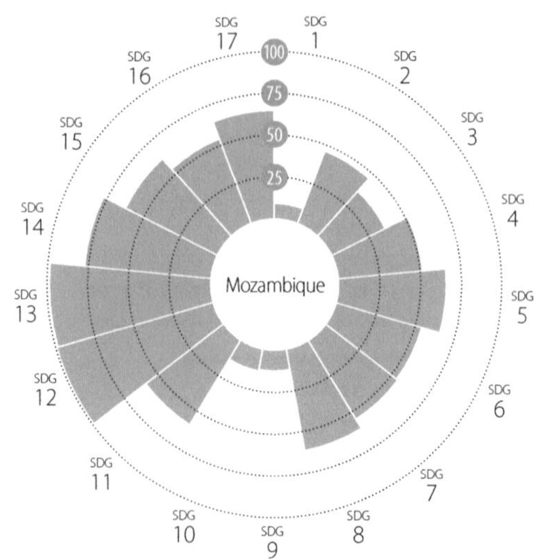

SDG DASHBOARDS AND TRENDS

Note: The full title of each SDG is available here: https://sustainabledevelopment.un.org/topics/sustainabledevelopmentgoals

INTERNATIONAL SPILLOVER INDEX

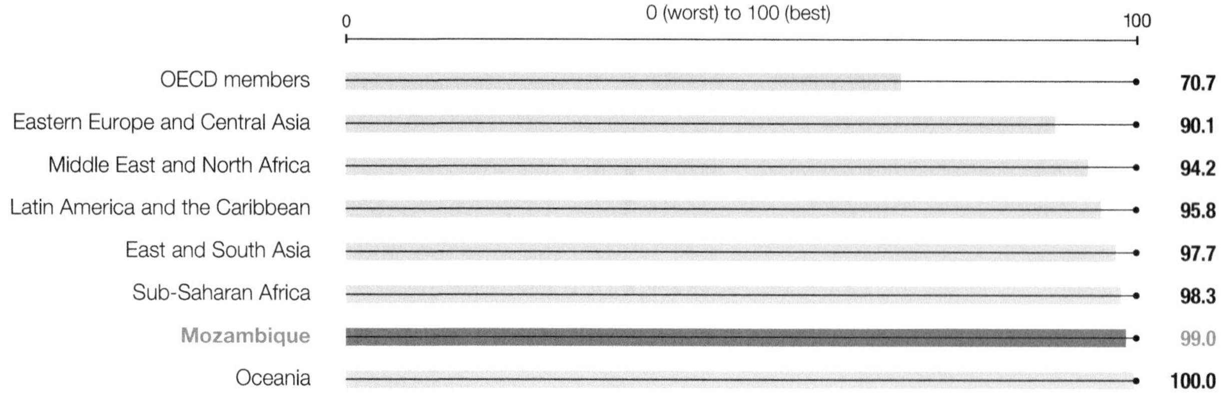

STATISTICAL PERFORMANCE INDEX

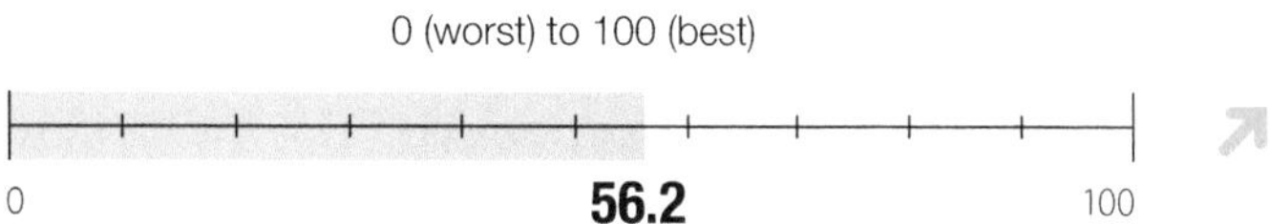

MISSING DATA IN SDG INDEX

3%

MOZAMBIQUE

Performance by Indicator

SDG1 – No Poverty	Value	Year	Rating	Trend
Poverty headcount ratio at \$1.90/day (%)	59.9	2022	●	→
Poverty headcount ratio at \$3.20/day (%)	80.4	2022	●	→
SDG2 – Zero Hunger				
Prevalence of undernourishment (%)	31.2	2019	●	↓
Prevalence of stunting in children under 5 years of age (%)	42.3	2015	●	→
Prevalence of wasting in children under 5 years of age (%)	4.4	2015	●	↑
Prevalence of obesity, BMI ≥ 30 (% of adult population)	7.2	2016	●	↑
Human Trophic Level (best 2–3 worst)	2.1	2017	●	↑
Cereal yield (tonnes per hectare of harvested land)	0.8	2018	●	→
Sustainable Nitrogen Management Index (best 0–1.41 worst)	0.9	2015	●	→
Exports of hazardous pesticides (tonnes per million population)	NA	NA	●	●
SDG3 – Good Health and Well-Being				
Maternal mortality rate (per 100,000 live births)	289	2017	●	↗
Neonatal mortality rate (per 1,000 live births)	28.3	2020	●	→
Mortality rate, under-5 (per 1,000 live births)	70.6	2020	●	↗
Incidence of tuberculosis (per 100,000 population)	368.0	2020	●	↓
New HIV infections (per 1,000 uninfected population)	3.5	2020	●	↗
Age-standardized death rate due to cardiovascular disease, cancer, diabetes, or chronic respiratory disease in adults aged 30–70 years (%)	30.6	2019	●	→
Age-standardized death rate attributable to household air pollution and ambient air pollution (per 100,000 population)	110	2016	●	●
Traffic deaths (per 100,000 population)	30.0	2019	●	→
Life expectancy at birth (years)	58.1	2019	●	→
Adolescent fertility rate (births per 1,000 females aged 15 to 19)	180.0	2016	●	●
Births attended by skilled health personnel (%)	73.0	2015	●	●
Surviving infants who received 2 WHO-recommended vaccines (%)	79	2020	●	↓
Universal health coverage (UHC) index of service coverage (worst 0–100 best)	47	2019	●	→
Subjective well-being (average ladder score, worst 0–10 best)	5.2	2021	●	↑
SDG4 – Quality Education				
Participation rate in pre-primary organized learning (% of children aged 4 to 6)	NA	NA	●	●
Net primary enrollment rate (%)	99.1	2020	●	↑
Lower secondary completion rate (%)	24.2	2019	●	→
Literacy rate (% of population aged 15 to 24)	70.9	2017	●	●
SDG5 – Gender Equality				
Demand for family planning satisfied by modern methods (% of females aged 15 to 49)	55.5	2015	●	↗
Ratio of female-to-male mean years of education received (%)	60.0	2019	●	→
Ratio of female-to-male labor force participation rate (%)	98.7	2020	●	↑
Seats held by women in national parliament (%)	42.4	2020	●	↑
SDG6 – Clean Water and Sanitation				
Population using at least basic drinking water services (%)	63.4	2020	●	↗
Population using at least basic sanitation services (%)	37.2	2020	●	→
Freshwater withdrawal (% of available freshwater resources)	1.8	2018	●	●
Anthropogenic wastewater that receives treatment (%)	0.2	2018	●	●
Scarce water consumption embodied in imports (m^3 H_2O eq/capita)	295.7	2018	●	●
SDG7 – Affordable and Clean Energy				
Population with access to electricity (%)	29.6	2019	●	→
Population with access to clean fuels and technology for cooking (%)	4.9	2019	●	→
CO_2 emissions from fuel combustion per total electricity output ($MtCO_2$/TWh)	0.5	2019	●	↑
Share of renewable energy in total primary energy supply (%)	80.1	2019	●	↑
SDG8 – Decent Work and Economic Growth				
Adjusted GDP growth (%)	-7.3	2020	●	●
Victims of modern slavery (per 1,000 population)	5.4	2018	●	●
Adults with an account at a bank or other financial institution or with a mobile-money-service provider (% of population aged 15 or over)	41.7	2017	●	●
Unemployment rate (% of total labor force)	3.8	2022	●	↑
Fundamental labor rights are effectively guaranteed (worst 0–1 best)	0.5	2020	●	●
Fatal work-related accidents embodied in imports (per 100,000 population)	0.0	2015	●	↑

* Imputed data point

SDG9 – Industry, Innovation and Infrastructure		Value	Year	Rating	Trend
Population using the internet (%)		16.5	2020	●	→
Mobile broadband subscriptions (per 100 population)		17.7	2019	●	↓
Logistics Performance Index: Quality of trade and transport-related infrastructure (worst 1–5 best)		2.2	2016	●	●
The Times Higher Education Universities Ranking: Average score of top 3 universities (worst 0–100 best)	*	0.0	2022	●	●
Articles published in academic journals (per 1,000 population)		0.0	2020	●	→
Expenditure on research and development (% of GDP)		0.3	2015	●	●
SDG10 – Reduced Inequalities					
Gini coefficient		54.0	2014	●	●
Palma ratio		3.9	2018	●	●
SDG11 – Sustainable Cities and Communities					
Proportion of urban population living in slums (%)		76.9	2018	●	→
Annual mean concentration of particulate matter of less than 2.5 microns in diameter (PM2.5) (μg/m^3)		20.5	2019	●	→
Access to improved water source, piped (% of urban population)		77.7	2020	●	↗
Satisfaction with public transport (%)		59.0	2021	●	↗
SDG12 – Responsible Consumption and Production					
Municipal solid waste (kg/capita/day)		0.3	2014	●	●
Electronic waste (kg/capita)		0.5	2019	●	●
Production-based SO_2 emissions (kg/capita)		1.2	2018	●	●
SO_2 emissions embodied in imports (kg/capita)		0.5	2018	●	●
Production-based nitrogen emissions (kg/capita)		3.2	2015	●	↑
Nitrogen emissions embodied in imports (kg/capita)		0.2	2015	●	↑
Exports of plastic waste (kg/capita)		0.0	2020	●	●
SDG13 – Climate Action					
CO_2 emissions from fossil fuel combustion and cement production (tCO_2/capita)		0.2	2020	●	↑
CO_2 emissions embodied in imports (tCO_2/capita)		0.1	2018	●	↑
CO_2 emissions embodied in fossil fuel exports (kg/capita)		343.4	2020	●	●
SDG14 – Life Below Water					
Mean area that is protected in marine sites important to biodiversity (%)		75.4	2020	●	→
Ocean Health Index: Clean Waters score (worst 0–100 best)		54.4	2020	●	↓
Fish caught from overexploited or collapsed stocks (% of total catch)		1.1	2018	●	↑
Fish caught by trawling or dredging (%)		0.0	2018	●	↑
Fish caught that are then discarded (%)		9.8	2018	●	→
Marine biodiversity threats embodied in imports (per million population)		0.0	2018	●	●
SDG15 – Life on Land					
Mean area that is protected in terrestrial sites important to biodiversity (%)		38.0	2020	●	→
Mean area that is protected in freshwater sites important to biodiversity (%)		52.3	2020	●	→
Red List Index of species survival (worst 0–1 best)		0.8	2021	●	↓
Permanent deforestation (% of forest area, 5-year average)		0.4	2020	●	↗
Terrestrial and freshwater biodiversity threats embodied in imports (per million population)		0.0	2018	●	●
SDG16 – Peace, Justice and Strong Institutions					
Homicides (per 100,000 population)		3.5	2011	●	●
Unsentenced detainees (% of prison population)		34.8	2017	●	●
Population who feel safe walking alone at night in the city or area where they live (%)		46	2021	●	↓
Property Rights (worst 1–7 best)		3.4	2020	●	↓
Birth registrations with civil authority (% of children under age 5)		55.0	2020	●	●
Corruption Perception Index (worst 0–100 best)		26	2021	●	↓
Children involved in child labor (% of population aged 5 to 14)		NA	NA	●	●
Exports of major conventional weapons (TIV constant million USD per 100,000 population)	*	0.0	2020	●	●
Press Freedom Index (best 0–100 worst)		35.4	2021	●	↓
Access to and affordability of justice (worst 0–1 best)		0.4	2020	●	●
SDG17 – Partnerships for the Goals					
Government spending on health and education (% of GDP)		7.9	2019	●	→
For high-income and all OECD DAC countries: International concessional public finance, including official development assistance (% of GNI)		NA	NA	●	●
Other countries: Government revenue excluding grants (% of GDP)		28.7	2019	●	↑
Corporate Tax Haven Score (best 0–100 worst)	*	0.0	2019	●	●
Statistical Performance Index (worst 0–100 best)		56.2	2019	●	↗

MYANMAR

East and South Asia

OVERALL PERFORMANCE

COUNTRY RANKING

MYANMAR

103 /163

COUNTRY SCORE

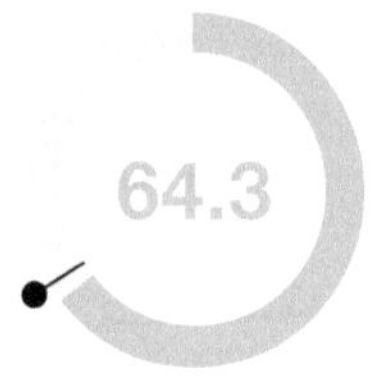

REGIONAL AVERAGE: 65.9

AVERAGE PERFORMANCE BY SDG

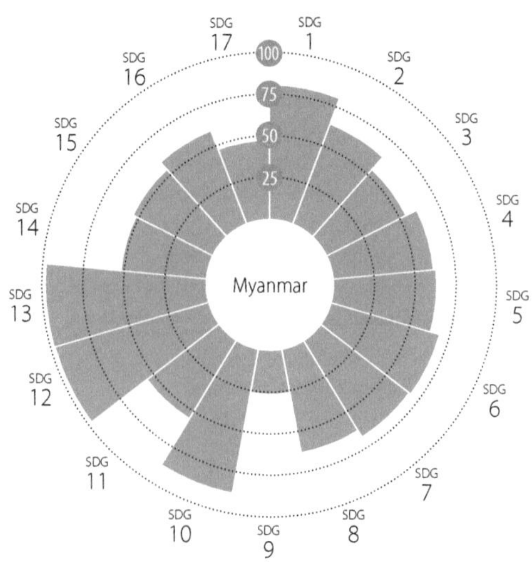

SDG DASHBOARDS AND TRENDS

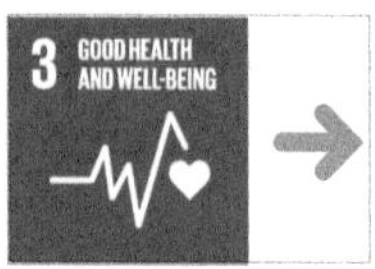

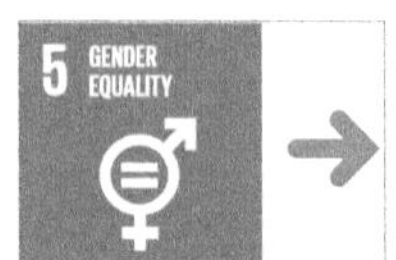

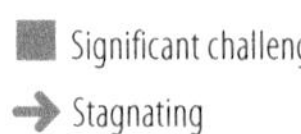

Major challenges · Significant challenges · Challenges remain · SDG achieved · Information unavailable

Decreasing · Stagnating · Moderately improving · On track or maintaining SDG achievement · Information unavailable

Note: The full title of each SDG is available here: https://sustainabledevelopment.un.org/topics/sustainabledevelopmentgoals

INTERNATIONAL SPILLOVER INDEX

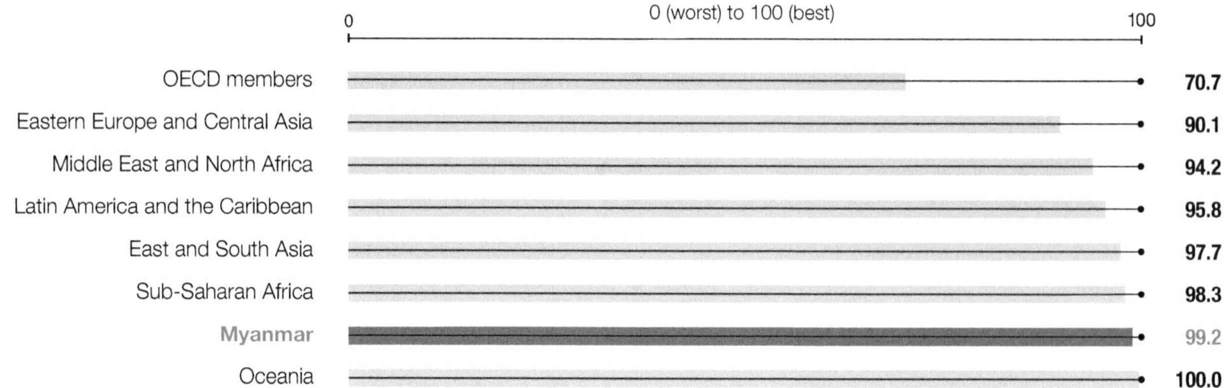

STATISTICAL PERFORMANCE INDEX

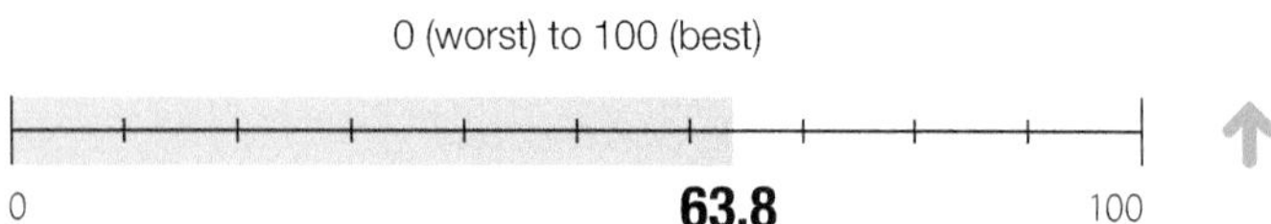

MISSING DATA IN SDG INDEX

3%

MYANMAR

Performance by Indicator

SDG1 – No Poverty	Value	Year	Rating	Trend
Poverty headcount ratio at \$1.90/day (%)	1.7	2022	●	↑
Poverty headcount ratio at \$3.20/day (%)	19.3	2022	●	→
SDG2 – Zero Hunger				
Prevalence of undernourishment (%)	7.6	2019	●	↑
Prevalence of stunting in children under 5 years of age (%)	26.7	2018	●	→
Prevalence of wasting in children under 5 years of age (%)	6.7	2018	●	→
Prevalence of obesity, BMI ≥ 30 (% of adult population)	5.8	2016	●	↑
Human Trophic Level (best 2–3 worst)	2.3	2017	●	→
Cereal yield (tonnes per hectare of harvested land)	3.6	2018	●	↑
Sustainable Nitrogen Management Index (best 0–1.41 worst)	0.6	2015	●	↓
Exports of hazardous pesticides (tonnes per million population)	0.2	2019	●	●
SDG3 – Good Health and Well-Being				
Maternal mortality rate (per 100,000 live births)	250	2017	●	→
Neonatal mortality rate (per 1,000 live births)	22.3	2020	●	↗
Mortality rate, under-5 (per 1,000 live births)	43.7	2020	●	↗
Incidence of tuberculosis (per 100,000 population)	308.0	2020	●	↗
New HIV infections (per 1,000 uninfected population)	1.0	2020	●	→
Age-standardized death rate due to cardiovascular disease, cancer, diabetes, or chronic respiratory disease in adults aged 30–70 years (%)	24.9	2019	●	→
Age-standardized death rate attributable to household air pollution and ambient air pollution (per 100,000 population)	156	2016	●	●
Traffic deaths (per 100,000 population)	20.4	2019	●	↓
Life expectancy at birth (years)	69.1	2019	●	→
Adolescent fertility rate (births per 1,000 females aged 15 to 19)	28.0	2015	●	●
Births attended by skilled health personnel (%)	60.2	2016	●	●
Surviving infants who received 2 WHO-recommended vaccines (%)	84	2020	●	→
Universal health coverage (UHC) index of service coverage (worst 0–100 best)	61	2019	●	↑
Subjective well-being (average ladder score, worst 0–10 best)	4.3	2021	●	→
SDG4 – Quality Education				
Participation rate in pre-primary organized learning (% of children aged 4 to 6)	11.8	2018	●	●
Net primary enrollment rate (%)	98.1	2018	●	●
Lower secondary completion rate (%)	64.8	2018	●	↑
Literacy rate (% of population aged 15 to 24)	95.4	2019	●	↑
SDG5 – Gender Equality				
Demand for family planning satisfied by modern methods (% of females aged 15 to 49)	74.9	2016	●	●
Ratio of female-to-male mean years of education received (%)	102.0	2019	●	↑
Ratio of female-to-male labor force participation rate (%)	59.9	2020	●	↓
Seats held by women in national parliament (%)	16.8	2020	●	→
SDG6 – Clean Water and Sanitation				
Population using at least basic drinking water services (%)	83.7	2020	●	↑
Population using at least basic sanitation services (%)	73.6	2020	●	→
Freshwater withdrawal (% of available freshwater resources)	5.8	2018	●	●
Anthropogenic wastewater that receives treatment (%)	0.0	2018	●	●
Scarce water consumption embodied in imports (m^3 H_2O eq/capita)	245.5	2018	●	●
SDG7 – Affordable and Clean Energy				
Population with access to electricity (%)	68.4	2019	●	↗
Population with access to clean fuels and technology for cooking (%)	30.3	2019	●	↗
CO_2 emissions from fuel combustion per total electricity output ($MtCO_2$/TWh)	1.3	2019	●	↗
Share of renewable energy in total primary energy supply (%)	49.8	2019	●	↑
SDG8 – Decent Work and Economic Growth				
Adjusted GDP growth (%)	0.8	2020	●	●
Victims of modern slavery (per 1,000 population)	11.0	2018	●	●
Adults with an account at a bank or other financial institution or with a mobile-money-service provider (% of population aged 15 or over)	26.0	2017	●	→
Unemployment rate (% of total labor force)	2.3	2022	●	↑
Fundamental labor rights are effectively guaranteed (worst 0–1 best)	0.5	2020	●	↗
Fatal work-related accidents embodied in imports (per 100,000 population)	0.0	2015	●	↑

* Imputed data point

SDG9 – Industry, Innovation and Infrastructure	Value	Year	Rating	Trend
Population using the internet (%)	35.1	2020	●	↑
Mobile broadband subscriptions (per 100 population)	120.8	2019	●	↑
Logistics Performance Index: Quality of trade and transport-related infrastructure (worst 1–5 best)	2.0	2018	●	↓
The Times Higher Education Universities Ranking: Average score of top 3 universities (worst 0–100 best)	* 0.0	2022	●	●
Articles published in academic journals (per 1,000 population)	0.0	2020	●	→
Expenditure on research and development (% of GDP)	0.0	2017	●	●
SDG10 – Reduced Inequalities				
Gini coefficient	30.7	2017	●	↑
Palma ratio	1.2	2018	●	●
SDG11 – Sustainable Cities and Communities				
Proportion of urban population living in slums (%)	57.1	2018	●	↓
Annual mean concentration of particulate matter of less than 2.5 microns in diameter (PM2.5) (μg/m^3)	34.2	2019	●	↗
Access to improved water source, piped (% of urban population)	66.2	2020	●	↗
Satisfaction with public transport (%)	53.0	2021	●	↓
SDG12 – Responsible Consumption and Production				
Municipal solid waste (kg/capita/day)	0.3	2000	●	●
Electronic waste (kg/capita)	1.6	2019	●	●
Production-based SO_2 emissions (kg/capita)	1.5	2018	●	●
SO_2 emissions embodied in imports (kg/capita)	0.3	2018	●	●
Production-based nitrogen emissions (kg/capita)	9.5	2015	●	↑
Nitrogen emissions embodied in imports (kg/capita)	0.0	2015	●	↑
Exports of plastic waste (kg/capita)	0.3	2020	●	●
SDG13 – Climate Action				
CO_2 emissions from fossil fuel combustion and cement production (tCO_2/capita)	0.7	2020	●	↑
CO_2 emissions embodied in imports (tCO_2/capita)	0.1	2018	●	↑
CO_2 emissions embodied in fossil fuel exports (kg/capita)	571.6	2020	●	●
SDG14 – Life Below Water				
Mean area that is protected in marine sites important to biodiversity (%)	19.2	2020	●	→
Ocean Health Index: Clean Waters score (worst 0–100 best)	48.6	2020	●	↓
Fish caught from overexploited or collapsed stocks (% of total catch)	20.2	2018	●	↑
Fish caught by trawling or dredging (%)	47.7	2018	●	↓
Fish caught that are then discarded (%)	3.0	2018	●	↑
Marine biodiversity threats embodied in imports (per million population)	NA	NA	●	●
SDG15 – Life on Land				
Mean area that is protected in terrestrial sites important to biodiversity (%)	25.1	2020	●	→
Mean area that is protected in freshwater sites important to biodiversity (%)	27.1	2020	●	→
Red List Index of species survival (worst 0–1 best)	0.8	2021	●	↓
Permanent deforestation (% of forest area, 5-year average)	0.5	2020	●	→
Terrestrial and freshwater biodiversity threats embodied in imports (per million population)	0.0	2018	●	●
SDG16 – Peace, Justice and Strong Institutions				
Homicides (per 100,000 population)	2.3	2016	●	●
Unsentenced detainees (% of prison population)	NA	NA	●	●
Population who feel safe walking alone at night in the city or area where they live (%)	44	2021	●	↓
Property Rights (worst 1–7 best)	NA	NA	●	●
Birth registrations with civil authority (% of children under age 5)	81.3	2020	●	●
Corruption Perception Index (worst 0–100 best)	28	2021	●	→
Children involved in child labor (% of population aged 5 to 14)	9.9	2019	●	●
Exports of major conventional weapons (TIV constant million USD per 100,000 population)	* 0.0	2020	●	●
Press Freedom Index (best 0–100 worst)	46.1	2021	●	↓
Access to and affordability of justice (worst 0–1 best)	0.3	2020	●	↓
SDG17 – Partnerships for the Goals				
Government spending on health and education (% of GDP)	2.7	2019	●	↓
For high-income and all OECD DAC countries: International concessional public finance, including official development assistance (% of GNI)	NA	NA	●	●
Other countries: Government revenue excluding grants (% of GDP)	15.4	2019	●	↓
Corporate Tax Haven Score (best 0–100 worst)	* 0.0	2019	●	●
Statistical Performance Index (worst 0–100 best)	63.8	2019	●	↑

5. Country Profiles

NAMIBIA

Sub-Saharan Africa

OVERALL PERFORMANCE

COUNTRY RANKING

NAMIBIA

114 **/163**

COUNTRY SCORE

AVERAGE PERFORMANCE BY SDG

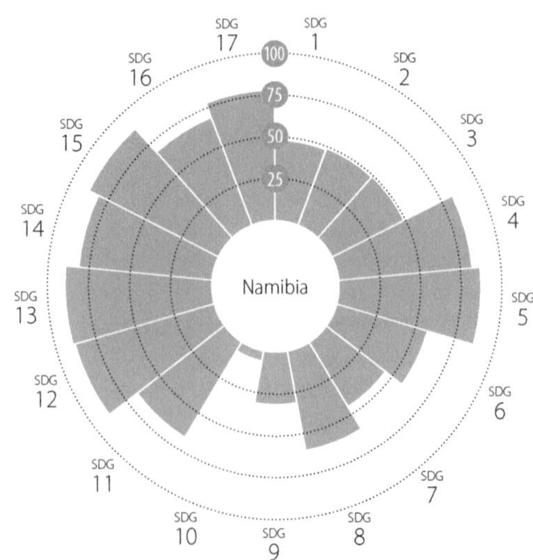

SDG DASHBOARDS AND TRENDS

Major challenges · Significant challenges · Challenges remain · SDG achieved · Information unavailable

Decreasing · Stagnating · Moderately improving · On track or maintaining SDG achievement · Information unavailable

Note: The full title of each SDG is available here: https://sustainabledevelopment.un.org/topics/sustainabledevelopmentgoals

INTERNATIONAL SPILLOVER INDEX

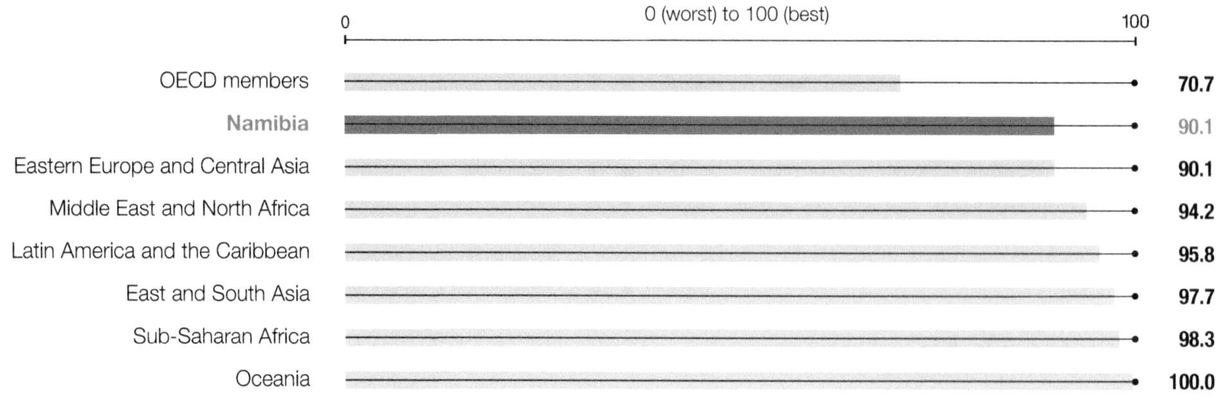

STATISTICAL PERFORMANCE INDEX

0 (worst) to 100 (best)

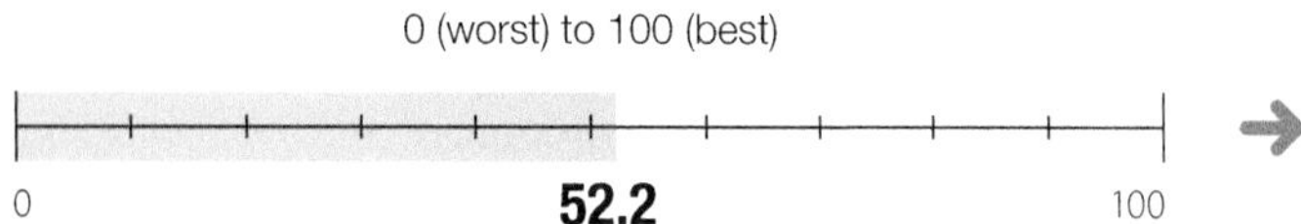

MISSING DATA IN SDG INDEX

2%

Performance by Indicator

SDG1 – No Poverty

Indicator	Value	Year	Rating	Trend
Poverty headcount ratio at $1.90/day (%)	24.0	2022	●	↓
Poverty headcount ratio at $3.20/day (%)	37.5	2022	●	↓

SDG2 – Zero Hunger

Indicator	Value	Year	Rating	Trend
Prevalence of undernourishment (%)	19.8	2019	●	→
Prevalence of stunting in children under 5 years of age (%)	22.7	2013	●	→
Prevalence of wasting in children under 5 years of age (%)	7.1	2013	●	→
Prevalence of obesity, BMI ≥ 30 (% of adult population)	17.2	2016	●	↓
Human Trophic Level (best 2–3 worst)	2.2	2017	●	→
Cereal yield (tonnes per hectare of harvested land)	0.5	2018	●	→
Sustainable Nitrogen Management Index (best 0–1.41 worst)	1.2	2015	●	↓
Exports of hazardous pesticides (tonnes per million population)	6.0	2019	●	●

SDG3 – Good Health and Well-Being

Indicator	Value	Year	Rating	Trend
Maternal mortality rate (per 100,000 live births)	195	2017	●	↗
Neonatal mortality rate (per 1,000 live births)	20.1	2020	●	→
Mortality rate, under-5 (per 1,000 live births)	40.2	2020	●	↗
Incidence of tuberculosis (per 100,000 population)	460.0	2020	●	↗
New HIV infections (per 1,000 uninfected population)	2.4	2020	●	↑
Age-standardized death rate due to cardiovascular disease, cancer, diabetes, or chronic respiratory disease in adults aged 30–70 years (%)	22.6	2019	●	↗
Age-standardized death rate attributable to household air pollution and ambient air pollution (per 100,000 population)	145	2016	●	●
Traffic deaths (per 100,000 population)	34.8	2019	●	↓
Life expectancy at birth (years)	64.6	2019	●	→
Adolescent fertility rate (births per 1,000 females aged 15 to 19)	63.9	2016	●	●
Births attended by skilled health personnel (%)	88.2	2013	●	●
Surviving infants who received 2 WHO-recommended vaccines (%)	80	2019	●	↓
Universal health coverage (UHC) index of service coverage (worst 0–100 best)	62	2019	●	↗
Subjective well-being (average ladder score, worst 0–10 best)	4.5	2021	●	↓

SDG4 – Quality Education

Indicator	Value	Year	Rating	Trend
Participation rate in pre-primary organized learning (% of children aged 4 to 6)	72.1	2019	●	↑
Net primary enrollment rate (%)	98.5	2018	●	●
Lower secondary completion rate (%)	85.2	2018	●	↑
Literacy rate (% of population aged 15 to 24)	95.2	2018	●	●

SDG5 – Gender Equality

Indicator	Value	Year	Rating	Trend
Demand for family planning satisfied by modern methods (% of females aged 15 to 49)	80.4	2013	●	↑
Ratio of female-to-male mean years of education received (%)	109.0	2019	●	↑
Ratio of female-to-male labor force participation rate (%)	87.6	2020	●	↑
Seats held by women in national parliament (%)	43.3	2020	●	↑

SDG6 – Clean Water and Sanitation

Indicator	Value	Year	Rating	Trend
Population using at least basic drinking water services (%)	84.3	2020	●	→
Population using at least basic sanitation services (%)	35.3	2020	●	→
Freshwater withdrawal (% of available freshwater resources)	0.9	2018	●	●
Anthropogenic wastewater that receives treatment (%)	6.3	2018	●	●
Scarce water consumption embodied in imports (m^3 H_2O eq/capita)	2501.1	2018	●	●

SDG7 – Affordable and Clean Energy

Indicator	Value	Year	Rating	Trend
Population with access to electricity (%)	55.2	2019	●	→
Population with access to clean fuels and technology for cooking (%)	46.3	2019	●	→
CO_2 emissions from fuel combustion per total electricity output ($MtCO_2$/TWh)	3.5	2019	●	→
Share of renewable energy in total primary energy supply (%)	23.2	2019	●	↑

SDG8 – Decent Work and Economic Growth

Indicator	Value	Year	Rating	Trend
Adjusted GDP growth (%)	-7.5	2020	●	●
Victims of modern slavery (per 1,000 population)	3.3	2018	●	●
Adults with an account at a bank or other financial institution or with a mobile-money-service provider (% of population aged 15 or over)	80.6	2017	●	↑
Unemployment rate (% of total labor force)	21.1	2022	●	↓
Fundamental labor rights are effectively guaranteed (worst 0–1 best)	0.6	2020	●	●
Fatal work-related accidents embodied in imports (per 100,000 population)	0.6	2015	●	↑

* Imputed data point

SDG9 – Industry, Innovation and Infrastructure

Indicator	Value	Year	Rating	Trend
Population using the internet (%)	41.0	2020	●	↗
Mobile broadband subscriptions (per 100 population)	66.2	2019	●	↑
Logistics Performance Index: Quality of trade and transport-related infrastructure (worst 1–5 best)	2.8	2016	●	●
The Times Higher Education Universities Ranking: Average score of top 3 universities (worst 0–100 best)	* 0.0	2022	●	●
Articles published in academic journals (per 1,000 population)	0.2	2020	●	→
Expenditure on research and development (% of GDP)	0.4	2014	●	●

SDG10 – Reduced Inequalities

Indicator	Value	Year	Rating	Trend
Gini coefficient	59.1	2015	●	●
Palma ratio	5.5	2018	●	●

SDG11 – Sustainable Cities and Communities

Indicator	Value	Year	Rating	Trend
Proportion of urban population living in slums (%)	42.8	2018	●	↓
Annual mean concentration of particulate matter of less than 2.5 microns in diameter (PM2.5) (μg/m^3)	25.8	2019	●	→
Access to improved water source, piped (% of urban population)	96.9	2020	●	→
Satisfaction with public transport (%)	46.0	2021	●	↓

SDG12 – Responsible Consumption and Production

Indicator	Value	Year	Rating	Trend
Municipal solid waste (kg/capita/day)	NA	NA	●	●
Electronic waste (kg/capita)	6.4	2019	●	●
Production-based SO_2 emissions (kg/capita)	8.1	2018	●	●
SO_2 emissions embodied in imports (kg/capita)	3.5	2018	●	●
Production-based nitrogen emissions (kg/capita)	26.0	2015	●	↗
Nitrogen emissions embodied in imports (kg/capita)	3.1	2015	●	↑
Exports of plastic waste (kg/capita)	0.4	2020	●	●

SDG13 – Climate Action

Indicator	Value	Year	Rating	Trend
CO_2 emissions from fossil fuel combustion and cement production (tCO_2/capita)	1.5	2020	●	↑
CO_2 emissions embodied in imports (tCO_2/capita)	0.8	2018	●	↑
CO_2 emissions embodied in fossil fuel exports (kg/capita)	0.0	2020	●	●

SDG14 – Life Below Water

Indicator	Value	Year	Rating	Trend
Mean area that is protected in marine sites important to biodiversity (%)	83.0	2020	●	→
Ocean Health Index: Clean Waters score (worst 0–100 best)	83.6	2020	●	↑
Fish caught from overexploited or collapsed stocks (% of total catch)	5.2	2018	●	↑
Fish caught by trawling or dredging (%)	33.5	2018	●	↓
Fish caught that are then discarded (%)	3.9	2018	●	↑
Marine biodiversity threats embodied in imports (per million population)	0.3	2018	●	●

SDG15 – Life on Land

Indicator	Value	Year	Rating	Trend
Mean area that is protected in terrestrial sites important to biodiversity (%)	86.2	2020	●	↑
Mean area that is protected in freshwater sites important to biodiversity (%)	85.7	2020	●	↑
Red List Index of species survival (worst 0–1 best)	1.0	2021	●	↑
Permanent deforestation (% of forest area, 5-year average)	0.2	2020	●	↓
Terrestrial and freshwater biodiversity threats embodied in imports (per million population)	1.3	2018	●	●

SDG16 – Peace, Justice and Strong Institutions

Indicator	Value	Year	Rating	Trend
Homicides (per 100,000 population)	11.9	2020	●	●
Unsentenced detainees (% of prison population)	3.2	2016	●	●
Population who feel safe walking alone at night in the city or area where they live (%)	41	2021	●	↓
Property Rights (worst 1–7 best)	4.9	2020	●	↑
Birth registrations with civil authority (% of children under age 5)	78.1	2020	●	●
Corruption Perception Index (worst 0–100 best)	49	2021	●	↓
Children involved in child labor (% of population aged 5 to 14)	NA	NA	●	●
Exports of major conventional weapons (TIV constant million USD per 100,000 population)	* 0.0	2020	●	●
Press Freedom Index (best 0–100 worst)	19.7	2021	●	↑
Access to and affordability of justice (worst 0–1 best)	0.5	2020	●	●

SDG17 – Partnerships for the Goals

Indicator	Value	Year	Rating	Trend
Government spending on health and education (% of GDP)	13.4	2020	●	↑
For high-income and all OECD DAC countries: International concessional public finance, including official development assistance (% of GNI)	NA	NA	●	●
Other countries: Government revenue excluding grants (% of GDP)	34.8	2019	●	↑
Corporate Tax Haven Score (best 0–100 worst)	* 0.0	2019	●	●
Statistical Performance Index (worst 0–100 best)	52.2	2019	●	→

NAURU

Oceania

OVERALL PERFORMANCE

COUNTRY RANKING

NAURU

NA /163

COUNTRY SCORE

AVERAGE PERFORMANCE BY SDG

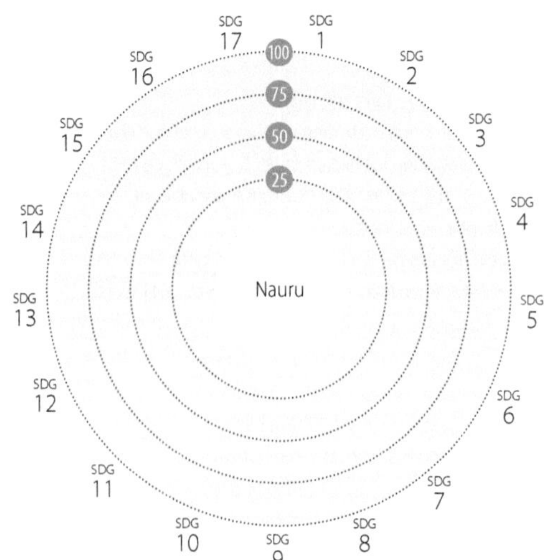

SDG DASHBOARDS AND TRENDS

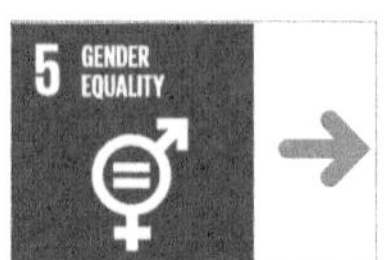

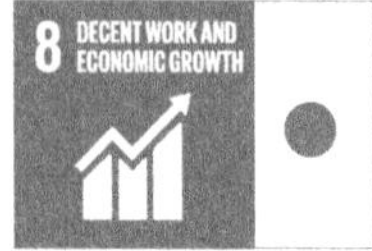

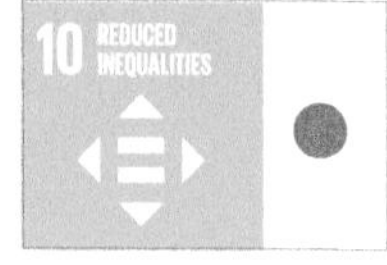

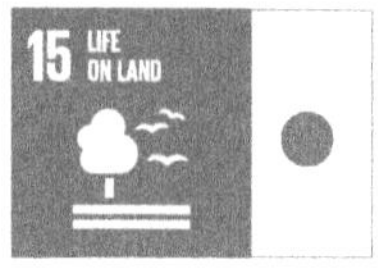

Major challenges · Significant challenges · Challenges remain · SDG achieved · Information unavailable

Decreasing · Stagnating · Moderately improving · On track or maintaining SDG achievement · Information unavailable

Note: The full title of each SDG is available here: https://sustainabledevelopment.un.org/topics/sustainabledevelopmentgoals

INTERNATIONAL SPILLOVER INDEX

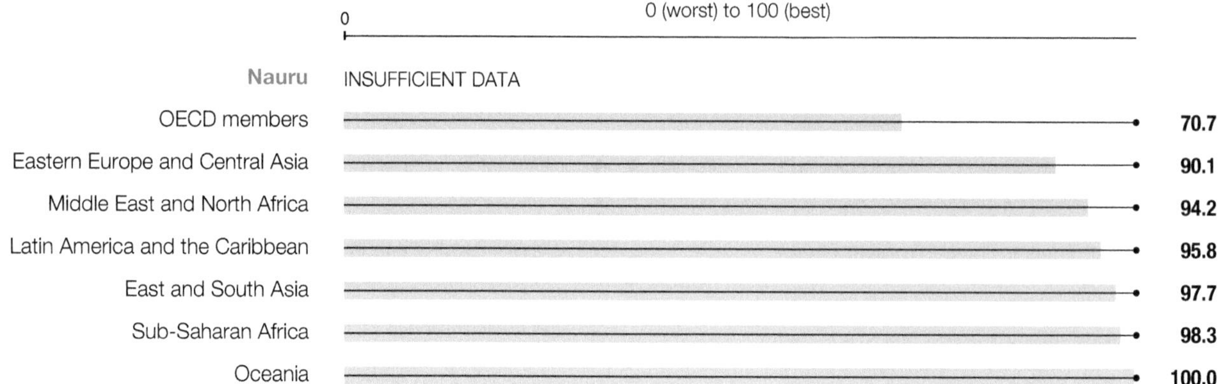

STATISTICAL PERFORMANCE INDEX

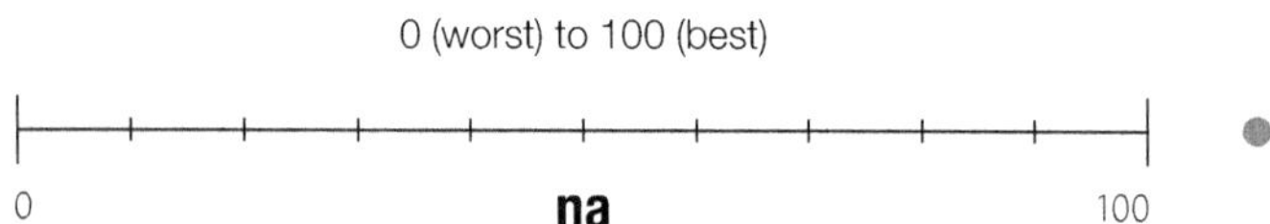

MISSING DATA IN SDG INDEX

54%

SDG1 – No Poverty	Value	Year	Rating	Trend
Poverty headcount ratio at $1.90/day (%)	NA	NA	●	●
Poverty headcount ratio at $3.20/day (%)	NA	NA	●	●
SDG2 – Zero Hunger				
Prevalence of undernourishment (%)	* 1.2	2019	●	●
Prevalence of stunting in children under 5 years of age (%)	24.0	2007	●	↑
Prevalence of wasting in children under 5 years of age (%)	1.0	2007	●	↑
Prevalence of obesity, BMI ≥ 30 (% of adult population)	61.0	2016	●	↓
Human Trophic Level (best 2–3 worst)	NA	NA	●	●
Cereal yield (tonnes per hectare of harvested land)	NA	NA	●	●
Sustainable Nitrogen Management Index (best 0–1.41 worst)	1.0	2015	●	→
Exports of hazardous pesticides (tonnes per million population)	NA	NA	●	●
SDG3 – Good Health and Well-Being				
Maternal mortality rate (per 100,000 live births)	NA	NA	●	●
Neonatal mortality rate (per 1,000 live births)	18.3	2020	●	↗
Mortality rate, under-5 (per 1,000 live births)	28.5	2020	●	↑
Incidence of tuberculosis (per 100,000 population)	180.0	2020	●	↓
New HIV infections (per 1,000 uninfected population)	NA	NA	●	●
Age-standardized death rate due to cardiovascular disease, cancer, diabetes, or chronic respiratory disease in adults aged 30–70 years (%)	NA	NA	●	●
Age-standardized death rate attributable to household air pollution and ambient air pollution (per 100,000 population)	NA	NA	●	●
Traffic deaths (per 100,000 population)	NA	NA	●	●
Life expectancy at birth (years)	NA	NA	●	●
Adolescent fertility rate (births per 1,000 females aged 15 to 19)	94.0	2015	●	●
Births attended by skilled health personnel (%)	97.4	2007	●	●
Surviving infants who received 2 WHO-recommended vaccines (%)	95	2020	●	↑
Universal health coverage (UHC) index of service coverage (worst 0–100 best)	NA	NA	●	●
Subjective well-being (average ladder score, worst 0–10 best)	NA	NA	●	●
SDG4 – Quality Education				
Participation rate in pre-primary organized learning (% of children aged 4 to 6)	96.0	2020	●	↑
Net primary enrollment rate (%)	95.7	2020	●	↓
Lower secondary completion rate (%)	86.6	2019	●	●
Literacy rate (% of population aged 15 to 24)	NA	NA	●	●
SDG5 – Gender Equality				
Demand for family planning satisfied by modern methods (% of females aged 15 to 49)	42.5	2007	●	●
Ratio of female-to-male mean years of education received (%)	NA	NA	●	●
Ratio of female-to-male labor force participation rate (%)	NA	NA	●	●
Seats held by women in national parliament (%)	10.5	2020	●	→
SDG6 – Clean Water and Sanitation				
Population using at least basic drinking water services (%)	100.0	2020	●	↑
Population using at least basic sanitation services (%)	65.6	2017	●	●
Freshwater withdrawal (% of available freshwater resources)	NA	NA	●	●
Anthropogenic wastewater that receives treatment (%)	0.9	2018	●	●
Scarce water consumption embodied in imports (m^3 H_2O eq/capita)	NA	NA	●	●
SDG7 – Affordable and Clean Energy				
Population with access to electricity (%)	100.0	2019	●	↑
Population with access to clean fuels and technology for cooking (%)	100.0	2019	●	↑
CO_2 emissions from fuel combustion per total electricity output ($MtCO_2$/TWh)	2.0	2019	●	→
Share of renewable energy in total primary energy supply (%)	NA	NA	●	●
SDG8 – Decent Work and Economic Growth				
Adjusted GDP growth (%)	-0.8	2020	●	●
Victims of modern slavery (per 1,000 population)	NA	NA	●	●
Adults with an account at a bank or other financial institution or with a mobile-money-service provider (% of population aged 15 or over)	NA	NA	●	●
Unemployment rate (% of total labor force)	NA	NA	●	●
Fundamental labor rights are effectively guaranteed (worst 0–1 best)	NA	NA	●	●
Fatal work-related accidents embodied in imports (per 100,000 population)	NA	NA	●	●

* Imputed data point

SDG9 – Industry, Innovation and Infrastructure	Value	Year	Rating	Trend
Population using the internet (%)	62.4	2017	●	●
Mobile broadband subscriptions (per 100 population)	37.2	2019	●	↗
Logistics Performance Index: Quality of trade and transport-related infrastructure (worst 1–5 best)	NA	NA	●	●
The Times Higher Education Universities Ranking: Average score of top 3 universities (worst 0–100 best)	* 0.0	2022	●	●
Articles published in academic journals (per 1,000 population)	0.3	2020	●	→
Expenditure on research and development (% of GDP)	NA	NA	●	●
SDG10 – Reduced Inequalities				
Gini coefficient	34.8	2012	●	●
Palma ratio	NA	NA	●	●
SDG11 – Sustainable Cities and Communities				
Proportion of urban population living in slums (%)	NA	NA	●	●
Annual mean concentration of particulate matter of less than 2.5 microns in diameter (PM2.5) (μg/m³)	11.8	2019	●	↑
Access to improved water source, piped (% of urban population)	52.8	2019	●	→
Satisfaction with public transport (%)	NA	NA	●	●
SDG12 – Responsible Consumption and Production				
Municipal solid waste (kg/capita/day)	1.6	2016	●	●
Electronic waste (kg/capita)	NA	NA	●	●
Production-based SO_2 emissions (kg/capita)	NA	NA	●	●
SO_2 emissions embodied in imports (kg/capita)	NA	NA	●	●
Production-based nitrogen emissions (kg/capita)	NA	NA	●	●
Nitrogen emissions embodied in imports (kg/capita)	NA	NA	●	●
Exports of plastic waste (kg/capita)	NA	NA	●	●
SDG13 – Climate Action				
CO_2 emissions from fossil fuel combustion and cement production (tCO_2/capita)	5.2	2020	●	→
CO_2 emissions embodied in imports (tCO_2/capita)	NA	NA	●	●
CO_2 emissions embodied in fossil fuel exports (kg/capita)	0.0	2020	●	●
SDG14 – Life Below Water				
Mean area that is protected in marine sites important to biodiversity (%)	0.0	2020	●	→
Ocean Health Index: Clean Waters score (worst 0–100 best)	24.2	2020	●	→
Fish caught from overexploited or collapsed stocks (% of total catch)	0.0	2018	●	↑
Fish caught by trawling or dredging (%)	0.0	2018	●	↑
Fish caught that are then discarded (%)	0.0	2003	●	●
Marine biodiversity threats embodied in imports (per million population)	NA	NA	●	●
SDG15 – Life on Land				
Mean area that is protected in terrestrial sites important to biodiversity (%)	0.0	2020	●	→
Mean area that is protected in freshwater sites important to biodiversity (%)	NA	NA	●	●
Red List Index of species survival (worst 0–1 best)	0.8	2021	●	↓
Permanent deforestation (% of forest area, 5-year average)	NA	NA	●	●
Terrestrial and freshwater biodiversity threats embodied in imports (per million population)	NA	NA	●	●
SDG16 – Peace, Justice and Strong Institutions				
Homicides (per 100,000 population)	NA	NA	●	●
Unsentenced detainees (% of prison population)	NA	NA	●	●
Population who feel safe walking alone at night in the city or area where they live (%)	NA	NA	●	●
Property Rights (worst 1–7 best)	NA	NA	●	●
Birth registrations with civil authority (% of children under age 5)	95.9	2020	●	●
Corruption Perception Index (worst 0–100 best)	NA	NA	●	●
Children involved in child labor (% of population aged 5 to 14)	NA	NA	●	●
Exports of major conventional weapons (TIV constant million USD per 100,000 population)	* 0.0	2020	●	●
Press Freedom Index (best 0–100 worst)	NA	NA	●	●
Access to and affordability of justice (worst 0–1 best)	NA	NA	●	●
SDG17 – Partnerships for the Goals				
Government spending on health and education (% of GDP)	12.7	2019	●	↑
For high-income and all OECD DAC countries: International concessional public finance, including official development assistance (% of GNI)	NA	NA	●	●
Other countries: Government revenue excluding grants (% of GDP)	NA	NA	●	●
Corporate Tax Haven Score (best 0–100 worst)	* NA	NA	●	●
Statistical Performance Index (worst 0–100 best)	NA	NA	●	●

NEPAL

AVERAGE PERFORMANCE BY SDG

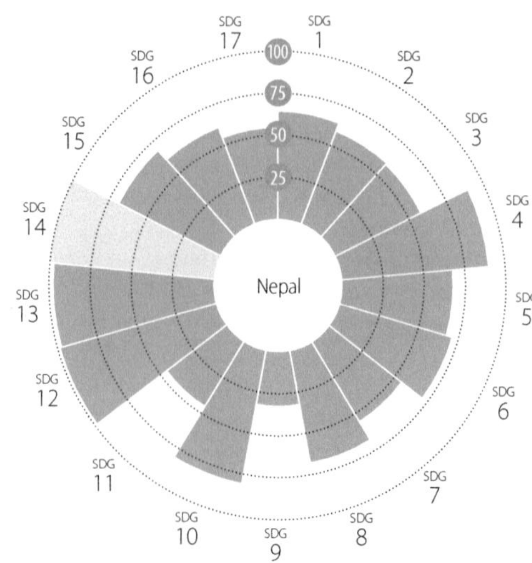

OVERALL PERFORMANCE

COUNTRY RANKING

NEPAL

98/163

COUNTRY SCORE

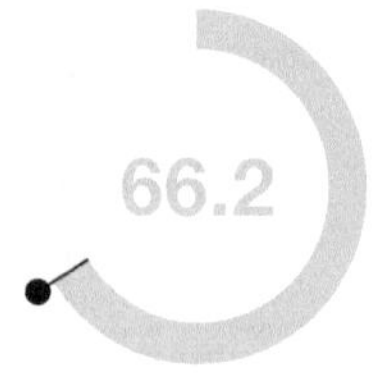

REGIONAL AVERAGE: 65.9

SDG DASHBOARDS AND TRENDS

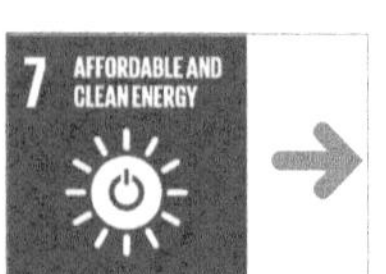

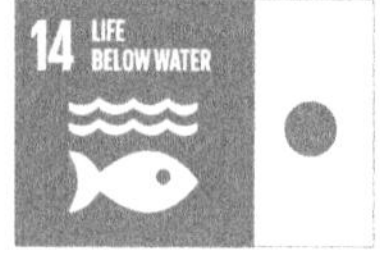

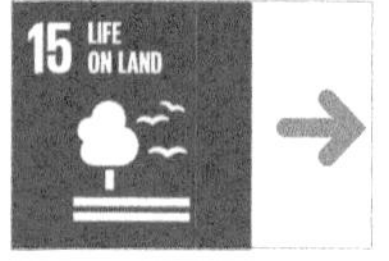

Major challenges | Significant challenges | Challenges remain | SDG achieved | Information unavailable

Decreasing | Stagnating | Moderately improving | On track or maintaining SDG achievement | Information unavailable

Note: The full title of each SDG is available here: https://sustainabledevelopment.un.org/topics/sustainabledevelopmentgoals

INTERNATIONAL SPILLOVER INDEX

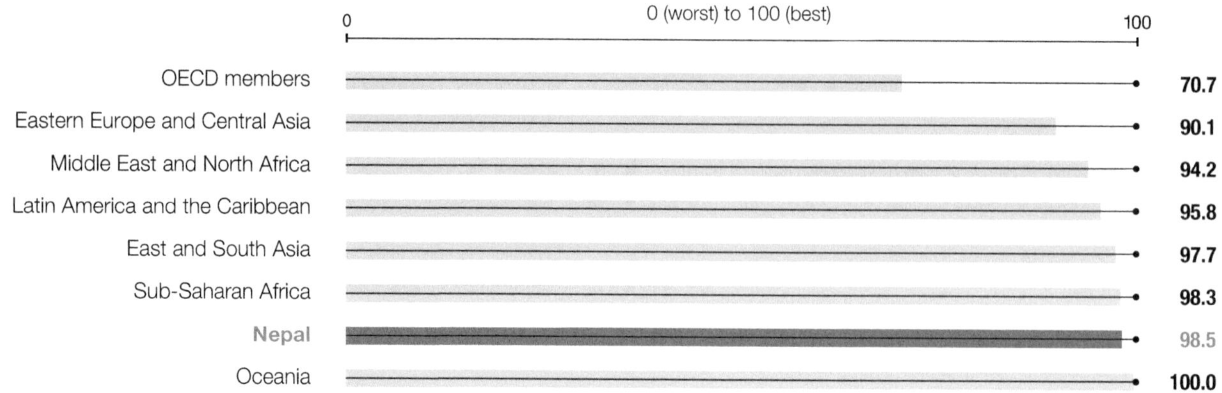

STATISTICAL PERFORMANCE INDEX

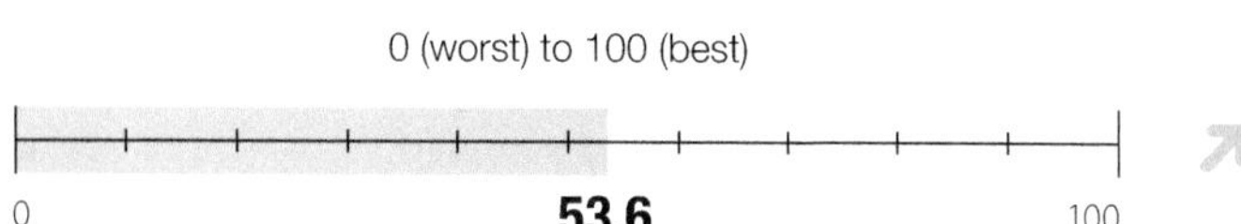

MISSING DATA IN SDG INDEX

3%

SDG1 – No Poverty	Value	Year	Rating	Trend
Poverty headcount ratio at \$1.90/day (%)	6.7	2022	●	↑
Poverty headcount ratio at \$3.20/day (%)	32.8	2022	●	↗
SDG2 – Zero Hunger				
Prevalence of undernourishment (%)	4.8	2019	●	↑
Prevalence of stunting in children under 5 years of age (%)	31.5	2019	●	→
Prevalence of wasting in children under 5 years of age (%)	12.0	2019	●	→
Prevalence of obesity, BMI ≥ 30 (% of adult population)	4.1	2016	●	↑
Human Trophic Level (best 2–3 worst)	2.1	2017	●	↑
Cereal yield (tonnes per hectare of harvested land)	2.9	2018	●	↑
Sustainable Nitrogen Management Index (best 0–1.41 worst)	0.7	2015	●	↓
Exports of hazardous pesticides (tonnes per million population)	NA	NA	●	●
SDG3 – Good Health and Well-Being				
Maternal mortality rate (per 100,000 live births)	186	2017	●	↑
Neonatal mortality rate (per 1,000 live births)	16.9	2020	●	↑
Mortality rate, under-5 (per 1,000 live births)	28.2	2020	●	↑
Incidence of tuberculosis (per 100,000 population)	235.0	2020	●	→
New HIV infections (per 1,000 uninfected population)	0.0	2020	●	↑
Age-standardized death rate due to cardiovascular disease, cancer, diabetes, or chronic respiratory disease in adults aged 30–70 years (%)	21.5	2019	●	↓
Age-standardized death rate attributable to household air pollution and ambient air pollution (per 100,000 population)	194	2016	●	●
Traffic deaths (per 100,000 population)	16.3	2019	●	→
Life expectancy at birth (years)	70.9	2019	●	↗
Adolescent fertility rate (births per 1,000 females aged 15 to 19)	63.0	2018	●	↑
Births attended by skilled health personnel (%)	58.0	2017	●	→
Surviving infants who received 2 WHO-recommended vaccines (%)	84	2020	●	→
Universal health coverage (UHC) index of service coverage (worst 0–100 best)	53	2019	●	↗
Subjective well-being (average ladder score, worst 0–10 best)	4.6	2021	●	↓
SDG4 – Quality Education				
Participation rate in pre-primary organized learning (% of children aged 4 to 6)	87.0	2019	●	↑
Net primary enrollment rate (%)	96.3	2019	●	↓
Lower secondary completion rate (%)	99.5	2020	●	↑
Literacy rate (% of population aged 15 to 24)	92.4	2018	●	●
SDG5 – Gender Equality				
Demand for family planning satisfied by modern methods (% of females aged 15 to 49)	61.9	2019	●	→
Ratio of female-to-male mean years of education received (%)	74.1	2019	●	↑
Ratio of female-to-male labor force participation rate (%)	95.2	2020	●	↑
Seats held by women in national parliament (%)	32.7	2020	●	↗
SDG6 – Clean Water and Sanitation				
Population using at least basic drinking water services (%)	90.1	2020	●	↗
Population using at least basic sanitation services (%)	76.6	2020	●	↑
Freshwater withdrawal (% of available freshwater resources)	8.3	2018	●	●
Anthropogenic wastewater that receives treatment (%)	0.0	2018	●	●
Scarce water consumption embodied in imports (m^3 H_2O eq/capita)	486.9	2018	●	●
SDG7 – Affordable and Clean Energy				
Population with access to electricity (%)	89.9	2019	●	↑
Population with access to clean fuels and technology for cooking (%)	31.0	2019	●	→
CO_2 emissions from fuel combustion per total electricity output ($MtCO_2$/TWh)	3.2	2019	●	→
Share of renewable energy in total primary energy supply (%)	NA	NA	●	●
SDG8 – Decent Work and Economic Growth				
Adjusted GDP growth (%)	-2.1	2020	●	●
Victims of modern slavery (per 1,000 population)	6.0	2018	●	●
Adults with an account at a bank or other financial institution or with a mobile-money-service provider (% of population aged 15 or over)	45.4	2017	●	↑
Unemployment rate (% of total labor force)	5.2	2022	●	↓
Fundamental labor rights are effectively guaranteed (worst 0–1 best)	0.6	2020	●	→
Fatal work-related accidents embodied in imports (per 100,000 population)	0.1	2015	●	↑

* Imputed data point

SDG9 – Industry, Innovation and Infrastructure	Value	Year	Rating	Trend
Population using the internet (%)	37.7	2020	●	↗
Mobile broadband subscriptions (per 100 population)	54.6	2019	●	↑
Logistics Performance Index: Quality of trade and transport-related infrastructure (worst 1–5 best)	2.2	2018	●	↓
The Times Higher Education Universities Ranking: Average score of top 3 universities (worst 0–100 best)	29.6	2022	●	●
Articles published in academic journals (per 1,000 population)	0.1	2020	●	→
Expenditure on research and development (% of GDP)	0.3	2010	●	●
SDG10 – Reduced Inequalities				
Gini coefficient	32.8	2010	●	●
Palma ratio	1.3	2018	●	●
SDG11 – Sustainable Cities and Communities				
Proportion of urban population living in slums (%)	49.3	2018	●	→
Annual mean concentration of particulate matter of less than 2.5 microns in diameter (PM2.5) (μg/m³)	95.7	2019	●	↓
Access to improved water source, piped (% of urban population)	52.9	2020	●	↓
Satisfaction with public transport (%)	73.0	2021	●	↑
SDG12 – Responsible Consumption and Production				
Municipal solid waste (kg/capita/day)	0.2	2016	●	●
Electronic waste (kg/capita)	0.9	2019	●	●
Production-based SO_2 emissions (kg/capita)	1.3	2018	●	●
SO_2 emissions embodied in imports (kg/capita)	0.7	2018	●	●
Production-based nitrogen emissions (kg/capita)	7.9	2015	●	↑
Nitrogen emissions embodied in imports (kg/capita)	0.3	2015	●	↑
Exports of plastic waste (kg/capita)	0.0	2019	●	●
SDG13 – Climate Action				
CO_2 emissions from fossil fuel combustion and cement production (tCO_2/capita)	0.6	2020	●	↑
CO_2 emissions embodied in imports (tCO_2/capita)	0.2	2018	●	↑
CO_2 emissions embodied in fossil fuel exports (kg/capita)	0.0	2018	●	●
SDG14 – Life Below Water				
Mean area that is protected in marine sites important to biodiversity (%)	NA	NA	●	●
Ocean Health Index: Clean Waters score (worst 0–100 best)	NA	NA	●	●
Fish caught from overexploited or collapsed stocks (% of total catch)	NA	NA	●	●
Fish caught by trawling or dredging (%)	NA	NA	●	●
Fish caught that are then discarded (%)	NA	NA	●	●
Marine biodiversity threats embodied in imports (per million population)	0.0	2018	●	●
SDG15 – Life on Land				
Mean area that is protected in terrestrial sites important to biodiversity (%)	50.7	2020	●	→
Mean area that is protected in freshwater sites important to biodiversity (%)	32.4	2020	●	→
Red List Index of species survival (worst 0–1 best)	0.8	2021	●	→
Permanent deforestation (% of forest area, 5-year average)	0.0	2020	●	↑
Terrestrial and freshwater biodiversity threats embodied in imports (per million population)	0.0	2018	●	●
SDG16 – Peace, Justice and Strong Institutions				
Homicides (per 100,000 population)	2.1	2014	●	●
Unsentenced detainees (% of prison population)	NA	NA	●	●
Population who feel safe walking alone at night in the city or area where they live (%)	59	2021	●	↓
Property Rights (worst 1–7 best)	4.0	2020	●	↓
Birth registrations with civil authority (% of children under age 5)	77.2	2020	●	●
Corruption Perception Index (worst 0–100 best)	33	2021	●	→
Children involved in child labor (% of population aged 5 to 14)	21.7	2019	●	●
Exports of major conventional weapons (TIV constant million USD per 100,000 population)	* 0.0	2020	●	●
Press Freedom Index (best 0–100 worst)	34.6	2021	●	↓
Access to and affordability of justice (worst 0–1 best)	0.5	2020	●	↗
SDG17 – Partnerships for the Goals				
Government spending on health and education (% of GDP)	5.5	2019	●	↗
For high-income and all OECD DAC countries: International concessional public finance, including official development assistance (% of GNI)	NA	NA	●	●
Other countries: Government revenue excluding grants (% of GDP)	22.4	2019	●	↑
Corporate Tax Haven Score (best 0–100 worst)	* 0.0	2019	●	●
Statistical Performance Index (worst 0–100 best)	53.6	2019	●	↗

NETHERLANDS

OECD Countries

OVERALL PERFORMANCE

COUNTRY RANKING

NETHERLANDS

17 **/163**

COUNTRY SCORE

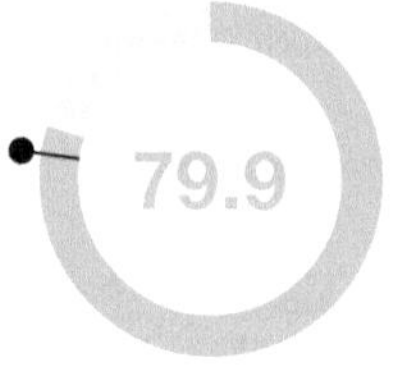

REGIONAL AVERAGE: 77.2

AVERAGE PERFORMANCE BY SDG

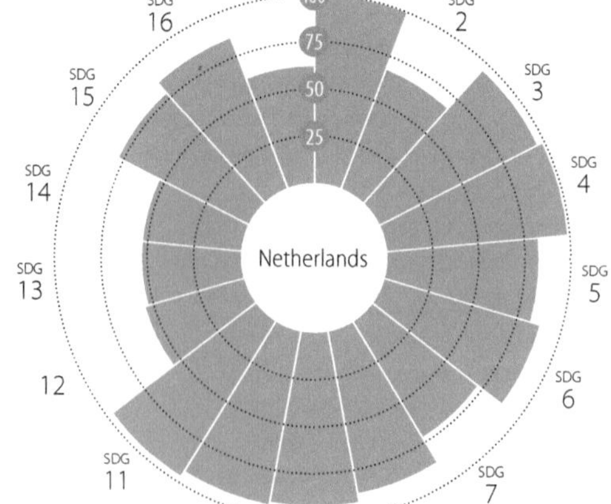

SDG DASHBOARDS AND TRENDS

Major challenges · Significant challenges · Challenges remain · SDG achieved · Information unavailable

Decreasing · Stagnating · Moderately improving · On track or maintaining SDG achievement · Information unavailable

Note: The full title of each SDG is available here: https://sustainabledevelopment.un.org/topics/sustainabledevelopmentgoals

INTERNATIONAL SPILLOVER INDEX

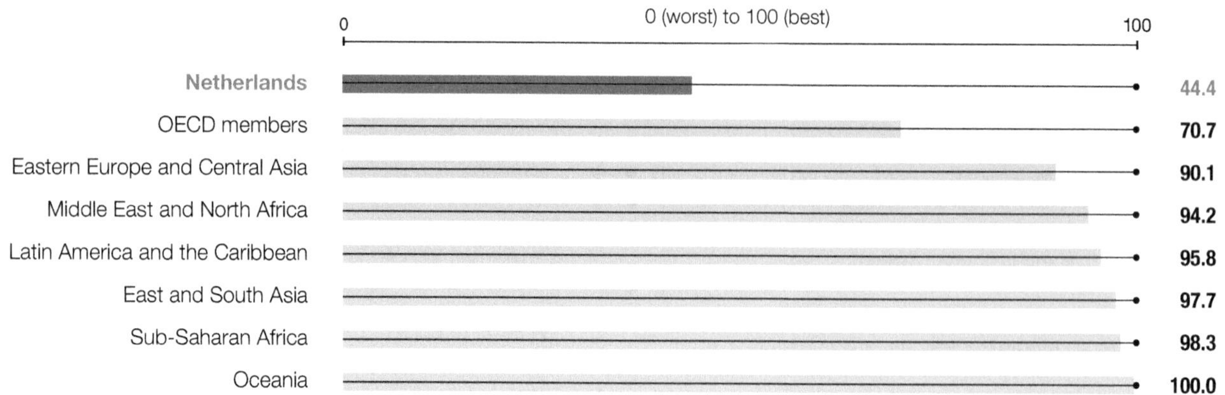

Region	Score
Netherlands	44.4
OECD members	70.7
Eastern Europe and Central Asia	90.1
Middle East and North Africa	94.2
Latin America and the Caribbean	95.8
East and South Asia	97.7
Sub-Saharan Africa	98.3
Oceania	100.0

STATISTICAL PERFORMANCE INDEX

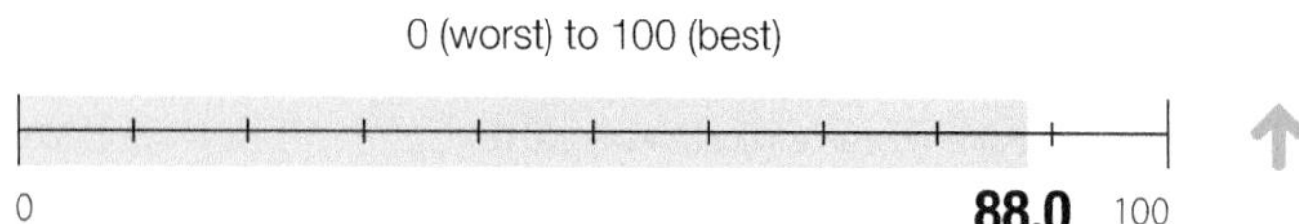

MISSING DATA IN SDG INDEX

1%

NETHERLANDS

Performance by Indicator

SDG1 – No Poverty	Value	Year	Rating	Trend
Poverty headcount ratio at $1.90/day (%)	0.2	2022	●	↑
Poverty headcount ratio at $3.20/day (%)	0.2	2022	●	↑
Poverty rate after taxes and transfers (%)	8.2	2019	●	↑
SDG2 – Zero Hunger				
Prevalence of undernourishment (%)	2.5	2019	●	↑
Prevalence of stunting in children under 5 years of age (%)	1.5	2009	●	↑
Prevalence of wasting in children under 5 years of age (%)	1.0	2009	●	↑
Prevalence of obesity, BMI ≥ 30 (% of adult population)	20.4	2016	●	↓
Human Trophic Level (best 2–3 worst)	2.5	2017	●	↓
Cereal yield (tonnes per hectare of harvested land)	8.3	2018	●	↑
Sustainable Nitrogen Management Index (best 0–1.41 worst)	0.8	2015	●	↓
Yield gap closure (% of potential yield)	76.2	2018	●	●
Exports of hazardous pesticides (tonnes per million population)	63.8	2019	●	●
SDG3 – Good Health and Well-Being				
Maternal mortality rate (per 100,000 live births)	5	2017	●	↑
Neonatal mortality rate (per 1,000 live births)	2.7	2020	●	↑
Mortality rate, under-5 (per 1,000 live births)	4.2	2020	●	↑
Incidence of tuberculosis (per 100,000 population)	4.1	2020	●	↑
New HIV infections (per 1,000 uninfected population)	0.0	2020	●	↑
Age-standardized death rate due to cardiovascular disease, cancer, diabetes, or chronic respiratory disease in adults aged 30–70 years (%)	10.4	2019	●	↑
Age-standardized death rate attributable to household air pollution and ambient air pollution (per 100,000 population)	14	2016	●	●
Traffic deaths (per 100,000 population)	4.0	2019	●	↑
Life expectancy at birth (years)	81.8	2019	●	↑
Adolescent fertility rate (births per 1,000 females aged 15 to 19)	2.6	2018	●	↑
Births attended by skilled health personnel (%)	100.0	2003	●	●
Surviving infants who received 2 WHO-recommended vaccines (%)	94	2020	●	↑
Universal health coverage (UHC) index of service coverage (worst 0–100 best)	86	2019	●	↑
Subjective well-being (average ladder score, worst 0–10 best)	7.3	2021	●	↑
Gap in life expectancy at birth among regions (years)	1.4	2019	●	↑
Gap in self-reported health status by income (percentage points)	24.8	2020	●	↓
Daily smokers (% of population aged 15 and over)	15.4	2019	●	↑
SDG4 – Quality Education				
Participation rate in pre-primary organized learning (% of children aged 4 to 6)	97.5	2019	●	↑
Net primary enrollment rate (%)	99.6	2019	●	↑
Lower secondary completion rate (%)	* 99.8	2019	●	↑
Literacy rate (% of population aged 15 to 24)	NA	NA	●	●
Tertiary educational attainment (% of population aged 25 to 34)	52.3	2020	●	↑
PISA score (worst 0–600 best)	502.3	2018	●	↑
Variation in science performance explained by socio-economic status (%)	12.9	2018	●	↓
Underachievers in science (% of 15-year-olds)	20.0	2018	●	↓
SDG5 – Gender Equality				
Demand for family planning satisfied by modern methods (% of females aged 15 to 49)	* 88.9	2022	●	↑
Ratio of female-to-male mean years of education received (%)	96.1	2019	●	↑
Ratio of female-to-male labor force participation rate (%)	86.4	2020	●	↑
Seats held by women in national parliament (%)	33.3	2020	●	↓
Gender wage gap (% of male median wage)	12.7	2018	●	↑
SDG6 – Clean Water and Sanitation				
Population using at least basic drinking water services (%)	100.0	2020	●	↑
Population using at least basic sanitation services (%)	97.7	2020	●	↑
Freshwater withdrawal (% of available freshwater resources)	15.4	2018	●	●
Anthropogenic wastewater that receives treatment (%)	100.0	2018	●	●
Scarce water consumption embodied in imports (m^3 H_2O eq/capita)	6241.6	2018	●	●
Population using safely managed water services (%)	100.0	2020	●	↑
Population using safely managed sanitation services (%)	97.5	2020	●	↑
SDG7 – Affordable and Clean Energy				
Population with access to electricity (%)	100.0	2019	●	↑
Population with access to clean fuels and technology for cooking (%)	100.0	2019	●	↑
CO_2 emissions from fuel combustion per total electricity output ($MtCO_2$/TWh)	1.3	2019	●	↑
Share of renewable energy in total primary energy supply (%)	7.2	2019	●	↗
SDG8 – Decent Work and Economic Growth				
Adjusted GDP growth (%)	0.4	2020	●	●
Victims of modern slavery (per 1,000 population)	1.8	2018	●	●
Adults with an account at a bank or other financial institution or with a mobile-money-service provider (% of population aged 15 or over)	99.6	2017	●	↑
Fundamental labor rights are effectively guaranteed (worst 0–1 best)	0.8	2020	●	↑
Fatal work-related accidents embodied in imports (per 100,000 population)	1.9	2015	●	↑
Employment-to-population ratio (%)	79.3	2020	●	↑
Youth not in employment, education or training (NEET) (% of population aged 15 to 29)	7.2	2020	●	↑

SDG9 – Industry, Innovation and Infrastructure	Value	Year	Rating	Trend
Population using the internet (%)	91.3	2020	●	↑
Mobile broadband subscriptions (per 100 population)	128.4	2019	●	↑
Logistics Performance Index: Quality of trade and transport-related infrastructure (worst 1–5 best)	4.2	2018	●	↑
The Times Higher Education Universities Ranking: Average score of top 3 universities (worst 0–100 best)	68.9	2022	●	●
Articles published in academic journals (per 1,000 population)	3.6	2020	●	↑
Expenditure on research and development (% of GDP)	2.2	2018	●	↑
Researchers (per 1,000 employed population)	10.2	2019	●	↑
Triadic patent families filed (per million population)	56.0	2019	●	↑
Gap in internet access by income (percentage points)	6.1	2020	●	↑
Female share of graduates from STEM fields at the tertiary level (%)	29.3	2017	●	↑
SDG10 – Reduced Inequalities				
Gini coefficient	28.1	2018	●	↑
Palma ratio	1.1	2019	●	→
Elderly poverty rate (% of population aged 66 or over)	5.2	2019	●	↓
SDG11 – Sustainable Cities and Communities				
Proportion of urban population living in slums (%)	* 0.0	2018	●	↑
Annual mean concentration of particulate matter of less than 2.5 microns in diameter (PM2.5) ($\mu g/m^3$)	11.4	2019	●	↑
Access to improved water source, piped (% of urban population)	100.0	2020	●	↑
Satisfaction with public transport (%)	78.0	2021	●	↑
Population with rent overburden (%)	6.1	2019	●	↑
SDG12 – Responsible Consumption and Production				
Electronic waste (kg/capita)	21.6	2019	●	●
Production-based SO_2 emissions (kg/capita)	15.0	2018	●	●
SO_2 emissions embodied in imports (kg/capita)	8.8	2018	●	●
Production-based nitrogen emissions (kg/capita)	12.7	2015	●	↑
Nitrogen emissions embodied in imports (kg/capita)	19.5	2015	●	↓
Exports of plastic waste (kg/capita)	22.2	2021	●	●
Non-recycled municipal solid waste (kg/capita/day)	0.6	2019	●	↑
SDG13 – Climate Action				
CO_2 emissions from fossil fuel combustion and cement production (tCO_2/capita)	8.1	2020	●	↗
CO_2 emissions embodied in imports (tCO_2/capita)	3.3	2018	●	↓
CO_2 emissions embodied in fossil fuel exports (kg/capita)	68.9	2021	●	●
Carbon Pricing Score at EUR60/tCO_2 (%, worst 0–100 best)	49.6	2018	●	↑
SDG14 – Life Below Water				
Mean area that is protected in marine sites important to biodiversity (%)	96.6	2020	●	↑
Ocean Health Index: Clean Waters score (worst 0–100 best)	45.5	2020	●	→
Fish caught from overexploited or collapsed stocks (% of total catch)	53.1	2018	●	↓
Fish caught by trawling or dredging (%)	31.4	2018	●	→
Fish caught that are then discarded (%)	19.1	2018	●	↓
Marine biodiversity threats embodied in imports (per million population)	0.3	2018	●	●
SDG15 – Life on Land				
Mean area that is protected in terrestrial sites important to biodiversity (%)	79.6	2020	●	↑
Mean area that is protected in freshwater sites important to biodiversity (%)	87.3	2020	●	↑
Red List Index of species survival (worst 0–1 best)	0.9	2021	●	↑
Permanent deforestation (% of forest area, 5-year average)	0.0	2020	●	↑
Terrestrial and freshwater biodiversity threats embodied in imports (per million population)	6.0	2018	●	●
SDG16 – Peace, Justice and Strong Institutions				
Homicides (per 100,000 population)	0.6	2020	●	↑
Unsentenced detainees (% of prison population)	26.6	2019	●	↑
Population who feel safe walking alone at night in the city or area where they live (%)	83	2021	●	↑
Property Rights (worst 1–7 best)	6.1	2020	●	↑
Birth registrations with civil authority (% of children under age 5)	100.0	2020	●	●
Corruption Perception Index (worst 0–100 best)	82	2021	●	↑
Children involved in child labor (% of population aged 5 to 14)	* 0.0	2019	●	●
Exports of major conventional weapons (TIV constant million USD per 100,000 population)	3.1	2020	●	●
Press Freedom Index (best 0–100 worst)	9.7	2021	●	↑
Access to and affordability of justice (worst 0–1 best)	0.8	2020	●	↑
Persons held in prison (per 100,000 population)	68.3	2019	●	↑
SDG17 – Partnerships for the Goals				
Government spending on health and education (% of GDP)	12.0	2019	●	↑
For high-income and all OECD DAC countries: International concessional public finance, including official development assistance (% of GNI)	0.5	2021	●	↓
Other countries: Government revenue excluding grants (% of GDP)	NA	NA	●	●
Corporate Tax Haven Score (best 0–100 worst)	78.0	2019	●	●
Financial Secrecy Score (best 0–100 worst)	71.8	2020	●	●
Shifted profits of multinationals (US$ billion)	105.9	2018	●	↓
Statistical Performance Index (worst 0–100 best)	88.0	2019	●	↑

* Imputed data point

NEW ZEALAND

OECD Countries

OVERALL PERFORMANCE

COUNTRY RANKING

NEW ZEALAND

26/163

COUNTRY SCORE

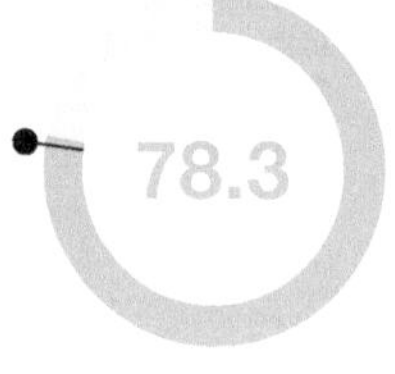

REGIONAL AVERAGE: 77.2

AVERAGE PERFORMANCE BY SDG

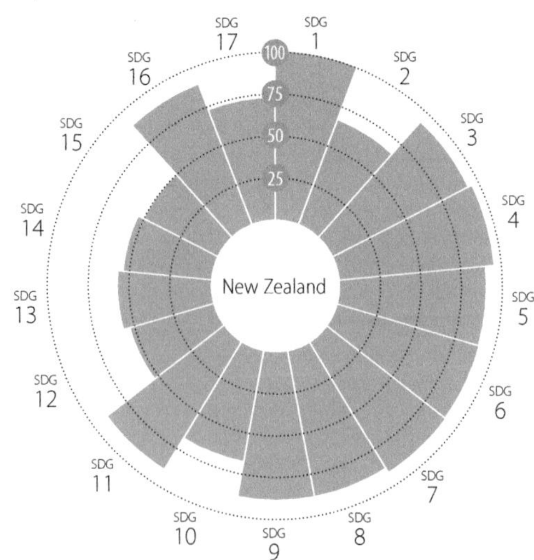

SDG DASHBOARDS AND TRENDS

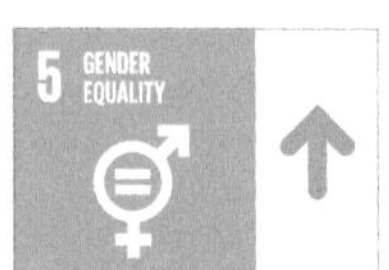

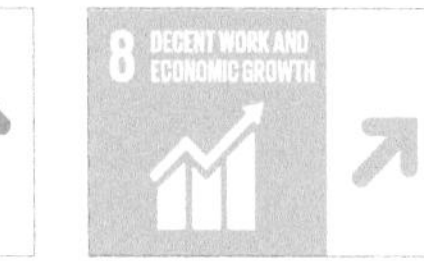

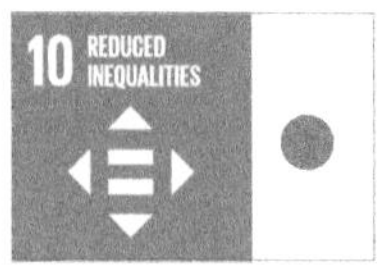

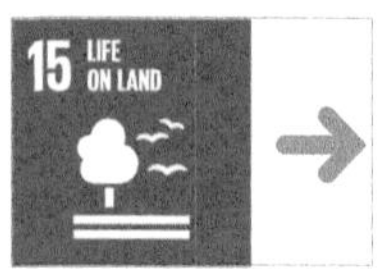

Major challenges | Significant challenges | Challenges remain | SDG achieved | Information unavailable

Decreasing | Stagnating | Moderately improving | On track or maintaining SDG achievement | Information unavailable

Note: The full title of each SDG is available here: https://sustainabledevelopment.un.org/topics/sustainabledevelopmentgoals

INTERNATIONAL SPILLOVER INDEX

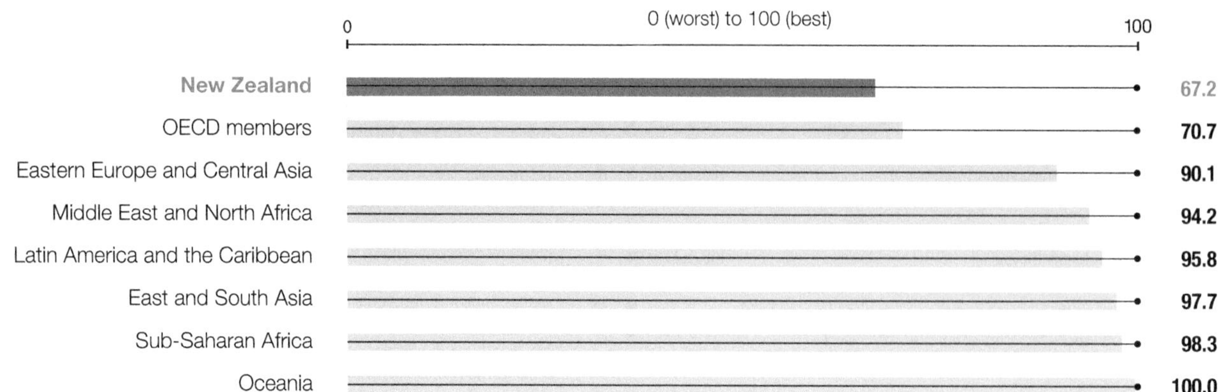

STATISTICAL PERFORMANCE INDEX

0 (worst) to 100 (best)

0 **85.3** 100

MISSING DATA IN SDG INDEX

3%

NEW ZEALAND

Performance by Indicator

SDG1 – No Poverty		Value	Year	Rating	Trend
Poverty headcount ratio at \$1.90/day (%)		0.0	2022	●	↑
Poverty headcount ratio at \$3.20/day (%)		0.0	2022	●	↑
Poverty rate after taxes and transfers (%)		10.9	2014	●	●
SDG2 – Zero Hunger					
Prevalence of undernourishment (%)		2.5	2019	●	↑
Prevalence of stunting in children under 5 years of age (%)	*	2.6	2019	●	↑
Prevalence of wasting in children under 5 years of age (%)	*	0.7	2019	●	↑
Prevalence of obesity, BMI ≥ 30 (% of adult population)		30.8	2016	●	↓
Human Trophic Level (best 2–3 worst)		2.4	2017	●	↓
Cereal yield (tonnes per hectare of harvested land)		8.1	2018	●	↑
Sustainable Nitrogen Management Index (best 0–1.41 worst)		0.6	2015	●	→
Yield gap closure (% of potential yield)		NA	NA	●	●
Exports of hazardous pesticides (tonnes per million population)		NA	NA	●	●
SDG3 – Good Health and Well-Being					
Maternal mortality rate (per 100,000 live births)		9	2017	●	↑
Neonatal mortality rate (per 1,000 live births)		2.6	2020	●	↑
Mortality rate, under-5 (per 1,000 live births)		4.7	2020	●	↑
Incidence of tuberculosis (per 100,000 population)		7.5	2020	●	↑
New HIV infections (per 1,000 uninfected population)		0.0	2020	●	↑
Age-standardized death rate due to cardiovascular disease, cancer, diabetes, or chronic respiratory disease in adults aged 30–70 years (%)		10.3	2019	●	↑
Age-standardized death rate attributable to household air pollution and ambient air pollution (per 100,000 population)		7	2016	●	●
Traffic deaths (per 100,000 population)		9.6	2019	●	↓
Life expectancy at birth (years)		82.0	2019	●	↑
Adolescent fertility rate (births per 1,000 females aged 15 to 19)		13.3	2019	●	↑
Births attended by skilled health personnel (%)		96.6	2017	●	↑
Surviving infants who received 2 WHO-recommended vaccines (%)		91	2020	●	↑
Universal health coverage (UHC) index of service coverage (worst 0–100 best)		86	2019	●	↑
Subjective well-being (average ladder score, worst 0–10 best)		7.1	2021	●	↑
Gap in life expectancy at birth among regions (years)		4.0	2013	●	●
Gap in self-reported health status by income (percentage points)		8.5	2020	●	↑
Daily smokers (% of population aged 15 and over)		11.6	2020	●	↑
SDG4 – Quality Education					
Participation rate in pre-primary organized learning (% of children aged 4 to 6)		91.5	2019	●	↑
Net primary enrollment rate (%)		100.0	2019	●	↑
Lower secondary completion rate (%)	*	99.0	2019	●	↑
Literacy rate (% of population aged 15 to 24)		NA	NA	●	●
Tertiary educational attainment (% of population aged 25 to 34)		43.9	2020	●	↑
PISA score (worst 0–600 best)		502.7	2018	●	↑
Variation in science performance explained by socio-economic status (%)		13.9	2018	●	↓
Underachievers in science (% of 15-year-olds)		18.0	2018	●	→
SDG5 – Gender Equality					
Demand for family planning satisfied by modern methods (% of females aged 15 to 49)		85.6	2021	●	↑
Ratio of female-to-male mean years of education received (%)		98.5	2019	●	↑
Ratio of female-to-male labor force participation rate (%)		86.4	2020	●	↑
Seats held by women in national parliament (%)		48.3	2020	●	↑
Gender wage gap (% of male median wage)		4.6	2020	●	↑
SDG6 – Clean Water and Sanitation					
Population using at least basic drinking water services (%)		100.0	2020	●	↑
Population using at least basic sanitation services (%)		100.0	2020	●	↑
Freshwater withdrawal (% of available freshwater resources)		8.1	2018	●	●
Anthropogenic wastewater that receives treatment (%)		79.9	2018	●	●
Scarce water consumption embodied in imports (m^3 H_2O eq/capita)		3180.8	2018	●	●
Population using safely managed water services (%)		100.0	2020	●	↑
Population using safely managed sanitation services (%)		82.2	2020	●	→
SDG7 – Affordable and Clean Energy					
Population with access to electricity (%)		100.0	2019	●	↑
Population with access to clean fuels and technology for cooking (%)		100.0	2019	●	↑
CO_2 emissions from fuel combustion per total electricity output ($MtCO_2$/TWh)		0.8	2019	●	↑
Share of renewable energy in total primary energy supply (%)		40.4	2019	●	↑
SDG8 – Decent Work and Economic Growth					
Adjusted GDP growth (%)		-0.7	2020	●	●
Victims of modern slavery (per 1,000 population)		0.6	2018	●	●
Adults with an account at a bank or other financial institution or with a mobile-money-service provider (% of population aged 15 or over)		99.2	2017	●	↑
Fundamental labor rights are effectively guaranteed (worst 0–1 best)		0.8	2020	●	↑
Fatal work-related accidents embodied in imports (per 100,000 population)		0.9	2015	●	↑
Employment-to-population ratio (%)		78.3	2021	●	↑
Youth not in employment, education or training (NEET) (% of population aged 15 to 29)		12.4	2020	●	↗

* Imputed data point

SDG9 – Industry, Innovation and Infrastructure		Value	Year	Rating	Trend
Population using the internet (%)		91.5	2020	●	↑
Mobile broadband subscriptions (per 100 population)		107.1	2019	●	↑
Logistics Performance Index: Quality of trade and transport-related infrastructure (worst 1–5 best)		4.0	2018	●	↑
The Times Higher Education Universities Ranking: Average score of top 3 universities (worst 0–100 best)		54.2	2022	●	●
Articles published in academic journals (per 1,000 population)		3.5	2020	●	↑
Expenditure on research and development (% of GDP)		1.3	2017	●	↑
Researchers (per 1,000 employed population)		10.8	2019	●	↑
Triadic patent families filed (per million population)		12.9	2019	●	↓
Gap in internet access by income (percentage points)		19.0	2012	●	●
Female share of graduates from STEM fields at the tertiary level (%)		35.0	2017	●	↑
SDG10 – Reduced Inequalities					
Gini coefficient		NA	NA	●	●
Palma ratio		1.4	2014	●	●
Elderly poverty rate (% of population aged 66 or over)		10.6	2014	●	●
SDG11 – Sustainable Cities and Communities					
Proportion of urban population living in slums (%)	*	0.0	2018	●	↑
Annual mean concentration of particulate matter of less than 2.5 microns in diameter (PM2.5) (μg/m³)		5.6	2019	●	↑
Access to improved water source, piped (% of urban population)		100.0	2020	●	↑
Satisfaction with public transport (%)		56.0	2021	●	↗
Population with rent overburden (%)		NA	NA	●	●
SDG12 – Responsible Consumption and Production					
Electronic waste (kg/capita)		19.2	2019	●	●
Production-based SO_2 emissions (kg/capita)		13.6	2018	●	●
SO_2 emissions embodied in imports (kg/capita)		9.0	2018	●	●
Production-based nitrogen emissions (kg/capita)		120.0	2015	●	↓
Nitrogen emissions embodied in imports (kg/capita)		7.1	2015	●	→
Exports of plastic waste (kg/capita)		6.0	2021	●	●
Non-recycled municipal solid waste (kg/capita/day)		NA	NA	●	●
SDG13 – Climate Action					
CO_2 emissions from fossil fuel combustion and cement production (tCO_2/capita)		6.9	2020	●	→
CO_2 emissions embodied in imports (tCO_2/capita)		3.0	2018	●	→
CO_2 emissions embodied in fossil fuel exports (kg/capita)		533.6	2020	●	●
Carbon Pricing Score at EUR60/tCO_2 (%, worst 0–100 best)		33.2	2018	●	↑
SDG14 – Life Below Water					
Mean area that is protected in marine sites important to biodiversity (%)		47.1	2020	●	→
Ocean Health Index: Clean Waters score (worst 0–100 best)		78.4	2020	●	→
Fish caught from overexploited or collapsed stocks (% of total catch)		60.4	2018	●	↓
Fish caught by trawling or dredging (%)		44.9	2018	●	→
Fish caught that are then discarded (%)		12.3	2018	●	↓
Marine biodiversity threats embodied in imports (per million population)		0.4	2018	●	●
SDG15 – Life on Land					
Mean area that is protected in terrestrial sites important to biodiversity (%)		46.5	2020	●	→
Mean area that is protected in freshwater sites important to biodiversity (%)		24.6	2020	●	→
Red List Index of species survival (worst 0–1 best)		0.6	2021	●	↓
Permanent deforestation (% of forest area, 5-year average)		0.0	2020	●	↑
Terrestrial and freshwater biodiversity threats embodied in imports (per million population)		2.6	2018	●	●
SDG16 – Peace, Justice and Strong Institutions					
Homicides (per 100,000 population)		2.6	2019	●	↓
Unsentenced detainees (% of prison population)		36.3	2019	●	↓
Population who feel safe walking alone at night in the city or area where they live (%)		65	2021	●	→
Property Rights (worst 1–7 best)		6.0	2020	●	↑
Birth registrations with civil authority (% of children under age 5)		100.0	2020	●	●
Corruption Perception Index (worst 0–100 best)		88	2021	●	↑
Children involved in child labor (% of population aged 5 to 14)	*	0.0	2019	●	●
Exports of major conventional weapons (TIV constant million USD per 100,000 population)		0.1	2020	●	●
Press Freedom Index (best 0–100 worst)		10.0	2021	●	↑
Access to and affordability of justice (worst 0–1 best)		0.7	2020	●	↑
Persons held in prison (per 100,000 population)		204.4	2019	●	↓
SDG17 – Partnerships for the Goals					
Government spending on health and education (% of GDP)		13.4	2019	●	↑
For high-income and all OECD DAC countries: International concessional public finance, including official development assistance (% of GNI)		0.3	2021	●	→
Other countries: Government revenue excluding grants (% of GDP)		NA	NA	●	●
Corporate Tax Haven Score (best 0–100 worst)	*	0.0	2019	●	●
Financial Secrecy Score (best 0–100 worst)		64.8	2020	●	●
Shifted profits of multinationals (US\$ billion)		2.7	2018	●	↑
Statistical Performance Index (worst 0–100 best)		85.3	2019	●	↑

NICARAGUA

Latin America and the Caribbean

OVERALL PERFORMANCE

COUNTRY RANKING

NICARAGUA

92/163

COUNTRY SCORE

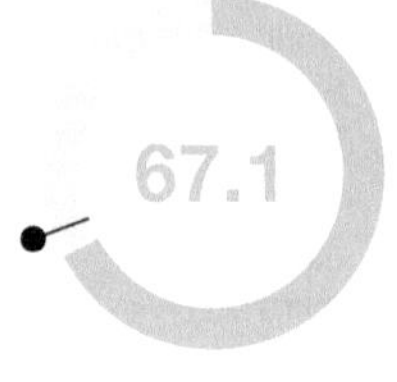

REGIONAL AVERAGE: 69.5

AVERAGE PERFORMANCE BY SDG

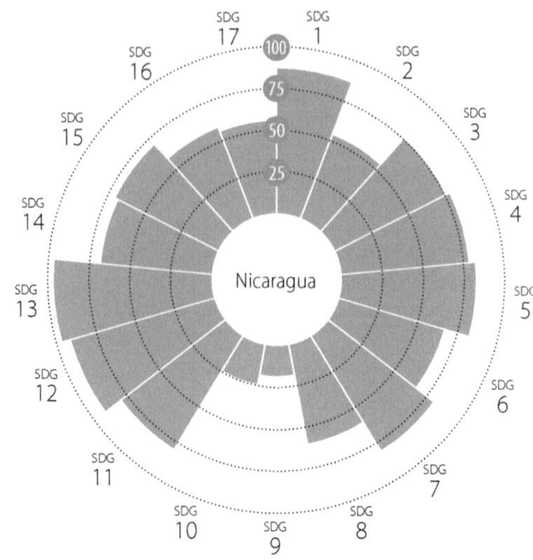

SDG DASHBOARDS AND TRENDS

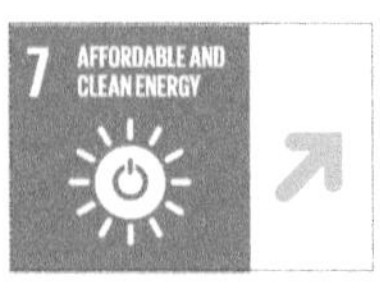

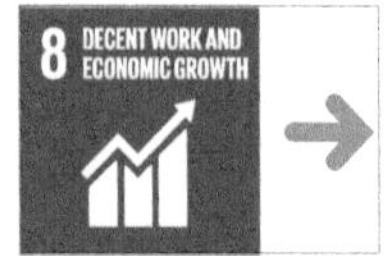

Major challenges | Significant challenges | Challenges remain | SDG achieved | Information unavailable

Decreasing | Stagnating | Moderately improving | On track or maintaining SDG achievement | Information unavailable

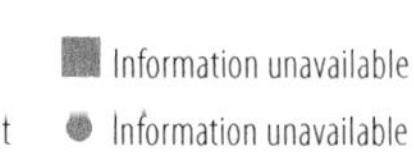

Note: The full title of each SDG is available here: https://sustainabledevelopment.un.org/topics/sustainabledevelopmentgoals

INTERNATIONAL SPILLOVER INDEX

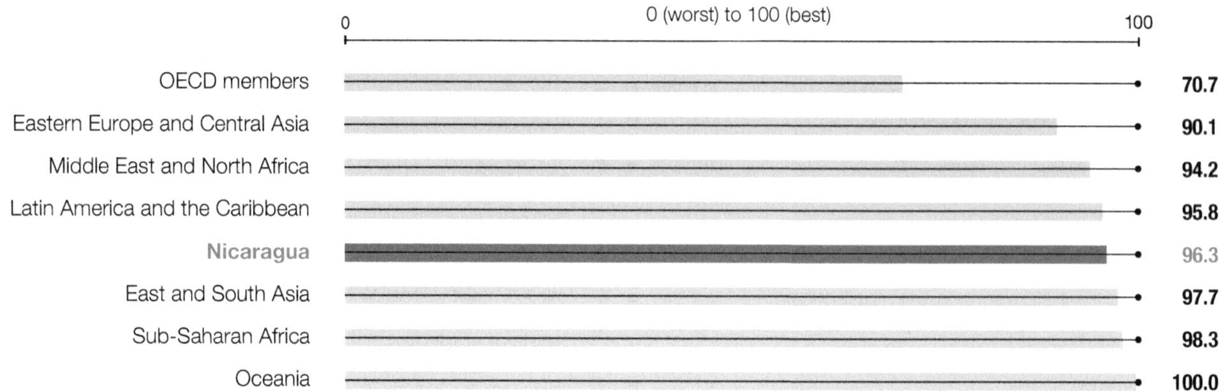

STATISTICAL PERFORMANCE INDEX

0 (worst) to 100 (best)

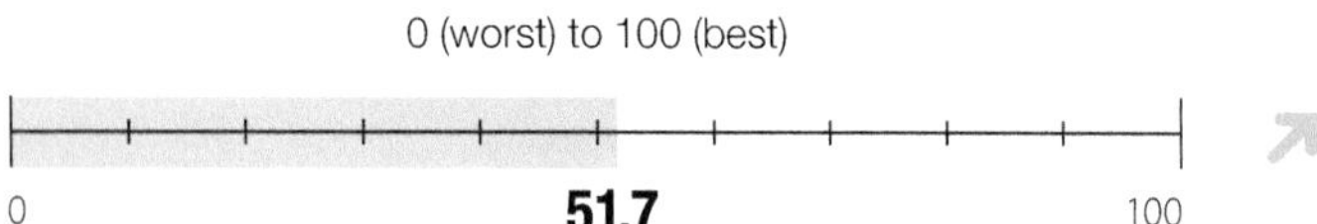

MISSING DATA IN SDG INDEX

1%

SDG1 – No Poverty

Indicator	Value	Year	Rating	Trend
Poverty headcount ratio at $1.90/day (%)	2.4	2022	●	↗
Poverty headcount ratio at $3.20/day (%)	11.8	2022	●	→

SDG2 – Zero Hunger

Indicator	Value	Year	Rating	Trend
Prevalence of undernourishment (%)	19.3	2019	●	↓
Prevalence of stunting in children under 5 years of age (%)	17.3	2012	●	→
Prevalence of wasting in children under 5 years of age (%)	2.2	2012	●	↑
Prevalence of obesity, BMI ≥ 30 (% of adult population)	23.7	2016	●	↓
Human Trophic Level (best 2–3 worst)	2.3	2017	●	↗
Cereal yield (tonnes per hectare of harvested land)	2.1	2018	●	↑
Sustainable Nitrogen Management Index (best 0–1.41 worst)	1.0	2015	●	↓
Exports of hazardous pesticides (tonnes per million population)	0.5	2019	●	●

SDG3 – Good Health and Well-Being

Indicator	Value	Year	Rating	Trend
Maternal mortality rate (per 100,000 live births)	98	2017	●	↗
Neonatal mortality rate (per 1,000 live births)	9.4	2020	●	↑
Mortality rate, under-5 (per 1,000 live births)	16.0	2020	●	↑
Incidence of tuberculosis (per 100,000 population)	42.0	2020	●	↗
New HIV infections (per 1,000 uninfected population)	0.1	2020	●	↑
Age-standardized death rate due to cardiovascular disease, cancer, diabetes, or chronic respiratory disease in adults aged 30–70 years (%)	15.3	2019	●	↓
Age-standardized death rate attributable to household air pollution and ambient air pollution (per 100,000 population)	56	2016	●	●
Traffic deaths (per 100,000 population)	16.9	2019	●	↓
Life expectancy at birth (years)	75.0	2019	●	→
Adolescent fertility rate (births per 1,000 females aged 15 to 19)	102.6	2018	●	●
Births attended by skilled health personnel (%)	96.0	2017	●	↑
Surviving infants who received 2 WHO-recommended vaccines (%)	92	2020	●	↑
Universal health coverage (UHC) index of service coverage (worst 0–100 best)	70	2019	●	↗
Subjective well-being (average ladder score, worst 0–10 best)	6.1	2021	●	↑

SDG4 – Quality Education

Indicator	Value	Year	Rating	Trend
Participation rate in pre-primary organized learning (% of children aged 4 to 6)	84.6	2010	●	●
Net primary enrollment rate (%)	96.3	2010	●	●
Lower secondary completion rate (%)	66.4	2010	●	●
Literacy rate (% of population aged 15 to 24)	91.6	2015	●	●

SDG5 – Gender Equality

Indicator	Value	Year	Rating	Trend
Demand for family planning satisfied by modern methods (% of females aged 15 to 49)	89.8	2012	●	↑
Ratio of female-to-male mean years of education received (%)	109.1	2019	●	↑
Ratio of female-to-male labor force participation rate (%)	57.4	2020	●	↓
Seats held by women in national parliament (%)	47.3	2020	●	↑

SDG6 – Clean Water and Sanitation

Indicator	Value	Year	Rating	Trend
Population using at least basic drinking water services (%)	81.7	2020	●	→
Population using at least basic sanitation services (%)	73.0	2020	●	→
Freshwater withdrawal (% of available freshwater resources)	2.7	2018	●	●
Anthropogenic wastewater that receives treatment (%)	0.0	2018	●	●
Scarce water consumption embodied in imports (m^3 H_2O eq/capita)	964.9	2018	●	●

SDG7 – Affordable and Clean Energy

Indicator	Value	Year	Rating	Trend
Population with access to electricity (%)	88.2	2019	●	↑
Population with access to clean fuels and technology for cooking (%)	55.4	2019	●	↗
CO_2 emissions from fuel combustion per total electricity output ($MtCO_2/TWh$)	1.3	2019	●	→
Share of renewable energy in total primary energy supply (%)	57.4	2019	●	↑

SDG8 – Decent Work and Economic Growth

Indicator	Value	Year	Rating	Trend
Adjusted GDP growth (%)	-7.8	2020	●	●
Victims of modern slavery (per 1,000 population)	2.9	2018	●	●
Adults with an account at a bank or other financial institution or with a mobile-money-service provider (% of population aged 15 or over)	30.9	2017	●	↑
Unemployment rate (% of total labor force)	5.7	2022	●	↓
Fundamental labor rights are effectively guaranteed (worst 0–1 best)	0.5	2020	●	↓
Fatal work-related accidents embodied in imports (per 100,000 population)	0.1	2015	●	↑

* Imputed data point

SDG9 – Industry, Innovation and Infrastructure

Indicator	Value	Year	Rating	Trend
Population using the internet (%)	45.2	2020	●	↑
Mobile broadband subscriptions (per 100 population)	18.0	2019	●	↗
Logistics Performance Index: Quality of trade and transport-related infrastructure (worst 1–5 best)	2.5	2016	●	●
The Times Higher Education Universities Ranking: Average score of top 3 universities (worst 0–100 best)	* 0.0	2022	●	●
Articles published in academic journals (per 1,000 population)	0.0	2020	●	→
Expenditure on research and development (% of GDP)	0.1	2015	●	●

SDG10 – Reduced Inequalities

Indicator	Value	Year	Rating	Trend
Gini coefficient	46.2	2014	●	●
Palma ratio	2.6	2018	●	●

SDG11 – Sustainable Cities and Communities

Indicator	Value	Year	Rating	Trend
Proportion of urban population living in slums (%)	41.8	2018	●	→
Annual mean concentration of particulate matter of less than 2.5 microns in diameter (PM2.5) ($\mu g/m^3$)	16.2	2019	●	↗
Access to improved water source, piped (% of urban population)	95.5	2020	●	→
Satisfaction with public transport (%)	70.0	2021	●	↓

SDG12 – Responsible Consumption and Production

Indicator	Value	Year	Rating	Trend
Municipal solid waste (kg/capita/day)	0.7	2010	●	●
Electronic waste (kg/capita)	2.5	2019	●	●
Production-based SO_2 emissions (kg/capita)	7.3	2018	●	●
SO_2 emissions embodied in imports (kg/capita)	0.7	2018	●	●
Production-based nitrogen emissions (kg/capita)	18.8	2015	●	↑
Nitrogen emissions embodied in imports (kg/capita)	0.8	2015	●	↑
Exports of plastic waste (kg/capita)	1.7	2020	●	●

SDG13 – Climate Action

Indicator	Value	Year	Rating	Trend
CO_2 emissions from fossil fuel combustion and cement production (tCO_2/capita)	0.8	2020	●	↑
CO_2 emissions embodied in imports (tCO_2/capita)	0.2	2018	●	↑
CO_2 emissions embodied in fossil fuel exports (kg/capita)	0.0	2020	●	●

SDG14 – Life Below Water

Indicator	Value	Year	Rating	Trend
Mean area that is protected in marine sites important to biodiversity (%)	49.9	2020	●	→
Ocean Health Index: Clean Waters score (worst 0–100 best)	65.0	2020	●	→
Fish caught from overexploited or collapsed stocks (% of total catch)	28.4	2018	●	↓
Fish caught by trawling or dredging (%)	0.0	2018	●	↑
Fish caught that are then discarded (%)	12.2	2018	●	→
Marine biodiversity threats embodied in imports (per million population)	0.0	2018	●	●

SDG15 – Life on Land

Indicator	Value	Year	Rating	Trend
Mean area that is protected in terrestrial sites important to biodiversity (%)	69.7	2020	●	→
Mean area that is protected in freshwater sites important to biodiversity (%)	73.7	2020	●	→
Red List Index of species survival (worst 0–1 best)	0.8	2021	●	↓
Permanent deforestation (% of forest area, 5-year average)	0.6	2020	●	↑
Terrestrial and freshwater biodiversity threats embodied in imports (per million population)	0.5	2018	●	●

SDG16 – Peace, Justice and Strong Institutions

Indicator	Value	Year	Rating	Trend
Homicides (per 100,000 population)	7.9	2019	●	→
Unsentenced detainees (% of prison population)	14.6	2018	●	↑
Population who feel safe walking alone at night in the city or area where they live (%)	59	2021	●	↗
Property Rights (worst 1–7 best)	2.6	2020	●	↓
Birth registrations with civil authority (% of children under age 5)	84.7	2020	●	●
Corruption Perception Index (worst 0–100 best)	20	2021	●	↓
Children involved in child labor (% of population aged 5 to 14)	NA	NA	●	●
Exports of major conventional weapons (TIV constant million USD per 100,000 population)	* 0.0	2020	●	●
Press Freedom Index (best 0–100 worst)	40.0	2021	●	↓
Access to and affordability of justice (worst 0–1 best)	0.5	2020	●	↑

SDG17 – Partnerships for the Goals

Indicator	Value	Year	Rating	Trend
Government spending on health and education (% of GDP)	8.6	2019	●	→
For high-income and all OECD DAC countries: International concessional public finance, including official development assistance (% of GNI)	NA	NA	●	●
Other countries: Government revenue excluding grants (% of GDP)	19.0	2019	●	↗
Corporate Tax Haven Score (best 0–100 worst)	* 0.0	2019	●	●
Statistical Performance Index (worst 0–100 best)	51.7	2019	●	↗

NIGER

Sub-Saharan Africa

OVERALL PERFORMANCE

COUNTRY RANKING

NIGER

149/163

COUNTRY SCORE

AVERAGE PERFORMANCE BY SDG

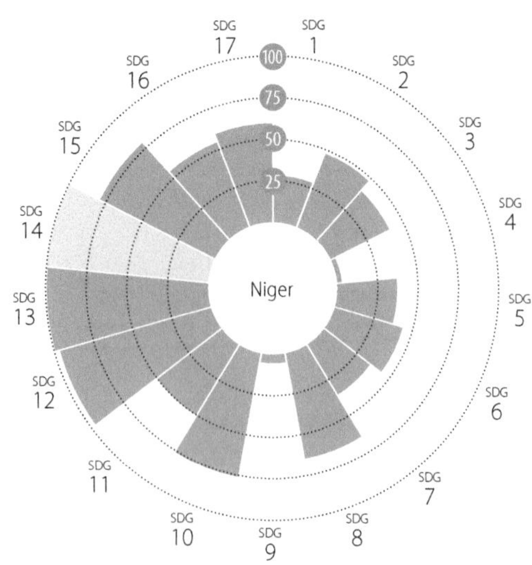

SDG DASHBOARDS AND TRENDS

Note: The full title of each SDG is available here: https://sustainabledevelopment.un.org/topics/sustainabledevelopmentgoals

INTERNATIONAL SPILLOVER INDEX

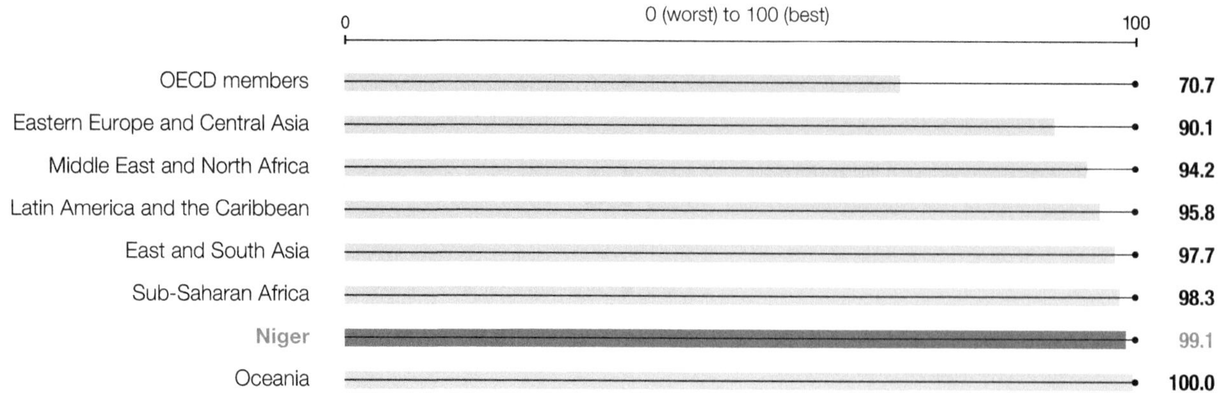

STATISTICAL PERFORMANCE INDEX

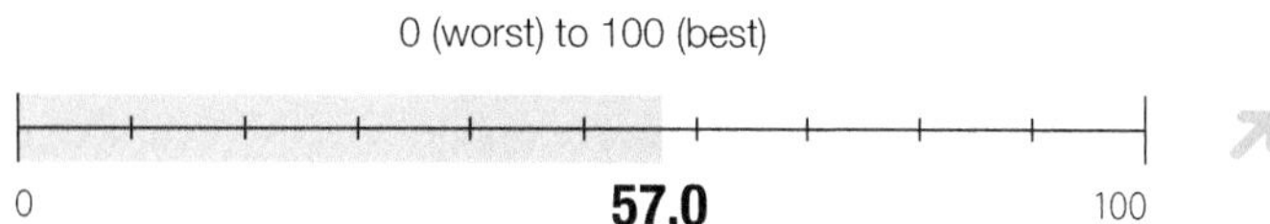

MISSING DATA IN SDG INDEX

4%

SDG1 – No Poverty	Value	Year	Rating	Trend
Poverty headcount ratio at $1.90/day (%)	31.4	2022	●	↗
Poverty headcount ratio at $3.20/day (%)	63.7	2022	●	→
SDG2 – Zero Hunger				
Prevalence of undernourishment (%)	NA	NA	●	●
Prevalence of stunting in children under 5 years of age (%)	47.1	2019	●	→
Prevalence of wasting in children under 5 years of age (%)	9.8	2019	●	→
Prevalence of obesity, BMI ≥ 30 (% of adult population)	5.5	2016	●	↑
Human Trophic Level (best 2–3 worst)	2.1	2017	●	↑
Cereal yield (tonnes per hectare of harvested land)	0.6	2018	●	→
Sustainable Nitrogen Management Index (best 0–1.41 worst)	0.9	2015	●	→
Exports of hazardous pesticides (tonnes per million population)	14.2	2019	●	●
SDG3 – Good Health and Well-Being				
Maternal mortality rate (per 100,000 live births)	509	2017	●	↗
Neonatal mortality rate (per 1,000 live births)	24.1	2020	●	↗
Mortality rate, under-5 (per 1,000 live births)	77.5	2020	●	↗
Incidence of tuberculosis (per 100,000 population)	83.0	2020	●	→
New HIV infections (per 1,000 uninfected population)	0.1	2020	●	↑
Age-standardized death rate due to cardiovascular disease, cancer, diabetes, or chronic respiratory disease in adults aged 30–70 years (%)	21.0	2019	●	→
Age-standardized death rate attributable to household air pollution and ambient air pollution (per 100,000 population)	252	2016	●	●
Traffic deaths (per 100,000 population)	25.5	2019	●	→
Life expectancy at birth (years)	63.3	2019	●	→
Adolescent fertility rate (births per 1,000 females aged 15 to 19)	154.0	2016	●	●
Births attended by skilled health personnel (%)	39.1	2016	●	●
Surviving infants who received 2 WHO-recommended vaccines (%)	79	2020	●	↓
Universal health coverage (UHC) index of service coverage (worst 0–100 best)	37	2019	●	→
Subjective well-being (average ladder score, worst 0–10 best)	5.0	2019	●	●
SDG4 – Quality Education				
Participation rate in pre-primary organized learning (% of children aged 4 to 6)	23.8	2019	●	→
Net primary enrollment rate (%)	59.0	2019	●	↓
Lower secondary completion rate (%)	17.7	2019	●	→
Literacy rate (% of population aged 15 to 24)	43.5	2018	●	●
SDG5 – Gender Equality				
Demand for family planning satisfied by modern methods (% of females aged 15 to 49)	45.5	2018	●	→
Ratio of female-to-male mean years of education received (%)	50.0	2019	●	↓
Ratio of female-to-male labor force participation rate (%)	73.5	2020	●	↑
Seats held by women in national parliament (%)	17.0	2020	●	→
SDG6 – Clean Water and Sanitation				
Population using at least basic drinking water services (%)	46.9	2020	●	→
Population using at least basic sanitation services (%)	14.8	2020	●	→
Freshwater withdrawal (% of available freshwater resources)	7.5	2018	●	●
Anthropogenic wastewater that receives treatment (%)	0.0	2018	●	●
Scarce water consumption embodied in imports (m[3] H_2O eq/capita)	163.2	2018	●	●
SDG7 – Affordable and Clean Energy				
Population with access to electricity (%)	18.8	2019	●	→
Population with access to clean fuels and technology for cooking (%)	2.4	2019	●	→
CO_2 emissions from fuel combustion per total electricity output ($MtCO_2$/TWh)	4.2	2019	●	→
Share of renewable energy in total primary energy supply (%)	75.9	2019	●	↑
SDG8 – Decent Work and Economic Growth				
Adjusted GDP growth (%)	-4.4	2020	●	●
Victims of modern slavery (per 1,000 population)	6.7	2018	●	●
Adults with an account at a bank or other financial institution or with a mobile-money-service provider (% of population aged 15 or over)	15.5	2017	●	↗
Unemployment rate (% of total labor force)	0.8	2022	●	↑
Fundamental labor rights are effectively guaranteed (worst 0–1 best)	0.6	2020	●	●
Fatal work-related accidents embodied in imports (per 100,000 population)	0.0	2015	●	↑

* Imputed data point

SDG9 – Industry, Innovation and Infrastructure	Value	Year	Rating	Trend
Population using the internet (%)	10.2	2017	●	●
Mobile broadband subscriptions (per 100 population)	5.0	2019	●	→
Logistics Performance Index: Quality of trade and transport-related infrastructure (worst 1–5 best)	2.0	2018	●	↓
The Times Higher Education Universities Ranking: Average score of top 3 universities (worst 0–100 best)	* 0.0	2022	●	●
Articles published in academic journals (per 1,000 population)	0.0	2020	●	↓
Expenditure on research and development (% of GDP)	* 0.0	2018	●	●
SDG10 – Reduced Inequalities				
Gini coefficient	34.3	2014	●	●
Palma ratio	1.4	2018	●	●
SDG11 – Sustainable Cities and Communities				
Proportion of urban population living in slums (%)	61.1	2018	●	↗
Annual mean concentration of particulate matter of less than 2.5 microns in diameter (PM2.5) (μg/m[3])	106.1	2019	●	↓
Access to improved water source, piped (% of urban population)	93.6	2020	●	↑
Satisfaction with public transport (%)	67.0	2019	●	●
SDG12 – Responsible Consumption and Production				
Municipal solid waste (kg/capita/day)	NA	NA	●	●
Electronic waste (kg/capita)	0.5	2019	●	●
Production-based SO_2 emissions (kg/capita)	0.4	2018	●	●
SO_2 emissions embodied in imports (kg/capita)	0.1	2018	●	●
Production-based nitrogen emissions (kg/capita)	19.2	2015	●	↑
Nitrogen emissions embodied in imports (kg/capita)	0.4	2015	●	↑
Exports of plastic waste (kg/capita)	0.0	2018	●	●
SDG13 – Climate Action				
CO_2 emissions from fossil fuel combustion and cement production (tCO_2/capita)	0.1	2020	●	↑
CO_2 emissions embodied in imports (tCO_2/capita)	0.0	2018	●	↑
CO_2 emissions embodied in fossil fuel exports (kg/capita)	0.0	2020	●	●
SDG14 – Life Below Water				
Mean area that is protected in marine sites important to biodiversity (%)	NA	NA	●	●
Ocean Health Index: Clean Waters score (worst 0–100 best)	NA	NA	●	●
Fish caught from overexploited or collapsed stocks (% of total catch)	NA	NA	●	●
Fish caught by trawling or dredging (%)	NA	NA	●	●
Fish caught that are then discarded (%)	NA	NA	●	●
Marine biodiversity threats embodied in imports (per million population)	0.0	2018	●	●
SDG15 – Life on Land				
Mean area that is protected in terrestrial sites important to biodiversity (%)	54.7	2020	●	↑
Mean area that is protected in freshwater sites important to biodiversity (%)	58.2	2020	●	↑
Red List Index of species survival (worst 0–1 best)	0.9	2021	●	↑
Permanent deforestation (% of forest area, 5-year average)	0.0	2020	●	↑
Terrestrial and freshwater biodiversity threats embodied in imports (per million population)	0.0	2018	●	●
SDG16 – Peace, Justice and Strong Institutions				
Homicides (per 100,000 population)	4.4	2012	●	●
Unsentenced detainees (% of prison population)	53.8	2017	●	●
Population who feel safe walking alone at night in the city or area where they live (%)	60	2019	●	●
Property Rights (worst 1–7 best)	NA	NA	●	●
Birth registrations with civil authority (% of children under age 5)	63.9	2020	●	●
Corruption Perception Index (worst 0–100 best)	31	2021	●	↓
Children involved in child labor (% of population aged 5 to 14)	34.4	2019	●	●
Exports of major conventional weapons (TIV constant million USD per 100,000 population)	* 0.0	2020	●	●
Press Freedom Index (best 0–100 worst)	28.4	2021	●	↑
Access to and affordability of justice (worst 0–1 best)	0.5	2020	●	●
SDG17 – Partnerships for the Goals				
Government spending on health and education (% of GDP)	5.5	2019	●	↓
For high-income and all OECD DAC countries: International concessional public finance, including official development assistance (% of GNI)	NA	NA	●	●
Other countries: Government revenue excluding grants (% of GDP)	NA	NA	●	●
Corporate Tax Haven Score (best 0–100 worst)	* 0.0	2019	●	●
Statistical Performance Index (worst 0–100 best)	57.0	2019	●	↗

NIGERIA

Sub-Saharan Africa

OVERALL PERFORMANCE

COUNTRY RANKING

NIGERIA

139/163

COUNTRY SCORE

REGIONAL AVERAGE: 53.6

AVERAGE PERFORMANCE BY SDG

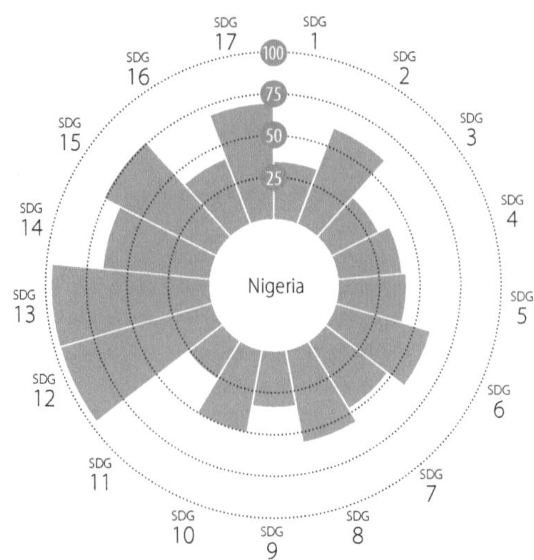

SDG DASHBOARDS AND TRENDS

Note: The full title of each SDG is available here: https://sustainabledevelopment.un.org/topics/sustainabledevelopmentgoals

INTERNATIONAL SPILLOVER INDEX

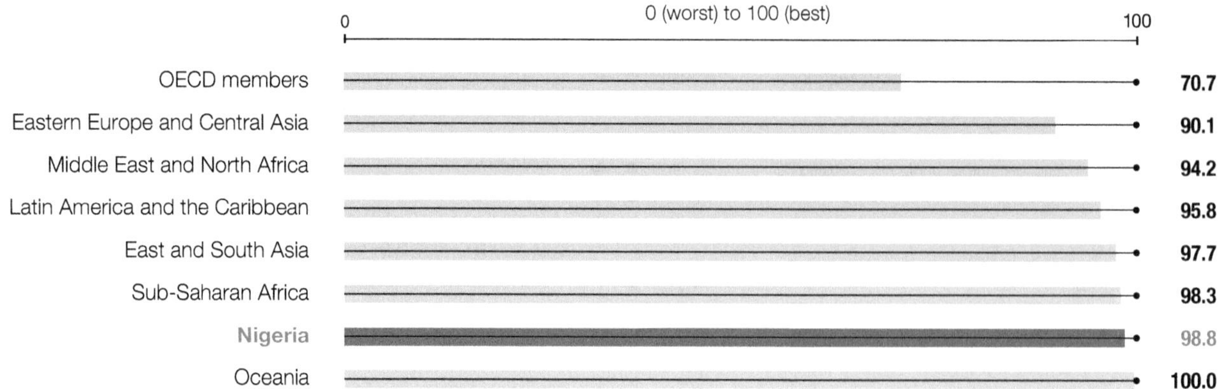

STATISTICAL PERFORMANCE INDEX

0 (worst) to 100 (best)

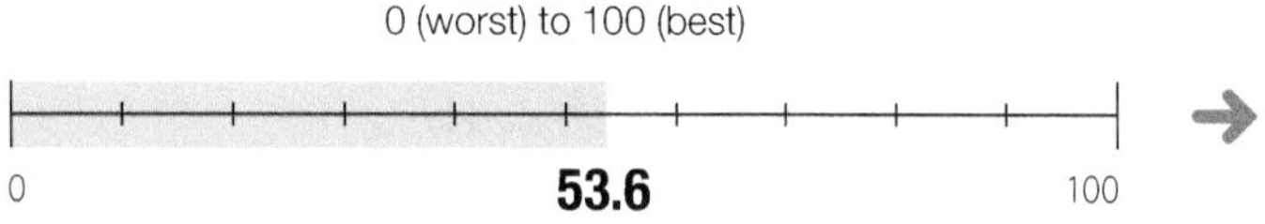

MISSING DATA IN SDG INDEX

5%

SDG1 – No Poverty	Value	Year	Rating	Trend
Poverty headcount ratio at \$1.90/day (%)	32.8	2022	●	↓
Poverty headcount ratio at \$3.20/day (%)	44.4	2022	●	↓

SDG2 – Zero Hunger	Value	Year	Rating	Trend
Prevalence of undernourishment (%)	14.6	2019	●	↓
Prevalence of stunting in children under 5 years of age (%)	31.5	2020	●	→
Prevalence of wasting in children under 5 years of age (%)	6.8	2018	●	→
Prevalence of obesity, BMI ≥ 30 (% of adult population)	8.9	2016	●	↑
Human Trophic Level (best 2–3 worst)	2.0	2017	●	↑
Cereal yield (tonnes per hectare of harvested land)	1.5	2018	●	→
Sustainable Nitrogen Management Index (best 0–1.41 worst)	0.8	2015	●	↓
Exports of hazardous pesticides (tonnes per million population)	2.4	2019	●	●

SDG3 – Good Health and Well-Being	Value	Year	Rating	Trend
Maternal mortality rate (per 100,000 live births)	917	2017	●	→
Neonatal mortality rate (per 1,000 live births)	35.5	2020	●	→
Mortality rate, under-5 (per 1,000 live births)	113.8	2020	●	→
Incidence of tuberculosis (per 100,000 population)	219.0	2020	●	→
New HIV infections (per 1,000 uninfected population)	0.4	2020	●	↗
Age-standardized death rate due to cardiovascular disease, cancer, diabetes, or chronic respiratory disease in adults aged 30–70 years (%)	16.9	2019	●	↑
Age-standardized death rate attributable to household air pollution and ambient air pollution (per 100,000 population)	307	2016	●	●
Traffic deaths (per 100,000 population)	20.8	2019	●	→
Life expectancy at birth (years)	62.6	2019	●	→
Adolescent fertility rate (births per 1,000 females aged 15 to 19)	106.0	2017	●	●
Births attended by skilled health personnel (%)	43.3	2018	●	●
Surviving infants who received 2 WHO-recommended vaccines (%)	54	2020	●	↗
Universal health coverage (UHC) index of service coverage (worst 0–100 best)	44	2019	●	→
Subjective well-being (average ladder score, worst 0–10 best)	4.5	2021	●	↓

SDG4 – Quality Education	Value	Year	Rating	Trend
Participation rate in pre-primary organized learning (% of children aged 4 to 6)	NA	NA	●	●
Net primary enrollment rate (%)	66.0	2010	●	●
Lower secondary completion rate (%)	47.1	2010	●	●
Literacy rate (% of population aged 15 to 24)	75.0	2018	●	●

SDG5 – Gender Equality	Value	Year	Rating	Trend
Demand for family planning satisfied by modern methods (% of females aged 15 to 49)	35.6	2018	●	→
Ratio of female-to-male mean years of education received (%)	74.0	2019	●	↗
Ratio of female-to-male labor force participation rate (%)	80.4	2020	●	↑
Seats held by women in national parliament (%)	7.2	2020	●	→

SDG6 – Clean Water and Sanitation	Value	Year	Rating	Trend
Population using at least basic drinking water services (%)	77.6	2020	●	↗
Population using at least basic sanitation services (%)	42.7	2020	●	→
Freshwater withdrawal (% of available freshwater resources)	9.7	2018	●	●
Anthropogenic wastewater that receives treatment (%)	0.2	2018	●	●
Scarce water consumption embodied in imports (m^3 H_2O eq/capita)	177.1	2018	●	●

SDG7 – Affordable and Clean Energy	Value	Year	Rating	Trend
Population with access to electricity (%)	55.4	2019	●	→
Population with access to clean fuels and technology for cooking (%)	13.0	2019	●	→
CO_2 emissions from fuel combustion per total electricity output ($MtCO_2$/TWh)	4.4	2019	●	→
Share of renewable energy in total primary energy supply (%)	75.1	2019	●	↑

SDG8 – Decent Work and Economic Growth	Value	Year	Rating	Trend
Adjusted GDP growth (%)	-5.6	2020	●	●
Victims of modern slavery (per 1,000 population)	* NA	NA	●	●
Adults with an account at a bank or other financial institution or with a mobile-money-service provider (% of population aged 15 or over)	39.7	2017	●	↓
Unemployment rate (% of total labor force)	9.6	2022	●	↓
Fundamental labor rights are effectively guaranteed (worst 0–1 best)	0.5	2020	●	↗
Fatal work-related accidents embodied in imports (per 100,000 population)	0.1	2015	●	↑

SDG9 – Industry, Innovation and Infrastructure	Value	Year	Rating	Trend
Population using the internet (%)	35.5	2020	●	↗
Mobile broadband subscriptions (per 100 population)	35.9	2019	●	↑
Logistics Performance Index: Quality of trade and transport-related infrastructure (worst 1–5 best)	2.6	2018	●	→
The Times Higher Education Universities Ranking: Average score of top 3 universities (worst 0–100 best)	39.0	2022	●	●
Articles published in academic journals (per 1,000 population)	0.1	2020	●	→
Expenditure on research and development (% of GDP)	0.1	2007	●	●

SDG10 – Reduced Inequalities	Value	Year	Rating	Trend
Gini coefficient	35.1	2018	●	●
Palma ratio	2.2	2018	●	●

SDG11 – Sustainable Cities and Communities	Value	Year	Rating	Trend
Proportion of urban population living in slums (%)	53.3	2018	●	↓
Annual mean concentration of particulate matter of less than 2.5 microns in diameter (PM2.5) (μg/m^3)	83.6	2019	●	↓
Access to improved water source, piped (% of urban population)	12.0	2020	●	↓
Satisfaction with public transport (%)	54.0	2021	●	→

SDG12 – Responsible Consumption and Production	Value	Year	Rating	Trend
Municipal solid waste (kg/capita/day)	0.5	2009	●	●
Electronic waste (kg/capita)	2.3	2019	●	●
Production-based SO_2 emissions (kg/capita)	0.4	2018	●	●
SO_2 emissions embodied in imports (kg/capita)	0.7	2018	●	●
Production-based nitrogen emissions (kg/capita)	6.7	2015	●	↑
Nitrogen emissions embodied in imports (kg/capita)	0.3	2015	●	↑
Exports of plastic waste (kg/capita)	0.1	2020	●	●

SDG13 – Climate Action	Value	Year	Rating	Trend
CO_2 emissions from fossil fuel combustion and cement production (tCO_2/capita)	0.6	2020	●	↑
CO_2 emissions embodied in imports (tCO_2/capita)	0.2	2018	●	↑
CO_2 emissions embodied in fossil fuel exports (kg/capita)	1060.8	2020	●	●

SDG14 – Life Below Water	Value	Year	Rating	Trend
Mean area that is protected in marine sites important to biodiversity (%)	0.0	2020	●	→
Ocean Health Index: Clean Waters score (worst 0–100 best)	37.1	2020	●	↓
Fish caught from overexploited or collapsed stocks (% of total catch)	10.2	2018	●	↑
Fish caught by trawling or dredging (%)	8.2	2018	●	↓
Fish caught that are then discarded (%)	0.5	2018	●	↑
Marine biodiversity threats embodied in imports (per million population)	0.0	2018	●	●

SDG15 – Life on Land	Value	Year	Rating	Trend
Mean area that is protected in terrestrial sites important to biodiversity (%)	80.4	2020	●	→
Mean area that is protected in freshwater sites important to biodiversity (%)	73.7	2020	●	→
Red List Index of species survival (worst 0–1 best)	0.9	2021	●	→
Permanent deforestation (% of forest area, 5-year average)	0.6	2020	●	↓
Terrestrial and freshwater biodiversity threats embodied in imports (per million population)	0.0	2018	●	●

SDG16 – Peace, Justice and Strong Institutions	Value	Year	Rating	Trend
Homicides (per 100,000 population)	NA	NA	●	●
Unsentenced detainees (% of prison population)	67.8	2017	●	●
Population who feel safe walking alone at night in the city or area where they live (%)	52	2021	●	↓
Property Rights (worst 1–7 best)	3.5	2020	●	↓
Birth registrations with civil authority (% of children under age 5)	42.6	2020	●	●
Corruption Perception Index (worst 0–100 best)	24	2021	●	↓
Children involved in child labor (% of population aged 5 to 14)	31.5	2019	●	●
Exports of major conventional weapons (TIV constant million USD per 100,000 population)	* 0.0	2020	●	●
Press Freedom Index (best 0–100 worst)	39.7	2021	●	↓
Access to and affordability of justice (worst 0–1 best)	0.6	2020	●	↑

SDG17 – Partnerships for the Goals	Value	Year	Rating	Trend
Government spending on health and education (% of GDP)	NA	NA	●	●
For high-income and all OECD DAC countries: International concessional public finance, including official development assistance (% of GNI)	NA	NA	●	●
Other countries: Government revenue excluding grants (% of GDP)	NA	NA	●	●
Corporate Tax Haven Score (best 0–100 worst)	* 0.0	2019	●	●
Statistical Performance Index (worst 0–100 best)	53.6	2019	●	→

* Imputed data point

5. Country Profiles

NORTH MACEDONIA

Eastern Europe and Central Asia

OVERALL PERFORMANCE

COUNTRY RANKING

NORTH MACEDONIA

57 **/163**

COUNTRY SCORE

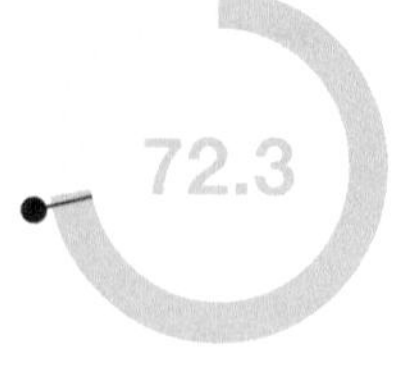

REGIONAL AVERAGE: 71.6

AVERAGE PERFORMANCE BY SDG

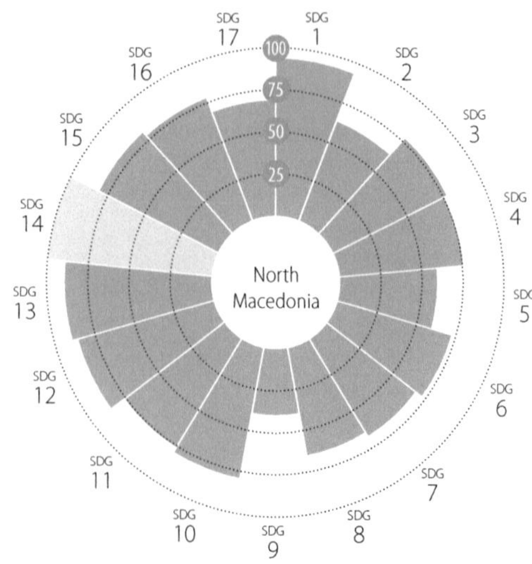

SDG DASHBOARDS AND TRENDS

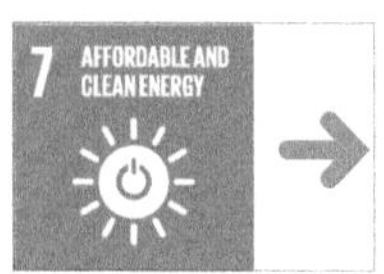

Major challenges | Significant challenges | Challenges remain | SDG achieved | Information unavailable

Decreasing | Stagnating | Moderately improving | On track or maintaining SDG achievement | Information unavailable

Note: The full title of each SDG is available here: https://sustainabledevelopment.un.org/topics/sustainabledevelopmentgoals

INTERNATIONAL SPILLOVER INDEX

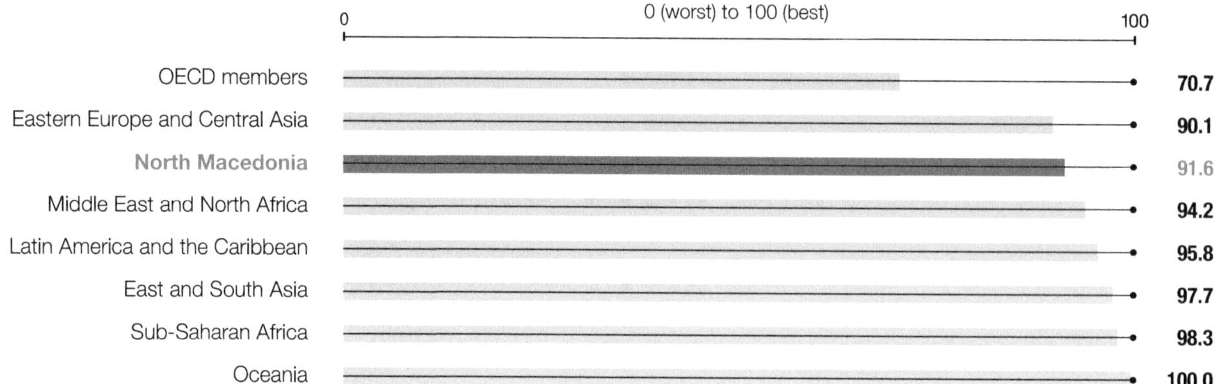

STATISTICAL PERFORMANCE INDEX

0 (worst) to 100 (best)

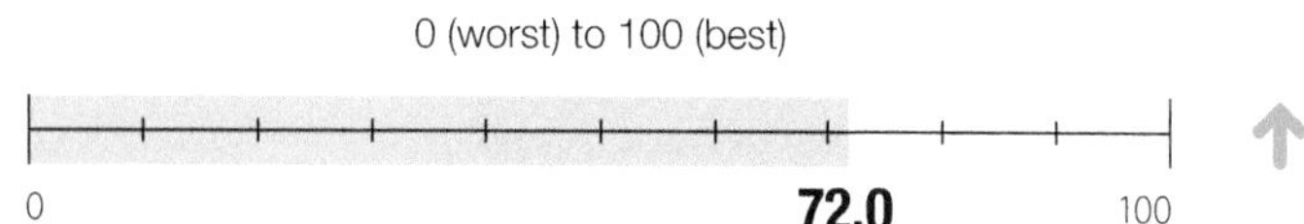

MISSING DATA IN SDG INDEX

1%

NORTH MACEDONIA

Performance by Indicator

SDG1 – No Poverty	Value	Year	Rating	Trend
Poverty headcount ratio at $1.90/day (%)	2.0	2022	●	↑
Poverty headcount ratio at $3.20/day (%)	5.5	2022	●	↑
SDG2 – Zero Hunger				
Prevalence of undernourishment (%)	2.7	2019	●	↑
Prevalence of stunting in children under 5 years of age (%)	4.3	2019	●	↑
Prevalence of wasting in children under 5 years of age (%)	3.4	2019	●	↑
Prevalence of obesity, BMI ≥ 30 (% of adult population)	22.4	2016	●	↓
Human Trophic Level (best 2–3 worst)	2.3	2017	●	→
Cereal yield (tonnes per hectare of harvested land)	3.7	2018	●	↑
Sustainable Nitrogen Management Index (best 0–1.41 worst)	0.7	2015	●	→
Exports of hazardous pesticides (tonnes per million population)	NA	NA	●	●
SDG3 – Good Health and Well-Being				
Maternal mortality rate (per 100,000 live births)	7	2017	●	↑
Neonatal mortality rate (per 1,000 live births)	3.9	2020	●	↑
Mortality rate, under-5 (per 1,000 live births)	5.9	2020	●	↑
Incidence of tuberculosis (per 100,000 population)	12.0	2020	●	↑
New HIV infections (per 1,000 uninfected population)	1.0	2020	●	→
Age-standardized death rate due to cardiovascular disease, cancer, diabetes, or chronic respiratory disease in adults aged 30–70 years (%)	22.7	2019	●	↗
Age-standardized death rate attributable to household air pollution and ambient air pollution (per 100,000 population)	82	2016	●	●
Traffic deaths (per 100,000 population)	5.2	2019	●	↑
Life expectancy at birth (years)	74.8	2019	●	↗
Adolescent fertility rate (births per 1,000 females aged 15 to 19)	15.1	2018	●	↑
Births attended by skilled health personnel (%)	99.9	2018	●	↑
Surviving infants who received 2 WHO-recommended vaccines (%)	63	2020	●	↓
Universal health coverage (UHC) index of service coverage (worst 0–100 best)	68	2019	●	↗
Subjective well-being (average ladder score, worst 0–10 best)	5.5	2021	●	↑
SDG4 – Quality Education				
Participation rate in pre-primary organized learning (% of children aged 4 to 6)	48.7	2018	●	●
Net primary enrollment rate (%)	99.3	2018	●	●
Lower secondary completion rate (%)	86.2	2018	●	↓
Literacy rate (% of population aged 15 to 24)	99.1	2020	●	↑
SDG5 – Gender Equality				
Demand for family planning satisfied by modern methods (% of females aged 15 to 49)	29.6	2019	●	●
Ratio of female-to-male mean years of education received (%)	92.2	2019	●	↗
Ratio of female-to-male labor force participation rate (%)	66.3	2020	●	↗
Seats held by women in national parliament (%)	39.2	2020	●	↑
SDG6 – Clean Water and Sanitation				
Population using at least basic drinking water services (%)	97.7	2020	●	↑
Population using at least basic sanitation services (%)	98.3	2020	●	↑
Freshwater withdrawal (% of available freshwater resources)	25.3	2018	●	●
Anthropogenic wastewater that receives treatment (%)	0.9	2018	●	●
Scarce water consumption embodied in imports (m^3 H_2O eq/capita)	2349.8	2018	●	●
SDG7 – Affordable and Clean Energy				
Population with access to electricity (%)	100.0	2019	●	↑
Population with access to clean fuels and technology for cooking (%)	76.0	2019	●	↑
CO_2 emissions from fuel combustion per total electricity output ($MtCO_2$/TWh)	1.4	2019	●	→
Share of renewable energy in total primary energy supply (%)	11.4	2019	●	↓
SDG8 – Decent Work and Economic Growth				
Adjusted GDP growth (%)	-1.3	2020	●	●
Victims of modern slavery (per 1,000 population)	8.7	2018	●	●
Adults with an account at a bank or other financial institution or with a mobile-money-service provider (% of population aged 15 or over)	76.6	2017	●	↑
Unemployment rate (% of total labor force)	16.1	2022	●	↑
Fundamental labor rights are effectively guaranteed (worst 0–1 best)	0.6	2020	●	↑
Fatal work-related accidents embodied in imports (per 100,000 population)	0.2	2015	●	↑

SDG9 – Industry, Innovation and Infrastructure	Value	Year	Rating	Trend
Population using the internet (%)	81.4	2020	●	↑
Mobile broadband subscriptions (per 100 population)	64.9	2019	●	↑
Logistics Performance Index: Quality of trade and transport-related infrastructure (worst 1–5 best)	2.5	2018	●	↓
The Times Higher Education Universities Ranking: Average score of top 3 universities (worst 0–100 best)	* 0.0	2022	●	●
Articles published in academic journals (per 1,000 population)	0.5	2020	●	→
Expenditure on research and development (% of GDP)	0.4	2018	●	↓
SDG10 – Reduced Inequalities				
Gini coefficient	33.0	2018	●	↑
Palma ratio	1.3	2018	●	●
SDG11 – Sustainable Cities and Communities				
Proportion of urban population living in slums (%)	6.4	2018	●	●
Annual mean concentration of particulate matter of less than 2.5 microns in diameter (PM2.5) (μg/m^3)	29.2	2019	●	↗
Access to improved water source, piped (% of urban population)	99.2	2020	●	↑
Satisfaction with public transport (%)	45.0	2021	●	↓
SDG12 – Responsible Consumption and Production				
Municipal solid waste (kg/capita/day)	0.8	2018	●	●
Electronic waste (kg/capita)	7.9	2019	●	●
Production-based SO_2 emissions (kg/capita)	27.1	2018	●	●
SO_2 emissions embodied in imports (kg/capita)	1.8	2018	●	●
Production-based nitrogen emissions (kg/capita)	8.1	2015	●	↑
Nitrogen emissions embodied in imports (kg/capita)	3.2	2015	●	↑
Exports of plastic waste (kg/capita)	2.7	2020	●	●
SDG13 – Climate Action				
CO_2 emissions from fossil fuel combustion and cement production (tCO_2/capita)	3.4	2020	●	→
CO_2 emissions embodied in imports (tCO_2/capita)	0.5	2018	●	↓
CO_2 emissions embodied in fossil fuel exports (kg/capita)	1.0	2020	●	●
SDG14 – Life Below Water				
Mean area that is protected in marine sites important to biodiversity (%)	NA	NA	●	●
Ocean Health Index: Clean Waters score (worst 0–100 best)	NA	NA	●	●
Fish caught from overexploited or collapsed stocks (% of total catch)	NA	NA	●	●
Fish caught by trawling or dredging (%)	NA	NA	●	●
Fish caught that are then discarded (%)	NA	NA	●	●
Marine biodiversity threats embodied in imports (per million population)	0.0	2018	●	●
SDG15 – Life on Land				
Mean area that is protected in terrestrial sites important to biodiversity (%)	24.4	2020	●	→
Mean area that is protected in freshwater sites important to biodiversity (%)	93.6	2020	●	↑
Red List Index of species survival (worst 0–1 best)	1.0	2021	●	↑
Permanent deforestation (% of forest area, 5-year average)	0.0	2020	●	↑
Terrestrial and freshwater biodiversity threats embodied in imports (per million population)	0.7	2018	●	●
SDG16 – Peace, Justice and Strong Institutions				
Homicides (per 100,000 population)	1.2	2019	●	↑
Unsentenced detainees (% of prison population)	8.4	2018	●	↑
Population who feel safe walking alone at night in the city or area where they live (%)	75	2021	●	↑
Property Rights (worst 1–7 best)	3.9	2020	●	↑
Birth registrations with civil authority (% of children under age 5)	99.8	2020	●	●
Corruption Perception Index (worst 0–100 best)	39	2021	●	↓
Children involved in child labor (% of population aged 5 to 14)	2.9	2019	●	●
Exports of major conventional weapons (TIV constant million USD per 100,000 population)	* 0.0	2020	●	●
Press Freedom Index (best 0–100 worst)	31.7	2021	●	↑
Access to and affordability of justice (worst 0–1 best)	0.6	2020	●	→
SDG17 – Partnerships for the Goals				
Government spending on health and education (% of GDP)	7.6	2019	●	→
For high-income and all OECD DAC countries: International concessional public finance, including official development assistance (% of GNI)	NA	NA	●	●
Other countries: Government revenue excluding grants (% of GDP)	28.3	2019	●	↑
Corporate Tax Haven Score (best 0–100 worst)	* 0.0	2019	●	●
Statistical Performance Index (worst 0–100 best)	72.0	2019	●	↑

* Imputed data point

5. Country Profiles

NORWAY

OECD Countries

OVERALL PERFORMANCE

COUNTRY RANKING

NORWAY

4 /163

COUNTRY SCORE

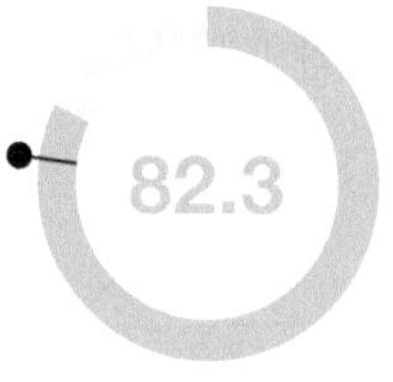

REGIONAL AVERAGE: 77.2

AVERAGE PERFORMANCE BY SDG

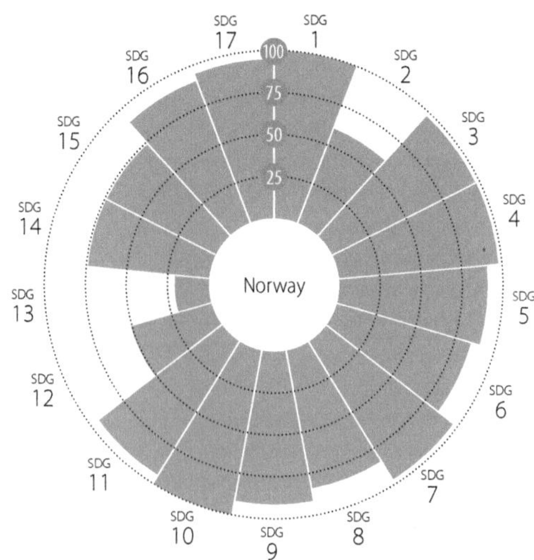

SDG DASHBOARDS AND TRENDS

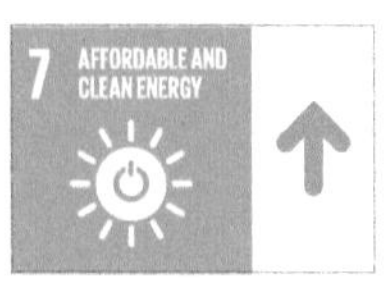

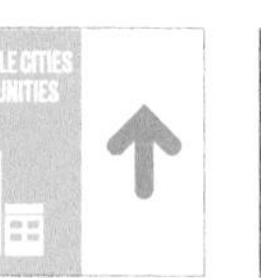

Information unavailable
Information unavailable

Note: The full title of each SDG is available here: https://sustainabledevelopment.un.org/topics/sustainabledevelopmentgoals

INTERNATIONAL SPILLOVER INDEX

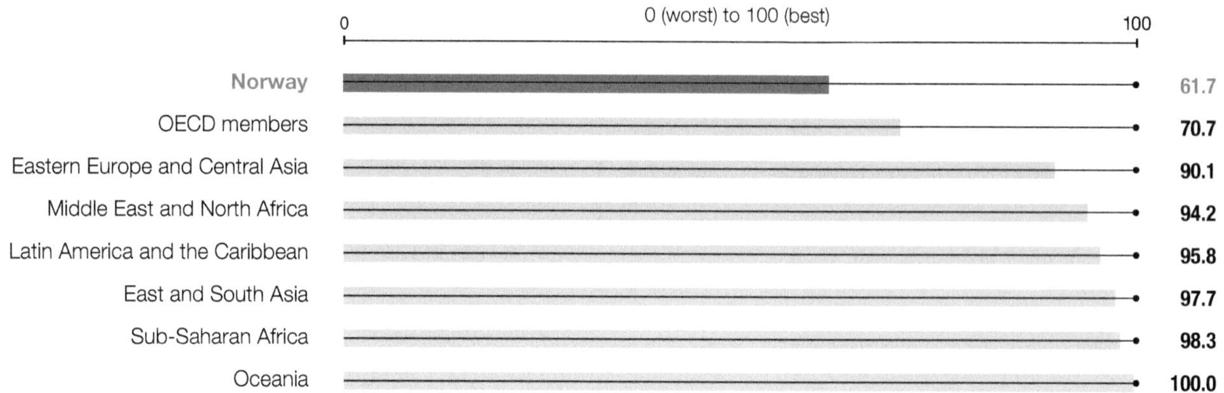

STATISTICAL PERFORMANCE INDEX

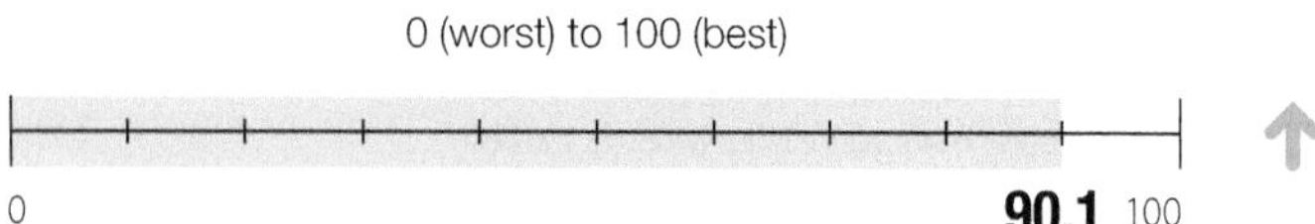

MISSING DATA IN SDG INDEX

1%

Performance by Indicator

SDG1 – No Poverty		Value	Year	Rating	Trend
Poverty headcount ratio at $1.90/day (%)		0.3	2022	●	↑
Poverty headcount ratio at $3.20/day (%)		0.3	2022	●	↑
Poverty rate after taxes and transfers (%)		8.4	2019	●	↑

SDG2 – Zero Hunger		Value	Year	Rating	Trend
Prevalence of undernourishment (%)		2.5	2019	●	↑
Prevalence of stunting in children under 5 years of age (%)	*	2.6	2019	●	↑
Prevalence of wasting in children under 5 years of age (%)	*	0.7	2019	●	↑
Prevalence of obesity, BMI ≥ 30 (% of adult population)		23.1	2016	●	↓
Human Trophic Level (best 2–3 worst)		2.5	2017	●	→
Cereal yield (tonnes per hectare of harvested land)		2.4	2018	●	↓
Sustainable Nitrogen Management Index (best 0–1.41 worst)		0.8	2015	●	↓
Yield gap closure (% of potential yield)		57.0	2018	●	●
Exports of hazardous pesticides (tonnes per million population)		2.9	2019	●	●

SDG3 – Good Health and Well-Being		Value	Year	Rating	Trend
Maternal mortality rate (per 100,000 live births)		2	2017	●	↑
Neonatal mortality rate (per 1,000 live births)		1.3	2020	●	↑
Mortality rate, under-5 (per 1,000 live births)		2.2	2020	●	↑
Incidence of tuberculosis (per 100,000 population)		3.1	2020	●	↑
New HIV infections (per 1,000 uninfected population)		0.0	2020	●	↑
Age-standardized death rate due to cardiovascular disease, cancer, diabetes, or chronic respiratory disease in adults aged 30–70 years (%)		8.7	2019	●	↑
Age-standardized death rate attributable to household air pollution and ambient air pollution (per 100,000 population)		9	2016	●	●
Traffic deaths (per 100,000 population)		2.1	2019	●	↑
Life expectancy at birth (years)		82.6	2019	●	↑
Adolescent fertility rate (births per 1,000 females aged 15 to 19)		2.6	2018	●	↑
Births attended by skilled health personnel (%)		99.2	2018	●	↑
Surviving infants who received 2 WHO-recommended vaccines (%)		97	2020	●	↑
Universal health coverage (UHC) index of service coverage (worst 0–100 best)		86	2019	●	↑
Subjective well-being (average ladder score, worst 0–10 best)		7.4	2021	●	↑
Gap in life expectancy at birth among regions (years)		4.9	2019	●	↓
Gap in self-reported health status by income (percentage points)		16.3	2019	●	↑
Daily smokers (% of population aged 15 and over)		9.0	2020	●	↑

SDG4 – Quality Education		Value	Year	Rating	Trend
Participation rate in pre-primary organized learning (% of children aged 4 to 6)		95.6	2019	●	↑
Net primary enrollment rate (%)		100.0	2019	●	↑
Lower secondary completion rate (%)		99.7	2019	●	↑
Literacy rate (% of population aged 15 to 24)		NA	NA	●	●
Tertiary educational attainment (% of population aged 25 to 34)		50.8	2020	●	↑
PISA score (worst 0–600 best)		496.7	2018	●	↑
Variation in science performance explained by socio-economic status (%)		8.9	2018	●	↑
Underachievers in science (% of 15-year-olds)		20.8	2018	●	↓

SDG5 – Gender Equality		Value	Year	Rating	Trend
Demand for family planning satisfied by modern methods (% of females aged 15 to 49)	*	88.5	2022	●	↑
Ratio of female-to-male mean years of education received (%)		101.6	2019	●	↑
Ratio of female-to-male labor force participation rate (%)		94.6	2020	●	↑
Seats held by women in national parliament (%)		41.4	2020	●	↑
Gender wage gap (% of male median wage)		4.8	2020	●	↑

SDG6 – Clean Water and Sanitation		Value	Year	Rating	Trend
Population using at least basic drinking water services (%)		100.0	2020	●	↑
Population using at least basic sanitation services (%)		98.1	2020	●	↑
Freshwater withdrawal (% of available freshwater resources)		2.1	2018	●	●
Anthropogenic wastewater that receives treatment (%)		64.3	2018	●	●
Scarce water consumption embodied in imports (m^3 H_2O eq/capita)		4197.5	2018	●	●
Population using safely managed water services (%)		98.6	2020	●	↑
Population using safely managed sanitation services (%)		65.4	2020	●	→

SDG7 – Affordable and Clean Energy		Value	Year	Rating	Trend
Population with access to electricity (%)		100.0	2019	●	↑
Population with access to clean fuels and technology for cooking (%)		100.0	2019	●	↑
CO_2 emissions from fuel combustion per total electricity output ($MtCO_2$/TWh)		0.3	2019	●	↑
Share of renewable energy in total primary energy supply (%)		47.6	2019	●	↑

SDG8 – Decent Work and Economic Growth		Value	Year	Rating	Trend
Adjusted GDP growth (%)		-2.5	2020	●	●
Victims of modern slavery (per 1,000 population)		1.8	2018	●	●
Adults with an account at a bank or other financial institution or with a mobile-money-service provider (% of population aged 15 or over)		99.7	2017	●	↑
Fundamental labor rights are effectively guaranteed (worst 0–1 best)		0.9	2020	●	↑
Fatal work-related accidents embodied in imports (per 100,000 population)		2.0	2015	●	↗
Employment-to-population ratio (%)		74.7	2020	●	↑
Youth not in employment, education or training (NEET) (% of population aged 15 to 29)		7.9	2020	●	↑

* Imputed data point

SDG9 – Industry, Innovation and Infrastructure		Value	Year	Rating	Trend
Population using the internet (%)		97.0	2020	●	↑
Mobile broadband subscriptions (per 100 population)		101.7	2019	●	↑
Logistics Performance Index: Quality of trade and transport-related infrastructure (worst 1–5 best)		3.7	2018	●	↑
The Times Higher Education Universities Ranking: Average score of top 3 universities (worst 0–100 best)		52.4	2022	●	●
Articles published in academic journals (per 1,000 population)		4.6	2020	●	↑
Expenditure on research and development (% of GDP)		2.1	2018	●	↑
Researchers (per 1,000 employed population)		12.6	2019	●	↑
Triadic patent families filed (per million population)		27.8	2019	●	↑
Gap in internet access by income (percentage points)		8.2	2020	●	↓
Female share of graduates from STEM fields at the tertiary level (%)		28.5	2017	●	↑

SDG10 – Reduced Inequalities		Value	Year	Rating	Trend
Gini coefficient		27.6	2018	●	↑
Palma ratio		0.9	2019	●	↑
Elderly poverty rate (% of population aged 66 or over)		4.3	2019	●	↑

SDG11 – Sustainable Cities and Communities		Value	Year	Rating	Trend
Proportion of urban population living in slums (%)	*	0.0	2018	●	↑
Annual mean concentration of particulate matter of less than 2.5 microns in diameter (PM2.5) (μg/m³)		6.5	2019	●	↑
Access to improved water source, piped (% of urban population)		100.0	2020	●	↑
Satisfaction with public transport (%)		68.0	2021	●	↑
Population with rent overburden (%)		7.7	2019	●	↑

SDG12 – Responsible Consumption and Production		Value	Year	Rating	Trend
Electronic waste (kg/capita)		26.0	2019	●	●
Production-based SO_2 emissions (kg/capita)		19.7	2018	●	●
SO_2 emissions embodied in imports (kg/capita)		11.5	2018	●	●
Production-based nitrogen emissions (kg/capita)		13.7	2015	●	↑
Nitrogen emissions embodied in imports (kg/capita)		17.2	2015	●	↓
Exports of plastic waste (kg/capita)		11.6	2020	●	●
Non-recycled municipal solid waste (kg/capita/day)		1.3	2019	●	↓

SDG13 – Climate Action		Value	Year	Rating	Trend
CO_2 emissions from fossil fuel combustion and cement production (tCO_2/capita)		7.6	2020	●	↗
CO_2 emissions embodied in imports (tCO_2/capita)		6.0	2018	●	→
CO_2 emissions embodied in fossil fuel exports (kg/capita)		83152.7	2020	●	●
Carbon Pricing Score at EUR60/tCO_2 (%, worst 0–100 best)		67.8	2018	●	↑

SDG14 – Life Below Water		Value	Year	Rating	Trend
Mean area that is protected in marine sites important to biodiversity (%)		55.1	2020	●	→
Ocean Health Index: Clean Waters score (worst 0–100 best)		77.0	2020	●	↓
Fish caught from overexploited or collapsed stocks (% of total catch)		18.3	2018	●	↑
Fish caught by trawling or dredging (%)		33.6	2018	●	↗
Fish caught that are then discarded (%)		0.3	2018	●	↑
Marine biodiversity threats embodied in imports (per million population)		0.4	2018	●	●

SDG15 – Life on Land		Value	Year	Rating	Trend
Mean area that is protected in terrestrial sites important to biodiversity (%)		56.5	2020	●	→
Mean area that is protected in freshwater sites important to biodiversity (%)		64.3	2020	●	↗
Red List Index of species survival (worst 0–1 best)		0.9	2021	●	↑
Permanent deforestation (% of forest area, 5-year average)		0.0	2020	●	↑
Terrestrial and freshwater biodiversity threats embodied in imports (per million population)		3.8	2018	●	●

SDG16 – Peace, Justice and Strong Institutions		Value	Year	Rating	Trend
Homicides (per 100,000 population)		0.6	2020	●	↑
Unsentenced detainees (% of prison population)		23.7	2018	●	↑
Population who feel safe walking alone at night in the city or area where they live (%)		93	2021	●	↑
Property Rights (worst 1–7 best)		5.8	2020	●	↑
Birth registrations with civil authority (% of children under age 5)		100.0	2020	●	●
Corruption Perception Index (worst 0–100 best)		85	2021	●	↑
Children involved in child labor (% of population aged 5 to 14)	*	0.0	2019	●	●
Exports of major conventional weapons (TIV constant million USD per 100,000 population)		1.6	2020	●	●
Press Freedom Index (best 0–100 worst)		6.7	2021	●	↑
Access to and affordability of justice (worst 0–1 best)		0.7	2020	●	↑
Persons held in prison (per 100,000 population)		71.0	2018	●	↑

SDG17 – Partnerships for the Goals		Value	Year	Rating	Trend
Government spending on health and education (% of GDP)		16.7	2019	●	↑
For high-income and all OECD DAC countries: International concessional public finance, including official development assistance (% of GNI)		0.9	2021	●	↑
Other countries: Government revenue excluding grants (% of GDP)		NA	NA	●	●
Corporate Tax Haven Score (best 0–100 worst)	*	0.0	2019	●	●
Financial Secrecy Score (best 0–100 worst)		44.3	2020	●	●
Shifted profits of multinationals (US$ billion)		7.2	2018	●	↑
Statistical Performance Index (worst 0–100 best)		90.1	2019	●	↑

OMAN

Middle East and North Africa

OVERALL PERFORMANCE

COUNTRY RANKING

OMAN

81 /163

COUNTRY SCORE

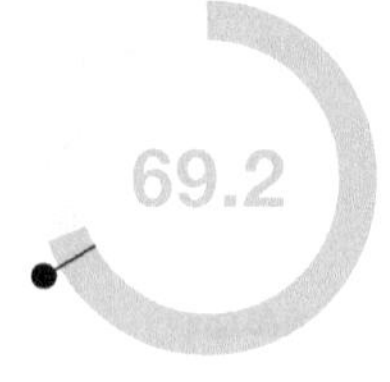

REGIONAL AVERAGE: 66.7

AVERAGE PERFORMANCE BY SDG

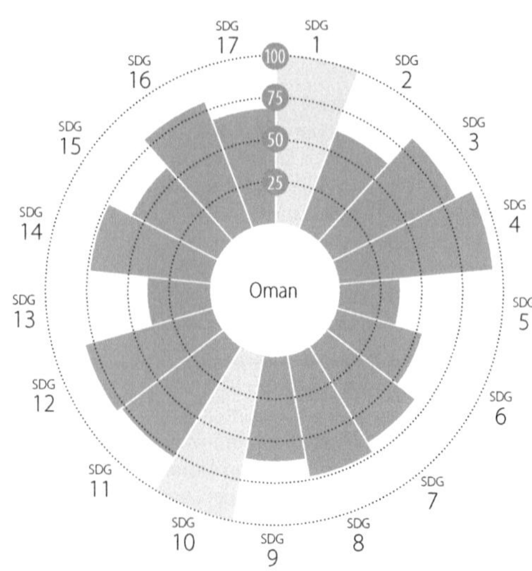

SDG DASHBOARDS AND TRENDS

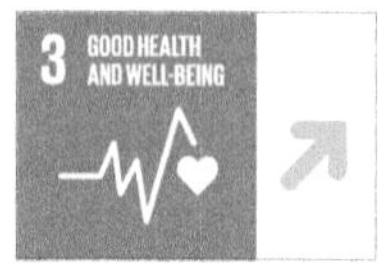

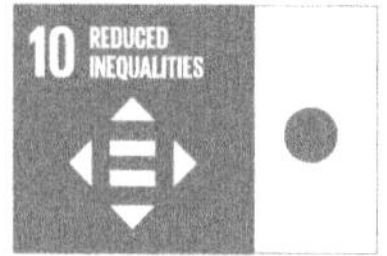

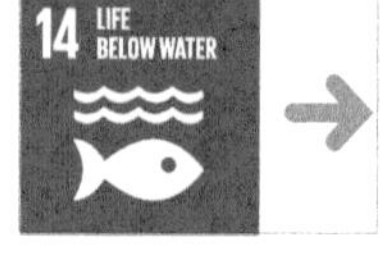
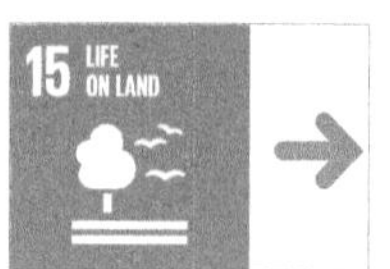

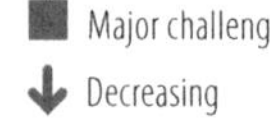

Major challenges · Significant challenges · Challenges remain · SDG achieved · Information unavailable

Decreasing · Stagnating · Moderately improving · On track or maintaining SDG achievement · Information unavailable

Note: The full title of each SDG is available here: https://sustainabledevelopment.un.org/topics/sustainabledevelopmentgoals

INTERNATIONAL SPILLOVER INDEX

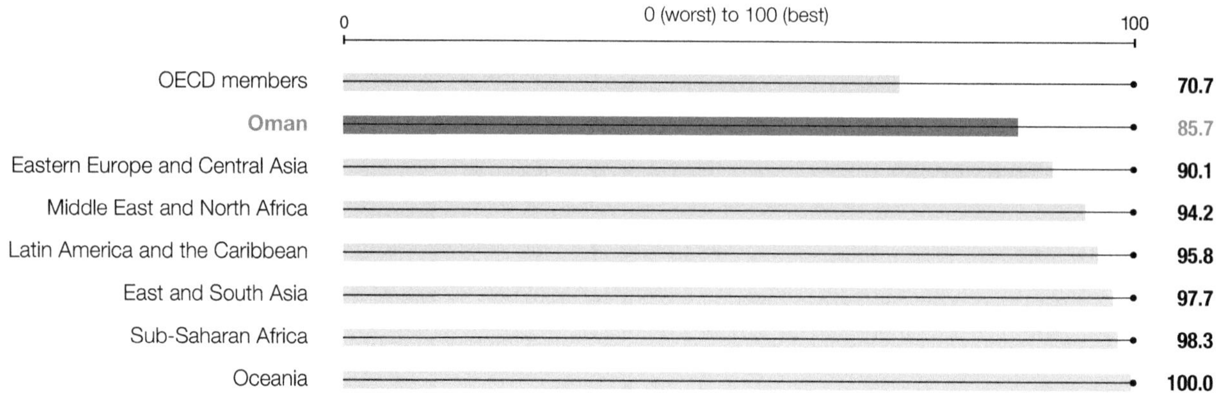

STATISTICAL PERFORMANCE INDEX

0 (worst) to 100 (best)

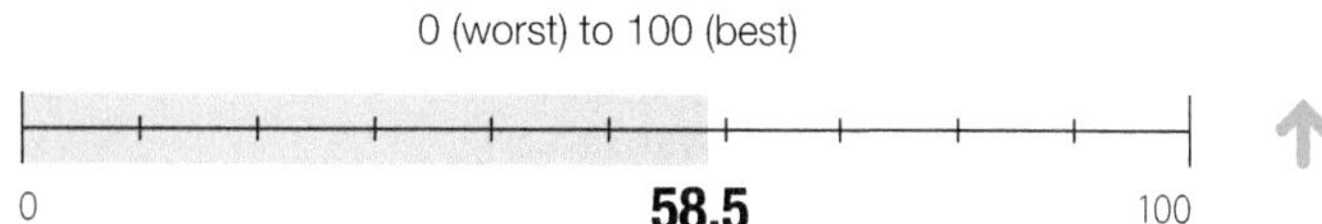

MISSING DATA IN SDG INDEX

15%

SDG1 – No Poverty	Value	Year	Rating	Trend
Poverty headcount ratio at $1.90/day (%)	* NA	NA	●	●
Poverty headcount ratio at $3.20/day (%)	* NA	NA	●	●

SDG2 – Zero Hunger	Value	Year	Rating	Trend
Prevalence of undernourishment (%)	8.2	2019	●	→
Prevalence of stunting in children under 5 years of age (%)	11.4	2017	●	→
Prevalence of wasting in children under 5 years of age (%)	9.3	2017	●	→
Prevalence of obesity, BMI ≥ 30 (% of adult population)	27.0	2016	●	↓
Human Trophic Level (best 2–3 worst)	2.3	2017	●	↗
Cereal yield (tonnes per hectare of harvested land)	13.4	2018	●	↑
Sustainable Nitrogen Management Index (best 0–1.41 worst)	0.7	2015	●	↗
Exports of hazardous pesticides (tonnes per million population)	8.8	2019	●	●

SDG3 – Good Health and Well-Being	Value	Year	Rating	Trend
Maternal mortality rate (per 100,000 live births)	19	2017	●	↑
Neonatal mortality rate (per 1,000 live births)	4.9	2020	●	↑
Mortality rate, under-5 (per 1,000 live births)	11.0	2020	●	↑
Incidence of tuberculosis (per 100,000 population)	7.0	2020	●	↑
New HIV infections (per 1,000 uninfected population)	1.0	2020	●	→
Age-standardized death rate due to cardiovascular disease, cancer, diabetes, or chronic respiratory disease in adults aged 30–70 years (%)	21.5	2019	●	↗
Age-standardized death rate attributable to household air pollution and ambient air pollution (per 100,000 population)	54	2016	●	●
Traffic deaths (per 100,000 population)	10.6	2019	●	↑
Life expectancy at birth (years)	73.9	2019	●	↗
Adolescent fertility rate (births per 1,000 females aged 15 to 19)	8.1	2019	●	↑
Births attended by skilled health personnel (%)	98.6	2018	●	↑
Surviving infants who received 2 WHO-recommended vaccines (%)	99	2020	●	↑
Universal health coverage (UHC) index of service coverage (worst 0–100 best)	69	2019	●	↗
Subjective well-being (average ladder score, worst 0–10 best)	6.9	2011	●	●

SDG4 – Quality Education	Value	Year	Rating	Trend
Participation rate in pre-primary organized learning (% of children aged 4 to 6)	86.3	2020	●	↑
Net primary enrollment rate (%)	98.4	2020	●	↑
Lower secondary completion rate (%)	112.7	2020	●	↑
Literacy rate (% of population aged 15 to 24)	98.6	2018	●	↑

SDG5 – Gender Equality	Value	Year	Rating	Trend
Demand for family planning satisfied by modern methods (% of females aged 15 to 49)	39.6	2014	●	→
Ratio of female-to-male mean years of education received (%)	112.8	2019	●	↑
Ratio of female-to-male labor force participation rate (%)	33.1	2020	●	↓
Seats held by women in national parliament (%)	2.3	2020	●	→

SDG6 – Clean Water and Sanitation	Value	Year	Rating	Trend
Population using at least basic drinking water services (%)	92.2	2020	●	↗
Population using at least basic sanitation services (%)	99.3	2020	●	↑
Freshwater withdrawal (% of available freshwater resources)	116.7	2018	●	●
Anthropogenic wastewater that receives treatment (%)	13.4	2018	●	●
Scarce water consumption embodied in imports (m^3 H_2O eq/capita)	3789.9	2018	●	●

SDG7 – Affordable and Clean Energy	Value	Year	Rating	Trend
Population with access to electricity (%)	100.0	2019	●	↑
Population with access to clean fuels and technology for cooking (%)	100.0	2019	●	↑
CO_2 emissions from fuel combustion per total electricity output ($MtCO_2$/TWh)	1.9	2019	●	→
Share of renewable energy in total primary energy supply (%)	0.0	2019	●	→

SDG8 – Decent Work and Economic Growth	Value	Year	Rating	Trend
Adjusted GDP growth (%)	-5.0	2020	●	●
Victims of modern slavery (per 1,000 population)	* NA	NA	●	●
Adults with an account at a bank or other financial institution or with a mobile-money-service provider (% of population aged 15 or over)	73.6	2011	●	●
Unemployment rate (% of total labor force)	3.1	2022	●	↑
Fundamental labor rights are effectively guaranteed (worst 0–1 best)	NA	NA	●	●
Fatal work-related accidents embodied in imports (per 100,000 population)	1.1	2015	●	↑

* Imputed data point

SDG9 – Industry, Innovation and Infrastructure	Value	Year	Rating	Trend
Population using the internet (%)	95.2	2020	●	↑
Mobile broadband subscriptions (per 100 population)	109.1	2019	●	↑
Logistics Performance Index: Quality of trade and transport-related infrastructure (worst 1–5 best)	3.2	2018	●	↑
The Times Higher Education Universities Ranking: Average score of top 3 universities (worst 0–100 best)	29.6	2022	●	●
Articles published in academic journals (per 1,000 population)	0.5	2020	●	↑
Expenditure on research and development (% of GDP)	0.2	2018	●	↓

SDG10 – Reduced Inequalities	Value	Year	Rating	Trend
Gini coefficient	NA	NA	●	●
Palma ratio	NA	NA	●	●

SDG11 – Sustainable Cities and Communities	Value	Year	Rating	Trend
Proportion of urban population living in slums (%)	NA	NA	●	●
Annual mean concentration of particulate matter of less than 2.5 microns in diameter (PM2.5) (μg/m³)	45.1	2019	●	↓
Access to improved water source, piped (% of urban population)	97.3	2020	●	↑
Satisfaction with public transport (%)	73.0	2011	●	●

SDG12 – Responsible Consumption and Production	Value	Year	Rating	Trend
Municipal solid waste (kg/capita/day)	1.2	2014	●	●
Electronic waste (kg/capita)	15.8	2019	●	●
Production-based SO_2 emissions (kg/capita)	8.7	2018	●	●
SO_2 emissions embodied in imports (kg/capita)	4.4	2018	●	●
Production-based nitrogen emissions (kg/capita)	6.1	2015	●	↑
Nitrogen emissions embodied in imports (kg/capita)	5.8	2015	●	↑
Exports of plastic waste (kg/capita)	0.5	2018	●	●

SDG13 – Climate Action	Value	Year	Rating	Trend
CO_2 emissions from fossil fuel combustion and cement production (tCO_2/capita)	12.2	2020	●	↗
CO_2 emissions embodied in imports (tCO_2/capita)	1.7	2018	●	↑
CO_2 emissions embodied in fossil fuel exports (kg/capita)	30968.1	2018	●	●

SDG14 – Life Below Water	Value	Year	Rating	Trend
Mean area that is protected in marine sites important to biodiversity (%)	7.1	2020	●	→
Ocean Health Index: Clean Waters score (worst 0–100 best)	66.2	2020	●	↓
Fish caught from overexploited or collapsed stocks (% of total catch)	3.3	2018	●	↑
Fish caught by trawling or dredging (%)	3.1	2011	●	●
Fish caught that are then discarded (%)	1.0	2018	●	↑
Marine biodiversity threats embodied in imports (per million population)	0.1	2018	●	●

SDG15 – Life on Land	Value	Year	Rating	Trend
Mean area that is protected in terrestrial sites important to biodiversity (%)	11.8	2020	●	→
Mean area that is protected in freshwater sites important to biodiversity (%)	NA	NA	●	●
Red List Index of species survival (worst 0–1 best)	0.9	2021	●	→
Permanent deforestation (% of forest area, 5-year average)	NA	NA	●	●
Terrestrial and freshwater biodiversity threats embodied in imports (per million population)	0.7	2018	●	●

SDG16 – Peace, Justice and Strong Institutions	Value	Year	Rating	Trend
Homicides (per 100,000 population)	0.5	2019	●	↑
Unsentenced detainees (% of prison population)	NA	NA	●	●
Population who feel safe walking alone at night in the city or area where they live (%)	NA	NA	●	●
Property Rights (worst 1–7 best)	5.5	2020	●	↑
Birth registrations with civil authority (% of children under age 5)	100.0	2020	●	●
Corruption Perception Index (worst 0–100 best)	52	2021	●	↑
Children involved in child labor (% of population aged 5 to 14)	NA	NA	●	●
Exports of major conventional weapons (TIV constant million USD per 100,000 population)	0.1	2020	●	●
Press Freedom Index (best 0–100 worst)	43.4	2021	●	↓
Access to and affordability of justice (worst 0–1 best)	NA	NA	●	●

SDG17 – Partnerships for the Goals	Value	Year	Rating	Trend
Government spending on health and education (% of GDP)	8.9	2019	●	→
For high-income and all OECD DAC countries: International concessional public finance, including official development assistance (% of GNI)	NA	NA	●	●
Other countries: Government revenue excluding grants (% of GDP)	NA	NA	●	●
Corporate Tax Haven Score (best 0–100 worst)	* 0.0	2019	●	●
Statistical Performance Index (worst 0–100 best)	58.5	2019	●	↑

PAKISTAN

East and South Asia

AVERAGE PERFORMANCE BY SDG

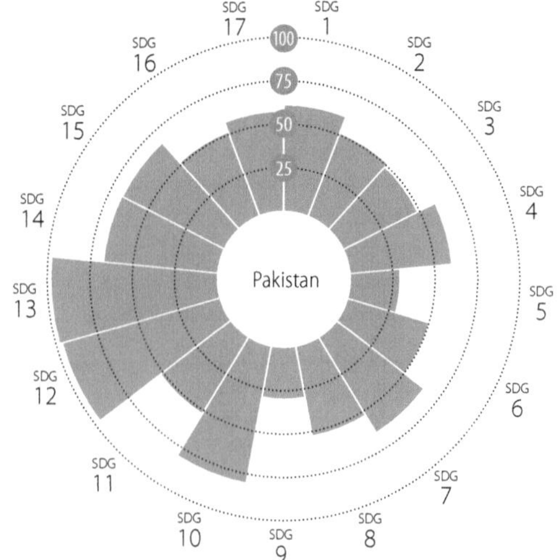

OVERALL PERFORMANCE

COUNTRY RANKING

PAKISTAN

125 **/163**

COUNTRY SCORE

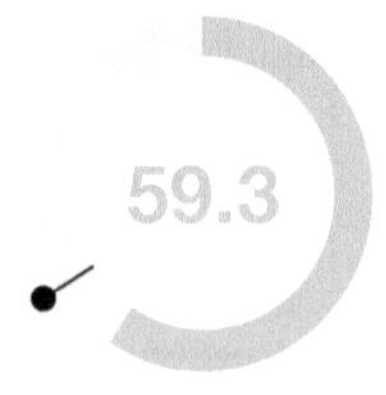

REGIONAL AVERAGE: 65.9

SDG DASHBOARDS AND TRENDS

Major challenges | Significant challenges | Challenges remain | SDG achieved | Information unavailable

Decreasing | Stagnating | Moderately improving | On track or maintaining SDG achievement | Information unavailable

Note: The full title of each SDG is available here: https://sustainabledevelopment.un.org/topics/sustainabledevelopmentgoals

INTERNATIONAL SPILLOVER INDEX

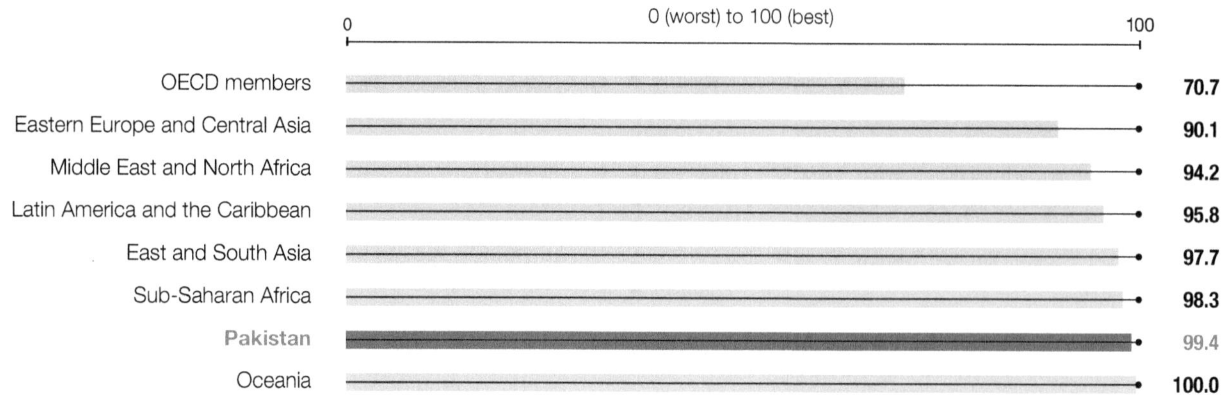

STATISTICAL PERFORMANCE INDEX

0 (worst) to 100 (best)

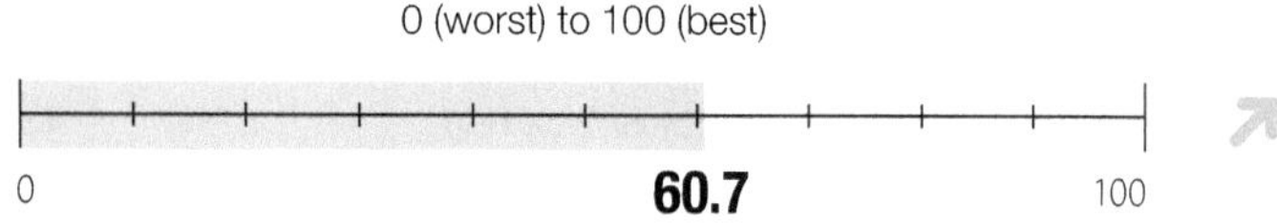

MISSING DATA IN SDG INDEX

3%

SDG1 – No Poverty		Value	Year	Rating	Trend
Poverty headcount ratio at $1.90/day (%)		4.8	2022	●	→
Poverty headcount ratio at $3.20/day (%)		37.0	2022	●	→
SDG2 – Zero Hunger					
Prevalence of undernourishment (%)		12.9	2019	●	→
Prevalence of stunting in children under 5 years of age (%)		37.6	2018	●	→
Prevalence of wasting in children under 5 years of age (%)		7.1	2018	●	→
Prevalence of obesity, BMI ≥ 30 (% of adult population)		8.6	2016	●	↑
Human Trophic Level (best 2–3 worst)		2.5	2017	●	↓
Cereal yield (tonnes per hectare of harvested land)		3.1	2018	●	↑
Sustainable Nitrogen Management Index (best 0–1.41 worst)		0.9	2015	●	→
Exports of hazardous pesticides (tonnes per million population)		0.0	2019	●	●
SDG3 – Good Health and Well-Being					
Maternal mortality rate (per 100,000 live births)		140	2017	●	↑
Neonatal mortality rate (per 1,000 live births)		40.4	2020	●	→
Mortality rate, under-5 (per 1,000 live births)		65.2	2020	●	↗
Incidence of tuberculosis (per 100,000 population)		259.0	2020	●	→
New HIV infections (per 1,000 uninfected population)		0.1	2020	●	↑
Age-standardized death rate due to cardiovascular disease, cancer, diabetes, or chronic respiratory disease in adults aged 30–70 years (%)		29.4	2019	●	→
Age-standardized death rate attributable to household air pollution and ambient air pollution (per 100,000 population)		174	2016	●	●
Traffic deaths (per 100,000 population)		13.0	2019	●	→
Life expectancy at birth (years)		65.6	2019	●	→
Adolescent fertility rate (births per 1,000 females aged 15 to 19)		54.0	2017	●	●
Births attended by skilled health personnel (%)		69.3	2018	●	●
Surviving infants who received 2 WHO-recommended vaccines (%)		77	2020	●	↗
Universal health coverage (UHC) index of service coverage (worst 0–100 best)		45	2019	●	→
Subjective well-being (average ladder score, worst 0–10 best)		4.5	2021	●	↓
SDG4 – Quality Education					
Participation rate in pre-primary organized learning (% of children aged 4 to 6)		94.3	2019	●	↑
Net primary enrollment rate (%)		NA	NA	●	●
Lower secondary completion rate (%)		49.0	2019	●	→
Literacy rate (% of population aged 15 to 24)		72.7	2019	●	↓
SDG5 – Gender Equality					
Demand for family planning satisfied by modern methods (% of females aged 15 to 49)		48.6	2018	●	→
Ratio of female-to-male mean years of education received (%)		60.3	2019	●	→
Ratio of female-to-male labor force participation rate (%)		26.5	2020	●	↓
Seats held by women in national parliament (%)		20.2	2020	●	↓
SDG6 – Clean Water and Sanitation					
Population using at least basic drinking water services (%)		90.1	2020	●	→
Population using at least basic sanitation services (%)		68.4	2020	●	↗
Freshwater withdrawal (% of available freshwater resources)		118.2	2018	●	●
Anthropogenic wastewater that receives treatment (%)		0.1	2018	●	●
Scarce water consumption embodied in imports (m^3 H_2O eq/capita)		256.6	2018	●	●
SDG7 – Affordable and Clean Energy					
Population with access to electricity (%)		73.9	2019	●	→
Population with access to clean fuels and technology for cooking (%)		49.1	2019	●	↗
CO_2 emissions from fuel combustion per total electricity output ($MtCO_2$/TWh)		1.9	2019	●	→
Share of renewable energy in total primary energy supply (%)		35.7	2019	●	↑
SDG8 – Decent Work and Economic Growth					
Adjusted GDP growth (%)		-4.0	2020	●	●
Victims of modern slavery (per 1,000 population)	*	NA	NA	●	●
Adults with an account at a bank or other financial institution or with a mobile-money-service provider (% of population aged 15 or over)		21.3	2017	●	↗
Unemployment rate (% of total labor force)		4.2	2022	●	↑
Fundamental labor rights are effectively guaranteed (worst 0–1 best)		0.3	2020	●	↗
Fatal work-related accidents embodied in imports (per 100,000 population)		0.0	2015	●	↑

SDG9 – Industry, Innovation and Infrastructure		Value	Year	Rating	Trend
Population using the internet (%)		25.0	2020	●	↗
Mobile broadband subscriptions (per 100 population)		35.1	2019	●	↑
Logistics Performance Index: Quality of trade and transport-related infrastructure (worst 1–5 best)		2.2	2018	●	↓
The Times Higher Education Universities Ranking: Average score of top 3 universities (worst 0–100 best)		36.5	2022	●	●
Articles published in academic journals (per 1,000 population)		0.1	2020	●	→
Expenditure on research and development (% of GDP)		0.2	2017	●	↓
SDG10 – Reduced Inequalities					
Gini coefficient		31.6	2018	●	↑
Palma ratio		1.4	2018	●	●
SDG11 – Sustainable Cities and Communities					
Proportion of urban population living in slums (%)		38.0	2018	●	↗
Annual mean concentration of particulate matter of less than 2.5 microns in diameter (PM2.5) (μg/m^3)		57.7	2019	●	→
Access to improved water source, piped (% of urban population)		45.0	2020	●	↓
Satisfaction with public transport (%)		64.0	2021	●	↑
SDG12 – Responsible Consumption and Production					
Municipal solid waste (kg/capita/day)		0.4	2017	●	●
Electronic waste (kg/capita)		2.1	2019	●	●
Production-based SO_2 emissions (kg/capita)		4.9	2018	●	●
SO_2 emissions embodied in imports (kg/capita)		0.2	2018	●	●
Production-based nitrogen emissions (kg/capita)		11.2	2015	●	↑
Nitrogen emissions embodied in imports (kg/capita)		0.1	2015	●	↑
Exports of plastic waste (kg/capita)		0.1	2021	●	●
SDG13 – Climate Action					
CO_2 emissions from fossil fuel combustion and cement production (tCO_2/capita)		1.1	2020	●	↑
CO_2 emissions embodied in imports (tCO_2/capita)		0.1	2018	●	↑
CO_2 emissions embodied in fossil fuel exports (kg/capita)		5.6	2021	●	●
SDG14 – Life Below Water					
Mean area that is protected in marine sites important to biodiversity (%)		14.6	2020	●	→
Ocean Health Index: Clean Waters score (worst 0–100 best)		45.6	2020	●	→
Fish caught from overexploited or collapsed stocks (% of total catch)		30.1	2018	●	↑
Fish caught by trawling or dredging (%)		0.0	2018	●	↑
Fish caught that are then discarded (%)		0.6	2018	●	↑
Marine biodiversity threats embodied in imports (per million population)		0.0	2018	●	●
SDG15 – Life on Land					
Mean area that is protected in terrestrial sites important to biodiversity (%)		34.8	2020	●	→
Mean area that is protected in freshwater sites important to biodiversity (%)		35.9	2020	●	→
Red List Index of species survival (worst 0–1 best)		0.9	2021	●	↓
Permanent deforestation (% of forest area, 5-year average)		0.0	2020	●	↑
Terrestrial and freshwater biodiversity threats embodied in imports (per million population)		0.0	2018	●	●
SDG16 – Peace, Justice and Strong Institutions					
Homicides (per 100,000 population)		3.8	2019	●	↑
Unsentenced detainees (% of prison population)		65.7	2016	●	●
Population who feel safe walking alone at night in the city or area where they live (%)		63	2021	●	↑
Property Rights (worst 1–7 best)		3.9	2020	●	↑
Birth registrations with civil authority (% of children under age 5)		42.2	2020	●	●
Corruption Perception Index (worst 0–100 best)		28	2021	●	↓
Children involved in child labor (% of population aged 5 to 14)		11.4	2019	●	●
Exports of major conventional weapons (TIV constant million USD per 100,000 population)		0.0	2020	●	●
Press Freedom Index (best 0–100 worst)		46.9	2021	●	→
Access to and affordability of justice (worst 0–1 best)		0.4	2020	●	→
SDG17 – Partnerships for the Goals					
Government spending on health and education (% of GDP)		3.6	2019	●	→
For high-income and all OECD DAC countries: International concessional public finance, including official development assistance (% of GNI)		NA	NA	●	●
Other countries: Government revenue excluding grants (% of GDP)		NA	NA	●	●
Corporate Tax Haven Score (best 0–100 worst)	*	0.0	2019	●	●
Statistical Performance Index (worst 0–100 best)		60.7	2019	●	↗

* Imputed data point

PALAU

Oceania

OVERALL PERFORMANCE

COUNTRY RANKING

PALAU

NA /163

COUNTRY SCORE

AVERAGE PERFORMANCE BY SDG

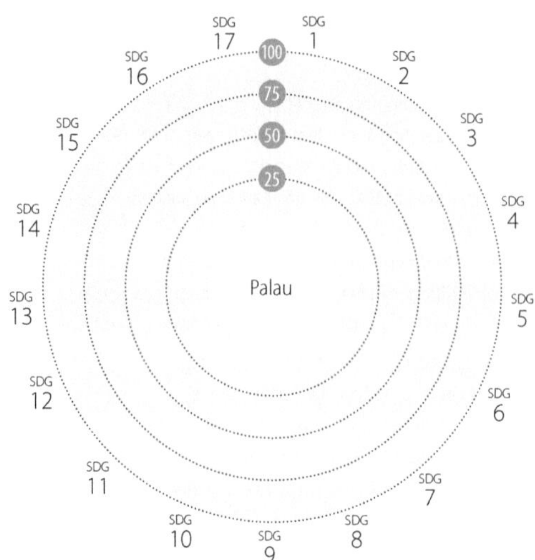

SDG DASHBOARDS AND TRENDS

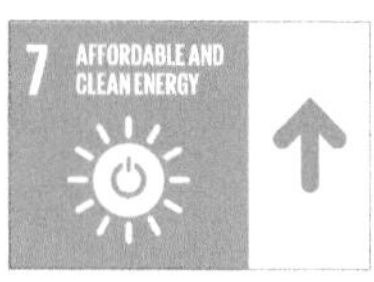

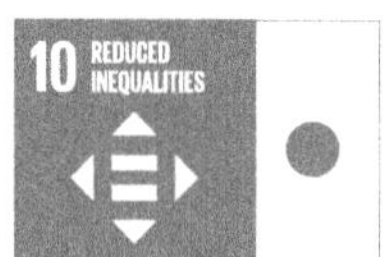

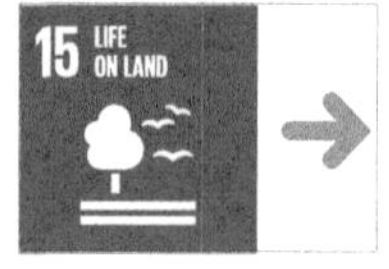

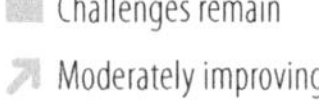

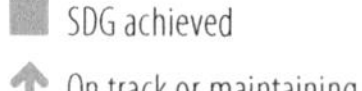

On track or maintaining SDG achievement

Information unavailable

Information unavailable

Note: The full title of each SDG is available here: https://sustainabledevelopment.un.org/topics/sustainabledevelopmentgoals

INTERNATIONAL SPILLOVER INDEX

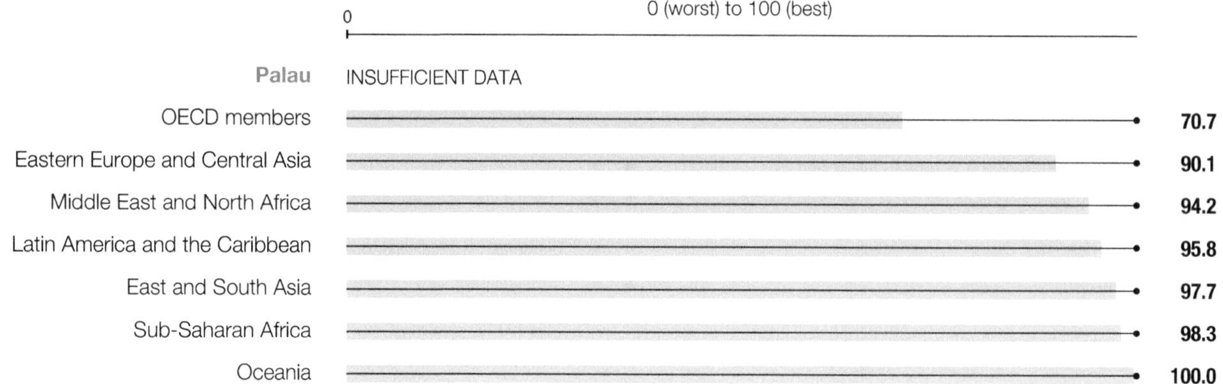

STATISTICAL PERFORMANCE INDEX

MISSING DATA IN SDG INDEX

54%

SDG1 – No Poverty		Value	Year	Rating	Trend
Poverty headcount ratio at $1.90/day (%)		NA	NA	●	●
Poverty headcount ratio at $3.20/day (%)		NA	NA	●	●
SDG2 – Zero Hunger					
Prevalence of undernourishment (%)	*	1.2	2019	●	●
Prevalence of stunting in children under 5 years of age (%)	*	2.6	2019	●	↑
Prevalence of wasting in children under 5 years of age (%)	*	0.7	2019	●	↑
Prevalence of obesity, BMI ≥ 30 (% of adult population)		55.3	2016	●	↓
Human Trophic Level (best 2–3 worst)		NA	NA	●	●
Cereal yield (tonnes per hectare of harvested land)		NA	NA	●	●
Sustainable Nitrogen Management Index (best 0–1.41 worst)		NA	NA	●	●
Exports of hazardous pesticides (tonnes per million population)		NA	NA	●	●
SDG3 – Good Health and Well-Being					
Maternal mortality rate (per 100,000 live births)		NA	NA	●	●
Neonatal mortality rate (per 1,000 live births)		8.9	2020	●	↑
Mortality rate, under-5 (per 1,000 live births)		16.9	2020	●	↑
Incidence of tuberculosis (per 100,000 population)		64.0	2020	●	↑
New HIV infections (per 1,000 uninfected population)		NA	NA	●	●
Age-standardized death rate due to cardiovascular disease, cancer, diabetes, or chronic respiratory disease in adults aged 30–70 years (%)		NA	NA	●	●
Age-standardized death rate attributable to household air pollution and ambient air pollution (per 100,000 population)		NA	NA	●	●
Traffic deaths (per 100,000 population)		NA	NA	●	●
Life expectancy at birth (years)		NA	NA	●	●
Adolescent fertility rate (births per 1,000 females aged 15 to 19)		33.8	2017	●	●
Births attended by skilled health personnel (%)		100.0	2018	●	↑
Surviving infants who received 2 WHO-recommended vaccines (%)		93	2020	●	↑
Universal health coverage (UHC) index of service coverage (worst 0–100 best)		NA	NA	●	●
Subjective well-being (average ladder score, worst 0–10 best)		NA	NA	●	●
SDG4 – Quality Education					
Participation rate in pre-primary organized learning (% of children aged 4 to 6)		89.3	2020	●	↓
Net primary enrollment rate (%)		96.1	2020	●	↑
Lower secondary completion rate (%)		108.5	2014	●	●
Literacy rate (% of population aged 15 to 24)		98.7	2015	●	●
SDG5 – Gender Equality					
Demand for family planning satisfied by modern methods (% of females aged 15 to 49)		NA	NA	●	●
Ratio of female-to-male mean years of education received (%)		NA	NA	●	●
Ratio of female-to-male labor force participation rate (%)		NA	NA	●	●
Seats held by women in national parliament (%)		6.3	2020	●	→
SDG6 – Clean Water and Sanitation					
Population using at least basic drinking water services (%)		99.7	2020	●	↑
Population using at least basic sanitation services (%)		99.6	2020	●	↑
Freshwater withdrawal (% of available freshwater resources)		NA	NA	●	●
Anthropogenic wastewater that receives treatment (%)		40.0	2018	●	●
Scarce water consumption embodied in imports (m^3 H_2O eq/capita)		NA	NA	●	●
SDG7 – Affordable and Clean Energy					
Population with access to electricity (%)		100.0	2019	●	↑
Population with access to clean fuels and technology for cooking (%)		100.0	2019	●	↑
CO_2 emissions from fuel combustion per total electricity output ($MtCO_2$/TWh)		NA	NA	●	●
Share of renewable energy in total primary energy supply (%)		NA	NA	●	●
SDG8 – Decent Work and Economic Growth					
Adjusted GDP growth (%)		-6.5	2020	●	●
Victims of modern slavery (per 1,000 population)		NA	NA	●	●
Adults with an account at a bank or other financial institution or with a mobile-money-service provider (% of population aged 15 or over)		NA	NA	●	●
Unemployment rate (% of total labor force)		NA	NA	●	●
Fundamental labor rights are effectively guaranteed (worst 0–1 best)		NA	NA	●	●
Fatal work-related accidents embodied in imports (per 100,000 population)		NA	NA	●	●

* Imputed data point

SDG9 – Industry, Innovation and Infrastructure		Value	Year	Rating	Trend
Population using the internet (%)		27.0	2004	●	●
Mobile broadband subscriptions (per 100 population)		0.0	2013	●	●
Logistics Performance Index: Quality of trade and transport-related infrastructure (worst 1–5 best)		NA	NA	●	●
The Times Higher Education Universities Ranking: Average score of top 3 universities (worst 0–100 best)	*	0.0	2022	●	●
Articles published in academic journals (per 1,000 population)		1.2	2020	●	↑
Expenditure on research and development (% of GDP)		NA	NA	●	●
SDG10 – Reduced Inequalities					
Gini coefficient		NA	NA	●	●
Palma ratio		NA	NA	●	●
SDG11 – Sustainable Cities and Communities					
Proportion of urban population living in slums (%)		NA	NA	●	●
Annual mean concentration of particulate matter of less than 2.5 microns in diameter (PM2.5) (μg/m³)		11.5	2019	●	↑
Access to improved water source, piped (% of urban population)		94.3	2020	●	↑
Satisfaction with public transport (%)		NA	NA	●	●
SDG12 – Responsible Consumption and Production					
Municipal solid waste (kg/capita/day)		1.5	2016	●	●
Electronic waste (kg/capita)		9.1	2019	●	●
Production-based SO_2 emissions (kg/capita)		NA	NA	●	●
SO_2 emissions embodied in imports (kg/capita)		NA	NA	●	●
Production-based nitrogen emissions (kg/capita)		NA	NA	●	●
Nitrogen emissions embodied in imports (kg/capita)		NA	NA	●	●
Exports of plastic waste (kg/capita)		5.8	2018	●	●
SDG13 – Climate Action					
CO_2 emissions from fossil fuel combustion and cement production (tCO_2/capita)		12.1	2020	●	↓
CO_2 emissions embodied in imports (tCO_2/capita)		NA	NA	●	●
CO_2 emissions embodied in fossil fuel exports (kg/capita)		NA	NA	●	●
SDG14 – Life Below Water					
Mean area that is protected in marine sites important to biodiversity (%)		72.3	2020	●	→
Ocean Health Index: Clean Waters score (worst 0–100 best)		71.9	2020	●	→
Fish caught from overexploited or collapsed stocks (% of total catch)		5.0	2018	●	↑
Fish caught by trawling or dredging (%)		0.0	2018	●	↑
Fish caught that are then discarded (%)		0.0	2011	●	●
Marine biodiversity threats embodied in imports (per million population)		NA	NA	●	●
SDG15 – Life on Land					
Mean area that is protected in terrestrial sites important to biodiversity (%)		48.1	2020	●	→
Mean area that is protected in freshwater sites important to biodiversity (%)		NA	NA	●	●
Red List Index of species survival (worst 0–1 best)		0.7	2021	●	↓
Permanent deforestation (% of forest area, 5-year average)		0.0	2020	●	↑
Terrestrial and freshwater biodiversity threats embodied in imports (per million population)		NA	NA	●	●
SDG16 – Peace, Justice and Strong Institutions					
Homicides (per 100,000 population)		11.2	2018	●	↑
Unsentenced detainees (% of prison population)		NA	NA	●	●
Population who feel safe walking alone at night in the city or area where they live (%)		NA	NA	●	●
Property Rights (worst 1–7 best)		NA	NA	●	●
Birth registrations with civil authority (% of children under age 5)		NA	NA	●	●
Corruption Perception Index (worst 0–100 best)		NA	NA	●	●
Children involved in child labor (% of population aged 5 to 14)		NA	NA	●	●
Exports of major conventional weapons (TIV constant million USD per 100,000 population)	*	0.0	2020	●	●
Press Freedom Index (best 0–100 worst)		NA	NA	●	●
Access to and affordability of justice (worst 0–1 best)		NA	NA	●	●
SDG17 – Partnerships for the Goals					
Government spending on health and education (% of GDP)		14.3	2019	●	↑
For high-income and all OECD DAC countries: International concessional public finance, including official development assistance (% of GNI)		NA	NA	●	●
Other countries: Government revenue excluding grants (% of GDP)		NA	NA	●	●
Corporate Tax Haven Score (best 0–100 worst)	*	0.0	2019	●	●
Statistical Performance Index (worst 0–100 best)		NA	NA	●	●

PANAMA

Latin America and the Caribbean

OVERALL PERFORMANCE

COUNTRY RANKING

PANAMA

105/163

COUNTRY SCORE

REGIONAL AVERAGE: 69.5

AVERAGE PERFORMANCE BY SDG

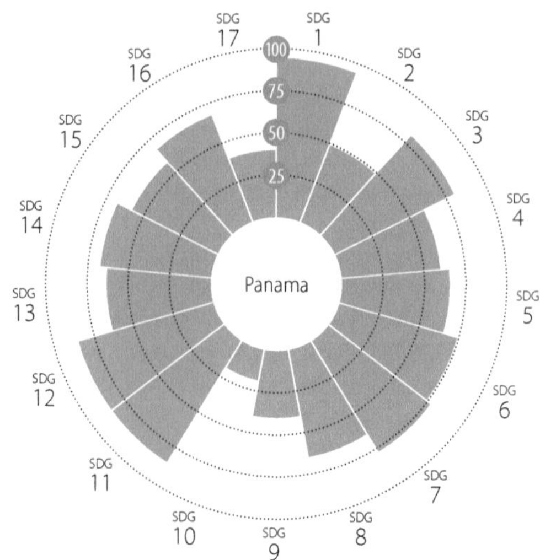

SDG DASHBOARDS AND TRENDS

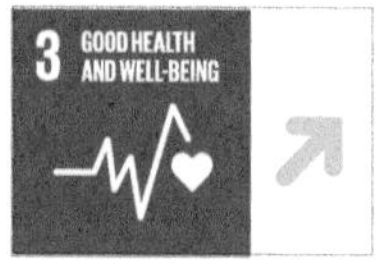

Major challenges | Significant challenges | Challenges remain | SDG achieved | Information unavailable

Decreasing | Stagnating | Moderately improving | On track or maintaining SDG achievement | Information unavailable

Note: The full title of each SDG is available here: https://sustainabledevelopment.un.org/topics/sustainabledevelopmentgoals

INTERNATIONAL SPILLOVER INDEX

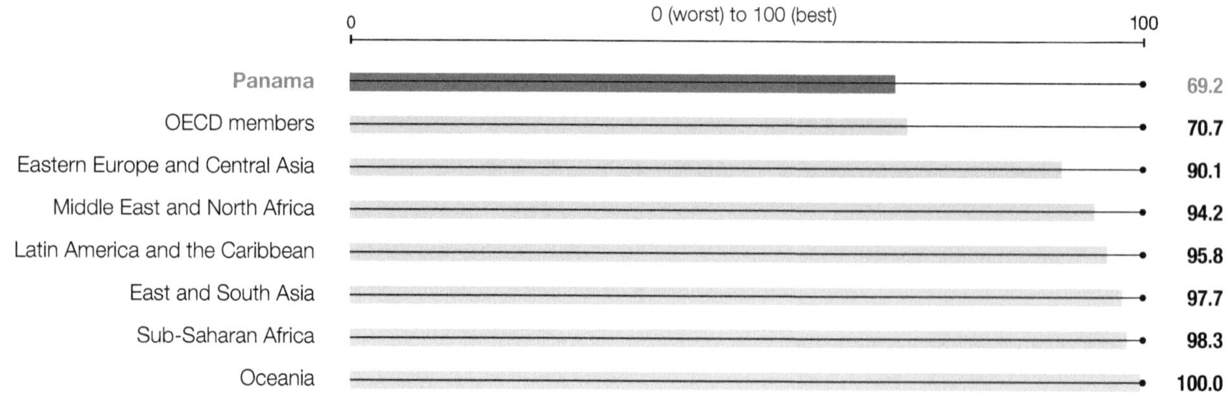

STATISTICAL PERFORMANCE INDEX

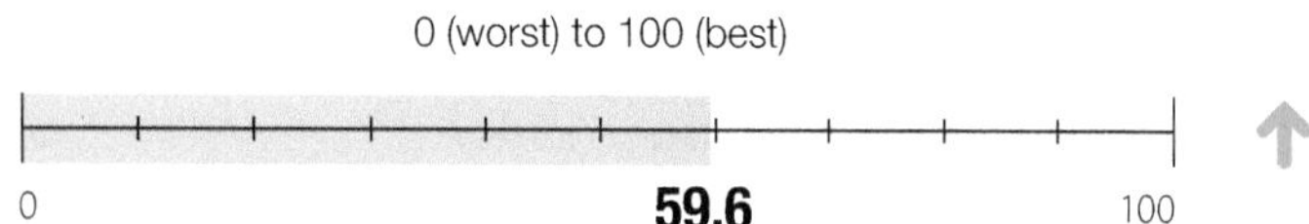

MISSING DATA IN SDG INDEX

0%

SDG1 – No Poverty	Value	Year	Rating	Trend
Poverty headcount ratio at $1.90/day (%)	0.8	2022	●	↑
Poverty headcount ratio at $3.20/day (%)	5.3	2022	●	↗
SDG2 – Zero Hunger				
Prevalence of undernourishment (%)	7.5	2019	●	↑
Prevalence of stunting in children under 5 years of age (%)	15.8	2019	●	↗
Prevalence of wasting in children under 5 years of age (%)	1.2	2008	●	↑
Prevalence of obesity, BMI ≥ 30 (% of adult population)	22.7	2016	●	↓
Human Trophic Level (best 2–3 worst)	2.3	2017	●	↗
Cereal yield (tonnes per hectare of harvested land)	2.9	2018	●	↑
Sustainable Nitrogen Management Index (best 0–1.41 worst)	1.0	2015	●	↓
Exports of hazardous pesticides (tonnes per million population)	224.5	2019	●	●
SDG3 – Good Health and Well-Being				
Maternal mortality rate (per 100,000 live births)	52	2017	●	↑
Neonatal mortality rate (per 1,000 live births)	8.0	2020	●	↑
Mortality rate, under-5 (per 1,000 live births)	14.3	2020	●	↑
Incidence of tuberculosis (per 100,000 population)	32.0	2020	●	↑
New HIV infections (per 1,000 uninfected population)	0.4	2020	●	→
Age-standardized death rate due to cardiovascular disease, cancer, diabetes, or chronic respiratory disease in adults aged 30–70 years (%)	10.7	2019	●	↑
Age-standardized death rate attributable to household air pollution and ambient air pollution (per 100,000 population)	26	2016	●	●
Traffic deaths (per 100,000 population)	13.9	2019	●	→
Life expectancy at birth (years)	79.3	2019	●	↑
Adolescent fertility rate (births per 1,000 females aged 15 to 19)	74.1	2018	●	↗
Births attended by skilled health personnel (%)	92.9	2018	●	↓
Surviving infants who received 2 WHO-recommended vaccines (%)	74	2020	●	→
Universal health coverage (UHC) index of service coverage (worst 0–100 best)	77	2019	●	↑
Subjective well-being (average ladder score, worst 0–10 best)	6.6	2021	●	↑
SDG4 – Quality Education				
Participation rate in pre-primary organized learning (% of children aged 4 to 6)	14.3	2020	●	↓
Net primary enrollment rate (%)	88.7	2020	●	↓
Lower secondary completion rate (%)	71.6	2020	●	●
Literacy rate (% of population aged 15 to 24)	98.9	2019	●	●
SDG5 – Gender Equality				
Demand for family planning satisfied by modern methods (% of females aged 15 to 49)	65.2	2015	●	↗
Ratio of female-to-male mean years of education received (%)	112.0	2019	●	↑
Ratio of female-to-male labor force participation rate (%)	67.5	2020	●	↑
Seats held by women in national parliament (%)	22.5	2020	●	↗
SDG6 – Clean Water and Sanitation				
Population using at least basic drinking water services (%)	94.4	2020	●	↗
Population using at least basic sanitation services (%)	84.6	2020	●	↑
Freshwater withdrawal (% of available freshwater resources)	0.9	2018	●	●
Anthropogenic wastewater that receives treatment (%)	23.1	2018	●	●
Scarce water consumption embodied in imports (m^3 H_2O eq/capita)	3038.8	2018	●	●
SDG7 – Affordable and Clean Energy				
Population with access to electricity (%)	95.8	2019	●	↑
Population with access to clean fuels and technology for cooking (%)	100.0	2019	●	↑
CO_2 emissions from fuel combustion per total electricity output ($MtCO_2$/TWh)	1.0	2019	●	↑
Share of renewable energy in total primary energy supply (%)	17.2	2019	●	↓
SDG8 – Decent Work and Economic Growth				
Adjusted GDP growth (%)	-7.1	2020	●	●
Victims of modern slavery (per 1,000 population)	2.1	2018	●	●
Adults with an account at a bank or other financial institution or with a mobile-money-service provider (% of population aged 15 or over)	46.5	2017	●	→
Unemployment rate (% of total labor force)	11.7	2022	●	↓
Fundamental labor rights are effectively guaranteed (worst 0–1 best)	0.7	2020	●	↑
Fatal work-related accidents embodied in imports (per 100,000 population)	0.5	2015	●	↑

* Imputed data point

SDG9 – Industry, Innovation and Infrastructure	Value	Year	Rating	Trend
Population using the internet (%)	64.3	2020	●	↑
Mobile broadband subscriptions (per 100 population)	79.3	2019	●	↑
Logistics Performance Index: Quality of trade and transport-related infrastructure (worst 1–5 best)	3.1	2018	●	↑
The Times Higher Education Universities Ranking: Average score of top 3 universities (worst 0–100 best)	* 3.4	2019	●	●
Articles published in academic journals (per 1,000 population)	0.2	2020	●	→
Expenditure on research and development (% of GDP)	0.1	2017	●	→
SDG10 – Reduced Inequalities				
Gini coefficient	49.8	2019	●	→
Palma ratio	3.1	2018	●	●
SDG11 – Sustainable Cities and Communities				
Proportion of urban population living in slums (%)	21.3	2018	●	↗
Annual mean concentration of particulate matter of less than 2.5 microns in diameter (PM2.5) ($\mu g/m^3$)	10.5	2019	●	↑
Access to improved water source, piped (% of urban population)	98.7	2020	●	↑
Satisfaction with public transport (%)	64.0	2021	●	↑
SDG12 – Responsible Consumption and Production				
Municipal solid waste (kg/capita/day)	1.0	2015	●	●
Electronic waste (kg/capita)	9.4	2019	●	●
Production-based SO_2 emissions (kg/capita)	18.4	2018	●	●
SO_2 emissions embodied in imports (kg/capita)	6.6	2018	●	●
Production-based nitrogen emissions (kg/capita)	8.1	2015	●	↑
Nitrogen emissions embodied in imports (kg/capita)	3.7	2015	●	↑
Exports of plastic waste (kg/capita)	0.0	2017	●	●
SDG13 – Climate Action				
CO_2 emissions from fossil fuel combustion and cement production (tCO_2/capita)	2.5	2020	●	↗
CO_2 emissions embodied in imports (tCO_2/capita)	3.1	2018	●	↓
CO_2 emissions embodied in fossil fuel exports (kg/capita)	0.0	2020	●	●
SDG14 – Life Below Water				
Mean area that is protected in marine sites important to biodiversity (%)	23.5	2020	●	→
Ocean Health Index: Clean Waters score (worst 0–100 best)	65.0	2020	●	↗
Fish caught from overexploited or collapsed stocks (% of total catch)	6.1	2018	●	↑
Fish caught by trawling or dredging (%)	0.3	2018	●	↑
Fish caught that are then discarded (%)	8.9	2018	●	↓
Marine biodiversity threats embodied in imports (per million population)	0.4	2018	●	●
SDG15 – Life on Land				
Mean area that is protected in terrestrial sites important to biodiversity (%)	33.2	2020	●	→
Mean area that is protected in freshwater sites important to biodiversity (%)	55.3	2020	●	→
Red List Index of species survival (worst 0–1 best)	0.7	2021	●	↓
Permanent deforestation (% of forest area, 5-year average)	0.3	2020	●	↓
Terrestrial and freshwater biodiversity threats embodied in imports (per million population)	1.4	2018	●	●
SDG16 – Peace, Justice and Strong Institutions				
Homicides (per 100,000 population)	11.1	2020	●	→
Unsentenced detainees (% of prison population)	47.3	2018	●	↑
Population who feel safe walking alone at night in the city or area where they live (%)	57	2021	●	↗
Property Rights (worst 1–7 best)	4.7	2020	●	↑
Birth registrations with civil authority (% of children under age 5)	96.7	2020	●	●
Corruption Perception Index (worst 0–100 best)	36	2021	●	↓
Children involved in child labor (% of population aged 5 to 14)	2.3	2019	●	●
Exports of major conventional weapons (TIV constant million USD per 100,000 population)	0.0	2020	●	●
Press Freedom Index (best 0–100 worst)	29.9	2021	●	↑
Access to and affordability of justice (worst 0–1 best)	0.6	2020	●	↓
SDG17 – Partnerships for the Goals				
Government spending on health and education (% of GDP)	8.1	2019	●	↑
For high-income and all OECD DAC countries: International concessional public finance, including official development assistance (% of GNI)	NA	NA	●	●
Other countries: Government revenue excluding grants (% of GDP)	13.7	2018	●	→
Corporate Tax Haven Score (best 0–100 worst)	71.8	2019	●	●
Statistical Performance Index (worst 0–100 best)	59.6	2019	●	↑

PAPUA NEW GUINEA

Oceania

OVERALL PERFORMANCE

COUNTRY RANKING

PAPUA NEW GUINEA

144/163

COUNTRY SCORE

AVERAGE PERFORMANCE BY SDG

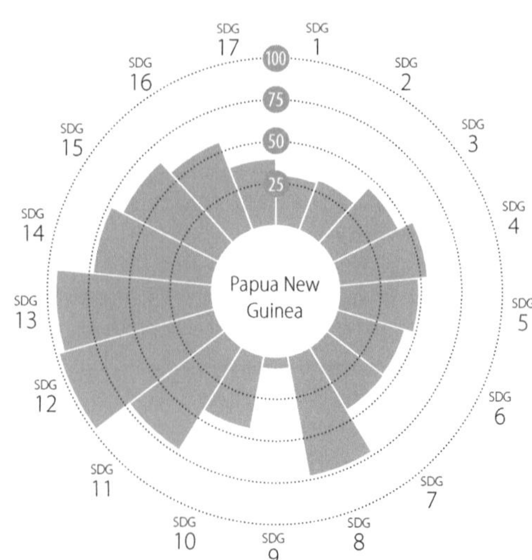

SDG DASHBOARDS AND TRENDS

Major challenges | Significant challenges | Challenges remain | SDG achieved | Information unavailable

Decreasing | Stagnating | Moderately improving | On track or maintaining SDG achievement | Information unavailable

Note: The full title of each SDG is available here: https://sustainabledevelopment.un.org/topics/sustainabledevelopmentgoals

INTERNATIONAL SPILLOVER INDEX

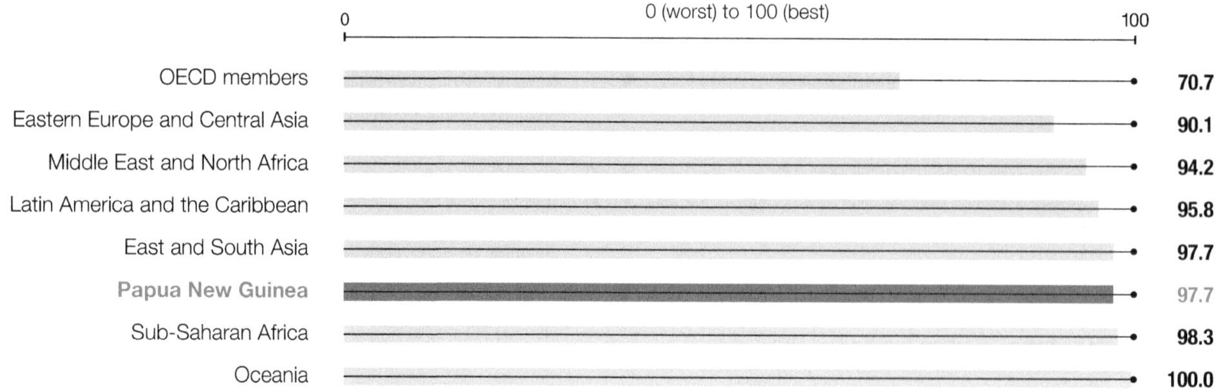

STATISTICAL PERFORMANCE INDEX

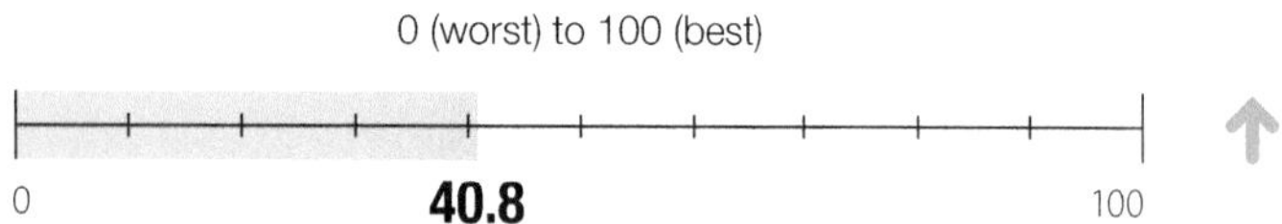

MISSING DATA IN SDG INDEX

16%

PAPUA NEW GUINEA

Performance by Indicator

SDG1 – No Poverty	Value	Year	Rating	Trend
Poverty headcount ratio at \$1.90/day (%)	29.8	2022	●	→
Poverty headcount ratio at \$3.20/day (%)	53.4	2022	●	→

SDG2 – Zero Hunger	Value	Year	Rating	Trend
Prevalence of undernourishment (%)	24.6	2019	●	→
Prevalence of stunting in children under 5 years of age (%)	49.5	2010	●	→
Prevalence of wasting in children under 5 years of age (%)	14.1	2010	●	→
Prevalence of obesity, BMI ≥ 30 (% of adult population)	21.3	2016	●	↓
Human Trophic Level (best 2–3 worst)	NA	NA	●	●
Cereal yield (tonnes per hectare of harvested land)	4.7	2018	●	↑
Sustainable Nitrogen Management Index (best 0–1.41 worst)	0.9	2015	●	→
Exports of hazardous pesticides (tonnes per million population)	NA	NA	●	●

SDG3 – Good Health and Well-Being	Value	Year	Rating	Trend
Maternal mortality rate (per 100,000 live births)	145	2017	●	↗
Neonatal mortality rate (per 1,000 live births)	21.5	2020	●	↗
Mortality rate, under-5 (per 1,000 live births)	43.9	2020	●	↗
Incidence of tuberculosis (per 100,000 population)	441.0	2020	●	↓
New HIV infections (per 1,000 uninfected population)	0.4	2020	●	→
Age-standardized death rate due to cardiovascular disease, cancer, diabetes, or chronic respiratory disease in adults aged 30–70 years (%)	36.0	2019	●	→
Age-standardized death rate attributable to household air pollution and ambient air pollution (per 100,000 population)	152	2016	●	●
Traffic deaths (per 100,000 population)	12.6	2019	●	↗
Life expectancy at birth (years)	65.3	2019	●	→
Adolescent fertility rate (births per 1,000 females aged 15 to 19)	68.0	2016	●	●
Births attended by skilled health personnel (%)	56.4	2018	●	●
Surviving infants who received 2 WHO-recommended vaccines (%)	39	2020	●	↓
Universal health coverage (UHC) index of service coverage (worst 0–100 best)	33	2019	●	↓
Subjective well-being (average ladder score, worst 0–10 best)	NA	NA	●	●

SDG4 – Quality Education	Value	Year	Rating	Trend
Participation rate in pre-primary organized learning (% of children aged 4 to 6)	71.4	2018	●	●
Net primary enrollment rate (%)	97.6	2018	●	●
Lower secondary completion rate (%)	37.2	2018	●	●
Literacy rate (% of population aged 15 to 24)	67.9	2010	●	●

SDG5 – Gender Equality	Value	Year	Rating	Trend
Demand for family planning satisfied by modern methods (% of females aged 15 to 49)	49.2	2018	●	→
Ratio of female-to-male mean years of education received (%)	75.5	2019	●	↗
Ratio of female-to-male labor force participation rate (%)	96.6	2020	●	↑
Seats held by women in national parliament (%)	0.0	2020	●	↓

SDG6 – Clean Water and Sanitation	Value	Year	Rating	Trend
Population using at least basic drinking water services (%)	45.3	2020	●	→
Population using at least basic sanitation services (%)	19.2	2020	●	→
Freshwater withdrawal (% of available freshwater resources)	0.1	2018	●	●
Anthropogenic wastewater that receives treatment (%)	0.0	2018	●	●
Scarce water consumption embodied in imports (m^3 H_2O eq/capita)	864.4	2018	●	●

SDG7 – Affordable and Clean Energy	Value	Year	Rating	Trend
Population with access to electricity (%)	63.5	2019	●	↑
Population with access to clean fuels and technology for cooking (%)	9.3	2019	●	→
CO_2 emissions from fuel combustion per total electricity output ($MtCO_2$/TWh)	2.2	2019	●	→
Share of renewable energy in total primary energy supply (%)	NA	NA	●	●

SDG8 – Decent Work and Economic Growth	Value	Year	Rating	Trend
Adjusted GDP growth (%)	-5.8	2020	●	●
Victims of modern slavery (per 1,000 population)	10.3	2018	●	●
Adults with an account at a bank or other financial institution or with a mobile-money-service provider (% of population aged 15 or over)	NA	NA	●	●
Unemployment rate (% of total labor force)	2.6	2022	●	↑
Fundamental labor rights are effectively guaranteed (worst 0–1 best)	NA	NA	●	●
Fatal work-related accidents embodied in imports (per 100,000 population)	0.1	2015	●	↑

SDG9 – Industry, Innovation and Infrastructure	Value	Year	Rating	Trend
Population using the internet (%)	11.2	2017	●	●
Mobile broadband subscriptions (per 100 population)	11.8	2019	●	→
Logistics Performance Index: Quality of trade and transport-related infrastructure (worst 1–5 best)	2.0	2018	●	↓
The Times Higher Education Universities Ranking: Average score of top 3 universities (worst 0–100 best)	* 0.0	2022	●	●
Articles published in academic journals (per 1,000 population)	0.0	2020	●	→
Expenditure on research and development (% of GDP)	0.0	2016	●	●

SDG10 – Reduced Inequalities	Value	Year	Rating	Trend
Gini coefficient	41.9	2009	●	●
Palma ratio	2.1	2018	●	●

SDG11 – Sustainable Cities and Communities	Value	Year	Rating	Trend
Proportion of urban population living in slums (%)	NA	NA	●	●
Annual mean concentration of particulate matter of less than 2.5 microns in diameter (PM2.5) (μg/m^3)	11.0	2019	●	↑
Access to improved water source, piped (% of urban population)	52.6	2020	●	↓
Satisfaction with public transport (%)	NA	NA	●	●

SDG12 – Responsible Consumption and Production	Value	Year	Rating	Trend
Municipal solid waste (kg/capita/day)	0.3	2014	●	●
Electronic waste (kg/capita)	1.1	2019	●	●
Production-based SO_2 emissions (kg/capita)	3.4	2018	●	●
SO_2 emissions embodied in imports (kg/capita)	0.6	2018	●	●
Production-based nitrogen emissions (kg/capita)	1.7	2015	●	↑
Nitrogen emissions embodied in imports (kg/capita)	0.4	2015	●	↑
Exports of plastic waste (kg/capita)	NA	NA	●	●

SDG13 – Climate Action	Value	Year	Rating	Trend
CO_2 emissions from fossil fuel combustion and cement production (tCO_2/capita)	0.7	2020	●	↑
CO_2 emissions embodied in imports (tCO_2/capita)	0.2	2018	●	↑
CO_2 emissions embodied in fossil fuel exports (kg/capita)	NA	NA	●	●

SDG14 – Life Below Water	Value	Year	Rating	Trend
Mean area that is protected in marine sites important to biodiversity (%)	1.9	2020	●	→
Ocean Health Index: Clean Waters score (worst 0–100 best)	65.2	2020	●	→
Fish caught from overexploited or collapsed stocks (% of total catch)	5.0	2018	●	↑
Fish caught by trawling or dredging (%)	0.0	2018	●	↑
Fish caught that are then discarded (%)	2.6	2018	●	↑
Marine biodiversity threats embodied in imports (per million population)	0.0	2018	●	●

SDG15 – Life on Land	Value	Year	Rating	Trend
Mean area that is protected in terrestrial sites important to biodiversity (%)	7.3	2020	●	→
Mean area that is protected in freshwater sites important to biodiversity (%)	NA	NA	●	●
Red List Index of species survival (worst 0–1 best)	0.8	2021	●	↓
Permanent deforestation (% of forest area, 5-year average)	0.1	2020	●	↑
Terrestrial and freshwater biodiversity threats embodied in imports (per million population)	0.0	2018	●	●

SDG16 – Peace, Justice and Strong Institutions	Value	Year	Rating	Trend
Homicides (per 100,000 population)	9.8	2010	●	●
Unsentenced detainees (% of prison population)	38.3	2016	●	●
Population who feel safe walking alone at night in the city or area where they live (%)	NA	NA	●	●
Property Rights (worst 1–7 best)	NA	NA	●	●
Birth registrations with civil authority (% of children under age 5)	13.4	2020	●	●
Corruption Perception Index (worst 0–100 best)	31	2021	●	→
Children involved in child labor (% of population aged 5 to 14)	NA	NA	●	●
Exports of major conventional weapons (TIV constant million USD per 100,000 population)	* 0.0	2020	●	●
Press Freedom Index (best 0–100 worst)	24.9	2021	●	↑
Access to and affordability of justice (worst 0–1 best)	NA	NA	●	●

SDG17 – Partnerships for the Goals	Value	Year	Rating	Trend
Government spending on health and education (% of GDP)	3.2	2019	●	●
For high-income and all OECD DAC countries: International concessional public finance, including official development assistance (% of GNI)	NA	NA	●	●
Other countries: Government revenue excluding grants (% of GDP)	14.2	2019	●	↓
Corporate Tax Haven Score (best 0–100 worst)	* 0.0	2019	●	●
Statistical Performance Index (worst 0–100 best)	40.8	2019	●	↑

* Imputed data point

5. Country Profiles

PARAGUAY

Latin America and the Caribbean

OVERALL PERFORMANCE

COUNTRY RANKING

PARAGUAY

91 **/163**

COUNTRY SCORE

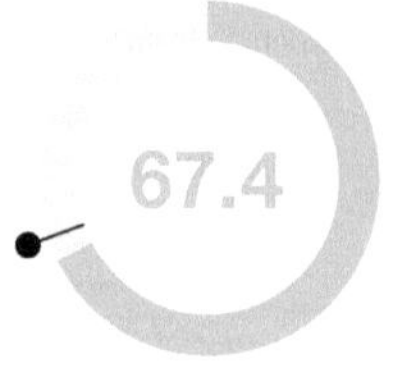

REGIONAL AVERAGE: 69.5

AVERAGE PERFORMANCE BY SDG

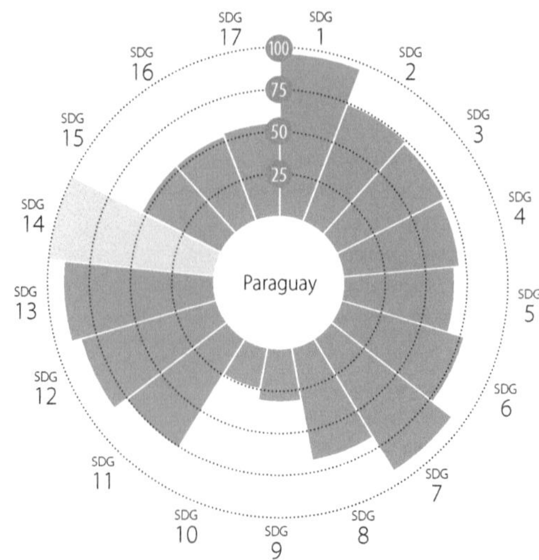

SDG DASHBOARDS AND TRENDS

Major challenges | Significant challenges | Challenges remain | SDG achieved | Information unavailable

Decreasing | Stagnating | Moderately improving | On track or maintaining SDG achievement | Information unavailable

Note: The full title of each SDG is available here: https://sustainabledevelopment.un.org/topics/sustainabledevelopmentgoals

INTERNATIONAL SPILLOVER INDEX

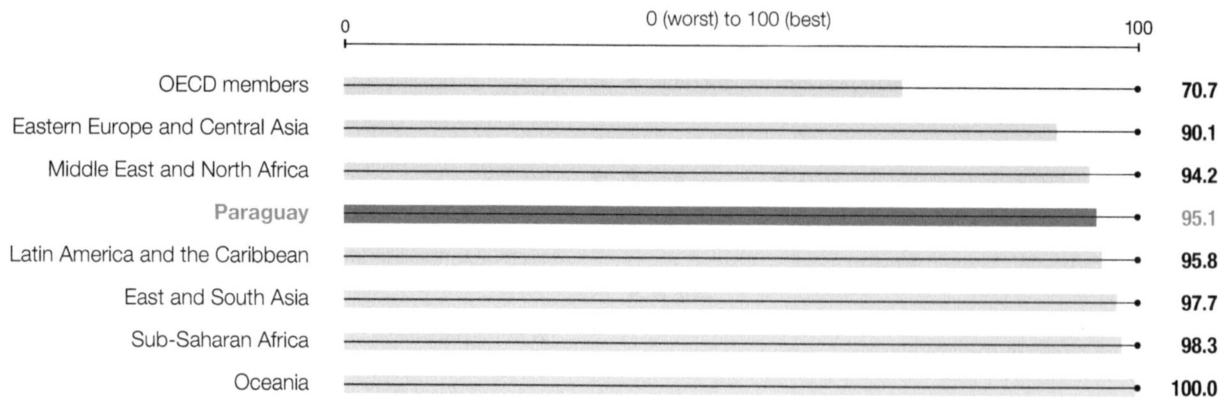

STATISTICAL PERFORMANCE INDEX

0 (worst) to 100 (best)

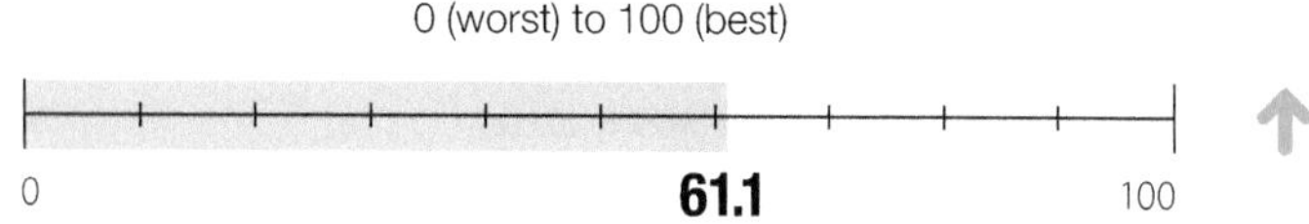

MISSING DATA IN SDG INDEX

2%

PARAGUAY

SDG1 – No Poverty		Value	Year	Rating	Trend
Poverty headcount ratio at \$1.90/day (%)		0.6	2022	●	↑
Poverty headcount ratio at \$3.20/day (%)		4.2	2022	●	↑
SDG2 – Zero Hunger					
Prevalence of undernourishment (%)		9.2	2019	●	↓
Prevalence of stunting in children under 5 years of age (%)		5.6	2016	●	↑
Prevalence of wasting in children under 5 years of age (%)		1.0	2016	●	↑
Prevalence of obesity, BMI ≥ 30 (% of adult population)		20.3	2016	●	↓
Human Trophic Level (best 2–3 worst)		2.2	2017	●	↑
Cereal yield (tonnes per hectare of harvested land)		4.2	2018	●	↑
Sustainable Nitrogen Management Index (best 0–1.41 worst)		0.3	2015	●	↑
Exports of hazardous pesticides (tonnes per million population)		17.7	2019	●	●
SDG3 – Good Health and Well-Being					
Maternal mortality rate (per 100,000 live births)		129	2017	●	→
Neonatal mortality rate (per 1,000 live births)		10.0	2020	●	↑
Mortality rate, under-5 (per 1,000 live births)		18.9	2020	●	↑
Incidence of tuberculosis (per 100,000 population)		48.0	2020	●	→
New HIV infections (per 1,000 uninfected population)		0.1	2020	●	↑
Age-standardized death rate due to cardiovascular disease, cancer, diabetes, or chronic respiratory disease in adults aged 30–70 years (%)		16.0	2019	●	→
Age-standardized death rate attributable to household air pollution and ambient air pollution (per 100,000 population)		57	2016	●	●
Traffic deaths (per 100,000 population)		22.0	2019	●	↓
Life expectancy at birth (years)		75.8	2019	●	→
Adolescent fertility rate (births per 1,000 females aged 15 to 19)		72.0	2015	●	●
Births attended by skilled health personnel (%)		97.7	2018	●	↑
Surviving infants who received 2 WHO-recommended vaccines (%)		79	2020	●	→
Universal health coverage (UHC) index of service coverage (worst 0–100 best)		61	2019	●	→
Subjective well-being (average ladder score, worst 0–10 best)		5.6	2021	●	→
SDG4 – Quality Education					
Participation rate in pre-primary organized learning (% of children aged 4 to 6)		77.4	2020	●	↑
Net primary enrollment rate (%)		80.3	2020	●	●
Lower secondary completion rate (%)		65.8	2020	●	↓
Literacy rate (% of population aged 15 to 24)		98.6	2020	●	↑
SDG5 – Gender Equality					
Demand for family planning satisfied by modern methods (% of females aged 15 to 49)		78.9	2016	●	↑
Ratio of female-to-male mean years of education received (%)		100.0	2019	●	↑
Ratio of female-to-male labor force participation rate (%)		68.6	2020	●	↑
Seats held by women in national parliament (%)		16.3	2020	●	→
SDG6 – Clean Water and Sanitation					
Population using at least basic drinking water services (%)		99.6	2020	●	↑
Population using at least basic sanitation services (%)		92.7	2020	●	↑
Freshwater withdrawal (% of available freshwater resources)		1.8	2018	●	●
Anthropogenic wastewater that receives treatment (%)		0.7	2018	●	●
Scarce water consumption embodied in imports (m[3] H_2O eq/capita)		1045.5	2018	●	●
SDG7 – Affordable and Clean Energy					
Population with access to electricity (%)		100.0	2019	●	↑
Population with access to clean fuels and technology for cooking (%)		68.2	2019	●	↗
CO_2 emissions from fuel combustion per total electricity output ($MtCO_2$/TWh)		0.1	2019	●	↑
Share of renewable energy in total primary energy supply (%)		101.5	2019	●	↑
SDG8 – Decent Work and Economic Growth					
Adjusted GDP growth (%)		-3.0	2020	●	●
Victims of modern slavery (per 1,000 population)		1.6	2018	●	●
Adults with an account at a bank or other financial institution or with a mobile-money-service provider (% of population aged 15 or over)		48.6	2017	●	●
Unemployment rate (% of total labor force)		7.1	2022	●	↓
Fundamental labor rights are effectively guaranteed (worst 0–1 best)		0.5	2020	●	●
Fatal work-related accidents embodied in imports (per 100,000 population)		0.3	2015	●	↑

* Imputed data point

SDG9 – Industry, Innovation and Infrastructure		Value	Year	Rating	Trend
Population using the internet (%)		74.0	2020	●	↑
Mobile broadband subscriptions (per 100 population)		61.2	2019	●	↑
Logistics Performance Index: Quality of trade and transport-related infrastructure (worst 1–5 best)		2.5	2018	●	↗
The Times Higher Education Universities Ranking: Average score of top 3 universities (worst 0–100 best)	*	0.0	2022	●	●
Articles published in academic journals (per 1,000 population)		0.1	2020	●	→
Expenditure on research and development (% of GDP)		0.1	2018	●	→
SDG10 – Reduced Inequalities					
Gini coefficient		45.7	2019	●	→
Palma ratio		2.6	2018	●	●
SDG11 – Sustainable Cities and Communities					
Proportion of urban population living in slums (%)		NA	NA	●	●
Annual mean concentration of particulate matter of less than 2.5 microns in diameter (PM2.5) (μg/m[3])		10.7	2019	●	↑
Access to improved water source, piped (% of urban population)		100.0	2020	●	↑
Satisfaction with public transport (%)		41.0	2021	●	↓
SDG12 – Responsible Consumption and Production					
Municipal solid waste (kg/capita/day)		0.7	2015	●	●
Electronic waste (kg/capita)		7.1	2019	●	●
Production-based SO_2 emissions (kg/capita)		2.4	2018	●	●
SO_2 emissions embodied in imports (kg/capita)		1.3	2018	●	●
Production-based nitrogen emissions (kg/capita)		46.0	2015	●	↓
Nitrogen emissions embodied in imports (kg/capita)		3.3	2015	●	↑
Exports of plastic waste (kg/capita)		0.2	2021	●	●
SDG13 – Climate Action					
CO_2 emissions from fossil fuel combustion and cement production (tCO_2/capita)		1.1	2020	●	↑
CO_2 emissions embodied in imports (tCO_2/capita)		0.4	2018	●	↑
CO_2 emissions embodied in fossil fuel exports (kg/capita)		NA	NA	●	●
SDG14 – Life Below Water					
Mean area that is protected in marine sites important to biodiversity (%)		NA	NA	●	●
Ocean Health Index: Clean Waters score (worst 0–100 best)		NA	NA	●	●
Fish caught from overexploited or collapsed stocks (% of total catch)		NA	NA	●	●
Fish caught by trawling or dredging (%)		NA	NA	●	●
Fish caught that are then discarded (%)		NA	NA	●	●
Marine biodiversity threats embodied in imports (per million population)		0.0	2018	●	●
SDG15 – Life on Land					
Mean area that is protected in terrestrial sites important to biodiversity (%)		36.3	2020	●	→
Mean area that is protected in freshwater sites important to biodiversity (%)		38.8	2020	●	→
Red List Index of species survival (worst 0–1 best)		1.0	2021	●	↑
Permanent deforestation (% of forest area, 5-year average)		1.4	2020	●	↗
Terrestrial and freshwater biodiversity threats embodied in imports (per million population)		0.4	2018	●	●
SDG16 – Peace, Justice and Strong Institutions					
Homicides (per 100,000 population)		6.7	2020	●	↗
Unsentenced detainees (% of prison population)		83.1	2019	●	↓
Population who feel safe walking alone at night in the city or area where they live (%)		48	2021	●	↗
Property Rights (worst 1–7 best)		4.2	2020	●	↑
Birth registrations with civil authority (% of children under age 5)		69.1	2020	●	●
Corruption Perception Index (worst 0–100 best)		30	2021	●	→
Children involved in child labor (% of population aged 5 to 14)		17.9	2019	●	●
Exports of major conventional weapons (TIV constant million USD per 100,000 population)	*	0.0	2020	●	●
Press Freedom Index (best 0–100 worst)		33.5	2021	●	→
Access to and affordability of justice (worst 0–1 best)		0.5	2020	●	●
SDG17 – Partnerships for the Goals					
Government spending on health and education (% of GDP)		6.8	2019	●	→
For high-income and all OECD DAC countries: International concessional public finance, including official development assistance (% of GNI)		NA	NA	●	●
Other countries: Government revenue excluding grants (% of GDP)		17.6	2019	●	↓
Corporate Tax Haven Score (best 0–100 worst)	*	0.0	2019	●	●
Statistical Performance Index (worst 0–100 best)		61.1	2019	●	↑

PERU

Latin America and the Caribbean

AVERAGE PERFORMANCE BY SDG

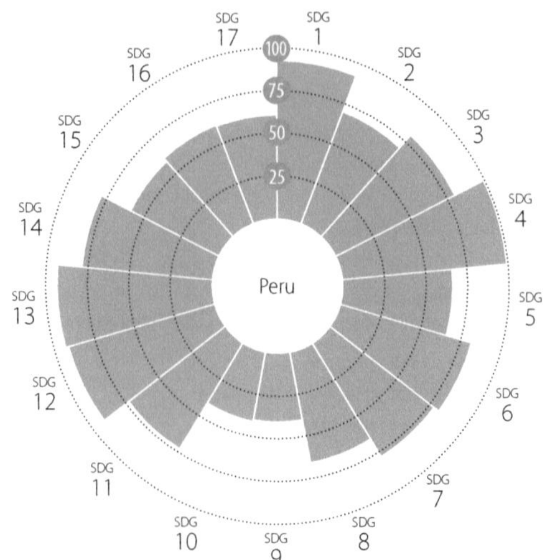

OVERALL PERFORMANCE

COUNTRY RANKING

PERU

58/163

COUNTRY SCORE

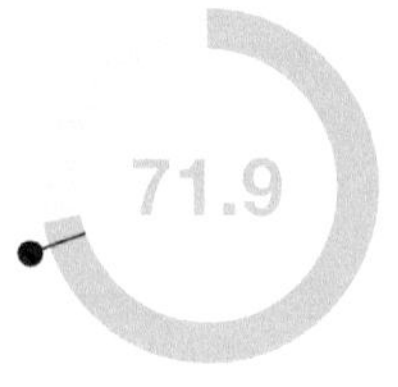

REGIONAL AVERAGE: 69.5

SDG DASHBOARDS AND TRENDS

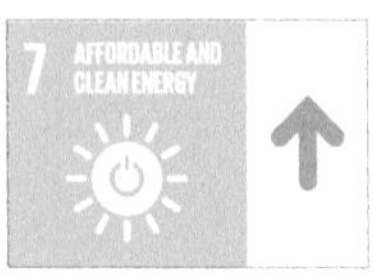

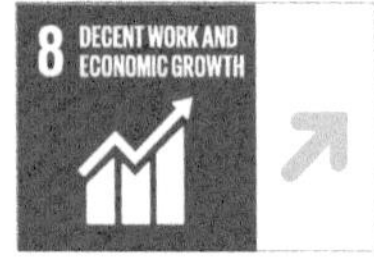

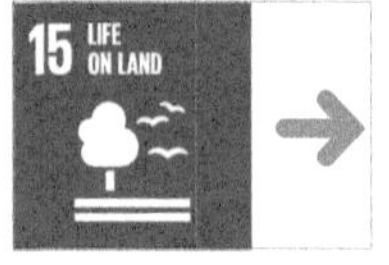

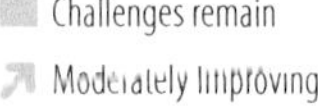

Major challenges | Significant challenges | Challenges remain | SDG achieved | Information unavailable

Decreasing | Stagnating | Moderately improving | On track or maintaining SDG achievement | Information unavailable

Note: The full title of each SDG is available here: https://sustainabledevelopment.un.org/topics/sustainabledevelopmentgoals

INTERNATIONAL SPILLOVER INDEX

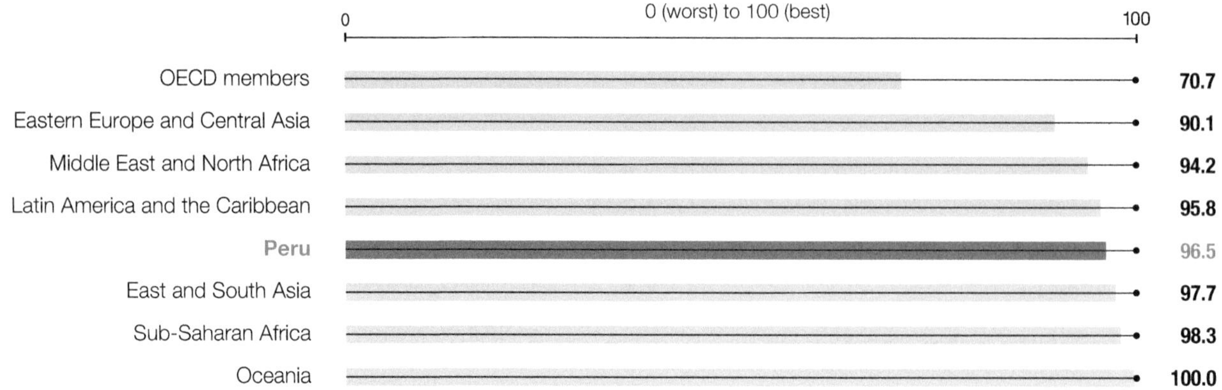

STATISTICAL PERFORMANCE INDEX

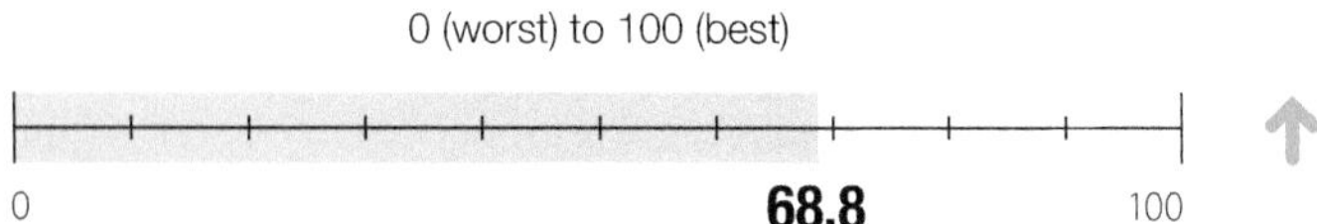

MISSING DATA IN SDG INDEX

0%

SDG1 – No Poverty	Value	Year	Rating	Trend
Poverty headcount ratio at $1.90/day (%)	1.6	2022	●	↑
Poverty headcount ratio at $3.20/day (%)	7.1	2022	●	↗
SDG2 – Zero Hunger				
Prevalence of undernourishment (%)	8.7	2019	●	↓
Prevalence of stunting in children under 5 years of age (%)	12.2	2019	●	→
Prevalence of wasting in children under 5 years of age (%)	0.4	2019	●	↑
Prevalence of obesity, BMI ≥ 30 (% of adult population)	19.7	2016	●	↓
Human Trophic Level (best 2–3 worst)	2.2	2017	●	↓
Cereal yield (tonnes per hectare of harvested land)	4.5	2018	●	↑
Sustainable Nitrogen Management Index (best 0–1.41 worst)	0.8	2015	●	→
Exports of hazardous pesticides (tonnes per million population)	2.2	2019	●	●
SDG3 – Good Health and Well-Being				
Maternal mortality rate (per 100,000 live births)	88	2017	●	↑
Neonatal mortality rate (per 1,000 live births)	6.7	2020	●	↑
Mortality rate, under-5 (per 1,000 live births)	12.8	2020	●	↑
Incidence of tuberculosis (per 100,000 population)	116.0	2020	●	→
New HIV infections (per 1,000 uninfected population)	0.1	2020	●	↑
Age-standardized death rate due to cardiovascular disease, cancer, diabetes, or chronic respiratory disease in adults aged 30–70 years (%)	9.7	2019	●	↑
Age-standardized death rate attributable to household air pollution and ambient air pollution (per 100,000 population)	64	2016	●	●
Traffic deaths (per 100,000 population)	13.6	2019	●	→
Life expectancy at birth (years)	79.9	2019	●	↑
Adolescent fertility rate (births per 1,000 females aged 15 to 19)	44.0	2017	●	●
Births attended by skilled health personnel (%)	92.1	2019	●	→
Surviving infants who received 2 WHO-recommended vaccines (%)	72	2020	●	↓
Universal health coverage (UHC) index of service coverage (worst 0–100 best)	78	2019	●	↑
Subjective well-being (average ladder score, worst 0–10 best)	5.7	2021	●	↗
SDG4 – Quality Education				
Participation rate in pre-primary organized learning (% of children aged 4 to 6)	99.7	2020	●	↑
Net primary enrollment rate (%)	98.2	2020	●	↑
Lower secondary completion rate (%)	101.6	2019	●	↑
Literacy rate (% of population aged 15 to 24)	99.4	2020	●	↑
SDG5 – Gender Equality				
Demand for family planning satisfied by modern methods (% of females aged 15 to 49)	66.6	2018	●	↗
Ratio of female-to-male mean years of education received (%)	88.4	2019	●	↓
Ratio of female-to-male labor force participation rate (%)	77.2	2020	●	↑
Seats held by women in national parliament (%)	26.2	2020	●	↗
SDG6 – Clean Water and Sanitation				
Population using at least basic drinking water services (%)	93.1	2020	●	↑
Population using at least basic sanitation services (%)	78.6	2020	●	↗
Freshwater withdrawal (% of available freshwater resources)	6.5	2018	●	●
Anthropogenic wastewater that receives treatment (%)	46.4	2018	●	●
Scarce water consumption embodied in imports (m^3 H_2O eq/capita)	701.5	2018	●	●
SDG7 – Affordable and Clean Energy				
Population with access to electricity (%)	98.3	2019	●	↑
Population with access to clean fuels and technology for cooking (%)	83.3	2019	●	↑
CO_2 emissions from fuel combustion per total electricity output ($MtCO_2$/TWh)	0.9	2019	●	↑
Share of renewable energy in total primary energy supply (%)	24.5	2019	●	↑
SDG8 – Decent Work and Economic Growth				
Adjusted GDP growth (%)	-6.0	2020	●	●
Victims of modern slavery (per 1,000 population)	2.6	2018	●	●
Adults with an account at a bank or other financial institution or with a mobile-money-service provider (% of population aged 15 or over)	42.6	2017	●	↑
Unemployment rate (% of total labor force)	4.2	2022	●	↑
Fundamental labor rights are effectively guaranteed (worst 0–1 best)	0.5	2020	●	↓
Fatal work-related accidents embodied in imports (per 100,000 population)	0.2	2015	●	↑

SDG9 – Industry, Innovation and Infrastructure	Value	Year	Rating	Trend
Population using the internet (%)	65.3	2020	●	↑
Mobile broadband subscriptions (per 100 population)	74.5	2019	●	↑
Logistics Performance Index: Quality of trade and transport-related infrastructure (worst 1–5 best)	2.3	2018	●	↓
The Times Higher Education Universities Ranking: Average score of top 3 universities (worst 0–100 best)	25.4	2022	●	●
Articles published in academic journals (per 1,000 population)	0.2	2020	●	→
Expenditure on research and development (% of GDP)	0.1	2018	●	→
SDG10 – Reduced Inequalities				
Gini coefficient	41.5	2019	●	↗
Palma ratio	2.2	2018	●	●
SDG11 – Sustainable Cities and Communities				
Proportion of urban population living in slums (%)	33.1	2018	●	→
Annual mean concentration of particulate matter of less than 2.5 microns in diameter (PM2.5) (μg/m^3)	23.3	2019	●	↗
Access to improved water source, piped (% of urban population)	94.5	2020	●	↑
Satisfaction with public transport (%)	54.0	2021	●	→
SDG12 – Responsible Consumption and Production				
Municipal solid waste (kg/capita/day)	0.8	2014	●	●
Electronic waste (kg/capita)	6.3	2019	●	●
Production-based SO_2 emissions (kg/capita)	5.6	2018	●	●
SO_2 emissions embodied in imports (kg/capita)	1.4	2018	●	●
Production-based nitrogen emissions (kg/capita)	11.9	2015	●	↑
Nitrogen emissions embodied in imports (kg/capita)	1.4	2015	●	↑
Exports of plastic waste (kg/capita)	0.0	2020	●	●
SDG13 – Climate Action				
CO_2 emissions from fossil fuel combustion and cement production (tCO_2/capita)	1.4	2020	●	↑
CO_2 emissions embodied in imports (tCO_2/capita)	0.5	2018	●	↑
CO_2 emissions embodied in fossil fuel exports (kg/capita)	389.9	2020	●	●
SDG14 – Life Below Water				
Mean area that is protected in marine sites important to biodiversity (%)	51.6	2020	●	→
Ocean Health Index: Clean Waters score (worst 0–100 best)	57.1	2020	●	→
Fish caught from overexploited or collapsed stocks (% of total catch)	1.2	2018	●	↑
Fish caught by trawling or dredging (%)	1.3	2018	●	↑
Fish caught that are then discarded (%)	4.2	2018	●	↑
Marine biodiversity threats embodied in imports (per million population)	0.0	2018	●	●
SDG15 – Life on Land				
Mean area that is protected in terrestrial sites important to biodiversity (%)	29.6	2020	●	→
Mean area that is protected in freshwater sites important to biodiversity (%)	49.6	2020	●	→
Red List Index of species survival (worst 0–1 best)	0.7	2021	●	→
Permanent deforestation (% of forest area, 5-year average)	0.2	2020	●	→
Terrestrial and freshwater biodiversity threats embodied in imports (per million population)	0.7	2018	●	●
SDG16 – Peace, Justice and Strong Institutions				
Homicides (per 100,000 population)	7.5	2019	●	→
Unsentenced detainees (% of prison population)	35.7	2019	●	↑
Population who feel safe walking alone at night in the city or area where they live (%)	48	2021	●	↗
Property Rights (worst 1–7 best)	3.6	2020	●	↓
Birth registrations with civil authority (% of children under age 5)	97.7	2020	●	●
Corruption Perception Index (worst 0–100 best)	36	2021	●	→
Children involved in child labor (% of population aged 5 to 14)	14.5	2019	●	●
Exports of major conventional weapons (TIV constant million USD per 100,000 population)	0.0	2020	●	●
Press Freedom Index (best 0–100 worst)	31.7	2021	●	↓
Access to and affordability of justice (worst 0–1 best)	0.5	2020	●	↗
SDG17 – Partnerships for the Goals				
Government spending on health and education (% of GDP)	7.5	2020	●	↗
For high-income and all OECD DAC countries: International concessional public finance, including official development assistance (% of GNI)	NA	NA	●	●
Other countries: Government revenue excluding grants (% of GDP)	19.5	2019	●	↓
Corporate Tax Haven Score (best 0–100 worst)	* 0.0	2019	●	●
Statistical Performance Index (worst 0–100 best)	68.8	2019	●	↑

* Imputed data point

5. Country Profiles

PHILIPPINES

East and South Asia

OVERALL PERFORMANCE

COUNTRY RANKING

PHILIPPINES

95/163

COUNTRY SCORE

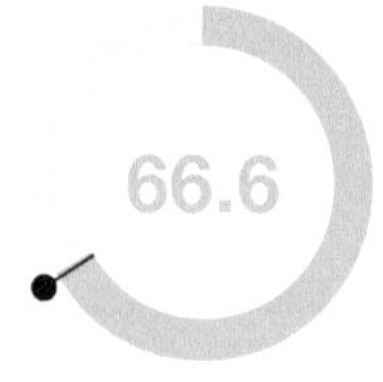

REGIONAL AVERAGE: 65.9

AVERAGE PERFORMANCE BY SDG

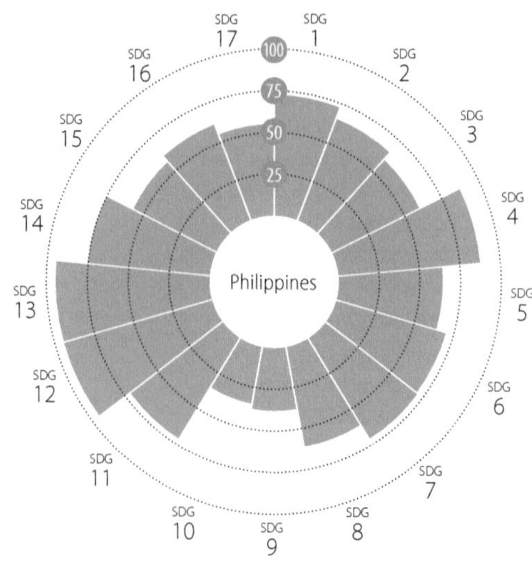

SDG DASHBOARDS AND TRENDS

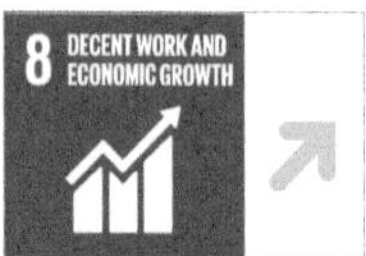

Information unavailable
Information unavailable

Note: The full title of each SDG is available here: https://sustainabledevelopment.un.org/topics/sustainabledevelopmentgoals

INTERNATIONAL SPILLOVER INDEX

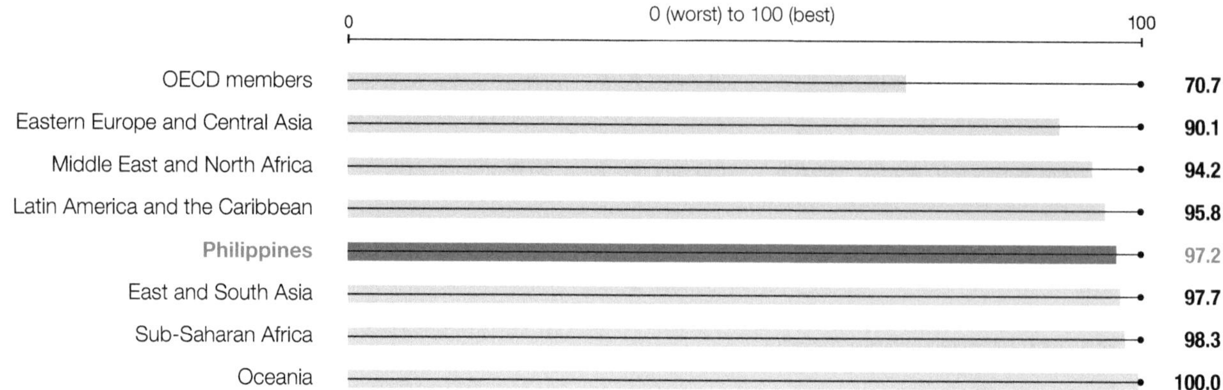

STATISTICAL PERFORMANCE INDEX

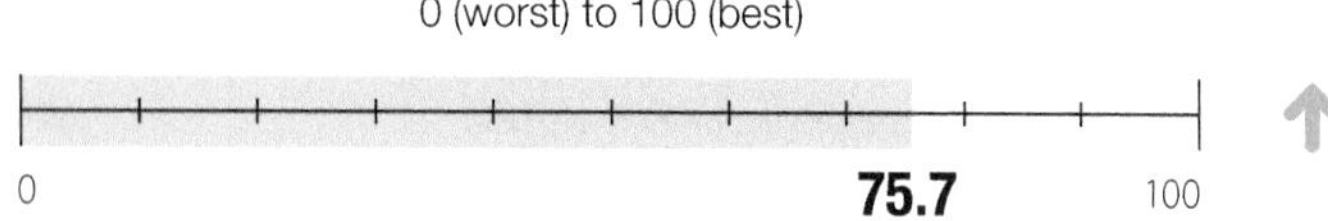

MISSING DATA IN SDG INDEX

1%

PHILIPPINES

Performance by Indicator

SDG1 – No Poverty	Value	Year	Rating	Trend
Poverty headcount ratio at $1.90/day (%)	4.5	2022	●	↑
Poverty headcount ratio at $3.20/day (%)	25.3	2022	●	→

SDG2 – Zero Hunger	Value	Year	Rating	Trend
Prevalence of undernourishment (%)	9.4	2019	●	↑
Prevalence of stunting in children under 5 years of age (%)	30.3	2018	●	→
Prevalence of wasting in children under 5 years of age (%)	5.6	2018	●	→
Prevalence of obesity, BMI ≥ 30 (% of adult population)	6.4	2016	●	↑
Human Trophic Level (best 2–3 worst)	2.2	2017	●	↑
Cereal yield (tonnes per hectare of harvested land)	3.7	2018	●	↑
Sustainable Nitrogen Management Index (best 0–1.41 worst)	0.8	2015	●	↓
Exports of hazardous pesticides (tonnes per million population)	7.6	2019	●	●

SDG3 – Good Health and Well-Being	Value	Year	Rating	Trend
Maternal mortality rate (per 100,000 live births)	121	2017	●	↗
Neonatal mortality rate (per 1,000 live births)	12.6	2020	●	↑
Mortality rate, under-5 (per 1,000 live births)	26.4	2020	●	↑
Incidence of tuberculosis (per 100,000 population)	539.0	2020	●	→
New HIV infections (per 1,000 uninfected population)	0.2	2020	●	↑
Age-standardized death rate due to cardiovascular disease, cancer, diabetes, or chronic respiratory disease in adults aged 30–70 years (%)	24.5	2019	●	→
Age-standardized death rate attributable to household air pollution and ambient air pollution (per 100,000 population)	185	2016	●	●
Traffic deaths (per 100,000 population)	12.0	2019	●	→
Life expectancy at birth (years)	70.4	2019	●	→
Adolescent fertility rate (births per 1,000 females aged 15 to 19)	36.4	2018	●	↑
Births attended by skilled health personnel (%)	84.4	2017	●	●
Surviving infants who received 2 WHO-recommended vaccines (%)	71	2020	●	↑
Universal health coverage (UHC) index of service coverage (worst 0–100 best)	55	2019	●	↗
Subjective well-being (average ladder score, worst 0–10 best)	6.0	2021	●	↑

SDG4 – Quality Education	Value	Year	Rating	Trend
Participation rate in pre-primary organized learning (% of children aged 4 to 6)	86.3	2019	●	↑
Net primary enrollment rate (%)	96.9	2019	●	↓
Lower secondary completion rate (%)	83.1	2019	●	↗
Literacy rate (% of population aged 15 to 24)	98.4	2019	●	↑

SDG5 – Gender Equality	Value	Year	Rating	Trend
Demand for family planning satisfied by modern methods (% of females aged 15 to 49)	56.0	2017	●	→
Ratio of female-to-male mean years of education received (%)	104.3	2019	●	↑
Ratio of female-to-male labor force participation rate (%)	63.6	2020	●	↓
Seats held by women in national parliament (%)	28.0	2020	●	→

SDG6 – Clean Water and Sanitation	Value	Year	Rating	Trend
Population using at least basic drinking water services (%)	94.1	2020	●	↑
Population using at least basic sanitation services (%)	82.3	2020	●	↑
Freshwater withdrawal (% of available freshwater resources)	28.7	2018	●	●
Anthropogenic wastewater that receives treatment (%)	0.7	2018	●	●
Scarce water consumption embodied in imports (m^3 H_2O eq/capita)	421.7	2018	●	●

SDG7 – Affordable and Clean Energy	Value	Year	Rating	Trend
Population with access to electricity (%)	95.6	2019	●	↑
Population with access to clean fuels and technology for cooking (%)	47.4	2019	●	→
CO_2 emissions from fuel combustion per total electricity output ($MtCO_2$/TWh)	1.4	2019	●	→
Share of renewable energy in total primary energy supply (%)	34.0	2019	●	↑

SDG8 – Decent Work and Economic Growth	Value	Year	Rating	Trend
Adjusted GDP growth (%)	-3.8	2020	●	●
Victims of modern slavery (per 1,000 population)	7.7	2018	●	●
Adults with an account at a bank or other financial institution or with a mobile-money-service provider (% of population aged 15 or over)	34.5	2017	●	→
Unemployment rate (% of total labor force)	2.3	2022	●	↑
Fundamental labor rights are effectively guaranteed (worst 0–1 best)	0.4	2020	●	→
Fatal work-related accidents embodied in imports (per 100,000 population)	0.1	2015	●	↑

SDG9 – Industry, Innovation and Infrastructure	Value	Year	Rating	Trend
Population using the internet (%)	49.8	2020	●	↗
Mobile broadband subscriptions (per 100 population)	67.2	2019	●	↑
Logistics Performance Index: Quality of trade and transport-related infrastructure (worst 1–5 best)	2.7	2018	●	↑
The Times Higher Education Universities Ranking: Average score of top 3 universities (worst 0–100 best)	25.7	2022	●	●
Articles published in academic journals (per 1,000 population)	0.1	2020	●	→
Expenditure on research and development (% of GDP)	0.2	2015	●	●

SDG10 – Reduced Inequalities	Value	Year	Rating	Trend
Gini coefficient	42.3	2018	●	↗
Palma ratio	2.3	2018	●	●

SDG11 – Sustainable Cities and Communities	Value	Year	Rating	Trend
Proportion of urban population living in slums (%)	44.3	2018	●	↓
Annual mean concentration of particulate matter of less than 2.5 microns in diameter (PM2.5) (μg/m³)	16.9	2019	●	↑
Access to improved water source, piped (% of urban population)	82.3	2020	●	↗
Satisfaction with public transport (%)	62.0	2021	●	↓

SDG12 – Responsible Consumption and Production	Value	Year	Rating	Trend
Municipal solid waste (kg/capita/day)	0.4	2016	●	●
Electronic waste (kg/capita)	3.9	2019	●	●
Production-based SO_2 emissions (kg/capita)	5.0	2018	●	●
SO_2 emissions embodied in imports (kg/capita)	0.9	2018	●	●
Production-based nitrogen emissions (kg/capita)	4.2	2015	●	↑
Nitrogen emissions embodied in imports (kg/capita)	0.6	2015	●	↑
Exports of plastic waste (kg/capita)	0.8	2020	●	●

SDG13 – Climate Action	Value	Year	Rating	Trend
CO_2 emissions from fossil fuel combustion and cement production (tCO_2/capita)	1.2	2020	●	↑
CO_2 emissions embodied in imports (tCO_2/capita)	0.3	2018	●	↑
CO_2 emissions embodied in fossil fuel exports (kg/capita)	140.4	2020	●	●

SDG14 – Life Below Water	Value	Year	Rating	Trend
Mean area that is protected in marine sites important to biodiversity (%)	38.0	2020	●	→
Ocean Health Index: Clean Waters score (worst 0–100 best)	54.2	2020	●	→
Fish caught from overexploited or collapsed stocks (% of total catch)	12.5	2018	●	↑
Fish caught by trawling or dredging (%)	3.4	2018	●	↑
Fish caught that are then discarded (%)	1.0	2018	●	↑
Marine biodiversity threats embodied in imports (per million population)	0.0	2018	●	●

SDG15 – Life on Land	Value	Year	Rating	Trend
Mean area that is protected in terrestrial sites important to biodiversity (%)	41.6	2020	●	→
Mean area that is protected in freshwater sites important to biodiversity (%)	49.8	2020	●	→
Red List Index of species survival (worst 0–1 best)	0.7	2021	●	↓
Permanent deforestation (% of forest area, 5-year average)	0.3	2020	●	↑
Terrestrial and freshwater biodiversity threats embodied in imports (per million population)	0.1	2018	●	●

SDG16 – Peace, Justice and Strong Institutions	Value	Year	Rating	Trend
Homicides (per 100,000 population)	4.4	2019	●	↑
Unsentenced detainees (% of prison population)	59.2	2019	●	↗
Population who feel safe walking alone at night in the city or area where they live (%)	68	2021	●	↑
Property Rights (worst 1–7 best)	4.4	2020	●	↑
Birth registrations with civil authority (% of children under age 5)	91.8	2020	●	●
Corruption Perception Index (worst 0–100 best)	33	2021	●	↓
Children involved in child labor (% of population aged 5 to 14)	NA	NA	●	●
Exports of major conventional weapons (TIV constant million USD per 100,000 population)	0.0	2020	●	●
Press Freedom Index (best 0–100 worst)	45.6	2021	●	↓
Access to and affordability of justice (worst 0–1 best)	0.5	2020	●	↑

SDG17 – Partnerships for the Goals	Value	Year	Rating	Trend
Government spending on health and education (% of GDP)	4.9	2019	●	→
For high-income and all OECD DAC countries: International concessional public finance, including official development assistance (% of GNI)	NA	NA	●	●
Other countries: Government revenue excluding grants (% of GDP)	16.1	2019	●	→
Corporate Tax Haven Score (best 0–100 worst)	* 0.0	2019	●	●
Statistical Performance Index (worst 0–100 best)	75.7	2019	●	↑

* Imputed data point

5. Country Profiles

OVERALL PERFORMANCE

COUNTRY RANKING

POLAND

12 **/163**

COUNTRY SCORE

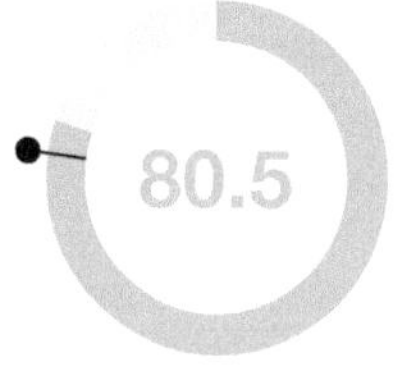

REGIONAL AVERAGE: 77.2

AVERAGE PERFORMANCE BY SDG

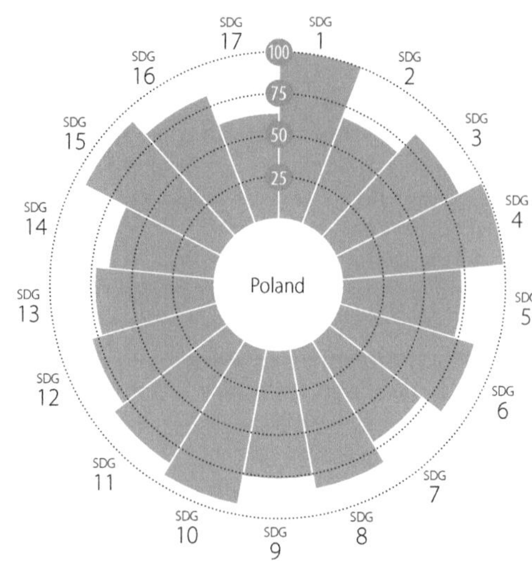

SDG DASHBOARDS AND TRENDS

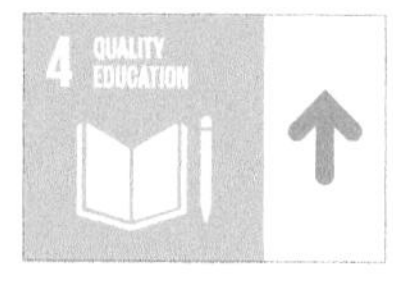

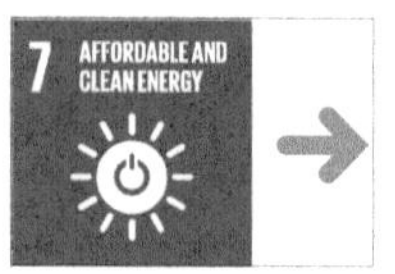

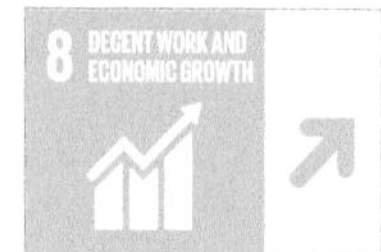

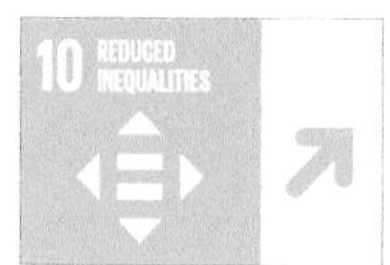

Note: The full title of each SDG is available here: https://sustainabledevelopment.un.org/topics/sustainabledevelopmentgoals

INTERNATIONAL SPILLOVER INDEX

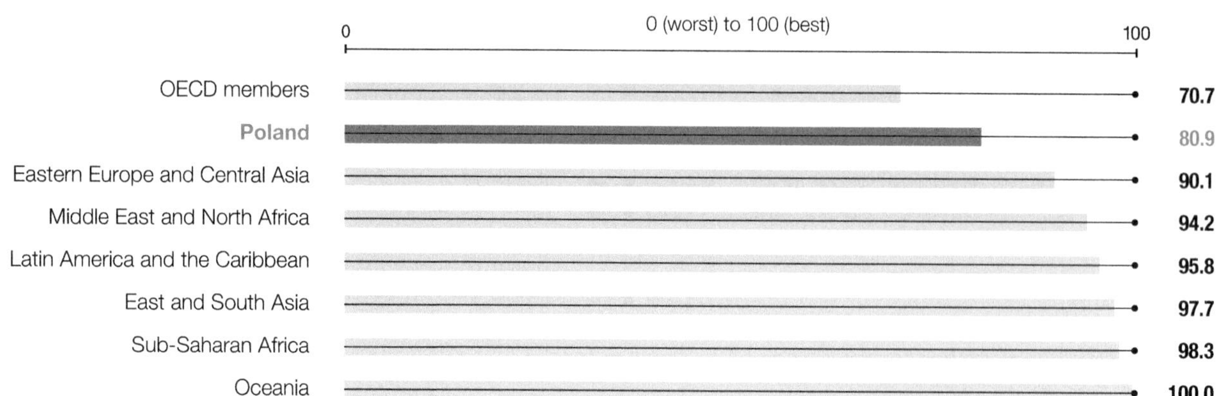

STATISTICAL PERFORMANCE INDEX

0 (worst) to 100 (best)

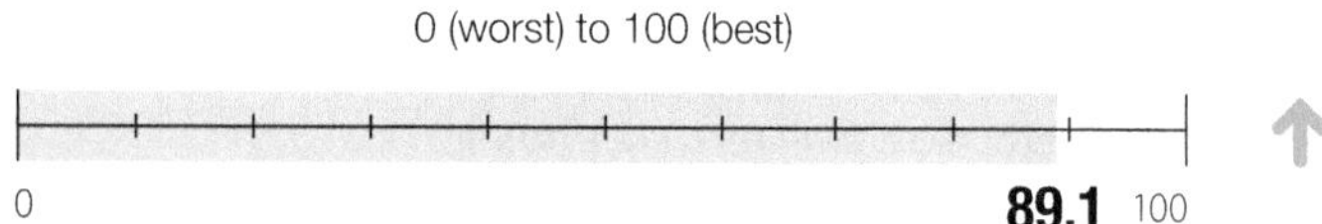

MISSING DATA IN SDG INDEX

POLAND

SDG1 – No Poverty

Indicator	Value	Year	Rating	Trend
Poverty headcount ratio at $1.90/day (%)	0.0	2022	●	↑
Poverty headcount ratio at $3.20/day (%)	0.1	2022	●	↑
Poverty rate after taxes and transfers (%)	9.8	2018	●	↑

SDG2 – Zero Hunger

Indicator	Value	Year	Rating	Trend
Prevalence of undernourishment (%)	2.5	2019	●	↑
Prevalence of stunting in children under 5 years of age (%)	2.6	2014	●	↑
Prevalence of wasting in children under 5 years of age (%)	0.7	2011	●	↑
Prevalence of obesity, BMI ≥ 30 (% of adult population)	23.1	2016	●	↓
Human Trophic Level (best 2–3 worst)	2.4	2017	●	↓
Cereal yield (tonnes per hectare of harvested land)	3.4	2018	●	↑
Sustainable Nitrogen Management Index (best 0–1.41 worst)	0.6	2015	●	→
Yield gap closure (% of potential yield)	44.0	2018	●	●
Exports of hazardous pesticides (tonnes per million population)	2.3	2019	●	●

SDG3 – Good Health and Well-Being

Indicator	Value	Year	Rating	Trend
Maternal mortality rate (per 100,000 live births)	2	2017	●	↑
Neonatal mortality rate (per 1,000 live births)	2.7	2020	●	↑
Mortality rate, under-5 (per 1,000 live births)	4.4	2020	●	↑
Incidence of tuberculosis (per 100,000 population)	9.6	2020	●	↑
New HIV infections (per 1,000 uninfected population)	1.0	2020	●	→
Age-standardized death rate due to cardiovascular disease, cancer, diabetes, or chronic respiratory disease in adults aged 30–70 years (%)	17.0	2019	●	↑
Age-standardized death rate attributable to household air pollution and ambient air pollution (per 100,000 population)	38	2016	●	●
Traffic deaths (per 100,000 population)	9.4	2019	●	→
Life expectancy at birth (years)	78.3	2019	●	↑
Adolescent fertility rate (births per 1,000 females aged 15 to 19)	10.3	2018	●	↑
Births attended by skilled health personnel (%)	99.8	2018	●	↑
Surviving infants who received 2 WHO-recommended vaccines (%)	80	2020	●	↓
Universal health coverage (UHC) index of service coverage (worst 0–100 best)	74	2019	●	↗
Subjective well-being (average ladder score, worst 0–10 best)	6.0	2021	●	↑
Gap in life expectancy at birth among regions (years)	2.6	2019	●	↑
Gap in self-reported health status by income (percentage points)	25.7	2019	●	↓
Daily smokers (% of population aged 15 and over)	17.1	2019	●	↑

SDG4 – Quality Education

Indicator	Value	Year	Rating	Trend
Participation rate in pre-primary organized learning (% of children aged 4 to 6)	98.8	2019	●	↑
Net primary enrollment rate (%)	98.9	2019	●	↑
Lower secondary completion rate (%)	103.3	2019	●	↑
Literacy rate (% of population aged 15 to 24)	99.8	2008	●	●
Tertiary educational attainment (% of population aged 25 to 34)	42.4	2020	●	↑
PISA score (worst 0–600 best)	513.0	2018	●	↑
Variation in science performance explained by socio-economic status (%)	12.6	2018	●	↑
Underachievers in science (% of 15-year-olds)	13.8	2018	●	↑

SDG5 – Gender Equality

Indicator	Value	Year	Rating	Trend
Demand for family planning satisfied by modern methods (% of females aged 15 to 49)	* 72.9	2022	●	↗
Ratio of female-to-male mean years of education received (%)	100.8	2019	●	↑
Ratio of female-to-male labor force participation rate (%)	73.6	2020	●	↑
Seats held by women in national parliament (%)	28.7	2020	●	→
Gender wage gap (% of male median wage)	8.7	2020	●	↑

SDG6 – Clean Water and Sanitation

Indicator	Value	Year	Rating	Trend
Population using at least basic drinking water services (%)	100.0	2020	●	↑
Population using at least basic sanitation services (%)	100.0	2020	●	↑
Freshwater withdrawal (% of available freshwater resources)	33.2	2018	●	●
Anthropogenic wastewater that receives treatment (%)	60.9	2018	●	●
Scarce water consumption embodied in imports (m^3 H_2O eq/capita)	1347.9	2018	●	●
Population using safely managed water services (%)	98.3	2020	●	↑
Population using safely managed sanitation services (%)	90.5	2020	●	↑

SDG7 – Affordable and Clean Energy

Indicator	Value	Year	Rating	Trend
Population with access to electricity (%)	100.0	2019	●	↑
Population with access to clean fuels and technology for cooking (%)	100.0	2019	●	↑
CO_2 emissions from fuel combustion per total electricity output ($MtCO_2$/TWh)	1.9	2019	●	→
Share of renewable energy in total primary energy supply (%)	9.4	2019	●	↓

SDG8 – Decent Work and Economic Growth

Indicator	Value	Year	Rating	Trend
Adjusted GDP growth (%)	1.5	2020	●	●
Victims of modern slavery (per 1,000 population)	3.4	2018	●	●
Adults with an account at a bank or other financial institution or with a mobile-money-service provider (% of population aged 15 or over)	86.7	2017	●	↑
Fundamental labor rights are effectively guaranteed (worst 0–1 best)	0.7	2020	●	↓
Fatal work-related accidents embodied in imports (per 100,000 population)	0.4	2015	●	↑
Employment-to-population ratio (%)	67.8	2020	●	↑
Youth not in employment, education or training (NEET) (% of population aged 15 to 29)	13.5	2020	●	↑

* Imputed data point

SDG9 – Industry, Innovation and Infrastructure

Indicator	Value	Year	Rating	Trend
Population using the internet (%)	83.2	2020	●	↑
Mobile broadband subscriptions (per 100 population)	185.8	2019	●	↑
Logistics Performance Index: Quality of trade and transport-related infrastructure (worst 1–5 best)	3.2	2018	●	↑
The Times Higher Education Universities Ranking: Average score of top 3 universities (worst 0–100 best)	33.1	2022	●	●
Articles published in academic journals (per 1,000 population)	1.4	2020	●	↑
Expenditure on research and development (% of GDP)	1.2	2018	●	↑
Researchers (per 1,000 employed population)	7.4	2019	●	↑
Triadic patent families filed (per million population)	2.3	2019	●	→
Gap in internet access by income (percentage points)	24.2	2020	●	↑
Female share of graduates from STEM fields at the tertiary level (%)	43.4	2017	●	↑

SDG10 – Reduced Inequalities

Indicator	Value	Year	Rating	Trend
Gini coefficient	30.2	2018	●	↑
Palma ratio	1.0	2018	●	↑
Elderly poverty rate (% of population aged 66 or over)	12.8	2018	●	↓

SDG11 – Sustainable Cities and Communities

Indicator	Value	Year	Rating	Trend
Proportion of urban population living in slums (%)	* 0.0	2018	●	↑
Annual mean concentration of particulate matter of less than 2.5 microns in diameter (PM2.5) (μg/m³)	19.7	2019	●	↗
Access to improved water source, piped (% of urban population)	96.6	2020	●	→
Satisfaction with public transport (%)	60.0	2021	●	↓
Population with rent overburden (%)	7.0	2019	●	↓

SDG12 – Responsible Consumption and Production

Indicator	Value	Year	Rating	Trend
Electronic waste (kg/capita)	11.7	2019	●	●
Production-based SO_2 emissions (kg/capita)	14.2	2018	●	●
SO_2 emissions embodied in imports (kg/capita)	4.7	2018	●	●
Production-based nitrogen emissions (kg/capita)	16.2	2015	●	↑
Nitrogen emissions embodied in imports (kg/capita)	3.8	2015	●	↑
Exports of plastic waste (kg/capita)	4.3	2021	●	●
Non-recycled municipal solid waste (kg/capita/day)	0.6	2019	●	↑

SDG13 – Climate Action

Indicator	Value	Year	Rating	Trend
CO_2 emissions from fossil fuel combustion and cement production (tCO_2/capita)	7.9	2020	●	→
CO_2 emissions embodied in imports (tCO_2/capita)	1.4	2018	●	↓
CO_2 emissions embodied in fossil fuel exports (kg/capita)	324.6	2020	●	●
Carbon Pricing Score at EUR60/tCO_2 (%, worst 0–100 best)	35.4	2018	●	↑

SDG14 – Life Below Water

Indicator	Value	Year	Rating	Trend
Mean area that is protected in marine sites important to biodiversity (%)	87.3	2020	●	↑
Ocean Health Index: Clean Waters score (worst 0–100 best)	44.4	2020	●	→
Fish caught from overexploited or collapsed stocks (% of total catch)	51.0	2018	●	↓
Fish caught by trawling or dredging (%)	38.8	2018	●	↓
Fish caught that are then discarded (%)	4.8	2018	●	↑
Marine biodiversity threats embodied in imports (per million population)	0.0	2018	●	●

SDG15 – Life on Land

Indicator	Value	Year	Rating	Trend
Mean area that is protected in terrestrial sites important to biodiversity (%)	87.3	2020	●	↑
Mean area that is protected in freshwater sites important to biodiversity (%)	91.1	2020	●	↑
Red List Index of species survival (worst 0–1 best)	1.0	2021	●	↑
Permanent deforestation (% of forest area, 5-year average)	0.0	2020	●	↑
Terrestrial and freshwater biodiversity threats embodied in imports (per million population)	1.0	2018	●	●

SDG16 – Peace, Justice and Strong Institutions

Indicator	Value	Year	Rating	Trend
Homicides (per 100,000 population)	0.7	2020	●	↑
Unsentenced detainees (% of prison population)	11.5	2019	●	↑
Population who feel safe walking alone at night in the city or area where they live (%)	71	2021	●	↑
Property Rights (worst 1–7 best)	4.1	2020	●	↓
Birth registrations with civil authority (% of children under age 5)	100.0	2020	●	●
Corruption Perception Index (worst 0–100 best)	56	2021	●	↓
Children involved in child labor (% of population aged 5 to 14)	* 0.0	2019	●	●
Exports of major conventional weapons (TIV constant million USD per 100,000 population)	0.0	2020	●	●
Press Freedom Index (best 0–100 worst)	28.8	2021	●	↑
Access to and affordability of justice (worst 0–1 best)	0.7	2020	●	↑
Persons held in prison (per 100,000 population)	196.9	2019	●	↓

SDG17 – Partnerships for the Goals

Indicator	Value	Year	Rating	Trend
Government spending on health and education (% of GDP)	9.2	2019	●	↓
For high-income and all OECD DAC countries: International concessional public finance, including official development assistance (% of GNI)	0.1	2021	●	→
Other countries: Government revenue excluding grants (% of GDP)	NA	NA	●	●
Corporate Tax Haven Score (best 0–100 worst)	40.4	2019	●	●
Financial Secrecy Score (best 0–100 worst)	55.6	2020	●	●
Shifted profits of multinationals (US$ billion)	5.9	2018	●	↑
Statistical Performance Index (worst 0–100 best)	89.1	2019	●	↑

5. Country Profiles

PORTUGAL

OECD Countries

OVERALL PERFORMANCE

COUNTRY RANKING

PORTUGAL

20/163

COUNTRY SCORE

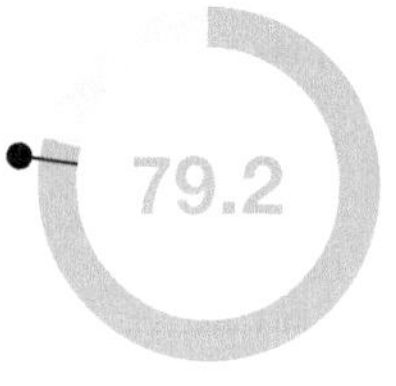

REGIONAL AVERAGE: 77.2

AVERAGE PERFORMANCE BY SDG

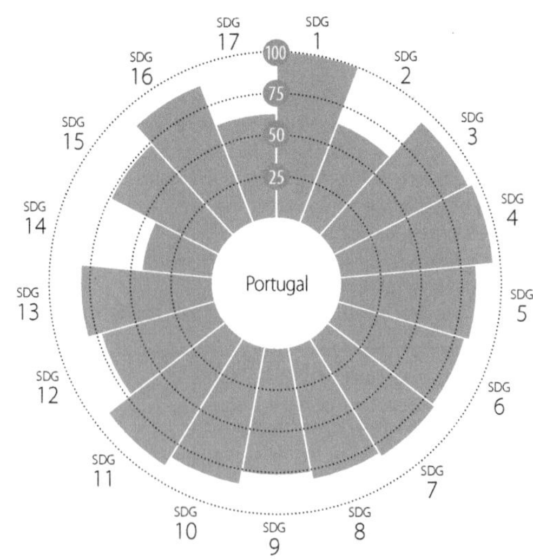

SDG DASHBOARDS AND TRENDS

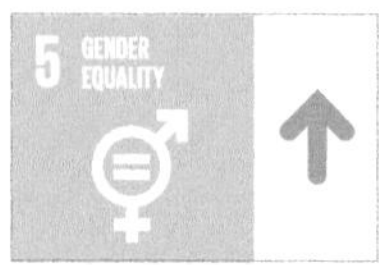

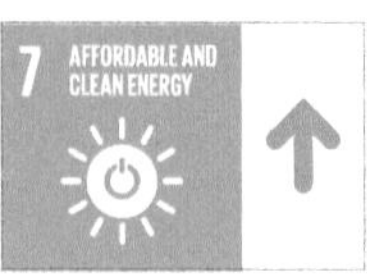

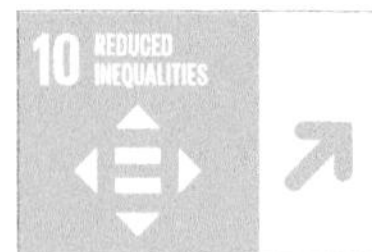

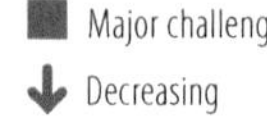

Major challenges | Significant challenges | Challenges remain | SDG achieved | Information unavailable

Decreasing | Stagnating | Moderately improving | On track or maintaining SDG achievement | Information unavailable

Note: The full title of each SDG is available here: https://sustainabledevelopment.un.org/topics/sustainabledevelopmentgoals

INTERNATIONAL SPILLOVER INDEX

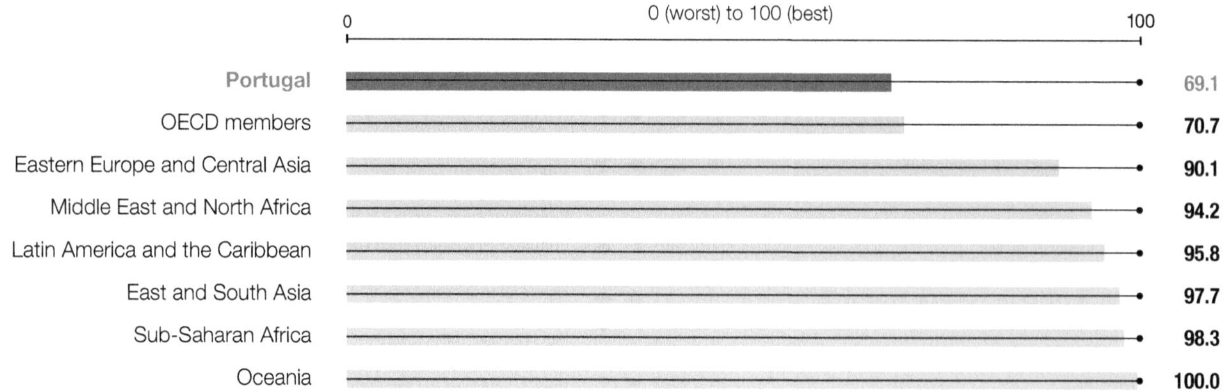

STATISTICAL PERFORMANCE INDEX

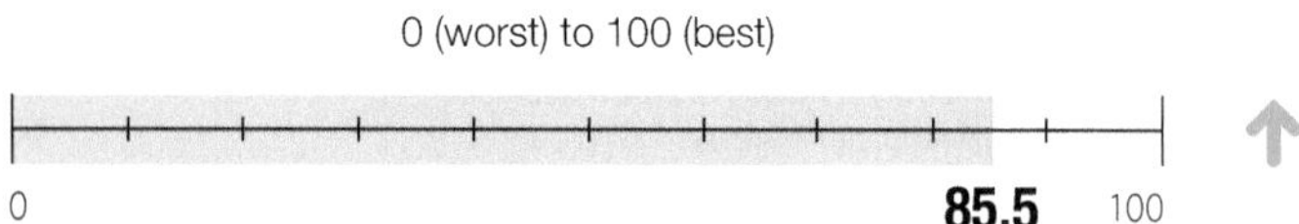

MISSING DATA IN SDG INDEX

0%

SDG1 – No Poverty	Value	Year	Rating	Trend
Poverty headcount ratio at $1.90/day (%)	0.3	2022	●	↑
Poverty headcount ratio at $3.20/day (%)	0.5	2022	●	↑
Poverty rate after taxes and transfers (%)	10.6	2019	●	↑
SDG2 – Zero Hunger				
Prevalence of undernourishment (%)	2.5	2019	●	↑
Prevalence of stunting in children under 5 years of age (%)	3.2	2016	●	↑
Prevalence of wasting in children under 5 years of age (%)	0.6	2016	●	↑
Prevalence of obesity, BMI ≥ 30 (% of adult population)	20.8	2016	●	↓
Human Trophic Level (best 2–3 worst)	2.4	2017	●	→
Cereal yield (tonnes per hectare of harvested land)	4.8	2018	●	↑
Sustainable Nitrogen Management Index (best 0–1.41 worst)	1.1	2015	●	→
Yield gap closure (% of potential yield)	NA	NA	●	●
Exports of hazardous pesticides (tonnes per million population)	0.8	2019	●	●
SDG3 – Good Health and Well-Being				
Maternal mortality rate (per 100,000 live births)	8	2017	●	↑
Neonatal mortality rate (per 1,000 live births)	1.8	2020	●	↑
Mortality rate, under-5 (per 1,000 live births)	3.3	2020	●	↑
Incidence of tuberculosis (per 100,000 population)	16.0	2020	●	↑
New HIV infections (per 1,000 uninfected population)	0.1	2020	●	↑
Age-standardized death rate due to cardiovascular disease, cancer, diabetes, or chronic respiratory disease in adults aged 30–70 years (%)	11.0	2019	●	↑
Age-standardized death rate attributable to household air pollution and ambient air pollution (per 100,000 population)	10	2016	●	●
Traffic deaths (per 100,000 population)	8.2	2019	●	↑
Life expectancy at birth (years)	81.6	2019	●	↑
Adolescent fertility rate (births per 1,000 females aged 15 to 19)	7.3	2018	●	↑
Births attended by skilled health personnel (%)	98.7	2018	●	↑
Surviving infants who received 2 WHO-recommended vaccines (%)	99	2020	●	↑
Universal health coverage (UHC) index of service coverage (worst 0–100 best)	84	2019	●	↑
Subjective well-being (average ladder score, worst 0–10 best)	6.2	2021	●	↑
Gap in life expectancy at birth among regions (years)	4.5	2019	●	→
Gap in self-reported health status by income (percentage points)	25.2	2019	●	↓
Daily smokers (% of population aged 15 and over)	14.2	2019	●	↑
SDG4 – Quality Education				
Participation rate in pre-primary organized learning (% of children aged 4 to 6)	92.8	2019	●	↑
Net primary enrollment rate (%)	99.6	2019	●	↑
Lower secondary completion rate (%)	93.6	2019	●	●
Literacy rate (% of population aged 15 to 24)	99.7	2018	●	●
Tertiary educational attainment (% of population aged 25 to 34)	41.9	2020	●	↑
PISA score (worst 0–600 best)	492.0	2018	●	↓
Variation in science performance explained by socio-economic status (%)	15.9	2018	●	↓
Underachievers in science (% of 15-year-olds)	19.6	2018	●	↓
SDG5 – Gender Equality				
Demand for family planning satisfied by modern methods (% of females aged 15 to 49)	* 79.0	2022	●	↑
Ratio of female-to-male mean years of education received (%)	103.3	2019	●	↑
Ratio of female-to-male labor force participation rate (%)	85.0	2020	●	↑
Seats held by women in national parliament (%)	40.0	2020	●	↑
Gender wage gap (% of male median wage)	11.7	2020	●	↑
SDG6 – Clean Water and Sanitation				
Population using at least basic drinking water services (%)	99.9	2020	●	↑
Population using at least basic sanitation services (%)	99.6	2020	●	↑
Freshwater withdrawal (% of available freshwater resources)	12.3	2018	●	●
Anthropogenic wastewater that receives treatment (%)	55.0	2018	●	●
Scarce water consumption embodied in imports (m^3 H_2O eq/capita)	5551.8	2018	●	●
Population using safely managed water services (%)	95.4	2020	●	↑
Population using safely managed sanitation services (%)	85.1	2020	●	↑
SDG7 – Affordable and Clean Energy				
Population with access to electricity (%)	100.0	2019	●	↑
Population with access to clean fuels and technology for cooking (%)	100.0	2019	●	↑
CO_2 emissions from fuel combustion per total electricity output ($MtCO_2$/TWh)	0.9	2019	●	↑
Share of renewable energy in total primary energy supply (%)	24.7	2019	●	↑
SDG8 – Decent Work and Economic Growth				
Adjusted GDP growth (%)	-1.7	2020	●	●
Victims of modern slavery (per 1,000 population)	2.5	2018	●	●
Adults with an account at a bank or other financial institution or with a mobile-money-service provider (% of population aged 15 or over)	92.3	2017	●	↑
Fundamental labor rights are effectively guaranteed (worst 0–1 best)	0.7	2020	●	→
Fatal work-related accidents embodied in imports (per 100,000 population)	0.8	2015	●	↑
Employment-to-population ratio (%)	68.5	2020	●	↑
Youth not in employment, education or training (NEET) (% of population aged 15 to 29)	11.1	2020	●	↑

* Imputed data point

SDG9 – Industry, Innovation and Infrastructure	Value	Year	Rating	Trend
Population using the internet (%)	78.3	2020	●	↑
Mobile broadband subscriptions (per 100 population)	79.1	2019	●	↑
Logistics Performance Index: Quality of trade and transport-related infrastructure (worst 1–5 best)	3.2	2018	●	↑
The Times Higher Education Universities Ranking: Average score of top 3 universities (worst 0–100 best)	43.3	2022	●	●
Articles published in academic journals (per 1,000 population)	2.9	2020	●	↑
Expenditure on research and development (% of GDP)	1.3	2018	●	↑
Researchers (per 1,000 employed population)	10.1	2019	●	↑
Triadic patent families filed (per million population)	5.3	2019	●	→
Gap in internet access by income (percentage points)	35.3	2020	●	↑
Female share of graduates from STEM fields at the tertiary level (%)	37.8	2017	●	↑
SDG10 – Reduced Inequalities				
Gini coefficient	33.5	2018	●	↑
Palma ratio	1.2	2019	●	↑
Elderly poverty rate (% of population aged 66 or over)	10.7	2019	●	→
SDG11 – Sustainable Cities and Communities				
Proportion of urban population living in slums (%)	0.0	2018	●	↑
Annual mean concentration of particulate matter of less than 2.5 microns in diameter (PM2.5) (μg/m^3)	7.5	2019	●	↑
Access to improved water source, piped (% of urban population)	100.0	2020	●	↑
Satisfaction with public transport (%)	58.0	2021	●	↗
Population with rent overburden (%)	5.7	2019	●	↑
SDG12 – Responsible Consumption and Production				
Electronic waste (kg/capita)	16.6	2019	●	●
Production-based SO_2 emissions (kg/capita)	8.3	2018	●	●
SO_2 emissions embodied in imports (kg/capita)	3.2	2018	●	●
Production-based nitrogen emissions (kg/capita)	7.6	2015	●	↑
Nitrogen emissions embodied in imports (kg/capita)	13.1	2015	●	↓
Exports of plastic waste (kg/capita)	5.1	2021	●	●
Non-recycled municipal solid waste (kg/capita/day)	1.0	2019	●	↓
SDG13 – Climate Action				
CO_2 emissions from fossil fuel combustion and cement production (tCO_2/capita)	4.0	2020	●	↑
CO_2 emissions embodied in imports (tCO_2/capita)	1.3	2018	●	↓
CO_2 emissions embodied in fossil fuel exports (kg/capita)	0.0	2021	●	●
Carbon Pricing Score at EUR60/tCO_2 (%, worst 0–100 best)	43.8	2018	●	↑
SDG14 – Life Below Water				
Mean area that is protected in marine sites important to biodiversity (%)	68.3	2020	●	→
Ocean Health Index: Clean Waters score (worst 0–100 best)	52.3	2020	●	↓
Fish caught from overexploited or collapsed stocks (% of total catch)	68.9	2018	●	↓
Fish caught by trawling or dredging (%)	35.4	2018	●	↓
Fish caught that are then discarded (%)	28.1	2018	●	↓
Marine biodiversity threats embodied in imports (per million population)	0.6	2018	●	●
SDG15 – Life on Land				
Mean area that is protected in terrestrial sites important to biodiversity (%)	75.4	2020	●	→
Mean area that is protected in freshwater sites important to biodiversity (%)	68.6	2020	●	→
Red List Index of species survival (worst 0–1 best)	0.9	2021	●	↓
Permanent deforestation (% of forest area, 5-year average)	0.0	2020	●	↑
Terrestrial and freshwater biodiversity threats embodied in imports (per million population)	4.0	2018	●	●
SDG16 – Peace, Justice and Strong Institutions				
Homicides (per 100,000 population)	0.9	2020	●	●
Unsentenced detainees (% of prison population)	17.5	2019	●	↑
Population who feel safe walking alone at night in the city or area where they live (%)	83	2021	●	↑
Property Rights (worst 1–7 best)	5.1	2020	●	↑
Birth registrations with civil authority (% of children under age 5)	100.0	2020	●	●
Corruption Perception Index (worst 0–100 best)	62	2021	●	↑
Children involved in child labor (% of population aged 5 to 14)	* 0.0	2019	●	●
Exports of major conventional weapons (TIV constant million USD per 100,000 population)	0.5	2020	●	●
Press Freedom Index (best 0–100 worst)	10.1	2021	●	↑
Access to and affordability of justice (worst 0–1 best)	0.7	2020	●	↑
Persons held in prison (per 100,000 population)	126.6	2019	●	↑
SDG17 – Partnerships for the Goals				
Government spending on health and education (% of GDP)	10.5	2019	●	↑
For high-income and all OECD DAC countries: International concessional public finance, including official development assistance (% of GNI)	0.2	2021	●	→
Other countries: Government revenue excluding grants (% of GDP)	NA	NA	●	●
Corporate Tax Haven Score (best 0–100 worst)	45.8	2019	●	●
Financial Secrecy Score (best 0–100 worst)	54.0	2020	●	●
Shifted profits of multinationals (US$ billion)	3.8	2018	●	↑
Statistical Performance Index (worst 0–100 best)	85.5	2019	●	↑

5. Country Profiles

QATAR

Middle East and North Africa

AVERAGE PERFORMANCE BY SDG

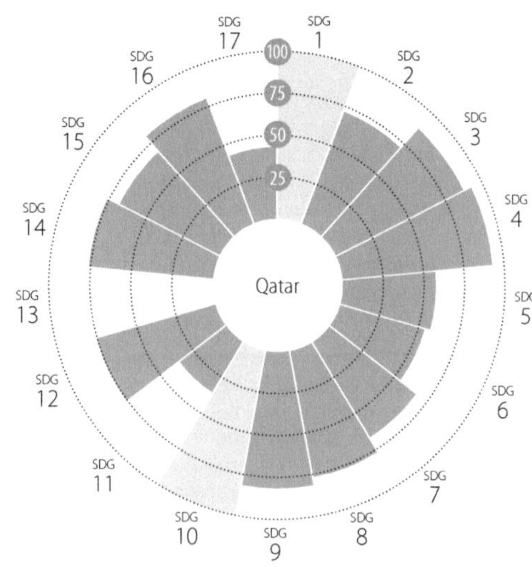

OVERALL PERFORMANCE

COUNTRY RANKING

QATAR

94/163

COUNTRY SCORE

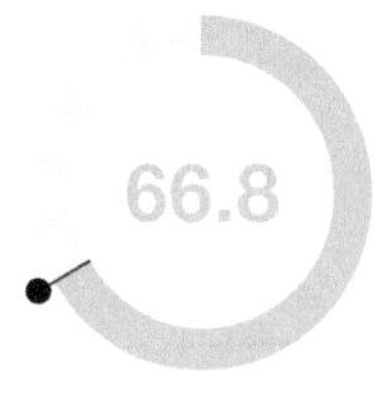

REGIONAL AVERAGE: 66.7

SDG DASHBOARDS AND TRENDS

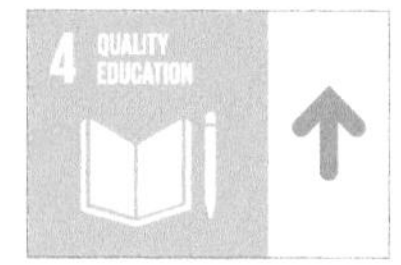

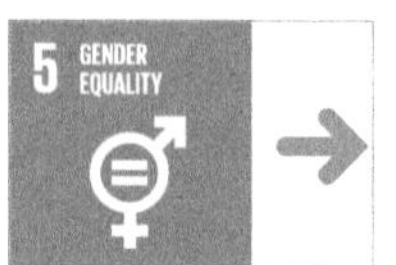

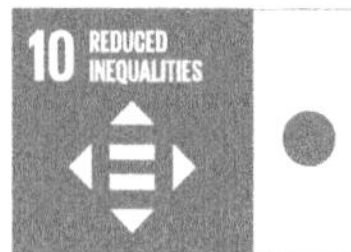

Major challenges · Significant challenges · Challenges remain · SDG achieved · Information unavailable

Decreasing · Stagnating · Moderately improving · On track or maintaining SDG achievement · Information unavailable

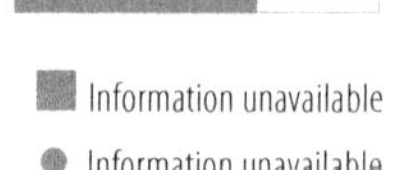

Note: The full title of each SDG is available here: https://sustainabledevelopment.un.org/topics/sustainabledevelopmentgoals

INTERNATIONAL SPILLOVER INDEX

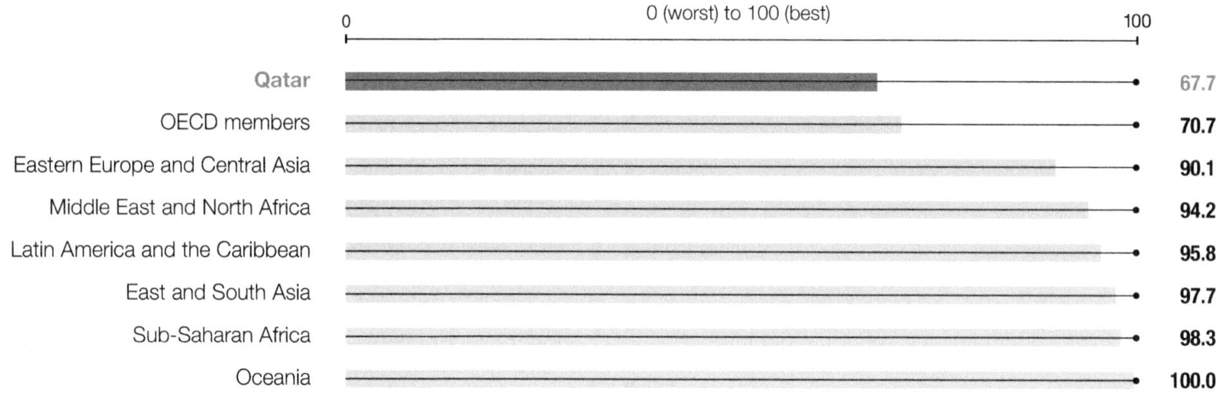

STATISTICAL PERFORMANCE INDEX

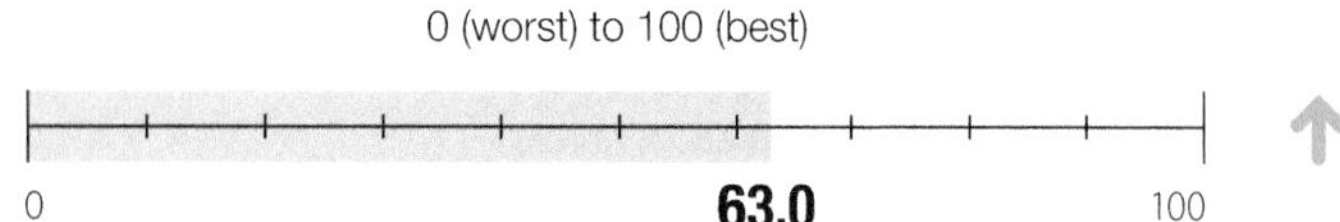

MISSING DATA IN SDG INDEX

17%

Performance by Indicator

Indicator		Value	Year	Rating	Trend
SDG1 – No Poverty					
Poverty headcount ratio at $1.90/day (%)	*	NA	NA	●	●
Poverty headcount ratio at $3.20/day (%)	*	NA	NA	●	●
SDG2 – Zero Hunger					
Prevalence of undernourishment (%)	*	1.2	2019	●	●
Prevalence of stunting in children under 5 years of age (%)	*	2.6	2019	●	↑
Prevalence of wasting in children under 5 years of age (%)	*	0.7	2019	●	↑
Prevalence of obesity, BMI ≥ 30 (% of adult population)		35.1	2016	●	↓
Human Trophic Level (best 2–3 worst)		NA	NA	●	●
Cereal yield (tonnes per hectare of harvested land)		8.7	2018	●	↑
Sustainable Nitrogen Management Index (best 0–1.41 worst)		1.0	2015	●	↓
Exports of hazardous pesticides (tonnes per million population)		0.0	2019	●	●
SDG3 – Good Health and Well-Being					
Maternal mortality rate (per 100,000 live births)		9	2017	●	↑
Neonatal mortality rate (per 1,000 live births)		3.5	2020	●	↑
Mortality rate, under-5 (per 1,000 live births)		5.8	2020	●	↑
Incidence of tuberculosis (per 100,000 population)		34.0	2020	●	→
New HIV infections (per 1,000 uninfected population)		0.1	2020	●	↑
Age-standardized death rate due to cardiovascular disease, cancer, diabetes, or chronic respiratory disease in adults aged 30–70 years (%)		10.7	2019	●	↑
Age-standardized death rate attributable to household air pollution and ambient air pollution (per 100,000 population)		47	2016	●	●
Traffic deaths (per 100,000 population)		7.3	2019	●	↑
Life expectancy at birth (years)		77.2	2019	●	↗
Adolescent fertility rate (births per 1,000 females aged 15 to 19)		7.2	2018	●	↑
Births attended by skilled health personnel (%)		100.0	2017	●	↑
Surviving infants who received 2 WHO-recommended vaccines (%)		82	2020	●	↓
Universal health coverage (UHC) index of service coverage (worst 0–100 best)		74	2019	●	↑
Subjective well-being (average ladder score, worst 0–10 best)		6.4	2014	●	●
SDG4 – Quality Education					
Participation rate in pre-primary organized learning (% of children aged 4 to 6)		94.9	2020	●	↑
Net primary enrollment rate (%)		98.2	2020	●	↑
Lower secondary completion rate (%)		93.7	2020	●	↑
Literacy rate (% of population aged 15 to 24)		94.6	2017	●	●
SDG5 – Gender Equality					
Demand for family planning satisfied by modern methods (% of females aged 15 to 49)		68.9	2012	●	→
Ratio of female-to-male mean years of education received (%)		120.2	2019	●	↑
Ratio of female-to-male labor force participation rate (%)		60.1	2020	●	↓
Seats held by women in national parliament (%)		9.8	2020	●	↗
SDG6 – Clean Water and Sanitation					
Population using at least basic drinking water services (%)		99.6	2020	●	↑
Population using at least basic sanitation services (%)		100.0	2020	●	↑
Freshwater withdrawal (% of available freshwater resources)		431.0	2018	●	●
Anthropogenic wastewater that receives treatment (%)		70.0	2018	●	●
Scarce water consumption embodied in imports (m^3 H_2O eq/capita)		10937.6	2018	●	●
SDG7 – Affordable and Clean Energy					
Population with access to electricity (%)		100.0	2019	●	↑
Population with access to clean fuels and technology for cooking (%)		100.0	2019	●	↑
CO_2 emissions from fuel combustion per total electricity output ($MtCO_2$/TWh)		2.0	2019	●	↑
Share of renewable energy in total primary energy supply (%)		0.0	2019	●	↓
SDG8 – Decent Work and Economic Growth					
Adjusted GDP growth (%)		-1.9	2020	●	●
Victims of modern slavery (per 1,000 population)	*	NA	NA	●	●
Adults with an account at a bank or other financial institution or with a mobile-money-service provider (% of population aged 15 or over)		65.9	2011	●	●
Unemployment rate (% of total labor force)		0.1	2022	●	↑
Fundamental labor rights are effectively guaranteed (worst 0–1 best)		NA	NA	●	●
Fatal work-related accidents embodied in imports (per 100,000 population)		1.3	2015	●	↑

* Imputed data point

Indicator		Value	Year	Rating	Trend
SDG9 – Industry, Innovation and Infrastructure					
Population using the internet (%)		99.7	2020	●	↑
Mobile broadband subscriptions (per 100 population)		124.8	2019	●	↑
Logistics Performance Index: Quality of trade and transport-related infrastructure (worst 1–5 best)		3.4	2018	●	↑
The Times Higher Education Universities Ranking: Average score of top 3 universities (worst 0–100 best)		47.1	2022	●	●
Articles published in academic journals (per 1,000 population)		1.8	2020	●	↑
Expenditure on research and development (% of GDP)		0.5	2018	●	↓
SDG10 – Reduced Inequalities					
Gini coefficient		NA	NA	●	●
Palma ratio		NA	NA	●	●
SDG11 – Sustainable Cities and Communities					
Proportion of urban population living in slums (%)		NA	NA	●	●
Annual mean concentration of particulate matter of less than 2.5 microns in diameter (PM2.5) (μg/m^3)		93.8	2019	●	→
Access to improved water source, piped (% of urban population)		NA	NA	●	●
Satisfaction with public transport (%)		65.0	2012	●	●
SDG12 – Responsible Consumption and Production					
Municipal solid waste (kg/capita/day)		1.2	2012	●	●
Electronic waste (kg/capita)		13.6	2019	●	●
Production-based SO_2 emissions (kg/capita)		17.1	2018	●	●
SO_2 emissions embodied in imports (kg/capita)		17.5	2018	●	●
Production-based nitrogen emissions (kg/capita)		2.7	2015	●	↑
Nitrogen emissions embodied in imports (kg/capita)		9.6	2015	●	↑
Exports of plastic waste (kg/capita)		0.0	2020	●	●
SDG13 – Climate Action					
CO_2 emissions from fossil fuel combustion and cement production (tCO_2/capita)		37.0	2020	●	↓
CO_2 emissions embodied in imports (tCO_2/capita)		6.8	2018	●	↓
CO_2 emissions embodied in fossil fuel exports (kg/capita)		61175.7	2020	●	●
SDG14 – Life Below Water					
Mean area that is protected in marine sites important to biodiversity (%)		60.0	2020	●	→
Ocean Health Index: Clean Waters score (worst 0–100 best)		62.3	2020	●	→
Fish caught from overexploited or collapsed stocks (% of total catch)		NA	NA	●	●
Fish caught by trawling or dredging (%)		0.0	2018	●	↑
Fish caught that are then discarded (%)		4.5	2018	●	↑
Marine biodiversity threats embodied in imports (per million population)		0.1	2018	●	●
SDG15 – Life on Land					
Mean area that is protected in terrestrial sites important to biodiversity (%)		60.0	2020	●	→
Mean area that is protected in freshwater sites important to biodiversity (%)		NA	NA	●	●
Red List Index of species survival (worst 0–1 best)		0.8	2021	●	↓
Permanent deforestation (% of forest area, 5-year average)		NA	NA	●	●
Terrestrial and freshwater biodiversity threats embodied in imports (per million population)		1.0	2018	●	●
SDG16 – Peace, Justice and Strong Institutions					
Homicides (per 100,000 population)		0.4	2014	●	●
Unsentenced detainees (% of prison population)		43.5	2016	●	●
Population who feel safe walking alone at night in the city or area where they live (%)		92	2012	●	●
Property Rights (worst 1–7 best)		5.6	2020	●	↑
Birth registrations with civil authority (% of children under age 5)		100.0	2020	●	●
Corruption Perception Index (worst 0–100 best)		63	2021	●	↑
Children involved in child labor (% of population aged 5 to 14)		NA	NA	●	●
Exports of major conventional weapons (TIV constant million USD per 100,000 population)		0.2	2020	●	●
Press Freedom Index (best 0–100 worst)		42.6	2021	●	↓
Access to and affordability of justice (worst 0–1 best)		NA	NA	●	●
SDG17 – Partnerships for the Goals					
Government spending on health and education (% of GDP)		5.3	2020	●	↓
For high-income and all OECD DAC countries: International concessional public finance, including official development assistance (% of GNI)		NA	NA	●	●
Other countries: Government revenue excluding grants (% of GDP)		NA	NA	●	●
Corporate Tax Haven Score (best 0–100 worst)	*	NA	NA	●	●
Statistical Performance Index (worst 0–100 best)		63.0	2019	●	↑

ROMANIA

Eastern Europe and Central Asia

OVERALL PERFORMANCE

COUNTRY RANKING

ROMANIA

30/163

COUNTRY SCORE

REGIONAL AVERAGE: 71.6

AVERAGE PERFORMANCE BY SDG

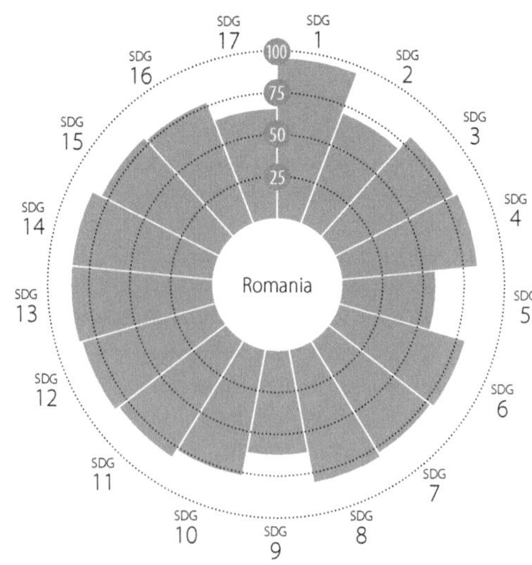

SDG DASHBOARDS AND TRENDS

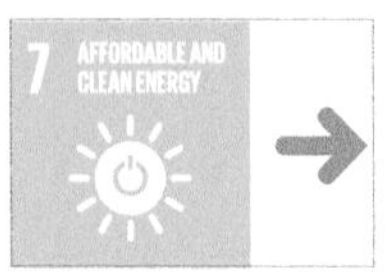

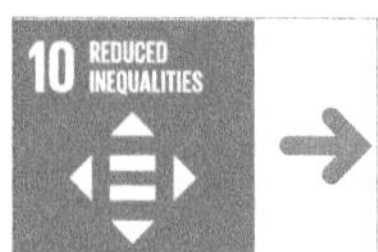

Note: The full title of each SDG is available here: https://sustainabledevelopment.un.org/topics/sustainabledevelopmentgoals

INTERNATIONAL SPILLOVER INDEX

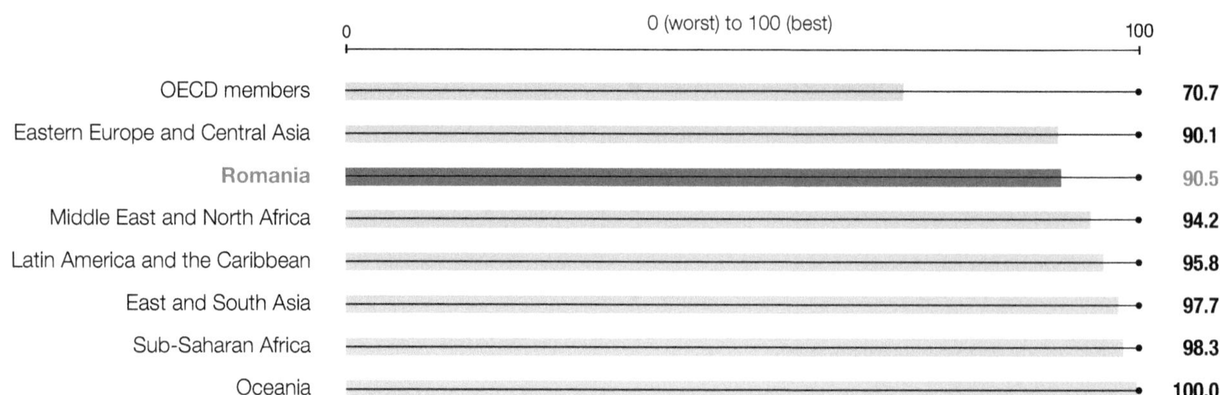

STATISTICAL PERFORMANCE INDEX

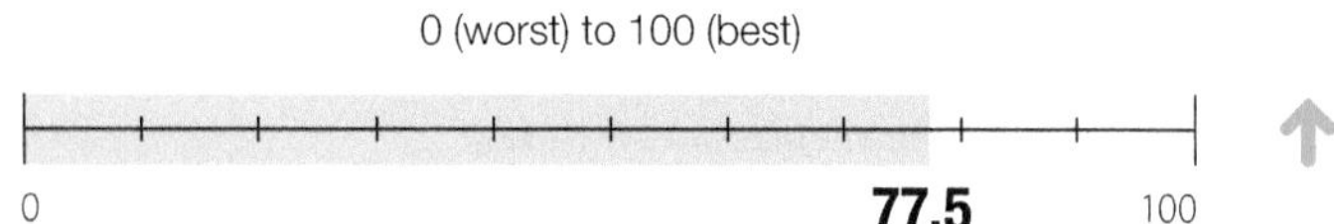

MISSING DATA IN SDG INDEX

2%

SDG1 – No Poverty	Value	Year	Rating	Trend
Poverty headcount ratio at $1.90/day (%)	1.4	2022	●	↑
Poverty headcount ratio at $3.20/day (%)	3.1	2022	●	↑

SDG2 – Zero Hunger	Value	Year	Rating	Trend
Prevalence of undernourishment (%)	2.5	2019	●	↑
Prevalence of stunting in children under 5 years of age (%)	12.8	2002	●	→
Prevalence of wasting in children under 5 years of age (%)	3.5	2002	●	↑
Prevalence of obesity, BMI ≥ 30 (% of adult population)	22.5	2016	●	↓
Human Trophic Level (best 2–3 worst)	2.3	2017	●	→
Cereal yield (tonnes per hectare of harvested land)	6.0	2018	●	↑
Sustainable Nitrogen Management Index (best 0–1.41 worst)	0.5	2015	●	↑
Exports of hazardous pesticides (tonnes per million population)	1.6	2019	●	●

SDG3 – Good Health and Well-Being	Value	Year	Rating	Trend
Maternal mortality rate (per 100,000 live births)	19	2017	●	↑
Neonatal mortality rate (per 1,000 live births)	3.5	2020	●	↑
Mortality rate, under-5 (per 1,000 live births)	6.9	2020	●	↑
Incidence of tuberculosis (per 100,000 population)	64.0	2020	●	↗
New HIV infections (per 1,000 uninfected population)	0.0	2020	●	↑
Age-standardized death rate due to cardiovascular disease, cancer, diabetes, or chronic respiratory disease in adults aged 30–70 years (%)	21.0	2019	●	→
Age-standardized death rate attributable to household air pollution and ambient air pollution (per 100,000 population)	59	2016	●	●
Traffic deaths (per 100,000 population)	10.3	2019	●	→
Life expectancy at birth (years)	75.6	2019	●	↗
Adolescent fertility rate (births per 1,000 females aged 15 to 19)	36.4	2018	●	→
Births attended by skilled health personnel (%)	97.1	2018	●	↑
Surviving infants who received 2 WHO-recommended vaccines (%)	87	2020	●	↗
Universal health coverage (UHC) index of service coverage (worst 0–100 best)	71	2019	●	→
Subjective well-being (average ladder score, worst 0–10 best)	6.5	2021	●	↑

SDG4 – Quality Education	Value	Year	Rating	Trend
Participation rate in pre-primary organized learning (% of children aged 4 to 6)	84.5	2019	●	→
Net primary enrollment rate (%)	87.3	2019	●	↓
Lower secondary completion rate (%)	88.5	2019	●	↓
Literacy rate (% of population aged 15 to 24)	99.4	2018	●	●

SDG5 – Gender Equality	Value	Year	Rating	Trend
Demand for family planning satisfied by modern methods (% of females aged 15 to 49)	46.5	2004	●	↑
Ratio of female-to-male mean years of education received (%)	94.7	2019	●	↑
Ratio of female-to-male labor force participation rate (%)	69.3	2020	●	↓
Seats held by women in national parliament (%)	21.9	2020	●	↗

SDG6 – Clean Water and Sanitation	Value	Year	Rating	Trend
Population using at least basic drinking water services (%)	100.0	2020	●	↑
Population using at least basic sanitation services (%)	87.1	2020	●	↑
Freshwater withdrawal (% of available freshwater resources)	6.0	2018	●	●
Anthropogenic wastewater that receives treatment (%)	30.4	2018	●	●
Scarce water consumption embodied in imports (m^3 H_2O eq/capita)	1948.6	2018	●	●

SDG7 – Affordable and Clean Energy	Value	Year	Rating	Trend
Population with access to electricity (%)	100.0	2019	●	↑
Population with access to clean fuels and technology for cooking (%)	100.0	2019	●	↑
CO_2 emissions from fuel combustion per total electricity output ($MtCO_2$/TWh)	1.2	2019	●	→
Share of renewable energy in total primary energy supply (%)	18.3	2019	●	↓

SDG8 – Decent Work and Economic Growth	Value	Year	Rating	Trend
Adjusted GDP growth (%)	2.7	2020	●	●
Victims of modern slavery (per 1,000 population)	4.3	2018	●	●
Adults with an account at a bank or other financial institution or with a mobile-money-service provider (% of population aged 15 or over)	57.8	2017	●	↓
Unemployment rate (% of total labor force)	4.7	2022	●	↑
Fundamental labor rights are effectively guaranteed (worst 0–1 best)	0.7	2020	●	↑
Fatal work-related accidents embodied in imports (per 100,000 population)	0.2	2015	●	↑

SDG9 – Industry, Innovation and Infrastructure	Value	Year	Rating	Trend
Population using the internet (%)	78.5	2020	●	↑
Mobile broadband subscriptions (per 100 population)	87.7	2019	●	↑
Logistics Performance Index: Quality of trade and transport-related infrastructure (worst 1–5 best)	2.9	2018	●	↑
The Times Higher Education Universities Ranking: Average score of top 3 universities (worst 0–100 best)	31.3	2022	●	●
Articles published in academic journals (per 1,000 population)	0.8	2020	●	↑
Expenditure on research and development (% of GDP)	0.5	2018	●	→

SDG10 – Reduced Inequalities	Value	Year	Rating	Trend
Gini coefficient	35.8	2018	●	→
Palma ratio	1.3	2019	●	●

SDG11 – Sustainable Cities and Communities	Value	Year	Rating	Trend
Proportion of urban population living in slums (%)	14.4	2018	●	●
Annual mean concentration of particulate matter of less than 2.5 microns in diameter (PM2.5) (μg/m³)	14.2	2019	●	↗
Access to improved water source, piped (% of urban population)	89.8	2018	●	●
Satisfaction with public transport (%)	58.0	2021	●	↓

SDG12 – Responsible Consumption and Production	Value	Year	Rating	Trend
Municipal solid waste (kg/capita/day)	0.8	2019	●	●
Electronic waste (kg/capita)	11.4	2019	●	●
Production-based SO_2 emissions (kg/capita)	17.0	2018	●	●
SO_2 emissions embodied in imports (kg/capita)	2.8	2018	●	●
Production-based nitrogen emissions (kg/capita)	20.2	2015	●	↓
Nitrogen emissions embodied in imports (kg/capita)	2.9	2015	●	↑
Exports of plastic waste (kg/capita)	1.2	2020	●	●

SDG13 – Climate Action	Value	Year	Rating	Trend
CO_2 emissions from fossil fuel combustion and cement production (tCO_2/capita)	3.7	2020	●	→
CO_2 emissions embodied in imports (tCO_2/capita)	0.8	2018	●	↓
CO_2 emissions embodied in fossil fuel exports (kg/capita)	10.0	2020	●	●

SDG14 – Life Below Water	Value	Year	Rating	Trend
Mean area that is protected in marine sites important to biodiversity (%)	88.6	2020	●	↑
Ocean Health Index: Clean Waters score (worst 0–100 best)	58.2	2020	●	→
Fish caught from overexploited or collapsed stocks (% of total catch)	NA	NA	●	●
Fish caught by trawling or dredging (%)	2.3	2012	●	●
Fish caught that are then discarded (%)	0.1	2018	●	↑
Marine biodiversity threats embodied in imports (per million population)	0.0	2018	●	●

SDG15 – Life on Land	Value	Year	Rating	Trend
Mean area that is protected in terrestrial sites important to biodiversity (%)	76.0	2020	●	→
Mean area that is protected in freshwater sites important to biodiversity (%)	60.8	2020	●	→
Red List Index of species survival (worst 0–1 best)	0.9	2021	●	→
Permanent deforestation (% of forest area, 5-year average)	0.0	2020	●	↑
Terrestrial and freshwater biodiversity threats embodied in imports (per million population)	0.5	2018	●	●

SDG16 – Peace, Justice and Strong Institutions	Value	Year	Rating	Trend
Homicides (per 100,000 population)	1.5	2020	●	↑
Unsentenced detainees (% of prison population)	7.7	2019	●	↑
Population who feel safe walking alone at night in the city or area where they live (%)	66	2021	●	↑
Property Rights (worst 1–7 best)	4.3	2020	●	↓
Birth registrations with civil authority (% of children under age 5)	100.0	2020	●	●
Corruption Perception Index (worst 0–100 best)	45	2021	●	↓
Children involved in child labor (% of population aged 5 to 14)	NA	NA	●	●
Exports of major conventional weapons (TIV constant million USD per 100,000 population)	0.0	2020	●	●
Press Freedom Index (best 0–100 worst)	24.9	2021	●	↑
Access to and affordability of justice (worst 0–1 best)	0.6	2020	●	↑

SDG17 – Partnerships for the Goals	Value	Year	Rating	Trend
Government spending on health and education (% of GDP)	7.9	2019	●	↑
For high-income and all OECD DAC countries: International concessional public finance, including official development assistance (% of GNI)	NA	NA	●	●
Other countries: Government revenue excluding grants (% of GDP)	29.7	2019	●	↓
Corporate Tax Haven Score (best 0–100 worst)	55.6	2019	●	●
Statistical Performance Index (worst 0–100 best)	77.5	2019	●	↑

* Imputed data point

RUSSIAN FEDERATION

Eastern Europe and Central Asia

OVERALL PERFORMANCE

COUNTRY RANKING

RUSSIAN FEDERATION

45/163

COUNTRY SCORE

REGIONAL AVERAGE: 71.6

AVERAGE PERFORMANCE BY SDG

SDG DASHBOARDS AND TRENDS

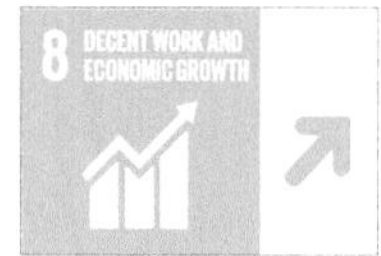

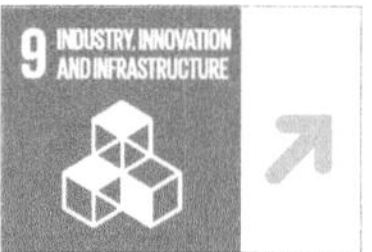

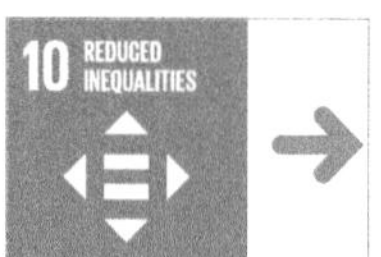

Major challenges | Significant challenges | Challenges remain | SDG achieved | Information unavailable

Decreasing | Stagnating | Moderately improving | On track or maintaining SDG achievement | Information unavailable

Note: The full title of each SDG is available here: https://sustainabledevelopment.un.org/topics/sustainabledevelopmentgoals

INTERNATIONAL SPILLOVER INDEX

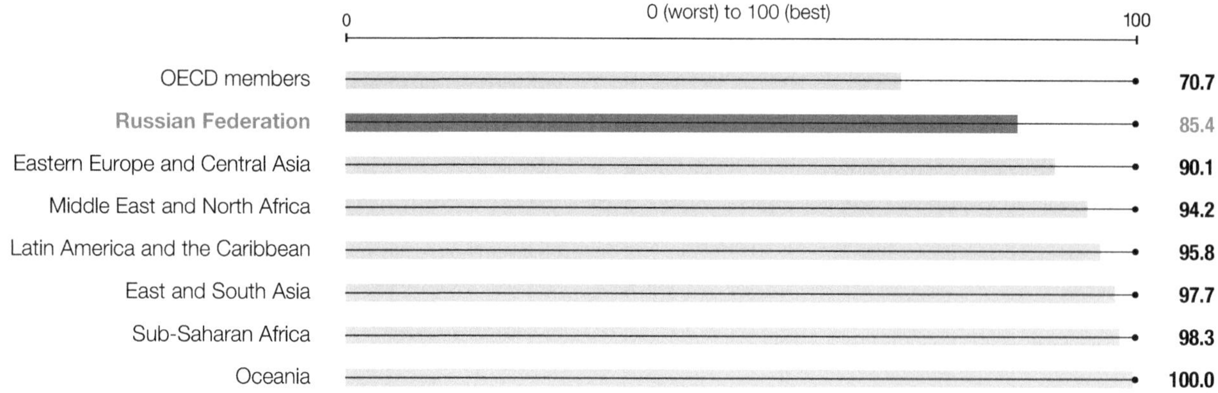

STATISTICAL PERFORMANCE INDEX

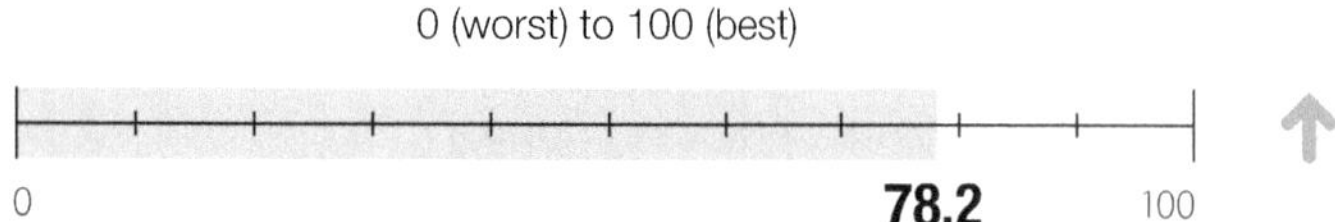

MISSING DATA IN SDG INDEX

4%

RUSSIAN FEDERATION

Performance by Indicator

	Value	Year	Rating	Trend
SDG1 – No Poverty				
Poverty headcount ratio at $1.90/day (%)	0.0	2022	●	↑
Poverty headcount ratio at $3.20/day (%)	0.1	2022	●	↑
SDG2 – Zero Hunger				
Prevalence of undernourishment (%)	2.5	2019	●	↑
Prevalence of stunting in children under 5 years of age (%)	NA	NA	●	●
Prevalence of wasting in children under 5 years of age (%)	NA	NA	●	●
Prevalence of obesity, BMI ≥ 30 (% of adult population)	23.1	2016	●	↓
Human Trophic Level (best 2–3 worst)	2.4	2017	●	→
Cereal yield (tonnes per hectare of harvested land)	2.6	2018	●	↑
Sustainable Nitrogen Management Index (best 0–1.41 worst)	0.6	2015	●	→
Exports of hazardous pesticides (tonnes per million population)	0.2	2019	●	●
SDG3 – Good Health and Well-Being				
Maternal mortality rate (per 100,000 live births)	17	2017	●	↑
Neonatal mortality rate (per 1,000 live births)	2.3	2020	●	↑
Mortality rate, under-5 (per 1,000 live births)	5.4	2020	●	↑
Incidence of tuberculosis (per 100,000 population)	46.0	2020	●	↑
New HIV infections (per 1,000 uninfected population)	1.0	2020	●	→
Age-standardized death rate due to cardiovascular disease, cancer, diabetes, or chronic respiratory disease in adults aged 30–70 years (%)	24.2	2019	●	↗
Age-standardized death rate attributable to household air pollution and ambient air pollution (per 100,000 population)	49	2016	●	●
Traffic deaths (per 100,000 population)	12.0	2019	●	↑
Life expectancy at birth (years)	73.2	2019	●	↗
Adolescent fertility rate (births per 1,000 females aged 15 to 19)	21.5	2016	●	●
Births attended by skilled health personnel (%)	99.7	2014	●	●
Surviving infants who received 2 WHO-recommended vaccines (%)	97	2020	●	↑
Universal health coverage (UHC) index of service coverage (worst 0–100 best)	75	2019	●	↑
Subjective well-being (average ladder score, worst 0–10 best)	5.4	2021	●	↓
SDG4 – Quality Education				
Participation rate in pre-primary organized learning (% of children aged 4 to 6)	93.0	2019	●	↑
Net primary enrollment rate (%)	99.9	2019	●	↑
Lower secondary completion rate (%)	104.0	2019	●	↑
Literacy rate (% of population aged 15 to 24)	99.7	2018	●	●
SDG5 – Gender Equality				
Demand for family planning satisfied by modern methods (% of females aged 15 to 49)	72.4	2011	●	↗
Ratio of female-to-male mean years of education received (%)	98.3	2019	●	↑
Ratio of female-to-male labor force participation rate (%)	78.7	2020	●	↑
Seats held by women in national parliament (%)	15.8	2020	●	→
SDG6 – Clean Water and Sanitation				
Population using at least basic drinking water services (%)	97.0	2020	●	↗
Population using at least basic sanitation services (%)	89.4	2020	●	↗
Freshwater withdrawal (% of available freshwater resources)	4.0	2018	●	●
Anthropogenic wastewater that receives treatment (%)	18.5	2018	●	●
Scarce water consumption embodied in imports (m^3 H_2O eq/capita)	1384.0	2018	●	●
SDG7 – Affordable and Clean Energy				
Population with access to electricity (%)	100.0	2019	●	↑
Population with access to clean fuels and technology for cooking (%)	90.1	2019	●	↑
CO_2 emissions from fuel combustion per total electricity output ($MtCO_2$/TWh)	1.7	2019	●	→
Share of renewable energy in total primary energy supply (%)	2.6	2019	●	→
SDG8 – Decent Work and Economic Growth				
Adjusted GDP growth (%)	1.6	2020	●	●
Victims of modern slavery (per 1,000 population)	5.5	2018	●	●
Adults with an account at a bank or other financial institution or with a mobile-money-service provider (% of population aged 15 or over)	75.8	2017	●	↑
Unemployment rate (% of total labor force)	4.7	2022	●	↑
Fundamental labor rights are effectively guaranteed (worst 0–1 best)	0.6	2020	●	↓
Fatal work-related accidents embodied in imports (per 100,000 population)	0.3	2015	●	↑

	Value	Year	Rating	Trend
SDG9 – Industry, Innovation and Infrastructure				
Population using the internet (%)	85.0	2020	●	↑
Mobile broadband subscriptions (per 100 population)	97.4	2019	●	↑
Logistics Performance Index: Quality of trade and transport-related infrastructure (worst 1–5 best)	2.8	2018	●	↑
The Times Higher Education Universities Ranking: Average score of top 3 universities (worst 0–100 best)	52.0	2022	●	●
Articles published in academic journals (per 1,000 population)	0.8	2020	●	↑
Expenditure on research and development (% of GDP)	1.0	2018	●	↓
SDG10 – Reduced Inequalities				
Gini coefficient	37.5	2018	●	→
Palma ratio	1.2	2017	●	●
SDG11 – Sustainable Cities and Communities				
Proportion of urban population living in slums (%)	NA	NA	●	●
Annual mean concentration of particulate matter of less than 2.5 microns in diameter (PM2.5) (μg/m^3)	15.6	2019	●	↗
Access to improved water source, piped (% of urban population)	96.9	2020	●	↑
Satisfaction with public transport (%)	65.0	2021	●	↑
SDG12 – Responsible Consumption and Production				
Municipal solid waste (kg/capita/day)	1.1	2012	●	●
Electronic waste (kg/capita)	11.3	2019	●	●
Production-based SO_2 emissions (kg/capita)	13.2	2018	●	●
SO_2 emissions embodied in imports (kg/capita)	1.4	2018	●	●
Production-based nitrogen emissions (kg/capita)	11.6	2015	●	↑
Nitrogen emissions embodied in imports (kg/capita)	5.6	2015	●	→
Exports of plastic waste (kg/capita)	0.1	2020	●	●
SDG13 – Climate Action				
CO_2 emissions from fossil fuel combustion and cement production (tCO_2/capita)	10.8	2020	●	→
CO_2 emissions embodied in imports (tCO_2/capita)	0.4	2018	●	↑
CO_2 emissions embodied in fossil fuel exports (kg/capita)	9224.4	2020	●	●
SDG14 – Life Below Water				
Mean area that is protected in marine sites important to biodiversity (%)	23.6	2020	●	→
Ocean Health Index: Clean Waters score (worst 0–100 best)	68.1	2020	●	→
Fish caught from overexploited or collapsed stocks (% of total catch)	35.6	2018	●	↓
Fish caught by trawling or dredging (%)	4.5	2018	●	↑
Fish caught that are then discarded (%)	24.4	2018	●	↓
Marine biodiversity threats embodied in imports (per million population)	0.1	2018	●	●
SDG15 – Life on Land				
Mean area that is protected in terrestrial sites important to biodiversity (%)	25.1	2020	●	→
Mean area that is protected in freshwater sites important to biodiversity (%)	26.2	2020	●	→
Red List Index of species survival (worst 0–1 best)	1.0	2021	●	↑
Permanent deforestation (% of forest area, 5-year average)	0.0	2020	●	↑
Terrestrial and freshwater biodiversity threats embodied in imports (per million population)	0.9	2018	●	●
SDG16 – Peace, Justice and Strong Institutions				
Homicides (per 100,000 population)	7.3	2020	●	↑
Unsentenced detainees (% of prison population)	9.7	2019	●	↑
Population who feel safe walking alone at night in the city or area where they live (%)	65	2021	●	↑
Property Rights (worst 1–7 best)	3.6	2020	●	→
Birth registrations with civil authority (% of children under age 5)	100.0	2020	●	●
Corruption Perception Index (worst 0–100 best)	29	2021	●	→
Children involved in child labor (% of population aged 5 to 14)	NA	NA	●	●
Exports of major conventional weapons (TIV constant million USD per 100,000 population)	3.8	2020	●	●
Press Freedom Index (best 0–100 worst)	48.7	2021	●	→
Access to and affordability of justice (worst 0–1 best)	0.6	2020	●	↑
SDG17 – Partnerships for the Goals				
Government spending on health and education (% of GDP)	8.1	2019	●	↑
For high-income and all OECD DAC countries: International concessional public finance, including official development assistance (% of GNI)	NA	NA	●	●
Other countries: Government revenue excluding grants (% of GDP)	27.6	2019	●	↑
Corporate Tax Haven Score (best 0–100 worst)	* 0.0	2019	●	●
Statistical Performance Index (worst 0–100 best)	78.2	2019	●	↑

* Imputed data point

RWANDA

Sub-Saharan Africa

OVERALL PERFORMANCE

COUNTRY RANKING

RWANDA

124/163

COUNTRY SCORE

REGIONAL AVERAGE: 53.6

AVERAGE PERFORMANCE BY SDG

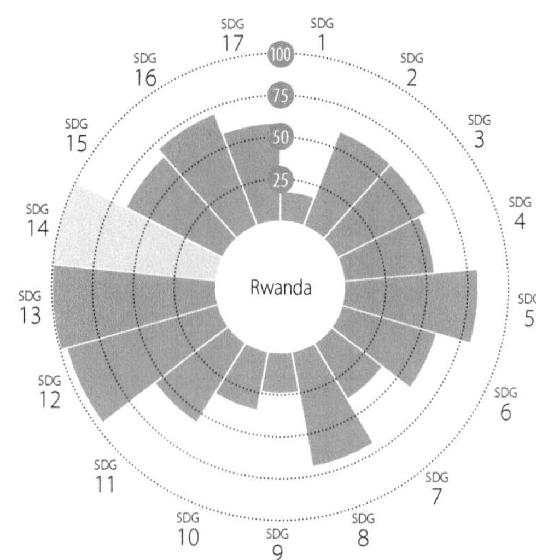

SDG DASHBOARDS AND TRENDS

Major challenges · Significant challenges · Challenges remain · SDG achieved · Information unavailable

Decreasing · Stagnating · Moderately improving · On track or maintaining SDG achievement · Information unavailable

Note: The full title of each SDG is available here: https://sustainabledevelopment.un.org/topics/sustainabledevelopmentgoals

INTERNATIONAL SPILLOVER INDEX

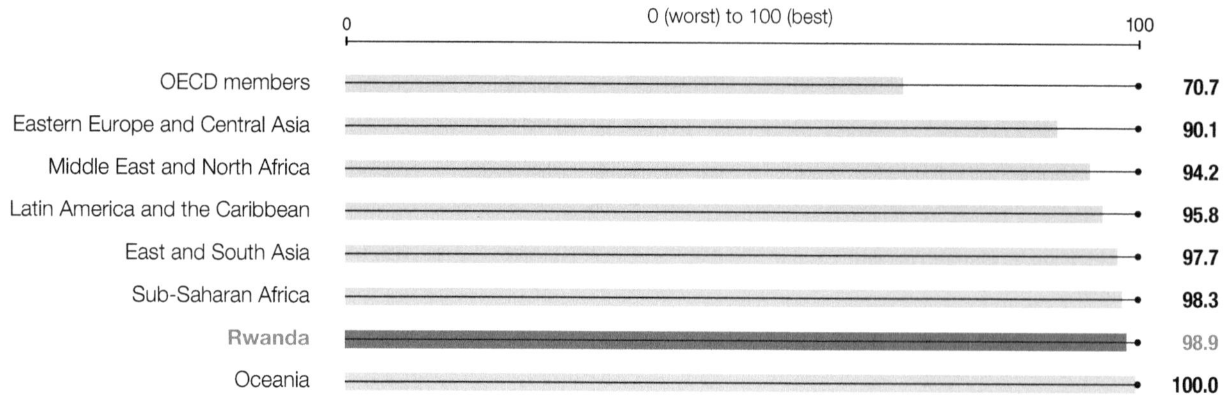

Region	Score
OECD members	70.7
Eastern Europe and Central Asia	90.1
Middle East and North Africa	94.2
Latin America and the Caribbean	95.8
East and South Asia	97.7
Sub-Saharan Africa	98.3
Rwanda	98.9
Oceania	100.0

STATISTICAL PERFORMANCE INDEX

0 (worst) to 100 (best)

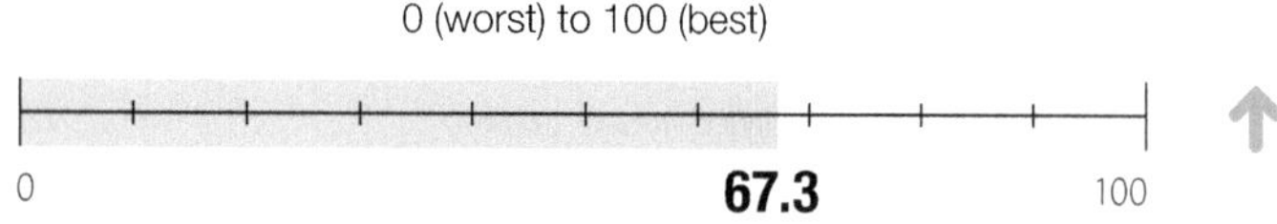

MISSING DATA IN SDG INDEX

2%

SDG1 – No Poverty	Value	Year	Rating	Trend
Poverty headcount ratio at $1.90/day (%)	47.5	2022	●	→
Poverty headcount ratio at $3.20/day (%)	74.4	2022	●	→

SDG2 – Zero Hunger	Value	Year	Rating	Trend
Prevalence of undernourishment (%)	35.2	2019	●	→
Prevalence of stunting in children under 5 years of age (%)	33.1	2020	●	→
Prevalence of wasting in children under 5 years of age (%)	2.0	2018	●	↑
Prevalence of obesity, BMI ≥ 30 (% of adult population)	5.8	2016	●	↑
Human Trophic Level (best 2–3 worst)	2.1	2017	●	↑
Cereal yield (tonnes per hectare of harvested land)	1.4	2018	●	↓
Sustainable Nitrogen Management Index (best 0–1.41 worst)	0.8	2015	●	→
Exports of hazardous pesticides (tonnes per million population)	0.0	2019	●	●

SDG3 – Good Health and Well-Being	Value	Year	Rating	Trend
Maternal mortality rate (per 100,000 live births)	248	2017	●	↑
Neonatal mortality rate (per 1,000 live births)	17.9	2020	●	↗
Mortality rate, under-5 (per 1,000 live births)	40.5	2020	●	↗
Incidence of tuberculosis (per 100,000 population)	58.0	2020	●	→
New HIV infections (per 1,000 uninfected population)	0.3	2020	●	↑
Age-standardized death rate due to cardiovascular disease, cancer, diabetes, or chronic respiratory disease in adults aged 30–70 years (%)	20.2	2019	●	→
Age-standardized death rate attributable to household air pollution and ambient air pollution (per 100,000 population)	121	2016	●	●
Traffic deaths (per 100,000 population)	29.5	2019	●	→
Life expectancy at birth (years)	69.1	2019	●	→
Adolescent fertility rate (births per 1,000 females aged 15 to 19)	41.0	2016	●	●
Births attended by skilled health personnel (%)	90.7	2015	●	●
Surviving infants who received 2 WHO-recommended vaccines (%)	91	2020	●	↑
Universal health coverage (UHC) index of service coverage (worst 0–100 best)	54	2019	●	→
Subjective well-being (average ladder score, worst 0–10 best)	3.3	2019	●	●

SDG4 – Quality Education	Value	Year	Rating	Trend
Participation rate in pre-primary organized learning (% of children aged 4 to 6)	52.7	2019	●	↑
Net primary enrollment rate (%)	93.7	2019	●	↓
Lower secondary completion rate (%)	42.5	2019	●	↗
Literacy rate (% of population aged 15 to 24)	86.5	2018	●	↗

SDG5 – Gender Equality	Value	Year	Rating	Trend
Demand for family planning satisfied by modern methods (% of females aged 15 to 49)	62.9	2015	●	↗
Ratio of female-to-male mean years of education received (%)	81.6	2019	●	↗
Ratio of female-to-male labor force participation rate (%)	100.3	2020	●	↑
Seats held by women in national parliament (%)	61.3	2020	●	↑

SDG6 – Clean Water and Sanitation	Value	Year	Rating	Trend
Population using at least basic drinking water services (%)	60.4	2020	●	→
Population using at least basic sanitation services (%)	68.8	2020	●	→
Freshwater withdrawal (% of available freshwater resources)	6.1	2018	●	●
Anthropogenic wastewater that receives treatment (%)	0.0	2018	●	●
Scarce water consumption embodied in imports (m^3 H_2O eq/capita)	312.8	2018	●	●

SDG7 – Affordable and Clean Energy	Value	Year	Rating	Trend
Population with access to electricity (%)	37.8	2019	●	↗
Population with access to clean fuels and technology for cooking (%)	1.5	2019	●	→
CO_2 emissions from fuel combustion per total electricity output ($MtCO_2$/TWh)	0.9	2019	●	↑
Share of renewable energy in total primary energy supply (%)	NA	NA	●	●

SDG8 – Decent Work and Economic Growth	Value	Year	Rating	Trend
Adjusted GDP growth (%)	-3.1	2020	●	●
Victims of modern slavery (per 1,000 population)	11.6	2018	●	●
Adults with an account at a bank or other financial institution or with a mobile-money-service provider (% of population aged 15 or over)	50.0	2017	●	↑
Unemployment rate (% of total labor force)	1.5	2022	●	↑
Fundamental labor rights are effectively guaranteed (worst 0–1 best)	0.7	2020	●	●
Fatal work-related accidents embodied in imports (per 100,000 population)	0.1	2015	●	↑

* Imputed data point

SDG9 – Industry, Innovation and Infrastructure	Value	Year	Rating	Trend
Population using the internet (%)	26.5	2020	●	→
Mobile broadband subscriptions (per 100 population)	42.3	2019	●	↑
Logistics Performance Index: Quality of trade and transport-related infrastructure (worst 1–5 best)	2.8	2018	●	↑
The Times Higher Education Universities Ranking: Average score of top 3 universities (worst 0–100 best)	* 0.0	2022	●	●
Articles published in academic journals (per 1,000 population)	0.1	2020	●	→
Expenditure on research and development (% of GDP)	0.6	2016	●	●

SDG10 – Reduced Inequalities	Value	Year	Rating	Trend
Gini coefficient	43.7	2016	●	●
Palma ratio	2.3	2018	●	●

SDG11 – Sustainable Cities and Communities	Value	Year	Rating	Trend
Proportion of urban population living in slums (%)	44.1	2018	●	↗
Annual mean concentration of particulate matter of less than 2.5 microns in diameter (PM2.5) (μg/m^3)	42.3	2019	●	↓
Access to improved water source, piped (% of urban population)	75.8	2020	●	→
Satisfaction with public transport (%)	47.0	2019	●	●

SDG12 – Responsible Consumption and Production	Value	Year	Rating	Trend
Municipal solid waste (kg/capita/day)	1.0	2016	●	●
Electronic waste (kg/capita)	0.6	2019	●	●
Production-based SO_2 emissions (kg/capita)	0.6	2018	●	●
SO_2 emissions embodied in imports (kg/capita)	0.2	2018	●	●
Production-based nitrogen emissions (kg/capita)	4.6	2015	●	↑
Nitrogen emissions embodied in imports (kg/capita)	0.6	2015	●	↑
Exports of plastic waste (kg/capita)	0.0	2019	●	●

SDG13 – Climate Action	Value	Year	Rating	Trend
CO_2 emissions from fossil fuel combustion and cement production (tCO_2/capita)	0.1	2020	●	↑
CO_2 emissions embodied in imports (tCO_2/capita)	0.1	2018	●	↑
CO_2 emissions embodied in fossil fuel exports (kg/capita)	0.0	2019	●	●

SDG14 – Life Below Water	Value	Year	Rating	Trend
Mean area that is protected in marine sites important to biodiversity (%)	NA	NA	●	●
Ocean Health Index: Clean Waters score (worst 0–100 best)	NA	NA	●	●
Fish caught from overexploited or collapsed stocks (% of total catch)	NA	NA	●	●
Fish caught by trawling or dredging (%)	NA	NA	●	●
Fish caught that are then discarded (%)	NA	NA	●	●
Marine biodiversity threats embodied in imports (per million population)	0.0	2018	●	●

SDG15 – Life on Land	Value	Year	Rating	Trend
Mean area that is protected in terrestrial sites important to biodiversity (%)	51.7	2020	●	→
Mean area that is protected in freshwater sites important to biodiversity (%)	29.2	2020	●	→
Red List Index of species survival (worst 0–1 best)	0.9	2021	●	→
Permanent deforestation (% of forest area, 5-year average)	0.3	2020	●	↓
Terrestrial and freshwater biodiversity threats embodied in imports (per million population)	0.3	2018	●	●

SDG16 – Peace, Justice and Strong Institutions	Value	Year	Rating	Trend
Homicides (per 100,000 population)	2.6	2015	●	●
Unsentenced detainees (% of prison population)	NA	NA	●	●
Population who feel safe walking alone at night in the city or area where they live (%)	80	2019	●	●
Property Rights (worst 1–7 best)	5.2	2020	●	↑
Birth registrations with civil authority (% of children under age 5)	56.0	2020	●	●
Corruption Perception Index (worst 0–100 best)	53	2021	●	↓
Children involved in child labor (% of population aged 5 to 14)	19.0	2019	●	●
Exports of major conventional weapons (TIV constant million USD per 100,000 population)	* 0.0	2020	●	●
Press Freedom Index (best 0–100 worst)	50.7	2021	●	→
Access to and affordability of justice (worst 0–1 best)	0.7	2020	●	●

SDG17 – Partnerships for the Goals	Value	Year	Rating	Trend
Government spending on health and education (% of GDP)	6.0	2020	●	→
For high-income and all OECD DAC countries: International concessional public finance, including official development assistance (% of GNI)	NA	NA	●	●
Other countries: Government revenue excluding grants (% of GDP)	20.7	2019	●	↗
Corporate Tax Haven Score (best 0–100 worst)	* 0.0	2019	●	●
Statistical Performance Index (worst 0–100 best)	67.3	2019	●	↑

SAMOA

Oceania

OVERALL PERFORMANCE

COUNTRY RANKING

SAMOA

NA /163

COUNTRY SCORE

AVERAGE PERFORMANCE BY SDG

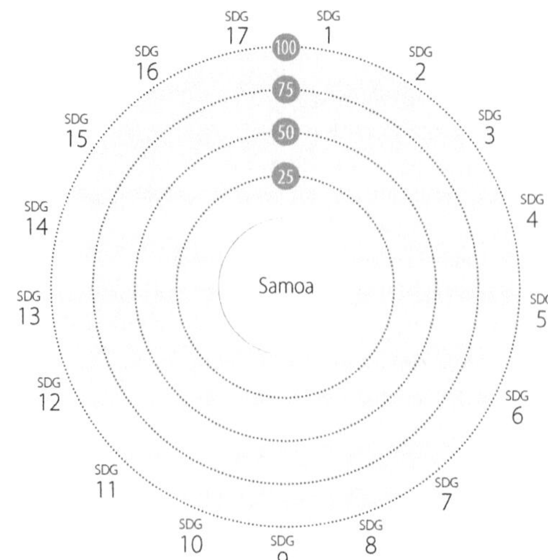

SDG DASHBOARDS AND TRENDS

Major challenges · Significant challenges · Challenges remain · SDG achieved · Information unavailable

Decreasing · Stagnating · Moderately improving · On track or maintaining SDG achievement · Information unavailable

Note: The full title of each SDG is available here: https://sustainabledevelopment.un.org/topics/sustainabledevelopmentgoals

INTERNATIONAL SPILLOVER INDEX

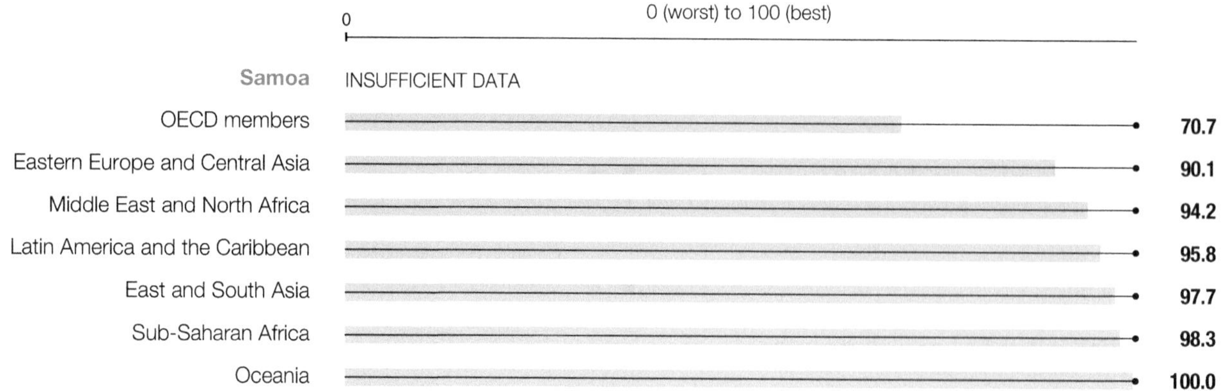

STATISTICAL PERFORMANCE INDEX

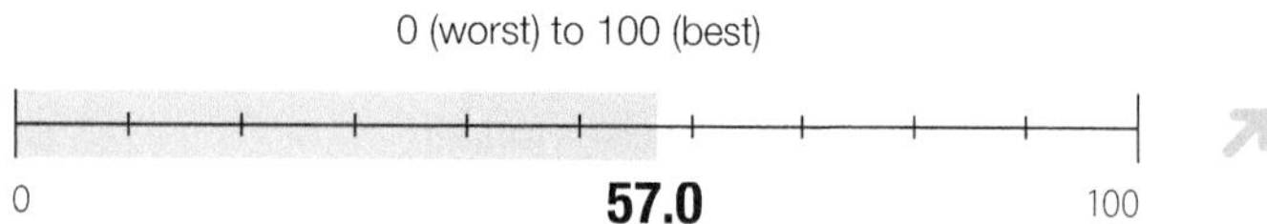

MISSING DATA IN SDG INDEX

28%

SAMOA

SDG1 – No Poverty	Value	Year	Rating	Trend
Poverty headcount ratio at $1.90/day (%)	0.6	2022	●	↑
Poverty headcount ratio at $3.20/day (%)	9.0	2022	●	→

SDG2 – Zero Hunger	Value	Year	Rating	Trend
Prevalence of undernourishment (%)	4.6	2019	●	↑
Prevalence of stunting in children under 5 years of age (%)	7.3	2019	●	↑
Prevalence of wasting in children under 5 years of age (%)	3.1	2019	●	↑
Prevalence of obesity, BMI ≥ 30 (% of adult population)	47.3	2016	●	↓
Human Trophic Level (best 2–3 worst)	2.3	2017	●	→
Cereal yield (tonnes per hectare of harvested land)	NA	NA	●	●
Sustainable Nitrogen Management Index (best 0–1.41 worst)	1.0	2015	●	→
Exports of hazardous pesticides (tonnes per million population)	NA	NA	●	●

SDG3 – Good Health and Well-Being	Value	Year	Rating	Trend
Maternal mortality rate (per 100,000 live births)	43	2017	●	↑
Neonatal mortality rate (per 1,000 live births)	6.7	2020	●	↑
Mortality rate, under-5 (per 1,000 live births)	17.0	2020	●	↑
Incidence of tuberculosis (per 100,000 population)	6.1	2020	●	↑
New HIV infections (per 1,000 uninfected population)	NA	NA	●	●
Age-standardized death rate due to cardiovascular disease, cancer, diabetes, or chronic respiratory disease in adults aged 30–70 years (%)	31.2	2019	●	→
Age-standardized death rate attributable to household air pollution and ambient air pollution (per 100,000 population)	85	2016	●	●
Traffic deaths (per 100,000 population)	13.0	2019	●	↓
Life expectancy at birth (years)	70.5	2019	●	→
Adolescent fertility rate (births per 1,000 females aged 15 to 19)	39.2	2011	●	●
Births attended by skilled health personnel (%)	82.5	2014	●	●
Surviving infants who received 2 WHO-recommended vaccines (%)	57	2020	●	↓
Universal health coverage (UHC) index of service coverage (worst 0–100 best)	53	2019	●	→
Subjective well-being (average ladder score, worst 0–10 best)	NA	NA	●	●

SDG4 – Quality Education	Value	Year	Rating	Trend
Participation rate in pre-primary organized learning (% of children aged 4 to 6)	35.1	2019	●	→
Net primary enrollment rate (%)	99.5	2020	●	↑
Lower secondary completion rate (%)	104.1	2020	●	↑
Literacy rate (% of population aged 15 to 24)	99.1	2018	●	●

SDG5 – Gender Equality	Value	Year	Rating	Trend
Demand for family planning satisfied by modern methods (% of females aged 15 to 49)	39.4	2014	●	●
Ratio of female-to-male mean years of education received (%)	NA	NA	●	●
Ratio of female-to-male labor force participation rate (%)	56.7	2020	●	↓
Seats held by women in national parliament (%)	10.0	2020	●	→

SDG6 – Clean Water and Sanitation	Value	Year	Rating	Trend
Population using at least basic drinking water services (%)	91.8	2020	●	→
Population using at least basic sanitation services (%)	96.8	2020	●	↑
Freshwater withdrawal (% of available freshwater resources)	NA	NA	●	●
Anthropogenic wastewater that receives treatment (%)	0.3	2018	●	●
Scarce water consumption embodied in imports (m^3 H_2O eq/capita)	NA	NA	●	●

SDG7 – Affordable and Clean Energy	Value	Year	Rating	Trend
Population with access to electricity (%)	99.2	2019	●	↑
Population with access to clean fuels and technology for cooking (%)	35.5	2019	●	→
CO_2 emissions from fuel combustion per total electricity output ($MtCO_2$/TWh)	2.6	2019	●	→
Share of renewable energy in total primary energy supply (%)	NA	NA	●	●

SDG8 – Decent Work and Economic Growth	Value	Year	Rating	Trend
Adjusted GDP growth (%)	-3.8	2020	●	●
Victims of modern slavery (per 1,000 population)	NA	NA	●	●
Adults with an account at a bank or other financial institution or with a mobile-money-service provider (% of population aged 15 or over)	NA	NA	●	●
Unemployment rate (% of total labor force)	9.9	2022	●	↓
Fundamental labor rights are effectively guaranteed (worst 0–1 best)	NA	NA	●	●
Fatal work-related accidents embodied in imports (per 100,000 population)	0.2	2015	●	↑

SDG9 – Industry, Innovation and Infrastructure	Value	Year	Rating	Trend
Population using the internet (%)	33.6	2017	●	●
Mobile broadband subscriptions (per 100 population)	17.8	2019	●	→
Logistics Performance Index: Quality of trade and transport-related infrastructure (worst 1–5 best)	NA	NA	●	●
The Times Higher Education Universities Ranking: Average score of top 3 universities (worst 0–100 best)	* 0.0	2022	●	●
Articles published in academic journals (per 1,000 population)	0.4	2020	●	↑
Expenditure on research and development (% of GDP)	NA	NA	●	●

SDG10 – Reduced Inequalities	Value	Year	Rating	Trend
Gini coefficient	38.7	2013	●	●
Palma ratio	1.7	2018	●	●

SDG11 – Sustainable Cities and Communities	Value	Year	Rating	Trend
Proportion of urban population living in slums (%)	NA	NA	●	●
Annual mean concentration of particulate matter of less than 2.5 microns in diameter (PM2.5) (μg/m^3)	10.8	2019	●	↑
Access to improved water source, piped (% of urban population)	86.8	2020	●	↓
Satisfaction with public transport (%)	NA	NA	●	●

SDG12 – Responsible Consumption and Production	Value	Year	Rating	Trend
Municipal solid waste (kg/capita/day)	0.4	2011	●	●
Electronic waste (kg/capita)	3.1	2019	●	●
Production-based SO_2 emissions (kg/capita)	NA	NA	●	●
SO_2 emissions embodied in imports (kg/capita)	NA	NA	●	●
Production-based nitrogen emissions (kg/capita)	9.3	2015	●	↑
Nitrogen emissions embodied in imports (kg/capita)	4.6	2015	●	↑
Exports of plastic waste (kg/capita)	0.0	2019	●	●

SDG13 – Climate Action	Value	Year	Rating	Trend
CO_2 emissions from fossil fuel combustion and cement production (tCO_2/capita)	1.2	2020	●	↑
CO_2 emissions embodied in imports (tCO_2/capita)	NA	NA	●	●
CO_2 emissions embodied in fossil fuel exports (kg/capita)	0.0	2019	●	●

SDG14 – Life Below Water	Value	Year	Rating	Trend
Mean area that is protected in marine sites important to biodiversity (%)	54.2	2020	●	→
Ocean Health Index: Clean Waters score (worst 0–100 best)	92.4	2020	●	↑
Fish caught from overexploited or collapsed stocks (% of total catch)	49.9	2018	●	↓
Fish caught by trawling or dredging (%)	0.0	2018	●	↑
Fish caught that are then discarded (%)	6.4	2018	●	↓
Marine biodiversity threats embodied in imports (per million population)	NA	NA	●	●

SDG15 – Life on Land	Value	Year	Rating	Trend
Mean area that is protected in terrestrial sites important to biodiversity (%)	47.1	2020	●	→
Mean area that is protected in freshwater sites important to biodiversity (%)	NA	NA	●	●
Red List Index of species survival (worst 0–1 best)	0.8	2021	●	↓
Permanent deforestation (% of forest area, 5-year average)	NA	NA	●	●
Terrestrial and freshwater biodiversity threats embodied in imports (per million population)	0.4	2018	●	●

SDG16 – Peace, Justice and Strong Institutions	Value	Year	Rating	Trend
Homicides (per 100,000 population)	6.6	2018	●	●
Unsentenced detainees (% of prison population)	6.5	2017	●	●
Population who feel safe walking alone at night in the city or area where they live (%)	NA	NA	●	●
Property Rights (worst 1–7 best)	NA	NA	●	●
Birth registrations with civil authority (% of children under age 5)	66.9	2020	●	●
Corruption Perception Index (worst 0–100 best)	NA	NA	●	●
Children involved in child labor (% of population aged 5 to 14)	NA	NA	●	●
Exports of major conventional weapons (TIV constant million USD per 100,000 population)	* 0.0	2020	●	●
Press Freedom Index (best 0–100 worst)	19.2	2021	●	↑
Access to and affordability of justice (worst 0–1 best)	NA	NA	●	●

SDG17 – Partnerships for the Goals	Value	Year	Rating	Trend
Government spending on health and education (% of GDP)	9.4	2020	●	→
For high-income and all OECD DAC countries: International concessional public finance, including official development assistance (% of GNI)	NA	NA	●	●
Other countries: Government revenue excluding grants (% of GDP)	35.6	2019	●	↑
Corporate Tax Haven Score (best 0–100 worst)	* 0.0	2019	●	●
Statistical Performance Index (worst 0–100 best)	57.0	2019	●	↗

* Imputed data point

5. Country Profiles

SAN MARINO

Western Europe

OVERALL PERFORMANCE

COUNTRY RANKING

SAN MARINO

NA /163

COUNTRY SCORE

na

REGIONAL AVERAGE: 71.6

AVERAGE PERFORMANCE BY SDG

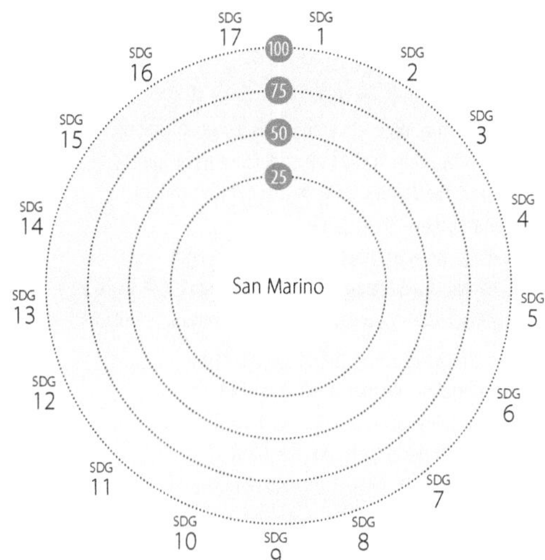

SDG DASHBOARDS AND TRENDS

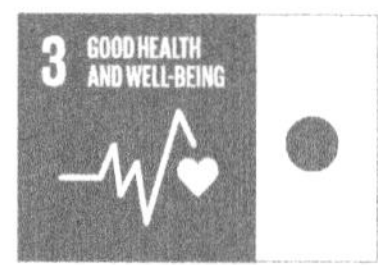

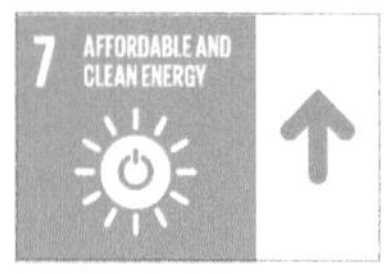

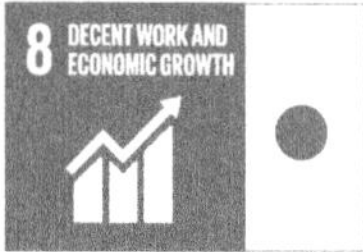

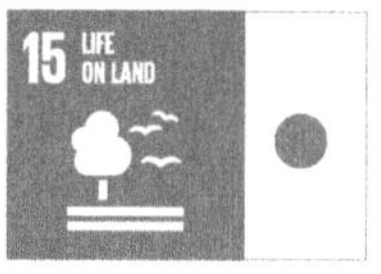

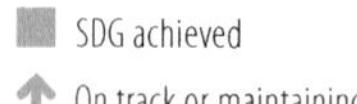

Major challenges · Significant challenges · Challenges remain · SDG achieved · Information unavailable

Decreasing · Stagnating · Moderately improving · On track or maintaining SDG achievement · Information unavailable

Note: The full title of each SDG is available here: https://sustainabledevelopment.un.org/topics/sustainabledevelopmentgoals

INTERNATIONAL SPILLOVER INDEX

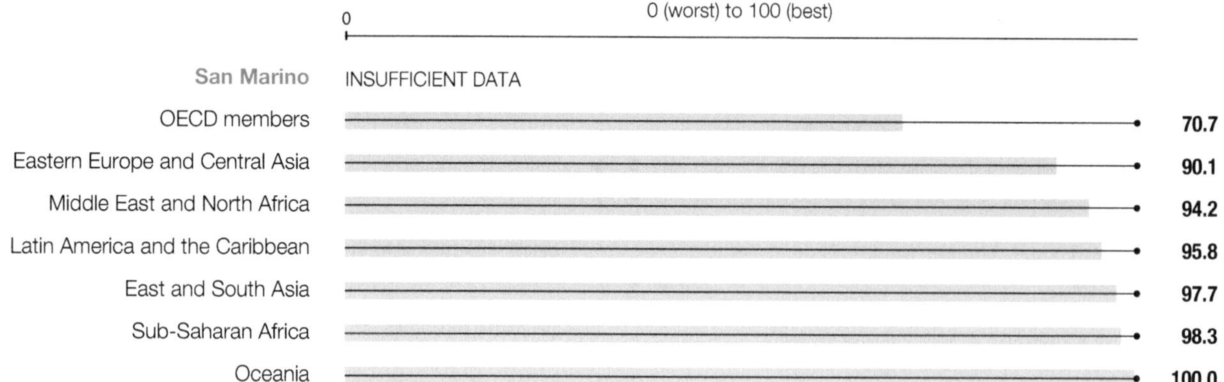

STATISTICAL PERFORMANCE INDEX

0 (worst) to 100 (best)

0 **na** 100

MISSING DATA IN SDG INDEX

61%

SAN MARINO

SDG1 – No Poverty

Indicator	Value	Year	Rating	Trend
Poverty headcount ratio at $1.90/day (%)	NA	NA	●	●
Poverty headcount ratio at $3.20/day (%)	NA	NA	●	●

SDG2 – Zero Hunger

Indicator	Value	Year	Rating	Trend
Prevalence of undernourishment (%)	* 1.2	2019	●	●
Prevalence of stunting in children under 5 years of age (%)	* 2.6	2019	●	↑
Prevalence of wasting in children under 5 years of age (%)	* 0.7	2019	●	↑
Prevalence of obesity, BMI ≥ 30 (% of adult population)	NA	NA	●	●
Human Trophic Level (best 2–3 worst)	NA	NA	●	●
Cereal yield (tonnes per hectare of harvested land)	NA	NA	●	●
Sustainable Nitrogen Management Index (best 0–1.41 worst)	NA	NA	●	●
Exports of hazardous pesticides (tonnes per million population)	NA	NA	●	●

SDG3 – Good Health and Well-Being

Indicator	Value	Year	Rating	Trend
Maternal mortality rate (per 100,000 live births)	NA	NA	●	●
Neonatal mortality rate (per 1,000 live births)	0.8	2020	●	↑
Mortality rate, under-5 (per 1,000 live births)	1.8	2020	●	↑
Incidence of tuberculosis (per 100,000 population)	0.0	2020	●	↑
New HIV infections (per 1,000 uninfected population)	NA	NA	●	●
Age-standardized death rate due to cardiovascular disease, cancer, diabetes, or chronic respiratory disease in adults aged 30–70 years (%)	NA	NA	●	●
Age-standardized death rate attributable to household air pollution and ambient air pollution (per 100,000 population)	NA	NA	●	●
Traffic deaths (per 100,000 population)	NA	NA	●	●
Life expectancy at birth (years)	NA	NA	●	●
Adolescent fertility rate (births per 1,000 females aged 15 to 19)	1.4	2017	●	●
Births attended by skilled health personnel (%)	NA	NA	●	●
Surviving infants who received 2 WHO-recommended vaccines (%)	89	2020	●	↑
Universal health coverage (UHC) index of service coverage (worst 0–100 best)	NA	NA	●	●
Subjective well-being (average ladder score, worst 0–10 best)	NA	NA	●	●

SDG4 – Quality Education

Indicator	Value	Year	Rating	Trend
Participation rate in pre-primary organized learning (% of children aged 4 to 6)	92.0	2020	●	●
Net primary enrollment rate (%)	96.3	2020	●	●
Lower secondary completion rate (%)	88.8	2020	●	●
Literacy rate (% of population aged 15 to 24)	NA	NA	●	●

SDG5 – Gender Equality

Indicator	Value	Year	Rating	Trend
Demand for family planning satisfied by modern methods (% of females aged 15 to 49)	NA	NA	●	●
Ratio of female-to-male mean years of education received (%)	NA	NA	●	●
Ratio of female-to-male labor force participation rate (%)	NA	NA	●	●
Seats held by women in national parliament (%)	33.3	2020	●	↑

SDG6 – Clean Water and Sanitation

Indicator	Value	Year	Rating	Trend
Population using at least basic drinking water services (%)	100.0	2020	●	↑
Population using at least basic sanitation services (%)	100.0	2020	●	↑
Freshwater withdrawal (% of available freshwater resources)	NA	NA	●	●
Anthropogenic wastewater that receives treatment (%)	6.2	2018	●	●
Scarce water consumption embodied in imports (m^3 H_2O eq/capita)	NA	NA	●	●

SDG7 – Affordable and Clean Energy

Indicator	Value	Year	Rating	Trend
Population with access to electricity (%)	100.0	2019	●	↑
Population with access to clean fuels and technology for cooking (%)	100.0	2019	●	↑
CO_2 emissions from fuel combustion per total electricity output ($MtCO_2$/TWh)	NA	NA	●	●
Share of renewable energy in total primary energy supply (%)	NA	NA	●	●

SDG8 – Decent Work and Economic Growth

Indicator	Value	Year	Rating	Trend
Adjusted GDP growth (%)	-0.7	2019	●	●
Victims of modern slavery (per 1,000 population)	NA	NA	●	●
Adults with an account at a bank or other financial institution or with a mobile-money-service provider (% of population aged 15 or over)	NA	NA	●	●
Unemployment rate (% of total labor force)	NA	NA	●	●
Fundamental labor rights are effectively guaranteed (worst 0–1 best)	NA	NA	●	●
Fatal work-related accidents embodied in imports (per 100,000 population)	11.0	2015	●	↓

* Imputed data point

SDG9 – Industry, Innovation and Infrastructure

Indicator	Value	Year	Rating	Trend
Population using the internet (%)	60.2	2017	●	●
Mobile broadband subscriptions (per 100 population)	131.4	2019	●	↑
Logistics Performance Index: Quality of trade and transport-related infrastructure (worst 1–5 best)	NA	NA	●	●
The Times Higher Education Universities Ranking: Average score of top 3 universities (worst 0–100 best)	* 0.0	2022	●	●
Articles published in academic journals (per 1,000 population)	1.5	2020	●	↑
Expenditure on research and development (% of GDP)	NA	NA	●	●

SDG10 – Reduced Inequalities

Indicator	Value	Year	Rating	Trend
Gini coefficient	NA	NA	●	●
Palma ratio	NA	NA	●	●

SDG11 – Sustainable Cities and Communities

Indicator	Value	Year	Rating	Trend
Proportion of urban population living in slums (%)	NA	NA	●	●
Annual mean concentration of particulate matter of less than 2.5 microns in diameter (PM2.5) (μg/m^3)	13.3	2019	●	↑
Access to improved water source, piped (% of urban population)	NA	NA	●	●
Satisfaction with public transport (%)	NA	NA	●	●

SDG12 – Responsible Consumption and Production

Indicator	Value	Year	Rating	Trend
Municipal solid waste (kg/capita/day)	1.4	2016	●	●
Electronic waste (kg/capita)	NA	NA	●	●
Production-based SO_2 emissions (kg/capita)	NA	NA	●	●
SO_2 emissions embodied in imports (kg/capita)	NA	NA	●	●
Production-based nitrogen emissions (kg/capita)	0.0	2015	●	↑
Nitrogen emissions embodied in imports (kg/capita)	150.5	2015	●	↓
Exports of plastic waste (kg/capita)	NA	NA	●	●

SDG13 – Climate Action

Indicator	Value	Year	Rating	Trend
CO_2 emissions from fossil fuel combustion and cement production (tCO_2/capita)	NA	NA	●	●
CO_2 emissions embodied in imports (tCO_2/capita)	NA	NA	●	●
CO_2 emissions embodied in fossil fuel exports (kg/capita)	NA	NA	●	●

SDG14 – Life Below Water

Indicator	Value	Year	Rating	Trend
Mean area that is protected in marine sites important to biodiversity (%)	NA	NA	●	●
Ocean Health Index: Clean Waters score (worst 0–100 best)	NA	NA	●	●
Fish caught from overexploited or collapsed stocks (% of total catch)	NA	NA	●	●
Fish caught by trawling or dredging (%)	0.0	2018	●	↑
Fish caught that are then discarded (%)	0.0	2018	●	↑
Marine biodiversity threats embodied in imports (per million population)	6.5	2018	●	●

SDG15 – Life on Land

Indicator	Value	Year	Rating	Trend
Mean area that is protected in terrestrial sites important to biodiversity (%)	NA	NA	●	●
Mean area that is protected in freshwater sites important to biodiversity (%)	NA	NA	●	●
Red List Index of species survival (worst 0–1 best)	1.0	2021	●	↑
Permanent deforestation (% of forest area, 5-year average)	NA	NA	●	●
Terrestrial and freshwater biodiversity threats embodied in imports (per million population)	59.1	2018	●	●

SDG16 – Peace, Justice and Strong Institutions

Indicator	Value	Year	Rating	Trend
Homicides (per 100,000 population)	0.0	2011	●	●
Unsentenced detainees (% of prison population)	NA	NA	●	●
Population who feel safe walking alone at night in the city or area where they live (%)	NA	NA	●	●
Property Rights (worst 1–7 best)	NA	NA	●	●
Birth registrations with civil authority (% of children under age 5)	100.0	2020	●	●
Corruption Perception Index (worst 0–100 best)	NA	NA	●	●
Children involved in child labor (% of population aged 5 to 14)	NA	NA	●	●
Exports of major conventional weapons (TIV constant million USD per 100,000 population)	* 0.0	2020	●	●
Press Freedom Index (best 0–100 worst)	NA	NA	●	●
Access to and affordability of justice (worst 0–1 best)	NA	NA	●	●

SDG17 – Partnerships for the Goals

Indicator	Value	Year	Rating	Trend
Government spending on health and education (% of GDP)	8.6	2019	●	→
For high-income and all OECD DAC countries: International concessional public finance, including official development assistance (% of GNI)	NA	NA	●	●
Other countries: Government revenue excluding grants (% of GDP)	NA	NA	●	●
Corporate Tax Haven Score (best 0–100 worst)	61.5	2019	●	●
Statistical Performance Index (worst 0–100 best)	NA	NA	●	●

SÃO TOMÉ AND PRÍNCIPE

Sub-Saharan Africa

OVERALL PERFORMANCE

COUNTRY RANKING

SÃO TOMÉ AND PRÍNCIPE

123/163

COUNTRY SCORE

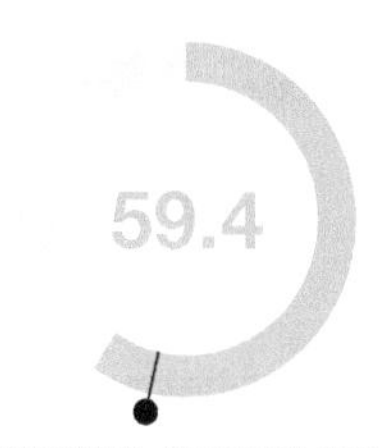

AVERAGE PERFORMANCE BY SDG

SDG DASHBOARDS AND TRENDS

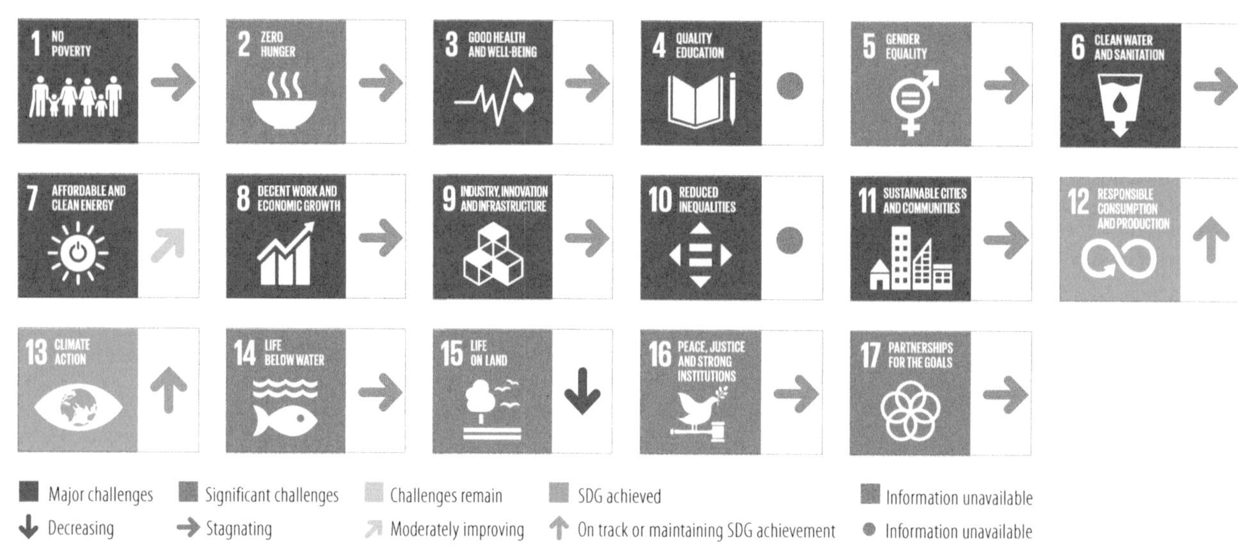

Major challenges | Significant challenges | Challenges remain | SDG achieved | Information unavailable

Decreasing | Stagnating | Moderately improving | On track or maintaining SDG achievement | Information unavailable

Note: The full title of each SDG is available here: https://sustainabledevelopment.un.org/topics/sustainabledevelopmentgoals

INTERNATIONAL SPILLOVER INDEX

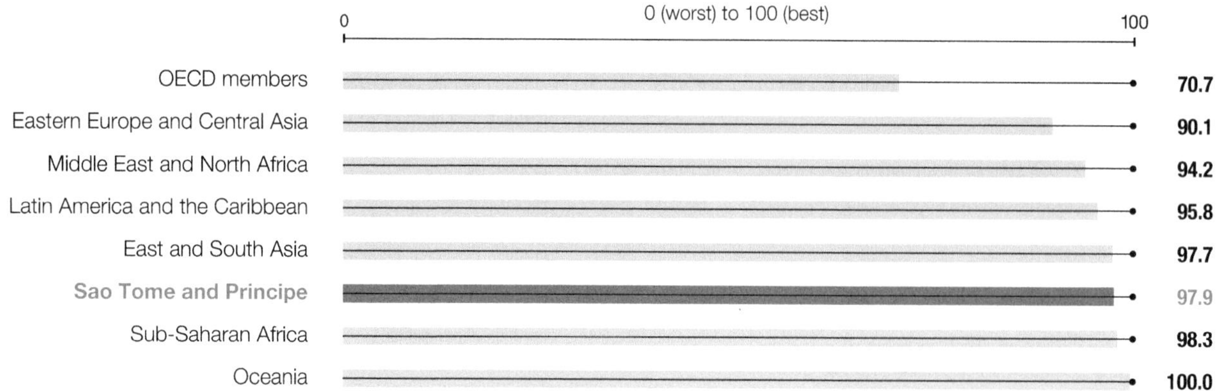

STATISTICAL PERFORMANCE INDEX

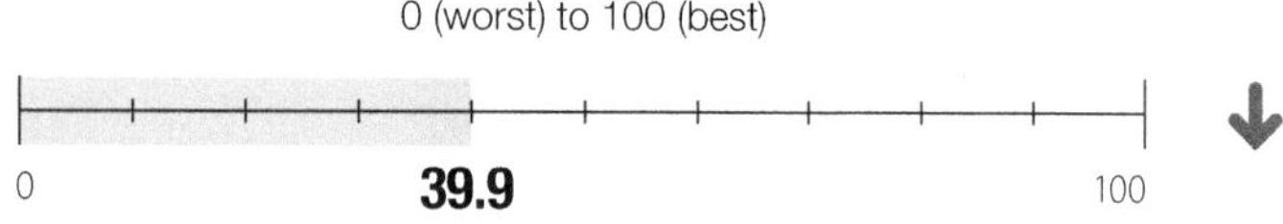

MISSING DATA IN SDG INDEX

19%

SÃO TOMÉ AND PRÍNCIPE

Performance by Indicator

SDG1 – No Poverty	Value	Year	Rating	Trend
Poverty headcount ratio at $1.90/day (%)	33.8	2022	●	→
Poverty headcount ratio at $3.20/day (%)	63.4	2022	●	→

SDG2 – Zero Hunger	Value	Year	Rating	Trend
Prevalence of undernourishment (%)	11.9	2019	●	↗
Prevalence of stunting in children under 5 years of age (%)	11.7	2019	●	→
Prevalence of wasting in children under 5 years of age (%)	4.1	2019	●	↑
Prevalence of obesity, BMI ≥ 30 (% of adult population)	12.4	2016	●	↓
Human Trophic Level (best 2–3 worst)	2.1	2017	●	↑
Cereal yield (tonnes per hectare of harvested land)	2.0	2018	●	↓
Sustainable Nitrogen Management Index (best 0–1.41 worst)	1.1	2015	●	↓
Exports of hazardous pesticides (tonnes per million population)	NA	NA	●	●

SDG3 – Good Health and Well-Being	Value	Year	Rating	Trend
Maternal mortality rate (per 100,000 live births)	130	2017	●	→
Neonatal mortality rate (per 1,000 live births)	7.8	2020	●	↑
Mortality rate, under-5 (per 1,000 live births)	16.1	2020	●	↑
Incidence of tuberculosis (per 100,000 population)	118.0	2020	●	↗
New HIV infections (per 1,000 uninfected population)	1.0	2020	●	→
Age-standardized death rate due to cardiovascular disease, cancer, diabetes, or chronic respiratory disease in adults aged 30–70 years (%)	21.0	2019	●	→
Age-standardized death rate attributable to household air pollution and ambient air pollution (per 100,000 population)	162	2016	●	●
Traffic deaths (per 100,000 population)	27.9	2019	●	↓
Life expectancy at birth (years)	70.4	2019	●	→
Adolescent fertility rate (births per 1,000 females aged 15 to 19)	86.0	2017	●	●
Births attended by skilled health personnel (%)	92.5	2014	●	●
Surviving infants who received 2 WHO-recommended vaccines (%)	95	2019	●	↑
Universal health coverage (UHC) index of service coverage (worst 0–100 best)	60	2019	●	→
Subjective well-being (average ladder score, worst 0–10 best)	NA	NA	●	●

SDG4 – Quality Education	Value	Year	Rating	Trend
Participation rate in pre-primary organized learning (% of children aged 4 to 6)	52.4	2015	●	●
Net primary enrollment rate (%)	94.0	2017	●	●
Lower secondary completion rate (%)	73.5	2017	●	●
Literacy rate (% of population aged 15 to 24)	97.8	2018	●	●

SDG5 – Gender Equality	Value	Year	Rating	Trend
Demand for family planning satisfied by modern methods (% of females aged 15 to 49)	57.7	2019	●	→
Ratio of female-to-male mean years of education received (%)	81.7	2019	●	→
Ratio of female-to-male labor force participation rate (%)	52.8	2020	●	→
Seats held by women in national parliament (%)	23.6	2020	●	↗

SDG6 – Clean Water and Sanitation	Value	Year	Rating	Trend
Population using at least basic drinking water services (%)	78.2	2020	●	→
Population using at least basic sanitation services (%)	47.6	2020	●	→
Freshwater withdrawal (% of available freshwater resources)	1.9	2018	●	●
Anthropogenic wastewater that receives treatment (%)	0.2	2018	●	●
Scarce water consumption embodied in imports (m^3 H_2O eq/capita)	NA	NA	●	●

SDG7 – Affordable and Clean Energy	Value	Year	Rating	Trend
Population with access to electricity (%)	75.2	2019	●	↗
Population with access to clean fuels and technology for cooking (%)	3.2	2019	●	→
CO_2 emissions from fuel combustion per total electricity output ($MtCO_2$/TWh)	1.2	2019	●	↑
Share of renewable energy in total primary energy supply (%)	NA	NA	●	●

SDG8 – Decent Work and Economic Growth	Value	Year	Rating	Trend
Adjusted GDP growth (%)	-3.3	2020	●	●
Victims of modern slavery (per 1,000 population)	NA	NA	●	●
Adults with an account at a bank or other financial institution or with a mobile-money-service provider (% of population aged 15 or over)	NA	NA	●	●
Unemployment rate (% of total labor force)	15.7	2022	●	↓
Fundamental labor rights are effectively guaranteed (worst 0–1 best)	NA	NA	●	●
Fatal work-related accidents embodied in imports (per 100,000 population)	0.2	2015	●	↑

SDG9 – Industry, Innovation and Infrastructure	Value	Year	Rating	Trend
Population using the internet (%)	33.0	2020	●	→
Mobile broadband subscriptions (per 100 population)	34.3	2019	●	↑
Logistics Performance Index: Quality of trade and transport-related infrastructure (worst 1–5 best)	2.3	2018	●	↓
The Times Higher Education Universities Ranking: Average score of top 3 universities (worst 0–100 best)	* 0.0	2022	●	●
Articles published in academic journals (per 1,000 population)	0.0	2020	●	→
Expenditure on research and development (% of GDP)	NA	NA	●	●

SDG10 – Reduced Inequalities	Value	Year	Rating	Trend
Gini coefficient	56.3	2017	●	●
Palma ratio	4.3	2018	●	●

SDG11 – Sustainable Cities and Communities	Value	Year	Rating	Trend
Proportion of urban population living in slums (%)	86.6	2018	●	→
Annual mean concentration of particulate matter of less than 2.5 microns in diameter (PM2.5) (μg/m³)	29.0	2019	●	↓
Access to improved water source, piped (% of urban population)	100.0	2020	●	↑
Satisfaction with public transport (%)	NA	NA	●	●

SDG12 – Responsible Consumption and Production	Value	Year	Rating	Trend
Municipal solid waste (kg/capita/day)	0.4	2014	●	●
Electronic waste (kg/capita)	1.5	2019	●	●
Production-based SO_2 emissions (kg/capita)	NA	NA	●	●
SO_2 emissions embodied in imports (kg/capita)	NA	NA	●	●
Production-based nitrogen emissions (kg/capita)	1.6	2015	●	↑
Nitrogen emissions embodied in imports (kg/capita)	4.0	2015	●	↑
Exports of plastic waste (kg/capita)	0.0	2018	●	●

SDG13 – Climate Action	Value	Year	Rating	Trend
CO_2 emissions from fossil fuel combustion and cement production (tCO_2/capita)	0.5	2020	●	↑
CO_2 emissions embodied in imports (tCO_2/capita)	NA	NA	●	●
CO_2 emissions embodied in fossil fuel exports (kg/capita)	0.0	2020	●	●

SDG14 – Life Below Water	Value	Year	Rating	Trend
Mean area that is protected in marine sites important to biodiversity (%)	82.5	2020	●	→
Ocean Health Index: Clean Waters score (worst 0–100 best)	57.9	2020	●	→
Fish caught from overexploited or collapsed stocks (% of total catch)	32.4	2018	●	↓
Fish caught by trawling or dredging (%)	2.0	2018	●	↑
Fish caught that are then discarded (%)	0.0	2017	●	↑
Marine biodiversity threats embodied in imports (per million population)	0.0	2018	●	●

SDG15 – Life on Land	Value	Year	Rating	Trend
Mean area that is protected in terrestrial sites important to biodiversity (%)	79.5	2020	●	→
Mean area that is protected in freshwater sites important to biodiversity (%)	72.9	2020	●	→
Red List Index of species survival (worst 0–1 best)	0.8	2021	●	↓
Permanent deforestation (% of forest area, 5-year average)	NA	NA	●	●
Terrestrial and freshwater biodiversity threats embodied in imports (per million population)	0.1	2018	●	●

SDG16 – Peace, Justice and Strong Institutions	Value	Year	Rating	Trend
Homicides (per 100,000 population)	3.3	2011	●	●
Unsentenced detainees (% of prison population)	32.8	2018	●	↓
Population who feel safe walking alone at night in the city or area where they live (%)	NA	NA	●	●
Property Rights (worst 1–7 best)	NA	NA	●	●
Birth registrations with civil authority (% of children under age 5)	98.6	2020	●	●
Corruption Perception Index (worst 0–100 best)	45	2021	●	→
Children involved in child labor (% of population aged 5 to 14)	18.2	2019	●	●
Exports of major conventional weapons (TIV constant million USD per 100,000 population)	* 0.0	2020	●	●
Press Freedom Index (best 0–100 worst)	NA	NA	●	●
Access to and affordability of justice (worst 0–1 best)	NA	NA	●	●

SDG17 – Partnerships for the Goals	Value	Year	Rating	Trend
Government spending on health and education (% of GDP)	8.5	2019	●	↑
For high-income and all OECD DAC countries: International concessional public finance, including official development assistance (% of GNI)	NA	NA	●	●
Other countries: Government revenue excluding grants (% of GDP)	NA	NA	●	●
Corporate Tax Haven Score (best 0–100 worst)	* 0.0	2019	●	●
Statistical Performance Index (worst 0–100 best)	39.9	2019	●	↓

* Imputed data point

SAUDI ARABIA

Middle East and North Africa

OVERALL PERFORMANCE

COUNTRY RANKING

SAUDI ARABIA

96/163

COUNTRY SCORE

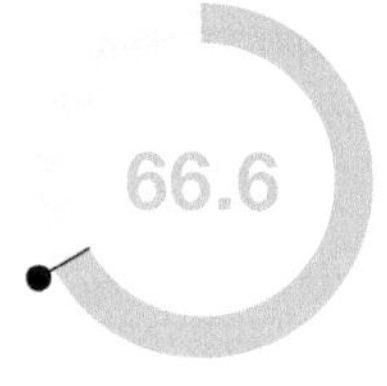

REGIONAL AVERAGE: 66.7

AVERAGE PERFORMANCE BY SDG

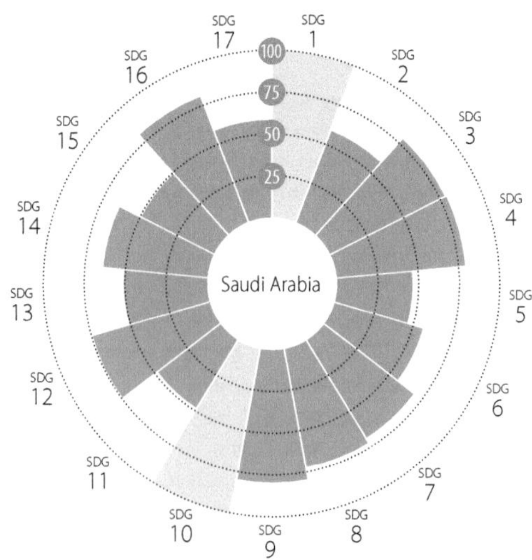

SDG DASHBOARDS AND TRENDS

Note: The full title of each SDG is available here: https://sustainabledevelopment.un.org/topics/sustainabledevelopmentgoals

INTERNATIONAL SPILLOVER INDEX

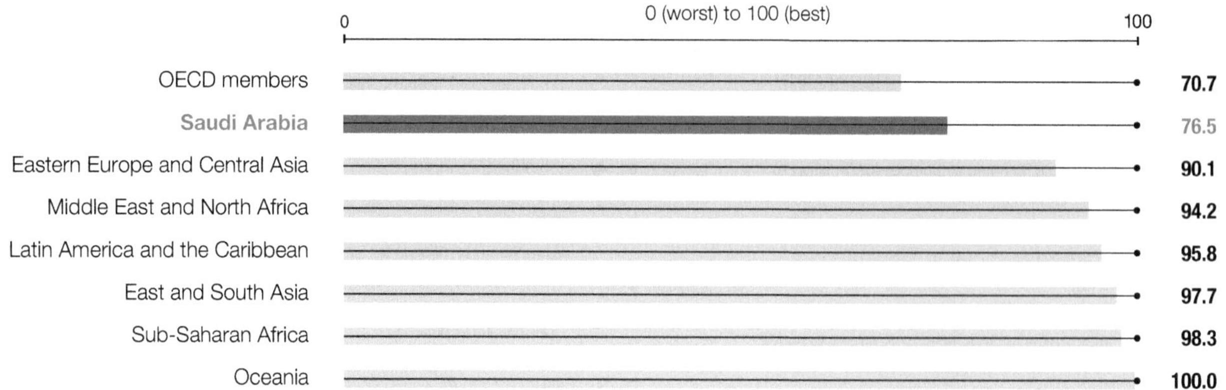

STATISTICAL PERFORMANCE INDEX

0 (worst) to 100 (best)

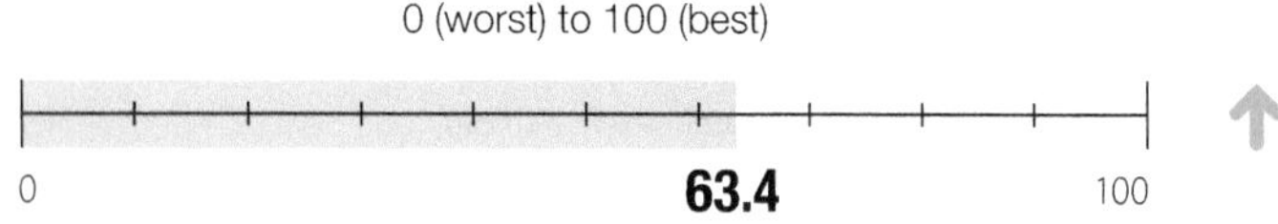

MISSING DATA IN SDG INDEX

12%

SDG1 – No Poverty		Value	Year	Rating	Trend
Poverty headcount ratio at \$1.90/day (%)	*	NA	NA	●	●
Poverty headcount ratio at \$3.20/day (%)	*	NA	NA	●	●
SDG2 – Zero Hunger					
Prevalence of undernourishment (%)		3.9	2019	●	↑
Prevalence of stunting in children under 5 years of age (%)		9.3	2004	●	↗
Prevalence of wasting in children under 5 years of age (%)		11.8	2004	●	→
Prevalence of obesity, BMI ≥ 30 (% of adult population)		35.4	2016	●	↓
Human Trophic Level (best 2–3 worst)		2.3	2017	●	→
Cereal yield (tonnes per hectare of harvested land)		5.6	2018	●	↑
Sustainable Nitrogen Management Index (best 0–1.41 worst)		0.6	2015	●	↑
Exports of hazardous pesticides (tonnes per million population)		1.2	2019	●	●
SDG3 – Good Health and Well-Being					
Maternal mortality rate (per 100,000 live births)		17	2017	●	↑
Neonatal mortality rate (per 1,000 live births)		3.5	2020	●	↑
Mortality rate, under-5 (per 1,000 live births)		7.0	2020	●	↑
Incidence of tuberculosis (per 100,000 population)		8.1	2020	●	↑
New HIV infections (per 1,000 uninfected population)		0.1	2020	●	↑
Age-standardized death rate due to cardiovascular disease, cancer, diabetes, or chronic respiratory disease in adults aged 30–70 years (%)		20.9	2019	●	↗
Age-standardized death rate attributable to household air pollution and ambient air pollution (per 100,000 population)		84	2016	●	●
Traffic deaths (per 100,000 population)		35.9	2019	●	↓
Life expectancy at birth (years)		74.3	2019	●	↗
Adolescent fertility rate (births per 1,000 females aged 15 to 19)		8.7	2009	●	●
Births attended by skilled health personnel (%)		99.4	2018	●	●
Surviving infants who received 2 WHO-recommended vaccines (%)		95	2020	●	↑
Universal health coverage (UHC) index of service coverage (worst 0–100 best)		73	2019	●	↗
Subjective well-being (average ladder score, worst 0–10 best)		6.4	2021	●	↑
SDG4 – Quality Education					
Participation rate in pre-primary organized learning (% of children aged 4 to 6)		53.0	2020	●	↗
Net primary enrollment rate (%)		94.8	2020	●	↓
Lower secondary completion rate (%)		104.1	2020	●	↑
Literacy rate (% of population aged 15 to 24)		99.5	2020	●	●
SDG5 – Gender Equality					
Demand for family planning satisfied by modern methods (% of females aged 15 to 49)	*	45.5	2022	●	→
Ratio of female-to-male mean years of education received (%)		93.3	2019	●	↑
Ratio of female-to-male labor force participation rate (%)		39.8	2020	●	↗
Seats held by women in national parliament (%)		19.9	2020	●	→
SDG6 – Clean Water and Sanitation					
Population using at least basic drinking water services (%)		100.0	2020	●	↑
Population using at least basic sanitation services (%)		100.0	2020	●	↑
Freshwater withdrawal (% of available freshwater resources)		992.8	2018	●	●
Anthropogenic wastewater that receives treatment (%)		11.8	2018	●	●
Scarce water consumption embodied in imports (m^3 H_2O eq/capita)		3509.3	2018	●	●
SDG7 – Affordable and Clean Energy					
Population with access to electricity (%)		100.0	2019	●	↑
Population with access to clean fuels and technology for cooking (%)		100.0	2019	●	↑
CO_2 emissions from fuel combustion per total electricity output ($MtCO_2$/TWh)		1.5	2019	●	↑
Share of renewable energy in total primary energy supply (%)		0.0	2019	●	→
SDG8 – Decent Work and Economic Growth					
Adjusted GDP growth (%)		-2.6	2020	●	●
Victims of modern slavery (per 1,000 population)	*	NA	NA	●	●
Adults with an account at a bank or other financial institution or with a mobile-money-service provider (% of population aged 15 or over)		71.7	2017	●	↑
Unemployment rate (% of total labor force)		6.7	2022	●	→
Fundamental labor rights are effectively guaranteed (worst 0–1 best)		NA	NA	●	●
Fatal work-related accidents embodied in imports (per 100,000 population)		1.2	2015	●	↑

SDG9 – Industry, Innovation and Infrastructure		Value	Year	Rating	Trend
Population using the internet (%)		97.9	2020	●	↑
Mobile broadband subscriptions (per 100 population)		116.9	2019	●	↑
Logistics Performance Index: Quality of trade and transport-related infrastructure (worst 1–5 best)		3.1	2018	●	↑
The Times Higher Education Universities Ranking: Average score of top 3 universities (worst 0–100 best)		50.6	2022	●	●
Articles published in academic journals (per 1,000 population)		1.0	2020	●	↑
Expenditure on research and development (% of GDP)		0.8	2013	●	●
SDG10 – Reduced Inequalities					
Gini coefficient		NA	NA	●	●
Palma ratio		NA	NA	●	●
SDG11 – Sustainable Cities and Communities					
Proportion of urban population living in slums (%)		NA	NA	●	●
Annual mean concentration of particulate matter of less than 2.5 microns in diameter (PM2.5) (μg/m³)		88.3	2019	●	→
Access to improved water source, piped (% of urban population)		NA	NA	●	●
Satisfaction with public transport (%)		80.0	2021	●	↑
SDG12 – Responsible Consumption and Production					
Municipal solid waste (kg/capita/day)		1.4	2015	●	●
Electronic waste (kg/capita)		17.6	2019	●	●
Production-based SO_2 emissions (kg/capita)		89.6	2018	●	●
SO_2 emissions embodied in imports (kg/capita)		4.8	2018	●	●
Production-based nitrogen emissions (kg/capita)		5.2	2015	●	↑
Nitrogen emissions embodied in imports (kg/capita)		10.2	2015	●	→
Exports of plastic waste (kg/capita)		1.3	2020	●	●
SDG13 – Climate Action					
CO_2 emissions from fossil fuel combustion and cement production (tCO_2/capita)		18.0	2020	●	↗
CO_2 emissions embodied in imports (tCO_2/capita)		1.9	2018	●	↑
CO_2 emissions embodied in fossil fuel exports (kg/capita)		0.0	2020	●	●
SDG14 – Life Below Water					
Mean area that is protected in marine sites important to biodiversity (%)		25.3	2020	●	→
Ocean Health Index: Clean Waters score (worst 0–100 best)		62.6	2020	●	→
Fish caught from overexploited or collapsed stocks (% of total catch)		15.8	2018	●	↑
Fish caught by trawling or dredging (%)		13.8	2018	●	↑
Fish caught that are then discarded (%)		6.6	2018	●	→
Marine biodiversity threats embodied in imports (per million population)		0.5	2018	●	●
SDG15 – Life on Land					
Mean area that is protected in terrestrial sites important to biodiversity (%)		22.0	2020	●	→
Mean area that is protected in freshwater sites important to biodiversity (%)		17.7	2020	●	→
Red List Index of species survival (worst 0–1 best)		0.9	2021	●	↑
Permanent deforestation (% of forest area, 5-year average)		NA	NA	●	●
Terrestrial and freshwater biodiversity threats embodied in imports (per million population)		1.8	2018	●	●
SDG16 – Peace, Justice and Strong Institutions					
Homicides (per 100,000 population)		0.8	2019	●	●
Unsentenced detainees (% of prison population)		20.0	2019	●	●
Population who feel safe walking alone at night in the city or area where they live (%)		91	2021	●	●
Property Rights (worst 1–7 best)		5.8	2020	●	↑
Birth registrations with civil authority (% of children under age 5)		99.2	2020	●	●
Corruption Perception Index (worst 0–100 best)		53	2021	●	→
Children involved in child labor (% of population aged 5 to 14)		NA	NA	●	●
Exports of major conventional weapons (TIV constant million USD per 100,000 population)		0.0	2020	●	●
Press Freedom Index (best 0–100 worst)		62.7	2021	●	↓
Access to and affordability of justice (worst 0–1 best)		NA	NA	●	●
SDG17 – Partnerships for the Goals					
Government spending on health and education (% of GDP)		9.1	2019	●	↓
For high-income and all OECD DAC countries: International concessional public finance, including official development assistance (% of GNI)		0.3	2021	●	●
Other countries: Government revenue excluding grants (% of GDP)		NA	NA	●	●
Corporate Tax Haven Score (best 0–100 worst)	*	0.0	2019	●	●
Statistical Performance Index (worst 0–100 best)		63.4	2019	●	↑

* Imputed data point

SENEGAL

Sub-Saharan Africa

OVERALL PERFORMANCE

COUNTRY RANKING

SENEGAL

126 **/163**

COUNTRY SCORE

REGIONAL AVERAGE: 53.6

AVERAGE PERFORMANCE BY SDG

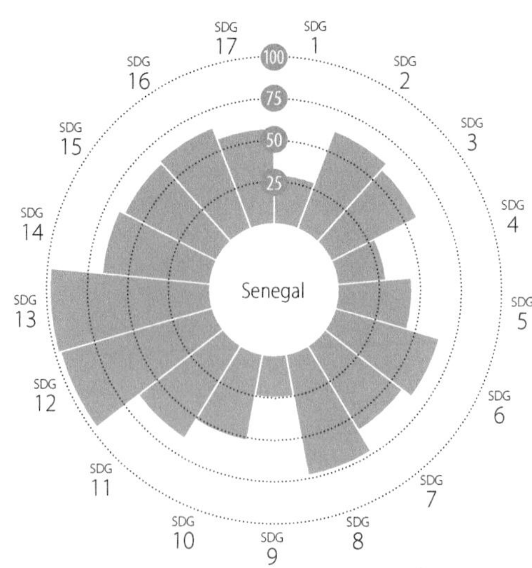

SDG DASHBOARDS AND TRENDS

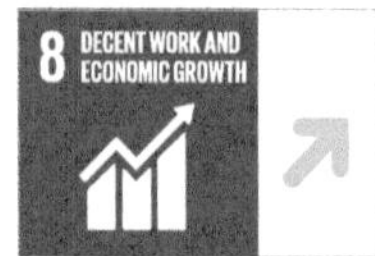

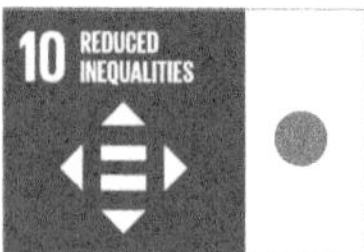

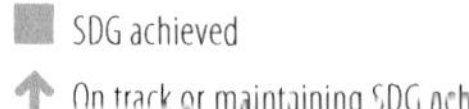

Information unavailable

Information unavailable

Note: The full title of each SDG is available here: https://sustainabledevelopment.un.org/topics/sustainabledevelopmentgoals

INTERNATIONAL SPILLOVER INDEX

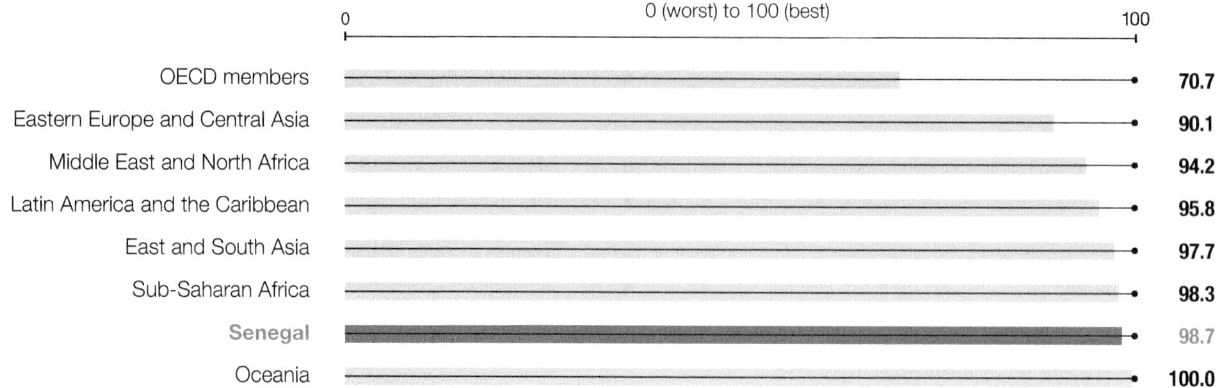

STATISTICAL PERFORMANCE INDEX

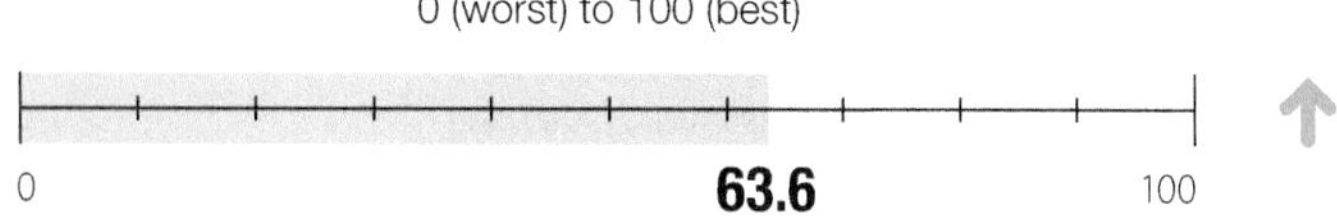

MISSING DATA IN SDG INDEX

0%

SENEGAL

Performance by Indicator

SDG1 – No Poverty	Value	Year	Rating	Trend
Poverty headcount ratio at $1.90/day (%)	30.7	2022	●	→
Poverty headcount ratio at $3.20/day (%)	57.2	2022	●	→
SDG2 – Zero Hunger				
Prevalence of undernourishment (%)	7.5	2019	●	↑
Prevalence of stunting in children under 5 years of age (%)	17.9	2019	●	↗
Prevalence of wasting in children under 5 years of age (%)	8.1	2019	●	→
Prevalence of obesity, BMI ≥ 30 (% of adult population)	8.8	2016	●	↑
Human Trophic Level (best 2–3 worst)	2.1	2017	●	↑
Cereal yield (tonnes per hectare of harvested land)	1.3	2018	●	↓
Sustainable Nitrogen Management Index (best 0–1.41 worst)	0.9	2015	●	↓
Exports of hazardous pesticides (tonnes per million population)	0.2	2019	●	●
SDG3 – Good Health and Well-Being				
Maternal mortality rate (per 100,000 live births)	315	2017	●	↗
Neonatal mortality rate (per 1,000 live births)	20.6	2020	●	↗
Mortality rate, under-5 (per 1,000 live births)	38.1	2020	●	↑
Incidence of tuberculosis (per 100,000 population)	117.0	2020	●	→
New HIV infections (per 1,000 uninfected population)	0.1	2020	●	↑
Age-standardized death rate due to cardiovascular disease, cancer, diabetes, or chronic respiratory disease in adults aged 30–70 years (%)	19.5	2019	●	↗
Age-standardized death rate attributable to household air pollution and ambient air pollution (per 100,000 population)	161	2016	●	●
Traffic deaths (per 100,000 population)	23.5	2019	●	→
Life expectancy at birth (years)	68.6	2019	●	→
Adolescent fertility rate (births per 1,000 females aged 15 to 19)	68.0	2017	●	●
Births attended by skilled health personnel (%)	74.5	2019	●	↑
Surviving infants who received 2 WHO-recommended vaccines (%)	88	2020	●	↑
Universal health coverage (UHC) index of service coverage (worst 0–100 best)	49	2019	●	→
Subjective well-being (average ladder score, worst 0–10 best)	4.9	2021	●	↗
SDG4 – Quality Education				
Participation rate in pre-primary organized learning (% of children aged 4 to 6)	15.9	2020	●	↓
Net primary enrollment rate (%)	75.4	2020	●	↓
Lower secondary completion rate (%)	37.1	2020	●	↓
Literacy rate (% of population aged 15 to 24)	69.5	2017	●	●
SDG5 – Gender Equality				
Demand for family planning satisfied by modern methods (% of females aged 15 to 49)	53.2	2019	●	↗
Ratio of female-to-male mean years of education received (%)	41.3	2019	●	↓
Ratio of female-to-male labor force participation rate (%)	58.8	2020	●	↓
Seats held by women in national parliament (%)	43.0	2020	●	↑
SDG6 – Clean Water and Sanitation				
Population using at least basic drinking water services (%)	84.9	2020	●	↗
Population using at least basic sanitation services (%)	56.8	2020	●	→
Freshwater withdrawal (% of available freshwater resources)	11.8	2018	●	●
Anthropogenic wastewater that receives treatment (%)	0.5	2018	●	●
Scarce water consumption embodied in imports (m^3 H_2O eq/capita)	418.3	2018	●	●
SDG7 – Affordable and Clean Energy				
Population with access to electricity (%)	70.4	2019	●	↗
Population with access to clean fuels and technology for cooking (%)	24.5	2019	●	↓
CO_2 emissions from fuel combustion per total electricity output ($MtCO_2$/TWh)	1.7	2019	●	↑
Share of renewable energy in total primary energy supply (%)	36.9	2019	●	↑
SDG8 – Decent Work and Economic Growth				
Adjusted GDP growth (%)	-3.3	2020	●	●
Victims of modern slavery (per 1,000 population)	2.9	2018	●	●
Adults with an account at a bank or other financial institution or with a mobile-money-service provider (% of population aged 15 or over)	42.3	2017	●	↑
Unemployment rate (% of total labor force)	3.6	2022	●	↑
Fundamental labor rights are effectively guaranteed (worst 0–1 best)	0.7	2020	●	→
Fatal work-related accidents embodied in imports (per 100,000 population)	0.1	2015	●	↑

SDG9 – Industry, Innovation and Infrastructure	Value	Year	Rating	Trend
Population using the internet (%)	42.6	2020	●	↑
Mobile broadband subscriptions (per 100 population)	54.2	2019	●	↑
Logistics Performance Index: Quality of trade and transport-related infrastructure (worst 1–5 best)	2.2	2018	●	↓
The Times Higher Education Universities Ranking: Average score of top 3 universities (worst 0–100 best)	* 0.0	2022	●	●
Articles published in academic journals (per 1,000 population)	0.1	2020	●	→
Expenditure on research and development (% of GDP)	0.6	2015	●	●
SDG10 – Reduced Inequalities				
Gini coefficient	40.3	2011	●	●
Palma ratio	1.9	2018	●	●
SDG11 – Sustainable Cities and Communities				
Proportion of urban population living in slums (%)	28.4	2018	●	↑
Annual mean concentration of particulate matter of less than 2.5 microns in diameter (PM2.5) (μg/m^3)	41.6	2019	●	→
Access to improved water source, piped (% of urban population)	85.4	2020	●	→
Satisfaction with public transport (%)	50.0	2021	●	↗
SDG12 – Responsible Consumption and Production				
Municipal solid waste (kg/capita/day)	0.4	2016	●	●
Electronic waste (kg/capita)	1.2	2019	●	●
Production-based SO_2 emissions (kg/capita)	3.7	2018	●	●
SO_2 emissions embodied in imports (kg/capita)	0.5	2018	●	●
Production-based nitrogen emissions (kg/capita)	9.6	2015	●	↑
Nitrogen emissions embodied in imports (kg/capita)	0.4	2015	●	↑
Exports of plastic waste (kg/capita)	0.2	2020	●	●
SDG13 – Climate Action				
CO_2 emissions from fossil fuel combustion and cement production (tCO_2/capita)	0.6	2020	●	↑
CO_2 emissions embodied in imports (tCO_2/capita)	0.1	2018	●	↑
CO_2 emissions embodied in fossil fuel exports (kg/capita)	0.0	2020	●	●
SDG14 – Life Below Water				
Mean area that is protected in marine sites important to biodiversity (%)	25.3	2020	●	→
Ocean Health Index: Clean Waters score (worst 0–100 best)	46.6	2020	●	→
Fish caught from overexploited or collapsed stocks (% of total catch)	14.4	2018	●	↑
Fish caught by trawling or dredging (%)	8.0	2018	●	↑
Fish caught that are then discarded (%)	6.3	2018	●	↑
Marine biodiversity threats embodied in imports (per million population)	0.0	2018	●	●
SDG15 – Life on Land				
Mean area that is protected in terrestrial sites important to biodiversity (%)	37.8	2020	●	→
Mean area that is protected in freshwater sites important to biodiversity (%)	23.7	2020	●	→
Red List Index of species survival (worst 0–1 best)	0.9	2021	●	↑
Permanent deforestation (% of forest area, 5-year average)	0.5	2020	●	↓
Terrestrial and freshwater biodiversity threats embodied in imports (per million population)	0.1	2018	●	●
SDG16 – Peace, Justice and Strong Institutions				
Homicides (per 100,000 population)	0.3	2015	●	●
Unsentenced detainees (% of prison population)	42.1	2017	●	●
Population who feel safe walking alone at night in the city or area where they live (%)	53	2021	●	→
Property Rights (worst 1–7 best)	4.4	2020	●	↑
Birth registrations with civil authority (% of children under age 5)	78.7	2020	●	●
Corruption Perception Index (worst 0–100 best)	43	2021	●	↓
Children involved in child labor (% of population aged 5 to 14)	22.8	2019	●	●
Exports of major conventional weapons (TIV constant million USD per 100,000 population)	* 0.0	2020	●	●
Press Freedom Index (best 0–100 worst)	25.2	2021	●	↑
Access to and affordability of justice (worst 0–1 best)	0.6	2020	●	↑
SDG17 – Partnerships for the Goals				
Government spending on health and education (% of GDP)	6.3	2019	●	↓
For high-income and all OECD DAC countries: International concessional public finance, including official development assistance (% of GNI)	NA	NA	●	●
Other countries: Government revenue excluding grants (% of GDP)	19.8	2018	●	→
Corporate Tax Haven Score (best 0–100 worst)	* 0.0	2019	●	●
Statistical Performance Index (worst 0–100 best)	63.6	2019	●	↑

* Imputed data point

SERBIA

Eastern Europe and Central Asia

AVERAGE PERFORMANCE BY SDG

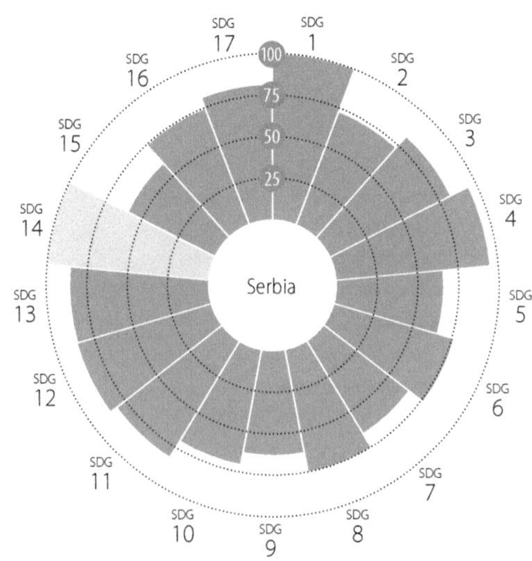

OVERALL PERFORMANCE

COUNTRY RANKING

SERBIA

35/163

COUNTRY SCORE

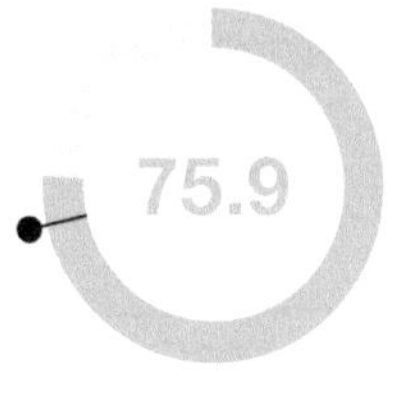

REGIONAL AVERAGE: 71.6

SDG DASHBOARDS AND TRENDS

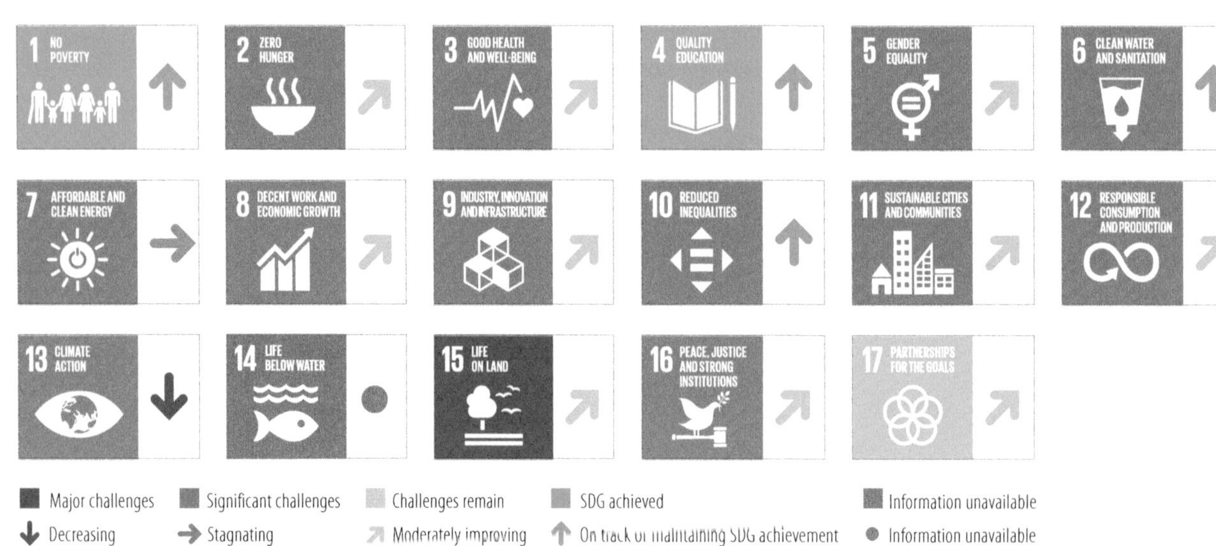

Note: The full title of each SDG is available here: https://sustainabledevelopment.un.org/topics/sustainabledevelopmentgoals

INTERNATIONAL SPILLOVER INDEX

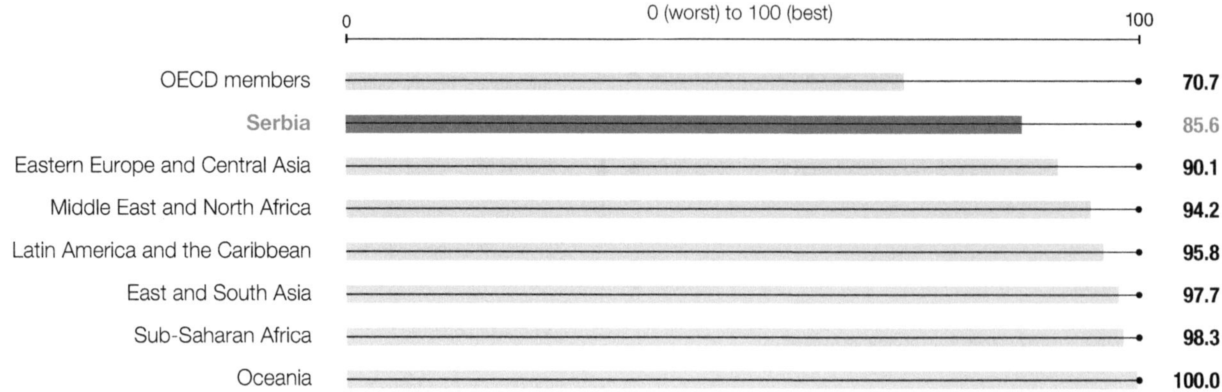

STATISTICAL PERFORMANCE INDEX

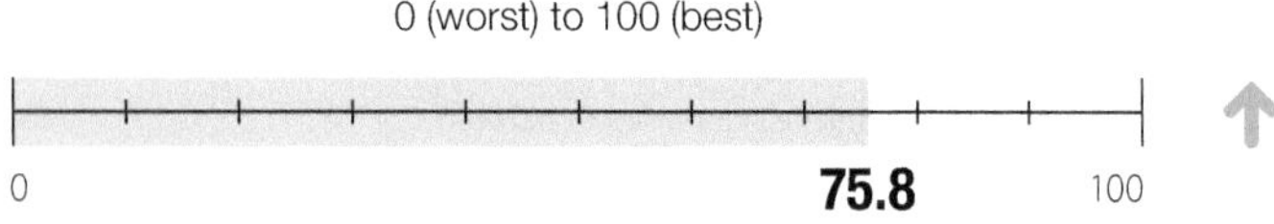

MISSING DATA IN SDG INDEX

0%

SERBIA

SDG1 – No Poverty	Value	Year	Rating	Trend
Poverty headcount ratio at \$1.90/day (%)	0.0	2022	●	↑
Poverty headcount ratio at \$3.20/day (%)	0.2	2022	●	↑
SDG2 – Zero Hunger				
Prevalence of undernourishment (%)	3.9	2019	●	↑
Prevalence of stunting in children under 5 years of age (%)	5.4	2019	●	↑
Prevalence of wasting in children under 5 years of age (%)	2.6	2019	●	↑
Prevalence of obesity, BMI ≥ 30 (% of adult population)	21.5	2016	●	↓
Human Trophic Level (best 2–3 worst)	2.3	2017	●	→
Cereal yield (tonnes per hectare of harvested land)	6.1	2018	●	↑
Sustainable Nitrogen Management Index (best 0–1.41 worst)	0.5	2015	●	↑
Exports of hazardous pesticides (tonnes per million population)	1.9	2019	●	●
SDG3 – Good Health and Well-Being				
Maternal mortality rate (per 100,000 live births)	12	2017	●	↑
Neonatal mortality rate (per 1,000 live births)	3.6	2020	●	↑
Mortality rate, under-5 (per 1,000 live births)	5.6	2020	●	↑
Incidence of tuberculosis (per 100,000 population)	13.0	2020	●	↑
New HIV infections (per 1,000 uninfected population)	0.0	2020	●	↑
Age-standardized death rate due to cardiovascular disease, cancer, diabetes, or chronic respiratory disease in adults aged 30–70 years (%)	22.0	2019	●	→
Age-standardized death rate attributable to household air pollution and ambient air pollution (per 100,000 population)	62	2016	●	●
Traffic deaths (per 100,000 population)	7.5	2019	●	↑
Life expectancy at birth (years)	75.9	2019	●	↗
Adolescent fertility rate (births per 1,000 females aged 15 to 19)	12.0	2019	●	↑
Births attended by skilled health personnel (%)	98.4	2014	●	●
Surviving infants who received 2 WHO-recommended vaccines (%)	78	2020	●	↓
Universal health coverage (UHC) index of service coverage (worst 0–100 best)	71	2019	●	↗
Subjective well-being (average ladder score, worst 0–10 best)	6.2	2021	●	↑
SDG4 – Quality Education				
Participation rate in pre-primary organized learning (% of children aged 4 to 6)	92.7	2020	●	↑
Net primary enrollment rate (%)	97.1	2020	●	↑
Lower secondary completion rate (%)	95.2	2020	●	↑
Literacy rate (% of population aged 15 to 24)	100.0	2019	●	↑
SDG5 – Gender Equality				
Demand for family planning satisfied by modern methods (% of females aged 15 to 49)	38.4	2019	●	→
Ratio of female-to-male mean years of education received (%)	93.1	2019	●	↗
Ratio of female-to-male labor force participation rate (%)	75.1	2020	●	↑
Seats held by women in national parliament (%)	38.8	2020	●	↑
SDG6 – Clean Water and Sanitation				
Population using at least basic drinking water services (%)	95.3	2020	●	↑
Population using at least basic sanitation services (%)	97.9	2020	●	↑
Freshwater withdrawal (% of available freshwater resources)	6.3	2018	●	●
Anthropogenic wastewater that receives treatment (%)	1.7	2018	●	●
Scarce water consumption embodied in imports (m^3 H_2O eq/capita)	1693.5	2018	●	●
SDG7 – Affordable and Clean Energy				
Population with access to electricity (%)	99.8	2019	●	↑
Population with access to clean fuels and technology for cooking (%)	66.1	2019	●	↓
CO_2 emissions from fuel combustion per total electricity output ($MtCO_2$/TWh)	1.7	2019	●	→
Share of renewable energy in total primary energy supply (%)	13.3	2019	●	→
SDG8 – Decent Work and Economic Growth				
Adjusted GDP growth (%)	1.0	2020	●	●
Victims of modern slavery (per 1,000 population)	3.3	2018	●	●
Adults with an account at a bank or other financial institution or with a mobile-money-service provider (% of population aged 15 or over)	71.4	2017	●	↓
Unemployment rate (% of total labor force)	10.6	2022	●	↑
Fundamental labor rights are effectively guaranteed (worst 0–1 best)	0.6	2020	●	↑
Fatal work-related accidents embodied in imports (per 100,000 population)	0.6	2015	●	↑

SDG9 – Industry, Innovation and Infrastructure	Value	Year	Rating	Trend
Population using the internet (%)	78.4	2020	●	↑
Mobile broadband subscriptions (per 100 population)	90.3	2019	●	↑
Logistics Performance Index: Quality of trade and transport-related infrastructure (worst 1–5 best)	2.6	2018	●	↓
The Times Higher Education Universities Ranking: Average score of top 3 universities (worst 0–100 best)	29.5	2022	●	●
Articles published in academic journals (per 1,000 population)	0.9	2020	●	↑
Expenditure on research and development (% of GDP)	0.9	2018	●	↗
SDG10 – Reduced Inequalities				
Gini coefficient	36.2	2017	●	↑
Palma ratio	1.5	2018	●	●
SDG11 – Sustainable Cities and Communities				
Proportion of urban population living in slums (%)	3.6	2018	●	●
Annual mean concentration of particulate matter of less than 2.5 microns in diameter (PM2.5) ($\mu g/m^3$)	23.8	2019	●	↗
Access to improved water source, piped (% of urban population)	97.7	2020	●	↗
Satisfaction with public transport (%)	54.0	2021	●	↑
SDG12 – Responsible Consumption and Production				
Municipal solid waste (kg/capita/day)	0.7	2019	●	●
Electronic waste (kg/capita)	9.4	2019	●	●
Production-based SO_2 emissions (kg/capita)	4.0	2018	●	●
SO_2 emissions embodied in imports (kg/capita)	1.9	2018	●	●
Production-based nitrogen emissions (kg/capita)	14.3	2015	●	↑
Nitrogen emissions embodied in imports (kg/capita)	6.6	2015	●	→
Exports of plastic waste (kg/capita)	0.8	2021	●	●
SDG13 – Climate Action				
CO_2 emissions from fossil fuel combustion and cement production (tCO_2/capita)	4.9	2020	●	→
CO_2 emissions embodied in imports (tCO_2/capita)	0.6	2018	●	↓
CO_2 emissions embodied in fossil fuel exports (kg/capita)	10.6	2021	●	●
SDG14 – Life Below Water				
Mean area that is protected in marine sites important to biodiversity (%)	NA	NA	●	●
Ocean Health Index: Clean Waters score (worst 0–100 best)	NA	NA	●	●
Fish caught from overexploited or collapsed stocks (% of total catch)	NA	NA	●	●
Fish caught by trawling or dredging (%)	NA	NA	●	●
Fish caught that are then discarded (%)	NA	NA	●	●
Marine biodiversity threats embodied in imports (per million population)	0.8	2018	●	●
SDG15 – Life on Land				
Mean area that is protected in terrestrial sites important to biodiversity (%)	26.8	2020	●	→
Mean area that is protected in freshwater sites important to biodiversity (%)	23.2	2020	●	→
Red List Index of species survival (worst 0–1 best)	1.0	2021	●	↑
Permanent deforestation (% of forest area, 5-year average)	0.0	2020	●	↑
Terrestrial and freshwater biodiversity threats embodied in imports (per million population)	3.8	2018	●	●
SDG16 – Peace, Justice and Strong Institutions				
Homicides (per 100,000 population)	1.0	2020	●	↑
Unsentenced detainees (% of prison population)	17.2	2019	●	↑
Population who feel safe walking alone at night in the city or area where they live (%)	76	2021	●	↑
Property Rights (worst 1–7 best)	4.1	2020	●	↑
Birth registrations with civil authority (% of children under age 5)	99.9	2020	●	●
Corruption Perception Index (worst 0–100 best)	38	2021	●	↓
Children involved in child labor (% of population aged 5 to 14)	9.5	2019	●	●
Exports of major conventional weapons (TIV constant million USD per 100,000 population)	0.3	2020	●	●
Press Freedom Index (best 0–100 worst)	32.0	2021	●	↓
Access to and affordability of justice (worst 0–1 best)	0.6	2020	●	↑
SDG17 – Partnerships for the Goals				
Government spending on health and education (% of GDP)	8.7	2019	●	↓
For high-income and all OECD DAC countries: International concessional public finance, including official development assistance (% of GNI)	NA	NA	●	●
Other countries: Government revenue excluding grants (% of GDP)	41.1	2019	●	↑
Corporate Tax Haven Score (best 0–100 worst)	* 0.0	2019	●	●
Statistical Performance Index (worst 0–100 best)	75.8	2019	●	↑

* Imputed data point

SEYCHELLES

Sub-Saharan Africa

AVERAGE PERFORMANCE BY SDG

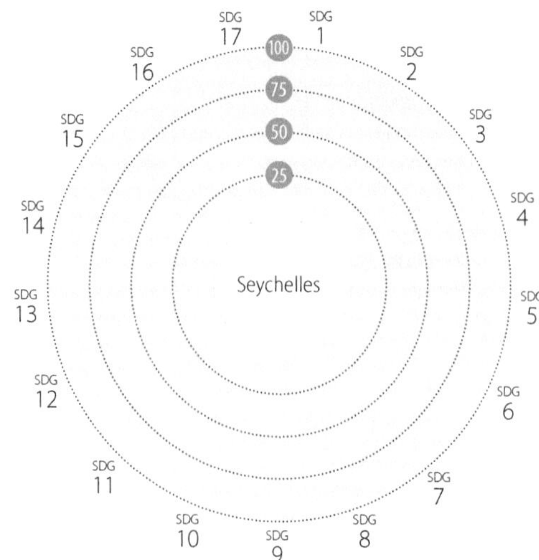

OVERALL PERFORMANCE

COUNTRY RANKING

SEYCHELLES

NA /163

COUNTRY SCORE

SDG DASHBOARDS AND TRENDS

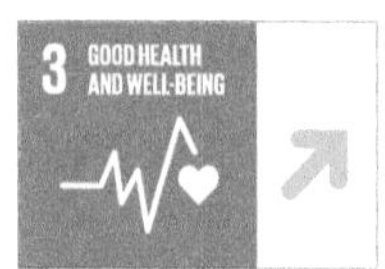

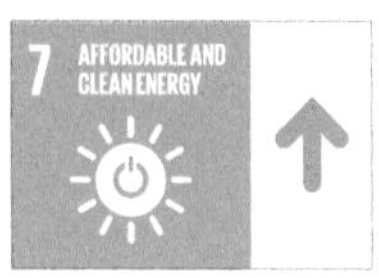

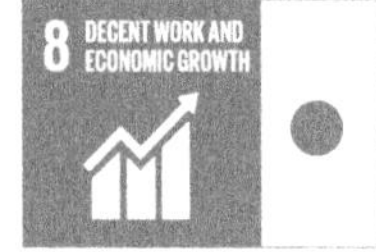

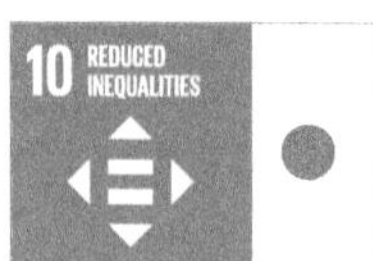

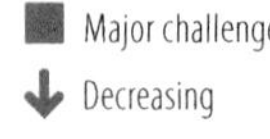 Major challenges / Decreasing
 Significant challenges / Stagnating
 Challenges remain / Moderately improving
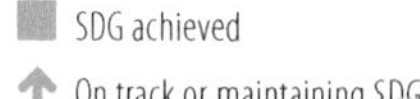 SDG achieved / On track or maintaining SDG achievement
Information unavailable / Information unavailable

Note: The full title of each SDG is available here: https://sustainabledevelopment.un.org/topics/sustainabledevelopmentgoals

INTERNATIONAL SPILLOVER INDEX

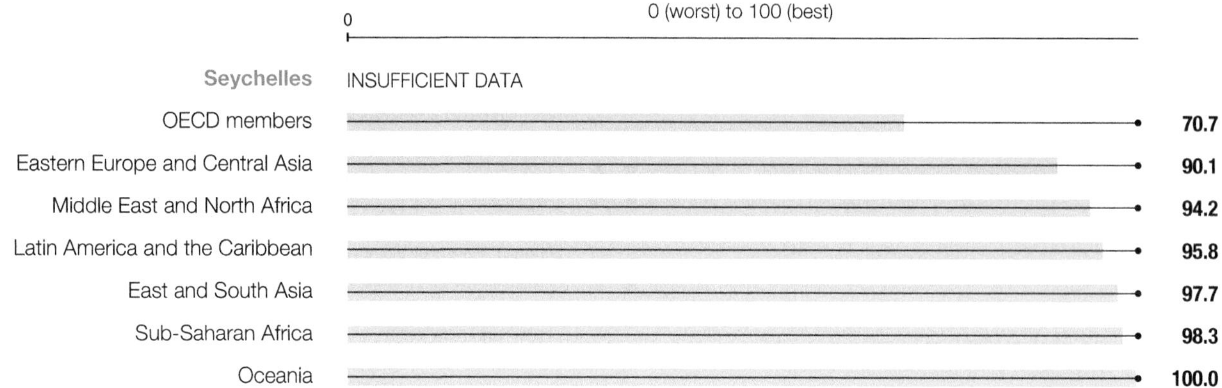

STATISTICAL PERFORMANCE INDEX

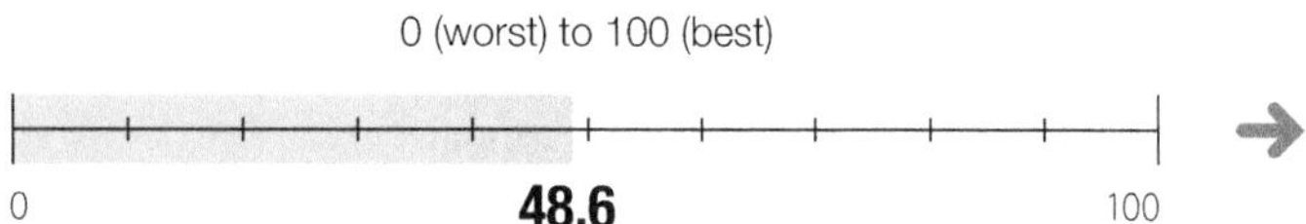

MISSING DATA IN SDG INDEX

32%

SEYCHELLES

Performance by Indicator

		Value	Year	Rating	Trend
SDG1 – No Poverty					
Poverty headcount ratio at $1.90/day (%)		NA	NA	●	●
Poverty headcount ratio at $3.20/day (%)		NA	NA	●	●
SDG2 – Zero Hunger					
Prevalence of undernourishment (%)	*	1.2	2019	●	●
Prevalence of stunting in children under 5 years of age (%)		7.9	2012	●	↑
Prevalence of wasting in children under 5 years of age (%)		4.3	2012	●	↑
Prevalence of obesity, BMI ≥ 30 (% of adult population)		14.0	2016	●	↓
Human Trophic Level (best 2–3 worst)		2.4	2007	●	●
Cereal yield (tonnes per hectare of harvested land)		NA	NA	●	●
Sustainable Nitrogen Management Index (best 0–1.41 worst)		1.2	2015	●	→
Exports of hazardous pesticides (tonnes per million population)		NA	NA	●	●
SDG3 – Good Health and Well-Being					
Maternal mortality rate (per 100,000 live births)		53	2017	●	↑
Neonatal mortality rate (per 1,000 live births)		8.4	2020	●	↑
Mortality rate, under-5 (per 1,000 live births)		13.9	2020	●	↑
Incidence of tuberculosis (per 100,000 population)		11.0	2020	●	↓
New HIV infections (per 1,000 uninfected population)		NA	NA	●	●
Age-standardized death rate due to cardiovascular disease, cancer, diabetes, or chronic respiratory disease in adults aged 30–70 years (%)		21.1	2019	●	↓
Age-standardized death rate attributable to household air pollution and ambient air pollution (per 100,000 population)		49	2016	●	●
Traffic deaths (per 100,000 population)		11.3	2019	●	↑
Life expectancy at birth (years)		73.3	2019	●	→
Adolescent fertility rate (births per 1,000 females aged 15 to 19)		68.3	2018	●	↓
Births attended by skilled health personnel (%)		99.0	2012	●	●
Surviving infants who received 2 WHO-recommended vaccines (%)		97	2020	●	↑
Universal health coverage (UHC) index of service coverage (worst 0–100 best)		70	2019	●	↑
Subjective well-being (average ladder score, worst 0–10 best)		NA	NA	●	●
SDG4 – Quality Education					
Participation rate in pre-primary organized learning (% of children aged 4 to 6)		97.0	2020	●	↑
Net primary enrollment rate (%)		98.6	2020	●	↑
Lower secondary completion rate (%)		101.5	2020	●	↑
Literacy rate (% of population aged 15 to 24)		99.1	2018	●	●
SDG5 – Gender Equality					
Demand for family planning satisfied by modern methods (% of females aged 15 to 49)		NA	NA	●	●
Ratio of female-to-male mean years of education received (%)		98.0	2019	●	●
Ratio of female-to-male labor force participation rate (%)		NA	NA	●	●
Seats held by women in national parliament (%)		24.2	2020	●	↓
SDG6 – Clean Water and Sanitation					
Population using at least basic drinking water services (%)		96.9	2019	●	↑
Population using at least basic sanitation services (%)		100.0	2020	●	↑
Freshwater withdrawal (% of available freshwater resources)		NA	NA	●	●
Anthropogenic wastewater that receives treatment (%)		1.7	2018	●	●
Scarce water consumption embodied in imports (m^3 H_2O eq/capita)		NA	NA	●	●
SDG7 – Affordable and Clean Energy					
Population with access to electricity (%)		100.0	2019	●	↑
Population with access to clean fuels and technology for cooking (%)		100.0	2019	●	↑
CO_2 emissions from fuel combustion per total electricity output ($MtCO_2$/TWh)		0.8	2019	●	↑
Share of renewable energy in total primary energy supply (%)		NA	NA	●	●
SDG8 – Decent Work and Economic Growth					
Adjusted GDP growth (%)		-5.0	2020	●	●
Victims of modern slavery (per 1,000 population)		NA	NA	●	●
Adults with an account at a bank or other financial institution or with a mobile-money-service provider (% of population aged 15 or over)		NA	NA	●	●
Unemployment rate (% of total labor force)		NA	NA	●	●
Fundamental labor rights are effectively guaranteed (worst 0–1 best)		NA	NA	●	●
Fatal work-related accidents embodied in imports (per 100,000 population)		1.6	2015	●	↗

		Value	Year	Rating	Trend
SDG9 – Industry, Innovation and Infrastructure					
Population using the internet (%)		79.0	2020	●	↑
Mobile broadband subscriptions (per 100 population)		92.0	2019	●	↑
Logistics Performance Index: Quality of trade and transport-related infrastructure (worst 1–5 best)		NA	NA	●	●
The Times Higher Education Universities Ranking: Average score of top 3 universities (worst 0–100 best)	*	0.0	2022	●	●
Articles published in academic journals (per 1,000 population)		1.1	2020	●	↑
Expenditure on research and development (% of GDP)		0.2	2016	●	●
SDG10 – Reduced Inequalities					
Gini coefficient		32.1	2018	●	●
Palma ratio		2.6	2018	●	●
SDG11 – Sustainable Cities and Communities					
Proportion of urban population living in slums (%)		NA	NA	●	●
Annual mean concentration of particulate matter of less than 2.5 microns in diameter (PM2.5) (μg/m³)		19.8	2019	●	→
Access to improved water source, piped (% of urban population)		NA	NA	●	●
Satisfaction with public transport (%)		NA	NA	●	●
SDG12 – Responsible Consumption and Production					
Municipal solid waste (kg/capita/day)		1.4	2012	●	●
Electronic waste (kg/capita)		12.6	2019	●	●
Production-based SO_2 emissions (kg/capita)		NA	NA	●	●
SO_2 emissions embodied in imports (kg/capita)		NA	NA	●	●
Production-based nitrogen emissions (kg/capita)		0.9	2015	●	↑
Nitrogen emissions embodied in imports (kg/capita)		13.7	2015	●	→
Exports of plastic waste (kg/capita)		NA	NA	●	●
SDG13 – Climate Action					
CO_2 emissions from fossil fuel combustion and cement production (tCO_2/capita)		5.0	2020	●	→
CO_2 emissions embodied in imports (tCO_2/capita)		NA	NA	●	●
CO_2 emissions embodied in fossil fuel exports (kg/capita)		0.0	2017	●	●
SDG14 – Life Below Water					
Mean area that is protected in marine sites important to biodiversity (%)		71.9	2020	●	↑
Ocean Health Index: Clean Waters score (worst 0–100 best)		78.8	2020	●	↓
Fish caught from overexploited or collapsed stocks (% of total catch)		23.9	2018	●	↑
Fish caught by trawling or dredging (%)		0.0	2018	●	↑
Fish caught that are then discarded (%)		4.8	2018	●	↑
Marine biodiversity threats embodied in imports (per million population)		NA	NA	●	●
SDG15 – Life on Land					
Mean area that is protected in terrestrial sites important to biodiversity (%)		52.8	2020	●	↑
Mean area that is protected in freshwater sites important to biodiversity (%)		98.9	2020	●	↑
Red List Index of species survival (worst 0–1 best)		0.7	2021	●	↓
Permanent deforestation (% of forest area, 5-year average)		NA	NA	●	●
Terrestrial and freshwater biodiversity threats embodied in imports (per million population)		0.5	2018	●	●
SDG16 – Peace, Justice and Strong Institutions					
Homicides (per 100,000 population)		10.2	2019	●	↓
Unsentenced detainees (% of prison population)		13.4	2018	●	↑
Population who feel safe walking alone at night in the city or area where they live (%)		NA	NA	●	●
Property Rights (worst 1–7 best)		4.7	2020	●	↑
Birth registrations with civil authority (% of children under age 5)		NA	NA	●	●
Corruption Perception Index (worst 0–100 best)		70	2021	●	↑
Children involved in child labor (% of population aged 5 to 14)		NA	NA	●	●
Exports of major conventional weapons (TIV constant million USD per 100,000 population)	*	0.0	2020	●	●
Press Freedom Index (best 0–100 worst)		25.7	2021	●	↑
Access to and affordability of justice (worst 0–1 best)		NA	NA	●	●
SDG17 – Partnerships for the Goals					
Government spending on health and education (% of GDP)		7.7	2019	●	→
For high-income and all OECD DAC countries: International concessional public finance, including official development assistance (% of GNI)		NA	NA	●	●
Other countries: Government revenue excluding grants (% of GDP)		NA	NA	●	●
Corporate Tax Haven Score (best 0–100 worst)		68.1	2019	●	●
Statistical Performance Index (worst 0–100 best)		48.6	2019	●	→

* Imputed data point

SIERRA LEONE

Sub-Saharan Africa

OVERALL PERFORMANCE

COUNTRY RANKING

SIERRA LEONE

146/163

COUNTRY SCORE

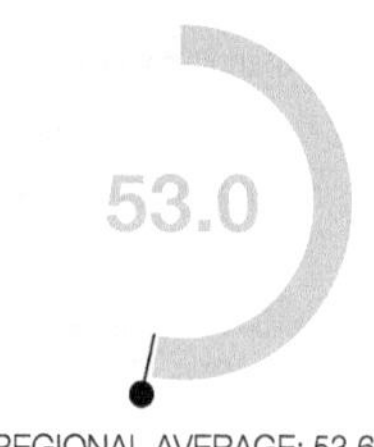

REGIONAL AVERAGE: 53.6

AVERAGE PERFORMANCE BY SDG

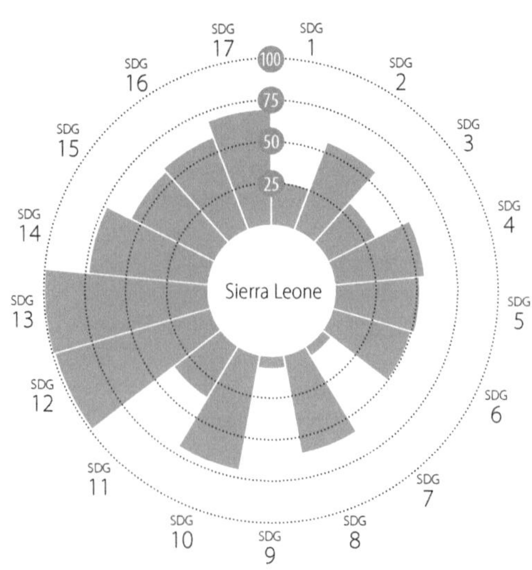

SDG DASHBOARDS AND TRENDS

Major challenges | Significant challenges | Challenges remain | SDG achieved | Information unavailable

Decreasing | Stagnating | Moderately improving | On track or maintaining SDG achievement | Information unavailable

Note: The full title of each SDG is available here: https://sustainabledevelopment.un.org/topics/sustainabledevelopmentgoals

INTERNATIONAL SPILLOVER INDEX

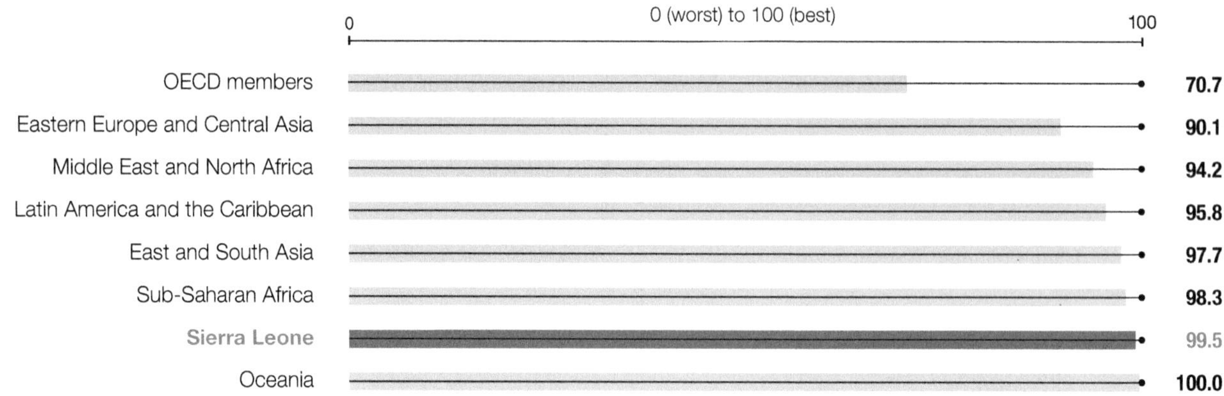

STATISTICAL PERFORMANCE INDEX

0 (worst) to 100 (best)

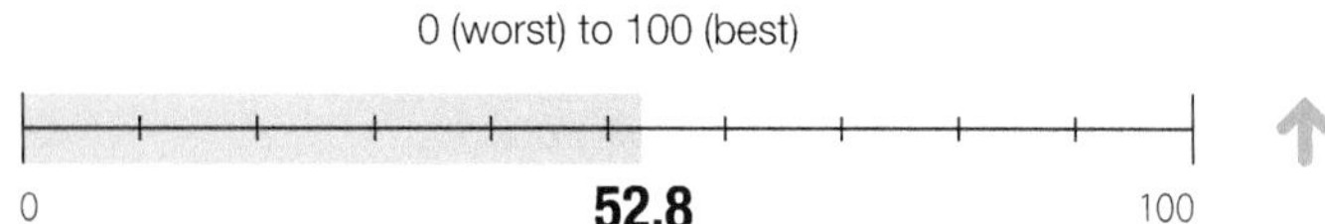

MISSING DATA IN SDG INDEX

2%

SDG1 – No Poverty

Indicator	Value	Year	Rating	Trend
Poverty headcount ratio at $1.90/day (%)	36.1	2022	●	→
Poverty headcount ratio at $3.20/day (%)	70.0	2022	●	→

SDG2 – Zero Hunger

Indicator	Value	Year	Rating	Trend
Prevalence of undernourishment (%)	26.2	2019	●	↓
Prevalence of stunting in children under 5 years of age (%)	29.5	2019	●	→
Prevalence of wasting in children under 5 years of age (%)	5.4	2019	●	→
Prevalence of obesity, BMI ≥ 30 (% of adult population)	8.7	2016	●	↑
Human Trophic Level (best 2–3 worst)	2.2	2017	●	↑
Cereal yield (tonnes per hectare of harvested land)	1.1	2018	●	↓
Sustainable Nitrogen Management Index (best 0–1.41 worst)	0.8	2015	●	→
Exports of hazardous pesticides (tonnes per million population)	0.0	2019	●	●

SDG3 – Good Health and Well-Being

Indicator	Value	Year	Rating	Trend
Maternal mortality rate (per 100,000 live births)	1120	2017	●	→
Neonatal mortality rate (per 1,000 live births)	31.4	2020	●	→
Mortality rate, under-5 (per 1,000 live births)	107.8	2020	●	↗
Incidence of tuberculosis (per 100,000 population)	298.0	2020	●	→
New HIV infections (per 1,000 uninfected population)	0.7	2020	●	↗
Age-standardized death rate due to cardiovascular disease, cancer, diabetes, or chronic respiratory disease in adults aged 30–70 years (%)	23.6	2019	●	↓
Age-standardized death rate attributable to household air pollution and ambient air pollution (per 100,000 population)	324	2016	●	●
Traffic deaths (per 100,000 population)	33.0	2019	●	↓
Life expectancy at birth (years)	60.8	2019	●	↗
Adolescent fertility rate (births per 1,000 females aged 15 to 19)	102.0	2018	●	↑
Births attended by skilled health personnel (%)	86.9	2019	●	●
Surviving infants who received 2 WHO-recommended vaccines (%)	87	2020	●	↑
Universal health coverage (UHC) index of service coverage (worst 0–100 best)	39	2019	●	→
Subjective well-being (average ladder score, worst 0–10 best)	3.7	2021	●	↓

SDG4 – Quality Education

Indicator	Value	Year	Rating	Trend
Participation rate in pre-primary organized learning (% of children aged 4 to 6)	41.7	2018	●	●
Net primary enrollment rate (%)	98.4	2020	●	↑
Lower secondary completion rate (%)	77.6	2020	●	↑
Literacy rate (% of population aged 15 to 24)	66.6	2018	●	●

SDG5 – Gender Equality

Indicator	Value	Year	Rating	Trend
Demand for family planning satisfied by modern methods (% of females aged 15 to 49)	53.0	2019	●	→
Ratio of female-to-male mean years of education received (%)	64.4	2019	●	→
Ratio of female-to-male labor force participation rate (%)	100.6	2020	●	↑
Seats held by women in national parliament (%)	12.3	2020	●	↓

SDG6 – Clean Water and Sanitation

Indicator	Value	Year	Rating	Trend
Population using at least basic drinking water services (%)	63.8	2020	●	→
Population using at least basic sanitation services (%)	16.5	2020	●	→
Freshwater withdrawal (% of available freshwater resources)	0.5	2018	●	●
Anthropogenic wastewater that receives treatment (%)	0.0	2018	●	●
Scarce water consumption embodied in imports (m^3 H_2O eq/capita)	285.5	2018	●	●

SDG7 – Affordable and Clean Energy

Indicator	Value	Year	Rating	Trend
Population with access to electricity (%)	22.7	2019	●	→
Population with access to clean fuels and technology for cooking (%)	0.7	2019	●	→
CO_2 emissions from fuel combustion per total electricity output ($MtCO_2$/TWh)	5.7	2019	●	→
Share of renewable energy in total primary energy supply (%)	NA	NA	●	●

SDG8 – Decent Work and Economic Growth

Indicator	Value	Year	Rating	Trend
Adjusted GDP growth (%)	-5.4	2020	●	●
Victims of modern slavery (per 1,000 population)	5.0	2018	●	●
Adults with an account at a bank or other financial institution or with a mobile-money-service provider (% of population aged 15 or over)	19.8	2017	●	→
Unemployment rate (% of total labor force)	5.0	2022	●	↓
Fundamental labor rights are effectively guaranteed (worst 0–1 best)	0.5	2020	●	↗
Fatal work-related accidents embodied in imports (per 100,000 population)	0.0	2015	●	↑

* Imputed data point

SDG9 – Industry, Innovation and Infrastructure

Indicator	Value	Year	Rating	Trend
Population using the internet (%)	18.0	2020	●	→
Mobile broadband subscriptions (per 100 population)	14.7	2019	●	→
Logistics Performance Index: Quality of trade and transport-related infrastructure (worst 1–5 best)	1.8	2018	●	●
The Times Higher Education Universities Ranking: Average score of top 3 universities (worst 0–100 best)	* 0.0	2022	●	●
Articles published in academic journals (per 1,000 population)	0.0	2020	●	→
Expenditure on research and development (% of GDP)	* 0.0	2018	●	●

SDG10 – Reduced Inequalities

Indicator	Value	Year	Rating	Trend
Gini coefficient	35.7	2018	●	●
Palma ratio	1.5	2018	●	●

SDG11 – Sustainable Cities and Communities

Indicator	Value	Year	Rating	Trend
Proportion of urban population living in slums (%)	59.6	2018	●	↗
Annual mean concentration of particulate matter of less than 2.5 microns in diameter (PM2.5) (μg/m^3)	22.9	2019	●	↓
Access to improved water source, piped (% of urban population)	33.0	2020	●	↓
Satisfaction with public transport (%)	22.0	2021	●	↓

SDG12 – Responsible Consumption and Production

Indicator	Value	Year	Rating	Trend
Municipal solid waste (kg/capita/day)	0.3	2004	●	●
Electronic waste (kg/capita)	0.5	2019	●	●
Production-based SO_2 emissions (kg/capita)	0.8	2018	●	●
SO_2 emissions embodied in imports (kg/capita)	0.1	2018	●	●
Production-based nitrogen emissions (kg/capita)	5.3	2015	●	↑
Nitrogen emissions embodied in imports (kg/capita)	0.4	2015	●	↑
Exports of plastic waste (kg/capita)	0.0	2017	●	●

SDG13 – Climate Action

Indicator	Value	Year	Rating	Trend
CO_2 emissions from fossil fuel combustion and cement production (tCO_2/capita)	0.1	2020	●	↑
CO_2 emissions embodied in imports (tCO_2/capita)	0.1	2018	●	↑
CO_2 emissions embodied in fossil fuel exports (kg/capita)	0.0	2018	●	●

SDG14 – Life Below Water

Indicator	Value	Year	Rating	Trend
Mean area that is protected in marine sites important to biodiversity (%)	33.3	2020	●	→
Ocean Health Index: Clean Waters score (worst 0–100 best)	43.4	2020	●	→
Fish caught from overexploited or collapsed stocks (% of total catch)	2.2	2018	●	↑
Fish caught by trawling or dredging (%)	13.3	2018	●	↑
Fish caught that are then discarded (%)	0.2	2018	●	↑
Marine biodiversity threats embodied in imports (per million population)	0.0	2018	●	●

SDG15 – Life on Land

Indicator	Value	Year	Rating	Trend
Mean area that is protected in terrestrial sites important to biodiversity (%)	49.2	2020	●	→
Mean area that is protected in freshwater sites important to biodiversity (%)	51.5	2020	●	→
Red List Index of species survival (worst 0–1 best)	0.9	2021	●	↑
Permanent deforestation (% of forest area, 5-year average)	2.2	2020	●	→
Terrestrial and freshwater biodiversity threats embodied in imports (per million population)	0.0	2018	●	●

SDG16 – Peace, Justice and Strong Institutions

Indicator	Value	Year	Rating	Trend
Homicides (per 100,000 population)	1.7	2015	●	●
Unsentenced detainees (% of prison population)	30.1	2018	●	↑
Population who feel safe walking alone at night in the city or area where they live (%)	46	2021	●	↓
Property Rights (worst 1–7 best)	3.3	2020	●	●
Birth registrations with civil authority (% of children under age 5)	90.4	2020	●	●
Corruption Perception Index (worst 0–100 best)	34	2021	●	→
Children involved in child labor (% of population aged 5 to 14)	25.2	2019	●	●
Exports of major conventional weapons (TIV constant million USD per 100,000 population)	* 0.0	2020	●	●
Press Freedom Index (best 0–100 worst)	29.6	2021	●	↑
Access to and affordability of justice (worst 0–1 best)	0.5	2020	●	↓

SDG17 – Partnerships for the Goals

Indicator	Value	Year	Rating	Trend
Government spending on health and education (% of GDP)	10.5	2020	●	↑
For high-income and all OECD DAC countries: International concessional public finance, including official development assistance (% of GNI)	NA	NA	●	●
Other countries: Government revenue excluding grants (% of GDP)	NA	NA	●	●
Corporate Tax Haven Score (best 0–100 worst)	* 0.0	2019	●	●
Statistical Performance Index (worst 0–100 best)	52.8	2019	●	↑

SINGAPORE

East and South Asia

OVERALL PERFORMANCE

COUNTRY RANKING

SINGAPORE

60/163

COUNTRY SCORE

REGIONAL AVERAGE: 65.9

AVERAGE PERFORMANCE BY SDG

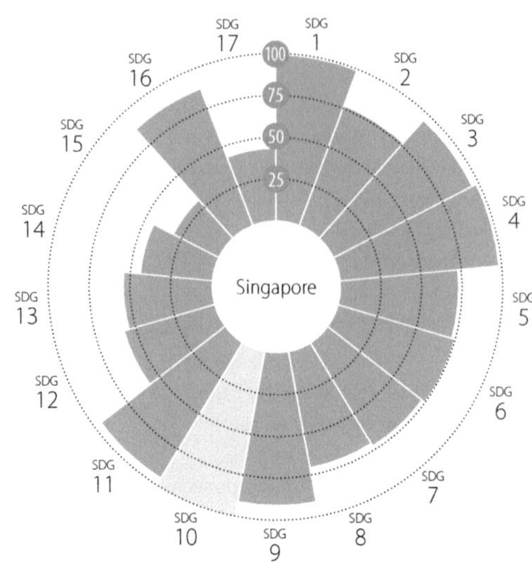

SDG DASHBOARDS AND TRENDS

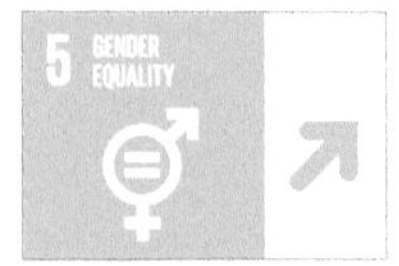

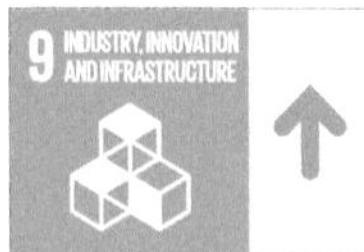

Note: The full title of each SDG is available here: https://sustainabledevelopment.un.org/topics/sustainabledevelopmentgoals

INTERNATIONAL SPILLOVER INDEX

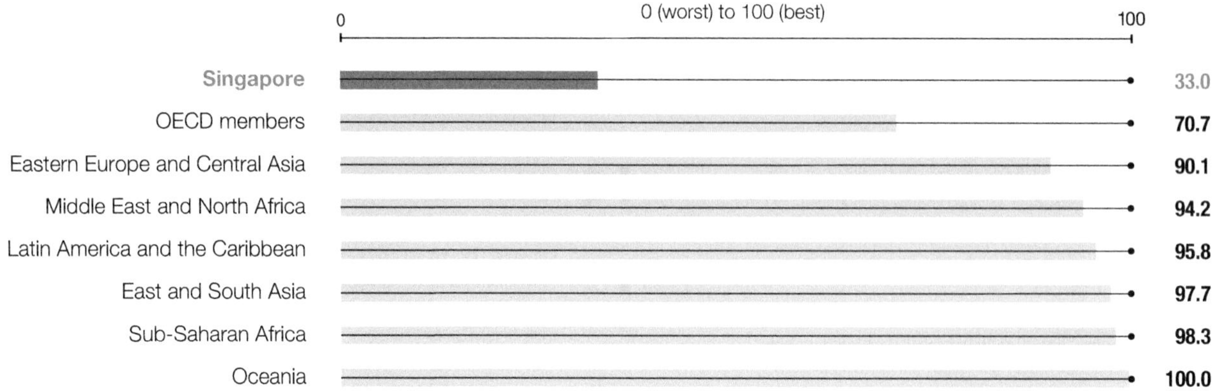

STATISTICAL PERFORMANCE INDEX

0 (worst) to 100 (best)

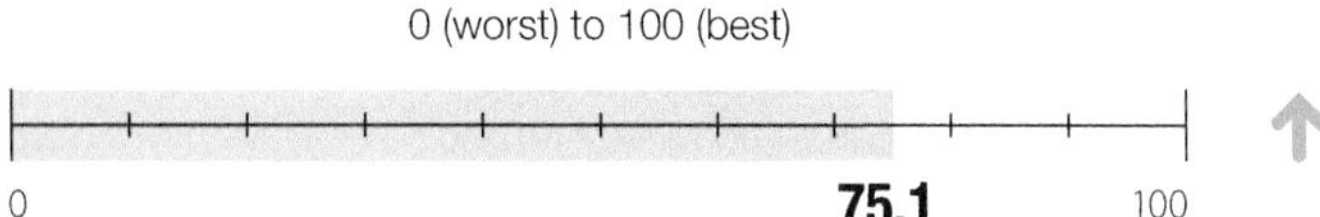

MISSING DATA IN SDG INDEX

10%

SDG1 – No Poverty	Value	Year	Rating	Trend
Poverty headcount ratio at $1.90/day (%)	0.8	2022	●	↑
Poverty headcount ratio at $3.20/day (%)	1.0	2022	●	↑
SDG2 – Zero Hunger				
Prevalence of undernourishment (%)	* 1.2	2019	●	●
Prevalence of stunting in children under 5 years of age (%)	4.4	2000	●	↑
Prevalence of wasting in children under 5 years of age (%)	3.6	2000	●	↑
Prevalence of obesity, BMI ≥ 30 (% of adult population)	6.1	2016	●	↑
Human Trophic Level (best 2–3 worst)	NA	NA	●	●
Cereal yield (tonnes per hectare of harvested land)	NA	NA	●	●
Sustainable Nitrogen Management Index (best 0–1.41 worst)	1.1	2015	●	↓
Exports of hazardous pesticides (tonnes per million population)	14.6	2019	●	●
SDG3 – Good Health and Well-Being				
Maternal mortality rate (per 100,000 live births)	8	2017	●	↑
Neonatal mortality rate (per 1,000 live births)	0.8	2020	●	↑
Mortality rate, under-5 (per 1,000 live births)	2.2	2020	●	↑
Incidence of tuberculosis (per 100,000 population)	46.0	2020	●	→
New HIV infections (per 1,000 uninfected population)	0.0	2020	●	↑
Age-standardized death rate due to cardiovascular disease, cancer, diabetes, or chronic respiratory disease in adults aged 30–70 years (%)	9.5	2019	●	↑
Age-standardized death rate attributable to household air pollution and ambient air pollution (per 100,000 population)	26	2016	●	●
Traffic deaths (per 100,000 population)	2.1	2019	●	↑
Life expectancy at birth (years)	83.2	2019	●	↑
Adolescent fertility rate (births per 1,000 females aged 15 to 19)	2.1	2019	●	↑
Births attended by skilled health personnel (%)	99.5	2018	●	↑
Surviving infants who received 2 WHO-recommended vaccines (%)	95	2019	●	↑
Universal health coverage (UHC) index of service coverage (worst 0–100 best)	86	2019	●	↑
Subjective well-being (average ladder score, worst 0–10 best)	6.6	2021	●	↑
SDG4 – Quality Education				
Participation rate in pre-primary organized learning (% of children aged 4 to 6)	94.2	2019	●	↑
Net primary enrollment rate (%)	99.9	2019	●	↑
Lower secondary completion rate (%)	100.2	2019	●	↑
Literacy rate (% of population aged 15 to 24)	99.9	2019	●	↑
SDG5 – Gender Equality				
Demand for family planning satisfied by modern methods (% of females aged 15 to 49)	* 77.4	2022	●	↗
Ratio of female-to-male mean years of education received (%)	92.6	2019	●	↗
Ratio of female-to-male labor force participation rate (%)	77.4	2020	●	↑
Seats held by women in national parliament (%)	29.5	2020	●	↑
SDG6 – Clean Water and Sanitation				
Population using at least basic drinking water services (%)	100.0	2020	●	↑
Population using at least basic sanitation services (%)	100.0	2020	●	↑
Freshwater withdrawal (% of available freshwater resources)	82.0	2018	●	●
Anthropogenic wastewater that receives treatment (%)	100.0	2018	●	●
Scarce water consumption embodied in imports (m^3 H_2O eq/capita)	5508.5	2018	●	●
SDG7 – Affordable and Clean Energy				
Population with access to electricity (%)	100.0	2019	●	↑
Population with access to clean fuels and technology for cooking (%)	100.0	2019	●	↑
CO_2 emissions from fuel combustion per total electricity output ($MtCO_2$/TWh)	0.7	2019	●	↑
Share of renewable energy in total primary energy supply (%)	1.2	2019	●	→
SDG8 – Decent Work and Economic Growth				
Adjusted GDP growth (%)	-0.1	2020	●	●
Victims of modern slavery (per 1,000 population)	3.4	2018	●	●
Adults with an account at a bank or other financial institution or with a mobile-money-service provider (% of population aged 15 or over)	97.9	2017	●	↑
Unemployment rate (% of total labor force)	3.9	2022	●	↑
Fundamental labor rights are effectively guaranteed (worst 0–1 best)	0.7	2020	●	↑
Fatal work-related accidents embodied in imports (per 100,000 population)	6.6	2015	●	↗

* Imputed data point

SDG9 – Industry, Innovation and Infrastructure	Value	Year	Rating	Trend
Population using the internet (%)	92.0	2020	●	↑
Mobile broadband subscriptions (per 100 population)	155.6	2019	●	↑
Logistics Performance Index: Quality of trade and transport-related infrastructure (worst 1–5 best)	4.1	2018	●	↑
The Times Higher Education Universities Ranking: Average score of top 3 universities (worst 0–100 best)	79.1	2022	●	●
Articles published in academic journals (per 1,000 population)	3.9	2020	●	↑
Expenditure on research and development (% of GDP)	1.9	2017	●	↑
SDG10 – Reduced Inequalities				
Gini coefficient	NA	NA	●	●
Palma ratio	NA	NA	●	●
SDG11 – Sustainable Cities and Communities				
Proportion of urban population living in slums (%)	NA	NA	●	●
Annual mean concentration of particulate matter of less than 2.5 microns in diameter (PM2.5) (μg/m³)	19.0	2019	●	↗
Access to improved water source, piped (% of urban population)	100.0	2020	●	↑
Satisfaction with public transport (%)	93.0	2021	●	↑
SDG12 – Responsible Consumption and Production				
Municipal solid waste (kg/capita/day)	0.9	2019	●	●
Electronic waste (kg/capita)	19.9	2019	●	●
Production-based SO_2 emissions (kg/capita)	34.7	2018	●	●
SO_2 emissions embodied in imports (kg/capita)	20.4	2018	●	●
Production-based nitrogen emissions (kg/capita)	0.1	2015	●	↑
Nitrogen emissions embodied in imports (kg/capita)	32.5	2015	●	↓
Exports of plastic waste (kg/capita)	5.7	2020	●	●
SDG13 – Climate Action				
CO_2 emissions from fossil fuel combustion and cement production (tCO_2/capita)	7.8	2020	●	↑
CO_2 emissions embodied in imports (tCO_2/capita)	7.5	2018	●	↑
CO_2 emissions embodied in fossil fuel exports (kg/capita)	0.0	2020	●	●
SDG14 – Life Below Water				
Mean area that is protected in marine sites important to biodiversity (%)	3.3	2020	●	→
Ocean Health Index: Clean Waters score (worst 0–100 best)	38.8	2020	●	↓
Fish caught from overexploited or collapsed stocks (% of total catch)	NA	NA	●	●
Fish caught by trawling or dredging (%)	0.0	2018	●	↑
Fish caught that are then discarded (%)	0.0	2018	●	↑
Marine biodiversity threats embodied in imports (per million population)	3.2	2018	●	●
SDG15 – Life on Land				
Mean area that is protected in terrestrial sites important to biodiversity (%)	21.1	2020	●	→
Mean area that is protected in freshwater sites important to biodiversity (%)	NA	NA	●	●
Red List Index of species survival (worst 0–1 best)	0.8	2021	●	↓
Permanent deforestation (% of forest area, 5-year average)	0.9	2020	●	↓
Terrestrial and freshwater biodiversity threats embodied in imports (per million population)	12.6	2018	●	●
SDG16 – Peace, Justice and Strong Institutions				
Homicides (per 100,000 population)	0.2	2020	●	↑
Unsentenced detainees (% of prison population)	10.5	2019	●	↑
Population who feel safe walking alone at night in the city or area where they live (%)	95	2021	●	↑
Property Rights (worst 1–7 best)	6.5	2020	●	↑
Birth registrations with civil authority (% of children under age 5)	99.9	2020	●	●
Corruption Perception Index (worst 0–100 best)	85	2021	●	↑
Children involved in child labor (% of population aged 5 to 14)	NA	NA	●	●
Exports of major conventional weapons (TIV constant million USD per 100,000 population)	0.8	2020	●	●
Press Freedom Index (best 0–100 worst)	55.2	2021	●	↓
Access to and affordability of justice (worst 0–1 best)	0.6	2020	●	→
SDG17 – Partnerships for the Goals				
Government spending on health and education (% of GDP)	4.6	2020	●	↓
For high-income and all OECD DAC countries: International concessional public finance, including official development assistance (% of GNI)	NA	NA	●	●
Other countries: Government revenue excluding grants (% of GDP)	NA	NA	●	●
Corporate Tax Haven Score (best 0–100 worst)	81.4	2019	●	●
Statistical Performance Index (worst 0–100 best)	75.1	2019	●	↑

SLOVAK REPUBLIC

OECD Countries

OVERALL PERFORMANCE

COUNTRY RANKING

SLOVAK REPUBLIC

24/163

COUNTRY SCORE

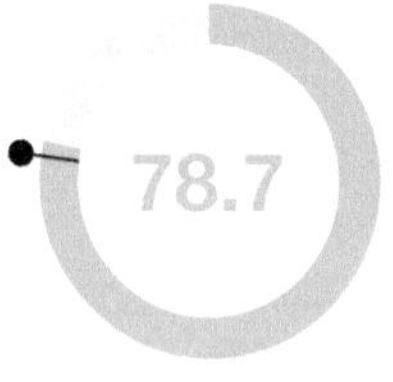

REGIONAL AVERAGE: 77.2

AVERAGE PERFORMANCE BY SDG

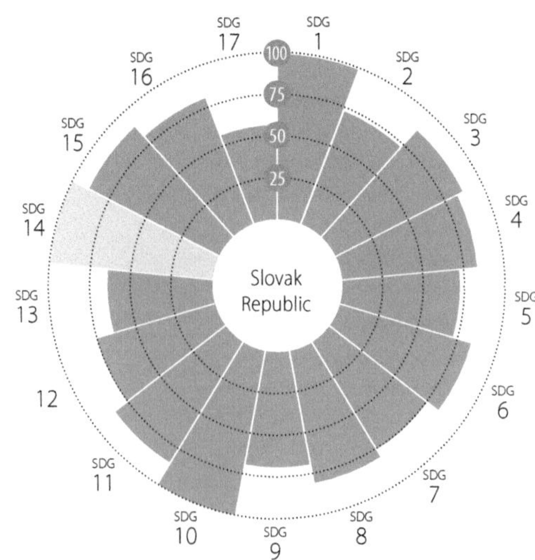

SDG DASHBOARDS AND TRENDS

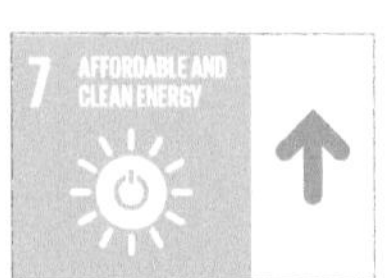

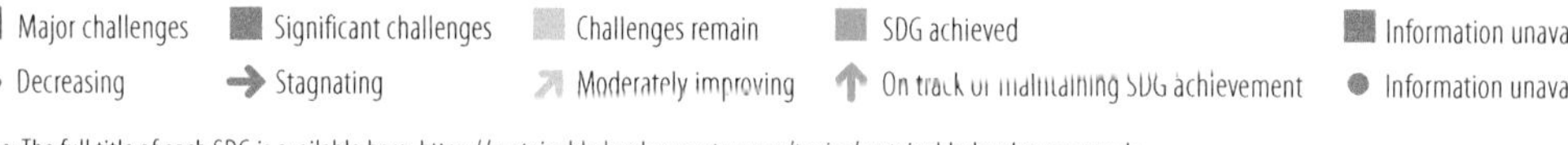

Note: The full title of each SDG is available here: https://sustainabledevelopment.un.org/topics/sustainabledevelopmentgoals

INTERNATIONAL SPILLOVER INDEX

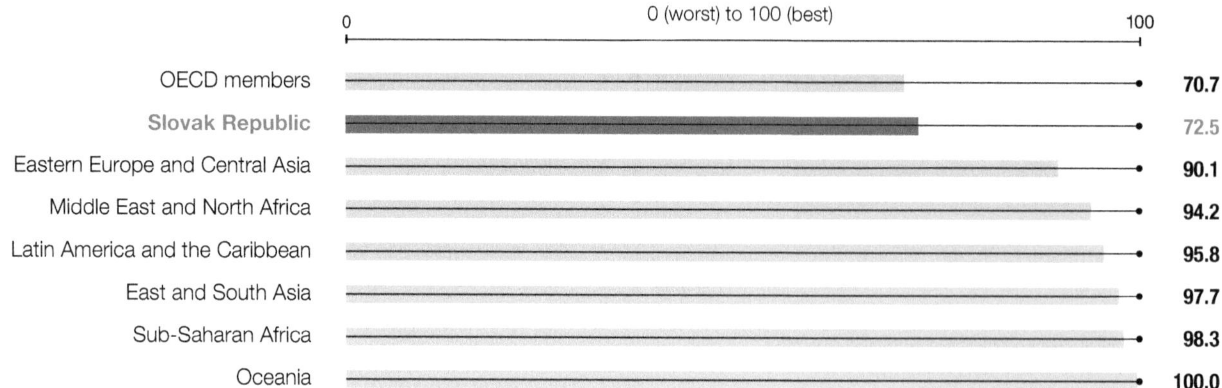

STATISTICAL PERFORMANCE INDEX

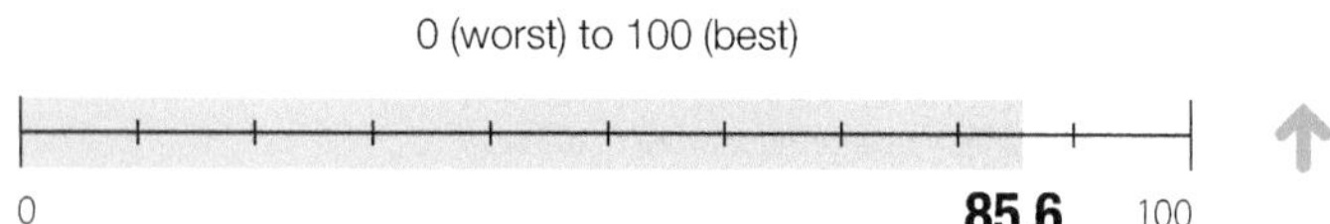

MISSING DATA IN SDG INDEX

1%

SLOVAK REPUBLIC

SDG1 – No Poverty		Value	Year	Rating	Trend
Poverty headcount ratio at $1.90/day (%)		0.6	2022	●	↑
Poverty headcount ratio at $3.20/day (%)		0.8	2022	●	↑
Poverty rate after taxes and transfers (%)		7.8	2019	●	↑
SDG2 – Zero Hunger					
Prevalence of undernourishment (%)		4.0	2019	●	↑
Prevalence of stunting in children under 5 years of age (%)	*	2.6	2019	●	↑
Prevalence of wasting in children under 5 years of age (%)	*	0.7	2019	●	↑
Prevalence of obesity, BMI ≥ 30 (% of adult population)		20.5	2016	●	↓
Human Trophic Level (best 2–3 worst)		2.4	2017	●	↓
Cereal yield (tonnes per hectare of harvested land)		5.4	2018	●	↑
Sustainable Nitrogen Management Index (best 0–1.41 worst)		0.5	2015	●	↓
Yield gap closure (% of potential yield)		48.7	2018	●	●
Exports of hazardous pesticides (tonnes per million population)		0.4	2019	●	●
SDG3 – Good Health and Well-Being					
Maternal mortality rate (per 100,000 live births)		5	2017	●	↑
Neonatal mortality rate (per 1,000 live births)		3.0	2020	●	↑
Mortality rate, under-5 (per 1,000 live births)		5.8	2020	●	↑
Incidence of tuberculosis (per 100,000 population)		3.2	2020	●	↑
New HIV infections (per 1,000 uninfected population)		1.0	2020	●	→
Age-standardized death rate due to cardiovascular disease, cancer, diabetes, or chronic respiratory disease in adults aged 30–70 years (%)		15.5	2019	●	↑
Age-standardized death rate attributable to household air pollution and ambient air pollution (per 100,000 population)		34	2016	●	●
Traffic deaths (per 100,000 population)		6.1	2019	●	↑
Life expectancy at birth (years)		78.2	2019	●	↑
Adolescent fertility rate (births per 1,000 females aged 15 to 19)		26.3	2018	●	↓
Births attended by skilled health personnel (%)		98.0	2018	●	↑
Surviving infants who received 2 WHO-recommended vaccines (%)		96	2020	●	↑
Universal health coverage (UHC) index of service coverage (worst 0–100 best)		77	2019	●	↑
Subjective well-being (average ladder score, worst 0–10 best)		6.4	2021	●	↑
Gap in life expectancy at birth among regions (years)		2.1	2019	●	↑
Gap in self-reported health status by income (percentage points)		20.4	2019	●	↓
Daily smokers (% of population aged 15 and over)		21.0	2019	●	↑
SDG4 – Quality Education					
Participation rate in pre-primary organized learning (% of children aged 4 to 6)		84.9	2019	●	→
Net primary enrollment rate (%)		96.7	2019	●	↑
Lower secondary completion rate (%)		83.2	2019	●	↓
Literacy rate (% of population aged 15 to 24)		NA	NA	●	●
Tertiary educational attainment (% of population aged 25 to 34)		39.0	2020	●	↑
PISA score (worst 0–600 best)		469.3	2018	●	↑
Variation in science performance explained by socio-economic status (%)		18.5	2018	●	↓
Underachievers in science (% of 15-year-olds)		29.3	2018	●	→
SDG5 – Gender Equality					
Demand for family planning satisfied by modern methods (% of females aged 15 to 49)	*	78.9	2022	●	↑
Ratio of female-to-male mean years of education received (%)		98.4	2019	●	↑
Ratio of female-to-male labor force participation rate (%)		77.9	2020	●	↑
Seats held by women in national parliament (%)		22.7	2020	●	↗
Gender wage gap (% of male median wage)		11.0	2020	●	↑
SDG6 – Clean Water and Sanitation					
Population using at least basic drinking water services (%)		99.8	2020	●	↑
Population using at least basic sanitation services (%)		97.5	2020	●	↑
Freshwater withdrawal (% of available freshwater resources)		2.4	2018	●	●
Anthropogenic wastewater that receives treatment (%)		43.7	2018	●	●
Scarce water consumption embodied in imports (m^3 H_2O eq/capita)		2602.6	2018	●	●
Population using safely managed water services (%)		99.2	2020	●	↑
Population using safely managed sanitation services (%)		81.9	2020	●	↓
SDG7 – Affordable and Clean Energy					
Population with access to electricity (%)		100.0	2019	●	↑
Population with access to clean fuels and technology for cooking (%)		100.0	2019	●	↑
CO_2 emissions from fuel combustion per total electricity output ($MtCO_2$/TWh)		1.1	2019	●	↑
Share of renewable energy in total primary energy supply (%)		12.7	2019	●	↑
SDG8 – Decent Work and Economic Growth					
Adjusted GDP growth (%)		-1.5	2020	●	●
Victims of modern slavery (per 1,000 population)		2.9	2018	●	●
Adults with an account at a bank or other financial institution or with a mobile-money-service provider (% of population aged 15 or over)		84.2	2017	●	↑
Fundamental labor rights are effectively guaranteed (worst 0–1 best)		0.7	2020	●	●
Fatal work-related accidents embodied in imports (per 100,000 population)		0.6	2015	●	↑
Employment-to-population ratio (%)		69.5	2020	●	↑
Youth not in employment, education or training (NEET) (% of population aged 15 to 29)		14.2	2020	●	↑

* Imputed data point

SDG9 – Industry, Innovation and Infrastructure		Value	Year	Rating	Trend
Population using the internet (%)		89.9	2020	●	↑
Mobile broadband subscriptions (per 100 population)		89.1	2019	●	↑
Logistics Performance Index: Quality of trade and transport-related infrastructure (worst 1–5 best)		3.0	2018	●	↑
The Times Higher Education Universities Ranking: Average score of top 3 universities (worst 0–100 best)		24.8	2022	●	●
Articles published in academic journals (per 1,000 population)		1.6	2020	●	↑
Expenditure on research and development (% of GDP)		0.8	2018	●	↓
Researchers (per 1,000 employed population)		6.9	2019	●	↑
Triadic patent families filed (per million population)		2.1	2019	●	→
Gap in internet access by income (percentage points)		10.5	2020	●	↑
Female share of graduates from STEM fields at the tertiary level (%)		35.2	2017	●	↑
SDG10 – Reduced Inequalities					
Gini coefficient		25.0	2018	●	↑
Palma ratio		0.7	2019	●	↑
Elderly poverty rate (% of population aged 66 or over)		6.6	2019	●	↓
SDG11 – Sustainable Cities and Communities					
Proportion of urban population living in slums (%)	*	0.0	2018	●	↑
Annual mean concentration of particulate matter of less than 2.5 microns in diameter (PM2.5) (μg/m^3)		16.9	2019	●	↗
Access to improved water source, piped (% of urban population)		97.2	2018	●	●
Satisfaction with public transport (%)		56.0	2021	●	↗
Population with rent overburden (%)		3.4	2019	●	↑
SDG12 – Responsible Consumption and Production					
Electronic waste (kg/capita)		12.8	2019	●	●
Production-based SO_2 emissions (kg/capita)		14.1	2018	●	●
SO_2 emissions embodied in imports (kg/capita)		6.2	2018	●	●
Production-based nitrogen emissions (kg/capita)		13.4	2015	●	↑
Nitrogen emissions embodied in imports (kg/capita)		9.8	2015	●	↓
Exports of plastic waste (kg/capita)		3.6	2020	●	●
Non-recycled municipal solid waste (kg/capita/day)		0.7	2019	●	↑
SDG13 – Climate Action					
CO_2 emissions from fossil fuel combustion and cement production (tCO_2/capita)		5.6	2020	●	→
CO_2 emissions embodied in imports (tCO_2/capita)		2.5	2018	●	↓
CO_2 emissions embodied in fossil fuel exports (kg/capita)		90.0	2020	●	●
Carbon Pricing Score at EUR60/tCO_2 (%, worst 0–100 best)		36.0	2018	●	↗
SDG14 – Life Below Water					
Mean area that is protected in marine sites important to biodiversity (%)		NA	NA	●	●
Ocean Health Index: Clean Waters score (worst 0–100 best)		NA	NA	●	●
Fish caught from overexploited or collapsed stocks (% of total catch)		NA	NA	●	●
Fish caught by trawling or dredging (%)		NA	NA	●	●
Fish caught that are then discarded (%)		NA	NA	●	●
Marine biodiversity threats embodied in imports (per million population)		0.1	2018	●	●
SDG15 – Life on Land					
Mean area that is protected in terrestrial sites important to biodiversity (%)		85.8	2020	●	↑
Mean area that is protected in freshwater sites important to biodiversity (%)		86.3	2020	●	↑
Red List Index of species survival (worst 0–1 best)		1.0	2021	●	↑
Permanent deforestation (% of forest area, 5-year average)		0.0	2020	●	↑
Terrestrial and freshwater biodiversity threats embodied in imports (per million population)		1.4	2018	●	●
SDG16 – Peace, Justice and Strong Institutions					
Homicides (per 100,000 population)		1.2	2020	●	↑
Unsentenced detainees (% of prison population)		15.5	2019	●	↑
Population who feel safe walking alone at night in the city or area where they live (%)		75	2021	●	↑
Property Rights (worst 1–7 best)		4.3	2020	●	↑
Birth registrations with civil authority (% of children under age 5)		100.0	2020	●	●
Corruption Perception Index (worst 0–100 best)		52	2021	●	→
Children involved in child labor (% of population aged 5 to 14)	*	0.0	2019	●	●
Exports of major conventional weapons (TIV constant million USD per 100,000 population)		0.2	2020	●	●
Press Freedom Index (best 0–100 worst)		23.0	2021	●	↑
Access to and affordability of justice (worst 0–1 best)		0.6	2020	●	●
Persons held in prison (per 100,000 population)		193.4	2019	●	↓
SDG17 – Partnerships for the Goals					
Government spending on health and education (% of GDP)		9.5	2019	●	↓
For high-income and all OECD DAC countries: International concessional public finance, including official development assistance (% of GNI)		0.1	2021	●	→
Other countries: Government revenue excluding grants (% of GDP)		NA	NA	●	●
Corporate Tax Haven Score (best 0–100 worst)		53.0	2019	●	●
Financial Secrecy Score (best 0–100 worst)		50.9	2020	●	●
Shifted profits of multinationals (US$ billion)		1.1	2018	●	↑
Statistical Performance Index (worst 0–100 best)		85.6	2019	●	↑

SLOVENIA

OECD Countries

OVERALL PERFORMANCE

COUNTRY RANKING

SLOVENIA

15 /163

COUNTRY SCORE

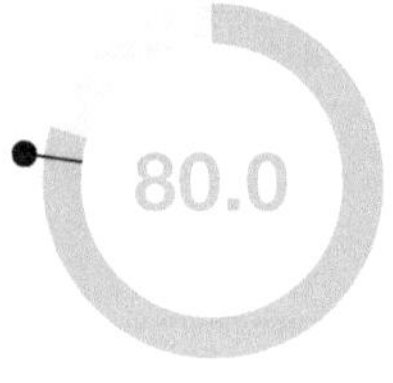

REGIONAL AVERAGE: 77.2

AVERAGE PERFORMANCE BY SDG

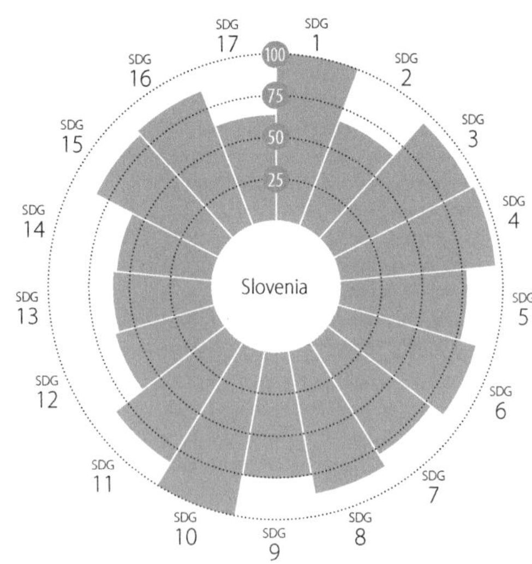

SDG DASHBOARDS AND TRENDS

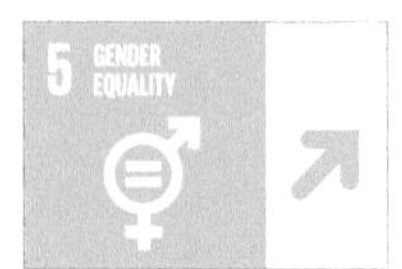

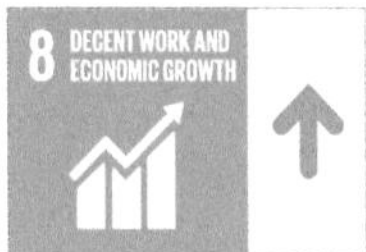

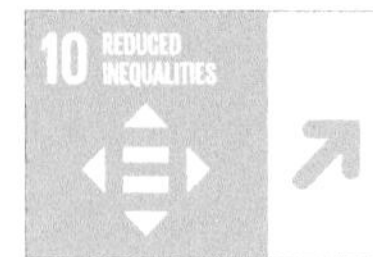

Major challenges | Significant challenges | Challenges remain | SDG achieved | Information unavailable

Decreasing | Stagnating | Moderately improving | On track or maintaining SDG achievement | Information unavailable

Note: The full title of each SDG is available here: https://sustainabledevelopment.un.org/topics/sustainabledevelopmentgoals

INTERNATIONAL SPILLOVER INDEX

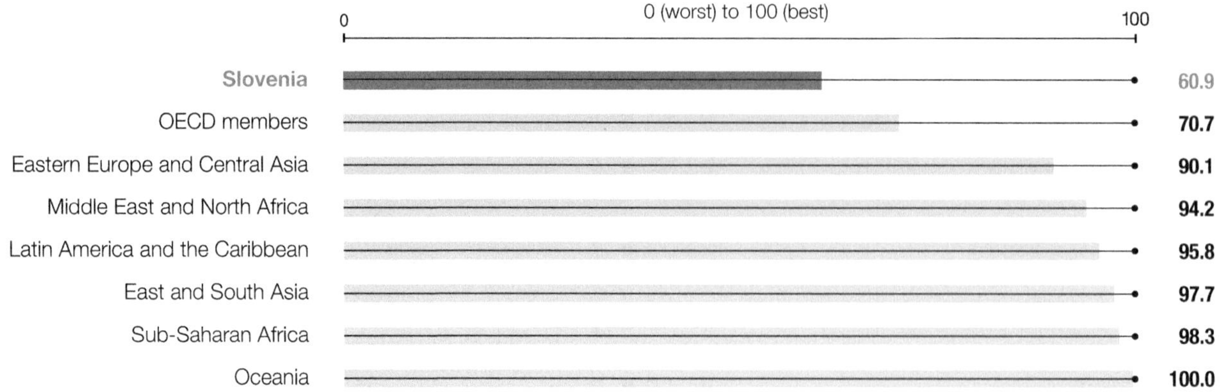

STATISTICAL PERFORMANCE INDEX

0 (worst) to 100 (best)

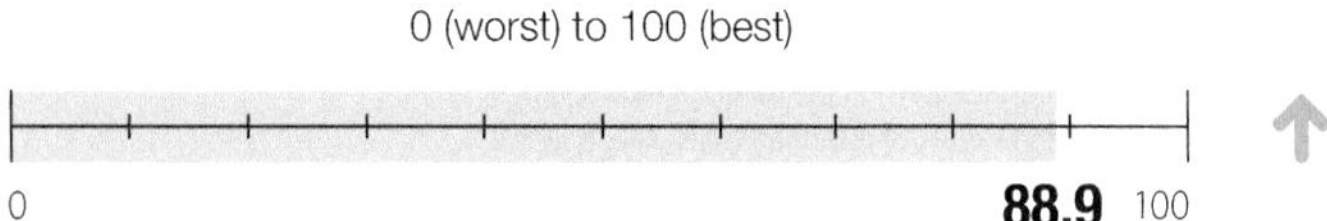

MISSING DATA IN SDG INDEX

2%

SDG1 – No Poverty

	Value	Year	Rating	Trend
Poverty headcount ratio at $1.90/day (%)	0.1	2022	●	↑
Poverty headcount ratio at $3.20/day (%)	0.1	2022	●	↑
Poverty rate after taxes and transfers (%)	7.4	2019	●	↑

SDG2 – Zero Hunger

	Value	Year	Rating	Trend
Prevalence of undernourishment (%)	2.5	2019	●	↑
Prevalence of stunting in children under 5 years of age (%) *	2.6	2019	●	↑
Prevalence of wasting in children under 5 years of age (%) *	0.7	2019	●	↑
Prevalence of obesity, BMI ≥ 30 (% of adult population)	20.2	2016	●	↓
Human Trophic Level (best 2–3 worst)	2.4	2017	●	↓
Cereal yield (tonnes per hectare of harvested land)	6.1	2018	●	↑
Sustainable Nitrogen Management Index (best 0–1.41 worst)	0.7	2015	●	→
Yield gap closure (% of potential yield)	57.5	2018	●	●
Exports of hazardous pesticides (tonnes per million population)	92.1	2019	●	●

SDG3 – Good Health and Well-Being

	Value	Year	Rating	Trend
Maternal mortality rate (per 100,000 live births)	7	2017	●	↑
Neonatal mortality rate (per 1,000 live births)	1.2	2020	●	↑
Mortality rate, under-5 (per 1,000 live births)	2.2	2020	●	↑
Incidence of tuberculosis (per 100,000 population)	4.1	2020	●	↑
New HIV infections (per 1,000 uninfected population)	0.0	2020	●	↑
Age-standardized death rate due to cardiovascular disease, cancer, diabetes, or chronic respiratory disease in adults aged 30–70 years (%)	11.5	2019	●	↑
Age-standardized death rate attributable to household air pollution and ambient air pollution (per 100,000 population)	23	2016	●	●
Traffic deaths (per 100,000 population)	5.1	2019	●	↑
Life expectancy at birth (years)	81.3	2019	●	↑
Adolescent fertility rate (births per 1,000 females aged 15 to 19)	3.8	2018	●	↑
Births attended by skilled health personnel (%)	99.8	2012	●	●
Surviving infants who received 2 WHO-recommended vaccines (%)	94	2020	●	↑
Universal health coverage (UHC) index of service coverage (worst 0–100 best)	80	2019	●	↑
Subjective well-being (average ladder score, worst 0–10 best)	6.8	2021	●	↑
Gap in life expectancy at birth among regions (years)	2.1	2019	●	↑
Gap in self-reported health status by income (percentage points)	30.3	2019	●	↓
Daily smokers (% of population aged 15 and over)	17.4	2019	●	↑

SDG4 – Quality Education

	Value	Year	Rating	Trend
Participation rate in pre-primary organized learning (% of children aged 4 to 6)	91.6	2019	●	↑
Net primary enrollment rate (%)	99.9	2019	●	↑
Lower secondary completion rate (%)	96.2	2019	●	↑
Literacy rate (% of population aged 15 to 24)	99.8	2014	●	●
Tertiary educational attainment (% of population aged 25 to 34)	45.4	2020	●	↑
PISA score (worst 0–600 best)	503.7	2018	●	↑
Variation in science performance explained by socio-economic status (%)	13.0	2018	●	↗
Underachievers in science (% of 15-year-olds)	14.6	2018	●	↑

SDG5 – Gender Equality

	Value	Year	Rating	Trend
Demand for family planning satisfied by modern methods (% of females aged 15 to 49) *	78.8	2022	●	↑
Ratio of female-to-male mean years of education received (%)	99.2	2019	●	↑
Ratio of female-to-male labor force participation rate (%)	85.3	2020	●	↑
Seats held by women in national parliament (%)	27.8	2020	●	↓
Gender wage gap (% of male median wage)	8.2	2018	●	↓

SDG6 – Clean Water and Sanitation

	Value	Year	Rating	Trend
Population using at least basic drinking water services (%)	99.5	2020	●	↑
Population using at least basic sanitation services (%)	98.1	2020	●	↑
Freshwater withdrawal (% of available freshwater resources)	6.5	2018	●	●
Anthropogenic wastewater that receives treatment (%)	89.1	2018	●	●
Scarce water consumption embodied in imports (m^3 H_2O eq/capita)	5416.0	2018	●	●
Population using safely managed water services (%)	98.3	2020	●	↑
Population using safely managed sanitation services (%)	71.5	2020	●	↑

SDG7 – Affordable and Clean Energy

	Value	Year	Rating	Trend
Population with access to electricity (%)	100.0	2019	●	↑
Population with access to clean fuels and technology for cooking (%)	100.0	2019	●	↑
CO_2 emissions from fuel combustion per total electricity output ($MtCO_2$/TWh)	0.8	2019	●	↑
Share of renewable energy in total primary energy supply (%)	16.2	2019	●	↓

SDG8 – Decent Work and Economic Growth

	Value	Year	Rating	Trend
Adjusted GDP growth (%)	0.2	2020	●	●
Victims of modern slavery (per 1,000 population)	2.2	2018	●	●
Adults with an account at a bank or other financial institution or with a mobile-money-service provider (% of population aged 15 or over)	97.5	2017	●	↑
Fundamental labor rights are effectively guaranteed (worst 0–1 best)	0.8	2020	●	↑
Fatal work-related accidents embodied in imports (per 100,000 population)	0.9	2015	●	↑
Employment-to-population ratio (%)	70.1	2020	●	↑
Youth not in employment, education or training (NEET) (% of population aged 15 to 29)	9.1	2020	●	↑

* Imputed data point

SDG9 – Industry, Innovation and Infrastructure

	Value	Year	Rating	Trend
Population using the internet (%)	86.6	2020	●	↑
Mobile broadband subscriptions (per 100 population)	84.1	2019	●	↑
Logistics Performance Index: Quality of trade and transport-related infrastructure (worst 1–5 best)	3.3	2018	●	↑
The Times Higher Education Universities Ranking: Average score of top 3 universities (worst 0–100 best)	26.4	2022	●	●
Articles published in academic journals (per 1,000 population)	3.3	2020	●	↑
Expenditure on research and development (% of GDP)	2.0	2018	●	↑
Researchers (per 1,000 employed population)	10.0	2019	●	↑
Triadic patent families filed (per million population)	4.6	2019	●	→
Gap in internet access by income (percentage points)	25.7	2020	●	↑
Female share of graduates from STEM fields at the tertiary level (%)	33.3	2017	●	↑

SDG10 – Reduced Inequalities

	Value	Year	Rating	Trend
Gini coefficient	24.6	2018	●	↑
Palma ratio	0.8	2019	●	↑
Elderly poverty rate (% of population aged 66 or over)	13.0	2019	●	→

SDG11 – Sustainable Cities and Communities

	Value	Year	Rating	Trend
Proportion of urban population living in slums (%)	0.0	2018	●	↑
Annual mean concentration of particulate matter of less than 2.5 microns in diameter (PM2.5) (μg/m^3)	15.4	2019	●	↑
Access to improved water source, piped (% of urban population)	NA	NA	●	●
Satisfaction with public transport (%)	60.0	2021	●	↓
Population with rent overburden (%)	3.4	2019	●	↑

SDG12 – Responsible Consumption and Production

	Value	Year	Rating	Trend
Electronic waste (kg/capita)	15.1	2019	●	●
Production-based SO_2 emissions (kg/capita)	11.6	2018	●	●
SO_2 emissions embodied in imports (kg/capita)	8.0	2018	●	●
Production-based nitrogen emissions (kg/capita)	10.3	2015	●	↑
Nitrogen emissions embodied in imports (kg/capita)	9.9	2015	●	↓
Exports of plastic waste (kg/capita)	65.6	2020	●	●
Non-recycled municipal solid waste (kg/capita/day)	0.4	2019	●	↑

SDG13 – Climate Action

	Value	Year	Rating	Trend
CO_2 emissions from fossil fuel combustion and cement production (tCO_2/capita)	6.0	2020	●	→
CO_2 emissions embodied in imports (tCO_2/capita)	2.8	2018	●	↓
CO_2 emissions embodied in fossil fuel exports (kg/capita)	18.6	2020	●	●
Carbon Pricing Score at EUR60/tCO_2 (%, worst 0–100 best)	57.1	2018	●	↑

SDG14 – Life Below Water

	Value	Year	Rating	Trend
Mean area that is protected in marine sites important to biodiversity (%)	62.4	2020	●	→
Ocean Health Index: Clean Waters score (worst 0–100 best)	28.4	2020	●	↓
Fish caught from overexploited or collapsed stocks (% of total catch)	NA	NA	●	●
Fish caught by trawling or dredging (%)	41.8	2018	●	↓
Fish caught that are then discarded (%)	4.1	2018	●	↑
Marine biodiversity threats embodied in imports (per million population)	0.1	2018	●	●

SDG15 – Life on Land

	Value	Year	Rating	Trend
Mean area that is protected in terrestrial sites important to biodiversity (%)	73.5	2020	●	→
Mean area that is protected in freshwater sites important to biodiversity (%)	84.0	2020	●	→
Red List Index of species survival (worst 0–1 best)	0.9	2021	●	↑
Permanent deforestation (% of forest area, 5-year average)	0.0	2020	●	↑
Terrestrial and freshwater biodiversity threats embodied in imports (per million population)	2.2	2018	●	●

SDG16 – Peace, Justice and Strong Institutions

	Value	Year	Rating	Trend
Homicides (per 100,000 population)	0.5	2020	●	↑
Unsentenced detainees (% of prison population)	23.8	2019	●	↑
Population who feel safe walking alone at night in the city or area where they live (%)	89	2021	●	↑
Property Rights (worst 1–7 best)	4.8	2020	●	↑
Birth registrations with civil authority (% of children under age 5)	100.0	2020	●	●
Corruption Perception Index (worst 0–100 best)	57	2021	●	↓
Children involved in child labor (% of population aged 5 to 14) *	0.0	2019	●	●
Exports of major conventional weapons (TIV constant million USD per 100,000 population)	0.0	2020	●	●
Press Freedom Index (best 0–100 worst)	23.1	2021	●	↑
Access to and affordability of justice (worst 0–1 best)	0.7	2020	●	↑
Persons held in prison (per 100,000 population)	67.2	2019	●	↑

SDG17 – Partnerships for the Goals

	Value	Year	Rating	Trend
Government spending on health and education (% of GDP)	11.1	2019	●	↑
For high-income and all OECD DAC countries: International concessional public finance, including official development assistance (% of GNI)	0.2	2021	●	→
Other countries: Government revenue excluding grants (% of GDP)	NA	NA	●	●
Corporate Tax Haven Score (best 0–100 worst)	49.6	2019	●	●
Financial Secrecy Score (best 0–100 worst)	37.6	2020	●	●
Shifted profits of multinationals (US$ billion)	0.5	2018	●	↑
Statistical Performance Index (worst 0–100 best)	88.9	2019	●	↑

SOLOMON ISLANDS

Oceania

OVERALL PERFORMANCE

COUNTRY RANKING

SOLOMON ISLANDS

NA /163

COUNTRY SCORE

AVERAGE PERFORMANCE BY SDG

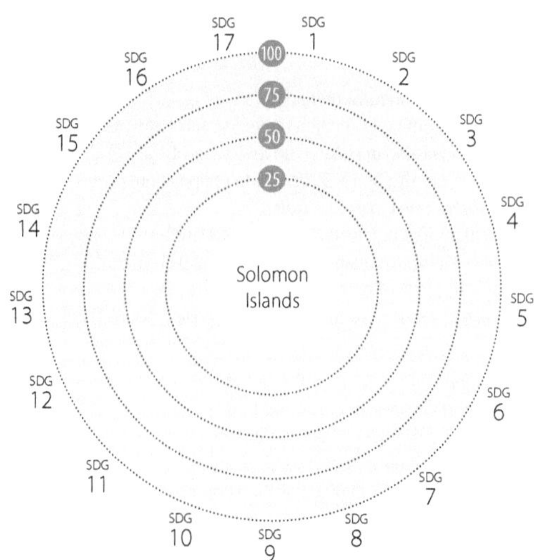

SDG DASHBOARDS AND TRENDS

Major challenges | Significant challenges | Challenges remain | SDG achieved | Information unavailable

Decreasing | Stagnating | Moderately improving | On track or maintaining SDG achievement | Information unavailable

Note: The full title of each SDG is available here: https://sustainabledevelopment.un.org/topics/sustainabledevelopmentgoals

INTERNATIONAL SPILLOVER INDEX

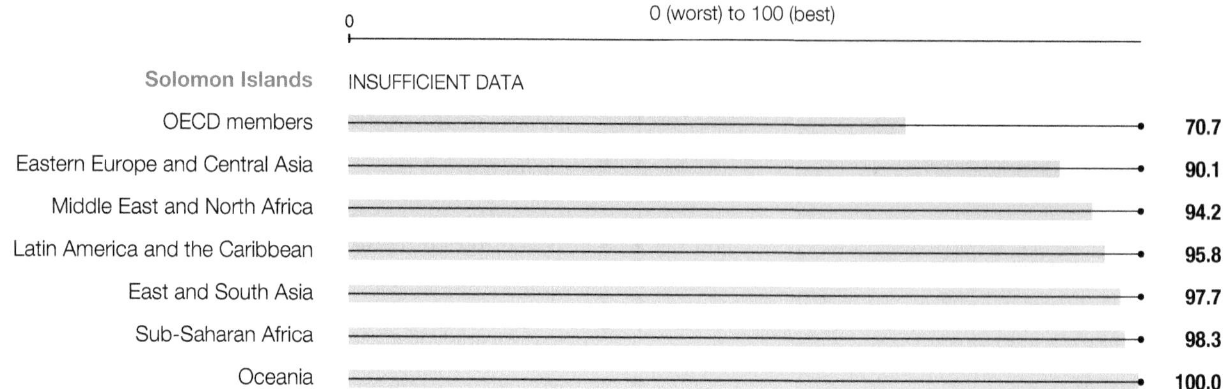

STATISTICAL PERFORMANCE INDEX

0 (worst) to 100 (best)

0 **41.7** 100

MISSING DATA IN SDG INDEX

30%

SOLOMON ISLANDS

SDG1 – No Poverty	Value	Year	Rating	Trend
Poverty headcount ratio at \$1.90/day (%)	25.2	2022	●	→
Poverty headcount ratio at \$3.20/day (%)	55.6	2022	●	→
SDG2 – Zero Hunger				
Prevalence of undernourishment (%)	16.5	2019	●	↗
Prevalence of stunting in children under 5 years of age (%)	31.7	2015	●	→
Prevalence of wasting in children under 5 years of age (%)	8.5	2015	●	→
Prevalence of obesity, BMI ≥ 30 (% of adult population)	22.5	2016	●	↓
Human Trophic Level (best 2–3 worst)	2.1	2017	●	↑
Cereal yield (tonnes per hectare of harvested land)	1.7	2018	●	↓
Sustainable Nitrogen Management Index (best 0–1.41 worst)	1.2	2015	●	↓
Exports of hazardous pesticides (tonnes per million population)	NA	NA	●	●
SDG3 – Good Health and Well-Being				
Maternal mortality rate (per 100,000 live births)	104	2017	●	↑
Neonatal mortality rate (per 1,000 live births)	7.8	2020	●	↑
Mortality rate, under-5 (per 1,000 live births)	19.4	2020	●	↑
Incidence of tuberculosis (per 100,000 population)	65.0	2020	●	↗
New HIV infections (per 1,000 uninfected population)	NA	NA	●	●
Age-standardized death rate due to cardiovascular disease, cancer, diabetes, or chronic respiratory disease in adults aged 30–70 years (%)	39.2	2019	●	→
Age-standardized death rate attributable to household air pollution and ambient air pollution (per 100,000 population)	137	2016	●	●
Traffic deaths (per 100,000 population)	16.5	2019	●	→
Life expectancy at birth (years)	65.3	2019	●	→
Adolescent fertility rate (births per 1,000 females aged 15 to 19)	78.0	2013	●	●
Births attended by skilled health personnel (%)	86.2	2015	●	●
Surviving infants who received 2 WHO-recommended vaccines (%)	81	2020	●	↑
Universal health coverage (UHC) index of service coverage (worst 0–100 best)	50	2019	●	→
Subjective well-being (average ladder score, worst 0–10 best)	NA	NA	●	●
SDG4 – Quality Education				
Participation rate in pre-primary organized learning (% of children aged 4 to 6)	65.6	2019	●	→
Net primary enrollment rate (%)	93.4	2019	●	↓
Lower secondary completion rate (%)	70.5	2019	●	↓
Literacy rate (% of population aged 15 to 24)	NA	NA	●	●
SDG5 – Gender Equality				
Demand for family planning satisfied by modern methods (% of females aged 15 to 49)	38.0	2015	●	●
Ratio of female-to-male mean years of education received (%)	NA	NA	●	●
Ratio of female-to-male labor force participation rate (%)	95.3	2020	●	↑
Seats held by women in national parliament (%)	6.4	2020	●	→
SDG6 – Clean Water and Sanitation				
Population using at least basic drinking water services (%)	67.3	2020	●	↓
Population using at least basic sanitation services (%)	34.8	2020	●	→
Freshwater withdrawal (% of available freshwater resources)	NA	NA	●	●
Anthropogenic wastewater that receives treatment (%)	0.0	2018	●	●
Scarce water consumption embodied in imports (m^3 H_2O eq/capita)	NA	NA	●	●
SDG7 – Affordable and Clean Energy				
Population with access to electricity (%)	70.3	2019	●	↑
Population with access to clean fuels and technology for cooking (%)	9.0	2019	●	→
CO_2 emissions from fuel combustion per total electricity output ($MtCO_2$/TWh)	3.8	2019	●	→
Share of renewable energy in total primary energy supply (%)	NA	NA	●	●
SDG8 – Decent Work and Economic Growth				
Adjusted GDP growth (%)	-7.1	2020	●	●
Victims of modern slavery (per 1,000 population)	NA	NA	●	●
Adults with an account at a bank or other financial institution or with a mobile-money-service provider (% of population aged 15 or over)	NA	NA	●	●
Unemployment rate (% of total labor force)	0.9	2022	●	↑
Fundamental labor rights are effectively guaranteed (worst 0–1 best)	NA	NA	●	●
Fatal work-related accidents embodied in imports (per 100,000 population)	NA	NA	●	●

SDG9 – Industry, Innovation and Infrastructure	Value	Year	Rating	Trend
Population using the internet (%)	11.9	2017	●	●
Mobile broadband subscriptions (per 100 population)	19.3	2019	●	→
Logistics Performance Index: Quality of trade and transport-related infrastructure (worst 1–5 best)	2.2	2018	●	↓
The Times Higher Education Universities Ranking: Average score of top 3 universities (worst 0–100 best)	* 0.0	2022	●	●
Articles published in academic journals (per 1,000 population)	0.1	2020	●	→
Expenditure on research and development (% of GDP)	NA	NA	●	●
SDG10 – Reduced Inequalities				
Gini coefficient	37.1	2012	●	●
Palma ratio	1.6	2018	●	●
SDG11 – Sustainable Cities and Communities				
Proportion of urban population living in slums (%)	NA	NA	●	●
Annual mean concentration of particulate matter of less than 2.5 microns in diameter (PM2.5) (μg/m³)	11.2	2019	●	↑
Access to improved water source, piped (% of urban population)	70.5	2020	●	↓
Satisfaction with public transport (%)	NA	NA	●	●
SDG12 – Responsible Consumption and Production				
Municipal solid waste (kg/capita/day)	0.9	2013	●	●
Electronic waste (kg/capita)	0.8	2019	●	●
Production-based SO_2 emissions (kg/capita)	NA	NA	●	●
SO_2 emissions embodied in imports (kg/capita)	NA	NA	●	●
Production-based nitrogen emissions (kg/capita)	NA	NA	●	●
Nitrogen emissions embodied in imports (kg/capita)	NA	NA	●	●
Exports of plastic waste (kg/capita)	NA	NA	●	●
SDG13 – Climate Action				
CO_2 emissions from fossil fuel combustion and cement production (tCO_2/capita)	0.4	2020	●	↑
CO_2 emissions embodied in imports (tCO_2/capita)	NA	NA	●	●
CO_2 emissions embodied in fossil fuel exports (kg/capita)	0.0	2020	●	●
SDG14 – Life Below Water				
Mean area that is protected in marine sites important to biodiversity (%)	3.2	2020	●	→
Ocean Health Index: Clean Waters score (worst 0–100 best)	72.9	2020	●	↑
Fish caught from overexploited or collapsed stocks (% of total catch)	54.1	2018	●	↓
Fish caught by trawling or dredging (%)	0.0	2018	●	↑
Fish caught that are then discarded (%)	0.0	2018	●	↑
Marine biodiversity threats embodied in imports (per million population)	NA	NA	●	●
SDG15 – Life on Land				
Mean area that is protected in terrestrial sites important to biodiversity (%)	4.6	2020	●	→
Mean area that is protected in freshwater sites important to biodiversity (%)	NA	NA	●	●
Red List Index of species survival (worst 0–1 best)	0.8	2021	●	↓
Permanent deforestation (% of forest area, 5-year average)	0.3	2020	●	→
Terrestrial and freshwater biodiversity threats embodied in imports (per million population)	NA	NA	●	●
SDG16 – Peace, Justice and Strong Institutions				
Homicides (per 100,000 population)	3.8	2008	●	●
Unsentenced detainees (% of prison population)	48.2	2017	●	●
Population who feel safe walking alone at night in the city or area where they live (%)	NA	NA	●	●
Property Rights (worst 1–7 best)	NA	NA	●	●
Birth registrations with civil authority (% of children under age 5)	88.0	2020	●	●
Corruption Perception Index (worst 0–100 best)	43	2021	●	→
Children involved in child labor (% of population aged 5 to 14)	17.9	2019	●	●
Exports of major conventional weapons (TIV constant million USD per 100,000 population)	* 0.0	2020	●	●
Press Freedom Index (best 0–100 worst)	NA	NA	●	●
Access to and affordability of justice (worst 0–1 best)	NA	NA	●	●
SDG17 – Partnerships for the Goals				
Government spending on health and education (% of GDP)	13.7	2019	●	↑
For high-income and all OECD DAC countries: International concessional public finance, including official development assistance (% of GNI)	NA	NA	●	●
Other countries: Government revenue excluding grants (% of GDP)	24.4	2020	●	↓
Corporate Tax Haven Score (best 0–100 worst)	* 0.0	2019	●	●
Statistical Performance Index (worst 0–100 best)	41.7	2019	●	↗

* Imputed data point

SOMALIA

Sub-Saharan Africa

OVERALL PERFORMANCE

COUNTRY RANKING

SOMALIA

160/163

COUNTRY SCORE

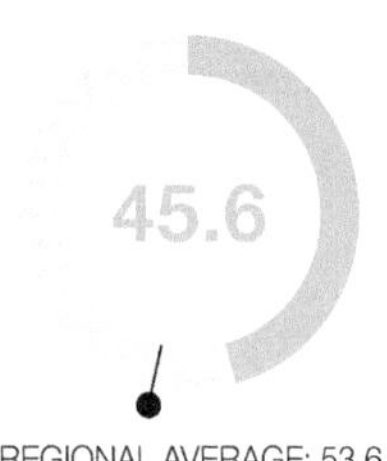

AVERAGE PERFORMANCE BY SDG

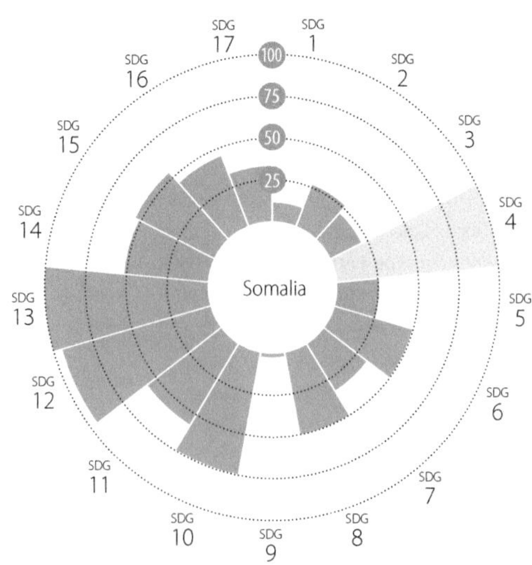

SDG DASHBOARDS AND TRENDS

Note: The full title of each SDG is available here: https://sustainabledevelopment.un.org/topics/sustainabledevelopmentgoals

INTERNATIONAL SPILLOVER INDEX

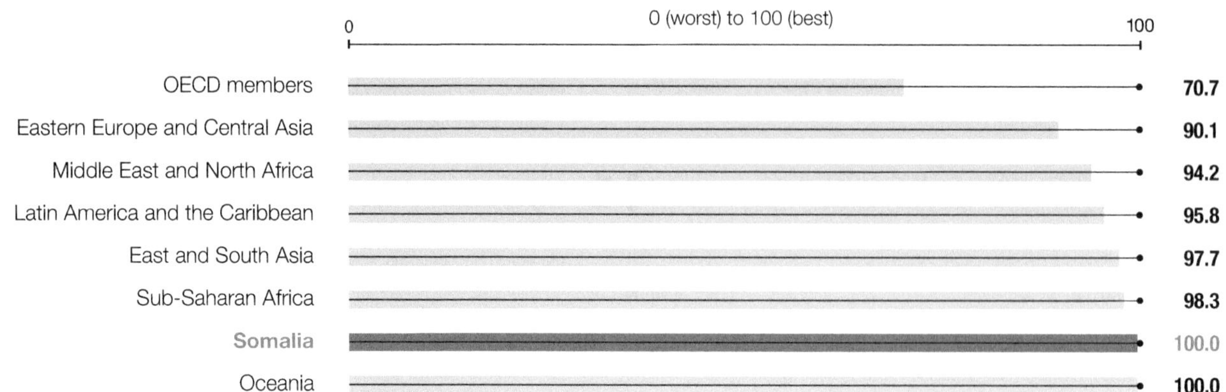

STATISTICAL PERFORMANCE INDEX

0 (worst) to 100 (best)

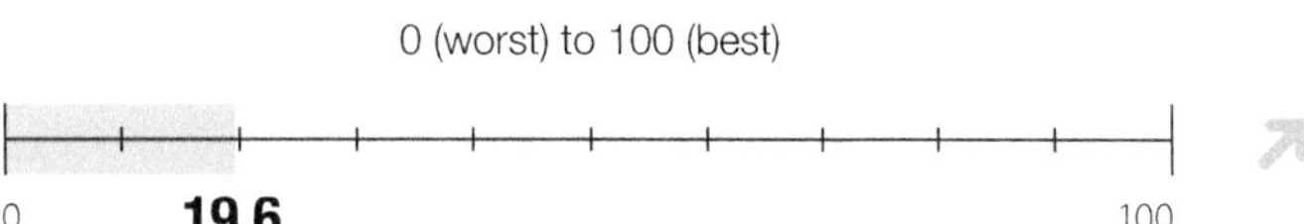

MISSING DATA IN SDG INDEX

20%

SOMALIA

Performance by Indicator

SDG1 – No Poverty	Value	Year	Rating	Trend
Poverty headcount ratio at $1.90/day (%)	55.5	2022	●	↓
Poverty headcount ratio at $3.20/day (%)	82.3	2022	●	↓
SDG2 – Zero Hunger				
Prevalence of undernourishment (%)	59.5	2019	●	→
Prevalence of stunting in children under 5 years of age (%)	25.3	2009	●	→
Prevalence of wasting in children under 5 years of age (%)	14.3	2009	●	→
Prevalence of obesity, BMI ≥ 30 (% of adult population)	8.3	2016	●	↑
Human Trophic Level (best 2–3 worst)	NA	NA	●	●
Cereal yield (tonnes per hectare of harvested land)	0.8	2018	●	↗
Sustainable Nitrogen Management Index (best 0–1.41 worst)	1.1	2015	●	→
Exports of hazardous pesticides (tonnes per million population)	NA	NA	●	●
SDG3 – Good Health and Well-Being				
Maternal mortality rate (per 100,000 live births)	829	2017	●	→
Neonatal mortality rate (per 1,000 live births)	36.8	2020	●	→
Mortality rate, under-5 (per 1,000 live births)	114.6	2020	●	↗
Incidence of tuberculosis (per 100,000 population)	259.0	2020	●	→
New HIV infections (per 1,000 uninfected population)	0.0	2020	●	↑
Age-standardized death rate due to cardiovascular disease, cancer, diabetes, or chronic respiratory disease in adults aged 30–70 years (%)	30.4	2019	●	→
Age-standardized death rate attributable to household air pollution and ambient air pollution (per 100,000 population)	213	2016	●	●
Traffic deaths (per 100,000 population)	27.4	2019	●	↓
Life expectancy at birth (years)	56.5	2019	●	→
Adolescent fertility rate (births per 1,000 females aged 15 to 19)	118.0	2017	●	●
Births attended by skilled health personnel (%)	9.4	2006	●	●
Surviving infants who received 2 WHO-recommended vaccines (%)	42	2020	●	→
Universal health coverage (UHC) index of service coverage (worst 0–100 best)	27	2019	●	→
Subjective well-being (average ladder score, worst 0–10 best)	4.7	2016	●	●
SDG4 – Quality Education				
Participation rate in pre-primary organized learning (% of children aged 4 to 6)	NA	NA	●	●
Net primary enrollment rate (%)	NA	NA	●	●
Lower secondary completion rate (%)	NA	NA	●	●
Literacy rate (% of population aged 15 to 24)	NA	NA	●	●
SDG5 – Gender Equality				
Demand for family planning satisfied by modern methods (% of females aged 15 to 49)	2.1	2019	●	→
Ratio of female-to-male mean years of education received (%)	NA	NA	●	●
Ratio of female-to-male labor force participation rate (%)	44.5	2020	●	→
Seats held by women in national parliament (%)	24.4	2020	●	↑
SDG6 – Clean Water and Sanitation				
Population using at least basic drinking water services (%)	56.5	2020	●	→
Population using at least basic sanitation services (%)	39.3	2020	●	→
Freshwater withdrawal (% of available freshwater resources)	24.5	2018	●	●
Anthropogenic wastewater that receives treatment (%)	0.0	2018	●	●
Scarce water consumption embodied in imports (m^3 H_2O eq/capita)	85.9	2018	●	●
SDG7 – Affordable and Clean Energy				
Population with access to electricity (%)	36.0	2019	●	→
Population with access to clean fuels and technology for cooking (%)	3.0	2019	●	→
CO_2 emissions from fuel combustion per total electricity output ($MtCO_2$/TWh)	2.0	2019	●	→
Share of renewable energy in total primary energy supply (%)	NA	NA	●	●
SDG8 – Decent Work and Economic Growth				
Adjusted GDP growth (%)	-3.0	2020	●	●
Victims of modern slavery (per 1,000 population)	15.5	2018	●	●
Adults with an account at a bank or other financial institution or with a mobile-money-service provider (% of population aged 15 or over)	38.7	2014	●	●
Unemployment rate (% of total labor force)	19.6	2022	●	↓
Fundamental labor rights are effectively guaranteed (worst 0–1 best)	NA	NA	●	●
Fatal work-related accidents embodied in imports (per 100,000 population)	0.0	2015	●	↑

* Imputed data point

SDG9 – Industry, Innovation and Infrastructure	Value	Year	Rating	Trend
Population using the internet (%)	2.0	2017	●	●
Mobile broadband subscriptions (per 100 population)	2.7	2019	●	→
Logistics Performance Index: Quality of trade and transport-related infrastructure (worst 1–5 best)	1.8	2018	●	↗
The Times Higher Education Universities Ranking: Average score of top 3 universities (worst 0–100 best)	* 0.0	2022	●	●
Articles published in academic journals (per 1,000 population)	0.0	2020	●	→
Expenditure on research and development (% of GDP)	* 0.0	2018	●	●
SDG10 – Reduced Inequalities				
Gini coefficient	36.8	2017	●	●
Palma ratio	NA	NA	●	●
SDG11 – Sustainable Cities and Communities				
Proportion of urban population living in slums (%)	73.6	2018	●	→
Annual mean concentration of particulate matter of less than 2.5 microns in diameter (PM2.5) (μg/m³)	32.9	2019	●	↓
Access to improved water source, piped (% of urban population)	76.2	2020	●	↑
Satisfaction with public transport (%)	62.0	2016	●	●
SDG12 – Responsible Consumption and Production				
Municipal solid waste (kg/capita/day)	0.4	2016	●	●
Electronic waste (kg/capita)	NA	NA	●	●
Production-based SO_2 emissions (kg/capita)	0.3	2018	●	●
SO_2 emissions embodied in imports (kg/capita)	0.0	2018	●	●
Production-based nitrogen emissions (kg/capita)	19.7	2015	●	↑
Nitrogen emissions embodied in imports (kg/capita)	0.1	2015	●	↑
Exports of plastic waste (kg/capita)	NA	NA	●	●
SDG13 – Climate Action				
CO_2 emissions from fossil fuel combustion and cement production (tCO_2/capita)	0.0	2020	●	↑
CO_2 emissions embodied in imports (tCO_2/capita)	0.0	2018	●	↑
CO_2 emissions embodied in fossil fuel exports (kg/capita)	0.0	2020	●	●
SDG14 – Life Below Water				
Mean area that is protected in marine sites important to biodiversity (%)	0.0	2020	●	→
Ocean Health Index: Clean Waters score (worst 0–100 best)	61.1	2020	●	→
Fish caught from overexploited or collapsed stocks (% of total catch)	14.0	2018	●	↑
Fish caught by trawling or dredging (%)	0.0	2018	●	↑
Fish caught that are then discarded (%)	14.7	2018	●	↓
Marine biodiversity threats embodied in imports (per million population)	NA	NA	●	●
SDG15 – Life on Land				
Mean area that is protected in terrestrial sites important to biodiversity (%)	0.0	2020	●	→
Mean area that is protected in freshwater sites important to biodiversity (%)	0.0	2020	●	→
Red List Index of species survival (worst 0–1 best)	0.9	2021	●	↓
Permanent deforestation (% of forest area, 5-year average)	0.1	2020	●	↓
Terrestrial and freshwater biodiversity threats embodied in imports (per million population)	0.0	2018	●	●
SDG16 – Peace, Justice and Strong Institutions				
Homicides (per 100,000 population)	NA	NA	●	●
Unsentenced detainees (% of prison population)	NA	NA	●	●
Population who feel safe walking alone at night in the city or area where they live (%)	85	2016	●	●
Property Rights (worst 1–7 best)	NA	NA	●	●
Birth registrations with civil authority (% of children under age 5)	3.5	2020	●	●
Corruption Perception Index (worst 0–100 best)	13	2021	●	→
Children involved in child labor (% of population aged 5 to 14)	NA	NA	●	●
Exports of major conventional weapons (TIV constant million USD per 100,000 population)	* 0.0	2020	●	●
Press Freedom Index (best 0–100 worst)	55.5	2021	●	↗
Access to and affordability of justice (worst 0–1 best)	NA	NA	●	●
SDG17 – Partnerships for the Goals				
Government spending on health and education (% of GDP)	NA	NA	●	●
For high-income and all OECD DAC countries: International concessional public finance, including official development assistance (% of GNI)	NA	NA	●	●
Other countries: Government revenue excluding grants (% of GDP)	0.0	2019	●	●
Corporate Tax Haven Score (best 0–100 worst)	* 0.0	2019	●	●
Statistical Performance Index (worst 0–100 best)	19.6	2019	●	↗

5. Country Profiles

SOUTH AFRICA

Sub-Saharan Africa

OVERALL PERFORMANCE

COUNTRY RANKING

SOUTH AFRICA

108/163

COUNTRY SCORE

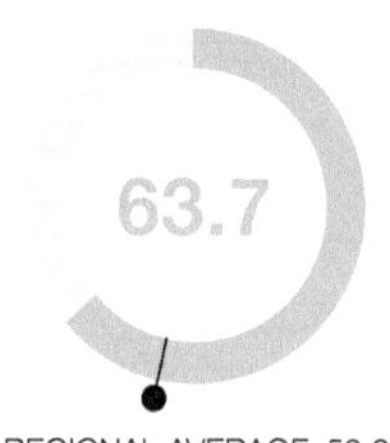

AVERAGE PERFORMANCE BY SDG

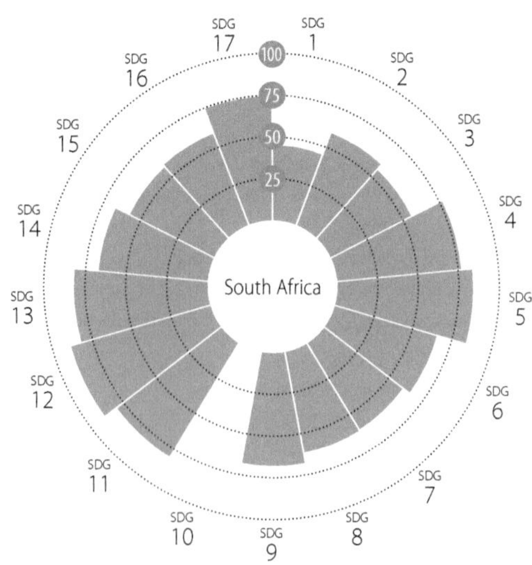

SDG DASHBOARDS AND TRENDS

Major challenges · Significant challenges · Challenges remain · SDG achieved · Information unavailable

Decreasing · Stagnating · Moderately improving · On track or maintaining SDG achievement · Information unavailable

Note: The full title of each SDG is available here: https://sustainabledevelopment.un.org/topics/sustainabledevelopmentgoals

INTERNATIONAL SPILLOVER INDEX

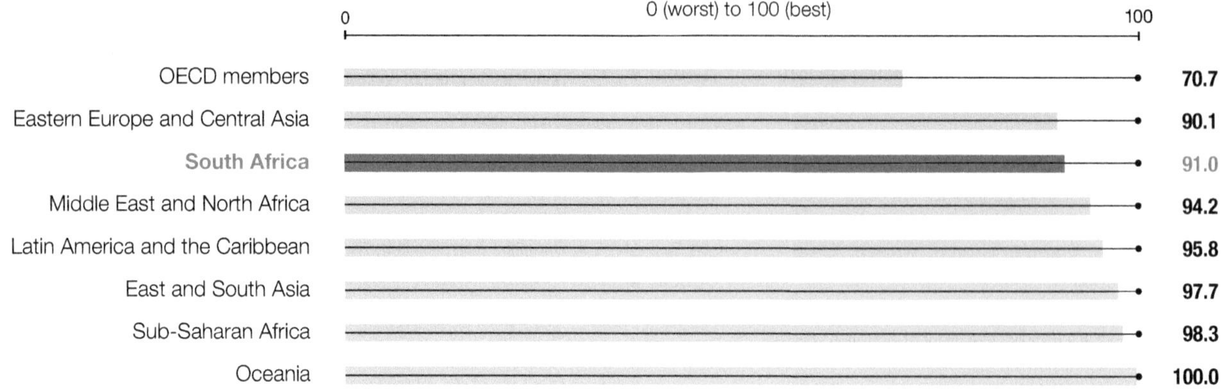

STATISTICAL PERFORMANCE INDEX

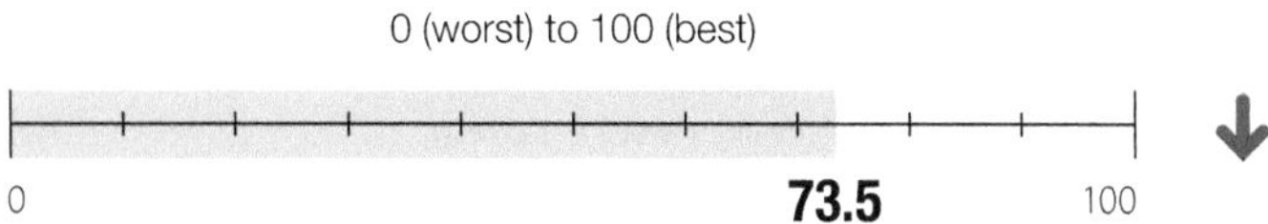

MISSING DATA IN SDG INDEX

0%

SDG1 – No Poverty	Value	Year	Rating	Trend
Poverty headcount ratio at $1.90/day (%)	26.7	2022	●	↓
Poverty headcount ratio at $3.20/day (%)	37.1	2022	●	↓
SDG2 – Zero Hunger				
Prevalence of undernourishment (%)	6.5	2019	●	↑
Prevalence of stunting in children under 5 years of age (%)	21.4	2017	●	→
Prevalence of wasting in children under 5 years of age (%)	3.4	2017	●	↑
Prevalence of obesity, BMI ≥ 30 (% of adult population)	28.3	2016	●	↓
Human Trophic Level (best 2–3 worst)	2.3	2017	●	→
Cereal yield (tonnes per hectare of harvested land)	4.9	2018	●	↑
Sustainable Nitrogen Management Index (best 0–1.41 worst)	0.5	2015	●	↗
Exports of hazardous pesticides (tonnes per million population)	98.8	2019	●	●
SDG3 – Good Health and Well-Being				
Maternal mortality rate (per 100,000 live births)	119	2017	●	↗
Neonatal mortality rate (per 1,000 live births)	10.6	2020	●	↑
Mortality rate, under-5 (per 1,000 live births)	32.2	2020	●	↑
Incidence of tuberculosis (per 100,000 population)	554.0	2020	●	↑
New HIV infections (per 1,000 uninfected population)	4.6	2020	●	↗
Age-standardized death rate due to cardiovascular disease, cancer, diabetes, or chronic respiratory disease in adults aged 30–70 years (%)	24.1	2019	●	↑
Age-standardized death rate attributable to household air pollution and ambient air pollution (per 100,000 population)	87	2016	●	●
Traffic deaths (per 100,000 population)	22.2	2019	●	→
Life expectancy at birth (years)	65.3	2019	●	↗
Adolescent fertility rate (births per 1,000 females aged 15 to 19)	40.9	2017	●	●
Births attended by skilled health personnel (%)	96.7	2016	●	●
Surviving infants who received 2 WHO-recommended vaccines (%)	84	2020	●	→
Universal health coverage (UHC) index of service coverage (worst 0–100 best)	67	2019	●	↗
Subjective well-being (average ladder score, worst 0–10 best)	5.6	2021	●	↑
SDG4 – Quality Education				
Participation rate in pre-primary organized learning (% of children aged 4 to 6)	72.0	2019	●	↓
Net primary enrollment rate (%)	89.2	2019	●	↓
Lower secondary completion rate (%)	80.4	2019	●	↓
Literacy rate (% of population aged 15 to 24)	98.4	2019	●	↑
SDG5 – Gender Equality				
Demand for family planning satisfied by modern methods (% of females aged 15 to 49)	79.7	2016	●	↑
Ratio of female-to-male mean years of education received (%)	97.1	2019	●	↑
Ratio of female-to-male labor force participation rate (%)	76.7	2020	●	↑
Seats held by women in national parliament (%)	46.8	2020	●	↑
SDG6 – Clean Water and Sanitation				
Population using at least basic drinking water services (%)	93.9	2020	●	↗
Population using at least basic sanitation services (%)	78.5	2020	●	↗
Freshwater withdrawal (% of available freshwater resources)	63.6	2018	●	●
Anthropogenic wastewater that receives treatment (%)	21.7	2018	●	●
Scarce water consumption embodied in imports (m^3 H_2O eq/capita)	455.1	2018	●	●
SDG7 – Affordable and Clean Energy				
Population with access to electricity (%)	85.0	2019	●	↓
Population with access to clean fuels and technology for cooking (%)	86.3	2019	●	↑
CO_2 emissions from fuel combustion per total electricity output ($MtCO_2$/TWh)	2.1	2019	●	→
Share of renewable energy in total primary energy supply (%)	6.6	2019	●	→
SDG8 – Decent Work and Economic Growth				
Adjusted GDP growth (%)	-5.3	2020	●	●
Victims of modern slavery (per 1,000 population)	2.8	2018	●	●
Adults with an account at a bank or other financial institution or with a mobile-money-service provider (% of population aged 15 or over)	69.2	2017	●	↓
Unemployment rate (% of total labor force)	33.5	2022	●	↓
Fundamental labor rights are effectively guaranteed (worst 0–1 best)	0.7	2020	●	↑
Fatal work-related accidents embodied in imports (per 100,000 population)	0.3	2015	●	↑

* Imputed data point

SDG9 – Industry, Innovation and Infrastructure	Value	Year	Rating	Trend
Population using the internet (%)	70.0	2020	●	↑
Mobile broadband subscriptions (per 100 population)	102.2	2019	●	↑
Logistics Performance Index: Quality of trade and transport-related infrastructure (worst 1–5 best)	3.2	2018	●	↑
The Times Higher Education Universities Ranking: Average score of top 3 universities (worst 0–100 best)	51.1	2022	●	●
Articles published in academic journals (per 1,000 population)	0.5	2020	●	↑
Expenditure on research and development (% of GDP)	0.8	2017	●	→
SDG10 – Reduced Inequalities				
Gini coefficient	63.0	2014	●	●
Palma ratio	6.9	2017	●	●
SDG11 – Sustainable Cities and Communities				
Proportion of urban population living in slums (%)	26.4	2018	●	↓
Annual mean concentration of particulate matter of less than 2.5 microns in diameter (PM2.5) (μg/m^3)	24.3	2019	●	→
Access to improved water source, piped (% of urban population)	98.2	2020	●	↑
Satisfaction with public transport (%)	66.0	2021	●	↑
SDG12 – Responsible Consumption and Production				
Municipal solid waste (kg/capita/day)	1.0	2011	●	●
Electronic waste (kg/capita)	7.1	2019	●	●
Production-based SO_2 emissions (kg/capita)	38.7	2018	●	●
SO_2 emissions embodied in imports (kg/capita)	1.3	2018	●	●
Production-based nitrogen emissions (kg/capita)	9.5	2015	●	↑
Nitrogen emissions embodied in imports (kg/capita)	2.3	2015	●	↑
Exports of plastic waste (kg/capita)	0.2	2020	●	●
SDG13 – Climate Action				
CO_2 emissions from fossil fuel combustion and cement production (tCO_2/capita)	7.6	2020	●	→
CO_2 emissions embodied in imports (tCO_2/capita)	0.4	2018	●	↑
CO_2 emissions embodied in fossil fuel exports (kg/capita)	1642.8	2020	●	●
SDG14 – Life Below Water				
Mean area that is protected in marine sites important to biodiversity (%)	46.6	2020	●	→
Ocean Health Index: Clean Waters score (worst 0–100 best)	55.7	2020	●	→
Fish caught from overexploited or collapsed stocks (% of total catch)	20.8	2018	●	↑
Fish caught by trawling or dredging (%)	23.1	2018	●	→
Fish caught that are then discarded (%)	6.2	2018	●	→
Marine biodiversity threats embodied in imports (per million population)	0.1	2018	●	●
SDG15 – Life on Land				
Mean area that is protected in terrestrial sites important to biodiversity (%)	33.1	2020	●	→
Mean area that is protected in freshwater sites important to biodiversity (%)	36.5	2020	●	→
Red List Index of species survival (worst 0–1 best)	0.8	2021	●	↓
Permanent deforestation (% of forest area, 5-year average)	0.2	2020	●	→
Terrestrial and freshwater biodiversity threats embodied in imports (per million population)	0.8	2018	●	●
SDG16 – Peace, Justice and Strong Institutions				
Homicides (per 100,000 population)	33.5	2020	●	→
Unsentenced detainees (% of prison population)	28.2	2018	●	↑
Population who feel safe walking alone at night in the city or area where they live (%)	32	2021	●	↓
Property Rights (worst 1–7 best)	4.3	2020	●	↓
Birth registrations with civil authority (% of children under age 5)	88.6	2020	●	●
Corruption Perception Index (worst 0–100 best)	44	2021	●	→
Children involved in child labor (% of population aged 5 to 14)	3.6	2019	●	●
Exports of major conventional weapons (TIV constant million USD per 100,000 population)	0.1	2020	●	●
Press Freedom Index (best 0–100 worst)	21.6	2021	●	↑
Access to and affordability of justice (worst 0–1 best)	0.5	2020	●	↑
SDG17 – Partnerships for the Goals				
Government spending on health and education (% of GDP)	12.2	2020	●	↑
For high-income and all OECD DAC countries: International concessional public finance, including official development assistance (% of GNI)	NA	NA	●	●
Other countries: Government revenue excluding grants (% of GDP)	29.4	2019	●	↑
Corporate Tax Haven Score (best 0–100 worst)	47.1	2019	●	●
Statistical Performance Index (worst 0–100 best)	73.5	2019	●	↓

SOUTH SUDAN

Sub-Saharan Africa

OVERALL PERFORMANCE

COUNTRY RANKING

SOUTH SUDAN

163 /163

COUNTRY SCORE

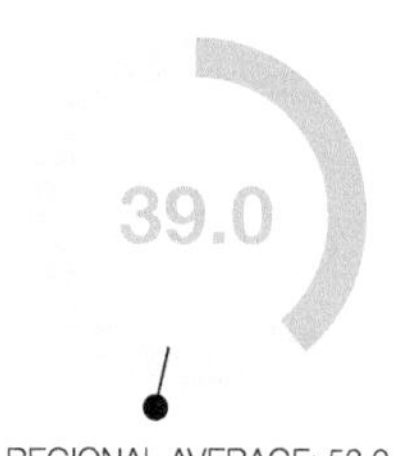

AVERAGE PERFORMANCE BY SDG

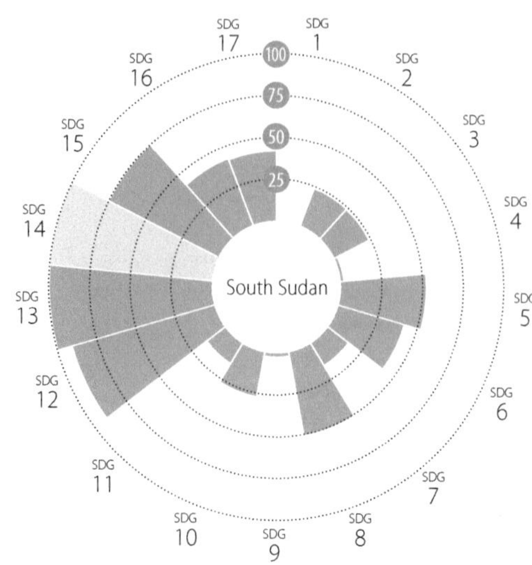

SDG DASHBOARDS AND TRENDS

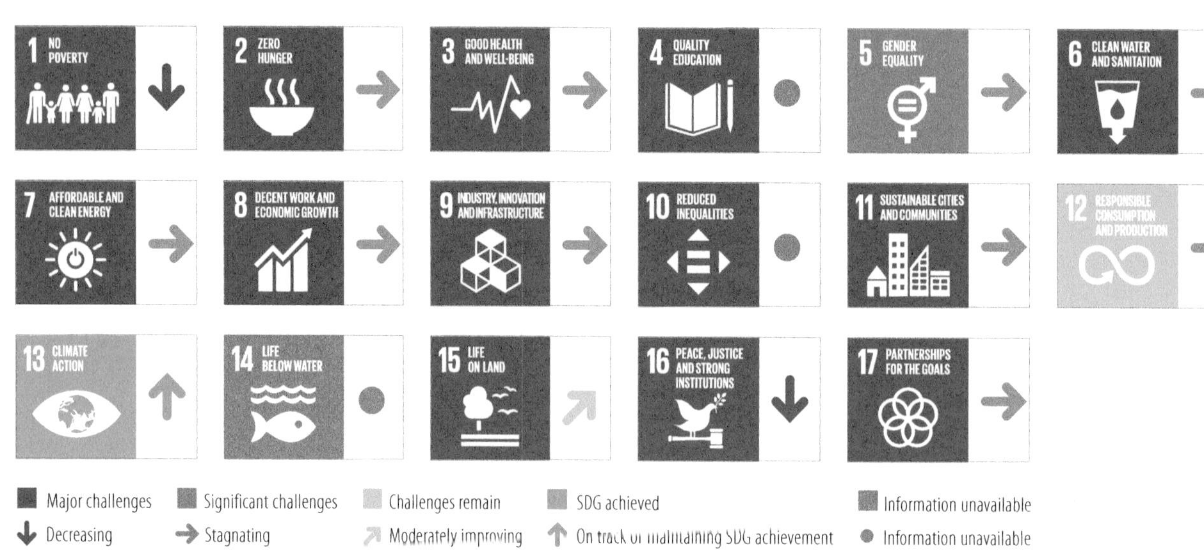

Major challenges · Significant challenges · Challenges remain · SDG achieved · Information unavailable

Decreasing · Stagnating · Moderately improving · On track or maintaining SDG achievement · Information unavailable

Note: The full title of each SDG is available here: https://sustainabledevelopment.un.org/topics/sustainabledevelopmentgoals

INTERNATIONAL SPILLOVER INDEX

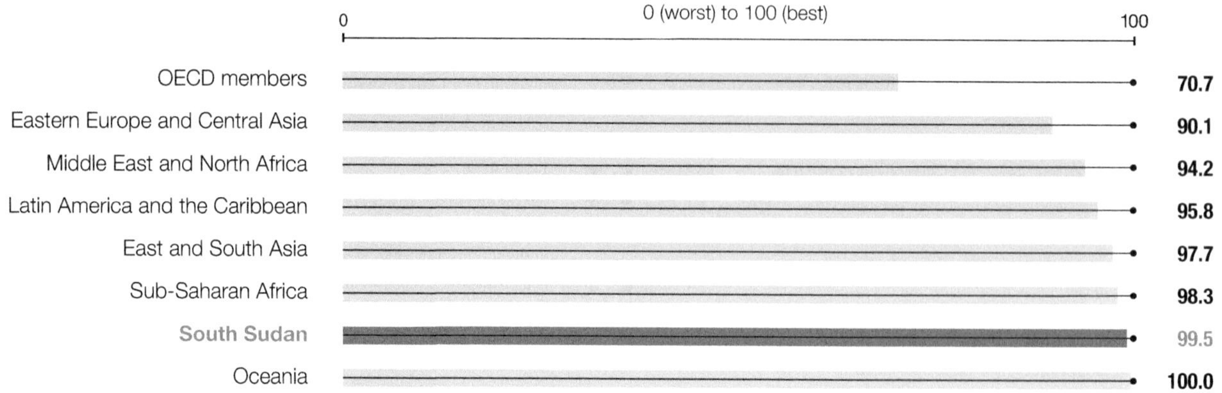

STATISTICAL PERFORMANCE INDEX

0 (worst) to 100 (best)

0 30.5 100

MISSING DATA IN SDG INDEX

19%

SDG1 – No Poverty		Value	Year	Rating	Trend
Poverty headcount ratio at $1.90/day (%)		84.5	2022	●	↓
Poverty headcount ratio at $3.20/day (%)		95.5	2022	●	↓
SDG2 – Zero Hunger					
Prevalence of undernourishment (%)		NA	NA	●	●
Prevalence of stunting in children under 5 years of age (%)		31.3	2010	●	→
Prevalence of wasting in children under 5 years of age (%)		22.7	2010	●	→
Prevalence of obesity, BMI ≥ 30 (% of adult population)		NA	NA	●	●
Human Trophic Level (best 2–3 worst)		2.3	2017	●	↑
Cereal yield (tonnes per hectare of harvested land)		0.7	2018	●	→
Sustainable Nitrogen Management Index (best 0–1.41 worst)		NA	NA	●	●
Exports of hazardous pesticides (tonnes per million population)		NA	NA	●	●
SDG3 – Good Health and Well-Being					
Maternal mortality rate (per 100,000 live births)		1150	2017	●	↓
Neonatal mortality rate (per 1,000 live births)		40.2	2020	●	→
Mortality rate, under-5 (per 1,000 live births)		97.9	2020	●	→
Incidence of tuberculosis (per 100,000 population)		232.0	2020	●	↓
New HIV infections (per 1,000 uninfected population)		1.4	2020	●	→
Age-standardized death rate due to cardiovascular disease, cancer, diabetes, or chronic respiratory disease in adults aged 30–70 years (%)		16.8	2019	●	→
Age-standardized death rate attributable to household air pollution and ambient air pollution (per 100,000 population)		165	2016	●	●
Traffic deaths (per 100,000 population)		36.7	2019	●	↓
Life expectancy at birth (years)		62.8	2019	●	→
Adolescent fertility rate (births per 1,000 females aged 15 to 19)		158.1	2008	●	●
Births attended by skilled health personnel (%)		19.4	2010	●	●
Surviving infants who received 2 WHO-recommended vaccines (%)		49	2020	●	→
Universal health coverage (UHC) index of service coverage (worst 0–100 best)		32	2019	●	→
Subjective well-being (average ladder score, worst 0–10 best)		2.8	2017	●	●
SDG4 – Quality Education					
Participation rate in pre-primary organized learning (% of children aged 4 to 6)		20.5	2015	●	●
Net primary enrollment rate (%)		37.6	2015	●	●
Lower secondary completion rate (%)		18.0	2011	●	●
Literacy rate (% of population aged 15 to 24)		47.9	2018	●	●
SDG5 – Gender Equality					
Demand for family planning satisfied by modern methods (% of females aged 15 to 49)		4.0	2010	●	→
Ratio of female-to-male mean years of education received (%)		75.0	2019	●	↓
Ratio of female-to-male labor force participation rate (%)		94.6	2020	●	↑
Seats held by women in national parliament (%)		28.5	2020	●	→
SDG6 – Clean Water and Sanitation					
Population using at least basic drinking water services (%)		41.0	2020	●	↓
Population using at least basic sanitation services (%)		15.8	2020	●	→
Freshwater withdrawal (% of available freshwater resources)		4.2	2018	●	●
Anthropogenic wastewater that receives treatment (%)		0.0	2018	●	●
Scarce water consumption embodied in imports (m^3 H_2O eq/capita)		447.4	2018	●	●
SDG7 – Affordable and Clean Energy					
Population with access to electricity (%)		6.7	2019	●	→
Population with access to clean fuels and technology for cooking (%)		0.0	2019	●	→
CO_2 emissions from fuel combustion per total electricity output ($MtCO_2$/TWh)		3.2	2019	●	↗
Share of renewable energy in total primary energy supply (%)		NA	NA	●	●
SDG8 – Decent Work and Economic Growth					
Adjusted GDP growth (%)		NA	NA	●	●
Victims of modern slavery (per 1,000 population)	*	NA	NA	●	●
Adults with an account at a bank or other financial institution or with a mobile-money-service provider (% of population aged 15 or over)		8.6	2017	●	●
Unemployment rate (% of total labor force)		13.3	2022	●	↓
Fundamental labor rights are effectively guaranteed (worst 0–1 best)		NA	NA	●	●
Fatal work-related accidents embodied in imports (per 100,000 population)		0.0	2015	●	↑

* Imputed data point

SDG9 – Industry, Innovation and Infrastructure		Value	Year	Rating	Trend
Population using the internet (%)		6.5	2020	●	→
Mobile broadband subscriptions (per 100 population)		6.0	2019	●	→
Logistics Performance Index: Quality of trade and transport-related infrastructure (worst 1–5 best)		NA	NA	●	●
The Times Higher Education Universities Ranking: Average score of top 3 universities (worst 0–100 best)	*	0.0	2022	●	●
Articles published in academic journals (per 1,000 population)		0.0	2020	●	→
Expenditure on research and development (% of GDP)	*	0.0	2018	●	●
SDG10 – Reduced Inequalities					
Gini coefficient		44.1	2016	●	●
Palma ratio		2.7	2018	●	●
SDG11 – Sustainable Cities and Communities					
Proportion of urban population living in slums (%)		97.3	2018	●	↓
Annual mean concentration of particulate matter of less than 2.5 microns in diameter (PM2.5) (μg/m^3)		46.1	2019	●	→
Access to improved water source, piped (% of urban population)		10.5	2020	●	↓
Satisfaction with public transport (%)		18.0	2017	●	●
SDG12 – Responsible Consumption and Production					
Municipal solid waste (kg/capita/day)		0.7	2013	●	●
Electronic waste (kg/capita)		NA	NA	●	●
Production-based SO_2 emissions (kg/capita)		0.8	2018	●	●
SO_2 emissions embodied in imports (kg/capita)		0.0	2018	●	●
Production-based nitrogen emissions (kg/capita)		32.1	2015	●	↓
Nitrogen emissions embodied in imports (kg/capita)		0.1	2015	●	↑
Exports of plastic waste (kg/capita)		NA	NA	●	●
SDG13 – Climate Action					
CO_2 emissions from fossil fuel combustion and cement production (tCO_2/capita)		0.1	2020	●	↑
CO_2 emissions embodied in imports (tCO_2/capita)		0.0	2018	●	↑
CO_2 emissions embodied in fossil fuel exports (kg/capita)		NA	NA	●	●
SDG14 – Life Below Water					
Mean area that is protected in marine sites important to biodiversity (%)		NA	NA	●	●
Ocean Health Index: Clean Waters score (worst 0–100 best)		NA	NA	●	●
Fish caught from overexploited or collapsed stocks (% of total catch)		NA	NA	●	●
Fish caught by trawling or dredging (%)		NA	NA	●	●
Fish caught that are then discarded (%)		NA	NA	●	●
Marine biodiversity threats embodied in imports (per million population)		0.0	2018	●	●
SDG15 – Life on Land					
Mean area that is protected in terrestrial sites important to biodiversity (%)		33.6	2020	●	→
Mean area that is protected in freshwater sites important to biodiversity (%)		58.6	2020	●	→
Red List Index of species survival (worst 0–1 best)		0.9	2021	●	↑
Permanent deforestation (% of forest area, 5-year average)		0.0	2020	●	↑
Terrestrial and freshwater biodiversity threats embodied in imports (per million population)		0.0	2018	●	●
SDG16 – Peace, Justice and Strong Institutions					
Homicides (per 100,000 population)		14.9	2012	●	●
Unsentenced detainees (% of prison population)		NA	NA	●	●
Population who feel safe walking alone at night in the city or area where they live (%)		42	2017	●	●
Property Rights (worst 1–7 best)		NA	NA	●	●
Birth registrations with civil authority (% of children under age 5)		35.4	2020	●	●
Corruption Perception Index (worst 0–100 best)		11	2021	●	↓
Children involved in child labor (% of population aged 5 to 14)		NA	NA	●	●
Exports of major conventional weapons (TIV constant million USD per 100,000 population)	*	0.0	2020	●	●
Press Freedom Index (best 0–100 worst)		45.8	2021	●	↓
Access to and affordability of justice (worst 0–1 best)		NA	NA	●	●
SDG17 – Partnerships for the Goals					
Government spending on health and education (% of GDP)		2.5	2019	●	●
For high-income and all OECD DAC countries: International concessional public finance, including official development assistance (% of GNI)		NA	NA	●	●
Other countries: Government revenue excluding grants (% of GDP)		NA	NA	●	●
Corporate Tax Haven Score (best 0–100 worst)	*	0.0	2019	●	●
Statistical Performance Index (worst 0–100 best)		30.5	2019	●	→

SPAIN

OVERALL PERFORMANCE

COUNTRY RANKING

SPAIN

16 /163

COUNTRY SCORE

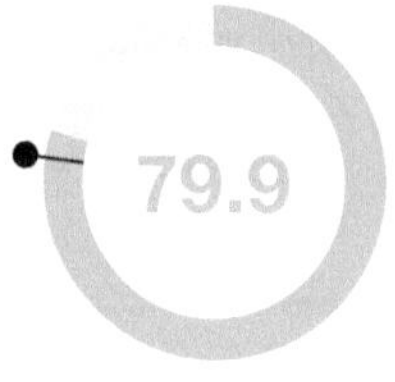

REGIONAL AVERAGE: 77.2

AVERAGE PERFORMANCE BY SDG

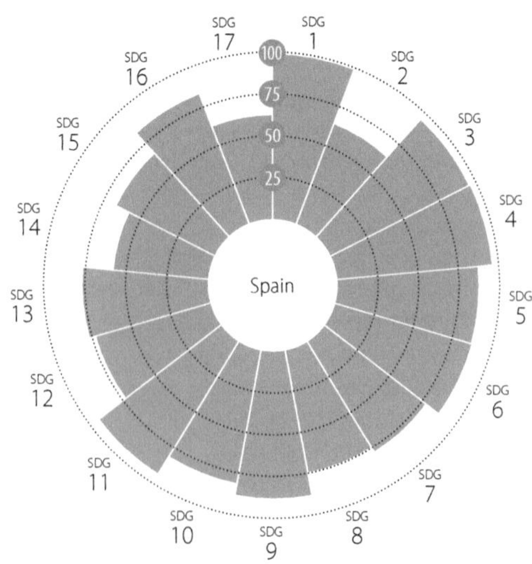

SDG DASHBOARDS AND TRENDS

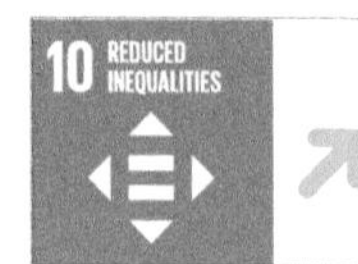

■ Major challenges ■ Significant challenges ■ Challenges remain ■ SDG achieved ■ Information unavailable

↓ Decreasing → Stagnating ↗ Moderately improving ↑ On track or maintaining SDG achievement ● Information unavailable

Note: The full title of each SDG is available here: https://sustainabledevelopment.un.org/topics/sustainabledevelopmentgoals

INTERNATIONAL SPILLOVER INDEX

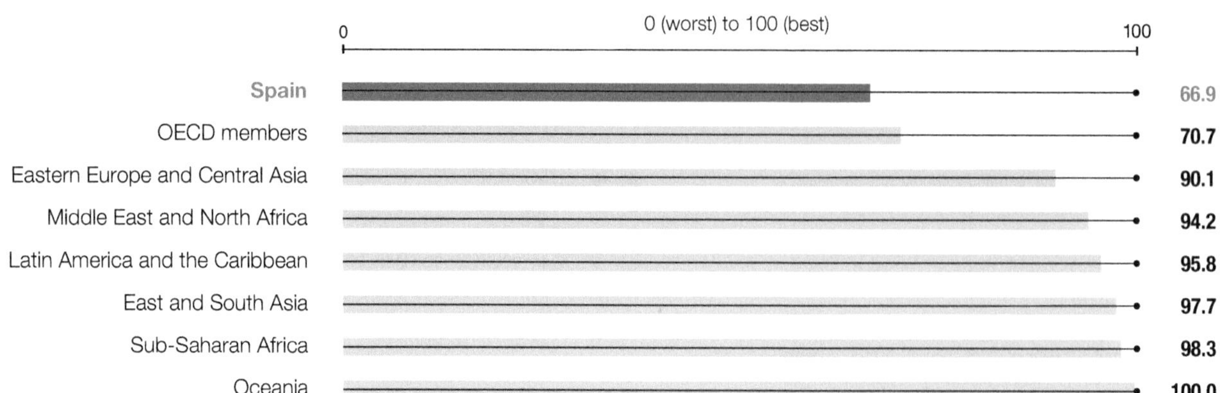

STATISTICAL PERFORMANCE INDEX

0 (worst) to 100 (best)

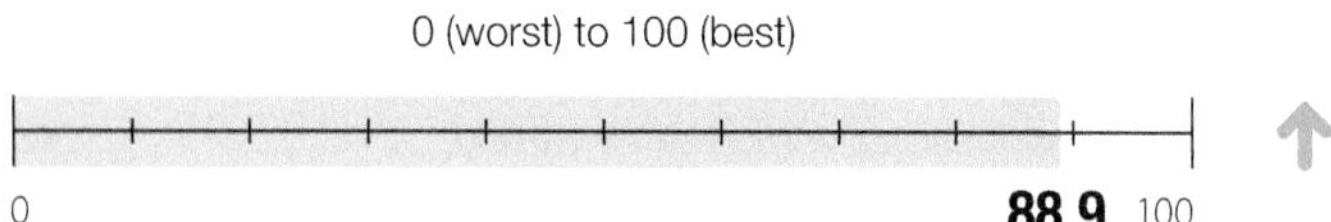

MISSING DATA IN SDG INDEX

1%

SDG1 – No Poverty		Value	Year	Rating	Trend
Poverty headcount ratio at \$1.90/day (%)		0.7	2022	●	↑
Poverty headcount ratio at \$3.20/day (%)		1.0	2022	●	↑
Poverty rate after taxes and transfers (%)		14.7	2019	●	→
SDG2 – Zero Hunger					
Prevalence of undernourishment (%)		2.5	2019	●	↑
Prevalence of stunting in children under 5 years of age (%)	*	2.6	2019	●	↑
Prevalence of wasting in children under 5 years of age (%)	*	0.7	2019	●	↑
Prevalence of obesity, BMI ≥ 30 (% of adult population)		23.8	2016	●	↓
Human Trophic Level (best 2–3 worst)		2.4	2017	●	↓
Cereal yield (tonnes per hectare of harvested land)		4.1	2018	●	↑
Sustainable Nitrogen Management Index (best 0–1.41 worst)		0.8	2015	●	↓
Yield gap closure (% of potential yield)		45.7	2018	●	●
Exports of hazardous pesticides (tonnes per million population)		20.0	2019	●	●
SDG3 – Good Health and Well-Being					
Maternal mortality rate (per 100,000 live births)		4	2017	●	↑
Neonatal mortality rate (per 1,000 live births)		1.7	2020	●	↑
Mortality rate, under-5 (per 1,000 live births)		3.2	2020	●	↑
Incidence of tuberculosis (per 100,000 population)		7.3	2020	●	↑
New HIV infections (per 1,000 uninfected population)		0.1	2020	●	↑
Age-standardized death rate due to cardiovascular disease, cancer, diabetes, or chronic respiratory disease in adults aged 30–70 years (%)		9.6	2019	●	↑
Age-standardized death rate attributable to household air pollution and ambient air pollution (per 100,000 population)		10	2016	●	●
Traffic deaths (per 100,000 population)		3.9	2019	●	↑
Life expectancy at birth (years)		83.2	2019	●	↑
Adolescent fertility rate (births per 1,000 females aged 15 to 19)		6.2	2018	●	↑
Births attended by skilled health personnel (%)		NA	NA	●	●
Surviving infants who received 2 WHO-recommended vaccines (%)		98	2020	●	↑
Universal health coverage (UHC) index of service coverage (worst 0–100 best)		86	2019	●	↑
Subjective well-being (average ladder score, worst 0–10 best)		6.5	2021	●	↑
Gap in life expectancy at birth among regions (years)		5.3	2019	●	↓
Gap in self-reported health status by income (percentage points)		13.4	2019	●	↑
Daily smokers (% of population aged 15 and over)		19.8	2020	●	↑
SDG4 – Quality Education					
Participation rate in pre-primary organized learning (% of children aged 4 to 6)		94.9	2019	●	↑
Net primary enrollment rate (%)		97.2	2019	●	↑
Lower secondary completion rate (%)		97.6	2019	●	↑
Literacy rate (% of population aged 15 to 24)		99.6	2020	●	↑
Tertiary educational attainment (% of population aged 25 to 34)		47.4	2020	●	↑
PISA score (worst 0–600 best)		486.7	2018	●	↓
Variation in science performance explained by socio-economic status (%)		10.0	2018	●	↑
Underachievers in science (% of 15-year-olds)		21.3	2018	●	↓
SDG5 – Gender Equality					
Demand for family planning satisfied by modern methods (% of females aged 15 to 49)	*	85.4	2022	●	↑
Ratio of female-to-male mean years of education received (%)		99.0	2019	●	↑
Ratio of female-to-male labor force participation rate (%)		83.2	2020	●	↑
Seats held by women in national parliament (%)		44.0	2020	●	↑
Gender wage gap (% of male median wage)		8.6	2018	●	↑
SDG6 – Clean Water and Sanitation					
Population using at least basic drinking water services (%)		99.9	2020	●	↑
Population using at least basic sanitation services (%)		99.9	2020	●	↑
Freshwater withdrawal (% of available freshwater resources)		42.6	2018	●	●
Anthropogenic wastewater that receives treatment (%)		91.5	2018	●	●
Scarce water consumption embodied in imports (m^3 H_2O eq/capita)		2384.5	2018	●	●
Population using safely managed water services (%)		99.6	2020	●	↑
Population using safely managed sanitation services (%)		95.7	2020	●	↑
SDG7 – Affordable and Clean Energy					
Population with access to electricity (%)		100.0	2019	●	↑
Population with access to clean fuels and technology for cooking (%)		100.0	2019	●	↑
CO_2 emissions from fuel combustion per total electricity output ($MtCO_2$/TWh)		0.9	2019	●	↑
Share of renewable energy in total primary energy supply (%)		14.8	2019	●	→
SDG8 – Decent Work and Economic Growth					
Adjusted GDP growth (%)		-4.0	2020	●	●
Victims of modern slavery (per 1,000 population)		2.3	2018	●	●
Adults with an account at a bank or other financial institution or with a mobile-money-service provider (% of population aged 15 or over)		93.8	2017	●	↑
Fundamental labor rights are effectively guaranteed (worst 0–1 best)		0.8	2020	●	↑
Fatal work-related accidents embodied in imports (per 100,000 population)		1.4	2015	●	↑
Employment-to-population ratio (%)		61.0	2020	●	↑
Youth not in employment, education or training (NEET) (% of population aged 15 to 29)		18.5	2020	●	↑

* Imputed data point

SDG9 – Industry, Innovation and Infrastructure		Value	Year	Rating	Trend
Population using the internet (%)		93.2	2020	●	↑
Mobile broadband subscriptions (per 100 population)		102.9	2019	●	↑
Logistics Performance Index: Quality of trade and transport-related infrastructure (worst 1–5 best)		3.8	2018	●	↑
The Times Higher Education Universities Ranking: Average score of top 3 universities (worst 0–100 best)		55.8	2022	●	●
Articles published in academic journals (per 1,000 population)		2.2	2020	●	↑
Expenditure on research and development (% of GDP)		1.2	2018	●	→
Researchers (per 1,000 employed population)		7.1	2019	●	↑
Triadic patent families filed (per million population)		7.3	2019	●	→
Gap in internet access by income (percentage points)		14.0	2020	●	↑
Female share of graduates from STEM fields at the tertiary level (%)		29.6	2017	●	↑
SDG10 – Reduced Inequalities					
Gini coefficient		34.7	2018	●	↑
Palma ratio		1.2	2019	●	↑
Elderly poverty rate (% of population aged 66 or over)		11.6	2019	●	↓
SDG11 – Sustainable Cities and Communities					
Proportion of urban population living in slums (%)		0.0	2018	●	↑
Annual mean concentration of particulate matter of less than 2.5 microns in diameter (PM2.5) (μg/m^3)		9.4	2019	●	↑
Access to improved water source, piped (% of urban population)		99.9	2020	●	↑
Satisfaction with public transport (%)		68.0	2021	●	→
Population with rent overburden (%)		11.1	2019	●	↑
SDG12 – Responsible Consumption and Production					
Electronic waste (kg/capita)		19.0	2019	●	●
Production-based SO_2 emissions (kg/capita)		10.1	2018	●	●
SO_2 emissions embodied in imports (kg/capita)		5.0	2018	●	●
Production-based nitrogen emissions (kg/capita)		15.2	2015	●	↑
Nitrogen emissions embodied in imports (kg/capita)		9.8	2015	●	↓
Exports of plastic waste (kg/capita)		3.0	2021	●	●
Non-recycled municipal solid waste (kg/capita/day)		0.9	2019	●	↗
SDG13 – Climate Action					
CO_2 emissions from fossil fuel combustion and cement production (tCO_2/capita)		4.5	2020	●	↑
CO_2 emissions embodied in imports (tCO_2/capita)		1.6	2018	●	↓
CO_2 emissions embodied in fossil fuel exports (kg/capita)		105.1	2021	●	●
Carbon Pricing Score at EUR60/tCO_2 (%, worst 0–100 best)		45.9	2018	●	↑
SDG14 – Life Below Water					
Mean area that is protected in marine sites important to biodiversity (%)		85.7	2020	●	↑
Ocean Health Index: Clean Waters score (worst 0–100 best)		48.7	2020	●	↓
Fish caught from overexploited or collapsed stocks (% of total catch)		32.1	2018	●	↗
Fish caught by trawling or dredging (%)		42.8	2018	●	↗
Fish caught that are then discarded (%)		10.8	2018	●	↑
Marine biodiversity threats embodied in imports (per million population)		0.6	2018	●	●
SDG15 – Life on Land					
Mean area that is protected in terrestrial sites important to biodiversity (%)		57.6	2020	●	→
Mean area that is protected in freshwater sites important to biodiversity (%)		51.3	2020	●	→
Red List Index of species survival (worst 0–1 best)		0.8	2021	●	↓
Permanent deforestation (% of forest area, 5-year average)		0.0	2020	●	↑
Terrestrial and freshwater biodiversity threats embodied in imports (per million population)		3.6	2018	●	●
SDG16 – Peace, Justice and Strong Institutions					
Homicides (per 100,000 population)		0.6	2020	●	↑
Unsentenced detainees (% of prison population)		16.2	2019	●	↑
Population who feel safe walking alone at night in the city or area where they live (%)		81	2021	●	↑
Property Rights (worst 1–7 best)		5.2	2020	●	↑
Birth registrations with civil authority (% of children under age 5)		100.0	2020	●	●
Corruption Perception Index (worst 0–100 best)		61	2021	●	↑
Children involved in child labor (% of population aged 5 to 14)	*	0.0	2019	●	●
Exports of major conventional weapons (TIV constant million USD per 100,000 population)		1.9	2020	●	●
Press Freedom Index (best 0–100 worst)		20.4	2021	●	↑
Access to and affordability of justice (worst 0–1 best)		0.7	2020	●	↑
Persons held in prison (per 100,000 population)		125.2	2019	●	↗
SDG17 – Partnerships for the Goals					
Government spending on health and education (% of GDP)		10.6	2019	●	↑
For high-income and all OECD DAC countries: International concessional public finance, including official development assistance (% of GNI)		0.3	2021	●	↗
Other countries: Government revenue excluding grants (% of GDP)		NA	NA	●	●
Corporate Tax Haven Score (best 0–100 worst)		54.5	2019	●	●
Financial Secrecy Score (best 0–100 worst)		44.0	2020	●	●
Shifted profits of multinationals (US\$ billion)		23.1	2018	●	↑
Statistical Performance Index (worst 0–100 best)		88.9	2019	●	↑

SRI LANKA

East and South Asia

OVERALL PERFORMANCE

COUNTRY RANKING

SRI LANKA

76/163

COUNTRY SCORE

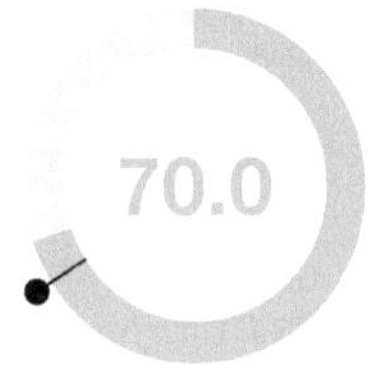

REGIONAL AVERAGE: 65.9

AVERAGE PERFORMANCE BY SDG

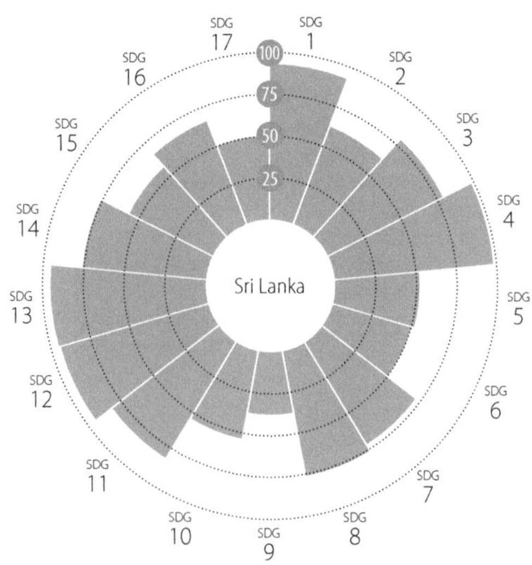

SDG DASHBOARDS AND TRENDS

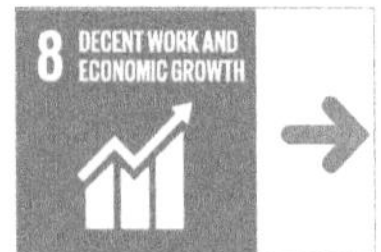

Major challenges · Significant challenges · Challenges remain · SDG achieved · Information unavailable

Decreasing · Stagnating · Moderately improving · On track or maintaining SDG achievement · Information unavailable

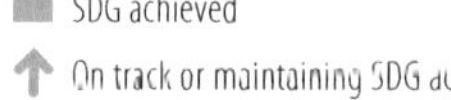

Note: The full title of each SDG is available here: https://sustainabledevelopment.un.org/topics/sustainabledevelopmentgoals

INTERNATIONAL SPILLOVER INDEX

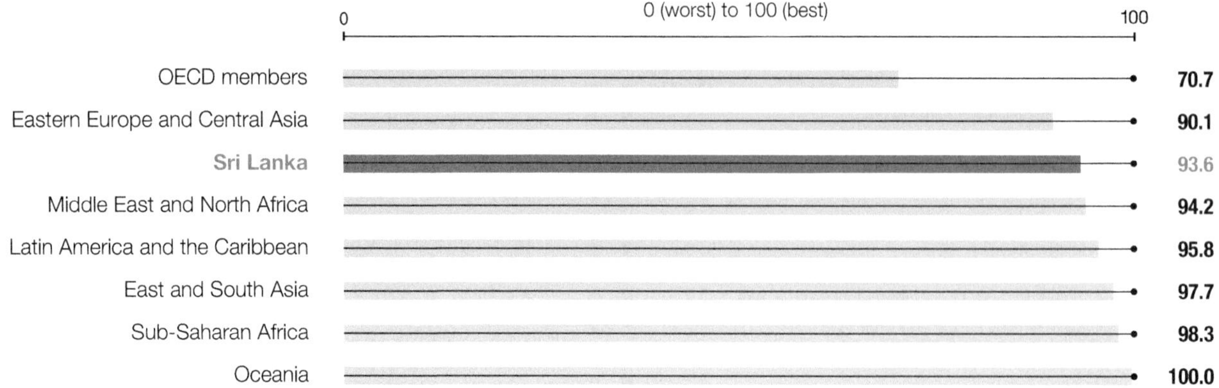

STATISTICAL PERFORMANCE INDEX

0 (worst) to 100 (best)

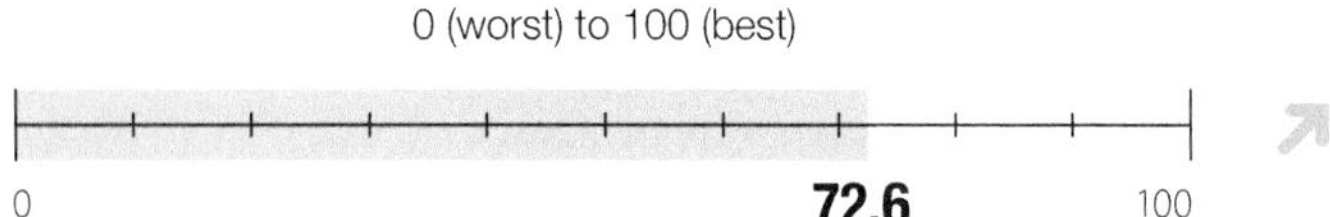

MISSING DATA IN SDG INDEX

2%

SDG1 – No Poverty	Value	Year	Rating	Trend
Poverty headcount ratio at \$1.90/day (%)	0.3	2022	●	↑
Poverty headcount ratio at \$3.20/day (%)	7.4	2022	●	↑
SDG2 – Zero Hunger				
Prevalence of undernourishment (%)	6.8	2019	●	↑
Prevalence of stunting in children under 5 years of age (%)	17.3	2016	●	↗
Prevalence of wasting in children under 5 years of age (%)	15.1	2016	●	→
Prevalence of obesity, BMI ≥ 30 (% of adult population)	5.2	2016	●	↑
Human Trophic Level (best 2–3 worst)	2.2	2017	●	↑
Cereal yield (tonnes per hectare of harvested land)	3.8	2018	●	↑
Sustainable Nitrogen Management Index (best 0–1.41 worst)	0.9	2015	●	→
Exports of hazardous pesticides (tonnes per million population)	9.4	2019	●	●
SDG3 – Good Health and Well-Being				
Maternal mortality rate (per 100,000 live births)	36	2017	●	↑
Neonatal mortality rate (per 1,000 live births)	4.0	2020	●	↑
Mortality rate, under-5 (per 1,000 live births)	6.9	2020	●	↑
Incidence of tuberculosis (per 100,000 population)	64.0	2020	●	→
New HIV infections (per 1,000 uninfected population)	0.0	2020	●	↑
Age-standardized death rate due to cardiovascular disease, cancer, diabetes, or chronic respiratory disease in adults aged 30–70 years (%)	13.2	2019	●	↑
Age-standardized death rate attributable to household air pollution and ambient air pollution (per 100,000 population)	80	2016	●	●
Traffic deaths (per 100,000 population)	19.7	2019	●	↓
Life expectancy at birth (years)	76.9	2019	●	↗
Adolescent fertility rate (births per 1,000 females aged 15 to 19)	21.0	2015	●	●
Births attended by skilled health personnel (%)	99.5	2016	●	●
Surviving infants who received 2 WHO-recommended vaccines (%)	96	2020	●	↑
Universal health coverage (UHC) index of service coverage (worst 0–100 best)	67	2019	●	↑
Subjective well-being (average ladder score, worst 0–10 best)	4.1	2021	●	↓
SDG4 – Quality Education				
Participation rate in pre-primary organized learning (% of children aged 4 to 6)	NA	NA	●	●
Net primary enrollment rate (%)	99.5	2018	●	●
Lower secondary completion rate (%)	98.0	2019	●	↑
Literacy rate (% of population aged 15 to 24)	99.0	2019	●	↑
SDG5 – Gender Equality				
Demand for family planning satisfied by modern methods (% of females aged 15 to 49)	74.3	2016	●	●
Ratio of female-to-male mean years of education received (%)	100.0	2019	●	↑
Ratio of female-to-male labor force participation rate (%)	45.1	2020	●	↓
Seats held by women in national parliament (%)	5.4	2020	●	→
SDG6 – Clean Water and Sanitation				
Population using at least basic drinking water services (%)	92.2	2020	●	↗
Population using at least basic sanitation services (%)	93.7	2020	●	↑
Freshwater withdrawal (% of available freshwater resources)	90.8	2018	●	●
Anthropogenic wastewater that receives treatment (%)	0.0	2018	●	●
Scarce water consumption embodied in imports (m^3 H_2O eq/capita)	4413.6	2018	●	●
SDG7 – Affordable and Clean Energy				
Population with access to electricity (%)	100.0	2019	●	↑
Population with access to clean fuels and technology for cooking (%)	31.2	2019	●	→
CO_2 emissions from fuel combustion per total electricity output ($MtCO_2$/TWh)	1.5	2019	●	→
Share of renewable energy in total primary energy supply (%)	43.1	2019	●	↑
SDG8 – Decent Work and Economic Growth				
Adjusted GDP growth (%)	-2.6	2020	●	●
Victims of modern slavery (per 1,000 population)	2.1	2018	●	●
Adults with an account at a bank or other financial institution or with a mobile-money-service provider (% of population aged 15 or over)	73.6	2017	●	↓
Unemployment rate (% of total labor force)	4.9	2022	●	↑
Fundamental labor rights are effectively guaranteed (worst 0–1 best)	0.6	2020	●	↓
Fatal work-related accidents embodied in imports (per 100,000 population)	0.3	2015	●	↑

* Imputed data point

SDG9 – Industry, Innovation and Infrastructure	Value	Year	Rating	Trend
Population using the internet (%)	35.0	2020	●	↑
Mobile broadband subscriptions (per 100 population)	64.9	2019	●	↑
Logistics Performance Index: Quality of trade and transport-related infrastructure (worst 1–5 best)	2.5	2018	●	↑
The Times Higher Education Universities Ranking: Average score of top 3 universities (worst 0–100 best)	36.0	2022	●	●
Articles published in academic journals (per 1,000 population)	0.1	2020	●	→
Expenditure on research and development (% of GDP)	0.1	2017	●	→
SDG10 – Reduced Inequalities				
Gini coefficient	39.3	2016	●	●
Palma ratio	1.9	2018	●	●
SDG11 – Sustainable Cities and Communities				
Proportion of urban population living in slums (%)	NA	NA	●	●
Annual mean concentration of particulate matter of less than 2.5 microns in diameter (PM2.5) (μg/m³)	7.2	2019	●	↑
Access to improved water source, piped (% of urban population)	79.0	2020	●	→
Satisfaction with public transport (%)	63.0	2021	●	↓
SDG12 – Responsible Consumption and Production				
Municipal solid waste (kg/capita/day)	0.3	2016	●	●
Electronic waste (kg/capita)	6.3	2019	●	●
Production-based SO_2 emissions (kg/capita)	6.1	2018	●	●
SO_2 emissions embodied in imports (kg/capita)	1.1	2018	●	●
Production-based nitrogen emissions (kg/capita)	5.1	2015	●	↑
Nitrogen emissions embodied in imports (kg/capita)	0.8	2015	●	↑
Exports of plastic waste (kg/capita)	0.0	2020	●	●
SDG13 – Climate Action				
CO_2 emissions from fossil fuel combustion and cement production (tCO_2/capita)	1.0	2020	●	↑
CO_2 emissions embodied in imports (tCO_2/capita)	0.3	2018	●	↑
CO_2 emissions embodied in fossil fuel exports (kg/capita)	0.0	2019	●	●
SDG14 – Life Below Water				
Mean area that is protected in marine sites important to biodiversity (%)	50.0	2020	●	→
Ocean Health Index: Clean Waters score (worst 0–100 best)	58.3	2020	●	→
Fish caught from overexploited or collapsed stocks (% of total catch)	11.7	2018	●	↑
Fish caught by trawling or dredging (%)	0.0	2018	●	↑
Fish caught that are then discarded (%)	4.2	2018	●	↑
Marine biodiversity threats embodied in imports (per million population)	0.1	2018	●	●
SDG15 – Life on Land				
Mean area that is protected in terrestrial sites important to biodiversity (%)	43.7	2020	●	→
Mean area that is protected in freshwater sites important to biodiversity (%)	43.9	2020	●	→
Red List Index of species survival (worst 0–1 best)	0.6	2021	●	↓
Permanent deforestation (% of forest area, 5-year average)	0.1	2020	●	↑
Terrestrial and freshwater biodiversity threats embodied in imports (per million population)	0.1	2018	●	●
SDG16 – Peace, Justice and Strong Institutions				
Homicides (per 100,000 population)	3.5	2019	●	→
Unsentenced detainees (% of prison population)	53.4	2017	●	●
Population who feel safe walking alone at night in the city or area where they live (%)	63	2021	●	↓
Property Rights (worst 1–7 best)	4.2	2020	●	→
Birth registrations with civil authority (% of children under age 5)	97.2	2020	●	●
Corruption Perception Index (worst 0–100 best)	37	2021	●	→
Children involved in child labor (% of population aged 5 to 14)	0.8	2019	●	●
Exports of major conventional weapons (TIV constant million USD per 100,000 population) *	0.0	2020	●	●
Press Freedom Index (best 0–100 worst)	42.2	2021	●	→
Access to and affordability of justice (worst 0–1 best)	0.5	2020	●	↗
SDG17 – Partnerships for the Goals				
Government spending on health and education (% of GDP)	4.1	2019	●	→
For high-income and all OECD DAC countries: International concessional public finance, including official development assistance (% of GNI)	NA	NA	●	●
Other countries: Government revenue excluding grants (% of GDP)	12.6	2019	●	↓
Corporate Tax Haven Score (best 0–100 worst) *	0.0	2019	●	●
Statistical Performance Index (worst 0–100 best)	72.6	2019	●	↗

5. Country Profiles

ST. KITTS AND NEVIS

Latin America and the Caribbean

OVERALL PERFORMANCE

COUNTRY RANKING

ST. KITTS AND NEVIS

NA /163

COUNTRY SCORE

REGIONAL AVERAGE: 69.5

AVERAGE PERFORMANCE BY SDG

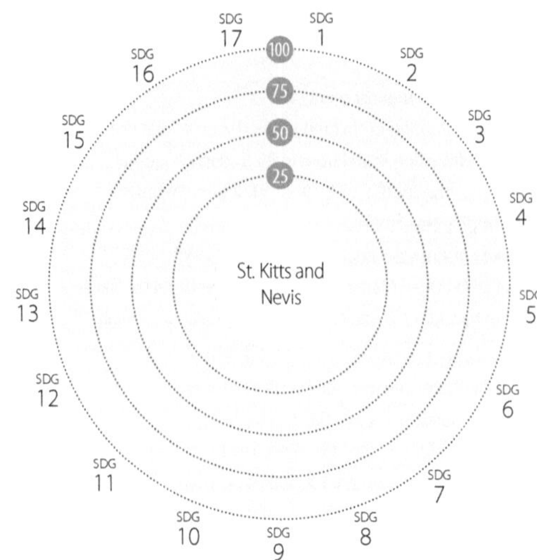

SDG DASHBOARDS AND TRENDS

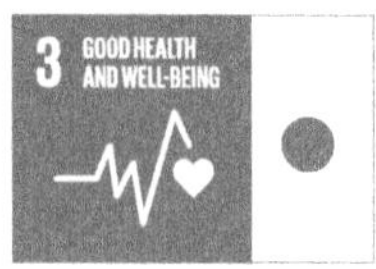

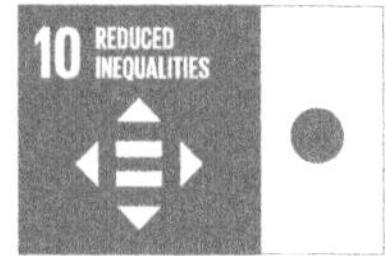

Challenges remain | SDG achieved | Information unavailable

On track or maintaining SDG achievement | Information unavailable

Note: The full title of each SDG is available here: https://sustainabledevelopment.un.org/topics/sustainabledevelopmentgoals

INTERNATIONAL SPILLOVER INDEX

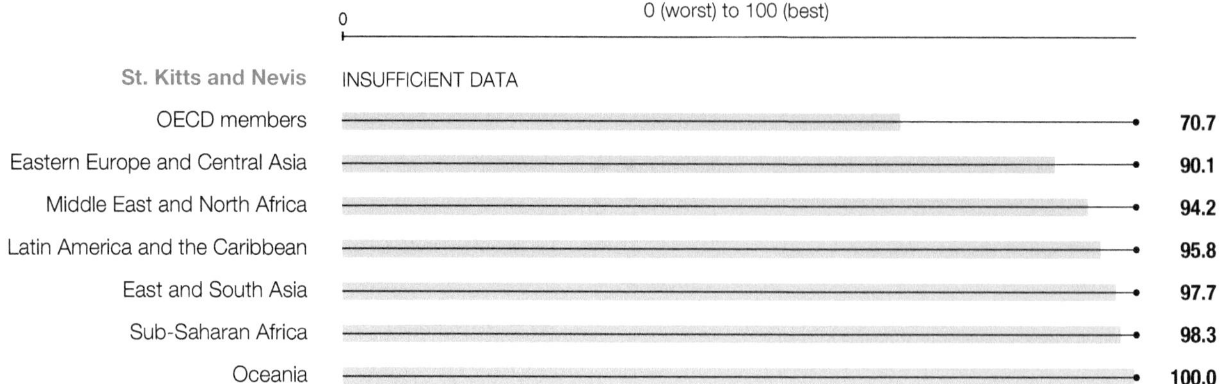

STATISTICAL PERFORMANCE INDEX

0 (worst) to 100 (best)

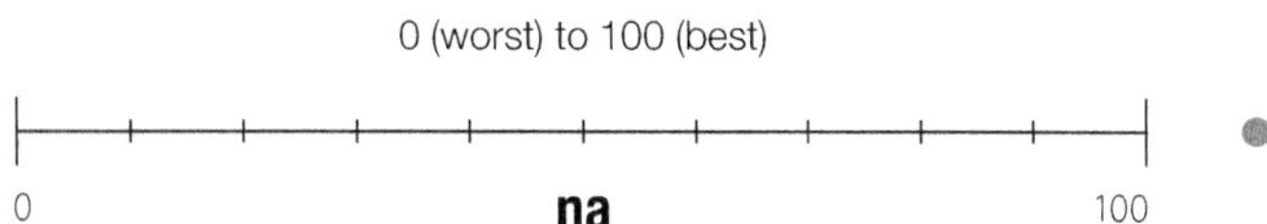

MISSING DATA IN SDG INDEX

50%

ST. KITTS AND NEVIS

Performance by Indicator

SDG1 – No Poverty		Value	Year	Rating	Trend
Poverty headcount ratio at \$1.90/day (%)		NA	NA	●	●
Poverty headcount ratio at \$3.20/day (%)		NA	NA	●	●
SDG2 – Zero Hunger					
Prevalence of undernourishment (%)	*	1.2	2019	●	●
Prevalence of stunting in children under 5 years of age (%)	*	2.6	2019	●	↑
Prevalence of wasting in children under 5 years of age (%)	*	0.7	2019	●	↑
Prevalence of obesity, BMI ≥ 30 (% of adult population)		22.9	2016	●	↓
Human Trophic Level (best 2–3 worst)		2.4	2017	●	↗
Cereal yield (tonnes per hectare of harvested land)		NA	NA	●	●
Sustainable Nitrogen Management Index (best 0–1.41 worst)		1.2	2015	●	→
Exports of hazardous pesticides (tonnes per million population)		NA	NA	●	●
SDG3 – Good Health and Well-Being					
Maternal mortality rate (per 100,000 live births)		NA	NA	●	●
Neonatal mortality rate (per 1,000 live births)		10.0	2020	●	↑
Mortality rate, under-5 (per 1,000 live births)		15.0	2020	●	↑
Incidence of tuberculosis (per 100,000 population)		4.3	2020	●	↑
New HIV infections (per 1,000 uninfected population)		NA	NA	●	●
Age-standardized death rate due to cardiovascular disease, cancer, diabetes, or chronic respiratory disease in adults aged 30–70 years (%)		NA	NA	●	●
Age-standardized death rate attributable to household air pollution and ambient air pollution (per 100,000 population)		NA	NA	●	●
Traffic deaths (per 100,000 population)		NA	NA	●	●
Life expectancy at birth (years)		NA	NA	●	●
Adolescent fertility rate (births per 1,000 females aged 15 to 19)		46.1	2007	●	●
Births attended by skilled health personnel (%)		100.0	2015	●	●
Surviving infants who received 2 WHO-recommended vaccines (%)		99	2020	●	↑
Universal health coverage (UHC) index of service coverage (worst 0–100 best)		NA	NA	●	●
Subjective well-being (average ladder score, worst 0–10 best)		NA	NA	●	●
SDG4 – Quality Education					
Participation rate in pre-primary organized learning (% of children aged 4 to 6)		89.3	2016	●	●
Net primary enrollment rate (%)		98.9	2016	●	●
Lower secondary completion rate (%)		111.2	2016	●	●
Literacy rate (% of population aged 15 to 24)		NA	NA	●	●
SDG5 – Gender Equality					
Demand for family planning satisfied by modern methods (% of females aged 15 to 49)		NA	NA	●	●
Ratio of female-to-male mean years of education received (%)		NA	NA	●	●
Ratio of female-to-male labor force participation rate (%)		NA	NA	●	●
Seats held by women in national parliament (%)		25.0	2020	●	↑
SDG6 – Clean Water and Sanitation					
Population using at least basic drinking water services (%)		98.6	2017	●	●
Population using at least basic sanitation services (%)		95.0	2017	●	●
Freshwater withdrawal (% of available freshwater resources)		50.8	2018	●	●
Anthropogenic wastewater that receives treatment (%)		0.6	2018	●	●
Scarce water consumption embodied in imports (m^3 H_2O eq/capita)		NA	NA	●	●
SDG7 – Affordable and Clean Energy					
Population with access to electricity (%)		100.0	2019	●	↑
Population with access to clean fuels and technology for cooking (%)		100.0	2019	●	↑
CO_2 emissions from fuel combustion per total electricity output ($MtCO_2$/TWh)		1.2	2019	●	→
Share of renewable energy in total primary energy supply (%)		NA	NA	●	●
SDG8 – Decent Work and Economic Growth					
Adjusted GDP growth (%)		-4.8	2020	●	●
Victims of modern slavery (per 1,000 population)		NA	NA	●	●
Adults with an account at a bank or other financial institution or with a mobile-money-service provider (% of population aged 15 or over)		NA	NA	●	●
Unemployment rate (% of total labor force)		NA	NA	●	●
Fundamental labor rights are effectively guaranteed (worst 0–1 best)		0.8	2020	●	↑
Fatal work-related accidents embodied in imports (per 100,000 population)		NA	NA	●	●

* Imputed data point

SDG9 – Industry, Innovation and Infrastructure		Value	Year	Rating	Trend
Population using the internet (%)		80.7	2017	●	●
Mobile broadband subscriptions (per 100 population)		92.5	2019	●	↑
Logistics Performance Index: Quality of trade and transport-related infrastructure (worst 1–5 best)		NA	NA	●	●
The Times Higher Education Universities Ranking: Average score of top 3 universities (worst 0–100 best)	*	0.0	2022	●	●
Articles published in academic journals (per 1,000 population)		2.3	2020	●	↑
Expenditure on research and development (% of GDP)		NA	NA	●	●
SDG10 – Reduced Inequalities					
Gini coefficient		NA	NA	●	●
Palma ratio		NA	NA	●	●
SDG11 – Sustainable Cities and Communities					
Proportion of urban population living in slums (%)		NA	NA	●	●
Annual mean concentration of particulate matter of less than 2.5 microns in diameter (PM2.5) (μg/m^3)		11.8	2019	●	↑
Access to improved water source, piped (% of urban population)		NA	NA	●	●
Satisfaction with public transport (%)		NA	NA	●	●
SDG12 – Responsible Consumption and Production					
Municipal solid waste (kg/capita/day)		1.8	2015	●	●
Electronic waste (kg/capita)		12.4	2019	●	●
Production-based SO_2 emissions (kg/capita)		NA	NA	●	●
SO_2 emissions embodied in imports (kg/capita)		NA	NA	●	●
Production-based nitrogen emissions (kg/capita)		NA	NA	●	●
Nitrogen emissions embodied in imports (kg/capita)		NA	NA	●	●
Exports of plastic waste (kg/capita)		NA	NA	●	●
SDG13 – Climate Action					
CO_2 emissions from fossil fuel combustion and cement production (tCO_2/capita)		4.0	2020	●	↗
CO_2 emissions embodied in imports (tCO_2/capita)		NA	NA	●	●
CO_2 emissions embodied in fossil fuel exports (kg/capita)		0.0	2020	●	●
SDG14 – Life Below Water					
Mean area that is protected in marine sites important to biodiversity (%)		51.7	2020	●	↑
Ocean Health Index: Clean Waters score (worst 0–100 best)		56.7	2020	●	→
Fish caught from overexploited or collapsed stocks (% of total catch)		NA	NA	●	●
Fish caught by trawling or dredging (%)		96.7	2018	●	↓
Fish caught that are then discarded (%)		41.2	2018	●	↓
Marine biodiversity threats embodied in imports (per million population)		NA	NA	●	●
SDG15 – Life on Land					
Mean area that is protected in terrestrial sites important to biodiversity (%)		56.8	2020	●	↑
Mean area that is protected in freshwater sites important to biodiversity (%)		NA	NA	●	●
Red List Index of species survival (worst 0–1 best)		0.7	2021	●	↓
Permanent deforestation (% of forest area, 5-year average)		0.0	2020	●	↑
Terrestrial and freshwater biodiversity threats embodied in imports (per million population)		NA	NA	●	●
SDG16 – Peace, Justice and Strong Institutions					
Homicides (per 100,000 population)		22.7	2019	●	↑
Unsentenced detainees (% of prison population)		30.5	2017	●	●
Population who feel safe walking alone at night in the city or area where they live (%)		NA	NA	●	●
Property Rights (worst 1–7 best)		NA	NA	●	●
Birth registrations with civil authority (% of children under age 5)		NA	NA	●	●
Corruption Perception Index (worst 0–100 best)		NA	NA	●	●
Children involved in child labor (% of population aged 5 to 14)		NA	NA	●	●
Exports of major conventional weapons (TIV constant million USD per 100,000 population)	*	0.0	2020	●	●
Press Freedom Index (best 0–100 worst)		NA	NA	●	●
Access to and affordability of justice (worst 0–1 best)		0.7	2020	●	↑
SDG17 – Partnerships for the Goals					
Government spending on health and education (% of GDP)		5.3	2019	●	→
For high-income and all OECD DAC countries: International concessional public finance, including official development assistance (% of GNI)		NA	NA	●	●
Other countries: Government revenue excluding grants (% of GDP)		NA	NA	●	●
Corporate Tax Haven Score (best 0–100 worst)	*	0.0	2019	●	●
Statistical Performance Index (worst 0–100 best)		NA	NA	●	●

5. Country Profiles

ST. LUCIA

Latin America and the Caribbean

OVERALL PERFORMANCE

COUNTRY RANKING

ST. LUCIA

NA /163

COUNTRY SCORE

REGIONAL AVERAGE: 69.5

AVERAGE PERFORMANCE BY SDG

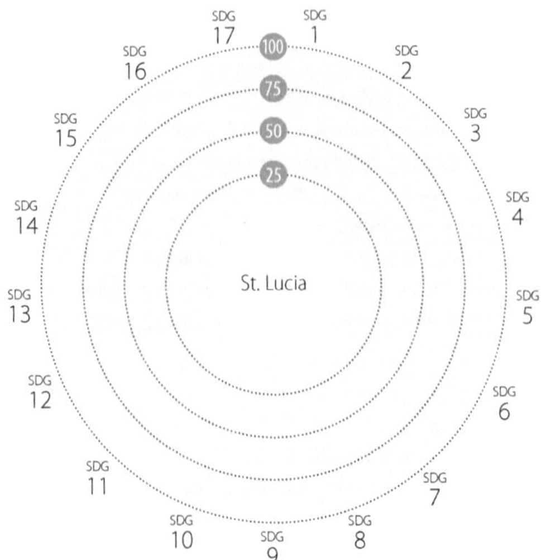

SDG DASHBOARDS AND TRENDS

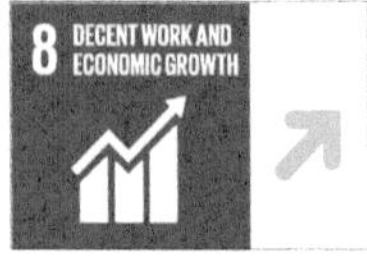

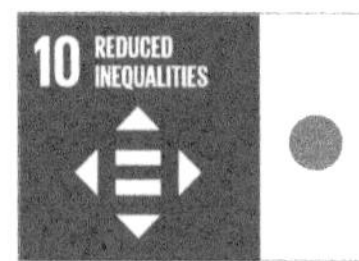

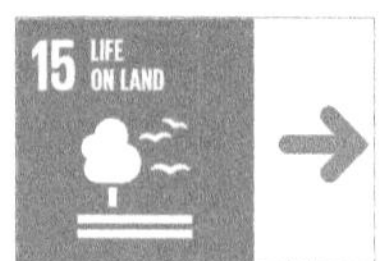

Major challenges | Significant challenges | Challenges remain | SDG achieved | Information unavailable

Decreasing | Stagnating | Moderately improving | On track or maintaining SDG achievement | Information unavailable

Note: The full title of each SDG is available here: https://sustainabledevelopment.un.org/topics/sustainabledevelopmentgoals

INTERNATIONAL SPILLOVER INDEX

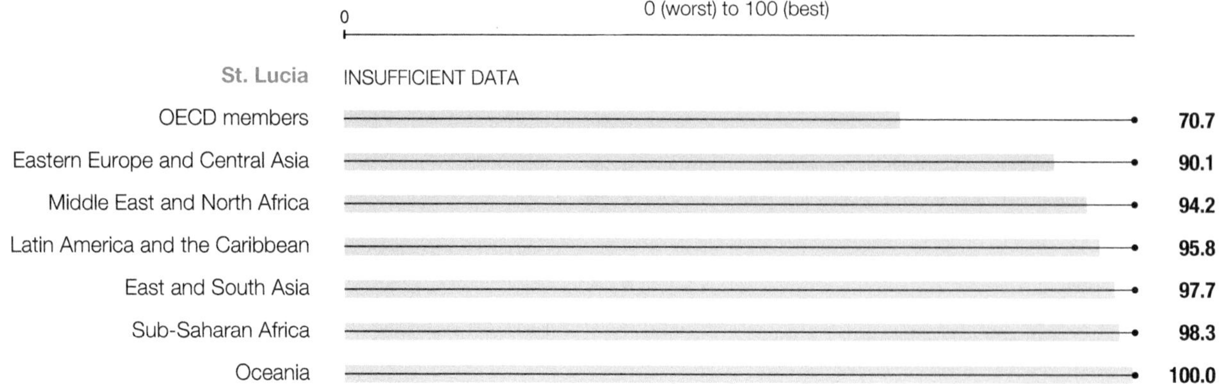

STATISTICAL PERFORMANCE INDEX

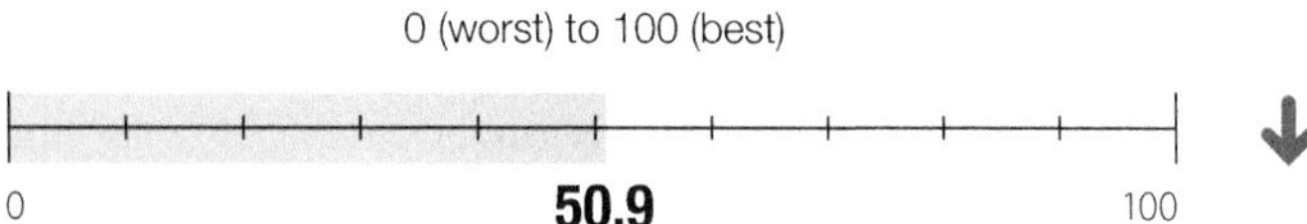

MISSING DATA IN SDG INDEX

27%

ST. LUCIA

Performance by Indicator

SDG1 – No Poverty		Value	Year	Rating	Trend
Poverty headcount ratio at $1.90/day (%)		4.8	2022	•	↗
Poverty headcount ratio at $3.20/day (%)		10.4	2022	•	→
SDG2 – Zero Hunger					
Prevalence of undernourishment (%)		NA	NA	•	•
Prevalence of stunting in children under 5 years of age (%)		2.5	2012	•	↑
Prevalence of wasting in children under 5 years of age (%)		3.7	2012	•	↑
Prevalence of obesity, BMI ≥ 30 (% of adult population)		19.7	2016	•	↓
Human Trophic Level (best 2–3 worst)		2.4	2017	•	↗
Cereal yield (tonnes per hectare of harvested land)		NA	NA	•	•
Sustainable Nitrogen Management Index (best 0–1.41 worst)		1.3	2015	•	↓
Exports of hazardous pesticides (tonnes per million population)		5.5	2019	•	•
SDG3 – Good Health and Well-Being					
Maternal mortality rate (per 100,000 live births)		117	2017	•	→
Neonatal mortality rate (per 1,000 live births)		12.9	2020	•	→
Mortality rate, under-5 (per 1,000 live births)		24.4	2020	•	↑
Incidence of tuberculosis (per 100,000 population)		2.2	2020	•	↑
New HIV infections (per 1,000 uninfected population)		NA	NA	•	•
Age-standardized death rate due to cardiovascular disease, cancer, diabetes, or chronic respiratory disease in adults aged 30–70 years (%)		17.7	2019	•	→
Age-standardized death rate attributable to household air pollution and ambient air pollution (per 100,000 population)		30	2016	•	•
Traffic deaths (per 100,000 population)		29.8	2019	•	↓
Life expectancy at birth (years)		74.3	2019	•	↓
Adolescent fertility rate (births per 1,000 females aged 15 to 19)		25.3	2020	•	↑
Births attended by skilled health personnel (%)		100.0	2017	•	↑
Surviving infants who received 2 WHO-recommended vaccines (%)		86	2020	•	↓
Universal health coverage (UHC) index of service coverage (worst 0–100 best)		72	2019	•	→
Subjective well-being (average ladder score, worst 0–10 best)		NA	NA	•	•
SDG4 – Quality Education					
Participation rate in pre-primary organized learning (% of children aged 4 to 6)		99.0	2020	•	↑
Net primary enrollment rate (%)		96.8	2020	•	↓
Lower secondary completion rate (%)		81.3	2020	•	↓
Literacy rate (% of population aged 15 to 24)		NA	NA	•	•
SDG5 – Gender Equality					
Demand for family planning satisfied by modern methods (% of females aged 15 to 49)		72.0	2012	•	↗
Ratio of female-to-male mean years of education received (%)		107.3	2019	•	↑
Ratio of female-to-male labor force participation rate (%)		85.8	2020	•	↑
Seats held by women in national parliament (%)		16.7	2020	•	→
SDG6 – Clean Water and Sanitation					
Population using at least basic drinking water services (%)		96.9	2020	•	↑
Population using at least basic sanitation services (%)		83.4	2020	•	→
Freshwater withdrawal (% of available freshwater resources)		14.3	2018	•	•
Anthropogenic wastewater that receives treatment (%)		0.9	2018	•	•
Scarce water consumption embodied in imports (m^3 H_2O eq/capita)		NA	NA	•	•
SDG7 – Affordable and Clean Energy					
Population with access to electricity (%)		99.5	2019	•	↑
Population with access to clean fuels and technology for cooking (%)		96.6	2019	•	↑
CO_2 emissions from fuel combustion per total electricity output ($MtCO_2$/TWh)		1.1	2019	•	↓
Share of renewable energy in total primary energy supply (%)		NA	NA	•	•
SDG8 – Decent Work and Economic Growth					
Adjusted GDP growth (%)		-9.2	2020	•	•
Victims of modern slavery (per 1,000 population)		NA	NA	•	•
Adults with an account at a bank or other financial institution or with a mobile-money-service provider (% of population aged 15 or over)		NA	NA	•	•
Unemployment rate (% of total labor force)		15.8	2022	•	↗
Fundamental labor rights are effectively guaranteed (worst 0–1 best)		0.7	2020	•	↗
Fatal work-related accidents embodied in imports (per 100,000 population)		NA	NA	•	•

* Imputed data point

SDG9 – Industry, Innovation and Infrastructure		Value	Year	Rating	Trend
Population using the internet (%)		53.3	2020	•	↗
Mobile broadband subscriptions (per 100 population)		48.9	2019	•	↑
Logistics Performance Index: Quality of trade and transport-related infrastructure (worst 1–5 best)		NA	NA	•	•
The Times Higher Education Universities Ranking: Average score of top 3 universities (worst 0–100 best)	*	0.0	2022	•	•
Articles published in academic journals (per 1,000 population)		0.1	2020	•	→
Expenditure on research and development (% of GDP)		NA	NA	•	•
SDG10 – Reduced Inequalities					
Gini coefficient		51.2	2016	•	•
Palma ratio		3.5	2018	•	•
SDG11 – Sustainable Cities and Communities					
Proportion of urban population living in slums (%)		11.9	2018	•	→
Annual mean concentration of particulate matter of less than 2.5 microns in diameter (PM2.5) (μg/m^3)		21.0	2019	•	↗
Access to improved water source, piped (% of urban population)		98.5	2020	•	↑
Satisfaction with public transport (%)		NA	NA	•	•
SDG12 – Responsible Consumption and Production					
Municipal solid waste (kg/capita/day)		1.2	2015	•	•
Electronic waste (kg/capita)		9.7	2019	•	•
Production-based SO_2 emissions (kg/capita)		NA	NA	•	•
SO_2 emissions embodied in imports (kg/capita)		NA	NA	•	•
Production-based nitrogen emissions (kg/capita)		NA	NA	•	•
Nitrogen emissions embodied in imports (kg/capita)		NA	NA	•	•
Exports of plastic waste (kg/capita)		0.2	2018	•	•
SDG13 – Climate Action					
CO_2 emissions from fossil fuel combustion and cement production (tCO_2/capita)		2.4	2020	•	↑
CO_2 emissions embodied in imports (tCO_2/capita)		NA	NA	•	•
CO_2 emissions embodied in fossil fuel exports (kg/capita)		0.0	2018	•	•
SDG14 – Life Below Water					
Mean area that is protected in marine sites important to biodiversity (%)		26.2	2020	•	→
Ocean Health Index: Clean Waters score (worst 0–100 best)		53.2	2020	•	↓
Fish caught from overexploited or collapsed stocks (% of total catch)		NA	NA	•	•
Fish caught by trawling or dredging (%)		0.2	2018	•	•
Fish caught that are then discarded (%)		0.6	2018	•	•
Marine biodiversity threats embodied in imports (per million population)		NA	NA	•	•
SDG15 – Life on Land					
Mean area that is protected in terrestrial sites important to biodiversity (%)		45.6	2020	•	→
Mean area that is protected in freshwater sites important to biodiversity (%)		NA	NA	•	•
Red List Index of species survival (worst 0–1 best)		0.8	2021	•	↓
Permanent deforestation (% of forest area, 5-year average)		0.0	2020	•	↑
Terrestrial and freshwater biodiversity threats embodied in imports (per million population)		NA	NA	•	•
SDG16 – Peace, Justice and Strong Institutions					
Homicides (per 100,000 population)		25.2	2019	•	↓
Unsentenced detainees (% of prison population)		53.3	2017	•	•
Population who feel safe walking alone at night in the city or area where they live (%)		NA	NA	•	•
Property Rights (worst 1–7 best)		NA	NA	•	•
Birth registrations with civil authority (% of children under age 5)		92.0	2020	•	•
Corruption Perception Index (worst 0–100 best)		56	2021	•	↓
Children involved in child labor (% of population aged 5 to 14)		3.3	2019	•	•
Exports of major conventional weapons (TIV constant million USD per 100,000 population)	*	0.0	2020	•	•
Press Freedom Index (best 0–100 worst)		NA	NA	•	•
Access to and affordability of justice (worst 0–1 best)		0.7	2020	•	↑
SDG17 – Partnerships for the Goals					
Government spending on health and education (% of GDP)		5.6	2020	•	↓
For high-income and all OECD DAC countries: International concessional public finance, including official development assistance (% of GNI)		NA	NA	•	•
Other countries: Government revenue excluding grants (% of GDP)		19.4	2017	•	•
Corporate Tax Haven Score (best 0–100 worst)	*	0.0	2019	•	•
Statistical Performance Index (worst 0–100 best)		50.9	2019	•	↓

ST. VINCENT AND THE GRENADINES

OVERALL PERFORMANCE

COUNTRY RANKING

ST. VINCENT AND THE GRENADINES

NA /163

COUNTRY SCORE

REGIONAL AVERAGE: 69.5

AVERAGE PERFORMANCE BY SDG

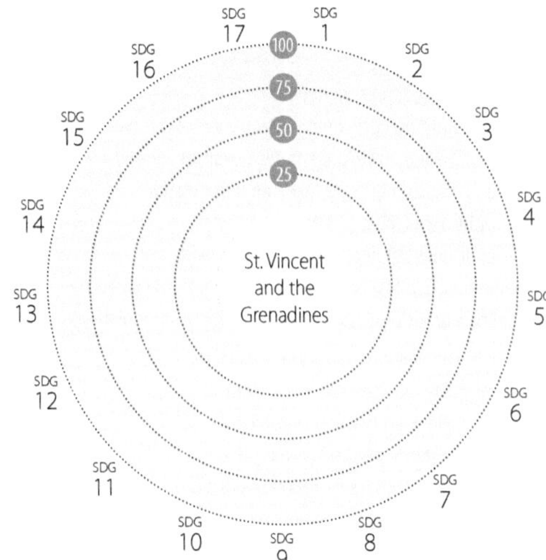

SDG DASHBOARDS AND TRENDS

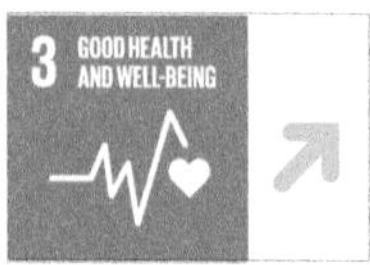

Major challenges | Significant challenges | Challenges remain | SDG achieved | Information unavailable

Decreasing | Stagnating | Moderately improving | On track or maintaining SDG achievement | Information unavailable

Note: The full title of each SDG is available here: https://sustainabledevelopment.un.org/topics/sustainabledevelopmentgoals

INTERNATIONAL SPILLOVER INDEX

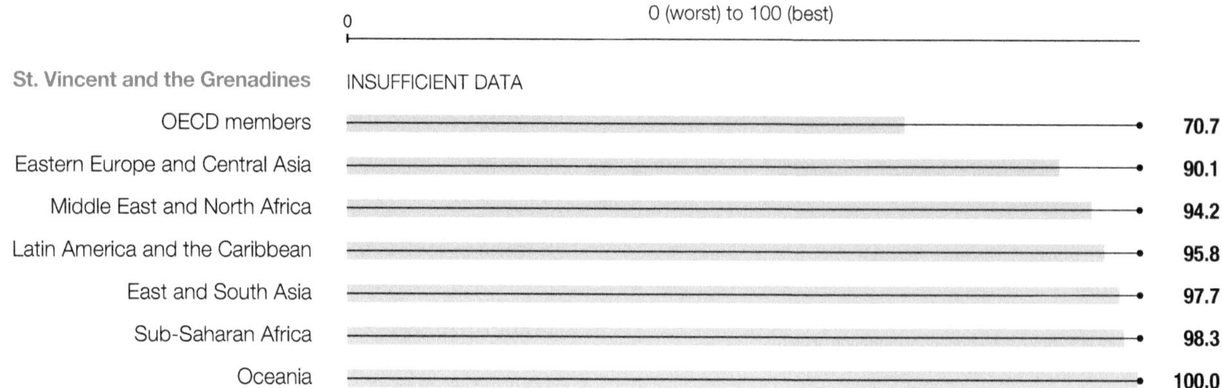

STATISTICAL PERFORMANCE INDEX

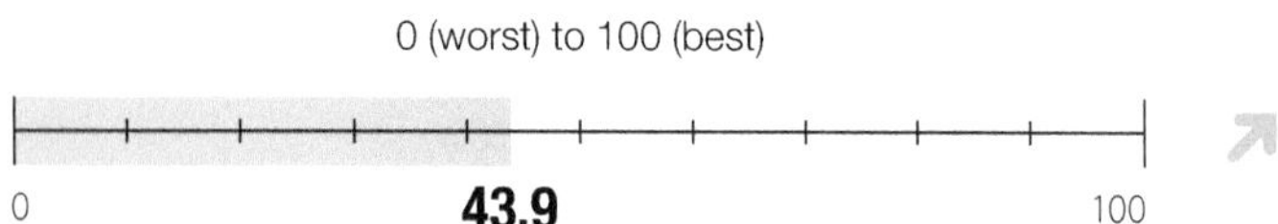

MISSING DATA IN SDG INDEX

35%

ST. VINCENT AND THE GRENADINES Performance by Indicator

SDG1 – No Poverty

Indicator		Value	Year	Rating	Trend
Poverty headcount ratio at \$1.90/day (%)	*	NA	NA	●	●
Poverty headcount ratio at \$3.20/day (%)	*	NA	NA	●	●

SDG2 – Zero Hunger

Indicator		Value	Year	Rating	Trend
Prevalence of undernourishment (%)		5.6	2019	●	↑
Prevalence of stunting in children under 5 years of age (%)		NA	NA	●	●
Prevalence of wasting in children under 5 years of age (%)		NA	NA	●	●
Prevalence of obesity, BMI ≥ 30 (% of adult population)		23.7	2016	●	↓
Human Trophic Level (best 2–3 worst)		2.3	2017	●	→
Cereal yield (tonnes per hectare of harvested land)		27.8	2018	●	↑
Sustainable Nitrogen Management Index (best 0–1.41 worst)		0.9	2015	●	→
Exports of hazardous pesticides (tonnes per million population)		NA	NA	●	●

SDG3 – Good Health and Well-Being

Indicator		Value	Year	Rating	Trend
Maternal mortality rate (per 100,000 live births)		68	2017	●	↑
Neonatal mortality rate (per 1,000 live births)		8.8	2020	●	↑
Mortality rate, under-5 (per 1,000 live births)		14.1	2020	●	↑
Incidence of tuberculosis (per 100,000 population)		6.7	2020	●	↑
New HIV infections (per 1,000 uninfected population)		NA	NA	●	●
Age-standardized death rate due to cardiovascular disease, cancer, diabetes, or chronic respiratory disease in adults aged 30–70 years (%)		20.7	2019	●	↗
Age-standardized death rate attributable to household air pollution and ambient air pollution (per 100,000 population)		48	2016	●	●
Traffic deaths (per 100,000 population)		7.4	2019	●	↑
Life expectancy at birth (years)		73.2	2019	●	→
Adolescent fertility rate (births per 1,000 females aged 15 to 19)		52.3	2017	●	●
Births attended by skilled health personnel (%)		98.6	2016	●	●
Surviving infants who received 2 WHO-recommended vaccines (%)		97	2020	●	↑
Universal health coverage (UHC) index of service coverage (worst 0–100 best)		73	2019	●	↗
Subjective well-being (average ladder score, worst 0–10 best)		NA	NA	●	●

SDG4 – Quality Education

Indicator		Value	Year	Rating	Trend
Participation rate in pre-primary organized learning (% of children aged 4 to 6)		99.8	2018	●	●
Net primary enrollment rate (%)		97.2	2018	●	●
Lower secondary completion rate (%)		92.0	2018	●	↑
Literacy rate (% of population aged 15 to 24)		NA	NA	●	●

SDG5 – Gender Equality

Indicator		Value	Year	Rating	Trend
Demand for family planning satisfied by modern methods (% of females aged 15 to 49)	*	80.0	2022	●	↑
Ratio of female-to-male mean years of education received (%)		102.3	2019	●	●
Ratio of female-to-male labor force participation rate (%)		71.1	2020	●	↑
Seats held by women in national parliament (%)		18.2	2020	●	↗

SDG6 – Clean Water and Sanitation

Indicator		Value	Year	Rating	Trend
Population using at least basic drinking water services (%)		95.1	2018	●	●
Population using at least basic sanitation services (%)		87.2	2018	●	●
Freshwater withdrawal (% of available freshwater resources)		7.9	2018	●	●
Anthropogenic wastewater that receives treatment (%)		0.7	2018	●	●
Scarce water consumption embodied in imports (m^3 H_2O eq/capita)		NA	NA	●	●

SDG7 – Affordable and Clean Energy

Indicator		Value	Year	Rating	Trend
Population with access to electricity (%)		100.0	2019	●	↑
Population with access to clean fuels and technology for cooking (%)		94.2	2019	●	↑
CO_2 emissions from fuel combustion per total electricity output ($MtCO_2$/TWh)		1.9	2019	●	→
Share of renewable energy in total primary energy supply (%)		NA	NA	●	●

SDG8 – Decent Work and Economic Growth

Indicator		Value	Year	Rating	Trend
Adjusted GDP growth (%)		-3.0	2020	●	●
Victims of modern slavery (per 1,000 population)		NA	NA	●	●
Adults with an account at a bank or other financial institution or with a mobile-money-service provider (% of population aged 15 or over)		NA	NA	●	●
Unemployment rate (% of total labor force)		21.0	2022	●	↓
Fundamental labor rights are effectively guaranteed (worst 0–1 best)		0.6	2020	●	↓
Fatal work-related accidents embodied in imports (per 100,000 population)		NA	NA	●	●

* Imputed data point

SDG9 – Industry, Innovation and Infrastructure

Indicator		Value	Year	Rating	Trend
Population using the internet (%)		56.0	2018	●	●
Mobile broadband subscriptions (per 100 population)		58.2	2019	●	↑
Logistics Performance Index: Quality of trade and transport-related infrastructure (worst 1–5 best)		NA	NA	●	●
The Times Higher Education Universities Ranking: Average score of top 3 universities (worst 0–100 best)	*	0.0	2022	●	●
Articles published in academic journals (per 1,000 population)		0.3	2020	●	↑
Expenditure on research and development (% of GDP)		0.1	2002	●	●

SDG10 – Reduced Inequalities

Indicator		Value	Year	Rating	Trend
Gini coefficient		NA	NA	●	●
Palma ratio		NA	NA	●	●

SDG11 – Sustainable Cities and Communities

Indicator		Value	Year	Rating	Trend
Proportion of urban population living in slums (%)		NA	NA	●	●
Annual mean concentration of particulate matter of less than 2.5 microns in diameter (PM2.5) (μg/m^3)		21.1	2019	●	↗
Access to improved water source, piped (% of urban population)		NA	NA	●	●
Satisfaction with public transport (%)		NA	NA	●	●

SDG12 – Responsible Consumption and Production

Indicator		Value	Year	Rating	Trend
Municipal solid waste (kg/capita/day)		0.8	2015	●	●
Electronic waste (kg/capita)		8.3	2019	●	●
Production-based SO_2 emissions (kg/capita)		NA	NA	●	●
SO_2 emissions embodied in imports (kg/capita)		NA	NA	●	●
Production-based nitrogen emissions (kg/capita)		NA	NA	●	●
Nitrogen emissions embodied in imports (kg/capita)		NA	NA	●	●
Exports of plastic waste (kg/capita)		1.9	2019	●	●

SDG13 – Climate Action

Indicator		Value	Year	Rating	Trend
CO_2 emissions from fossil fuel combustion and cement production (tCO_2/capita)		1.9	2020	●	↑
CO_2 emissions embodied in imports (tCO_2/capita)		NA	NA	●	●
CO_2 emissions embodied in fossil fuel exports (kg/capita)		0.0	2017	●	●

SDG14 – Life Below Water

Indicator		Value	Year	Rating	Trend
Mean area that is protected in marine sites important to biodiversity (%)		26.3	2020	●	→
Ocean Health Index: Clean Waters score (worst 0–100 best)		59.2	2020	●	→
Fish caught from overexploited or collapsed stocks (% of total catch)		NA	NA	●	●
Fish caught by trawling or dredging (%)		0.2	2018	●	●
Fish caught that are then discarded (%)		11.2	2018	●	↗
Marine biodiversity threats embodied in imports (per million population)		NA	NA	●	●

SDG15 – Life on Land

Indicator		Value	Year	Rating	Trend
Mean area that is protected in terrestrial sites important to biodiversity (%)		45.6	2020	●	→
Mean area that is protected in freshwater sites important to biodiversity (%)		NA	NA	●	●
Red List Index of species survival (worst 0–1 best)		0.8	2021	●	↓
Permanent deforestation (% of forest area, 5-year average)		0.0	2020	●	↑
Terrestrial and freshwater biodiversity threats embodied in imports (per million population)		NA	NA	●	●

SDG16 – Peace, Justice and Strong Institutions

Indicator		Value	Year	Rating	Trend
Homicides (per 100,000 population)		17.2	2019	●	↑
Unsentenced detainees (% of prison population)		57.1	2019	●	↑
Population who feel safe walking alone at night in the city or area where they live (%)		NA	NA	●	●
Property Rights (worst 1–7 best)		NA	NA	●	●
Birth registrations with civil authority (% of children under age 5)		NA	NA	●	●
Corruption Perception Index (worst 0–100 best)		59	2021	●	↓
Children involved in child labor (% of population aged 5 to 14)		NA	NA	●	●
Exports of major conventional weapons (TIV constant million USD per 100,000 population)	*	0.0	2020	●	●
Press Freedom Index (best 0–100 worst)		NA	NA	●	●
Access to and affordability of justice (worst 0–1 best)		0.7	2020	●	↑

SDG17 – Partnerships for the Goals

Indicator		Value	Year	Rating	Trend
Government spending on health and education (% of GDP)		8.8	2019	●	↑
For high-income and all OECD DAC countries: International concessional public finance, including official development assistance (% of GNI)		NA	NA	●	●
Other countries: Government revenue excluding grants (% of GDP)		27.2	2017	●	●
Corporate Tax Haven Score (best 0–100 worst)	*	0.0	2019	●	●
Statistical Performance Index (worst 0–100 best)		43.9	2019	●	↗

5. Country Profiles

SUDAN

Sub-Saharan Africa

OVERALL PERFORMANCE

COUNTRY RANKING

SUDAN

159/163

COUNTRY SCORE

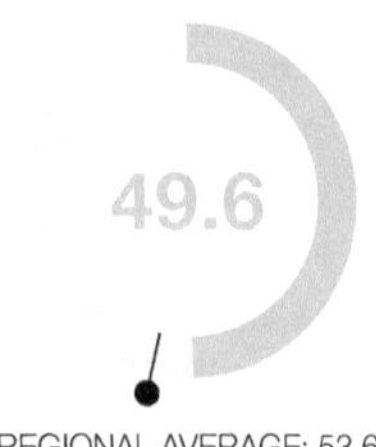

REGIONAL AVERAGE: 53.6

AVERAGE PERFORMANCE BY SDG

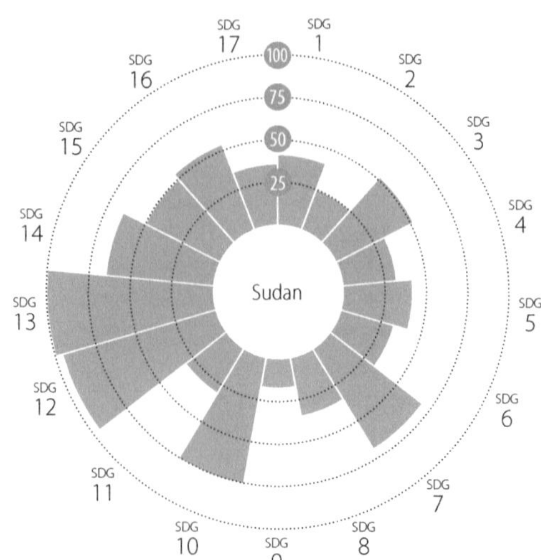

SDG DASHBOARDS AND TRENDS

Major challenges | Significant challenges | Challenges remain | SDG achieved | Information unavailable

Decreasing | Stagnating | Moderately improving | On track or maintaining SDG achievement | Information unavailable

Note: The full title of each SDG is available here: https://sustainabledevelopment.un.org/topics/sustainabledevelopmentgoals

INTERNATIONAL SPILLOVER INDEX

STATISTICAL PERFORMANCE INDEX

0 (worst) to 100 (best)

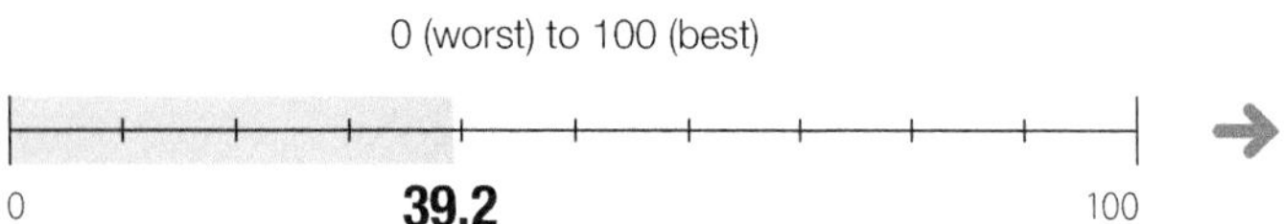

MISSING DATA IN SDG INDEX

9%

SUDAN

Performance by Indicator

SDG1 – No Poverty	Value	Year	Rating	Trend
Poverty headcount ratio at $1.90/day (%)	16.3	2022	●	↓
Poverty headcount ratio at $3.20/day (%)	49.4	2022	●	↓

SDG2 – Zero Hunger	Value	Year	Rating	Trend
Prevalence of undernourishment (%)	12.3	2019	●	→
Prevalence of stunting in children under 5 years of age (%)	38.2	2014	●	→
Prevalence of wasting in children under 5 years of age (%)	16.3	2014	●	→
Prevalence of obesity, BMI ≥ 30 (% of adult population)	NA	NA	●	●
Human Trophic Level (best 2–3 worst)	2.4	2011	●	●
Cereal yield (tonnes per hectare of harvested land)	0.7	2018	●	→
Sustainable Nitrogen Management Index (best 0–1.41 worst)	NA	NA	●	●
Exports of hazardous pesticides (tonnes per million population)	NA	NA	●	●

SDG3 – Good Health and Well-Being	Value	Year	Rating	Trend
Maternal mortality rate (per 100,000 live births)	295	2017	●	↗
Neonatal mortality rate (per 1,000 live births)	26.8	2020	●	→
Mortality rate, under-5 (per 1,000 live births)	56.6	2020	●	↗
Incidence of tuberculosis (per 100,000 population)	63.0	2020	●	↗
New HIV infections (per 1,000 uninfected population)	0.1	2020	●	↑
Age-standardized death rate due to cardiovascular disease, cancer, diabetes, or chronic respiratory disease in adults aged 30–70 years (%)	22.8	2019	●	→
Age-standardized death rate attributable to household air pollution and ambient air pollution (per 100,000 population)	185	2016	●	●
Traffic deaths (per 100,000 population)	26.8	2019	●	↓
Life expectancy at birth (years)	69.2	2019	●	→
Adolescent fertility rate (births per 1,000 females aged 15 to 19)	86.8	2013	●	●
Births attended by skilled health personnel (%)	77.7	2014	●	●
Surviving infants who received 2 WHO-recommended vaccines (%)	86	2020	●	→
Universal health coverage (UHC) index of service coverage (worst 0–100 best)	44	2019	●	→
Subjective well-being (average ladder score, worst 0–10 best)	4.1	2014	●	●

SDG4 – Quality Education	Value	Year	Rating	Trend
Participation rate in pre-primary organized learning (% of children aged 4 to 6)	39.9	2018	●	●
Net primary enrollment rate (%)	67.1	2018	●	●
Lower secondary completion rate (%)	50.8	2018	●	↓
Literacy rate (% of population aged 15 to 24)	73.0	2018	●	●

SDG5 – Gender Equality	Value	Year	Rating	Trend
Demand for family planning satisfied by modern methods (% of females aged 15 to 49)	30.1	2014	●	→
Ratio of female-to-male mean years of education received (%)	78.6	2019	●	↗
Ratio of female-to-male labor force participation rate (%)	41.8	2020	●	→
Seats held by women in national parliament (%)	30.5	2018	●	●

SDG6 – Clean Water and Sanitation	Value	Year	Rating	Trend
Population using at least basic drinking water services (%)	60.4	2020	●	→
Population using at least basic sanitation services (%)	36.9	2020	●	→
Freshwater withdrawal (% of available freshwater resources)	118.7	2018	●	●
Anthropogenic wastewater that receives treatment (%)	0.0	2018	●	●
Scarce water consumption embodied in imports (m^3 H_2O eq/capita)	230.2	2018	●	●

SDG7 – Affordable and Clean Energy	Value	Year	Rating	Trend
Population with access to electricity (%)	53.8	2019	●	↗
Population with access to clean fuels and technology for cooking (%)	53.2	2019	●	↗
CO_2 emissions from fuel combustion per total electricity output ($MtCO_2$/TWh)	1.6	2019	●	→
Share of renewable energy in total primary energy supply (%)	65.3	2019	●	↑

SDG8 – Decent Work and Economic Growth	Value	Year	Rating	Trend
Adjusted GDP growth (%)	-9.2	2020	●	●
Victims of modern slavery (per 1,000 population)	12.0	2018	●	●
Adults with an account at a bank or other financial institution or with a mobile-money-service provider (% of population aged 15 or over)	15.3	2014	●	●
Unemployment rate (% of total labor force)	19.5	2022	●	↓
Fundamental labor rights are effectively guaranteed (worst 0–1 best)	0.3	2020	●	●
Fatal work-related accidents embodied in imports (per 100,000 population)	0.0	2015	●	↑

* Imputed data point

SDG9 – Industry, Innovation and Infrastructure	Value	Year	Rating	Trend
Population using the internet (%)	28.4	2020	●	↗
Mobile broadband subscriptions (per 100 population)	37.9	2019	●	↗
Logistics Performance Index: Quality of trade and transport-related infrastructure (worst 1–5 best)	2.2	2018	●	↑
The Times Higher Education Universities Ranking: Average score of top 3 universities (worst 0–100 best)	* 0.0	2022	●	●
Articles published in academic journals (per 1,000 population)	0.0	2020	●	→
Expenditure on research and development (% of GDP)	0.3	2005	●	●

SDG10 – Reduced Inequalities	Value	Year	Rating	Trend
Gini coefficient	34.2	2014	●	●
Palma ratio	1.4	2018	●	●

SDG11 – Sustainable Cities and Communities	Value	Year	Rating	Trend
Proportion of urban population living in slums (%)	93.7	2018	●	↓
Annual mean concentration of particulate matter of less than 2.5 microns in diameter (PM2.5) (μg/m³)	58.7	2019	●	↓
Access to improved water source, piped (% of urban population)	68.6	2020	●	→
Satisfaction with public transport (%)	33.0	2014	●	●

SDG12 – Responsible Consumption and Production	Value	Year	Rating	Trend
Municipal solid waste (kg/capita/day)	0.2	2015	●	●
Electronic waste (kg/capita)	2.1	2019	●	●
Production-based SO_2 emissions (kg/capita)	2.4	2018	●	●
SO_2 emissions embodied in imports (kg/capita)	0.0	2018	●	●
Production-based nitrogen emissions (kg/capita)	22.5	2015	●	→
Nitrogen emissions embodied in imports (kg/capita)	0.0	2015	●	↑
Exports of plastic waste (kg/capita)	0.3	2018	●	●

SDG13 – Climate Action	Value	Year	Rating	Trend
CO_2 emissions from fossil fuel combustion and cement production (tCO_2/capita)	0.4	2020	●	↑
CO_2 emissions embodied in imports (tCO_2/capita)	0.0	2018	●	↑
CO_2 emissions embodied in fossil fuel exports (kg/capita)	40.1	2018	●	●

SDG14 – Life Below Water	Value	Year	Rating	Trend
Mean area that is protected in marine sites important to biodiversity (%)	48.0	2020	●	↑
Ocean Health Index: Clean Waters score (worst 0–100 best)	45.3	2020	●	↓
Fish caught from overexploited or collapsed stocks (% of total catch)	38.2	2018	●	↓
Fish caught by trawling or dredging (%)	0.0	2018	●	↑
Fish caught that are then discarded (%)	1.6	2009	●	●
Marine biodiversity threats embodied in imports (per million population)	NA	NA	●	●

SDG15 – Life on Land	Value	Year	Rating	Trend
Mean area that is protected in terrestrial sites important to biodiversity (%)	17.8	2020	●	→
Mean area that is protected in freshwater sites important to biodiversity (%)	0.0	2020	●	→
Red List Index of species survival (worst 0–1 best)	0.9	2021	●	↑
Permanent deforestation (% of forest area, 5-year average)	0.0	2020	●	↑
Terrestrial and freshwater biodiversity threats embodied in imports (per million population)	NA	NA	●	●

SDG16 – Peace, Justice and Strong Institutions	Value	Year	Rating	Trend
Homicides (per 100,000 population)	NA	NA	●	●
Unsentenced detainees (% of prison population)	NA	NA	●	●
Population who feel safe walking alone at night in the city or area where they live (%)	71	2014	●	●
Property Rights (worst 1–7 best)	NA	NA	●	●
Birth registrations with civil authority (% of children under age 5)	67.3	2020	●	●
Corruption Perception Index (worst 0–100 best)	20	2021	●	→
Children involved in child labor (% of population aged 5 to 14)	18.1	2019	●	●
Exports of major conventional weapons (TIV constant million USD per 100,000 population)	0.0	2020	●	●
Press Freedom Index (best 0–100 worst)	52.9	2021	●	↑
Access to and affordability of justice (worst 0–1 best)	0.4	2020	●	●

SDG17 – Partnerships for the Goals	Value	Year	Rating	Trend
Government spending on health and education (% of GDP)	3.3	2019	●	↓
For high-income and all OECD DAC countries: International concessional public finance, including official development assistance (% of GNI)	NA	NA	●	●
Other countries: Government revenue excluding grants (% of GDP)	8.8	2016	●	●
Corporate Tax Haven Score (best 0–100 worst)	* 0.0	2019	●	●
Statistical Performance Index (worst 0–100 best)	39.2	2019	●	→

SURINAME

Latin America and the Caribbean

OVERALL PERFORMANCE

COUNTRY RANKING

SURINAME

62/163

COUNTRY SCORE

REGIONAL AVERAGE: 69.5

AVERAGE PERFORMANCE BY SDG

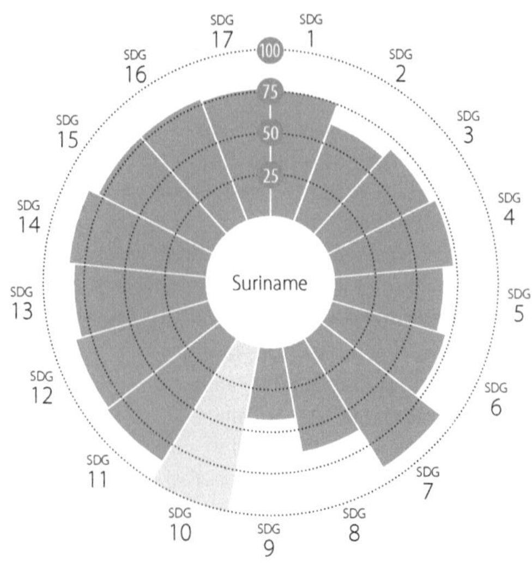

SDG DASHBOARDS AND TRENDS

Major challenges | Significant challenges | Challenges remain | SDG achieved | Information unavailable

Decreasing | Stagnating | Moderately improving | On track or maintaining SDG achievement | Information unavailable

Note: The full title of each SDG is available here: https://sustainabledevelopment.un.org/topics/sustainabledevelopmentgoals

INTERNATIONAL SPILLOVER INDEX

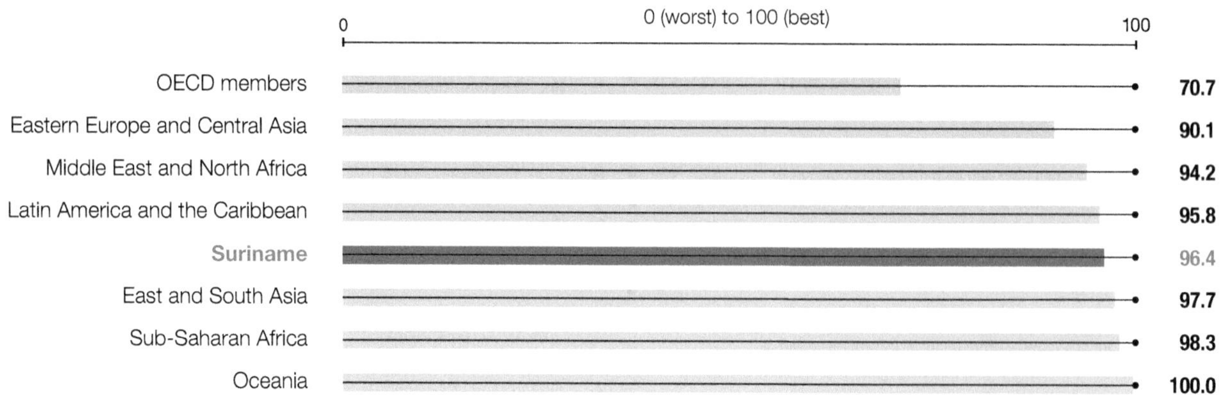

STATISTICAL PERFORMANCE INDEX

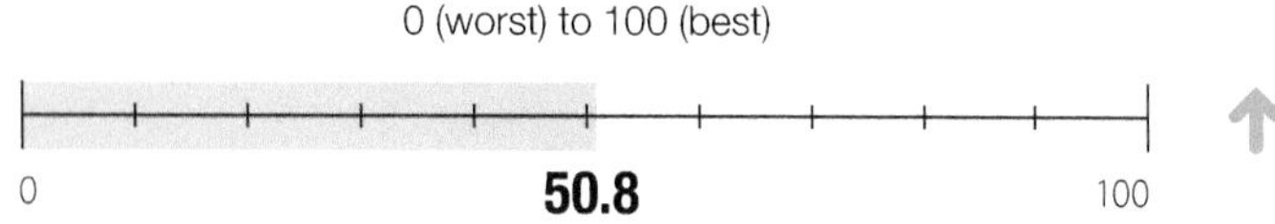

MISSING DATA IN SDG INDEX

16%

SURINAME

SDG1 – No Poverty		Value	Year	Rating	Trend
Poverty headcount ratio at $1.90/day (%)		8.6	2022	●	→
Poverty headcount ratio at $3.20/day (%)		19.3	2022	●	↓
SDG2 – Zero Hunger					
Prevalence of undernourishment (%)		8.7	2019	●	→
Prevalence of stunting in children under 5 years of age (%)		8.3	2018	●	↗
Prevalence of wasting in children under 5 years of age (%)		5.5	2018	●	→
Prevalence of obesity, BMI ≥ 30 (% of adult population)		26.4	2016	●	↓
Human Trophic Level (best 2–3 worst)		2.2	2017	●	↑
Cereal yield (tonnes per hectare of harvested land)		4.9	2018	●	↑
Sustainable Nitrogen Management Index (best 0–1.41 worst)		0.7	2015	●	→
Exports of hazardous pesticides (tonnes per million population)		NA	NA	●	●
SDG3 – Good Health and Well-Being					
Maternal mortality rate (per 100,000 live births)		120	2017	●	→
Neonatal mortality rate (per 1,000 live births)		10.9	2020	●	↑
Mortality rate, under-5 (per 1,000 live births)		17.6	2020	●	↑
Incidence of tuberculosis (per 100,000 population)		29.0	2020	●	→
New HIV infections (per 1,000 uninfected population)		0.3	2020	●	↑
Age-standardized death rate due to cardiovascular disease, cancer, diabetes, or chronic respiratory disease in adults aged 30–70 years (%)		22.7	2019	●	↓
Age-standardized death rate attributable to household air pollution and ambient air pollution (per 100,000 population)		57	2016	●	●
Traffic deaths (per 100,000 population)		15.3	2019	●	↓
Life expectancy at birth (years)		71.5	2019	●	↓
Adolescent fertility rate (births per 1,000 females aged 15 to 19)		53.9	2018	●	↗
Births attended by skilled health personnel (%)		98.4	2018	●	↑
Surviving infants who received 2 WHO-recommended vaccines (%)		45	2020	●	↓
Universal health coverage (UHC) index of service coverage (worst 0–100 best)		67	2019	●	→
Subjective well-being (average ladder score, worst 0–10 best)		6.3	2012	●	●
SDG4 – Quality Education					
Participation rate in pre-primary organized learning (% of children aged 4 to 6)		88.9	2019	●	↓
Net primary enrollment rate (%)		87.7	2019	●	↓
Lower secondary completion rate (%)		47.4	2019	●	↓
Literacy rate (% of population aged 15 to 24)		98.6	2018	●	●
SDG5 – Gender Equality					
Demand for family planning satisfied by modern methods (% of females aged 15 to 49)		57.5	2018	●	→
Ratio of female-to-male mean years of education received (%)		103.3	2019	●	↑
Ratio of female-to-male labor force participation rate (%)		66.2	2020	●	→
Seats held by women in national parliament (%)		29.4	2020	●	↗
SDG6 – Clean Water and Sanitation					
Population using at least basic drinking water services (%)		98.0	2020	●	↑
Population using at least basic sanitation services (%)		90.0	2020	●	↑
Freshwater withdrawal (% of available freshwater resources)		4.0	2018	●	●
Anthropogenic wastewater that receives treatment (%)		0.0	2018	●	●
Scarce water consumption embodied in imports (m^3 H_2O eq/capita)		NA	NA	●	●
SDG7 – Affordable and Clean Energy					
Population with access to electricity (%)		97.9	2019	●	↑
Population with access to clean fuels and technology for cooking (%)		94.1	2019	●	↑
CO_2 emissions from fuel combustion per total electricity output ($MtCO_2$/TWh)		1.2	2019	●	↑
Share of renewable energy in total primary energy supply (%)		NA	NA	●	●
SDG8 – Decent Work and Economic Growth					
Adjusted GDP growth (%)		-6.6	2020	●	●
Victims of modern slavery (per 1,000 population)		2.3	2018	●	●
Adults with an account at a bank or other financial institution or with a mobile-money-service provider (% of population aged 15 or over)		NA	NA	●	●
Unemployment rate (% of total labor force)		9.9	2022	●	↓
Fundamental labor rights are effectively guaranteed (worst 0–1 best)		0.5	2020	●	↓
Fatal work-related accidents embodied in imports (per 100,000 population)		0.5	2015	●	↑

* Imputed data point

SDG9 – Industry, Innovation and Infrastructure		Value	Year	Rating	Trend
Population using the internet (%)		70.1	2020	●	↑
Mobile broadband subscriptions (per 100 population)		91.2	2019	●	↑
Logistics Performance Index: Quality of trade and transport-related infrastructure (worst 1–5 best)		NA	NA	●	●
The Times Higher Education Universities Ranking: Average score of top 3 universities (worst 0–100 best)	*	0.0	2022	●	●
Articles published in academic journals (per 1,000 population)		0.1	2020	●	→
Expenditure on research and development (% of GDP)		NA	NA	●	●
SDG10 – Reduced Inequalities					
Gini coefficient		NA	NA	●	●
Palma ratio		NA	NA	●	●
SDG11 – Sustainable Cities and Communities					
Proportion of urban population living in slums (%)		5.5	2018	●	↑
Annual mean concentration of particulate matter of less than 2.5 microns in diameter (PM2.5) (μg/m^3)		23.6	2019	●	↗
Access to improved water source, piped (% of urban population)		88.7	2020	●	→
Satisfaction with public transport (%)		73.0	2012	●	●
SDG12 – Responsible Consumption and Production					
Municipal solid waste (kg/capita/day)		0.4	2010	●	●
Electronic waste (kg/capita)		9.4	2019	●	●
Production-based SO_2 emissions (kg/capita)		NA	NA	●	●
SO_2 emissions embodied in imports (kg/capita)		NA	NA	●	●
Production-based nitrogen emissions (kg/capita)		4.5	2015	●	↑
Nitrogen emissions embodied in imports (kg/capita)		4.4	2015	●	↑
Exports of plastic waste (kg/capita)		NA	NA	●	●
SDG13 – Climate Action					
CO_2 emissions from fossil fuel combustion and cement production (tCO_2/capita)		3.8	2020	●	↑
CO_2 emissions embodied in imports (tCO_2/capita)		NA	NA	●	●
CO_2 emissions embodied in fossil fuel exports (kg/capita)		NA	NA	●	●
SDG14 – Life Below Water					
Mean area that is protected in marine sites important to biodiversity (%)		74.2	2020	●	→
Ocean Health Index: Clean Waters score (worst 0–100 best)		79.0	2020	●	→
Fish caught from overexploited or collapsed stocks (% of total catch)		7.7	2018	●	↑
Fish caught by trawling or dredging (%)		0.0	2018	●	↑
Fish caught that are then discarded (%)		5.8	2018	●	→
Marine biodiversity threats embodied in imports (per million population)		0.0	2018	●	●
SDG15 – Life on Land					
Mean area that is protected in terrestrial sites important to biodiversity (%)		51.2	2020	●	→
Mean area that is protected in freshwater sites important to biodiversity (%)		49.4	2020	●	→
Red List Index of species survival (worst 0–1 best)		1.0	2021	●	↑
Permanent deforestation (% of forest area, 5-year average)		0.1	2020	●	→
Terrestrial and freshwater biodiversity threats embodied in imports (per million population)		0.3	2018	●	●
SDG16 – Peace, Justice and Strong Institutions					
Homicides (per 100,000 population)		5.2	2019	●	↗
Unsentenced detainees (% of prison population)		3.4	2018	●	↑
Population who feel safe walking alone at night in the city or area where they live (%)		60	2012	●	●
Property Rights (worst 1–7 best)		NA	NA	●	●
Birth registrations with civil authority (% of children under age 5)		98.3	2020	●	●
Corruption Perception Index (worst 0–100 best)		39	2021	●	→
Children involved in child labor (% of population aged 5 to 14)		4.3	2019	●	●
Exports of major conventional weapons (TIV constant million USD per 100,000 population)	*	0.0	2020	●	●
Press Freedom Index (best 0–100 worst)		17.0	2021	●	↑
Access to and affordability of justice (worst 0–1 best)		0.5	2020	●	↓
SDG17 – Partnerships for the Goals					
Government spending on health and education (% of GDP)		14.2	2019	●	↑
For high-income and all OECD DAC countries: International concessional public finance, including official development assistance (% of GNI)		NA	NA	●	●
Other countries: Government revenue excluding grants (% of GDP)		NA	NA	●	●
Corporate Tax Haven Score (best 0–100 worst)	*	0.0	2019	●	●
Statistical Performance Index (worst 0–100 best)		50.8	2019	●	↑

SWEDEN

OECD Countries

AVERAGE PERFORMANCE BY SDG

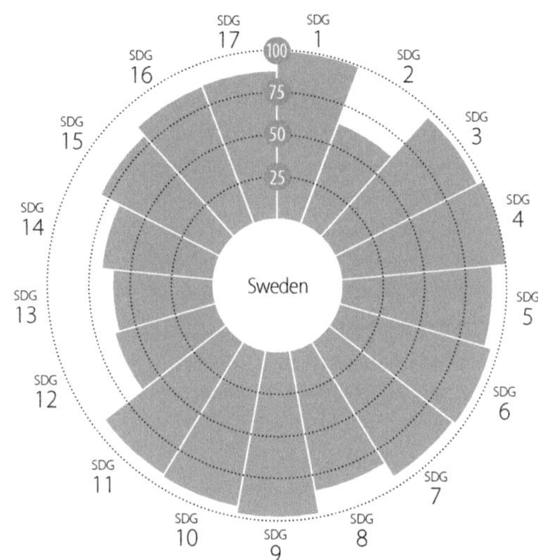

OVERALL PERFORMANCE

COUNTRY RANKING

SWEDEN

3 **/163**

COUNTRY SCORE

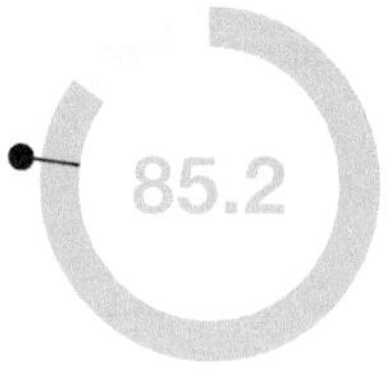

REGIONAL AVERAGE: 77.2

SDG DASHBOARDS AND TRENDS

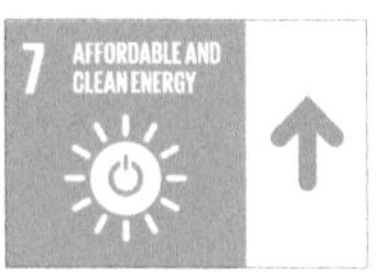

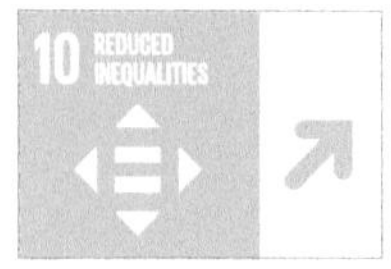

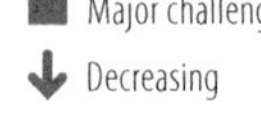

Major challenges | Significant challenges | Challenges remain | SDG achieved | Information unavailable

Decreasing | Stagnating | Moderately improving | On track or maintaining SDG achievement | Information unavailable

Note: The full title of each SDG is available here: https://sustainabledevelopment.un.org/topics/sustainabledevelopmentgoals

INTERNATIONAL SPILLOVER INDEX

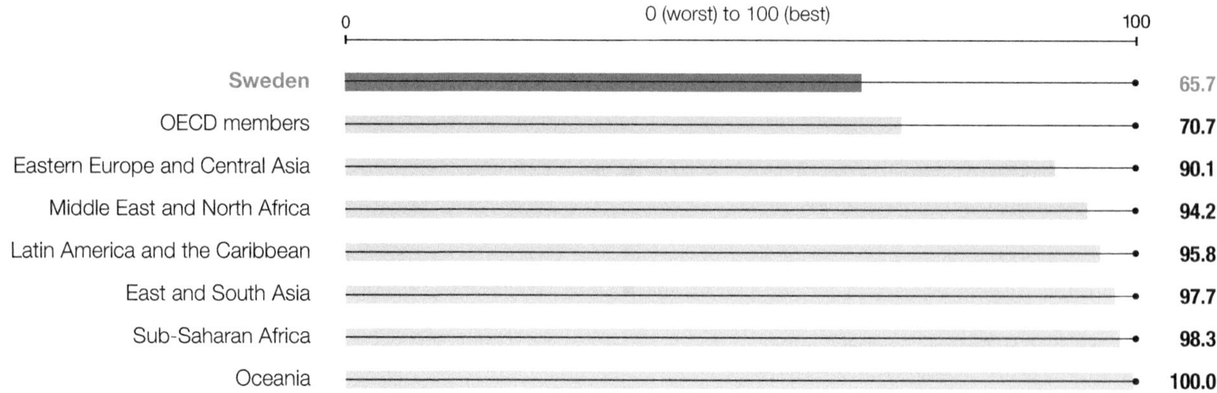

Region	Score
Sweden	65.7
OECD members	70.7
Eastern Europe and Central Asia	90.1
Middle East and North Africa	94.2
Latin America and the Caribbean	95.8
East and South Asia	97.7
Sub-Saharan Africa	98.3
Oceania	100.0

STATISTICAL PERFORMANCE INDEX

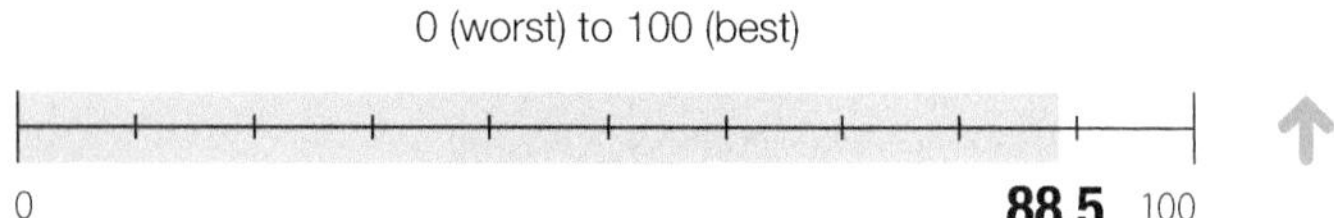

MISSING DATA IN SDG INDEX

2%

SDG1 – No Poverty	Value	Year	Rating	Trend
Poverty headcount ratio at $1.90/day (%)	0.6	2022	●	↑
Poverty headcount ratio at $3.20/day (%)	0.7	2022	●	↑
Poverty rate after taxes and transfers (%)	9.3	2019	●	↑
SDG2 – Zero Hunger				
Prevalence of undernourishment (%)	2.5	2019	●	↑
Prevalence of stunting in children under 5 years of age (%)	* 2.6	2019	●	↑
Prevalence of wasting in children under 5 years of age (%)	* 0.7	2019	●	↑
Prevalence of obesity, BMI ≥ 30 (% of adult population)	20.6	2016	●	↓
Human Trophic Level (best 2–3 worst)	2.5	2017	●	→
Cereal yield (tonnes per hectare of harvested land)	3.5	2018	●	↑
Sustainable Nitrogen Management Index (best 0–1.41 worst)	0.5	2015	●	↓
Yield gap closure (% of potential yield)	68.0	2018	●	●
Exports of hazardous pesticides (tonnes per million population)	75.8	2019	●	●
SDG3 – Good Health and Well-Being				
Maternal mortality rate (per 100,000 live births)	4	2017	●	↑
Neonatal mortality rate (per 1,000 live births)	1.4	2020	●	↑
Mortality rate, under-5 (per 1,000 live births)	2.6	2020	●	↑
Incidence of tuberculosis (per 100,000 population)	3.6	2020	●	↑
New HIV infections (per 1,000 uninfected population)	1.0	2020	●	→
Age-standardized death rate due to cardiovascular disease, cancer, diabetes, or chronic respiratory disease in adults aged 30–70 years (%)	8.4	2019	●	↑
Age-standardized death rate attributable to household air pollution and ambient air pollution (per 100,000 population)	7	2016	●	●
Traffic deaths (per 100,000 population)	3.1	2019	●	↑
Life expectancy at birth (years)	82.4	2019	●	↑
Adolescent fertility rate (births per 1,000 females aged 15 to 19)	4.2	2018	●	↑
Births attended by skilled health personnel (%)	NA	NA	●	●
Surviving infants who received 2 WHO-recommended vaccines (%)	97	2020	●	↑
Universal health coverage (UHC) index of service coverage (worst 0–100 best)	87	2019	●	↑
Subjective well-being (average ladder score, worst 0–10 best)	7.4	2021	●	↑
Gap in life expectancy at birth among regions (years)	1.8	2019	●	↑
Gap in self-reported health status by income (percentage points)	22.5	2019	●	↓
Daily smokers (% of population aged 15 and over)	10.4	2019	●	↑
SDG4 – Quality Education				
Participation rate in pre-primary organized learning (% of children aged 4 to 6)	99.9	2019	●	↑
Net primary enrollment rate (%)	99.9	2019	●	↑
Lower secondary completion rate (%)	107.6	2019	●	↑
Literacy rate (% of population aged 15 to 24)	NA	NA	●	●
Tertiary educational attainment (% of population aged 25 to 34)	49.1	2020	●	↑
PISA score (worst 0–600 best)	502.3	2018	●	↑
Variation in science performance explained by socio-economic status (%)	12.7	2018	●	↓
Underachievers in science (% of 15-year-olds)	19.0	2018	●	↑
SDG5 – Gender Equality				
Demand for family planning satisfied by modern methods (% of females aged 15 to 49)	86.7	2017	●	↑
Ratio of female-to-male mean years of education received (%)	102.4	2019	●	↑
Ratio of female-to-male labor force participation rate (%)	89.0	2020	●	↑
Seats held by women in national parliament (%)	47.0	2020	●	↑
Gender wage gap (% of male median wage)	7.4	2020	●	↑
SDG6 – Clean Water and Sanitation				
Population using at least basic drinking water services (%)	99.8	2020	●	↑
Population using at least basic sanitation services (%)	99.3	2020	●	↑
Freshwater withdrawal (% of available freshwater resources)	3.4	2018	●	●
Anthropogenic wastewater that receives treatment (%)	100.0	2018	●	●
Scarce water consumption embodied in imports (m^3 H_2O eq/capita)	2676.0	2018	●	●
Population using safely managed water services (%)	99.8	2020	●	↑
Population using safely managed sanitation services (%)	94.9	2020	●	↑
SDG7 – Affordable and Clean Energy				
Population with access to electricity (%)	100.0	2019	●	↑
Population with access to clean fuels and technology for cooking (%)	100.0	2019	●	↑
CO_2 emissions from fuel combustion per total electricity output ($MtCO_2$/TWh)	0.2	2019	●	↑
Share of renewable energy in total primary energy supply (%)	40.1	2019	●	↑
SDG8 – Decent Work and Economic Growth				
Adjusted GDP growth (%)	0.2	2020	●	●
Victims of modern slavery (per 1,000 population)	1.6	2018	●	●
Adults with an account at a bank or other financial institution or with a mobile-money-service provider (% of population aged 15 or over)	99.7	2017	●	↑
Fundamental labor rights are effectively guaranteed (worst 0–1 best)	0.8	2020	●	↑
Fatal work-related accidents embodied in imports (per 100,000 population)	1.2	2015	●	↑
Employment-to-population ratio (%)	74.9	2020	●	↑
Youth not in employment, education or training (NEET) (% of population aged 15 to 29)	7.6	2020	●	↑

SDG9 – Industry, Innovation and Infrastructure	Value	Year	Rating	Trend
Population using the internet (%)	94.5	2020	●	↑
Mobile broadband subscriptions (per 100 population)	128.8	2019	●	↑
Logistics Performance Index: Quality of trade and transport-related infrastructure (worst 1–5 best)	4.2	2018	●	↑
The Times Higher Education Universities Ranking: Average score of top 3 universities (worst 0–100 best)	64.7	2022	●	●
Articles published in academic journals (per 1,000 population)	4.3	2020	●	↑
Expenditure on research and development (% of GDP)	3.3	2018	●	↑
Researchers (per 1,000 employed population)	15.1	2019	●	↑
Triadic patent families filed (per million population)	84.9	2019	●	↑
Gap in internet access by income (percentage points)	15.1	2020	●	↓
Female share of graduates from STEM fields at the tertiary level (%)	35.5	2017	●	↑
SDG10 – Reduced Inequalities				
Gini coefficient	30.0	2018	●	↑
Palma ratio	1.0	2019	●	↑
Elderly poverty rate (% of population aged 66 or over)	11.4	2019	●	→
SDG11 – Sustainable Cities and Communities				
Proportion of urban population living in slums (%)	* 0.0	2018	●	↑
Annual mean concentration of particulate matter of less than 2.5 microns in diameter (PM2.5) (μg/m^3)	6.0	2019	●	↑
Access to improved water source, piped (% of urban population)	89.2	2020	●	→
Satisfaction with public transport (%)	70.0	2021	●	↑
Population with rent overburden (%)	9.5	2019	●	→
SDG12 – Responsible Consumption and Production				
Electronic waste (kg/capita)	20.1	2019	●	●
Production-based SO_2 emissions (kg/capita)	15.7	2018	●	●
SO_2 emissions embodied in imports (kg/capita)	7.7	2018	●	●
Production-based nitrogen emissions (kg/capita)	12.7	2015	●	↑
Nitrogen emissions embodied in imports (kg/capita)	11.8	2015	●	↓
Exports of plastic waste (kg/capita)	9.0	2021	●	●
Non-recycled municipal solid waste (kg/capita/day)	0.7	2019	●	↑
SDG13 – Climate Action				
CO_2 emissions from fossil fuel combustion and cement production (tCO_2/capita)	3.8	2020	●	↗
CO_2 emissions embodied in imports (tCO_2/capita)	3.3	2018	●	→
CO_2 emissions embodied in fossil fuel exports (kg/capita)	67.5	2020	●	●
Carbon Pricing Score at EUR60/tCO_2 (%, worst 0–100 best)	29.0	2018	●	→
SDG14 – Life Below Water				
Mean area that is protected in marine sites important to biodiversity (%)	60.2	2020	●	→
Ocean Health Index: Clean Waters score (worst 0–100 best)	63.5	2020	●	↓
Fish caught from overexploited or collapsed stocks (% of total catch)	39.2	2018	●	↓
Fish caught by trawling or dredging (%)	22.8	2018	●	↑
Fish caught that are then discarded (%)	6.7	2018	●	↑
Marine biodiversity threats embodied in imports (per million population)	0.1	2018	●	●
SDG15 – Life on Land				
Mean area that is protected in terrestrial sites important to biodiversity (%)	59.1	2020	●	→
Mean area that is protected in freshwater sites important to biodiversity (%)	59.4	2020	●	→
Red List Index of species survival (worst 0–1 best)	1.0	2021	●	↑
Permanent deforestation (% of forest area, 5-year average)	0.0	2020	●	↑
Terrestrial and freshwater biodiversity threats embodied in imports (per million population)	1.6	2018	●	●
SDG16 – Peace, Justice and Strong Institutions				
Homicides (per 100,000 population)	1.2	2020	●	↑
Unsentenced detainees (% of prison population)	28.1	2019	●	↑
Population who feel safe walking alone at night in the city or area where they live (%)	81	2021	●	↑
Property Rights (worst 1–7 best)	5.4	2020	●	↑
Birth registrations with civil authority (% of children under age 5)	100.0	2020	●	●
Corruption Perception Index (worst 0–100 best)	85	2021	●	↑
Children involved in child labor (% of population aged 5 to 14)	* 0.0	2019	●	●
Exports of major conventional weapons (TIV constant million USD per 100,000 population)	1.9	2020	●	●
Press Freedom Index (best 0–100 worst)	7.2	2021	●	↑
Access to and affordability of justice (worst 0–1 best)	0.8	2020	●	↑
Persons held in prison (per 100,000 population)	66.9	2019	●	↑
SDG17 – Partnerships for the Goals				
Government spending on health and education (% of GDP)	16.9	2019	●	↑
For high-income and all OECD DAC countries: International concessional public finance, including official development assistance (% of GNI)	0.9	2021	●	↑
Other countries: Government revenue excluding grants (% of GDP)	NA	NA	●	●
Corporate Tax Haven Score (best 0–100 worst)	56.0	2019	●	●
Financial Secrecy Score (best 0–100 worst)	45.7	2020	●	●
Shifted profits of multinationals (US$ billion)	13.7	2018	●	↑
Statistical Performance Index (worst 0–100 best)	88.5	2019	●	↑

* Imputed data point

5. Country Profiles

SWITZERLAND

OECD Countries

OVERALL PERFORMANCE

COUNTRY RANKING

SWITZERLAND

8 **/163**

COUNTRY SCORE

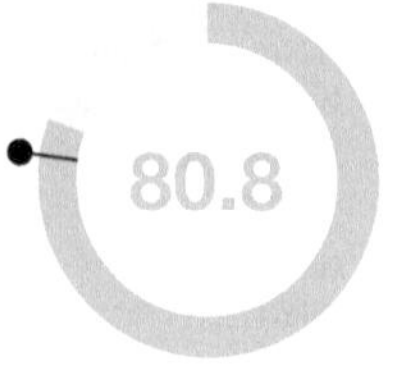

REGIONAL AVERAGE: 77.2

AVERAGE PERFORMANCE BY SDG

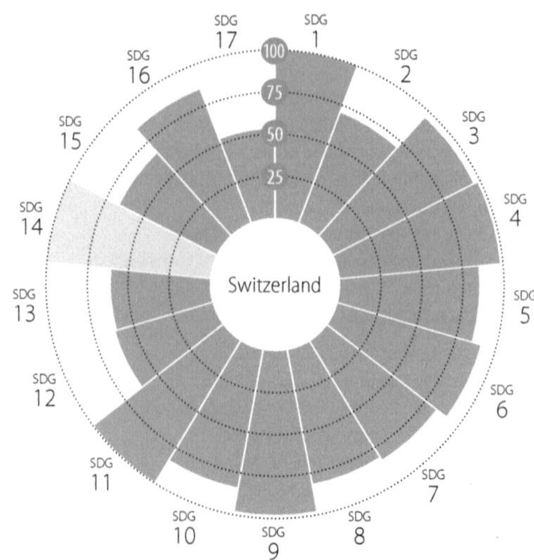

SDG DASHBOARDS AND TRENDS

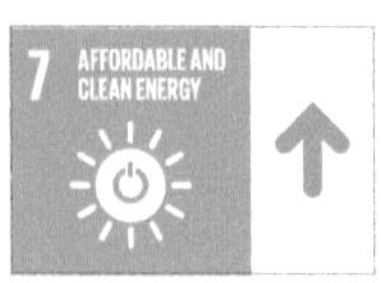
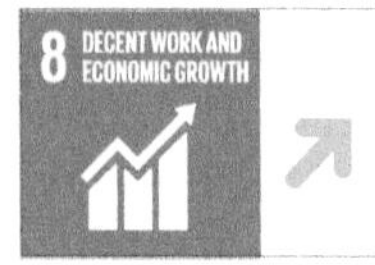

Major challenges · Significant challenges · Challenges remain · SDG achieved · Information unavailable

Decreasing · Stagnating · Moderately improving · On track or maintaining SDG achievement · Information unavailable

Note: The full title of each SDG is available here: https://sustainabledevelopment.un.org/topics/sustainabledevelopmentgoals

INTERNATIONAL SPILLOVER INDEX

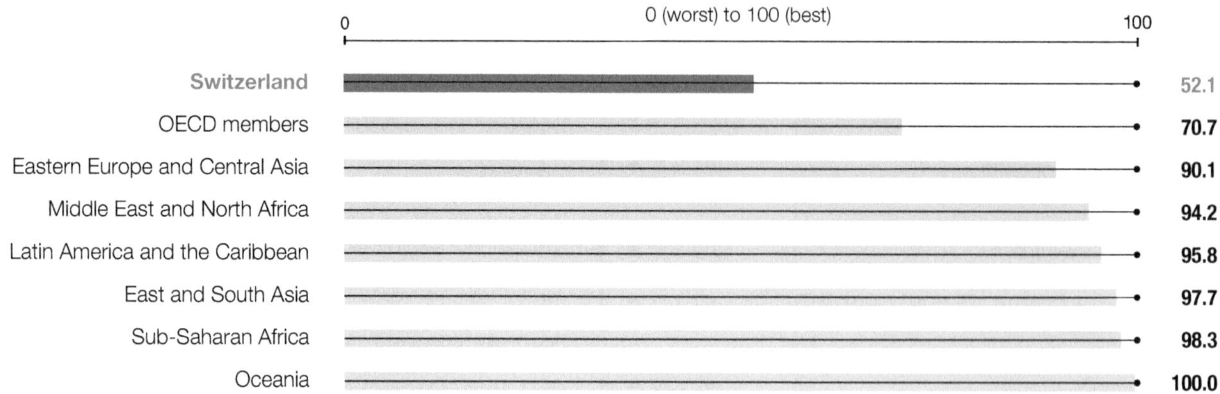

STATISTICAL PERFORMANCE INDEX

0 (worst) to 100 (best)

0 **87.0** 100

MISSING DATA IN SDG INDEX

3%

SWITZERLAND

Performance by Indicator

SDG1 – No Poverty	Value	Year	Rating	Trend
Poverty headcount ratio at \$1.90/day (%)	0.2	2022	●	↑
Poverty headcount ratio at \$3.20/day (%)	0.2	2022	●	↑
Poverty rate after taxes and transfers (%)	10.5	2018	●	↓

SDG2 – Zero Hunger	Value	Year	Rating	Trend
Prevalence of undernourishment (%)	2.5	2019	●	↑
Prevalence of stunting in children under 5 years of age (%)	* 2.6	2019	●	↑
Prevalence of wasting in children under 5 years of age (%)	* 0.7	2019	●	↑
Prevalence of obesity, BMI ≥ 30 (% of adult population)	19.5	2016	●	↓
Human Trophic Level (best 2–3 worst)	2.5	2017	●	→
Cereal yield (tonnes per hectare of harvested land)	6.2	2018	●	↑
Sustainable Nitrogen Management Index (best 0–1.41 worst)	0.7	2015	●	↓
Yield gap closure (% of potential yield)	64.2	2018	●	●
Exports of hazardous pesticides (tonnes per million population)	0.3	2019	●	●

SDG3 – Good Health and Well-Being	Value	Year	Rating	Trend
Maternal mortality rate (per 100,000 live births)	5	2017	●	↑
Neonatal mortality rate (per 1,000 live births)	2.8	2020	●	↑
Mortality rate, under-5 (per 1,000 live births)	4.0	2020	●	↑
Incidence of tuberculosis (per 100,000 population)	4.7	2020	●	↑
New HIV infections (per 1,000 uninfected population)	1.0	2020	●	↓
Age-standardized death rate due to cardiovascular disease, cancer, diabetes, or chronic respiratory disease in adults aged 30–70 years (%)	7.9	2019	●	↑
Age-standardized death rate attributable to household air pollution and ambient air pollution (per 100,000 population)	10	2016	●	●
Traffic deaths (per 100,000 population)	2.3	2019	●	↑
Life expectancy at birth (years)	83.5	2019	●	↑
Adolescent fertility rate (births per 1,000 females aged 15 to 19)	2.3	2018	●	↑
Births attended by skilled health personnel (%)	100.0	2006	●	●
Surviving infants who received 2 WHO-recommended vaccines (%)	96	2020	●	↑
Universal health coverage (UHC) index of service coverage (worst 0–100 best)	87	2019	●	↑
Subjective well-being (average ladder score, worst 0–10 best)	7.3	2021	●	↑
Gap in life expectancy at birth among regions (years)	1.4	2019	●	↑
Gap in self-reported health status by income (percentage points)	18.8	2019	●	↑
Daily smokers (% of population aged 15 and over)	19.1	2017	●	●

SDG4 – Quality Education	Value	Year	Rating	Trend
Participation rate in pre-primary organized learning (% of children aged 4 to 6)	99.6	2019	●	↑
Net primary enrollment rate (%)	99.9	2019	●	↑
Lower secondary completion rate (%)	95.6	2019	●	↑
Literacy rate (% of population aged 15 to 24)	NA	NA	●	●
Tertiary educational attainment (% of population aged 25 to 34)	53.0	2020	●	↑
PISA score (worst 0–600 best)	498.0	2018	●	↑
Variation in science performance explained by socio-economic status (%)	16.3	2018	●	↓
Underachievers in science (% of 15-year-olds)	20.2	2018	●	↓

SDG5 – Gender Equality	Value	Year	Rating	Trend
Demand for family planning satisfied by modern methods (% of females aged 15 to 49)	* 88.9	2022	●	↑
Ratio of female-to-male mean years of education received (%)	93.4	2019	●	↓
Ratio of female-to-male labor force participation rate (%)	85.2	2020	●	↑
Seats held by women in national parliament (%)	41.5	2020	●	↑
Gender wage gap (% of male median wage)	13.8	2020	●	↗

SDG6 – Clean Water and Sanitation	Value	Year	Rating	Trend
Population using at least basic drinking water services (%)	100.0	2020	●	↑
Population using at least basic sanitation services (%)	99.9	2020	●	↑
Freshwater withdrawal (% of available freshwater resources)	6.5	2018	●	●
Anthropogenic wastewater that receives treatment (%)	96.7	2018	●	●
Scarce water consumption embodied in imports (m^3 H_2O eq/capita)	4868.1	2018	●	●
Population using safely managed water services (%)	94.2	2020	●	→
Population using safely managed sanitation services (%)	99.7	2020	●	↑

SDG7 – Affordable and Clean Energy	Value	Year	Rating	Trend
Population with access to electricity (%)	100.0	2019	●	↑
Population with access to clean fuels and technology for cooking (%)	100.0	2019	●	↑
CO_2 emissions from fuel combustion per total electricity output ($MtCO_2$/TWh)	0.5	2019	●	↑
Share of renewable energy in total primary energy supply (%)	22.5	2019	●	↑

SDG8 – Decent Work and Economic Growth	Value	Year	Rating	Trend
Adjusted GDP growth (%)	0.4	2020	●	●
Victims of modern slavery (per 1,000 population)	1.7	2018	●	●
Adults with an account at a bank or other financial institution or with a mobile-money-service provider (% of population aged 15 or over)	98.4	2017	●	↑
Fundamental labor rights are effectively guaranteed (worst 0–1 best)	NA	NA	●	●
Fatal work-related accidents embodied in imports (per 100,000 population)	2.4	2015	●	↗
Employment-to-population ratio (%)	79.9	2020	●	↑
Youth not in employment, education or training (NEET) (% of population aged 15 to 29)	7.0	2020	●	●

SDG9 – Industry, Innovation and Infrastructure	Value	Year	Rating	Trend
Population using the internet (%)	94.2	2020	●	↑
Mobile broadband subscriptions (per 100 population)	100.4	2019	●	↑
Logistics Performance Index: Quality of trade and transport-related infrastructure (worst 1–5 best)	4.0	2018	●	↑
The Times Higher Education Universities Ranking: Average score of top 3 universities (worst 0–100 best)	76.0	2022	●	●
Articles published in academic journals (per 1,000 population)	5.5	2020	●	↑
Expenditure on research and development (% of GDP)	3.4	2017	●	↑
Researchers (per 1,000 employed population)	9.2	2017	●	●
Triadic patent families filed (per million population)	142.6	2019	●	↑
Gap in internet access by income (percentage points)	26.7	2014	●	●
Female share of graduates from STEM fields at the tertiary level (%)	22.3	2017	●	→

SDG10 – Reduced Inequalities	Value	Year	Rating	Trend
Gini coefficient	33.1	2018	●	↓
Palma ratio	1.2	2018	●	↓
Elderly poverty rate (% of population aged 66 or over)	21.4	2018	●	↓

SDG11 – Sustainable Cities and Communities	Value	Year	Rating	Trend
Proportion of urban population living in slums (%)	* 0.0	2018	●	↑
Annual mean concentration of particulate matter of less than 2.5 microns in diameter (PM2.5) (μg/m^3)	9.3	2019	●	↑
Access to improved water source, piped (% of urban population)	100.0	2020	●	↑
Satisfaction with public transport (%)	87.0	2021	●	↑
Population with rent overburden (%)	7.6	2019	●	↓

SDG12 – Responsible Consumption and Production	Value	Year	Rating	Trend
Electronic waste (kg/capita)	23.4	2019	●	●
Production-based SO_2 emissions (kg/capita)	17.9	2018	●	●
SO_2 emissions embodied in imports (kg/capita)	11.7	2018	●	●
Production-based nitrogen emissions (kg/capita)	6.7	2015	●	↑
Nitrogen emissions embodied in imports (kg/capita)	21.9	2015	●	↓
Exports of plastic waste (kg/capita)	2.6	2021	●	●
Non-recycled municipal solid waste (kg/capita/day)	0.9	2019	●	↗

SDG13 – Climate Action	Value	Year	Rating	Trend
CO_2 emissions from fossil fuel combustion and cement production (tCO_2/capita)	3.7	2020	●	↑
CO_2 emissions embodied in imports (tCO_2/capita)	4.4	2018	●	↗
CO_2 emissions embodied in fossil fuel exports (kg/capita)	0.0	2021	●	●
Carbon Pricing Score at EUR60/tCO_2 (%, worst 0–100 best)	69.3	2018	●	→

SDG14 – Life Below Water	Value	Year	Rating	Trend
Mean area that is protected in marine sites important to biodiversity (%)	NA	NA	●	●
Ocean Health Index: Clean Waters score (worst 0–100 best)	NA	NA	●	●
Fish caught from overexploited or collapsed stocks (% of total catch)	NA	NA	●	●
Fish caught by trawling or dredging (%)	NA	NA	●	●
Fish caught that are then discarded (%)	NA	NA	●	●
Marine biodiversity threats embodied in imports (per million population)	0.5	2018	●	●

SDG15 – Life on Land	Value	Year	Rating	Trend
Mean area that is protected in terrestrial sites important to biodiversity (%)	37.0	2020	●	→
Mean area that is protected in freshwater sites important to biodiversity (%)	60.2	2020	●	→
Red List Index of species survival (worst 0–1 best)	1.0	2021	●	↑
Permanent deforestation (% of forest area, 5-year average)	0.0	2020	●	↑
Terrestrial and freshwater biodiversity threats embodied in imports (per million population)	5.8	2018	●	●

SDG16 – Peace, Justice and Strong Institutions	Value	Year	Rating	Trend
Homicides (per 100,000 population)	0.5	2020	●	↑
Unsentenced detainees (% of prison population)	44.2	2019	●	↓
Population who feel safe walking alone at night in the city or area where they live (%)	89	2021	●	↑
Property Rights (worst 1–7 best)	6.4	2020	●	↑
Birth registrations with civil authority (% of children under age 5)	100.0	2020	●	●
Corruption Perception Index (worst 0–100 best)	84	2021	●	↑
Children involved in child labor (% of population aged 5 to 14)	* 0.0	2019	●	●
Exports of major conventional weapons (TIV constant million USD per 100,000 population)	2.4	2020	●	●
Press Freedom Index (best 0–100 worst)	10.6	2021	●	↑
Access to and affordability of justice (worst 0–1 best)	NA	NA	●	●
Persons held in prison (per 100,000 population)	76.6	2019	●	↑

SDG17 – Partnerships for the Goals	Value	Year	Rating	Trend
Government spending on health and education (% of GDP)	8.5	2019	●	→
For high-income and all OECD DAC countries: International concessional public finance, including official development assistance (% of GNI)	0.5	2021	●	↓
Other countries: Government revenue excluding grants (% of GDP)	NA	NA	●	●
Corporate Tax Haven Score (best 0–100 worst)	83.3	2019	●	●
Financial Secrecy Score (best 0–100 worst)	74.1	2020	●	●
Shifted profits of multinationals (US\$ billion)	102.3	2018	●	↓
Statistical Performance Index (worst 0–100 best)	87.0	2019	●	↑

* Imputed data point

5. Country Profiles

SYRIAN ARAB REPUBLIC Middle East and North Africa

OVERALL PERFORMANCE

COUNTRY RANKING

SYRIAN ARAB REPUBLIC

129 **/163**

COUNTRY SCORE

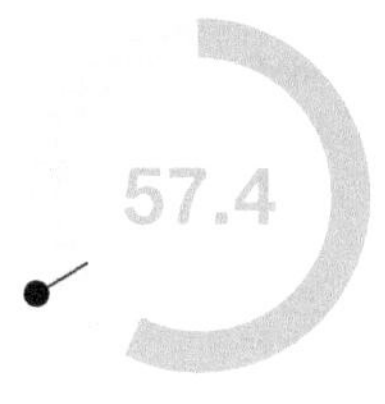

REGIONAL AVERAGE: 66.7

AVERAGE PERFORMANCE BY SDG

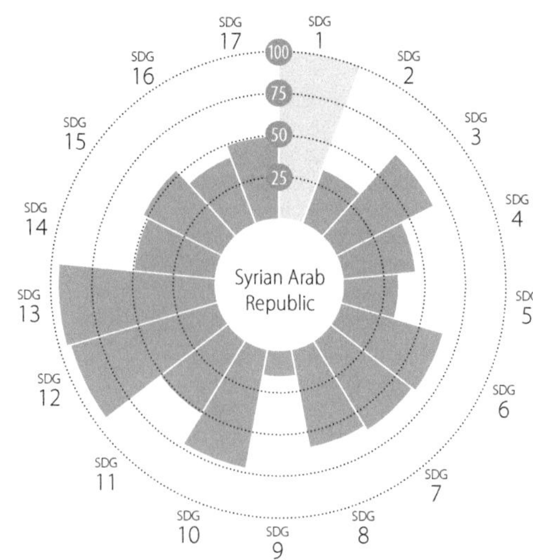

SDG DASHBOARDS AND TRENDS

Major challenges · Significant challenges · Challenges remain · SDG achieved · Information unavailable

Decreasing · Stagnating · Moderately improving · On track or maintaining SDG achievement · Information unavailable

Note: The full title of each SDG is available here: https://sustainabledevelopment.un.org/topics/sustainabledevelopmentgoals

INTERNATIONAL SPILLOVER INDEX

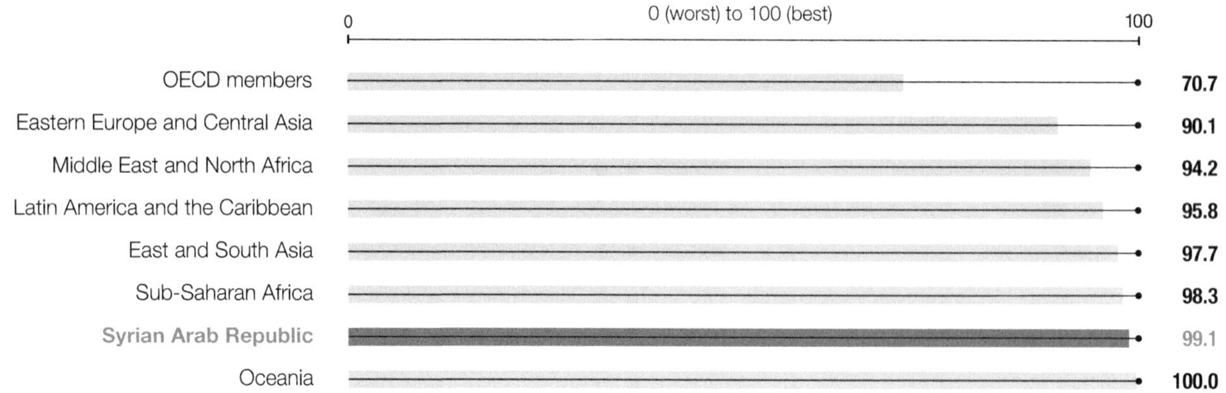

STATISTICAL PERFORMANCE INDEX

0 (worst) to 100 (best)

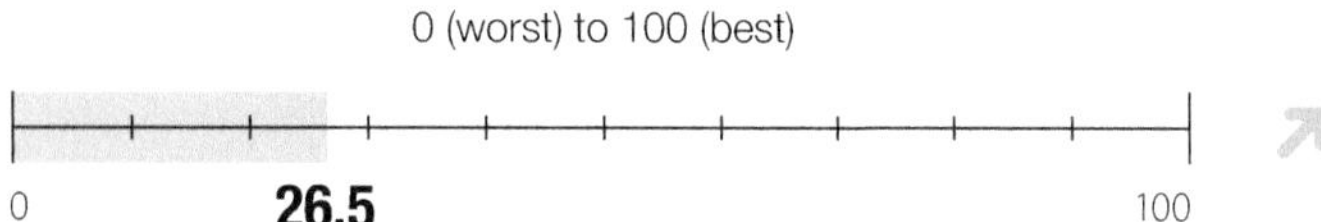

MISSING DATA IN SDG INDEX

16%

SYRIAN ARAB REPUBLIC

Performance by Indicator

SDG1 – No Poverty	Value	Year	Rating	Trend
Poverty headcount ratio at $1.90/day (%)	NA	NA	●	●
Poverty headcount ratio at $3.20/day (%)	NA	NA	●	●

SDG2 – Zero Hunger	Value	Year	Rating	Trend
Prevalence of undernourishment (%)	NA	NA	●	●
Prevalence of stunting in children under 5 years of age (%)	27.9	2010	●	→
Prevalence of wasting in children under 5 years of age (%)	11.5	2010	●	→
Prevalence of obesity, BMI ≥ 30 (% of adult population)	27.8	2016	●	↓
Human Trophic Level (best 2–3 worst)	2.2	2007	●	●
Cereal yield (tonnes per hectare of harvested land)	1.2	2018	●	→
Sustainable Nitrogen Management Index (best 0–1.41 worst)	0.7	2015	●	→
Exports of hazardous pesticides (tonnes per million population)	NA	NA	●	●

SDG3 – Good Health and Well-Being	Value	Year	Rating	Trend
Maternal mortality rate (per 100,000 live births)	31	2017	●	↑
Neonatal mortality rate (per 1,000 live births)	10.7	2020	●	↑
Mortality rate, under-5 (per 1,000 live births)	22.4	2020	●	↑
Incidence of tuberculosis (per 100,000 population)	19.0	2020	●	→
New HIV infections (per 1,000 uninfected population)	0.0	2020	●	↑
Age-standardized death rate due to cardiovascular disease, cancer, diabetes, or chronic respiratory disease in adults aged 30–70 years (%)	22.1	2019	●	↓
Age-standardized death rate attributable to household air pollution and ambient air pollution (per 100,000 population)	75	2016	●	●
Traffic deaths (per 100,000 population)	14.9	2019	●	↑
Life expectancy at birth (years)	72.7	2019	●	↑
Adolescent fertility rate (births per 1,000 females aged 15 to 19)	21.9	2004	●	●
Births attended by skilled health personnel (%)	96.2	2009	●	●
Surviving infants who received 2 WHO-recommended vaccines (%)	49	2020	●	→
Universal health coverage (UHC) index of service coverage (worst 0–100 best)	56	2019	●	→
Subjective well-being (average ladder score, worst 0–10 best)	3.5	2015	●	●

SDG4 – Quality Education	Value	Year	Rating	Trend
Participation rate in pre-primary organized learning (% of children aged 4 to 6)	39.6	2013	●	●
Net primary enrollment rate (%)	72.4	2013	●	●
Lower secondary completion rate (%)	53.8	2013	●	●
Literacy rate (% of population aged 15 to 24)	92.5	2004	●	●

SDG5 – Gender Equality	Value	Year	Rating	Trend
Demand for family planning satisfied by modern methods (% of females aged 15 to 49)	53.3	2009	●	●
Ratio of female-to-male mean years of education received (%)	82.1	2019	●	→
Ratio of female-to-male labor force participation rate (%)	21.9	2020	●	↓
Seats held by women in national parliament (%)	11.2	2020	●	↓

SDG6 – Clean Water and Sanitation	Value	Year	Rating	Trend
Population using at least basic drinking water services (%)	93.9	2020	●	→
Population using at least basic sanitation services (%)	89.7	2020	●	→
Freshwater withdrawal (% of available freshwater resources)	124.4	2018	●	●
Anthropogenic wastewater that receives treatment (%)	48.0	2018	●	●
Scarce water consumption embodied in imports (m^3 H_2O eq/capita)	412.1	2018	●	●

SDG7 – Affordable and Clean Energy	Value	Year	Rating	Trend
Population with access to electricity (%)	89.3	2019	●	→
Population with access to clean fuels and technology for cooking (%)	97.4	2019	●	↑
CO_2 emissions from fuel combustion per total electricity output ($MtCO_2$/TWh)	2.2	2019	●	→
Share of renewable energy in total primary energy supply (%)	0.8	2019	●	→

SDG8 – Decent Work and Economic Growth	Value	Year	Rating	Trend
Adjusted GDP growth (%)	NA	NA	●	●
Victims of modern slavery (per 1,000 population)	* NA	NA	●	●
Adults with an account at a bank or other financial institution or with a mobile-money-service provider (% of population aged 15 or over)	23.3	2011	●	●
Unemployment rate (% of total labor force)	10.0	2022	●	↓
Fundamental labor rights are effectively guaranteed (worst 0–1 best)	NA	NA	●	●
Fatal work-related accidents embodied in imports (per 100,000 population)	0.1	2015	●	↑

SDG9 – Industry, Innovation and Infrastructure	Value	Year	Rating	Trend
Population using the internet (%)	35.8	2020	●	→
Mobile broadband subscriptions (per 100 population)	11.5	2019	●	↓
Logistics Performance Index: Quality of trade and transport-related infrastructure (worst 1–5 best)	2.5	2018	●	↑
The Times Higher Education Universities Ranking: Average score of top 3 universities (worst 0–100 best)	* 0.0	2022	●	●
Articles published in academic journals (per 1,000 population)	0.0	2020	●	→
Expenditure on research and development (% of GDP)	0.0	2015	●	●

SDG10 – Reduced Inequalities	Value	Year	Rating	Trend
Gini coefficient	37.5	2003	●	●
Palma ratio	NA	NA	●	●

SDG11 – Sustainable Cities and Communities	Value	Year	Rating	Trend
Proportion of urban population living in slums (%)	13.8	2018	●	↑
Annual mean concentration of particulate matter of less than 2.5 microns in diameter (PM2.5) (μg/m^3)	46.2	2019	●	↓
Access to improved water source, piped (% of urban population)	70.5	2020	●	↓
Satisfaction with public transport (%)	15.0	2015	●	●

SDG12 – Responsible Consumption and Production	Value	Year	Rating	Trend
Municipal solid waste (kg/capita/day)	0.6	2009	●	●
Electronic waste (kg/capita)	5.2	2019	●	●
Production-based SO_2 emissions (kg/capita)	7.7	2018	●	●
SO_2 emissions embodied in imports (kg/capita)	0.1	2018	●	●
Production-based nitrogen emissions (kg/capita)	7.2	2015	●	↑
Nitrogen emissions embodied in imports (kg/capita)	0.5	2015	●	↑
Exports of plastic waste (kg/capita)	NA	NA	●	●

SDG13 – Climate Action	Value	Year	Rating	Trend
CO_2 emissions from fossil fuel combustion and cement production (tCO_2/capita)	1.7	2020	●	↑
CO_2 emissions embodied in imports (tCO_2/capita)	0.0	2018	●	↑
CO_2 emissions embodied in fossil fuel exports (kg/capita)	NA	NA	●	●

SDG14 – Life Below Water	Value	Year	Rating	Trend
Mean area that is protected in marine sites important to biodiversity (%)	0.0	2020	●	→
Ocean Health Index: Clean Waters score (worst 0–100 best)	37.3	2020	●	→
Fish caught from overexploited or collapsed stocks (% of total catch)	NA	NA	●	●
Fish caught by trawling or dredging (%)	34.2	2018	●	↓
Fish caught that are then discarded (%)	5.8	2018	●	→
Marine biodiversity threats embodied in imports (per million population)	0.0	2018	●	●

SDG15 – Life on Land	Value	Year	Rating	Trend
Mean area that is protected in terrestrial sites important to biodiversity (%)	0.0	2020	●	→
Mean area that is protected in freshwater sites important to biodiversity (%)	0.0	2020	●	→
Red List Index of species survival (worst 0–1 best)	0.9	2021	●	↑
Permanent deforestation (% of forest area, 5-year average)	0.3	2020	●	↓
Terrestrial and freshwater biodiversity threats embodied in imports (per million population)	0.1	2018	●	●

SDG16 – Peace, Justice and Strong Institutions	Value	Year	Rating	Trend
Homicides (per 100,000 population)	19.7	2019	●	●
Unsentenced detainees (% of prison population)	50.5	2004	●	●
Population who feel safe walking alone at night in the city or area where they live (%)	32	2015	●	●
Property Rights (worst 1–7 best)	NA	NA	●	●
Birth registrations with civil authority (% of children under age 5)	96.0	2020	●	●
Corruption Perception Index (worst 0–100 best)	13	2021	●	↓
Children involved in child labor (% of population aged 5 to 14)	NA	NA	●	●
Exports of major conventional weapons (TIV constant million USD per 100,000 population)	0.0	2020	●	●
Press Freedom Index (best 0–100 worst)	70.6	2021	●	↗
Access to and affordability of justice (worst 0–1 best)	NA	NA	●	●

SDG17 – Partnerships for the Goals	Value	Year	Rating	Trend
Government spending on health and education (% of GDP)	6.7	2012	●	●
For high-income and all OECD DAC countries: International concessional public finance, including official development assistance (% of GNI)	NA	NA	●	●
Other countries: Government revenue excluding grants (% of GDP)	NA	NA	●	●
Corporate Tax Haven Score (best 0–100 worst)	* 0.0	2019	●	●
Statistical Performance Index (worst 0–100 best)	26.5	2019	●	↗

* Imputed data point

TAJIKISTAN

Eastern Europe and Central Asia

OVERALL PERFORMANCE

COUNTRY RANKING

TAJIKISTAN

78/163

COUNTRY SCORE

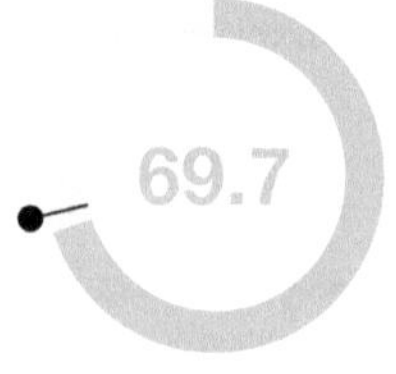

REGIONAL AVERAGE: 71.6

AVERAGE PERFORMANCE BY SDG

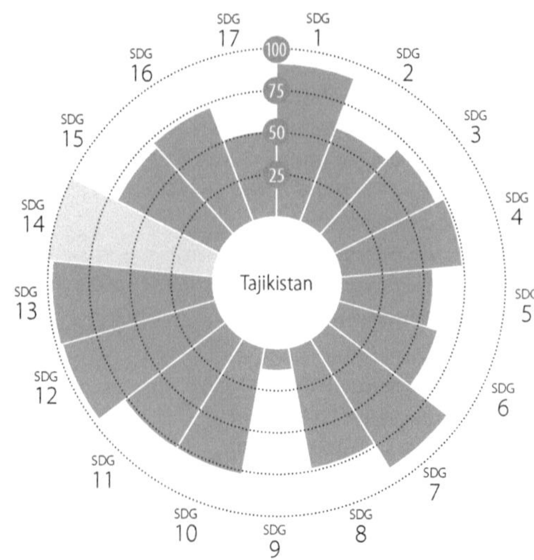

SDG DASHBOARDS AND TRENDS

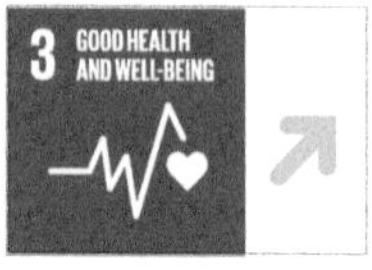

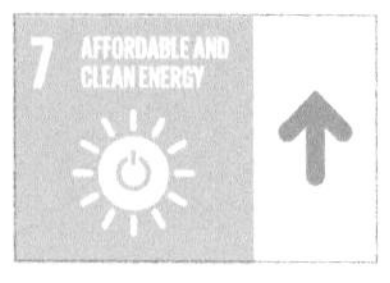

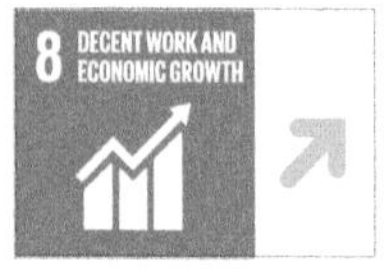

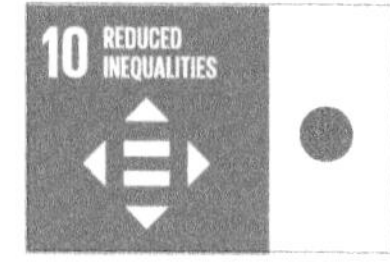

Major challenges · Significant challenges · Challenges remain · SDG achieved · Information unavailable

Decreasing · Stagnating · Moderately improving · On track or maintaining SDG achievement · Information unavailable

Note: The full title of each SDG is available here: https://sustainabledevelopment.un.org/topics/sustainabledevelopmentgoals

INTERNATIONAL SPILLOVER INDEX

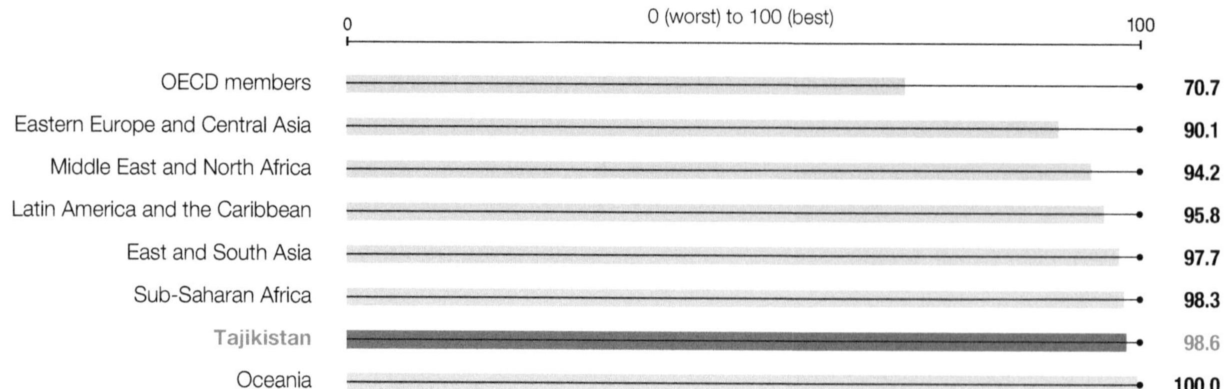

OECD members	70.7
Eastern Europe and Central Asia	90.1
Middle East and North Africa	94.2
Latin America and the Caribbean	95.8
East and South Asia	97.7
Sub-Saharan Africa	98.3
Tajikistan	98.6
Oceania	100.0

STATISTICAL PERFORMANCE INDEX

0 (worst) to 100 (best)

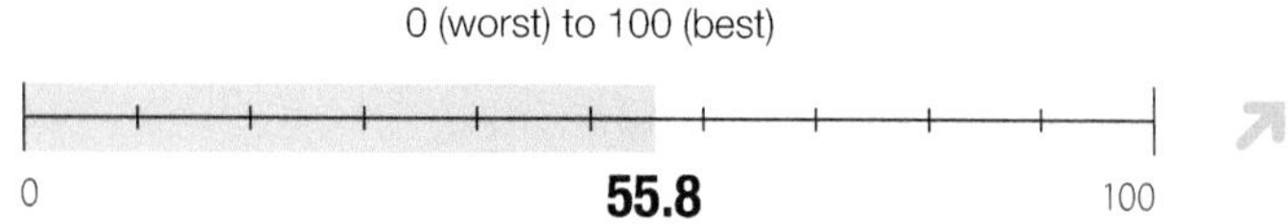

MISSING DATA IN SDG INDEX

8%

TAJIKISTAN

SDG1 – No Poverty

Indicator	Value	Year	Rating	Trend
Poverty headcount ratio at $1.90/day (%)	1.0	2022	●	↑
Poverty headcount ratio at $3.20/day (%)	8.6	2022	●	↑

SDG2 – Zero Hunger

Indicator	Value	Year	Rating	Trend
Prevalence of undernourishment (%)	NA	NA	●	●
Prevalence of stunting in children under 5 years of age (%)	17.5	2017	●	→
Prevalence of wasting in children under 5 years of age (%)	5.6	2017	●	→
Prevalence of obesity, BMI ≥ 30 (% of adult population)	14.2	2016	●	↓
Human Trophic Level (best 2–3 worst)	2.1	2017	●	↑
Cereal yield (tonnes per hectare of harvested land)	3.4	2018	●	↑
Sustainable Nitrogen Management Index (best 0–1.41 worst)	0.7	2015	●	→
Exports of hazardous pesticides (tonnes per million population)	NA	NA	●	●

SDG3 – Good Health and Well-Being

Indicator	Value	Year	Rating	Trend
Maternal mortality rate (per 100,000 live births)	17	2017	●	↑
Neonatal mortality rate (per 1,000 live births)	14.0	2020	●	↑
Mortality rate, under-5 (per 1,000 live births)	32.3	2020	●	↑
Incidence of tuberculosis (per 100,000 population)	84.0	2020	●	→
New HIV infections (per 1,000 uninfected population)	0.1	2020	●	↑
Age-standardized death rate due to cardiovascular disease, cancer, diabetes, or chronic respiratory disease in adults aged 30–70 years (%)	28.3	2019	●	→
Age-standardized death rate attributable to household air pollution and ambient air pollution (per 100,000 population)	129	2016	●	●
Traffic deaths (per 100,000 population)	15.7	2019	●	↑
Life expectancy at birth (years)	69.5	2019	●	→
Adolescent fertility rate (births per 1,000 females aged 15 to 19)	54.3	2016	●	●
Births attended by skilled health personnel (%)	94.8	2017	●	↓
Surviving infants who received 2 WHO-recommended vaccines (%)	97	2020	●	↑
Universal health coverage (UHC) index of service coverage (worst 0–100 best)	66	2019	●	↗
Subjective well-being (average ladder score, worst 0–10 best)	5.3	2021	●	↗

SDG4 – Quality Education

Indicator	Value	Year	Rating	Trend
Participation rate in pre-primary organized learning (% of children aged 4 to 6)	12.5	2017	●	●
Net primary enrollment rate (%)	99.5	2017	●	●
Lower secondary completion rate (%)	96.2	2017	●	●
Literacy rate (% of population aged 15 to 24)	99.9	2014	●	●

SDG5 – Gender Equality

Indicator	Value	Year	Rating	Trend
Demand for family planning satisfied by modern methods (% of females aged 15 to 49)	52.1	2017	●	●
Ratio of female-to-male mean years of education received (%)	90.3	2019	●	→
Ratio of female-to-male labor force participation rate (%)	60.0	2020	●	↓
Seats held by women in national parliament (%)	23.8	2020	●	↗

SDG6 – Clean Water and Sanitation

Indicator	Value	Year	Rating	Trend
Population using at least basic drinking water services (%)	81.9	2020	●	↗
Population using at least basic sanitation services (%)	96.8	2020	●	↑
Freshwater withdrawal (% of available freshwater resources)	61.5	2018	●	●
Anthropogenic wastewater that receives treatment (%)	2.3	2018	●	●
Scarce water consumption embodied in imports (m³ H_2O eq/capita)	424.0	2018	●	●

SDG7 – Affordable and Clean Energy

Indicator	Value	Year	Rating	Trend
Population with access to electricity (%)	99.6	2019	●	↑
Population with access to clean fuels and technology for cooking (%)	82.0	2019	●	↑
CO_2 emissions from fuel combustion per total electricity output ($MtCO_2$/TWh)	0.2	2019	●	↑
Share of renewable energy in total primary energy supply (%)	42.7	2019	●	↑

SDG8 – Decent Work and Economic Growth

Indicator	Value	Year	Rating	Trend
Adjusted GDP growth (%)	-0.4	2020	●	●
Victims of modern slavery (per 1,000 population)	4.5	2018	●	●
Adults with an account at a bank or other financial institution or with a mobile-money-service provider (% of population aged 15 or over)	47.0	2017	●	↑
Unemployment rate (% of total labor force)	7.7	2022	●	→
Fundamental labor rights are effectively guaranteed (worst 0–1 best)	NA	NA	●	●
Fatal work-related accidents embodied in imports (per 100,000 population)	0.1	2015	●	↑

* Imputed data point

SDG9 – Industry, Innovation and Infrastructure

Indicator	Value	Year	Rating	Trend
Population using the internet (%)	22.0	2017	●	●
Mobile broadband subscriptions (per 100 population)	24.1	2019	●	↗
Logistics Performance Index: Quality of trade and transport-related infrastructure (worst 1–5 best)	2.2	2018	●	↓
The Times Higher Education Universities Ranking: Average score of top 3 universities (worst 0–100 best)	* 0.0	2022	●	●
Articles published in academic journals (per 1,000 population)	0.0	2020	●	→
Expenditure on research and development (% of GDP)	0.1	2018	●	↓

SDG10 – Reduced Inequalities

Indicator	Value	Year	Rating	Trend
Gini coefficient	34.0	2015	●	●
Palma ratio	1.4	2018	●	●

SDG11 – Sustainable Cities and Communities

Indicator	Value	Year	Rating	Trend
Proportion of urban population living in slums (%)	23.6	2018	●	●
Annual mean concentration of particulate matter of less than 2.5 microns in diameter (PM2.5) (µg/m³)	44.6	2019	●	→
Access to improved water source, piped (% of urban population)	89.9	2020	●	→
Satisfaction with public transport (%)	77.0	2021	●	↑

SDG12 – Responsible Consumption and Production

Indicator	Value	Year	Rating	Trend
Municipal solid waste (kg/capita/day)	0.6	2013	●	●
Electronic waste (kg/capita)	NA	NA	●	●
Production-based SO_2 emissions (kg/capita)	1.2	2018	●	●
SO_2 emissions embodied in imports (kg/capita)	0.4	2018	●	●
Production-based nitrogen emissions (kg/capita)	7.5	2015	●	↑
Nitrogen emissions embodied in imports (kg/capita)	0.5	2015	●	↑
Exports of plastic waste (kg/capita)	0.3	2020	●	●

SDG13 – Climate Action

Indicator	Value	Year	Rating	Trend
CO_2 emissions from fossil fuel combustion and cement production (tCO_2/capita)	1.0	2020	●	↑
CO_2 emissions embodied in imports (tCO_2/capita)	0.1	2018	●	↑
CO_2 emissions embodied in fossil fuel exports (kg/capita)	3.3	2020	●	●

SDG14 – Life Below Water

Indicator	Value	Year	Rating	Trend
Mean area that is protected in marine sites important to biodiversity (%)	NA	NA	●	●
Ocean Health Index: Clean Waters score (worst 0–100 best)	NA	NA	●	●
Fish caught from overexploited or collapsed stocks (% of total catch)	NA	NA	●	●
Fish caught by trawling or dredging (%)	NA	NA	●	●
Fish caught that are then discarded (%)	NA	NA	●	●
Marine biodiversity threats embodied in imports (per million population)	0.0	2018	●	●

SDG15 – Life on Land

Indicator	Value	Year	Rating	Trend
Mean area that is protected in terrestrial sites important to biodiversity (%)	16.8	2020	●	→
Mean area that is protected in freshwater sites important to biodiversity (%)	30.5	2020	●	→
Red List Index of species survival (worst 0–1 best)	1.0	2021	●	↑
Permanent deforestation (% of forest area, 5-year average)	0.0	2020	●	↑
Terrestrial and freshwater biodiversity threats embodied in imports (per million population)	0.0	2018	●	●

SDG16 – Peace, Justice and Strong Institutions

Indicator	Value	Year	Rating	Trend
Homicides (per 100,000 population)	0.9	2020	●	●
Unsentenced detainees (% of prison population)	NA	NA	●	●
Population who feel safe walking alone at night in the city or area where they live (%)	93	2021	●	↑
Property Rights (worst 1–7 best)	4.8	2020	●	↑
Birth registrations with civil authority (% of children under age 5)	95.8	2020	●	●
Corruption Perception Index (worst 0–100 best)	25	2021	●	↓
Children involved in child labor (% of population aged 5 to 14)	NA	NA	●	●
Exports of major conventional weapons (TIV constant million USD per 100,000 population)	* 0.0	2020	●	●
Press Freedom Index (best 0–100 worst)	55.5	2021	●	↓
Access to and affordability of justice (worst 0–1 best)	NA	NA	●	●

SDG17 – Partnerships for the Goals

Indicator	Value	Year	Rating	Trend
Government spending on health and education (% of GDP)	7.7	2019	●	↗
For high-income and all OECD DAC countries: International concessional public finance, including official development assistance (% of GNI)	NA	NA	●	●
Other countries: Government revenue excluding grants (% of GDP)	13.5	2004	●	●
Corporate Tax Haven Score (best 0–100 worst)	* 0.0	2019	●	●
Statistical Performance Index (worst 0–100 best)	55.8	2019	●	↗

TANZANIA

Sub-Saharan Africa

OVERALL PERFORMANCE

COUNTRY RANKING

TANZANIA

130/163

COUNTRY SCORE

AVERAGE PERFORMANCE BY SDG

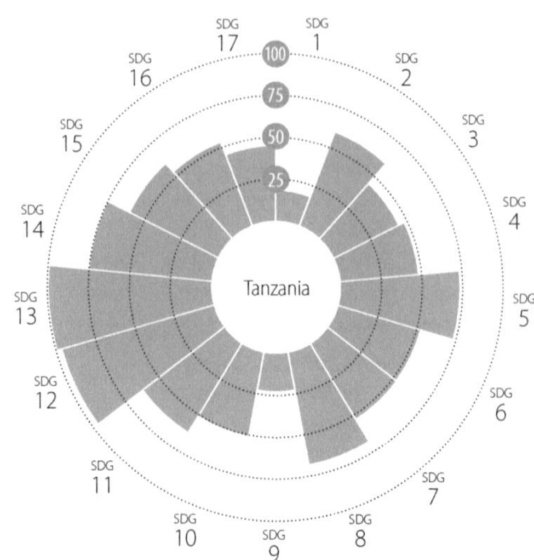

SDG DASHBOARDS AND TRENDS

Note: The full title of each SDG is available here: https://sustainabledevelopment.un.org/topics/sustainabledevelopmentgoals

INTERNATIONAL SPILLOVER INDEX

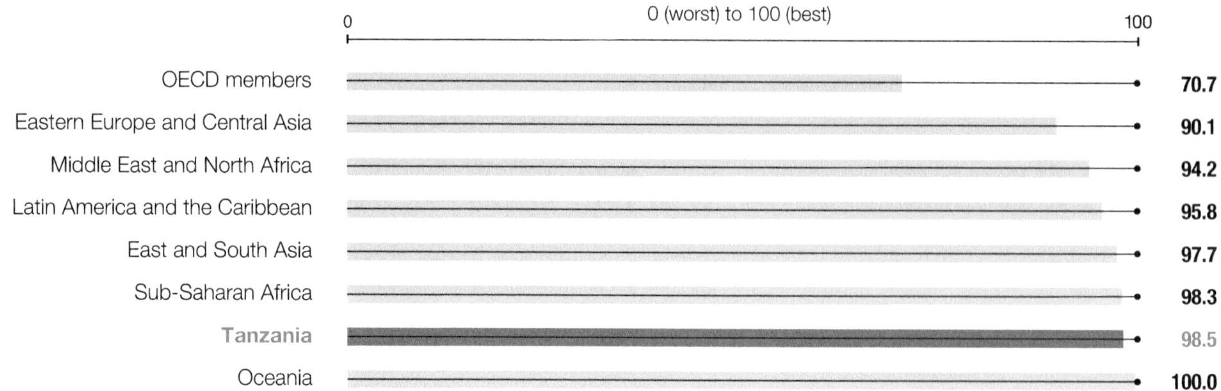

STATISTICAL PERFORMANCE INDEX

0 (worst) to 100 (best)

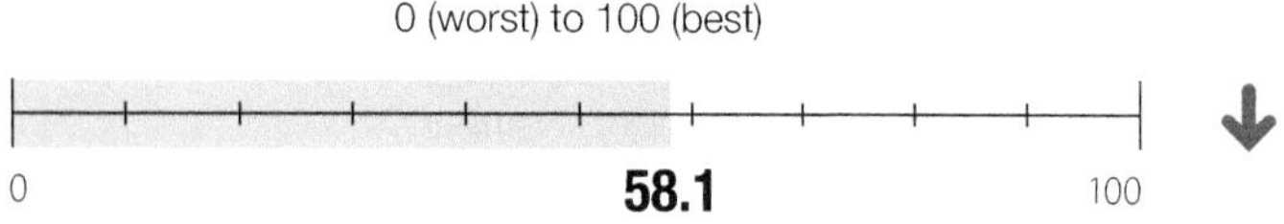

MISSING DATA IN SDG INDEX

TANZANIA

SDG1 – No Poverty

Indicator	Value	Year	Rating	Trend
Poverty headcount ratio at \$1.90/day (%)	46.5	2022	●	→
Poverty headcount ratio at \$3.20/day (%)	75.2	2022	●	→

SDG2 – Zero Hunger

Indicator	Value	Year	Rating	Trend
Prevalence of undernourishment (%)	25.1	2019	●	↓
Prevalence of stunting in children under 5 years of age (%)	31.8	2018	●	→
Prevalence of wasting in children under 5 years of age (%)	3.5	2018	●	↑
Prevalence of obesity, BMI ≥ 30 (% of adult population)	8.4	2016	●	↑
Human Trophic Level (best 2–3 worst)	2.1	2017	●	↑
Cereal yield (tonnes per hectare of harvested land)	1.6	2018	●	↓
Sustainable Nitrogen Management Index (best 0–1.41 worst)	0.8	2015	●	→
Exports of hazardous pesticides (tonnes per million population)	0.4	2019	●	●

SDG3 – Good Health and Well-Being

Indicator	Value	Year	Rating	Trend
Maternal mortality rate (per 100,000 live births)	524	2017	●	↗
Neonatal mortality rate (per 1,000 live births)	20.1	2020	●	↗
Mortality rate, under-5 (per 1,000 live births)	48.9	2020	●	↗
Incidence of tuberculosis (per 100,000 population)	222.0	2020	●	↗
New HIV infections (per 1,000 uninfected population)	1.3	2020	●	↑
Age-standardized death rate due to cardiovascular disease, cancer, diabetes, or chronic respiratory disease in adults aged 30–70 years (%)	17.4	2019	●	→
Age-standardized death rate attributable to household air pollution and ambient air pollution (per 100,000 population)	139	2016	●	●
Traffic deaths (per 100,000 population)	31.1	2019	●	↓
Life expectancy at birth (years)	67.3	2019	●	↗
Adolescent fertility rate (births per 1,000 females aged 15 to 19)	138.9	2016	●	●
Births attended by skilled health personnel (%)	63.5	2016	●	●
Surviving infants who received 2 WHO-recommended vaccines (%)	84	2020	●	↓
Universal health coverage (UHC) index of service coverage (worst 0–100 best)	46	2019	●	→
Subjective well-being (average ladder score, worst 0–10 best)	3.7	2021	●	→

SDG4 – Quality Education

Indicator	Value	Year	Rating	Trend
Participation rate in pre-primary organized learning (% of children aged 4 to 6)	56.3	2020	●	↗
Net primary enrollment rate (%)	83.9	2020	●	↓
Lower secondary completion rate (%)	33.2	2020	●	→
Literacy rate (% of population aged 15 to 24)	85.8	2015	●	●

SDG5 – Gender Equality

Indicator	Value	Year	Rating	Trend
Demand for family planning satisfied by modern methods (% of females aged 15 to 49)	55.1	2016	●	●
Ratio of female-to-male mean years of education received (%)	90.6	2019	●	↑
Ratio of female-to-male labor force participation rate (%)	91.4	2020	●	↑
Seats held by women in national parliament (%)	36.7	2020	●	↗

SDG6 – Clean Water and Sanitation

Indicator	Value	Year	Rating	Trend
Population using at least basic drinking water services (%)	60.7	2020	●	↗
Population using at least basic sanitation services (%)	31.8	2020	●	→
Freshwater withdrawal (% of available freshwater resources)	13.0	2018	●	●
Anthropogenic wastewater that receives treatment (%)	1.4	2018	●	●
Scarce water consumption embodied in imports (m^3 H_2O eq/capita)	111.5	2018	●	●

SDG7 – Affordable and Clean Energy

Indicator	Value	Year	Rating	Trend
Population with access to electricity (%)	37.7	2019	●	↗
Population with access to clean fuels and technology for cooking (%)	4.3	2019	●	→
CO_2 emissions from fuel combustion per total electricity output ($MtCO_2$/TWh)	1.5	2019	●	→
Share of renewable energy in total primary energy supply (%)	83.6	2019	●	↑

SDG8 – Decent Work and Economic Growth

Indicator	Value	Year	Rating	Trend
Adjusted GDP growth (%)	-3.5	2020	●	●
Victims of modern slavery (per 1,000 population)	6.2	2018	●	●
Adults with an account at a bank or other financial institution or with a mobile-money-service provider (% of population aged 15 or over)	46.8	2017	●	↗
Unemployment rate (% of total labor force)	2.6	2022	●	↑
Fundamental labor rights are effectively guaranteed (worst 0–1 best)	0.5	2020	●	↗
Fatal work-related accidents embodied in imports (per 100,000 population)	0.0	2015	●	↑

* Imputed data point

SDG9 – Industry, Innovation and Infrastructure

Indicator	Value	Year	Rating	Trend
Population using the internet (%)	22.0	2020	●	↗
Mobile broadband subscriptions (per 100 population)	9.8	2019	●	→
Logistics Performance Index: Quality of trade and transport-related infrastructure (worst 1–5 best)	2.8	2016	●	●
The Times Higher Education Universities Ranking: Average score of top 3 universities (worst 0–100 best)	16.5	2022	●	●
Articles published in academic journals (per 1,000 population)	0.0	2020	●	→
Expenditure on research and development (% of GDP)	0.5	2013	●	●

SDG10 – Reduced Inequalities

Indicator	Value	Year	Rating	Trend
Gini coefficient	40.5	2017	●	●
Palma ratio	1.9	2018	●	●

SDG11 – Sustainable Cities and Communities

Indicator	Value	Year	Rating	Trend
Proportion of urban population living in slums (%)	40.2	2018	●	↗
Annual mean concentration of particulate matter of less than 2.5 microns in diameter (PM2.5) (μg/m^3)	28.5	2019	●	↓
Access to improved water source, piped (% of urban population)	59.6	2020	●	↓
Satisfaction with public transport (%)	60.0	2021	●	↑

SDG12 – Responsible Consumption and Production

Indicator	Value	Year	Rating	Trend
Municipal solid waste (kg/capita/day)	0.5	2012	●	●
Electronic waste (kg/capita)	1.0	2019	●	●
Production-based SO_2 emissions (kg/capita)	0.8	2018	●	●
SO_2 emissions embodied in imports (kg/capita)	0.2	2018	●	●
Production-based nitrogen emissions (kg/capita)	11.6	2015	●	↑
Nitrogen emissions embodied in imports (kg/capita)	0.2	2015	●	↑
Exports of plastic waste (kg/capita)	0.2	2021	●	●

SDG13 – Climate Action

Indicator	Value	Year	Rating	Trend
CO_2 emissions from fossil fuel combustion and cement production (tCO_2/capita)	0.2	2020	●	↑
CO_2 emissions embodied in imports (tCO_2/capita)	0.1	2018	●	↑
CO_2 emissions embodied in fossil fuel exports (kg/capita)	2.6	2021	●	●

SDG14 – Life Below Water

Indicator	Value	Year	Rating	Trend
Mean area that is protected in marine sites important to biodiversity (%)	52.1	2020	●	→
Ocean Health Index: Clean Waters score (worst 0–100 best)	50.6	2020	●	→
Fish caught from overexploited or collapsed stocks (% of total catch)	23.5	2018	●	↑
Fish caught by trawling or dredging (%)	0.0	2018	●	↑
Fish caught that are then discarded (%)	1.9	2018	●	↑
Marine biodiversity threats embodied in imports (per million population)	0.0	2018	●	●

SDG15 – Life on Land

Indicator	Value	Year	Rating	Trend
Mean area that is protected in terrestrial sites important to biodiversity (%)	63.0	2020	●	↗
Mean area that is protected in freshwater sites important to biodiversity (%)	36.2	2020	●	→
Red List Index of species survival (worst 0–1 best)	0.7	2021	●	↓
Permanent deforestation (% of forest area, 5-year average)	0.3	2020	●	↓
Terrestrial and freshwater biodiversity threats embodied in imports (per million population)	0.0	2018	●	●

SDG16 – Peace, Justice and Strong Institutions

Indicator	Value	Year	Rating	Trend
Homicides (per 100,000 population)	6.5	2016	●	●
Unsentenced detainees (% of prison population)	50.0	2016	●	●
Population who feel safe walking alone at night in the city or area where they live (%)	67	2021	●	↑
Property Rights (worst 1–7 best)	4.3	2020	●	↑
Birth registrations with civil authority (% of children under age 5)	26.4	2020	●	●
Corruption Perception Index (worst 0–100 best)	39	2021	●	↗
Children involved in child labor (% of population aged 5 to 14)	24.8	2019	●	●
Exports of major conventional weapons (TIV constant million USD per 100,000 population)	* 0.0	2020	●	●
Press Freedom Index (best 0–100 worst)	40.7	2021	●	↓
Access to and affordability of justice (worst 0–1 best)	0.5	2020	●	↗

SDG17 – Partnerships for the Goals

Indicator	Value	Year	Rating	Trend
Government spending on health and education (% of GDP)	4.7	2020	●	↓
For high-income and all OECD DAC countries: International concessional public finance, including official development assistance (% of GNI)	NA	NA	●	●
Other countries: Government revenue excluding grants (% of GDP)	13.9	2018	●	↗
Corporate Tax Haven Score (best 0–100 worst)	46.1	2019	●	●
Statistical Performance Index (worst 0–100 best)	58.1	2019	●	↓

THAILAND

OVERALL PERFORMANCE

COUNTRY RANKING

THAILAND

44/163

COUNTRY SCORE

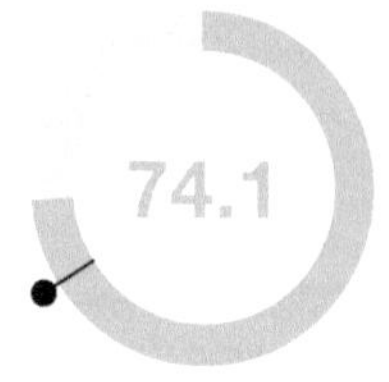

REGIONAL AVERAGE: 65.9

AVERAGE PERFORMANCE BY SDG

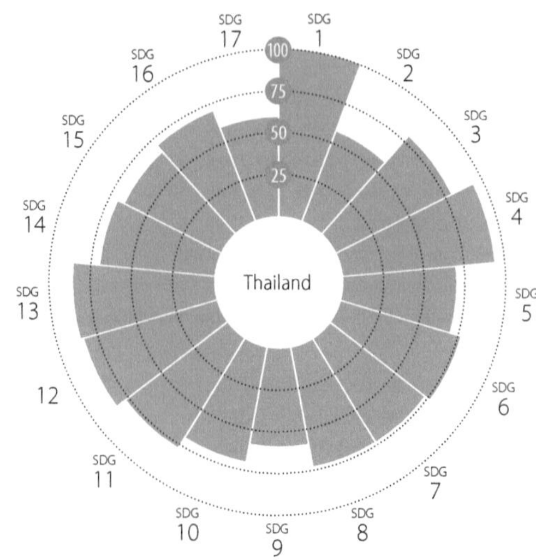

SDG DASHBOARDS AND TRENDS

Major challenges | Significant challenges | Challenges remain | SDG achieved | Information unavailable

Decreasing | Stagnating | Moderately improving | On track or maintaining SDG achievement | Information unavailable

Note: The full title of each SDG is available here: https://sustainabledevelopment.un.org/topics/sustainabledevelopmentgoals

INTERNATIONAL SPILLOVER INDEX

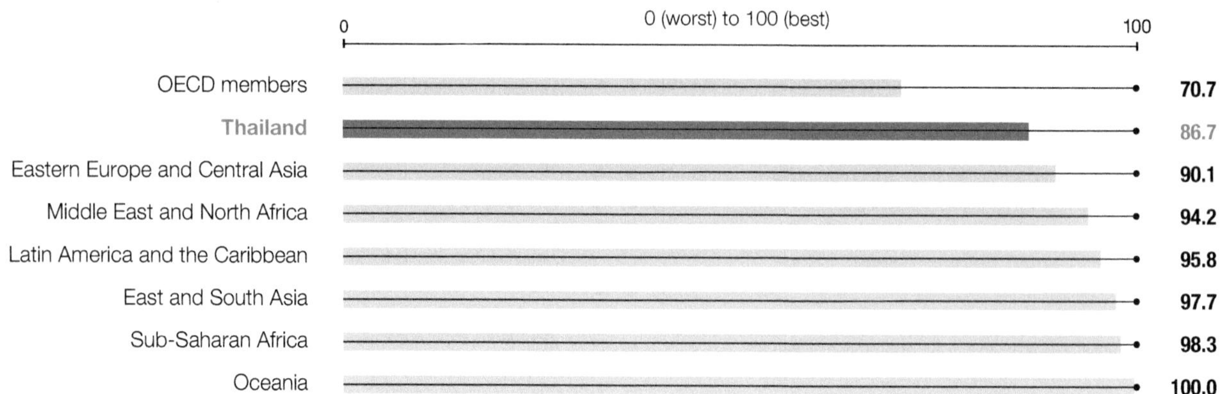

STATISTICAL PERFORMANCE INDEX

0 (worst) to 100 (best)

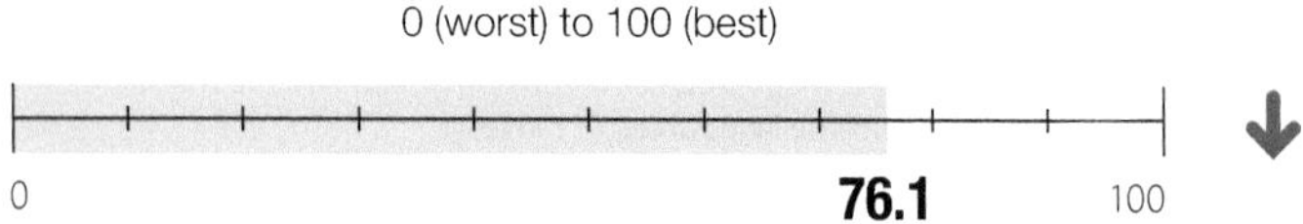

MISSING DATA IN SDG INDEX

1%

Performance by Indicator

SDG1 – No Poverty	Value	Year	Rating	Trend
Poverty headcount ratio at \$1.90/day (%)	0.0	2022	●	↑
Poverty headcount ratio at \$3.20/day (%)	0.0	2022	●	↑
SDG2 – Zero Hunger				
Prevalence of undernourishment (%)	8.2	2019	●	↓
Prevalence of stunting in children under 5 years of age (%)	13.4	2019	●	→
Prevalence of wasting in children under 5 years of age (%)	7.7	2019	●	→
Prevalence of obesity, BMI ≥ 30 (% of adult population)	10.0	2016	●	↑
Human Trophic Level (best 2–3 worst)	2.2	2017	●	↑
Cereal yield (tonnes per hectare of harvested land)	3.2	2018	●	↑
Sustainable Nitrogen Management Index (best 0–1.41 worst)	0.9	2015	●	↓
Exports of hazardous pesticides (tonnes per million population)	151.1	2019	●	●
SDG3 – Good Health and Well-Being				
Maternal mortality rate (per 100,000 live births)	37	2017	●	↑
Neonatal mortality rate (per 1,000 live births)	4.9	2020	●	↑
Mortality rate, under-5 (per 1,000 live births)	8.7	2020	●	↑
Incidence of tuberculosis (per 100,000 population)	150.0	2020	●	→
New HIV infections (per 1,000 uninfected population)	0.1	2020	●	↑
Age-standardized death rate due to cardiovascular disease, cancer, diabetes, or chronic respiratory disease in adults aged 30–70 years (%)	13.7	2019	●	↑
Age-standardized death rate attributable to household air pollution and ambient air pollution (per 100,000 population)	61	2016	●	●
Traffic deaths (per 100,000 population)	32.2	2019	●	→
Life expectancy at birth (years)	77.7	2019	●	→
Adolescent fertility rate (births per 1,000 females aged 15 to 19)	23.0	2019	●	↑
Births attended by skilled health personnel (%)	99.1	2016	●	●
Surviving infants who received 2 WHO-recommended vaccines (%)	96	2020	●	↑
Universal health coverage (UHC) index of service coverage (worst 0–100 best)	83	2019	●	↑
Subjective well-being (average ladder score, worst 0–10 best)	5.6	2021	●	↓
SDG4 – Quality Education				
Participation rate in pre-primary organized learning (% of children aged 4 to 6)	99.7	2020	●	↑
Net primary enrollment rate (%)	98.3	2009	●	●
Lower secondary completion rate (%)	85.2	2020	●	↑
Literacy rate (% of population aged 15 to 24)	98.1	2018	●	↑
SDG5 – Gender Equality				
Demand for family planning satisfied by modern methods (% of females aged 15 to 49)	88.2	2019	●	●
Ratio of female-to-male mean years of education received (%)	93.9	2019	●	→
Ratio of female-to-male labor force participation rate (%)	78.5	2020	●	↑
Seats held by women in national parliament (%)	15.7	2020	●	↗
SDG6 – Clean Water and Sanitation				
Population using at least basic drinking water services (%)	100.0	2020	●	↑
Population using at least basic sanitation services (%)	98.7	2020	●	↑
Freshwater withdrawal (% of available freshwater resources)	23.0	2018	●	●
Anthropogenic wastewater that receives treatment (%)	2.0	2018	●	●
Scarce water consumption embodied in imports (m^3 H_2O eq/capita)	810.1	2018	●	●
SDG7 – Affordable and Clean Energy				
Population with access to electricity (%)	99.9	2019	●	↑
Population with access to clean fuels and technology for cooking (%)	79.5	2019	●	↗
CO_2 emissions from fuel combustion per total electricity output ($MtCO_2$/TWh)	1.5	2019	●	↗
Share of renewable energy in total primary energy supply (%)	20.7	2019	●	↑
SDG8 – Decent Work and Economic Growth				
Adjusted GDP growth (%)	-2.2	2020	●	●
Victims of modern slavery (per 1,000 population)	8.9	2018	●	●
Adults with an account at a bank or other financial institution or with a mobile-money-service provider (% of population aged 15 or over)	81.6	2017	●	↑
Unemployment rate (% of total labor force)	1.0	2022	●	↑
Fundamental labor rights are effectively guaranteed (worst 0–1 best)	0.5	2020	●	↓
Fatal work-related accidents embodied in imports (per 100,000 population)	0.3	2015	●	↑

* Imputed data point

SDG9 – Industry, Innovation and Infrastructure	Value	Year	Rating	Trend
Population using the internet (%)	77.8	2020	●	↑
Mobile broadband subscriptions (per 100 population)	86.7	2019	●	↑
Logistics Performance Index: Quality of trade and transport-related infrastructure (worst 1–5 best)	3.1	2018	●	↑
The Times Higher Education Universities Ranking: Average score of top 3 universities (worst 0–100 best)	33.2	2022	●	●
Articles published in academic journals (per 1,000 population)	0.3	2020	●	↗
Expenditure on research and development (% of GDP)	1.0	2017	●	↑
SDG10 – Reduced Inequalities				
Gini coefficient	34.9	2019	●	↗
Palma ratio	1.5	2018	●	●
SDG11 – Sustainable Cities and Communities				
Proportion of urban population living in slums (%)	24.5	2018	●	→
Annual mean concentration of particulate matter of less than 2.5 microns in diameter (PM2.5) ($\mu g/m^3$)	24.2	2019	●	↗
Access to improved water source, piped (% of urban population)	90.6	2020	●	↑
Satisfaction with public transport (%)	63.0	2021	●	↓
SDG12 – Responsible Consumption and Production				
Municipal solid waste (kg/capita/day)	1.1	2015	●	●
Electronic waste (kg/capita)	9.2	2019	●	●
Production-based SO_2 emissions (kg/capita)	9.9	2018	●	●
SO_2 emissions embodied in imports (kg/capita)	2.1	2018	●	●
Production-based nitrogen emissions (kg/capita)	11.6	2015	●	↑
Nitrogen emissions embodied in imports (kg/capita)	2.7	2015	●	↑
Exports of plastic waste (kg/capita)	2.9	2020	●	●
SDG13 – Climate Action				
CO_2 emissions from fossil fuel combustion and cement production (tCO_2/capita)	3.7	2020	●	↗
CO_2 emissions embodied in imports (tCO_2/capita)	0.8	2018	●	→
CO_2 emissions embodied in fossil fuel exports (kg/capita)	70.8	2020	●	●
SDG14 – Life Below Water				
Mean area that is protected in marine sites important to biodiversity (%)	47.5	2020	●	→
Ocean Health Index: Clean Waters score (worst 0–100 best)	60.3	2020	●	↗
Fish caught from overexploited or collapsed stocks (% of total catch)	46.3	2018	●	↗
Fish caught by trawling or dredging (%)	16.3	2018	●	↓
Fish caught that are then discarded (%)	0.8	2018	●	↑
Marine biodiversity threats embodied in imports (per million population)	0.1	2018	●	●
SDG15 – Life on Land				
Mean area that is protected in terrestrial sites important to biodiversity (%)	71.1	2020	●	→
Mean area that is protected in freshwater sites important to biodiversity (%)	40.7	2020	●	→
Red List Index of species survival (worst 0–1 best)	0.8	2021	●	↓
Permanent deforestation (% of forest area, 5-year average)	0.3	2020	●	↑
Terrestrial and freshwater biodiversity threats embodied in imports (per million population)	1.0	2018	●	●
SDG16 – Peace, Justice and Strong Institutions				
Homicides (per 100,000 population)	4.9	2011	●	●
Unsentenced detainees (% of prison population)	11.9	2019	●	↑
Population who feel safe walking alone at night in the city or area where they live (%)	61	2021	●	↓
Property Rights (worst 1–7 best)	4.3	2020	●	↑
Birth registrations with civil authority (% of children under age 5)	99.8	2020	●	●
Corruption Perception Index (worst 0–100 best)	35	2021	●	↓
Children involved in child labor (% of population aged 5 to 14)	NA	NA	●	●
Exports of major conventional weapons (TIV constant million USD per 100,000 population)	0.0	2020	●	●
Press Freedom Index (best 0–100 worst)	45.2	2021	●	↓
Access to and affordability of justice (worst 0–1 best)	0.6	2020	●	↑
SDG17 – Partnerships for the Goals				
Government spending on health and education (% of GDP)	5.7	2019	●	↓
For high-income and all OECD DAC countries: International concessional public finance, including official development assistance (% of GNI)	NA	NA	●	●
Other countries: Government revenue excluding grants (% of GDP)	19.3	2019	●	↓
Corporate Tax Haven Score (best 0–100 worst)	* 0.0	2019	●	●
Statistical Performance Index (worst 0–100 best)	76.1	2019	●	↓

TIMOR-LESTE

East and South Asia

OVERALL PERFORMANCE

COUNTRY RANKING

TIMOR-LESTE

NA /163

COUNTRY SCORE

REGIONAL AVERAGE: 65.9

AVERAGE PERFORMANCE BY SDG

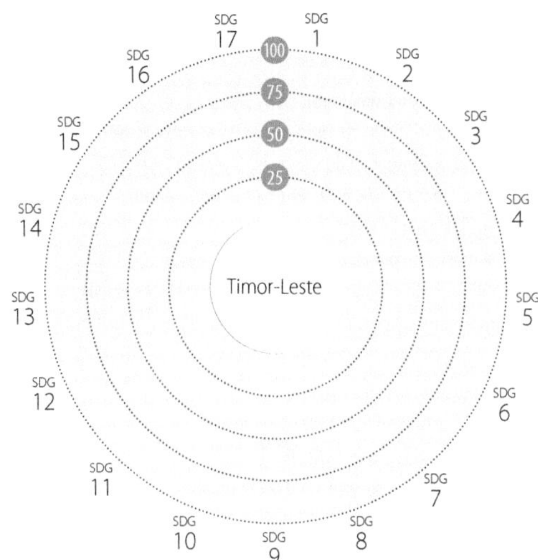

SDG DASHBOARDS AND TRENDS

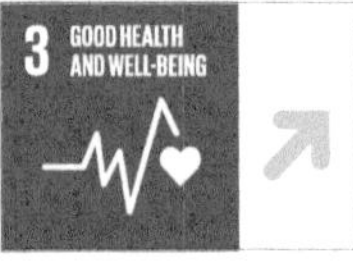

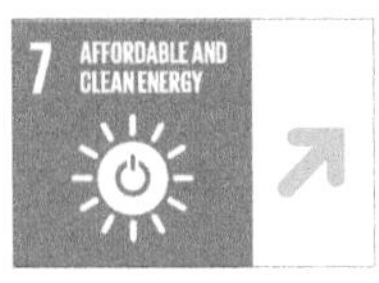

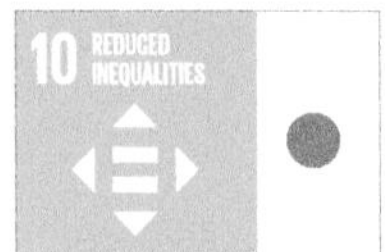

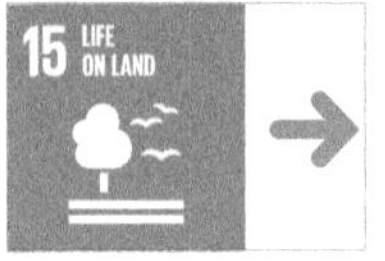

Major challenges · Significant challenges · Challenges remain · SDG achieved · Information unavailable

Decreasing · Stagnating · Moderately improving · On track or maintaining SDG achievement · Information unavailable

Note: The full title of each SDG is available here: https://sustainabledevelopment.un.org/topics/sustainabledevelopmentgoals

INTERNATIONAL SPILLOVER INDEX

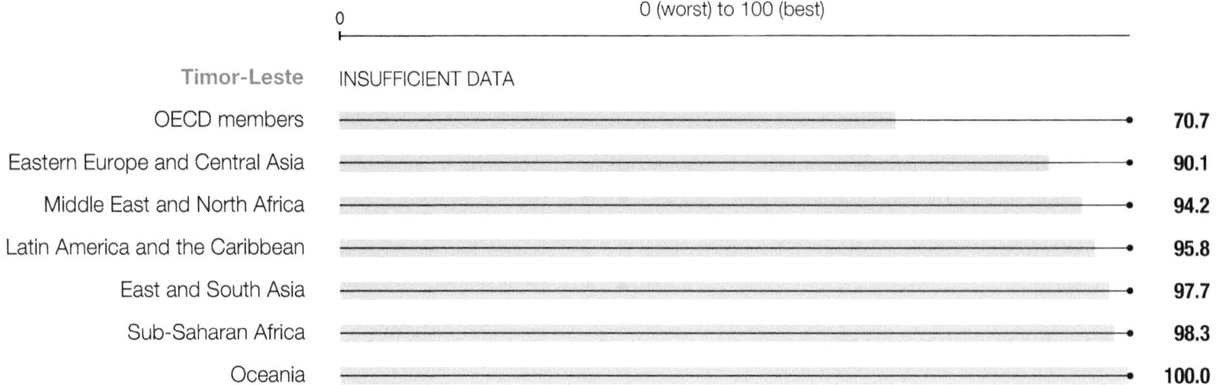

STATISTICAL PERFORMANCE INDEX

0 (worst) to 100 (best)

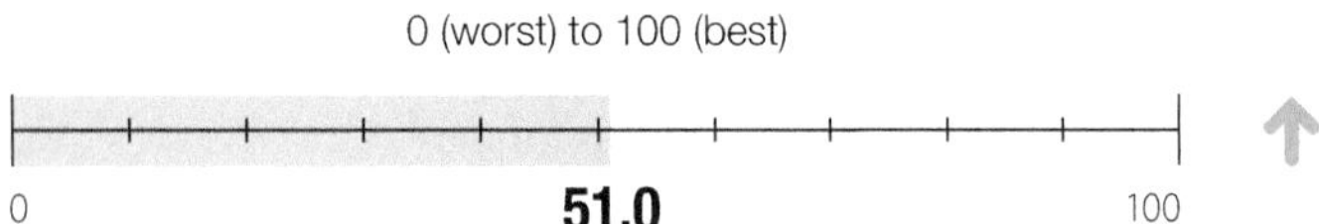

MISSING DATA IN SDG INDEX

27%

TIMOR-LESTE

Performance by Indicator

SDG1 – No Poverty	Value	Year	Rating	Trend
Poverty headcount ratio at $1.90/day (%)	26.6	2022	●	↓
Poverty headcount ratio at $3.20/day (%)	67.6	2022	●	↓

SDG2 – Zero Hunger	Value	Year	Rating	Trend
Prevalence of undernourishment (%)	22.6	2019	●	→
Prevalence of stunting in children under 5 years of age (%)	51.7	2013	●	→
Prevalence of wasting in children under 5 years of age (%)	9.9	2013	●	→
Prevalence of obesity, BMI ≥ 30 (% of adult population)	3.8	2016	●	↑
Human Trophic Level (best 2–3 worst)	2.1	2017	●	↑
Cereal yield (tonnes per hectare of harvested land)	2.6	2018	●	↑
Sustainable Nitrogen Management Index (best 0–1.41 worst)	0.9	2015	●	→
Exports of hazardous pesticides (tonnes per million population)	NA	NA	●	●

SDG3 – Good Health and Well-Being	Value	Year	Rating	Trend
Maternal mortality rate (per 100,000 live births)	142	2017	●	↑
Neonatal mortality rate (per 1,000 live births)	19.4	2020	●	↗
Mortality rate, under-5 (per 1,000 live births)	42.3	2020	●	↗
Incidence of tuberculosis (per 100,000 population)	508.0	2020	●	↓
New HIV infections (per 1,000 uninfected population)	0.1	2020	●	↑
Age-standardized death rate due to cardiovascular disease, cancer, diabetes, or chronic respiratory disease in adults aged 30–70 years (%)	20.0	2019	●	↓
Age-standardized death rate attributable to household air pollution and ambient air pollution (per 100,000 population)	140	2016	●	●
Traffic deaths (per 100,000 population)	11.9	2019	●	↗
Life expectancy at birth (years)	69.6	2019	●	→
Adolescent fertility rate (births per 1,000 females aged 15 to 19)	41.9	2015	●	●
Births attended by skilled health personnel (%)	56.7	2016	●	●
Surviving infants who received 2 WHO-recommended vaccines (%)	79	2020	●	↑
Universal health coverage (UHC) index of service coverage (worst 0–100 best)	53	2019	●	→
Subjective well-being (average ladder score, worst 0–10 best)	NA	NA	●	●

SDG4 – Quality Education	Value	Year	Rating	Trend
Participation rate in pre-primary organized learning (% of children aged 4 to 6)	50.2	2019	●	↓
Net primary enrollment rate (%)	95.1	2019	●	↗
Lower secondary completion rate (%)	90.8	2019	●	↑
Literacy rate (% of population aged 15 to 24)	83.5	2018	●	●

SDG5 – Gender Equality	Value	Year	Rating	Trend
Demand for family planning satisfied by modern methods (% of females aged 15 to 49)	45.9	2016	●	→
Ratio of female-to-male mean years of education received (%)	67.9	2019	●	→
Ratio of female-to-male labor force participation rate (%)	84.7	2020	●	↑
Seats held by women in national parliament (%)	38.5	2020	●	→

SDG6 – Clean Water and Sanitation	Value	Year	Rating	Trend
Population using at least basic drinking water services (%)	85.5	2020	●	↑
Population using at least basic sanitation services (%)	56.8	2020	●	→
Freshwater withdrawal (% of available freshwater resources)	28.3	2018	●	●
Anthropogenic wastewater that receives treatment (%)	0.3	2018	●	●
Scarce water consumption embodied in imports (m^3 H_2O eq/capita)	NA	NA	●	●

SDG7 – Affordable and Clean Energy	Value	Year	Rating	Trend
Population with access to electricity (%)	94.7	2019	●	↑
Population with access to clean fuels and technology for cooking (%)	12.6	2019	●	→
CO_2 emissions from fuel combustion per total electricity output ($MtCO_2$/TWh)	NA	NA	●	●
Share of renewable energy in total primary energy supply (%)	NA	NA	●	●

SDG8 – Decent Work and Economic Growth	Value	Year	Rating	Trend
Adjusted GDP growth (%)	2.9	2020	●	●
Victims of modern slavery (per 1,000 population)	7.7	2018	●	●
Adults with an account at a bank or other financial institution or with a mobile-money-service provider (% of population aged 15 or over)	NA	NA	●	●
Unemployment rate (% of total labor force)	4.8	2022	●	↑
Fundamental labor rights are effectively guaranteed (worst 0–1 best)	NA	NA	●	●
Fatal work-related accidents embodied in imports (per 100,000 population)	NA	NA	●	●

* Imputed data point

SDG9 – Industry, Innovation and Infrastructure	Value	Year	Rating	Trend
Population using the internet (%)	29.1	2020	●	↗
Mobile broadband subscriptions (per 100 population)	31.0	2019	●	↓
Logistics Performance Index: Quality of trade and transport-related infrastructure (worst 1–5 best)	NA	NA	●	●
The Times Higher Education Universities Ranking: Average score of top 3 universities (worst 0–100 best)	* 0.0	2022	●	●
Articles published in academic journals (per 1,000 population)	0.0	2020	●	→
Expenditure on research and development (% of GDP)	NA	NA	●	●

SDG10 – Reduced Inequalities	Value	Year	Rating	Trend
Gini coefficient	28.7	2014	●	●
Palma ratio	1.1	2018	●	●

SDG11 – Sustainable Cities and Communities	Value	Year	Rating	Trend
Proportion of urban population living in slums (%)	30.1	2018	●	●
Annual mean concentration of particulate matter of less than 2.5 microns in diameter (PM2.5) (μg/m³)	18.5	2019	●	↗
Access to improved water source, piped (% of urban population)	81.6	2020	●	↗
Satisfaction with public transport (%)	NA	NA	●	●

SDG12 – Responsible Consumption and Production	Value	Year	Rating	Trend
Municipal solid waste (kg/capita/day)	0.1	2016	●	●
Electronic waste (kg/capita)	2.9	2019	●	●
Production-based SO_2 emissions (kg/capita)	NA	NA	●	●
SO_2 emissions embodied in imports (kg/capita)	NA	NA	●	●
Production-based nitrogen emissions (kg/capita)	NA	NA	●	●
Nitrogen emissions embodied in imports (kg/capita)	NA	NA	●	●
Exports of plastic waste (kg/capita)	NA	NA	●	●

SDG13 – Climate Action	Value	Year	Rating	Trend
CO_2 emissions from fossil fuel combustion and cement production (tCO_2/capita)	0.4	2020	●	↑
CO_2 emissions embodied in imports (tCO_2/capita)	NA	NA	●	●
CO_2 emissions embodied in fossil fuel exports (kg/capita)	NA	NA	●	●

SDG14 – Life Below Water	Value	Year	Rating	Trend
Mean area that is protected in marine sites important to biodiversity (%)	19.6	2020	●	→
Ocean Health Index: Clean Waters score (worst 0–100 best)	NA	NA	●	●
Fish caught from overexploited or collapsed stocks (% of total catch)	9.6	2018	●	↑
Fish caught by trawling or dredging (%)	0.0	2018	●	↑
Fish caught that are then discarded (%)	0.0	2018	●	↑
Marine biodiversity threats embodied in imports (per million population)	NA	NA	●	●

SDG15 – Life on Land	Value	Year	Rating	Trend
Mean area that is protected in terrestrial sites important to biodiversity (%)	45.6	2020	●	→
Mean area that is protected in freshwater sites important to biodiversity (%)	NA	NA	●	●
Red List Index of species survival (worst 0–1 best)	0.8	2021	●	↓
Permanent deforestation (% of forest area, 5-year average)	0.1	2020	●	→
Terrestrial and freshwater biodiversity threats embodied in imports (per million population)	NA	NA	●	●

SDG16 – Peace, Justice and Strong Institutions	Value	Year	Rating	Trend
Homicides (per 100,000 population)	4.1	2015	●	●
Unsentenced detainees (% of prison population)	23.8	2017	●	●
Population who feel safe walking alone at night in the city or area where they live (%)	NA	NA	●	●
Property Rights (worst 1–7 best)	NA	NA	●	●
Birth registrations with civil authority (% of children under age 5)	60.4	2020	●	●
Corruption Perception Index (worst 0–100 best)	41	2021	●	↑
Children involved in child labor (% of population aged 5 to 14)	9.2	2019	●	●
Exports of major conventional weapons (TIV constant million USD per 100,000 population)	* 0.0	2020	●	●
Press Freedom Index (best 0–100 worst)	29.1	2021	●	↑
Access to and affordability of justice (worst 0–1 best)	NA	NA	●	●

SDG17 – Partnerships for the Goals	Value	Year	Rating	Trend
Government spending on health and education (% of GDP)	10.8	2019	●	↑
For high-income and all OECD DAC countries: International concessional public finance, including official development assistance (% of GNI)	NA	NA	●	●
Other countries: Government revenue excluding grants (% of GDP)	67.0	2019	●	↑
Corporate Tax Haven Score (best 0–100 worst)	* 0.0	2019	●	●
Statistical Performance Index (worst 0–100 best)	51.0	2019	●	↑

5. Country Profiles

TOGO

Sub-Saharan Africa

OVERALL PERFORMANCE

COUNTRY RANKING

TOGO

133/163

COUNTRY SCORE

REGIONAL AVERAGE: 53.6

AVERAGE PERFORMANCE BY SDG

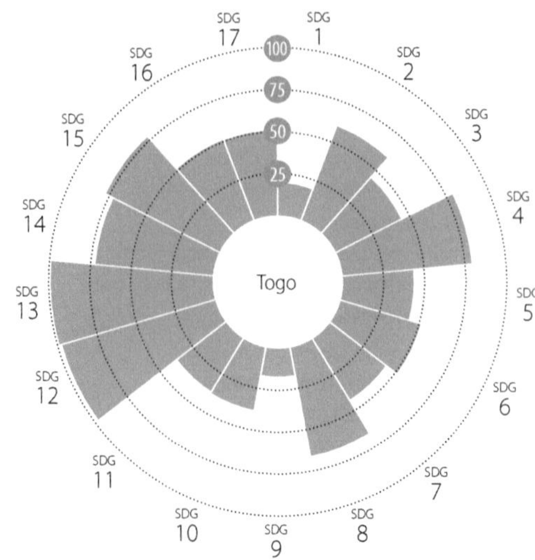

SDG DASHBOARDS AND TRENDS

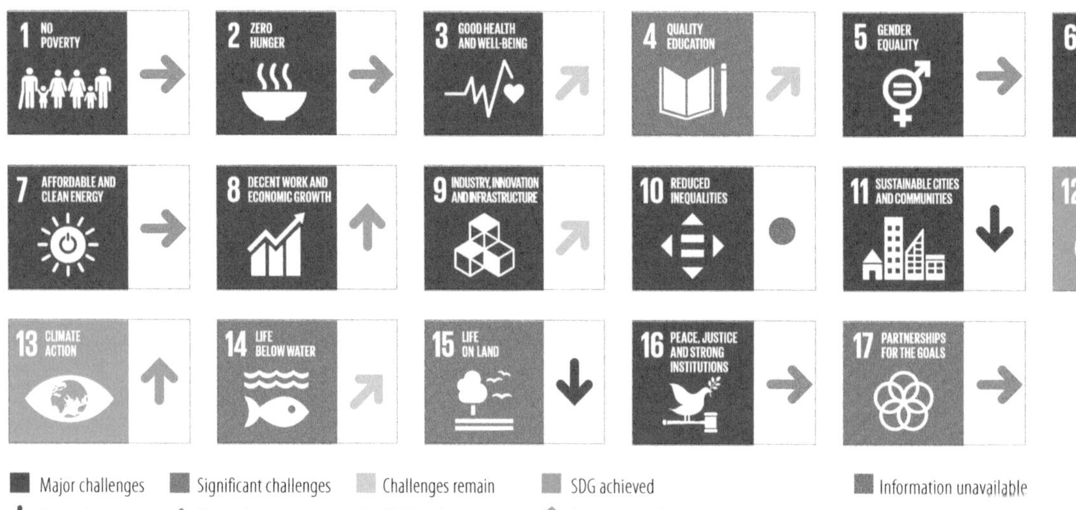

Major challenges | Significant challenges | Challenges remain | SDG achieved | Information unavailable

Decreasing | Stagnating | Moderately improving | On track or maintaining SDG achievement | Information unavailable

Note: The full title of each SDG is available here: https://sustainabledevelopment.un.org/topics/sustainabledevelopmentgoals

INTERNATIONAL SPILLOVER INDEX

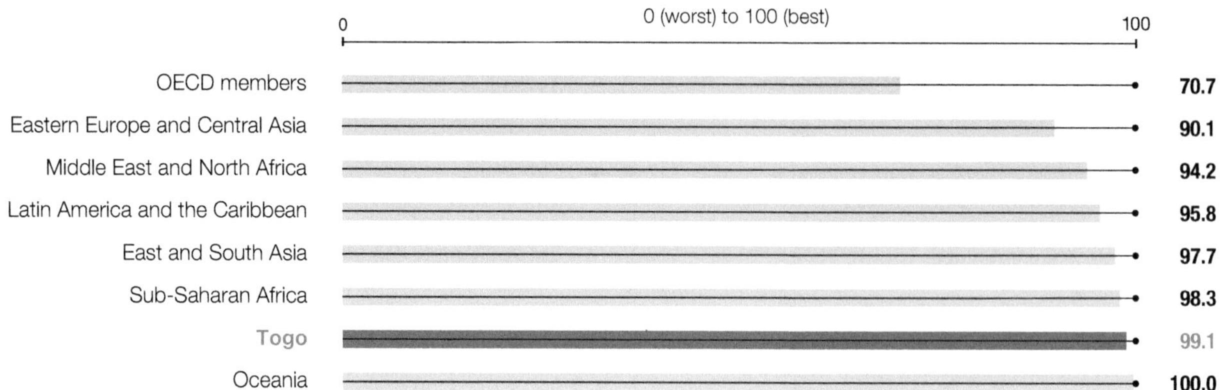

STATISTICAL PERFORMANCE INDEX

0 (worst) to 100 (best)

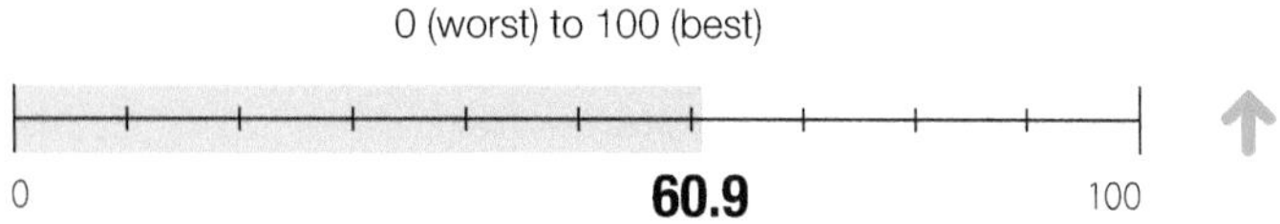

MISSING DATA IN SDG INDEX

5%

TOGO

Performance by Indicator

Indicator	Value	Year	Rating	Trend
SDG1 – No Poverty				
Poverty headcount ratio at \$1.90/day (%)	44.4	2022	●	→
Poverty headcount ratio at \$3.20/day (%)	69.3	2022	●	→
SDG2 – Zero Hunger				
Prevalence of undernourishment (%)	20.4	2019	●	→
Prevalence of stunting in children under 5 years of age (%)	23.8	2017	●	↗
Prevalence of wasting in children under 5 years of age (%)	5.7	2017	●	→
Prevalence of obesity, BMI ≥ 30 (% of adult population)	8.4	2016	●	↑
Human Trophic Level (best 2–3 worst)	2.1	2017	●	↑
Cereal yield (tonnes per hectare of harvested land)	1.1	2018	●	↓
Sustainable Nitrogen Management Index (best 0–1.41 worst)	0.9	2015	●	→
Exports of hazardous pesticides (tonnes per million population)	2.5	2019	●	●
SDG3 – Good Health and Well-Being				
Maternal mortality rate (per 100,000 live births)	396	2017	●	→
Neonatal mortality rate (per 1,000 live births)	24.5	2020	●	→
Mortality rate, under-5 (per 1,000 live births)	64.4	2020	●	↗
Incidence of tuberculosis (per 100,000 population)	36.0	2020	●	↑
New HIV infections (per 1,000 uninfected population)	0.5	2020	●	↑
Age-standardized death rate due to cardiovascular disease, cancer, diabetes, or chronic respiratory disease in adults aged 30–70 years (%)	23.9	2019	●	↗
Age-standardized death rate attributable to household air pollution and ambient air pollution (per 100,000 population)	250	2016	●	●
Traffic deaths (per 100,000 population)	28.7	2019	●	→
Life expectancy at birth (years)	64.3	2019	●	→
Adolescent fertility rate (births per 1,000 females aged 15 to 19)	79.0	2016	●	●
Births attended by skilled health personnel (%)	69.4	2017	●	↑
Surviving infants who received 2 WHO-recommended vaccines (%)	69	2020	●	↓
Universal health coverage (UHC) index of service coverage (worst 0–100 best)	44	2019	●	→
Subjective well-being (average ladder score, worst 0–10 best)	4.0	2021	●	→
SDG4 – Quality Education				
Participation rate in pre-primary organized learning (% of children aged 4 to 6)	99.4	2020	●	●
Net primary enrollment rate (%)	98.8	2020	●	↑
Lower secondary completion rate (%)	51.9	2020	●	↗
Literacy rate (% of population aged 15 to 24)	87.9	2019	●	↑
SDG5 – Gender Equality				
Demand for family planning satisfied by modern methods (% of females aged 15 to 49)	39.6	2017	●	●
Ratio of female-to-male mean years of education received (%)	52.2	2019	●	→
Ratio of female-to-male labor force participation rate (%)	93.7	2020	●	↑
Seats held by women in national parliament (%)	18.7	2020	●	→
SDG6 – Clean Water and Sanitation				
Population using at least basic drinking water services (%)	68.6	2020	●	→
Population using at least basic sanitation services (%)	18.6	2020	●	→
Freshwater withdrawal (% of available freshwater resources)	3.4	2018	●	●
Anthropogenic wastewater that receives treatment (%)	0.0	2018	●	●
Scarce water consumption embodied in imports (m^3 H_2O eq/capita)	430.6	2018	●	●
SDG7 – Affordable and Clean Energy				
Population with access to electricity (%)	52.4	2019	●	↗
Population with access to clean fuels and technology for cooking (%)	9.3	2019	●	→
CO_2 emissions from fuel combustion per total electricity output ($MtCO_2$/TWh)	4.9	2019	●	→
Share of renewable energy in total primary energy supply (%)	83.1	2019	●	↑
SDG8 – Decent Work and Economic Growth				
Adjusted GDP growth (%)	-3.6	2020	●	●
Victims of modern slavery (per 1,000 population)	6.8	2018	●	●
Adults with an account at a bank or other financial institution or with a mobile-money-service provider (% of population aged 15 or over)	45.3	2017	●	↑
Unemployment rate (% of total labor force)	3.9	2022	●	↑
Fundamental labor rights are effectively guaranteed (worst 0–1 best)	0.5	2020	●	●
Fatal work-related accidents embodied in imports (per 100,000 population)	0.0	2015	●	↑

* Imputed data point

Indicator	Value	Year	Rating	Trend
SDG9 – Industry, Innovation and Infrastructure				
Population using the internet (%)	24.0	2020	●	↗
Mobile broadband subscriptions (per 100 population)	41.1	2019	●	↑
Logistics Performance Index: Quality of trade and transport-related infrastructure (worst 1–5 best)	2.2	2018	●	↗
The Times Higher Education Universities Ranking: Average score of top 3 universities (worst 0–100 best)	* 0.0	2022	●	●
Articles published in academic journals (per 1,000 population)	0.0	2020	●	→
Expenditure on research and development (% of GDP)	0.3	2014	●	●
SDG10 – Reduced Inequalities				
Gini coefficient	43.1	2015	●	●
Palma ratio	2.2	2018	●	●
SDG11 – Sustainable Cities and Communities				
Proportion of urban population living in slums (%)	53.3	2018	●	↓
Annual mean concentration of particulate matter of less than 2.5 microns in diameter (PM2.5) ($\mu g/m^3$)	41.1	2019	●	↓
Access to improved water source, piped (% of urban population)	41.8	2020	●	↓
Satisfaction with public transport (%)	29.0	2021	●	→
SDG12 – Responsible Consumption and Production				
Municipal solid waste (kg/capita/day)	0.4	2014	●	●
Electronic waste (kg/capita)	0.9	2019	●	●
Production-based SO_2 emissions (kg/capita)	0.4	2018	●	●
SO_2 emissions embodied in imports (kg/capita)	0.2	2018	●	●
Production-based nitrogen emissions (kg/capita)	6.6	2015	●	↑
Nitrogen emissions embodied in imports (kg/capita)	0.7	2015	●	↑
Exports of plastic waste (kg/capita)	0.0	2020	●	●
SDG13 – Climate Action				
CO_2 emissions from fossil fuel combustion and cement production (tCO_2/capita)	0.3	2020	●	↑
CO_2 emissions embodied in imports (tCO_2/capita)	0.1	2018	●	↑
CO_2 emissions embodied in fossil fuel exports (kg/capita)	0.0	2017	●	●
SDG14 – Life Below Water				
Mean area that is protected in marine sites important to biodiversity (%)	NA	NA	●	●
Ocean Health Index: Clean Waters score (worst 0–100 best)	21.4	2020	●	→
Fish caught from overexploited or collapsed stocks (% of total catch)	NA	NA	●	●
Fish caught by trawling or dredging (%)	11.2	2018	●	↑
Fish caught that are then discarded (%)	0.0	2018	●	↑
Marine biodiversity threats embodied in imports (per million population)	0.0	2018	●	●
SDG15 – Life on Land				
Mean area that is protected in terrestrial sites important to biodiversity (%)	79.5	2020	●	→
Mean area that is protected in freshwater sites important to biodiversity (%)	NA	NA	●	●
Red List Index of species survival (worst 0–1 best)	0.9	2021	●	→
Permanent deforestation (% of forest area, 5-year average)	0.5	2020	●	↓
Terrestrial and freshwater biodiversity threats embodied in imports (per million population)	0.0	2018	●	●
SDG16 – Peace, Justice and Strong Institutions				
Homicides (per 100,000 population)	NA	NA	●	●
Unsentenced detainees (% of prison population)	62.7	2012	●	●
Population who feel safe walking alone at night in the city or area where they live (%)	57	2021	●	→
Property Rights (worst 1–7 best)	NA	NA	●	●
Birth registrations with civil authority (% of children under age 5)	82.9	2020	●	●
Corruption Perception Index (worst 0–100 best)	30	2021	●	↓
Children involved in child labor (% of population aged 5 to 14)	38.5	2019	●	●
Exports of major conventional weapons (TIV constant million USD per 100,000 population)	* 0.0	2020	●	●
Press Freedom Index (best 0–100 worst)	29.6	2021	●	↑
Access to and affordability of justice (worst 0–1 best)	0.6	2020	●	●
SDG17 – Partnerships for the Goals				
Government spending on health and education (% of GDP)	5.8	2019	●	↓
For high-income and all OECD DAC countries: International concessional public finance, including official development assistance (% of GNI)	NA	NA	●	●
Other countries: Government revenue excluding grants (% of GDP)	14.8	2019	●	↓
Corporate Tax Haven Score (best 0–100 worst)	* 0.0	2019	●	●
Statistical Performance Index (worst 0–100 best)	60.9	2019	●	↑

TONGA

Oceania

OVERALL PERFORMANCE

COUNTRY RANKING

TONGA

NA /163

COUNTRY SCORE

na

REGIONAL AVERAGE: 52.3

AVERAGE PERFORMANCE BY SDG

SDG 1, SDG 2, SDG 3, SDG 4, SDG 5, SDG 6, SDG 7, SDG 8, SDG 9, SDG 10, SDG 11, SDG 12, SDG 13, SDG 14, SDG 15, SDG 16, SDG 17

100, 75, 50, 25

Tonga

SDG DASHBOARDS AND TRENDS

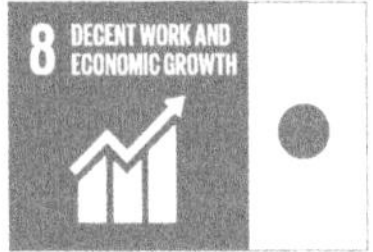

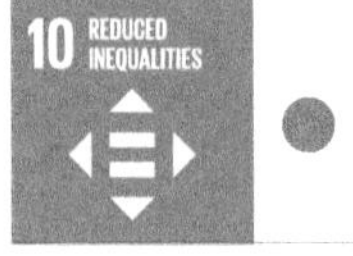

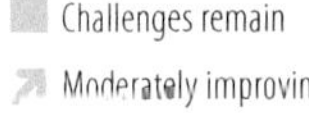

Major challenges · Significant challenges · Challenges remain · SDG achieved · Information unavailable

Decreasing · Stagnating · Moderately improving · On track or maintaining SDG achievement · Information unavailable

Note: The full title of each SDG is available here: https://sustainabledevelopment.un.org/topics/sustainabledevelopmentgoals

INTERNATIONAL SPILLOVER INDEX

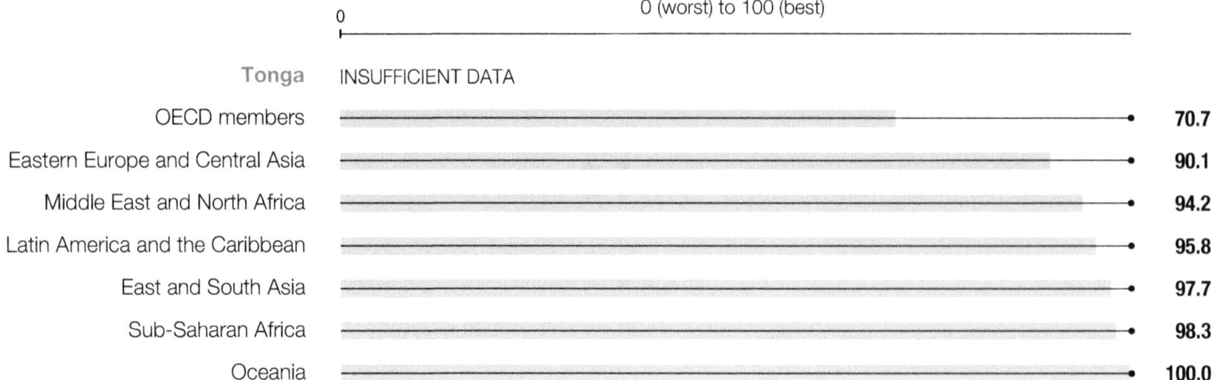

STATISTICAL PERFORMANCE INDEX

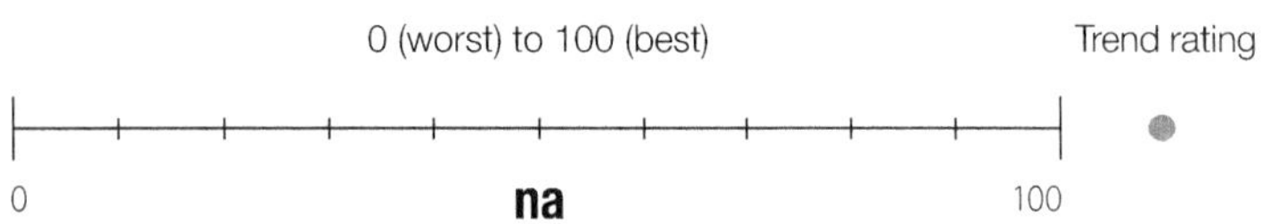

MISSING DATA IN SDG INDEX

35%

Performance by Indicator

SDG1 – No Poverty	Value	Year	Rating	Trend
Poverty headcount ratio at \$1.90/day (%)	0.1	2022	●	↑
Poverty headcount ratio at \$3.20/day (%)	5.0	2022	●	↑
SDG2 – Zero Hunger				
Prevalence of undernourishment (%)	NA	NA	●	●
Prevalence of stunting in children under 5 years of age (%)	2.2	2019	●	↑
Prevalence of wasting in children under 5 years of age (%)	1.1	2019	●	↑
Prevalence of obesity, BMI ≥ 30 (% of adult population)	48.2	2016	●	↓
Human Trophic Level (best 2–3 worst)	NA	NA	●	●
Cereal yield (tonnes per hectare of harvested land)	NA	NA	●	●
Sustainable Nitrogen Management Index (best 0–1.41 worst)	1.0	2015	●	↓
Exports of hazardous pesticides (tonnes per million population)	NA	NA	●	●
SDG3 – Good Health and Well-Being				
Maternal mortality rate (per 100,000 live births)	52	2017	●	↑
Neonatal mortality rate (per 1,000 live births)	5.0	2020	●	↑
Mortality rate, under-5 (per 1,000 live births)	11.4	2020	●	↑
Incidence of tuberculosis (per 100,000 population)	10.0	2020	●	↑
New HIV infections (per 1,000 uninfected population)	NA	NA	●	●
Age-standardized death rate due to cardiovascular disease, cancer, diabetes, or chronic respiratory disease in adults aged 30–70 years (%)	24.8	2019	●	→
Age-standardized death rate attributable to household air pollution and ambient air pollution (per 100,000 population)	73	2016	●	●
Traffic deaths (per 100,000 population)	33.0	2019	●	↓
Life expectancy at birth (years)	72.6	2019	●	→
Adolescent fertility rate (births per 1,000 females aged 15 to 19)	30.0	2016	●	●
Births attended by skilled health personnel (%)	95.5	2012	●	●
Surviving infants who received 2 WHO-recommended vaccines (%)	99	2020	●	↑
Universal health coverage (UHC) index of service coverage (worst 0–100 best)	56	2019	●	→
Subjective well-being (average ladder score, worst 0–10 best)	NA	NA	●	●
SDG4 – Quality Education				
Participation rate in pre-primary organized learning (% of children aged 4 to 6)	94.6	2020	●	●
Net primary enrollment rate (%)	99.4	2020	●	↑
Lower secondary completion rate (%)	76.4	2020	●	●
Literacy rate (% of population aged 15 to 24)	99.4	2018	●	●
SDG5 – Gender Equality				
Demand for family planning satisfied by modern methods (% of females aged 15 to 49)	49.9	2019	●	●
Ratio of female-to-male mean years of education received (%)	100.9	2019	●	↑
Ratio of female-to-male labor force participation rate (%)	67.6	2020	●	↗
Seats held by women in national parliament (%)	7.4	2020	●	↗
SDG6 – Clean Water and Sanitation				
Population using at least basic drinking water services (%)	98.7	2020	●	↑
Population using at least basic sanitation services (%)	92.9	2020	●	→
Freshwater withdrawal (% of available freshwater resources)	NA	NA	●	●
Anthropogenic wastewater that receives treatment (%)	0.3	2018	●	●
Scarce water consumption embodied in imports (m^3 H_2O eq/capita)	NA	NA	●	●
SDG7 – Affordable and Clean Energy				
Population with access to electricity (%)	98.4	2019	●	↑
Population with access to clean fuels and technology for cooking (%)	76.4	2019	●	↑
CO_2 emissions from fuel combustion per total electricity output ($MtCO_2$/TWh)	3.8	2019	●	→
Share of renewable energy in total primary energy supply (%)	NA	NA	●	●
SDG8 – Decent Work and Economic Growth				
Adjusted GDP growth (%)	-4.1	2020	●	●
Victims of modern slavery (per 1,000 population)	NA	NA	●	●
Adults with an account at a bank or other financial institution or with a mobile-money-service provider (% of population aged 15 or over)	NA	NA	●	●
Unemployment rate (% of total labor force)	3.8	2022	●	↑
Fundamental labor rights are effectively guaranteed (worst 0–1 best)	NA	NA	●	●
Fatal work-related accidents embodied in imports (per 100,000 population)	NA	NA	●	●

SDG9 – Industry, Innovation and Infrastructure	Value	Year	Rating	Trend
Population using the internet (%)	41.2	2017	●	●
Mobile broadband subscriptions (per 100 population)	59.4	2019	●	↑
Logistics Performance Index: Quality of trade and transport-related infrastructure (worst 1–5 best)	NA	NA	●	●
The Times Higher Education Universities Ranking: Average score of top 3 universities (worst 0–100 best)	* 0.0	2022	●	●
Articles published in academic journals (per 1,000 population)	0.3	2020	●	↗
Expenditure on research and development (% of GDP)	NA	NA	●	●
SDG10 – Reduced Inequalities				
Gini coefficient	37.6	2015	●	●
Palma ratio	1.6	2018	●	●
SDG11 – Sustainable Cities and Communities				
Proportion of urban population living in slums (%)	NA	NA	●	●
Annual mean concentration of particulate matter of less than 2.5 microns in diameter (PM2.5) (μg/m^3)	10.1	2019	●	↑
Access to improved water source, piped (% of urban population)	99.8	2020	●	↑
Satisfaction with public transport (%)	NA	NA	●	●
SDG12 – Responsible Consumption and Production				
Municipal solid waste (kg/capita/day)	0.5	2012	●	●
Electronic waste (kg/capita)	3.3	2019	●	●
Production-based SO_2 emissions (kg/capita)	NA	NA	●	●
SO_2 emissions embodied in imports (kg/capita)	NA	NA	●	●
Production-based nitrogen emissions (kg/capita)	NA	NA	●	●
Nitrogen emissions embodied in imports (kg/capita)	NA	NA	●	●
Exports of plastic waste (kg/capita)	NA	NA	●	●
SDG13 – Climate Action				
CO_2 emissions from fossil fuel combustion and cement production (tCO_2/capita)	1.4	2020	●	↑
CO_2 emissions embodied in imports (tCO_2/capita)	NA	NA	●	●
CO_2 emissions embodied in fossil fuel exports (kg/capita)	0.0	2020	●	●
SDG14 – Life Below Water				
Mean area that is protected in marine sites important to biodiversity (%)	19.2	2020	●	→
Ocean Health Index: Clean Waters score (worst 0–100 best)	67.3	2020	●	↑
Fish caught from overexploited or collapsed stocks (% of total catch)	0.7	2018	●	↑
Fish caught by trawling or dredging (%)	0.0	2018	●	↑
Fish caught that are then discarded (%)	0.1	2009	●	●
Marine biodiversity threats embodied in imports (per million population)	NA	NA	●	●
SDG15 – Life on Land				
Mean area that is protected in terrestrial sites important to biodiversity (%)	26.1	2020	●	→
Mean area that is protected in freshwater sites important to biodiversity (%)	NA	NA	●	●
Red List Index of species survival (worst 0–1 best)	0.7	2021	●	↓
Permanent deforestation (% of forest area, 5-year average)	NA	NA	●	●
Terrestrial and freshwater biodiversity threats embodied in imports (per million population)	NA	NA	●	●
SDG16 – Peace, Justice and Strong Institutions				
Homicides (per 100,000 population)	2.9	2019	●	●
Unsentenced detainees (% of prison population)	7.4	2016	●	●
Population who feel safe walking alone at night in the city or area where they live (%)	NA	NA	●	●
Property Rights (worst 1–7 best)	NA	NA	●	●
Birth registrations with civil authority (% of children under age 5)	97.7	2020	●	●
Corruption Perception Index (worst 0–100 best)	NA	NA	●	●
Children involved in child labor (% of population aged 5 to 14)	26.1	2019	●	●
Exports of major conventional weapons (TIV constant million USD per 100,000 population)	* 0.0	2020	●	●
Press Freedom Index (best 0–100 worst)	24.6	2021	●	↑
Access to and affordability of justice (worst 0–1 best)	NA	NA	●	●
SDG17 – Partnerships for the Goals				
Government spending on health and education (% of GDP)	10.9	2019	●	↑
For high-income and all OECD DAC countries: International concessional public finance, including official development assistance (% of GNI)	NA	NA	●	●
Other countries: Government revenue excluding grants (% of GDP)	NA	NA	●	●
Corporate Tax Haven Score (best 0–100 worst)	* 0.0	2019	●	●
Statistical Performance Index (worst 0–100 best)	NA	NA	●	●

* Imputed data point

5. Country Profiles

TRINIDAD AND TOBAGO Latin America and the Caribbean

OVERALL PERFORMANCE

COUNTRY RANKING

TRINIDAD AND TOBAGO

119/163

COUNTRY SCORE

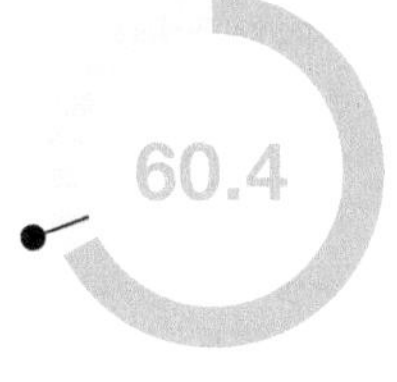

REGIONAL AVERAGE: 69.5

AVERAGE PERFORMANCE BY SDG

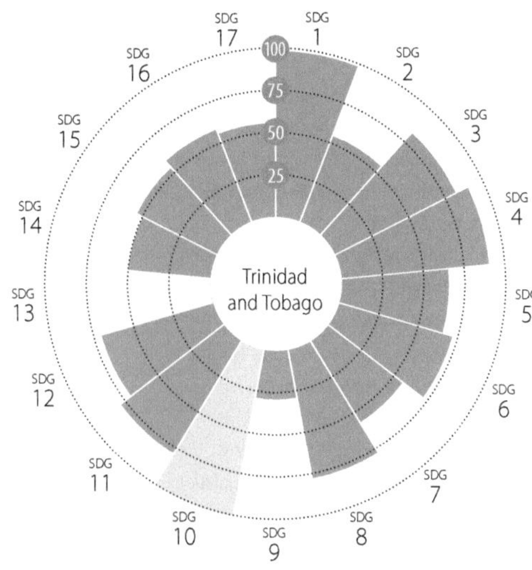

SDG DASHBOARDS AND TRENDS

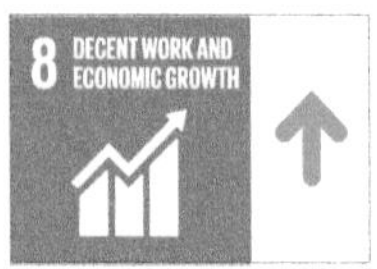

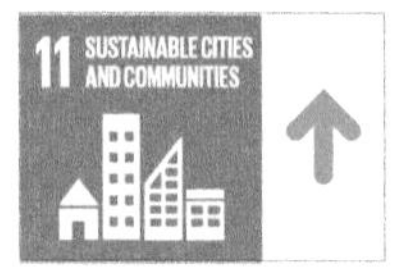

Major challenges · Significant challenges · Challenges remain · SDG achieved · Information unavailable

Decreasing · Stagnating · Moderately improving · On track or maintaining SDG achievement · Information unavailable

Note: The full title of each SDG is available here: https://sustainabledevelopment.un.org/topics/sustainabledevelopmentgoals

INTERNATIONAL SPILLOVER INDEX

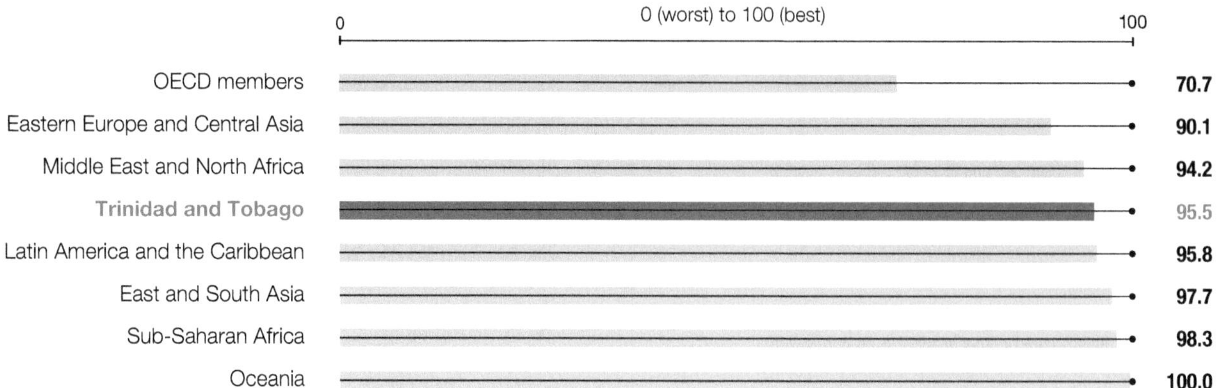

STATISTICAL PERFORMANCE INDEX

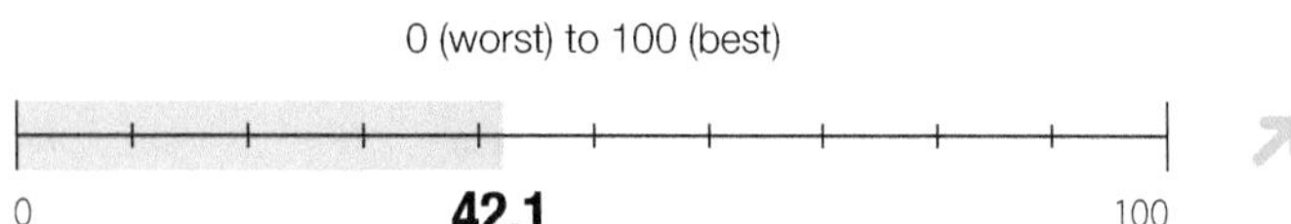

MISSING DATA IN SDG INDEX

11%

TRINIDAD AND TOBAGO

Performance by Indicator

SDG1 – No Poverty	Value	Year	Rating	Trend
Poverty headcount ratio at \$1.90/day (%)	0.3	2022	●	↑
Poverty headcount ratio at \$3.20/day (%)	1.4	2022	●	↑

SDG2 – Zero Hunger	Value	Year	Rating	Trend
Prevalence of undernourishment (%)	6.7	2019	●	↑
Prevalence of stunting in children under 5 years of age (%)	9.2	2011	●	↑
Prevalence of wasting in children under 5 years of age (%)	6.4	2011	●	↑
Prevalence of obesity, BMI ≥ 30 (% of adult population)	18.6	2016	●	↓
Human Trophic Level (best 2–3 worst)	2.3	2017	●	→
Cereal yield (tonnes per hectare of harvested land)	2.0	2018	●	↑
Sustainable Nitrogen Management Index (best 0–1.41 worst)	1.3	2015	●	↓
Exports of hazardous pesticides (tonnes per million population)	0.0	2019	●	●

SDG3 – Good Health and Well-Being	Value	Year	Rating	Trend
Maternal mortality rate (per 100,000 live births)	67	2017	●	↑
Neonatal mortality rate (per 1,000 live births)	10.6	2020	●	↑
Mortality rate, under-5 (per 1,000 live births)	16.6	2020	●	↑
Incidence of tuberculosis (per 100,000 population)	18.0	2020	●	→
New HIV infections (per 1,000 uninfected population)	0.1	2020	●	↑
Age-standardized death rate due to cardiovascular disease, cancer, diabetes, or chronic respiratory disease in adults aged 30–70 years (%)	17.1	2019	●	↑
Age-standardized death rate attributable to household air pollution and ambient air pollution (per 100,000 population)	39	2016	●	●
Traffic deaths (per 100,000 population)	9.3	2019	●	↑
Life expectancy at birth (years)	76.1	2019	●	↑
Adolescent fertility rate (births per 1,000 females aged 15 to 19)	32.0	2011	●	●
Births attended by skilled health personnel (%)	100.0	2017	●	↑
Surviving infants who received 2 WHO-recommended vaccines (%)	93	2019	●	↑
Universal health coverage (UHC) index of service coverage (worst 0–100 best)	73	2019	●	→
Subjective well-being (average ladder score, worst 0–10 best)	6.2	2017	●	●

SDG4 – Quality Education	Value	Year	Rating	Trend
Participation rate in pre-primary organized learning (% of children aged 4 to 6)	91.8	2007	●	●
Net primary enrollment rate (%)	98.8	2010	●	●
Lower secondary completion rate (%)	80.9	2010	●	●
Literacy rate (% of population aged 15 to 24)	99.6	2010	●	●

SDG5 – Gender Equality	Value	Year	Rating	Trend
Demand for family planning satisfied by modern methods (% of females aged 15 to 49)	58.2	2011	●	●
Ratio of female-to-male mean years of education received (%)	101.8	2019	●	↑
Ratio of female-to-male labor force participation rate (%)	68.5	2020	●	→
Seats held by women in national parliament (%)	26.2	2020	●	↓

SDG6 – Clean Water and Sanitation	Value	Year	Rating	Trend
Population using at least basic drinking water services (%)	98.9	2020	●	↑
Population using at least basic sanitation services (%)	93.9	2020	●	↗
Freshwater withdrawal (% of available freshwater resources)	20.3	2018	●	●
Anthropogenic wastewater that receives treatment (%)	3.2	2018	●	●
Scarce water consumption embodied in imports (m^3 H_2O eq/capita)	NA	NA	●	●

SDG7 – Affordable and Clean Energy	Value	Year	Rating	Trend
Population with access to electricity (%)	100.0	2019	●	↑
Population with access to clean fuels and technology for cooking (%)	100.0	2019	●	↑
CO_2 emissions from fuel combustion per total electricity output ($MtCO_2$/TWh)	4.4	2019	●	↗
Share of renewable energy in total primary energy supply (%)	0.1	2019	●	→

SDG8 – Decent Work and Economic Growth	Value	Year	Rating	Trend
Adjusted GDP growth (%)	-4.8	2020	●	●
Victims of modern slavery (per 1,000 population)	3.0	2018	●	●
Adults with an account at a bank or other financial institution or with a mobile-money-service provider (% of population aged 15 or over)	80.8	2017	●	●
Unemployment rate (% of total labor force)	4.3	2022	●	↑
Fundamental labor rights are effectively guaranteed (worst 0–1 best)	0.7	2020	●	↑
Fatal work-related accidents embodied in imports (per 100,000 population)	0.6	2015	●	↑

SDG9 – Industry, Innovation and Infrastructure	Value	Year	Rating	Trend
Population using the internet (%)	70.6	2017	●	●
Mobile broadband subscriptions (per 100 population)	37.6	2019	●	→
Logistics Performance Index: Quality of trade and transport-related infrastructure (worst 1–5 best)	2.4	2018	●	●
The Times Higher Education Universities Ranking: Average score of top 3 universities (worst 0–100 best)	* 0.0	2022	●	●
Articles published in academic journals (per 1,000 population)	0.3	2020	●	↗
Expenditure on research and development (% of GDP)	0.1	2018	●	↓

SDG10 – Reduced Inequalities	Value	Year	Rating	Trend
Gini coefficient	NA	NA	●	●
Palma ratio	NA	NA	●	●

SDG11 – Sustainable Cities and Communities	Value	Year	Rating	Trend
Proportion of urban population living in slums (%)	1.9	2018	●	↑
Annual mean concentration of particulate matter of less than 2.5 microns in diameter (PM2.5) (μg/m^3)	22.9	2019	●	↗
Access to improved water source, piped (% of urban population)	NA	NA	●	●
Satisfaction with public transport (%)	56.0	2017	●	●

SDG12 – Responsible Consumption and Production	Value	Year	Rating	Trend
Municipal solid waste (kg/capita/day)	1.5	2010	●	●
Electronic waste (kg/capita)	15.7	2019	●	●
Production-based SO_2 emissions (kg/capita)	NA	NA	●	●
SO_2 emissions embodied in imports (kg/capita)	NA	NA	●	●
Production-based nitrogen emissions (kg/capita)	5.4	2015	●	↑
Nitrogen emissions embodied in imports (kg/capita)	4.7	2015	●	↑
Exports of plastic waste (kg/capita)	NA	NA	●	●

SDG13 – Climate Action	Value	Year	Rating	Trend
CO_2 emissions from fossil fuel combustion and cement production (tCO_2/capita)	25.4	2020	●	↗
CO_2 emissions embodied in imports (tCO_2/capita)	NA	NA	●	●
CO_2 emissions embodied in fossil fuel exports (kg/capita)	NA	NA	●	●

SDG14 – Life Below Water	Value	Year	Rating	Trend
Mean area that is protected in marine sites important to biodiversity (%)	8.5	2020	●	→
Ocean Health Index: Clean Waters score (worst 0–100 best)	62.5	2020	●	↓
Fish caught from overexploited or collapsed stocks (% of total catch)	37.7	2018	●	↓
Fish caught by trawling or dredging (%)	9.7	2018	●	→
Fish caught that are then discarded (%)	29.2	2018	●	↓
Marine biodiversity threats embodied in imports (per million population)	0.1	2018	●	●

SDG15 – Life on Land	Value	Year	Rating	Trend
Mean area that is protected in terrestrial sites important to biodiversity (%)	32.0	2020	●	→
Mean area that is protected in freshwater sites important to biodiversity (%)	0.0	2020	●	→
Red List Index of species survival (worst 0–1 best)	0.8	2021	●	↓
Permanent deforestation (% of forest area, 5-year average)	0.1	2020	●	↗
Terrestrial and freshwater biodiversity threats embodied in imports (per million population)	0.6	2018	●	●

SDG16 – Peace, Justice and Strong Institutions	Value	Year	Rating	Trend
Homicides (per 100,000 population)	38.6	2019	●	↓
Unsentenced detainees (% of prison population)	59.7	2018	●	↑
Population who feel safe walking alone at night in the city or area where they live (%)	52	2017	●	●
Property Rights (worst 1–7 best)	4.1	2020	●	↓
Birth registrations with civil authority (% of children under age 5)	96.5	2020	●	●
Corruption Perception Index (worst 0–100 best)	41	2021	●	→
Children involved in child labor (% of population aged 5 to 14)	0.8	2019	●	●
Exports of major conventional weapons (TIV constant million USD per 100,000 population)	* 0.0	2020	●	●
Press Freedom Index (best 0–100 worst)	21.6	2021	●	↑
Access to and affordability of justice (worst 0–1 best)	0.6	2020	●	↑

SDG17 – Partnerships for the Goals	Value	Year	Rating	Trend
Government spending on health and education (% of GDP)	6.8	2019	●	→
For high-income and all OECD DAC countries: International concessional public finance, including official development assistance (% of GNI)	NA	NA	●	●
Other countries: Government revenue excluding grants (% of GDP)	NA	NA	●	●
Corporate Tax Haven Score (best 0–100 worst)	* 0.0	2019	●	●
Statistical Performance Index (worst 0–100 best)	42.1	2019	●	↗

* Imputed data point

5. Country Profiles

TUNISIA

Middle East and North Africa

OVERALL PERFORMANCE

COUNTRY RANKING

TUNISIA

69/163

COUNTRY SCORE

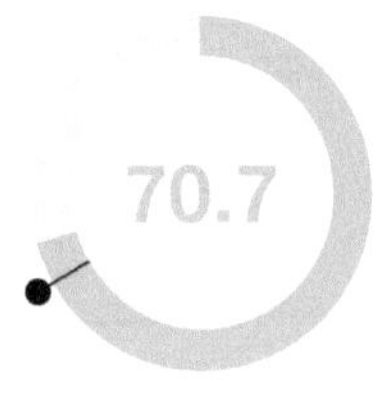

REGIONAL AVERAGE: 66.7

AVERAGE PERFORMANCE BY SDG

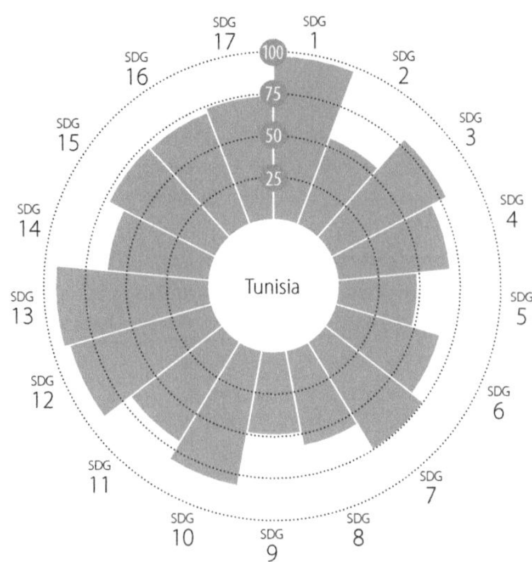

SDG DASHBOARDS AND TRENDS

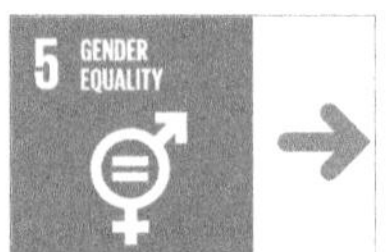

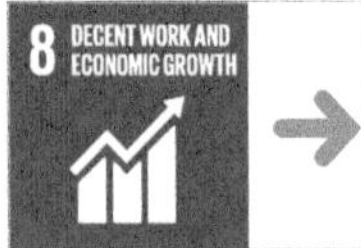

Note: The full title of each SDG is available here: https://sustainabledevelopment.un.org/topics/sustainabledevelopmentgoals

INTERNATIONAL SPILLOVER INDEX

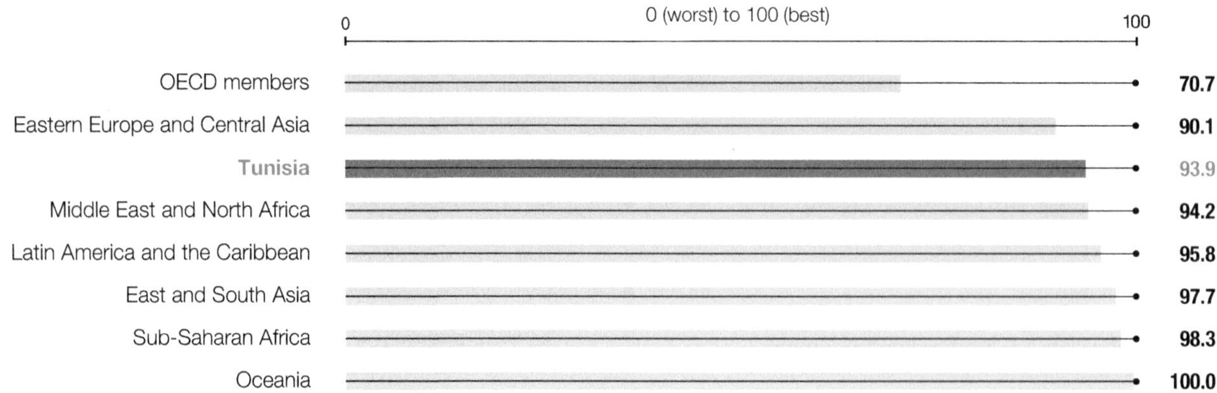

STATISTICAL PERFORMANCE INDEX

0 (worst) to 100 (best)

0 **64.1** 100

MISSING DATA IN SDG INDEX

1%

SDG1 – No Poverty	Value	Year	Rating	Trend
Poverty headcount ratio at $1.90/day (%)	0.2	2022	●	↑
Poverty headcount ratio at $3.20/day (%)	2.8	2022	●	→
SDG2 – Zero Hunger				
Prevalence of undernourishment (%)	3.0	2019	●	↑
Prevalence of stunting in children under 5 years of age (%)	8.4	2018	●	↗
Prevalence of wasting in children under 5 years of age (%)	2.1	2018	●	↑
Prevalence of obesity, BMI ≥ 30 (% of adult population)	26.9	2016	●	↓
Human Trophic Level (best 2–3 worst)	2.2	2017	●	→
Cereal yield (tonnes per hectare of harvested land)	1.4	2018	●	↑
Sustainable Nitrogen Management Index (best 0–1.41 worst)	1.0	2015	●	↓
Exports of hazardous pesticides (tonnes per million population)	NA	NA	●	●
SDG3 – Good Health and Well-Being				
Maternal mortality rate (per 100,000 live births)	43	2017	●	↑
Neonatal mortality rate (per 1,000 live births)	11.8	2020	●	↑
Mortality rate, under-5 (per 1,000 live births)	16.6	2020	●	↑
Incidence of tuberculosis (per 100,000 population)	36.0	2020	●	→
New HIV infections (per 1,000 uninfected population)	0.0	2020	●	↑
Age-standardized death rate due to cardiovascular disease, cancer, diabetes, or chronic respiratory disease in adults aged 30–70 years (%)	15.7	2019	●	↑
Age-standardized death rate attributable to household air pollution and ambient air pollution (per 100,000 population)	56	2016	●	●
Traffic deaths (per 100,000 population)	16.5	2019	●	↑
Life expectancy at birth (years)	77.0	2019	●	→
Adolescent fertility rate (births per 1,000 females aged 15 to 19)	7.0	2017	●	●
Births attended by skilled health personnel (%)	99.5	2018	●	●
Surviving infants who received 2 WHO-recommended vaccines (%)	92	2020	●	↑
Universal health coverage (UHC) index of service coverage (worst 0–100 best)	70	2019	●	↑
Subjective well-being (average ladder score, worst 0–10 best)	4.5	2021	●	↓
SDG4 – Quality Education				
Participation rate in pre-primary organized learning (% of children aged 4 to 6)	42.1	2002	●	●
Net primary enrollment rate (%)	99.2	2020	●	↑
Lower secondary completion rate (%)	77.4	2018	●	↑
Literacy rate (% of population aged 15 to 24)	96.2	2014	●	●
SDG5 – Gender Equality				
Demand for family planning satisfied by modern methods (% of females aged 15 to 49)	62.7	2018	●	●
Ratio of female-to-male mean years of education received (%)	81.3	2019	●	→
Ratio of female-to-male labor force participation rate (%)	37.9	2020	●	→
Seats held by women in national parliament (%)	24.9	2020	●	↓
SDG6 – Clean Water and Sanitation				
Population using at least basic drinking water services (%)	97.5	2020	●	↑
Population using at least basic sanitation services (%)	97.4	2020	●	↑
Freshwater withdrawal (% of available freshwater resources)	96.0	2018	●	●
Anthropogenic wastewater that receives treatment (%)	43.0	2018	●	●
Scarce water consumption embodied in imports (m^3 H_2O eq/capita)	1292.0	2018	●	●
SDG7 – Affordable and Clean Energy				
Population with access to electricity (%)	100.0	2019	●	↑
Population with access to clean fuels and technology for cooking (%)	99.8	2019	●	↑
CO_2 emissions from fuel combustion per total electricity output ($MtCO_2$/TWh)	1.1	2019	●	↑
Share of renewable energy in total primary energy supply (%)	10.9	2019	●	→
SDG8 – Decent Work and Economic Growth				
Adjusted GDP growth (%)	-5.6	2020	●	●
Victims of modern slavery (per 1,000 population)	2.2	2018	●	●
Adults with an account at a bank or other financial institution or with a mobile-money-service provider (% of population aged 15 or over)	36.9	2017	●	↗
Unemployment rate (% of total labor force)	16.2	2022	●	↓
Fundamental labor rights are effectively guaranteed (worst 0–1 best)	0.5	2020	●	↓
Fatal work-related accidents embodied in imports (per 100,000 population)	0.3	2015	●	↑

* Imputed data point

SDG9 – Industry, Innovation and Infrastructure	Value	Year	Rating	Trend
Population using the internet (%)	71.9	2020	●	↑
Mobile broadband subscriptions (per 100 population)	77.8	2019	●	↑
Logistics Performance Index: Quality of trade and transport-related infrastructure (worst 1–5 best)	2.1	2018	●	↓
The Times Higher Education Universities Ranking: Average score of top 3 universities (worst 0–100 best)	22.0	2022	●	●
Articles published in academic journals (per 1,000 population)	0.7	2020	●	↑
Expenditure on research and development (% of GDP)	0.6	2018	●	↓
SDG10 – Reduced Inequalities				
Gini coefficient	32.8	2015	●	●
Palma ratio	1.3	2018	●	●
SDG11 – Sustainable Cities and Communities				
Proportion of urban population living in slums (%)	8.0	2018	●	→
Annual mean concentration of particulate matter of less than 2.5 microns in diameter (PM2.5) (μg/m³)	40.3	2019	●	↓
Access to improved water source, piped (% of urban population)	99.2	2020	●	↑
Satisfaction with public transport (%)	38.0	2021	●	↓
SDG12 – Responsible Consumption and Production				
Municipal solid waste (kg/capita/day)	0.7	2014	●	●
Electronic waste (kg/capita)	6.4	2019	●	●
Production-based SO_2 emissions (kg/capita)	4.4	2018	●	●
SO_2 emissions embodied in imports (kg/capita)	0.9	2018	●	●
Production-based nitrogen emissions (kg/capita)	8.9	2015	●	↑
Nitrogen emissions embodied in imports (kg/capita)	2.0	2015	●	↑
Exports of plastic waste (kg/capita)	2.2	2019	●	●
SDG13 – Climate Action				
CO_2 emissions from fossil fuel combustion and cement production (tCO_2/capita)	2.4	2020	●	↑
CO_2 emissions embodied in imports (tCO_2/capita)	0.3	2018	●	↑
CO_2 emissions embodied in fossil fuel exports (kg/capita)	321.3	2019	●	●
SDG14 – Life Below Water				
Mean area that is protected in marine sites important to biodiversity (%)	39.6	2020	●	→
Ocean Health Index: Clean Waters score (worst 0–100 best)	49.2	2020	●	→
Fish caught from overexploited or collapsed stocks (% of total catch)	22.3	2018	●	↑
Fish caught by trawling or dredging (%)	18.8	2018	●	→
Fish caught that are then discarded (%)	9.6	2018	●	→
Marine biodiversity threats embodied in imports (per million population)	0.1	2018	●	●
SDG15 – Life on Land				
Mean area that is protected in terrestrial sites important to biodiversity (%)	39.5	2020	●	→
Mean area that is protected in freshwater sites important to biodiversity (%)	43.4	2020	●	→
Red List Index of species survival (worst 0–1 best)	1.0	2021	●	↑
Permanent deforestation (% of forest area, 5-year average)	0.2	2020	●	↑
Terrestrial and freshwater biodiversity threats embodied in imports (per million population)	0.3	2018	●	●
SDG16 – Peace, Justice and Strong Institutions				
Homicides (per 100,000 population)	4.8	2020	●	●
Unsentenced detainees (% of prison population)	51.6	2017	●	●
Population who feel safe walking alone at night in the city or area where they live (%)	64	2021	●	↗
Property Rights (worst 1–7 best)	4.5	2020	●	↓
Birth registrations with civil authority (% of children under age 5)	99.9	2020	●	●
Corruption Perception Index (worst 0–100 best)	44	2021	●	↗
Children involved in child labor (% of population aged 5 to 14)	2.3	2019	●	●
Exports of major conventional weapons (TIV constant million USD per 100,000 population)	* 0.0	2020	●	●
Press Freedom Index (best 0–100 worst)	29.5	2021	●	↑
Access to and affordability of justice (worst 0–1 best)	0.6	2020	●	↑
SDG17 – Partnerships for the Goals				
Government spending on health and education (% of GDP)	11.3	2019	●	↑
For high-income and all OECD DAC countries: International concessional public finance, including official development assistance (% of GNI)	NA	NA	●	●
Other countries: Government revenue excluding grants (% of GDP)	29.9	2012	●	●
Corporate Tax Haven Score (best 0–100 worst)	* 0.0	2019	●	●
Statistical Performance Index (worst 0–100 best)	64.1	2019	●	↗

TURKEY

OECD Countries

OVERALL PERFORMANCE

COUNTRY RANKING

TURKEY

71 **/163**

COUNTRY SCORE

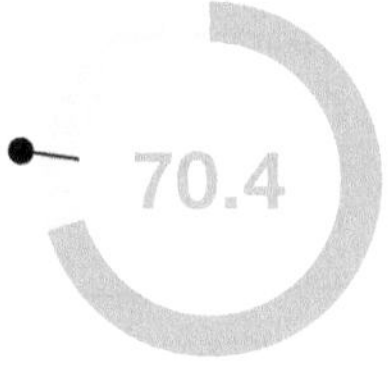

REGIONAL AVERAGE: 77.2

AVERAGE PERFORMANCE BY SDG

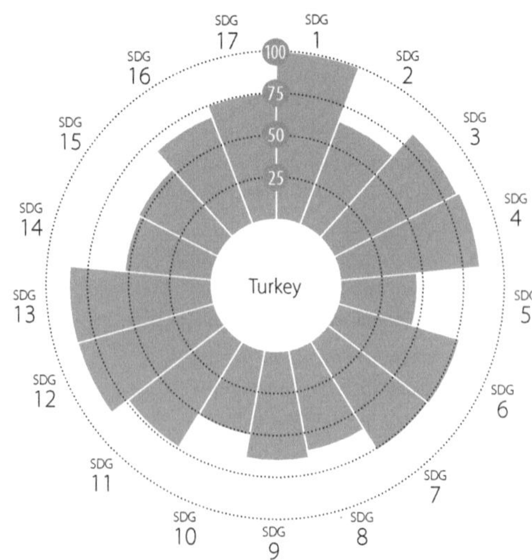

SDG DASHBOARDS AND TRENDS

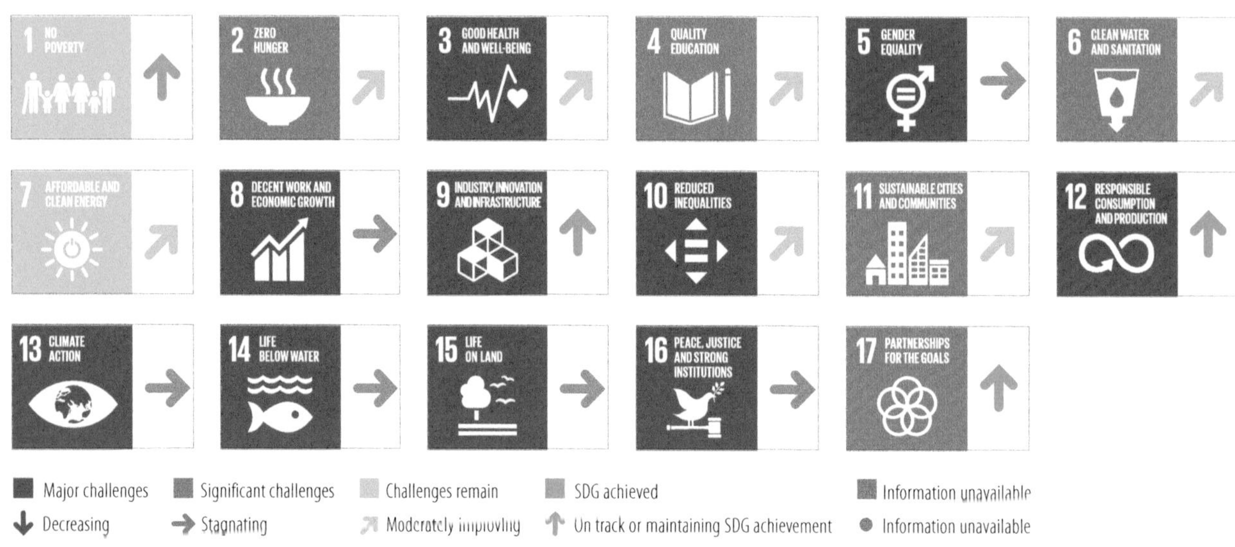

Major challenges   Significant challenges   Challenges remain   SDG achieved   Information unavailable

Decreasing   Stagnating   Moderately improving   On track or maintaining SDG achievement   Information unavailable

Note: The full title of each SDG is available here: https://sustainabledevelopment.un.org/topics/sustainabledevelopmentgoals

INTERNATIONAL SPILLOVER INDEX

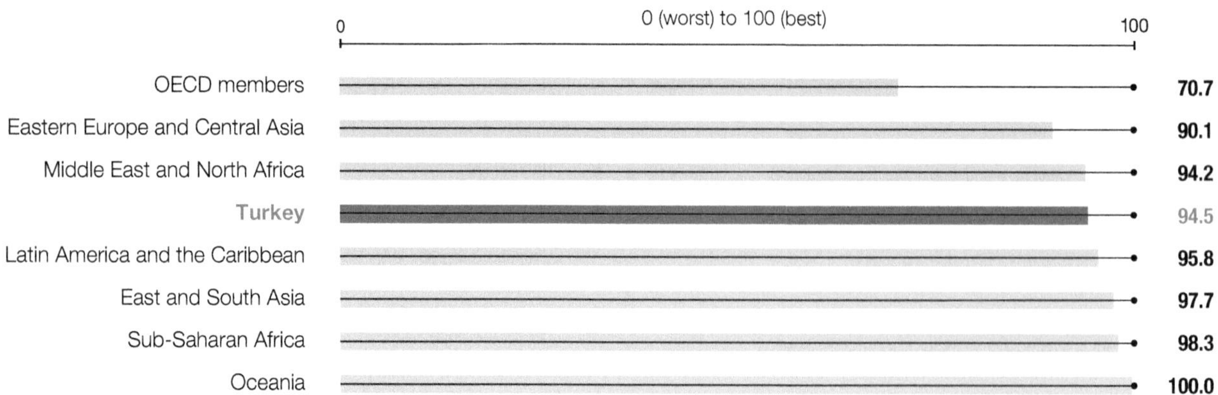

STATISTICAL PERFORMANCE INDEX

0 (worst) to 100 (best)

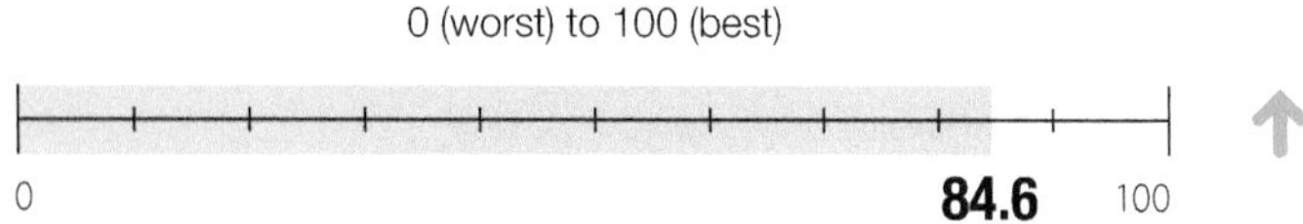

MISSING DATA IN SDG INDEX

1%

SDG1 – No Poverty	Value	Year	Rating	Trend
Poverty headcount ratio at $1.90/day (%)	0.0	2022	●	↑
Poverty headcount ratio at $3.20/day (%)	0.6	2022	●	↑
Poverty rate after taxes and transfers (%)	14.4	2018	●	↑
SDG2 – Zero Hunger				
Prevalence of undernourishment (%)	2.5	2019	●	↑
Prevalence of stunting in children under 5 years of age (%)	6.0	2018	●	↑
Prevalence of wasting in children under 5 years of age (%)	1.7	2018	●	↑
Prevalence of obesity, BMI ≥ 30 (% of adult population)	32.1	2016	●	↓
Human Trophic Level (best 2–3 worst)	2.3	2017	●	↗
Cereal yield (tonnes per hectare of harvested land)	3.2	2018	●	↑
Sustainable Nitrogen Management Index (best 0–1.41 worst)	0.6	2015	●	→
Yield gap closure (% of potential yield)	NA	NA	●	●
Exports of hazardous pesticides (tonnes per million population)	4.6	2019	●	●
SDG3 – Good Health and Well-Being				
Maternal mortality rate (per 100,000 live births)	17	2017	●	↑
Neonatal mortality rate (per 1,000 live births)	5.0	2020	●	↑
Mortality rate, under-5 (per 1,000 live births)	9.5	2020	●	↑
Incidence of tuberculosis (per 100,000 population)	15.0	2020	●	↑
New HIV infections (per 1,000 uninfected population)	1.0	2020	●	→
Age-standardized death rate due to cardiovascular disease, cancer, diabetes, or chronic respiratory disease in adults aged 30–70 years (%)	15.6	2019	●	↑
Age-standardized death rate attributable to household air pollution and ambient air pollution (per 100,000 population)	47	2016	●	●
Traffic deaths (per 100,000 population)	6.7	2019	●	↑
Life expectancy at birth (years)	78.6	2019	●	↑
Adolescent fertility rate (births per 1,000 females aged 15 to 19)	19.2	2018	●	↑
Births attended by skilled health personnel (%)	98.0	2018	●	↑
Surviving infants who received 2 WHO-recommended vaccines (%)	95	2020	●	↑
Universal health coverage (UHC) index of service coverage (worst 0–100 best)	79	2019	●	↑
Subjective well-being (average ladder score, worst 0–10 best)	4.4	2021	●	↓
Gap in life expectancy at birth among regions (years)	8.6	2019	●	↓
Gap in self-reported health status by income (percentage points)	10.5	2019	●	↑
Daily smokers (% of population aged 15 and over)	28.0	2019	●	↓
SDG4 – Quality Education				
Participation rate in pre-primary organized learning (% of children aged 4 to 6)	75.9	2019	●	↑
Net primary enrollment rate (%)	95.2	2019	●	↗
Lower secondary completion rate (%)	88.8	2019	●	↓
Literacy rate (% of population aged 15 to 24)	99.9	2019	●	↑
Tertiary educational attainment (% of population aged 25 to 34)	35.3	2019	●	↑
PISA score (worst 0–600 best)	462.7	2018	●	↑
Variation in science performance explained by socio-economic status (%)	11.0	2018	●	↓
Underachievers in science (% of 15-year-olds)	25.2	2018	●	↑
SDG5 – Gender Equality				
Demand for family planning satisfied by modern methods (% of females aged 15 to 49)	60.1	2018	●	●
Ratio of female-to-male mean years of education received (%)	81.1	2019	●	→
Ratio of female-to-male labor force participation rate (%)	45.2	2020	●	→
Seats held by women in national parliament (%)	17.3	2020	●	→
Gender wage gap (% of male median wage)	10.0	2018	●	↓
SDG6 – Clean Water and Sanitation				
Population using at least basic drinking water services (%)	97.0	2020	●	↑
Population using at least basic sanitation services (%)	99.2	2020	●	↑
Freshwater withdrawal (% of available freshwater resources)	45.4	2018	●	●
Anthropogenic wastewater that receives treatment (%)	30.4	2018	●	●
Scarce water consumption embodied in imports (m^3 H_2O eq/capita)	974.3	2018	●	●
Population using safely managed water services (%)	NA	NA	●	●
Population using safely managed sanitation services (%)	78.4	2020	●	↗
SDG7 – Affordable and Clean Energy				
Population with access to electricity (%)	100.0	2019	●	↑
Population with access to clean fuels and technology for cooking (%)	95.1	2019	●	↑
CO_2 emissions from fuel combustion per total electricity output ($MtCO_2$/TWh)	1.3	2019	●	→
Share of renewable energy in total primary energy supply (%)	15.9	2019	●	↑
SDG8 – Decent Work and Economic Growth				
Adjusted GDP growth (%)	-3.9	2020	●	●
Victims of modern slavery (per 1,000 population)	6.5	2018	●	●
Adults with an account at a bank or other financial institution or with a mobile-money-service provider (% of population aged 15 or over)	68.6	2017	●	↑
Fundamental labor rights are effectively guaranteed (worst 0–1 best)	0.4	2020	●	→
Fatal work-related accidents embodied in imports (per 100,000 population)	0.2	2015	●	↑
Employment-to-population ratio (%)	47.5	2020	●	↓
Youth not in employment, education or training (NEET) (% of population aged 15 to 29)	28.8	2019	●	→

* Imputed data point

SDG9 – Industry, Innovation and Infrastructure	Value	Year	Rating	Trend
Population using the internet (%)	77.7	2020	●	↑
Mobile broadband subscriptions (per 100 population)	74.8	2019	●	↑
Logistics Performance Index: Quality of trade and transport-related infrastructure (worst 1–5 best)	3.2	2018	●	↑
The Times Higher Education Universities Ranking: Average score of top 3 universities (worst 0–100 best)	40.5	2022	●	●
Articles published in academic journals (per 1,000 population)	0.6	2020	●	↑
Expenditure on research and development (% of GDP)	1.0	2017	●	↗
Researchers (per 1,000 employed population)	4.9	2019	●	↑
Triadic patent families filed (per million population)	1.0	2019	●	→
Gap in internet access by income (percentage points)	NA	NA	●	●
Female share of graduates from STEM fields at the tertiary level (%)	34.7	2014	●	●
SDG10 – Reduced Inequalities				
Gini coefficient	41.9	2019	●	→
Palma ratio	1.8	2018	●	→
Elderly poverty rate (% of population aged 66 or over)	11.1	2018	●	↑
SDG11 – Sustainable Cities and Communities				
Proportion of urban population living in slums (%)	7.0	2018	●	↑
Annual mean concentration of particulate matter of less than 2.5 microns in diameter (PM2.5) (μg/m^3)	45.2	2019	●	→
Access to improved water source, piped (% of urban population)	98.3	2020	●	↑
Satisfaction with public transport (%)	52.0	2021	●	↓
Population with rent overburden (%)	NA	NA	●	●
SDG12 – Responsible Consumption and Production				
Electronic waste (kg/capita)	10.2	2019	●	●
Production-based SO_2 emissions (kg/capita)	15.1	2018	●	●
SO_2 emissions embodied in imports (kg/capita)	1.7	2018	●	●
Production-based nitrogen emissions (kg/capita)	14.5	2015	●	↑
Nitrogen emissions embodied in imports (kg/capita)	2.9	2015	●	↑
Exports of plastic waste (kg/capita)	0.2	2020	●	●
Non-recycled municipal solid waste (kg/capita/day)	1.0	2019	●	↑
SDG13 – Climate Action				
CO_2 emissions from fossil fuel combustion and cement production (tCO_2/capita)	4.7	2020	●	→
CO_2 emissions embodied in imports (tCO_2/capita)	0.6	2018	●	↑
CO_2 emissions embodied in fossil fuel exports (kg/capita)	1.0	2020	●	●
Carbon Pricing Score at EUR60/tCO_2 (%, worst 0–100 best)	23.6	2018	●	→
SDG14 – Life Below Water				
Mean area that is protected in marine sites important to biodiversity (%)	3.8	2020	●	→
Ocean Health Index: Clean Waters score (worst 0–100 best)	50.5	2020	●	↓
Fish caught from overexploited or collapsed stocks (% of total catch)	57.5	2018	●	→
Fish caught by trawling or dredging (%)	25.5	2018	●	↗
Fish caught that are then discarded (%)	5.5	2018	●	↑
Marine biodiversity threats embodied in imports (per million population)	0.0	2018	●	●
SDG15 – Life on Land				
Mean area that is protected in terrestrial sites important to biodiversity (%)	2.3	2020	●	→
Mean area that is protected in freshwater sites important to biodiversity (%)	4.2	2020	●	→
Red List Index of species survival (worst 0–1 best)	0.9	2021	●	→
Permanent deforestation (% of forest area, 5-year average)	0.0	2020	●	↑
Terrestrial and freshwater biodiversity threats embodied in imports (per million population)	0.7	2018	●	●
SDG16 – Peace, Justice and Strong Institutions				
Homicides (per 100,000 population)	2.4	2019	●	↑
Unsentenced detainees (% of prison population)	15.9	2019	●	↑
Population who feel safe walking alone at night in the city or area where they live (%)	55	2021	●	↓
Property Rights (worst 1–7 best)	4.6	2020	●	↑
Birth registrations with civil authority (% of children under age 5)	98.4	2020	●	●
Corruption Perception Index (worst 0–100 best)	38	2021	●	↓
Children involved in child labor (% of population aged 5 to 14)	NA	NA	●	●
Exports of major conventional weapons (TIV constant million USD per 100,000 population)	0.2	2020	●	●
Press Freedom Index (best 0–100 worst)	49.8	2021	●	→
Access to and affordability of justice (worst 0–1 best)	0.6	2020	●	↑
Persons held in prison (per 100,000 population)	349.5	2019	●	↓
SDG17 – Partnerships for the Goals				
Government spending on health and education (% of GDP)	7.7	2019	●	↑
For high-income and all OECD DAC countries: International concessional public finance, including official development assistance (% of GNI)	NA	NA	●	●
Other countries: Government revenue excluding grants (% of GDP)	30.4	2020	●	↑
Corporate Tax Haven Score (best 0–100 worst)	* 0.0	2019	●	●
Financial Secrecy Score (best 0–100 worst)	59.5	2020	●	●
Shifted profits of multinationals (US$ billion)	5.0	2018	●	↑
Statistical Performance Index (worst 0–100 best)	84.6	2019	●	↑

TURKMENISTAN

Eastern Europe and Central Asia

OVERALL PERFORMANCE

COUNTRY RANKING

TURKMENISTAN

99/163

COUNTRY SCORE

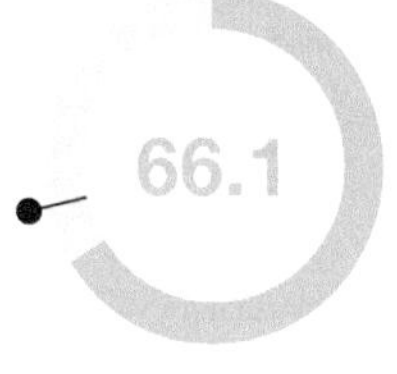

REGIONAL AVERAGE: 71.6

AVERAGE PERFORMANCE BY SDG

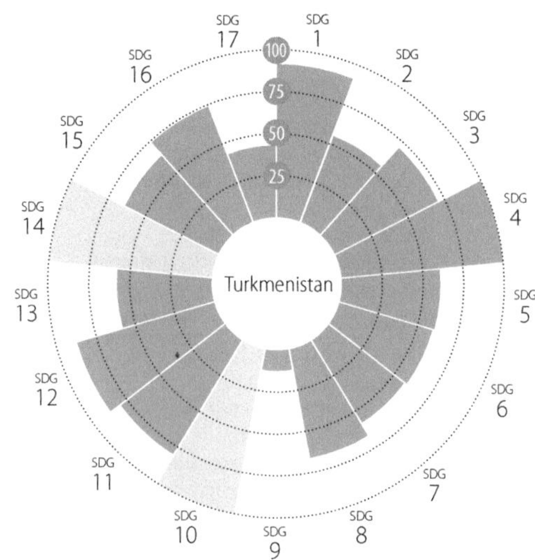

SDG DASHBOARDS AND TRENDS

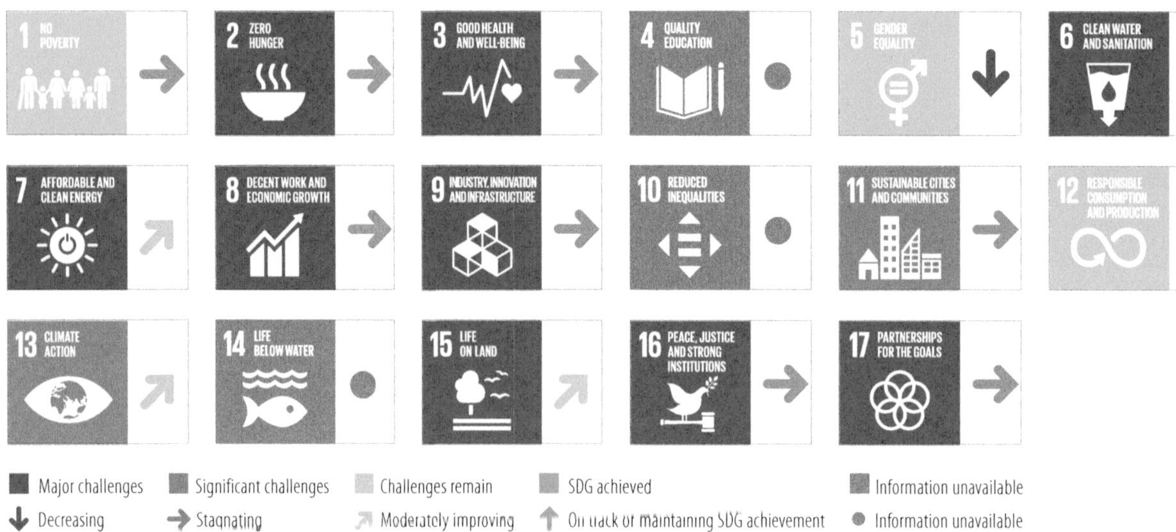

Major challenges · Significant challenges · Challenges remain · SDG achieved · Information unavailable

Decreasing · Stagnating · Moderately improving · On track or maintaining SDG achievement · Information unavailable

Note: The full title of each SDG is available here: https://sustainabledevelopment.un.org/topics/sustainabledevelopmentgoals

INTERNATIONAL SPILLOVER INDEX

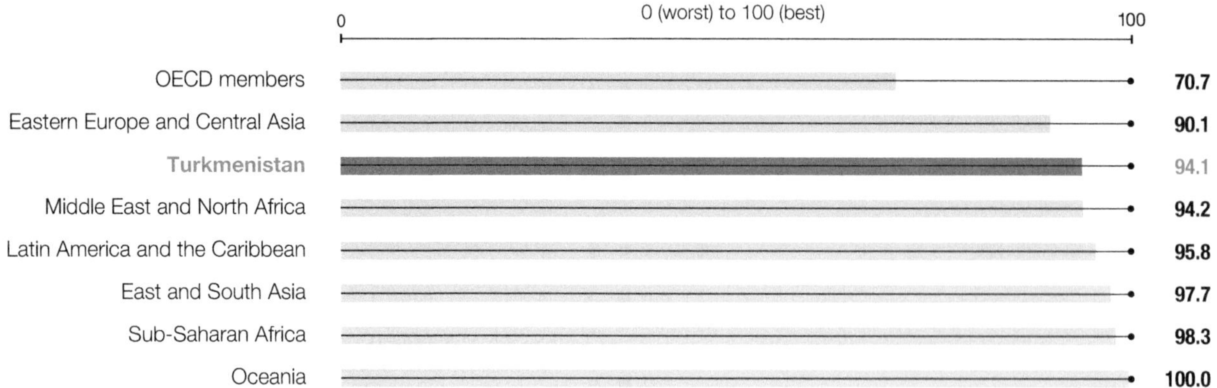

STATISTICAL PERFORMANCE INDEX

0 (worst) to 100 (best)

0 **23.5** 100

MISSING DATA IN SDG INDEX

17%

TURKMENISTAN

Performance by Indicator

SDG1 – No Poverty	Value	Year	Rating	Trend
Poverty headcount ratio at \$1.90/day (%)	0.6	2022	●	↑
Poverty headcount ratio at \$3.20/day (%)	8.8	2022	●	↓
SDG2 – Zero Hunger				
Prevalence of undernourishment (%)	4.1	2019	●	↑
Prevalence of stunting in children under 5 years of age (%)	7.2	2019	●	↑
Prevalence of wasting in children under 5 years of age (%)	4.1	2019	●	↑
Prevalence of obesity, BMI ≥ 30 (% of adult population)	18.6	2016	●	↓
Human Trophic Level (best 2–3 worst)	2.3	2017	●	→
Cereal yield (tonnes per hectare of harvested land)	1.1	2018	●	↓
Sustainable Nitrogen Management Index (best 0–1.41 worst)	0.7	2015	●	↓
Exports of hazardous pesticides (tonnes per million population)	NA	NA	●	●
SDG3 – Good Health and Well-Being				
Maternal mortality rate (per 100,000 live births)	7	2017	●	↑
Neonatal mortality rate (per 1,000 live births)	23.5	2020	●	↓
Mortality rate, under-5 (per 1,000 live births)	41.8	2020	●	→
Incidence of tuberculosis (per 100,000 population)	47.0	2020	●	→
New HIV infections (per 1,000 uninfected population)	1.0	2020	●	→
Age-standardized death rate due to cardiovascular disease, cancer, diabetes, or chronic respiratory disease in adults aged 30–70 years (%)	27.7	2019	●	→
Age-standardized death rate attributable to household air pollution and ambient air pollution (per 100,000 population)	79	2016	●	●
Traffic deaths (per 100,000 population)	13.5	2019	●	↑
Life expectancy at birth (years)	69.8	2019	●	→
Adolescent fertility rate (births per 1,000 females aged 15 to 19)	22.0	2017	●	●
Births attended by skilled health personnel (%)	100.0	2016	●	●
Surviving infants who received 2 WHO-recommended vaccines (%)	98	2020	●	↑
Universal health coverage (UHC) index of service coverage (worst 0–100 best)	73	2019	●	↑
Subjective well-being (average ladder score, worst 0–10 best)	5.5	2019	●	●
SDG4 – Quality Education				
Participation rate in pre-primary organized learning (% of children aged 4 to 6)	NA	NA	●	●
Net primary enrollment rate (%)	NA	NA	●	●
Lower secondary completion rate (%)	NA	NA	●	●
Literacy rate (% of population aged 15 to 24)	99.8	2014	●	●
SDG5 – Gender Equality				
Demand for family planning satisfied by modern methods (% of females aged 15 to 49)	79.6	2019	●	●
Ratio of female-to-male mean years of education received (%)	NA	NA	●	●
Ratio of female-to-male labor force participation rate (%)	66.1	2020	●	→
Seats held by women in national parliament (%)	25.0	2020	●	↓
SDG6 – Clean Water and Sanitation				
Population using at least basic drinking water services (%)	100.0	2020	●	↑
Population using at least basic sanitation services (%)	99.4	2020	●	↑
Freshwater withdrawal (% of available freshwater resources)	143.6	2018	●	●
Anthropogenic wastewater that receives treatment (%)	9.8	2018	●	●
Scarce water consumption embodied in imports (m^3 H_2O eq/capita)	1513.1	2018	●	●
SDG7 – Affordable and Clean Energy				
Population with access to electricity (%)	99.9	2019	●	↑
Population with access to clean fuels and technology for cooking (%)	99.9	2019	●	↑
CO_2 emissions from fuel combustion per total electricity output ($MtCO_2$/TWh)	4.0	2019	●	→
Share of renewable energy in total primary energy supply (%)	0.0	2019	●	→
SDG8 – Decent Work and Economic Growth				
Adjusted GDP growth (%)	-0.8	2019	●	●
Victims of modern slavery (per 1,000 population)	11.2	2018	●	●
Adults with an account at a bank or other financial institution or with a mobile-money-service provider (% of population aged 15 or over)	40.6	2017	●	●
Unemployment rate (% of total labor force)	5.1	2022	●	↓
Fundamental labor rights are effectively guaranteed (worst 0–1 best)	NA	NA	●	●
Fatal work-related accidents embodied in imports (per 100,000 population)	0.4	2015	●	↑

* Imputed data point

SDG9 – Industry, Innovation and Infrastructure	Value	Year	Rating	Trend
Population using the internet (%)	21.3	2017	●	●
Mobile broadband subscriptions (per 100 population)	14.8	2019	●	→
Logistics Performance Index: Quality of trade and transport-related infrastructure (worst 1–5 best)	2.2	2018	●	↗
The Times Higher Education Universities Ranking: Average score of top 3 universities (worst 0–100 best)	* 0.0	2022	●	●
Articles published in academic journals (per 1,000 population)	0.0	2020	●	↓
Expenditure on research and development (% of GDP)	NA	NA	●	●
SDG10 – Reduced Inequalities				
Gini coefficient	NA	NA	●	●
Palma ratio	NA	NA	●	●
SDG11 – Sustainable Cities and Communities				
Proportion of urban population living in slums (%)	NA	NA	●	●
Annual mean concentration of particulate matter of less than 2.5 microns in diameter (PM2.5) (μg/m^3)	19.9	2019	●	↗
Access to improved water source, piped (% of urban population)	77.4	2020	●	↓
Satisfaction with public transport (%)	71.0	2019	●	●
SDG12 – Responsible Consumption and Production				
Municipal solid waste (kg/capita/day)	0.3	2013	●	●
Electronic waste (kg/capita)	6.5	2019	●	●
Production-based SO_2 emissions (kg/capita)	5.7	2018	●	●
SO_2 emissions embodied in imports (kg/capita)	1.8	2018	●	●
Production-based nitrogen emissions (kg/capita)	35.7	2015	●	↓
Nitrogen emissions embodied in imports (kg/capita)	1.6	2015	●	↑
Exports of plastic waste (kg/capita)	NA	NA	●	●
SDG13 – Climate Action				
CO_2 emissions from fossil fuel combustion and cement production (tCO_2/capita)	12.5	2020	●	→
CO_2 emissions embodied in imports (tCO_2/capita)	0.7	2018	●	↑
CO_2 emissions embodied in fossil fuel exports (kg/capita)	NA	NA	●	●
SDG14 – Life Below Water				
Mean area that is protected in marine sites important to biodiversity (%)	NA	NA	●	●
Ocean Health Index: Clean Waters score (worst 0–100 best)	NA	NA	●	●
Fish caught from overexploited or collapsed stocks (% of total catch)	NA	NA	●	●
Fish caught by trawling or dredging (%)	NA	NA	●	●
Fish caught that are then discarded (%)	NA	NA	●	●
Marine biodiversity threats embodied in imports (per million population)	0.0	2018	●	●
SDG15 – Life on Land				
Mean area that is protected in terrestrial sites important to biodiversity (%)	14.0	2020	●	→
Mean area that is protected in freshwater sites important to biodiversity (%)	12.7	2020	●	→
Red List Index of species survival (worst 0–1 best)	1.0	2021	●	↑
Permanent deforestation (% of forest area, 5-year average)	0.0	2020	●	↑
Terrestrial and freshwater biodiversity threats embodied in imports (per million population)	0.2	2018	●	●
SDG16 – Peace, Justice and Strong Institutions				
Homicides (per 100,000 population)	4.2	2006	●	●
Unsentenced detainees (% of prison population)	10.9	2006	●	●
Population who feel safe walking alone at night in the city or area where they live (%)	93	2019	●	●
Property Rights (worst 1–7 best)	NA	NA	●	●
Birth registrations with civil authority (% of children under age 5)	99.9	2020	●	●
Corruption Perception Index (worst 0–100 best)	19	2021	●	→
Children involved in child labor (% of population aged 5 to 14)	0.3	2019	●	●
Exports of major conventional weapons (TIV constant million USD per 100,000 population)	* 0.0	2020	●	●
Press Freedom Index (best 0–100 worst)	80.0	2021	●	→
Access to and affordability of justice (worst 0–1 best)	NA	NA	●	●
SDG17 – Partnerships for the Goals				
Government spending on health and education (% of GDP)	4.3	2019	●	↓
For high-income and all OECD DAC countries: International concessional public finance, including official development assistance (% of GNI)	NA	NA	●	●
Other countries: Government revenue excluding grants (% of GDP)	NA	NA	●	●
Corporate Tax Haven Score (best 0–100 worst)	* 0.0	2019	●	●
Statistical Performance Index (worst 0–100 best)	23.5	2019	●	→

5. Country Profiles

TUVALU

Oceania

AVERAGE PERFORMANCE BY SDG

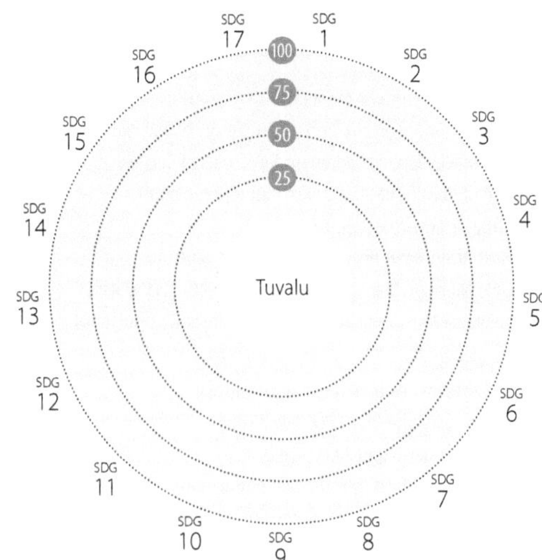

OVERALL PERFORMANCE

COUNTRY RANKING

TUVALU

NA /163

COUNTRY SCORE

REGIONAL AVERAGE: 52.3

SDG DASHBOARDS AND TRENDS

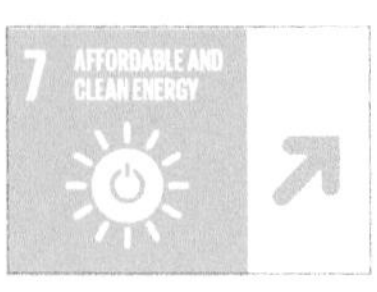

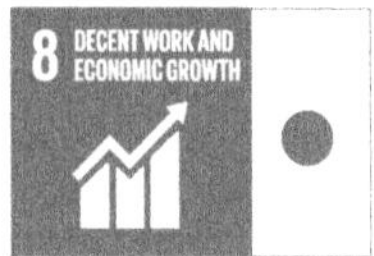

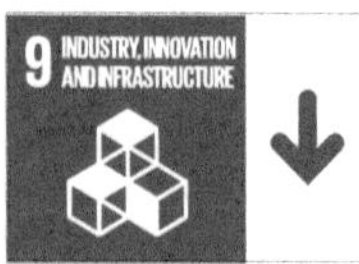

Major challenges | Significant challenges | Challenges remain | SDG achieved | Information unavailable

Decreasing | Stagnating | Moderately improving | On track or maintaining SDG achievement | Information unavailable

Note: The full title of each SDG is available here: https://sustainabledevelopment.un.org/topics/sustainabledevelopmentgoals

INTERNATIONAL SPILLOVER INDEX

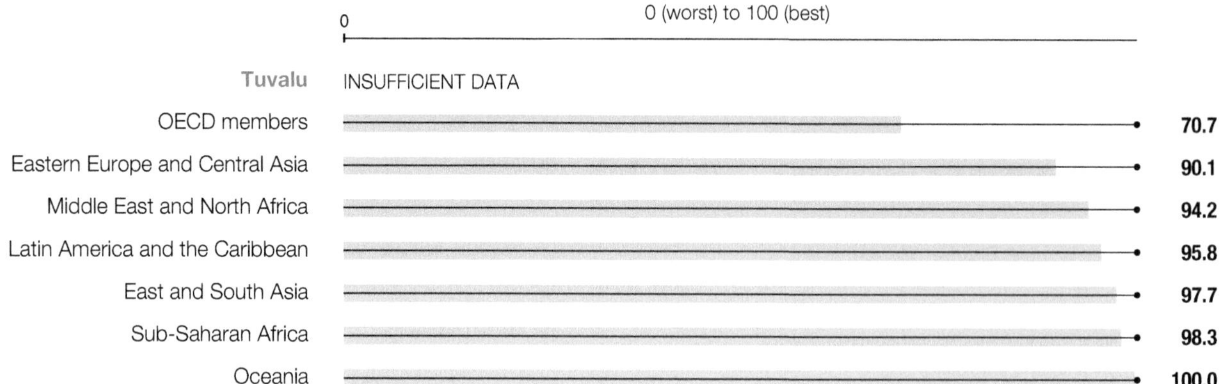

STATISTICAL PERFORMANCE INDEX

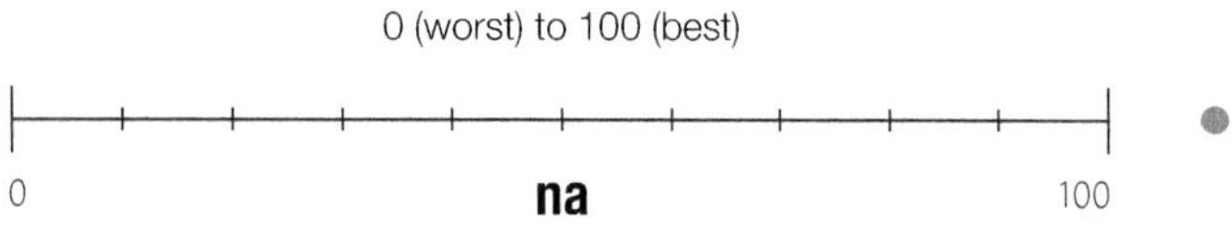

MISSING DATA IN SDG INDEX

54%

Performance by Indicator

SDG1 – No Poverty	Value	Year	Rating	Trend
Poverty headcount ratio at $1.90/day (%)	NA	NA	●	●
Poverty headcount ratio at $3.20/day (%)	NA	NA	●	●
SDG2 – Zero Hunger				
Prevalence of undernourishment (%)	NA	NA	●	●
Prevalence of stunting in children under 5 years of age (%)	10.0	2007	●	→
Prevalence of wasting in children under 5 years of age (%)	3.3	2007	●	↑
Prevalence of obesity, BMI ≥ 30 (% of adult population)	51.6	2016	●	↓
Human Trophic Level (best 2–3 worst)	NA	NA	●	●
Cereal yield (tonnes per hectare of harvested land)	NA	NA	●	●
Sustainable Nitrogen Management Index (best 0–1.41 worst)	1.3	2015	●	↓
Exports of hazardous pesticides (tonnes per million population)	NA	NA	●	●
SDG3 – Good Health and Well-Being				
Maternal mortality rate (per 100,000 live births)	NA	NA	●	●
Neonatal mortality rate (per 1,000 live births)	10.1	2020	●	↑
Mortality rate, under-5 (per 1,000 live births)	22.0	2020	●	↑
Incidence of tuberculosis (per 100,000 population)	296.0	2020	●	↓
New HIV infections (per 1,000 uninfected population)	NA	NA	●	●
Age-standardized death rate due to cardiovascular disease, cancer, diabetes, or chronic respiratory disease in adults aged 30–70 years (%)	NA	NA	●	●
Age-standardized death rate attributable to household air pollution and ambient air pollution (per 100,000 population)	NA	NA	●	●
Traffic deaths (per 100,000 population)	NA	NA	●	●
Life expectancy at birth (years)	NA	NA	●	●
Adolescent fertility rate (births per 1,000 females aged 15 to 19)	26.6	2016	●	●
Births attended by skilled health personnel (%)	93.1	2007	●	●
Surviving infants who received 2 WHO-recommended vaccines (%)	93	2020	●	↑
Universal health coverage (UHC) index of service coverage (worst 0–100 best)	NA	NA	●	●
Subjective well-being (average ladder score, worst 0–10 best)	NA	NA	●	●
SDG4 – Quality Education				
Participation rate in pre-primary organized learning (% of children aged 4 to 6)	95.0	2019	●	↑
Net primary enrollment rate (%)	82.6	2020	●	↓
Lower secondary completion rate (%)	62.7	2020	●	↓
Literacy rate (% of population aged 15 to 24)	NA	NA	●	●
SDG5 – Gender Equality				
Demand for family planning satisfied by modern methods (% of females aged 15 to 49)	41.0	2007	●	●
Ratio of female-to-male mean years of education received (%)	NA	NA	●	●
Ratio of female-to-male labor force participation rate (%)	NA	NA	●	●
Seats held by women in national parliament (%)	6.3	2020	●	↓
SDG6 – Clean Water and Sanitation				
Population using at least basic drinking water services (%)	100.0	2020	●	↑
Population using at least basic sanitation services (%)	83.7	2018	●	●
Freshwater withdrawal (% of available freshwater resources)	NA	NA	●	●
Anthropogenic wastewater that receives treatment (%)	0.1	2018	●	●
Scarce water consumption embodied in imports (m^3 H_2O eq/capita)	NA	NA	●	●
SDG7 – Affordable and Clean Energy				
Population with access to electricity (%)	100.0	2019	●	↑
Population with access to clean fuels and technology for cooking (%)	68.9	2019	●	↗
CO_2 emissions from fuel combustion per total electricity output ($MtCO_2$/TWh)	NA	NA	●	●
Share of renewable energy in total primary energy supply (%)	NA	NA	●	●
SDG8 – Decent Work and Economic Growth				
Adjusted GDP growth (%)	0.1	2020	●	●
Victims of modern slavery (per 1,000 population)	NA	NA	●	●
Adults with an account at a bank or other financial institution or with a mobile-money-service provider (% of population aged 15 or over)	NA	NA	●	●
Unemployment rate (% of total labor force)	NA	NA	●	●
Fundamental labor rights are effectively guaranteed (worst 0–1 best)	NA	NA	●	●
Fatal work-related accidents embodied in imports (per 100,000 population)	NA	NA	●	●

* Imputed data point

SDG9 – Industry, Innovation and Infrastructure	Value	Year	Rating	Trend
Population using the internet (%)	35.2	2017	●	●
Mobile broadband subscriptions (per 100 population)	0.0	2017	●	●
Logistics Performance Index: Quality of trade and transport-related infrastructure (worst 1–5 best)	NA	NA	●	●
The Times Higher Education Universities Ranking: Average score of top 3 universities (worst 0–100 best)	* 0.0	2022	●	●
Articles published in academic journals (per 1,000 population)	0.2	2020	●	↓
Expenditure on research and development (% of GDP)	NA	NA	●	●
SDG10 – Reduced Inequalities				
Gini coefficient	39.1	2010	●	●
Palma ratio	1.8	2018	●	●
SDG11 – Sustainable Cities and Communities				
Proportion of urban population living in slums (%)	NA	NA	●	●
Annual mean concentration of particulate matter of less than 2.5 microns in diameter (PM2.5) (μg/m^3)	10.3	2019	●	↑
Access to improved water source, piped (% of urban population)	100.0	2020	●	↑
Satisfaction with public transport (%)	NA	NA	●	●
SDG12 – Responsible Consumption and Production				
Municipal solid waste (kg/capita/day)	1.0	2016	●	●
Electronic waste (kg/capita)	1.5	2019	●	●
Production-based SO_2 emissions (kg/capita)	NA	NA	●	●
SO_2 emissions embodied in imports (kg/capita)	NA	NA	●	●
Production-based nitrogen emissions (kg/capita)	NA	NA	●	●
Nitrogen emissions embodied in imports (kg/capita)	NA	NA	●	●
Exports of plastic waste (kg/capita)	NA	NA	●	●
SDG13 – Climate Action				
CO_2 emissions from fossil fuel combustion and cement production (tCO_2/capita)	0.6	2020	●	↑
CO_2 emissions embodied in imports (tCO_2/capita)	NA	NA	●	●
CO_2 emissions embodied in fossil fuel exports (kg/capita)	0.0	2020	●	●
SDG14 – Life Below Water				
Mean area that is protected in marine sites important to biodiversity (%)	NA	NA	●	●
Ocean Health Index: Clean Waters score (worst 0–100 best)	52.6	2020	●	→
Fish caught from overexploited or collapsed stocks (% of total catch)	0.0	2018	●	↑
Fish caught by trawling or dredging (%)	0.0	2018	●	↑
Fish caught that are then discarded (%)	1.4	2018	●	↑
Marine biodiversity threats embodied in imports (per million population)	NA	NA	●	●
SDG15 – Life on Land				
Mean area that is protected in terrestrial sites important to biodiversity (%)	NA	NA	●	●
Mean area that is protected in freshwater sites important to biodiversity (%)	NA	NA	●	●
Red List Index of species survival (worst 0–1 best)	0.8	2021	●	↓
Permanent deforestation (% of forest area, 5-year average)	NA	NA	●	●
Terrestrial and freshwater biodiversity threats embodied in imports (per million population)	NA	NA	●	●
SDG16 – Peace, Justice and Strong Institutions				
Homicides (per 100,000 population)	0.0	2019	●	●
Unsentenced detainees (% of prison population)	NA	NA	●	●
Population who feel safe walking alone at night in the city or area where they live (%)	NA	NA	●	●
Property Rights (worst 1–7 best)	NA	NA	●	●
Birth registrations with civil authority (% of children under age 5)	49.9	2020	●	●
Corruption Perception Index (worst 0–100 best)	NA	NA	●	●
Children involved in child labor (% of population aged 5 to 14)	NA	NA	●	●
Exports of major conventional weapons (TIV constant million USD per 100,000 population)	* 0.0	2020	●	●
Press Freedom Index (best 0–100 worst)	NA	NA	●	●
Access to and affordability of justice (worst 0–1 best)	NA	NA	●	●
SDG17 – Partnerships for the Goals				
Government spending on health and education (% of GDP)	21.5	2019	●	↑
For high-income and all OECD DAC countries: International concessional public finance, including official development assistance (% of GNI)	NA	NA	●	●
Other countries: Government revenue excluding grants (% of GDP)	NA	NA	●	●
Corporate Tax Haven Score (best 0–100 worst)	* 0.0	2019	●	●
Statistical Performance Index (worst 0–100 best)	NA	NA	●	●

UGANDA

Sub-Saharan Africa

OVERALL PERFORMANCE

COUNTRY RANKING

UGANDA

136/163

COUNTRY SCORE

AVERAGE PERFORMANCE BY SDG

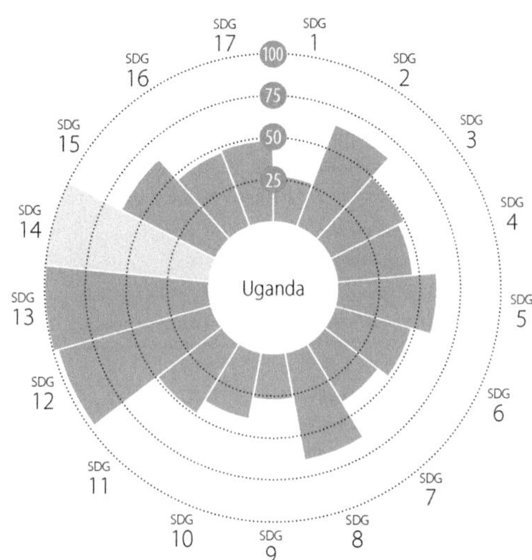

SDG DASHBOARDS AND TRENDS

Major challenges | Significant challenges | Challenges remain | SDG achieved | Information unavailable

Decreasing | Stagnating | Moderately improving | On track or maintaining SDG achievement | Information unavailable

Note: The full title of each SDG is available here: https://sustainabledevelopment.un.org/topics/sustainabledevelopmentgoals

INTERNATIONAL SPILLOVER INDEX

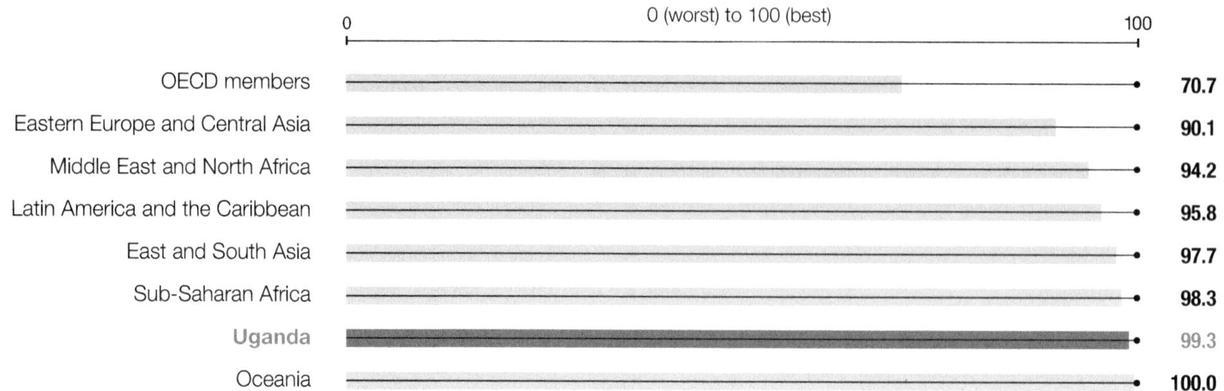

STATISTICAL PERFORMANCE INDEX

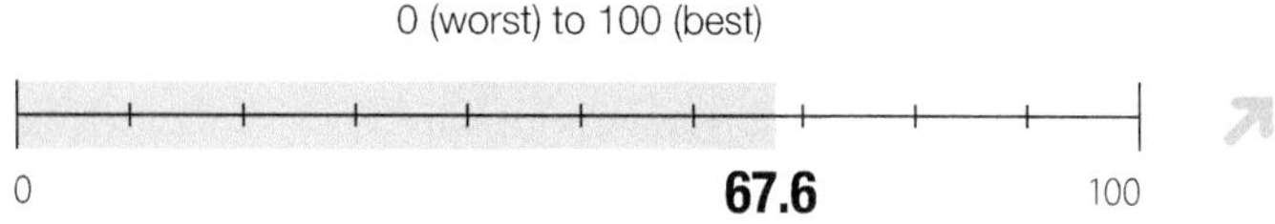

MISSING DATA IN SDG INDEX

UGANDA

Performance by Indicator

SDG1 – No Poverty

Indicator	Value	Year	Rating	Trend
Poverty headcount ratio at $1.90/day (%)	34.4	2022	●	→
Poverty headcount ratio at $3.20/day (%)	61.5	2022	●	→

SDG2 – Zero Hunger

Indicator	Value	Year	Rating	Trend
Prevalence of undernourishment (%)	NA	NA	●	●
Prevalence of stunting in children under 5 years of age (%)	28.9	2016	●	→
Prevalence of wasting in children under 5 years of age (%)	3.5	2016	●	↑
Prevalence of obesity, BMI ≥ 30 (% of adult population)	5.3	2016	●	↑
Human Trophic Level (best 2–3 worst)	2.1	2017	●	↑
Cereal yield (tonnes per hectare of harvested land)	2.1	2018	●	↑
Sustainable Nitrogen Management Index (best 0–1.41 worst)	0.8	2015	●	→
Exports of hazardous pesticides (tonnes per million population)	0.1	2019	●	●

SDG3 – Good Health and Well-Being

Indicator	Value	Year	Rating	Trend
Maternal mortality rate (per 100,000 live births)	375	2017	●	→
Neonatal mortality rate (per 1,000 live births)	19.2	2020	●	↗
Mortality rate, under-5 (per 1,000 live births)	43.3	2020	●	↑
Incidence of tuberculosis (per 100,000 population)	196.0	2020	●	→
New HIV infections (per 1,000 uninfected population)	1.0	2020	●	↑
Age-standardized death rate due to cardiovascular disease, cancer, diabetes, or chronic respiratory disease in adults aged 30–70 years (%)	21.2	2019	●	→
Age-standardized death rate attributable to household air pollution and ambient air pollution (per 100,000 population)	156	2016	●	●
Traffic deaths (per 100,000 population)	29.4	2019	●	→
Life expectancy at birth (years)	66.7	2019	●	↗
Adolescent fertility rate (births per 1,000 females aged 15 to 19)	111.4	2017	●	●
Births attended by skilled health personnel (%)	74.2	2016	●	●
Surviving infants who received 2 WHO-recommended vaccines (%)	87	2020	●	↑
Universal health coverage (UHC) index of service coverage (worst 0–100 best)	50	2019	●	↗
Subjective well-being (average ladder score, worst 0–10 best)	4.2	2021	●	→

SDG4 – Quality Education

Indicator	Value	Year	Rating	Trend
Participation rate in pre-primary organized learning (% of children aged 4 to 6)	34.1	2010	●	●
Net primary enrollment rate (%)	95.6	2013	●	●
Lower secondary completion rate (%)	26.4	2017	●	●
Literacy rate (% of population aged 15 to 24)	89.4	2018	●	●

SDG5 – Gender Equality

Indicator	Value	Year	Rating	Trend
Demand for family planning satisfied by modern methods (% of females aged 15 to 49)	55.1	2018	●	●
Ratio of female-to-male mean years of education received (%)	64.5	2019	●	↓
Ratio of female-to-male labor force participation rate (%)	89.1	2020	●	↑
Seats held by women in national parliament (%)	34.9	2020	●	↓

SDG6 – Clean Water and Sanitation

Indicator	Value	Year	Rating	Trend
Population using at least basic drinking water services (%)	55.9	2020	●	→
Population using at least basic sanitation services (%)	19.8	2020	●	→
Freshwater withdrawal (% of available freshwater resources)	5.8	2018	●	●
Anthropogenic wastewater that receives treatment (%)	0.4	2018	●	●
Scarce water consumption embodied in imports (m^3 H_2O eq/capita)	169.1	2018	●	●

SDG7 – Affordable and Clean Energy

Indicator	Value	Year	Rating	Trend
Population with access to electricity (%)	41.3	2019	●	↑
Population with access to clean fuels and technology for cooking (%)	0.5	2019	●	↓
CO_2 emissions from fuel combustion per total electricity output ($MtCO_2$/TWh)	0.9	2019	●	↑
Share of renewable energy in total primary energy supply (%)	NA	NA	●	●

SDG8 – Decent Work and Economic Growth

Indicator	Value	Year	Rating	Trend
Adjusted GDP growth (%)	-3.5	2020	●	●
Victims of modern slavery (per 1,000 population)	7.6	2018	●	●
Adults with an account at a bank or other financial institution or with a mobile-money-service provider (% of population aged 15 or over)	59.2	2017	●	↑
Unemployment rate (% of total labor force)	2.9	2022	●	↑
Fundamental labor rights are effectively guaranteed (worst 0–1 best)	0.4	2020	●	→
Fatal work-related accidents embodied in imports (per 100,000 population)	0.1	2015	●	↑

* Imputed data point

SDG9 – Industry, Innovation and Infrastructure

Indicator	Value	Year	Rating	Trend
Population using the internet (%)	19.9	2020	●	↗
Mobile broadband subscriptions (per 100 population)	38.3	2019	●	↑
Logistics Performance Index: Quality of trade and transport-related infrastructure (worst 1–5 best)	2.2	2018	●	●
The Times Higher Education Universities Ranking: Average score of top 3 universities (worst 0–100 best)	35.0	2022	●	●
Articles published in academic journals (per 1,000 population)	0.0	2020	●	→
Expenditure on research and development (% of GDP)	0.1	2014	●	●

SDG10 – Reduced Inequalities

Indicator	Value	Year	Rating	Trend
Gini coefficient	42.8	2016	●	●
Palma ratio	2.2	2018	●	●

SDG11 – Sustainable Cities and Communities

Indicator	Value	Year	Rating	Trend
Proportion of urban population living in slums (%)	46.0	2018	●	↗
Annual mean concentration of particulate matter of less than 2.5 microns in diameter (PM2.5) (μg/m³)	52.5	2019	●	↓
Access to improved water source, piped (% of urban population)	53.0	2020	●	↓
Satisfaction with public transport (%)	53.0	2021	●	↗

SDG12 – Responsible Consumption and Production

Indicator	Value	Year	Rating	Trend
Municipal solid waste (kg/capita/day)	0.6	2011	●	●
Electronic waste (kg/capita)	0.8	2019	●	●
Production-based SO_2 emissions (kg/capita)	0.6	2018	●	●
SO_2 emissions embodied in imports (kg/capita)	0.2	2018	●	●
Production-based nitrogen emissions (kg/capita)	8.8	2015	●	↑
Nitrogen emissions embodied in imports (kg/capita)	0.2	2015	●	↑
Exports of plastic waste (kg/capita)	0.1	2020	●	●

SDG13 – Climate Action

Indicator	Value	Year	Rating	Trend
CO_2 emissions from fossil fuel combustion and cement production (tCO_2/capita)	0.1	2020	●	↑
CO_2 emissions embodied in imports (tCO_2/capita)	0.1	2018	●	↑
CO_2 emissions embodied in fossil fuel exports (kg/capita)	0.0	2020	●	●

SDG14 – Life Below Water

Indicator	Value	Year	Rating	Trend
Mean area that is protected in marine sites important to biodiversity (%)	NA	NA	●	●
Ocean Health Index: Clean Waters score (worst 0–100 best)	NA	NA	●	●
Fish caught from overexploited or collapsed stocks (% of total catch)	NA	NA	●	●
Fish caught by trawling or dredging (%)	NA	NA	●	●
Fish caught that are then discarded (%)	NA	NA	●	●
Marine biodiversity threats embodied in imports (per million population)	0.0	2018	●	●

SDG15 – Life on Land

Indicator	Value	Year	Rating	Trend
Mean area that is protected in terrestrial sites important to biodiversity (%)	72.2	2020	●	→
Mean area that is protected in freshwater sites important to biodiversity (%)	48.5	2020	●	→
Red List Index of species survival (worst 0–1 best)	0.7	2021	●	↓
Permanent deforestation (% of forest area, 5-year average)	0.6	2020	●	→
Terrestrial and freshwater biodiversity threats embodied in imports (per million population)	0.2	2018	●	●

SDG16 – Peace, Justice and Strong Institutions

Indicator	Value	Year	Rating	Trend
Homicides (per 100,000 population)	9.8	2020	●	↗
Unsentenced detainees (% of prison population)	51.2	2017	●	●
Population who feel safe walking alone at night in the city or area where they live (%)	45	2021	●	↓
Property Rights (worst 1–7 best)	4.0	2020	●	→
Birth registrations with civil authority (% of children under age 5)	32.2	2020	●	●
Corruption Perception Index (worst 0–100 best)	27	2021	●	→
Children involved in child labor (% of population aged 5 to 14)	18.1	2019	●	●
Exports of major conventional weapons (TIV constant million USD per 100,000 population)	0.0	2020	●	●
Press Freedom Index (best 0–100 worst)	41.2	2021	●	↓
Access to and affordability of justice (worst 0–1 best)	0.4	2020	●	→

SDG17 – Partnerships for the Goals

Indicator	Value	Year	Rating	Trend
Government spending on health and education (% of GDP)	3.6	2020	●	→
For high-income and all OECD DAC countries: International concessional public finance, including official development assistance (% of GNI)	NA	NA	●	●
Other countries: Government revenue excluding grants (% of GDP)	13.1	2019	●	→
Corporate Tax Haven Score (best 0–100 worst)	* 0.0	2019	●	●
Statistical Performance Index (worst 0–100 best)	67.6	2019	●	↗

UKRAINE

Eastern Europe and Central Asia

OVERALL PERFORMANCE

COUNTRY RANKING

UKRAINE

37 **/163**

COUNTRY SCORE

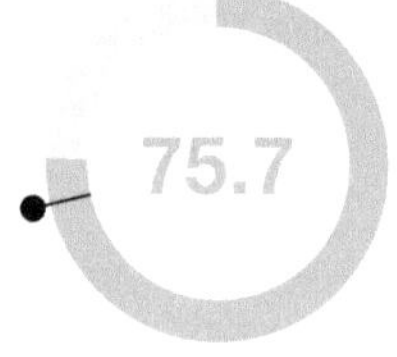

REGIONAL AVERAGE: 71.6

AVERAGE PERFORMANCE BY SDG

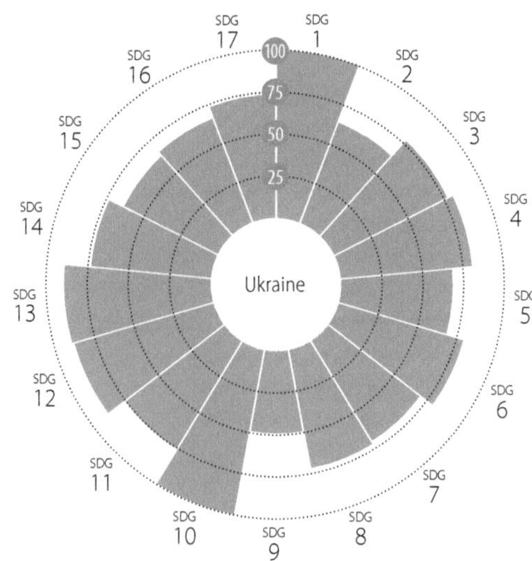

SDG DASHBOARDS AND TRENDS

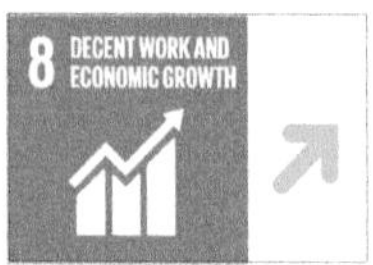

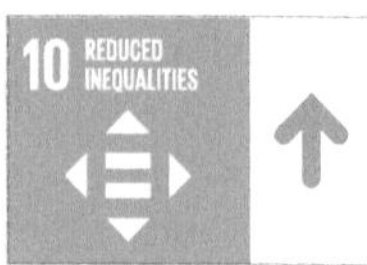

Major challenges | Significant challenges | Challenges remain | SDG achieved | Information unavailable

Decreasing | Stagnating | Moderately improving | On track or maintaining SDG achievement | Information unavailable

Note: The full title of each SDG is available here: https://sustainabledevelopment.un.org/topics/sustainabledevelopmentgoals

INTERNATIONAL SPILLOVER INDEX

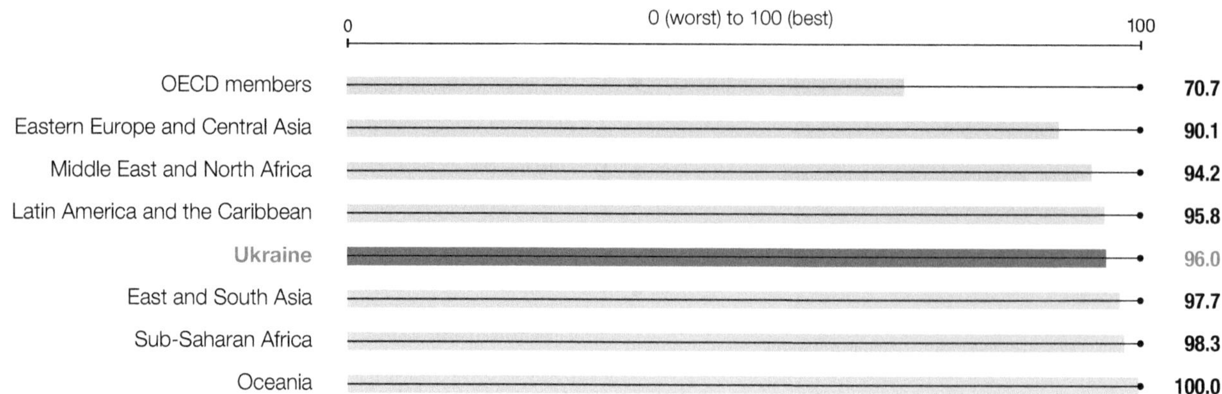

STATISTICAL PERFORMANCE INDEX

0 (worst) to 100 (best)

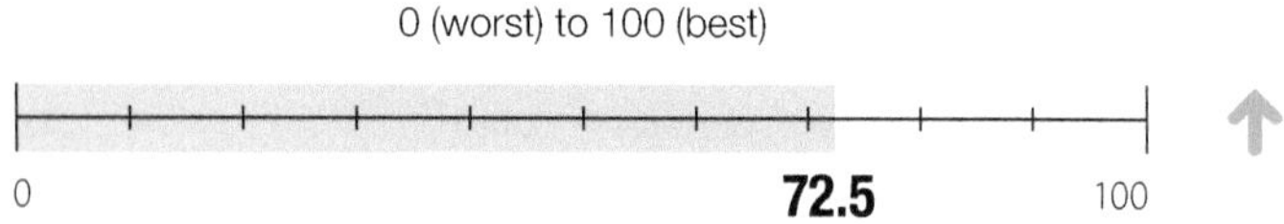

MISSING DATA IN SDG INDEX

0%

UKRAINE

SDG1 – No Poverty

Indicator	Value	Year	Rating	Trend
Poverty headcount ratio at $1.90/day (%)	0.0	2022	●	↑
Poverty headcount ratio at $3.20/day (%)	0.1	2022	●	↑

SDG2 – Zero Hunger

Indicator	Value	Year	Rating	Trend
Prevalence of undernourishment (%)	2.5	2019	●	↑
Prevalence of stunting in children under 5 years of age (%)	22.9	2000	●	↗
Prevalence of wasting in children under 5 years of age (%)	8.2	2000	●	→
Prevalence of obesity, BMI ≥ 30 (% of adult population)	24.1	2016	●	↓
Human Trophic Level (best 2–3 worst)	2.3	2017	●	→
Cereal yield (tonnes per hectare of harvested land)	4.9	2018	●	↑
Sustainable Nitrogen Management Index (best 0–1.41 worst)	0.4	2015	●	↑
Exports of hazardous pesticides (tonnes per million population)	0.1	2019	●	●

SDG3 – Good Health and Well-Being

Indicator	Value	Year	Rating	Trend
Maternal mortality rate (per 100,000 live births)	19	2017	●	↑
Neonatal mortality rate (per 1,000 live births)	4.8	2020	●	↑
Mortality rate, under-5 (per 1,000 live births)	8.1	2020	●	↑
Incidence of tuberculosis (per 100,000 population)	73.0	2020	●	↗
New HIV infections (per 1,000 uninfected population)	0.2	2020	●	↑
Age-standardized death rate due to cardiovascular disease, cancer, diabetes, or chronic respiratory disease in adults aged 30–70 years (%)	25.5	2019	●	→
Age-standardized death rate attributable to household air pollution and ambient air pollution (per 100,000 population)	71	2016	●	●
Traffic deaths (per 100,000 population)	10.2	2019	●	↑
Life expectancy at birth (years)	73.0	2019	●	→
Adolescent fertility rate (births per 1,000 females aged 15 to 19)	18.0	2018	●	↑
Births attended by skilled health personnel (%)	99.9	2014	●	●
Surviving infants who received 2 WHO-recommended vaccines (%)	81	2020	●	↑
Universal health coverage (UHC) index of service coverage (worst 0–100 best)	73	2019	●	↑
Subjective well-being (average ladder score, worst 0–10 best)	5.3	2021	●	↑

SDG4 – Quality Education

Indicator	Value	Year	Rating	Trend
Participation rate in pre-primary organized learning (% of children aged 4 to 6)	64.2	2017	●	●
Net primary enrollment rate (%)	92.0	2014	●	●
Lower secondary completion rate (%)	94.4	2014	●	●
Literacy rate (% of population aged 15 to 24)	100.0	2012	●	●

SDG5 – Gender Equality

Indicator	Value	Year	Rating	Trend
Demand for family planning satisfied by modern methods (% of females aged 15 to 49)	68.0	2012	●	●
Ratio of female-to-male mean years of education received (%)	100.0	2019	●	↑
Ratio of female-to-male labor force participation rate (%)	75.9	2020	●	↑
Seats held by women in national parliament (%)	20.8	2020	●	↗

SDG6 – Clean Water and Sanitation

Indicator	Value	Year	Rating	Trend
Population using at least basic drinking water services (%)	93.9	2020	●	→
Population using at least basic sanitation services (%)	97.7	2020	●	↑
Freshwater withdrawal (% of available freshwater resources)	13.9	2018	●	●
Anthropogenic wastewater that receives treatment (%)	14.1	2018	●	●
Scarce water consumption embodied in imports (m^3 H_2O eq/capita)	720.9	2018	●	●

SDG7 – Affordable and Clean Energy

Indicator	Value	Year	Rating	Trend
Population with access to electricity (%)	100.0	2019	●	↑
Population with access to clean fuels and technology for cooking (%)	95.2	2019	●	↑
CO_2 emissions from fuel combustion per total electricity output ($MtCO_2$/TWh)	1.2	2019	●	↑
Share of renewable energy in total primary energy supply (%)	4.9	2019	●	→

SDG8 – Decent Work and Economic Growth

Indicator	Value	Year	Rating	Trend
Adjusted GDP growth (%)	-1.1	2020	●	●
Victims of modern slavery (per 1,000 population)	6.4	2018	●	●
Adults with an account at a bank or other financial institution or with a mobile-money-service provider (% of population aged 15 or over)	62.9	2017	●	↑
Unemployment rate (% of total labor force)	8.5	2022	●	→
Fundamental labor rights are effectively guaranteed (worst 0–1 best)	0.7	2020	●	↓
Fatal work-related accidents embodied in imports (per 100,000 population)	0.2	2015	●	↑

* Imputed data point

SDG9 – Industry, Innovation and Infrastructure

Indicator	Value	Year	Rating	Trend
Population using the internet (%)	75.0	2020	●	↑
Mobile broadband subscriptions (per 100 population)	77.3	2019	●	↑
Logistics Performance Index: Quality of trade and transport-related infrastructure (worst 1–5 best)	2.2	2018	●	↓
The Times Higher Education Universities Ranking: Average score of top 3 universities (worst 0–100 best)	33.1	2022	●	●
Articles published in academic journals (per 1,000 population)	0.4	2020	●	↑
Expenditure on research and development (% of GDP)	0.5	2018	●	↓

SDG10 – Reduced Inequalities

Indicator	Value	Year	Rating	Trend
Gini coefficient	26.6	2019	●	↑
Palma ratio	0.9	2018	●	●

SDG11 – Sustainable Cities and Communities

Indicator	Value	Year	Rating	Trend
Proportion of urban population living in slums (%)	18.0	2018	●	●
Annual mean concentration of particulate matter of less than 2.5 microns in diameter (PM2.5) ($\mu g/m^3$)	19.0	2019	●	↗
Access to improved water source, piped (% of urban population)	79.0	2020	●	↓
Satisfaction with public transport (%)	58.0	2021	●	→

SDG12 – Responsible Consumption and Production

Indicator	Value	Year	Rating	Trend
Municipal solid waste (kg/capita/day)	0.9	2016	●	●
Electronic waste (kg/capita)	7.7	2019	●	●
Production-based SO_2 emissions (kg/capita)	16.9	2018	●	●
SO_2 emissions embodied in imports (kg/capita)	0.7	2018	●	●
Production-based nitrogen emissions (kg/capita)	18.2	2015	●	↑
Nitrogen emissions embodied in imports (kg/capita)	2.4	2015	●	↑
Exports of plastic waste (kg/capita)	0.0	2020	●	●

SDG13 – Climate Action

Indicator	Value	Year	Rating	Trend
CO_2 emissions from fossil fuel combustion and cement production (tCO_2/capita)	4.9	2020	●	→
CO_2 emissions embodied in imports (tCO_2/capita)	0.2	2018	●	↑
CO_2 emissions embodied in fossil fuel exports (kg/capita)	13.8	2020	●	●

SDG14 – Life Below Water

Indicator	Value	Year	Rating	Trend
Mean area that is protected in marine sites important to biodiversity (%)	30.7	2020	●	→
Ocean Health Index: Clean Waters score (worst 0–100 best)	59.2	2020	●	↓
Fish caught from overexploited or collapsed stocks (% of total catch)	8.0	2018	●	↑
Fish caught by trawling or dredging (%)	15.2	2018	●	↑
Fish caught that are then discarded (%)	1.6	2018	●	↑
Marine biodiversity threats embodied in imports (per million population)	0.0	2018	●	●

SDG15 – Life on Land

Indicator	Value	Year	Rating	Trend
Mean area that is protected in terrestrial sites important to biodiversity (%)	21.7	2020	●	→
Mean area that is protected in freshwater sites important to biodiversity (%)	16.2	2020	●	→
Red List Index of species survival (worst 0–1 best)	0.9	2021	●	↑
Permanent deforestation (% of forest area, 5-year average)	0.0	2020	●	↑
Terrestrial and freshwater biodiversity threats embodied in imports (per million population)	0.3	2018	●	●

SDG16 – Peace, Justice and Strong Institutions

Indicator	Value	Year	Rating	Trend
Homicides (per 100,000 population)	6.2	2017	●	→
Unsentenced detainees (% of prison population)	33.8	2017	●	●
Population who feel safe walking alone at night in the city or area where they live (%)	62	2021	●	↑
Property Rights (worst 1–7 best)	3.2	2020	●	↓
Birth registrations with civil authority (% of children under age 5)	99.8	2020	●	●
Corruption Perception Index (worst 0–100 best)	32	2021	●	→
Children involved in child labor (% of population aged 5 to 14)	3.2	2019	●	●
Exports of major conventional weapons (TIV constant million USD per 100,000 population)	0.5	2020	●	●
Press Freedom Index (best 0–100 worst)	33.0	2021	●	→
Access to and affordability of justice (worst 0–1 best)	0.6	2020	●	↑

SDG17 – Partnerships for the Goals

Indicator	Value	Year	Rating	Trend
Government spending on health and education (% of GDP)	8.6	2019	●	↓
For high-income and all OECD DAC countries: International concessional public finance, including official development assistance (% of GNI)	NA	NA	●	●
Other countries: Government revenue excluding grants (% of GDP)	31.9	2019	●	↑
Corporate Tax Haven Score (best 0–100 worst)	* 0.0	2019	●	●
Statistical Performance Index (worst 0–100 best)	72.5	2019	●	↑

UNITED ARAB EMIRATES

Middle East and North Africa

OVERALL PERFORMANCE

COUNTRY RANKING

UNITED ARAB EMIRATES

85/163

COUNTRY SCORE

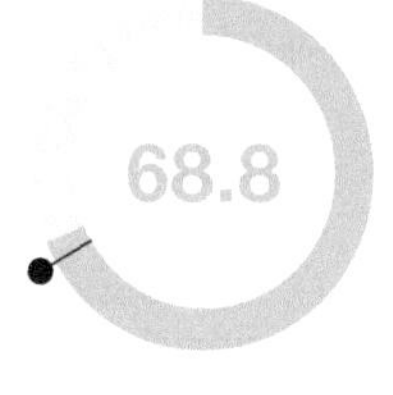

REGIONAL AVERAGE: 66.7

AVERAGE PERFORMANCE BY SDG

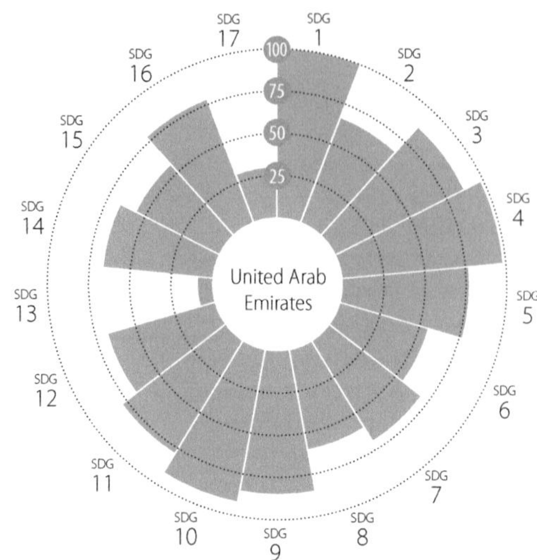

SDG DASHBOARDS AND TRENDS

Note: The full title of each SDG is available here: https://sustainabledevelopment.un.org/topics/sustainabledevelopmentgoals

INTERNATIONAL SPILLOVER INDEX

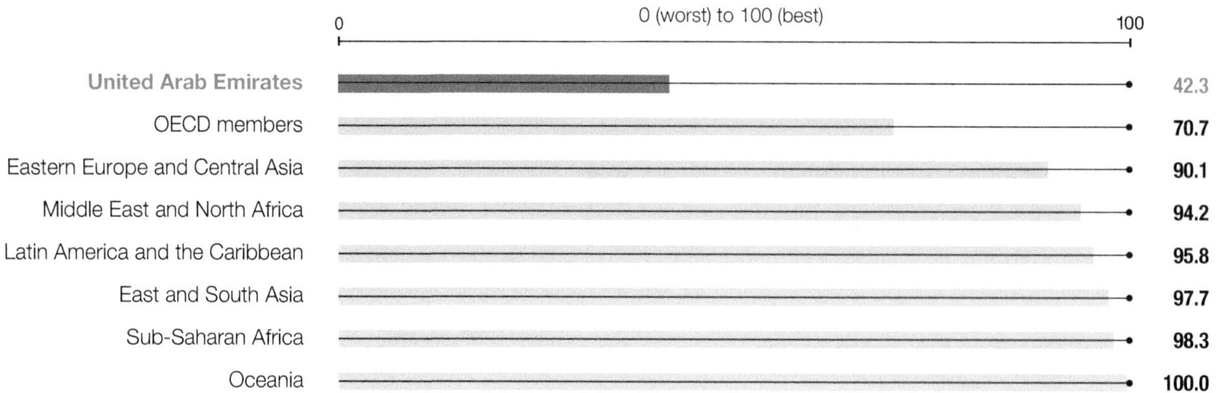

STATISTICAL PERFORMANCE INDEX

0 (worst) to 100 (best)

0 **59.7** 100

MISSING DATA IN SDG INDEX

7%

UNITED ARAB EMIRATES

Performance by Indicator

SDG1 – No Poverty		Value	Year	Rating	Trend
Poverty headcount ratio at $1.90/day (%)		0.2	2022	●	↑
Poverty headcount ratio at $3.20/day (%)		0.3	2022	●	↑
SDG2 – Zero Hunger					
Prevalence of undernourishment (%)		3.7	2019	●	↑
Prevalence of stunting in children under 5 years of age (%)	*	2.6	2019	●	↑
Prevalence of wasting in children under 5 years of age (%)	*	0.7	2019	●	↑
Prevalence of obesity, BMI ≥ 30 (% of adult population)		31.7	2016	●	↓
Human Trophic Level (best 2–3 worst)		2.3	2017	●	↑
Cereal yield (tonnes per hectare of harvested land)		27.6	2018	●	↑
Sustainable Nitrogen Management Index (best 0–1.41 worst)		1.2	2015	●	→
Exports of hazardous pesticides (tonnes per million population)		27.8	2019	●	●
SDG3 – Good Health and Well-Being					
Maternal mortality rate (per 100,000 live births)		3	2017	●	↑
Neonatal mortality rate (per 1,000 live births)		3.6	2020	●	↑
Mortality rate, under-5 (per 1,000 live births)		6.6	2020	●	↑
Incidence of tuberculosis (per 100,000 population)		0.8	2020	●	↑
New HIV infections (per 1,000 uninfected population)		0.1	2020	●	↑
Age-standardized death rate due to cardiovascular disease, cancer, diabetes, or chronic respiratory disease in adults aged 30–70 years (%)		18.5	2019	●	↑
Age-standardized death rate attributable to household air pollution and ambient air pollution (per 100,000 population)		55	2016	●	●
Traffic deaths (per 100,000 population)		8.9	2019	●	↑
Life expectancy at birth (years)		76.1	2019	●	↗
Adolescent fertility rate (births per 1,000 females aged 15 to 19)		3.8	2018	●	↑
Births attended by skilled health personnel (%)		99.9	2015	●	●
Surviving infants who received 2 WHO-recommended vaccines (%)		90	2020	●	↑
Universal health coverage (UHC) index of service coverage (worst 0–100 best)		78	2019	●	→
Subjective well-being (average ladder score, worst 0–10 best)		6.7	2021	●	↑
SDG4 – Quality Education					
Participation rate in pre-primary organized learning (% of children aged 4 to 6)		99.7	2020	●	↑
Net primary enrollment rate (%)		99.8	2020	●	↑
Lower secondary completion rate (%)		96.9	2020	●	↑
Literacy rate (% of population aged 15 to 24)		98.2	2019	●	●
SDG5 – Gender Equality					
Demand for family planning satisfied by modern methods (% of females aged 15 to 49)		NA	NA	●	●
Ratio of female-to-male mean years of education received (%)		94.4	2019	●	↓
Ratio of female-to-male labor force participation rate (%)		52.4	2020	●	↓
Seats held by women in national parliament (%)		50.0	2020	●	↑
SDG6 – Clean Water and Sanitation					
Population using at least basic drinking water services (%)		100.0	2020	●	↑
Population using at least basic sanitation services (%)		99.2	2020	●	↑
Freshwater withdrawal (% of available freshwater resources)		1667.3	2018	●	●
Anthropogenic wastewater that receives treatment (%)		76.8	2018	●	●
Scarce water consumption embodied in imports (m^3 H_2O eq/capita)		26346.4	2018	●	●
SDG7 – Affordable and Clean Energy					
Population with access to electricity (%)		100.0	2019	●	↑
Population with access to clean fuels and technology for cooking (%)		100.0	2019	●	↑
CO_2 emissions from fuel combustion per total electricity output ($MtCO_2$/TWh)		1.4	2019	●	↑
Share of renewable energy in total primary energy supply (%)		0.8	2019	●	→
SDG8 – Decent Work and Economic Growth					
Adjusted GDP growth (%)		-1.9	2020	●	●
Victims of modern slavery (per 1,000 population)	*	NA	NA	●	●
Adults with an account at a bank or other financial institution or with a mobile-money-service provider (% of population aged 15 or over)		88.2	2017	●	↑
Unemployment rate (% of total labor force)		3.3	2022	●	↑
Fundamental labor rights are effectively guaranteed (worst 0–1 best)		0.4	2020	●	↓
Fatal work-related accidents embodied in imports (per 100,000 population)		4.0	2015	●	↗

* Imputed data point

SDG9 – Industry, Innovation and Infrastructure	Value	Year	Rating	Trend
Population using the internet (%)	100.0	2020	●	↑
Mobile broadband subscriptions (per 100 population)	239.9	2019	●	↑
Logistics Performance Index: Quality of trade and transport-related infrastructure (worst 1–5 best)	4.0	2018	●	↑
The Times Higher Education Universities Ranking: Average score of top 3 universities (worst 0–100 best)	44.2	2022	●	●
Articles published in academic journals (per 1,000 population)	1.0	2020	●	↑
Expenditure on research and development (% of GDP)	1.3	2018	●	↑
SDG10 – Reduced Inequalities				
Gini coefficient	26.0	2018	●	●
Palma ratio	1.2	2018	●	●
SDG11 – Sustainable Cities and Communities				
Proportion of urban population living in slums (%)	NA	NA	●	●
Annual mean concentration of particulate matter of less than 2.5 microns in diameter (PM2.5) (μg/m^3)	41.7	2019	●	→
Access to improved water source, piped (% of urban population)	NA	NA	●	●
Satisfaction with public transport (%)	84.0	2021	●	↑
SDG12 – Responsible Consumption and Production				
Municipal solid waste (kg/capita/day)	1.6	2019	●	●
Electronic waste (kg/capita)	15.0	2019	●	●
Production-based SO_2 emissions (kg/capita)	42.0	2018	●	●
SO_2 emissions embodied in imports (kg/capita)	19.1	2018	●	●
Production-based nitrogen emissions (kg/capita)	3.7	2015	●	↑
Nitrogen emissions embodied in imports (kg/capita)	18.9	2015	●	↓
Exports of plastic waste (kg/capita)	1.2	2020	●	●
SDG13 – Climate Action				
CO_2 emissions from fossil fuel combustion and cement production (tCO_2/capita)	15.2	2020	●	↑
CO_2 emissions embodied in imports (tCO_2/capita)	5.5	2018	●	↓
CO_2 emissions embodied in fossil fuel exports (kg/capita)	43151.2	2020	●	●
SDG14 – Life Below Water				
Mean area that is protected in marine sites important to biodiversity (%)	48.6	2020	●	→
Ocean Health Index: Clean Waters score (worst 0–100 best)	68.3	2020	●	→
Fish caught from overexploited or collapsed stocks (% of total catch)	49.5	2018	●	↓
Fish caught by trawling or dredging (%)	0.0	2018	●	↑
Fish caught that are then discarded (%)	0.5	2018	●	↑
Marine biodiversity threats embodied in imports (per million population)	1.0	2018	●	●
SDG15 – Life on Land				
Mean area that is protected in terrestrial sites important to biodiversity (%)	51.6	2020	●	↗
Mean area that is protected in freshwater sites important to biodiversity (%)	NA	NA	●	●
Red List Index of species survival (worst 0–1 best)	0.8	2021	●	↓
Permanent deforestation (% of forest area, 5-year average)	NA	NA	●	●
Terrestrial and freshwater biodiversity threats embodied in imports (per million population)	4.6	2018	●	●
SDG16 – Peace, Justice and Strong Institutions				
Homicides (per 100,000 population)	0.7	2019	●	↑
Unsentenced detainees (% of prison population)	38.2	2016	●	●
Population who feel safe walking alone at night in the city or area where they live (%)	92	2021	●	●
Property Rights (worst 1–7 best)	5.6	2020	●	↑
Birth registrations with civil authority (% of children under age 5)	100.0	2020	●	●
Corruption Perception Index (worst 0–100 best)	69	2021	●	↑
Children involved in child labor (% of population aged 5 to 14)	NA	NA	●	●
Exports of major conventional weapons (TIV constant million USD per 100,000 population)	1.3	2020	●	●
Press Freedom Index (best 0–100 worst)	43.1	2021	●	↓
Access to and affordability of justice (worst 0–1 best)	0.6	2020	●	↑
SDG17 – Partnerships for the Goals				
Government spending on health and education (% of GDP)	5.3	2019	●	●
For high-income and all OECD DAC countries: International concessional public finance, including official development assistance (% of GNI)	0.4	2021	●	↓
Other countries: Government revenue excluding grants (% of GDP)	NA	NA	●	●
Corporate Tax Haven Score (best 0–100 worst)	98.3	2019	●	●
Statistical Performance Index (worst 0–100 best)	59.7	2019	●	↑

5. Country Profiles

UNITED KINGDOM

OECD Countries

OVERALL PERFORMANCE

COUNTRY RANKING

UNITED KINGDOM

11 **/163**

COUNTRY SCORE

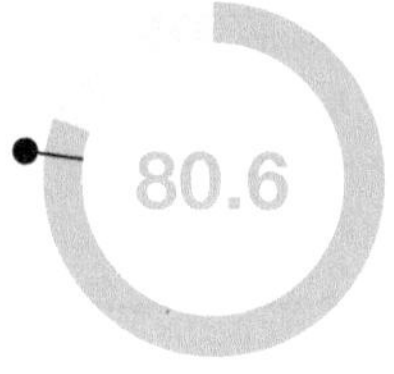

REGIONAL AVERAGE: 77.2

AVERAGE PERFORMANCE BY SDG

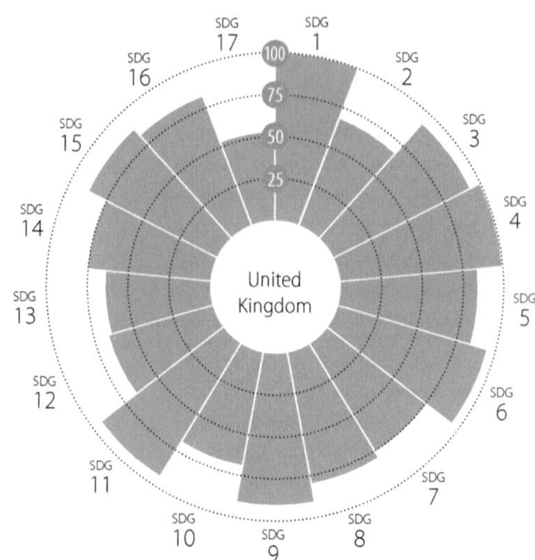

SDG DASHBOARDS AND TRENDS

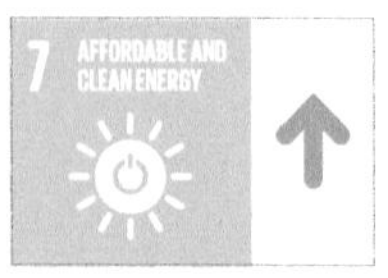

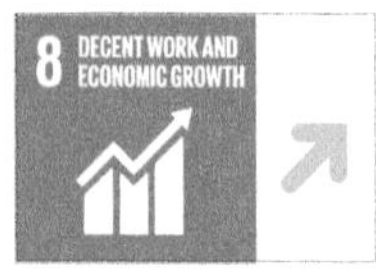

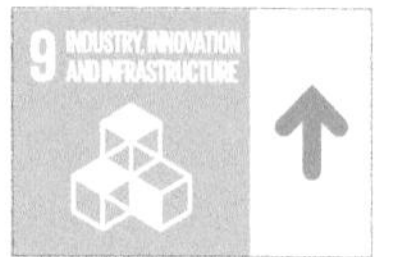

Major challenges | Significant challenges | Challenges remain | SDG achieved | Information unavailable

Decreasing | Stagnating | Moderately improving | On track or maintaining SDG achievement | Information unavailable

Note: The full title of each SDG is available here: https://sustainabledevelopment.un.org/topics/sustainabledevelopmentgoals

INTERNATIONAL SPILLOVER INDEX

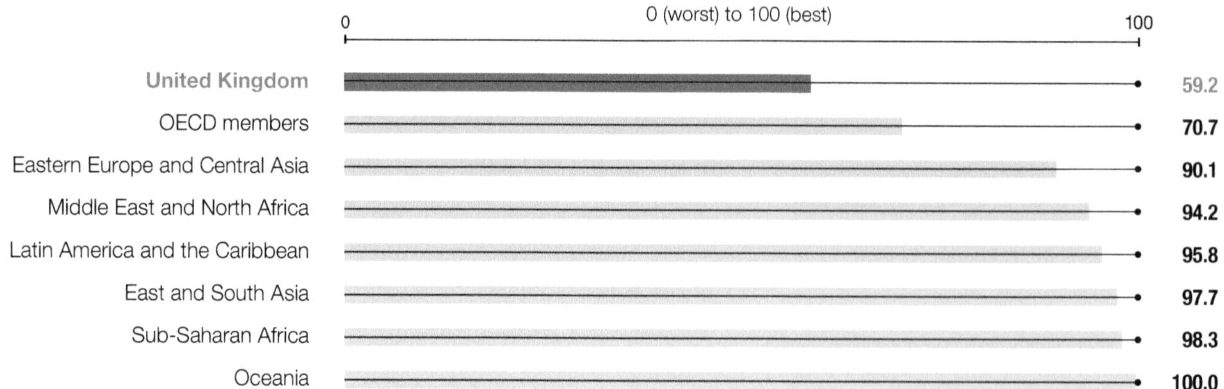

STATISTICAL PERFORMANCE INDEX

0 (worst) to 100 (best)

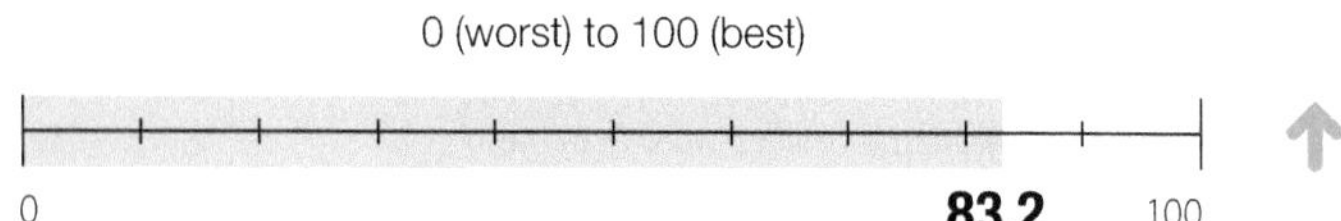

MISSING DATA IN SDG INDEX

2%

UNITED KINGDOM

Performance by Indicator

SDG1 – No Poverty	Value	Year	Rating	Trend
Poverty headcount ratio at \$1.90/day (%)	0.2	2022	●	↑
Poverty headcount ratio at \$3.20/day (%)	0.3	2022	●	↑
Poverty rate after taxes and transfers (%)	12.4	2019	●	↓

SDG2 – Zero Hunger	Value	Year	Rating	Trend
Prevalence of undernourishment (%)	2.5	2019	●	↑
Prevalence of stunting in children under 5 years of age (%)	* 2.6	2019	●	↑
Prevalence of wasting in children under 5 years of age (%)	* 0.7	2019	●	↑
Prevalence of obesity, BMI ≥ 30 (% of adult population)	27.8	2016	●	↓
Human Trophic Level (best 2–3 worst)	2.4	2017	●	→
Cereal yield (tonnes per hectare of harvested land)	6.8	2018	●	↑
Sustainable Nitrogen Management Index (best 0–1.41 worst)	0.6	2015	●	↓
Yield gap closure (% of potential yield)	67.8	2018	●	●
Exports of hazardous pesticides (tonnes per million population)	60.6	2019	●	●

SDG3 – Good Health and Well-Being	Value	Year	Rating	Trend
Maternal mortality rate (per 100,000 live births)	7	2017	●	↑
Neonatal mortality rate (per 1,000 live births)	2.7	2020	●	↑
Mortality rate, under-5 (per 1,000 live births)	4.2	2020	●	↑
Incidence of tuberculosis (per 100,000 population)	6.9	2020	●	↑
New HIV infections (per 1,000 uninfected population)	1.0	2020	●	→
Age-standardized death rate due to cardiovascular disease, cancer, diabetes, or chronic respiratory disease in adults aged 30–70 years (%)	10.3	2019	●	↑
Age-standardized death rate attributable to household air pollution and ambient air pollution (per 100,000 population)	14	2016	●	●
Traffic deaths (per 100,000 population)	3.2	2019	●	↑
Life expectancy at birth (years)	81.4	2019	●	↑
Adolescent fertility rate (births per 1,000 females aged 15 to 19)	11.9	2018	●	↑
Births attended by skilled health personnel (%)	NA	NA	●	●
Surviving infants who received 2 WHO-recommended vaccines (%)	91	2020	●	↑
Universal health coverage (UHC) index of service coverage (worst 0–100 best)	88	2019	●	↑
Subjective well-being (average ladder score, worst 0–10 best)	6.9	2021	●	↑
Gap in life expectancy at birth among regions (years)	3.6	2018	●	↓
Gap in self-reported health status by income (percentage points)	20.4	2019	●	↑
Daily smokers (% of population aged 15 and over)	15.8	2019	●	↑

SDG4 – Quality Education	Value	Year	Rating	Trend
Participation rate in pre-primary organized learning (% of children aged 4 to 6)	100.0	2019	●	↑
Net primary enrollment rate (%)	98.9	2019	●	↑
Lower secondary completion rate (%)	100.0	2019	●	●
Literacy rate (% of population aged 15 to 24)	NA	NA	●	●
Tertiary educational attainment (% of population aged 25 to 34)	55.8	2020	●	↑
PISA score (worst 0–600 best)	503.7	2018	●	↑
Variation in science performance explained by socio-economic status (%)	10.7	2018	●	↓
Underachievers in science (% of 15-year-olds)	17.4	2018	●	→

SDG5 – Gender Equality	Value	Year	Rating	Trend
Demand for family planning satisfied by modern methods (% of females aged 15 to 49)	86.5	2012	●	●
Ratio of female-to-male mean years of education received (%)	100.0	2019	●	↑
Ratio of female-to-male labor force participation rate (%)	87.3	2020	●	↑
Seats held by women in national parliament (%)	33.8	2020	●	↑
Gender wage gap (% of male median wage)	12.3	2020	●	↑

SDG6 – Clean Water and Sanitation	Value	Year	Rating	Trend
Population using at least basic drinking water services (%)	100.0	2020	●	↑
Population using at least basic sanitation services (%)	99.1	2020	●	↑
Freshwater withdrawal (% of available freshwater resources)	14.4	2018	●	●
Anthropogenic wastewater that receives treatment (%)	98.5	2018	●	●
Scarce water consumption embodied in imports (m^3 H_2O eq/capita)	2688.5	2018	●	●
Population using safely managed water services (%)	99.8	2020	●	↑
Population using safely managed sanitation services (%)	98.1	2020	●	↑

SDG7 – Affordable and Clean Energy	Value	Year	Rating	Trend
Population with access to electricity (%)	100.0	2019	●	↑
Population with access to clean fuels and technology for cooking (%)	100.0	2019	●	↑
CO_2 emissions from fuel combustion per total electricity output ($MtCO_2$/TWh)	1.1	2019	●	↑
Share of renewable energy in total primary energy supply (%)	12.2	2019	●	↑

SDG8 – Decent Work and Economic Growth	Value	Year	Rating	Trend
Adjusted GDP growth (%)	-2.2	2020	●	●
Victims of modern slavery (per 1,000 population)	2.1	2018	●	●
Adults with an account at a bank or other financial institution or with a mobile-money-service provider (% of population aged 15 or over)	96.4	2017	●	↑
Fundamental labor rights are effectively guaranteed (worst 0–1 best)	0.7	2020	●	↓
Fatal work-related accidents embodied in imports (per 100,000 population)	1.5	2015	●	↑
Employment-to-population ratio (%)	75.2	2021	●	↑
Youth not in employment, education or training (NEET) (% of population aged 15 to 29)	11.8	2021	●	↑

* Imputed data point

SDG9 – Industry, Innovation and Infrastructure	Value	Year	Rating	Trend
Population using the internet (%)	94.8	2020	●	↑
Mobile broadband subscriptions (per 100 population)	103.8	2019	●	↑
Logistics Performance Index: Quality of trade and transport-related infrastructure (worst 1–5 best)	4.0	2018	●	↑
The Times Higher Education Universities Ranking: Average score of top 3 universities (worst 0–100 best)	93.2	2022	●	●
Articles published in academic journals (per 1,000 population)	2.9	2020	●	↑
Expenditure on research and development (% of GDP)	1.7	2018	●	↑
Researchers (per 1,000 employed population)	9.7	2019	●	↑
Triadic patent families filed (per million population)	25.0	2019	●	↑
Gap in internet access by income (percentage points)	36.5	2008	●	●
Female share of graduates from STEM fields at the tertiary level (%)	38.1	2016	●	↑

SDG10 – Reduced Inequalities	Value	Year	Rating	Trend
Gini coefficient	35.1	2017	●	↓
Palma ratio	1.6	2019	●	↓
Elderly poverty rate (% of population aged 66 or over)	15.5	2019	●	↓

SDG11 – Sustainable Cities and Communities	Value	Year	Rating	Trend
Proportion of urban population living in slums (%)	* 0.0	2018	●	↑
Annual mean concentration of particulate matter of less than 2.5 microns in diameter (PM2.5) (μg/m^3)	10.0	2019	●	↑
Access to improved water source, piped (% of urban population)	100.0	2020	●	↑
Satisfaction with public transport (%)	68.0	2021	●	↓
Population with rent overburden (%)	12.9	2018	●	↓

SDG12 – Responsible Consumption and Production	Value	Year	Rating	Trend
Electronic waste (kg/capita)	23.9	2019	●	●
Production-based SO_2 emissions (kg/capita)	8.1	2018	●	●
SO_2 emissions embodied in imports (kg/capita)	7.9	2018	●	●
Production-based nitrogen emissions (kg/capita)	12.4	2015	●	↑
Nitrogen emissions embodied in imports (kg/capita)	13.3	2015	●	↓
Exports of plastic waste (kg/capita)	4.8	2021	●	●
Non-recycled municipal solid waste (kg/capita/day)	0.7	2018	●	↑

SDG13 – Climate Action	Value	Year	Rating	Trend
CO_2 emissions from fossil fuel combustion and cement production (tCO_2/capita)	4.9	2020	●	↑
CO_2 emissions embodied in imports (tCO_2/capita)	2.6	2018	●	↑
CO_2 emissions embodied in fossil fuel exports (kg/capita)	1425.2	2021	●	●
Carbon Pricing Score at EUR60/tCO_2 (%, worst 0–100 best)	46.9	2018	●	↗

SDG14 – Life Below Water	Value	Year	Rating	Trend
Mean area that is protected in marine sites important to biodiversity (%)	85.3	2020	●	↑
Ocean Health Index: Clean Waters score (worst 0–100 best)	64.1	2020	●	→
Fish caught from overexploited or collapsed stocks (% of total catch)	24.8	2018	●	↑
Fish caught by trawling or dredging (%)	23.7	2018	●	↓
Fish caught that are then discarded (%)	4.2	2018	●	↑
Marine biodiversity threats embodied in imports (per million population)	0.2	2018	●	●

SDG15 – Life on Land	Value	Year	Rating	Trend
Mean area that is protected in terrestrial sites important to biodiversity (%)	86.4	2020	●	↑
Mean area that is protected in freshwater sites important to biodiversity (%)	91.2	2020	●	↑
Red List Index of species survival (worst 0–1 best)	1.0	2021	●	↑
Permanent deforestation (% of forest area, 5-year average)	0.0	2020	●	↑
Terrestrial and freshwater biodiversity threats embodied in imports (per million population)	3.2	2018	●	●

SDG16 – Peace, Justice and Strong Institutions	Value	Year	Rating	Trend
Homicides (per 100,000 population)	1.9	2002	●	●
Unsentenced detainees (% of prison population)	9.0	2018	●	↑
Population who feel safe walking alone at night in the city or area where they live (%)	68	2021	●	↓
Property Rights (worst 1–7 best)	5.3	2020	●	↑
Birth registrations with civil authority (% of children under age 5)	100.0	2020	●	●
Corruption Perception Index (worst 0–100 best)	78	2021	●	↑
Children involved in child labor (% of population aged 5 to 14)	* 0.0	2019	●	●
Exports of major conventional weapons (TIV constant million USD per 100,000 population)	1.4	2020	●	●
Press Freedom Index (best 0–100 worst)	21.6	2021	●	↑
Access to and affordability of justice (worst 0–1 best)	0.5	2020	●	↓
Persons held in prison (per 100,000 population)	137.1	2018	●	↗

SDG17 – Partnerships for the Goals	Value	Year	Rating	Trend
Government spending on health and education (% of GDP)	13.3	2019	●	↑
For high-income and all OECD DAC countries: International concessional public finance, including official development assistance (% of GNI)	0.5	2021	●	↓
Other countries: Government revenue excluding grants (% of GDP)	NA	NA	●	●
Corporate Tax Haven Score (best 0–100 worst)	100.0	2019	●	●
Financial Secrecy Score (best 0–100 worst)	70.8	2020	●	●
Shifted profits of multinationals (US\$ billion)	-41.2	2018	●	●
Statistical Performance Index (worst 0–100 best)	83.2	2019	●	↑

UNITED STATES

OECD Countries

OVERALL PERFORMANCE

COUNTRY RANKING

UNITED STATES

41 /163

COUNTRY SCORE

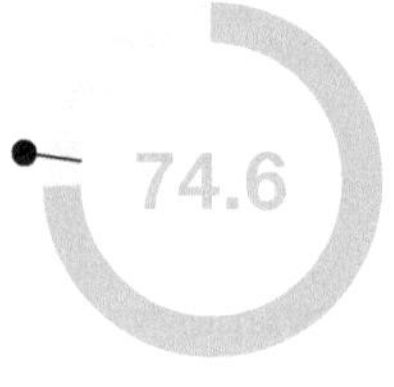

REGIONAL AVERAGE: 77.2

AVERAGE PERFORMANCE BY SDG

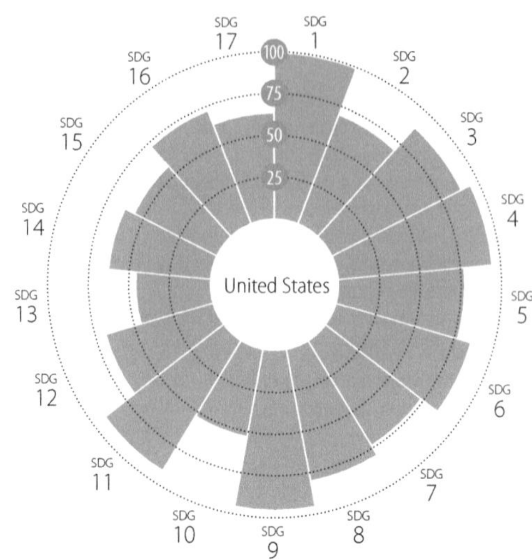

SDG DASHBOARDS AND TRENDS

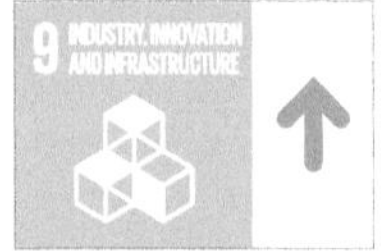

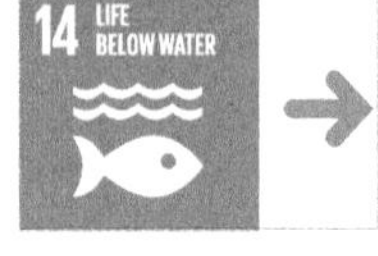

Major challenges | Significant challenges | Challenges remain | SDG achieved | Information unavailable

Decreasing | Stagnating | Moderately improving | On track or maintaining SDG achievement | Information unavailable

Note: The full title of each SDG is available here: https://sustainabledevelopment.un.org/topics/sustainabledevelopmentgoals

INTERNATIONAL SPILLOVER INDEX

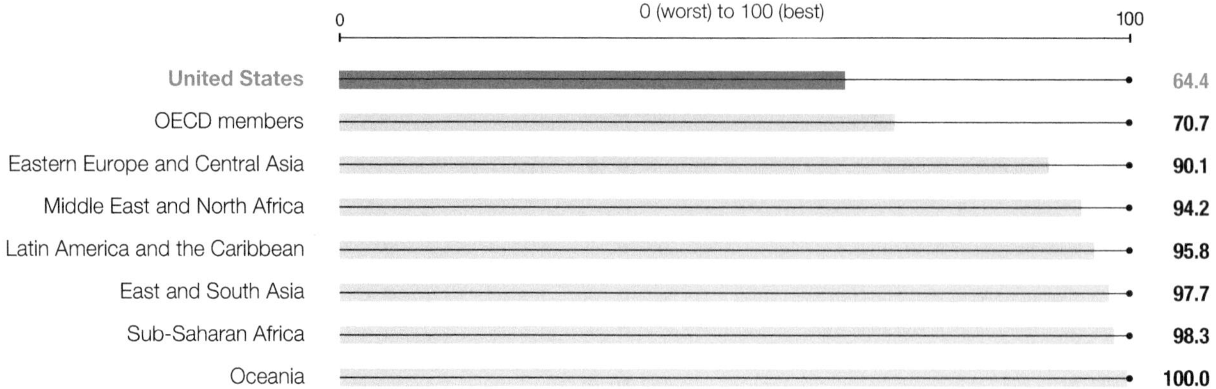

STATISTICAL PERFORMANCE INDEX

0 (worst) to 100 (best)

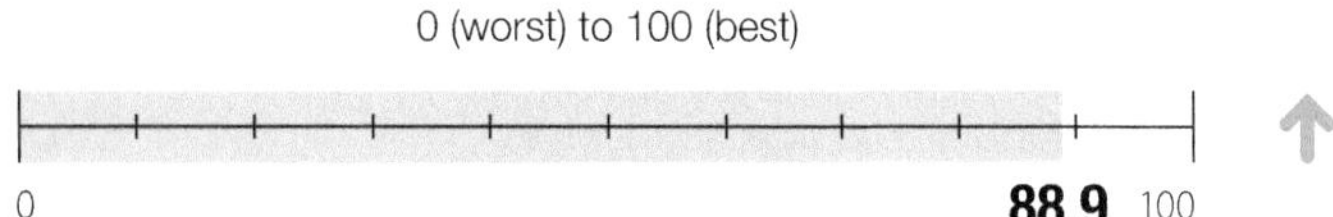

MISSING DATA IN SDG INDEX

2%

UNITED STATES

Performance by Indicator

SDG1 – No Poverty

Indicator	Value	Year	Rating	Trend
Poverty headcount ratio at \$1.90/day (%)	0.4	2022	●	↑
Poverty headcount ratio at \$3.20/day (%)	0.6	2022	●	↑
Poverty rate after taxes and transfers (%)	18.0	2019	●	↓

SDG2 – Zero Hunger

Indicator	Value	Year	Rating	Trend
Prevalence of undernourishment (%)	2.5	2019	●	↑
Prevalence of stunting in children under 5 years of age (%)	3.4	2018	●	↑
Prevalence of wasting in children under 5 years of age (%)	0.1	2018	●	↑
Prevalence of obesity, BMI ≥ 30 (% of adult population)	36.2	2016	●	↓
Human Trophic Level (best 2–3 worst)	2.5	2017	●	↓
Cereal yield (tonnes per hectare of harvested land)	8.7	2018	●	↑
Sustainable Nitrogen Management Index (best 0–1.41 worst)	0.3	2015	●	→
Yield gap closure (% of potential yield)	68.0	2018	●	●
Exports of hazardous pesticides (tonnes per million population)	18.6	2019	●	●

SDG3 – Good Health and Well-Being

Indicator	Value	Year	Rating	Trend
Maternal mortality rate (per 100,000 live births)	19	2017	●	↑
Neonatal mortality rate (per 1,000 live births)	3.4	2020	●	↑
Mortality rate, under-5 (per 1,000 live births)	6.3	2020	●	↑
Incidence of tuberculosis (per 100,000 population)	2.4	2020	●	↑
New HIV infections (per 1,000 uninfected population)	1.0	2020	●	↓
Age-standardized death rate due to cardiovascular disease, cancer, diabetes, or chronic respiratory disease in adults aged 30–70 years (%)	13.6	2019	●	↑
Age-standardized death rate attributable to household air pollution and ambient air pollution (per 100,000 population)	13	2016	●	●
Traffic deaths (per 100,000 population)	12.7	2019	●	↓
Life expectancy at birth (years)	78.5	2019	●	↓
Adolescent fertility rate (births per 1,000 females aged 15 to 19)	17.4	2018	●	↑
Births attended by skilled health personnel (%)	99.1	2018	●	↑
Surviving infants who received 2 WHO-recommended vaccines (%)	91	2020	●	↑
Universal health coverage (UHC) index of service coverage (worst 0–100 best)	83	2019	●	↑
Subjective well-being (average ladder score, worst 0–10 best)	7.0	2021	●	↑
Gap in life expectancy at birth among regions (years)	6.3	2010	●	●
Gap in self-reported health status by income (percentage points)	24.2	2019	●	↓
Daily smokers (% of population aged 15 and over)	10.9	2019	●	↑

SDG4 – Quality Education

Indicator	Value	Year	Rating	Trend
Participation rate in pre-primary organized learning (% of children aged 4 to 6)	89.8	2019	●	↓
Net primary enrollment rate (%)	99.1	2019	●	↑
Lower secondary completion rate (%)	103.4	2019	●	●
Literacy rate (% of population aged 15 to 24)	NA	NA	●	●
Tertiary educational attainment (% of population aged 25 to 34)	51.9	2020	●	↑
PISA score (worst 0–600 best)	495.0	2018	●	↑
Variation in science performance explained by socio-economic status (%)	12.3	2018	●	↓
Underachievers in science (% of 15-year-olds)	18.6	2018	●	↑

SDG5 – Gender Equality

Indicator	Value	Year	Rating	Trend
Demand for family planning satisfied by modern methods (% of females aged 15 to 49)	78.4	2019	●	●
Ratio of female-to-male mean years of education received (%)	100.7	2019	●	↑
Ratio of female-to-male labor force participation rate (%)	83.2	2020	●	↑
Seats held by women in national parliament (%)	27.5	2020	●	↑
Gender wage gap (% of male median wage)	17.7	2020	●	→

SDG6 – Clean Water and Sanitation

Indicator	Value	Year	Rating	Trend
Population using at least basic drinking water services (%)	99.9	2020	●	↑
Population using at least basic sanitation services (%)	99.7	2020	●	↑
Freshwater withdrawal (% of available freshwater resources)	28.2	2018	●	●
Anthropogenic wastewater that receives treatment (%)	58.9	2018	●	●
Scarce water consumption embodied in imports (m^3 H_2O eq/capita)	1741.3	2018	●	●
Population using safely managed water services (%)	97.3	2020	●	↑
Population using safely managed sanitation services (%)	98.3	2020	●	↑

SDG7 – Affordable and Clean Energy

Indicator	Value	Year	Rating	Trend
Population with access to electricity (%)	100.0	2019	●	↑
Population with access to clean fuels and technology for cooking (%)	100.0	2019	●	↑
CO_2 emissions from fuel combustion per total electricity output ($MtCO_2$/TWh)	1.2	2019	●	↗
Share of renewable energy in total primary energy supply (%)	7.9	2019	●	→

SDG8 – Decent Work and Economic Growth

Indicator	Value	Year	Rating	Trend
Adjusted GDP growth (%)	0.0	2020	●	●
Victims of modern slavery (per 1,000 population)	1.3	2018	●	●
Adults with an account at a bank or other financial institution or with a mobile-money-service provider (% of population aged 15 or over)	93.1	2017	●	↑
Fundamental labor rights are effectively guaranteed (worst 0–1 best)	0.6	2020	●	↓
Fatal work-related accidents embodied in imports (per 100,000 population)	1.1	2015	●	↑
Employment-to-population ratio (%)	69.4	2021	●	↑
Youth not in employment, education or training (NEET) (% of population aged 15 to 29)	13.4	2020	●	↑

* Imputed data point

SDG9 – Industry, Innovation and Infrastructure

Indicator	Value	Year	Rating	Trend
Population using the internet (%)	90.9	2020	●	↑
Mobile broadband subscriptions (per 100 population)	149.8	2019	●	↑
Logistics Performance Index: Quality of trade and transport-related infrastructure (worst 1–5 best)	4.0	2018	●	↑
The Times Higher Education Universities Ranking: Average score of top 3 universities (worst 0–100 best)	95.0	2022	●	●
Articles published in academic journals (per 1,000 population)	1.9	2020	●	↑
Expenditure on research and development (% of GDP)	2.8	2018	●	↑
Researchers (per 1,000 employed population)	9.8	2018	●	↑
Triadic patent families filed (per million population)	39.1	2019	●	↑
Gap in internet access by income (percentage points)	26.9	2019	●	↑
Female share of graduates from STEM fields at the tertiary level (%)	34.0	2016	●	↑

SDG10 – Reduced Inequalities

Indicator	Value	Year	Rating	Trend
Gini coefficient	41.4	2018	●	↓
Palma ratio	1.8	2019	●	↓
Elderly poverty rate (% of population aged 66 or over)	23.0	2019	●	↓

SDG11 – Sustainable Cities and Communities

Indicator	Value	Year	Rating	Trend
Proportion of urban population living in slums (%)	* 0.0	2018	●	↑
Annual mean concentration of particulate matter of less than 2.5 microns in diameter (PM2.5) (μg/m^3)	6.8	2019	●	↑
Access to improved water source, piped (% of urban population)	99.6	2020	●	↑
Satisfaction with public transport (%)	60.0	2021	●	↗
Population with rent overburden (%)	11.0	2019	●	↗

SDG12 – Responsible Consumption and Production

Indicator	Value	Year	Rating	Trend
Electronic waste (kg/capita)	21.0	2019	●	●
Production-based SO_2 emissions (kg/capita)	30.4	2018	●	●
SO_2 emissions embodied in imports (kg/capita)	8.4	2018	●	●
Production-based nitrogen emissions (kg/capita)	24.3	2015	●	↓
Nitrogen emissions embodied in imports (kg/capita)	7.5	2015	●	→
Exports of plastic waste (kg/capita)	0.5	2021	●	●
Non-recycled municipal solid waste (kg/capita/day)	1.5	2018	●	↓

SDG13 – Climate Action

Indicator	Value	Year	Rating	Trend
CO_2 emissions from fossil fuel combustion and cement production (tCO_2/capita)	14.2	2020	●	↗
CO_2 emissions embodied in imports (tCO_2/capita)	2.8	2018	●	→
CO_2 emissions embodied in fossil fuel exports (kg/capita)	2409.5	2021	●	●
Carbon Pricing Score at EUR60/tCO_2 (%, worst 0–100 best)	22.1	2018	●	●

SDG14 – Life Below Water

Indicator	Value	Year	Rating	Trend
Mean area that is protected in marine sites important to biodiversity (%)	31.8	2020	●	→
Ocean Health Index: Clean Waters score (worst 0–100 best)	72.7	2020	●	→
Fish caught from overexploited or collapsed stocks (% of total catch)	22.1	2018	●	↑
Fish caught by trawling or dredging (%)	19.0	2018	●	↓
Fish caught that are then discarded (%)	10.5	2018	●	→
Marine biodiversity threats embodied in imports (per million population)	0.5	2018	●	●

SDG15 – Life on Land

Indicator	Value	Year	Rating	Trend
Mean area that is protected in terrestrial sites important to biodiversity (%)	34.9	2020	●	→
Mean area that is protected in freshwater sites important to biodiversity (%)	28.6	2020	●	→
Red List Index of species survival (worst 0–1 best)	0.8	2021	●	↓
Permanent deforestation (% of forest area, 5-year average)	0.1	2020	●	↑
Terrestrial and freshwater biodiversity threats embodied in imports (per million population)	3.7	2018	●	●

SDG16 – Peace, Justice and Strong Institutions

Indicator	Value	Year	Rating	Trend
Homicides (per 100,000 population)	6.3	2020	●	→
Unsentenced detainees (% of prison population)	24.3	2019	●	↑
Population who feel safe walking alone at night in the city or area where they live (%)	73	2021	●	↑
Property Rights (worst 1–7 best)	5.5	2020	●	↑
Birth registrations with civil authority (% of children under age 5)	100.0	2020	●	●
Corruption Perception Index (worst 0–100 best)	67	2021	●	↑
Children involved in child labor (% of population aged 5 to 14)	* 0.0	2019	●	●
Exports of major conventional weapons (TIV constant million USD per 100,000 population)	3.1	2020	●	●
Press Freedom Index (best 0–100 worst)	23.9	2021	●	↑
Access to and affordability of justice (worst 0–1 best)	0.4	2020	●	→
Persons held in prison (per 100,000 population)	630.1	2019	●	→

SDG17 – Partnerships for the Goals

Indicator	Value	Year	Rating	Trend
Government spending on health and education (% of GDP)	NA	NA	●	●
For high-income and all OECD DAC countries: International concessional public finance, including official development assistance (% of GNI)	0.2	2021	●	→
Other countries: Government revenue excluding grants (% of GDP)	NA	NA	●	●
Corporate Tax Haven Score (best 0–100 worst)	43.2	2019	●	●
Financial Secrecy Score (best 0–100 worst)	70.0	2020	●	●
Shifted profits of multinationals (US\$ billion)	186.4	2018	●	↑
Statistical Performance Index (worst 0–100 best)	88.9	2019	●	↑

5. Country Profiles

URUGUAY

Latin America and the Caribbean

OVERALL PERFORMANCE

COUNTRY RANKING

URUGUAY

31 /163

COUNTRY SCORE

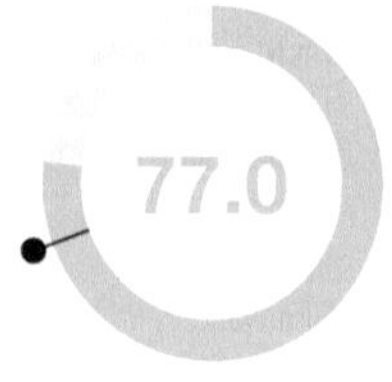

REGIONAL AVERAGE: 69.5

AVERAGE PERFORMANCE BY SDG

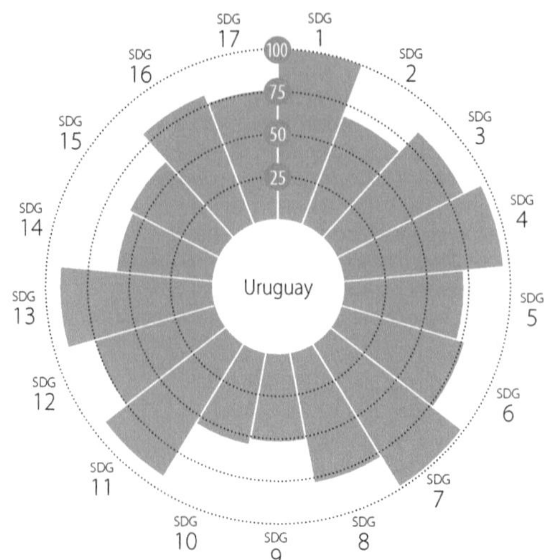

SDG DASHBOARDS AND TRENDS

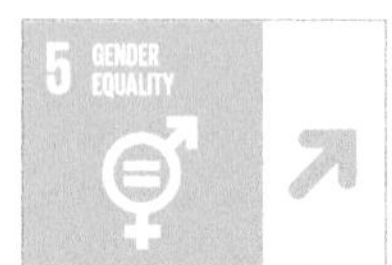

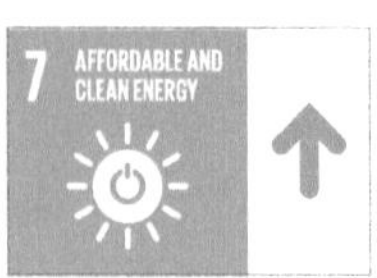

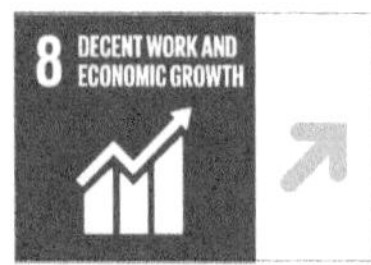

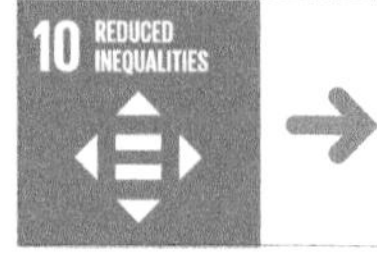

■ Major challenges ■ Significant challenges ■ Challenges remain ■ SDG achieved ■ Information unavailable

↓ Decreasing → Stagnating ↗ Moderately improving ↑ On track or maintaining SDG achievement ● Information unavailable

Note: The full title of each SDG is available here: https://sustainabledevelopment.un.org/topics/sustainabledevelopmentgoals

INTERNATIONAL SPILLOVER INDEX

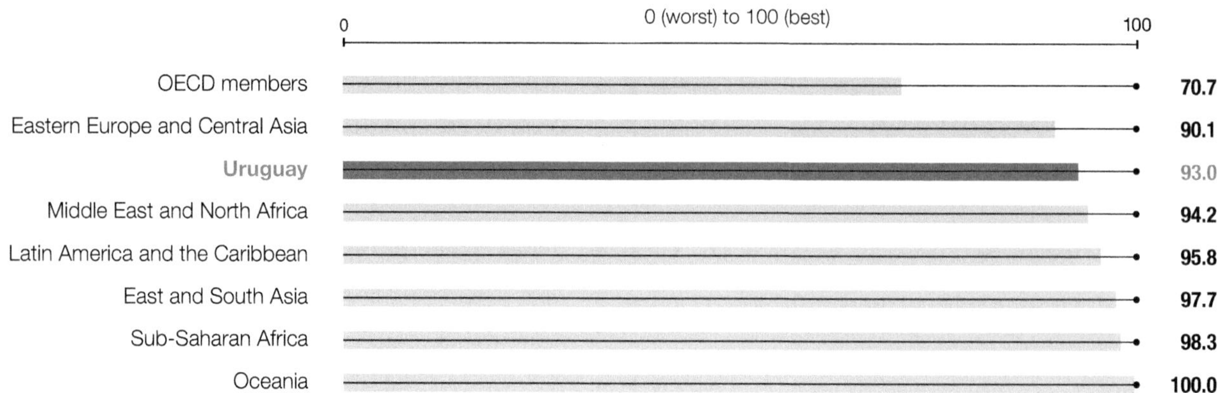

STATISTICAL PERFORMANCE INDEX

0 (worst) to 100 (best)

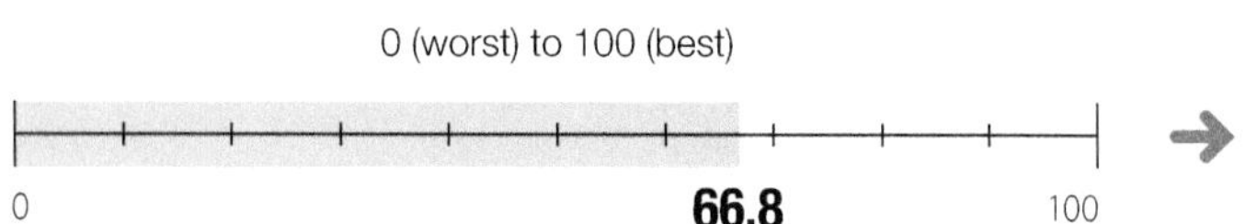

MISSING DATA IN SDG INDEX

3%

SDG1 – No Poverty

Indicator	Value	Year	Rating	Trend
Poverty headcount ratio at $1.90/day (%)	0.0	2022	●	↑
Poverty headcount ratio at $3.20/day (%)	0.1	2022	●	↑

SDG2 – Zero Hunger

Indicator	Value	Year	Rating	Trend
Prevalence of undernourishment (%)	2.5	2019	●	↑
Prevalence of stunting in children under 5 years of age (%)	6.9	2018	●	↑
Prevalence of wasting in children under 5 years of age (%)	1.4	2018	●	↑
Prevalence of obesity, BMI ≥ 30 (% of adult population)	27.9	2016	●	↓
Human Trophic Level (best 2–3 worst)	2.4	2017	●	↗
Cereal yield (tonnes per hectare of harvested land)	5.0	2018	●	↑
Sustainable Nitrogen Management Index (best 0–1.41 worst)	0.5	2015	●	↓
Exports of hazardous pesticides (tonnes per million population)	0.6	2019	●	●

SDG3 – Good Health and Well-Being

Indicator	Value	Year	Rating	Trend
Maternal mortality rate (per 100,000 live births)	17	2017	●	↑
Neonatal mortality rate (per 1,000 live births)	4.1	2020	●	↑
Mortality rate, under-5 (per 1,000 live births)	6.2	2020	●	↑
Incidence of tuberculosis (per 100,000 population)	32.0	2020	●	→
New HIV infections (per 1,000 uninfected population)	0.2	2020	●	↑
Age-standardized death rate due to cardiovascular disease, cancer, diabetes, or chronic respiratory disease in adults aged 30–70 years (%)	16.5	2019	●	↑
Age-standardized death rate attributable to household air pollution and ambient air pollution (per 100,000 population)	18	2016	●	●
Traffic deaths (per 100,000 population)	14.8	2019	●	→
Life expectancy at birth (years)	77.1	2019	●	→
Adolescent fertility rate (births per 1,000 females aged 15 to 19)	35.8	2018	●	↑
Births attended by skilled health personnel (%)	100.0	2017	●	↑
Surviving infants who received 2 WHO-recommended vaccines (%)	92	2020	●	↑
Universal health coverage (UHC) index of service coverage (worst 0–100 best)	79	2019	●	↑
Subjective well-being (average ladder score, worst 0–10 best)	6.5	2021	●	↑

SDG4 – Quality Education

Indicator	Value	Year	Rating	Trend
Participation rate in pre-primary organized learning (% of children aged 4 to 6)	95.6	2019	●	↑
Net primary enrollment rate (%)	99.4	2019	●	↑
Lower secondary completion rate (%)	94.6	2019	●	●
Literacy rate (% of population aged 15 to 24)	99.0	2019	●	↑

SDG5 – Gender Equality

Indicator	Value	Year	Rating	Trend
Demand for family planning satisfied by modern methods (% of females aged 15 to 49)	NA	NA	●	●
Ratio of female-to-male mean years of education received (%)	107.0	2019	●	↑
Ratio of female-to-male labor force participation rate (%)	79.0	2020	●	↑
Seats held by women in national parliament (%)	21.2	2020	●	↗

SDG6 – Clean Water and Sanitation

Indicator	Value	Year	Rating	Trend
Population using at least basic drinking water services (%)	99.5	2020	●	↑
Population using at least basic sanitation services (%)	98.1	2020	●	↑
Freshwater withdrawal (% of available freshwater resources)	9.8	2018	●	●
Anthropogenic wastewater that receives treatment (%)	2.2	2018	●	●
Scarce water consumption embodied in imports (m^3 H_2O eq/capita)	2066.5	2018	●	●

SDG7 – Affordable and Clean Energy

Indicator	Value	Year	Rating	Trend
Population with access to electricity (%)	99.9	2019	●	↑
Population with access to clean fuels and technology for cooking (%)	100.0	2019	●	↑
CO_2 emissions from fuel combustion per total electricity output ($MtCO_2$/TWh)	0.5	2019	●	↑
Share of renewable energy in total primary energy supply (%)	63.4	2019	●	↑

SDG8 – Decent Work and Economic Growth

Indicator	Value	Year	Rating	Trend
Adjusted GDP growth (%)	-3.7	2020	●	●
Victims of modern slavery (per 1,000 population)	1.0	2018	●	●
Adults with an account at a bank or other financial institution or with a mobile-money-service provider (% of population aged 15 or over)	63.9	2017	●	↑
Unemployment rate (% of total labor force)	10.3	2022	●	↓
Fundamental labor rights are effectively guaranteed (worst 0–1 best)	0.8	2020	●	↑
Fatal work-related accidents embodied in imports (per 100,000 population)	0.5	2015	●	↑

* Imputed data point

SDG9 – Industry, Innovation and Infrastructure

Indicator	Value	Year	Rating	Trend
Population using the internet (%)	86.1	2020	●	↑
Mobile broadband subscriptions (per 100 population)	101.1	2019	●	↑
Logistics Performance Index: Quality of trade and transport-related infrastructure (worst 1–5 best)	2.4	2018	●	↓
The Times Higher Education Universities Ranking: Average score of top 3 universities (worst 0–100 best)	* 12.0	2019	●	●
Articles published in academic journals (per 1,000 population)	0.5	2020	●	↑
Expenditure on research and development (% of GDP)	0.4	2018	●	→

SDG10 – Reduced Inequalities

Indicator	Value	Year	Rating	Trend
Gini coefficient	39.7	2019	●	→
Palma ratio	1.8	2018	●	●

SDG11 – Sustainable Cities and Communities

Indicator	Value	Year	Rating	Trend
Proportion of urban population living in slums (%)	NA	NA	●	●
Annual mean concentration of particulate matter of less than 2.5 microns in diameter (PM2.5) (μg/m^3)	8.7	2019	●	↑
Access to improved water source, piped (% of urban population)	100.0	2020	●	↑
Satisfaction with public transport (%)	68.0	2021	●	↑

SDG12 – Responsible Consumption and Production

Indicator	Value	Year	Rating	Trend
Municipal solid waste (kg/capita/day)	1.0	2015	●	●
Electronic waste (kg/capita)	10.5	2019	●	●
Production-based SO_2 emissions (kg/capita)	14.4	2018	●	●
SO_2 emissions embodied in imports (kg/capita)	1.6	2018	●	●
Production-based nitrogen emissions (kg/capita)	79.2	2015	●	↓
Nitrogen emissions embodied in imports (kg/capita)	7.0	2015	●	→
Exports of plastic waste (kg/capita)	0.3	2020	●	●

SDG13 – Climate Action

Indicator	Value	Year	Rating	Trend
CO_2 emissions from fossil fuel combustion and cement production (tCO_2/capita)	1.7	2020	●	↑
CO_2 emissions embodied in imports (tCO_2/capita)	0.6	2018	●	↓
CO_2 emissions embodied in fossil fuel exports (kg/capita)	0.0	2018	●	●

SDG14 – Life Below Water

Indicator	Value	Year	Rating	Trend
Mean area that is protected in marine sites important to biodiversity (%)	53.8	2020	●	→
Ocean Health Index: Clean Waters score (worst 0–100 best)	58.5	2020	●	→
Fish caught from overexploited or collapsed stocks (% of total catch)	42.5	2018	●	↓
Fish caught by trawling or dredging (%)	60.5	2018	●	↓
Fish caught that are then discarded (%)	6.5	2018	●	→
Marine biodiversity threats embodied in imports (per million population)	0.0	2018	●	●

SDG15 – Life on Land

Indicator	Value	Year	Rating	Trend
Mean area that is protected in terrestrial sites important to biodiversity (%)	23.3	2020	●	→
Mean area that is protected in freshwater sites important to biodiversity (%)	28.3	2020	●	→
Red List Index of species survival (worst 0–1 best)	0.9	2021	●	→
Permanent deforestation (% of forest area, 5-year average)	0.1	2020	●	↑
Terrestrial and freshwater biodiversity threats embodied in imports (per million population)	0.7	2018	●	●

SDG16 – Peace, Justice and Strong Institutions

Indicator	Value	Year	Rating	Trend
Homicides (per 100,000 population)	11.3	2019	●	↓
Unsentenced detainees (% of prison population)	22.0	2019	●	↑
Population who feel safe walking alone at night in the city or area where they live (%)	51	2021	●	↗
Property Rights (worst 1–7 best)	5.3	2020	●	↑
Birth registrations with civil authority (% of children under age 5)	99.8	2020	●	●
Corruption Perception Index (worst 0–100 best)	73	2021	●	↑
Children involved in child labor (% of population aged 5 to 14)	4.2	2019	●	●
Exports of major conventional weapons (TIV constant million USD per 100,000 population)	0.0	2020	●	●
Press Freedom Index (best 0–100 worst)	16.4	2021	●	↑
Access to and affordability of justice (worst 0–1 best)	0.8	2020	●	↑

SDG17 – Partnerships for the Goals

Indicator	Value	Year	Rating	Trend
Government spending on health and education (% of GDP)	10.9	2019	●	↑
For high-income and all OECD DAC countries: International concessional public finance, including official development assistance (% of GNI)	NA	NA	●	●
Other countries: Government revenue excluding grants (% of GDP)	NA	NA	●	●
Corporate Tax Haven Score (best 0–100 worst)	* 0.0	2019	●	●
Statistical Performance Index (worst 0–100 best)	66.8	2019	●	→

UZBEKISTAN

Eastern Europe and Central Asia

AVERAGE PERFORMANCE BY SDG

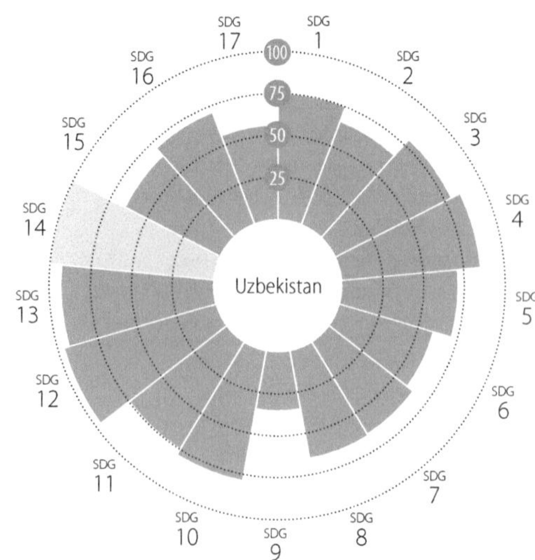

OVERALL PERFORMANCE

COUNTRY RANKING

UZBEKISTAN

77 /163

COUNTRY SCORE

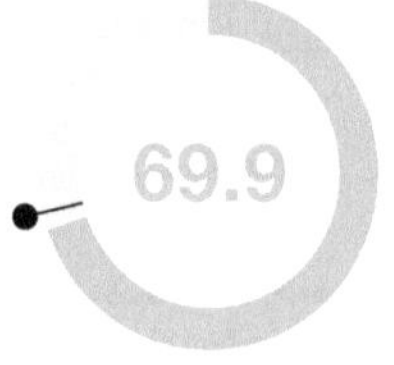

REGIONAL AVERAGE: 71.6

SDG DASHBOARDS AND TRENDS

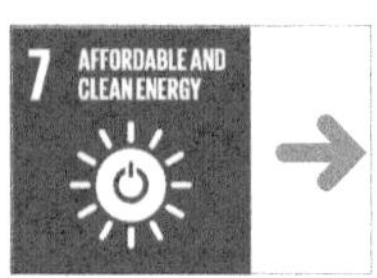

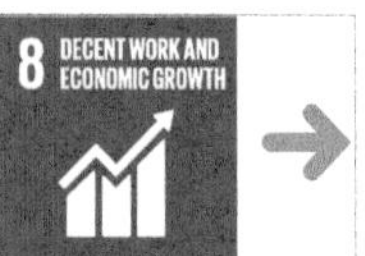

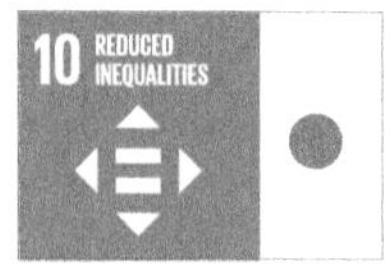

Major challenges · Significant challenges · Challenges remain · SDG achieved · Information unavailable

Decreasing · Stagnating · Moderately improving · On track or maintaining SDG achievement · Information unavailable

Note: The full title of each SDG is available here: https://sustainabledevelopment.un.org/topics/sustainabledevelopmentgoals

INTERNATIONAL SPILLOVER INDEX

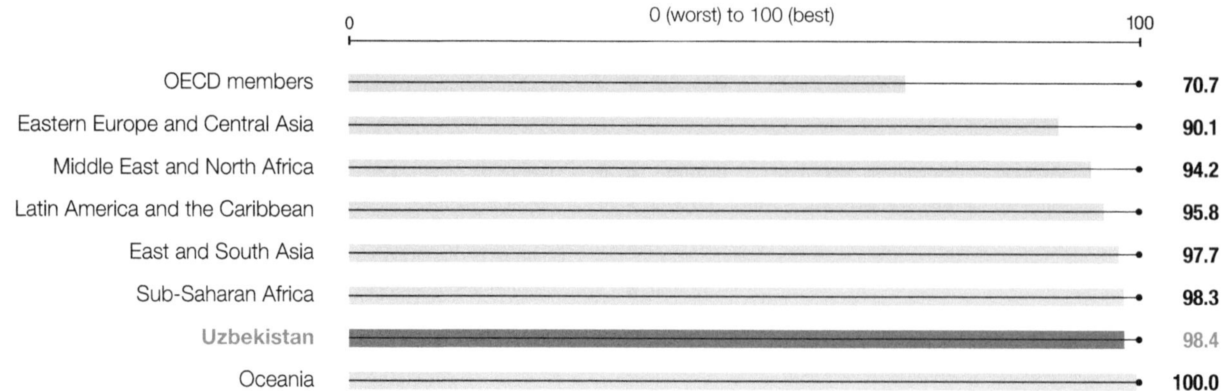

STATISTICAL PERFORMANCE INDEX

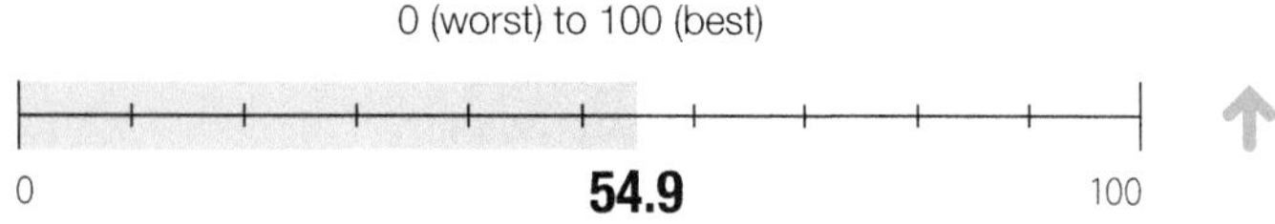

MISSING DATA IN SDG INDEX

SDG1 – No Poverty

Indicator	Value	Year	Rating	Trend
Poverty headcount ratio at $1.90/day (%)	4.6	2022	●	↑
Poverty headcount ratio at $3.20/day (%)	22.9	2022	●	↗

SDG2 – Zero Hunger

Indicator	Value	Year	Rating	Trend
Prevalence of undernourishment (%)	2.5	2019	●	↑
Prevalence of stunting in children under 5 years of age (%)	10.8	2017	●	→
Prevalence of wasting in children under 5 years of age (%)	1.8	2017	●	↑
Prevalence of obesity, BMI ≥ 30 (% of adult population)	16.6	2016	●	↓
Human Trophic Level (best 2–3 worst)	2.3	2017	●	→
Cereal yield (tonnes per hectare of harvested land)	4.1	2018	●	↑
Sustainable Nitrogen Management Index (best 0–1.41 worst)	0.7	2015	●	↓
Exports of hazardous pesticides (tonnes per million population)	NA	NA	●	●

SDG3 – Good Health and Well-Being

Indicator	Value	Year	Rating	Trend
Maternal mortality rate (per 100,000 live births)	29	2017	●	↑
Neonatal mortality rate (per 1,000 live births)	7.6	2020	●	↑
Mortality rate, under-5 (per 1,000 live births)	13.9	2020	●	↑
Incidence of tuberculosis (per 100,000 population)	66.0	2020	●	↗
New HIV infections (per 1,000 uninfected population)	0.1	2020	●	↑
Age-standardized death rate due to cardiovascular disease, cancer, diabetes, or chronic respiratory disease in adults aged 30–70 years (%)	25.3	2019	●	↗
Age-standardized death rate attributable to household air pollution and ambient air pollution (per 100,000 population)	81	2016	●	●
Traffic deaths (per 100,000 population)	11.7	2019	●	→
Life expectancy at birth (years)	73.0	2019	●	↗
Adolescent fertility rate (births per 1,000 females aged 15 to 19)	18.9	2017	●	●
Births attended by skilled health personnel (%)	100.0	2018	●	↑
Surviving infants who received 2 WHO-recommended vaccines (%)	95	2020	●	↑
Universal health coverage (UHC) index of service coverage (worst 0–100 best)	71	2019	●	↑
Subjective well-being (average ladder score, worst 0–10 best)	6.2	2021	●	↑

SDG4 – Quality Education

Indicator	Value	Year	Rating	Trend
Participation rate in pre-primary organized learning (% of children aged 4 to 6)	62.8	2020	●	↑
Net primary enrollment rate (%)	99.1	2020	●	↑
Lower secondary completion rate (%)	97.5	2020	●	↑
Literacy rate (% of population aged 15 to 24)	100.0	2019	●	↑

SDG5 – Gender Equality

Indicator	Value	Year	Rating	Trend
Demand for family planning satisfied by modern methods (% of females aged 15 to 49)	NA	NA	●	●
Ratio of female-to-male mean years of education received (%)	96.7	2019	●	→
Ratio of female-to-male labor force participation rate (%)	63.3	2020	●	↓
Seats held by women in national parliament (%)	32.0	2020	●	↑

SDG6 – Clean Water and Sanitation

Indicator	Value	Year	Rating	Trend
Population using at least basic drinking water services (%)	97.8	2020	●	↑
Population using at least basic sanitation services (%)	100.0	2020	●	↑
Freshwater withdrawal (% of available freshwater resources)	168.9	2018	●	●
Anthropogenic wastewater that receives treatment (%)	0.0	2018	●	●
Scarce water consumption embodied in imports (m^3 H_2O eq/capita)	356.8	2018	●	●

SDG7 – Affordable and Clean Energy

Indicator	Value	Year	Rating	Trend
Population with access to electricity (%)	100.0	2019	●	↑
Population with access to clean fuels and technology for cooking (%)	84.6	2019	●	↓
CO_2 emissions from fuel combustion per total electricity output ($MtCO_2$/TWh)	1.8	2019	●	→
Share of renewable energy in total primary energy supply (%)	1.2	2019	●	↓

SDG8 – Decent Work and Economic Growth

Indicator	Value	Year	Rating	Trend
Adjusted GDP growth (%)	-1.0	2020	●	●
Victims of modern slavery (per 1,000 population)	5.2	2018	●	●
Adults with an account at a bank or other financial institution or with a mobile-money-service provider (% of population aged 15 or over)	37.1	2017	●	↓
Unemployment rate (% of total labor force)	7.0	2022	●	↓
Fundamental labor rights are effectively guaranteed (worst 0–1 best)	0.5	2020	●	↓
Fatal work-related accidents embodied in imports (per 100,000 population)	0.1	2015	●	↑

* Imputed data point

SDG9 – Industry, Innovation and Infrastructure

Indicator	Value	Year	Rating	Trend
Population using the internet (%)	71.1	2020	●	↑
Mobile broadband subscriptions (per 100 population)	79.4	2019	●	↑
Logistics Performance Index: Quality of trade and transport-related infrastructure (worst 1–5 best)	2.6	2018	●	↑
The Times Higher Education Universities Ranking: Average score of top 3 universities (worst 0–100 best)	* 0.0	2022	●	●
Articles published in academic journals (per 1,000 population)	0.1	2020	●	→
Expenditure on research and development (% of GDP)	0.1	2018	●	↓

SDG10 – Reduced Inequalities

Indicator	Value	Year	Rating	Trend
Gini coefficient	35.3	2003	●	●
Palma ratio	NA	NA	●	●

SDG11 – Sustainable Cities and Communities

Indicator	Value	Year	Rating	Trend
Proportion of urban population living in slums (%)	58.5	2018	●	●
Annual mean concentration of particulate matter of less than 2.5 microns in diameter (PM2.5) ($\mu g/m^3$)	26.9	2019	●	↗
Access to improved water source, piped (% of urban population)	88.1	2020	●	↓
Satisfaction with public transport (%)	84.0	2021	●	↑

SDG12 – Responsible Consumption and Production

Indicator	Value	Year	Rating	Trend
Municipal solid waste (kg/capita/day)	0.4	2012	●	●
Electronic waste (kg/capita)	NA	NA	●	●
Production-based SO_2 emissions (kg/capita)	2.4	2018	●	●
SO_2 emissions embodied in imports (kg/capita)	0.3	2018	●	●
Production-based nitrogen emissions (kg/capita)	14.7	2015	●	↑
Nitrogen emissions embodied in imports (kg/capita)	0.6	2015	●	↑
Exports of plastic waste (kg/capita)	0.0	2020	●	●

SDG13 – Climate Action

Indicator	Value	Year	Rating	Trend
CO_2 emissions from fossil fuel combustion and cement production (tCO_2/capita)	3.4	2020	●	→
CO_2 emissions embodied in imports (tCO_2/capita)	0.1	2018	●	↑
CO_2 emissions embodied in fossil fuel exports (kg/capita)	441.8	2020	●	●

SDG14 – Life Below Water

Indicator	Value	Year	Rating	Trend
Mean area that is protected in marine sites important to biodiversity (%)	NA	NA	●	●
Ocean Health Index: Clean Waters score (worst 0–100 best)	NA	NA	●	●
Fish caught from overexploited or collapsed stocks (% of total catch)	NA	NA	●	●
Fish caught by trawling or dredging (%)	NA	NA	●	●
Fish caught that are then discarded (%)	NA	NA	●	●
Marine biodiversity threats embodied in imports (per million population)	0.0	2018	●	●

SDG15 – Life on Land

Indicator	Value	Year	Rating	Trend
Mean area that is protected in terrestrial sites important to biodiversity (%)	17.7	2020	●	→
Mean area that is protected in freshwater sites important to biodiversity (%)	13.4	2020	●	→
Red List Index of species survival (worst 0–1 best)	1.0	2021	●	↑
Permanent deforestation (% of forest area, 5-year average)	0.0	2020	●	↑
Terrestrial and freshwater biodiversity threats embodied in imports (per million population)	0.0	2018	●	●

SDG16 – Peace, Justice and Strong Institutions

Indicator	Value	Year	Rating	Trend
Homicides (per 100,000 population)	1.2	2019	●	↑
Unsentenced detainees (% of prison population)	NA	NA	●	●
Population who feel safe walking alone at night in the city or area where they live (%)	81	2021	●	↑
Property Rights (worst 1–7 best)	NA	NA	●	●
Birth registrations with civil authority (% of children under age 5)	99.9	2020	●	●
Corruption Perception Index (worst 0–100 best)	28	2021	●	↗
Children involved in child labor (% of population aged 5 to 14)	NA	NA	●	●
Exports of major conventional weapons (TIV constant million USD per 100,000 population)	0.2	2020	●	●
Press Freedom Index (best 0–100 worst)	50.7	2021	●	↗
Access to and affordability of justice (worst 0–1 best)	0.5	2020	●	↑

SDG17 – Partnerships for the Goals

Indicator	Value	Year	Rating	Trend
Government spending on health and education (% of GDP)	7.4	2020	●	↓
For high-income and all OECD DAC countries: International concessional public finance, including official development assistance (% of GNI)	NA	NA	●	●
Other countries: Government revenue excluding grants (% of GDP)	20.3	2019	●	→
Corporate Tax Haven Score (best 0–100 worst)	* 0.0	2019	●	●
Statistical Performance Index (worst 0–100 best)	54.9	2019	●	↑

VANUATU

Oceania

OVERALL PERFORMANCE

COUNTRY RANKING

VANUATU

NA /163

COUNTRY SCORE

AVERAGE PERFORMANCE BY SDG

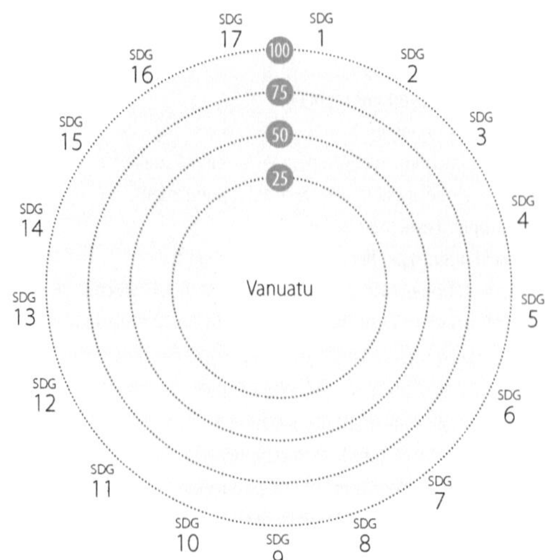

SDG DASHBOARDS AND TRENDS

Major challenges   Significant challenges   Challenges remain   SDG achieved   Information unavailable

Decreasing   Stagnating   Moderately improving   On track or maintaining SDG achievement   Information unavailable

Note: The full title of each SDG is available here: https://sustainabledevelopment.un.org/topics/sustainabledevelopmentgoals

INTERNATIONAL SPILLOVER INDEX

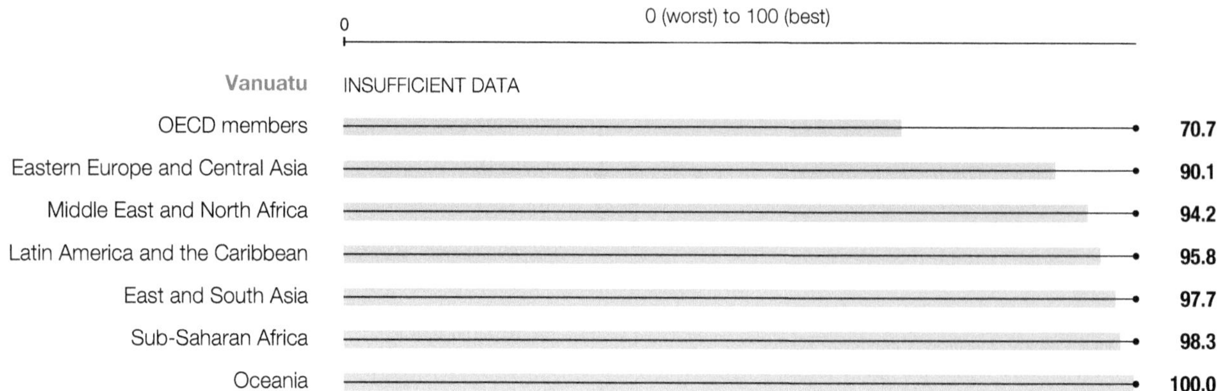

STATISTICAL PERFORMANCE INDEX

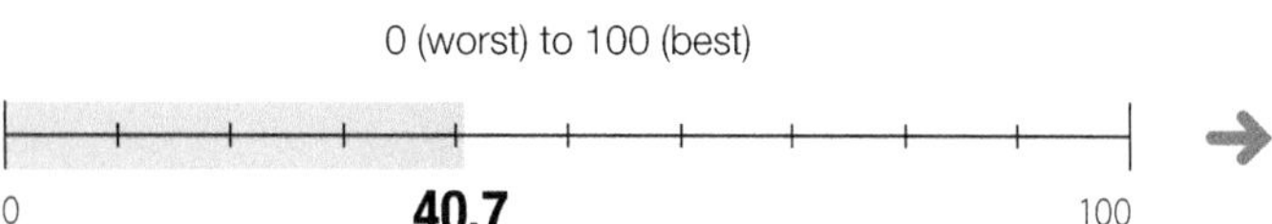

MISSING DATA IN SDG INDEX

24%

VANUATU

Performance by Indicator

SDG1 – No Poverty	Value	Year	Rating	Trend
Poverty headcount ratio at $1.90/day (%)	13.8	2022	●	↓
Poverty headcount ratio at $3.20/day (%)	38.7	2022	●	↓
SDG2 – Zero Hunger				
Prevalence of undernourishment (%)	9.3	2019	●	→
Prevalence of stunting in children under 5 years of age (%)	28.9	2013	●	→
Prevalence of wasting in children under 5 years of age (%)	4.7	2013	●	↑
Prevalence of obesity, BMI ≥ 30 (% of adult population)	25.2	2016	●	↓
Human Trophic Level (best 2–3 worst)	2.2	2017	●	↑
Cereal yield (tonnes per hectare of harvested land)	0.6	2018	●	→
Sustainable Nitrogen Management Index (best 0–1.41 worst)	0.9	2015	●	→
Exports of hazardous pesticides (tonnes per million population)	NA	NA	●	●
SDG3 – Good Health and Well-Being				
Maternal mortality rate (per 100,000 live births)	72	2017	●	↑
Neonatal mortality rate (per 1,000 live births)	10.5	2020	●	↑
Mortality rate, under-5 (per 1,000 live births)	24.9	2020	●	↑
Incidence of tuberculosis (per 100,000 population)	38.0	2020	●	↑
New HIV infections (per 1,000 uninfected population)	NA	NA	●	●
Age-standardized death rate due to cardiovascular disease, cancer, diabetes, or chronic respiratory disease in adults aged 30–70 years (%)	39.7	2019	●	→
Age-standardized death rate attributable to household air pollution and ambient air pollution (per 100,000 population)	136	2016	●	●
Traffic deaths (per 100,000 population)	14.9	2019	●	→
Life expectancy at birth (years)	65.3	2019	●	→
Adolescent fertility rate (births per 1,000 females aged 15 to 19)	51.2	2013	●	●
Births attended by skilled health personnel (%)	89.4	2013	●	●
Surviving infants who received 2 WHO-recommended vaccines (%)	78	2020	●	→
Universal health coverage (UHC) index of service coverage (worst 0–100 best)	52	2019	●	→
Subjective well-being (average ladder score, worst 0–10 best)	NA	NA	●	●
SDG4 – Quality Education				
Participation rate in pre-primary organized learning (% of children aged 4 to 6)	98.0	2020	●	↑
Net primary enrollment rate (%)	96.6	2020	●	↑
Lower secondary completion rate (%)	51.1	2020	●	↓
Literacy rate (% of population aged 15 to 24)	96.3	2018	●	↑
SDG5 – Gender Equality				
Demand for family planning satisfied by modern methods (% of females aged 15 to 49)	50.7	2013	●	→
Ratio of female-to-male mean years of education received (%)	NA	NA	●	●
Ratio of female-to-male labor force participation rate (%)	76.6	2020	●	↑
Seats held by women in national parliament (%)	0.0	2020	●	→
SDG6 – Clean Water and Sanitation				
Population using at least basic drinking water services (%)	91.2	2020	●	→
Population using at least basic sanitation services (%)	52.7	2020	●	↓
Freshwater withdrawal (% of available freshwater resources)	NA	NA	●	●
Anthropogenic wastewater that receives treatment (%)	0.0	2018	●	●
Scarce water consumption embodied in imports (m^3 H_2O eq/capita)	NA	NA	●	●
SDG7 – Affordable and Clean Energy				
Population with access to electricity (%)	64.7	2019	●	↑
Population with access to clean fuels and technology for cooking (%)	7.8	2019	●	↓
CO_2 emissions from fuel combustion per total electricity output ($MtCO_2$/TWh)	3.0	2019	●	→
Share of renewable energy in total primary energy supply (%)	NA	NA	●	●
SDG8 – Decent Work and Economic Growth				
Adjusted GDP growth (%)	-7.1	2020	●	●
Victims of modern slavery (per 1,000 population)	NA	NA	●	●
Adults with an account at a bank or other financial institution or with a mobile-money-service provider (% of population aged 15 or over)	NA	NA	●	●
Unemployment rate (% of total labor force)	2.1	2022	●	↑
Fundamental labor rights are effectively guaranteed (worst 0–1 best)	NA	NA	●	●
Fatal work-related accidents embodied in imports (per 100,000 population)	0.2	2015	●	↑

SDG9 – Industry, Innovation and Infrastructure	Value	Year	Rating	Trend
Population using the internet (%)	25.7	2017	●	●
Mobile broadband subscriptions (per 100 population)	237.1	2019	●	↑
Logistics Performance Index: Quality of trade and transport-related infrastructure (worst 1–5 best)	NA	NA	●	●
The Times Higher Education Universities Ranking: Average score of top 3 universities (worst 0–100 best)	* 0.0	2022	●	●
Articles published in academic journals (per 1,000 population)	0.2	2020	●	→
Expenditure on research and development (% of GDP)	NA	NA	●	●
SDG10 – Reduced Inequalities				
Gini coefficient	37.6	2010	●	●
Palma ratio	1.7	2018	●	●
SDG11 – Sustainable Cities and Communities				
Proportion of urban population living in slums (%)	NA	NA	●	●
Annual mean concentration of particulate matter of less than 2.5 microns in diameter (PM2.5) (μg/m^3)	11.1	2019	●	↑
Access to improved water source, piped (% of urban population)	78.3	2020	●	↓
Satisfaction with public transport (%)	NA	NA	●	●
SDG12 – Responsible Consumption and Production				
Municipal solid waste (kg/capita/day)	0.7	2016	●	●
Electronic waste (kg/capita)	1.1	2019	●	●
Production-based SO_2 emissions (kg/capita)	NA	NA	●	●
SO_2 emissions embodied in imports (kg/capita)	NA	NA	●	●
Production-based nitrogen emissions (kg/capita)	15.6	2015	●	↑
Nitrogen emissions embodied in imports (kg/capita)	3.8	2015	●	↑
Exports of plastic waste (kg/capita)	NA	NA	●	●
SDG13 – Climate Action				
CO_2 emissions from fossil fuel combustion and cement production (tCO_2/capita)	0.6	2020	●	↑
CO_2 emissions embodied in imports (tCO_2/capita)	NA	NA	●	●
CO_2 emissions embodied in fossil fuel exports (kg/capita)	0.0	2020	●	●
SDG14 – Life Below Water				
Mean area that is protected in marine sites important to biodiversity (%)	3.3	2020	●	→
Ocean Health Index: Clean Waters score (worst 0–100 best)	62.0	2020	●	↓
Fish caught from overexploited or collapsed stocks (% of total catch)	34.6	2018	●	↓
Fish caught by trawling or dredging (%)	0.3	2018	●	↑
Fish caught that are then discarded (%)	13.9	2018	●	↑
Marine biodiversity threats embodied in imports (per million population)	0.0	2018	●	●
SDG15 – Life on Land				
Mean area that is protected in terrestrial sites important to biodiversity (%)	2.9	2020	●	→
Mean area that is protected in freshwater sites important to biodiversity (%)	NA	NA	●	●
Red List Index of species survival (worst 0–1 best)	0.7	2021	●	↓
Permanent deforestation (% of forest area, 5-year average)	0.0	2020	●	↑
Terrestrial and freshwater biodiversity threats embodied in imports (per million population)	0.3	2018	●	●
SDG16 – Peace, Justice and Strong Institutions				
Homicides (per 100,000 population)	0.3	2020	●	●
Unsentenced detainees (% of prison population)	22.4	2016	●	●
Population who feel safe walking alone at night in the city or area where they live (%)	NA	NA	●	●
Property Rights (worst 1–7 best)	NA	NA	●	●
Birth registrations with civil authority (% of children under age 5)	43.4	2020	●	●
Corruption Perception Index (worst 0–100 best)	45	2021	●	●
Children involved in child labor (% of population aged 5 to 14)	15.6	2019	●	●
Exports of major conventional weapons (TIV constant million USD per 100,000 population)	* 0.0	2020	●	●
Press Freedom Index (best 0–100 worst)	NA	NA	●	●
Access to and affordability of justice (worst 0–1 best)	NA	NA	●	●
SDG17 – Partnerships for the Goals				
Government spending on health and education (% of GDP)	4.2	2020	●	↓
For high-income and all OECD DAC countries: International concessional public finance, including official development assistance (% of GNI)	NA	NA	●	●
Other countries: Government revenue excluding grants (% of GDP)	31.3	2019	●	↑
Corporate Tax Haven Score (best 0–100 worst)	* 0.0	2019	●	●
Statistical Performance Index (worst 0–100 best)	40.7	2019	●	→

* Imputed data point

5. Country Profiles

VENEZUELA, RB

Latin America and the Caribbean

OVERALL PERFORMANCE

COUNTRY RANKING

VENEZUELA, RB

120 **/163**

COUNTRY SCORE

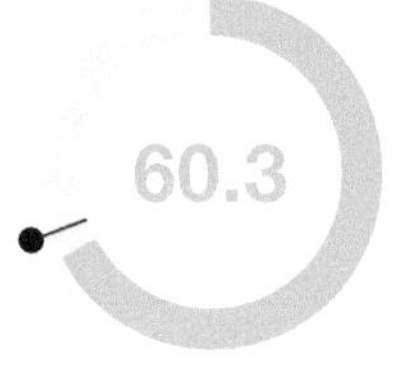

REGIONAL AVERAGE: 69.5

AVERAGE PERFORMANCE BY SDG

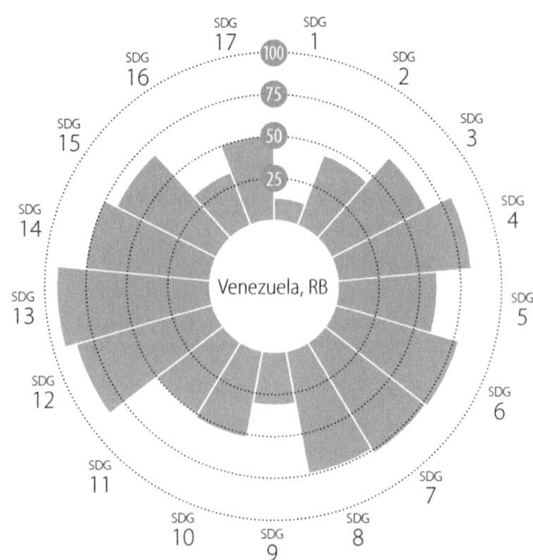

SDG DASHBOARDS AND TRENDS

Major challenges | Significant challenges | Challenges remain | SDG achieved | Information unavailable

Decreasing | Stagnating | Moderately improving | On track or maintaining SDG achievement | Information unavailable

Note: The full title of each SDG is available here: https://sustainabledevelopment.un.org/topics/sustainabledevelopmentgoals

INTERNATIONAL SPILLOVER INDEX

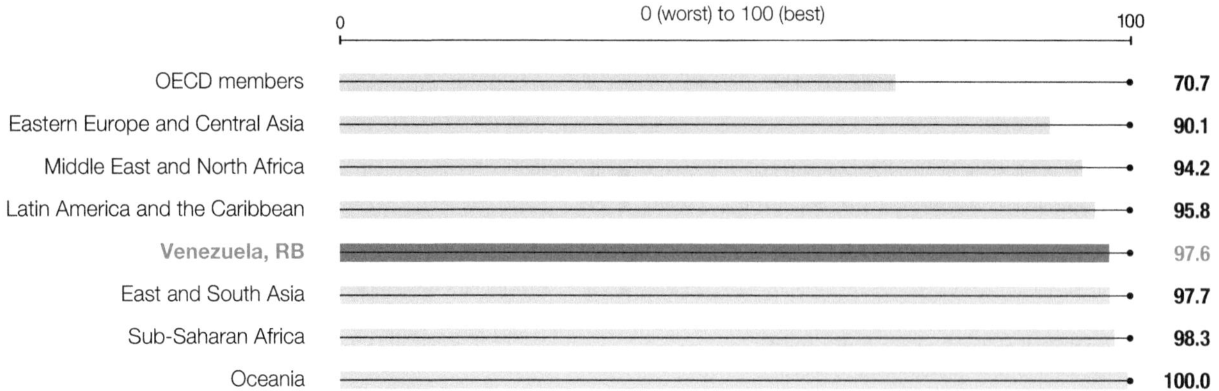

STATISTICAL PERFORMANCE INDEX

0 (worst) to 100 (best)

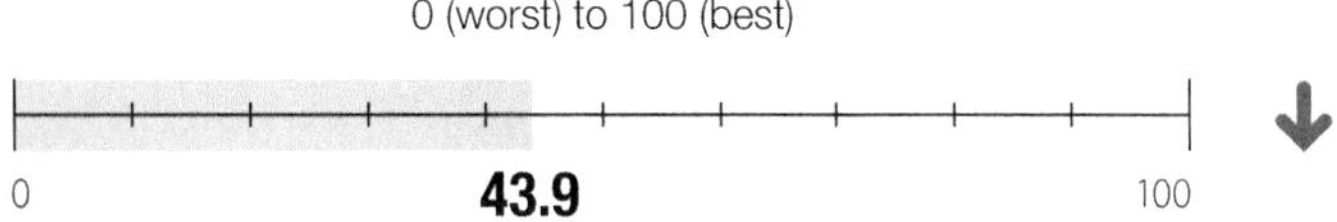

MISSING DATA IN SDG INDEX

10%

VENEZUELA, RB

Performance by Indicator

SDG1 – No Poverty	Value	Year	Rating	Trend
Poverty headcount ratio at $1.90/day (%)	53.5	2022	●	↓
Poverty headcount ratio at $3.20/day (%)	78.0	2022	●	↓
SDG2 – Zero Hunger				
Prevalence of undernourishment (%)	27.4	2019	●	↓
Prevalence of stunting in children under 5 years of age (%)	13.4	2009	●	↓
Prevalence of wasting in children under 5 years of age (%)	4.1	2009	●	↑
Prevalence of obesity, BMI ≥ 30 (% of adult population)	25.6	2016	●	↓
Human Trophic Level (best 2–3 worst)	2.3	2017	●	↑
Cereal yield (tonnes per hectare of harvested land)	3.4	2018	●	↑
Sustainable Nitrogen Management Index (best 0–1.41 worst)	1.0	2015	●	↓
Exports of hazardous pesticides (tonnes per million population)	NA	NA	●	●
SDG3 – Good Health and Well-Being				
Maternal mortality rate (per 100,000 live births)	125	2017	●	→
Neonatal mortality rate (per 1,000 live births)	14.6	2020	●	→
Mortality rate, under-5 (per 1,000 live births)	24.2	2020	●	↑
Incidence of tuberculosis (per 100,000 population)	47.0	2020	●	→
New HIV infections (per 1,000 uninfected population)	0.1	2020	●	↑
Age-standardized death rate due to cardiovascular disease, cancer, diabetes, or chronic respiratory disease in adults aged 30–70 years (%)	14.8	2019	●	↑
Age-standardized death rate attributable to household air pollution and ambient air pollution (per 100,000 population)	35	2016	●	●
Traffic deaths (per 100,000 population)	39.0	2019	●	↓
Life expectancy at birth (years)	74.0	2019	●	↓
Adolescent fertility rate (births per 1,000 females aged 15 to 19)	94.5	2012	●	●
Births attended by skilled health personnel (%)	99.1	2017	●	↑
Surviving infants who received 2 WHO-recommended vaccines (%)	54	2020	●	↓
Universal health coverage (UHC) index of service coverage (worst 0–100 best)	70	2019	●	↓
Subjective well-being (average ladder score, worst 0–10 best)	5.1	2021	●	↓
SDG4 – Quality Education				
Participation rate in pre-primary organized learning (% of children aged 4 to 6)	85.8	2017	●	●
Net primary enrollment rate (%)	90.4	2017	●	●
Lower secondary completion rate (%)	75.2	2017	●	●
Literacy rate (% of population aged 15 to 24)	98.8	2016	●	●
SDG5 – Gender Equality				
Demand for family planning satisfied by modern methods (% of females aged 15 to 49)	NA	NA	●	●
Ratio of female-to-male mean years of education received (%)	106.0	2019	●	↑
Ratio of female-to-male labor force participation rate (%)	50.8	2020	●	↓
Seats held by women in national parliament (%)	22.2	2020	●	↗
SDG6 – Clean Water and Sanitation				
Population using at least basic drinking water services (%)	93.7	2020	●	→
Population using at least basic sanitation services (%)	95.8	2020	●	↑
Freshwater withdrawal (% of available freshwater resources)	7.5	2018	●	●
Anthropogenic wastewater that receives treatment (%)	6.4	2018	●	●
Scarce water consumption embodied in imports (m^3 H_2O eq/capita)	463.6	2018	●	●
SDG7 – Affordable and Clean Energy				
Population with access to electricity (%)	100.0	2019	●	↑
Population with access to clean fuels and technology for cooking (%)	97.1	2019	●	↑
CO_2 emissions from fuel combustion per total electricity output ($MtCO_2$/TWh)	0.9	2019	●	↑
Share of renewable energy in total primary energy supply (%)	13.9	2019	●	↑
SDG8 – Decent Work and Economic Growth				
Adjusted GDP growth (%)	NA	NA	●	●
Victims of modern slavery (per 1,000 population)	5.6	2018	●	●
Adults with an account at a bank or other financial institution or with a mobile-money-service provider (% of population aged 15 or over)	73.5	2017	●	↑
Unemployment rate (% of total labor force)	5.5	2022	●	↑
Fundamental labor rights are effectively guaranteed (worst 0–1 best)	0.5	2020	●	↓
Fatal work-related accidents embodied in imports (per 100,000 population)	0.1	2015	●	↑

* Imputed data point

SDG9 – Industry, Innovation and Infrastructure	Value	Year	Rating	Trend
Population using the internet (%)	61.6	2017	●	●
Mobile broadband subscriptions (per 100 population)	54.0	2019	●	↑
Logistics Performance Index: Quality of trade and transport-related infrastructure (worst 1–5 best)	2.1	2018	●	↓
The Times Higher Education Universities Ranking: Average score of top 3 universities (worst 0–100 best)	16.5	2022	●	●
Articles published in academic journals (per 1,000 population)	0.0	2020	●	↓
Expenditure on research and development (% of GDP)	0.3	2014	●	●
SDG10 – Reduced Inequalities				
Gini coefficient	44.8	2006	●	●
Palma ratio	NA	NA	●	●
SDG11 – Sustainable Cities and Communities				
Proportion of urban population living in slums (%)	35.8	2018	●	↓
Annual mean concentration of particulate matter of less than 2.5 microns in diameter (PM2.5) (μg/m^3)	15.6	2019	●	↑
Access to improved water source, piped (% of urban population)	NA	NA	●	●
Satisfaction with public transport (%)	19.0	2021	●	↓
SDG12 – Responsible Consumption and Production				
Municipal solid waste (kg/capita/day)	0.9	2012	●	●
Electronic waste (kg/capita)	10.7	2019	●	●
Production-based SO_2 emissions (kg/capita)	12.3	2018	●	●
SO_2 emissions embodied in imports (kg/capita)	0.0	2018	●	●
Production-based nitrogen emissions (kg/capita)	13.1	2015	●	↑
Nitrogen emissions embodied in imports (kg/capita)	2.6	2015	●	↑
Exports of plastic waste (kg/capita)	NA	NA	●	●
SDG13 – Climate Action				
CO_2 emissions from fossil fuel combustion and cement production (tCO_2/capita)	3.0	2020	●	↑
CO_2 emissions embodied in imports (tCO_2/capita)	0.0	2018	●	↑
CO_2 emissions embodied in fossil fuel exports (kg/capita)	NA	NA	●	●
SDG14 – Life Below Water				
Mean area that is protected in marine sites important to biodiversity (%)	32.6	2020	●	→
Ocean Health Index: Clean Waters score (worst 0–100 best)	60.7	2020	●	→
Fish caught from overexploited or collapsed stocks (% of total catch)	16.8	2018	●	↑
Fish caught by trawling or dredging (%)	0.4	2018	●	↑
Fish caught that are then discarded (%)	0.8	2018	●	↑
Marine biodiversity threats embodied in imports (per million population)	0.0	2018	●	●
SDG15 – Life on Land				
Mean area that is protected in terrestrial sites important to biodiversity (%)	53.6	2020	●	→
Mean area that is protected in freshwater sites important to biodiversity (%)	42.1	2020	●	→
Red List Index of species survival (worst 0–1 best)	0.8	2021	●	↓
Permanent deforestation (% of forest area, 5-year average)	0.1	2020	●	↑
Terrestrial and freshwater biodiversity threats embodied in imports (per million population)	0.8	2018	●	●
SDG16 – Peace, Justice and Strong Institutions				
Homicides (per 100,000 population)	49.9	2017	●	→
Unsentenced detainees (% of prison population)	63.0	2017	●	●
Population who feel safe walking alone at night in the city or area where they live (%)	33	2021	●	↗
Property Rights (worst 1–7 best)	1.7	2020	●	↓
Birth registrations with civil authority (% of children under age 5)	81.3	2020	●	●
Corruption Perception Index (worst 0–100 best)	14	2021	●	↓
Children involved in child labor (% of population aged 5 to 14)	NA	NA	●	●
Exports of major conventional weapons (TIV constant million USD per 100,000 population)	0.0	2020	●	●
Press Freedom Index (best 0–100 worst)	47.6	2021	●	↓
Access to and affordability of justice (worst 0–1 best)	0.5	2020	●	↓
SDG17 – Partnerships for the Goals				
Government spending on health and education (% of GDP)	3.8	2019	●	↓
For high-income and all OECD DAC countries: International concessional public finance, including official development assistance (% of GNI)	NA	NA	●	●
Other countries: Government revenue excluding grants (% of GDP)	NA	NA	●	●
Corporate Tax Haven Score (best 0–100 worst)	* 0.0	2019	●	●
Statistical Performance Index (worst 0–100 best)	43.9	2019	●	↓

5. Country Profiles

VIETNAM

East and South Asia

OVERALL PERFORMANCE

COUNTRY RANKING

VIETNAM

55/163

COUNTRY SCORE

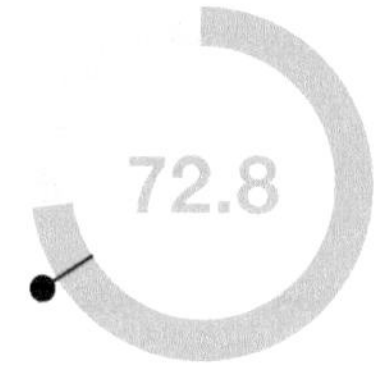

REGIONAL AVERAGE: 65.9

AVERAGE PERFORMANCE BY SDG

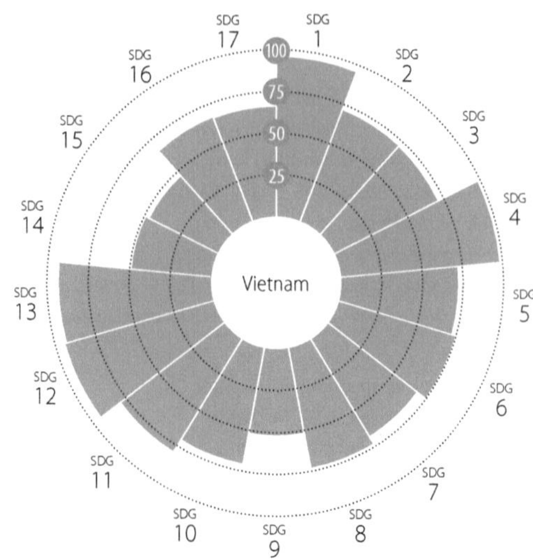

SDG DASHBOARDS AND TRENDS

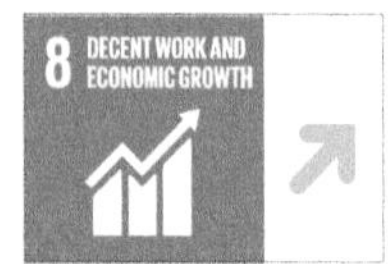

Major challenges · Significant challenges · Challenges remain · SDG achieved · Information unavailable

Decreasing · Stagnating · Moderately improving · On track or maintaining SDG achievement · Information unavailable

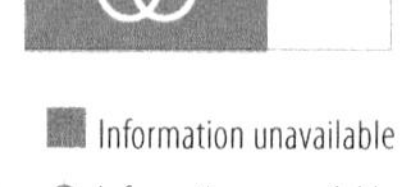

Note: The full title of each SDG is available here: https://sustainabledevelopment.un.org/topics/sustainabledevelopmentgoals

INTERNATIONAL SPILLOVER INDEX

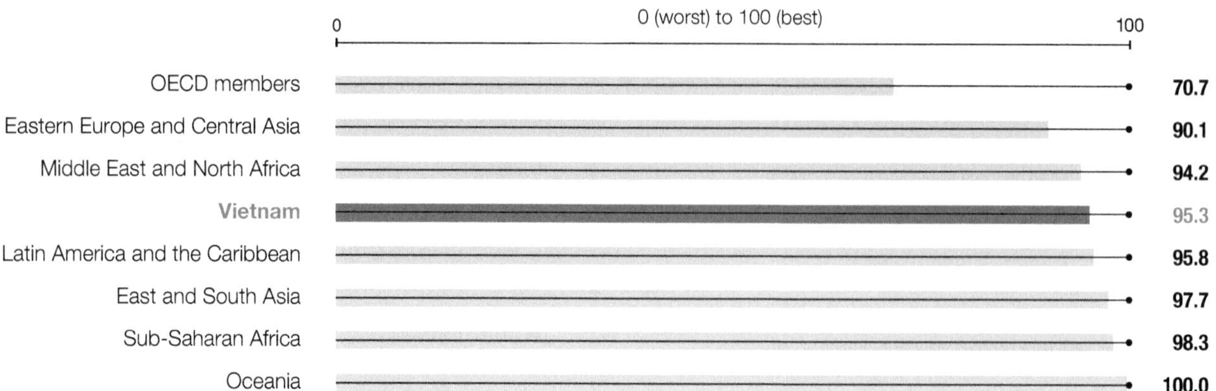

STATISTICAL PERFORMANCE INDEX

0 (worst) to 100 (best)

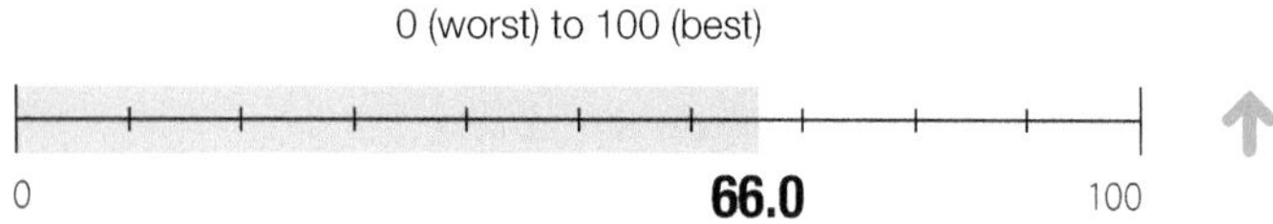

MISSING DATA IN SDG INDEX

1%

VIETNAM

SDG1 – No Poverty	Value	Year	Rating	Trend
Poverty headcount ratio at \$1.90/day (%)	0.8	2022	●	↑
Poverty headcount ratio at \$3.20/day (%)	4.0	2022	●	↑

SDG2 – Zero Hunger	Value	Year	Rating	Trend
Prevalence of undernourishment (%)	6.7	2019	●	↑
Prevalence of stunting in children under 5 years of age (%)	23.8	2017	●	→
Prevalence of wasting in children under 5 years of age (%)	5.8	2017	●	→
Prevalence of obesity, BMI ≥ 30 (% of adult population)	2.1	2016	●	↑
Human Trophic Level (best 2–3 worst)	2.2	2017	●	→
Cereal yield (tonnes per hectare of harvested land)	5.7	2018	●	↑
Sustainable Nitrogen Management Index (best 0–1.41 worst)	0.6	2015	●	→
Exports of hazardous pesticides (tonnes per million population)	43.7	2019	●	●

SDG3 – Good Health and Well-Being	Value	Year	Rating	Trend
Maternal mortality rate (per 100,000 live births)	43	2017	●	↑
Neonatal mortality rate (per 1,000 live births)	10.0	2020	●	↑
Mortality rate, under-5 (per 1,000 live births)	20.9	2020	●	↑
Incidence of tuberculosis (per 100,000 population)	176.0	2020	●	→
New HIV infections (per 1,000 uninfected population)	0.1	2020	●	↑
Age-standardized death rate due to cardiovascular disease, cancer, diabetes, or chronic respiratory disease in adults aged 30–70 years (%)	21.2	2019	●	→
Age-standardized death rate attributable to household air pollution and ambient air pollution (per 100,000 population)	64	2016	●	●
Traffic deaths (per 100,000 population)	30.6	2019	●	↓
Life expectancy at birth (years)	73.7	2019	●	→
Adolescent fertility rate (births per 1,000 females aged 15 to 19)	35.0	2019	●	→
Births attended by skilled health personnel (%)	93.8	2014	●	●
Surviving infants who received 2 WHO-recommended vaccines (%)	94	2020	●	↑
Universal health coverage (UHC) index of service coverage (worst 0–100 best)	70	2019	●	↑
Subjective well-being (average ladder score, worst 0–10 best)	5.5	2021	●	↑

SDG4 – Quality Education	Value	Year	Rating	Trend
Participation rate in pre-primary organized learning (% of children aged 4 to 6)	99.9	2018	●	●
Net primary enrollment rate (%)	98.5	2020	●	↑
Lower secondary completion rate (%)	97.7	2018	●	↑
Literacy rate (% of population aged 15 to 24)	98.6	2019	●	●

SDG5 – Gender Equality	Value	Year	Rating	Trend
Demand for family planning satisfied by modern methods (% of females aged 15 to 49)	69.6	2014	●	↑
Ratio of female-to-male mean years of education received (%)	93.0	2019	●	↓
Ratio of female-to-male labor force participation rate (%)	87.0	2020	●	↑
Seats held by women in national parliament (%)	26.7	2020	●	→

SDG6 – Clean Water and Sanitation	Value	Year	Rating	Trend
Population using at least basic drinking water services (%)	96.9	2020	●	↑
Population using at least basic sanitation services (%)	89.2	2020	●	↑
Freshwater withdrawal (% of available freshwater resources)	18.1	2018	●	●
Anthropogenic wastewater that receives treatment (%)	0.3	2018	●	●
Scarce water consumption embodied in imports (m^3 H_2O eq/capita)	665.2	2018	●	●

SDG7 – Affordable and Clean Energy	Value	Year	Rating	Trend
Population with access to electricity (%)	99.4	2019	●	↑
Population with access to clean fuels and technology for cooking (%)	64.7	2019	●	↗
CO_2 emissions from fuel combustion per total electricity output ($MtCO_2$/TWh)	1.1	2019	●	→
Share of renewable energy in total primary energy supply (%)	15.8	2019	●	↓

SDG8 – Decent Work and Economic Growth	Value	Year	Rating	Trend
Adjusted GDP growth (%)	1.4	2020	●	●
Victims of modern slavery (per 1,000 population)	4.5	2018	●	●
Adults with an account at a bank or other financial institution or with a mobile-money-service provider (% of population aged 15 or over)	30.8	2017	●	↓
Unemployment rate (% of total labor force)	2.3	2022	●	↑
Fundamental labor rights are effectively guaranteed (worst 0–1 best)	0.6	2020	●	↗
Fatal work-related accidents embodied in imports (per 100,000 population)	0.1	2015	●	↑

SDG9 – Industry, Innovation and Infrastructure	Value	Year	Rating	Trend
Population using the internet (%)	70.3	2020	●	↑
Mobile broadband subscriptions (per 100 population)	72.5	2019	●	↑
Logistics Performance Index: Quality of trade and transport-related infrastructure (worst 1–5 best)	3.0	2018	●	↑
The Times Higher Education Universities Ranking: Average score of top 3 universities (worst 0–100 best)	36.6	2022	●	●
Articles published in academic journals (per 1,000 population)	0.2	2020	●	↗
Expenditure on research and development (% of GDP)	0.5	2017	●	↗

SDG10 – Reduced Inequalities	Value	Year	Rating	Trend
Gini coefficient	35.7	2018	●	↓
Palma ratio	1.5	2018	●	●

SDG11 – Sustainable Cities and Communities	Value	Year	Rating	Trend
Proportion of urban population living in slums (%)	13.5	2018	●	↑
Annual mean concentration of particulate matter of less than 2.5 microns in diameter (PM2.5) (μg/m^3)	27.9	2019	●	↗
Access to improved water source, piped (% of urban population)	85.4	2020	●	↑
Satisfaction with public transport (%)	66.0	2021	●	→

SDG12 – Responsible Consumption and Production	Value	Year	Rating	Trend
Municipal solid waste (kg/capita/day)	0.3	2010	●	●
Electronic waste (kg/capita)	2.7	2019	●	●
Production-based SO_2 emissions (kg/capita)	10.4	2018	●	●
SO_2 emissions embodied in imports (kg/capita)	0.8	2018	●	●
Production-based nitrogen emissions (kg/capita)	10.1	2015	●	↑
Nitrogen emissions embodied in imports (kg/capita)	0.5	2015	●	↑
Exports of plastic waste (kg/capita)	1.5	2020	●	●

SDG13 – Climate Action	Value	Year	Rating	Trend
CO_2 emissions from fossil fuel combustion and cement production (tCO_2/capita)	2.6	2020	●	→
CO_2 emissions embodied in imports (tCO_2/capita)	0.3	2018	●	↑
CO_2 emissions embodied in fossil fuel exports (kg/capita)	195.8	2020	●	●

SDG14 – Life Below Water	Value	Year	Rating	Trend
Mean area that is protected in marine sites important to biodiversity (%)	23.9	2020	●	→
Ocean Health Index: Clean Waters score (worst 0–100 best)	45.4	2020	●	→
Fish caught from overexploited or collapsed stocks (% of total catch)	5.5	2018	●	↑
Fish caught by trawling or dredging (%)	64.8	2018	●	→
Fish caught that are then discarded (%)	15.4	2018	●	↓
Marine biodiversity threats embodied in imports (per million population)	0.0	2018	●	●

SDG15 – Life on Land	Value	Year	Rating	Trend
Mean area that is protected in terrestrial sites important to biodiversity (%)	40.0	2020	●	→
Mean area that is protected in freshwater sites important to biodiversity (%)	38.2	2020	●	→
Red List Index of species survival (worst 0–1 best)	0.7	2021	●	↓
Permanent deforestation (% of forest area, 5-year average)	1.1	2020	●	↗
Terrestrial and freshwater biodiversity threats embodied in imports (per million population)	0.1	2018	●	●

SDG16 – Peace, Justice and Strong Institutions	Value	Year	Rating	Trend
Homicides (per 100,000 population)	1.5	2011	●	●
Unsentenced detainees (% of prison population)	12.4	2018	●	●
Population who feel safe walking alone at night in the city or area where they live (%)	70	2021	●	↑
Property Rights (worst 1–7 best)	4.4	2020	●	↑
Birth registrations with civil authority (% of children under age 5)	96.1	2020	●	●
Corruption Perception Index (worst 0–100 best)	39	2021	●	↗
Children involved in child labor (% of population aged 5 to 14)	13.1	2019	●	●
Exports of major conventional weapons (TIV constant million USD per 100,000 population)	0.0	2020	●	●
Press Freedom Index (best 0–100 worst)	78.5	2021	●	↓
Access to and affordability of justice (worst 0–1 best)	0.5	2020	●	↗

SDG17 – Partnerships for the Goals	Value	Year	Rating	Trend
Government spending on health and education (% of GDP)	6.4	2019	●	↓
For high-income and all OECD DAC countries: International concessional public finance, including official development assistance (% of GNI)	NA	NA	●	●
Other countries: Government revenue excluding grants (% of GDP)	NA	NA	●	●
Corporate Tax Haven Score (best 0–100 worst)	* 0.0	2019	●	●
Statistical Performance Index (worst 0–100 best)	66.0	2019	●	↑

* Imputed data point

5. Country Profiles

YEMEN, REPUBLIC OF

Middle East and North Africa

OVERALL PERFORMANCE

COUNTRY RANKING

YEMEN, REPUBLIC OF

150/163

COUNTRY SCORE

REGIONAL AVERAGE: 66.7

AVERAGE PERFORMANCE BY SDG

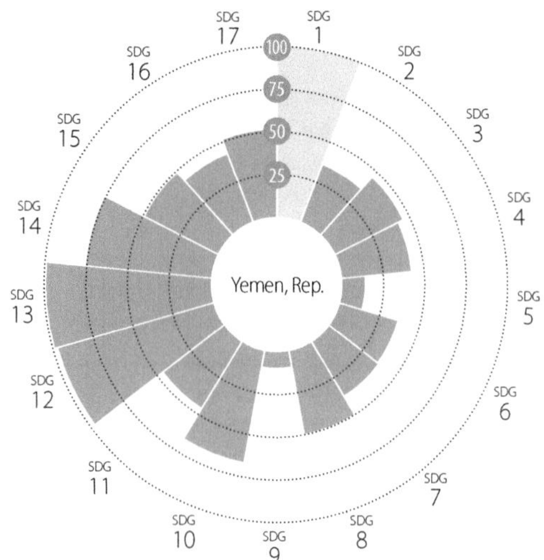

SDG DASHBOARDS AND TRENDS

Major challenges · Significant challenges · Challenges remain · SDG achieved · Information unavailable

Decreasing · Stagnating · Moderately improving · On track or maintaining SDG achievement · Information unavailable

Note: The full title of each SDG is available here: https://sustainabledevelopment.un.org/topics/sustainabledevelopmentgoals

INTERNATIONAL SPILLOVER INDEX

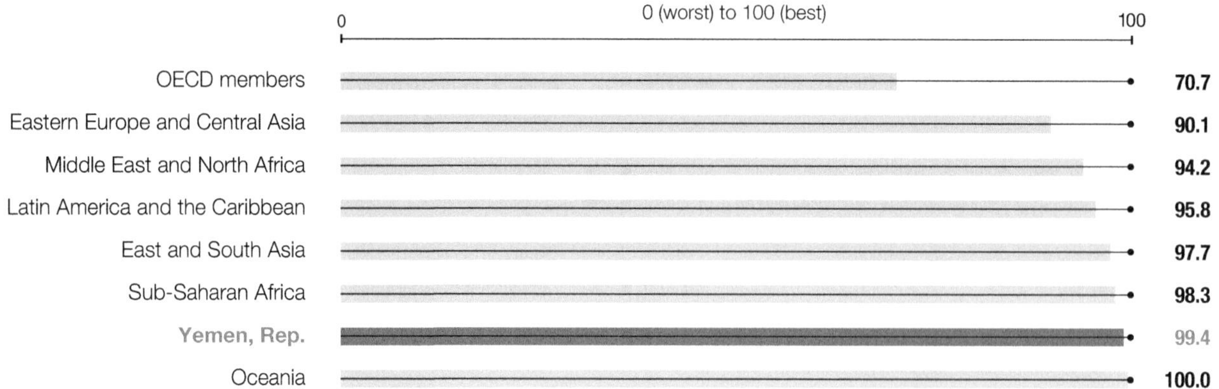

STATISTICAL PERFORMANCE INDEX

0 (worst) to 100 (best)

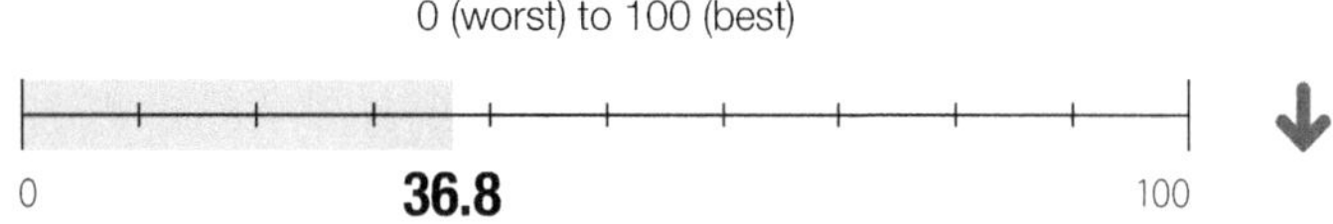

MISSING DATA IN SDG INDEX

11%

YEMEN, REPUBLIC OF

Performance by Indicator

SDG1 – No Poverty

Indicator		Value	Year	Rating	Trend
Poverty headcount ratio at $1.90/day (%)	*	NA	NA	●	●
Poverty headcount ratio at $3.20/day (%)	*	NA	NA	●	●

SDG2 – Zero Hunger

Indicator		Value	Year	Rating	Trend
Prevalence of undernourishment (%)		45.4	2019	●	↓
Prevalence of stunting in children under 5 years of age (%)		46.4	2013	●	→
Prevalence of wasting in children under 5 years of age (%)		16.4	2013	●	→
Prevalence of obesity, BMI ≥ 30 (% of adult population)		17.1	2016	●	↓
Human Trophic Level (best 2–3 worst)		2.1	2017	●	↑
Cereal yield (tonnes per hectare of harvested land)		0.8	2018	●	↓
Sustainable Nitrogen Management Index (best 0–1.41 worst)		0.8	2015	●	↓
Exports of hazardous pesticides (tonnes per million population)		0.1	2019	●	●

SDG3 – Good Health and Well-Being

Indicator		Value	Year	Rating	Trend
Maternal mortality rate (per 100,000 live births)		164	2017	●	↗
Neonatal mortality rate (per 1,000 live births)		28.1	2020	●	→
Mortality rate, under-5 (per 1,000 live births)		59.6	2020	●	→
Incidence of tuberculosis (per 100,000 population)		49.0	2020	●	→
New HIV infections (per 1,000 uninfected population)		0.0	2020	●	↑
Age-standardized death rate due to cardiovascular disease, cancer, diabetes, or chronic respiratory disease in adults aged 30–70 years (%)		27.6	2019	●	↓
Age-standardized death rate attributable to household air pollution and ambient air pollution (per 100,000 population)		194	2016	●	●
Traffic deaths (per 100,000 population)		29.4	2019	●	↓
Life expectancy at birth (years)		66.6	2019	●	↓
Adolescent fertility rate (births per 1,000 females aged 15 to 19)		67.2	2012	●	●
Births attended by skilled health personnel (%)		44.7	2013	●	●
Surviving infants who received 2 WHO-recommended vaccines (%)		68	2020	●	→
Universal health coverage (UHC) index of service coverage (worst 0–100 best)		44	2019	●	→
Subjective well-being (average ladder score, worst 0–10 best)		4.2	2019	●	●

SDG4 – Quality Education

Indicator		Value	Year	Rating	Trend
Participation rate in pre-primary organized learning (% of children aged 4 to 6)		4.1	2016	●	●
Net primary enrollment rate (%)		84.4	2016	●	●
Lower secondary completion rate (%)		53.1	2016	●	●
Literacy rate (% of population aged 15 to 24)		77.0	2004	●	●

SDG5 – Gender Equality

Indicator		Value	Year	Rating	Trend
Demand for family planning satisfied by modern methods (% of females aged 15 to 49)		40.5	2013	●	●
Ratio of female-to-male mean years of education received (%)		56.9	2019	●	↑
Ratio of female-to-male labor force participation rate (%)		9.0	2020	●	↓
Seats held by women in national parliament (%)		0.3	2020	●	→

SDG6 – Clean Water and Sanitation

Indicator		Value	Year	Rating	Trend
Population using at least basic drinking water services (%)		60.7	2020	●	→
Population using at least basic sanitation services (%)		54.1	2020	●	→
Freshwater withdrawal (% of available freshwater resources)		169.8	2018	●	●
Anthropogenic wastewater that receives treatment (%)		0.0	2018	●	●
Scarce water consumption embodied in imports (m^3 H_2O eq/capita)		369.3	2018	●	●

SDG7 – Affordable and Clean Energy

Indicator		Value	Year	Rating	Trend
Population with access to electricity (%)		72.8	2019	●	↗
Population with access to clean fuels and technology for cooking (%)		60.9	2019	●	→
CO_2 emissions from fuel combustion per total electricity output ($MtCO_2$/TWh)		5.0	2019	●	↓
Share of renewable energy in total primary energy supply (%)		4.1	2019	●	→

SDG8 – Decent Work and Economic Growth

Indicator		Value	Year	Rating	Trend
Adjusted GDP growth (%)		NA	NA	●	●
Victims of modern slavery (per 1,000 population)	*	NA	NA	●	●
Adults with an account at a bank or other financial institution or with a mobile-money-service provider (% of population aged 15 or over)		6.4	2014	●	●
Unemployment rate (% of total labor force)		13.3	2022	●	→
Fundamental labor rights are effectively guaranteed (worst 0–1 best)		NA	NA	●	●
Fatal work-related accidents embodied in imports (per 100,000 population)		0.1	2015	●	↑

* Imputed data point

SDG9 – Industry, Innovation and Infrastructure

Indicator		Value	Year	Rating	Trend
Population using the internet (%)		26.7	2017	●	●
Mobile broadband subscriptions (per 100 population)		5.7	2019	●	→
Logistics Performance Index: Quality of trade and transport-related infrastructure (worst 1–5 best)		2.1	2018	●	↗
The Times Higher Education Universities Ranking: Average score of top 3 universities (worst 0–100 best)	*	0.0	2022	●	●
Articles published in academic journals (per 1,000 population)		0.0	2020	●	→
Expenditure on research and development (% of GDP)	*	0.0	2018	●	●

SDG10 – Reduced Inequalities

Indicator		Value	Year	Rating	Trend
Gini coefficient		36.7	2014	●	●
Palma ratio		1.6	2018	●	●

SDG11 – Sustainable Cities and Communities

Indicator		Value	Year	Rating	Trend
Proportion of urban population living in slums (%)		56.0	2018	●	→
Annual mean concentration of particulate matter of less than 2.5 microns in diameter ($PM_{2.5}$) (μg/m^3)		51.9	2019	●	→
Access to improved water source, piped (% of urban population)		76.7	2020	●	→
Satisfaction with public transport (%)		37.0	2019	●	●

SDG12 – Responsible Consumption and Production

Indicator		Value	Year	Rating	Trend
Municipal solid waste (kg/capita/day)		0.5	2016	●	●
Electronic waste (kg/capita)		1.5	2019	●	●
Production-based SO_2 emissions (kg/capita)		2.0	2018	●	●
SO_2 emissions embodied in imports (kg/capita)		0.1	2018	●	●
Production-based nitrogen emissions (kg/capita)		6.2	2015	●	↑
Nitrogen emissions embodied in imports (kg/capita)		0.4	2015	●	↑
Exports of plastic waste (kg/capita)		0.0	2018	●	●

SDG13 – Climate Action

Indicator		Value	Year	Rating	Trend
CO_2 emissions from fossil fuel combustion and cement production (tCO_2/capita)		0.3	2020	●	↑
CO_2 emissions embodied in imports (tCO_2/capita)		0.0	2018	●	↑
CO_2 emissions embodied in fossil fuel exports (kg/capita)		NA	NA	●	●

SDG14 – Life Below Water

Indicator		Value	Year	Rating	Trend
Mean area that is protected in marine sites important to biodiversity (%)		30.6	2020	●	→
Ocean Health Index: Clean Waters score (worst 0–100 best)		53.5	2020	●	↓
Fish caught from overexploited or collapsed stocks (% of total catch)		6.7	2018	●	↑
Fish caught by trawling or dredging (%)		2.9	2018	●	↑
Fish caught that are then discarded (%)		0.6	2018	●	↑
Marine biodiversity threats embodied in imports (per million population)		0.0	2018	●	●

SDG15 – Life on Land

Indicator		Value	Year	Rating	Trend
Mean area that is protected in terrestrial sites important to biodiversity (%)		27.9	2020	●	→
Mean area that is protected in freshwater sites important to biodiversity (%)		8.2	2020	●	→
Red List Index of species survival (worst 0–1 best)		0.8	2021	●	↓
Permanent deforestation (% of forest area, 5-year average)		NA	NA	●	●
Terrestrial and freshwater biodiversity threats embodied in imports (per million population)		0.0	2018	●	●

SDG16 – Peace, Justice and Strong Institutions

Indicator		Value	Year	Rating	Trend
Homicides (per 100,000 population)		6.8	2013	●	●
Unsentenced detainees (% of prison population)		40.2	2009	●	●
Population who feel safe walking alone at night in the city or area where they live (%)		52	2019	●	●
Property Rights (worst 1–7 best)		3.2	2020	●	↗
Birth registrations with civil authority (% of children under age 5)		30.7	2020	●	●
Corruption Perception Index (worst 0–100 best)		16	2021	●	↓
Children involved in child labor (% of population aged 5 to 14)		NA	NA	●	●
Exports of major conventional weapons (TIV constant million USD per 100,000 population)	*	0.0	2020	●	●
Press Freedom Index (best 0–100 worst)		62.4	2021	●	→
Access to and affordability of justice (worst 0–1 best)		NA	NA	●	●

SDG17 – Partnerships for the Goals

Indicator		Value	Year	Rating	Trend
Government spending on health and education (% of GDP)		5.6	2015	●	●
For high-income and all OECD DAC countries: International concessional public finance, including official development assistance (% of GNI)		NA	NA	●	●
Other countries: Government revenue excluding grants (% of GDP)		NA	NA	●	●
Corporate Tax Haven Score (best 0–100 worst)	*	0.0	2019	●	●
Statistical Performance Index (worst 0–100 best)		36.8	2019	●	↓

ZAMBIA

Sub-Saharan Africa

OVERALL PERFORMANCE

COUNTRY RANKING

ZAMBIA

140/163

COUNTRY SCORE

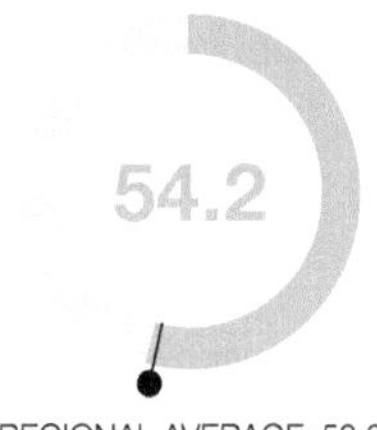

AVERAGE PERFORMANCE BY SDG

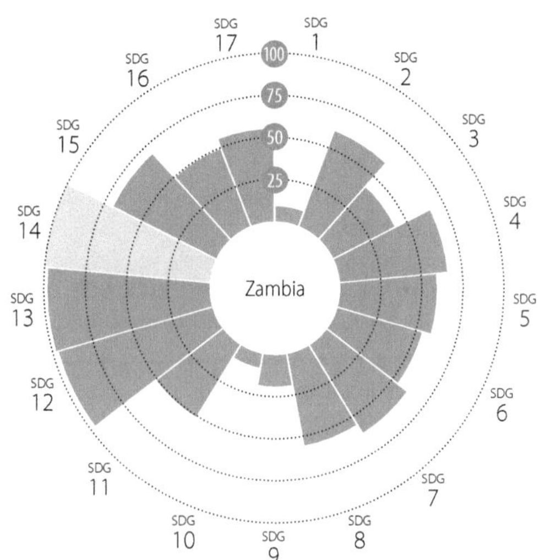

SDG DASHBOARDS AND TRENDS

Major challenges | Significant challenges | Challenges remain | SDG achieved | Information unavailable

Decreasing | Stagnating | Moderately improving | On track or maintaining SDG achievement | Information unavailable

Note: The full title of each SDG is available here: https://sustainabledevelopment.un.org/topics/sustainabledevelopmentgoals

INTERNATIONAL SPILLOVER INDEX

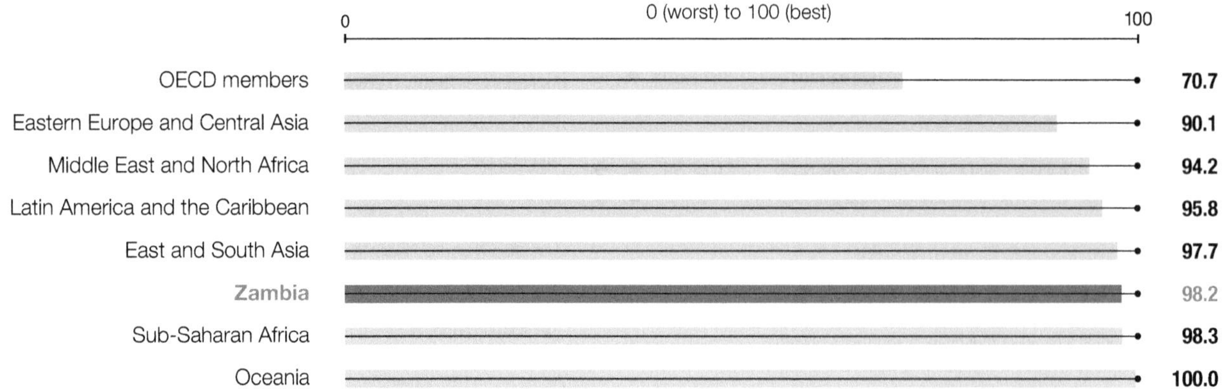

OECD members	70.7
Eastern Europe and Central Asia	90.1
Middle East and North Africa	94.2
Latin America and the Caribbean	95.8
East and South Asia	97.7
Zambia	98.2
Sub-Saharan Africa	98.3
Oceania	100.0

STATISTICAL PERFORMANCE INDEX

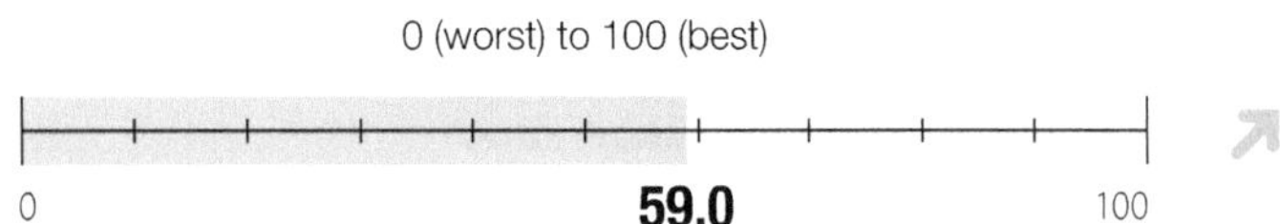

MISSING DATA IN SDG INDEX

2%

ZAMBIA

Performance by Indicator

SDG1 – No Poverty	Value	Year	Rating	Trend
Poverty headcount ratio at $1.90/day (%)	58.9	2022	●	↓
Poverty headcount ratio at $3.20/day (%)	76.8	2022	●	↓
SDG2 – Zero Hunger				
Prevalence of undernourishment (%)	NA	NA	●	●
Prevalence of stunting in children under 5 years of age (%)	34.6	2018	●	→
Prevalence of wasting in children under 5 years of age (%)	4.2	2018	●	↑
Prevalence of obesity, BMI ≥ 30 (% of adult population)	8.1	2016	●	↑
Human Trophic Level (best 2–3 worst)	2.1	2017	●	↑
Cereal yield (tonnes per hectare of harvested land)	2.2	2018	●	↓
Sustainable Nitrogen Management Index (best 0–1.41 worst)	0.8	2015	●	→
Exports of hazardous pesticides (tonnes per million population)	0.3	2019	●	●
SDG3 – Good Health and Well-Being				
Maternal mortality rate (per 100,000 live births)	213	2017	●	↗
Neonatal mortality rate (per 1,000 live births)	24.0	2020	●	→
Mortality rate, under-5 (per 1,000 live births)	61.4	2020	●	→
Incidence of tuberculosis (per 100,000 population)	319.0	2020	●	↗
New HIV infections (per 1,000 uninfected population)	3.6	2020	●	↗
Age-standardized death rate due to cardiovascular disease, cancer, diabetes, or chronic respiratory disease in adults aged 30–70 years (%)	24.6	2019	●	↗
Age-standardized death rate attributable to household air pollution and ambient air pollution (per 100,000 population)	127	2016	●	●
Traffic deaths (per 100,000 population)	20.5	2019	●	→
Life expectancy at birth (years)	62.5	2019	●	→
Adolescent fertility rate (births per 1,000 females aged 15 to 19)	135.0	2017	●	●
Births attended by skilled health personnel (%)	80.4	2018	●	↑
Surviving infants who received 2 WHO-recommended vaccines (%)	84	2020	●	↓
Universal health coverage (UHC) index of service coverage (worst 0–100 best)	55	2019	●	↗
Subjective well-being (average ladder score, worst 0–10 best)	3.1	2021	●	↓
SDG4 – Quality Education				
Participation rate in pre-primary organized learning (% of children aged 4 to 6)	NA	NA	●	●
Net primary enrollment rate (%)	85.1	2017	●	●
Lower secondary completion rate (%)	54.8	2013	●	●
Literacy rate (% of population aged 15 to 24)	92.1	2018	●	●
SDG5 – Gender Equality				
Demand for family planning satisfied by modern methods (% of females aged 15 to 49)	65.9	2018	●	●
Ratio of female-to-male mean years of education received (%)	76.8	2019	●	↓
Ratio of female-to-male labor force participation rate (%)	89.1	2020	●	↑
Seats held by women in national parliament (%)	16.8	2020	●	→
SDG6 – Clean Water and Sanitation				
Population using at least basic drinking water services (%)	65.4	2020	●	→
Population using at least basic sanitation services (%)	31.9	2020	●	→
Freshwater withdrawal (% of available freshwater resources)	2.8	2018	●	●
Anthropogenic wastewater that receives treatment (%)	4.2	2018	●	●
Scarce water consumption embodied in imports (m^3 H_2O eq/capita)	350.9	2018	●	●
SDG7 – Affordable and Clean Energy				
Population with access to electricity (%)	43.0	2019	●	↗
Population with access to clean fuels and technology for cooking (%)	15.7	2019	●	→
CO_2 emissions from fuel combustion per total electricity output ($MtCO_2$/TWh)	0.4	2019	●	↑
Share of renewable energy in total primary energy supply (%)	83.4	2019	●	↑
SDG8 – Decent Work and Economic Growth				
Adjusted GDP growth (%)	-6.4	2020	●	●
Victims of modern slavery (per 1,000 population)	5.7	2018	●	●
Adults with an account at a bank or other financial institution or with a mobile-money-service provider (% of population aged 15 or over)	45.9	2017	●	↑
Unemployment rate (% of total labor force)	13.0	2022	●	↓
Fundamental labor rights are effectively guaranteed (worst 0–1 best)	0.4	2020	●	→
Fatal work-related accidents embodied in imports (per 100,000 population)	0.1	2015	●	↑

SDG9 – Industry, Innovation and Infrastructure	Value	Year	Rating	Trend
Population using the internet (%)	19.8	2020	●	→
Mobile broadband subscriptions (per 100 population)	51.1	2019	●	↑
Logistics Performance Index: Quality of trade and transport-related infrastructure (worst 1–5 best)	2.3	2018	●	↓
The Times Higher Education Universities Ranking: Average score of top 3 universities (worst 0–100 best)	* 0.0	2022	●	●
Articles published in academic journals (per 1,000 population)	0.0	2020	●	→
Expenditure on research and development (% of GDP)	0.3	2008	●	●
SDG10 – Reduced Inequalities				
Gini coefficient	57.1	2015	●	●
Palma ratio	5.0	2018	●	●
SDG11 – Sustainable Cities and Communities				
Proportion of urban population living in slums (%)	63.3	2018	●	↓
Annual mean concentration of particulate matter of less than 2.5 microns in diameter (PM2.5) ($\mu g/m^3$)	26.3	2019	●	→
Access to improved water source, piped (% of urban population)	66.1	2020	●	↓
Satisfaction with public transport (%)	41.0	2021	●	→
SDG12 – Responsible Consumption and Production				
Municipal solid waste (kg/capita/day)	0.5	2011	●	●
Electronic waste (kg/capita)	1.0	2019	●	●
Production-based SO_2 emissions (kg/capita)	5.3	2018	●	●
SO_2 emissions embodied in imports (kg/capita)	0.7	2018	●	●
Production-based nitrogen emissions (kg/capita)	9.2	2015	●	↑
Nitrogen emissions embodied in imports (kg/capita)	0.4	2015	●	↑
Exports of plastic waste (kg/capita)	0.1	2020	●	●
SDG13 – Climate Action				
CO_2 emissions from fossil fuel combustion and cement production (tCO_2/capita)	0.4	2020	●	↑
CO_2 emissions embodied in imports (tCO_2/capita)	0.2	2018	●	↑
CO_2 emissions embodied in fossil fuel exports (kg/capita)	1.5	2020	●	●
SDG14 – Life Below Water				
Mean area that is protected in marine sites important to biodiversity (%)	NA	NA	●	●
Ocean Health Index: Clean Waters score (worst 0–100 best)	NA	NA	●	●
Fish caught from overexploited or collapsed stocks (% of total catch)	NA	NA	●	●
Fish caught by trawling or dredging (%)	NA	NA	●	●
Fish caught that are then discarded (%)	NA	NA	●	●
Marine biodiversity threats embodied in imports (per million population)	0.0	2018	●	●
SDG15 – Life on Land				
Mean area that is protected in terrestrial sites important to biodiversity (%)	46.1	2020	●	→
Mean area that is protected in freshwater sites important to biodiversity (%)	56.8	2020	●	→
Red List Index of species survival (worst 0–1 best)	0.9	2021	●	→
Permanent deforestation (% of forest area, 5-year average)	0.3	2020	●	↓
Terrestrial and freshwater biodiversity threats embodied in imports (per million population)	0.5	2018	●	●
SDG16 – Peace, Justice and Strong Institutions				
Homicides (per 100,000 population)	5.4	2015	●	●
Unsentenced detainees (% of prison population)	28.0	2017	●	●
Population who feel safe walking alone at night in the city or area where they live (%)	41	2021	●	↓
Property Rights (worst 1–7 best)	4.3	2020	●	↓
Birth registrations with civil authority (% of children under age 5)	14.1	2020	●	●
Corruption Perception Index (worst 0–100 best)	33	2021	●	↓
Children involved in child labor (% of population aged 5 to 14)	23.0	2019	●	●
Exports of major conventional weapons (TIV constant million USD per 100,000 population)	* 0.0	2020	●	●
Press Freedom Index (best 0–100 worst)	38.2	2021	●	↓
Access to and affordability of justice (worst 0–1 best)	0.4	2020	●	↓
SDG17 – Partnerships for the Goals				
Government spending on health and education (% of GDP)	6.6	2019	●	↓
For high-income and all OECD DAC countries: International concessional public finance, including official development assistance (% of GNI)	NA	NA	●	●
Other countries: Government revenue excluding grants (% of GDP)	19.6	2019	●	→
Corporate Tax Haven Score (best 0–100 worst)	* 0.0	2019	●	●
Statistical Performance Index (worst 0–100 best)	59.0	2019	●	↗

* Imputed data point

5. Country Profiles

ZIMBABWE

Sub-Saharan Africa

OVERALL PERFORMANCE

COUNTRY RANKING

ZIMBABWE

131/163

COUNTRY SCORE

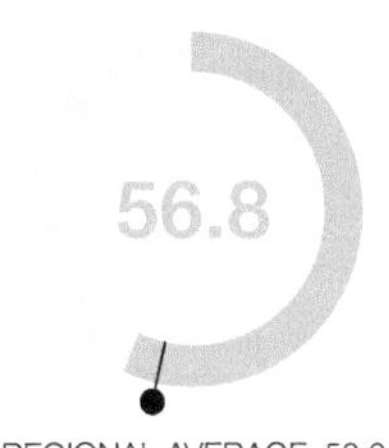

AVERAGE PERFORMANCE BY SDG

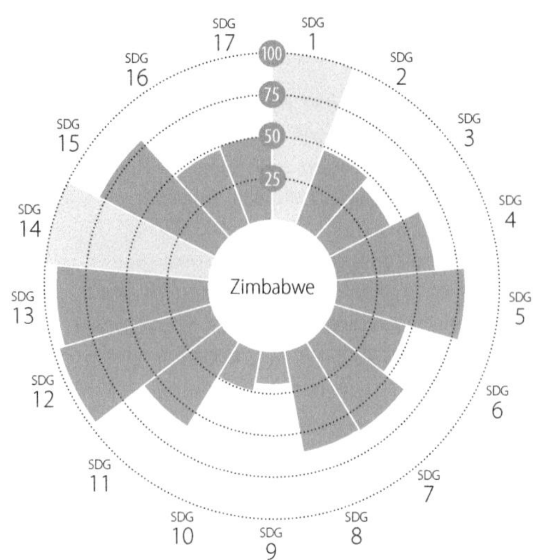

SDG DASHBOARDS AND TRENDS

Major challenges · Significant challenges · Challenges remain · SDG achieved · Information unavailable

Decreasing · Stagnating · Moderately improving · On track or maintaining SDG achievement · Information unavailable

Note: The full title of each SDG is available here: https://sustainabledevelopment.un.org/topics/sustainabledevelopmentgoals

INTERNATIONAL SPILLOVER INDEX

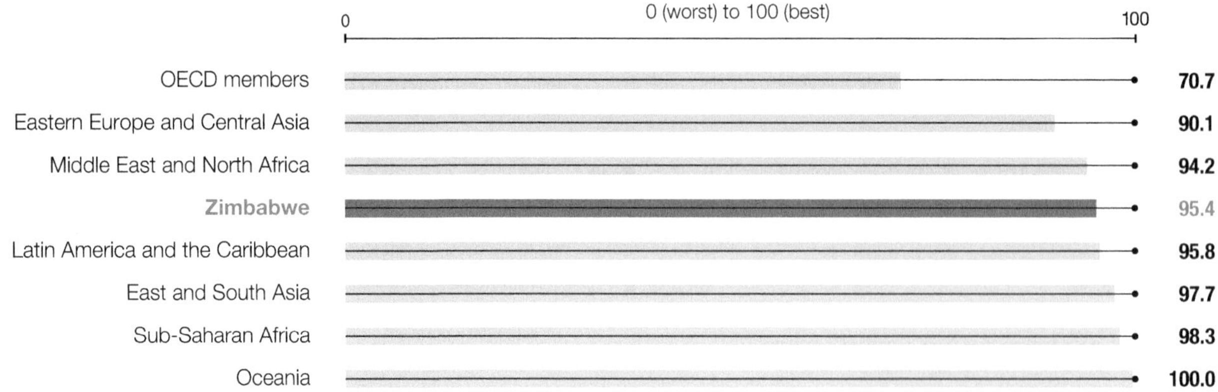

OECD members	70.7
Eastern Europe and Central Asia	90.1
Middle East and North Africa	94.2
Zimbabwe	95.4
Latin America and the Caribbean	95.8
East and South Asia	97.7
Sub-Saharan Africa	98.3
Oceania	100.0

STATISTICAL PERFORMANCE INDEX

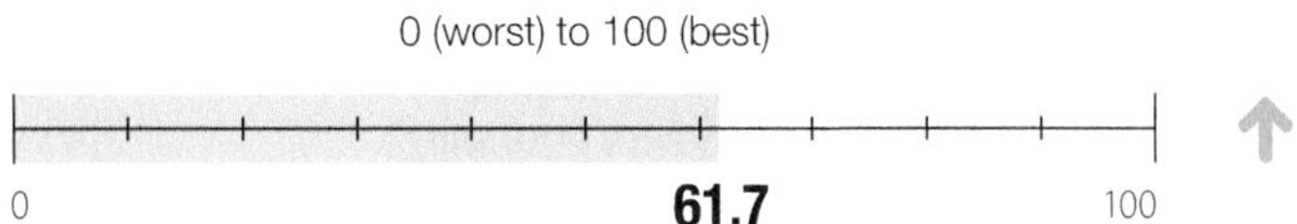

MISSING DATA IN SDG INDEX

ZIMBABWE

Performance by Indicator

SDG1 – No Poverty	Value	Year	Rating	Trend
Poverty headcount ratio at $1.90/day (%)	* NA	NA	●	●
Poverty headcount ratio at $3.20/day (%)	* NA	NA	●	●
SDG2 – Zero Hunger				
Prevalence of undernourishment (%)	NA	NA	●	●
Prevalence of stunting in children under 5 years of age (%)	23.5	2019	●	→
Prevalence of wasting in children under 5 years of age (%)	2.9	2019	●	↑
Prevalence of obesity, BMI ≥ 30 (% of adult population)	15.5	2016	●	↓
Human Trophic Level (best 2–3 worst)	2.2	2017	●	↑
Cereal yield (tonnes per hectare of harvested land)	0.6	2018	●	→
Sustainable Nitrogen Management Index (best 0–1.41 worst)	1.0	2015	●	→
Exports of hazardous pesticides (tonnes per million population)	NA	NA	●	●
SDG3 – Good Health and Well-Being				
Maternal mortality rate (per 100,000 live births)	458	2017	●	→
Neonatal mortality rate (per 1,000 live births)	25.7	2020	●	→
Mortality rate, under-5 (per 1,000 live births)	53.9	2020	●	↗
Incidence of tuberculosis (per 100,000 population)	193.0	2020	●	↗
New HIV infections (per 1,000 uninfected population)	1.7	2020	●	↑
Age-standardized death rate due to cardiovascular disease, cancer, diabetes, or chronic respiratory disease in adults aged 30–70 years (%)	28.4	2019	●	↗
Age-standardized death rate attributable to household air pollution and ambient air pollution (per 100,000 population)	133	2016	●	●
Traffic deaths (per 100,000 population)	41.2	2019	●	↓
Life expectancy at birth (years)	60.7	2019	●	→
Adolescent fertility rate (births per 1,000 females aged 15 to 19)	107.9	2017	●	●
Births attended by skilled health personnel (%)	86.0	2019	●	↑
Surviving infants who received 2 WHO-recommended vaccines (%)	85	2020	●	→
Universal health coverage (UHC) index of service coverage (worst 0–100 best)	55	2019	●	→
Subjective well-being (average ladder score, worst 0–10 best)	3.2	2021	●	↓
SDG4 – Quality Education				
Participation rate in pre-primary organized learning (% of children aged 4 to 6)	54.7	2019	●	→
Net primary enrollment rate (%)	86.4	2020	●	↓
Lower secondary completion rate (%)	68.0	2020	●	→
Literacy rate (% of population aged 15 to 24)	90.4	2014	●	●
SDG5 – Gender Equality				
Demand for family planning satisfied by modern methods (% of females aged 15 to 49)	84.8	2015	●	↑
Ratio of female-to-male mean years of education received (%)	91.0	2019	●	↑
Ratio of female-to-male labor force participation rate (%)	89.0	2020	●	↑
Seats held by women in national parliament (%)	31.9	2020	●	→
SDG6 – Clean Water and Sanitation				
Population using at least basic drinking water services (%)	62.7	2020	●	↓
Population using at least basic sanitation services (%)	35.2	2020	●	↓
Freshwater withdrawal (% of available freshwater resources)	35.4	2018	●	●
Anthropogenic wastewater that receives treatment (%)	0.0	2018	●	●
Scarce water consumption embodied in imports (m^3 H_2O eq/capita)	1251.5	2018	●	●
SDG7 – Affordable and Clean Energy				
Population with access to electricity (%)	41.1	2019	●	→
Population with access to clean fuels and technology for cooking (%)	30.0	2019	●	→
CO_2 emissions from fuel combustion per total electricity output ($MtCO_2$/TWh)	0.9	2019	●	↑
Share of renewable energy in total primary energy supply (%)	71.4	2019	●	↑
SDG8 – Decent Work and Economic Growth				
Adjusted GDP growth (%)	-8.4	2020	●	●
Victims of modern slavery (per 1,000 population)	6.7	2018	●	●
Adults with an account at a bank or other financial institution or with a mobile-money-service provider (% of population aged 15 or over)	55.3	2017	●	↑
Unemployment rate (% of total labor force)	5.0	2022	●	↓
Fundamental labor rights are effectively guaranteed (worst 0–1 best)	0.5	2020	●	↓
Fatal work-related accidents embodied in imports (per 100,000 population)	0.1	2015	●	↑

* Imputed data point

SDG9 – Industry, Innovation and Infrastructure	Value	Year	Rating	Trend
Population using the internet (%)	29.3	2020	●	→
Mobile broadband subscriptions (per 100 population)	51.7	2019	●	↑
Logistics Performance Index: Quality of trade and transport-related infrastructure (worst 1–5 best)	1.8	2018	●	↓
The Times Higher Education Universities Ranking: Average score of top 3 universities (worst 0–100 best)	* 0.0	2022	●	●
Articles published in academic journals (per 1,000 population)	0.1	2020	●	→
Expenditure on research and development (% of GDP)	NA	NA	●	●
SDG10 – Reduced Inequalities				
Gini coefficient	50.3	2019	●	●
Palma ratio	2.3	2018	●	●
SDG11 – Sustainable Cities and Communities				
Proportion of urban population living in slums (%)	29.0	2018	●	↓
Annual mean concentration of particulate matter of less than 2.5 microns in diameter (PM2.5) (μg/m^3)	21.3	2019	●	→
Access to improved water source, piped (% of urban population)	66.8	2020	●	↓
Satisfaction with public transport (%)	35.0	2021	●	↓
SDG12 – Responsible Consumption and Production				
Municipal solid waste (kg/capita/day)	0.3	2002	●	●
Electronic waste (kg/capita)	1.1	2019	●	●
Production-based SO_2 emissions (kg/capita)	2.6	2018	●	●
SO_2 emissions embodied in imports (kg/capita)	2.5	2018	●	●
Production-based nitrogen emissions (kg/capita)	8.9	2015	●	↑
Nitrogen emissions embodied in imports (kg/capita)	0.5	2015	●	↑
Exports of plastic waste (kg/capita)	0.1	2020	●	●
SDG13 – Climate Action				
CO_2 emissions from fossil fuel combustion and cement production (tCO_2/capita)	0.7	2020	●	↑
CO_2 emissions embodied in imports (tCO_2/capita)	0.6	2018	●	→
CO_2 emissions embodied in fossil fuel exports (kg/capita)	18.6	2020	●	●
SDG14 – Life Below Water				
Mean area that is protected in marine sites important to biodiversity (%)	NA	NA	●	●
Ocean Health Index: Clean Waters score (worst 0–100 best)	NA	NA	●	●
Fish caught from overexploited or collapsed stocks (% of total catch)	NA	NA	●	●
Fish caught by trawling or dredging (%)	NA	NA	●	●
Fish caught that are then discarded (%)	NA	NA	●	●
Marine biodiversity threats embodied in imports (per million population)	0.0	2018	●	●
SDG15 – Life on Land				
Mean area that is protected in terrestrial sites important to biodiversity (%)	81.2	2020	●	→
Mean area that is protected in freshwater sites important to biodiversity (%)	82.0	2020	●	→
Red List Index of species survival (worst 0–1 best)	0.8	2021	●	↓
Permanent deforestation (% of forest area, 5-year average)	0.2	2020	●	↑
Terrestrial and freshwater biodiversity threats embodied in imports (per million population)	0.3	2018	●	●
SDG16 – Peace, Justice and Strong Institutions				
Homicides (per 100,000 population)	7.5	2012	●	●
Unsentenced detainees (% of prison population)	17.1	2015	●	●
Population who feel safe walking alone at night in the city or area where they live (%)	43	2021	●	↓
Property Rights (worst 1–7 best)	2.8	2020	●	↗
Birth registrations with civil authority (% of children under age 5)	48.7	2020	●	●
Corruption Perception Index (worst 0–100 best)	23	2021	●	→
Children involved in child labor (% of population aged 5 to 14)	27.9	2019	●	●
Exports of major conventional weapons (TIV constant million USD per 100,000 population)	0.0	2020	●	●
Press Freedom Index (best 0–100 worst)	43.1	2021	●	↓
Access to and affordability of justice (worst 0–1 best)	0.4	2020	●	→
SDG17 – Partnerships for the Goals				
Government spending on health and education (% of GDP)	4.9	2019	●	↓
For high-income and all OECD DAC countries: International concessional public finance, including official development assistance (% of GNI)	NA	NA	●	●
Other countries: Government revenue excluding grants (% of GDP)	15.3	2018	●	↓
Corporate Tax Haven Score (best 0–100 worst)	* 0.0	2019	●	●
Statistical Performance Index (worst 0–100 best)	61.7	2019	●	↑

EAST AND SOUTH ASIA

OVERALL PERFORMANCE

RANKING

EAST AND SOUTH ASIA

NA

AVERAGE

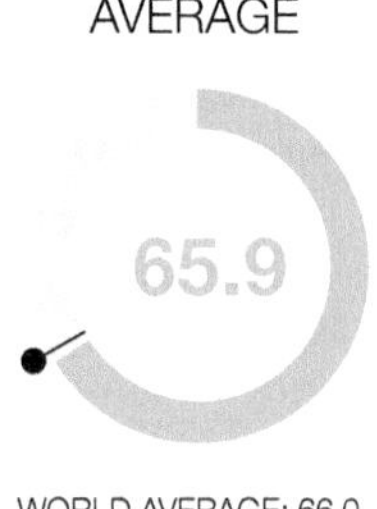

WORLD AVERAGE: 66.0

AVERAGE PERFORMANCE BY SDG

SDG DASHBOARDS AND TRENDS

Major challenges | Significant challenges | Challenges remain | SDG achieved | Information unavailable

Decreasing | Stagnating | Moderately improving | On track or maintaining SDG achievement | Information unavailable

Note: The full title of each SDG is available here: https://sustainabledevelopment.un.org/topics/sustainabledevelopmentgoals

INTERNATIONAL SPILLOVER INDEX

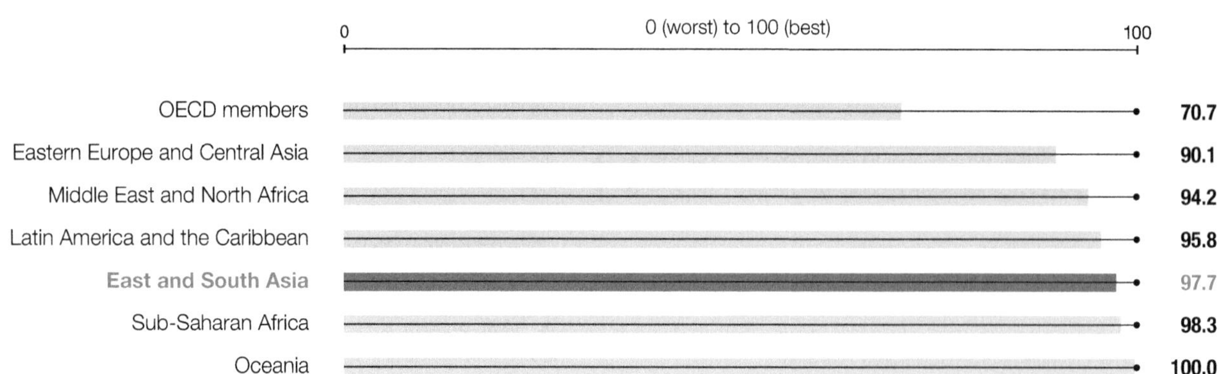

STATISTICAL PERFORMANCE INDEX

0 (worst) to 100 (best)

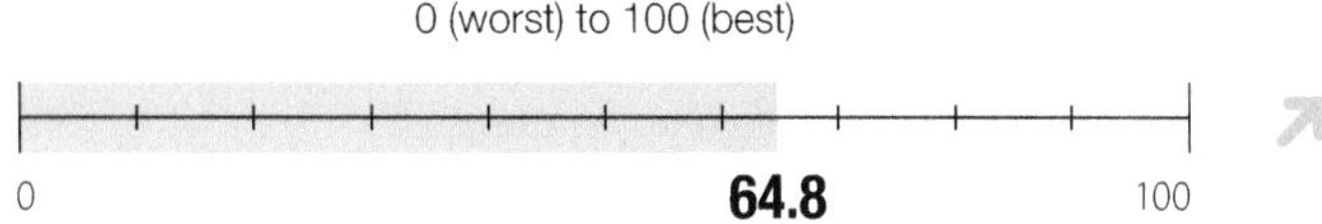

MISSING DATA IN SDG INDEX

0%

EAST AND SOUTH ASIA

SDG1 – No Poverty	Value	Year	Rating	Trend
Poverty headcount ratio at $1.90/day (%)	2.9	2022	●	↑
Poverty headcount ratio at $3.20/day (%)	19.2	2022	●	↗

SDG2 – Zero Hunger	Value	Year	Rating	Trend
Prevalence of undernourishment (%)	8.9	2019	●	→
Prevalence of stunting in children under 5 years of age (%)	22.2	2019	●	→
Prevalence of wasting in children under 5 years of age (%)	9.1	2019	●	→
Prevalence of obesity, BMI ≥ 30 (% of adult population)	5.5	2016	●	↑
Human Trophic Level (best 2–3 worst)	2.2	2017	●	→
Cereal yield (tonnes per hectare of harvested land)	4.6	2018	●	↑
Sustainable Nitrogen Management Index (best 0–1.41 worst)	0.8	2015	●	→
Exports of hazardous pesticides (tonnes per million population)	11.2	2019	●	●

SDG3 – Good Health and Well-Being	Value	Year	Rating	Trend
Maternal mortality rate (per 100,000 live births)	101	2017	●	↑
Neonatal mortality rate (per 1,000 live births)	13.5	2020	●	↑
Mortality rate, under-5 (per 1,000 live births)	23.2	2020	●	↑
Incidence of tuberculosis (per 100,000 population)	166.3	2020	●	→
New HIV infections (per 1,000 uninfected population)	0.5	2020	●	→
Age-standardized death rate due to cardiovascular disease, cancer, diabetes, or chronic respiratory disease in adults aged 30–70 years (%)	20.1	2019	●	→
Age-standardized death rate attributable to household air pollution and ambient air pollution (per 100,000 population)	144	2016	●	●
Traffic deaths (per 100,000 population)	16.5	2019	●	→
Life expectancy at birth (years)	73.3	2019	●	→
Adolescent fertility rate (births per 1,000 females aged 15 to 19)	19.9	2019	●	●
Births attended by skilled health personnel (%)	87.8	2018	●	↑
Surviving infants who received 2 WHO-recommended vaccines (%)	90	2020	●	↓
Universal health coverage (UHC) index of service coverage (worst 0–100 best)	68	2019	●	↑
Subjective well-being (average ladder score, worst 0–10 best)	4.9	2021	●	→

SDG4 – Quality Education	Value	Year	Rating	Trend
Participation rate in pre-primary organized learning (% of children aged 4 to 6)	86.2	2020	●	●
Net primary enrollment rate (%)	95.2	2020	●	↑
Lower secondary completion rate (%)	88.6	2020	●	→
Literacy rate (% of population aged 15 to 24)	94.9	2020	●	●

SDG5 – Gender Equality	Value	Year	Rating	Trend
Demand for family planning satisfied by modern methods (% of females aged 15 to 49)	80.1	2022	●	↑
Ratio of female-to-male mean years of education received (%)	79.5	2019	●	→
Ratio of female-to-male labor force participation rate (%)	56.3	2020	●	↓
Seats held by women in national parliament (%)	20.1	2020	●	→

SDG6 – Clean Water and Sanitation	Value	Year	Rating	Trend
Population using at least basic drinking water services (%)	92.6	2020	●	↗
Population using at least basic sanitation services (%)	80.9	2020	●	↑
Freshwater withdrawal (% of available freshwater resources)	50.5	2018	●	●
Anthropogenic wastewater that receives treatment (%)	4.5	2018	●	●
Scarce water consumption embodied in imports (m^3 H_2O eq/capita)	329.2	2018	●	●

SDG7 – Affordable and Clean Energy	Value	Year	Rating	Trend
Population with access to electricity (%)	96.3	2019	●	↑
Population with access to clean fuels and technology for cooking (%)	61.6	2019	●	↑
CO_2 emissions from fuel combustion per total electricity output ($MtCO_2$/TWh)	1.5	2019	●	↗
Share of renewable energy in total primary energy supply (%)	19.3	2019	●	→

SDG8 – Decent Work and Economic Growth	Value	Year	Rating	Trend
Adjusted GDP growth (%)	-0.8	2020	●	●
Victims of modern slavery (per 1,000 population)	5.5	2018	●	●
Adults with an account at a bank or other financial institution or with a mobile-money-service provider (% of population aged 15 or over)	69.5	2017	●	↑
Unemployment rate (% of total labor force)	4.6	2022	●	↑
Fundamental labor rights are effectively guaranteed (worst 0–1 best)	0.4	2020	●	→
Fatal work-related accidents embodied in imports (per 100,000 population)	0.1	2015	●	↑

SDG9 – Industry, Innovation and Infrastructure	Value	Year	Rating	Trend
Population using the internet (%)	53.3	2020	●	↑
Mobile broadband subscriptions (per 100 population)	70.9	2019	●	↑
Logistics Performance Index: Quality of trade and transport-related infrastructure (worst 1–5 best)	3.1	2018	●	↑
The Times Higher Education Universities Ranking: Average score of top 3 universities (worst 0–100 best)	53.5	2022	●	●
Articles published in academic journals (per 1,000 population)	0.3	2020	●	↗
Expenditure on research and development (% of GDP)	1.1	2018	●	●

SDG10 – Reduced Inequalities	Value	Year	Rating	Trend
Gini coefficient	36.7	2019	●	●
Palma ratio	3.0	2019	●	●

SDG11 – Sustainable Cities and Communities	Value	Year	Rating	Trend
Proportion of urban population living in slums (%)	35.4	2018	●	↓
Annual mean concentration of particulate matter of less than 2.5 microns in diameter (PM2.5) (μg/m^3)	59.5	2019	●	→
Access to improved water source, piped (% of urban population)	73.0	2020	●	↓
Satisfaction with public transport (%)	74.6	2021	●	↑

SDG12 – Responsible Consumption and Production	Value	Year	Rating	Trend
Municipal solid waste (kg/capita/day)	0.6	2019	●	●
Electronic waste (kg/capita)	4.6	2019	●	●
Production-based SO_2 emissions (kg/capita)	11.0	2018	●	●
SO_2 emissions embodied in imports (kg/capita)	0.5	2018	●	●
Production-based nitrogen emissions (kg/capita)	9.2	2015	●	↑
Nitrogen emissions embodied in imports (kg/capita)	0.9	2015	●	↑
Exports of plastic waste (kg/capita)	0.2	2021	●	●

SDG13 – Climate Action	Value	Year	Rating	Trend
CO_2 emissions from fossil fuel combustion and cement production (tCO_2/capita)	3.8	2020	●	→
CO_2 emissions embodied in imports (tCO_2/capita)	0.2	2018	●	↑
CO_2 emissions embodied in fossil fuel exports (kg/capita)	316.1	2021	●	●

SDG14 – Life Below Water	Value	Year	Rating	Trend
Mean area that is protected in marine sites important to biodiversity (%)	16.8	2020	●	→
Ocean Health Index: Clean Waters score (worst 0–100 best)	37.2	2020	●	→
Fish caught from overexploited or collapsed stocks (% of total catch)	17.3	2018	●	↑
Fish caught by trawling or dredging (%)	44.9	2018	●	↓
Fish caught that are then discarded (%)	4.3	2018	●	↑
Marine biodiversity threats embodied in imports (per million population)	0.0	2018	●	●

SDG15 – Life on Land	Value	Year	Rating	Trend
Mean area that is protected in terrestrial sites important to biodiversity (%)	21.4	2020	●	→
Mean area that is protected in freshwater sites important to biodiversity (%)	19.5	2020	●	→
Red List Index of species survival (worst 0–1 best)	0.7	2021	●	↓
Permanent deforestation (% of forest area, 5-year average)	0.2	2020	●	↑
Terrestrial and freshwater biodiversity threats embodied in imports (per million population)	0.3	2018	●	●

SDG16 – Peace, Justice and Strong Institutions	Value	Year	Rating	Trend
Homicides (per 100,000 population)	1.9	2020	●	●
Unsentenced detainees (% of prison population)	59.5	2019	●	●
Population who feel safe walking alone at night in the city or area where they live (%)	75	2021	●	↑
Property Rights (worst 1–7 best)	4.5	2020	●	↑
Birth registrations with civil authority (% of children under age 5)	76.3	2020	●	●
Corruption Perception Index (worst 0–100 best)	40	2021	●	→
Children involved in child labor (% of population aged 5 to 14)	10.4	2019	●	●
Exports of major conventional weapons (TIV constant million USD per 100,000 population)	0.0	2020	●	●
Press Freedom Index (best 0–100 worst)	58.5	2021	●	→
Access to and affordability of justice (worst 0–1 best)	0.5	2020	●	↗

SDG17 – Partnerships for the Goals	Value	Year	Rating	Trend
Government spending on health and education (% of GDP)	5.1	2020	●	↓
For high-income and all OECD DAC countries: International concessional public finance, including official development assistance (% of GNI)	NA	NA	●	●
Other countries: Government revenue excluding grants (% of GDP)	14.8	2019	●	→
Corporate Tax Haven Score (best 0–100 worst)	21.2	2019	●	●
Statistical Performance Index (worst 0–100 best)	64.8	2019	●	↗

* Imputed data point

EASTERN EUROPE AND CENTRAL ASIA

OVERALL PERFORMANCE

RANKING

EASTERN EUROPE AND CENTRAL ASIA

NA

AVERAGE

WORLD AVERAGE: 66.0

AVERAGE PERFORMANCE BY SDG

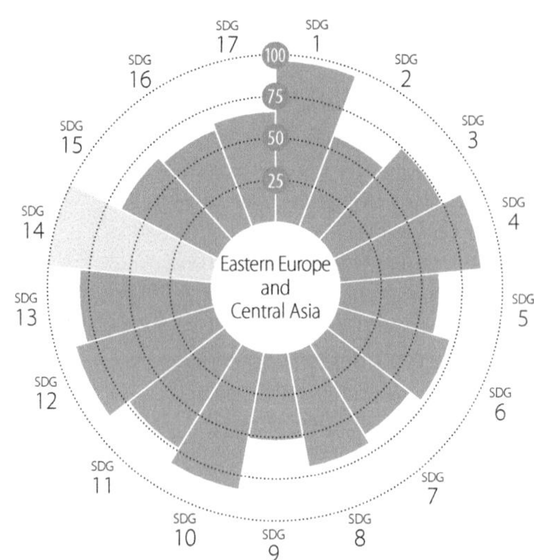

SDG DASHBOARDS AND TRENDS

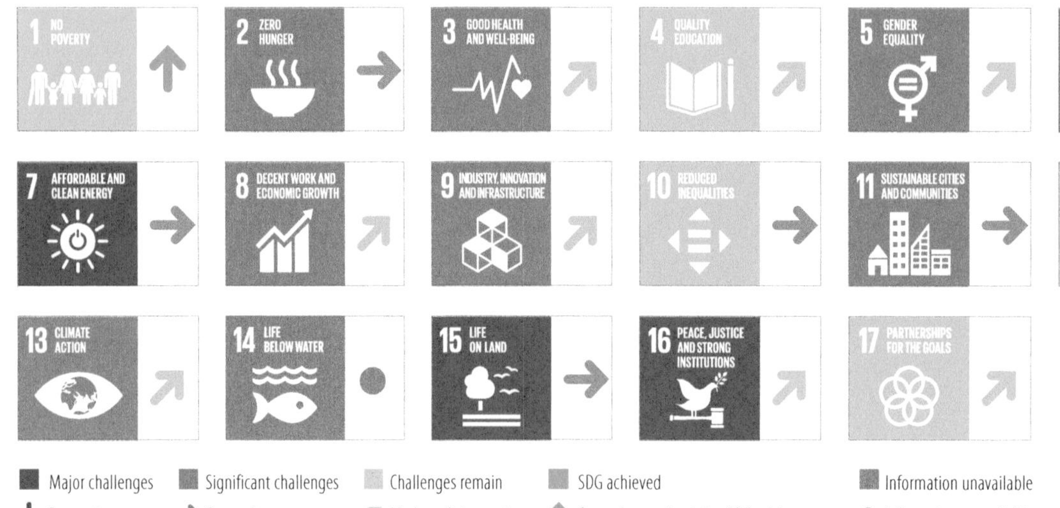

Major challenges · Significant challenges · Challenges remain · SDG achieved · Information unavailable

Decreasing · Stagnating · Moderately improving · On track or maintaining SDG achievement · Information unavailable

Note: The full title of each SDG is available here: https://sustainabledevelopment.un.org/topics/sustainabledevelopmentgoals

INTERNATIONAL SPILLOVER INDEX

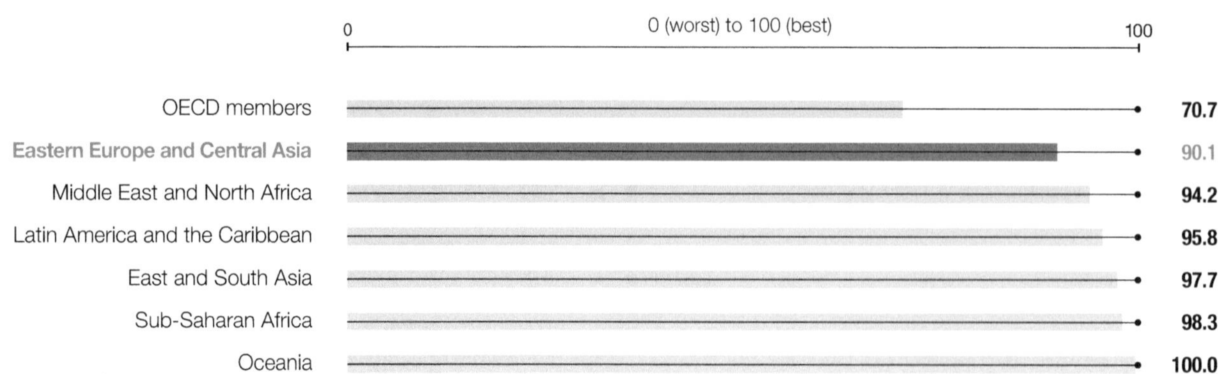

STATISTICAL PERFORMANCE INDEX

0 (worst) to 100 (best)

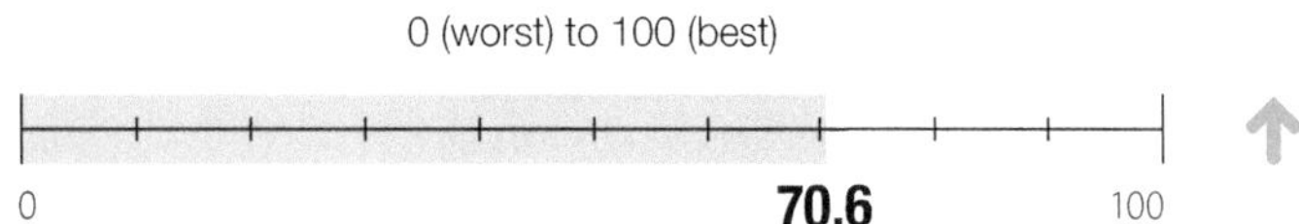

MISSING DATA IN SDG INDEX

7%

SDG1 – No Poverty	Value	Year	Rating	Trend
Poverty headcount ratio at $1.90/day (%)	0.7	2022	●	↑
Poverty headcount ratio at $3.20/day (%)	3.5	2022	●	↑
SDG2 – Zero Hunger				
Prevalence of undernourishment (%)	5.2	2019	●	↑
Prevalence of stunting in children under 5 years of age (%)	17.0	2019	●	→
Prevalence of wasting in children under 5 years of age (%)	4.2	2019	●	↑
Prevalence of obesity, BMI ≥ 30 (% of adult population)	20.1	2016	●	↓
Human Trophic Level (best 2–3 worst)	2.3	2017	●	→
Cereal yield (tonnes per hectare of harvested land)	3.3	2018	●	↑
Sustainable Nitrogen Management Index (best 0–1.41 worst)	0.6	2015	●	→
Exports of hazardous pesticides (tonnes per million population)	NA	NA	●	●
SDG3 – Good Health and Well-Being				
Maternal mortality rate (per 100,000 live births)	82	2017	●	↑
Neonatal mortality rate (per 1,000 live births)	7.9	2020	●	↑
Mortality rate, under-5 (per 1,000 live births)	14.2	2020	●	↑
Incidence of tuberculosis (per 100,000 population)	67.8	2020	●	↗
New HIV infections (per 1,000 uninfected population)	0.5	2020	●	→
Age-standardized death rate due to cardiovascular disease, cancer, diabetes, or chronic respiratory disease in adults aged 30–70 years (%)	25.1	2019	●	→
Age-standardized death rate attributable to household air pollution and ambient air pollution (per 100,000 population)	78	2016	●	●
Traffic deaths (per 100,000 population)	11.8	2019	●	↑
Life expectancy at birth (years)	72.5	2019	●	↗
Adolescent fertility rate (births per 1,000 females aged 15 to 19)	27.2	2019	●	↑
Births attended by skilled health personnel (%)	95.2	2018	●	●
Surviving infants who received 2 WHO-recommended vaccines (%)	89	2020	●	↑
Universal health coverage (UHC) index of service coverage (worst 0–100 best)	69	2019	●	↑
Subjective well-being (average ladder score, worst 0–10 best)	5.3	2021	●	↓
SDG4 – Quality Education				
Participation rate in pre-primary organized learning (% of children aged 4 to 6)	80.6	2020	●	↗
Net primary enrollment rate (%)	96.6	2020	●	↑
Lower secondary completion rate (%)	94.7	2020	●	↑
Literacy rate (% of population aged 15 to 24)	95.2	2020	●	●
SDG5 – Gender Equality				
Demand for family planning satisfied by modern methods (% of females aged 15 to 49)	61.9	2022	●	●
Ratio of female-to-male mean years of education received (%)	90.3	2019	●	→
Ratio of female-to-male labor force participation rate (%)	70.1	2020	●	↑
Seats held by women in national parliament (%)	22.2	2020	●	↗
SDG6 – Clean Water and Sanitation				
Population using at least basic drinking water services (%)	94.0	2020	●	↗
Population using at least basic sanitation services (%)	88.8	2020	●	↗
Freshwater withdrawal (% of available freshwater resources)	33.7	2018	●	●
Anthropogenic wastewater that receives treatment (%)	13.9	2018	●	●
Scarce water consumption embodied in imports (m^3 H_2O eq/capita)	1284.8	2018	●	●
SDG7 – Affordable and Clean Energy				
Population with access to electricity (%)	99.7	2019	●	↑
Population with access to clean fuels and technology for cooking (%)	84.7	2019	●	↓
CO_2 emissions from fuel combustion per total electricity output ($MtCO_2$/TWh)	2.3	2019	●	→
Share of renewable energy in total primary energy supply (%)	7.0	2019	●	→
SDG8 – Decent Work and Economic Growth				
Adjusted GDP growth (%)	-0.4	2020	●	●
Victims of modern slavery (per 1,000 population)	7.3	2018	●	●
Adults with an account at a bank or other financial institution or with a mobile-money-service provider (% of population aged 15 or over)	58.7	2017	●	↑
Unemployment rate (% of total labor force)	7.6	2022	●	→
Fundamental labor rights are effectively guaranteed (worst 0–1 best)	0.6	2020	●	↓
Fatal work-related accidents embodied in imports (per 100,000 population)	0.2	2015	●	↑

* Imputed data point

SDG9 – Industry, Innovation and Infrastructure	Value	Year	Rating	Trend
Population using the internet (%)	71.3	2020	●	↑
Mobile broadband subscriptions (per 100 population)	79.0	2019	●	↑
Logistics Performance Index: Quality of trade and transport-related infrastructure (worst 1–5 best)	2.5	2018	●	→
The Times Higher Education Universities Ranking: Average score of top 3 universities (worst 0–100 best)	28.3	2022	●	●
Articles published in academic journals (per 1,000 population)	0.5	2020	●	↑
Expenditure on research and development (% of GDP)	0.6	2018	●	↓
SDG10 – Reduced Inequalities				
Gini coefficient	33.9	2019	●	→
Palma ratio	1.2	2019	●	●
SDG11 – Sustainable Cities and Communities				
Proportion of urban population living in slums (%)	35.5	2018	●	●
Annual mean concentration of particulate matter of less than 2.5 microns in diameter (PM2.5) (μg/m^3)	22.6	2019	●	↗
Access to improved water source, piped (% of urban population)	87.6	2020	●	→
Satisfaction with public transport (%)	60.4	2021	●	→
SDG12 – Responsible Consumption and Production				
Municipal solid waste (kg/capita/day)	0.9	2019	●	●
Electronic waste (kg/capita)	8.8	2019	●	●
Production-based SO_2 emissions (kg/capita)	13.8	2018	●	●
SO_2 emissions embodied in imports (kg/capita)	1.4	2018	●	●
Production-based nitrogen emissions (kg/capita)	13.6	2015	●	↑
Nitrogen emissions embodied in imports (kg/capita)	3.3	2015	●	↑
Exports of plastic waste (kg/capita)	0.4	2021	●	●
SDG13 – Climate Action				
CO_2 emissions from fossil fuel combustion and cement production (tCO_2/capita)	6.9	2020	●	→
CO_2 emissions embodied in imports (tCO_2/capita)	0.5	2018	●	↑
CO_2 emissions embodied in fossil fuel exports (kg/capita)	4781.4	2021	●	●
SDG14 – Life Below Water				
Mean area that is protected in marine sites important to biodiversity (%)	NA	NA	●	●
Ocean Health Index: Clean Waters score (worst 0–100 best)	NA	NA	●	●
Fish caught from overexploited or collapsed stocks (% of total catch)	NA	NA	●	●
Fish caught by trawling or dredging (%)	NA	NA	●	●
Fish caught that are then discarded (%)	NA	NA	●	●
Marine biodiversity threats embodied in imports (per million population)	0.0	2018	●	●
SDG15 – Life on Land				
Mean area that is protected in terrestrial sites important to biodiversity (%)	26.6	2020	●	↓
Mean area that is protected in freshwater sites important to biodiversity (%)	25.9	2020	●	↓
Red List Index of species survival (worst 0–1 best)	0.9	2021	●	↑
Permanent deforestation (% of forest area, 5-year average)	0.0	2020	●	↑
Terrestrial and freshwater biodiversity threats embodied in imports (per million population)	0.6	2018	●	●
SDG16 – Peace, Justice and Strong Institutions				
Homicides (per 100,000 population)	4.9	2020	●	↑
Unsentenced detainees (% of prison population)	17.1	2019	●	↑
Population who feel safe walking alone at night in the city or area where they live (%)	64	2021	●	↑
Property Rights (worst 1–7 best)	3.8	2020	●	→
Birth registrations with civil authority (% of children under age 5)	93.6	2020	●	●
Corruption Perception Index (worst 0–100 best)	31	2021	●	→
Children involved in child labor (% of population aged 5 to 14)	NA	NA	●	●
Exports of major conventional weapons (TIV constant million USD per 100,000 population)	1.6	2020	●	●
Press Freedom Index (best 0–100 worst)	43.9	2021	●	→
Access to and affordability of justice (worst 0–1 best)	0.6	2020	●	↑
SDG17 – Partnerships for the Goals				
Government spending on health and education (% of GDP)	7.4	2020	●	↗
For high-income and all OECD DAC countries: International concessional public finance, including official development assistance (% of GNI)	NA	NA	●	●
Other countries: Government revenue excluding grants (% of GDP)	25.9	2019	●	↗
Corporate Tax Haven Score (best 0–100 worst)	4.7	2019	●	●
Statistical Performance Index (worst 0–100 best)	70.6	2019	●	↑

LATIN AMERICA AND THE CARIBBEAN

OVERALL PERFORMANCE

RANKING

LATIN AMERICA AND THE CARIBBEAN

NA

AVERAGE

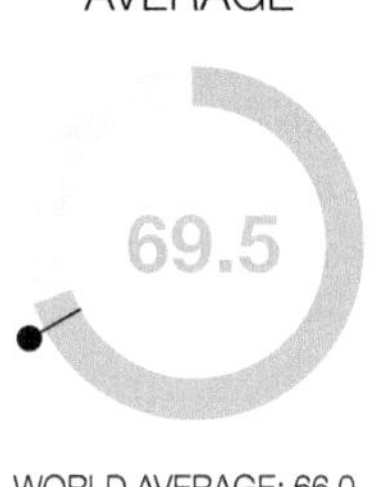

WORLD AVERAGE: 66.0

AVERAGE PERFORMANCE BY SDG

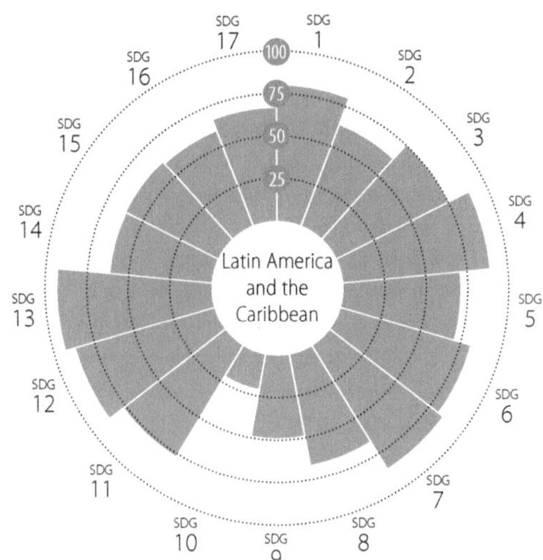

SDG DASHBOARDS AND TRENDS

Major challenges | Significant challenges | Challenges remain | SDG achieved | Information unavailable

Decreasing | Stagnating | Moderately improving | On track or maintaining SDG achievement | Information unavailable

Note: The full title of each SDG is available here: https://sustainabledevelopment.un.org/topics/sustainabledevelopmentgoals

INTERNATIONAL SPILLOVER INDEX

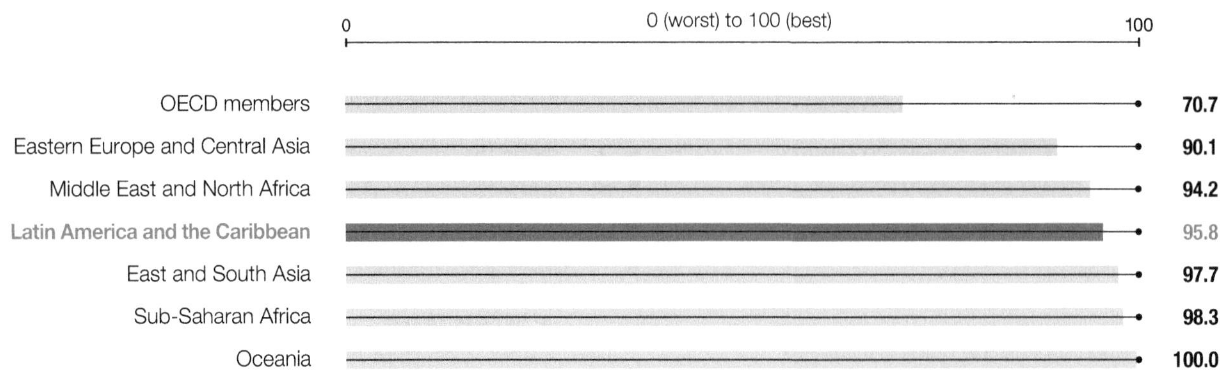

STATISTICAL PERFORMANCE INDEX

0 (worst) to 100 (best)

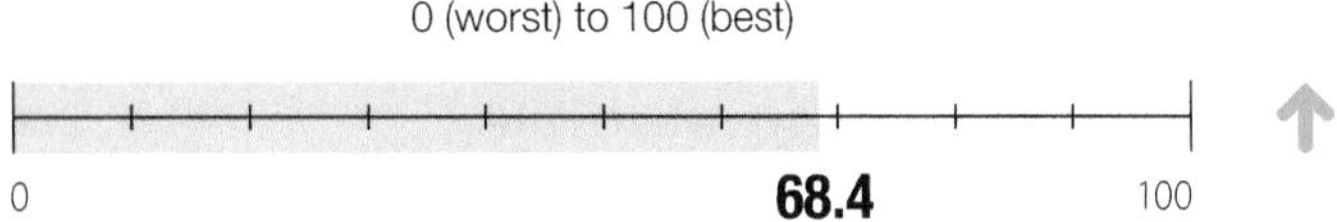

MISSING DATA IN SDG INDEX

0%

SDG1 – No Poverty	Value	Year	Rating	Trend
Poverty headcount ratio at $1.90/day (%)	7.3	2022	●	↓
Poverty headcount ratio at $3.20/day (%)	15.2	2022	●	↓
SDG2 – Zero Hunger				
Prevalence of undernourishment (%)	8.0	2019	●	↓
Prevalence of stunting in children under 5 years of age (%)	11.5	2019	●	→
Prevalence of wasting in children under 5 years of age (%)	2.0	2019	●	↑
Prevalence of obesity, BMI ≥ 30 (% of adult population)	22.9	2016	●	↓
Human Trophic Level (best 2–3 worst)	2.3	2017	●	→
Cereal yield (tonnes per hectare of harvested land)	4.1	2018	●	↑
Sustainable Nitrogen Management Index (best 0–1.41 worst)	0.7	2015	●	↓
Exports of hazardous pesticides (tonnes per million population)	26.9	2019	●	●
SDG3 – Good Health and Well-Being				
Maternal mortality rate (per 100,000 live births)	81	2017	●	↑
Neonatal mortality rate (per 1,000 live births)	9.3	2020	●	↑
Mortality rate, under-5 (per 1,000 live births)	16.6	2020	●	↑
Incidence of tuberculosis (per 100,000 population)	51.2	2020	●	→
New HIV infections (per 1,000 uninfected population)	0.2	2020	●	↑
Age-standardized death rate due to cardiovascular disease, cancer, diabetes, or chronic respiratory disease in adults aged 30–70 years (%)	15.5	2019	●	↑
Age-standardized death rate attributable to household air pollution and ambient air pollution (per 100,000 population)	42	2016	●	●
Traffic deaths (per 100,000 population)	18.9	2019	●	→
Life expectancy at birth (years)	75.6	2019	●	→
Adolescent fertility rate (births per 1,000 females aged 15 to 19)	56.8	2019	●	●
Births attended by skilled health personnel (%)	93.9	2018	●	↗
Surviving infants who received 2 WHO-recommended vaccines (%)	75	2020	●	↓
Universal health coverage (UHC) index of service coverage (worst 0–100 best)	73	2019	●	→
Subjective well-being (average ladder score, worst 0–10 best)	5.8	2021	●	●
SDG4 – Quality Education				
Participation rate in pre-primary organized learning (% of children aged 4 to 6)	94.3	2020	●	↑
Net primary enrollment rate (%)	96.9	2020	●	↑
Lower secondary completion rate (%)	77.8	2020	●	→
Literacy rate (% of population aged 15 to 24)	98.4	2020	●	●
SDG5 – Gender Equality				
Demand for family planning satisfied by modern methods (% of females aged 15 to 49)	81.2	2022	●	↑
Ratio of female-to-male mean years of education received (%)	101.9	2019	●	↑
Ratio of female-to-male labor force participation rate (%)	68.1	2020	●	→
Seats held by women in national parliament (%)	22.9	2020	●	↗
SDG6 – Clean Water and Sanitation				
Population using at least basic drinking water services (%)	96.5	2020	●	↑
Population using at least basic sanitation services (%)	86.8	2020	●	↗
Freshwater withdrawal (% of available freshwater resources)	6.9	2018	●	●
Anthropogenic wastewater that receives treatment (%)	28.9	2018	●	●
Scarce water consumption embodied in imports (m^3 H_2O eq/capita)	585.1	2018	●	●
SDG7 – Affordable and Clean Energy				
Population with access to electricity (%)	97.7	2019	●	↑
Population with access to clean fuels and technology for cooking (%)	88.0	2019	●	↑
CO_2 emissions from fuel combustion per total electricity output ($MtCO_2$/TWh)	1.0	2019	●	↑
Share of renewable energy in total primary energy supply (%)	36.6	2019	●	↑
SDG8 – Decent Work and Economic Growth				
Adjusted GDP growth (%)	-4.4	2020	●	●
Victims of modern slavery (per 1,000 population)	2.4	2018	●	●
Adults with an account at a bank or other financial institution or with a mobile-money-service provider (% of population aged 15 or over)	60.0	2017	●	↑
Unemployment rate (% of total labor force)	10.2	2022	●	↓
Fundamental labor rights are effectively guaranteed (worst 0–1 best)	0.5	2020	●	↓
Fatal work-related accidents embodied in imports (per 100,000 population)	0.2	2015	●	↑

SDG9 – Industry, Innovation and Infrastructure	Value	Year	Rating	Trend
Population using the internet (%)	73.0	2020	●	↑
Mobile broadband subscriptions (per 100 population)	71.4	2019	●	↑
Logistics Performance Index: Quality of trade and transport-related infrastructure (worst 1–5 best)	2.6	2018	●	↓
The Times Higher Education Universities Ranking: Average score of top 3 universities (worst 0–100 best)	27.1	2022	●	●
Articles published in academic journals (per 1,000 population)	0.3	2020	●	→
Expenditure on research and development (% of GDP)	0.7	2018	●	●
SDG10 – Reduced Inequalities				
Gini coefficient	48.6	2019	●	●
Palma ratio	2.6	2019	●	●
SDG11 – Sustainable Cities and Communities				
Proportion of urban population living in slums (%)	22.3	2018	●	↗
Annual mean concentration of particulate matter of less than 2.5 microns in diameter (PM2.5) (μg/m^3)	14.4	2019	●	↑
Access to improved water source, piped (% of urban population)	95.0	2020	●	↗
Satisfaction with public transport (%)	48.2	2021	●	●
SDG12 – Responsible Consumption and Production				
Municipal solid waste (kg/capita/day)	0.9	2019	●	●
Electronic waste (kg/capita)	8.8	2019	●	●
Production-based SO_2 emissions (kg/capita)	9.2	2018	●	●
SO_2 emissions embodied in imports (kg/capita)	1.0	2018	●	●
Production-based nitrogen emissions (kg/capita)	25.0	2015	●	↓
Nitrogen emissions embodied in imports (kg/capita)	2.1	2015	●	↑
Exports of plastic waste (kg/capita)	0.2	2021	●	●
SDG13 – Climate Action				
CO_2 emissions from fossil fuel combustion and cement production (tCO_2/capita)	2.2	2020	●	↑
CO_2 emissions embodied in imports (tCO_2/capita)	0.3	2018	●	↑
CO_2 emissions embodied in fossil fuel exports (kg/capita)	631.7	2021	●	●
SDG14 – Life Below Water				
Mean area that is protected in marine sites important to biodiversity (%)	57.1	2020	●	→
Ocean Health Index: Clean Waters score (worst 0–100 best)	60.5	2020	●	→
Fish caught from overexploited or collapsed stocks (% of total catch)	19.0	2018	●	↑
Fish caught by trawling or dredging (%)	13.1	2018	●	↓
Fish caught that are then discarded (%)	19.6	2018	●	↓
Marine biodiversity threats embodied in imports (per million population)	0.1	2018	●	●
SDG15 – Life on Land				
Mean area that is protected in terrestrial sites important to biodiversity (%)	42.0	2020	●	→
Mean area that is protected in freshwater sites important to biodiversity (%)	40.4	2020	●	→
Red List Index of species survival (worst 0–1 best)	0.8	2021	●	↓
Permanent deforestation (% of forest area, 5-year average)	0.4	2020	●	↑
Terrestrial and freshwater biodiversity threats embodied in imports (per million population)	0.5	2018	●	●
SDG16 – Peace, Justice and Strong Institutions				
Homicides (per 100,000 population)	18.6	2020	●	↗
Unsentenced detainees (% of prison population)	39.4	2019	●	↑
Population who feel safe walking alone at night in the city or area where they live (%)	48	2021	●	●
Property Rights (worst 1–7 best)	3.7	2020	●	↓
Birth registrations with civil authority (% of children under age 5)	94.0	2020	●	●
Corruption Perception Index (worst 0–100 best)	35	2021	●	→
Children involved in child labor (% of population aged 5 to 14)	8.1	2019	●	●
Exports of major conventional weapons (TIV constant million USD per 100,000 population)	0.0	2020	●	●
Press Freedom Index (best 0–100 worst)	35.9	2021	●	↓
Access to and affordability of justice (worst 0–1 best)	0.6	2020	●	↗
SDG17 – Partnerships for the Goals				
Government spending on health and education (% of GDP)	9.1	2020	●	↓
For high-income and all OECD DAC countries: International concessional public finance, including official development assistance (% of GNI)	NA	NA	●	●
Other countries: Government revenue excluding grants (% of GDP)	24.7	2019	●	●
Corporate Tax Haven Score (best 0–100 worst)	0.8	2019	●	●
Statistical Performance Index (worst 0–100 best)	68.4	2019	●	↑

* Imputed data point

MIDDLE EAST AND NORTH AFRICA

OVERALL PERFORMANCE

RANKING

MIDDLE EAST AND NORTH AFRICA

NA

AVERAGE

WORLD AVERAGE: 66.0

AVERAGE PERFORMANCE BY SDG

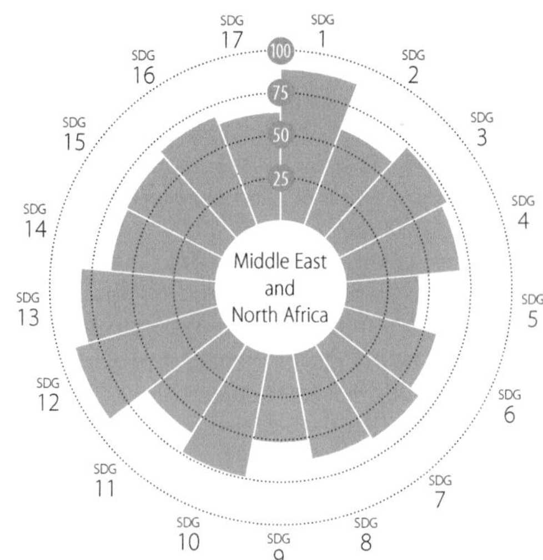

SDG DASHBOARDS AND TRENDS

Major challenges | Significant challenges | Challenges remain | SDG achieved | Information unavailable

Decreasing | Stagnating | Moderately improving | On track or maintaining SDG achievement | Information unavailable

Note: The full title of each SDG is available here: https://sustainabledevelopment.un.org/topics/sustainabledevelopmentgoals

INTERNATIONAL SPILLOVER INDEX

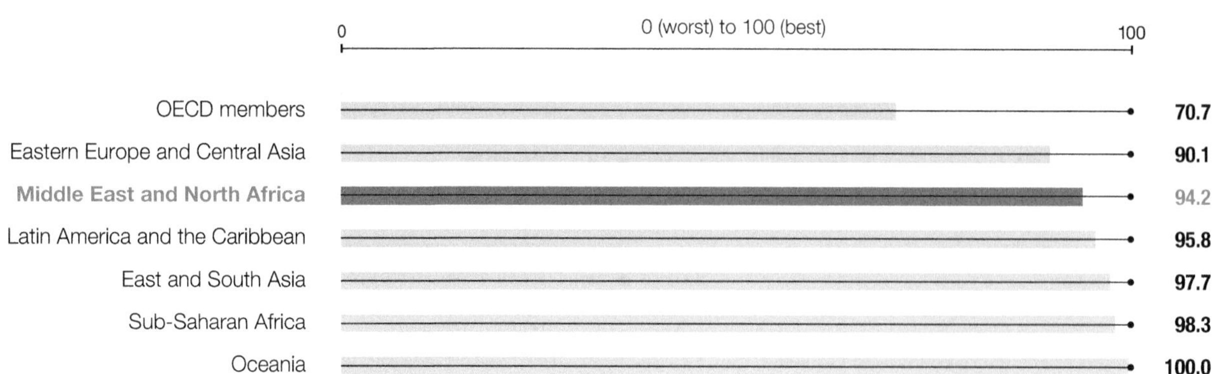

Region	Score
OECD members	70.7
Eastern Europe and Central Asia	90.1
Middle East and North Africa	94.2
Latin America and the Caribbean	95.8
East and South Asia	97.7
Sub-Saharan Africa	98.3
Oceania	100.0

STATISTICAL PERFORMANCE INDEX

0 (worst) to 100 (best)

0 **56.6** 100

MISSING DATA IN SDG INDEX

6%

SDG1 – No Poverty

Indicator	Value	Year	Rating	Trend
Poverty headcount ratio at $1.90/day (%)	1.1	2022	●	↑
Poverty headcount ratio at $3.20/day (%)	11.4	2022	●	↓

SDG2 – Zero Hunger

Indicator	Value	Year	Rating	Trend
Prevalence of undernourishment (%)	10.8	2019	●	→
Prevalence of stunting in children under 5 years of age (%)	16.1	2019	●	→
Prevalence of wasting in children under 5 years of age (%)	6.6	2019	●	→
Prevalence of obesity, BMI ≥ 30 (% of adult population)	28.8	2016	●	↓
Human Trophic Level (best 2–3 worst)	2.2	2017	●	↑
Cereal yield (tonnes per hectare of harvested land)	4.2	2018	●	↑
Sustainable Nitrogen Management Index (best 0–1.41 worst)	0.8	2015	●	↗
Exports of hazardous pesticides (tonnes per million population)	1.9	2019	●	●

SDG3 – Good Health and Well-Being

Indicator	Value	Year	Rating	Trend
Maternal mortality rate (per 100,000 live births)	53	2017	●	↑
Neonatal mortality rate (per 1,000 live births)	11.2	2020	●	↑
Mortality rate, under-5 (per 1,000 live births)	19.8	2020	●	↑
Incidence of tuberculosis (per 100,000 population)	28.5	2020	●	↗
New HIV infections (per 1,000 uninfected population)	0.1	2020	●	↑
Age-standardized death rate due to cardiovascular disease, cancer, diabetes, or chronic respiratory disease in adults aged 30–70 years (%)	21.2	2019	●	→
Age-standardized death rate attributable to household air pollution and ambient air pollution (per 100,000 population)	80	2016	●	●
Traffic deaths (per 100,000 population)	19.4	2019	●	→
Life expectancy at birth (years)	74.1	2019	●	↗
Adolescent fertility rate (births per 1,000 females aged 15 to 19)	34.1	2019	●	●
Births attended by skilled health personnel (%)	92.1	2018	●	●
Surviving infants who received 2 WHO-recommended vaccines (%)	87	2020	●	→
Universal health coverage (UHC) index of service coverage (worst 0–100 best)	68	2019	●	↑
Subjective well-being (average ladder score, worst 0–10 best)	4.8	2021	●	↓

SDG4 – Quality Education

Indicator	Value	Year	Rating	Trend
Participation rate in pre-primary organized learning (% of children aged 4 to 6)	48.0	2020	●	→
Net primary enrollment rate (%)	95.9	2020	●	●
Lower secondary completion rate (%)	79.9	2020	●	↗
Literacy rate (% of population aged 15 to 24)	93.8	2020	●	●

SDG5 – Gender Equality

Indicator	Value	Year	Rating	Trend
Demand for family planning satisfied by modern methods (% of females aged 15 to 49)	65.1	2022	●	→
Ratio of female-to-male mean years of education received (%)	86.2	2019	●	↗
Ratio of female-to-male labor force participation rate (%)	25.5	2020	●	↓
Seats held by women in national parliament (%)	18.4	2020	●	↗

SDG6 – Clean Water and Sanitation

Indicator	Value	Year	Rating	Trend
Population using at least basic drinking water services (%)	94.8	2020	●	↑
Population using at least basic sanitation services (%)	91.4	2020	●	↑
Freshwater withdrawal (% of available freshwater resources)	252.5	2018	●	●
Anthropogenic wastewater that receives treatment (%)	23.8	2018	●	●
Scarce water consumption embodied in imports (m^3 H_2O eq/capita)	1707.3	2018	●	●

SDG7 – Affordable and Clean Energy

Indicator	Value	Year	Rating	Trend
Population with access to electricity (%)	97.2	2019	●	↑
Population with access to clean fuels and technology for cooking (%)	96.2	2019	●	↑
CO_2 emissions from fuel combustion per total electricity output ($MtCO_2$/TWh)	2.0	2019	●	→
Share of renewable energy in total primary energy supply (%)	3.0	2019	●	→

SDG8 – Decent Work and Economic Growth

Indicator	Value	Year	Rating	Trend
Adjusted GDP growth (%)	-4.3	2020	●	●
Victims of modern slavery (per 1,000 population)	NA	NA	●	●
Adults with an account at a bank or other financial institution or with a mobile-money-service provider (% of population aged 15 or over)	48.3	2017	●	↗
Unemployment rate (% of total labor force)	10.7	2022	●	→
Fundamental labor rights are effectively guaranteed (worst 0–1 best)	NA	NA	●	●
Fatal work-related accidents embodied in imports (per 100,000 population)	0.4	2015	●	↑

* Imputed data point

SDG9 – Industry, Innovation and Infrastructure

Indicator	Value	Year	Rating	Trend
Population using the internet (%)	71.4	2020	●	↑
Mobile broadband subscriptions (per 100 population)	70.0	2019	●	↑
Logistics Performance Index: Quality of trade and transport-related infrastructure (worst 1–5 best)	2.6	2018	●	↓
The Times Higher Education Universities Ranking: Average score of top 3 universities (worst 0–100 best)	32.0	2022	●	●
Articles published in academic journals (per 1,000 population)	0.5	2020	●	↑
Expenditure on research and development (% of GDP)	0.6	2018	●	●

SDG10 – Reduced Inequalities

Indicator	Value	Year	Rating	Trend
Gini coefficient	34.5	2019	●	●
Palma ratio	1.4	2019	●	●

SDG11 – Sustainable Cities and Communities

Indicator	Value	Year	Rating	Trend
Proportion of urban population living in slums (%)	NA	NA	●	●
Annual mean concentration of particulate matter of less than 2.5 microns in diameter (PM2.5) (μg/m³)	58.6	2019	●	→
Access to improved water source, piped (% of urban population)	91.3	2020	●	→
Satisfaction with public transport (%)	56.6	2021	●	↓

SDG12 – Responsible Consumption and Production

Indicator	Value	Year	Rating	Trend
Municipal solid waste (kg/capita/day)	0.8	2019	●	●
Electronic waste (kg/capita)	7.9	2019	●	●
Production-based SO_2 emissions (kg/capita)	19.4	2018	●	●
SO_2 emissions embodied in imports (kg/capita)	1.7	2018	●	●
Production-based nitrogen emissions (kg/capita)	7.1	2015	●	↑
Nitrogen emissions embodied in imports (kg/capita)	2.4	2015	●	↑
Exports of plastic waste (kg/capita)	0.3	2021	●	●

SDG13 – Climate Action

Indicator	Value	Year	Rating	Trend
CO_2 emissions from fossil fuel combustion and cement production (tCO_2/capita)	5.8	2020	●	→
CO_2 emissions embodied in imports (tCO_2/capita)	0.6	2018	●	↑
CO_2 emissions embodied in fossil fuel exports (kg/capita)	4252.6	2021	●	●

SDG14 – Life Below Water

Indicator	Value	Year	Rating	Trend
Mean area that is protected in marine sites important to biodiversity (%)	41.5	2020	●	→
Ocean Health Index: Clean Waters score (worst 0–100 best)	53.5	2020	●	↓
Fish caught from overexploited or collapsed stocks (% of total catch)	21.6	2018	●	↑
Fish caught by trawling or dredging (%)	21.9	2018	●	↗
Fish caught that are then discarded (%)	9.0	2018	●	→
Marine biodiversity threats embodied in imports (per million population)	0.1	2018	●	●

SDG15 – Life on Land

Indicator	Value	Year	Rating	Trend
Mean area that is protected in terrestrial sites important to biodiversity (%)	31.3	2020	●	→
Mean area that is protected in freshwater sites important to biodiversity (%)	31.9	2020	●	→
Red List Index of species survival (worst 0–1 best)	0.9	2021	●	→
Permanent deforestation (% of forest area, 5-year average)	0.1	2020	●	↑
Terrestrial and freshwater biodiversity threats embodied in imports (per million population)	0.4	2018	●	●

SDG16 – Peace, Justice and Strong Institutions

Indicator	Value	Year	Rating	Trend
Homicides (per 100,000 population)	3.1	2020	●	→
Unsentenced detainees (% of prison population)	24.1	2019	●	●
Population who feel safe walking alone at night in the city or area where they live (%)	73	2021	●	↑
Property Rights (worst 1–7 best)	4.6	2020	●	↑
Birth registrations with civil authority (% of children under age 5)	94.2	2020	●	●
Corruption Perception Index (worst 0–100 best)	32	2021	●	↓
Children involved in child labor (% of population aged 5 to 14)	NA	NA	●	●
Exports of major conventional weapons (TIV constant million USD per 100,000 population)	0.0	2020	●	●
Press Freedom Index (best 0–100 worst)	56.8	2021	●	↓
Access to and affordability of justice (worst 0–1 best)	NA	NA	●	●

SDG17 – Partnerships for the Goals

Indicator	Value	Year	Rating	Trend
Government spending on health and education (% of GDP)	7.1	2020	●	→
For high-income and all OECD DAC countries: International concessional public finance, including official development assistance (% of GNI)	NA	NA	●	●
Other countries: Government revenue excluding grants (% of GDP)	NA	NA	●	●
Corporate Tax Haven Score (best 0–100 worst)	3.3	2019	●	●
Statistical Performance Index (worst 0–100 best)	56.6	2019	●	↗

OCEANIA

OVERALL PERFORMANCE

RANKING

OCEANIA

NA

AVERAGE

AVERAGE PERFORMANCE BY SDG

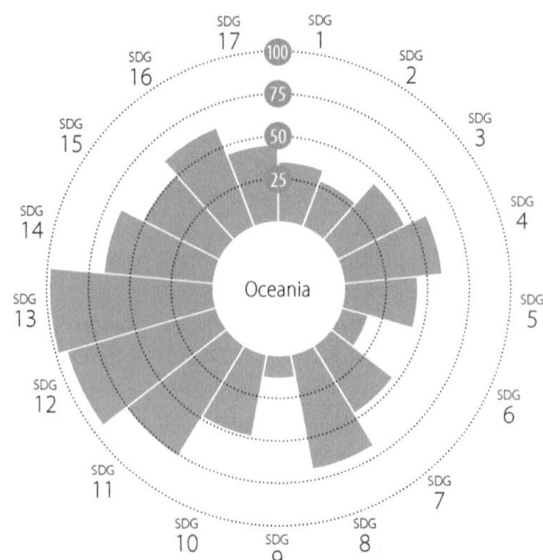

SDG DASHBOARDS AND TRENDS

Major challenges | Significant challenges | Challenges remain | SDG achieved | Information unavailable

Decreasing | Stagnating | Moderately improving | On track or maintaining SDG achievement | Information unavailable

Note: The full title of each SDG is available here: https://sustainabledevelopment.un.org/topics/sustainabledevelopmentgoals

INTERNATIONAL SPILLOVER INDEX

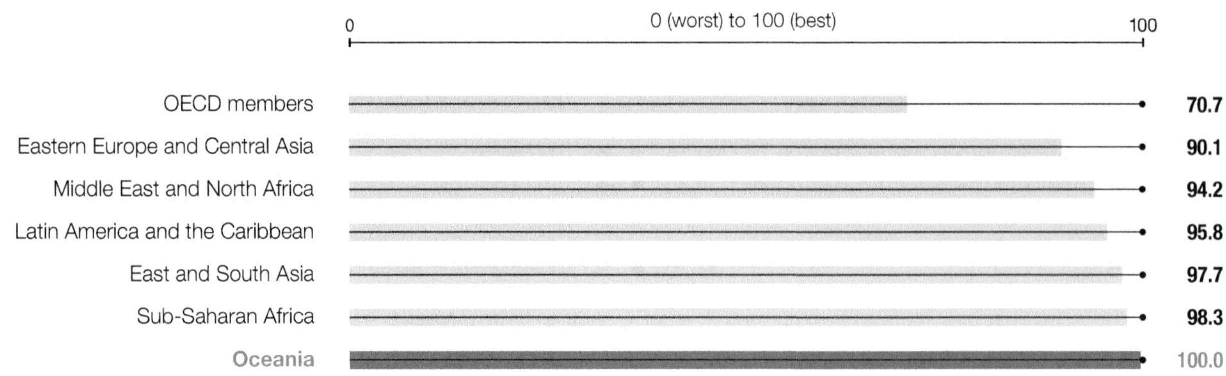

Region	Score
OECD members	70.7
Eastern Europe and Central Asia	90.1
Middle East and North Africa	94.2
Latin America and the Caribbean	95.8
East and South Asia	97.7
Sub-Saharan Africa	98.3
Oceania	100.0

STATISTICAL PERFORMANCE INDEX

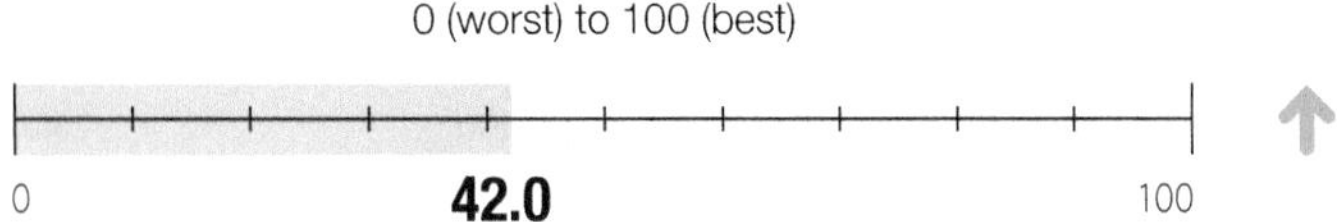

MISSING DATA IN SDG INDEX

34%

OCEANIA

SDG1 – No Poverty	Value	Year	Rating	Trend
Poverty headcount ratio at $1.90/day (%)	25.9	2022	●	→
Poverty headcount ratio at $3.20/day (%)	48.4	2022	●	→
SDG2 – Zero Hunger				
Prevalence of undernourishment (%)	21.5	2019	●	→
Prevalence of stunting in children under 5 years of age (%)	42.8	2019	●	→
Prevalence of wasting in children under 5 years of age (%)	12.4	2019	●	→
Prevalence of obesity, BMI ≥ 30 (% of adult population)	23.6	2016	●	↓
Human Trophic Level (best 2–3 worst)	NA	NA	●	●
Cereal yield (tonnes per hectare of harvested land)	NA	NA	●	●
Sustainable Nitrogen Management Index (best 0–1.41 worst)	1.0	2015	●	→
Exports of hazardous pesticides (tonnes per million population)	NA	NA	●	●
SDG3 – Good Health and Well-Being				
Maternal mortality rate (per 100,000 live births)	128	2017	●	↗
Neonatal mortality rate (per 1,000 live births)	19.1	2020	●	↗
Mortality rate, under-5 (per 1,000 live births)	39.6	2020	●	↗
Incidence of tuberculosis (per 100,000 population)	362.6	2020	●	↓
New HIV infections (per 1,000 uninfected population)	NA	NA	●	●
Age-standardized death rate due to cardiovascular disease, cancer, diabetes, or chronic respiratory disease in adults aged 30–70 years (%)	36.5	2019	●	→
Age-standardized death rate attributable to household air pollution and ambient air pollution (per 100,000 population)	145	2016	●	●
Traffic deaths (per 100,000 population)	12.9	2019	●	↗
Life expectancy at birth (years)	65.6	2019	●	→
Adolescent fertility rate (births per 1,000 females aged 15 to 19)	63.4	2019	●	●
Births attended by skilled health personnel (%)	64.4	2018	●	●
Surviving infants who received 2 WHO-recommended vaccines (%)	49	2020	●	↓
Universal health coverage (UHC) index of service coverage (worst 0–100 best)	38	2019	●	↓
Subjective well-being (average ladder score, worst 0–10 best)	NA	NA	●	●
SDG4 – Quality Education				
Participation rate in pre-primary organized learning (% of children aged 4 to 6)	73.8	2020	●	↗
Net primary enrollment rate (%)	97.1	2020	●	↑
Lower secondary completion rate (%)	47.7	2020	●	↓
Literacy rate (% of population aged 15 to 24)	70.0	2020	●	●
SDG5 – Gender Equality				
Demand for family planning satisfied by modern methods (% of females aged 15 to 49)	49.8	2022	●	●
Ratio of female-to-male mean years of education received (%)	NA	NA	●	●
Ratio of female-to-male labor force participation rate (%)	91.3	2020	●	↑
Seats held by women in national parliament (%)	2.3	2020	●	↓
SDG6 – Clean Water and Sanitation				
Population using at least basic drinking water services (%)	54.1	2020	●	→
Population using at least basic sanitation services (%)	30.8	2020	●	→
Freshwater withdrawal (% of available freshwater resources)	NA	NA	●	●
Anthropogenic wastewater that receives treatment (%)	0.4	2018	●	●
Scarce water consumption embodied in imports (m^3 H_2O eq/capita)	NA	NA	●	●
SDG7 – Affordable and Clean Energy				
Population with access to electricity (%)	68.5	2019	●	↑
Population with access to clean fuels and technology for cooking (%)	14.0	2019	●	→
CO_2 emissions from fuel combustion per total electricity output ($MtCO_2$/TWh)	2.4	2019	●	→
Share of renewable energy in total primary energy supply (%)	NA	NA	●	●
SDG8 – Decent Work and Economic Growth				
Adjusted GDP growth (%)	-6.0	2020	●	●
Victims of modern slavery (per 1,000 population)	NA	NA	●	●
Adults with an account at a bank or other financial institution or with a mobile-money-service provider (% of population aged 15 or over)	NA	NA	●	●
Unemployment rate (% of total labor force)	2.8	2022	●	↑
Fundamental labor rights are effectively guaranteed (worst 0–1 best)	NA	NA	●	●
Fatal work-related accidents embodied in imports (per 100,000 population)	NA	NA	●	●

SDG9 – Industry, Innovation and Infrastructure	Value	Year	Rating	Trend
Population using the internet (%)	17.5	2020	●	●
Mobile broadband subscriptions (per 100 population)	23.6	2019	●	↗
Logistics Performance Index: Quality of trade and transport-related infrastructure (worst 1–5 best)	NA	NA	●	●
The Times Higher Education Universities Ranking: Average score of top 3 universities (worst 0–100 best)	1.9	2022	●	●
Articles published in academic journals (per 1,000 population)	0.1	2020	●	→
Expenditure on research and development (% of GDP)	NA	NA	●	●
SDG10 – Reduced Inequalities				
Gini coefficient	40.9	2019	●	●
Palma ratio	2.0	2019	●	●
SDG11 – Sustainable Cities and Communities				
Proportion of urban population living in slums (%)	NA	NA	●	●
Annual mean concentration of particulate matter of less than 2.5 microns in diameter (PM2.5) (μg/m^3)	11.0	2019	●	↑
Access to improved water source, piped (% of urban population)	59.0	2020	●	↓
Satisfaction with public transport (%)	NA	NA	●	●
SDG12 – Responsible Consumption and Production				
Municipal solid waste (kg/capita/day)	0.4	2019	●	●
Electronic waste (kg/capita)	1.5	2019	●	●
Production-based SO_2 emissions (kg/capita)	NA	NA	●	●
SO_2 emissions embodied in imports (kg/capita)	NA	NA	●	●
Production-based nitrogen emissions (kg/capita)	NA	NA	●	●
Nitrogen emissions embodied in imports (kg/capita)	NA	NA	●	●
Exports of plastic waste (kg/capita)	NA	NA	●	●
SDG13 – Climate Action				
CO_2 emissions from fossil fuel combustion and cement production (tCO_2/capita)	0.8	2020	●	↑
CO_2 emissions embodied in imports (tCO_2/capita)	NA	NA	●	●
CO_2 emissions embodied in fossil fuel exports (kg/capita)	0.0	2021	●	●
SDG14 – Life Below Water				
Mean area that is protected in marine sites important to biodiversity (%)	4.7	2020	●	↓
Ocean Health Index: Clean Waters score (worst 0–100 best)	66.5	2020	●	→
Fish caught from overexploited or collapsed stocks (% of total catch)	10.8	2018	●	↑
Fish caught by trawling or dredging (%)	0.0	2018	●	↑
Fish caught that are then discarded (%)	3.4	2018	●	↑
Marine biodiversity threats embodied in imports (per million population)	NA	NA	●	●
SDG15 – Life on Land				
Mean area that is protected in terrestrial sites important to biodiversity (%)	8.5	2020	●	↓
Mean area that is protected in freshwater sites important to biodiversity (%)	NA	NA	●	●
Red List Index of species survival (worst 0–1 best)	0.8	2021	●	↓
Permanent deforestation (% of forest area, 5-year average)	0.1	2020	●	↑
Terrestrial and freshwater biodiversity threats embodied in imports (per million population)	NA	NA	●	●
SDG16 – Peace, Justice and Strong Institutions				
Homicides (per 100,000 population)	8.3	2020	●	●
Unsentenced detainees (% of prison population)	36.3	2019	●	●
Population who feel safe walking alone at night in the city or area where they live (%)	NA	NA	●	●
Property Rights (worst 1–7 best)	NA	NA	●	●
Birth registrations with civil authority (% of children under age 5)	22.5	2020	●	●
Corruption Perception Index (worst 0–100 best)	NA	NA	●	●
Children involved in child labor (% of population aged 5 to 14)	NA	NA	●	●
Exports of major conventional weapons (TIV constant million USD per 100,000 population)	0.0	2020	●	●
Press Freedom Index (best 0–100 worst)	NA	NA	●	●
Access to and affordability of justice (worst 0–1 best)	NA	NA	●	●
SDG17 – Partnerships for the Goals				
Government spending on health and education (% of GDP)	4.8	2020	●	↓
For high-income and all OECD DAC countries: International concessional public finance, including official development assistance (% of GNI)	NA	NA	●	●
Other countries: Government revenue excluding grants (% of GDP)	17.9	2019	●	↓
Corporate Tax Haven Score (best 0–100 worst)	0.0	2019	●	●
Statistical Performance Index (worst 0–100 best)	42.0	2019	●	↑

* Imputed data point

5. Country Profiles

OECD MEMBERS

OVERALL PERFORMANCE

RANKING

OECD MEMBERS

NA

AVERAGE

WORLD AVERAGE: 66.0

AVERAGE PERFORMANCE BY SDG

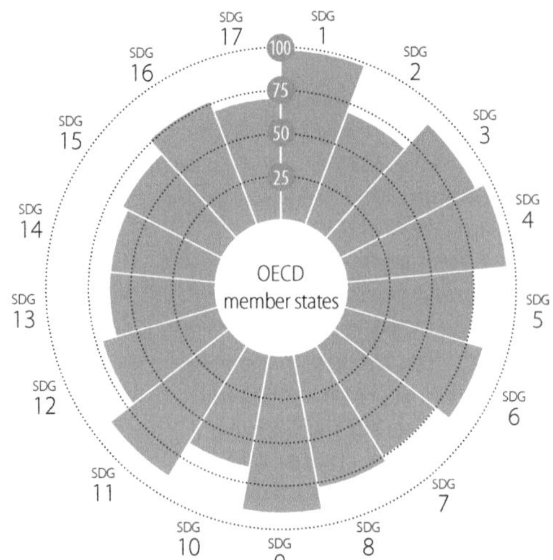

SDG DASHBOARDS AND TRENDS

Major challenges | Significant challenges | Challenges remain | SDG achieved | Information unavailable

Decreasing | Stagnating | Moderately improving | On track or maintaining SDG achievement | Information unavailable

Note: The full title of each SDG is available here: https://sustainabledevelopment.un.org/topics/sustainabledevelopmentgoals

INTERNATIONAL SPILLOVER INDEX

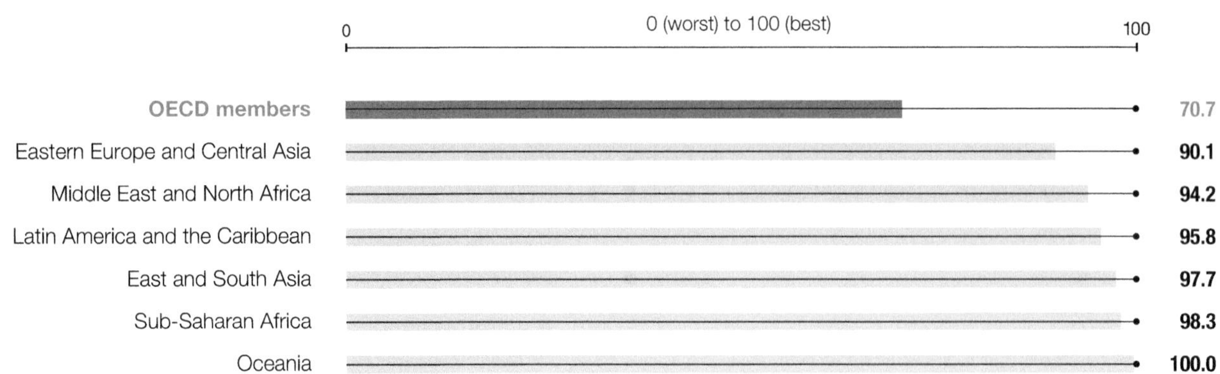

STATISTICAL PERFORMANCE INDEX

0 (worst) to 100 (best)

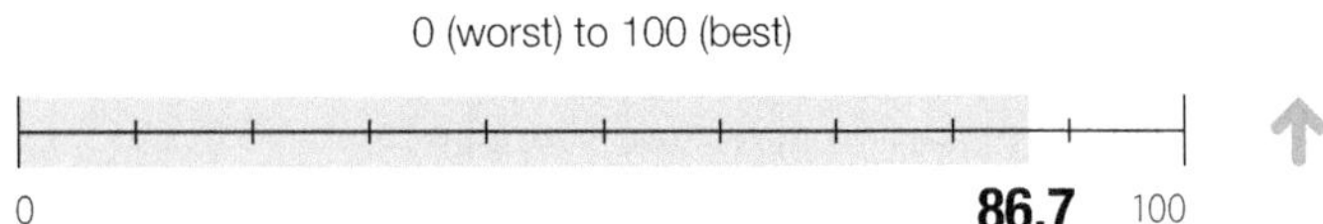

MISSING DATA IN SDG INDEX

1%

SDG1 – No Poverty	Value	Year	Rating	Trend
Poverty headcount ratio at $1.90/day (%)	0.6	2022	●	↑
Poverty headcount ratio at $3.20/day (%)	1.7	2022	●	↑

SDG2 – Zero Hunger	Value	Year	Rating	Trend
Prevalence of undernourishment (%)	3.2	2019	●	↑
Prevalence of stunting in children under 5 years of age (%)	4.8	2019	●	↑
Prevalence of wasting in children under 5 years of age (%)	0.9	2019	●	↑
Prevalence of obesity, BMI ≥ 30 (% of adult population)	25.3	2016	●	↓
Human Trophic Level (best 2–3 worst)	2.4	2017	●	↓
Cereal yield (tonnes per hectare of harvested land)	6.0	2018	●	↑
Sustainable Nitrogen Management Index (best 0–1.41 worst)	0.6	2015	●	↓
Exports of hazardous pesticides (tonnes per million population)	18.1	2019	●	●

SDG3 – Good Health and Well-Being	Value	Year	Rating	Trend
Maternal mortality rate (per 100,000 live births)	15	2017	●	↑
Neonatal mortality rate (per 1,000 live births)	3.4	2020	●	↑
Mortality rate, under-5 (per 1,000 live births)	6.0	2020	●	↑
Incidence of tuberculosis (per 100,000 population)	11.2	2020	●	↑
New HIV infections (per 1,000 uninfected population)	0.6	2020	●	→
Age-standardized death rate due to cardiovascular disease, cancer, diabetes, or chronic respiratory disease in adults aged 30–70 years (%)	11.9	2019	●	↑
Age-standardized death rate attributable to household air pollution and ambient air pollution (per 100,000 population)	20	2016	●	●
Traffic deaths (per 100,000 population)	8.2	2019	●	↑
Life expectancy at birth (years)	80.4	2019	●	↑
Adolescent fertility rate (births per 1,000 females aged 15 to 19)	17.5	2019	●	↑
Births attended by skilled health personnel (%)	98.8	2018	●	↑
Surviving infants who received 2 WHO-recommended vaccines (%)	91	2020	●	↑
Universal health coverage (UHC) index of service coverage (worst 0–100 best)	82	2019	●	↑
Subjective well-being (average ladder score, worst 0–10 best)	6.5	2021	●	↑

SDG4 – Quality Education	Value	Year	Rating	Trend
Participation rate in pre-primary organized learning (% of children aged 4 to 6)	93.3	2020	●	↑
Net primary enrollment rate (%)	98.6	2020	●	↑
Lower secondary completion rate (%)	97.6	2020	●	↑
Literacy rate (% of population aged 15 to 24)	NA	NA	●	●

SDG5 – Gender Equality	Value	Year	Rating	Trend
Demand for family planning satisfied by modern methods (% of females aged 15 to 49)	79.1	2022	●	↑
Ratio of female-to-male mean years of education received (%)	98.1	2019	●	↑
Ratio of female-to-male labor force participation rate (%)	76.1	2020	●	↑
Seats held by women in national parliament (%)	29.3	2020	●	↗

SDG6 – Clean Water and Sanitation	Value	Year	Rating	Trend
Population using at least basic drinking water services (%)	99.5	2020	●	↑
Population using at least basic sanitation services (%)	98.6	2020	●	↑
Freshwater withdrawal (% of available freshwater resources)	29.6	2018	●	●
Anthropogenic wastewater that receives treatment (%)	65.4	2018	●	●
Scarce water consumption embodied in imports (m^3 H_2O eq/capita)	2229.7	2018	●	●

SDG7 – Affordable and Clean Energy	Value	Year	Rating	Trend
Population with access to electricity (%)	100.0	2019	●	↑
Population with access to clean fuels and technology for cooking (%)	98.0	2019	●	↑
CO_2 emissions from fuel combustion per total electricity output ($MtCO_2$/TWh)	1.2	2019	●	↑
Share of renewable energy in total primary energy supply (%)	12.1	2019	●	→

SDG8 – Decent Work and Economic Growth	Value	Year	Rating	Trend
Adjusted GDP growth (%)	-1.6	2020	●	●
Victims of modern slavery (per 1,000 population)	2.1	2018	●	●
Adults with an account at a bank or other financial institution or with a mobile-money-service provider (% of population aged 15 or over)	85.5	2017	●	↑
Unemployment rate (% of total labor force)	5.8	2022	●	●
Fundamental labor rights are effectively guaranteed (worst 0–1 best)	0.6	2020	●	↓
Fatal work-related accidents embodied in imports (per 100,000 population)	1.0	2015	●	↑

* Imputed data point

SDG9 – Industry, Innovation and Infrastructure	Value	Year	Rating	Trend
Population using the internet (%)	86.3	2020	●	↑
Mobile broadband subscriptions (per 100 population)	118.6	2019	●	↑
Logistics Performance Index: Quality of trade and transport-related infrastructure (worst 1–5 best)	3.7	2018	●	↑
The Times Higher Education Universities Ranking: Average score of top 3 universities (worst 0–100 best)	65.5	2022	●	●
Articles published in academic journals (per 1,000 population)	1.8	2020	●	↑
Expenditure on research and development (% of GDP)	2.1	2018	●	↑

SDG10 – Reduced Inequalities	Value	Year	Rating	Trend
Gini coefficient	37.5	2019	●	→
Palma ratio	1.6	2019	●	●

SDG11 – Sustainable Cities and Communities	Value	Year	Rating	Trend
Proportion of urban population living in slums (%)	2.9	2018	●	↑
Annual mean concentration of particulate matter of less than 2.5 microns in diameter (PM2.5) ($\mu g/m^3$)	13.8	2019	●	↑
Access to improved water source, piped (% of urban population)	99.0	2020	●	↑
Satisfaction with public transport (%)	60.8	2021	●	→

SDG12 – Responsible Consumption and Production	Value	Year	Rating	Trend
Municipal solid waste (kg/capita/day)	1.5	2019	●	●
Electronic waste (kg/capita)	17.5	2019	●	●
Production-based SO_2 emissions (kg/capita)	17.2	2018	●	●
SO_2 emissions embodied in imports (kg/capita)	6.0	2018	●	●
Production-based nitrogen emissions (kg/capita)	17.2	2015	●	↑
Nitrogen emissions embodied in imports (kg/capita)	9.2	2015	●	→
Exports of plastic waste (kg/capita)	3.8	2021	●	●

SDG13 – Climate Action	Value	Year	Rating	Trend
CO_2 emissions from fossil fuel combustion and cement production (tCO_2/capita)	8.1	2020	●	↗
CO_2 emissions embodied in imports (tCO_2/capita)	2.1	2018	●	→
CO_2 emissions embodied in fossil fuel exports (kg/capita)	2529.0	2021	●	●

SDG14 – Life Below Water	Value	Year	Rating	Trend
Mean area that is protected in marine sites important to biodiversity (%)	55.0	2020	●	→
Ocean Health Index: Clean Waters score (worst 0–100 best)	62.2	2020	●	→
Fish caught from overexploited or collapsed stocks (% of total catch)	34.8	2018	●	↓
Fish caught by trawling or dredging (%)	21.3	2018	●	→
Fish caught that are then discarded (%)	10.1	2018	●	→
Marine biodiversity threats embodied in imports (per million population)	0.4	2018	●	●

SDG15 – Life on Land	Value	Year	Rating	Trend
Mean area that is protected in terrestrial sites important to biodiversity (%)	52.0	2020	●	→
Mean area that is protected in freshwater sites important to biodiversity (%)	52.3	2020	●	→
Red List Index of species survival (worst 0–1 best)	0.8	2021	●	↓
Permanent deforestation (% of forest area, 5-year average)	0.1	2020	●	→
Terrestrial and freshwater biodiversity threats embodied in imports (per million population)	3.3	2018	●	●

SDG16 – Peace, Justice and Strong Institutions	Value	Year	Rating	Trend
Homicides (per 100,000 population)	5.8	2020	●	→
Unsentenced detainees (% of prison population)	23.9	2019	●	↑
Population who feel safe walking alone at night in the city or area where they live (%)	69	2021	●	↑
Property Rights (worst 1–7 best)	5.2	2020	●	↑
Birth registrations with civil authority (% of children under age 5)	99.3	2020	●	●
Corruption Perception Index (worst 0–100 best)	62	2021	●	↑
Children involved in child labor (% of population aged 5 to 14)	0.7	2019	●	●
Exports of major conventional weapons (TIV constant million USD per 100,000 population)	1.5	2020	●	●
Press Freedom Index (best 0–100 worst)	27.0	2021	●	↑
Access to and affordability of justice (worst 0–1 best)	0.6	2020	●	↗

SDG17 – Partnerships for the Goals	Value	Year	Rating	Trend
Government spending on health and education (% of GDP)	10.9	2020	●	↑
For high-income and all OECD DAC countries: International concessional public finance, including official development assistance (% of GNI)	0.3	2021	●	→
Other countries: Government revenue excluding grants (% of GDP)	NA	NA	●	●
Corporate Tax Haven Score (best 0–100 worst)	32.2	2019	●	●
Statistical Performance Index (worst 0–100 best)	86.7	2019	●	↑

SMALL ISLAND DEVELOPING STATES

OVERALL PERFORMANCE

RANKING

Small Island Developing States

NA

AVERAGE

WORLD AVERAGE: 66.0

AVERAGE PERFORMANCE BY SDG

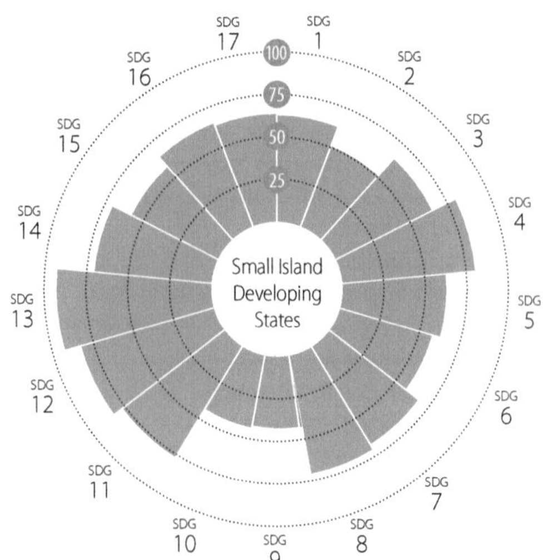

SDG DASHBOARDS AND TRENDS

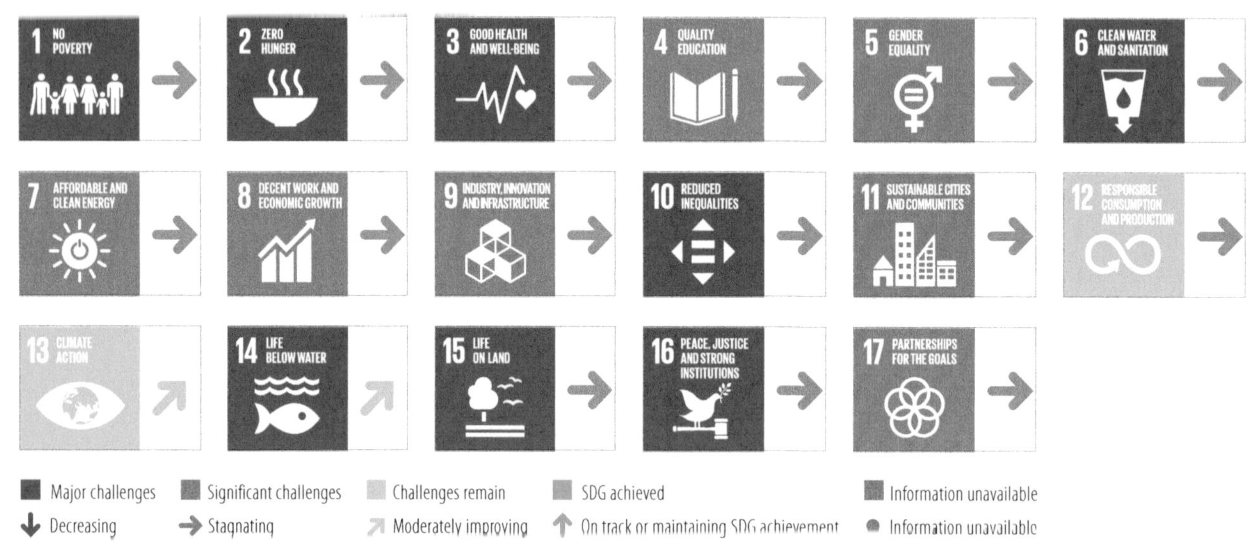

Note: The full title of each SDG is available here: https://sustainabledevelopment.un.org/topics/sustainabledevelopmentgoals

INTERNATIONAL SPILLOVER INDEX

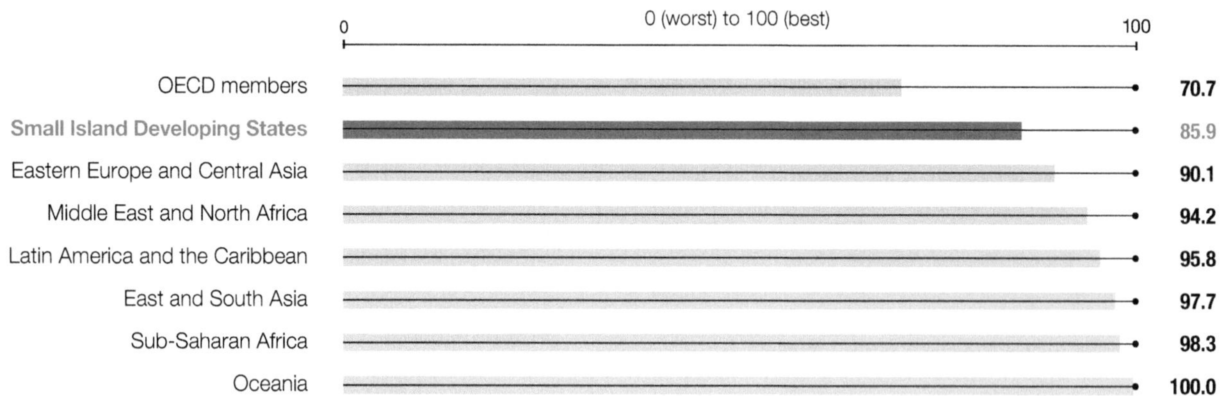

STATISTICAL PERFORMANCE INDEX

0 (worst) to 100 (best)

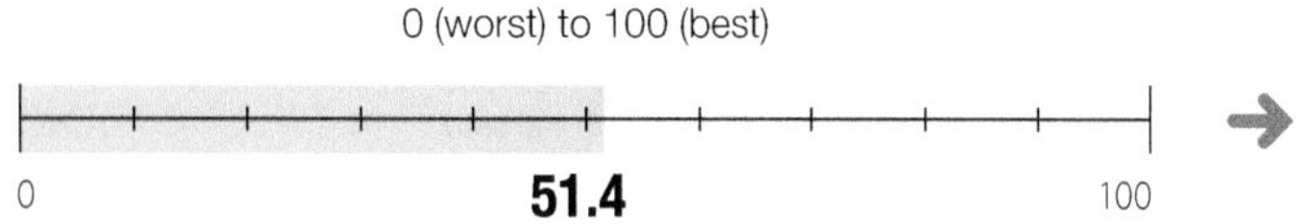

MISSING DATA IN SDG INDEX

21%

SDG1 – No Poverty	Value	Year	Rating	Trend
Poverty headcount ratio at $1.90/day (%)	14.4	2022	●	↓
Poverty headcount ratio at $3.20/day (%)	28.2	2022	●	→
SDG2 – Zero Hunger				
Prevalence of undernourishment (%)	15.9	2019	●	↓
Prevalence of stunting in children under 5 years of age (%)	17.9	2019	●	→
Prevalence of wasting in children under 5 years of age (%)	5.1	2019	●	→
Prevalence of obesity, BMI ≥ 30 (% of adult population)	21.3	2016	●	↓
Human Trophic Level (best 2–3 worst)	2.2	2017	●	↑
Cereal yield (tonnes per hectare of harvested land)	2.8	2018	●	↑
Sustainable Nitrogen Management Index (best 0–1.41 worst)	1.0	2015	●	→
Exports of hazardous pesticides (tonnes per million population)	NA	NA	●	●
SDG3 – Good Health and Well-Being				
Maternal mortality rate (per 100,000 live births)	165	2017	●	→
Neonatal mortality rate (per 1,000 live births)	15.2	2020	●	↗
Mortality rate, under-5 (per 1,000 live births)	30.2	2020	●	↗
Incidence of tuberculosis (per 100,000 population)	128.0	2020	●	→
New HIV infections (per 1,000 uninfected population)	0.4	2020	●	↗
Age-standardized death rate due to cardiovascular disease, cancer, diabetes, or chronic respiratory disease in adults aged 30–70 years (%)	23.1	2019	●	→
Age-standardized death rate attributable to household air pollution and ambient air pollution (per 100,000 population)	94	2016	●	●
Traffic deaths (per 100,000 population)	21.5	2019	●	↓
Life expectancy at birth (years)	71.6	2019	●	→
Adolescent fertility rate (births per 1,000 females aged 15 to 19)	49.0	2019	●	↗
Births attended by skilled health personnel (%)	80.8	2018	●	↓
Surviving infants who received 2 WHO-recommended vaccines (%)	76	2020	●	↓
Universal health coverage (UHC) index of service coverage (worst 0–100 best)	61	2019	●	→
Subjective well-being (average ladder score, worst 0–10 best)	NA	NA	●	●
SDG4 – Quality Education				
Participation rate in pre-primary organized learning (% of children aged 4 to 6)	84.5	2020	●	→
Net primary enrollment rate (%)	96.0	2020	●	↑
Lower secondary completion rate (%)	77.0	2020	●	↓
Literacy rate (% of population aged 15 to 24)	89.8	2020	●	↗
SDG5 – Gender Equality				
Demand for family planning satisfied by modern methods (% of females aged 15 to 49)	65.3	2022	●	→
Ratio of female-to-male mean years of education received (%)	88.9	2019	●	→
Ratio of female-to-male labor force participation rate (%)	74.6	2020	●	↑
Seats held by women in national parliament (%)	22.3	2020	●	→
SDG6 – Clean Water and Sanitation				
Population using at least basic drinking water services (%)	82.9	2020	●	→
Population using at least basic sanitation services (%)	68.0	2020	●	→
Freshwater withdrawal (% of available freshwater resources)	28.8	2018	●	●
Anthropogenic wastewater that receives treatment (%)	13.1	2018	●	●
Scarce water consumption embodied in imports (m^3 H_2O eq/capita)	NA	NA	●	●
SDG7 – Affordable and Clean Energy				
Population with access to electricity (%)	82.5	2019	●	↗
Population with access to clean fuels and technology for cooking (%)	56.3	2019	●	↓
CO_2 emissions from fuel combustion per total electricity output ($MtCO_2$/TWh)	2.0	2019	●	→
Share of renewable energy in total primary energy supply (%)	NA	NA	●	●
SDG8 – Decent Work and Economic Growth				
Adjusted GDP growth (%)	-4.2	2020	●	●
Victims of modern slavery (per 1,000 population)	NA	NA	●	●
Adults with an account at a bank or other financial institution or with a mobile-money-service provider (% of population aged 15 or over)	NA	NA	●	●
Unemployment rate (% of total labor force)	6.9	2022	●	→
Fundamental labor rights are effectively guaranteed (worst 0–1 best)	NA	NA	●	●
Fatal work-related accidents embodied in imports (per 100,000 population)	1.0	2015	●	↑

* Imputed data point

SDG9 – Industry, Innovation and Infrastructure	Value	Year	Rating	Trend
Population using the internet (%)	55.5	2020	●	↗
Mobile broadband subscriptions (per 100 population)	52.1	2019	●	↑
Logistics Performance Index: Quality of trade and transport-related infrastructure (worst 1–5 best)	NA	NA	●	●
The Times Higher Education Universities Ranking: Average score of top 3 universities (worst 0–100 best)	12.0	2022	●	●
Articles published in academic journals (per 1,000 population)	0.5	2020	●	↗
Expenditure on research and development (% of GDP)	NA	NA	●	●
SDG10 – Reduced Inequalities				
Gini coefficient	41.6	2019	●	→
Palma ratio	2.1	2019	●	●
SDG11 – Sustainable Cities and Communities				
Proportion of urban population living in slums (%)	NA	NA	●	●
Annual mean concentration of particulate matter of less than 2.5 microns in diameter (PM2.5) ($\mu g/m^3$)	17.6	2019	●	→
Access to improved water source, piped (% of urban population)	68.9	2020	●	↓
Satisfaction with public transport (%)	NA	NA	●	●
SDG12 – Responsible Consumption and Production				
Municipal solid waste (kg/capita/day)	0.8	2019	●	●
Electronic waste (kg/capita)	7.4	2019	●	●
Production-based SO_2 emissions (kg/capita)	NA	NA	●	●
SO_2 emissions embodied in imports (kg/capita)	NA	NA	●	●
Production-based nitrogen emissions (kg/capita)	7.3	2015	●	↑
Nitrogen emissions embodied in imports (kg/capita)	5.7	2015	●	→
Exports of plastic waste (kg/capita)	2.4	2021	●	→
SDG13 – Climate Action				
CO_2 emissions from fossil fuel combustion and cement production (tCO_2/capita)	3.0	2020	●	↗
CO_2 emissions embodied in imports (tCO_2/capita)	NA	NA	●	●
CO_2 emissions embodied in fossil fuel exports (kg/capita)	66.8	2021	●	●
SDG14 – Life Below Water				
Mean area that is protected in marine sites important to biodiversity (%)	36.9	2020	●	→
Ocean Health Index: Clean Waters score (worst 0–100 best)	53.6	2020	●	→
Fish caught from overexploited or collapsed stocks (% of total catch)	11.3	2018	●	↑
Fish caught by trawling or dredging (%)	1.8	2018	●	↑
Fish caught that are then discarded (%)	2.7	2018	●	↑
Marine biodiversity threats embodied in imports (per million population)	0.5	2018	●	●
SDG15 – Life on Land				
Mean area that is protected in terrestrial sites important to biodiversity (%)	36.9	2020	●	→
Mean area that is protected in freshwater sites important to biodiversity (%)	NA	NA	●	●
Red List Index of species survival (worst 0–1 best)	0.7	2021	●	↓
Permanent deforestation (% of forest area, 5-year average)	0.3	2020	●	↗
Terrestrial and freshwater biodiversity threats embodied in imports (per million population)	2.4	2018	●	●
SDG16 – Peace, Justice and Strong Institutions				
Homicides (per 100,000 population)	8.8	2020	●	↗
Unsentenced detainees (% of prison population)	45.9	2019	●	→
Population who feel safe walking alone at night in the city or area where they live (%)	NA	NA	●	●
Property Rights (worst 1–7 best)	NA	NA	●	●
Birth registrations with civil authority (% of children under age 5)	79.2	2020	●	●
Corruption Perception Index (worst 0–100 best)	39	2021	●	→
Children involved in child labor (% of population aged 5 to 14)	NA	NA	●	●
Exports of major conventional weapons (TIV constant million USD per 100,000 population)	0.1	2020	●	●
Press Freedom Index (best 0–100 worst)	36.4	2021	●	→
Access to and affordability of justice (worst 0–1 best)	NA	NA	●	●
SDG17 – Partnerships for the Goals				
Government spending on health and education (% of GDP)	8.3	2020	●	↓
For high-income and all OECD DAC countries: International concessional public finance, including official development assistance (% of GNI)	NA	NA	●	●
Other countries: Government revenue excluding grants (% of GDP)	NA	NA	●	●
Corporate Tax Haven Score (best 0–100 worst)	9.5	2019	●	●
Statistical Performance Index (worst 0–100 best)	51.4	2019	●	→

SUB-SAHARAN AFRICA

OVERALL PERFORMANCE

RANKING

SUB-SAHARAN AFRICA

NA

AVERAGE

WORLD AVERAGE: 66.0

AVERAGE PERFORMANCE BY SDG

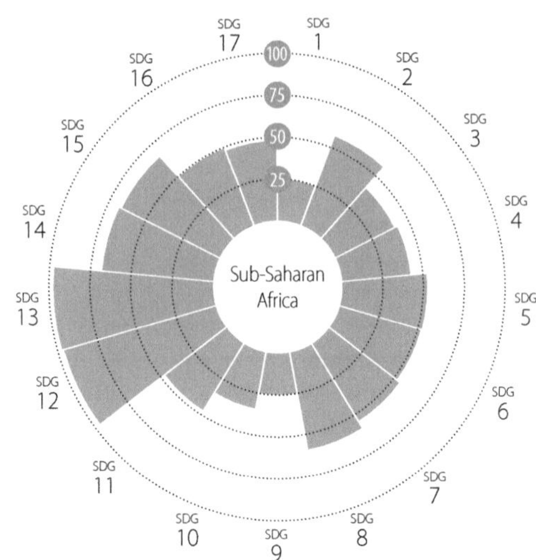

SDG DASHBOARDS AND TRENDS

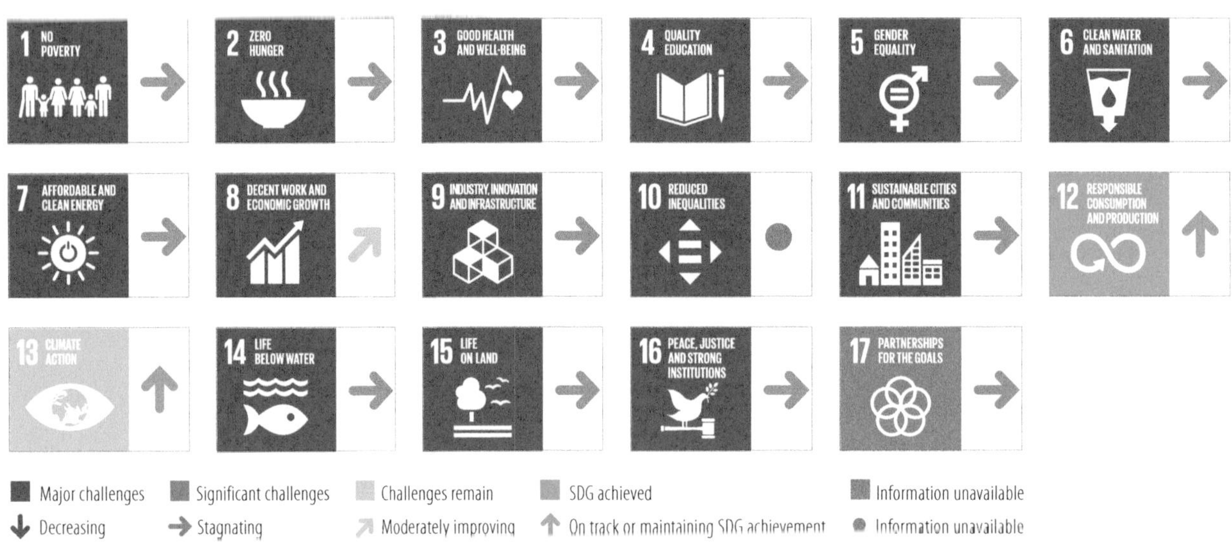

Major challenges | Significant challenges | Challenges remain | SDG achieved | Information unavailable

Decreasing | Stagnating | Moderately improving | On track or maintaining SDG achievement | Information unavailable

Note: The full title of each SDG is available here: https://sustainabledevelopment.un.org/topics/sustainabledevelopmentgoals

INTERNATIONAL SPILLOVER INDEX

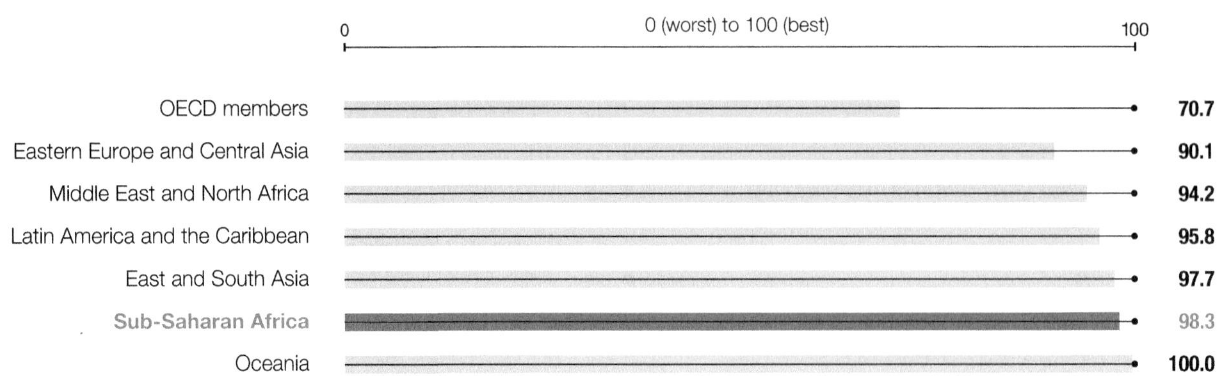

STATISTICAL PERFORMANCE INDEX

0 (worst) to 100 (best)

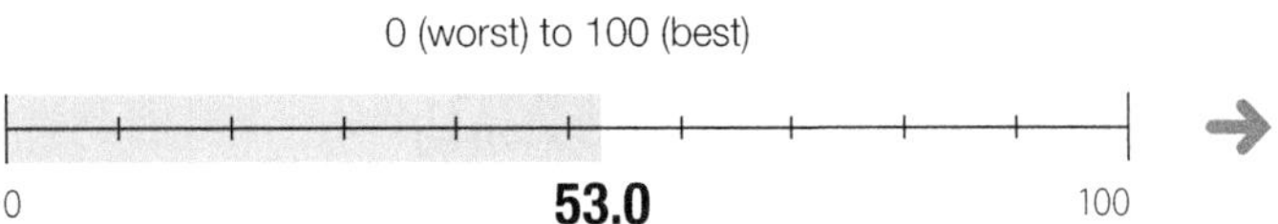

MISSING DATA IN SDG INDEX

SDG1 – No Poverty	Value	Year	Rating	Trend
Poverty headcount ratio at $1.90/day (%)	36.6	2022	●	→
Poverty headcount ratio at $3.20/day (%)	57.2	2022	●	→

SDG2 – Zero Hunger	Value	Year	Rating	Trend
Prevalence of undernourishment (%)	20.4	2019	●	↓
Prevalence of stunting in children under 5 years of age (%)	32.4	2019	●	→
Prevalence of wasting in children under 5 years of age (%)	6.6	2019	●	→
Prevalence of obesity, BMI ≥ 30 (% of adult population)	8.8	2016	●	↑
Human Trophic Level (best 2–3 worst)	2.1	2017	●	↑
Cereal yield (tonnes per hectare of harvested land)	1.7	2018	●	→
Sustainable Nitrogen Management Index (best 0–1.41 worst)	0.8	2015	●	→
Exports of hazardous pesticides (tonnes per million population)	8.7	2019	●	●

SDG3 – Good Health and Well-Being	Value	Year	Rating	Trend
Maternal mortality rate (per 100,000 live births)	514	2017	●	→
Neonatal mortality rate (per 1,000 live births)	26.5	2020	●	→
Mortality rate, under-5 (per 1,000 live births)	70.6	2020	●	↗
Incidence of tuberculosis (per 100,000 population)	220.1	2020	●	↗
New HIV infections (per 1,000 uninfected population)	0.8	2020	●	↑
Age-standardized death rate due to cardiovascular disease, cancer, diabetes, or chronic respiratory disease in adults aged 30–70 years (%)	21.3	2019	●	↗
Age-standardized death rate attributable to household air pollution and ambient air pollution (per 100,000 population)	187	2016	●	●
Traffic deaths (per 100,000 population)	27.4	2019	●	↓
Life expectancy at birth (years)	64.3	2019	●	→
Adolescent fertility rate (births per 1,000 females aged 15 to 19)	109.1	2019	●	●
Births attended by skilled health personnel (%)	60.7	2018	●	●
Surviving infants who received 2 WHO-recommended vaccines (%)	69	2020	●	→
Universal health coverage (UHC) index of service coverage (worst 0–100 best)	45	2019	●	→
Subjective well-being (average ladder score, worst 0–10 best)	4.4	2021	●	●

SDG4 – Quality Education	Value	Year	Rating	Trend
Participation rate in pre-primary organized learning (% of children aged 4 to 6)	47.8	2020	●	●
Net primary enrollment rate (%)	80.8	2020	●	→
Lower secondary completion rate (%)	44.7	2020	●	●
Literacy rate (% of population aged 15 to 24)	77.3	2020	●	●

SDG5 – Gender Equality	Value	Year	Rating	Trend
Demand for family planning satisfied by modern methods (% of females aged 15 to 49)	47.9	2022	●	→
Ratio of female-to-male mean years of education received (%)	69.7	2019	●	→
Ratio of female-to-male labor force participation rate (%)	82.9	2020	●	↑
Seats held by women in national parliament (%)	23.8	2020	●	→

SDG6 – Clean Water and Sanitation	Value	Year	Rating	Trend
Population using at least basic drinking water services (%)	64.4	2020	●	→
Population using at least basic sanitation services (%)	32.8	2020	●	→
Freshwater withdrawal (% of available freshwater resources)	18.4	2018	●	●
Anthropogenic wastewater that receives treatment (%)	1.4	2018	●	●
Scarce water consumption embodied in imports (m^3 H_2O eq/capita)	292.4	2018	●	●

SDG7 – Affordable and Clean Energy	Value	Year	Rating	Trend
Population with access to electricity (%)	46.6	2019	●	↗
Population with access to clean fuels and technology for cooking (%)	17.0	2019	●	→
CO_2 emissions from fuel combustion per total electricity output ($MtCO_2$/TWh)	2.4	2019	●	→
Share of renewable energy in total primary energy supply (%)	71.3	2019	●	↑

SDG8 – Decent Work and Economic Growth	Value	Year	Rating	Trend
Adjusted GDP growth (%)	-4.7	2020	●	●
Victims of modern slavery (per 1,000 population)	8.3	2018	●	●
Adults with an account at a bank or other financial institution or with a mobile-money-service provider (% of population aged 15 or over)	39.9	2017	●	↗
Unemployment rate (% of total labor force)	8.1	2022	●	↓
Fundamental labor rights are effectively guaranteed (worst 0–1 best)	0.5	2020	●	●
Fatal work-related accidents embodied in imports (per 100,000 population)	0.1	2015	●	↑

* Imputed data point

SDG9 – Industry, Innovation and Infrastructure	Value	Year	Rating	Trend
Population using the internet (%)	28.4	2020	●	↗
Mobile broadband subscriptions (per 100 population)	33.9	2019	●	↗
Logistics Performance Index: Quality of trade and transport-related infrastructure (worst 1–5 best)	2.4	2018	●	→
The Times Higher Education Universities Ranking: Average score of top 3 universities (worst 0–100 best)	19.0	2022	●	●
Articles published in academic journals (per 1,000 population)	0.1	2020	●	→
Expenditure on research and development (% of GDP)	0.3	2018	●	●

SDG10 – Reduced Inequalities	Value	Year	Rating	Trend
Gini coefficient	41.4	2019	●	●
Palma ratio	2.4	2019	●	●

SDG11 – Sustainable Cities and Communities	Value	Year	Rating	Trend
Proportion of urban population living in slums (%)	56.7	2018	●	→
Annual mean concentration of particulate matter of less than 2.5 microns in diameter (PM2.5) (μg/m^3)	47.8	2019	●	↓
Access to improved water source, piped (% of urban population)	58.8	2020	●	↓
Satisfaction with public transport (%)	48.8	2021	●	●

SDG12 – Responsible Consumption and Production	Value	Year	Rating	Trend
Municipal solid waste (kg/capita/day)	0.5	2019	●	●
Electronic waste (kg/capita)	1.7	2019	●	●
Production-based SO_2 emissions (kg/capita)	3.0	2018	●	●
SO_2 emissions embodied in imports (kg/capita)	0.5	2018	●	●
Production-based nitrogen emissions (kg/capita)	10.3	2015	●	↑
Nitrogen emissions embodied in imports (kg/capita)	0.5	2015	●	↑
Exports of plastic waste (kg/capita)	0.1	2021	●	●

SDG13 – Climate Action	Value	Year	Rating	Trend
CO_2 emissions from fossil fuel combustion and cement production (tCO_2/capita)	0.7	2020	●	↑
CO_2 emissions embodied in imports (tCO_2/capita)	0.2	2018	●	↑
CO_2 emissions embodied in fossil fuel exports (kg/capita)	365.5	2021	●	●

SDG14 – Life Below Water	Value	Year	Rating	Trend
Mean area that is protected in marine sites important to biodiversity (%)	32.7	2020	●	→
Ocean Health Index: Clean Waters score (worst 0–100 best)	44.4	2020	●	↓
Fish caught from overexploited or collapsed stocks (% of total catch)	18.7	2018	●	↑
Fish caught by trawling or dredging (%)	7.2	2018	●	↓
Fish caught that are then discarded (%)	4.0	2018	●	↑
Marine biodiversity threats embodied in imports (per million population)	0.0	2018	●	●

SDG15 – Life on Land	Value	Year	Rating	Trend
Mean area that is protected in terrestrial sites important to biodiversity (%)	50.4	2020	●	→
Mean area that is protected in freshwater sites important to biodiversity (%)	46.8	2020	●	→
Red List Index of species survival (worst 0–1 best)	0.8	2021	●	↓
Permanent deforestation (% of forest area, 5-year average)	0.4	2020	●	↓
Terrestrial and freshwater biodiversity threats embodied in imports (per million population)	0.2	2018	●	●

SDG16 – Peace, Justice and Strong Institutions	Value	Year	Rating	Trend
Homicides (per 100,000 population)	8.3	2020	●	●
Unsentenced detainees (% of prison population)	48.9	2019	●	●
Population who feel safe walking alone at night in the city or area where they live (%)	51	2021	●	●
Property Rights (worst 1–7 best)	3.7	2020	●	↓
Birth registrations with civil authority (% of children under age 5)	47.3	2020	●	●
Corruption Perception Index (worst 0–100 best)	30	2021	●	→
Children involved in child labor (% of population aged 5 to 14)	26.4	2019	●	●
Exports of major conventional weapons (TIV constant million USD per 100,000 population)	0.0	2020	●	●
Press Freedom Index (best 0–100 worst)	37.2	2021	●	→
Access to and affordability of justice (worst 0–1 best)	0.5	2020	●	●

SDG17 – Partnerships for the Goals	Value	Year	Rating	Trend
Government spending on health and education (% of GDP)	5.3	2020	●	↓
For high-income and all OECD DAC countries: International concessional public finance, including official development assistance (% of GNI)	NA	NA	●	●
Other countries: Government revenue excluding grants (% of GDP)	15.6	2019	●	↓
Corporate Tax Haven Score (best 0–100 worst)	9.1	2019	●	●
Statistical Performance Index (worst 0–100 best)	53.0	2019	●	→

5. Country Profiles

LOW-INCOME COUNTRIES

OVERALL PERFORMANCE

RANKING

LOW-INCOME COUNTRIES

NA

AVERAGE

WORLD AVERAGE: 66.0

AVERAGE PERFORMANCE BY SDG

SDG DASHBOARDS AND TRENDS

Note: The full title of each SDG is available here: https://sustainabledevelopment.un.org/topics/sustainabledevelopmentgoals

INTERNATIONAL SPILLOVER INDEX

STATISTICAL PERFORMANCE INDEX

0 (worst) to 100 (best)

0 **47.6** 100

MISSING DATA IN SDG INDEX

0%

LOW-INCOME COUNTRIES

SDG1 – No Poverty

Indicator	Value	Year	Rating	Trend
Poverty headcount ratio at $1.90/day (%)	41.7	2022	●	→
Poverty headcount ratio at $3.20/day (%)	65.5	2022	●	→

SDG2 – Zero Hunger

Indicator	Value	Year	Rating	Trend
Prevalence of undernourishment (%)	28.7	2019	●	↓
Prevalence of stunting in children under 5 years of age (%)	36.3	2019	●	→
Prevalence of wasting in children under 5 years of age (%)	7.9	2019	●	→
Prevalence of obesity, BMI ≥ 30 (% of adult population)	7.2	2016	●	↑
Human Trophic Level (best 2–3 worst)	2.1	2017	●	↑
Cereal yield (tonnes per hectare of harvested land)	1.6	2018	●	↓
Sustainable Nitrogen Management Index (best 0–1.41 worst)	0.8	2015	●	→
Exports of hazardous pesticides (tonnes per million population)	1.2	2019	●	●

SDG3 – Good Health and Well-Being

Indicator	Value	Year	Rating	Trend
Maternal mortality rate (per 100,000 live births)	440	2017	●	↗
Neonatal mortality rate (per 1,000 live births)	25.9	2020	●	↗
Mortality rate, under-5 (per 1,000 live births)	63.0	2020	●	↗
Incidence of tuberculosis (per 100,000 population)	187.2	2020	●	→
New HIV infections (per 1,000 uninfected population)	0.5	2020	●	↑
Age-standardized death rate due to cardiovascular disease, cancer, diabetes, or chronic respiratory disease in adults aged 30–70 years (%)	23.5	2019	●	→
Age-standardized death rate attributable to household air pollution and ambient air pollution (per 100,000 population)	175	2016	●	●
Traffic deaths (per 100,000 population)	28.7	2019	●	↓
Life expectancy at birth (years)	65.1	2019	●	→
Adolescent fertility rate (births per 1,000 females aged 15 to 19)	102.5	2019	●	●
Births attended by skilled health personnel (%)	60.5	2018	●	●
Surviving infants who received 2 WHO-recommended vaccines (%)	69	2020	●	→
Universal health coverage (UHC) index of service coverage (worst 0–100 best)	42	2019	●	→
Subjective well-being (average ladder score, worst 0–10 best)	4.2	2021	●	●

SDG4 – Quality Education

Indicator	Value	Year	Rating	Trend
Participation rate in pre-primary organized learning (% of children aged 4 to 6)	37.9	2020	●	●
Net primary enrollment rate (%)	83.4	2020	●	●
Lower secondary completion rate (%)	38.1	2020	●	●
Literacy rate (% of population aged 15 to 24)	72.7	2020	●	●

SDG5 – Gender Equality

Indicator	Value	Year	Rating	Trend
Demand for family planning satisfied by modern methods (% of females aged 15 to 49)	47.7	2022	●	→
Ratio of female-to-male mean years of education received (%)	60.1	2019	●	→
Ratio of female-to-male labor force participation rate (%)	74.3	2020	●	↑
Seats held by women in national parliament (%)	24.8	2020	●	→

SDG6 – Clean Water and Sanitation

Indicator	Value	Year	Rating	Trend
Population using at least basic drinking water services (%)	58.6	2020	●	→
Population using at least basic sanitation services (%)	29.2	2020	●	→
Freshwater withdrawal (% of available freshwater resources)	32.0	2018	●	●
Anthropogenic wastewater that receives treatment (%)	1.3	2018	●	●
Scarce water consumption embodied in imports (m^3 H_2O eq/capita)	218.7	2018	●	●

SDG7 – Affordable and Clean Energy

Indicator	Value	Year	Rating	Trend
Population with access to electricity (%)	40.8	2019	●	↗
Population with access to clean fuels and technology for cooking (%)	14.3	2019	●	→
CO_2 emissions from fuel combustion per total electricity output ($MtCO_2$/TWh)	2.1	2019	●	→
Share of renewable energy in total primary energy supply (%)	75.2	2019	●	●

SDG8 – Decent Work and Economic Growth

Indicator	Value	Year	Rating	Trend
Adjusted GDP growth (%)	-4.7	2020	●	●
Victims of modern slavery (per 1,000 population)	14.7	2018	●	●
Adults with an account at a bank or other financial institution or with a mobile-money-service provider (% of population aged 15 or over)	28.8	2017	●	↗
Unemployment rate (% of total labor force)	7.0	2022	●	↓
Fundamental labor rights are effectively guaranteed (worst 0–1 best)	0.5	2020	●	●
Fatal work-related accidents embodied in imports (per 100,000 population)	0.0	2015	●	↑

* Imputed data point

SDG9 – Industry, Innovation and Infrastructure

Indicator	Value	Year	Rating	Trend
Population using the internet (%)	18.6	2020	●	→
Mobile broadband subscriptions (per 100 population)	20.6	2019	●	↗
Logistics Performance Index: Quality of trade and transport-related infrastructure (worst 1–5 best)	2.1	2018	●	→
The Times Higher Education Universities Ranking: Average score of top 3 universities (worst 0–100 best)	9.7	2022	●	●
Articles published in academic journals (per 1,000 population)	0.0	2020	●	→
Expenditure on research and development (% of GDP)	0.2	2018	●	●

SDG10 – Reduced Inequalities

Indicator	Value	Year	Rating	Trend
Gini coefficient	39.4	2019	●	●
Palma ratio	1.9	2019	●	●

SDG11 – Sustainable Cities and Communities

Indicator	Value	Year	Rating	Trend
Proportion of urban population living in slums (%)	66.9	2018	●	→
Annual mean concentration of particulate matter of less than 2.5 microns in diameter (PM2.5) (μg/m^3)	44.3	2019	●	↓
Access to improved water source, piped (% of urban population)	69.5	2020	●	→
Satisfaction with public transport (%)	43.6	2021	●	●

SDG12 – Responsible Consumption and Production

Indicator	Value	Year	Rating	Trend
Municipal solid waste (kg/capita/day)	0.4	2019	●	●
Electronic waste (kg/capita)	1.0	2019	●	●
Production-based SO_2 emissions (kg/capita)	1.1	2018	●	●
SO_2 emissions embodied in imports (kg/capita)	0.2	2018	●	●
Production-based nitrogen emissions (kg/capita)	11.4	2015	●	↑
Nitrogen emissions embodied in imports (kg/capita)	0.2	2015	●	↑
Exports of plastic waste (kg/capita)	0.0	2021	●	●

SDG13 – Climate Action

Indicator	Value	Year	Rating	Trend
CO_2 emissions from fossil fuel combustion and cement production (tCO_2/capita)	0.2	2020	●	↑
CO_2 emissions embodied in imports (tCO_2/capita)	0.1	2018	●	↑
CO_2 emissions embodied in fossil fuel exports (kg/capita)	24.7	2021	●	●

SDG14 – Life Below Water

Indicator	Value	Year	Rating	Trend
Mean area that is protected in marine sites important to biodiversity (%)	34.6	2020	●	●
Ocean Health Index: Clean Waters score (worst 0–100 best)	47.0	2020	●	↓
Fish caught from overexploited or collapsed stocks (% of total catch)	17.4	2018	●	●
Fish caught by trawling or dredging (%)	6.4	2018	●	●
Fish caught that are then discarded (%)	3.9	2018	●	●
Marine biodiversity threats embodied in imports (per million population)	0.0	2018	●	●

SDG15 – Life on Land

Indicator	Value	Year	Rating	Trend
Mean area that is protected in terrestrial sites important to biodiversity (%)	35.6	2020	●	→
Mean area that is protected in freshwater sites important to biodiversity (%)	31.2	2020	●	→
Red List Index of species survival (worst 0–1 best)	0.9	2021	●	→
Permanent deforestation (% of forest area, 5-year average)	0.3	2020	●	→
Terrestrial and freshwater biodiversity threats embodied in imports (per million population)	0.1	2018	●	●

SDG16 – Peace, Justice and Strong Institutions

Indicator	Value	Year	Rating	Trend
Homicides (per 100,000 population)	7.2	2020	●	●
Unsentenced detainees (% of prison population)	44.6	2019	●	●
Population who feel safe walking alone at night in the city or area where they live (%)	49	2021	●	●
Property Rights (worst 1–7 best)	3.5	2020	●	●
Birth registrations with civil authority (% of children under age 5)	44.5	2020	●	●
Corruption Perception Index (worst 0–100 best)	26	2021	●	→
Children involved in child labor (% of population aged 5 to 14)	26.6	2019	●	●
Exports of major conventional weapons (TIV constant million USD per 100,000 population)	0.0	2020	●	●
Press Freedom Index (best 0–100 worst)	42.8	2021	●	↗
Access to and affordability of justice (worst 0–1 best)	0.4	2020	●	●

SDG17 – Partnerships for the Goals

Indicator	Value	Year	Rating	Trend
Government spending on health and education (% of GDP)	4.7	2020	●	↓
For high-income and all OECD DAC countries: International concessional public finance, including official development assistance (% of GNI)	NA	NA	●	●
Other countries: Government revenue excluding grants (% of GDP)	12.3	2019	●	●
Corporate Tax Haven Score (best 0–100 worst)	0.5	2019	●	●
Statistical Performance Index (worst 0–100 best)	47.6	2019	●	↗

LOWER-MIDDLE-INCOME COUNTRIES

OVERALL PERFORMANCE

RANKING

LOWER-MIDDLE-INCOME COUNTRIES

NA

AVERAGE

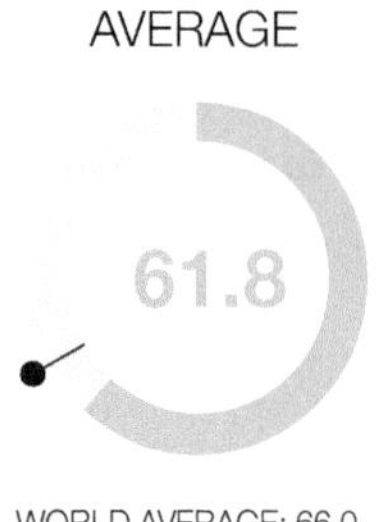

WORLD AVERAGE: 66.0

AVERAGE PERFORMANCE BY SDG

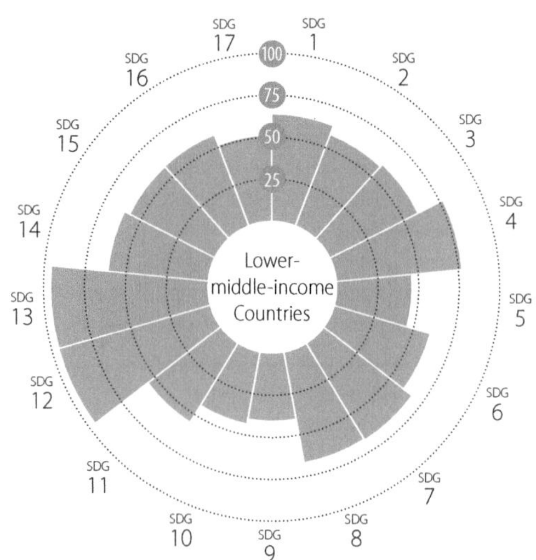

SDG DASHBOARDS AND TRENDS

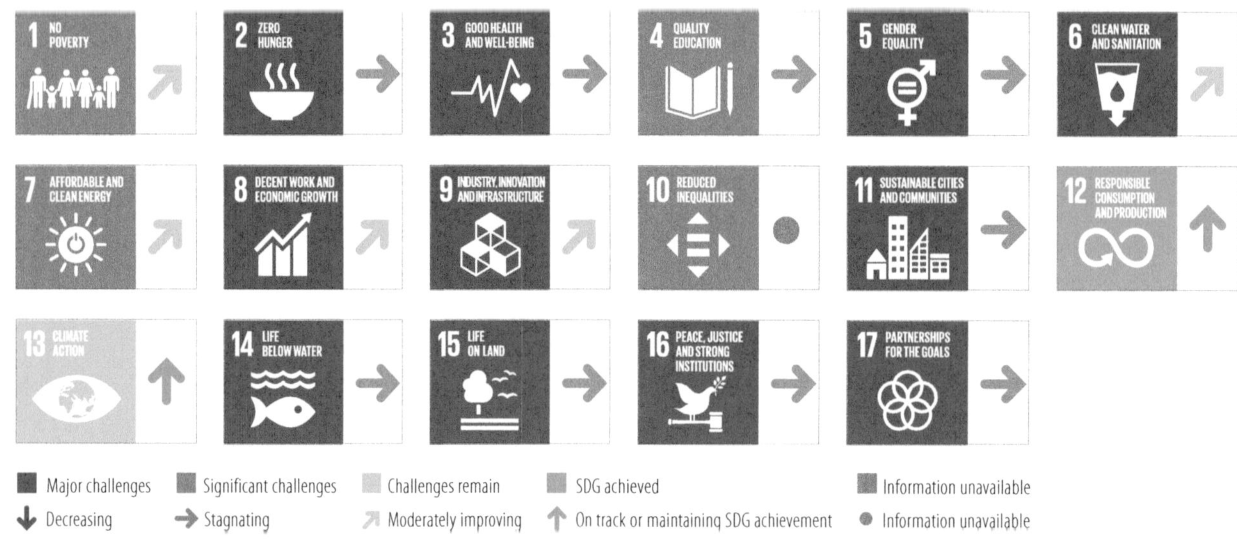

Major challenges · Significant challenges · Challenges remain · SDG achieved · Information unavailable

Decreasing · Stagnating · Moderately improving · On track or maintaining SDG achievement · Information unavailable

Note: The full title of each SDG is available here: https://sustainabledevelopment.un.org/topics/sustainabledevelopmentgoals

INTERNATIONAL SPILLOVER INDEX

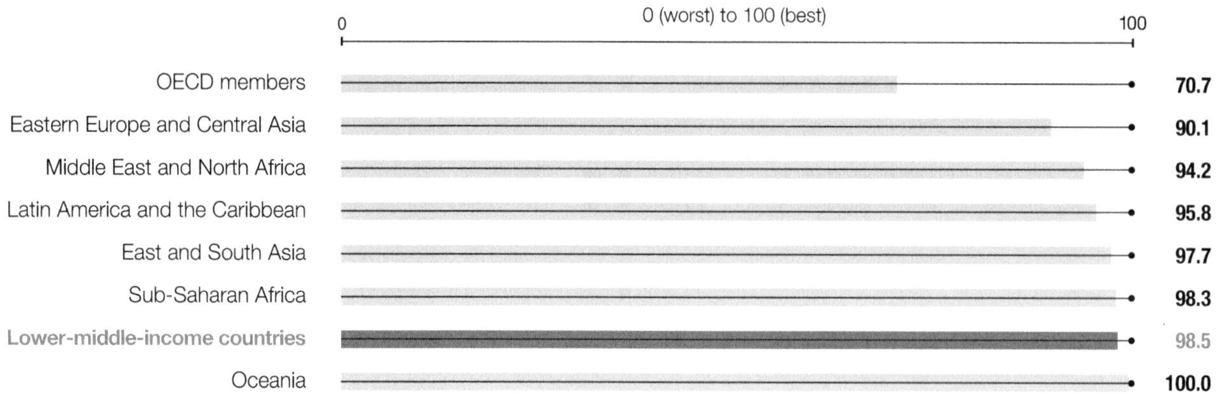

STATISTICAL PERFORMANCE INDEX

0 (worst) to 100 (best)

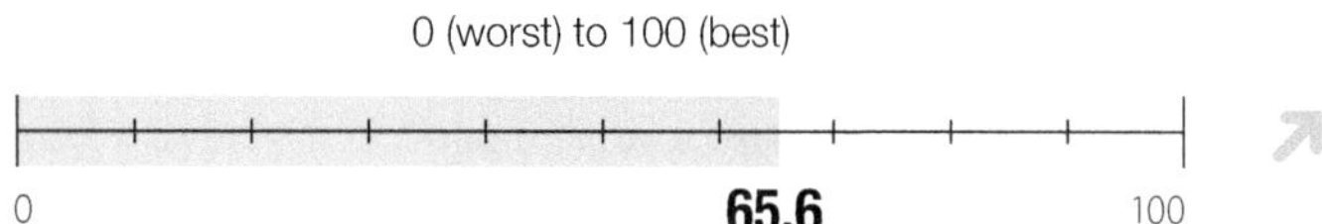

MISSING DATA IN SDG INDEX

0%

SDG1 – No Poverty	Value	Year	Rating	Trend
Poverty headcount ratio at $1.90/day (%)	8.7	2022	●	↗
Poverty headcount ratio at $3.20/day (%)	31.5	2022	●	→
SDG2 – Zero Hunger				
Prevalence of undernourishment (%)	12.3	2019	●	→
Prevalence of stunting in children under 5 years of age (%)	30.2	2019	●	→
Prevalence of wasting in children under 5 years of age (%)	11.3	2019	●	→
Prevalence of obesity, BMI ≥ 30 (% of adult population)	8.2	2016	●	↑
Human Trophic Level (best 2–3 worst)	2.2	2017	●	↓
Cereal yield (tonnes per hectare of harvested land)	3.4	2018	●	↑
Sustainable Nitrogen Management Index (best 0–1.41 worst)	0.8	2015	●	→
Exports of hazardous pesticides (tonnes per million population)	4.8	2019	●	●
SDG3 – Good Health and Well-Being				
Maternal mortality rate (per 100,000 live births)	208	2017	●	↗
Neonatal mortality rate (per 1,000 live births)	20.1	2020	●	↗
Mortality rate, under-5 (per 1,000 live births)	38.7	2020	●	↑
Incidence of tuberculosis (per 100,000 population)	204.4	2020	●	→
New HIV infections (per 1,000 uninfected population)	0.2	2020	●	↑
Age-standardized death rate due to cardiovascular disease, cancer, diabetes, or chronic respiratory disease in adults aged 30–70 years (%)	22.2	2019	●	→
Age-standardized death rate attributable to household air pollution and ambient air pollution (per 100,000 population)	162	2016	●	●
Traffic deaths (per 100,000 population)	17.0	2019	●	→
Life expectancy at birth (years)	70.0	2019	●	→
Adolescent fertility rate (births per 1,000 females aged 15 to 19)	41.2	2019	●	●
Births attended by skilled health personnel (%)	78.1	2018	●	●
Surviving infants who received 2 WHO-recommended vaccines (%)	82	2020	●	→
Universal health coverage (UHC) index of service coverage (worst 0–100 best)	58	2019	●	↗
Subjective well-being (average ladder score, worst 0–10 best)	4.3	2021	●	↓
SDG4 – Quality Education				
Participation rate in pre-primary organized learning (% of children aged 4 to 6)	78.7	2020	●	↗
Net primary enrollment rate (%)	92.5	2020	●	→
Lower secondary completion rate (%)	77.5	2020	●	→
Literacy rate (% of population aged 15 to 24)	90.4	2020	●	●
SDG5 – Gender Equality				
Demand for family planning satisfied by modern methods (% of females aged 15 to 49)	66.5	2022	●	→
Ratio of female-to-male mean years of education received (%)	74.3	2019	●	→
Ratio of female-to-male labor force participation rate (%)	46.3	2020	●	↓
Seats held by women in national parliament (%)	18.1	2020	●	→
SDG6 – Clean Water and Sanitation				
Population using at least basic drinking water services (%)	88.5	2020	●	↗
Population using at least basic sanitation services (%)	69.8	2020	●	↗
Freshwater withdrawal (% of available freshwater resources)	52.9	2018	●	●
Anthropogenic wastewater that receives treatment (%)	3.3	2018	●	●
Scarce water consumption embodied in imports (m^3 H_2O eq/capita)	358.5	2018	●	●
SDG7 – Affordable and Clean Energy				
Population with access to electricity (%)	88.9	2019	●	↑
Population with access to clean fuels and technology for cooking (%)	56.8	2019	●	↗
CO_2 emissions from fuel combustion per total electricity output ($MtCO_2$/TWh)	1.9	2019	●	→
Share of renewable energy in total primary energy supply (%)	30.4	2019	●	↑
SDG8 – Decent Work and Economic Growth				
Adjusted GDP growth (%)	-3.1	2020	●	●
Victims of modern slavery (per 1,000 population)	6.1	2018	●	●
Adults with an account at a bank or other financial institution or with a mobile-money-service provider (% of population aged 15 or over)	58.2	2017	●	↑
Unemployment rate (% of total labor force)	5.8	2022	●	→
Fundamental labor rights are effectively guaranteed (worst 0–1 best)	0.5	2020	●	↗
Fatal work-related accidents embodied in imports (per 100,000 population)	0.1	2015	●	↑

* Imputed data point

SDG9 – Industry, Innovation and Infrastructure	Value	Year	Rating	Trend
Population using the internet (%)	44.5	2020	●	↑
Mobile broadband subscriptions (per 100 population)	53.8	2019	●	↑
Logistics Performance Index: Quality of trade and transport-related infrastructure (worst 1–5 best)	2.7	2018	●	↓
The Times Higher Education Universities Ranking: Average score of top 3 universities (worst 0–100 best)	34.3	2022	●	●
Articles published in academic journals (per 1,000 population)	0.1	2020	●	→
Expenditure on research and development (% of GDP)	0.5	2018	●	●
SDG10 – Reduced Inequalities				
Gini coefficient	36.3	2019	●	●
Palma ratio	2.3	2019	●	●
SDG11 – Sustainable Cities and Communities				
Proportion of urban population living in slums (%)	35.9	2018	●	↓
Annual mean concentration of particulate matter of less than 2.5 microns in diameter (PM2.5) (μg/m^3)	63.1	2019	●	↓
Access to improved water source, piped (% of urban population)	61.5	2020	●	↓
Satisfaction with public transport (%)	64.9	2021	●	→
SDG12 – Responsible Consumption and Production				
Municipal solid waste (kg/capita/day)	0.4	2019	●	●
Electronic waste (kg/capita)	3.1	2019	●	●
Production-based SO_2 emissions (kg/capita)	6.1	2018	●	●
SO_2 emissions embodied in imports (kg/capita)	0.5	2018	●	●
Production-based nitrogen emissions (kg/capita)	8.4	2015	●	↑
Nitrogen emissions embodied in imports (kg/capita)	0.5	2015	●	↑
Exports of plastic waste (kg/capita)	0.2	2021	●	●
SDG13 – Climate Action				
CO_2 emissions from fossil fuel combustion and cement production (tCO_2/capita)	1.7	2020	●	↑
CO_2 emissions embodied in imports (tCO_2/capita)	0.2	2018	●	↑
CO_2 emissions embodied in fossil fuel exports (kg/capita)	604.1	2021	●	●
SDG14 – Life Below Water				
Mean area that is protected in marine sites important to biodiversity (%)	25.9	2020	●	→
Ocean Health Index: Clean Waters score (worst 0–100 best)	40.1	2020	●	→
Fish caught from overexploited or collapsed stocks (% of total catch)	13.4	2018	●	↑
Fish caught by trawling or dredging (%)	35.1	2018	●	↓
Fish caught that are then discarded (%)	5.0	2018	●	↑
Marine biodiversity threats embodied in imports (per million population)	0.0	2018	●	●
SDG15 – Life on Land				
Mean area that is protected in terrestrial sites important to biodiversity (%)	33.6	2020	●	→
Mean area that is protected in freshwater sites important to biodiversity (%)	31.6	2020	●	→
Red List Index of species survival (worst 0–1 best)	0.8	2021	●	↓
Permanent deforestation (% of forest area, 5-year average)	0.3	2020	●	↗
Terrestrial and freshwater biodiversity threats embodied in imports (per million population)	0.1	2018	●	●
SDG16 – Peace, Justice and Strong Institutions				
Homicides (per 100,000 population)	3.1	2020	●	●
Unsentenced detainees (% of prison population)	56.4	2019	●	●
Population who feel safe walking alone at night in the city or area where they live (%)	64	2021	●	↓
Property Rights (worst 1–7 best)	3.9	2020	●	↓
Birth registrations with civil authority (% of children under age 5)	73.8	2020	●	●
Corruption Perception Index (worst 0–100 best)	35	2021	●	→
Children involved in child labor (% of population aged 5 to 14)	15.8	2019	●	●
Exports of major conventional weapons (TIV constant million USD per 100,000 population)	0.0	2020	●	●
Press Freedom Index (best 0–100 worst)	45.8	2021	●	↓
Access to and affordability of justice (worst 0–1 best)	0.5	2020	●	↗
SDG17 – Partnerships for the Goals				
Government spending on health and education (% of GDP)	4.7	2020	●	→
For high-income and all OECD DAC countries: International concessional public finance, including official development assistance (% of GNI)	NA	NA	●	●
Other countries: Government revenue excluding grants (% of GDP)	15.2	2019	●	→
Corporate Tax Haven Score (best 0–100 worst)	2.1	2019	●	●
Statistical Performance Index (worst 0–100 best)	65.6	2019	●	↗

UPPER-MIDDLE-INCOME COUNTRIES

OVERALL PERFORMANCE

RANKING

UPPER-MIDDLE-INCOME COUNTRIES

NA

AVERAGE

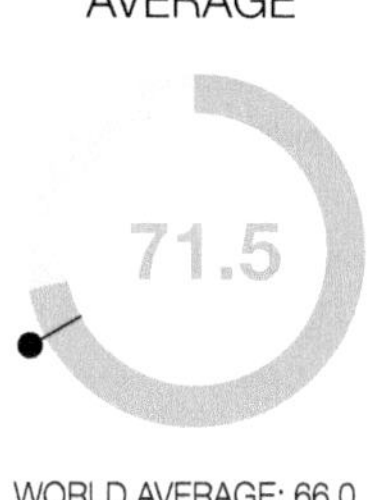

WORLD AVERAGE: 66.0

AVERAGE PERFORMANCE BY SDG

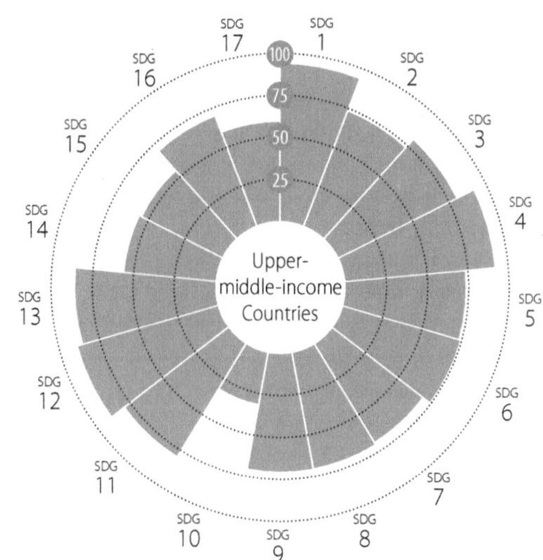

SDG DASHBOARDS AND TRENDS

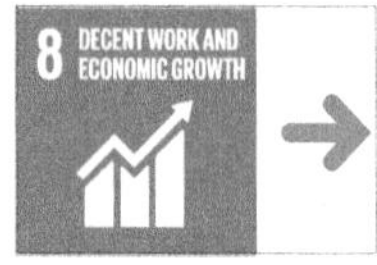

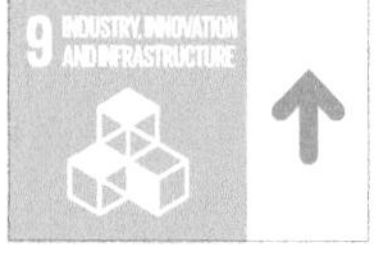

SDG achieved
On track or maintaining SDG achievement
Information unavailable
Information unavailable

Note: The full title of each SDG is available here: https://sustainabledevelopment.un.org/topics/sustainabledevelopmentgoals

INTERNATIONAL SPILLOVER INDEX

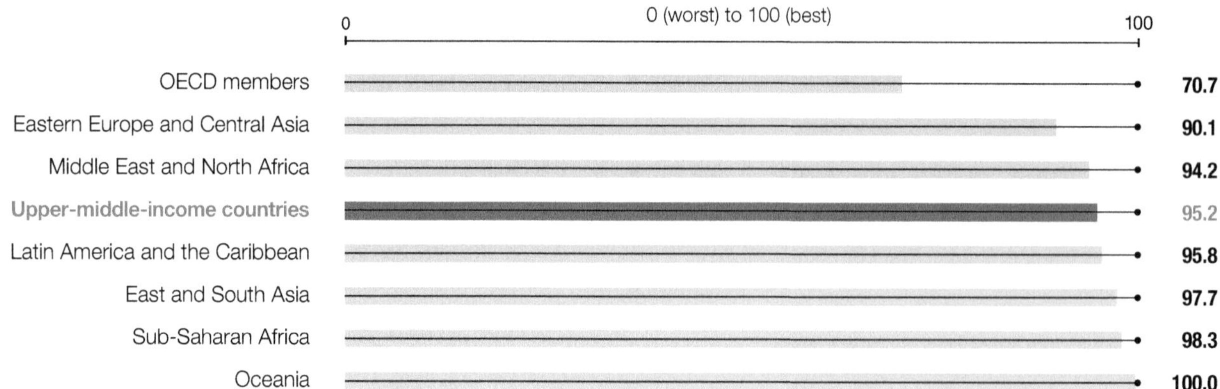

STATISTICAL PERFORMANCE INDEX

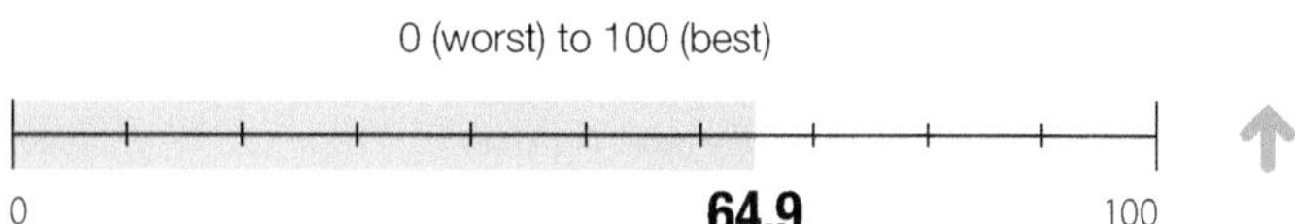

MISSING DATA IN SDG INDEX

0%

UPPER-MIDDLE-INCOME COUNTRIES

SDG1 – No Poverty	Value	Year	Rating	Trend
Poverty headcount ratio at $1.90/day (%)	2.1	2022	●	↓
Poverty headcount ratio at $3.20/day (%)	5.1	2022	●	↗

SDG2 – Zero Hunger	Value	Year	Rating	Trend
Prevalence of undernourishment (%)	4.4	2019	●	↑
Prevalence of stunting in children under 5 years of age (%)	7.9	2019	●	↗
Prevalence of wasting in children under 5 years of age (%)	2.3	2019	●	↑
Prevalence of obesity, BMI ≥ 30 (% of adult population)	14.1	2016	●	↓
Human Trophic Level (best 2–3 worst)	2.2	2017	●	→
Cereal yield (tonnes per hectare of harvested land)	5.0	2018	●	↑
Sustainable Nitrogen Management Index (best 0–1.41 worst)	0.7	2015	●	→
Exports of hazardous pesticides (tonnes per million population)	19.1	2019	●	●

SDG3 – Good Health and Well-Being	Value	Year	Rating	Trend
Maternal mortality rate (per 100,000 live births)	39	2017	●	↑
Neonatal mortality rate (per 1,000 live births)	5.2	2020	●	↑
Mortality rate, under-5 (per 1,000 live births)	10.2	2020	●	↑
Incidence of tuberculosis (per 100,000 population)	66.8	2020	●	↗
New HIV infections (per 1,000 uninfected population)	0.8	2020	●	→
Age-standardized death rate due to cardiovascular disease, cancer, diabetes, or chronic respiratory disease in adults aged 30–70 years (%)	16.6	2019	●	↑
Age-standardized death rate attributable to household air pollution and ambient air pollution (per 100,000 population)	84	2016	●	●
Traffic deaths (per 100,000 population)	17.2	2019	●	→
Life expectancy at birth (years)	76.4	2019	●	↗
Adolescent fertility rate (births per 1,000 females aged 15 to 19)	24.0	2019	●	↑
Births attended by skilled health personnel (%)	98.9	2018	●	●
Surviving infants who received 2 WHO-recommended vaccines (%)	92	2020	●	↑
Universal health coverage (UHC) index of service coverage (worst 0–100 best)	78	2019	●	↑
Subjective well-being (average ladder score, worst 0–10 best)	5.8	2021	●	↑

SDG4 – Quality Education	Value	Year	Rating	Trend
Participation rate in pre-primary organized learning (% of children aged 4 to 6)	88.6	2020	●	↑
Net primary enrollment rate (%)	96.7	2020	●	↓
Lower secondary completion rate (%)	93.0	2020	●	↑
Literacy rate (% of population aged 15 to 24)	99.4	2020	●	●

SDG5 – Gender Equality	Value	Year	Rating	Trend
Demand for family planning satisfied by modern methods (% of females aged 15 to 49)	87.1	2022	●	↑
Ratio of female-to-male mean years of education received (%)	94.1	2019	●	↑
Ratio of female-to-male labor force participation rate (%)	75.3	2020	●	↑
Seats held by women in national parliament (%)	24.9	2020	●	→

SDG6 – Clean Water and Sanitation	Value	Year	Rating	Trend
Population using at least basic drinking water services (%)	95.7	2020	●	↑
Population using at least basic sanitation services (%)	92.0	2020	●	↑
Freshwater withdrawal (% of available freshwater resources)	35.2	2018	●	●
Anthropogenic wastewater that receives treatment (%)	16.2	2018	●	●
Scarce water consumption embodied in imports (m^3 H_2O eq/capita)	613.5	2018	●	●

SDG7 – Affordable and Clean Energy	Value	Year	Rating	Trend
Population with access to electricity (%)	99.4	2019	●	↑
Population with access to clean fuels and technology for cooking (%)	75.8	2019	●	↗
CO_2 emissions from fuel combustion per total electricity output ($MtCO_2$/TWh)	1.3	2019	●	↑
Share of renewable energy in total primary energy supply (%)	13.7	2019	●	↗

SDG8 – Decent Work and Economic Growth	Value	Year	Rating	Trend
Adjusted GDP growth (%)	0.0	2020	●	●
Victims of modern slavery (per 1,000 population)	3.3	2018	●	●
Adults with an account at a bank or other financial institution or with a mobile-money-service provider (% of population aged 15 or over)	71.8	2017	●	↑
Unemployment rate (% of total labor force)	7.0	2022	●	→
Fundamental labor rights are effectively guaranteed (worst 0–1 best)	0.4	2020	●	↓
Fatal work-related accidents embodied in imports (per 100,000 population)	0.2	2015	●	↑

SDG9 – Industry, Innovation and Infrastructure	Value	Year	Rating	Trend
Population using the internet (%)	72.7	2020	●	↑
Mobile broadband subscriptions (per 100 population)	88.9	2019	●	↑
Logistics Performance Index: Quality of trade and transport-related infrastructure (worst 1–5 best)	3.3	2018	●	↑
The Times Higher Education Universities Ranking: Average score of top 3 universities (worst 0–100 best)	60.4	2022	●	●
Articles published in academic journals (per 1,000 population)	0.5	2020	●	↑
Expenditure on research and development (% of GDP)	1.5	2018	●	↑

SDG10 – Reduced Inequalities	Value	Year	Rating	Trend
Gini coefficient	40.9	2019	●	●
Palma ratio	3.2	2019	●	●

SDG11 – Sustainable Cities and Communities	Value	Year	Rating	Trend
Proportion of urban population living in slums (%)	20.2	2018	●	●
Annual mean concentration of particulate matter of less than 2.5 microns in diameter (PM2.5) (μg/m^3)	36.4	2019	●	↗
Access to improved water source, piped (% of urban population)	93.6	2020	●	↗
Satisfaction with public transport (%)	71.6	2021	●	↑

SDG12 – Responsible Consumption and Production	Value	Year	Rating	Trend
Municipal solid waste (kg/capita/day)	0.9	2019	●	●
Electronic waste (kg/capita)	8.1	2019	●	●
Production-based SO_2 emissions (kg/capita)	16.3	2018	●	●
SO_2 emissions embodied in imports (kg/capita)	1.0	2018	●	●
Production-based nitrogen emissions (kg/capita)	13.6	2015	●	↑
Nitrogen emissions embodied in imports (kg/capita)	2.0	2015	●	↑
Exports of plastic waste (kg/capita)	0.2	2021	●	●

SDG13 – Climate Action	Value	Year	Rating	Trend
CO_2 emissions from fossil fuel combustion and cement production (tCO_2/capita)	6.2	2020	●	→
CO_2 emissions embodied in imports (tCO_2/capita)	0.4	2018	●	↑
CO_2 emissions embodied in fossil fuel exports (kg/capita)	1147.8	2021	●	●

SDG14 – Life Below Water	Value	Year	Rating	Trend
Mean area that is protected in marine sites important to biodiversity (%)	23.1	2020	●	→
Ocean Health Index: Clean Waters score (worst 0–100 best)	45.9	2020	●	→
Fish caught from overexploited or collapsed stocks (% of total catch)	26.7	2018	●	↓
Fish caught by trawling or dredging (%)	35.2	2018	●	↓
Fish caught that are then discarded (%)	8.5	2018	●	→
Marine biodiversity threats embodied in imports (per million population)	0.1	2018	●	●

SDG15 – Life on Land	Value	Year	Rating	Trend
Mean area that is protected in terrestrial sites important to biodiversity (%)	21.3	2020	●	→
Mean area that is protected in freshwater sites important to biodiversity (%)	21.1	2020	●	→
Red List Index of species survival (worst 0–1 best)	0.8	2021	●	↓
Permanent deforestation (% of forest area, 5-year average)	0.1	2020	●	↑
Terrestrial and freshwater biodiversity threats embodied in imports (per million population)	0.7	2018	●	●

SDG16 – Peace, Justice and Strong Institutions	Value	Year	Rating	Trend
Homicides (per 100,000 population)	6.7	2020	●	→
Unsentenced detainees (% of prison population)	28.1	2019	●	↑
Population who feel safe walking alone at night in the city or area where they live (%)	76	2021	●	↑
Property Rights (worst 1–7 best)	4.8	2020	●	↑
Birth registrations with civil authority (% of children under age 5)	96.2	2020	●	●
Corruption Perception Index (worst 0–100 best)	41	2021	●	→
Children involved in child labor (% of population aged 5 to 14)	5.4	2019	●	●
Exports of major conventional weapons (TIV constant million USD per 100,000 population)	0.3	2020	●	●
Press Freedom Index (best 0–100 worst)	62.1	2021	●	→
Access to and affordability of justice (worst 0–1 best)	0.6	2020	●	↗

SDG17 – Partnerships for the Goals	Value	Year	Rating	Trend
Government spending on health and education (% of GDP)	7.3	2020	●	↓
For high-income and all OECD DAC countries: International concessional public finance, including official development assistance (% of GNI)	NA	NA	●	●
Other countries: Government revenue excluding grants (% of GDP)	20.3	2019	●	→
Corporate Tax Haven Score (best 0–100 worst)	34.5	2019	●	●
Statistical Performance Index (worst 0–100 best)	64.9	2019	●	↑

* Imputed data point

HIGH-INCOME COUNTRIES

OVERALL PERFORMANCE

RANKING

HIGH-INCOME COUNTRIES

NA

AVERAGE

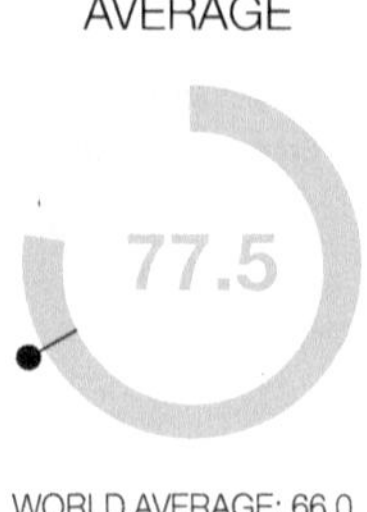

WORLD AVERAGE: 66.0

AVERAGE PERFORMANCE BY SDG

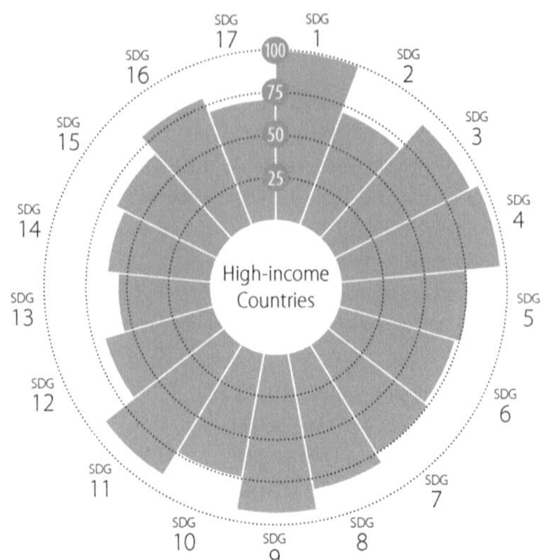

SDG DASHBOARDS AND TRENDS

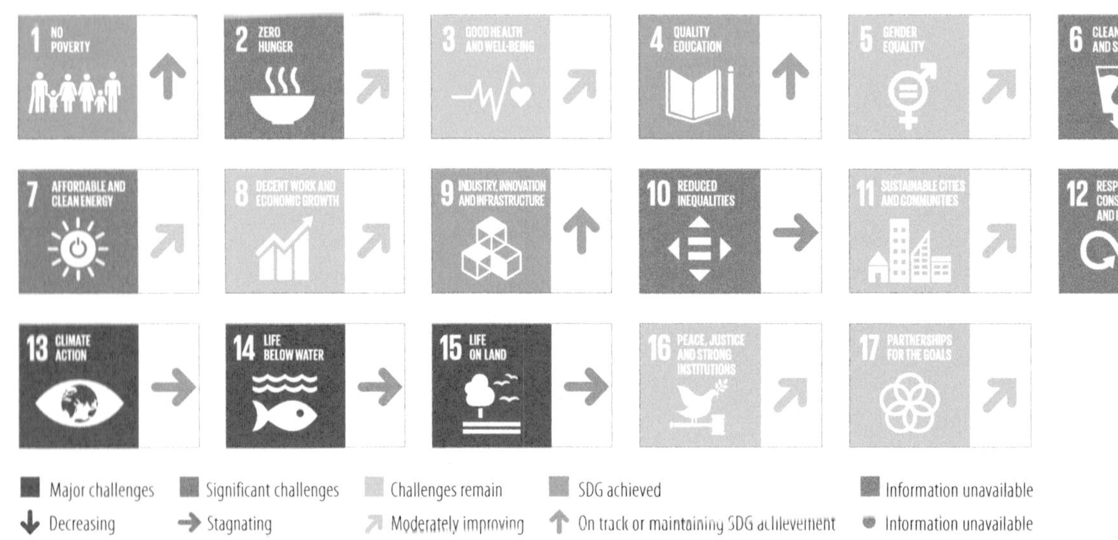

Major challenges · Significant challenges · Challenges remain · SDG achieved · Information unavailable

Decreasing · Stagnating · Moderately improving · On track or maintaining SDG achievement · Information unavailable

Note: The full title of each SDG is available here: https://sustainabledevelopment.un.org/topics/sustainabledevelopmentgoals

INTERNATIONAL SPILLOVER INDEX

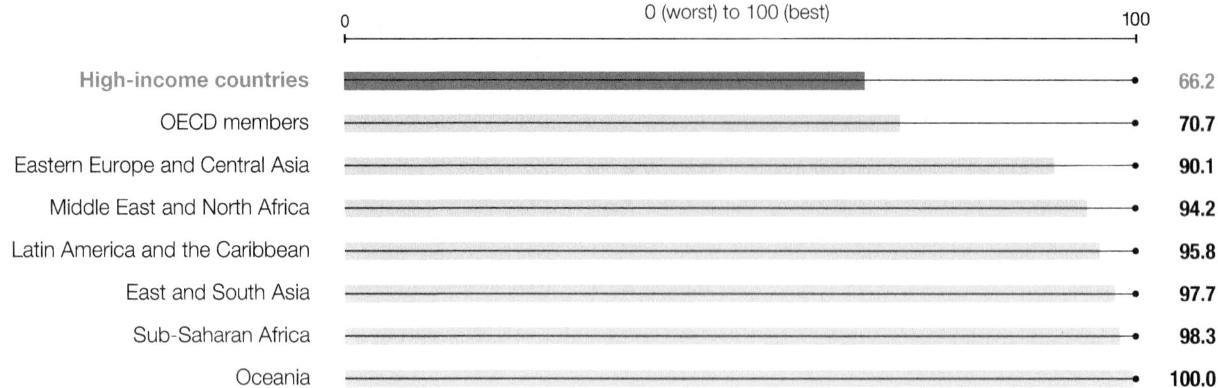

STATISTICAL PERFORMANCE INDEX

0 (worst) to 100 (best)

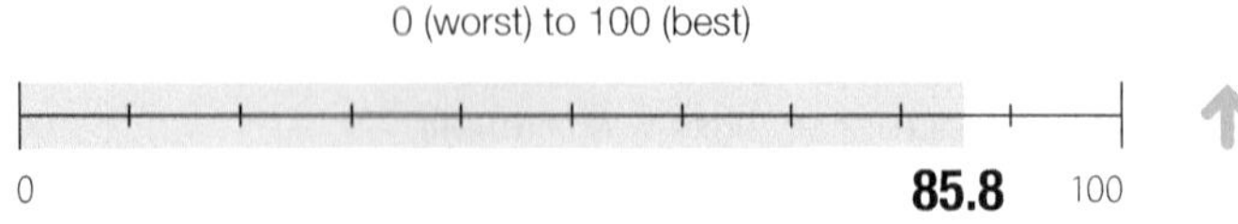

MISSING DATA IN SDG INDEX

HIGH-INCOME COUNTRIES

SDG1 – No Poverty	Value	Year	Rating	Trend
Poverty headcount ratio at $1.90/day (%)	0.4	2022	●	↑
Poverty headcount ratio at $3.20/day (%)	0.5	2022	●	↑
SDG2 – Zero Hunger				
Prevalence of undernourishment (%)	2.6	2019	●	↑
Prevalence of stunting in children under 5 years of age (%)	3.5	2019	●	↑
Prevalence of wasting in children under 5 years of age (%)	1.1	2019	●	↑
Prevalence of obesity, BMI ≥ 30 (% of adult population)	24.8	2016	●	↓
Human Trophic Level (best 2–3 worst)	2.4	2017	●	↓
Cereal yield (tonnes per hectare of harvested land)	6.7	2018	●	↑
Sustainable Nitrogen Management Index (best 0–1.41 worst)	0.5	2015	●	→
Exports of hazardous pesticides (tonnes per million population)	20.3	2019	●	●
SDG3 – Good Health and Well-Being				
Maternal mortality rate (per 100,000 live births)	10	2017	●	↑
Neonatal mortality rate (per 1,000 live births)	2.5	2020	●	↑
Mortality rate, under-5 (per 1,000 live births)	4.6	2020	●	↑
Incidence of tuberculosis (per 100,000 population)	8.5	2020	●	↑
New HIV infections (per 1,000 uninfected population)	0.6	2020	●	→
Age-standardized death rate due to cardiovascular disease, cancer, diabetes, or chronic respiratory disease in adults aged 30–70 years (%)	11.7	2019	●	↑
Age-standardized death rate attributable to household air pollution and ambient air pollution (per 100,000 population)	18	2016	●	●
Traffic deaths (per 100,000 population)	8.4	2019	●	↑
Life expectancy at birth (years)	80.8	2019	●	↑
Adolescent fertility rate (births per 1,000 females aged 15 to 19)	10.1	2019	●	↑
Births attended by skilled health personnel (%)	99.2	2018	●	↑
Surviving infants who received 2 WHO-recommended vaccines (%)	93	2020	●	↑
Universal health coverage (UHC) index of service coverage (worst 0–100 best)	83	2019	●	↑
Subjective well-being (average ladder score, worst 0–10 best)	6.7	2021	●	↑
SDG4 – Quality Education				
Participation rate in pre-primary organized learning (% of children aged 4 to 6)	92.2	2020	●	↑
Net primary enrollment rate (%)	98.7	2020	●	↑
Lower secondary completion rate (%)	100.2	2020	●	↑
Literacy rate (% of population aged 15 to 24)	99.5	2020	●	●
SDG5 – Gender Equality				
Demand for family planning satisfied by modern methods (% of females aged 15 to 49)	78.7	2022	●	↗
Ratio of female-to-male mean years of education received (%)	99.2	2019	●	↑
Ratio of female-to-male labor force participation rate (%)	79.2	2020	●	↑
Seats held by women in national parliament (%)	28.1	2020	●	↗
SDG6 – Clean Water and Sanitation				
Population using at least basic drinking water services (%)	99.8	2020	●	↑
Population using at least basic sanitation services (%)	99.5	2020	●	↑
Freshwater withdrawal (% of available freshwater resources)	87.7	2018	●	●
Anthropogenic wastewater that receives treatment (%)	71.6	2018	●	●
Scarce water consumption embodied in imports (m^3 H_2O eq/capita)	2812.1	2018	●	●
SDG7 – Affordable and Clean Energy				
Population with access to electricity (%)	100.0	2019	●	↑
Population with access to clean fuels and technology for cooking (%)	100.0	2019	●	↑
CO_2 emissions from fuel combustion per total electricity output ($MtCO_2$/TWh)	1.1	2019	●	↑
Share of renewable energy in total primary energy supply (%)	11.1	2019	●	→
SDG8 – Decent Work and Economic Growth				
Adjusted GDP growth (%)	-1.0	2020	●	●
Victims of modern slavery (per 1,000 population)	1.7	2018	●	●
Adults with an account at a bank or other financial institution or with a mobile-money-service provider (% of population aged 15 or over)	93.3	2017	●	↑
Unemployment rate (% of total labor force)	5.1	2022	●	●
Fundamental labor rights are effectively guaranteed (worst 0–1 best)	0.7	2020	●	↓
Fatal work-related accidents embodied in imports (per 100,000 population)	1.3	2015	●	↑

SDG9 – Industry, Innovation and Infrastructure	Value	Year	Rating	Trend
Population using the internet (%)	89.8	2020	●	↑
Mobile broadband subscriptions (per 100 population)	130.0	2019	●	↑
Logistics Performance Index: Quality of trade and transport-related infrastructure (worst 1–5 best)	3.9	2018	●	↑
The Times Higher Education Universities Ranking: Average score of top 3 universities (worst 0–100 best)	71.2	2022	●	●
Articles published in academic journals (per 1,000 population)	2.0	2020	●	↑
Expenditure on research and development (% of GDP)	2.4	2018	●	↑
SDG10 – Reduced Inequalities				
Gini coefficient	35.4	2019	●	→
Palma ratio	1.4	2019	●	●
SDG11 – Sustainable Cities and Communities				
Proportion of urban population living in slums (%)	0.0	2018	●	↑
Annual mean concentration of particulate matter of less than 2.5 microns in diameter (PM2.5) (μg/m³)	14.0	2019	●	↑
Access to improved water source, piped (% of urban population)	99.2	2020	●	↑
Satisfaction with public transport (%)	62.9	2021	●	→
SDG12 – Responsible Consumption and Production				
Municipal solid waste (kg/capita/day)	1.6	2019	●	●
Electronic waste (kg/capita)	19.4	2019	●	●
Production-based SO_2 emissions (kg/capita)	21.8	2018	●	●
SO_2 emissions embodied in imports (kg/capita)	7.1	2018	●	●
Production-based nitrogen emissions (kg/capita)	17.6	2015	●	↑
Nitrogen emissions embodied in imports (kg/capita)	10.9	2015	●	→
Exports of plastic waste (kg/capita)	4.5	2021	●	●
SDG13 – Climate Action				
CO_2 emissions from fossil fuel combustion and cement production (tCO_2/capita)	9.8	2020	●	↗
CO_2 emissions embodied in imports (tCO_2/capita)	2.5	2018	●	→
CO_2 emissions embodied in fossil fuel exports (kg/capita)	3297.9	2021	●	●
SDG14 – Life Below Water				
Mean area that is protected in marine sites important to biodiversity (%)	56.4	2020	●	→
Ocean Health Index: Clean Waters score (worst 0–100 best)	62.7	2020	●	→
Fish caught from overexploited or collapsed stocks (% of total catch)	33.8	2018	●	↓
Fish caught by trawling or dredging (%)	22.1	2018	●	→
Fish caught that are then discarded (%)	9.9	2018	●	→
Marine biodiversity threats embodied in imports (per million population)	0.5	2018	●	●
SDG15 – Life on Land				
Mean area that is protected in terrestrial sites important to biodiversity (%)	56.2	2020	●	→
Mean area that is protected in freshwater sites important to biodiversity (%)	55.1	2020	●	→
Red List Index of species survival (worst 0–1 best)	0.9	2021	●	→
Permanent deforestation (% of forest area, 5-year average)	0.0	2020	●	↑
Terrestrial and freshwater biodiversity threats embodied in imports (per million population)	3.8	2018	●	●
SDG16 – Peace, Justice and Strong Institutions				
Homicides (per 100,000 population)	2.6	2020	●	→
Unsentenced detainees (% of prison population)	22.5	2019	●	↑
Population who feel safe walking alone at night in the city or area where they live (%)	75	2021	●	↑
Property Rights (worst 1–7 best)	5.4	2020	●	↑
Birth registrations with civil authority (% of children under age 5)	100.0	2020	●	●
Corruption Perception Index (worst 0–100 best)	68	2021	●	↑
Children involved in child labor (% of population aged 5 to 14)	0.1	2019	●	●
Exports of major conventional weapons (TIV constant million USD per 100,000 population)	1.7	2020	●	●
Press Freedom Index (best 0–100 worst)	24.0	2021	●	↑
Access to and affordability of justice (worst 0–1 best)	0.6	2020	●	↗
SDG17 – Partnerships for the Goals				
Government spending on health and education (% of GDP)	11.6	2020	●	↑
For high-income and all OECD DAC countries: International concessional public finance, including official development assistance (% of GNI)	0.3	2021	●	→
Other countries: Government revenue excluding grants (% of GDP)	NA	NA	●	●
Corporate Tax Haven Score (best 0–100 worst)	39.2	2019	●	●
Statistical Performance Index (worst 0–100 best)	85.8	2019	●	↑

* Imputed data point

NOTES